Contemporary
Literary Criticism

Guide to Gale Literary Criticism Series

For criticism on	Consult these Gale series
Authors now living or who died after December 31, 1959	*CONTEMPORARY LITERARY CRITICISM (CLC)*
Authors who died between 1900 and 1959	*TWENTIETH-CENTURY LITERARY CRITICISM (TCLC)*
Authors who died between 1800 and 1899	*NINETEENTH-CENTURY LITERATURE CRITICISM (NCLC)*
Authors who died between 1400 and 1799	*LITERATURE CRITICISM FROM 1400 TO 1800 (LC)* *SHAKESPEAREAN CRITICISM (SC)*
Authors who died before 1400	*CLASSICAL AND MEDIEVAL LITERATURE CRITICISM (CMLC)*
Black writers of the past two hundred years	*BLACK LITERATURE CRITICISM (BLC)*
Authors of books for children and young adults	*CHILDREN'S LITERATURE REVIEW (CLR)*
Dramatists	*DRAMA CRITICISM (DC)*
Hispanic writers of the late nineteenth and twentieth centuries	*HISPANIC LITERATURE CRITICISM (HLC)*
Native North American writers and orators of the eighteenth, nineteenth, and twentieth centuries	*NATIVE NORTH AMERICAN LITERATURE (NNAL)*
Poets	*POETRY CRITICISM (PC)*
Short story writers	*SHORT STORY CRITICISM (SSC)*
Major authors from the Renaissance to the present	*WORLD LITERATURE CRITICISM, 1500 TO THE PRESENT (WLC)*

ISSN 0091-3421

Volume 95

Contemporary Literary Criticism

Excerpts from Criticism of the Works
of Today's Novelists, Poets, Playwrights,
Short Story Writers, Scriptwriters, and
Other Creative Writers

Brigham Narins
Deborah A. Stanley
EDITORS,

George H. Blair
Jeff Chapman
Pamela S. Dear
Daniel Jones
John D. Jorgenson
Aarti D. Stephens
Polly A. Vedder
Thomas Wiloch
Kathleen Wilson
Janet Witalec
ASSOCIATE EDITORS

GALE

DETROIT · NEW YORK · TORONTO · LONDON

STAFF

igham Narins and Deborah A. Stanley, *Editors*

Jeff Chapman, Pamela S. Dear, John D. Jorgenson, Aarti D. Stephens,
Kathleen Wilson, and Janet Witalec, *Contributing Editors*

George H. Blair, Daniel Jones, Polly A. Vedder, and Thomas Wiloch, *Associate Editors*

John P. Daniel, Christopher Giroux, Joshua Lauer, Janet Mullane,
Annette Petrusso, Linda Quigley, and John Stanley, *Assistant Editors*

Marlene S. Hurst, *Permissions Manager*
Margaret A. Chamberlain, Maria Franklin, and Kimberly F. Smilay, *Permissions Specialists*
Diane Cooper, Edna Hedblad, Michele Lonoconus, Maureen Puhl, Susan Salas, and Shalice Shah, *Permissions Associates*
Sarah Chesney and Jeffrey Hermann, *Permissions Assistants*

Victoria B. Cariappa, *Research Manager*
Julia C. Daniel, Tamara C. Nott, Michele P. Pica, Tracie A. Richardson,
Norma Sawaya, and Cheryl L. Warnock, *Research Associates*
Laura C. Bissey, Alfred A. Gardner I, and Sean R. Smith, *Research Assistants*

Mary Beth Trimper, *Production Director*
Deborah L. Milliken, *Production Assistant*

Barbara J. Yarrow, *Graphic Services Manager*
Sherrell Hobbs, *Macintosh Artist*
Randy Bassett, *Image Database Supervisor*
Robert Duncan and Mikal Ansari, *Scanner Operators*
Pamela Hayes, *Photography Coordinator*

Library of Congress Catalog Card Number 76-46132
ISBN 0-7876-1056-9
ISSN 0091-3421

Printed in the United States of America
10 9 8 7 6 5 4 3 2 1

Contents

Preface vii

Acknowledgments xi

Preface

A Comprehensive Information Source
on Contemporary Literature

Named "one of the twenty-five most distinguished reference titles published during the past twenty-five years" by *Reference Quarterly,* the *Contemporary Literary Criticism (CLC)* series provides readers with critical commentary and general information on more than 2,000 authors now living or who died after December 31, 1959. Previous to the publication of the first volume of *CLC* in 1973, there was no ongoing digest monitoring scholarly and popular sources of critical opinion and explication of modern literature. *CLC,* therefore, has fulfilled an essential need, particularly since the complexity and variety of contemporary literature makes the function of criticism especially important to today's reader.

Scope of the Series

CLC presents significant passages from published criticism of works by creative writers. Since many of the authors covered by *CLC* inspire continual critical commentary, writers are often represented in more than one volume. There is, of course, no duplication of reprinted criticism.

Authors are selected for inclusion for a variety of reasons, among them the publication or dramatic production of a critically acclaimed new work, the reception of a major literary award, revival of interest in past writings, or the adaptation of a literary work to film or television.

Attention is also given to several other groups of writers-authors of considerable public interest—about whose work criticism is often difficult to locate. These include mystery and science fiction writers, literary and social critics, foreign writers, and authors who represent particular ethnic groups within the United States.

Format of the Book

Each *CLC* volume contains about 500 individual excerpts taken from hundreds of book review periodicals, general magazines, scholarly journals, monographs, and books. Entries include critical evaluations spanning from the beginning of an author's career to the most current commentary. Interviews, feature articles, and other published writings that offer insight into the author's works are also presented. Students, teachers, librarians, and researchers will find that the generous excerpts and supplementary material in *CLC* provide them with vital information required to write a term paper, analyze a poem, or lead a book discussion group. In addition, complete bibliographical citations note the original source and all of the information necessary for a term paper footnote or bibliography.

Features

A *CLC* author entry consists of the following elements:

- The **Author Heading** cites the author's name in the form under which the author has most commonly published, followed by birth date, and death date when applicable. Uncertainty as to a birth or death date is indicated by a question mark.

■ A **Portrait** of the author is included when available.

■ A brief **Biographical and Critical Introduction** to the author and his or her work precedes the excerpted criticism. The first line of the introduction provides the author's full name, pseudonyms (if applicable), nationality, and a listing of genres in which the author has written. To provide users with easier access to information, the biographical and critical essay included in each author entry is divided into four categories: "Introduction," "Biographical Information," "Major Works," and "Critical Reception." The introductions to single-work entries—entries that focus on well known and frequently studied books, short stories, and poems—are similarly organized to quickly provide readers with information on the plot and major characters of the work being discussed, its major themes, and its critical reception. Previous volumes of *CLC* in which the author has been featured are also listed in the introduction.

■ A list of **Principal Works** notes the most important writings by the author. When foreign-language works have been translated into English, the English-language version of the title follows in brackets.

■ The **Excerpted Criticism** represents various kinds of critical writing, ranging in form from the brief review to the scholarly exegesis. Essays are selected by the editors to reflect the spectrum of opinion about a specific work or about an author's literary career in general. The excerpts are presented chronologically, adding a useful perspective to the entry. All titles by the author featured in the entry are printed in boldface type, which enables the reader to easily identify the works being discussed. Publication information (such as publisher names and book prices) and parenthetical numerical references (such as footnotes or page and line references to specific editions of a work) have been deleted at the editor's discretion to provide smoother reading of the text.

■ Critical essays are prefaced by **Explanatory Notes** as an additional aid to readers. These notes may provide several types of valuable information, including: the reputation of the critic, the importance of the work of criticism, the commentator's approach to the author's work, the purpose of the criticism, and changes in critical trends regarding the author.

■ A complete **Bibliographical Citation** designed to help the user find the original essay or book precedes each excerpt.

■ Whenever possible, a recent, previously unpublished **Author Interview** accompanies each entry.

■ A concise **Further Reading** section appears at the end of entries on authors for whom a significant amount of criticism exists in addition to the pieces reprinted in *CLC*. Each citation in this section is accompanied by a descriptive annotation describing the content of that article. Materials included in this section are grouped under various headings (e.g., Biography, Bibliography, Criticism, and Interviews) to aid users in their search for additional information. Cross-references to other useful sources published by Gale Research in which the author has appeared are also included: *Authors in the News, Black Writers, Children's Literature Review, Contemporary Authors, Dictionary of Literary Biography, DISCovering Authors, Drama Criticism, Hispanic Literature Criticism, Hispanic Writers, Native North American Literature, Poetry Criticism, Something about the Author, Short Story Criticism, Contemporary Authors Autobiography Series,* and *Something about the Author Autobiography Series.*

Other Features

CLC also includes the following features:

- An **Acknowledgments** section lists the copyright holders who have granted permission to reprint material in this volume of *CLC*. It does not, however, list every book or periodical reprinted or consulted during the preparation of the volume.

- Each new volume of *CLC* includes a **Cumulative Topic Index,** which lists all literary topics treated in *CLC, NCLC, TCLC,* and *LC 1400-1800.*

- A **Cumulative Author Index** lists all the authors who have appeared in the various literary criticism series published by Gale Research, with cross-references to Gale's biographical and autobiographical series. A full listing of the series referenced there appears on the first page of the indexes of this volume. Readers will welcome this cumulated author index as a useful tool for locating an author within the various series. The index, which lists birth and death dates when available, will be particularly valuable for those authors who are identified with a certain period but whose death dates cause them to be placed in another, or for those authors whose careers span two periods. For example, Ernest Hemingway is found in *CLC,* yet F. Scott Fitzgerald, a writer often associated with him, is found in *Twentieth-Century Literary Criticism.*

- A **Cumulative Nationality Index** alphabetically lists all authors featured in *CLC* by nationality, followed by numbers corresponding to the volumes in which the authors appear.

- An alphabetical **Title Index** accompanies each volume of *CLC*. Listings are followed by the author's name and the corresponding page numbers where the titles are discussed. English translations of foreign titles and variations of titles are cross-referenced to the title under which a work was originally published. Titles of novels, novellas, dramas, films, record albums, and poetry, short story, and essay collections are printed in italics, while all individual poems, short stories, essays, and songs are printed in roman type within quotation marks; when published separately (e.g., T. S. Eliot's poem *The Waste Land),* the titles of long poems are printed in italics.

- In response to numerous suggestions from librarians, Gale has also produced a **Special Paperbound Edition** of the *CLC* title index. This annual cumulation, which alphabetically lists all titles reviewed in the series, is available to all customers and is typically published with every fifth volume of *CLC*. Additional copies of the index are available upon request. Librarians and patrons will welcome this separate index: it saves shelf space, is easy to use, and is recyclable upon receipt of the next edition.

Citing *Contemporary Literary Criticism*

When writing papers, students who quote directly from any volume in the Literary Criticism Series may use the following general forms to footnote reprinted criticism. The first example pertains to material drawn from periodicals, the second to material reprinted in books:

[1]Alfred Cismaru, "Making the Best of It," *The New Republic,* 207, No. 24, (December 7, 1992), 30, 32; excerpted and reprinted in *Contemporary Literary Criticism,* Vol. 85, ed. Christopher Giroux (Detroit: Gale Research, 1995), pp. 73-4.

[2]Yvor Winters, *The Post-Symbolist Methods* (Allen Swallow, 1967); excerpted and reprinted in *Contemporary Literary Criticism,* Vol. 85, ed. Christopher Giroux (Detroit: Gale Research, 1995), pp. 223-26.

Suggestions Are Welcome

The editors hope that readers will find *CLC* a useful reference tool and welcome comments about the work. Send comments and suggestions to: Editors, *Contemporary Literary Criticism,* Gale Research, Penobscot Building, Detroit, MI 48226-4094.

Acknowledgments

The editors wish to thank the copyright holders of the excerpted criticism included in this volume and the permissions managers of many book and magazine publishing companies for assisting us in securing reprint rights. We are also grateful to the staffs of the Detroit Public Library, the Library of Congress, the University of Detroit Mercy Library, Wayne State University Purdy/Kresge Library Complex, and the University of Michigan Libraries for making their resources available to us. Following is a list of the copyright holders who have granted us permission to reprint material in this volume of *CLC*. Every effort has been made to trace copyright, but if omissions have been made, please let us know.

COPYRIGHTED EXCERPTS IN *CLC*, VOLUME 95, WERE REPRINTED FROM THE FOLLOWING PERIODICALS:

Jane Campion

1955(?)-

New Zealander filmmaker.

The following entry provides an overview of Campion's career through 1994.

INTRODUCTION

Campion is best known for films that feature strong, compelling female characters and realistic—while also somewhat oneiric—narratives. Her early works are characterized by highly stylized techniques and a nonlinear, experimental approach to storytelling. Her subsequent work—best exemplified by *The Piano* (1993)—rely less on technical flourishes and emphasize the development and subjective experiences of her protagonists.

Biographical Information

Campion was born in Wellington, New Zealand, to parents who were professionally involved in the theatre—her father was a director and her mother an actress and author. After unsuccessful attempts studying art in Venice and working with a documentary film producer in London, Campion attended the Sydney College of Arts in Australia. During her last year of study there she made her first short film, *Tissues* (1981). In 1984 she earned a diploma in directing from the prestigious Australian Film, Television, and Radio School. Campion's work first gained widespread critical attention at the 1986 Cannes International Film Festival, where her film *Peel* (1982)—made in her second year at the Australian Film, Television, and Radio School—won the Palme d'Or award in the short film category.

Major Works

Campion's early short works and the feature-length *Sweetie* (1989) are marked by what she has described as a maverick approach to filmmaking. *Sweetie,* considered Campion's first major work, blends the supernatural with the mundane, the comic with the tragic. The story focuses on the relationship between Kay—a somewhat emotionally disturbed young woman who is deathly afraid of trees—and her sister Sweetie—a loud, overweight, manic-depressive aspiring actress with a voracious appetite for drugs, alcohol, and sex. The theme of the tenuous distinction between sanity and insanity is explored when Kay's father, Sweetie, and Sweetie's boyfriend all move in with her. This theme is further developed in *An Angel at My Table* (1990), in which Campion fulfilled a long-held desire to make a film about novelist and fellow New Zealander Janet Frame. Based on Frame's three autobiographies—*To the Is-Land* (1982), *An Angel at My Table* (1984), and *The Envoy from the Mirror City* (1985)—the film features three actresses in the role of Frame from

childhood through adulthood. The story follows Frame from her isolated and uneventful childhood, her culture shock and emotional troubles upon going away to school, through her endurance of shock therapy after an inaccurate diagnosis of schizophrenia, and her eventual marginal assimilation into society and maturation into a respected author. *The Piano* begins when the willfully mute mail-order bride Ada (Holly Hunter), her illegitimate daughter Flora (Anna Paquin), and their belongings—including Ada's full-sized piano—are delivered from England to a deserted beach in New Zealand and left to wait for the arrival of Ada's new husband, Stewart (Sam Neill). Ignorant of the piano's importance to Ada, Stewart orders it left behind when he arrives the next day. The piano is later retrieved by Stewart's assistant, Baines (Harvey Keitel), who suspects its significance. The themes of interpersonal communication and marital relationships are developed as Baines, not Stewart, recognizes and exploits the fact that Ada's piano-playing is her most important means of self-expression.

Critical Reception

Critical opinions about Campion's work vary. While she

is generally recognized as a technically skilled filmmaker, some critics believe she emphasizes the purely stylistic aspects of her films at the expense of the cohesiveness of her stories. For example, Campion and the actresses from *Sweetie* were lambasted by critics at the Cannes film festival in 1989; later that year, however, the film received the Australian Film Critics' Circle awards for best film and best director. Noting the stylistic experimentation of her early work, several critics have stated that with *An Angel at My Table* Campion displayed a growing artistic maturity. The film received numerous awards in 1991, including the Toronto Film Festival Critics Award, the Otto Debelius Prize from the international jury at the Berlin Film Festival, the Elvira Notari Award for the best woman director, and eight awards from the Venice Film Festival. Critics observed that Campion was much more gentle in her treatment of the real-life Janet Frame than she had been toward her previous fictional characters, Sweetie in particular. Many reviewers of *The Piano* praised Campion's skill in accurately reproducing 19th-century period detail, acknowledged the artfully and technically impressive camera work in the film, and commended her ability to elicit impassioned performances from actors. Other commentators were made uncomfortable by her use of the camera, specifically the reliance on close-ups, and suggested that the film's narrative was too elliptical, requiring the viewer to draw connections and conclusions that the film should have depicted. *The Piano* was recognized by the Academy of Motion Picture Arts and Sciences with an Oscar for best original screenplay and a nomination for best director.

---

*PRINCIPAL WORKS

Tissues (film) 1981
Peel: An Exercise in Discipline (film) 1982
A Girl's Own Story (film) 1983
After Hours (film) 1984
Passionless Moments (film) 1984
Two Friends (film) 1986
Sweetie [with Gerard Lee] (film) 1989
An Angel at My Table [with Laura Jones] (film) 1990
The Piano (film) 1993
Portrait of a Lady [with Jones; based on the novel *The Portrait of a Lady* (1881) by Henry James] (film) 1996

*Campion directed all the films listed here. Bracketed information refers to screenwriting credit.

CRITICISM

Robert Seidenberg (review date January 1990)

SOURCE: "*Sweetie*: Jane Campion's Maverick Family," in *American Film*, Vol. XV, No. 4, January, 1990, pp. 59, 65.

[*In the following review, Seidenberg examines Campion's treatment of family life in* Sweetie.]

Dark, destructive forces simmer under the surface of everyday life, held at bay by repression and denial. Add a little pressure to the mix and those forces bubble over. In the offbeat comedy *Sweetie,* Jane Campion's feature debut, they erupt with volcanic force, bringing chaos to an Australian family.

"In families, like everything else, there's the good side and the sick side," explains Campion, a 35-year-old New Zealander living in Sydney. "In *Sweetie,* the family is in distress, and under stress things usually don't come out so well."

Fulfilling the prophecy of a fortune-teller, Kay (Karen Colston) falls for a man with "a question mark"—formed by a cowlick and mole—on his forehead. A year later, the road turns rocky. The brooding Kay turns frigid. Her romance dissolves. Even worse, she's visited by her manic sister, Sweetie (Genevieve Lemon).

Though she's an irresponsible, conniving adult, Sweetie still sees herself as daddy's little girl: a sweet, tap-dancing show-off with infinite potential. She'll stoop to anything to get attention, even barking and biting like an incensed hound. With her erratic behavior, she's detonated more than her fair share of family traumas.

"Sweetie has a powerful effect over the entire family," says Campion. "And her father doesn't help at all because he gives in to her. He loves the little girl she once was and is intimidated by the reality of her as she is now. He lives in a complete delusion about her."

Kay's equally deluded, but Sweetie's arrival inspires her to confront the truth. She examines her frigidity rather than rationalizing it away as "just a no-sex phase." She realizes that perhaps true love can't be found among gypsy-read tea leaves. And after a surprisingly bleak—yet hilarious—scene, she even begins to value her relationship with Sweetie.

Campion gracefully takes us on a private tour inside of Kay's mind—where it's evident that Kay herself is not well. Grainy black-and-white nightmares, haunting visions of strangulating tree roots, the disturbing memories and hallucinations that strike when eyes are closed—in these moments, captured in stunning compositions, Campion excels.

"I'm interested in the aspects of being human that aren't socialized—the undercurrent, the hidden agenda that we all live our lives by—because a lot of everyday life is like that," Campion explains.

In her quest to illuminate life beneath the surface, Campion's developing a distinctive style of her own. This first feature picks up where she left off in three shorts (*Passionless Moments, A Girl's Own Story* and *Peel*) that caused a stir at Cannes in 1986. The connection between these works, according to Campion, is their maverick approach. "It's obvious that I'm still working out how to put a film together," she half-jokes, "and that the normal way, the sort of seamless filmmaking that is basically American in origin, has totally eluded me. I'm obviously barking up some other completely separate tree.

"With *Sweetie,* we wanted to take a risk, but we also wanted people to have a relationship with the film somehow, to be touched and not just think, Hey, wow, this is weird."

Sheila Benson   (review date 14 February 1990)

SOURCE: "Move Over David Lynch, Here Comes Australia's 'Sweetie,' " in *Los Angeles Times,* February 14, 1990, pp. F2-F3.

[*In the following review of* Sweetie, *Benson focuses on the relationship between Kay and her sister, Sweetie.*]

We haven't had a movie as profoundly unsettling as *Sweetie* since *Blue Velvet.* David Lynch's dark metaphor created the same reactions as Jane Campion's first feature; both of them have been called masterly and disgusting, by turns. But while Campion's vision is no less precise and no less bizarre than Lynch's and while both directors deal in manifestations of the unconscious, the comparisons stop there.

Writer-director Campion has her own powerful identity and a far less ominous affect. *Sweetie* is warm, intense and wickedly funny, with a faint edge of danger that's never quite absent, but it has none of Lynch's psycho-sexual torment. Made with a post-Modernist's eye and a brilliant satiric ear, *Sweetie* is the announcement of a singular, smashing talent.

Campion's subject is families, pressure-cookers with no safety valves. She seems to have total recall for details of jealousy and score-keeping, unquestioned love and resentment as she sketches the pulls between two sisters, Sweetie, "Dad's real girl," who's had lifelong, unquestioning love, and her sister Kay, who's never felt loved at all.

The story is set in one of the bleaker suburbs in Sydney, Australia, as a family is pulled off-center by its most demanding member, the outrageous Sweetie (Genevieve Lemon), a sometimes mental patient and decidedly free spirit.

Sad-faced and repressed, Kay (Karen Colston) is at the center of the story. In her late 20s and fleetingly pretty, she's Sweetie's slightly older sister. It's a relationship that has taken its toll. Any number of things unnerve Kay, especially trees, whose roots—like her family's—seem profoundly unstable.

Sex is another disquieting subject, but it doesn't keep Kay from moving in with lightning speed on Louis (Tom Lycos), who seems to fit a psychic's prediction of the man she's destined for. The fact that he's just become engaged is totally irrelevant. Bewildered, vaguely flattered, Louis succumbs and moves in, bag and baggage.

Actually, both sisters are irresistible forces when they set their minds on something. It's just that Sweetie's mind has been set so irrevocably, so mistakenly and for so long. She's been fueled from the cradle by her father's vision of

her as a rare and God-given talent. We never quite know when Sweetie began to take this information onto another plane, when expectation became craziness, but the two are fused now.

Sweetie bursts back into Kay's life just as Kay and Louis's 13-month relationship has hit a particularly contemporary snag: they love each other, but at Kay's request they just don't make love. Kay's phobias have had a field day recently and the bombshell of Sweetie's midnight arrival doesn't soothe them.

Sweetie is roughly 60 pounds overweight, add an extra 10 pounds for makeup; the beautiful features of her Kewpie Doll face look as though they'd been inflated with a bicycle pump and her lace mitts probably cover sawed-up wrists. She arrives with Bob (Michael Lake), a drooling druggie she calls her producer and she has stopped her medication. However, success is only inches away. "Bob and I are gonna walk through some doors" she announces triumphantly. As soon as Bob stops nodding off midsentence.

What really perturbs Kay is the force of Sweetie's uninhibited sexuality, the other end of the spectrum from her own. It doesn't unclench Kay in the slightest.

Sweetie's fluctuating behavior has very nearly destroyed her parents' marriage. As we meet her mother, Flo (Dorothy Barry) she's calmly taken time off to get a breather from Sweetie and from her husband's sentimental uselessness about her.

Campion may not be sentimental but she's a nutsy romantic. The Outback sequence, where Flo has taken a job happily cooking for an outpost of Aussie cowboys, is pure, saturated longing. Kay, Louie and Gordon drive to this wilderness only to find the seven jackaroos, like something out of Agnes de Mille's *Rodeo,* spending yearning nights under the blue-purple skies, brushing up on their two-step. It's absolutely magical.

Deadpan funny as the script can be—to balance its horrific moments—its wit is matched by the director's visual style. Campion, with cinematographer Sally Bongers, uses an accumulation of images to build mood; a blizzard of them at first, slowing down as the film builds. Her character's claustrophobia and depressions are caught by subjective angles within rooms or landscapes, yet there's not an uninteresting image in the film.

The cast is breathtaking. Clearly, there would be no film without Genevieve Lemon's uncanny, unsparing Sweetie, touched with a sort of grandiosity of aberration; hers is an amazing creation. But in less flamboyant ways every actor, down to the maddening little boy next door (Andre Pataczek), is working with an equal measure of skill and delicacy.

Campion and Gerard Lee, her co-writer, regard Sweetie with a sort of detached amazement, refusing to sentimentalize her. She's the film's explosive humor, its sexuality, its pathos, and its reflective energy source. There's no question that she's deeply disturbing, yet it's clear that Campion regards this tyrant—who has held her entire family hostage emotionally for nearly 25 years—with equal love and clarity. And if there could be any question that Kay's love matches her fury at her mad sister, watch Kay's action in their closing scene together. It's the summation of their entire impossible relationship.

Stuart Klawans   (review date 19 February 1990)

SOURCE: A review of *Sweetie,* in *The Nation,* New York, Vol. 250, No. 7, February 19, 1990, p. 252.

[*In the following review, Klawans praises the narrative structure and visual style of* Sweetie.]

One of the first things you see in ***Sweetie*** is the muddy-hued, domestic equivalent of a Rorschach blot: the pattern in a carpet. The camera peers down on this floral invitation to daydreaming, which takes up most of the screen; to one side, a fragment of the narrator's body is visible. Kay (Karen Colston) begins to talk in voiceover about her fantasies, but you already know plenty about them from the image. ***Sweetie***—the utterly distinctive and assured first feature by Jane Campion—will be about the meanings people read into whatever they choose to see as clues: tea leaves, a tossed coin, a stray curl of hair, a little girl's aptitude for clowning. And just as the opening shot is off-center, so too are the characters. Not only do they spend their lives interpreting auguries, but they invariably look at them askew.

Kay begins by deciding that her auguries lead straight to Lou (Tom Lycos). He is the sort of earnest, not-too-bright young man who, believing whatever he's told, spends a lot of his time trying to understand pure nonsense. Though engaged to one of Kay's friends at work—a commitment that has lasted "for fifty-five minutes," as he points out—he yields immediately when Kay declares, "I'm destined to be with you." Within seconds, the two are grappling on the grease-stained floor of the parking garage where Kay has made her revelation. "Lou said there are seven spiritual planes," she explains later on the soundtrack, "and the love we had was somewhere near the top."

The next time Kay reads an omen, though, it makes her heartsick. When Lou plants a tree in the backyard, Kay fears that the sapling portends doom. She has nightmares about germination—eruptions of fierce cytoplasmic tendrils, which roar like dinosaurs as their maws break open. Kay uproots the sapling, which means, quite naturally, that she also stops sleeping with Lou.

In a less original film, this would probably be the first fifteen minutes of a drama about pregnancy, or the lack of it. In *Sweetie* it leads instead to the arrival of the title character, a woman even more fantastical than Kay: her disorderly, willful, half-cracked sister (Genevieve Lemon). Whereas Kay is pretty in a pert, dark, conventional way (dampened by an expression of perpetual worry), Sweetie has a fat, puppyish face under a butchery of greasy hair. She considers herself a theatrical star, though she has never worked; she dresses in a style that might be called thrift-shope glamour, except that her clothes look more like the discards from the alley behind the shop. When first seen, just after she has invaded Kay's house, she is in bed with her current boyfriend and "producer," Bob (Mi-

chael Lake), regaling him, herself and anyone within earshot with the pleasure of her ample flesh.

Again, a more conventional film would probably set about contrasting the riotously life-affirming Sweetie with the dour, frightened Kay. But *Sweetie* continues to mutate. Very soon, Kay and Sweetie's parents enter the picture, and we begin to see how *everyone* here is atilt. Though Kay disavows any connection with Sweetie—"She was just *born*," she tells Lou, "I don't have anything to do with her"—the eccentric branchings of love have entangled her, too, along with the rest of the family. Kay sometimes fights Sweetie, sometimes humors her, sometimes conspires with the others against her, all in an effort to cope with someone who is either crazy or just an impossible burden, depending on your point of view.

With a narrative structure as skillfully off-center as its characters and visual style, *Sweetie* keeps the viewer in delighted suspense through a swift ninety minutes. There is no way to predict the next turn of events or camera angle, though once something has crossed the screen, it invariably feels just right. With the collaboration of Gerard Lee as co-screenwriter and with the help of a winning cast—especially Genevieve Lemon, in a self-sacrificing performance—Jane Campion has made a droll, witty, moving, understated triumph of a feature-film debut. It's set in Australia, by the way. Don't let that keep you from seeing it.

Stanley Kauffmann   (review date 26 February 1990)

SOURCE: A review of *Sweetie,* in *New Republic,* Vol. 202, No. 3919, February 26, 1990, pp. 26-7.

[*Kauffmann is an American playwright, actor, director, and critic. In the following excerpt, he contends that Campion is more interested in her film's visual impact than its narrative.*]

Jane Campion is a newcomer, a New Zealander who works in Australia and is now loudly hailed in America. *Sweetie* is her first feature. She wrote it with Gerard Lee; but after the first five or six minutes, it's clear that her heart is not in the screenplay, it's in the pictures that she makes with her cinematographer Sally Bongers.

Still, there *is* a screenplay—about a young Australian factory worker named Kay, who believes in omens and hauntings. Tea leaves, for instance. A medium tells her that a question mark will figure in her life. She then meets Lou, a young man whose hair curls in a question mark on his forehead. Immediately she seduces him away from his fiancée. Then Sweetie arrives at the house that Kay shares with Lou. Sweetie is Kay's adipose, highly disturbed sister who thinks she's a pop singer and who brings along her drugged-out "producer." Sweetie immediately slovens up the house, in her neurotic way, and the parents can't help, because back in *their* house, Mom has just left Dad and has gone out west to become a cook on a ranch (as we'd call it).

A few questions. What did Lou's fiancée say or do to Kay after the latter stole her boyfriend? Why did Kay and Lou make love in an oil puddle on a garage floor? Why did

Mom leave Dad? Why do Mom and Dad become reconciled? What do Kay and Lou and Dad think will happen, other than disaster, when they leave Sweetie alone in Kay's house and drive out west to see Mom?

Answers are not expected. The questions themselves are the answer—the fact that they, and others, exist. They only underscore that Campion is more keen about photo opportunities than about dramatic or narrative cogency. Her screenplay is to her what a libretto was to a lesser 19th-century opera composer: a series of pegs for visual arias.

Corners of rooms, low angles, high angles, shots past large objects in the foreground, heightened light or lowered light—all these get a good workout. When we go to a cemetery, the first shot is of a row of cypress trees, through which we manage to glimpse one grave. This shot, like so many others, is not meant to epitomize the moment but to draw our attention to Campion. And Bongers.

Campion has been compared to Jim Jarmusch. This seems absurd. Jarmusch's spare screenplays are carefully measured to the necessary minimum, like good minimal design of every kind. His camera operates in the same precise, equivalently minimal way. Campion wants to deal much more conventionally with her characters, with more psychological probing and emotional interaction than Jarmusch cares about. At the same time she wants to indulge her painterly eye. The result is a deadlock between these two elements, dramatic and pictorial.

If Campion can accept that we now know about her eye and can concentrate on an integrated story, she might make a good traditional filmmaker. If that road doesn't interest her, she could diminish the emotional turbulence in her scripts so that it doesn't clamor for attention, and become something like a (minor) cinematic Robert Wilson. But whatever she does later, *Sweetie* is only a workshop along the way.

Maitland McDonagh   (review date 19 May 1991)

SOURCE: "Jane Campion's 'Angel' Is Another Quirky Soul," in *New York Times,* May 19, 1991, p. 22.

[*In the following review, McDonagh draws comparisons between* An Angel at My Table *and Campion's previous works, arguing that the director is kinder to her subject in the film under review.*]

"Just show me an ordinary person," says the director Jane Campion, "and I'll show you a troubled soul." And she should know; troubled souls are her stock in trade. Her first feature, *Sweetie,* revolved around two warring sisters: the dour Kay, who has nightmares about trees with human powers, and Sweetie, who is exuberant, impulsive and destructively out of control. The heroine of Miss Campion's new film, *An Angel at My Table*—adapted from the autobiography of the renowned New Zealand poet and novelist Janet Frame—is a prickly introvert who spent eight years in a mental institution and much of the rest of her life repairing her fragile sense of self. But where Miss Campion was casually hard on Kay in *Sweetie,* she

is gentle to the awkward, high-strung Miss Frame, kinder even than the author is to herself.

Like Miss Frame's autobiography [also titled *An Angel at My Table*], *An Angel at My Table,* opening today in New York City, is divided into three parts. Alexia Cox portrays Miss Frame as a little girl; Karen Fergusson plays her as a teen-ager, and Kerry Fox as an adult. From the beginning, Miss Campion wanted the length of a mini-series; *Angel* was made for Australian television. The director initially resisted theatrical release, but after seeing the film's reception at last year's Sydney Film Festival, she relented. Trimmed slightly, the movie runs just over two and a half hours.

Angel, which is packed with the minutiae of Miss Frame's life, at first in New Zealand, where she was born in 1924, and later in England and Spain, follows her from a childhood of rural poverty to middle age. It explores her family relationships, her extreme shyness—misdiagnosed as schizophrenia, with horrifying results—and her eventual success as a writer. *Angel* doesn't look like a television movie, except perhaps in the intimacy of its subject: the largely unremarkable but richly remembered life of a plain, intelligent woman with a startling head of frizzy ginger hair.

Forthright and sharp-witted, the 36-year-old Miss Campion is, like Miss Frame, a native New Zealander, and she has wanted to make *An Angel at My Table* for years. "I read her novel *Owls Do Cry,* when I was about 13," Miss Campion remembers. "It deals very poetically, lyrically, with the subject of madness in a young girl. I think it rang a note for me because at 13, you feel the potential for madness for the first time in your life." Curious about this woman who wrote so persuasively about insanity, Miss Campion inquired and first heard the party line about Miss Frame: she was reclusive, peculiar and "possibly quite mad."

Fifteen years later, while Miss Campion was at the Australian Film and Television School in Sydney, the first volume of Miss Frame's autobiography was published. "My mother sent it over to me, and I remember reading it in one night, just getting into bed and staying there until I finished it the next morning." Miss Campion said. She was enthralled by its directness and the intense detail of memory. "From that point I took on the idea that I would like to turn it into some kind of film."

Miss Campion's cinematic world is full of eccentrics because, she says, "I just don't know this elusive normal person, you know? I don't believe they exist."

—*Maitland McDonagh*

A visit to the author was encouraging. "She didn't seem to be concerned about whether or not I'd done anything before, which was just as well, since I hadn't," Miss Campion said. She joined forces with the producer Bridget Ikin, and "finally, when the three books came out, we re-approached Janet with a proper deal idea, and she agreed to it."

Laura Jones, the script editor on Miss Campion's 1984 short film *After Hours,* was recruited to write the screen-play, and the process of transforming Miss Frame's life into *An Angel at My Table* began.

"I felt a little inhibited by the fact that Janet was still very much alive," Miss Campion observes. "No matter what, I knew *Angel* wasn't going to be Janet Frame's story any-more. It was going to be my interpretation. But Janet was very generous: Her idea was that we should take it and re-invent it, be bold about it, and I had this confidence that since I really loved the material, I wouldn't do anything too wrong."

Miss Campion has established a reputation for making slightly off-kilter films in which regular folks get glimpses of the darkness that lurks beneath the surfaces of their lives. In the short *Passionless Moments,* suburban neigh-bors obsess about song lyrics and paper products; in *A Girl's Own Story,* teen-agers try to tease out the truth about love and sex from a tangle of pop culture myths and miserable examples set at home. In *Peel,* which is subtitled *An Exercise in Discipline,* a drive in the country turns into a pitched battle of wills when a small boy defiantly tosses orange peel out the window. The "peel" in the title refers to rind, but it also suggests skin, layer after layer of per-sonality and self-delusion, armor and exposed flesh.

Miss Campion's cinematic world is full of eccentrics be-cause, she says, "I just don't know this elusive normal per-son, you know? I don't believe they exist.

"I feel acknowledging the dark side of yourself, or the dark side of life is important," she continues. "Anyway, I'm curious. Anything and everything interests me . . . especially what I'm told not to look at."

Family relationships have been a constant in Miss Campi-on's work, but she denies that her films are autobiographi-cal. Nevertheless, she admits with a laugh, "I did borrow a dress once from my mother to use in *A Girl's Own Story.* Mum never noticed until my sister said 'Don't you see . . . we're all in that film.' Then she had another look and saw her dress. When she gets annoyed at me she often brings that one up.

"My mother writes," she says, "and anything we say is fair game. And my sister makes films, too. We're all after each other's skins, but we're also very close and loving."

American audiences, Miss Campion says, should have no trouble identifying with Miss Frame's struggles, despite the exotic settings. "We all sometimes feel very shy and apart from ourselves. I think everyone has had the feeling that he or she isn't acceptable. That's really what *An Angel at My Table* is all about."

And Miss Frame's hair, the unruly, carrot-colored mop she writes about with such despair: Is it really that alarm-ing? "It's distinctive," Miss Campion admits. "I can't say that Janet's hair looks that odd to me, but then, nothing much looks odd to me."

Stanley Kauffmann   (review date 3 June 1991)

SOURCE: Review of *An Angel at My Table,* in *New Re-public,* Vol. 204, No. 3985, June 3, 1991, pp. 28-9.

[*In the following review, Kauffmann asserts that Campion "has moved forward healthily" with* An Angel at My Table, *eschewing the "precious camera work" of* Sweetie *to put "her (considerable) pictorial skill at the service of Janet Frame."*]

Last year, reviewing Jane Campion's *Sweetie,* I said, "If Campion can accept that we now know about her [pictori-al] eye and can concentrate on an integrated story, she might make a good traditional filmmaker." She hadn't waited for my advice: she was already almost finished with *Angel at My Table,* which is traditional in approach, which employs her eye to present a narrative, and which is good.

Angel at My Table is a two-and-a-half-hour distillation, by the screenwriter Laura Jones, of Janet Frame's three volumes of autobiography. (The books are now available in one paperbound volume from George Braziller.) The film calls itself a trilogy, with one section devoted to each volume. For those who haven't read the books, the story may be surprising. We know that Frame is an eminent writer, and we know that she will move from ordinary be-ginnings to recognition and success. But we are not pre-pared for much of the dark texture that intervenes or for the odd, almost cheery tone in which even the worst mo-ments are couched.

Frame (b. 1924) is one of the five children of a New Zea-land railway worker and his hearty wife. Her childhood included the usual momentous initiations into the world but also into a world beyond the visible and tangible, dis-closed to her by imagination. Early on, she discovered that she liked to write and that she was shy. This shyness ap-parently had something to do with the fact that she was chunkily built, had a large mop of frizzy red hair, and had curious teeth.

When she was quite young, a sister drowned. (Ten years later, another sister drowned.) As a young teacher, she be-came stressed and depressed and made a feeble (aspirin) attempt at suicide. She was taken to a mental hospital, falsely diagnosed as schizophrenic, and was given electric shock therapy. In and out of hospitals, she was given 200 shock treatments in the next eight years—during which she also published a book of stories and won a prize.

With a travel grant, she went to London. She soon fell into a consciously arty set, who were somewhat nettled to find that this provincial had already published a book and had another forthcoming. She then went to Ibiza (along the way, her teeth were fixed), continued to write fiction and poetry, had her first sexual experience, returned to Lon-don where the diagnosis of schizophrenia was ruled false, then went home to New Zealand where she lives and writes. (To date, eleven novels, four story collections, a volume of poetry, and a children's book.)

The first part of the film is the fullest because childhood, though hardly simple, is simpler than what comes after. In the second and third parts, even those who don't know the books may sense synoptic touches. But Jones's screenplay, as treated by Campion, does the essential: it captures the straightforward, fresh tone.

For Frame's autobiography is suffused with appetite, with openness, even when she is beset by peculiar people, peculiar diagnoses, peculiar emotions. She is like an especially patient Candide, forging ahead with mixed purpose and acceptance, with ego (who could be a writer without ego?) but with wonder. The film understands all this.

Campion's prime and perfect move was in the casting of the three Janets: the child, Alexia Keogh, the adolescent, Karen Fergusson, and the young woman, Kerry Fox. Each of them has a third of the picture. That Campion was able to find three people with physical resemblances to one another and to Frame was possibly only good luck, though makeup and costuming doubtless helped. But, more important, what Campion achieved with her three Janets was a continuity of presence and person, of temperament: a manner of walking, of posture, of gesture, and, fundamentally, a continuity of inner self. The woman who has her first sexual experience in Ibiza is related to the child who, at the family dinner table, innocently uses a naughty word that a school chum taught her.

Everyone else in the cast helps substantially. The casting and behavior of the child's schoolteachers evoke time and place. K. J. Wilson is her sturdy father; Iris Churn is an Erda-like mother. David Letch dabs in a vivid sketch of Janet's Irish landlord in London, who is smitten with her. William Brandt is amusingly serious as her American lover in Ibiza. The score by Don McGlashan has a nice folk feeling, varied with a few uses of Schubert's "An die Musik," which enraptured Janet at first hearing.

Campion's previous film was burdened with precious camera work—high angles, low angles, weird vantage points. Not one bit of that is evident here. She was so concerned with her subject that she forgot about self-display and put her (considerable) pictorial skill at the service of Janet Frame. Oh, there are a couple of shots of a distant train chugging along past a sunset, but those are negligible if only because they are commonplace. Campion is so responsive to the currents of humanity in this story that she has found the exactly right general locus for her camera—close without close-ups. The camera is attentive, not intrusive.

The cinematography by Stuart Dryburgh adds something else, particularly in the first section—a homely grubbiness. At first it seems like inadequate color, a bit runny, or like slightly undefined focus; but soon it's apparent that Campion and Dryburgh want to suggest a social milieu, crowded, congenial, warmly though somewhat shabbily dressed. From the photography alone, we get some sense of what life is like for this segment of New Zealand society, getting the best out of what they had, in their pullovers and plain dresses, at close quarters.

Angel at My Table (it's the title of the second of Frame's three volumes) is not often exciting or deeply moving. It's simply interesting. Two qualities distinguish it. First, one female artist of a particular culture wanted to present the life of another female artist of that culture. I don't think it's wisdom after the event to say that certain bonds of sisterly sympathy are manifest throughout, certain avenues of understanding. (There's a cousinly relationship with *My Brilliant Career,* an Australian woman's film from an autobiographical novel by an Australian woman.) Second, the purpose here is to recount a life, rather than to create a drama. This was probably not a fresh film idea when Mark Donskoy made his *Gorky* trilogy (1938-40). Still, there is something full-souled about the venture, something respectful of the human enterprise as a whole and of art as its adjunct.

In any case, Campion has moved forward healthily. More, please.

Terrence Rafferty   (review date 3 June 1991)

SOURCE: "Outlaw Princesses," in *The New Yorker,* Vol. LXVII, No. 15, June 3, 1991, pp. 86-8.

[*In the following excerpt, Rafferty describes* An Angel at My Table *as a "perverse exercise in biographical filmmaking," faulting Campion for keeping viewers disoriented and withholding from them a sense of Frame's "inner life."*]

An Angel at My Table is based on the autobiography of the New Zealand novelist and poet Janet Frame. It covers the first forty years or so of the writer's life—she was born in 1924—and takes close to three hours to tell the story. When it's all over, you feel that you know far too little about Janet Frame and far too much about the film's director, Jane Campion. Frame's life doesn't seem to have been a particularly dramatic one. She grew up shy and literary, in a working-class family that moved around a lot, being shifted from town to town by the father's employer, the railroad. Her childhood and adolescence were, by her own account, spent in a kind of happy isolation from the world, within the safe confines of her affectionate family and her own imagination, which was fired by sentimental poetry and popular songs. Aside from the sudden death of her older sister, nothing much happened to Janet until she left home to go to teachers college in the city, where she found herself painfully ill-equipped to deal with the emotional demands of the outside world. In the autobiography she says, "Writing now, I am impatient with my student self that was so unformed, ungrownup, so cruelly innocent. Although I had no means of knowing if other students lived in such innocence, I have since learned that many, in timidity and shyness and ignorance, lived as bizarre a life as I. . . . Our lives were frail, full of agonies of embarrassment and regret, of misunderstood communication and strong with the intense feeling of wonder at the torrent of ideas released by books, music, art, other people; it was a time of finding shelter among the mightily capitalled abstractions of Love, Life, Time, Age, Youth, Imagination." Frame's struggle, as a writer and as a woman, was to find a way out of this tortured confinement in herself, and she took some giant steps backward before she was able to make any progress. While she was still a student, she suffered a breakdown, and was diagnosed (inaccurately) as schizophrenic; she spent years in mental institutions, where she received hundreds of shock treatments. The success of her writing helped her escape the institutions; eventually, she travelled to Europe, became more confident of her talent, and grew comfortable enough with people to be able to have a sexual relationship. (She was in her mid-thirties when she lost her virginity.)

The Janet Frame of Campion's film doesn't seem to have any inner life—not as a child, not as an adolescent, and not as an adult. And without that she has no life at all. The movie (which was made as a three-part miniseries for Australian television) is a succession of odd, mannered tableaux, more or less in the style of Campion's 1990 arthouse hit *Sweetie,* which was a static, self-conscious black comedy about an inarticulate young woman and her grotesquely infantile sister. Campion's compositions emphasize the peculiarities of Janet's appearance, especially in her childhood and awkward adolescence: she has a stiff, frizzy mop of bright-orange hair, and her teeth are badly decayed. Janet is played by three actresses: as a child, by Alexia Keogh; as a young teen-ager, by Karen Fergusson; and as an adult by Kerry Fox. As Campion has directed them, they're all morose and affectless; none of the performances gives us much of a clue to what Janet is thinking or feeling. You'd hardly know, for example, that Janet consciously adopted "schizophrenic" traits after her diagnosis: when it suited her, she used her supposed madness as a form of self-protection. Her breakdown and her periods of hospitalization are the pivotal dramatic events in this story, yet the movie's treatment of them is so flat and elliptical that we're unable to respond.

Throughout the film, Campion's imagery has a skewed, alienating quality that can be very effective: there's a distinctive strangeness in the way she places people in their environments, a trompe-l'oeil sense of unease. Unfortunately, her narrative technique has a similar effect. Time after time, we find ourselves unable to orient ourselves in crucial scenes, because the director hasn't bothered to establish the characters or the setting; whole sequences go by in which we're not sure where we are or whom we're watching. You might suspect that this is the filmmaker's way of forcing us to share her heroine's sense of dissociation from the world. But Janet couldn't possibly be as dissociated as the audience is; at times, we can't even identify the members of her family with any certainty. Writers' lives are weird enough without being subjected to this sort of willful disruption of their emotional continuity. Campion's perverse exercise in biographical filmmaking deserves a new title: "My Incomprehensible Career."

Elizabeth Drucker   (review date July 1991)

SOURCE: "*An Angel at My Table:* Jane Campion Throws a Curve," in *American Film,* Vol. XVI, No. 7, July, 1991, pp. 52-3.

[*In the following review, Drucker finds* An Angel at My Table "*as subtle and straightforward as* Sweetie *was startling and stylized.*"]

Director Jane Campion woke up the film world in 1989

with the bizarre, darkly comic vision of *Sweetie*. A tale about the rivalry between two sisters—one neurotic, the other psychotic—Campion's feature debut boasted eerie dream sequences, flamboyant characters and altogether odd behavior.

Just when critics thought they had Campion pegged (many referred to her as a female David Lynch), the 37-year-old filmmaker threw a curve. Campion's follow-up film, *An Angel at My Table,* is as subtle and straightforward as *Sweetie* was startling and stylized. The story of celebrated New Zealand author Janet Frame (played in turn by Alexia Keogh as the young Janet, Karen Fergusson as the teenager and, in an astonishingly controlled performance, Kerry Fox as the adult Janet), *Angel* is, in Campion's own words, a "gentler, more humanist piece."

Almost twice as long, slower-paced and less experimental than *Sweetie, Angel* does share one element with its predecessor: the theme of insanity. The title character of *Sweetie,* a gregarious madwoman, imagines herself a talented singer, and in *Angel,* Janet Frame, a shy but truly gifted writer, is mistakenly diagnosed as schizophrenic. Campion says that like Lynch, whom she admittedly hero-worships, she "is interested in the darker sides of the mind, those sorts of subconscious qualities that are happening to us."

Campion's desire to film Frame's story grew after she read the author's three-volume autobiography. "It was clear once I started reading that this was not the tale of a mad writer [but] of an ordinary person with a great gift for detail and frankness. It completely disarmed me."

The director felt so strongly about Frame's writing that she decided to give her own high-profile style a back seat. "I wanted to keep it really simple," explains Campion. "I felt that anything too flash would overload her story, and I thought the power of it would be in its simplicity. Her story should be unfettered by any overly stylistic concerns."

Mirroring Frame's books, the film, which was originally intended as a television miniseries, is divided into three sections: Frame's Depression-era childhood on the South Island of New Zealand; her college years when she retreats further into herself, eventually being misdiagnosed and institutionalized; and finally, her travels to Europe on a literary fellowship after gaining her release.

Campion was not involved in the scriptwriting for *Angel,* as she had been with *Sweetie,* but feels that had its benefits. "I think when you're working on someone else's idea, you feel protective toward them and their story," says Campion. "I feel very strong in defending Janet's writing, whereas I don't about my own. It's more frightening and challenging working from your own ideas, because you're saying, This is what I believe. With the Janet story, I wasn't so out on a limb. Instead, I was really developing other parts of myself that I hadn't before. Things like trying to support an actress in a sustained performance. Softer things, really."

The filming of *Angel* marked Campion's return to her native New Zealand after several years in Australia. Her experience with the New Zealand crew made her realize both what her homeland had given her and why she had instinctively wanted to leave. "Modesty and a strong work ethic are very New Zealand qualities. The crews were incredibly hardworking. But also I think that there's a sense of not liking individualism. It comes from the egalitarian beginnings of New Zealand. It was colonized as a kind of ideal state where people of lower-middle class background could share equal wealth and possibility. Which is great, but the downside of that is that excelling in anything is seen as showing off. There's a sense of not being accepted if you're trying to explore your individual qualities."

Campion, like Frame, left New Zealand to pursue her ambitions, going off to art school in London and finishing up with film school in Australia. Campion's background explains her sharp eye for detail and composition, whether the film is subtle in style or outrageous. "I think having the kind of keenness that people look with when they're doing an art study goes all the way through. You just can't go back to a kind of ignorant way of looking."

Mary Cantwell   (essay date 19 September 1993)

SOURCE: "Jane Campion's Lunatic Women," in *New York Times Magazine,* September 19, 1993, pp. 40-1, 44, 51.

[*Cantwell is an American editor, nonfiction writer, and critic. In the following essay, based on an interview with Campion, Cantwell surveys Campion's life and works, focusing on the female characters in Campion's films.*]

This October, a romantic epic titled *The Piano,* written and directed by a New Zealander named Jane Campion, will be the grand finale of the New York Film Festival at Lincoln Center. In November it will open all over the country. *The Piano,* which is set in 19th-century New Zealand, has already made Campion the first woman to win the Palme d'Or at the Cannes Film Festival, and the reviews so far—but for a cavil about its being too consciously an "art" film—have been ecstatic. Vincent Canby of *The New York Times,* for instance, described *The Piano* as "a triumph . . . so good, so tough, so moving and, especially, so original." Yet when I asked a friend, like me a great admirer of Campion's work, what she wanted to learn from my interview with the film maker, she replied, "First, I want to know if she's sane."

I had expected curiosity about why Australia, where Campion went to film school and lives, has produced what seems to be an inordinate number of world-class directors: Bruce Beresford and Peter Weir and George Miller among them. Or why, given the hen's tooth scarcity of prominent female directors anywhere in the world, three—Campion, Gillian Armstrong and Jocelyn Moorhouse—emerged from a country associated with a certain cheerful misogyny. But why be curious about Campion's sanity?

"Because," my friend answered, "she's obsessed with lunatic women."

In truth, only the eponymous protagonist of Campion's first feature film, the extraordinary *Sweetie,* is genuinely mad. The New Zealand novelist Janet Frame, whose auto-

biography, *An Angel at My Table,* became Campion's second film, was only *thought* to be mad. Diagnosed in her early 20's as a schizophrenic and institutionalized, she was within inches of a lobotomy when her doctors decided that a woman who had managed to write and publish distinguished fiction while in the bin was probably not in need of a brain correction. Ada in *The Piano* isn't mad either, but her mulishness approaches sublimity. That Ada doesn't speak, for instance, isn't because she can't but because she will not.

Lunatic women? Except for the simultaneously hilarious and tragic Sweetie, no. But powerful women, which in some minds may add up to the same thing? Yes. Sweetie has a tornado's destructiveness, Janet Frame stayed sane in the midst of madness and Ada's will is iron. What roles!

If artists looked like their creations, the progenitor of *The Piano* would resemble a Brontë sister or George Eliot. Instead, Campion looks like a commercial for Fun and Sun in Australia. Her hair is very fair, her eyes are very blue and her speech—typically antipodean in its narrow vowels and the upward curve of its sentences—is spattered with self-mockery and great bursts of laughter. "Mum" and "Dad" are a big part of her conversation; so are her friends, whom one half-expects her to call, as do most of the residents of her part of the world, "mates."

On a day in mid-June of this year, Campion was a month away from having won the Palme d'Or. She was two weeks away from giving birth to her first child, a son whose presence was already inescapable in the Sydney apartment she shares with her husband, Colin Englert, a television producer and director. The baby's crib was set up in Englert's small office, and Campion lifted her billowy white shirt once to stare at her swollen belly. "Is he kicking?" her visitor asked. "Mmmmm," she answered, lost for a moment in that curious bubble that encloses the pregnant.

Campion was, in brief, at the pinnacle of her particular world, at a place where the professional and the personal were about to meet in blessed convergence. And although she'd done her share of interviews, she wasn't yet weary of the same old questions because she hadn't yet heard them all. Chatty, spontaneous (once, she unexpectedly kissed my cheek), Campion in June of 1993 was, to an interviewer, equivalent to an unplowed field.

Campion was born 39 years ago, to parents whom she describes as having had "a strange life compared to most New Zealanders." They had a strange life compared with almost everybody's.

"My mother was an heiress, but an orphan at the same time, so she was brought up by different people and finally given her inheritance," she said. "She and my father met at university, then went to England to study at the Old Vic. When they came back, they started the first official touring company in New Zealand. It wasn't a financial success at all, and so they just started working in other established theaters. Mother retired when she had the three of us, but Dad's still doing a lot of things, like opera."

At Victoria University, where she majored in anthropology, Campion was interested in acting. "But I felt I had to distinguish myself from the family. You know? Besides, I thought acting quite frivolous. Now I'm grateful that I was raised in an atmosphere which had some sort of gaiety to it. But at the time, I thought that these people were . . . *insincere.*

"After that, the thing was to try and travel and take a look at where I came from, along with the rest of Europe. You know?"

Anyone who has ever run into Australians and New Zealanders on what they usually call "my trip" knows. The trip is their Wanderjahr, and analogous to the lazing-about-Europe-after-graduation done by countless young Americans in the days when a college degree was a guarantee of a job offer. To hear Campion talk about her trip is to be reminded of theirs: of the postcards detailing the wonders of Chartres, the mysteries of the bidet and a whole litany of missed trains and misunderstandings.

"My other aim was to go to art school. The first attempt was to go to one in Venice, but all sorts of complicated issues turned up. This boy I knew was arrested for cocaine trafficking. And I couldn't speak Italian very well. And I was going to the school, but I wasn't really enrolled because no one could work out who I was or what I was supposed to be doing there. And then it was winter, and they had the *agua alta,* the water that comes up over your gum boots. Then, of course, I was under suspicion, too, because I was a friend of his. He told me later that his mother had sent him some potato purée from Hungary and that it had been misinterpreted. But that sounds a little unlikely to me now, you know?"

Eventually Campion left Venice for London and a job assisting someone who made documentaries and commercials. Getting into an art school was still on her mind, but none were interested, mostly because her work was primitive, but partly, she suspects, because she may have looked like a ditz.

"I remember going to one of them, with a copy of *Cosmopolitan* magazine under my arm, and somebody coming to the door while I was still putting on lipstick. 'Uh, oh,' I thought. 'This isn't the right image.'

"I didn't like England. I couldn't take the look of the place or the style of friendship. I need more intimacy from people than is considered O.K. there, and I felt that my personality and my enthusiasms weren't understood. I had to put a big lid on myself. But I thought: 'You've just got to live with this. This is the rite of passage to being an adult—misery.'

"I have a complicated theory for why I was so depressed—that in the Southern Hemisphere you can use the weather to relate your moods with. If you did that in England, where it's continuously bleak, you'd just die.

"Also, there's a fury I have when I hear an English upper-class voice—that voice that speaks really loudly about its 'dahhhhggs.' Grrrr!"

There was nothing to do but go back: to the sun and the blue, blue skies and a society determined on classlessness.

It doesn't quite succeed, but never mind. The accent, so contagious that even the most recent immigrant is speaking "Strine" seemingly within minutes of arrival, is a great leveler.

This time, Campion went to Australia, to Sydney rather than Melbourne, because in the first city she had one friend and in the second, none. There a life that had been hitherto purposeless, if pleasant, finally took on a point.

"The art school I went to had young tutors who were into minimalist and conceptual art. They made everybody rethink their thinking about everything, which sent some people into sort of schizophrenic binges. But it was a brilliantly exciting atmosphere. You could do anything—installations, performance, whatever.

"First I was a bit at sea. Then, suddenly, for the first time in my life I really tried to do something. I'd never had a commitment to my ability; I knew there were people cleverer than me. What I was looking to do was to just learn enough so that I could in some way be supportive of somebody who really *was* gifted.

"There was another thing. About that stage I had a couple of boyfriends, and they both kind of disappeared. Being alone was a shock to me, and a good shock. Because I said: 'O.K., you've got nobody now. You're by yourself. So maybe it's time you had a look at what you can do if you really try, to find out what your potential really is.'

"I decided to try and make my artwork directly about the things that I'd rush home to ruminate about. Things like confusions about sex and intimacy, for instance.

"I was painting at the time, crude sexual paintings, I suppose, with some feminist imagery as well.

"There was a lot of performance stuff going on, too, so I used to put on little plays about women and sex—things like that. Pretty weird, really. Next, I decided that instead of being in a play I'd film it.

Campion's movies don't resemble anyone else's, and neither do they resemble one another.

—Mary Cantwell

"So, in my last year, I made this little film called *Tissues,* probably the only one I ever made that I loved. It was a very funny, rather crazy film about a father who'd been arrested for child molestation. The family tried to deal with it, and in every scene a tissue was used. Dum da dum!

"After that, I was just trying to get into the film industry in any way I could, and going through the usual stuff where everybody tells you, 'Yeah, maybe you can write, but you've got no directing skills.' And I thought, 'How on earth am I going to start?'"

By now the possessor of a B.A. in structural anthropology

and a diploma in fine arts, Campion started by going back. Once again, she went to school. Her father groaned.

Entering the Australian Film, Television and Radio School, however, is tantamount to becoming a part of the Australian film industry in that it's financed by the Government and gives its students—only 25 are chosen every year—a small stipend. For a prospective film maker, it is also a lot like going to heaven. "You could do any story you wanted to without having to argue for it. You had a chance to see how your ideas would turn out."

From the beginning, Campion's ideas were sui generis: the anthropologist sees coolly and dispassionately; the artist translates the spectacle into images unlike anyone else's.

In *Peel,* for instance, which she made in her second year and which eventually won an award at Cannes, a little boy is ordered by his father to pick up every piece of orange peel he's tossed from a car window. The boy looks like his father, his mother looks like her husband, the sun is merciless and the entire transaction is a ludicrous lesson in discipline. Like *Sweetie, Peel* is curiously mysterious in that Campion offers the viewer no clues as to what to think of it all. Herself averse to being told what to feel, she claims a corresponding reluctance to tell an audience what to feel.

The last of Campion's student films, *A Girl's Own Story,* is an intensely personal oddity about innocence, pubescence and childhood incest and, in a sense, a precursor to *The Piano*. In their frank acknowledgment of the awful power of sex, and, not incidentally, its awful messiness, both carry a disconcerting erotic charge. In *A Girl's Own Story,* a brother and sister embark on intercourse as casually as cats. In *The Piano,* in which petticoats and pantalets seem endless barriers to consummation, a mere half-inch of flesh is enough to tantalize.

After film school, Campion joined the Women's Film Unit, an Australian remedy for the imbalance between the number of men and women in Government-sponsored film programs (about even) and the number in the film industry (not even close). Her first assignment was a film on sexual harassment in the work place, which "I agree is a pain, but I'm so perverse I'm going the other way," she said. "I think everybody should be harassing each other a whole lot more. I'm averse to teaching messages— they're a load of rubbish."

The Women's Film Unit was also a bit of a pain. "Basically, the way film sets work is very undemocratic, whereas the idea behind the unit—the idealism—predisposed its members to expect a lot more say. On a normal set, the priority is the work; in a situation like the Women's Film Unit, the politics were the work.

"All the same, the unit did address a major inequality. Also, there was a radical feminist group, film makers and activists, who had a huge impact on the Australian Film Commission. They were astonishing in their ability to intimidate the bureaucracy into supporting more women. But I think it's quite clear in my work that my orientation isn't political or doesn't come out of modern politics."

There, of course, is the rub. Campion is, to a degree, the beneficiary of a group effort. But what makes her a remarkable director is a truly singular talent, which is why she squirms when asked about being the first woman to win the Palme d'Or. To mention her sex is, however inadvertently, to modify the accomplishment. But if art, as the singer K. D. Lang put it, "transcends the tools you carry," the fact remains that Campion's tools, especially when she is dealing with sexuality, are often splendidly, uniquely female.

It may also be her sex that allows Campion to confess that although she had received development money for *The Piano* from the Australian Film Commission, it was loneliness that drove her to accept the producer Jan Chapman's offer of work on Australian television.

The experience ballooned Campion's confidence to the point where she was bursting to speak with her own voice. But because she believed that neither her understanding nor her skills as a movie maker were yet up to *The Piano,* she chose instead to do "something wilder, a bit younger, a bit more obnoxious. Provocative, you know?" She did *Sweetie*.

Sweetie, which she cowrote with her then-boyfriend, Gerard Lee, is all those things. *Sweetie* is about a young woman whose burning desire to be in show business is predicated on her ability to ride a toppling chair until it (slowly) hits the ground. Sweetie was not supposed to be the star; her younger sister, a kind of walking recessive gene, was. But Sweetie, who is nuts, took over the film as surely as she took over her family.

An Angel at My Table came next. Originally, it was meant for New Zealand television. Had it not been, Laura Jones, who wrote the script, said she would have done it differently: "I might have thought of dealing with a smaller time frame. And one wouldn't normally have such discursive storytelling in a feature film. But it worked, which made me rethink what *does* work."

What works in *Angel* is Campion's eye. Every image is freighted with meaning. A teacher, an insignificant-looking young man bent on bonhomie, stretches himself along his desk. Janet Frame, shy, a virgin and irredeemably isolate, stares fixedly at his trousers' fly. There, under the buttons, is the means to connection. A student-teacher, Frame picks up the chalk. Suddenly, she doesn't know what it is, what it's for. "I write for Jane," Jones said, "in a way I couldn't write for any other director."

Finally, there is *The Piano. Sweetie* cost less than $1 million; *Angel,* very little more. *The Piano,* which had seed money from the Australian Film Commission and major money from its French producers, was big-budget and thus scary.

"I thought: 'I haven't got any excuses. I have enough money to do this film really well,' " Campion said. "But I soon realized the anxiety was stifling, that I had to throw it away and just be naughty.

"*The Piano,* like *A Girl's Own Story,* is my territory— things I know about, that nobody else could easily get access to. I'd become fascinated by early photographs of New Zealand, and especially by portraits of Europeans and married people, and I was dying to do my version of a period film. Also, I've always wanted to tell an erotic story, particularly from a woman's perspective."

The story is simple. Ada, a Scotswoman with an illegitimate child, is married by proxy to a New Zealand settler, Stewart, and shipped to the other side of the world. With her are her small daughter and her piano, which, together, are her voice. When Stewart refuses to transport the piano to his farm, another settler, Baines, buys it and makes a bargain. He will give the piano to Ada if she will give him piano lessons. In truth, he does not want to learn the piano. He wants to learn Ada.

Sam Neill plays Stewart, a more or less predictable piece of casting, since Neill, himself a New Zealander, specializes in projecting a certain innocent, albeit sexy, confusion. But Harvey Keitel, he of the terrier ferocity, is hardly the first person one would think of for a scarcely housebroken, illiterate English settler with a tattooed (Maori-style) nose. Nor does Holly Hunter, who won the best-actress award at Cannes, seem a natural for a 19th-century woman who's constrained not only by custom and corsets but also by her stubborn and seemingly intractable speechlessness. But Campion casts "according to whom I am attracted to, and some people can't understand at first glance why that would be. But if you can see the potential in that person's character, it's really more interesting that others cannot. Because they're going to learn through you."

Asked to describe working with Campion, Keitel said: "Jane Campion is a goddess, and it's difficult for a mere mortal to talk about a goddess. I fear being struck by lightning bolts." The next day he called to clarify, "What's unusual about her," he continued, "has to do with ethereal things. She is at play, like a warm breeze."

Fortunately for someone who prefers to build with concrete, there was Neill. "Jane works in an unusually intimate way with people," he said. "When you're an actor, you're always putting yourself in other people's hands anyway, and she repays the gesture many times over. Jane's interested in complexity, not reductiveness, and very sure of what she's doing. If you have an opinion contrary to hers, she listens with the greatest care and consideration, then does what she had in mind all along."

Genevieve Lemon, who played Sweetie and the silly, love-starved Nessie of *The Piano*, said of Campion: "She digs deep when she's working with an actor, and that can be pretty confronting. She's always saying, 'Strip, strip, give me less acting,' and you try to give her exactly what she wants because her instincts are so sound. Most of the time with a director you think, 'Stop! What's going on here? Where am I going?' But you trust Jane absolutely."

("Gen's method," Campion said, "is impenetrable by somebody else, but that's true of a lot of actors. How they do it is alarming for them. That's why you have to be very careful about interfering with their securities and their methods. I just contribute in however much room they leave for me to contribute.")

The Piano is intensely romantic on several counts. All three of its protagonists are sexual innocents (Stewart may even be a virgin), which is why their introduction to eroticism constitutes an inundation. Ada's music, which was composed by Michael Nyman and played by Hunter herself, is as somber and powerful as Ada is. And New Zealand's bush, albeit a very different landscape, seems as magical as the moors near Wuthering Heights.

Campion's movies don't resemble anyone else's, and neither do they resemble one another. The strange, skewed look of *Sweetie,* for example, was influenced by the work of certain American photographers, Diane Arbus in particular. The look of *Angel,* however, is simple, allusionless: it was Janet Frame's story, after all, and Campion "had to stay out of its way." But for *Piano,* Campion and the director of photography, Stuart Dryburgh, dove right in. Using as their starting point a mutual love of autochromes, an early color process based on potato dyes, they allowed some tints to completely drain scenes and turned the bush into a kind of underwater world.

"Only Stuart and I really liked what we liked," she said. "Everyone else was, 'Mmmmmmmmmm.' It's scary, you know? But to get a look you have to stick your foot out. You can't play it safe.

"I had this spooky psychological thing about *The Piano* before it began, which was how everybody was going to go nuts on the set. Because a film tends to set up the way people are going to behave. But then I said to myself, 'O.K., it doesn't actually matter what people do so long as you go through it, as long as you don't pull back, as long as you take responsibility.' In the end, the making of *The Piano* was an enormous pleasure, and it encouraged me to take some risks romantically which paid off very well."

"Getting married, you mean?" her visitor asked.

"Oh, no," Campion said. "I wanted to get married. Colin and I had been best friends for six or seven years. The big emotional risk was in becoming lovers."

Jan Chapman, who produced *The Piano,* works out of two large, airy rooms above a fish restaurant. Campion's apartment, though in a chic part of Sydney, is modest and does not feature an art collection. Laura Jones, upon entering a rather grand hotel for morning coffee, said, "This isn't my usual kind of place," and when asked about Robert Altman's film *The Player,* in which writers "pitch" and producers murder, replied, "Well, with us there's more chatting than pitching."

In June, Jones, Campion and Chapman were chatting about *The Portrait of a Lady,* the Henry James novel for which Jones is writing the adaptation, Campion is directing and Chapman is the script consultant. (Nicole Kidman will play the heroine, Isabel Archer, for whom self-creation and, indeed, self-perfection, is life's purpose.) Unlike Campion's other films, this one is large American dollars all the way—which at this point may make no difference in the final product. But it might have made a difference once. "The Government support here," Chapman said, "has enabled producers and directors to pursue their own talents early on. As soon as you start having big systems trying to simplify ideas you lose that spark." And although she is as reluctant as Campion to discuss sexual politics, she added: "And because of this Government assistance, nothing stopped us. There wasn't a male-based system that, consciously or unconsciously, we had to adapt ourselves to."

Portrait, Campion said, is one of her favorite books, partly because she herself feels "so Isabel Archerish. I think that coming from Australia or New Zealand now makes one more like Americans going to Europe were then than Americans going to Europe are now. They're much more sophisticated, whereas we have more of a colonial attitude about ourselves, a more can-do, anything's-possible attitude. I felt so much like Isabel as a young woman, a sense of having extraordinary potential without knowing what the hell to do with it. Before *Piano,* I wouldn't have had the guts to take on a big classic thing. But now I don't feel frightened at all.

"I seem to have been able to make a career out of doing what I feel like doing, so why not keep doing it? What's corrupting is wanting to be more important. You want to be more arty—you get your identity from that. Or you get your identity out of making more money. I get my pleasure, which is far more important to me, out of trying to follow my instincts."

In tracking those instincts, her film editor Veronika Jenet said, "Jane always surrounds herself with people who are very supportive and give her free range." If sanity lies in knowing your strengths and how to capitalize on them, then Campion is clearly a monument thereto.

By the middle of June, the chatting with Laura Jones and Jan Chapman about Isabel, her aunt Mrs. Touchett, her friend Henrietta Stackpole, the sinuous Madame Merle ("Great parts for women! But, of course, the point about Henry James is that all the parts are good") and Isabel's quartet of swains had more or less ceased. Jane had high blood pressure, and nobody could tell her and Colin precisely what that might mean. Still, they consoled themselves with the thought that, after having had three miscarriages, Jane had only two weeks to go to term. Two weeks to go—it was like being in a marathon and knowing you had only another ten yards to run.

"I was getting a bit sick of myself toward the end of my 30's, thinking, 'Is this all there is to know?'" she said. "Having a baby has completely distracted me from that. Now I have a big stake in the future because his will be part of mine. At the same time, I'll be forced back, because I'll be part of being a child again through him. And as he grows up and has his problems, I'll be part of that, too."

A few days later, Jane Campion's son, Jasper, was delivered by emergency Caesarean section. His parents were told almost immediately that he could not live outside an incubator, and that he would die soon. When, in fact, was up to them. Twelve days after his birth, Jane and Colin took Jasper home, where he died the following dawn.

The day after Jasper's cremation, 35 of his parents' family and friends gathered at Neilson Park, on the cliffs overlooking Sydney Harbor, to honor his brief life. Rugs were spread for the guests to sit upon, food was served and Jane

and Colin talked about their baby and what he had meant to them. There were other speakers, and some people read poems they had written.

To hear of that sad, brave ceremony was suddenly to remember Colette's harsh "Who said you should be happy? Do your work." It was also to hope that in special gifts lie special consolations.

Stella Bruzzi   (essay date October 1993)

SOURCE: "Bodyscape," in *Sight and Sound,* Vol. 3, No. 10, October, 1993, pp. 6-10.

[*In the following essay, Bruzzi compares* The Piano *to other dramatic works dealing with sexuality in the Victorian Age and argues that* The Piano *is a "cryptic and evocative exploration of how women's sexuality, clothes and lives interconnect."*]

At the beginning of *The Piano,* Ada (Holly Hunter), a mute Scottish woman, arrives in New Zealand with her nine-year-old daughter Flora. They disembark on a remote beach, where they are left by the sailors who accompanied them to await Ada's new husband Stewart (Sam Neill), a rich local landowner. Their strung-out possessions are silhouetted in a flimsy line against the evening sun. Another silhouetted, skeletal structure comes into shot: a tent, made from Ada's hoops and underskirts, beneath which they shelter for the night.

The Piano ends with a parallel scene as Ada, having left Stewart, returns to the beach and boards a boat with Flora, her lover Baines (Harvey Keitel) and the possessions she arrived with. To preserve the equilibrium of the boat she orders her prized piano to be discarded. As it is tipped overboard her foot is caught in the unravelling rope and she is dragged under. Her upturned hoops and skirts billow out against the luminous water. At this point, as at others through the film, Ada appears to be trapped and defeated by her clothes. At the last moment, however, she disentangles herself and swims to the surface, leaving her shoe behind; she has, as her voiceover says, "chosen life". Her clothes, as elsewhere, work for her.

The Piano is not a simple women's film about a woman's past, but rather a cryptic and evocative exploration of how women's sexuality, clothes and lives interconnect. It is set in New Zealand in the mid-1800s, and though the exact dates of events are never specified, the age which the costumes, morality and gender relations evoke is central to the way the film tackles its theme. Why has Jane Campion chosen to frame the story of Ada's sexual and emotional awakening in terms of the last century? The Victorian age is seen today as synonymous with the oppression of female sexuality; everything from the voluminous clothes to the many laws which deprived wives of financial autonomy legitimised a patriarchy which kept women in check. In order to express themselves, women were constrained to invent male pseudonyms, to 'ghost' music and art for husbands and brothers, to create elaborate metaphors for their experiences. Their voices were often heard only indirectly: they fabricated unruly, angry alter egos, such as Charlotte Brontë's "mad woman in the attic" or the monstrous creation of Mary Shelley's *Frankenstein,* or codified their anger against male brutality as did Artemesia Gentileschi in her violent depiction of *Judith Beheading Holofernes.*

In such a male-dominated history, the experiences of women have been almost entirely obscured, and women since have invaded the past to liberate the female imagination and sexuality, as well as to help them to make sense of the present. Since the 70s women have been unearthing forgotten literary works, creating an alternative cultural canon, reinterpreting male texts, and forefronting experiences deemed peripheral. The desire to articulate this forgotten past is perhaps the common impulse behind such diverse works as Jean Rhys' prequel to *Jane Eyre, Wide Sargasso Sea,* A. S. Byatt's *Possession,* Sally Potter's film version of *Orlando*—and Jane Campion's ***The Piano*** which empowers Ada with a 1990s strength and self-knowledge that enables her to transcend the limitations of such disempowered nineteenth-century heroines as Emily Brontë's Catherine.

The two most pervasive models of reclamation of the past used by women film-makers could be termed the 'liberal' and the 'sexual'. The liberal method concentrates on finding a political and ideological affinity between the struggles of women in the present and figures from the past. Campion's film about New Zealand writer Janet Frame, ***An Angel At My Table,*** Margarethe von Trotta's film biography *Rosa Luxemburg,* and the repeated feminist revivals of Ibsen's plays stem from a liberal impulse to utilise the juxtaposition between past and present to illuminate both. The 'sexual' model, by contrast, foregrounds the personal, more hidden aspects of past women's lives—their dormant passions, sexual frustrations and the process of denial which governed their relationships with (primarily) men. Although both types of looking back involve costume, in liberal films these are merely signifiers to carry information about country, class and period. Films interested in the emotive aspects of the past imbue the clothes themselves with sensuality, so they become essential components of the sexual dialogue.

The pioneering Australasian women's film of the 70s was Gillian Armstrong's *My Brilliant Career* (1979), a feminist reworking of the traditionally male genre of the big liberal history movie—Stanley Kramer's *Inherit the Wind,* Fred Zinnemann's *A Man for All Seasons* and so on. *My Brilliant Career,* a quintessential feminist fairy tale, is based on Miles Franklin's semi-biographical novel about Sybylla Melvyn, a teenage girl from the Bush who chooses a career over a husband. The headstrong Sybylla embodies the struggle for independence and emancipation which was taking place in Australia during the 1890s, but she is equally a construct of the late 1970s—a case of the second women's movement making sense of the first. *My Brilliant Career* was an important feel-good movie for women of my generation, who in 1979 were much the same age as Sybylla was in the late 1890s. Women were still uncertain about what they wanted, but were sure that it was not what was on offer. As Sybylla puts it: being "a wife out in the bush, having a baby every year."

More crucial to liberal movies than the superficial authenticity of meticulously costumed films such as Christine Edzard's *Little Dorritt* or *The Fool* is a broad awareness of contemporary events, which form a discrete backdrop to the narrative. *My Brilliant Career* spans five years; Sybylla's voiceover states that the film begins in "Possum Gully, Australia 1897", and at the end we are told that *My Brilliant Career* was published in "Edinburgh, 1901". Australia (far in advance of Britain, which did not grant women the vote until after the First World War) was then in the midst of a successful movement for universal suffrage; two states, South and Western Australia, had already changed the electoral system, while Sybylla's native New South Wales was on the verge of doing so. Sybylla epitomises the exhilaration of this era—her twitching anticipation as she stares into the dawn horizon after posting her manuscript is almost tangible.

The liberal film discerns patterns or draws out meanings which at the time may have been obscured. Sybylla is both historical and contemporary, her struggle (with herself, her family and men) both parochial and perennial. *My Brilliant Career* thus operates as a metaphor for a universal female dilemma. Sybylla remains such a positive role model for women (and paradoxically attractive to all the men in the film) because she pursues her own goals rather than those society would impose. Though she is repeatedly warned that "loneliness is a terrible price to pay for independence", she ultimately refuses all proposals of marriage and puts her own aspirations first. The straightforwardness of Sybylla's choice might in a modern context—such as the much untidier world of Armstrong's latest film *The Last Days of Chez Nous*—appear woefully naive. Placed within a historical context, however, the dilemma and decision gain strength from their very simplicity. The liberal analogy film functions best when the metaphor is less complex than the issues it raises about present-day society. Thus Sybylla's "wildness of spirit" and pursuit of a "career"—which at the start could be almost anything that got her out of the Bush—were points of identification for 1970s women with more specific concerns.

The Piano offers a more elliptical way of examining the past—one based on complex, hard-to-define emotions and attractions rather than concrete events. This is not to say that ***The Piano*** is apolitical, but that unlike *My Brilliant Career,* which carries its political commentary through its plot, ***The Piano*** does so through clothes and sexuality. Films which use sexuality to explore women's unspoken pasts are more personal, more challenging, more dangerous than their liberal counterparts. It is difficult to envisage women objecting to an uncomplicated liberal film like *My Brilliant Career,* but a sexual film such as Liliana Cavani's *The Night Porter* (1974), which examines Nazism through the sado-masochistic relationship between Max, an ex-camp officer, and Lucia, a survivor, frequently repels its audiences. Cavani confronts us with an ambiguous and unpalatable sexual history in which a woman chooses to reenter a violent relationship that eventually leads to her death. Perhaps the film says the unsayable: that Lucia is not Max's victim, but his equal; that brutal sexuality is not simply a male construct.

Campion's innovation in ***The Piano*** is to discover a language which articulates a radical opposition to the restrictions imposed on nineteenth-century women through the very means by which those restrictions are usually manifested—clothes. Throughout the film clothes function as agents to liberate rather than to constrain. Visually this is suggested by recurrent images that demonstrate how clothes are constructed, drawing a distinction between the harsh frames—Ada's hoops and the wired angel wings of Flora's Bluebeard costume—and the softness and fluidity of the fabrics stretched over them. Both Ada and Flora are seen adjusting to their clothes, exploring and adapting them and finally learning to feel comfortable in them. To return briefly to the mad woman in the attic and Frankenstein's monster: both Charlotte Brontë and Mary Shelley were impelled to create metaphors which externalised the internal 'demons' of their anger; Campion in **The Piano** finds a way for Ada to express herself through (rather than despite of) her Victorian persona.

Campion's reclamation of women's sexual pasts is exhilarating, but Ada's eventual liberation is presented as an arduous struggle against the systematic denial of the existence of female desire. As wife to Stewart and lover to Baines, she represents conflicting aspects of Victorian womanhood. On the one hand she is the trapped, unwilling wife—a New Zealand Madame Bovary with apparently as much chance of escape or fulfilment from her stifling bourgeois marriage. She is also, in her refusal to speak, representative of what the medical profession branded a 'hysterical' woman; catatonia, anorexia, chronic fatigue and other forms of self-imposed sensory deprivation were commonplace among dissatisfied and desperate Victorian wives, the majority of whom were regarded as dysfunctional rather than as unhappy. Through the elaborate clothes-language she formulates with Baines, however, Ada engineers her escape from Stewart, drudgery and sexual repression—a modern and radical reassessment of the options available to women in the 1850s.

Clothes traditionally signify restraint and conformity; they have covered our nakedness and hidden our shame. Joe Orton's black farce *What the Butler Saw*, for example, concludes with Rance's weary nod in the direction of respectability: "Let us put on our clothes and face the world." The Victorians were obsessed with hiding anything that could be deemed suggestive of sex or nakedness, daubing fig leaves on Adams and Eves and covering the bare legs of tables. The sexuality of Victorian women was repressed or presumed not to exist at all: Queen Victoria herself was so convinced that female sexuality was a dutiful response to men's demands that she denied the possibility of lesbianism.

Victorian women's clothes, as much as the way they were treated, made them inactive and vulnerable. At the start of Caryl Churchill's 1979 play *Cloud Nine*, set in a "British colony in Africa in Victorian times", the colonial's wife, Betty, complains to her husband because her servant has refused to get the book she requested, having snapped: "Fetch it yourself. You've got legs under that dress." *Cloud Nine* is an elaborate dissection of the sexual underworld of Victorian society. Largely through the use of cross-dressing, Churchill challenges and ridicules the ac-

cepted notions of Victorian morality and behaviour by inverting the assumption that what people look like and wear are straightforward indicators of who they are or what they are feeling. So Betty, the embodiment of what "a wife should be", is played by a bearded man, her son by a woman. Throughout Act I characters are rarely permitted to have sex with either the individual or the gender they desire, and the action culminates in the face-saving marriage between the lesbian governess and the intrepid gay explorer. Queen Victoria's model household is a fantasy, a flimsy front for confused morals and anarchic sexuality. Churchill's solution is to liberate the characters by transporting them into the permissive 1970s, because only now, *Cloud Nine* intimates, can clothes be truly compatible with gender and sexuality. In this instance, as in the final sequences of Potter's *Orlando,* the analogy between present and past is made explicit through direct juxtaposition.

The Piano enters into a much more complex dialogue with women's sexual histories, since the present-day consciousness remains embedded exclusively within the nineteenth-century narrative. The sexual experiences of the three protagonists—Ada, Baines and Stewart—are markedly different; Stewart, the stiff, bourgeois gentleman, represents respectability and ignorance, while Ada and Baines epitomise radicalism and liberation. Stewart, like head of household Clive in *Cloud Nine,* is frustrated by how far he is from unlocking the 'mystery' of sexuality and remains unable to break free of his social and gender stereotype. He is left stranded, yearning but unable to deal with the reality of closeness. We do not feel for Clive as his servant cocks his rifle and aims at him, but Stewart's isolation is painful. By the end, he realises that with Baines Ada has discovered an intimacy he, frozen in his social role, will always be excluded from. At this point, the only option he can see is violence: he hurls Ada against the wall and hacks off her finger when she refuses to deny her love for Baines.

Stewart's first appearance in the film—at the head of the welcoming party to greet his new wife—is in his muddied formal dark suit and top hat. He is embarrassed and puzzled to discover Ada and Flora sheltering under the hoops and underskirt, and awkwardly commences his rehearsed greeting. Images of a furtive, frustrated gentleman at a peep show spring to mind as Campion distances him from the female sexuality he can never understand or get close to through a series of classic male voyeur images: squinting through a camera eyepiece at Ada posing unhappily in her wedding dress, or sneaking a glance at her making love to Baines through the cracks in the walls or between the floorboards.

Stewart is clearly identified as a rigid masculine figure marooned in what becomes a feminine world. For much of the time he inhabits a different film from Ada. Stewart's sensibility and world view is closer to that of another Australasian Victorian costume drama, Peter Weir's *Picnic At Hanging Rock* (1975), in which three schoolgirls mysteriously disappear while on a Valentine's Day picnic. Here female sexuality is also consistently symbolised through clothes, but the film is built on the mystery rather than the attainment of female sexuality. Unable to articulate their desire, the men in the film become deviant voyeurs, transferring their sexual desire from the girls to their virginal dresses. Thus the dirty scrap of lace which the youthful Michael discovers during the search is invested with sexually charged significance, as is the fact that one girl is subsequently found "intact" minus her corset. *Picnic At Hanging Rock* is the crystallisation of the Victorian man's perception of intimacy as unobtainable, bewildering, and fascinating.

In *The Piano* Stewart's predicament is more ambiguous. Denied intimacy, he ultimately unleashes his pent-up sexuality by attempting to rape Ada in the woods. Ada struggles, falls over her skirts and is pulled to the ground. She seems defeated, but is eventually saved by her cumbersome, all-enveloping clothes. Stewart's aggression is deflected by the symbol of Victorian femininity—the hooped skirt—and she escapes. In one of the few scenes when he is alone with his wife, Ada awakens Stewart's desire by skimming his chest with the back of her hand, but when he asks to touch her she recoils. The following night, as Ada strokes his back and buttocks, it is Stewart who wants to stop. What sets Stewart apart from the men in *Picnic At Hanging Rock* is that he reaches the painful point of realising that there is more to sexual contact than sneaking glimpses, frustrated brutality and being touched.

Much of *The Piano* depicts a life which conforms to Stewart's masculine perception. New Zealand may have been the first country to grant women the vote, but little of this liberalism is manifested in the first part of the film. Often Ada is as quintessentially the Victorian woman as Stewart is the Victorian man; on the beach in the first scene, for example, she looks like a doll beneath the exaggerated hugeness of her travelling outfit and lampshade bonnet. Women's clothes are presented as constricting, ugly, absurd; the multiple skirts which trip Ada and Flora as they trudge through the mud, and which make it ludicrously difficult for Aunt Morag to relieve herself when "caught short" in the woods. Clothes seem liberating only when they come off, as when Flora dances and cartwheels across the beach in her petticoat. That is, until Ada starts to fall in love with Baines.

In this relationship, the modernity of Campion's response to the past dominates, the potential for sexual expression is realised, and clothes are no longer socially determined. Physically Baines is Stewart's opposite: he never appears dressed as a colonial master and his face is pricked with Maoriesque markings. It is this unconventionality which frees Ada.

The relationship begins when Baines saves Ada's prized piano by intimating a desire to learn how to play. The instrument is brought to his hut, and Stewart tells Ada she is to instruct him. Baines' fascination is not with learning, but with watching Ada play, so a bizarre bargain is struck whereby Ada is allowed to play and win back her piano, while he is permitted to watch, to touch and gradually to unclothe her. As spectators it is clear that we are entering—or rather intruding on—an intensely private world. This intrusion begins one evening after the piano has arrived at Baines' hut: Baines gets up from his bed, removes

his shirt and, naked, uses it indulgently to dust the piano, circling it, judging it, getting to know it. Baines considers himself alone, we really shouldn't be there, but we are intrigued by the ritual.

In this formal Victorian world, Harvey Keitel's proud nakedness is both shocking and liberating. Convention is inverted as the man is constructed as a sexual being before the woman. We the audience find ourselves privy to a private dialogue which imbues clothes with a potency beyond the bounds of fetishism and makes what follows an elaborate seduction rather than a cheap strip. This is partly due to the scenes' curious rhythm, a slow but relentless evolution as Ada reworks and refines repeated musical refrains while Baines tells her when to stop, what garment to remove or when he wants to kiss her or lie with her in response to a complex set of rules agreed beforehand. The rich obscurity of the clothes-language is counterbalanced by an incongruous matter-of-factness that puts the relationship on a different plane from anything else.

The language has to do with the sensuality of clothes: how they feel, smell and look, not just what they might signify, as in *Picnic At Hanging Rock*. Thus Baines' rapture can be contained within the minute act of smelling and burying his face in one of Ada's garments while she remains wrapped in her music. Campion's fascination with clothes is reminiscent of that described by the seventeenth-century poet and priest Robert Herrick, whose illicit passion for Julia is displaced on to her clothes—her lace is "erring", and beneath her "tempestuous petticoat" lurks "a careless shoestring in whose tie/ I see a wild civility." Herrick creates a clothes-eroticism so enticing that Julia becomes insignificant by comparison.

In *The Piano,* the point is not that the clothes are substitutes for Ada, but that they are part of her and her body's sensuality. Perhaps the film's most erotically charged moment is when Baines, crouched under the piano, discovers a tiny hole in Ada's stocking and slowly caresses it, skin touching skin. Later, when Ada is sitting at the piano in just her bodice and skirt, Baines stands behind her naked to the waist and glides his hands across her bare shoulders. Again the camera acts in collusion with the characters, skirting around them as Baines circles Ada, picking up the charge between them. Ada and Baines are gradually becoming equals, as the traditional striptease relationship of one person clothed watching another undress is supplanted. When they finally have sex, they undress together.

Why is this secret language not ludicrous like the adolescent heavings of *Picnic At Hanging Rock* or the misguided gay advances of *Cloud Nine*? The strength of the affair in the *The Piano* lies in Ada's responsiveness; she is no longer the passive Victorian woman, acted upon rather than acting. At first she remains wary and resentful of Baines' bargain, yet she gradually discovers that the relationship can offer her the freedom she, with her mute defiance, had been holding out for. Yet this is not an easy realisation: when Ada returns to Baines' hut having already acknowledged that she loves him, she slaps his cheek and pummels his chest before they kiss, as if she needs to repel him as she repelled Stewart. Then they have sex.

The relationship with Baines is the catalyst to Ada's sensual awakening. When she arrived in New Zealand her piano was her only liberation; she had not spoken since she was six and she had been married off to a stranger. Through *The Piano* Ada discovers the means to articulate what she wants—firstly through constructing an intimacy around clothes, through choosing Baines over Stewart, choosing not to be drowned by her sinking piano, and finally choosing to learn to speak when she and Baines have started a new life together in Nelson. The closing image is of a woman attached to the piano by a taut rope like a graceful helium balloon; beautiful in death but silent. But however momentarily enticing this ocean death may be, Ada chooses to reject it and to live. *The Piano* is primarily but not exclusively Ada's liberation; it is also the reclamation of women's desires, the sexual personae which the past silenced.

Lizzie Francke   (review date November 1993)

SOURCE: A review of *The Piano,* in *Sight and Sound,* Vol. 3, No. 11, November, 1993, pp. 50-1.

[*In the following excerpt, Francke comments on theme in* The Piano, *noting that the film "demands as much a physical and emotional response as an intellectual one."*]

For a while I could not think, let alone write, about *The Piano* without shaking. Precipitating a flood of feelings, *The Piano* demands as much a physical and emotional response as an intellectual one. As with the Maoris in the film who, believing the Bluebeard shadow play to be real, attempt to stop the old duke add another wife to his collection, I wanted to rush at the screen and shout and scream. Not since the early days of cinema, when audiences trampled over each other towards the exit to avoid the train emerging from the screen, could I imagine the medium of film to be so powerful. Like Ada's piano music, which is described as "a mood that passes through you . . . a sound that creeps into you", this is cinema that fills every sense. The opening shot of delicate pink skin smoothed over the screen, as fingers hide eyes, suggests the membrane that the audience must burst through to make the painful and traumatic trek into the film's dark, gnarled woods, finally to be released in the watery death/birth of an ending. Moving pictures indeed.

A film about silence and expression beyond language, *The Piano* resonates with the silences embedded deep in the texts of such 19th-century women writers as Emily Brontë or Emily Dickinson, women who hid scraps of their work under blotters, who hid themselves behind pseudonyms. They, like the strident composer Ada, were told that their creations were most irregular. In *The Piano,* Jane Campion feels her way around those echoing caves upon which they built their haunted houses of fiction. It is a virtuoso interpretation of that literary sensibility in a cinematic form, truer than any doggedly faithful adaptation of, say, *Wuthering Heights.* Indeed, *The Piano* puts us in the grip of the repressions of the 19th century—an era which saw polite society sheathing the ankles of piano legs with special socks in case they gave young men ideas. Such is the erotic object at the heart of the film.

Campion is playful with the period's more bizarre neuroses. The film flashes with moments of indignant humour, such as when Flora is ordered to whitewash some trees after she and her young friends are caught rubbing up against them in a playful—and unwitting—imitation of the sexual act. But Campion is careful not to let the comedy take hold. Under less thoughtful direction Stewart could have been the buffoonish patriarch, hauling his white man's burden behind him. He treats the Maoris like children, paying them in buttons and staking out his territory over their sacred burial grounds. After the shocking punishment he metes out to Ada, he informs her, "I only clipped your wings." He is, as one Maori dubs him, an emotionally shrivelled "old dry balls". Yet this awful paterfamilias is invested with some sympathy. He is a confused man, who attempts to guy his world down in the chaos of change, who wants his music—and his sex—played to a strict time, so fearful is he of the other rhythms that might move him. If only he could listen, like Ada's previous lover and the father of Flora, upon whom she could "lay thoughts on his mind like a sheet". It is the communication of the gentle caress, the smoothing of nimble fingers over sheets and scales.

Conventional language imprisons Ada like the crinoline, which ambiguously also marks out her private, silent space (the skirt provides an intimate tent for Ada and Flora to shelter in the beach). Crucially, it is the written word that finally betrays her as she sends her love note to Baines, who cannot read but who knows the languages of those around him. Her arrangement with Baines has previously been based on a sensuous play of touch, smell and sound.

Bodies become instruments of expression, while the piano smelling of scent and salt becomes corporeal. Baines' massaging of Ada's leg through a hole in her black worsted stocking is given the same erotic charge as her fingering of the scales. After such libidinous exchange, the marking down of her feelings for him with words only brings destruction, which is hastened by Flora, Ada's little echoing mouthpiece (who is also the most compulsive and intriguing of fabulists).

What to make, then, of Ada's sudden plunge after her lifeless piano, which can no longer sing, into the watery grave? Ada's bid to enter into the order of language brings only death. Her will moves her finally to wave, not drown, to take life.

But there is the disquieting shadow of death cast on to the coda of the film. Brighter than in any of the previous scenes, she is seen in mourning grey, her head covered in a black-edged veil, tapping out notes with the silver artificial finger, which now marks her as the town freak. She is learning to speak but her voice rings the knell—"death, death, death". At night she dreams of her husk, anchored to the piano, skirts billowing out like a balloon, floating in the silence of the deep, deep sea. Impossible to shake off, it is the final image in a film that weighs heavy on the heart and mind, that drags us down into our own shuddering silence.

Brian D. Johnson (review date 22 November 1993)

SOURCE: "Rain Forest Rhapsody: *The Piano* Is a Work of Passion and Beauty," in *Maclean's,* Vol. 106, No. 47, November 22, 1993, pp. 72, 74.

[*In the following review, Johnson praises* The Piano *on a number of counts, including its story and strong female leading role, and describes it as "a welcome antidote to almost everything that seems to be wrong with the movies."*]

Every now and then, a movie comes along that restores faith in the visionary power of cinema. **The Piano,** a haunting fable about a mute mail-order bride caught between two men in the wilds of 19th-century New Zealand, is that kind of film. It arrives as a welcome antidote to almost everything that seems to be wrong with the movies. People complain that there are no good stories, that there are no strong roles for women, that there is no eroticism, just sex—no magic, just manipulation. On all counts, **The Piano** serves as an exhilarating exception to the rule. And for New Zealand-born director Jane Campion, it marks a milestone. Last spring, she became the first woman in the 48-year history of the Cannes Film Festival to win the grand prize, the Palme d'Or. And her film—a wildly original work of passion, beauty and intelligence—confirms her status, at 39, as one of the best directors working today.

With **The Piano,** Campion expands her repertoire of strong-willed, unbalanced heroines. Her first feature, **Sweetie** (1989), was the offbeat tale of a young woman's lunatic spiral of self-destruction. Then, with **An Angel at My Table** (1990), Campion dramatized the true story of New Zealand novelist Janet Frame, who was wrongly institutionalized for schizophrenia. "I like working with extreme characters," the director told *Maclean's* recently, "characters that carry more extremely a lot of the syndromes that most of us share in a minor way." But unlike her first two movies, made for about $1 million each, **The Piano** is a sumptuous period saga with a name cast— Holly Hunter, Harvey Keitel and Sam Neill.

The drama of a love triangle among colonials in the bush, the movie has the romantic intensity of a Brontë novel. But despite its 19th-century setting, **The Piano** seems in tune with the times, resonant with contemporary obsessions ranging from gender confusion to aboriginal rights. And although the script was Campion's own invention, it has a timeless enchantment. "It does feel archetypal," she acknowledges. "It's like a Grimm's fairy tale—I don't even feel that it's quite mine."

The movie's spell is cast right from the opening scene, a sequence of breathtaking images filmed on a savage New Zealand shore: a woman in a bonnet and hoopskirt clambering out of a boat in rough seas with her daughter, men hauling a large crate on to the beach, mountains of surf crashing behind them, the woman's hand poking through a hole in the crate and caressing the keys of a piano.

The woman, a Scot named Ada (Hunter), has been imported to New Zealand for an arranged marriage with a settler, Stewart (Neill), whom she has never met. Ada is mute. For mysterious reasons, she has not spoken a word since the age of six. The piano belongs to her; it is her voice. And she becomes understandably distraught when Stewart decides to leave it on the beach, rather than drag it through the bush. Later, Ada persuades his neighbor, Baines (Keitel), to retrieve it. He is an illiterate colonist who has gone native, decorating his face with Maori tattoos. Baines is the 19th-century answer to the New Man.

After salvaging the piano, he buys it from Ada's husband in exchange for some land. Ada is furious. But Baines offers to sell the instrument back to her in return for "piano lessons"—one black key for every session. His proposal is merely a pretext for seduction. While she plays, he watches, and inch by inch, he prods her into stripping away her Victorian layers of inhibition. "She's an object of curiosity to him," says Campion. "But what he really wants is a sort of reciprocity. He wants her to feel for him the way she feels about her piano."

The adulterous romance, and its dire consequences, take place amid primeval surroundings, a claustrophobic world of rain and mud. Campion has filmed the forest in shades of ultramarine, giving it an underwater look that activates the central metaphor: drowning.

For a director with such a strong visual sense, Campion is exceptionally good with actors. In **The Piano,** she draws note-perfect performances from her cast. Without uttering a word (except in the narration), Hunter expresses herself with the kind of power and subtlety that wins Oscars. Neill modulates his character's insensitivity with touching strains of pathos. And as Ada's nine-year-old daughter, an impetuous sprite named Flora, New Zealand's Anna Paquin is amazing. Most remarkably, though, Keitel trades in his hard-boiled, urban persona to play a beguiling romantic lead with a soft Scottish burr.

Campion's stars, meanwhile, are rhapsodic about her talents. "I would have played the third Maori from the left for Jane," says Neill. "She's a fantastic woman and a great director." Kietel calls her "a goddess."

She is a vivacious woman, with blue eyes, waves of blond hair and a reckless laugh. One morning last month, weary from jet lag, Campion talked with *Maclean's* in a Manhattan hotel room, absently stirring a bowl of soggy granola and berries. It was her first round of interviews since Cannes, and stepping back into the public eye was not easy. Last June, just two months after winning the Palme d'Or, she gave birth to her first child, Jasper, who died 12 days later.

Campion now lives in Sydney, Australia, with husband Colin Englert, a TV producer and director. The child of two actors, she was raised in New Zealand, then attended Victoria University in Melbourne. She chose to study anthropology, she says, "because it seemed like the course where the greatest proportion of students passed. But it became quite a passion for me." After graduating, Campion dove into another obsession, enrolling in a Sydney art school where minimalism and performance art were all the rage. "It was unbelievably exciting," she recalls. "The school was run by really young artists who had incredibly tough standards. I was having nervous breakdowns. Trying to find your own personal vision—that was the challenge."

Campion found her vision by staging "little plays about women and sex," which led her to make her first short film. She went on to attend film school and work with Australia's Women's Film Unit. "But I am very influenced by painting," she says. "That's where I come into film-making. I do love films, but I'm not a film buff at all. When people go on about Preston Sturges and all that, I'm completely lost."

Influences of both painting and anthropology surface in *The Piano,* a sexual gothic tableau that Campion seems to have divined from her New Zealand roots. It is a primal tale of ancestral innocence. And the anthropology, she says, is intuitive—"it's behind me in the layering of meanings and cultural symbols."

She dreamt up the idea for *The Piano* well before making her first film. But it took time to work up the nerve, and the money, to execute it. "I really wanted to do a love story where you could see the growth from fetishism towards eroticism, and to more of a blend of love and sexuality," she says. "These characters are approaching sex with really no experience. Although Ada's had a child, we imagine it was from a pretty rudimentary experience."

The director takes issue with the way sex is usually portrayed in movies. "One of the obsessions, with men directing sex scenes, is to show sex as they would do it," she says, laughing at the idea. "So there's a sort of athleticism involved. And they try to turn the audience on in a softporn kind of way." She adds, "I don't mind if the sex in my film does titillate or arouse, but that's not the ambition in itself. The important thing is that it doesn't seem out of place for the characters."

An unspoken feminism seems to inform Campion's attitude, and her sense of humor. "But at the time I was writing *The Piano,*" she recalls, "I thought I wouldn't like to be pigeonholed as a feminist. Now I think that yes, I really am a strong feminist, in the sense that I like women a lot and I am curious about women. Also, men do seem to have the obvious, literal power and wealth." Campion appears unimpressed by the obvious. But, after improvising a career out of intangibles, with *The Piano* she has found her voice and taken her place as a diva among directors.

Stuart Klawans   (review date 6 December 1993)

SOURCE: Review of *The Piano,* in *The Nation,* New York, Vol. 257, No. 19, December 6, 1993, pp. 704-06.

[*In the following mixed review, Klawans finds* The Piano *contrived and allegorized, but acknowledges that most viewers will admire the film's eroticism and formal inventiveness.*]

A skeptic's notes on the most believed-in movie of the year:

No one will deny that Jane Campion's *The Piano* is a genuinely erotic picture. That alone would have made it stand out in any era; it glows all the brighter today, when screen couplings resemble either the Clash of the Titans (*Basic Instinct*) or a perfume ad (*Henry and June*). What a stimulus, what a relief, to see Holly Hunter and Harvey Keitel get naked in *The Piano,* in a scene with both heat *and* moisture; what delicious suspense later on, when Hunter explores the skittish body of Sam Neill. Poems will soon be written about the curves of the performers' buttocks as they're outlined in candlelight; about the atmosphere that surrounds the dropping away of each item of clothing; about the immediate tactile shock when flesh first touches flesh in the film, in closeup, as a fingertip covers a tiny hole in Hunter's stocking. Such moments are surely beyond even a skeptic's power to resist.

Nor could the most hardened skeptic doubt the beauty of *The Piano*. Campion has set the film in the wilds of New Zealand, where silver waves pound the beach beneath a misty, purplish horizon and lush greenery spouts from primordial muck. Yet Campion is such a formidable imagemaker that the landscape, for her, is more of a surplus than a necessity. In an early scene, for example, Hunter and her movie daughter (Anna Paquin) must camp out for one night on the beach. Campion has them take shelter beneath a hoop skirt, which, lit from within, shines on the screen like an improbable Chinese lantern. That's how good Jane Campion is—she transforms everything she sees. A teacup in Sam Neill's hand, abruptly shown from straight above, turns into a placid little pool, where the character's desires have been contained. A set of fingers, held close to the lens, turns into an abstract pattern of red lights and fuzzy shadows—the curtain of mystery that must part for the film to reveal itself.

That shot through the fingers functions as more than just a moment's decoration. Though Campion has an eye for sensual pleasures, she also (as an honest skeptic will admit) has a mind for themes and motifs; and so she thickens her film with multiple peekaboo shots and a continual wagging of fingers. Characters in *The Piano* are forever spying on one another; digits are always talking. You will also notice that a good many of the characters are easily influenced—they tend to ape one another's words and gestures and show a weakness for theatrical illusion. The heroine's daughter, having been cast in a church pageant, wears her angel's wings ever after and tries to live up to them. A group of Maoris, alarmed at a pantomime in the same pageant, storms the stage; though later, when a similar crisis erupts in real life, the same Maoris don't budge. People who are malleable and credulous, the film seems to argue, are likely to be undependable to boot.

Since that is one of the morals to be drawn from *The Piano,* I will assume I have Jane Campion's permission for skepticism. Her film is astonishing, even ravishing, in many ways. But why are so many people swallowing it whole, and why (in my case) did it not go down?

Here is the story:

A nineteenth-century Scotswoman, Ada, is sent off with her daughter to New Zealand, there to marry a settler named Stewart, whom she has never met. For reasons that Ada herself does not understand, she gave up speaking at age 6. Now she communicates only through writing, sign language, occasional feats of mental telepathy and (above all) piano playing. Her music, composed for the film by Michael Nyman, is supposed to be original, impassioned and wild. Actually, it's just a lot of modal noodling, in a style that goes over well today on sound-tracks and in the tonier Los Angeles restaurants but that in the nineteenth century would have been considered not so much eccentric as brain-damaged. Ada, however, is not brain-damaged. She is just inexplicably mute and intensely piano-dependent and indomitably strong-willed, though not so much as to prevent her husband (the one she's never met before) from abandoning her indispensable piano on the beach. It's too heavy, he says, to carry to their far-off home. But geography turns out to be variable in this movie. When a tattooed, gone-native neighbor named Baines later takes an interest in Ada, he not only has the piano delivered straight to his house but even contracts for a tuner to visit him in the inaccessible, photogenic wilds.

Sexy stuff then happens between Baines and the strong-willed Ada, who doesn't like him at first but then does—just as her daughter abruptly stops despising Stewart and comes to adore him. (As Darryl Zanuck used to decree in his celebrated script conferences, "Her love turns to hate!") Eventually, Stewart gets wise and locks up his wife, who responds by playing finger exercises on his spine. Now remember, Stewart is a thoroughly rigid, shuttered man—the kind who would abandon a large piece of symbolic furniture on the beach. He's so thick, he tries to buy a Maori burial ground with a jar of buttons as his payment. Yet he has the exquisite sensitivity to wait for a mail-order wife to come to his bed. When she does, he also has the spiritual refinement to hear her unvoiced words. Naturally, an experience of such depth and tenderness leads him to violence (his love turns to hate), in the course of which, though a clumsy man, he performs a feat requiring near-miraculous fine-motor control. After that, three more reversals occur without benefit of motivation, whereupon the film reaches as satisfying a happy ending as Zanuck himself might have engineered, or even Louis B. Mayer.

In brief, this skeptic thinks **The Piano** is a work of imagination but also of the will—not Ada's will, unfortunately, but Jane Campion's. Compared with **Sweetie,** her extraordinary first film, **The Piano** seems to me contrived, allegorized, rhetorical and altogether too eager to tell people what they want to hear. It's not so much an outburst of wild talent as it is the performance of wildness before an audience; not so much a waking dream as a melodrama.

Or, as true believers would have it, a fairy tale. Many of the viewers who give themselves up to **The Piano** will surely excuse its inconsistencies by appealing to Hans Christian Andersen and the Brothers Grimm; and yet the comparison doesn't work. **The Piano** is too bound up with specifics of time and place to be a fairy tale, though not enough so to be a historical drama. It's something in between—a reverie about the Victorian, colonial past—which means it's just close enough to realism to frustrate anybody who pauses to think about the plot. The same

holds true for the characters. The makers of fairy tales are pretty shrewd about human behavior; Freud himself never wrote a case study more acute than "The Princess and the Pea." But in The Piano, Campion's whim is the only law. You can't learn anything about the characters beyond what she chooses to tell you at the moment, because they are mere artifices—like Michael Nyman's music, which is neither convincing as a nineteenth-century imposture nor substantial enough to withstand scrutiny as part of our own era.

To the great majority of viewers, none of this means a damn. They're swept away by the eroticism, the beauty, the formal inventiveness and (no doubt) the easy allegory of **The Piano**. I yield to their judgment, bearing in mind the motto of the great art historian Ernst Gombrich: "There are no wrong reasons for liking a work of art." In fact, of all types of art, films are the most likely to overwhelm the carpings of reason—which means you could argue that **The Piano** has the added virtue of expressing an inherent quality of its medium. And yet . . .

The difference between admiring **The Piano** with reservations and believing in it wholeheartedly comes down to one's willingness to identify with the heroine. That's a tricky business. In current film criticism, especially the hard-core stuff, identification has become a key concept, as if it were general to narrative filmmaking. But with whom would you identify in *Citizen Kane? Pickpoket? Andrei Rublev? The Bank Dick?* Though it's undeniable that many narrative films encourage you to identify with a given character, others don't. So, to address the crudest form of identification theory, the "chick's movie" slur: Yes, I am willing to adopt the point of view of female protagonists. Because of certain oddities in my upbringing, I'm even more willing to identify with piano players. (Somebody once asked for a list of my ten favorite films. I came up with *Quai des Orfèvres, Shoot the Piano Player, Five Easy Pieces, Stroszek, Letter From an Unknown Woman, Hangover Square, A Song to Remember,* George Kuchar's *Pagan Rhapsody, The World of Henry Orient* and *El Dorado,* for the scene where Robert Mitchum shotguns a piano.) So my failure to plunge into the being of the piano player in this new movie very likely reflects some shortcoming in the production—perhaps Jane Campion's insistence that I should, I must, I *will* identify with Holly Hunter.

A sharper critic than I, Stephen Dedalus, has remarked that two types of identification are at work in the classic theory of drama. Aristotle's "pity," says Dedalus, moves the viewer to identify with the suffering character; but "terror" simultaneously incites us to identify "with the secret cause." To this, I would add only that the intuition of a secret cause of our sufferings, our attempt to know that cause by joining with it imaginatively, is the act that brings reason into play. My objection to **The Piano**? The film gives reason nothing to do. It intuits no secret cause. It offers only the occasion to feel pity, and for a character you're *right* to pity.

I bet you'll love it.

John Simon (review date 27 December 1993)

SOURCE: "Praise Jack, Shoot 'The Piano,' " in *National Review,* Vol. 45, No. 25, December 27, 1993, pp. 65-7.

[*Simon is a Yugoslavian-born American film and theater critic. In the following excerpt, he argues that* The Piano *contains numerous logical inconsistencies that detract from its quality.*]

At a New York Film Festival press conference, Jane Campion said she had originally intended to have the Cannes grand-prize-winning **The Piano** end with the drowning of the heroine. Instead, she has her going off to live happily ever after with her lover. I wonder about a writer-director who ends up making the opposite of what she set out to do.

The film starts with Ada, a Scottish mail-order bride, arriving on a desolate New Zealand coast with her small daughter, Flora. It's sometime in the nineteenth century, and there is no dock; the sailors unceremoniously dump people and their belongings on a deserted beach. Next day, Stewart, the husband, arrives with some Maori carriers. As the return trek leads through muddy jungles, Stewart decrees that Ada's most precious possession, her piano, be temporarily left behind, exposed to the mercy of the waves and weather. Ada, by the way, is mute, and communicates with her daughter in a home-made sign language; with others, via a notebook she wears around her neck, on whose pages she furiously scribbles the notes she hands out. Early sequences of the film have voiceover narration in Ada's voice at age six, when she voluntarily stopped speaking. Don't inner voices mature?

> Jane Campion prides herself on leaving much unexplained. She has every right to be proud: at leaving things unexplained, Miss Campion is a champion.
>
> —*John Simon*

We never find out anything about Ada's background, her first husband, and how Stewart acquired her in marriage. Or why she gave up speaking. Later, Flora will offer a wildly fanciful explanation that we, clearly, are not meant to believe. When mother and daughter spend that first cold night on the beach, they sleep under Ada's hoopskirt; who would have thought a crinoline could provide shelter for two? Why would a welcoming husband abandon his bride's beloved piano, her chief mode of self-expression, when there are enough porters to carry it; and why not at least move it out of the reach of the waves? Later, it is Stewart's less affluent partner, Baines—an Englishman gone native, who sports Maori tattoos on his face—who buys the piano from Stewart, and seems to have no problem hauling it to his homestead. That the piano should play perfectly after what it's been through is one of the film's most resounding lies.

Ada refuses to sleep with her husband, which he meekly accepts; he'll wait. Baines tells Ada he'll let her have the piano back in exchange for lessons. She goes to his house to give them, each session earning her a black key or, if she is particularly complaisant, more than one; the white keys, evidently, have no market value. Baines watches her from odd angles, including from below, often playing with her various extremities—with anything but the keyboard. Eventually, he presents himself to her naked and panting with desire; session by session, he has already removed quite a bit of her clothing. She succumbs, and they make wild, un-Victorian love. After that, things become rather more implausible.

Jane Campion prides herself on leaving much unexplained. She has every right to be proud: at leaving things unexplained, Miss Campion is a champion. We do not even get a sense of topography, of the distances between places, of what kind of settlement this is, of the reasons for the comings and goings of certain other white persons. As for the Maoris, they are lazy, giggling children, given to making rude jokes about the whites, which are sometimes, not always, translated by subtitles. Flora's actions consistently make no sense, but she at least has the excuse of being a child. What the adults do would make sense only as the wet dream of an inane woman, which **The Piano,** apparently, is not meant to be.

A final example. When Ada, who now plays teasing sexual games with her embarrassed husband (who had watched her through a window make love to Baines, and said nothing, only to keep her later under household arrest), decides to send a love message to Baines, she writes it on a key she rips from her piano—as if there were no paper, and as if Baines, who is illiterate, could read it. She entrusts the missive to Flora, who, perversely, walks miles to deliver it to Stewart instead, even though she bears him no particular allegiance. The consequences are dire, of course, but in an utterly loony way. Miss Campion claims kinship with Emily Brontë; but *Wuthering Heights,* another overheated spinsterish fantasy, makes a lot more sense, and has a little thing called genius going for it.

Even the music is absurd. Except for one piece of mauled Chopin, the score is by Michael Nyman, one of the most self-important, overrated, and, to my ears, worthless composers around; for this period piece, he has written his usual New Age claptrap. Yet, in other ways, Miss Campion is a stickler for accuracy, especially when such accuracy looks or sounds ridiculous to us, e.g., people wearing London street clothes and shoes to slosh through jungle mud.

Holly Hunter looks dismal and ghostly most of the time, her two white ears protruding through an oily, slicked-down carapace of black hair like a pair of stale shrimps. She plays piano and bizarre equally well. Harvey Keitel manages to act supremely randy in a childlike way, and wears his blue Morse-code-like tattoo with a straight face, which is an accomplishment. Sam Neill struggles with a role as unappetizing as it is thankless, and Anna Pacquin is an adorably precocious brat ripe for strangling. What possessed the Cannes judges to divide the Golden Palm between this and *Farewell My Concubine,* which is at least indisputably a film? The only similarity between the two lies in each having a main character one of whose fingers gets lustily chopped off.

Richard A. Blake   (review date 15 January 1994)

SOURCE: "Sound Effects," in *America,* Vol. 170, No. 2, January 15, 1994, p. 14.

[*Blake is an American educator, editor, film critic, and Roman Catholic priest. In the following review, he asserts that* The Piano *provides "a brilliant analysis" of human isolation and remarks on Campion's artistic development.*]

Traditionally, the holiday season works violence on the emotions. It offers images of happy family gatherings, but the sad reality is that many people eat Thanksgiving dinner alone in cafeterias, neither give nor receive Christmas presents and play solitaire on New Year's Eve. At a time when need for communication becomes obsessive, loneliness weighs like a Yule log on the heart. The January removal of Christmas decorations from shop windows comes as a blessed relief.

The Piano, written and directed by Jane Campion, offers a brilliant analysis of such poignant human isolation. Ada (Holly Hunter) cannot speak, Baines (Harvey Keitel) cannot read and Stewart (Sam Neill) cannot love. Despite their tragic solitude, masking its painful truth under a guise of self-sufficiency, each longs for the touch of another person. Since they cannot communicate directly, a piano mediates their relationships, thus assuming a symbolic, even mystical function throughout the film. It, rather than the human characters, is the center of the story.

Through voice-over narration, Ada, speaking with the voice of a young girl, explains that she simply stopped speaking at the age of six. This attractive young widow travels with her 9-year-old daughter Flora (Anna Paquin) from Scotland to New Zealand to marry Stewart, whom she has never met. Eager for a bride, Stewart accepts her muteness as an indication that she is "stunted." Her inability to communicate, however, becomes a sign of her own apparent inner strength. When she and Flora are dumped on the beach by the traders, she converts one of her huge hoop skirts into a tent so that she and Flora can survive until the groom arrives with his Maori porters to take her and her possessions to her new home. Her insistence on having them take her crated piano puts the new couple into immediate conflict. For him it is foolishness; for her it is life. When he leaves it on the beach, she is diminished, if only for a time.

In the mid-19th century, at this remote edge of the rain forest, European conventions have not yet taken root. Ada will have no wedding ceremony other than a photograph taken in a dripping shed with her soggy wedding gown draped loosely over her street clothes. Immediately after their wedding, Stewart announces his plans to be away for a prolonged period, and he will hear nothing more of the piano.

Baines, however, is more sympathetic. Tattooed with Maori markings on his forehead and nose, this rough-hewn neighbor gradually sees the piano as an opportunity to befriend Ada. His Maori workers, men and women both, engage in ribald conversation to tease him about his need for a wife. By offering Stewart a parcel of land, Baines takes possession of the piano, moves it into his own house and arranges to take lessons from Ada. At the end of a series of lessons, one for each black key on the keyboard, the piano will revert to Ada.

Eager to regain her only form of self-expression, Ada complies, knowing quite well that Baines is more interested in her than in music. At first he is content to watch her feet and to touch her shin through a hole in her stocking as she plies the pedals. In exchange for additional black keys she allows greater liberties, as Flora, not fully comprehending, watches them from the porch. What has begun as an eerie seduction for Baines and a business proposition for Ada, has, against their better judgment and good sense, matured into romance.

The erotic theme reinforces the frustration of failed communication. Ada soon realizes that Stewart cannot respond to her sexual overtures, and Baines cannot have the woman he loves. Thus both are sexually unfulfilled. Caught in an irresolvable triangle, Ada finds herself imprisoned in her own bedroom just as clearly as she is trapped in her own muteness. Her only form of expression is her piano, with its glorious music exposing the passion that rages in her heart. As it once gave her power over Baines, in her own home it provides a sense of emotional superiority over her uncomprehending, unfeeling husband.

The piano remains the focal point of the narrative as it twists through several abrupt, shocking developments. The love story stands on its own merits dramatically, but as the triangle sorts itself out, Ada and her piano acquire a significance that reaches far beyond the romantic conflict. The film enters into a dream mode, where images penetrate the subconscious, provoke, disturb and ultimately enlighten. In one of the final scenes, for example, Ada appears with a black veil over her face, and we must wonder how much of her we have actually seen or understood. She remains a mystery to the end. Ada's story speaks of love and survival, dignity and destruction, and especially of loneliness and communication.

As writer and director, Jane Campion has reached artistic maturity in a remarkably brief time. Her script holds all the elements of tragedy and pathos of the Victorian romance, but she refuses to offer her audience one moment of easy sentimentality. In Ada she has created a character of such strength that she evokes admiration rather than pity. Holly Hunter's features have sharpened since *Broadcast News* (1987), and her set jaw and tight lips speak more eloquently than any dialogue. Her silent rage during her arguments with Stewart, her comic negotiations with Baines and her tender exchanges with Flora show the expressiveness of silent images created by a talented director and actor working as one.

Harvey Keitel continues to grow as an actor. Baines is part brute and part lovesick fool, but Keitel and Campion make him neither frightening nor pathetic. In their telling, his strange behavior seems plausible, even inevitable. Sam

Neill creates a suitably bland Stewart, whose rage quietly builds until it explodes in a series of increasingly desperate, destructive acts. Stuart Dryburgh's photography is splendid without being showy. His presentation of the New Zealand forest is exquisite, while the dark interiors of the lantern-lit cabins provide an appropriate image of Ada's sense of confinement.

Does *The Piano* have the required happy ending? I'm not sure. I was certainly not elated, nor was I depressed—but I was profoundly disturbed. The memory of this film will last a long time, and that may be the true test of a work of art.

Sarah Kerr   (review date 3 February 1994)

SOURCE: "Shoot the Piano Player," in *The New York Review of Books,* Vol. XLI, No. 3, February 3, 1994, pp. 29-30.

[*In the following review, Kerr discusses the scenery, costumes, and narrative of* The Piano, *arguing that Campion creates an "immersion experience" rather than a dramatic narrative.*]

Several reviewers of her latest film [*The Piano*] have called Jane Campion a fourth Brontë sister. Campion, too, has dropped hints that this is where she got her inspiration. Attached to the book version of her screenplay, there is an appendix entitled "The Making of *The Piano*" in which she is quoted comparing "the kind of romance that Emily Brontë portrayed" to the perverse love affair in her film. This statement sent me paging through an old paperback of *Wuthering Heights,* where I came across a preface by Charlotte Brontë, an eloquent defense of her sister's novel written for the 1850 edition, two years after Emily's death. In it, Charlotte concedes that the central characters of Catherine and especially Heathcliff were perhaps too "tragic and terrible," and she finds the Yorkshire setting unrelievedly stark. But she counters that brightening the dialogue or adding a day trip to London would have subtracted from what was most true about the book. Emily's nature had, after all, been a brooding one. Bleak heaths and gnarled firs were the everyday view outside her window. Besides, according to Charlotte, she had possessed the true creative gift, the kind that "wills and works for itself," heedless of its owner's conscious intent.

The preface clarified a misgiving I'd had about comparing that particular mid-nineteenth-century novelist to this particular late-twentieth-century director. It is hard enough to reconcile the romantic picture, preserved since high school, of the solitary artist, in a naive trance-like state in her rural "wild workshop," with the multimillion-dollar, multinational, collaborative state of film making today. It is especially hard, though, to reconcile it with a film like *The Piano,* whose own trance-like quality seems not naive, but the result of cool, worldly calculation.

The appendix to the screenplay, part backstage visit with celebrities, part Cliff's Notes (and, by the way, pretty much the same as the press kits publicists handed to reviewers at advance screenings, hoping to jog memories and suggest a good hook for their reviews), documents a lot of hard planning. Holly Hunter, the star, tells how she took her acting cue from the restrictive corsets and stiff-hooped petticoats women wore during the 1850s, when the film takes place. Andrew McAlpine, the production designer, explains that he finessed the mood of certain scenes by layering an extra web of supplejack—a sinister, creeping black plant—over the New Zealand bush, where the movie was made. As if to underline the fact that this was not the view outside anyone's window, but a meticulously designed enterprise, the smallest eccentricities of which were deliberate, someone has supplied a glossary of terms like *moko* and *kumera*: Maori for facial tattoo and sweet potato.

The publisher has chosen this clinical-sounding quote from Campion as an epigraph: "I think that the romantic impulse is in all of us and that sometimes we live it for a short time," she says, "but it's not part of a sensible way of living." As an announcement of what the film is "about," this statement is remarkably bland and equivocal, but it does in an odd way capture the spirit of *The Piano*. The key word is not "romantic," but "impulse." The focus, quite accurately, is on "us," the rapt audience, whose breath Campion intends to quicken.

What we get in the movie is less a story than a situation, which is set up in the first few minutes, then turned loose. Ada, a mute Scottish woman, is promised in a match arranged by her father to Stewart, an English settler in New Zealand. She sails there to marry and live with him, bringing along her impish ten-year-old daughter, Flora (who the father was, we don't know), with whom she communicates in sign language, and her piano, which we are meant to understand as her surrogate voice. (She has played since she was five or six, around the time she stopped talking.)

From the beginning, Ada is a perverse heroine, indifferent to her stiff husband's shy request that she be more "affectionate," and, quite beyond her muteness (which, it is hinted, is willful), emotionally remote. When she plays the piano her eyes dilate, her cheeks twitch, and she looks disturbingly off, like a proud cat that has bathed and forgotten to stick its tongue back in. Any warmth she has is for her daughter, whose company at all times, including night-time, she prefers to that of Stewart. (There appears to be no incest here, but, as in her first film, *Sweetie,* Campion fixes on petting and power games between parents and children—on the thin line separating doting from coercion. The relationship of Ada and Flora is the most complicated one in the film.)

Stewart, recognizing the piano as a rival, trades it, against Ada's wishes, for a piece of land to another settler, a crude, illiterate Welshman named Baines. As part of the deal, she is to teach Baines how to play. A number of clichés get teased in *The Piano,* beginning with this throwing together of two unlikely people, a standard prelude to movie intimacy. Using his ownership of the piano as leverage, Baines arranges a deal with Ada, and the "lessons" in his cabin quickly turn into strange intimate sessions in which she lets him "do things" to her.

Whether it is love or power or jungle fever that motivates Baines is unclear. He politely notifies her in advance of what he is about to do each time he nuzzles her neck or peeks up her skirt (right in line with the Antioch rules), but there is an ugliness to their time together, because it is bought. His desire seems primitive. Alone, in between lessons, he lies in bed looking undone by lust; he gets up and in a slow, solo nude scene strips off his nightshirt and uses it to wipe down the piano. Harvey Keitel, bringing some Actor's Studio introspection to this scene (and, bravely, a squat body that makes him resemble a twisted balloon animal), keeps us in further suspense whether Baines is a feminist dreamboat or simply Tarzan beating on his chest.

Of course, this is exactly the question that Campion designed her film to provoke, and then, it seems, to duck. She presents Stewart as a "character" with a set of attributes (lonely, wants a family, something of a bore), and the actor, Sam Neill, plays him that way. But Ada and Baines are kept opaque in the way that real people we hardly know are opaque. Their histories are murky, and their motives, despite the surface emotionality, are unfathomable. Even Ada's muteness seems conceived as a disorienting device. The less readable her behavior, the more thrillingly her affair with Baines unfolds, before our eyes, free of distraction.

The same goes for her music. Piano-playing is said to be Ada's voice, but significantly, she plays mood rather than expressive music—not the truly romantic pieces she might have been expected to know, with a melody, a dramatic arc, a real *voice*. (The dreary score, like an étude in which the student works to make each new note sound as much as possible like the last, is by Michael Nyman, the composer for Peter Greenaway's baroque, impersonal films.) Music may be too articulate a form of expression for Campion's purposes. She does better with a baser stimulus, like touch: early on, Baines's thumb brushing the nickel-sized patch of Ada's thigh that shows through her stocking, and later, the consummation, which,

> STEWART *watches, stepping down to peer lower as* BAINES *buries into* ADA's *skirt. He does not seem to notice the dog licking his hand. Suddenly he pulls his hand away and looks at it, wet with dog saliva; he wipes it on the boards and continues watching as if mesmerized.*

The sex scenes are uncannily immediate, more purely sensual than any I have seen. This is sex in a different century, under a different set of rules—sex without a script, without particular characters. And Campion makes us into witnesses.

But twice in the second half of **The Piano,** we are jolted in a contradictory way. These moments are not plot twists in the conventional sense: no character is revealed, no confusion cleared up. Each one comes out of the blue, and neither seems to have real consequences. The first occurs when Stewart, after keeping her locked up for days, decides to trust Ada not to repeat the tryst with Baines and leaves the house to resume surveying his land. In his absence Ada attempts to send Baines a piano key as a love token. But instead of delivering the key to Baines as her mother ordered, Flora hands it to Stewart. Stewart returns in a rage, grabs Ada and throws her around, throws his

axe at the piano, and drags her to a tree stump outside and hacks off her index finger. He then goes to see Baines, holds a gun to Baines's throat, and confesses his torment.

Here arrives the other jolt, which is twofold. Presumably Baines calms Stewart down, because in the next scene he and Ada and Flora are departing in a boat. Ada impulsively orders the beloved piano thrown overboard:

> *As the piano splashes into the sea, the loose ropes speed their way after it. ADA watches them snake past her feet and then, out of a fatal curiosity, odd and undisciplined, she steps into a loop.*
>
> *The rope tightens and grips her foot so that she is snatched into the sea, and pulled by the piano down through the cold water.*

146. INT. SEA NEAR BEACH. DAY.
Bubbles tumble from her mouth. Down she falls, on and on, her eyes are open, her clothes twisting about her. The MAORIS diving after her cannot reach her in these depths. ADA begins to struggle. She kicks at the rope, but it holds tight around her boot. She kicks hard again and then, with her other foot, levers herself free from her shoe. The piano and her shoe continue their fall while ADA floats above, suspended in deep water, then suddenly her body awakes and fights, struggling upwards to the surface.

This harrowing sequence, done in slow-motion, captures the dumb desperation of trying to claw one's way out of a trap but being unable to move that one experiences in dreams. But this nightmare, regrettably, is followed by an epilogue, a sunlit scene on the porch of their new house which looks imported from a film version of *Pride and Prejudice*. In the screenplay they've ended up in the pretty town of Nelson, New Zealand. Ada explains in a voice-over that Baines has built her a new metal finger. She gives piano lessons. There she is, learning how to talk again, her daughter cartwheeling past in the garden, her lover reeling her in for a kiss.

The scene is a negation of everything that preceded it. The reckless logic of the film has prepared us to reject Baines and Ada as a happy domesticated couple, just as the more stoic logic of *Casablanca* would be ruined if Ingrid Bergman's getting on the plane with Paul Henreid to help him fight Nazis turned out to be a ruse. (Nobody really wanted to see her and Humphrey Bogart five years later, sitting down to breakfast in a tract home in New Rochelle.)

The Piano is different in offering no message whatsoever. Certain men have found it to be anti-man, and certain feminists have accused Campion of hating women. These opposite reactions point to a hollowness at the film's core.

—*Sarah Kerr*

In fact, the logic of *The Piano* would make any ending seem pat. The film makes its point by showing how time-bound and rhetoric-laden our expectations about sex are: how much we rate it, classify it as "casual" and "serious" and sometimes "rape," look for signs of love or lack of love, for an expression, in miniature, of a character's approach to life. We usually subordinate sex to a larger story, but the point of *The Piano is* the sex: there's no larger story to tell.

Campion has solved the usual problem with historical films, which is that everything on screen feels too familiar: the waistlines, the hairdos, the shade of lipstick are all from this month's magazines, and so, we suspect, is whatever dilemma the characters are grappling with. On the contrary, she has been unsparingly thorough. The blue-green, yellow, and amber tinges that at first seem mere mood heighteners actually mimic autochrome, a nineteenth-century stills process. Charred trees were placed just so to create a slashed-and-burned look around Stewart's house. In the production notes, Campion makes it a point of honor that Holly Hunter's hair was authentically greasy.

The vanished landscape was resurrected, however, not to be understood but as another field of tactile and visual opportunities to be mined. Campion makes a self-conscious point in the production notes of her determination to do a "Maori story." The movie takes place in the 1850s, and there is some oblique business here about contested land; in one scene the Maori complain about the takeover of a burial ground. By 1860, according to the *Encyclopedia Britannica* entry on New Zealand, the land gripes only hinted at here broke out into a full-fledged war that lasted ten years. Campion painstakingly avoids the usual traps; her Maori are neither especially savage nor excessively innocent. But sitting cross-legged in the forest, wearing their top hats, they come perilously close to being backdrop, like the cliffs and the waves, contributors to the estrangement the audience is supposed to feel. Mostly, they serve the purpose of being hipper to sex than the whites are. They dispense salty putdowns ("Old dry balls is getting touchy," one of them says about the uptight Stewart), and encourage young Flora, flustered from peeking in on one of Baines's "lessons," to make out with a tree.

Campion is a brilliant depicter of moods and reactions—a behaviorist, poking at her characters with a stick and showing us how they wriggle—and *The Piano* strings together a dozen or so memorable moments of great psychological truth. Its cumulative effect, though, is to induce a feverish pang, like lovesickness, in the audience.

In an essay on Bertolucci's film *1900,* Pauline Kael wrote about a point in mid-career when a great director experiences the almost missionary drive to express "what the artist thinks are the unconscious needs of the public." Kael was talking about films from *Intolerance* to *Apocalypse Now* which, like certain huge, layered, didactic nineteenth-century novels, attempt to diagnose the way we live now, often with great bitterness. Though the story of *The Piano* is tiny and confined, Campion directs it with the grave authority of one of these films, so that we reflexively look for a sermon in the sensations she thrusts in front of us.

But *The Piano* is different in offering no message whatsoever. Certain men have found it to be anti-man, and certain feminists have accused Campion of hating women. These opposite reactions point to a hollowness at the film's core. Its avoidance of judgment gives it an open-armed warmth, a slightly New Age quality that shows up at the end of the final credits, when Campion thanks everyone who tried out but didn't make it to the screen. It has another more remote, asocial side, though. Its goal is a private sensory charge—or, as Campion puts it in the production notes, describing what she can do now that Emily Brontë couldn't in her time, "the actual bodyscape of it . . . because the body has certain effects, like a drug almost." While it dangles in front of us intense images (the piano, the cut-off finger) that look as if they should work the way symbols in great novels do, *The Piano* has a peculiarly contemporary, almost technological dimension. The story of Ada and Baines's affair is, like the story of Spielberg's T-Rex, secondary to its physical representation. Instead of a dramatic narrative, we get an immersion experience: a Virtual Romance. We leave the theater more intensely aware of how tight or loose our clothes are hanging, how close the next person is standing, how damp the air is outside.

Right now Campion is completing a screenplay adaptation of *The Portrait of a Lady,* which she plans to shoot next year. She has enough specialties in common with James (willful heroines, charged glances) to make this something to stand in line to see. Still, I wonder whether her brand of insight isn't best suited to adapting not nineteenth-century novels, but biographies.

Real people rarely have been served well by the movies, which tend to camouflage physical and psychic flaws, and pound lives into the shape of a lesson. Campion's previous film, *An Angel at My Table,* is a beautiful exception to the rule. It is based on the autobiography of the New Zealand novelist Janet Frame, who because of extreme shyness was misdiagnosed as schizophrenic while in her early twenties, and confined to an asylum, where, over a period of eight years, she was dealt close to two hundred rounds of electric shock.

Campion's unsentimental grasp of period detail and shifting states of mind allow us to follow Janet from childhood tableaux through wrenching, particular adolescent hurdles and finally to an adult calm. There is an especially moving moment at the end, after Janet has left the asylum, done a European tour, established a small literary reputation, and returned to New Zealand, where she is staying with her one surviving sister, in a shed adjacent to the sister's trailer. From up in the night sky, we look down on Janet alone in the yard on a break from work, and hear the dim sound of a pop song coming from inside the trailer. We see her stand listening. She does a brief distracted dance, then after a moment goes still, waits, turns, walks back inside the shed, and as the camera descends and closes in on the window, first slowly and then picking up speed as if hurrying to catch something terribly elusive, we see her begin to type.

There is no obvious prettiness here: just a middle-aged woman with a red afro and rotting teeth and terrible social skills, typing. Yet the mix of concreteness and mystery seems almost medieval, like the confirmation of a sacred calling. It means nothing, and teaches nothing, but it reaches us in some intense and direct way.

Harvey Greenberg   (review date Spring 1994)

SOURCE: A review of *The Piano,* in *Film Quarterly,* Vol. 47, No. 3, Spring, 1994, pp. 46-50.

[*Greenberg is an American educator, psychiatrist, nonfiction writer, and author of* Screen Memories: Hollywood Cinema on the Psychoanalytic Couch *(1993). In the following review, he discusses the themes of* The Piano, *focusing on sexuality and identity.*]

Jane Campion's *Sweetie* (1989) described the calamitous impact of a raucous schizophrenic woman upon her relatives. *An Angel at My Table* (1990), based on the autobiography of Janet Frame, depicted the no less harrowing effects of institutionalization upon a female writer misdiagnosed as chronically schizophrenic. *The Piano,* directed from her own screenplay, comprises Campion's most extraordinary exploration of unsettled, unsettling feminine outsiders to date. Its heroine is Ada McGrath (Holly Hunter), a Victorian unwed mother of pallid countenance and somber dress, whose silent compliance conceals and protects a fiercely unconventional spirit.

Ada is not so much unable as *unwilling* to speak. She suffers, or, depending upon one's viewpoint, practices elective mutism. This rare, puzzling condition usually develops in early childhood and occurs rather more frequently in girls than boys. The electively mute child has been characterized as symbiotically bound to a powerfully possessive adult; as alternately clinging and shy, or intensely stubborn and negativistic; as terribly fearful of the sound of its own voice; as traumatized by abuse or non-abusive injury; as fighting intense family scapegoating with passive-aggressive silence. Interestingly enough, especially in light of Ada's character, the syndrome is thought by some to represent a strategy of active manipulation and control, rather than merely being a symptom of autistic withdrawal.

Campion compounds the enigma of Ada's condition by furnishing only the sparest details of her background or the early forces which have played upon her. She lives in a cloistered, mid-Victorian Glasgow home. *The Piano*'s establishing sequence begins out of focus, as in a hypnogogic state. The camera peers at the emerging world through the lattice of a child's fingers, while Ada's six-year-old voice tells us she ceased speaking at that age, and does not remember why. (One notes that *The Piano*'s narrative engine is propelled by the internal monologue of a character who cannot or will not speak—another compelling paradox spun out of Ada's mutism.)

She relates that her beloved father (neither he or any other family member is ever seen) has a strangely approving notion of her affliction as a "dark talent." He's arranged her marriage to a lonely expatriate English farmer in New Zealand. Quite possibly he is the recipient of her dowry.

In a trice Ada is whisked over the sea, dumped unceremoniously upon the New Zealand shore with her baggage, her precious piano, and her out-of-wedlock daughter Flora (Anna Paquin)—a precocious and voluble nine-year-old who is Ada's interpreter to the world. The two communicate through their own invented sign system.

Campion has kept the camera claustrophobically screwed down until now: Ada's instant voyage is literally *embodied* by the fragmented hands and torsos of the sailors carrying her from skiff to land (a locution the director used to underscore the heroine's schizoid isolation from an equally alienated husband in *Sweetie*). The mise-en-scène briefly opens out into a vista of stormswept grey sky, huge waves tumbling against a barren stretch of sand. One's view is then constricted again, and for the most part will remain so. Tight close-ups further accentuate the nuances of an unfolding and mute—or barely spoken—triangle of desire.

Stewart, Ada's new husband (Sam Neill), is stiff-upper-lip reticence personified: handsome, not unkind, but disastrously unimaginative. His narrow utilitarian purposes immediately oppress Ada's sensibility when he refuses to bring her instrument back to his plantation. In a breathtaking long shot the lone piano is limned starkly against the rolling surf: it's suddenly a vivid icon of cultural collision, of yet another stifling of Ada's voice, of her delivery into paltry domesticity in a startling alien environment.

Stewart's home is kept by gabbling, censorious female relatives. Ada and Flora retreat from a bizarre simulacrum of English gentility into their room and private world. The taciturn Stewart, unlike the rest of his clan (and much like Ada's father) accepts, even approves of Ada's disability ("There's something to be said for silence"). As frustration with his unconsummated marriage mounts, Stewart wonders if Ada might be mad as well as mute, yet grows ever more entranced with her.

Stewart's neighbor, Baines (Harvey Keitel), offers to purchase the beached piano from Stewart for 80 prime acres, with music instruction by Ada thrown into the bargain. (Campion permits an inference that the two men have previously done business, and—perhaps as a result—aren't altogether happy with each other.) Stewart agrees, hoping she can be drawn out of her shell. Baines makes an unprepossessing pupil. He's squat, illiterate, his face tattooed like the ribald Maoris who lounge about his ramshackle hut.

Baines offers to sell back the piano one key at a time in return for voyeuristic liberties with Ada's person. Apparently shocked at first, she nevertheless consents with her usual passivity; then piquantly shifts the grounds of what seems like a perverse, humiliating bargain, demanding more keys for each favor. Eventually the two lie together nude without making love; Hunter's unexpectedly voluptuous body is pressed against Keitel's compact, powerfully muscled, yet unglamorous frame—a moment both unutterably moving and incredibly erotic.

Baines grows disgusted with himself for engineering a degrading charade: he was instantly smitten with Ada, and could think of no other way to court her. When he proposes ending their "arrangement" and returning the piano to Stewart's house, she flies into a fury and quickly takes him to bed. One infers this is her first real passion. The relationship which engendered Flora seems to have been short-lived and cerebral, with a man Ada implies was too timorous to keep "listening" to the quicksilver mind and tumultuous roil of emotion hidden beneath her silence.

Stewart discovers the affair. In an exceptionally creepy scene, he peeps upon the trysting couple from underneath the floor of Baines' hut—*he,* not Baines, is revealed as the repressed voyeur. Enraged, he forbids her Baines' presence, literally penning her up in his house with the piano until she can be "good." Unaccountably, she appears to warm to her husband, and he gives her back her freedom.

Ada is next seen pressing her lips against her mirrored image, then caressing the piano's keys with a sensual backhand gesture. When she attempts to awaken Stewart with the same languours touch he cannot abide his arousal and rebuffs her. Rather than rejection, she feels release. It's subtly apparent that while one part of her has been dutifully attempting to shape herself to Stewart's limitations, the larger part has been using her husband as a substitute object—as well as her piano and her own reflected self. All are now metonyms of her rapturous infatuation with Baines.

She entrusts Flora to give Baines a piece of the piano's keyboard, upon which she has penned a testament of her love. In a jealous fit, Flora brings it to Stewart instead. At this moment, he represents the lesser of two evils, since he poses no threat to Flora's symbiotic attachment to her mother. But the child, caught up in fantasies of retaliation which are ultimately aimed at regaining her mother's affection, misgauges the potential for violence born out of Stewart's narcissistic injuries. Stewart takes an ax to the piano, then to Ada's hand. Amidst a welter of screams and blood, he awakens to a horrified recognition of his unleashed brutality—and to the impossibility of Ada's ever coming to heel, ever truly becoming his wife. Wishing only to be quit of her uncanny power over him—"I am afraid of her *will!*" —he relinquishes her to Baines.

Campion's tale sounds over-the-top penny-dreadful in the telling, but it's tremendously absorbing on the screen. The dark side of Eros is often diminished today: sexuality is chattered to death in the tabloids, on "Oprah," or in the clinic. *The Piano* restores the orphic power of sex. In the film's puritanical milieu, desire is filtered through murky Victorian notions about feminine purity or evil, through the era's fascination with the sway of the primitive, the savage imperatives of nature, the chilly balm of death.

The Piano's protagonists are intensely passionate. But Campion intimates they are also erotic naïfs (the men in particular), who confront sexuality as if it were newly minted in the disconcerting unfamiliarity of the New Zealand bush. Stewart can only follow the rulebook that stringently tutors him on patriarchal duty, feminine docility, the white man's imperial burden. Baines, who emigrated

after being abandoned by his wife for reasons never explicated, is discovered sunk in debauched despair.

Ada is the most daring of the three in her struggles with Eros. It is moot whether some ungovernable childhood abuse, some terrible skepticism of ever being understood or cherished has driven her behind her wall of stillness. Her sea change liberates the extraordinary "will" that so infuriates (and intimidates) her husband. It surges forth with a force so primal as to seem impersonal to her, spurring an unruly independence—and a tender carnality which finds its match in the bosom of the no-less-wounded (and nearly as inarticulate) Baines.

The Piano's literary antecedents include those lurid Gothic romances replete with frail heroines, exotic locales, and masterful/sinister noblemen; the *amours fous* of *Wuthering Heights* and *Tess of the D'Urbervilles*; fairy tales with *amour fou* preoccupations, notably *Beauty and the Beast* and *Bluebeard*. By design or unconscious intention, Campion has adroitly reinterpreted such sources. Her work exemplifies the unique spin on Gothic strategems, inflected by the surreal peculiarities of "down under" nature, which has distinguished the cinema of Australia and New Zealand at least since Peter Weir's *Picnic at Hanging Rock* (1975) and *The Last Wave* (1977). Stuart Dryburgh's photography of the deep aquamarine shade and rough, tangled vegetation of the New Zealand bush serves to highlight the protagonists' convoluted and excessive emotionality (as when the vengeful Stewart rushes upon Ada, and both become caught in a twisted mesh of ancient vine).

The Piano is true to its period in every respect (saving its music), while simultaneously addressing a host of issues dear to contemporary cultural critics and film scholars. Feminist theoreticians have notably explored the suppression of the feminine voice under patriarchy's insensible rule and the attendant possibility for recovering that voice at the very core of its suppression. In this context, Ada's muteness can be interpreted as a limit case of patriarchal domination, both symptom *and* countercoup.

In a much cited study, "Visual Pleasure and Narrative Cinema" [published in *Screen* (1975)], Laura Mulvey asserts that classic Hollywood cinema treats woman as the object of male gaze; her disruptive sexuality must be neutralized by transforming her into a docile fetish, marrying her off, or killing her. Ada's two suitors attempt to "objectify" her by all of these measures (Stewart stops just short of murder). Yet Campion has her turn the tables and make Stewart and Baines helplessly enthralled objects of *her* gaze, *her* desire.

The arrogance and ignorance of the colonizing consciousness toward native culture and the parallel bewilderment, silent contempt, and resentment of the Maoris toward their English masters constitute a less visible, but no less crucial ideological subtext of *The Piano*. Stewart is horrified when he sees Flora and her Maori friends in semi-masturbatory play. What he takes for licentiousness betokens the Maori absence of Victorian childhood sexual repression (their taboos lie elsewhere).

During the colonists' staging of *Bluebeard,* the horrified locals rush upon the stage to prevent the butchering of the wives (presaging Stewart's savage attack upon Ada). The Maoris are indeed untutored in Western drama, but Campion's chief point here is that Bluebeard's sadistic intention toward his wives is deeply offensive to them.

While her sympathies are tilted toward the Maoris, Campion's perspective on settler as well as indigenous tribe is for the most part coolly balanced. The Maoris are not glorified (or degraded) as noble primitives. The director shows that they and the English are equally capable of being wrongheadedly amused or appalled by each other's Otherness. Nor is Stewart an unregenerate villain. His hopefulness about winning Ada's love in the face of her fierce disdain is as pitiable as his violence upon her is odious.

Sam Neill poignantly captures Stewart's uncomprehending pain over Ada's disaffection as well as his repellent paternalism. Anna Pacquin's Flora is a radiant delight. Harvey Keitel has created a galaxy of Caliban-like characters; *The Piano* shows him evolving into the light, Baines' defensive brutishness yielding to an amazing, grave sweetness.

But the film's complex heart belongs to Hunter. Her perky American roles (*Broadcast News* and *Raising Arizona* [1987], *Always* and *Miss Firecracker* [1989]) do not prepare one for the acute intelligence and volcanic sensuality spoken by the actress's pale face, her flashing eye, and her exquisitely tuned gestures. She transforms Ada's perennial black dress, bonnet, camisole, and bustle into a prison for her character's body and soul.

Hunter is also an able pianist; her rendition of Michael Nyman's score heightens her verisimilitude in the role. Nyman has often reworked earlier styles with a kind of Brechtian defamiliarization (e. g., his brittle deconstruction of Purcell in *The Draughtman's Contract* [1982]). In *The Piano,* he refuses to dissect or defamiliarize mid-nineteenth-century Romanticism, indeed makes little reference at all to the musical idioms of the period. Using New Age harmonies and plangent arpeggios, he has composed an elegiac improvisation on wild Scottish folk themes which would have proven bathetic in less skillful hands.

Voyaging with Baines to resettlement in urban New Zealand, Ada pitches her piano overboard lest the boat capsize. She becomes entangled in a rope, and is herself pulled over the side. She sinks into the deep, but to her utter amazement decides to free herself—"my will has chosen life!" The image dissolves to scenes of that life; her now adult voiceover relates that Baines has repaired Stewart's assault and provided her with a curious metallic finger. She has taken up teaching piano, is learning to speak haltingly again, and muses that she is probably viewed as the "town freak."

The conclusion of this intricate fable of feminine identity is ambiguous. In *The Piano*'s enigmatic opening, a child peers at a world yet unborn through fingers which both hide and disclose. It's not precisely clear whether they belong to Ada or Flora. In retrospect, one speculates that Campion is meditating upon a Victorian girl's fascinated, terrified fantasies about her path toward sexual awakening.

For Ada, these fantasies unfold in an odyssey shot through with references to voyeurism, the primal scene, rape and castration fears—and an overarching anxiety over incestuous desire. It is moot whether Ada has been banished by her father to New Zealand in aid of improving his cash flow or has herself actively sought flight from an imperious, possibly seductive/abusive father who prized and perhaps enabled her loss of voice. Stewart may be interpreted as his neurotic reinvention; Baines, as embodying his gentler, more wholesome recuperation. One hopes Flora will find calmer seas. Campion offers subliminal hope that she may fare better than her mother, not least because Baines represents a father who can allow a woman a voice and space of her own.

But the director also intimates that her heroine's decision to voyage from the New Zealand wilds back to "civilized" life with Baines may constitute a sacrifice of her freer, darker nature, one that perhaps would not have occurred had there been no Flora. In jettisoning the piano, Ada seems compelled not only by the imperative of survival but also by the need to abjure the dangerous Dionysian thrust of her temperament. One is left with a ruling image of her eerily suspended in mid-ocean like some tenebrous, funereal blossom, before her "will" chooses a tamer Eros over the Thanatos which may well be the ultimate desire prefigured by her muteness.

Sara Halprin   (review date July 1994)

SOURCE: "A Key to *The Piano,*" in *The Women's Review of Books,* Vol. XI, Nos. 10-11, July, 1994, pp. 35-6.

[*In the following review, Halprin discusses* The Piano *in relation to the published screenplay and comments on the film's literary influences.*]

> I am frightened of my will, of what it might do,
> it is so strange and strong.

Jane Campion began writing the script for her acclaimed and controversial third feature film, *The Piano,* in 1984, nine years before it reached the screen. The published script, accompanied by production notes, monochrome stills and credits, is a literary oddity which owes its life and reason for being to the film. It serves as a study guide, clarifying and articulating the territory the film explores.

The Piano is marked by unusual visual perspective, strong acting and music-impelled narrative. Set in the 1850s, it tells the story of Ada McGrath, mute by her own decision from the age of six, and her illegitimate ten-year-old daughter Flora, who accompanies her from Scotland to the New Zealand bush to start a new home with Stewart, the mail-order husband procured by Ada's father. Flora shares a private sign language with her mother and serves as her voice in the world. Stewart, despite Flora's translation, is unable to understand Ada or her passion for her piano, her other voice. Awkward and earnest, he longs for her affection and fails to win it.

His more sensitive colleague, Baines, also longs for her,

and is more successful. He trades land to Stewart for the piano, then uses the piano to barter for sensual favors from Ada. He stops, however, when he perceives that the deal is making her into "a whore." "I want you to care for me," he says to her, "but you can't." Stewart is too busy trying to wrest more land from the Maoris to notice what is happening. His inability to understand the Maoris' passion for their land is equalled only by his incomprehension of Ada. Meanwhile, Ada realizes that she does care for Baines and, with characteristic impetuosity, goes to him.

When Stewart discovers that Ada and Baines are lovers, he is beside himself. Kept from Baines, Ada turns her newly awakened sexuality toward Stewart but still refuses him her affection. She sends a love message written on a piano key to Baines through Flora, who delivers it instead to Stewart. Driven beyond the bounds of his limited reason, Stewart takes violent revenge. In front of Flora, in a shocking scene, Stewart chops off one of Ada's fingers. Eventually, however, through a convoluted sequence of scenes, he is persuaded to allow Ada and Flora to go off with Baines. Seated in the Maori canoe that is taking them to another part of New Zealand, Ada orders her piano shoved overboard and apparently allows herself to be dragged in with it, but then frees herself and survives. The film ends with her "mind's voice" (heard once before at the beginning) reading lines from a poem by the nineteenthcentury writer Thomas Hood, which appear on screen:

> There is a silence where hath been no
> sound
> There is a silence where no sound may
> be
> In the cold grave, under the deep deep
> sea.

The Piano has been widely reviewed as a Victorian melodrama, influenced, depending on the interests of the critic, by the Brontës, Emily Dickinson, *The French Lieutenant's Woman,* the German filmmaker Lotte Reiniger, Victorian portrait photography, Virginia Woolf, D.H. Lawrence and Edward Lear. Insofar as the film depicts events that follow one another in time, it is a conventional narrative, but it does not explain why things happen or why characters behave the way they do, which has perplexed and infuriated some viewers. Critical responses to the film following the award of the Cannes Palme d'Or—the first time it has ever gone to a film by a woman—ranged from sublime to ridiculous to hostile, with feminist responses split down the middle.

Campion herself, in the production notes that follow the script, says:

> I feel a kinship between the kind of romance that Emily Brontë portrayed in *Wuthering Heights* and this film. Hers is not the notion of romance that we've come to use, it's very harsh and extreme, a gothic exploration of the romantic impulse. I wanted to respond to those ideas in my own century.

The script articulates crucial moments in the film that for some viewers may have passed too quickly to stick in the memory, but which were meant to help explain a charac-

ter's motivation. Some critics have questioned Flora's motivation for delivering the piano key to Stewart, which precipitates the action that leads to her mother's mutilation. Reading the script, we quickly realize that Flora is truly her mother's daughter, with a strange, even perverse will of her own. During one of Baines' early piano "lessons," she is described as "operating a merciless power game with [Baines'] dog, forcing it out of the verandah with a stick." In the next scene she "cradl[es] the poor confused dog, asking him what cruel miserable person sent him out into the cold and wet." When the betrayed Stewart barricades Ada and Flora in their hut, the child "joins in the spirit of the exercise, gaily pointing out any slats Stewart has missed." When her mother orders her to deliver the piano key to Baines, she "is shocked, stunned"; at the junction where the paths leading to Baines and to Stewart separate, she "looks back to see if her mother is watching; she's not"—and chooses her stepfather over her mother's lover.

The Piano is not a film for everyone; it is not for those committed to patriarchal concepts (see John Simon, for example, in the *National Review,* who called the film "the wet dream of an inane woman"), nor for every feminist. The violence against Ada, seen through the eyes of young Flora, is the focus of most feminist concern about the film; what is the function of this violence? The script is helpful here in articulating a sense of the inevitability of an explosion, one made so not only by Stewart's unimaginative insistence on his own pragmatic way, but also by Ada's remorseless use of the virginal Stewart as a sexual object.

> *The Piano* has been widely reviewed as a Victorian melodrama, influenced, depending on the interests of the critic, by the Brontës, Emily Dickinson, *The French Lieutenant's Woman,* the German filmmaker Lotte Reiniger, Victorian portrait photography, Virginia Woolf, D. H. Lawrence and Edward Lear.
>
> —Sara Halprin

The script also confirms that a performance of "Bluebeard" at the local mission center is meant to prefigure Stewart's attack on Ada. The silhouetted figure of Bluebeard brandishing an axe at his wife is echoed in the image of Stewart striding home with his ax; the script tells us that when Ada hands Flora the fateful piano key, "her black shadow behind the sheet recalls the macabre play." As used in this film, "Bluebeard" is the story of a man's attempt to subjugate a woman to his will by obliterating all traces of her own, even in his absence, and of her refusal to be subjugated.

The script makes clear Ada's role in creating the tension that culminates in Stewart's violence. Far from being a helpless, silent victim, Ada is depicted as a willful woman, at once courageous and foolhardy in pursuing her passion, whether for her piano or for Baines. The script explicitly compares these two: in one scene, Ada looks "down at Baines and his hut, in the exact same manner that she once looked at her piano. . . ." The production notes that follow the script explain Campion's view of Ada and Stewart's relationship:

> Ada actually uses her husband Stewart as a sexual object—this is the outrageous morality of the film—which seems very innocent but in fact has its power to be very surprising. I think many women have had the experience of feeling like a sexual object, and that's exactly what happens to Stewart. . . . It becomes a relationship of power, the power of those that care and those that don't care.

The Piano explores sexuality, intimacy and power in the complex relationships not only between women and men, mother and daughter, but also between colonizer and colonized. The Maori subplot is intended to function not as a colorful, exotic background to the white European romance but as a parallel example of power, its misuse and the resulting violence. In fact, the greater violence in *The Piano* is that done to the land itself: the film shows Stewart's hut "bleakly set among smoking stumps."

The script and accompanying notes make it clear that Campion wished to represent Maori frustration that they and the land they hold sacred are treated as objects by the colonist Stewart. However, this is an area that could have been strengthened in the film. Many of the scenes in the script that were deleted from the film have to do with the Maoris; they prefigure the war that was very soon to break out between the Maoris and the colonists.

Their deletion suggests that Campion may have had difficulty in realizing her intentions; ultimately, it will be Maori filmmakers who succeed with Maori perspectives on New Zealand. The lines by Thomas Hood can be seen to refer in part to the silence of those who survive systematic violence at great cost to their freedom of expression. I would have liked to learn the actual relationship of script to film—was this the actual working script? and were the deleted scenes shot and then dropped in editing, or were changes made before shooting took place?

Apart from *Wuthering Heights,* it is hard to say what the actual influences for *The Piano* were. Certainly it is possible to view the film and read the text and imagine all the influences critics have mentioned, and more: the work is grounded in a sophisticated sense of European and New Zealand culture and history. But a comparison comes immediately to my mind: the work of Marguerite Duras, who has done so much on women's silence, as a defense, as a weapon, as a language; and on issues of voice and perspective—in writing and in film. Duras was a pioneer in the field of multimedia; she understood that a story may have many lives, as a text, as a play, as a film. Her work—nonlinear and often shocking audiences used to more con-

ventional narrative—explores global as well as intimate perspectives on power relations. And her use of her childhood in French colonial Indochina/ Vietnam is comparable to Campion's use of her own background, her "strange heritage . . . as a *pakeha* New Zealander." Campion's comments in the production notes show she realized how the look of the film—its portrayal of the bush, the authenticity of the Victorian costumes, the greasiness of Holly Hunter's hair—would both document and construct a composite portrait of an era and its human relationships.

To construct that portrait, Campion pulled together an extraordinary collection of talents, briefly described in the notes. One of these was the composer Michael Nyman, whose comments appear in the notes along with those of Campion, her producer Jan Chapman and the actors. Nyman describes how he used Scottish folk songs as a base, and created a score especially adapted to lead actor Holly Hunter's ability as a pianist. "It's as though I've been writing the music of another composer," he says, "who happened to live in Scotland, then New Zealand in the mid 1850s."

I am disappointed that the book is not fuller because I have gained so much from what is there. I also would have liked the book to take more care in introducing its own materials: it is difficult to get a sense of who wrote the various parts. It seems there was no actual author; someone simply assembled Campion's script, Miro Bilborough's production notes, some sepia-tinted stills and a list of credits. The book lacks the film's cohesiveness, and compares unfavorably to other documentations of films, such as the book about Spike Lee's *Do the Right Thing* and the text and separately published production history of Marguerite Duras' *India Song.* (A novelization of the film by Jane Campion and Kate Pullinger has since been published, also by Hyperion.) The film itself is an instrument of great subtlety and power in depicting the scope and boundaries of a woman's will; the book provides a useful, if slight, accompaniment to the film's greater performance.

FURTHER READING

Criticism

Lane, Anthony. "Sheet Music." *The New Yorker,* No. 40 (29 November 1993): 148-51.

> Asserts that viewers will find *The Piano* somewhat forbidding and tedious but contends that it "easily outstrips most of what we see these days."

Lopate, Phillip. Review of *An Angel at My Table,* by Jane Campion. *Vogue* 181 (March 1991): 260, 266.

> Notes there is evidence of a broadening emotional range in *An Angel at My Table.*

Isak Dinesen

1885-1962

(Born Karen Christentze Dinesen; also known by her married name Karen Blixen; also wrote under the pseudonyms Tania Blixen, Osceola, and Pierre Andrézel). Danish short story writer, autobiographer, novelist, and translator.

The following entry presents an overview of Dinesen's career. For further information on her life and works, see *CLC*, Volumes 10 and 29.

INTRODUCTION

Dinesen is best known for *Seven Gothic Tales* (1934) and the autobiographical novel *Den afrikanske farm* (1937; *Out of Africa*). Acclaimed for her poetic prose style, complex characters, and intricate plots, Dinesen was concerned with such themes as the lives and values of aristocrats, the nature of fate and destiny, God and the supernatural, the artist, and the place of women in society. Hailed as a proto-feminist by some critics, scorned as a colonialist by others, Dinesen is chiefly regarded as a masterful storyteller. Ernest Hemingway once remarked that the Nobel Prize for Literature he received in 1954 should have been awarded to her.

Biographical Information

Born in Rungsted, Denmark, Dinesen was the daughter of an army officer who was a friend of Hans Christian Andersen and who wrote a book about his experiences as a fur trapper among the Indians of the northern United States. Dinesen studied English at Oxford University and painting at the Royal Academies in Copenhagen, Paris, and Rome. Following her marriage to Baron Bror Blixen-Finecke, a cousin, in 1914, Dinesen moved to East Africa as the owner and manager of a coffee plantation near present-day Nairobi, Kenya. Following the death of her lover Denys Finch-Hatton and the eventual sale of her farm in 1931—events that are dramatized in *Out of Africa*—Dinesen returned to Denmark, where she completed her first book, *Seven Gothic Tales.* Subsequent works included several more short story collections, and numerous essays and novels in both Danish and English. Although she suffered from chronic spinal syphilis, emaciation, and the physical frailty attendant to these conditions, she continued to lecture and give interviews. She became a founding member of the Danish Academy in 1960. Dinesen died in Rungsted in 1962.

Major Works

Seven Gothic Tales is a collection of short stories written in a romantic style, employing fantasy to explore aristocratic sensibilities and values. For example, in "The Deluge at Norderney," a Cardinal directs his high-born companions to give up their places on a boat to save peasants during a flood. *Out of Africa* presents Dinesen's experiences as a British East African coffee plantation owner, her relationship with the Africans who lived and worked on and around her plantation, her divorce from Baron Blixen, her affair with Denys Finch-Hatton, and the failure of her coffee enterprise, which precipitated her return to Denmark. The short stories in *Winter's Tales* (1942), with their simpler narrative style and attention to landscape, history, and life of Denmark, solidified Dinesen's standing in the Danish literary community. "Sorrow-Acre," for instance, is based on a medieval Danish folktale and is set in eighteenth-century Denmark. The story examines the inevitable social consequences of the master-servant relationship: how aristocratic values and traditions govern the attitudes and actions of a landlord toward a thieving serf and his mother. During the Nazi occupation of Denmark, Dinesen wrote *The Angelic Avengers* (1946), a mystery-thriller about two orphaned girls. The manuscript was smuggled out of Denmark and published under the pseudonymn Pierre Andrézel. Dinesen continually denied authorship of the book, however, because she was unsatisfied with its literary quality. *Last Tales* (1957) is a collection of short stories that are divided into three

sections—New Gothic Tales, New Winter's Tales, and Tales from *Albondocani.* These works represent a return to her earlier literary style, themes, and characters. In "Echoes," for instance, Pellegrina Leoni, who first appears in *Seven Gothic Tales,* is an ex-opera star, devastated by the loss of her voice. Consequently, a disgruntled Pellegrini uses elaborate disguises to ensure her anonymity. She remarks that when it comes to fate and life, God can be both a charlatan and "jokester" with his human creations. *Skygger paa Græsset* (1960; *Shadows on the Grass*) recalls Dinesen's African experiences. In this nonfiction work she focuses on the lives of several of the African servants and friends whom she first wrote about in *Out of Africa.* The novel *Ehrengard* (1963) was published posthumously and was Dinesen's last work. Its themes include the notion of the artist as creator and interpreter of life. The story follows the artist Cazotte's lust for Ehrengard, while she sits for a portrait. Cazotte's objective is to humiliate her, and in the process diabolically usurp God's role as the ultimate and defining artist of creation and master of life. Among Dinesen's other posthumously published works are *Carnival: Entertainments and Posthumous Tales* (1977); *Breve fra Afrika 1914-31* (1978; *Letters from Africa: 1914-1931*), which contain her correspondence with family and friends during her years in Africa; and *Daguerreotypes, and Other Essays* (1979), containing the well-known "Bonfire Speech," which presents her thoughts on many feminist issues.

Critical Reception

Dinesen's writings have been widely praised and enthusiastically received. Critics applaud her prose style, her facility with complicated plots and characters, and her "natural" gift for storytelling. While many scholars have claimed that her picture of Africa in *Out of Africa* is romanticized, they note that the story is engaging, well-structured, and presents a detailed picture of life among British expatriots in Africa. Several commentators have noted similarities between Dinesen's views on identity, spirituality, and meaning and those of Danish philosopher Søren Kierkegaard; others have detected the influence of Aldous Huxley and Sigmund Freud on the development of Dinesen's themes and characters, particularly in such works as "Carnival." Finally, many critics have recognized humor as an integral part of Dinesen's literary style and agree that her stories consistently reveal a positive attitude and "passion for life," which embraces life's challenges and adversities as well as its triumphs and joys.

PRINCIPAL WORKS

Seven Gothic Tales (short stories) 1934
Sanhedens Haevn [*The Revenge of Truth*] (drama) 1936
Out of Africa [*Den Afrikanske Farm*] (autobiography) 1937
Winter's Tales (short stories) 1942
Farah (novel) 1950

En Baaltale med 14 Aars Forsinkelse [*Bonfire Speech Fourteen Years Delayed*] (essay) 1953
Last Tales [*Sidste Fortaellinger*] (short stories) 1957
Anecdotes of Destiny [*Skaebne-Anekdoter*] (short stories) 1958
Skygger paa Graesset [*Shadows on the Grass*] (autobiography) 1960
Osceola (short stories and poetry) 1962
Ehrengard (novel) 1963
Essays (essays) 1965; also published as *Mit livs mottoer og andre essays* [enlarged edition], 1978
Breve fra Afrika 1914-31. 2 vols. [*Letter from Africa 1914-31*] (letters) 1978
Daguerreotypes, and Other Essays (essays) 1979
Samlede (essays) 1985

CRITICISM

Katherine Woods (review date 6 March 1938)

SOURCE: "Isak Dinesen's Fine Record of Life on an African Farm," in *The New York Times Book Review,* March 6, 1938, p. 3.

[*In the following review, Woods enthusiastically praises* Out of Africa.]

The book [*Out of Africa*] which Isak Dinesen has made from her life on an African farm is a surprising piece of writing to come from the author of *Seven Gothic Tales.* After dazzling the public with what Dorothy Canfield called "the strange slanting beauty and controlled fantasy" of the first book, this amazing Danish master of English prose has stepped now into the clearest reality, the utmost classic simplicity, the most direct—yet the most exquisitely restrained—truth. But it is an incandescent simplicity; the reality is of the spirit as well as of object and event; the truth is a cry from the heart. And after all the books that we have had out of Africa, I think this is the one we have been waiting for.

Like the Ngong hills—"which are amongst the most beautiful in the world"—this writing is without redundancies, bared to its lines of strength and beauty. "There was no fat on it, and no luxuriance anywhere," she says of her African landscape; so in the book there is no sentimentality, no elaboration. It is an autobiographical book: in one sense, only partly an autobiography; in another sense, doubly autobiographical. This is not a chronological record; and until close to the end it touches almost casually the course of the author's life. It is peopled with other characters, every one of them alive. And the author knows how the hills look just before the rains come; and how the bleak wind runs over the land and the scents and colors die when the rains fail; and how often the bright air will bring illusion, as if one were walking on the bottom of the sea. She can make a sudden parable of the resignation of the oxen, and understand the tragedy of the captured giraffes, so proud and innocent; and the ancient African forest, she says, is like an old tapestry. She knows the practical details, the hard work, of this farm life, too.

In this personal record out of Africa, so sincere and natural, so direct and clear, there is that penetration, restraint, simplicity and precision which, together, mark the highly civilized mind, and that compassion, courage and dignity which mark civilization.

—*Katherine Woods*

But before one has read many pages in her book one realizes how, in a deeper sense than that of mere chronicle, these clear objective details from a farm in Kenya are themselves wholly personal. Once, looking back on an evening errand in wartime in the Masai Reserve, she shows the reason:

> The plains with the thorntrees on them were already quite dark, but the air was filled with clarity—and over our heads, to the west, a single star which was to grow big and radiant in the course of the night was now just visible, like a silver point in the sky of citrine topaz. The air was cold to the lungs, the long grass dripping wet, and the herbs on it gave out their spiced astringent scent. In a little while on the sides the cicada would begin to sing. The grass was me, and the air, the distant invisible mountains were me, the tired oxen were me. I breathed with the slight wind in the thorntrees.

This is more than mere understanding. And Africa lives through all this beautiful and heart-stirring book because of that simple and unsought-for fusion of the spirit, lying behind the skill which can put the sense of Africa's being into clear, right, simple words, through the things and people of the farm.

The farm was a coffee plantation, but much of it was grass land and part was primeval forest, and native squatters lived, by law and custom, on 1,000 of its 6,000 acres and had their own gardens and herds there. Across the river was the country of the Masai, a proud people who had been great fighters but were now a dying race. Hunting country was roundabout, and two missions were a few miles away (in opposite directions), and it was not a long drive to Nairobi, even in the early days by cart. Other Europeans came and went, and some lived in these same hills. That complex scene, that unpredictable cast of characters, of the European colony in Africa, can be found in this book. But Baroness Blixen (not yet known under her pen-name of Isak Dinesen) was very close to the native peoples and to all the immemorial life of the African wild. It was not easy to get to know the natives, she says: they understood her better than she understood them; but she felt a great affection for them, from the first.

She used to doctor them, from her simple knowledge. She had an evening school for them, with a native schoolmaster. She studied their language, and told them stories to which they loved to listen. They came to her—even the Masai across the river—to complain when a lion was taking their cows, and she would go out and shoot it; one night she and Denys Finch-Hatton shot two of these marauding lions, and the children came out from their school near by and sang a little song of triumph, which ended "in an intoxicated refrain, 'A-B-C-D,' because they came straight from the school and had their heads filled with wisdom." And the little herd-boys brought their sheep to graze on her lawns. She was the friend of the Kikuyu chief, and he sent for her to come to him when he was dying. And once when a serious dispute among the Kikuyu on the farm had gone beyond the power of her peace-making, she asked the chief to render judgment for her on the important matter of cows and witchcraft; for she was a sort of judge among them, too; the Elders held their council meetings before her house, and used to ask her for final decisions.

So, as the years went by, she came to know them: their justice which is so different from the white man's justice; their untroubled acceptance of life's uncertainties which is so different from the white man's shrinking from risk; their courage, which is "unadulterated liking for danger"; their strange dancing imagination, and their stillness and their hardness and their mocking mirth; the way, too, in which they could be "unreliable and yet in the grand manner sincere." And she came to know how the African natives will make of some certain European, for some certain reason, a symbol—a brass serpent lifted up in the wilderness—and even to see that she had become such a symbol, herself. In these and other ways she knew the African peoples among whom she lived, and whose friend she was. And unforgettably, through her book, she draws the portraits, and tells or suggests the stories of individuals—natives, Europeans, animals.

In this personal record out of Africa, so sincere and natural, so direct and clear, there is that penetration, restraint, simplicity and precision which, together, mark the highly civilized mind, and that compassion, courage and dignity which mark civilization, in the best sense, in the human heart. This writing is poignant and exquisite, it has an echoing reticence, it is swift in profundity or insight or tenderness or irony. And no description of this book, highly as it may praise its solid substance, can in itself do justice to its effortless, expressive, wholly individual beauty of form, or even list the evocations and suggestions that lie within, or are touched by, its very simplicity. ***Out of Africa*** is something rare and lovely, to read again and again.

At the last, it tears the heart with its disaster and its simple gallantry. Isak Dinesen had planted her own deep roots in this soil, long years before. And the roots were broken at last. She had to sell the farm, and leave Africa. After tedious effort she was able to assure her villages being kept together, when she had gone. But the farm was lost and divided. She tells the story with quiet and noble beauty. And one knows that her wish for life as a whole has been fulfilled by Africa: she did not let it go until it blessed her.

Eric O. Johannesson   (essay date Winter 1962)

SOURCE: "Isak Dinesen, Søren Kierkegaard, and the Present Age," in *Books Abroad,* Vol. 36, No. 1, Winter, 1962, pp. 20-4.

[In the following essay, Johannesson examines the similarities between the philosophical views expressed in many of Dinesen's works and those of Danish philosopher Søren Kierkegaard, notably themes relating to human identity, human interdependence, and passion for life.]

To compare Isak Dinesen and Søren Kierkegaard may seem a rather frivolous undertaking particularly to those who see in the former a sophisticated and witty Danish Baroness who likes to tell decadent and bizarre tales about a bygone era or produce elegiac memorials to a vanished Africa. The world of Isak Dinesen whose stories grace the pages of *Harper's Bazaar* and *Ladies Home Journal* and whose histrionic face peers at us in *Life* magazine seems far removed from that of Søren Kierkegaard, whose efforts to reawaken the individual to a passionate awareness of his own existence drove him to martyrdom. Yet the two are not as far apart as it might seem. While Isak Dinesen has often been regarded as merely an expert in the elegant art of pastiche, Kierkegaard in the opinion of his age was a wealthy playboy with ambitions to become a writer. If the mask of Kierkegaard deceived his contemporaries and obscured the real significance of his works, the mask of Isak Dinesen has sometimes obscured the depth of feeling and meaningful order which underlies her fictional world. For though they chose to express their visions of life in very different modes, Kierkegaard in his "mimic essays" so well suited to his lyric-philosophical style and his desire to explore certain attitudes to life in their purest form, and Dinesen in her unique form of storytelling, both are essentially artists of the mask. Kierkegaard's masks were many: Victor Eremita, Johannes Climacus, Frater Taciturnus, Constantin Constantius. He showed an uninhibited love for literary mystifications, taking great pains not to have the identity of any one of his masks mistaken for his own. Isak Dinesen is, as everyone probably knows by now, a pseudonym for Karen Blixen-Finecke, but it is only one of Karen Blixen's masks. There are at least two others: Osceola, and Pierre Andrézel (author of the little known Gothic novel *The Angelic Avengers*).

Dinesen regards the adoption of a mask as an active, passionate and self-mastering state, making for greatness, while the contemplation of the self is seen as a source of passivity and melancholy.

—Eric O. Johannesson

What is the reason for this play of masks? The reason is, first of all, to be sought in a sense for the histrionic: a love of theater and opera. Kierkegaard wrote perceptive studies of several actors and actresses, as well as of the great archetypal figures of the stage, a Don Juan, a Faust. Isak Dinesen's heroes and heroines are often theatrical personalities, and the spirit of Shakespeare's comedies pervades the tales. But while this shared inclination to mask play has its simple motivation in a love for the stage, it is deeply rooted in a genuine sense for the multiple possibilities of the self. Thus Kierkegaard explored through the various pseudonyms pure forms or "stages" of existence: the aesthetic, the ethical, the demonic, the humorous, the religious. This mode of presentation he referred to as indirect communication, the only mode of expression suited to his purpose: to initiate the reader in the art of becoming subjective, of becoming an individual. By carrying the description of each stage to its extreme form, i.e., despair, he sought to awaken the individual to the necessity of choice and thus to that passionate sense of his own unique existence which characterizes the art of becoming subjective. In an age of reflection he sought a return to passion. Dinesen's mask play is also deeply rooted in her view of life. In her stories the adoption of a mask is contrasted to the contemplation of the self in a mirror. Like Yeats, Dinesen regards the adoption of a mask as an active, passionate and self-mastering state, making for greatness, while the contemplation of the self is seen as a source of passivity and melancholy. To don a mask is regarded as an aristocratic manner: to play the lover, the hero, the saint, requires the aristocratic virtues of courage and imagination, and a passionate affirmation of destiny. Thus it is opposed to the bourgeois virtues: being true to one's own self, sincerity, and security. Thus the mask play is a defense of the aristocratic virtues in a bourgeois age. It is here that Dinesen and Kierkegaard have their basic affinity: both view the present in the light of a vanishing age, whether from the vantage point of the revolutionary age of Napoleon or from the vantage point of *l'ancien régime.*

Kierkegaard's reflections on his age have found their most succinct and delightful expression in his review, written in 1846, of the novel *To tidsaldre (The Two Ages)* by Thomasine Gyllembourg. In this review Kierkegaard compares what he calls "the revolutionary age" with the present age, a comparison which does not present the latter in any favourable light. "Our age is essentially one of understanding and reflection, without passion, momentarily bursting into enthusiasm, and shrewdly relapsing into repose". [Søren Kierkegaard, *The Present Age,* 1940]. This is the beginning of the attack on the age of reflection, an age in which one is, as Kierkegaard puts it, "tempted to ask whether there is a single man left who, for once, commits an outrageous folly." It is an age in which "not even a suicide kills himself in desperation," but "deliberates so long and so carefully that he literally chokes with the thought." Being an age without passion it has no values, and produces "no hero, no lover, no thinker, no knight of the faith, no proud man, no man in despair" [*The Present Age*], since these cannot exist without complete personal commitment to a set of values. When a man of the present age happens to make a decision which saves him from evil one can no longer tell, says Kierkegaard, whether the decision is reached "after thorough consideration, or whether it is simply the exhaustion resulting from reflection which prevents him from doing wrong."

Dinesen has left us no doubt as to her aristocratic sympathies, sympathies molded by her own family background and by her years in Africa.

—Eric O. Johannesson

In this age the spirit of rebellion which characterizes a revolutionary age is transformed "into a feat of dialectics: it leaves everything standing but cunningly empties it of significance" [*The Present Age*]. Thus the state of tension which characterizes the interplay of opposites in a relationship is lost: "For example, the admirer no longer cheerfully and happily acknowledges greatness, promptly expressing his appreciation, and then rebelling against its pride and arrogance." To be a subject now means "to be a third party": the subject no longer has a "direct relation to the king but simply becomes an observer and deliberately works out the problem; i.e., the relation of a subject to his king." The young student is no longer afraid of his master, or going to school to learn: going to school "rather implies being interested in the problem of education." Thus the relationships of father and son, man and woman, and master and servant are destroyed from exhausted tension. The result is a general levelling, a loss of individuality, and a rule by the anonymous phantom called the public, and its organ, the press. In this situation, says Kierkegaard, the only salvation lies in religion, in becoming an individual.

Isak Dinesen has left us no doubt as to her aristocratic sympathies, sympathies molded by her own family background and by her years in Africa. They are reflected in many of her best tales, in **"The Deluge at Norderney,"** and in **"Sorrow Acre,"** for instance. In these and in several other tales the aristocratic figure is contrasted with either the Hamlet figure given to contemplating himself in the mirror or the anxious bourgeois, both shrinking from action either from excess of reflection or from fear or the lack of imagination.

In **"The Deluge at Norderney"** Dinesen has placed a few of her most delightful aristocratic figures on a precarious and symbolic hayloft where they carry on some interesting conversations and tell tales, most of them relating to mask play and the virtues of aristocracy. Here we are in the age of Louis Philippe (the year is 1835), and Kasparson does not hide his contempt for the bourgeois king. The trouble with Louis Philippe, says Kasparson, whose motto is "Disguise yourselves," is that he lacks charlatanry, "he is genuinely reliable all through" [**"The Deluge at Norderney"**]. In the modern world, Kasparson laments, greatness of imagination is sadly lacking. But on the Day of Judgment man is to be judged by his mask, that is, by the range of his imagination. To adopt a mask, play a great role, is the aristocratic way of life, requiring passion, courage, energy and imagination, leading to an affirmation of destiny. The mask is the destiny which the proud man chooses for himself.

With the others on the hayloft is also a young man, a bourgeois from Copenhagen, referred to as Timon of Assens. He is a Hamlet figure, the melancholy hero, so frequently the hero of Dinesen's tales. Like Count Augustus von Schimmelmann in **"The Roads Round Pisa,"** Axel Leth in **"The Invincible Slaveowners,"** Charles Despard of **"The Young Man with the Carnation,"** and Adam in **"Sorrow Acre,"** he is an observer of life, contemplating himself thoughtfully in the mirror, wondering about his identity, unable to commit himself to any course of action. The stories in which these melancholy and reflective heroes become involved, or the stories that are told to them, are often designed to present them with an insight, an insight which will help them regain their faith in life and embrace their destiny. Thus, Adam in **"Sorrow Acre,"** imbued with the new humanitarian and sentimental ideas of the nineteenth century, cannot abide the suffering of the old Marie who is trying to save the life of her son. When he upbraids the uncle for his inhumanity, telling him that he will go to the United States, the uncle says: "Take service, there, with the power that will give you an easier bargain than this: That with your own life you may buy the life of your son" [**"Sorrow Acre"**]. Adam finally comes to accept the values of the feudal aristocratic world, realizing that all which lives must suffer, that there are no easy bargains in life. He also realizes that suffering confers greatness, and comes to accept tragedy—not as a misfortune—but as a human privilege. Other bourgeois figures receive similar insight. Lady Carlotta in **"The Roads Round Pisa,"** the parson in **"Alkmene,"** Emilie Van Damm in **"The Dreaming Child,"** Jensine in **"The Pearl"**: they are made to realize that they have not had faith in life, they have been in the words of Prince Pozentiani, "too small for the ways of God," (*Seven Gothic Tales*), having tried to arrange matters so as to obtain maximum security instead of entrusting themselves to destiny.

Related to the aristocratic code in Dinesen's world is the principle of interdependence, the tension between opposites, as it is expressed in the relationship between master and servant, or between man and woman. In the account of her Somali servant Farah, in *Shadows on the Grass,* Dinesen speaks of the master-servant relationship that existed between them in Africa. The relationship was an ideal one, because she and Farah were separated by such great differences. The relationship was like that between Don Quixote and Sancho Panza, in which the noble knight was highly dependent upon his servant, but Sancho Panza would never have become immortal on his own. In a little fireside talk some years ago Dinesen also expressed her "faith in the importance of interaction and her conviction about the great riches and unlimited possibilities that are contained in the correspondence and interplay of two dissimilar entities." In this talk she spoke of the relationship between men and women, stressing that women should not try to imitate men: in Dinesen's words, women should *be,* men should *act*.

The theme of interdependence runs through many of Dinesen's tales. **"The Invincible Slaveowners"** deals with the master-servant relationship, and **"A Consolatory Tale"** and **"The Young Man with the Carnation"** deal with the relationship between the artist and his public, and between the artist and God. In **"The Deluge at Norderney"** Kasparson chides King Louis Philippe for trying to be "just like a plain ordinary citizen," abhors this "humane God" and feels a longing for the time "when in the nights of Mexico, I felt great traditions rise up again of a God who did not give a pin for our commandments" (**Seven Gothic Tales**).

The concept of interdependence is one of the basic concepts of Dinesen's world. As such it is no solution to the world's ills, but rather an attempt to preserve the tension of opposites which gives order, harmony and value to human relations. Its underlying principle is best expressed in the words of Baron Brackel in **"The Old Chevalier"**: "to love, or cherish, the pride of your partner, or of your adversary, as you will define it, as highly as or higher than your own."

Dinesen's world-view is aristocratic, but deep down it is aesthetic in nature. When the Baron in **"The Old Chevalier"** loses the young Nathalie as the result of his fidelity to the knightly code of chivalry, he observes the rules of an elegant game, and by respecting the pride of his partner he ends the relationship as it began: within a magic circle of freedom, grace, and beauty. Thus the aristocrat becomes an aesthetic type, and the laws governing human relations come to resemble the rules governing the composition of a fugue or a symphony. There is seemingly a gulf between this basically aesthetic view and Kierkegaard's belief that religion alone can restore individuality and prevent the abstract levelling process. And yet there is, once again, a deep affinity of outlook between the two writers. For, though Isak Dinesen rejects the doctrine of Christ's expiatory sacrifice, she often expresses her admiration for the Old Testament and its religious values, and, in particular, for the Book of Job, which has a central place in her work. Kierkegaard's religious views are also much closer to the spirit of the Old Testament, though he regards the belief in the paradox of Christ as the real criterion of a Christian. It is significant that Kierkegaard in his representation of the religious stage chose Abraham as his hero, and in his novel *Repetition* the figure of Job is constantly invoked by the young man. It is about the figure of Job that Dinesen's and Kierkegaard's views again converge.

Though the great theme of Dinesen's works is the theme of acceptance, this acceptance is usually preceded by rebellion. Her characters are often engaged in discussions like those between God and Job, or they are involved in stories in which they learn the art of acceptance. The God against whom the characters rebel is a God whose nature transcends human imagination, and from whom anything may be expected. He cannot be appeased if he is angry or cajoled into doing man's will. If he loves you, he may destroy you. If you are good, he sends you afflictions. In Africa Dinesen learned to know God as an arbitrary, gratuitous figure who does not "give a pin for our commandments," a God who does not justify himself by any arguments of right and wrong: whose argument is the whirlwind. To believe in this God on account of his righteousness or goodness is absurd, but then the primary distinction of a God is greatness, not goodness. Like the natives in Africa, Dinesen recognizes only a God who is gratu-

itous, who acts capriciously, and whose imagination always transcends human understanding, these being the virtues which make him great and set him apart from human beings. Thus the principle of interdependence is preserved in the religious sphere, for the relationship between God and man is one of tension. Man's greatness lies in his proud defiance of God and in his equally proud acceptance and yes-saying to whatever life might bring, in an affirmation of his essentially tragic destiny.

In Kierkegaard's *Repetition* the young friend of Constantin Constantius praises Job because there is passion in his speech, because he is "a mouth for the afflicted, and a cry for the contrite, and a shriek for the anguished," a voice that dares to contend with God. "The Lord is not afraid, He is well able to define himself, but how might He be able to speak in His defense if no one ventures to complain as it is seemly for a man to do? Speak, lift up thy voice, speak aloud, God surely can speak louder, He possesses the thunder—but that too is an answer, an explanation, reliable, trustworthy, genuine, an answer from God himself, an answer which even if it crush a man is more glorious than gossip and rumor about the righteousness of providence which are invented by human wisdom and circulated by effeminate creatures and eunuchs" [Søren Kierkegaard, *Repetition*]. The greatness of Job lies in his contention that he is in the right, and in his refusal to accept the fact that he has suffered because of his sins.

The story of Constantin Constantius in *Repetition* is, as Kierkegaard himself called it, a "story of suffering." So is the story of Quidam in *Stages on Life's Way,* and so is the story of Kierkegaard's own life. When Kierkegaard realized that he had to sacrifice his love for Regine Olsen he saw himself in the image of Job, and like Job he sought to retain his faith in the miraculous recovery of what he had lost. In his life as well as in his works, suffering and absolute faith in the paradox and the absurd point the way to the recovery of inwardness and passion in an age of reflection.

Donald Hannah (essay date October-December 1963)

SOURCE: "In Memoriam Karen Blixen: Some Aspects of Her Attitude of Life," in *The Sewanee Review,* Vol. LXXI, No. 4, October-December, 1963, pp. 585-604.

[*In the following essay, Hannah examines Dinesen's major works—the autobiography* Out of Africa *and several of the short stories—focusing on their depiction of the past and evocation of nostalgia.*]

It was perhaps typical of that elusive, even enigmatic figure, the late Baroness Karen Blixen-Finecke, that she was most widely known by her pseudonym, Isak Dinesen. But this is the least of the paradoxes with which the reader of her work is faced. Karen Blixen, a Dane, wrote most of her short stories first in English, and then "translated" them into her native language. The deep vein of fantasy and imagination in her work is matched by a rigorous process of selection and control. She was the great story-teller in an age where the story-element is considered one of the less important aspects of fiction. But possibly the most striking side of her work lies in her treatment of the past;

it exercised a very strong fascination for her, and it is the dimension in which her imagination seemed most at home. Nevertheless, although her stories are set in the past, in general, spanning the period from the end of the eighteenth century to the mid-nineteenth, they can be considered as historical fiction in only a very limited sense.

When one turns to the details of her work, the impression of paradox is strengthened. She was both Isak Dinesen, the detached, impersonal story-teller, seldom, if ever, entering into her work to comment upon the action, and Karen Blixen, the author of an autobiography in which comment and action are of equal importance. As Isak Dinesen, she published four collections of short stories, *Seven Gothic Tales* (1934), *Winter's Tales* (1942), *Last Tales* (1957), and *Anecdotes of Destiny* (1958). These are her chief works of fiction, but to these should be added her novel, *The Angelic Avengers,* published in 1947 under another pseudonym, Pierre Andrézel. This was written, as a diversion, during the German occupation of Denmark, but except for the fact that it too is set in the past, in mid-nineteenth century England, it lies outside the main scope of her work. Her autobiography, *Out of Africa,* was published under her own name in 1937. This was supplemented by a small volume, *Shadows on the Grass* (1960), published under her usual pseudonym.

Karen Blixen was born in 1885 at Rungstedlund in Denmark; just before the first World War she went out to Kenya. She spent the next seventeen years of her life there as the owner of a large farm near Nairobi. Then she returned to Denmark to begin a new life as a writer, living again at Rungstedlund until her death on September 7, 1962, after a long drawn-out illness which she bore with characteristic courage.

Karen Blixen and Isak Dinesen. Her own story and her tales. Her life and her art. How are these related to one another? Karen Blixen's work is, in fact, the expression of firmly held convictions and a sharply individual attitude to life, shaped and moulded by personal experience. To discover something of the basis of this experience, one must turn to *Out of Africa,* for it was during the period recorded there that the connecting link was forged between Karen Blixen's life and her art. During her latter years in Kenya, her life was shadowed by personal tragedy and by incessant struggle against debt and failure of harvests. From life she turned to fiction, from the present to the past:

> I began in the evenings to write stories, fairy-tales and romances, that would take my mind a long way off, to other countries and times.
> [*Out of Africa*]

In 1931 the farm had to be sold. The moving and restrained account of her grief at this and at the tragic death of her beloved friend, Denys Finch-Hatton, should be read in its entirety for no isolated quotation can do it justice.

But her life in Kenya was not all tragedy:

> Looking back on a sojourn in the African highlands, you are struck by your feeling of having lived for a time up in the air.. .. you breathed easily, drawing in a vital assurance and lightness of

heart. In the highlands you woke up in the morning and thought: Here I am, where I ought to be.

"Looking back. . . . where I ought to be." The two phrases suggest the whole tone of the book and the mood underlying it. For if the predominant impression left on the reader is one of the splendour of Karen Blixen's life in Africa, there is also a persistent undertone of deep sadness. *Out of Africa* has been written and is read in the shadow cast by the title.

The great attraction of Kenya for Karen Blixen was not only the splendour of the surroundings, but also the way of life on the farm. As the owner of much land, she had many duties to perform, as law-giver, doctor, hunter, for the Africans living on it. She carried these out with great sympathy and insight, as both *Out of Africa* and *Shadows on the Grass* bear witness, but she was also happy in doing so. "Life out there," she once said, "was, I believe, rather like 18th Century England: one might often be hard up for cash, but life was still rich in many ways." Not only the short stories are set in the past; *Out of Africa* too recalls a vanished epoch:

> The Colony is changing and has already changed since I lived there. When I write down as accurately as possible my experiences on the farm . . . it may have a sort of historical interest.

Writing of the death of Berkeley Cole, one of her close friends, she says, "When Berkeley died, the country changed. . . . Up till his death [it] had been the Happy Hunting Grounds, now it was slowly changing and turning into a business proposition." The book describes a society before the full effects of this change were felt. Inevitably, when the farm was sold, Karen Blixen's life in Kenya came to an end, and the Africans living on the farm were similarly uprooted when they were given six months' notice to get off the land. Seen from this point of view, the fact that the farm was parcelled out as building-plots, and that her house was turned into a club for the new residential quarter, acquires an almost symbolic meaning. The departure from the farm was the signal for the full establishment of the "business proposition" and the consequent disruption of the settled, determined, and ordered life of the past. The semi-feudal conditions of life on the farm meant that she had actually lived in the past and felt deeply attracted to it. It was natural, therefore, that Karen Blixen should return to the past in her fiction, although actually not with her mind "a long way off."

This is not to suggest, however, that, as a process of nostalgic wish-fulfilment, Karen Blixen simply transposed into her short stories the details of her own story in Africa. It is true that *Out of Africa* has some "sort of historical interest," but of equal importance is the way in which that historical interest is coloured by the personality of Karen Blixen herself. This is also true of the short stories. The paradox of the contrast between them and *Out of Africa* is not really so great, for despite the apparent elimination of the personality of the author by the technique adopted for the narration of the tales, despite the substitution of the figure of Isak Dinesen for the personality of Karen Blixen, the attitude to life and the personality behind them can be clearly traced, and it is that of the author of *Out of Africa.* In the stories an historical period is recorded; yet an imaginative world, based upon personal experience, is also created.

The ruling principles of this world are firmly held convictions which determine its every constituent element. Karen Blixen's short stories are the result of a completely disciplined and a completely conscious artistry. There is no chance or triviality in the world she creates; all irrelevant incident and detail is either eliminated or is later shown to be an integrated and connected strand woven into the total pattern and thus contributing its part to the completed design. There is no figure in the carpet; the figure is the carpet itself. The narrative pattern of the story and the life which is described and traced out by this pattern become one and the same thing. A world is created by her art, where it is possible for a character to play an accepted and ordained role, which is accepted by the character himself, is ordained by the demands of the story, and where the choice of the role is made both possible and necessary by the period in which the story is set. This conception of playing a role is fundamental both to Karen Blixen's art and to her attitude to life. The parallel which this offers with Karen Blixen's own life as the great landowner in Kenya does not need stressing. It was a role which she accepted for herself, and which the conditions in Kenya at that time made it possible to play and necessary to accept.

The world described in *Out of Africa,* set and rooted in the past, is intertwined with Karen Blixen's own; and this is also true of the stories. Nowhere do these aspects eventually become clearer than in the short story "Sorrow-Acre," included in *Winter's Tales.* This story represents in a small compass many of the major aspects of her work; it also marks what is probably Karen Blixen's greatest single achievement in fiction.

"Sorrow-Acre" is based on a folk-tale from the south of Jutland. The details of the folk-tale vary, but the most important version for our purpose is given in F. Ohrt's *Udvalgte Sönderiydske Folkesagn (Selected Folk-Tales from South Jutland),* published in 1919. This version runs as follows:

> During a flood with high tidal waves, a good deal of flotsam drifted ashore near Ballum. Amongst it, a young man from the town recognised some pieces belonging to his family and started salvaging them. Whilst he was doing this, one of the robbers from Skaerbaek came and wanted some of it. They started fighting and the young lad unfortunately killed his opponent. At that time, however, these beachrobbers were so powerful that they had him condemned to death at the court-house. His mother, deeply distressed by this, went to the Count at his castle of Skakkenborg, told him of her grief, and implored him to show mercy towards her son. The Count promised her to do so on the condition that she must mow a field of barley between sunrise and sunset. This field was so large that four men would have had much labour to cut it in one day. If she could do it, her son would be set free.

> The mother accepted the task, and did finish it. When she had cut the last handful with her sickle, she said,

> Now the sun will set
> Now God's mercy I will get.

> But at the very moment when she raised herself from her bent position, her back broke and she fell dead. The mother was buried in the churchyard at Ballum. On her grave, a stone has been laid on which she is drawn with a sheaf and sickle in her arm. The field where she cut the corn is still shown. To this day it is known as Sorrow-Acre.

The date of the events giving rise to the folk-tale can be determined with some accuracy, since the flood took place in 1634.

In March, 1931, the Danish writer Paul la Cour published a much longer version of the folk-tale in the periodical *Tilskueren.* The original version, as found in Ohrt's collection, was also included. Karen Blixen had already published some work in this periodical, which occupied a prominent place in Danish cultural life, but although this contribution to *Tilskueren* therefore was probably the actual source of "Sorrow-Acre," her short story, nevertheless, differs considerably from both la Cour's version and from the original folk-tale itself.

Paul la Cour follows the details of the original story very closely. But considering these bare details as "schematic and too condensed" he lengthens them very considerably, mainly by dwelling on the feelings of the mother, through whom much of the story is presented. The focus of the tale is consequently shifted, and the final result is an emotionally heightened elaboration in which the feelings receive as much emphasis as the events. Karen Blixen's short story, however, contrasts sharply with la Cour's, since the stress falls on the narration of the actual events, while the details of the narrative, as found in the folk-tale, are extensively changed.

In "Sorrow-Acre," a young man on the estate of a Danish lord has been accused of setting fire to one of the barns. Anne-Marie, his widowed mother, intercedes for him, and, like the mother in the folk-tale, is told that if she can cut a field of corn between sunrise and sunset her son will be set free. But if she fails, the case against her son will go through and she will never see him again. To this agreement the lord pledges his word and Anne-Marie accepts the conditions. We learn of this in retrospect, since "Sorrow-Acre" begins with the thoughts and reminiscences of the lord's young nephew, Adam, newly returned from a long stay in England. It is through his eyes that much of the action is presented, and the conflicting ideas forming the centre of the story emerge from the conversations which take place between the two men when Adam entreats the lord to retract his word, thereby annulling the agreement. He refuses to do this, and the rest of the story follows the folk-tale, with the mother dying just as she has completed her task. The son is freed, and the field afterwards is named "Sorrow-Acre."

From this, some of the changes made will be apparent;

two, in particular, are very significant. A completely new character, Adam, is introduced, and his importance in the story is stressed by the method of narration. The other major change from the folk-tale is that the date at which the events take place has been altered by well over a hundred years. This date is just as firmly given as it was in the folk-tale, though in a more indirect way. During the course of the story, Adam lends his uncle a book which has recently been published. Since it is described as a tragedy by Johannes Ewald dealing with the gods of Nordic mythology, it is clear that the work is *Balders Död,* first published in 1775. The introduction of a new main character and a shift in time from about 1634 to 1775—why are these changes made?

These two major alterations are connected and together they point to one of the major themes. The story is set in the period when the long-established, semi-feudal, landed society of the eighteenth century is beginning to face the challenge of new ideas. Moreover, the fact that *Balders Död* gives rise to the discussions is clearly intended by Karen Blixen, not only to give the period in which **"Sorrow-Acre"** is set, but also to cast further light upon the opposing attitudes. Ewald's drama centres on Balder, who in this work is a Nordic demi-god driven to his death by the irresistible force of his love for Nanna, a mortal woman; although a demi-god, he is powerless to control his emotions. The main significance of *Balders Död* for the old lord is that it marks the emergence of a new era, which "has made to itself a God in its own image, an emotional God" [**"Sorrow-Acre"**]. and is thus in complete opposition to his own ideal of omnipotence upon which he bases his conduct and which is represented for him by the ancient gods of classical mythology. The setting of the folk-tale has been deliberately transferred by Karen Blixen, so that now her short story stands near one of the great turning-points in Danish and European social and cultural history, and the figure of Adam is introduced to be the voice of the new age. The two ways of life confront each other in the impassioned appeal made by Adam:

> "This woman is ready to die for her son, —will it ever happen to you or me that a woman willingly gives up her life for us? And if it did indeed come to pass, should we make so light of it as not to give up a dogma in return?"

> "You are young," said the old Lord. "A new age will undoubtedly applaud you. I am old-fashioned, I have been quoting to you texts a thousand years old. We do not, perhaps, quite understand one another."

> ["Sorrow-Acre"]

A ready sympathy is aroused by the views here expressed by Adam. But, perhaps, the sympathy is felt a little too readily and the identification with one character made too swiftly. For part of the greatness of **"Sorrow-Acre"** lies in the fact that the reader is gradually forced from this identification with one character to a clearer perception and imaginative understanding of the old lord's role, and everything which this represents. In particular, we are made to realize the full implications of what is merely "a dogma" or "a whim" for Adam. The conflicting issues in **"Sorrow-Acre"** are not simply presented in abstract terms in discussions; they take on a life of their own and are embodied by the complete story. They are strands which are woven into the completed pattern, and which must be related to the whole; indeed, we are compelled to relate them by the narrative method adopted, the deceptive simplicity of which really conceals much artistry.

The artistry by which we are made to look on the old lord's role with a maturing sympathy and a gradually quickened understanding needs to be stressed, since it can be so easily overlooked. The method of narration is actually used in order to weight the scales against the lord, since we see him mainly through the eyes of a highly critical Adam. It is a criticism which is presented with scrupulous honesty and to which full weight is given. And although Anne-Marie dies at the supreme moment of her love and glory, her sacrifice, which has been exacted by the conditions imposed by the lord, is not minimized in any way. On the contrary, it has been counted against him in the beautifully rendered description of Anne-Marie's death at the end:

> At the sound of [her son's] voice she lifted her face to him, a faint, bland shadow of surprise ran over it, but still she gave no sign of having heard what he said, so that the people round them began to wonder if the exhaustion had turned her deaf. But after a moment she slowly and waveringly raised her hand, fumbling in the air as she aimed at his face, and with her fingers touched his cheek. The cheek was wet with tears, so that at the contact her finger-tips lightly stuck to it, and she seemed unable to overcome the infinitely slight resistance or to withdraw her hand. For a minute the two looked one another in the face. Then, softly and lingeringly, like a sheaf of corn that falls to the ground, she sank forward on to the boy's shoulder, and he closed his arms round her.

With all these factors apparently weighing so heavily against the old lord, how is the reader brought to an understanding of the part he plays and the ideals he represents?

Behind Karen Blixen's attitude is the firm belief that there is a purpose in life, that we have been created with a particular design in mind.

—Donald Hannah

The simplest answer to this question is to consider the way in which his character is conceived and presented by Karen Blixen. His attributes of firmness, stateliness, and nobility are clearly brought out by the manner and style with which his speech and his actions are presented. They compel the reader's admiration. But he is not really individualized in the story, not even given a name; he remains from first to last "the old lord." And this lack of individualization in terms of the story reflects his position in the particular period of history in which the story is set. Describing the life of the great country houses, the author remarks:

> To the King and the country, to his family and to the individual Lord of the manor himself it was a matter of minor consequence which particular Rosenkrantz, Juel or Skeel, out of a long row of Fathers and Sons, at the moment in his person incarnated the fields and woods, the peasants, cattle and game of the estate.

The reader's understanding of the character of the old lord also extends to the part he has to play. His character in the story is his part in life; the two cannot be separated, for they are made one by the way in which he is presented. An understanding of the lord's character clarifies what he stands for; by her way of representing him, Karen Blixen has succeeded, against all modern predilections, and against all odds, in investing his duties with nobility, grandeur, and understanding. He is seen as the embodiment of the duties of the great land-owners of the past, both to their land and to the people living on it. This fact offers an indication of the part which the superb evocation of the Danish landscape at the beginning of the story contributes to the whole. The pen in Karen Blixen's hand is here used like a brush (as a young girl she attended courses in painting and art in Copenhagen and Paris), but the details painted in so deftly and delicately, stroke by stroke, are not merely there to provide local colour. Like the splendour of the description of the surroundings in *Out of Africa* which convey something of the same quality to the account of her life there, these details in **"Sorrow-Acre"** contribute to the total effect of the story. The description is of a landscape—but of a landscape with figures; rendered in terms of the people and society which inhabit it, it ceases to be merely this, and becomes a land where life falls into an ordered pattern, drawn by generations of people, traced by stability, marked by tradition and order, and maintained throughout the centuries by these same qualities:

> A child of the country would read this open landscape like a book. The irregular mosaic of meadows and cornlands was a picture, in timid green and yellow, of the people's struggle for its daily bread, —the centuries had taught it to plough and sow in this way. . . .
>
> . . . But where, amongst cupular woods and groves, the lordly, pyramidal silhouette of the cut lime-avenues rose in the air, there a big country-house lav . . . as firmly rooted in the soil of Denmark as the peasants' huts.

In this description and rendering of a way of life, country-house and peasant hut, peasant and lord, are parts which together form the complete whole. The old lord's word—to Adam only a dogma and a whim—is the principle of this land upon which the maintenance and continuation of this whole order and way of life rests. **"Sorrow-Acre"** itself is but one field in the whole pattern drawn in the landscape. Much more is at stake for the old lord than Anne-Marie's individual fate and destiny, or even his own.

None of the characters are individualized, standing out in bold relief from the story; instead they are made to play their parts which are fitted into the design depicted at the beginning. Representation of the complete pattern of this life becomes the total design of the story—design in every sense—which is reaffirmed at the close, when, in the evening-light, the people left in the field after Anne-Marie's death bind up the corn she has cut, "imitating and measuring her course from one end of the rye-field to the other." The unity between the old lord and the people has been maintained; "the old Lord stayed with them for a long time, stepping along a little, and again standing still. As it grew darker he could walk up quite close to them or move amongst them, without being recognised."

The old order has been re-affirmed and maintained, the unity of this life has been continued—but for how long? Ultimately history itself breaks into this stable world, set in the past and enclosed by the story. Adam too has his destiny to fulfill. There is no heir to the land; the lord's son has died, and while Adam was in England, it was predicted to him that a son of his would inherit the estate. His relationship to the lord's young wife and its implications are not elaborated, but they also form part of the events and point symbolically to the future. The setting in the past, which causes the conflict between the two ways of life, also indicates the way in which the issue will be decided. And it is one which heightens the stature of the old lord into that of an indomitable figure defending a dying order.

One final point remains to be made about the old lord, for behind this figure can be discerned much of the attitude which shaped Karen Blixen's whole life and work. For him, "tragedy is the privilege of man, his highest privilege," whereas "the true art of the Gods is the comic." He develops this belief by saying, that here on earth, "we, who stand in lieu of the Gods . . . should leave to our vassals their monopoly of tragedy, and for ourselves accept the comic with grace," and he acts accordingly by leaving to Anne-Marie her monopoly of tragedy. But if she is made a tragic figure by the old lord's actions, he, in turn, is made into something rather different by the author. By implying that the old lord will be made a cuckold by his young wife and Adam, Karen Blixen has thus turned him into one of the most traditional figures of comedy; moreover, by doing so, she has implicitly endorsed the validity of his attitude and belief. In fact, she has revealed, simply through the narrative events of the story and the turn given to them, how closely she herself is to be identified with his ideas. The old lord remarks that "the very same fatality which, in striking the burgher or peasant will become tragedy, with the aristocrat is exalted to the comic. By the grace and wit of our acceptance hereof our aristocracy is known." If these beliefs govern his attitude and behaviour in **"Sorrow-Acre,"** they also define, with equal force, the attitude and behaviour of Karen Blixen herself as revealed in *Out of Africa.*

Adam, however, remains unconvinced by his uncle's point of view, as indeed he must as a character in the story with an historical role. Nevertheless, there is a point, where suddenly, he seems to perceive the meaning of life, and to see a concord arising out of the conflict:

> All that lived must suffer, the old man, whom he had judged hardly, had suffered, as he had watched his son die, and had dreaded the obliteration of his being, —he himself would come to know ache, tears and remorse, and, even through these, the fullness of life. So might now, to the woman in the rye-field, her ordeal be a triumphant procession. For to die for the one you loved was an effort too sweet for words. . . . As the song is one with the voice that sings it, as the road is one with the goal, as lovers are made one in their embrace, so is man one with his destiny, and he shall love it as himself.

> [**"Sorrow-Acre"**]

The concept of destiny expressed here is a theme which echoes again and again in Karen Blixen's work, for it voices some of her most deeply felt convictions. In *Out of Africa,* a passage which has rightly been described as "quintessential Blixen," offers a close parallel to Adam's thoughts:

> Pride is faith in the idea that God had, when he made us. A proud man is conscious of the idea, and aspires to realize it. He does not strive towards a happiness, or comfort, which may be irrelevant to God's idea of him. His success is the idea of God, successfully carried through, and he is in love with his destiny. As the good citizen finds his happiness in the fulfilment of his duty to the community so does the proud man find his happiness in the fulfilment of his fate.

> People who have no pride are not aware of any idea of God in the making of them, and sometimes they make you doubt that there has ever been much of an idea, or else it has been lost, and who shall find it again? They have got to accept as success what others warrant to be so, and to take their happiness, and even their own selves, at the quotation of the day. They tremble, with reason, before their fate.

> [*Out of Africa*]

This passage illustrates very clearly the attitude and beliefs which have created the figures in **"Sorrow-Acre,"** and accounts for the way in which they are conceived and presented. Their role is their destiny successfully carried though and they become at one with it. Adam sees the actions of the people in **"Sorrow-Acre"** as an illustration of the general destiny of human life. Because the story is set in a particular period, the conflicts, reflected in it, cannot be reconciled in those particular historical terms. Nevertheless, they *are* brought into concord; not, however, in terms of the past, but in those of Karen Blixen's own attitude to life. The old lord, Anne-Marie, Adam, all fulfil their destiny, and just as these characters are not individuals, but part of a total whole, so too are the events in the field, **"Sorrow-Acre."** "All that lived must suffer" . . . ; man is "one with his destiny." The story illustrates the general law of human existence for Karen Blixen, and one which is independent of a particular time and a localized place. As in other stories, she establishes the world of this story in an age and society of the past, but uses it to illustrate the law of her own world. **"Sorrow-Acre"** is only one short story and one small field; it is, however, large enough to stretch out to a farm in Africa and to span the world of Karen Blixen's fiction.

To realize fully how much of this world it does span, one must go back at least a decade further than *Out of Africa* to a short play, *Sandhedens Hævn (Revenge of Truth),* first published in *Tilskueren* in May, 1926, but probably written many years before. In a letter to me, Karen Blixen once said, "I wrote it when I was a young girl, my sisters and brothers and myself acted it here at Rungstedlund."

The play is short, it was written in Danish, and it has not been translated into English. It is subtitled "A Marionette Comedy," but this description can be misleading. As Karen Blixen's letter indicated, it was originally performed by her brothers and sisters and herself. The play, therefore, was not written for puppets acting as human beings; it is, rather, the human beings in it who act as puppets. They are turned into marionettes by the plot, which tells how a witch casts a spell over the characters staying at an inn so that any lie they tell eventually becomes the truth, and they are unable to prevent this from happening. Thus the subtitle, "A Marionette Comedy," does not so much describe the type of play as indicate its major theme. Undoubtedly, here in this early play can be seen the genesis of much of her later work.

Sandhedens Hoevn itself is brought quite explicitly into a short story, **"The Roads round Pisa,"** included in *Seven Gothic Tales.* In that story, the main figures, like those in the play, are brought together at an inn, and during the evening some of them watch the performance of a marionette comedy. This play is actually Karen Blixen's own earlier work:

> The play which was being acted was the immortal *Revenge of Truth,* that most charming of marionette comedies. Every body will remember how the plot is created by a witch pronouncing, upon the house wherein all the characters are collected, a curse to the effect that any lie told within it will become true. . . . At the end the witch appears again, and on being asked what is really the truth, answers: "The truth, my children, is that we are, all of us, acting in a marionette comedy. What is important more than anything else in a marionette comedy, is keeping the ideas of the author clear. This is the real happiness of life, and now that I have at last come into a marionette play, I will never go out of it again. But you, my fellow actors, keep the ideas of the author clear. Aye, drive them to their utmost consequences."

> [*Seven Gothic Tales*]

If the three passages, Adam's thoughts in **"Sorrow-Acre,"** Karen Blixen's own attitude as expressed in *Out of Africa,* and this last extract, where two works overlap into one, are compared, some striking parallels immediately become apparent. Man is "one with his destiny—and he shall love it as himself. . . ."—"His success is the idea of God, successfully carried through, and he is in love with his destiny"—"keep the ideas of the author clear. Aye, drive them to their utmost consequences." Obviously, these are much more than verbal echoes. What we witness here, in fact, is the intersection for Karen Blixen of her life and her art, the point where her attitude to life becomes her attitude to her art, Isak Dinesen and Karen Blixen merge into one figure, and life and literature meet and become one single entity.

"The truth," says the witch in *Sanhedens Hoevn,* "is that we are, all of us, acting in a marionette comedy." And this is true, not only for that particular play, but also for Karen Blixen's work in general—with one essential qualification. The choice for her figures is not whether they should be in a marionette comedy; they are already in it, by being figures in the stories. The choice lies in whether they should *act* in it or not. The persons in Karen Blixen's stories can be divided into two main categories. There are, first, those who choose a role and play it so successfully that they become their role. We have already seen this process in **"Sorrow-Acre,"** and similar figures can be found in many other stories. In several tales, the parts which they succeed in playing are even suggested by the titles— **"The Invincible Slave-Owners," "The Old Chevalier," "The Heroine."** The persons in this category are those who have "faith in the idea that God had, when he made us," and having faith, they "keep the ideas of the author clear." Secondly, there are those who are unable to play a role, who "are not aware of any idea of God in the making of them," persons such as **"The Dreamers,"** who do nothing to choose their own ways, or like Count Augustus von Schimmelmann in **"The Poet,"** who has "to accept his happiness according to the quotation of the day."

Even from this brief summary, several implications will be clear. The two main categories, to which Karen Blixen's characters conform, are those set out in the two paragraphs on pride in *Out of Africa.* If these paragraphs are "quintessential Blixen," they also establish the central tenets of Isak Dinesen. They not only record an attitude to life, they are also the expression of an artistic creed.

Behind Karen Blixen's attitude is the firm belief that there is a purpose in life, that we have been created with a particular design in mind. Our function in life is to realize what this design is, and to carry it through. It is also possible, however, to refuse this role, by being unaware of the idea underlying our creation, in which case we lose any sense of purpose in life. This is precisely the choice with which the persons in her stories are confronted; we have already noted how the figures in **"Sorrow-Acre"** accept their roles and play them to a conclusion. The persons in her stories are not individualized; they are stylized to a type and simplified to a basic idea—their role. They are personifications of the ideas of the author, and their purpose is to trace out her design.

This conception of fulfiling one's destiny by playing an allotted role, however, is not one of passive resignation. Although there is little choice of the type of part, nevertheless, the true choice for Karen Blixen, both in her own life, and for the figures in her stories, is always one between active acceptance and passive refusal. Both persons in real life, and the figures in the stories, may be marionettes—but it is also possible for marionettes to get the strings entangled. Her stories are concerned with the attempt to unravel them.

Possibly, by thus analyzing Karen Blixen's attitude and beliefs, one has also reached the position from which the true perspective of the setting in the past can be seen. The world of her short stories is both the reflection of a particular historical period, and, at the same time, a mirror in which can be discerned her attitude to life. And this is true even for **"Sorrow-Acre,"** possibly the short story where the historical setting figures most prominently. As important as the historical past, in which the stories take place, are the past years of Karen Blixen's own life spent in Africa.

Finally, there is a rather curious analogy with Karen Blixen's attitude to life, particularly towards her life in Africa, which may also help to define her beliefs more clearly; the analogy is with that of W. B. Yeats in some of his poetry. If she had her farm in Africa, Yeats also stayed often at Coole Park, and for both of them, these places represented much more than simply large landed estates. Yeats's feeling that here "Life overflows without ambitious pains; / And rains down life until the basin spills" ["Meditations in Time of Civil War—Ancestral Houses," in *Collected Poems of W.B. Yeats,* 1950] is also a constant theme in the account of Karen Blixen's life in Africa, and it is one which gives the book some of its characteristic tone. Even the fate of both estates was the same; Coole Park was also sold. "All that great glory spent" ["Coole Park and Ballylee, 1931," *Collected Poems*]; Yeats's remark could easily afford an epigraph to *Out of Africa.* There is also an analogy between Karen Blixen's idea of choosing a role and Yeats's theory of the "Mask," even though in his work, of course, the theory is much more complex. Moreover, if Yeats, as a poet, felt himself to be one of the last Romantics, in a poetic tradition going back many thousands of years:

> We were the last romantics—chose for theme
> Traditional sanctity and loveliness;
> Whatever's written in what poets name
> The book of the people; whatever most can bless
> The mind of man or elevate a rhyme;
> But all is changed, that high horse riderless,
> Though mounted in that saddle Homer rode
> Where the swan drifts upon a darkening flood.
> ["Coole Park and Ballylee, 1931"]

Karen Blixen was equally conscious, as a story-teller, of belonging to an age-old tradition, of possibly being one of the last representatives of it. On a record, which she made in Denmark, she prefaced telling some of her stories by saying:

> I belong to an ancient, idle, wild and useless tribe, perhaps I am even one of the last members of it, who, for many thousands of years, in all countries and parts of the world, has, now and again, stayed for a time among the hardworking, honest people in real life, and sometimes has thus been fortunate enough to create another sort of reality for them, which, in some way or another, has satisfied them. I am a story-teller.

["Karen Blixer Fortaeller . . . ," *Louisiana Grammofonplader*]

If the passage on pride in *Out of Africa* was the key-stone of Karen Blixen's life and work, Yeats's own "pride like that of the morn" ["The Tower," *Collected Poems*] is part of the foundations upon which "The Tower" is established. And what better summary of Karen Blixen's work is there, than Yeats's own epitaph?

> Cast a cold eye
> On life, on death.
> Horseman, pass by!

It is obvious that Karen Blixen's short stories, based on these beliefs, will never gain an easy popularity—nor do they court it. They are the expression of an attitude and controlled by certain convictions, which are, perhaps, hard and uncomforting; indeed, they reflect a world where happiness, ease, and comfort are simply irrelevant considerations. No one reading *Out of Africa* can doubt that these beliefs were reached at the cost of much personal suffering and endurance. Formed and confirmed by hard and bitter experience, they were tenaciously and uncompromisingly carried through until the end both in life and in fiction. But the result is an achievement which wins our respect—and deserves our admiration.

Janet Lewis   (essay date March 1966)

SOURCE: "Isak Dinesen: An Appreciation," in *The Southern Review,* Vol. 2, No. 2, March, 1966, pp. 297-314.

[*Lewis is a novelist, poet, editor, educator, and librettist. In the following essay, she discusses* Out of Africa *and the short stories in* Seven Gothic Tales, Winter's Tales, *and* Last Tales, *noting the thematic and stylistic differences between Dinesen's fiction and nonfiction.*]

When you have read *Out of Africa* you will have learned a great deal about Isak Dinesen. There remains a certain amount of mystery, however. She centers her attention on the African aspects of the farm. Even the account of that down-at-the-heels, fugitive actor Emmanuelson, which seems at first to be an episode concerning the Baroness and her European guest, turns out to be primarily a comment on the Masai, those natives who were at once both aristocrat and proletarian, and therefore capable of recognizing and sympathizing with tragedy. But, although the Natives and the African world appear under special scrutiny, and it is upon these that the intensity and the illumination of her nostalgia falls, the picture of a young Danish woman of noble birth becomes increasingly complete with every page. She seems to be alone, save for an occasional visitor, and one wonders how this came to be.

Her maiden name was Karen Christence Dinesen; she is sometimes called, and sometimes has signed herself Tanya. She was born in Denmark, April 17, 1885, and in 1914 she married the Swedish Baron Bror von Blixen-Finecke, her second cousin, who was also a cousin of the King of Denmark. Before that she had studied to be a painter, in Paris and in Rome. She wrote a little comedy for marionettes—just when, I don't know. It was not published, I think, until 1960, and then only in Danish. From

the world of Paris, Copenhagen, Rome, she went with her husband to British East Africa, which later became the Kenya Colony; there her family had bought for her a coffee plantation. In 1921, after a divorce from the Baron, she took over the management of the plantation. In 1931, the year of the Depression, she was forced to sell the farm because of financial losses, and she returned to Denmark, to her family home of Rungstedlund, where she died at the age of seventy-seven, September 7, 1962. Her father, "an officer in the Danish and French army," was also once for three years a trapper in Minnesota; the Indians there gave him the name of Boganis, which he used as a pseudonym to sign his book about these adventures. This was in 1872. His Indians were the Pawnee and the Chippewa.

Out of Africa, Mr. Wescott says in his *Images of Truth,* is her only "truthful" book, that is to say, the only book of hers which is not fiction. To this must be added the volume called *Shadows on the Grass* (English edition, 1960), which consists of four stories or sketches which become marvellous footnotes to the first work. It is hardly just to call them footnotes. They are properly a part of *Out of Africa,* and the reader who comes to them without knowing *Out of Africa* will lose a great part of their value and poignancy. This book is illustrated not only by photographs of Isak Dinesen, but by line drawings and paintings from her hand of a number of her people at the farm. Her training in Rome and Paris was not wasted.

We learn in *Out of Africa* that she began to write on the farm to lessen the loneliness. What she wrote on the sheets which Farah thought could never be brought together into anything solid, like a real book with blue covers, was published in 1934 as *Seven Gothic Tales.* In these she returns to Europe, to a world of infinite conversation. The scene is almost purely European, except for the framework, or setting, for the story told in **"The Dreamers."** Here the setting is aboard an Arab dhow as it approaches Mombasa. It carries a wandering Englishman and a Mohammedan storyteller. Yet even here the story which is told is of Europe, and the teller is the Englishman. In all these tales, it seems to me, there are many things, many ways of thinking, which she learned at the farm. If she observed Africa with the eyes of a European, she also remembered Europe with a wisdom not unrelated to the wisdom of the Kikuyu, and it becomes a fascination to trace the interweaving of thought between these two books.

Out of Africa was written in Denmark. She spent seventeen years in Africa. The book is written at a great distance in time and space from its scene and its events. It has been filtered through memory, and suffused with longing. "'Tis more than love that looketh on / What it no longer hath." I am quoting from a poem by Elizabeth Daryush. The book partakes therefore of the quality of fiction, not because it is untrue, but because it is the result of the creative method of which Henry James spoke, to distinguish it from the method of the reporter. Details which have been filtered through the memory have more truth in them than facts in general because they carry an emotional content; because they are the essential things to be remembered.

When I again read *Out of Africa* after a very long time this was what struck me more sharply than before, this immense nostalgia for what was gone, and the awareness of change. For the change had begun around and about Nairobi even before Karen Blixen left the farm. In **"The Dreamers,"** which is one of the *Seven Gothic Tales,* Mira, the Arabian story-teller, says, "I have been trying for a long time to understand God. Now I have made friends with him. To love him truly you must love change, and you must love a joke, these being the true inclinations of his own heart." Change was not easy to love when what was being changed was the park of Africa, the forest within view of her house into the suburbs of Nairobi.

In the autumn of 1963 I was talking with an Englishman, a man in his eighties, who had come out to Canada many years before, and had been living for a long time in British Columbia. He had a brother in Africa—this is the story of the British Empire, this dissemination of families. He said that his brother had experienced no trouble with the Natives so far; he lived in Kenya, and there he was on good terms with the Natives. His brother had, in fact, a coffee plantation about twelve miles out of Nairobi. He had bought it from a Baroness, about 1931. My friend had not heard of Baroness Blixen, but his brother surely must have known whose acres he bought, for in 1951, when Bernardine Kielty visited the farm, although it had become in part a suburb of Nairobi, it was called Karen Estates, and Karen House was the center of it. It is pleasant to think that in 1963, at least, the descendants of Isak Dinesen's friends, the Kikuyu, were friends with the new occupants of the farm.

When Dinesen says, in the person of the Arabian, Mira, "to love God you must love a joke," I seem to hear the laughter of the Kikuyu of which she tells us in *Out of Africa,* their "shrill delight in things going wrong." They expected not the reasonable of God, or of Fate, but the impossible, the imaginative, the unexpected. They expected Him to act in a large way, and without regard for their personal convenience. She relates this feeling of the Kikuyu to the latter part of the Book of Job. I don't know whether her deep understanding and empathy—if we hesitate to call it sympathy—with the Kikuyu was a natural thing to her, and a part of her own disposition and training, but I have a feeling that she learned some of this fortitude and gallantry from the Natives of Africa. Perhaps also some of it from the thinking of the Arabs, which had filtered into the tribal thought of many Africans. The old Kikuyu women who had walked many miles to her house for a gift of tobacco on a day when she had no *tombacco* for them, laughed uncontrollably at the joke on themselves, and for a long time after, when they met her, they said, "Do you remember, no tombacco, Msabu? Ha, ha."

When the bad days came on the farm, and Kinanjui was dead, and her great friend Denys Finch-Hatton was dead, with the lions pacing or lying above his grave, and she had come to the end of her courage, she asked for a sign from the Powers of the universe. Then came that battle between the white cock and the chameleon, when the cock snatched the tongue from the mouth of the chameleon, leaving it more than disarmed—leaving it doomed, unable to catch the insects which were its food. She was frightened, this woman who had faced lions. Farah brought her tea at the stone table before the house.

"I looked down on the stone and dared not look up, such a dangerous place did the world seem to me. Very slowly only, in the course of the next few days, it came upon me that I had had the most spiritual answer possible to my call. . . . The powers to which I cried had stood on my dignity more than I had done myself, and what other answer could they then give? This was clearly not the hour for coddling, and they had chosen to connive at my invocation of it. Great powers had laughed to me, with an echo from the hills to follow the laughter, they said among the trumpets, among the cocks and chameleons, Ha, ha."

Whether learned from the Natives of Africa or the peasants and pastors of Denmark, courage can do no more than this. Whoever said that the universe was a safe place for Man? Jehovah did indeed make some promises to some special people, and Kamante, after he became a Christian, put a little faith in them—not too much. He talked a good deal about setting his heel upon the serpent's head; when the serpent appeared it seemed better to call for help and have it shot. After all, as he remarked, it was on the roof, an inconvenient spot in which to set his heel.

Though *Out of Africa* was written in Denmark the *Seven Gothic Tales,* her first book, was for the most part written in Africa. In these she dreamed of Europe, and to Dinesen in Denmark the memory of writing the *Seven Tales* must of necessity have been a part of her experience on the farm. When in *Out of Africa* she wrote of Farah's women and their wonderful clothing—ten yards of material to a single dress—and when she quoted Baudelaire (I think it is Baudelaire) on how their bodies moved under all that drapery, was she not remembering The Old Chevalier, and his comments on the dress of women in her own story of that name? When she wrote the words of the Old Chevalier, was she not writing with Farah's women under her eyes?

Neither the *Tales* nor *Out of Africa* could be what they are, unless their author had seen each world through the eyes of the other. And probably it would be true to say that you could not have a full appreciation of Dinesen without reading at least the *Seven Gothic Tales* as well as *Out of Africa.* But *Out of Africa* remains for me, and for most of us, her best book. This is not merely, I think, because we like to know that it is "true"—and she vouches elsewhere for its complete factual truth—and because it is personal, but because it is simpler, closer to the bare bone of what she wanted most to say. It is about the things that mattered most to her, the problems projected upon the people and things nearest to her, nearest in every way. God knows it is not a simple book in the sense of being simpleminded. It is more simple in structure, more economical in thought and language than any of the *Tales.* There is less of that elaborateness with which she amused herself in the lonely evenings on the farm. It is almost completely objective.

Linguistically she disproves Jespersen's theory that truly bilingual people never become great writers in either language. She grew up learning French and English, by preceptors, as well as her mother tongue of Danish. I mean that she was tutored in these languages, while, presumably, she drank in Danish with her mother's milk. But I can detect practically nothing of the foreigner in her use of English, and she surely is a master stylist. She does ungrammatically misuse *lay* for *laid,* and so do many English speaking persons. And she does invent words, which have an odd and delightful sound, as for instance, instead of *salvaged* she invents *salved,* with slightly medicinal overtones. Almost all her work exists in both English and Danish. Some of it, I think, was translated into Danish by her secretary, Clara Svendsen. I cannot imagine that anyone but Dinesen herself translated any of it into English. Very likely the scholarship of Mr. Robert Langbaum (*The Gayety of Vision,* Random House, 1965), can identify which work was written first in which language. Certainly none of it which I have read in English bears the stamp of being a translation. This alone is an extraordinary achievement.

The style is that of the storyteller. The voice is quiet. The rhythm is the long easy one of an unhurried narrative, spoken aloud. It almost has the long easy lope of a runner across a great plain. It never, that I can remember, becomes breathless. What she tells us of the beginning of her stories, how she told them to Denys Finch-Hatton, herself seated cross-legged on the floor like Scheherazade, makes this observation easy to arrive at; but I think one would come to that observation anyway without difficulty. You have only to read a page of it aloud, and you might begin with page 43 in the Modern Library Edition of *Out of Africa,* where in three paragraphs she gives us a poem about the rain, except that it is in prose, true prose, and not in verse, either scannable or so-called free.

The structure of this book at first seems casual and accidental—just sketches, strung together as her fancy pleased. On a second look we see that it is really not so. The fact that we can pick from it, like plums from a pudding, at almost any page, an anecdote, an epigram, a fine phrase, tempts one to think that it is loosely put together. The progress of the book, which is roughly that of a progress through time, intensifies the nostalgia, the affection which Dinesen felt for the farm. She looks more and more closely at what she will come to lose, at what she has lost. The book ends as a tragedy, almost a five act tragedy, but it is also triumphant. She sums up this strange feeling of triumph in a short bit in the chapter she calls "From an Immigrant's Notebook." The short bit is called: "I will not let thee go, except thou bless me," and it is to the house that she is speaking, to begin with. But she says this too, of the things and people on the farm, remembering a year of drought: "You also were there. You also were part of the Ngong Farm. That bad time blessed us and went away." And in the end she says, "My life, I will not let you go except you bless me, but then I will let you go."

Upon consideration one says, this is a very sad book surely; and yet its sadness is equalled only by its joy. For Dinesen as for Colette, sorrow, pain, joy, were all great treasures of experience, all to be valued, perhaps equally. Colette said, during her last illness, when the pain from arthritis was constant, "Par chance, j'ai douleur." Fortunately, I suffer. As if she said, "I still feel; therefore I still live."

Dinesen is like Colette in this appreciation of the experience of being alive, unlike her in her great concern with the metaphysical, and unlike her in the long narrative rhythm, which makes every episode into a recounting, a story told, not an action presented *en scène;* on stage. If you wish an example in contrast of the extraordinary ability of Colette to present her subject *en scène,* you might consider the opening of almost any chapter in *The Other One (La Seconde)* by Colette, scenes which usually begin with a voice, the speaker unnamed, for the moment, so that you mentally prick up your ears, turn your head and listen, being there in person as audience. Or remember the first words in the first story in *My Mother's House (La Maison de Claudine)*—"Where are the children?" Or think of the child in the garden at nightfall seeing through the window in the safe circle of the lamplight, a hand, her mother's hand, moving back and forth, the middle finger capped with a silver thimble. The immediacy is poignant. In Dinesen, we hear the voice of the narrator, and the remoteness of the subject is poignant.

When **Seven Gothic Tales** was first published in this country the pseudonym of Isak Dinesen was a great mystery, and Dorothy Canfield Fisher, writing the introduction to this book, apparently did not know whether the author was a man or a woman. Mrs. Fisher was almost equally mystified by the stories, in their quality of being unclassifiable. Her praise was rapturous, although she endeavored to speak like a Vermonter in her last sentence, when she said: "It will be worth your while to read them." The English edition of **Out of Africa** appeared under the signature of Karen Blixen, and from then on the pseudonym remained as a kind of *décor,* which did not attempt to conceal anything. However, she remained for a long time a mystery in this country, and when she did appear in person, in 1959, finally, she caused a good bit of a sensation. She was much photographed for the news magazines, and her fragile, elegant, heavily wrinkled face with the great luminous eyes reminded the reviewers and interviewers of spells and enchantments. One article about her began with a quotation from her story, **"The Old Chevalier."**

"I myself," said the Old Chevalier, "do not think I could really love a woman who had not, at some time or another, been up on a broomstick." In her last years she lived almost exclusively on raw oysters and champagne, and she was so frail that she did not move about without the supporting arm of an escort. And if, Mr. Wescott reported, that arm failed her for any reason, she simply sank to the floor. But she was no great weight to lift again.

She came to this country to raise funds for the future of Rungstedlund, which she planned to leave to the state as a bird sanctuary, and also as a sanctuary for certain literary memories beyond her own life, because the Danish poet Ewald had once lived there, before her time. "I hear his steps," she said, "as he wanders from room to room."

Her visit to this country was not a lecture tour but a tour of storytelling, and she did not range very far from New York, no farther than to Washington and to Cambridge, I believe. Mr. Wescott accompanied her a part of the time, and he reported that the story which she told most often was that of the King's letter. It is the second story in **Shad-**

ows on the Grass, and it is called **"Barua a Soldani."** It takes about forty-five minutes to read aloud. The first time he heard her tell it he had the impression that she was inventing word by word as she spoke. After that, since she told it in almost exactly the same words each time, he realized that she had memorized it. Perhaps in the writing it had memorized itself for her, or perhaps she had told it many times before she wrote it down, thus putting a high finish on it in the time-honored manner of true folk tale tellers. It is a fine story, and I will not spoil it by trying to retell it in a reduced form.

The first story in **Shadows** is the story of Farah, her Somali servant, who was with her for almost eighteen years, walking, she says, five feet behind her, a vigilant shadow; or, on a safari, handing her a gun, or, on the farm, managing her household and her finances. Leaving him, when she left the farm for Denmark, was like losing her right hand.

In this account of Farah she has a good deal to say about the time-honored relationship between servant and master. This theme of the felicitous relationship between servant and master runs through all her work. It is an essentially feudal point of view; it belongs to a time gone past. I cannot think of this point of view in Dinesen as condescending or—crime of crimes, as undemocratic—because of her profound appreciation of what the master owes the servant, that is, for all that for which the master is truly indebted to the servant. The servant takes pride in the relationship equally with the master. This attitude of hers is part of an aristocratic turn of mind. It is this quality of mind that must have suggested to her that a letter from the King might have a curative power. It is moreover a part of her metaphysics of the universe, a metaphysic of relationships, in which opposites are paired, and become one.

> A major theme of Dinesen's which fascinates her almost as much as the feudal lord and servant theme, is that of disguise, the assumed role, the form-changing, and, . . . the power of vicarious experience.
>
> —*Janet Lewis*

In what she has to report of Africa, it is natural to find this master-servant relationship in existence continually. She was the lady of the manor, the healer, the director, the European. Her devotion to her servants is always accompanied by her realization of the beauty and strangeness they brought into her life. Indeed, she speaks of this at length at the very beginning of her story of the farm. In the *Tales*—[*Seven Gothic Tales* or *Last Tales*]—when she is writing of an invented world, a world of fantasy in the highest form, the theme underlies some of her strongest and finest stories—**"Sorrow Acre"** is a most notable example—and almost all these stories are removed from us,

backward in time by a generation or so, if not father. In Africa she found herself moved backward in time in her actual living. She might not find in Africa today that paradisiacal relationship. In the United States she would find it but rarely; but one can hardly consider the history of Europe (the literary history) without brushing against it in one form or another. Don Giovanni and Leporello, Don Quixote and Sancho Panza are the literary descendants of Arthur and his Knights, Charlemagne and his Peers.

One should not let oneself be put off by a remark which Dinesen is quoted as having made during a conversation: "If I were rich I think that slaves would be the great thing to have." She also said, at the same time, "I do believe in democracy, although I think it has been misused." She understands quite well that the age of the slave owners is past—she would not have it any other way—and she writes of it as a part of the past.

Another major theme of Dinesen's which fascinates her almost as much as the feudal lord and servant theme, is that of the disguise, the assumed role, the form-changing, and, what is in itself a form of the assumed role, the power of vicarious experience. This theme turns up constantly in the *Tales,* more than in the "true" stories, and it assumes most devious and changing aspects, as indeed one might expect it to do. **"Sorrow Acre"** is a combination of these two major preoccupations of her imagination. I don't know whether it is absolutely the finest of her Tales, but it is probably the most haunting, and certainly as characteristic a piece of work as one could find. It is from *Winter's Tales.*

She begins this story with a description of the earth of Denmark; she gives us immediately the theme of the peasant and the feudal lord, and she presents this relationship as giving strength to the country, the people, the very earth. The land, the church, the big house, the people appear in this order. She says: "A human race had lived on this land for a thousand years, had been formed by its soil and its weather, and had marked it with its thoughts, so that now no one could tell where the existence of the one ceased and the other began."

We are well prepared, by the time the young man Adam appears, for his feeling about the land which he had almost inherited, and for the grief of the old Lord, who had no living issue to inherit that land. The cousin of Adam, the son of the old Lord, had died before reaching manhood. The old Lord has married the destined bride of his son.

We have in the understanding of Adam, who has been abroad, in England, an answer to all the protests that will arise in the mind of a non-feudal reader; that is to say, it is Adam who will realize and resent the seeming blasphemy of the old Lord before he will succumb to his own feeling for the land, and agree with the ultimate action of the old Lord. That action is one of vicarious experience. The son of one of the peasants of the old Lord, an old woman called Anne-Marie, has been accused of arson. The Lord has it in his power to forgive the boy or to send him away to rot in prison, and he has promised Anne-Marie that he will spare her son if she will harvest all alone in the space of one day an acre of rye. He is quite aware that this is one day's work for three men, and he is aware that the labor will certainly kill the old woman. He gives her this great chance to die for her son, which is the great chance that his own life denied him.

She completes her harvest just as the sun dips below the horizon. She is assured by the old Lord that she has saved her son, and she dies. The old Lord, like a kind of spiritual vampire, absorbs into his own spirit the joy of her sacrifice and triumph. I doubt if Dinesen would care to have me use the phrase, spiritual vampire. I think she means to say that even at the cost of being cruel the old Lord has been magnificently kind.

Meanwhile Adam, who is not idly called by this name, remembers the song which the young bride of his uncle has been singing—essentially a love song, and of sexual love. "Mourir pour ce qu'on aime, c'est un trop doux effort." It is too sweet a struggle, to die for what (or whom) one loves. And he thinks: "the ways of life . . . are as a twined and tangled design . . . it was not given to him or any mortal to command or control it. Life and death, happiness and woe, the past and the present, were interlaced within that pattern." Then there comes to him a moment in which he feels that he perceives the unity of things. "As the song is one with the voice that sings it, as the road is one with the goal, as lovers are one in their embrace, so is man one with his destiny, and he shall love it as himself."

He terminates with this his quarrel with his uncle the old Lord. He does not depart for America in anger and disillusion, as he had intended. He accepts the old woman's death for what the old Lord meant it, a moment of triumph and sweetness for her, and he accepts his destiny, which is to marry the young bride after the death of his uncle, to remain and carry on the tradition of his land.

Now I read this story without the shock of protest that I first felt, but I hold it at a certain distance from me. I think I understand and credit Dinesen's intention; but I also still feel that no human being is justified in making such a tremendous decision over the life of another, in playing God, in directing destiny. The action of the old Lord, although indicative of the depth of his personal loss, is tyrannical; his assumption of power, to me, blasphemous. None of this invalidates the story as a work of art. We are not required to approve of the conduct of King Lear. We remain quite free to disapprove of the action of the old Lord.

There is in Adam's vision of unity, especially the unity of lovers, a theme that carries us back to *Out of Africa.* In the Modern Library edition, on page 230, she tells of finding, in company with Denys Finch-Hatton, the carcass of a giraffe on which a lioness was feasting. Denys killed the lioness, and a little later, on that same day before dawn he handed his gun to Karen Blixen so that she might kill the lion which had succeeded the lioness at the feast. She says:

"I was never keen to shoot with his rifle, which was too long and heavy for me. . . . still here the shot was a declaration of love." And this declaration was by no means a declaration from Denys to Karen Blixen. It was the declaration of the hunter to the quarry. The entire passage, with the description of the magnificence of the lion makes this quite clear. She concludes, "should not the rifle then be of the biggest calibre?"

This sort of thinking may have come to her from the Far East.

The idea of the efficacy of the vicarious experience occurs notably in the story of **"Alkmene".** In this tale Alkmene, a child of unknown and mysterious origin, brought up by good, sober foster parents in the country, a child of gay, imaginative, and alien temperament, destroys her true self in order to become what she believes her foster parents wish her to be. To this end she requests her friend, the young man who is the narrator of the story, to escort her to a public execution. As the unfortunate condemned man loses his head, Alkmene grows very pale, and it is understood that she has herself died vicariously at that moment, and by her own will. Thereafter in the story she speaks of Alkmene in the third person, as of some one who no longer exists. This is too bare an account of the plot. There is also the matter of the girl's devotion to the young man, who, unaware at the time of his true feelings, rejects her. But it is not merely a story of unrequited love.

Again, in the character of the great diva, Pellegrina Leoni, we have both the theme of the disguise and the theme of the vicarious experience operating, and in more than one story. Pellegrina appears first in **"The Dreamers,"** in *Seven Gothic Tales,* in the story within a story told by the young Englishman who has been her lover, not knowing at that time who she was. He tells the story to Mira, the Arabian, on the dhow approaching Mombasa, which I mentioned earlier. Pellegrina lost her voice in an illness following a fire on stage, and although she did not die then, she had it given out that she had died, since Pellegrina the singer was in fact dead. She wandered incognita thereafter all over Europe, existing as many different personalities, and disappearing whenever the danger of discovery became close. In this story she meets her actual death, also. In *Last Tales* Dinesen gives us one more of her adventures during the period between the professed death and the actual one. The story is called **"Echoes".**

In the time of her wanderings, just after she had fled from the young Englishman in order to retain her anonymity, she comes to a village in the Italian mountains, and there she hears a young boy sing with the voice that had once been hers. She becomes his teacher, determined to send back to the world her lost voice, and to make of the boy a great and successful artist. She adores the boy, and he, knowing her to be the great Pellegrina, adores her also. She absorbs him in her will, in her great plans for him, until suddenly, through a clever and symbolic device in the plot, he becomes convinced that she is a witch; and he revolts over her dominion of him. When he runs away from her, she follows him, and he hurls a rock at her.

This is, again, an unjustly bare account of the plot; but this is the essential of it. The vicarious experience this time is for the sake of life, not death. The servant-master relationship has become the teacher-pupil relationship, and the relationship of the enchanter and enchanted. And it is very sad that the beautiful relationship could not continue. But there is more going on in this story than the episode between Pellegrina and the boy with her voice. There is also the story of Niccolo, the fisherman, who once ate human flesh, and his relationship with God, and Pellegrina's ideas about God, which recall the remark by Mira the Arabian.

If we are to believe, as the psychiatrists tell us, that the dreamer himself is all the characters in his dream, those who frighten him as well as those who help him, then even more certainly we can trust that all the characters in a story are in a way the writer himself. Therefore the boy who was in danger of being taken over by the personality of Pellegrina is as much Dinesen's spokesman as is Pellegrina. And it occurs to Pellegrina that she had no right to take over the privilege to which every human creature should be born, that of creating himself, or at least of assisting at the creation of himself. Like the old Lord in **"Sorrow Acre,"** she was taking upon herself a part of the prerogative of God. This intricate story, **"Echoes,"** ends with Pellegrina's quoting to herself the words of Niccolo, the fisherman. "One can take many liberties with God which one cannot take with men. One may allow oneself many things toward Him which one cannot allow oneself toward man. And, because He is God, in doing so one will even be honoring Him."

The theme of God as artist, poet, creator, is constant throughout her work, and of God the aristocrat, the unreasonable, whose ways must not be questioned, for if He were always reasonable, He would be merely human. Shakespeare and Goethe are the Gods of the worlds which they created.

These favorite themes of hers, and others which I have not space to discuss here, reappear together with many characters in story after story, so that it needs an effort, after much reading of her work, to keep the stories, all of them, distinct. They tend to merge, but, when you return from them to reading *Out of Africa,* you find it illuminated by the stories. After the many tales of actors, the story of the fugitive actor Emmanuelson, in *Out of Africa,* has a greater significance. You are more aware of her understanding of Old Knudsen and of how he played the part of Old Knudsen, almost to his last breath. Old Knudsen of the farm, and the Cardinal who was in fact a valet, in **"The Deluge at Norderney";** the Prioress who was from time to time a monkey; and the old Councillor, in the story called **"The Poet,"** who stumbled, dying, into the world of the poet Goethe and there was safe, as Lear was safe in the hands of Shakespeare, these are all of the same stuff.

The theme of God as artist, poet, creator, is constant throughout her work, and of God the unreasonable, whose ways must not be questioned.

—Janet Lewis

Whether *Out of Africa* is her greatest book I am not prepared to state flatly, but I prefer it, still, and so do most

readers of whose opinion I'm aware. It is, as I've suggested, her most nearly objective book. In the *Tales* she seems to move in a world almost purely the creation of her own imagination. In *Out of Africa* she is meeting directly a world created outside herself and by a greater imagination, the last, the final Imagination. I have a feeling that she would not object to this comment. In the *Tales* there seems to me often a faint note of mockery; it is the voice of Scheherazade seeking to entertain herself, and her listener. It is in the last words of **"The Deluge at Norderney,"** which seem to leave us forever ignorant of the fate of these people in the loft, although we know their triumph which would be impossible without their death. "À ce moment de sa narration, Schéhérazade vit paraître le matin, et, discrète, se tut."

Once this mockery is accepted, the *Tales* remain as serious as you like, to the point of heartbreak.

There is one more work by Karen Blixen which should be taken into consideration in any total picture of her strange and fascinating genius. She mentions it briefly in *Shadows on the Grass,* pages ninety-four and ninety-five. This is a Gothic novel to end all Gothic novels, called *The Angelic Avengers,* and published first to the best of my knowledge in 1944 and almost certainly in Danish. It appeared in English in this country in 1946, under the pseudonym of Pierre Andrézel. The dates are significant, especially in the light of the foreword to the story, which is a quotation from the story itself. Thus:

> "You serious people must not be too hard on human beings for what they choose to amuse themselves with when they are shut up as in a prison, and are not even allowed to say that they are prisoners. If I do not soon get a little bit of fun, I shall die."

These are the words of the more rebellious of the two young girls of the story, the more vengeful, righteously, of the two angelic avengers, and she speaks in this fashion at a time when the girls have become aware that they are prisoners, detained by two evil persons, and treated very kindly, like imprisoned canaries, in order to become witnesses unwittingly against the truth, that is, against the evil of their captors. The kindness of these evil people is to be their defense, their moral alibi, against any accusation of evil deeds committed by them earlier.

This is a characteristically devious situation for a story by Karen Blixen. Everyone is pretending. The face of evil is kind, the face of vengeance, is submissive and innocent. No one knows quite who is who, but never fear. The author will untangle everything in due time, evil will be vanquished by grace. The enemy is destroyed by forgiveness. But the book was written, as indicated, to give the author a little bit of fun. It was written in Denmark under the Nazi occupation, and the words quoted give one a little chill along the spine, quite apart from the Gothic tale. "Shut up as in a prison and not even allowed to say that they are prisoners."

She says, in *Shadows on the Grass,* that when she began the story she had no intention in mind, no idea what form it might take, and that when the Nazi persecution of the

Danish Jews began, she abandoned it, having no heart to compete with greater and actual horrors. When the Danish Resistance began to take force, she regained courage, gave the book a happy ending, and published it. For us the book stands as a demonstration of those compelling interests and attitudes which underly all her work, and the very fact that she had no plans at all for the book when she began it, indicates how freely she let those interests take possession.

For the rest, —the story begins with a heroine and a situation so standard that it was long since given over to the most deplorable and innocuous works of fiction. A heroine excessively young and pure, with long golden ringlets, an orphan and a governess in the house of a rich man to his little blind son. The language, though correct, is also pure cliché for a while. It is so good an imitation of the impossibly dull that I almost lacked the courage to go on with it. I would not have read beyond the first chapter except for the knowledge that Andrézel was Blixen, and except for the foreword which warned the reader that this book was a spoof. However, it soon turned out to be much more than that. Somewhere along the line it became a genuine thriller. It remains in my memory as a sort of Christmas pantomime, an allegory of good and evil, truly a fairy tale for adults. It is filled with impossible coincidences; it contains most of Dinesen's favorite tricks, of disguises. The theme of the devoted servant is there, witchcraft is there, the truly noble aristocrat is there; and paradox upon paradox. The reader has only to keep the foreword firmly in mind, and to read on, trusting to the wit and integrity of the author. All will be well in the end.

And this leads me back to the phrase so often employed by commentators on Dinesen—fairy tales for adults. When she leaves the world of fact, as she writes of it in *Out of Africa,* she becomes closer to her compatriot, Hans Christian Andersen, than to any other writer I can think of, except in a way, to Shakespeare. When one remembers the vast world of fantasy of Shakespeare, his divine disregard for historical fact, for geography, his lighthearted trust, even in his greatest tragedies, in the efficacy of disguise, it is easy to see a relationship with the *Gothic Tales.*

In conclusion, I return to *Out of Africa* as my preferred book; I read it with the greater pleasure, and I trust, with the greater comprehension, because of the privilege of having shared in the diversions of her imagination, the *Tales.*

Thomas R. Whissen   (essay date Winter 1974)

SOURCE: "The Bow of the Lord: Isak Dinesen's 'Portrait of the Artist,'" in *Scandinavian Studies,* Vol. 46, No. 1, Winter, 1974, pp. 47-58.

[*In the following essay, Whissen examines the theme of the artist in several of Dinesen's works. He contends that she sees the artist as God-like, but that the human artist "is not the master of the situation, for he has an adversary in the greater artist, God."*]

In a little play, *The Revenge of Truth,* written long before she was to achieve fame with her first collection of tales,

Isak Dinesen expresses an idea that most critics have interpreted as the governing principle behind her attitude towards life and art. At the end of the play, the witch comes forth to state this idea in a speech which is also included in **"The Roads Round Pisa"** (*Seven Gothic Tales*) as the central motif of that story.

> The truth, my children, is that we are, all of us, acting in a marionette comedy. What is important more than anything else in a marionette comedy, is keeping the ideas of the author clear. This is the real happiness of life, and now that I have at last come into a marionette play, I will never go out of it again. But you, my fellow actors, keep the ideas of the author clear. Aye, drive them to their utmost consequences.

Such critics as Aage Henriksen, Eric Johannesson, and Robert Langbaum have explored the ramifications of this statement, have noted its indebtedness to Heinrich von Kleist's "Dialogue on the Marionette Theater," and have argued convincingly against the oversimplified interpretation of the statement as advocating either determinism or blind acceptance. I mention it here, not to add unnecessarily to that discussion, but to point out that Isak Dinesen does believe that man has a primary possibility in life which it is his duty to discover and to exploit. He is equally free not to discover this possibility and not to exploit it, but his greatest happiness comes from believing that there is an author and a play and that the role he is to assume is the only possible one for him.

The author to whom the witch refers is specifically the human author of the marionette comedy, but it is obvious that she is also referring to God as the author of life. The fusion of the two meanings in the single word is the beginning of Isak Dinesen's critical thinking, for stemming from this comparison between God and the artist are all the principles by which she judges art. Although both God and the artist are authors, the artist is not master of the situation, for he has an adversary in the greater artist, God. The artist is, himself, a character in God's greater story, and as such he is as much obliged as anyone else to "keep the ideas of the author clear." For Isak Dinesen, God is the greatest artist; it is He who will finally read the last proof. As Johannes Rosendahl puts it: "God is the poet, the artist in whom man must put himself" [in *Karen Blixen: Fire Foredray,* 1957].

It is not surprising, then, that Isak Dinesen should see the offices of priest and poet as reverse sides of the same coin. In **"The Cardinal's First Tale"** (*Last Tales*) she affirms the inseparableness of the two offices in the character of Cardinal Salviati whose personality contains a strong mixture of both. When the lady in black asks him, "Who are you?", he must tell her a strange story in the midst of which he asks: "Who, Madame, is the man who is placed, in his life on earth, with his back to God and his face to man, because he is God's mouthpiece, and through him the voice of God is given forth? Who is the man who has no existence of his own—because the existence of each human being is his—and who has neither home nor friends nor wife—because his hearth is the hearth of and he himself is the friend and lover of all human beings?"

The lady's reply to this question is "the artist," to which the Cardinal adds that it is also the priest.

The Cardinal is well qualified to talk about the poet-priest relationship because he was trained to be both. He and his twin brother were intended at birth to be, one an artist and the other a priest. But the death of one brother in a fire and the resulting confusion of identities led to the other's being educated officially for the priesthood but unofficially as an artist. Through this man Isak Dinesen is able to express not only the Apollonian-Dionysian tension in both artist and priest but also to reveal how both share, along with the aristocrat, a separation from ordinary society as well as an obligation to a destiny that differs significantly from that of the rest of humanity. In fulfilling their own destinies, these are the only persons who consciously lead others to fulfill theirs. In a world where all destinies were obvious, the artist, the priest, and the aristocrat would have no reason to exist.

For Isak Dinesen, God is the greatest artist.

—Thomas R. Whissen

Because his back is to God and he serves as God's mouthpiece, the artist, as well as the priest and the aristocrat, must share something of God's loneliness and risk; and he is denied certain advantages that other men are free to enjoy, among these the possibility of remorse and the possession of honor. "Certain spiritual benefits granted to other human beings, are indeed withheld," says the Cardinal, but he also reminds the lady in black that the Lord indemnifies his mouthpiece. "If he is without potency, he has been given a small bit of omnipotence." And he adds:

> Calmly, like a child in his father's house binding and loosening his favorite dogs, he will bind the influence of Pleiades and loose the bands of Orion. Like a child in his father's house ordering about his servants, he will send lightnings, that they may go and say to him: 'Here we are.' Just as the gate of the citadel is opened to the viceregent, the gates of death have been opened to him. And as the heir apparent will have been entrusted with the regalia of the King, he knows where light dwells, and as to darkness, where is the place thereof.

It is in such stories as **"Sorrow-Acre"** (*Winter's Tales*) and **"Converse at Night in Copenhagen"** (*Last Tales*) that Isak Dinesen includes the aristocrat in her category of God's mouthpieces. "Of all people in Copenhagen," says the poet, Johannes Ewald, in **"Converse,"** "very likely you and I, the monarch and the poet, are the two who come nearest to being almighty." Lonely and slightly mad, young King Christian VII, whom Ewald is addressing, is the poet's perfect counterpart. In their vastly different ways both men bear a burden of responsibility to man and God that is not shared by either man or God. The inclu-

sion of the aristocrat in the triumvirate of those who stand in lieu of God is important because it points up the fact that even those who rule in God's place are not free from the exigencies of mortality. The old lord in **"Sorrow-Acre"** explains patiently to his impatient nephew Adam that although the aristocrat bears the same responsibility to those beneath him as the gods do to those beneath them, the aristocrat is still subject, like all men, to the will of the gods.

Isak Dinesen makes the sharpest distinction between the functions of God and the artist when, in **"The Deluge at Norderney"** (*Seven Gothic Tales*), the valet disguised as a Cardinal refers to God as the arbiter of the masquerade and to the artist as the arbiter on reality. As arbiter of the masquerade, God has a taste for disguises and prefers his creatures to respect his mask and their own rather than attempt to give back to him the truth which he knows already. To reveal the truth is his prerogative, and the day on which he chooses to reveal the truth will be the day of judgment—"the hour in which the Almighty God himself lets fall the mask," as the disguised valet puts it. The masks behind which God conceals the truth are everywhere present in nature, but they are not always readily apparent to man. The person best equipped to perceive the masks that pervade reality is the artist; and it is his function, as the arbiter on reality, to make these masks apparent as masks, in a way that leads not to any explicable truth behind the masks, but rather to an acceptance of the presence behind the masks of a truth which we are not privileged to understand.

The process of discovering the masks within reality is somewhat like the children's game in which one is asked to study a drawing and find as many faces as he can in what looks at first glance to be merely a landscape. It is the artist who is most adept at discerning these faces, and when he points them out to us to our satisfaction, we find that we can no longer look at the landscape without seeing the faces. After a while it may even be difficult for us to see the landscape at all or believe that we ever could have seen it and nothing else. The faces then become more important than the landscape; the landscape exists only to contain the faces; and although we know no more about the truth behind the drawing than we did before, we cannot deny the presence of the masks nor the effect they give to the drawing, which is to make it seem whole and proper only when they are in it. God, as arbiter of the masquerade, draws the faces and then obscures them in the landscape; and the artist, as arbiter on reality, fills in the drawing in such a way that the landscape reveals the faces.

Part of the risk inherent in this distinction is that of failure on the part of the artist to perceive the mask or, perceiving it, not to re-create it authentically. Or he may go the other way and see more faces than are really there, thus misrepresenting God with false images. A much greater risk, however, stems from the artist's disadvantage of not knowing any more of the truth behind the mask than any other man. As Johannes Rosendahl says, the decisive factor is: will the artist tell his own story or God's? The artist is not master of the situation as God is; thus he must work without the assurance that God has that he is doing the right thing.

The weight of the risk is heavy, and in a character such as Charlie Despard who appears both in **"The Young Man with the Carnation"** *Winter's Tales* and **"A Consolatory Tale"** *Winter's Tales,* Isak Dinesen portrays the artist in the throes of wrestling with his responsibility and in danger of lapsing into despair. "I have had to read the Book of Job, to get strength to bear my responsibility at all," says Despard to Aeneas Snell in **"A Consolatory Tale."** "Do you see yourself in the place of Job, Charlie?" asks Aeneas. "No," says Despard solemnly and proudly, "in the place of the Lord."

Hans Brix, in *Blixens Eventyr,* feels that Isak Dinesen identified very closely with the character of Charlie Despard. His very initials suggest her own (Karen Christentze Dinesen), and his situation in **"The Young Man with the Carnation,"** the story that introduces her second volume of stories, *Winter's Tales,* resembles her own just prior to its publication. He is a writer whose first book was a success and who is now worried about his second. **"A Consolatory Tale,"** which concludes *Winter's Tales,* shows a still questioning but more confident Despard fusing his ideas with those of the equally adept story-teller, Aeneas Snell. Their ideas about story-telling, although different, are really merely two ways of arriving at the same end.

By identifying the artist with the Lord in the story of Job, Isak Dinesen further isolates him from the society of common men and establishes him as a person of extraordinary obligations. Developing his analogy, Despard explains his theory to Aeneas Snell. "I have behaved to my reader as the Lord behaves to Job," he says. "I have laid a wager with Satan about the soul of my reader. I have marred his path and turned terrors upon him, caused him to ride on the wind and dissolved his substance, and when he waited for light there was darkness."

What Despard does not say, but what we, as readers, remember, is that the artist as man is not spared Job's lot. There is, therefore, a double burden upon him. For while he may hold with the valet/Cardinal in **"Deluge"** that the mask of God will fall away on the day of judgment and the voice in the whirlwind take on meaning, he knows that the answer to the mysteries which his art presents are also locked in that voice and behind that mask, and it is not in his power either to know or to dispense secrets.

When the lady in black, in **"The Cardinal's First Tale"**, sighs at the lot of the artist, the Cardinal tells her not to have pity on him.

> The servant was neither forced nor lured into service. Before taking him on, his Master spoke straightly and fairly to him. 'You are aware,' he said, 'that I am almighty. And you have before you the world which I have created. Now give me your opinion on it. Do you take it that I have meant to create a peaceful world?' 'No, my Lord,' the candidate replied. 'Or that I have,' the Lord asked, 'meant to create a pretty and neat world?' 'No, indeed,' answered the youth. 'Or a world easy to live in?' asked the Lord. 'O good Lord, no!' said the candidate. 'Or do you,' the

Lord asked for the last time, 'hold and believe that I have resolved to create a sublime world, with all things necessary to the purpose in it, and none left out?' 'I do,' said the young man. 'Then,' said the Master, 'then, my servant and mouthpiece, take the oath!'

A similar dialogue with the Lord in **"The Young Man with the Carnation"** brings Despard to the point where he is ready to accept the Lord's covenant. Again, the Lord's preliminary questioning is rendered by Isak Dinesen in the manner of God's dialogue with Job.

> "Who made the ships, Charlie?" he asked. "Nay, I know not," said Charlie, "did you make them?" "Yes," said the Lord, "I made the ships on their keels, and all floating things. The moon that sails in the sky, the orbs that swing in the universe, the tides, the generations, the fashions. You make me laugh, for I have given you all the world to sail and float in, and you have run aground here, in a room of the Queen's Hotel to seek a quarrel."

It is at this point that the Lord makes it clear to Despard that the artist creates not for himself or his public but for God because, as Peter says, in **"Peter and Rosa"** (*Winter's Tales*): "If the work of God does not glorify him, how can God be glorious?" Aage Henriksen says that this question is an assertion and that the assertion immediately has consequences for the poet who, in his works, has put himself in the place of God. The story-teller, says Henriksen, is providence for the persons that he tells about and can see to it that they get what they deserve. "However," Henriksen asks, "what does man deserve, and what can he in reality get? An explanation? Justice? Grace?" These questions, Henriksen goes on to say, cannot be answered except by what he calls "artistic evidence" [Aage Henriksen, *Guder og gulgefugie,* 1956].

Artistic evidence is much like the Lord's answer to Charlie Despard. It is not an answer at all, really, but an injunction not to expect answers; and before it Despard is silenced. With the discussion thus ended, Despard is ready to enter into a pact with the Lord in which the Lord makes it clear that the purpose of art is not to explain Him but to glorify Him.

> "Come," said the Lord again, "I will make a covenant between me and you. I, I will not measure you out any more distress than you need to write your books." "Oh, indeed!" said Charlie. "What did you say?" asked the Lord. "Do you want any less than that?" "I said nothing," said Charlie. "But you are to write the books," said the Lord. "For it is I who want them written. Not the public, not by any means the critics, but ME!" "Can I be certain of that?" Charlie asked. "Not always," said the Lord. "You will not be certain of it at all times. But I tell you now that it is so. You will have to hold on to that." "O good God," said Charlie. "Are you going," said the Lord, "to thank me for what I have done for you tonight?" "I think," said Charlie, "that we will leave it at what it is, and say no more about it."

> **["The Young Man with the Carnation"]**

In addition to the Lord's insistence that Despard write for Him, there are two important points in this last dialogue that are fundamental to Isak Dinesen's concept of the artist. One has to do with the "measure of distress" that the Lord promises to dispense in quantities just sufficient to result in the production of art. The other is Despard's reluctance to thank the Lord for what the Lord has agreed to do. This last point is pertinent here in clarification of the relationship between God and artist. In not allowing Despard to show gratitude to God, Isak Dinesen is denying the artist the comfort of common piety. What she implies is that the distresses measured out to the artist balance any rewards. One does not show gratitude for a dearly purchased gift.

Besides bestowing the gift of creativity on the artist, God also supplies him with the raw material out of which he can create fictional characters that can outlive God's own mortal ones. In a story within the story, **"The Roads Round Pisa",** the librettist Monti is replying to a Monsignor Talbot who has just asked Monti if he really does believe himself to be a creator in the same sense as God.

> " 'God!' Monti cried, 'God! Do you not know that what God really wants to create is my Don Giovanni, and the Odysseus of Homer, and Cervantes's knight? Very likely those are the only people for whom heaven and hell have ever been made, for you cannot imagine that an Almighty God would go on forever and ever, world without end, with my mother-in-law and the Emperor of Austria? Humanity, the men and women of this earth, are only the plaster of God, and we, the artists, are his tools, and when the statue is finished in marble or bronze, he breaks us all up. When you die you will probably go out like a candle, with nothing left, but in the mansions of eternity will walk Orlando, the Misanthrope and my Donna Elvira. Such is God's plan of work, and if we find it somehow slow, who are we that we should criticize him, seeing that we know nothing whatever of time or eternity?'

In creating such imaginative and enduring characters, the artist is, however, not exceeding God's imagination but rather entering into it. Erik O. Johannesson says that in Isak Dinesen's world "God is the greatest artist because He has the greatest imagination. . . . When her characters . . . recognize their limitations and affirm the power of God, they affirm the artist and the story, for God is the greatest story-teller of them all" [*The World of Isak Dinesen,* 1961].

When an artist is at his best, he is exhibiting what the valet disguised as a Cardinal in **"Deluge"** calls the "tremendous courage of the Creator of this world." The artist is closest to God and to the creative spirit when he is exercising, in the words of Adam in **"Sorrow-Acre,"** "Imagination, daring, and passion." "Your stories are over our stories," says Charlie Despard; and this acknowledgment leads Johannes Rosendahl to note the obligation on the part of the artist to rise above the triviality of life and its banal claims and to make his stories rival God's own.

God's envy of man's creation as expressed by Monti in

"Roads" is balanced by what the valet/Cardinal goes on to say about man's envy of God.

> Every human being has, I believe, at times given room to the idea of creating a world himself. The Pope, in a flattering way, encouraged these thoughts in me when I was a young man. I reflected then that I might, had I been given omnipotence and a free hand, have made a fine world. I might have bethought me of the trees and rivers, of the different keys in music, of friendship, and innocence; but upon my word and honor, I should not have dared to arrange these matters of love and marriage as they are, and my world should have lost sadly thereby. What an overwhelming lesson to all artists! Be not afraid of absurdity; do not shrink from the fantastic. Within a dilemma, choose the most unheard-of, the most dangerous, solution. Be brave, be brave! Ah, Madame, we have got much to learn.

The idea of creating a world himself occurred also, we know, to Satan who did not shrink from absurdity or the fantastic. In Isak Dinesen's concept of the artist there is a trace of the diabolical, and Louis E. Grandjean points out in *Blixens Animus* that she shared with Nietzsche the belief that the Satanic are preferable to the good who do not create, since the diabolical create more than they destroy. Even Cardinal Salviati in **"The Cardinal's First Tale"** must confess to the lady in black that he is not sure it is God he serves.

It is probably the painter Cazotte in *Ehrengard* who best illustrates the presence of the diabolical in the artist. While in the midst of a scheme to humiliate Ehrengard, he betrays his peculiarly mixed loyalties in a letter to the Countess von Gassner.

> P.S. Walking in the garden this evening Prince Lothar said to Princess Ludmilla: "So here is Paradise." And with her head upon his shoulder his young wife echoed: "Paradise." I smiled benevolence on them, like an archangel assisting the Lord in laying out the garden of Eden, and smiling on the first human male and female. But the great landscape architect himself, when his work had been completed, on looking at it and listening to the Gloria and Hallelujah of his angelic chorus, will have felt the craving for a clear, unbiased eye to view it with him, the eye of a critic, a connoisseur and an arbiter. With what creature, in all Paradise, will he have found that eye, Madame? Madame—with the Serpent!

If the Serpent had been content to be nothing more than critic, connoisseur, and arbiter, he would very much have resembled the artist who, as the old artist in **"Copenhagen Season"** (*Last Tales*) tells his drawingroom audience, would not have been shocked by the nakedness of Adam and Eve. But there is a vital difference between the two. The artist turns his passive observations into action by recreating what he sees; the Serpent steps out of his role as passive observer into the role of active manipulator by interfering in what he sees.

Thus, Cazotte might resemble an archangel when he is busily arranging the Eden-like retreat at Rosenbad, and he is the balanced artist when he is painting scenes and portraits; but the diabolical begins to overpower him at the time he is painting Ehrengard's portrait without her knowledge and for impure reasons; and it consumes him completely once his plan to seduce Ehrengard—albeit symbolically—is put into practice. In so doing, however, Cazotte leaves himself vulnerable to the prophecy in the Garden which foretells that the woman shall conquer. His plan fails, and the victory goes to Ehrengard.

To say that Cazotte has confused life with art, has tried to mix the two, has endeavored to alchemize art into life is to say that he has tried to usurp God's role as arbiter of the masquerade. Life, Isak Dinesen insists, is God's story, and he will dress it as he sees fit and with greater imagination. Any attempt to invade his domain will result in surprise and failure for the interloper. Out of the raw material of His imagination God has fashioned creation and given it to man as the raw material out of which man, as artist, may fashion art. As God respects the artist by refusing to turn reality into art, so must the artist respect God by resisting the temptation to turn art into reality.

The efficacy of this mandate is the express concern not only of **Ehrengard** but also of **"The Immortal Story"** (*Anecdotes of Destiny*) and **"The Poet"** (*Seven Gothic Tales*). "The Immortal Story" is the tale of an old man, Mr. Clay, who deliberately sets about turning a traditional sailor's yarn into reality. For years sailors have told each other about how, during shore leave, they were picked up by an elderly man, carried to his lavish home, plied with the finest food and wines and then given five pounds to sleep with the old man's lovely young wife. When Mr. Clay is told this story by his faithful clerk, Elishama, and it is explained to him that the story has no truth in it, Mr. Clay will not rest until he sees the story enacted before his eyes with himself in the role of the impotent old man.

With the able assistance of his clerk, Mr. Clay manages, not without some difficulty, to hire the services of a prostitute and to pick up a young sailor from the waterfront. The fact that old Mr. Clay must hire a prostitute because he does not have a wife is only the first of many ways in which the story changes as it is brought to life. Two attempts to pick up a sailor fail, and when they finally do find one who will cooperate, it is one who is more interested in the money than in the adventure. The sailor is on the point of leaving several times during dinner, but he is persuaded to stay only to surprise everyone by falling in love with the prostitute. The following morning he finds it difficult to see any resemblance between what has just happened to him and the story he has heard (and told) many times at sea. But once he does see the connection, he insists that he will never tell what happened to him because surely no one would ever believe it.

The yarn as it has always been told is a mask visible by the story teller through his arbitrary use of reality. But once that mask is violated, is forced to become real, it vanishes and a different mask takes its place. The new story is a totally different story. It is not the story of a sailor's dream but of an old man's desire to impose his will upon life. Ironically, the old man dies during the night, and his

death reveals that a greater imagination than his is directing the story.

As an imaginary arrangement of incidents and characters to conform to the ideas of the story-teller, the story is safe. But the moment the story takes life, the moment the imagination of the artist comes in conflict with the imagination of God, the artist loses control over it and usually suffers in the bargain. I think the evidence is clear that Isak Dinesen would scorn those who would take her views on aristocracy and acceptance too personally and try to pattern their lives in accordance with those of any of her characters. The artist's job, as she sees it, is not to show man how to live but to heighten his consciousness of the life he is already living.

Councilor Mathiesen in **"The Poet"** (*Seven Gothic Tales*) repeats Cazotte's and Mr. Clay's mistake but with direr consequences. To compensate for his own failure as a poet, Mathiesen meddles in the life of the genuine young poet, Anders Kube. He hopes by interfering to guide Kube towards higher poetic powers and thereby experience vicariously the fruits of success. In order to accomplish this end, Mathiesen decides to marry the young widow, Fransine, because he knows that she and Kube have fallen in love, and he feels that such a melancholy romantic situation will stimulate Kube to new lyrical heights. As his plan takes shape, however, a greater imagination than his assumes control and brings about a quite different story. Mathiesen does not know that Kube plans to commit suicide on the day of the wedding. Nor does he anticipate that his scheme to have Fransine disrobe before her lover on the night before the wedding will result in disaster and death.

The death scene in "The Poet" is Isak Dinesen's most graphic illustration of her assertion of the evil of exceeding the limits of art.

—Thomas R. Whissen

The idea for the midnight disrobing is an idea which Mathiesen has taken from a currently popular and highly controversial German romance. By so doing, Mathiesen is giving another turn of the screw to the theme of life imitating art. Life, of course, departs radically from art when Kube spurns Fransine and then uses the suicide gun to shoot the voyeur Mathiesen. Bleeding profusely, the Councilor crawls back to the house to which Fransine has fled and tries to convince her with his dying breath that the world is still beautiful and good. Because it suits him that the world should be lovely, he means to conjure it into being so. But Fransine knows that the world of which he speaks is really the world in which Anders Kube will be hanged for murder, and in her anguish she lifts up a large stone and crushes Mathiesen's head. "You," she cries at him. "You Poet!"

The epithet is bitterly ironic because Mathiesen is the antithesis of Isak Dinesen's true artist. He has usurped God's role by taking Kube into his own hands, and he has violated the mask by forcing reality upon it. Mathiesen dies with his hand outstretched to touch Fransine's heel while she stands above him, the conquering woman. The scene is Isak Dinesen's most graphic illustration of the Biblical prophecy and her own relentless assertion of the evil of exceeding the limits of art. In *Ehrengard* and **"The Immortal Story"** only the perpetrators suffer, but in **"The Poet"** the suffering extends to others. The innocent lovers become murderers.

The true artist keeps the ideas of the author clear. Once he has found his way into a marionette play, he will never go out of it again.

Anthony Burgess   (review date 6 September 1981)

SOURCE: "A Saga of Africa," in *The Observer Review*, September 6, 1981, p. 29.

[*Burgess was an esteemed English novelist, essayist, playwright, and short story writer best known for his novel* A Clockwork Orange *(1962). In the following review of* Letters from Africa: 1914-1931, *he favorably assesses Dinesen's writing style, contending that she "never fails in grace, sharpness, and humanity."*]

At the end of 1913, Karen Dinesen left Denmark and sailed to Mombasa. She disembarked to marry immediately Baron Bror Blixen-Finecke of Näsbyholm, to whom she had been engaged for a year. Baroness Karen Blixen and her husband then went to Nairobi to manage a Swedish-owned coffee plantation called MBagathi.

They were not the only Scandinavians in East Africa, and the tradition of sending the skills of the Northmen, and their Lutheran conscientiousness, to Kenya continues: at a dinner table last night in Oslo I heard good Swahili spoken. But only Karen Blixen, under the name of Isak Dinesen, has enriched Scandinavian literature with a classic book made out of the impact of Africa on a complex Nordic sensibility. As she wrote an English as well as a Danish version of *Out of Africa* (in Denmark 'The African Farm'), she may also be said to have enriched Anglo-American literature. These letters [in *Letters from Africa, 1914-1931*] are the immediate record of the African life she not only enjoyed but endured. The book is mostly lyrical; the letters are both lyrical and sombre.

Shortly after her marriage to Blixen-Finecke, the 29-year-old Karen discovered that he had infected her with syphilis. Mercury treatment proved ineffectual. The First World War began, and she and her husband, despite their work for the Allied effort, were accused of pro-German sympathies. The Baron was inefficient as an estate manager and unreliable over money. The marriage broke up but the legacy of disease continued. Karen struggled, with little success, to become a published writer. She took an English lover, Denys Finch Hatton, and this relationship engendered fresh agonies as well as social problems, especially when the Baron reappeared in the tight gossipy English colony with a new Baroness.

> ***Letters from Africa* contains mostly family letters, long and lucid, full of information and atmosphere.**
>
> *—Anthony Burgess*

Hatton was killed in an air crash in Tanganyika. Karen wound up the coffee enterprise, which was in financial chaos, and went back to Denmark to live in poverty with her mother. In 1934 she published *Seven Gothic Tales* under the pseudonym Isak Dinesen. It was a Book of the Month Club choice in America, and her position as a major writer was established. In 1954 Ernest Hemingway named her as the most suitable candidate for the Nobel Prize: she did not get it, though, of course, he did. How much she is now read in Britain I do not know; in the rest of the world, meaning mostly America, she is considered a major voice of the century.

These are mostly family letters, long and lucid, full of information and atmosphere. Anne Born has translated them from the Danish, underlining the many English phrases and thus giving a typographical impression of emphasis alien to the unemphatic style. Young Karen, not yet a writer, has the unifying gift of the writer, finding something of the Danish landscape in Kenya and hearing in remembered Danish folksongs a lyricism appropriate to the African scene.

In 1928 she is writing to her mother about the 'concept of Angst . . . with due respect to Kierkegaard,' and proclaiming (in English) that there is nothing to be afraid of, not even the belligerent natives who could enter the house and kill her with the indifference proper to the killing of a deer. 'All terror is more or less terror of the dark: bring light, and it must of necessity pass.' But there was plenty to fear—disease, the failure of an estate, the collapse of love, loneliness. In 1931, when the letters come to an end, aware of near-total defeat, she is still able to write: —

> Of all the idiots I have met in my life—and the Lord knows that they have not been few or little—I think that I have been the biggest. But a certain love of greatness, which could not be quelled, has kept a hold on me, has been 'my daimon.' And I have had so infinitely much that was wonderful. She may be more gentle to others, but I hold to the belief that I am one of Africa's favourite children. A great world of poetry has revealed itself to me and taken me to itself here, and I have loved it. I have looked into the eyes of lions and slept under the Southern Cross, I have seen the grass of the great plains ablaze and covered with delicate green after the rains, I have been the friend of Somali, Kikuyu and Masai, I have flown over the Ngong Hills—'I plucked the best rose of life, and Freja be praised.'

Not God but a Northern goddess. This is the lyricism of the great memoir written five years later.

Hemingway had the effrontery to consider himself a fellow-African, but for him Kenya was only a safari park, with twilight opportunities for 'feeling good' after the day's slaughter and contemplating patches of false lyricism for a book inferior to hers. Karen Dinesen was no mere tourist with a gun. She had a stake in Kenya, though she knew from the start it was a false one. In 1914, a few months after her arrival, she saw the 'end approaching—chiefly through the influence of Christianity.' The mission schools turn out thieves and liars, she says, but Islam instils a stoic fatalism which denies the need for fear.

> A few days ago when a man at Swedo fell ill and died, of plague it was thought, all except the Somalis ran away. I asked Fara if they were not afraid of infection; he shrugged his shoulders and replied that they knew better; if God decided they were to die, they would die—if they were to live, they would live. . . .

The English, as one expected, do not come out well; they evince less intelligence than the natives. They cannot distinguish between the tribes, they don't trouble to learn Swahili. At the Oslo dinner party the other evening my blonde companion went into great philological detail about the language, a thing I have never heard an English Kenyan do. The English have never, I suppose, been sufficiently serious. The seriousness of this young Danish woman in Africa is undoubted, but it is not stodgy. How beautiful she was, before disease gnawed at her. . . . The letters themselves never fail in grace, sharpness and humanity

Sara Stambaugh   (essay date Summer 1983)

SOURCE: "Witch as Quintessential Woman: A Context for Isak Dinesen's Fiction," in *Mosaic,* Vol. XVI, No. 3, Summer, 1983, pp. 87-100.

[*Stambaugh is an educator, novelist, and critic whose works include* The Witch and the Goddess in the Stories of Isak Dinesen *(1988). In the following essay, she examines Dinesen's "complex" relationship to feminism, drawing mainly on her letters published in* Letters from Africa, 1914-1931.]

In Isak Dinesen's **"The Dreamers"** Lincoln Forsner begins his tale of Pellegrina Leoni by saying, "You must take in whatever you can, and leave the rest outside. It is not a bad thing in a tale that you understand only half of it." The major approaches to Dinesen's work so far, I think, have taken in "only half of it"; by focusing upon esthetic issues, critics have overlooked the fact that her subject is almost always the role of women. Eric Johannesson perceived it when he observed: "The Gothic tales of Dinesen deal with individuals who are trapped in one way or another, by sex, by class, by history. . . . [They reveal] a strong feeling on behalf of the author for those who are trapped by life, particularly for women who are forced by social conventions to live on the edge of life" [*The World of Isak Dinesen,* 1961]. Writing in 1961, however, Johannesson was not equipped to realize just how important the conditioning of her sex is to the female writer or the extent to which women of Dinesen's generation had learned to disguise their real concerns. Nor was it until 1981 and the

publication of Karen Blixen's **Letters from Africa** that Hans Lasson called for a study of "Karen Blixen's opinions on the liberation of women and the relationship between the sexes. . ." [from the introduction to **Letters**].

Lasson's call for a feminist approach might have jolted Karen Blixen, as Dinesen is known in Denmark, because she was caught between two worlds and had a complicated opinion about women's role. She examined it again and again—if only as the bottom layer in fiction of the sort Sandra Gilbert and Susan Gubar describe in *The Madwoman in the Attic:* "a palimpsestic or encoded artwork, concealing female secrets within male-devised genres and conventions" [*The Madwoman in the Attic: The Woman Writer and the Nineteenth-Century Literary Imagination,* 1979]. Similarly, what Anthea Zeman says about serious women writers of earlier generations applies to Dinesen as well: "these writers held fast to their subject, [which was] not society, but women's relationship to it" [*Presumptuous Girls: Women and Their World in the Serious Woman's Novel,* 1974]. Although Dinesen's fiction derives its strength from the fact that she does not ignore the larger context, her ultimate concern is with "what a woman is faced with in her time because she is a woman" (Zeman).

It may therefore be well to begin this discussion by examining the way in which some of Isak Dinesen's subjects have typically been treated by male critics. **"The Blank Page,"** for example, is perhaps her central esthetic statement about the art of storytelling. It ends the first section of *Last Tales,* the opening story of which—**"The Cardinal's First Tale"**—is also concerned with the nature of art. Robert Langbaum examines the opening story in some detail, describing it "as Isak Dinesen's explicit defense of her own apparently anachronistic art" [*The Gayety of Vision: A Study of Isak Dinesen's Art,* 1964]. His treatment of **"The Blank Page,"** however, is limited to two sentences, in which he mentions that it deals with the same theme as the opening story and that it "offers a diagram of the perfect story as the exceptional and enigmatic case, as the story written upon the blank page." Johannesson ignores the story, and Thomas Whissen—though he discusses it in some detail because his subject is Dinesen's esthetics—concludes that it makes a comment about "the fall of man and his subsequent suffering" [*Isak Dinesen's Aesthetics,* 1973]. Diametrically opposed to such interpretations, therefore, is the recent reading of the tale by Susan Gubar. Focusing upon the Freudian implications, Gubar regards the story as central to her thesis that women resent being treated as blank page/vagina by the male pen/penis. Her discussion emphasizes female resentment of male "rending" and of "the blood of menstruation which presumably defiles like a curse . . ." [" 'The Blank Page,' and the Issues of Female Creativity," *Critical Inquiry,* No. 8 (Winter 1981)]. In spite of its value in placing Dinesen within the tradition of women who write about women, however, Gubar's reading would probably have made Dinesen uneasy.

The story of **"The Blank Page"** is told by an ancient woman who has "told many tales, one more than a thousand," and who is thus associated with the archetypal female storyteller Scheherazade, as well as with Dinesen herself. She relates her storytelling to the time after "I first let young men tell me, myself, tales of a red rose, two smooth lily buds, and four silky, supple, deadly entwining snakes." The art of storytelling has been passed down to her, she says, from her grandmother, who learned it in turn from her grandmother, who "as a little girl was the pet of an old Jewish rabbi, and the learning she received from him has been kept and passed on in our family." She describes the art of the blank page as representing the highest art of storytelling, the point at which "silence will speak"; it is "the old women who tell stories, [who] know the story of the blank page." In other words, the female can become the highest kind of artist after she has undergone her apprenticeship in sex and living and mastered esoteric knowledge passed down the female line.

Dinesen presents the subject of her art as explicitly female and connected with women's private sexuality: stories written in the blood of women's "nether springs."

—*Sara Stambaugh*

To explain the meaning of the "blank page," the old woman describes a convent where "labor-hardened virginal hands" grow and weave the finest linen in Portugal whose seed came from the lands which Caleb's daughter begged of her father along with "the upper springs and the nether springs." The sheets woven by the nuns are given to the royal house and displayed after a royal wedding to prove that the bride was a virgin, after which the stained sections are returned to the convent and framed. The old storyteller continues, "Within the faded markings of the canvases people of some imagination and sensibility may read all the signs of the zodiac: the Scales, the Scorpion, the Lion, the Twins. Or they may there find pictures from their own world of ideas: a rose, a heart, a sword—or even a heart pierced through with a sword." Again, "Each separate canvas with its coroneted name-plate has a story to tell, and each has been set up in loyalty to the story," although the one framed, unstained square tells the most powerful story of all and is "The Blank Page" of the title.

Dinesen, then, has presented the subject of her art as explicitly female and connected with women's private sexuality: stories written in the blood of women's "nether springs." It is also noteworthy that the convent is "High up in the blue mountains" and reflects a totally female society permeated with stories from which men are excluded. Besides the nuns who live there, the convent is visited only by royal ladies and occasional old maids, who come here "on a pilgrimage which was by nature both sacred and secretly gay."

Pride in female sexuality is also shown in other stories in *Last Tales.* In the opening story, for example, the Cardinal remarks to his listener, "But your sex possesses sources and resources of its own; it changes its blood at

celestial order, and to a fair woman her beauty will be the one unfailing and indisputable reality." **"Tales of Two Old Gentlemen"** goes further. As they consider "the complexity of the universe in general," one of the old gentlemen presents his grandfather's theory that the "originator and upholder" "of the Cosmos" is female and describes God as a shepherdess, to whom

> tears are convenient and precious, like rain—as in the old song *il pleut, il pleut, bergére*—like pearls, or like falling stars running over the firmament—all phenomena in themselves divine, and symbolic of the highest and the deepest spheres of human knowledge. And as to the shedding of blood, this to our shepherdess—as to any lady—is a high privilege and is inseparably united with the sublimest moments of existence, with promotion and beatification. What little girl will not joyously shed her blood in order to become a virgin, what bride not hers in order to become a wife, what young wife not hers to become a mother?

Even though the speakers in these two stories are male, both see female sexuality as completely admirable, and in the second story as closely associated with divinity.

A central problem in approaching the subject of Dinesen's feminism is her own complex attitude toward women's role and what it should be—which is perhaps one of the reasons she returns to the subject time and again as if to examine it from every possible angle. The complexity of her stance is reflected in the only essay she published about feminism, **"Oration at a Bonfire, Fourteen Years Late."** According to Langbaum, this essay was originally a speech delivered at a Women's Rights Congress in 1953; it was fourteen years late because, as Dinesen explains, she had been asked to speak about feminism to an international women's congress in 1939 and had declined:

> "I cannot accept this assignment, for I am not a feminist." "Are you against feminism?" asked Mrs. Hein. "No," I said, "I can't say that I'm that, either." "How do you stand upon feminism?" asked Mrs. Hein again. "Well, I never thought of it," I answered. "Well, think of it now," said Mrs. Hein.

A letter written to her Aunt Bess during Dinesen's African years provides an interesting gloss on this description: "Like most people I am too slow witted to have my arguments ready at hand in a discussion and am therefore often obliged . . . to resort to the excuse of saying: I haven't thought about it. But afterward, of course, one tries to give the subject serious thought and to clarify it, and then one may wish to resume the discussion . . ." (*Letters*). Dinesen's disclaimer, therefore, should not be taken to mean that she had not previously thought about feminism.

In fact, the thrust of her speech repeats a point made in *Out of Africa* in which she discusses "the fascination of things wholly different from themselves," a point she later elaborates in *Shadows on the Grass* when she describes her relationship with her servant Farah: "In order to form and make up a Unity, in particular a creative Unity, the individual components must needs be of different nature, they should even be in a sense contrasts. Two homogeneous units will never be capable of forming a whole, or their whole at its best will remain barren." As she comments later in the same passage, "A community of but one sex would be a blind world."

The point of her belated Bonfire Speech is that men and women are different and should not try to be alike. She speaks of "my old belief in the significance of interaction, and . . . my conviction regarding the opulent and unlimited possibilities which arise from the fellowship and interplay of two different individuals," an interplay she describes as "the reciprocity between man and woman." What makes them different is that "A man's center of gravity, the substance of his being, consists in what he has executed and performed in life; the woman's, in what she is." As she sees it, therefore, "woman's function is to expand her own being," and she gives as examples Maria Theresa, Elizabeth I, Queen Victoria, the Maid of Orleans, and the Virgin Mary, all of whom, she says, are known for what they were rather than for what they did. Paradoxically, this means that "the average woman is more of an artist than the average man," for even though "few women have been great artists," if "they do not *create* a work of art, they can themselves be said to *become* works of art—that is, as actresses, singers, or dancers."

Apparently aware of the offense she may be giving to her feminist audience, Dinesen pauses to give a kind of apology in which she praises "the older women of the women's movement now in their graves" and acknowledges that her own freedom "to study what I wished and where I wished . . . to travel around the world alone . . . put my ideas freely into print . . . [and] stand here at the lectern" stems from "the grand old women [who] struck the first blow for us." But Dinesen's point is that the battle has been won, and women no longer have to act like men: the woman of today "has certainly such a firm footing in the old strongholds that she can confidently open her visor and show the world that she is a woman and no disguised rogue."

Simone de Beauvoir denounces Dinesen's contention that women exist for what they are, because dependence upon an indefinable essence makes women too lazy to be, for example, serious literary artists.

—Sara Stambaugh

Her assumption, of course, would be opposed by many feminists. In *The Second Sex* Simone de Beauvoir specifically denounces several of Dinesen's stances. In her introduction, de Beauvoir uses Dinesen's favorite analogy of master and servant, which de Beauvoir presents as "master and slave [who], also, are united by a reciprocal need, in this case economic, which does not liberate the slave." She concludes that "Even if the need is at bottom equally urgent for both, it always works in favor of the oppressor against the oppressed."

De Beauvoir also denounces Dinesen's contention that women exist for what they are, because, according to de Beauvoir, dependence upon an indefinable essence makes women too lazy to be, for example, serious literary artists. De Beauvoir says about traditional women: "In order to seduce, they know only the method of showing themselves; then their charm either works or does not work, they have no real hand in its success or failure. They suppose that in analogous fashion it is sufficient for expression, communication, to show what one is. . . ."

But if Isak Dinesen rejected some feminist stances, a further look at her Bonfire Speech shows that she cared about women and insisted upon their right to be different from men because of her strong assumption that the sexes were equal. She describes the early feminists as "sly" because, in effect, they disguised themselves as men to break down sexual barriers and enter the professions. But now that they are free to be doctors, she wonders why women should not bring to that profession their traditional skills as midwives and clairvoyants. The implication is that women have special talents which transcend the roles devised by men.

A key phrase in the Bonfire Speech is Dinesen's reference to "the reciprocity between man and woman," because reciprocity can exist only between equals. Dinesen is wickedly witty, for example, in dismissing "the attitude of various past eras" that "one half of the race should devote itself to preservation and procreation while the other half took on the task of development and progress." To illustrate her point, she describes Kaiser Wilhelm's view that woman's place was "*Kirche, Kinder, Küche*—the church, the children and the kitchen." Commenting on the Kaiser's view, she says:

> Personally I would say that, were this seriously meant, it would be an offer worth considering. But it never *was* seriously meant. Had the church really been a woman's field of endeavor we might naturally have had woman priests and bishops and also woman popes—but about such one knows only of Pope Joan, who is unfortunately said not to have been a favorable representative of her sex and has been sadly reduced by later, skeptical times to a legendary figure. The officials of the church have always been exclusively male and the woman's role has been limited to that of the churchgoer—which nobody could very well refuse her. Had *Kinder* been put into the hands of women, had schools and the educational system been their domain, the world would probably look rather different than what Kaiser Wilhelm imagined or wished it to be. For him the concept was presumably most nearly associated with cradles and diapers, a realm for which there has never been any zealous male competition. As far as the third K, the kitchen, is concerned—the area where women can be assumed to have been more or less sovereign—they seem to have displayed an admirable unselfishness. It is the male taste which dominates both the family table and the restaurant— when women eat together and can themselves

decide the menu, it has quite a different, lighter, and more varied character. Here I may interpose the remark that Negro and Somali women are clever about poisoning their men by the dishes which they put before them, and that as a consequence they enjoy quite peculiar respect.

As this passage shows, however uncongenial her views might be to some feminists, Isak Dinesen was no simple reactionary.

In fact, the central point of her essay is that the world needs to be feminized. As she says, "our own time can be said to need a revision of its ambition from *doing* to *being*", in other words, from masculine to feminine values as she has defined them. She goes on to compare women to trees and men to machines in a feminist revision of a favorite figure of the nineteenth century:

> At times it can seem that our day, proud of its mighty achievements, would claim the superiority of the motor over the oak tree, the machine over growth. But it is also conceivable that in such an evaluation we have been misled by an interpretation of the theory of the survival of the fittest. It is clear that the motor can destroy the oak tree—while the oak tree cannot be thought capable of destroying the motor—but what follows? That which itself has no independent being—or is without any loyalty to such a being—is unable to create. Now I have not meant that women are trees and men are motors, but I wish to insinuate into the minds of the women of our time as well as those of the men, that they should meditate not only upon what they may accomplish but most profoundly upon what they are.

Her speech ends with a call for people "who *are* agriculturists," "who *are* sailors," "who *are* teachers," and "who *are* poets", in other words, for a world infused with the quality of "being" which she considers fundamentally feminine.

If Isak Dinesen rejected conventional feminism, it was not through lack of familiarity. In fact, she was raised in a family bristling with militant feminists. After her father's suicide when she was nine, she spent most of her life until her marriage at twenty-eight in a matriarchal society dominated by her maternal grandmother, her mother and her mother's sister, Mary Bess Westenholtz. All three had strong personalities. In addition, as Dinesen's brother Thomas comments, "All the Matrup family had always been involved in political problems and disputes of the day. They were all pronouncedly to the left, and amongst other things, were very much in favour of votes for women" [Thomas Dinesen, *My Sister, Isak Dinesen,* 1975]. Dinesen's Aunt Bess, for example, was known for her invasion of Parliament in 1909 when she seized the podium and denounced the male legislators as cowards—after which, Thomas comments, "a large deputation of women gathered at Folehave to thank her for her courage and resolution." Dinesen's mother was also a political activist. When Danish women were granted the vote in 1916 she was elected "to Hørsholm Parish Council, and when it turned out that she was the eldest of the elected members, for a few days she had the honour of being Den-

mark's first woman parish councillor." Isak Dinesen, then, grew up watching the fight for women's rights, because "the grand old women [who] struck the first blow for us" included her intimate relatives.

As her Bonfire Speech indicates, however, Dinesen apparently thought that in fighting for equality her female relatives had sacrificed something of their femininity; perhaps she had them in mind when she referred to early feminists as disguising themselves as men. Dinesen has been accused of disliking "her aunt, and the maternal wing of her family in general" [Judith Thurman, "Isak Dinesen/Karen Blixen: A Very Personal Memoir," *MS* II, No. 3 (September 1973)]. but as one might expect of Isak Dinesen, her letters indicate a more complex relationship. Her letters to her mother, for example, are filled with endearments such as "my beloved little Mother," "My own beloved Mother," and "My own beloved beloved wonderful little mother" (*Letters*). Writing to her grandmother, she wonders "whether . . . I'm not rather like you" (Thomas Dinesen), and in another letter to her mother she comments that she is certainly fonder of her Aunt Bess than her sisters are (*Letters*). In all, the letters show a warm family feeling on the part of Isak Dinesen—but not one which is uncritical.

Although Dinesen loves the members of the family matriarchy, she makes clear that she rejects their values. As she remarks to her mother, "I think that to a certain extent all of your family lack the ability to 'amuse themselves,' —or, to express it symbolically: 'to enjoy the *wine* of life,' and are inclined to think that happiness is to be found in a diet of bread and milk." Elsewhere she says to her mother, "recently I have come to see that your way of thinking is completely foreign to me; I will never belong to it." Of her grandmother, aunt and the maternal uncle largely responsible for financing her stay in Africa she complains: "They are always trying to change me into something quite different; they do not like the parts of me that I believe to be good." In a letter to her brother in which she discusses her plans to leave Africa and expresses her dislike of moving into her mother's house, she writes, "the atmosphere at home has never suited me," and she indicates that she "married and put all my efforts into emigrating in order to get away . . ." (*Letters*). It would seem that her rejection of feminism is part of a reaction against the wider system of values she associates with it.

Apparently Dinesen judged feminism to be bourgeois and rejected it along with the other maternal values she opposed to the aristocratic ones associated with her father. As she mentions in a radio talk, she was her father's "favorite child, and I know he thought I resembled him" ["**Rungstedlund: A Radio Address**," in *Daguerreotypes, and Other Essays*]. If she considered herself alien to the maternal world, one reason was her conviction that she was her father's daughter, so much so that her first pen name was Osceola, the Indian name of her father's dog [see Parmenia Migel, *Titania: The Biography of Isak Dinesen,* 1967], and her house in Africa was first called Bogani House in tribute to her father's pen name of Boganis. The idealized values she associates with him permeate her work, just as aspects of his life appear, for example, in the failed love affair described in **"Copenhagen Season."** As a result of her identification with her father, the values she embraces are those likely to be associated with a masculine system, the belief in risks, for example, or in the grand gesture. A friend says that when Dinesen was a girl, "She looked down upon the female—bearing, consoling, surviving—for in her experience, the female was only the survivor. . . . In most cases, she defined the difference between women and men as the difference between goodness and greatness: the prudence that respects life versus the extravagance that defies death. It was the same distinction she made, on another level, between the bourgeois and the aristocrat. .." (quoted by Thurman). Whether or not the friend is to be trusted, Isak Dinesen's identification with her father and rejection of her mother's values influenced her views of feminism.

To complicate things even more, the youthful Dinesen thought herself the victim of a sexist society, the instruments of which were her maternal relatives, whose concern that women should vote did not include a belief in equal education. In a fairly general way, Thomas deplores that in his sister's youth young women were not trained for anything but marriage, when "all that could be hoped for and helped with was to ensure that they found the right husband . . . ." In a 1927 letter his sister is more explicit in speaking of her own "bitterness where the old laws and ideals are concerned" and in assigning blame: "For instance, where the case of the emancipation of women is concerned, I myself feel, despite my affection for much that was beautiful and graceful in the old ideals, despite my gratitude toward those old women who struck the first blow for our freedom and independence, that the accounts have not been quite settled with a world, a system (not, of course, with any individuals at all), that with a perfectly clear conscience allowed practically all my abilities to lie fallow and passed me on to charity or prostitution in some shape or other . . ." (*Letters*). Whether or not her assessment is just, it helps to explain, for example, her reference in **"The Monkey"** (in **Seven Gothic Tales**) to the fury sealed in the breasts of old women "by the Solomonic wax of their education". It also illuminates what happens to the heroine of **"Alkmene,"** who is a good Greek scholar until her lessons are stopped when she is confirmed because masculine learning is unsuitable to a woman. Even if she grew up in a feminist household, Isak Dinesen had a fair share of grudges because of the repression she felt in it—one of the reasons, perhaps, that according to Thomas, "for years [she] looked with enthusiasm on the French Revolution and its characters: 'I wonder if I could ever be a person like Robespierre?' she said".

Isak Dinesen, then, was fully aware of the limitations she faced as a woman in the late nineteenth and early twentieth centuries, although just how resentful she was has been made clear only with the publication of her letters. In one, for example, she describes "the shooting parties at Näsbyholm," the estate of her paternal uncle, from which women were excluded and "did not exist until the men came home from shooting and they could begin to be charming for them at dinner" (*Letters*). (Apparently commenting on this letter, Naomi Bliven remarks that Dinesen's "pleasure in shooting wild animals [in Africa] . . .

arose at least in part from resentment of European shooting parties she recalls, from which women were excluded" ["A Woman and a Foreigner," *The New Yorker,* September 7, 1981]). Even more noteworthy is Dinesen's outspoken defense of women's independence, particularly in her epistolary debates with the more and more reactionary Aunt Bess and in her less defensive letters to her sister Ellen. Writing to the latter in 1928, she confided: "Incidentally, I think that there is a really fine time ahead for women and that the next hundred years will bring many glorious revelations to them. For there is hardly any other sphere in which prejudice and superstition of the most horrific kind have been retained so long as in that of women, and just as it must have been an inexpressible relief for humanity when it shook off the burden of religious prejudice and superstition, I think it will be truly glorious when women become real people and have the whole world open before them" (*Letters*). To her Aunt Bess she writes elaborate defenses of the current generation of women, who "desire and are striving to be human beings with a direct relationship with life in the same way as men have done and do this" (*Letters*). In a later passage—that must delight Gilbert and Gubar, who devote a chapter of *The Madwoman in the Attic* to "Milton's Bogey: Patriarchal Poetry and Women Readers"—Dinesen develops her argument by refuting Milton's " '*He all for God and she for God in him*' " (*Letters*). To her mother Dinesen writes of her delight in learning to drive a car and in cutting her hair: "For centuries long hair has been a sort of slavery; suddenly one feels freer than words can express. . . . And as nobody wears corsets out here you can really move as a man's equal" (*Letters*). She adds that she would wear shorts if she had better legs.

The letters I have quoted were written during Dinesen's African years and reflect her joy at independence, especially after her separation from her husband. But the marriage itself, as she indicates in a letter quoted above, was contracted as a bid for independence. Before her letters were published, her brother wrote: "To me it seems likely that Tanne [Dinesen's family name] had felt it absolutely vital to seek a totally new form of existence, perhaps different from the Victorian life imprinted on her home, which she had come to find intolerable". The joy she found in the freedom of her African life is beautifully attested to in **Out of Africa,** but her reaction at her freedom is perhaps most succinctly stated in an excerpt from an unpublished lecture of 1938: "Here at long last one was in a position not to give a damn for all conventions, here was a new kind of freedom which until then one had only found in dreams. It was like beginning to swim where one could stretch out in all directions, it was like beginning to fly where one seemed to have left the law of gravity behind. One might get a little dizzy, it was a little dangerous as well, it took courage, as it always does to recognize the truth. But it was glorious, intoxicating" [quoted by Donald Hannah, *Isak Dinesen and Karen Blixen: The Mask and the Reality,* 1971]. As Dinesen remarks to her brother in another letter, "I prize my freedom above everything else that I possess . . ." (*Letters*).

If Africa offered her freedom, however, it also allowed her to explore its limits. "Life here . . . has many features in common with life in Denmark two hundred years ago," she wrote; "the *roughness* of the conditions shows up the difference in the physical capacity of men and women . . ." (**Letters**). Although Dinesen ran a plantation in Africa (none too efficiently, it appears), she fell into the role of Victorian woman, raising flowers to please her anachronistic sixteenth-century gentlemen callers and apparently extending her being to entertain them, especially Denys Finch Hatton, whom, like Scherherazade, she amused by telling stories. Like her relationship with her father, the one with Finch Hatton may have contributed to the complexity of her sexual stance, because according to his biographer [Errol Trzebinski, in *Silence Will Speak: A Study of the Life of Denys Finch Hatton and His Relationship with Karen Blixen,* 1977], Denys "claimed to have inherited [his 'talent for writing verse'] from his bluestocking ancestor, Anne Finch, Lady Winchilsea"—a writer currently regarded by feminist critics as a pioneer feminist. According to Naomi Bliven, the idealized Denys is "like a more polished and magnetic version of her husband," with both being "a thousand years behind the times" but paradoxically, "agents of modernization" in East Africa. Bliven concludes that Dinesen "failed—perhaps inevitably—in her attempt to assert the rights of twentieth-century women in an existence imagined by nineteenth-century men."

Dinesen's stance on feminism is especially complex because on the one hand she wants absolute independence . . . and on the other she apparently enjoyed the idea that women embodied special qualities and deserved special tribute as women.

—Sara Stambaugh

Dinesen's stance on feminism, then, is especially complex because on the one hand she wants absolute independence and thinks that the relationship between the sexes will have to be revised in the twentieth century. She writes her brother that nineteenth-century versions of marriage and the relations of the sexes represented "a very brief and myopic period of exception in the history of man" probably brought about by Romanticism which managed to "[confuse] realities and feelings in a hitherto unknown manner" and ended by "[muddling] up a code that was probably none too clear previously" (**Letters**). She even wrote a monograph, *Modern Marriage and Other Considerations,* sent to her brother in November 1924 but so far—unless perhaps in Danish—unpublished (**Letters** [the work was published in 1986 as **On Modern Marriage, and Other Observations**]).

On the other hand, Dinesen apparently enjoyed the idea that women embodied special qualities and deserved special tribute as women. In a 1928 letter to her sister Ellen she laments "that the idea, so to speak, has disappeared

from womanliness, of what it is to be a woman." She continues:

> I think that the women of the old days, and especially the best of them, felt themselves to be representatives of something great and sacred, by virtue of which they possessed importance outside themselves and could feel great pride and dignity, and toward which they had a weighty responsibility. Neither the arrogance of the young and beautiful girl or the majesty of the old lady was, after all, felt on their own behalf; they were without any element of personal vanity, but were borne as something to take pride in, a shield or a banner. Where a personal affront might well be pardoned, a violation of that womanliness whose representatives they were could never be forgiven. . . .

> (**Letters**)

In her fiction, of course, Dinesen loves to examine such past attitudes, but to some extent, at least, she seems to have shared this one. She was personally vain. Migel, for example, comments upon her feminine vanity and "desire to charm and conquer, which was even more essential to her than to most women", and Eugene Walter describes an encounter in Rome between Dinesen and an Italian princess, who "achieved only an exquisite springtime chilliness with each other." He concludes, "both ladies, at heart, really liked to be surrounded only by males" ["Isak Dinesen Conquers Rome," *Harper's Magazine,* February, 1965].

Apparently Dinesen finally decided to enjoy independence yet at the same time to cultivate a special feminine mystique. The stance is uncomfortably close to the reactions against feminism by early twentieth-century writers as described by Elaine Showalter, who remarks that "many women writers of this generation seem to have retreated from social involvement into a leisurely examination of the sensibility, into the cultivation of a beautiful womanly Unlikeness" [*A Literature of Their Own: British Women Novelists from Brontë to Lessing,* 1977]. Dinesen certainly insists on "womanly Unlikeness." What separates her from such anti-feminists as Marie Corelli is that Dinesen rejects the idea that " 'the clever woman sits at home' " and controls men by her passivity [Corelli quoted by Showalter]. To the contrary, Dinesen's female characters as often as not are powerful, independent and free of sexual restraints, like the Danish noblewomen she often describes or, particularly, like Pellegrina Leoni. If from one perspective Dinesen's stance can be considered a reaction against feminism, from another it might be considered an example of what Showalter posits as the third and truly liberated stage of women's writing, the "phase of *self-discovery,* a turning inward freed from some of the dependency of opposition, a search for identity." More recently Judith Finlayson has suggested that "there may be means of achieving and using power that do not conform to the male model. . . ." ["An Introduction to *Women and Power,*" *Homemaker's Magazine,* No. 17, January-February, 1982.]

To Dinesen, the admirable men of the world are those who honor and acknowledge the superior wisdom of the one woman who never conformed and who never had to earn her independence, the witch. In the title work of her collected essays Dinesen speaks of three groups in which an "older generation [of men] viewed women," who "were for them either guardian angels or housewives or, in a third group . . . what I here, to use a nice word—for there are a good many that are not so nice—shall call the bayadères." After describing each type she adds that "the men of the nineteenth century viewed their women from these points of view, or in three groups, officially," but "in reality they had in their consciousness still another type of woman which for all of them was very much alive and present but was not mentioned or recognized by the light of day.. .. [L]ong before the words 'emancipation of women' came into use, [she] existed independently and had her own center of gravity. She was the witch" ["**Daguerreotypes**," in ***Daguerreotypes, and Other Essays***]. Describing the witch, Dinesen allegedly quotes a friend from Africa:

> "Even though the witch is a lonely figure," said my friend, "she has a good relationship with her sister witches. She is a black guardian angel, a bat on a dark night filled with Northern lights as a flickering reflection from the time that Lucifer was the morning star. She is a housewife to the hilt: fire and fireplace are precious to her and the cauldron is indispensable. She is a bayadère and a seductress even as a Sibyl or a mummy:
>
> black from Phoebus's pinch of love
> and wrinkled deep by time . . .
>
> And if the learned gentlemen feel their masculine dignity is affronted by the thought that she prefers the devil to a man, then the layman and outdoorsman find some compensation in another remark: the basis, indeed the prerequisite for the witch's entire activity is the circumstance that the devil is masculine.

The witch, then, embodies the characteristics Dinesen associated with ideal womanhood: friendship with other women, masculine independence, the rebelliousness associated with Lucifer, housewifely skills, seductiveness and a strong attraction to men. If her attitude toward feminism is complex, in the figure of the witch Dinesen found a means of expressing it.

It is not surprising that the witch is a central figure in her fiction. Not only is the witch quintessential woman, but she reflects as well the superior powers associated with women through the ancient moon goddesses and their descendants, the medieval practitioners of the Craft of the Wise. Like the moon goddesses, she has a double aspect and can appear as primordial mother, crone and loathly lady or else as Kore, captive princess and benevolent fairy. The witch Sunniva of **"The Sailor-Boy's Tale"** is both hag and, it can be argued, the nubile young Nora, who rewards the hero with a kiss. But like the Lapp witch Lahula of **"The Bear and the Kiss,"** she is most often misunderstood and reviled by men who fear the power of the independent woman. Thus she not only expresses the power of womanhood in a particularly feminine form but also reflects the difficulties the emancipated woman faces in the twentieth century.

Vivian Greene-Gantzberg and Arthur R. Gantzberg (essay date November 1983)

SOURCE: "Karen Blixen's 'Carnival,' " in *Scandinavica*, Vol. 22, No. 2, November, 1983, pp. 159-70.

[*In the following essay on the short story "Carnival," the critics examine Dinesen's literary style, characters, and use of fantasy, while exploring the themes of aristocratic life and the role of the artist. They also discuss the influence of Aldous Huxley, Sigmund Freud, Edgar Allan Poe, Guy de Maupassant, and E. T. A. Hoffman on Dinesen's work.*]

'Carnival', which is among the most recently published of Karen Blixen's tales, dates from the 1920s—presumably around 1926, just after she had completed the shorter marionette comedy entitled ***Sandhedens Hævn***. Originally, 'Carnival' too, was planned as a marionette comedy. The comedy was rewritten as a tale and was intended to be included in a collection to be entitled 'Nine Tales by Nozdref 's Cook', which contained the material for ***Seven Gothic Tales*** (1933). In 1961, the year before Karen Blixen's death, she contemplated revising the manuscript of **'Carnival'**. **'Carnival'** warrants close study because its thematic and structural patterns prefigure those of her subsequent tales.

With the publication of Karen Blixen's letters from Africa in 1978, much of the conjecture about her development during the years between 1914 and 1931—and consequently about her posthumous tales from that period—has been eliminated or is at least now based on a more reliable body of material. The background of her artistic achievement can now be understood in terms of her private life. In reading the letters, we realize how greatly her correspondence resembles ideas that are expressed in her essays and fiction, in particular, with regard to the individual's attitude toward social codes. Although Karen Blixen's letters comment relatively infrequently on her literary efforts, they nevertheless reveal the interplay of truth and fiction and relate the origins of her fantastic tales. Letters to her mother, Ingeborg Dinesen, her Aunt Mary Bess Westenholz, and her brother Thomas Dinesen contain references to persons, books, and events that have been helpful in restructuring the myriad of her personal and literary activities that were essential to the creation of **'Carnival'**.

The most difficult period for Karen Blixen coincides with the years that lead to the composition of **'Carnival'**. It is instructive to consider events in her personal life between 1919, the year in which it becomes certain that her marriage with her cousin Bror Blixen Finecke cannot continue, and 1926, when she returns to Kenya from Denmark and experiences a number of personal crises. In 1920, Karen Blixen returns to Africa after her second visit to Denmark. She is accompanied by her brother Thomas, who is to assess the financial state of the coffee farm of which she later is appointed manager. In 1921, she separates from her husband. She is disappointed in her first expectation of pregnancy by her English companion Denys Finch Hatton in 1926. The following year Karen Blixen begins to write a lengthy essay on the institution of marriage entitled **'Moderne AE gteskab og andre Betragtninger'** (first published in 1977). The finished manuscript is sent to Thomas Dinesen in 1924. Karen and Bror Blixen are divorced in 1925, after which she returns to Denmark in order to establish literary relations there. Her unsuccessful attempts lead her back to Kenya in 1926 when **Sandhedens Haevn** is published. During this year, Karen Blixen again takes up the tales and comedies begun in her youth, along with **'Carnival'**, one of the first gothic tales. In a letter to Thomas dated 16 May 1926, she writes, 'Jeg er ved at skrive paa to smaa nye Marionette Komedier for at trøste mig, men det er en daarlig Trøst. . . .'

Documents from the years between 1919 and 1926, that attest Karen Blixen's preoccupation with ethics are her comments in the letters from Africa on marriage, sexuality, and morals and her essay on marriage. The common theme in the letters, the essay, and the tale **'Carnival'** is society's axiomatic assumption that love—for which marriage is a symbol—represents a source of value. Karen Blixen believed that relationships between men and women had been construed traditionally as necessarily linked to sexual morality, so that morality associated with sexual behaviour also threatened to become one of the foundations of modern society. In reshaping her ideas about individuality and democracy, Karen Blixen protested traditions of the age that made eroticism the foundation of everyday life, 'som har regnet med at bygge virkelig praktiske og reale Forhold i Livet, —Hjem, Slægt, økonomiske Forhold, —op paa denne farlige og usikre Magt: Erotiken' [**Breve for Afrika, 1914-34,** edited by Frans Lasson, 1978]. In this connection Karen Blixen recommended to her brother Thomas, Bertrand Russell's book *Principles of Social Reconstruction* (first printed 1916), in which he discusses the weight that reactionary opinions carry in the consideration of moral problems. Russell's aim is to suggest a philosophy of politics that is based on creative impulse and not on materialistic values of human experience. In a chapter on marriage, Russell outlines the ills of this—to use his term—political institution. Karen Blixen's own essay on marriage is, incidentally, very much in tune with the ideas in Russell's book.

Karen Blixen confesses the unsuitability of marriage for herself and in this context, advances the theory that modern love is 'Homosexualite, —opfattet paa samme Maade som naar man bruger Udtrykket i homogen, —som mere tager Form som en lidenskabelig Sympathi, et Fællesskab i Kærlighed til Ideer eller Idealer, end som en personlig Opgaaen i, og Hengivelse til hinanden; . . .' 'Aldous Huxley', writes Karen Blixen, 'har et Udtryk: 'The love of the parallels,' som han rigtignok anvender i en temmelig tragisk Betydning, men som jeg vel kan have Lov til at opfatte som jeg vil.' (Blixen rephrases, incidentally, Huxley's title—'The Loves of the Parallels'—to her own advantage. Her interpretation of Huxley's phrase is that 'one does not "[løbe] 'ud i', gaar ikke 'op i' hinanden; men kommer maaske ikke hinanden saa nær som de Mennesker, der har Evener til en saadan Opgaaen i hinanden, og man er sletikke hinandens Maal i Livet, man mens man er sig selv og stræber mod sit eget fjerne Maal, finder man Lykken i Overbevisningen om i al Evighed at løbe parallelt"'.' She proposes that the relationship between men and women be one of 'parallel moving' beings.)

On 13 July 1927, Karen Blixen continues the discussion of man's search for values with her Aunt Bess by arguing that 'bourgeois happiness' is not what people search for in life; neither is it 'bourgeois happiness' which satisfies them. She feels that in determining one's *raison d'être,* misconceptions about marriage and the development of the self arise. Accordingly, she fails to understand why one cannot live for oneself in marriage. She finds the practice of free relations a more nourishing alternative. The configurations of free relationships in **'Carnival'** is, consequently, not a symbol for immorality, but rather for friendships that are void of the conflicts of marriage and that are maintained by the mutual tastes, work, and interest of spiritually self-sufficient individuals. That Karen Blixen should choose adventures of the heart as a central issue in the tale is consistent with her belief that society of her day substituted amorous inclinations for hazardous passions. In retrospect, she relates the idea of comfort to the style of life characteristic of 1925, thus borrowing from her contemporary Aldous Huxley ideas about the materialistic philosophy of 'le moderne comfort'.

In her letters from Africa, Karen Blixen cites Huxley as an author whom she liked very much. Her literary attraction to Huxley grew into a personal friendship that continued even after she had returned to Denmark permanently. (Karen Blixen's companion Denys Finch Hatton was, moreover, a personal friend of Aldous Huxley's brother Julian.) Huxley's popularity during the twenties, which presumably reached Karen Blixen through her circle of English friends in Kenya, was symptomatic of the times. Besides themes of decadence and materialistic philosophy, Huxley's works from the twenties—*Chrome Yellow* (1921), *Antic Hay* (1923), *Those Barren Leaves* (1925)—demonstrate a search for values. In these novels, Huxley draws references from various disciplines—science, philosophy, psychology, religions, art, and music.

We know that Karen Blixen did not always attempt to be original with regard to themes, symbols, and archetypes in her stories. Not only does she quote from individual authors—classical and contemporary—but she also consciously creates a mosaic of her sources. With **'Carnival'** Karen Blixen set out to write a certain kind of tale. Huxley's own discussion of his narrative technique throws some light on the spirit in which **'Carnival'** was created.

> All you need is a sufficiency of characters and parallel contrapuntal plots . . . You alternate the themes. More interesting, the modulations and variations are also more difficult. A novelist modulates by repudiating situations and characters. He shows several people falling in love . . . in different ways . . . In this way, you can modulate through all the aspects of your theme, you can write variations in any number of different moods. Another way: The novelist can assume the god-like creative privilege and simply elect to consider the events of the story of their various aspects—emotional, scientific, economic, religious, metaphysical, etc.

[Huxley, *Point Counter Point,* 1928]

An essayist and novelist, Huxley engages a fluidity of form that allows him to comment on a wide range of subjects.

Any given subject may serve as a starting point for discussing something else. His reader's task is to reconstruct order.

Comparisons and narrative devices used by Blixen and Huxley can be made with regard to the sudden shift of ideas and the repetition of themes and their variations. Karen Blixen writes, for example, in the tale **'Carnival'** about a diplomat's reassignment from Copenhagen to Egypt; this remark is followed by an excerpt from a fairy tale, an exchange in blank verse between lovers, and an artist's discussion of colours. All of this within a single paragraph. Throughout the tale, seemingly unmotivated anecdotes of events that occurred in remote lands interrupt the story. The recurrence of themes is observed in parallel love affairs, searchings for a source of value by all of the characters, dual personalities, and desires to experience seduction.

In this study, *Aldous Huxley, A Study of the Major Novels* (London, 1968), Peter Bowering points out that Huxley's first major novel (*Crome Yellow,* 1921) is a house party novel, that is (as we shall witness in **'Carnival'**), a tale which employs as its point of departure the meeting of a circle of social and artistic dilettantes at a secluded house party. In Huxley's tales, the characters, each of whose personalities characterizes a particular set of values, are exposed one by one. The polemical element of his narrative allows for a dialectical discussion that concerns the moral and intellectual bankruptcy of the postwar era. Like Huxley's, Karen Blixen's tales are intellectual dialogues couched in satirical moralities on love and art.

Although Baroness Blixen was not born into the aristocracy, she married into it and managed to enjoy the style of life it maintained. Blixen's characters were, too, at once themselves and impersonators in a world that was not their own.

—*Vivian Greene-Gantzberg and Arthur R. Gantzberg*

Up until the 1930s, the period of Karen Blixen's development that is of interest to us, public and private and morality was a chief consideration in Huxley's fiction and nonfiction. Karen Blixen and Huxley question love as a source of value. The relation between men and women, the social versus the personal self, the fruits of self-denial, the harsh gaiety of the twenties, and the overindulgence of aristocratic society were central issues in their tales.

A certain perception of the aristocratic world is inherent in Karen Blixen's metaphor 'carnival'. Although Baroness Blixen was not born into the aristocracy, she married into it and managed to enjoy the style of life it maintained. Blixen's characters were, too, 'rich, disillusioned, and hungry'. They were at once themselves and impersonators in a world that was not their own. The 'carnival' is a fitting

introduction to the tale, as the metaphor defines the scene ('the great Opera Carnival at Copenhagen of 1925') to which the players were to return after an evening in the manner of the past—masquerading as caricatures—superimposing a sense of substance on their own empty lives.

We are reminded of Thackeray's use of the carnival as a symbol of the warped state of society in his novel *Vanity Fair* (1847-48). Like the message in Blixen's tale, Thackeray's social novel of the previous century holds up hypocrisy, greed, pretence, and moral insensibility to ridicule. Both works strive to suggest that a lack of self-knowledge contributes to the superficiality of aristocratic society and that man can progress from moral insensibility to self-knowledge. Unlike **'Carnival'**, however, *Vanity Fair* is a social satire in which characters' weaknesses are unmasked. The strength of **'Carnival'** lies not in its derision of superficiality, but rather, in the simple statement that 'life itself is a true carnival'. Life of the aristocracy too, is a marionette comedy in which a player has no soul, no conscience, and no values. Karen Blixen regards the aristocracy as separate from ordinary society in that aristocratic and artistic values are much the same.

'Carnival' is set on the outskirts of Copenhagen in the mid-1920s. The story involves members of a supper party who decide to draw lots that will allow one of them to live on their pooled income for one year, while the others forfeit their wealth. The party takes an unexpected turn when an intruder who poses as a Negro page holds up the assembled group and demands money. The dinner guests persuade the intruder to take part in the lottery, that is ended when one of the original guests draws the winning card and elects to take on Zamor, the page, as an artificial shadow.

Personalities in **'Carnival'** are disentangled only through the reader's careful separation and matching of figurative and literary pseudonyms with given names. One is best served by arranging a list of characters subsumed under the headings: Christian name, masks, and relation (to the other characters). Masks and given names are referred to interchangeably in the tale. Females play male roles but also their own roles as women. The pronoun 'she', for example, may sometimes refer to the female masked figure, when, in fact, the actual male person is being referred to. Moreover, complex relations between marriage partners and friends may lead to confusion.

The nine characters in **'Carnival'** include four women and five men. Mimi ('Watteau Pierrot') and Polly ('Arlecchino') are sisters. Mimi is married to Julius ('The Venetian lady'), who has twice been in love with Fritze ('Camelia'). Tido, the male futuristic Harlequin is in love with Annelise ('Søren Kierkegaard'). Her divorced husband is, incidentally, married to his divorced wife. The foreigner among the dinner guests is Charlie ('The Magenta Domino'). Rosendaal, the painter, is the eldest among them. Finally, Zamor (whose actual given name is not imparted), Madame Rubenstein's salesman and adopted son, pretends to be a Negro page.

Much of the narration in the first half of the tale deals with the manner in which the disguise of the other self is manifested. Costumes have been carefully chosen, and persons who don them play the roles that are dictated by their masks. Camelia is dressed in pink satin that accentuates her indeterminate character—'at whatever place you cut her slim body . . . you would have got a perfectly circular transverse incision.' Søren Kierkegaard—'that brilliant, deep, and desperate Danish philosopher of the eighteen forties was admired for her rare grace.' The sisters 'Pierrot' and 'Arlecchino' are likened, not to 'a congenial upheap of heterogeneous atoms, but to a heterogeneous upheap of congenial atoms.' We witness with them 'a scoffing expression which one finds in the faces of Japanese dolls.' 'The Venetian lady' wears heavy luminous silver cloth and brocade. The futuristic Harlequin is dressed in clothes of soft metallic materials in pale shades of jade, mauve, and grey. The Magenta Domino, whose face is not fully concealed—is played by an Englishman; as a foreigner, he perceives the events with some degree of disinterest. Rosendaal is dressed in yellow to challenge the belief that 'yellow is a colour which has no depth.' Zamor's colour is 'unmistakably a fake.' The black of his skin is described as an 'unmixed, sooty darkness.'

'Carnival' convincingly recalls the traditions of *commedia dell' arte,* the theatre of improvisation originated in sixteenth-century Italy in which players—referred to as 'masks'—work from a plot outline and fulfill inherited or invented roles. Stock players generally wear disguises or comic make-up; they include among others, old men, lovers, and comic valets. Although Karen Blixen employs familiar stock types as well as historical figures, her general design in **'Carnival'** remains loyal to improvised theatre.

Two elements account for the fundamental structure of **'Carnival':** first, Karen Blixen's use of fantasy and second, her questioning of the compatibility of traditional ethics and modern society. The interplay of these elements (which underscores a convergence of the artistic, psychological, and social parts of Karen Blixen's philosophical convictions) is emphasised here. **'Carnival'** is a symbolic expression for how Karen Blixen dealt with the various forces that moulded her view of life. Metaphorically speaking, the tale is as well a sketch of her later paintings.

Some stories of Karen Blixen—or 'Isak Dinesen' to use her English pseudonym—dramatise a theme of ambiguous identity that is at first reminiscent of tales by E. T. A. Hoffmann or Edgar Allan Poe. The distinguishing motif in Karen Blixen's tales is, however, the theatrical quality of life that manifests itself in the mask. Her tales involving the mask range from the years before she was to achieve fame until recently when her posthumous tales were published. Karen Blixen's early fiction—some tales considered by her to be incomplete—contains basic ideas for her later, major stories. The marionette comedy *Sandhedens Hævn—The Revenge of Truth*—which was published in 1926 in the Danish cultural monthly *Tilskueren* illustrates her attempt to dispel the theatre's traditional verisimilitude. In the play, characters reveal consciousness of their roles and their audience. Comic awareness is emphasised by impromptu stage directions, improvisations, and the characters' ability to alter their established roles. As a re-

sult, the play can be perceived not merely as a world of marionettes, but also as a world in the tradition of *commedia dell'arte,* where players enjoy relative freedom of action—a freedom which conforms to Karen Blixen's idea that art and life are reconciled in the mask.

That Karen Blixen should employ the mask as one of her chief symbols is not arbitrary. The manner in which she herself chose private and public roles shows her own need to have had at her disposal various facets of personality. In the short story **'The Roads around Pisa'** (in *Seven Gothic Tales*), Karen Blixen—'Isak Dinesen'—epitomises consciousness that can tolerate ambiguous identity. The essence of this consciousness is the ability deliberately to choose among several roles or modes of behaviour. Such a choice is governed by the integrating force of a unique and permanent self. The capacity to assume a new role at will without losing the sense of continuity of the self (that is, without displaying signs of pathological processes that threaten the psyche) defines the attitude of the actor. In **'The Roads around Pisa',** the protagonist becomes an actor in a play within a play and the work's narrative structure is understood in terms of the theatre. In **'The Cardinal's First Tale'** (*Last Tales*) the reader is confronted by a character whose personality is a blend of a metaphorical God and of man, as it were, of priest and poet. The ambiguity of identity appears again in **'The Dreamers'** ('Drømmerne'), where the opera singer Pellegrina Leoni poses in a succession of diverse disguises, but also vows never again to limit herself to being only one person.

As Donald Hannah points out in an essay entitled 'The Latter Phase: "Isak Dinesen",' Karen Blixen considered the name 'Isak Dinesen' not a deception, but a mask [see Hannah, *'Isak Dinesen' and Karen Blixen,* 1962]. The public face was a mask that permitted and nourished her artistic concept of the self and was to superimpose the identity society had chosen for her. Karen Blixen's dissatisfaction with society's expectations—which defined the boundaries of her conventional identity—stemmed from an awareness that the exploration of the inner self constitutes artistic freedom. The idea of making explicit a hidden facet of one's self by creating a new role and a new outward appearance is illustrated vividly in Kasparson's words from **'The Deluge at Norderney'** (*Seven Gothic Tales*): 'the witty woman chooses a carnival costume which ingeniously reveals something in her spirit or heart which the conventions of everyday life conceal'. By using a mask deliberately, it is possible to become detached from one's assigned role on the 'stage of life'.

The donning of masks—as portrayed in Karen Blixen's tales—distinguishes itself from classic depictions of the double—or double identity—to be found in the works of Hoffmann, Poe, or Maupassant. Instead of allowing her characters to be intimidated by their alternate roles (as Hoffmann does in his tales), she allows the characters playfully to engage in conversation about the ability to create and choose roles. Instead of portraying incidents of pathological processes in which individuals are incapable of distinguishing their doubles from their permanent selves, Blixen injects an intentional contradiction of the consciousness of the artistically created identity (signified

> In 'Carnival,' The purpose of the mask is
> not motivated by a desire to escape fear.
> In Karen Blixen, the reader perceives an
> alternate spiritual identity. The ambiguity
> of identity may be contained in a single
> person.
>
> —*Vivian Greene-Gantzberg and Arthur R.*
> *Gantzberg*

by the mask) and the function of the created identity. Blixen's players as well as her readers are aware that the personae may simultaneously reveal multiple facets of their identities. The nature of disguise—costumes with half masks, no masks, or, as in the case of 'Pierrot', a floured face that reveals her conventional identity but that cannot be unmasked—enhances the idea of conscious conflict and the conflict of consciousness. In Karen Blixen's tale, the purpose of the mask is not motivated by a desire to escape fear. There are no doppelgänger among Blixen's multiple identities. In Karen Blixen, the reader perceives an alternate spiritual identity and not a physical double. 'Masks' in Karen Blixen's tales do not function as ethical contrasts, but rather as caricatures in their own right. The ambiguity of identity may be contained in a single person. The masks in **'Carnival'** are not used to obscure the identity of the wearers entirely; on the contrary, certain comic effects in the tale are attained by contrasting the wearer's still visible, banal appearance with the highmindedness revealed by the choice of the mask. The philosopher Søren Kierkegaard, for example, must coexist with the shallow figure of Annelise, whose brilliance is defined only by her outward appearance.

Among the most striking 'masks' in **'Carnival'** are the Chinese painter, Arlecchino and Pierrot. The painter assumes the personality of stock types known as 'the old men'; this type wears a mask of dignity, but Rosendaal, as Blixen states, would shed his skin 'with the ease of an old snake which believes it has got something better underneath.' 'Arlecchino' appears in **'Carnival'** as the 'genuine classic figure of the old Italian pantomime.' Blixen's 'Pierrot' is expressly labelled 'Watteau Pierrot', recognisable by admirers of works by Antoine Watteau. Karen Blixen, who herself studied art, achieves a refinement of the mask by attending to artistic principles that suggest three-dimensionality through the use of shadows and defined luminous sources.

The combination of light and colour, atmospheric effect, and linear drawing are essential to **'Carnival'**. The costume of the Venetian lady is compared to a great waterfall of moonlight. 'Moonshine' is the password of Blixen's sister masks and rivals, 'Arlecchino' and 'Pierrot', and is a symbol for the 'enhanced lustre, the gentle reflection of a coveted admiration with which the happy rival would shine in the unhappy rival's eye.' As the dinner party begins Karen Blixen remarks on a 'meeting and mating of light and colour.' Arlecchino complains of the vulgarity

of being three-dimensional and considers making a shadow theatre. Zamor is saved from an 'embarkment to Cythere', clearly an allusion to a painting that is characteristic of Watteau's style: *L'embarquement pour Cythere* is a delicate courtly fantasy represented in warm and shimmering tones.

Donning a mask is not only a matter of masquerading. All of the dinner guests are aware of their costumes; this makes it possible for them to develop conversation about the superficiality of their society—the ethos of Karen Blixen's tale. They talk of the fundamental falsity of the traditional idea of covering up the body and leaving the face bare. Pierrot remarks: 'but to be your own caricature—that is a true carnival', and thus concedes the theatrical qualities of our own age. Mimi considers taking a job as a mannequin—'[to be] twelve different mannequins to twelve different houses, and to create twelve different styles.' A preoccupation with masks—in defence of deception—is further revealed in Arlecchino's command to her sister: 'change your face now, for here comes your husband.' The mechanical act is to effect a change of disposition as well as a change of person. And in Julius' apology to Polly, 'I beg your pardon, it was your costume misleading me', the character's subconscious response becomes clear.

Karen Blixen also dramatises ambiguous identity in the character's adaptation to social forces. As in **'The Roads around Pisa'** in which the protagonist finds his identity mirrored in the minds of others, so too in **'Carnival'** do the *personae* find their traits reflected in objects that serve to complement—in concrete and abstract terms—the inadequacies of the ego. The reader is struck by the structural similarity of Karen Blixen's technique in portraying alternate identities with principal ideas in Freud's explanations in psychoanalysis; yet, there is not sufficient evidence among her biographical writings to confirm that Karen Blixen intended to write or have her works interpreted in light of Freud's teachings. When **'Carnival'** was written, Karen Blixen had been living in Africa, and except through a circle of European friends, had little opportunity to learn about contemporary movements in psychology in Western Europe. She complains frequently in her letters about her lack of current sources and books. That she is aware of Sigmund Freud's contribution is, however, clarified in at least one interview with the Danish journalist Bent Mohn. Mohn remarked: 'You spoke of the unconscious. What do you think of Freud?' Karen Blixen replied by saying, 'I really don't know enough about Freud to express myself about him . . . I believe that Freud did his time a great service by acknowledging complexes or facing up to them and thereby freeing people of much worry and anxiety. But I also believe that those who came after him frequently carried his ideas too far, or that they misunderstood him.'

The distinction that Karen Blixen makes between Freud and 'Freudian' is also fundamental to the present discussion. Karen Blixen's allusions to ideas historically associated with Freud illustrate merely that she was affected by the assumptions of her time. She was a contemporary of Freud and Carl Jung, as well as of authors of imaginative literature whose works reflected a consciousness of new perspectives inspired by psychoanalysis.

The source of Karen Blixen's allusion to Freud's teachings in a scene involving Tido and Camelia:

> Your mask would give you at least that release from self... Your centre of gravity is moved from the ego to the object; through true humility of self denial you arrive at an all comprehending unity with life.

is confirmed in Freud's explanation of the mechanism that involves a shift of energy from the ego to the object. In Freud's terms, the 'ego is regarded as a great reservoir of energy' that maintains a fluctuating balance between ego and object. Otto Rank, among the most prominent of lay theorists of psychoanalysis, provided a psychoanalytic interpretation where the ego is indistinct from its object; the imagined outward projection of the ego is, in other words, its 'double'. Infatuation of the ego with itself perpetuates an exact copy of itself in the outer world. The double relays guilt and death impulses toward the person. On a psychological level, resulting murderous and suicidal impulses are equivalent because object and ego are perceived as identical.

Karen Blixen's expansion of the self through the creation of a personality which reveals a hidden facet of the original self surpasses the idea of mere infatuation with the self. The confrontation of the social self and the artistic concept of the self provides a springboard for the question 'Who am I?' 'Masks' in **'Carnival'** are in each case visibly different personalities—even though the personalities represented by the masks contain psychic energy that has been displaced from the original self. The altered outward appearance of the 'masks' underlines Karen Blixen's attempt to utilise knowledge about the self by exploring its many possibilities.

The process of 'moving one's centre of gravity from the ego to the object' takes on thematic and structural importance in **'Carnival'.** The moral insufficiency that predominates in **'Carnival'**'s social institutions causes individuals to forfeit self-realisation. Early in the story Mimi and Polly discuss the advantages and disadvantages of marriage and, in general, relations between the sexes. By being married, Mimi denies her own desires for the sake of deception—deception that is assumed to bring about happiness. 'All my existence becomes nothing but being in love . . . nothing at all has got any meaning except for his sake and for the sake of what he thinks of me.' Mimi refers to her existence in terms that recall visual perspective; her life runs parallel with Julius'. Mimi shifts her interests to those of her husband. 'My thoughts turn around a single person.' Mimi compares her dilemma to that of nuns who live for God; she suggests that God dislikes their inability to find their own lives interesting. Mimi longs for a relation with Julius in which their lives intersect, that is, 'to be Julius' shadow.' She remarks to Polly, 'God, how sorry one ought to feel for all parallel lines which want to intersect as badly as I do.'

The conversation between 'Pierrot' and 'Arlecchino' foreshadows symbols and ideas explored philosophically in

the events leading to the lottery's execution. **'Carnival'**'s two-fold purpose—to contemplate human existence in a society that lacks values and to consider a means of acquiring moral sensibility—is expressed with references to colour, two-dimensional images such as the shadow and the silhouette, as well as mirror images. Superficiality and artificiality are the characteristics of aristocratic life symbolised. A striking aspect of Blixen's descriptions is her assignment of sensual qualities to colours. Pastels are 'flat and greasy'; 'they have no depth'. Black, by contrast, possessed substance—'a little piece of night itself, containing all its mystery, depth, and bliss . . . ;' black is hard, dry, and light. The pastels and black are frequently juxtaposed. Pierrot insists on not wanting to be black and remarks that had she known what to do with her legs, she would have come to the carnival as a rainbow. Blixen tells us that Camelia is dressed in pink satin and has blackened eyelashes. When speaking of her visit in Paris, Camelia refers to her moments there as glowing bits of black, against the flat pink faces of the new houses. And finally, Rosendaal explains to Zamor the treat of being the one central little shadow in a world of artificial rosy lights. Blixen's aim in each case is to impress upon the players and the reader the necessity of getting a little black into life. The street 'Vognmagergade' was the 'black spot upon the clean face of Copenhagen.' The time had almost come when it would be necessary to have government grants in order to protect society from pastel coloured 'fatty degeneration'.

The contrast of black and white in **'Carnival'** is discussed in conjunction with the shadow as a symbol for the conscience. The insinuation—in keeping with the painter's insistence on the superior nature of black—is, of course, contrary to traditional ideas. The paradox is, for example, witnessed in Arlecchino's remark 'Then are our beggars bodies, and our monarchs and outstretched heroes the beggars' shadows.' The shadow can be interpreted as the soul or alter ego; it may symbolise as well a split personality. Losing one's shadow, as recalled by Karen Blixen in the case of Peter Schlemihl, connotes a loss of one's soul. By contrast, the prospect of being able to acquire a shadow—'they must be marketable goods', says Arlecchino—results in her decision to take Zamor, who only pretends to be black, as her artificial shadow—her artificial conscience. Similarly, black and the shadow are employed in more subtle contrasts: the black mole at the small of Camelia's back is likened to 'the little shadow of a wick within the alabaster lamp'. The *verole* is described as a strong black, like a shadow throwing itself forward and backward.

Airiness and transience of life are intimated in Blixen's use of mirror images. The two sisters, dancing, stop before one of the long mirrors. The law of gravitation has been done away with for the night. In **'Carnival'** mirror images are enticing. They are able to bring out the inner significance of the person but do not grin back or frighten.

Karen Blixen's use of reflections as symbols is strengthened by manipulations of visual perspective. While the actors maintain a passive role—they do not react to each other's frequently nonchalant metaphors containing sudden changes of visual perspective—the reader realises that the subtle references to depth, direction, and intensity contain clues to the ethos of the tale. The watchful reader proceeds in active anticipation of such references. A frequent means of keeping the matter of perspective in the reader's mind is the juxtaposition of the concrete and the abstract or of the subjective and the objective. During the course of Polly's conversation with Mimi we are, for example, directed abruptly from subjective contemplation to a perceptible, trivial act.

> When I think, said Arlecchino very slowly, of all the people who envy you your modern silhouette. Yes, said Pierrot sadly. The silhouette of your mind, Arlecchino went on with great force, might be a Masaccio. Yes, said Pierrot. She dived into her large pocket for her cigarette case.

Later a moment of insight is compared to a sensation of distance. The idea of Zamor's taking part in the lottery

> suddenly gave new importance to their gamble . . . In Pierrot herself it produced the sensation when you get in an aeroplane, when you have for some time kept your eyes inside the machine, and then turn to look down—an apprehension of distance, a perspective.

In each of these examples there is a sharp contrast of subjective and objective realms of experience. Although the lottery really does take place, it initially involves a gamble of aristocratic possessions and not those of the lower class. The inclusion of Zamor redefines the effect of the lottery's outcome. The swift transition from the elevated to the mundane also speaks to the artificiality and shallowness of conversation and attitude in **'Carnival'.** Karen Blixen addresses the aristocratic society's superficiality as well in the physical features of the *persona:* Rosendaal—although 'a brilliant person'—has 'a little full-moon face, with no features, hair or expression to speak of, indeed most of all like the posterior of a baby.' And Julius had the capacity of drowning his observer's eye in his own being, and of remaining forever unseen.

The concept of the self is also a primary theme in Karen Blixen's later gothic tale **'The Deluge at Norderney'.** The story contains many metaphors derived from **'Carnival',** which Robert Langbaum suggests was the preliminary version of the gothic tale. One recalls among other themes and images, the tenuous line separating truth and deception, the practice of disguising the truth and of playing roles, the donning of the mask, the virtue of black, the contrast between the virtues of the bourgeoisie and the vices of the aristocracy, and characters who are by profession actors. Kasparson, the protagonist in **'The Deluge',** exemplifies yet another manifestation of ambiguous identity, achieved not through the alteration of the self or the transference of the self to an object or person, but rather, the replacement of the self; the individual takes on the identity of another but is at the same time conscious that he is playing a role. When Blixen remarks, 'I suppose you have understood that the two figures, the Cardinal and Kasparson, are really one and the same person' [Aage Henriksen, *Det quddmelige barn og andre Essays on Karen Blixen,* 1965], she implies not that Kasparson sees himself in the Cardinal, but rather, that Kasparson has played this par-

ticular role well. The earlier mentioned distinction that Karen Blixen makes between Freud and 'Freudian' is demonstrated by her use of multiple possibilities of the self—not for a pathological interpretation where characters are overwhelmed by distortions of the mind, but rather, as an exercise in self-knowledge for which the character's conscious recognition of his social and artistic roles is requisite. Karen Blixen is concerned less with the psychological mechanisms that lead to ambiguous identity than with the possibilities for behaviour granted by the mechanisms. Her portrayals, moreover, underscore the trend of her generation of writers to acknowledge subconscious processes as an explanation for some of our behaviour. Kasparson's impersonation of the Cardinal is psychologically distinct from that of the person who sees the double as a reflection of the ego—a threat to the integrity of the self—and who tries to kill the double in spite of his knowledge that he is simultaneously killing himself. Kasparson's murdering the Cardinal brings, in fact, the opposite result; indeed, his disguise and future existence depend on the Cardinal's death. Art and life are reconciled in the mask of the Cardinal. Reminiscent of sentiments expressed in **'Carnival',** Kasparson warns: 'Not by the face shall the man be known, but by the mask.'

Casey Bjerregaard Black   (essay date Autumn 1985)

SOURCE: "The Fantastic in Karen Blixen's *Osceola* Production," in *Scandinavian Studies,* Vol. 57, No. 4, Autumn, 1985, pp. 379-89.

[*In the following essay, Black describes* Osceola *as a collection of "three kinds of fantastic tales" whose "interrogations of reality" satirize bourgeois values and sensibilities.*]

Until recently, the only examples of Karen Blixen's juvenile works were to be found in the little known collection **Osceola,** in the marionette comedy **Sandhedens haevn,** and in the Karen Blixen Archives at the Royal Library in Copenhagen. In 1977, however, **"The De Cats Family"** and **"Uncle Theodore"** appeared, and in 1981 and 1983, several other stories in greater or lesser degrees of completion were made available through the pages of *Blixeniana.* Unfortunately, the newest material remains in its original Danish. And still more incomplete but lengthy fragments such as "Doris Alvarez. En spøgelseshistorie" remain in manuscript form. The relative obscurity and inaccessibility of these materials for American readers and scholars has served to effectively block a firsthand evaluation of their worth and their relevance to the rest of Blixen's authorship.

Osceola was a teller of ghost stories, thrillers, and love stories. These tales are not opaque but straightforward, and they are mainly either ironic and humorous or more serious and rather frightening. But the streak of supernaturalism that runs through them all and the sheer fun of Osceola's authorship links it to a curious quality about Karen Blixen's authorship that has either been quietly ignored or taken for granted.

Karen Blixen herself acknowledged that her production was made up of essentially two kinds of works: those she considered serious literature and those told for the sake of entertainment. That Karen Blixen's readers derive a great deal of pleasure from *Seven Gothic Tales, Out of Africa, Winter's Tales,* or the stories collected in *Last Tales* does not detract from the fact that she saw a fundamental qualitative difference between these works and the stories she wrote for the *Ladies' Home Journal.* It is a sad irony that the Baroness was dismayed when the sensational Gothic thriller *The Angelic Avengers,* which she had dictated off the cuff and published under the new pseudonym Pierre Andrézal, was accepted as a book of the month along with her serious contributions. In a newspaper article, Blixen, without acknowledging *Gengoedelsens veje* as her own, wrote that Pierre Andrézal perhaps wrote his book:

> [U]nder en Undtagelsestilstand, at lade sit eget Arbejde vaere, saa at sige, en Undtagelse. Hvis det skulde forholde sig saadan, at han før har skrevet og udgivet andre Bøger, under sit virkelige Navn, har han ikke villet have dem sammenstillet eller sammenlignet med 'Gengaedelsens Veje.' [D]uring a state of emergency, letting his own work be, as it were, an exception. If it should be the case that he has before written and published other books under his real name, he has not wanted to have them held up to or compared with *The Angelic Avengers.*
>
> [Karen Blixen, **"Om pseudonumerog Gengaedelsens veje,"** *Berlingske Aftenavis,* 23 November 1944, translated by Casey Bjerregaard Black]

In fact, critics have taken her at her word and until recently have either not been too concerned with the minor and lesser known works and very little with *The Angelic Avengers,* or they have glossed over the whole issue of Blixen's pseudonyms. For example, several stories that date from the Osceola period were collected in the volume entitled *Carnival* under the pseudonym Isak Dinesen. And in the most recent edition of *The Angelic Avengers,* the pseudonym Pierre Andrézal was replaced, again, by Isak Dinesen.

I do not mean to overemphasize this distinction even though it was recognized by Blixen herself. Nor should the pseudonymous character of the authorship be overexaggerated in light of the fact that, with the exception of *The Angelic Avengers,* Karen Blixen wrote under her own name in Denmark. After all, the authorship does not neatly divide into two camps. But the entire authorship could be said to balance between the classic desire to delight and instruct. The morality of the instruction may be suspect, especially in the mature works of Isak Dinesen, but the entertainment value is universally accepted. Writing in a fantastic mode allowed her to captivate and entertain by virtue of the gothic's appeal as a popular genre, but it also gave her the freedom to question, criticize and put into doubt the moral conventions of her age.

The most powerful synthesis of the two poles of Blixen's authorship remains *Seven Gothic Tales,* the first work published under the pseudonym Isak Dinesen. It was neither Blixen's first nor last attempt at writing in the Gothic style, for Karen Blixen's relationship with the fantastic stretches throughout her production. But if we look at the character of her authorship up to the time when she began

work on the tales that would eventually become *Seven Gothic Tales,* we see that Osceola's *Sandsynlige historier* were in fact very unlikely stories. Osceola was a writer of fantastic tales. Looking beyond the Osceola production and *Seven Gothic Tales,* however, it is clear that the mode of fantastic expression varies throughout the authorship. If it can be assumed that these differences are not merely due to a greater or lesser degree of indulgence in the art of pastiche, then we must know what the fantastic is and what it does if we are to account for the role of the fantastic not only in the Osceola production but throughout the entire authorship.

This task has been made considerably easier by contributions made on both sides of the Atlantic in the last decade or so by critics and researchers of fantastic literature. The breakthrough came in 1970, with Tzvetan Todorov's *Introduction à la littérature fantastique.* For Todorov, the genre of fantastic literature was a way for the nineteenth century to write about the unconscious and the taboo. It was a means of combatting personal and institutional censure.

Irène Bessière's *Le Récit fantastique* explains that the fantastic is more than a condition of hesitation on the part of the protagonist and the reader when confronted with the apparently supernatural. It is a language of uncertainty that attacks social norms but in the end reasserts them.

In *The Literature of Terror* David Punter concentrates on the double movement within Gothic terror that both attacks and reasserts predominently middle-class values. Punter includes a chapter on modern perceptions of the barbaric in which he treats Isak Dinesen as a maverick. He points to the irony in her use of the term "gothic." And even as he points out those qualities that make her archaic, he recognizes that they are countered by a pervasive and ironic female self-consciousness. Punter criticizes Blixen's terrorless fantastic as suffering from this inner contradiction between the archaic quality of her style and the modern tone of her subject matter. His reservations are puzzling because the crucial element in his definition of the gothic is that it is both a bourgeois and an anti-bourgeois literature. This very tension has long been recognized by Blixen scholarship, and the *Letters from Africa* further substantiate this conflict between Blixen's realms of Paradise and Lucifer.

Rosemary Jackson's *Fantasy: The Literature of Subversion,* concentrates on the fantastic as a mode of literature in counterpoint to realism. Just as realistic genres reflect the values and the reality of an age, so does its fantastic counterpart change in the expression of the unreal and the immoral. Its role in modern western culture is not escapism but subversion of middle-class values, sexual repression, and capitalism. It is a psychologically necessary antipode. The fantastic is not a retreat from reality, but an aggressive, revolutionary interrogation of it.

Tzvetan Todorov, Irène Bessière, David Punter, and Rosemary Jackson oppose the idea that fantastic literature is essentially a form of escapism, and they assign to it a more dynamic and generally more provocative role. In *The Romantic Fantastic,* Tobin Siebers links the fantastic to the logic of superstition so that the violence and exclusion directed towards the fantastic character and the Romantic poet herself are understood as mechanisms of self-identification.

For these critics, fantastic literature is not mere entertainment. Its essence, lies not in sensational Gothic gimmickry. The fantastic fascinates not through its ability to divert, but by its ability to subvert the laws of the real world, to express desire and oppression, and to act, as does the logic of superstition, as a mechanism of self-identification. It is with this understanding of the fantastic that we must approach Karen Blixen as not only a writer of Gothic tales but as a writer in the fantastic mode.

The fantastic is a highly malleable mode of expression, but its essence is transgression. In the March 1926 letter to her brother Thomas, Blixen claims Lucifer as her paradigm for enlightened rebellion. "Paradise" was the unlimited goodness, love, and kindness of her home which made it impossible for her to show opposition. Lucifer, rather than something wild and demonic, she conceived of as meaning:

> [T]ruth, or the search for truth, striving toward the light, a critical attitude, —indeed, what one means by *spirit*. The opposite of settling down believing that what one cares for is and must be best, indeed, settling into the studied calm, satisfaction and uncritical atmosphere of the Paradise. And in addition to this: work . . . —a *sense of humor* which is afraid of *nothing*, but has the *courage of its convictions* to make fun of everything, and life, new light, variety.

> [*Letters from Africa*]

She also describes her sense of failure and loss in her inability to live or write up to her luciferian ideal:

> Can you remember us talking about Lucifer in Knuthenborg Park? —Well, I am convinced that Lucifer is the angel whose wings should be hovering over me. And we know that the only solution for Lucifer was rebellion, and then the fall to his own kingdom. . . . Now I am able to see many opportunities when I ought to have made a break with that special Paradise. . . . I should have run away with some man or other in Rome. It was simply contemptible of me not to do so, and lack of Lucifer's vision; but at the time I could not see this. . . . The same is true of my pathetic "authorship." I cannot, I cannot *possibly* write anything of the slightest interest without breaking way from the Paradise and hurtling down to my kingdom. **"The Revenge of Truth"** is a miniature of that, you know; I wrote that in Rome.

> [*Letters from Africa*]

In her next letter to Thomas Dinesen she writes that she can now get on with her marionette plays: "I was feeling so uncertain and could not do anything about it until I had heard my own voice, seen myself in that mirror that is the person to whom one is speaking." She took up again the marionette comedy *La Valse mauve* and recast it as the story **"Carnival"** in English. It was to be included along with **"Caryatids"** and the seven other gothic tales in a collection called *Nine Tales by Nozdref's Cook*. But **"Carnival"** was never published until after her death.

"Carnival," then, is the product of a period of transition. Like **The Revenge of Truth** it has its origins in the Osceola period, and its plot structure is still a series of vignettes. But **"Carnival"** clearly belongs to the **Seven Gothic Tales** with respect to subject matter, characterization, and imagery. As her letters to her brother indicate. **"Carnival"** was recast after she had mastered her own uncertainty and found her own identity. The Lucifer ideal—the striving for truth and light, the critical attitude, the sense of humor and fearlessness—was not new to Blixen. Satire and rebellion to some degree and in some fashion are at the heart of the Osceola production. But in 1926, Blixen revolts against Paradise and hurtles herself down to her own kingdom. Henceforth, her authorship will bear the stamp of this sea-change. And conversely, her former "pathetic 'authorship' " is marked by the author's inability to see or to choose unequivocally the luciferian path.

The Osceola works are thus predictably different from the post-1926 period. They are not just less interesting, less intricate, shallower, less skillful, or less mature. They are fundamentally different because the nature of the fantastic in them is qualitatively different. Whereas the revolt, satire, humor, fearlessness, and the search for truth and self-knowledge is unrelieved in **"Carnival"** and in **Seven Gothic Tales,** in the Osceola stories, these transgressive and self-identifying qualities of the fantastic are recouped. The real world, that is, Blixen's Paradise, maintains the upper hand.

In **"Eneboerne"** Osceola tells the story of an eternal triangle consisting of Lucie and Eugene Vandamm and a ghost, Cristobal Christmas. When her husband abandons her for the book he is writing, Lucie draws ever closer to the world of the supernatural; she falls in love with Cristobal. The demon is associated with Christian love and rebirth while the new husband is associated with the satanic storm that rages about their deserted island. Just as Lucie succumbs to the ghost's embrace, she awakens from her dream world and turns to her husband and reality, but too late, for she dies the next morning, which happens to be Christmas. The ending is equivocal because we sense that Lucie by dying chooses the world and the man closest to her, namely the world of imagination and Cristobal Christmas. On the other hand, by giving up corporeal life she loses exactly what Christmas wishes he had and the husband whose reawakened attention she required. By dying, she opts for imagination just as she seems to have gained in reality what she imagined. Lucie's death becomes the embrace of imagination.

But such an evaluation of her fate runs counter to the overtly tragic and horrific nature of her death. On the surface level of the ghost story, Osceola condemns Lucie's death as a retreat from real life. However, the vacillation within the narrative voice places reality and imagination on an equally ambiguous footing. In this way Lucie is allowed to hold faith with the two sides of an ideal man whom she can not have in real life. With **"Eneboerne"**

Osceola's fantastic tales are interrogations of reality and of her own place and role in that reality.

—Casey Bjerreqaard Black

Osceola revolts against the male-dominated reality and embraces the world of imagination, but only in a fantastic space that is created beside the tale's plot. Thus the fantastic in **"Eneboerne"** functions as a release valve; the rebellion is within, dominated and overcome by objective life.

In **"Pløjeren"** [in *Osceola*] Lea is confronted by a man caught between two worlds. Anders Østrel is the son of a man and a witch. Because of his disappointment in a love affair, he curses the hour he was born and in turn is cursed by his mother. All his desires are to be fulfilled and his faults and wrongs will be loved equally with his good deeds. Thus he is both supernaturally powerful and tainted with human morality. He is the personification of the wild primeval forest evoked in the opening pages—a forest criss-crossed with roads and paths in the daytime but haunted at night. His power has given him wings and freedom, but an unfulfilled love has perverted his power into coldness, anger, bitterness, hate, and arrogance. For his crimes he begs Lea for judgment. She refuses. She tells him bluntly that error must be punished, but a wave of feeling for him prevents her from passing sentence.

Lea's confrontation with this spirit of the forest is nothing less than an emotional earthquake:

> [I] en ukendt Verden sank hendes gamle kendte og urokkelige Verden og gik tilbunds i et uhrye Mørke.

> (Her old familiar and unshakable world sank into an unknown world and went to the bottom of an immense darkness.)

["Pløjeren"]

She returns home in despair as towards her harbor. But shelter can no longer be found there:

> Hun havde troet, at i den varme oplyste Stue var Redning, og nu haendte det hende, som en ny Raedsel den Aften, idet de talte til hende, idet hun kom ind og følte den hjemlige Luft i Stuen, at noget i hende rejste sig og forvandledes, det var som om denne hjemlige Verden voldsomt og afgørende vendte sig fra hende, og som om hun vendte sig fra den. Imod hendes Vilje, imod hvad hun havde troet muligt, greb denne Følelse hende, hun kunde ikke holde det ud, hun troede, at hvis hun blev staaende et ørjeblik, vilde hun dø. Hvor var der Fred at finde, var den ikke herhjemme, saa var den ingensteds. . . . det var forfaerdeligt at vaere paa disse kendte Steder, i hendes Hjem, Verdens Grundvold og saa saaledes forstødt, forskudt.

> (She had thought that she would find refuge in the warm, lighted room, and now on this evening a new terror befell her, for as they spoke to her and as she felt the cozy feeling of home in the room, something in her rose up and was transformed. It was as if this familiar world turned violently and decisively away from her . . . and as if she turned away from it. This feeling came over her against her will and against what she would have thought possible. She couldn't stand it. She thought that she would die if she should remain there even a moment. If peace were not to be found at home, then it was not to be found anywhere. . . . It was horrible to be in these familiar places, in her home—the foundation of her world—and be so cast-off and displaced.)

["Pløjeren"]

What is most frightening to her is not the contact with supernatural powers but the necessity of thinking of her own feelings. She must fight for lucidity, and after a long sleepless night of the kind "forbeholdt Forbrydere og Folk med ond Samvittighed" [reserved for criminals and people with a bad conscience] she finds a foothold: "[I]mod alle den gamle Verdens Love og imod, hvad der havde vaeret muligt i den, tog hun sin stilling op og erklaerede sig tilfreds med den" (Against all of the laws of the old world and against what had been possible in it, she accepted her position and declared herself satisfied with it) [**"Pløjeren"**]. Her compassion is like that of her maternal ancestors who "havde ligget saaledes vaagne on Natten af Bekymring og Fortvivlelse over deres Maends Lidenskaber og var staaet saaledes op om Morgenen, for at hjaelpe dem" (had thus lain awake at night from worry and despair over the passions of their men and thus had risen in the morning to help them) [**"Pløjeren"**].

She is determined to help him, and without realizing it, an inherited maternal instinct instructs her to put Anders to work plowing the rolling fields. Peace, triumph, and calm come to her. She has been transformed, and he is cured and has found his equilibrium. He falls to his knees, kisses the hem of her dress, and calls her "Du velsignede" (blessed one). But the cure and the blessing have come from the earth. He claims her for his own. When he smiles her pride is overcome, the uncertainty in their relationship ends, and he kisses her.

"Pløjeren" is patently the story of an emotional crisis brought on by the confrontation between pride and sensuality, of everyday laws and morality versus wild freedom. Anders Østrel is clearly a fantastic projection of Lea's own feelings of desire, frustration, rebellion and guilt. That she has refused to confront these feelings until he appears is proof that not even to herself has she given voice to her dissatisfaction with her home and the old world's laws of what is possible. Her despair is not caused by her recognition of Anders, however; it is grounded in the disappearance of the foundations to her real life. The solidity of reality has given way to uncertainty. If Anders' despair is caused by his bad conscience and his salvation comes through Lea's compassion by way of the boundless pity of mother earth, then Lea's peace, too, is won through compassion. Not the self-pity that Anders displays, but a recognition of and a feeling for her own earthly passions and anti-paradisical longings.

In **"Pløjeren"** Osceola has again written a fantastic story that allows her to have her cake and eat it. The element of uncertainty in the story is both explicit and understood. On the one hand, the reality of the supernatural events is never questioned. The fantastic is consequently threatened by a shift towards the marvellous. On the other hand, a cursory analysis of the story reveals that the supernatural dimension is a mask for a psychological investigation, and when the fantastic is psychologized, the hesitation on the part of the reader vaporizes and the fantastic is replaced with the real. Passion, sensuality, pride, revolt, and guilt are all expressed, but only in indirect and archetypal forms. The reader must assemble the psychological puzzle; otherwise, the story ends as a simple gothic tale with a happy romantic ending. Thus the illuminating elements of the fantastic are placed within a frame of gothic romance whose distance from the real weakens their disruptive force. As in **"Eneboerne,"** Osceola shoots from cover.

"Familien de Cats" [in *Carnival: Entertainments and Posthumous Tales,* 1977] is even more straightforward than **"Eneboerne"** and **"Pløjeren."** Here the supernatural plays a relatively minor role. The extraordinary virtue of the de Cats family is due to the fateful circumstance that the entire sum of their vice is concentrated in a single member of the family. Unfortunately the current scapegoat, Jeremias, reforms, and the entire family begins to engage in scandalous behavior. The brothers Petrus and Coenraad endeavor to make him revert to his former state. They give him money, arrange for an actress named Jacobina to tempt him, and end up paying her yet more when she refuses to believe their fantastic scapegoat story. Jeremias interrupts a family council to volunteer that he take up again his role—for a princely sum. The family's honor is saved. When the scapegoat, true to his nature, voluntarily reassumes his naturally dishonorable role, he exchanges the family's bourgeois honor for an honor that is not of the Paradise, but which is, nonetheless, no less legitimate.

"Familien de Cats" relies on sustained irony. On the surface the narrator tells the story as if the wealthy bourgeois family really suffers from a demonic curse. But the irony is transparent. The outcasts, Jeremias and Jacobina, share in their names a prophetic and revolutionary character. The Old Testament Jeremiah made enemies even in his own family with his strict judgments, his preaching, and his continual prophecies of the fall of the kingdom and the temple. The significance of Jacobina's name is self-evident. These two are the characters who really belong to the "nobility consisting of honest people" [**"Familien de Cats"**]. Ironically it is they who are truly honorable, since they are true to their roles as the necessary evil antitheses to the family's bourgeois virtue. The family's virtue is no more than bourgeois reputation to be bought at will. Petrus's initial insistence on justice towards Jeremias—including punishment—without mercy is visited in full upon the family when Jeremias, the agent of Nemesis, demands his 100,000 guilders to take up his role as scapegoat and leave them to theirs.

The satire of bourgeois virtue is relentless. Family honor, chastity, sanctity, pecuniary responsibility, and pride are mercilessly ridiculed. Osceola saves her bitterest moment for the young Dina de Cats, who renounces her intended, Jeremias, if to take him means the ruin of the foundation of her life since childhood: "I will not betray my family which has stood firm for a century. . . . For Jeremias I could sacrifice my own happiness, yes, but not even for his sake will I lower myself to the level of the people I look down on." The attack on the bourgeois Paradise could not be more luciferian.

The polemic is blunted, nevertheless, by three mitigating circumstances. First, Jeremias and Jacobina are not actively retributive; they are agents of Nemesis. The de Cats brothers' machinations are unnecessary; they bring on their own miseries. Moreover, the notions of justice, mercy, and fate are enunciated by Petrus and Coenraad. Truth comes from the mouths of these pitiable, narrowminded men of the bourgeoisie. Thirdly, the narrator refuses to condemn these two members of the family and in general declines to pass judgment. The opening paragraph claims that the story has no other merit than an excellent moral. This moral can only be the virtue of mercy. Petrus and Coenraad deny Jeremias forgiveness for his past sins, and their seductive maneuvers deserve punishment, but fate is merciful. As Jeremias explains at the final family conference, he understands why Jacobina refused to believe their story: "[S]he believed there was something hidden behind it all, but that was because she does not know you. I who know you, I who (so to speak) am one of you, understood at once that there was nothing hidden behind it: you simply meant it." Jacobina expects deceit and unreliability where only literal reality is to be found. Jeremias—and Osceola—are yet members of the guilty party. They can see both the letter and the spirit of the World. The merciless satirical attack is moderated by Osceola's ultimate acknowledgment of her own place in the Paradise.

In the three original published Osceola stories, the young Karen Christentze Dinesen wrote three kinds of fantastic tales. **"Eneboerne"** is a ghost story; **"Pløjeren"** a gothic love story, and **"Familien de Cats"** a humorous and ironic anecdote. In all three she either attacks the bourgeois status quo, expresses an inner conflict between pride and sensuality, or revolts against the male order. But the fantastic in the texts is controlled and subordinate. Osceola's fantastic tales are interrogations of reality and of her own place and role in that reality. She yearns for Lucifer and rebellion, but her sympathy ties her to Paradise. It is not until Karen Blixen becomes Isak Dinesen that the luciferian rebellion breaks out and seeks revenge.

John Updike   (essay date 23 February 1986)

SOURCE: *"Seven Gothic Tales:* The Divine Swank of Isak Dinesen," in *The New York Times Book Review,* February 23, 1986, pp. 3, 37.

[Updike is a Pulitzer Prize-winning American novelist, short story writer, essayist, poet, dramatist, and critic. In the following essay, adapted from the "Introduction" to a spe-

cial edition of Seven Gothic Tales *published in honor of The Book-of-the-Month-Club's 60th anniversary, he presents an overview of Dinesen's life and discusses the main stylistic and thematic features of the collection.*]

When the Book-of-the-Month Club offered **Seven Gothic Tales,** by Isak Dinesen, as its selection for April of 1934, its newsletter said simply, "No clue is available as to the pseudonymic author." But even then, with some detective work by the newspapermen of Denmark, this utterly obscure author was emerging into the spotlight as one of the most picturesque and flamboyant literary personalities of the century, a woman who had "style" as well as a remarkably grave and luminous prose style, and whose works as they followed her veiled debut seemed successive enlargements of her dramatic persona. She relished what she called "the sweetness of fame" and the company of the great and glamorous; she received in her native Denmark and while traveling elsewhere the attention due a celebrity. In her frail last years, on her one trip to the United States, she went out of her way to meet Marilyn Monroe, and recently has herself become a movie heroine, as played by Meryl Streep in the stately adaptation of **Out of Africa.** Since her death in 1962—the cause of death was given as "emaciation"—the many-named woman known to the world as Isak Dinesen has been the subject of a number of biographies, including a truly excellent one by Judith Thurman [*Isak Dinesen: The Life of a Storyteller,* 1982], from which I have drawn most of the following clues.

Karen Christentze Dinesen was born in April of 1885, in a manor house near the coast, 15 miles north of Copenhagen. Her father, Wilhelm Dinesen, the younger son of a Jutland landowner (who had once traveled through Italy with Hans Christian Andersen), was a soldier, adventurer and writer, whose epistolary memoir, *Letters From the Hunt,* ranks as a minor classic of Danish literature. Karen's mother, Ingeborg, came from a family of wealthy traders and merchants. she married Wilhelm in 1881 and within five years was the mother of three daughters, of whom Karen, nicknamed Tanne, was the second. Two more children, both sons, followed in the next decade. Tanne was her father's favorite and confidante; all the greater the blow, then, to the little girl when Wilhelm, whose careers in both politics and literature had taken discouraging turns, and who had a history of restlessness and "soul-sickness," committed suicide, by hanging, shortly before Tanne's 10th birthday.

Karen grew up, in the strongly feminine company of her mother and sisters and servants and aunts, as the family fantastic, who from the age of 10 or 11 concocted plays that were performed within the domestic circle, the children and their friends taking the parts of Columbine and Harlequin, Blancheflor and Knight Orlando. In adolescence she became obsessed with the figure of her dead father and the notion that his ideals and romantic spirit had descended into her. When, in her early 20's, she published a few tales in Danish magazines, it was under the pen name Osceola. Osceola was the name of Wilhelm's dog, with whom the father and daughter used to take their walks. In 1934 Isak Dinesen explained to a Danish interviewer that she had taken a pen name "on the same

grounds my father hid behind the pseudonym Boganis . . . so he could express himself freely, give his imagination a free rein. . . . In many things I resemble my father." And when, in early 1914, at the near-spinsterish age of 28, she married, it was to a Swedish aristocrat, her cousin Bror Blixen, who like her father was restless, impractical and cavalier. Though he was to be an unfaithful husband, he gave her two wedding gifts beautifully faithful to her sense of herself: he made her a baroness, and he took her to Africa.

Baroness Blixen's time in Africa—1914 to 1931—has been much written about, most splendidly by her. Her main memoir, **Out of Africa,** published in 1937, has been called the greatest pastoral romance of modern times. It is a severely smoothed account of 17 bumpy years, her prime as a woman, spent coping with a recalcitrant and ill-conceived coffee plantation, with her rich Danish relations as they reluctantly financed this losing venture, with an errant and often absent big-game-hunting husband and then a lover (also a big-game hunter) even more elusive, and with a painful and persistent case of syphilis contracted from Bror in the first year of their marriage. From the standpoint of her writing, two crucial developments might be noted. In British East Africa, English became her daily language; and in the person of her handsome, Etonian, Oxonian lover, Denys Finch-Hatton, she for the first time encountered a fully involving intellectual partner, a brilliant and playful stimulant to her own intelligence and her storyteller's gift. She liked to think of herself as Scheherazade, and in Denys she met her Sultan. Also, in the Kenyan highlands she encountered two societies, the African and the white settlers', colorfully imbued with the aristocratic notions of honor, fatalism and daring that had always attracted her. Many of the 19th-century exotics of **Seven Gothic Tales,** in fact, are based on originals met in the semifeudal world, simultaneously raffish and posh, rough and luxurious, around Nairobi.

Her situation, when at the age of 46 she was at last compelled to return to Denmark, might be described as ignominious. Her marriage long ended, her farm bankrupt and sold to a real estate developer, her lover recently dead in the crash of his airplane, her body tormented by the complications of tabes dorsalis (syphilis of the spine), she was received into her mother's household as a prodigal daughter, a middle-aged adolescent. Setting up shop in her father's old office, she picked up notebooks and ideas she had been toying with for 10 years while in Africa.

The manuscript of **Seven Gothic Tales** was ready by the spring of 1933, but, rich and strange and free as it was, had difficulty getting into print. Several English publishers rejected it; Thomas Dinesen, however, had befriended an American writer, Dorothy Canfield, who was on the Book-of-the-Month Club's first board of judges, and sent his sister's manuscript to her in Vermont. Miss Canfield was impressed, and urged the book in turn upon her neighbor, Robert Haas, a publisher whose firm later merged with Random House. He published the book in January of 1934, and the Book-of-the-Month Club offered it to its members, Miss Canfield writing in the newsletter the report that memorably begins, "The person who has set his teeth into a kind of fruit new to him, is usually as eager as he is unable to tell you how it tastes." The new fruit met critical acclaim and, unexpectedly, commercial success as well. The club printed 50,000 copies, and was ultimately to select books by Isak Dinesen five times. This Danish woman who had lived among the English had her breakthrough in the United States, and a special warmth continued to exist between Isak Dinesen and her American audience. Not only were her American royalties much the most munificent, but the reviewers treated her without the note of cavil and suspicion often heard in England and Denmark. When at last, amid immense enthusiasm and excessive festivity, the wraithlike author visited the United States in 1959, she told a Danish reporter, "When I compare the American and Danish reviews of my first book I cannot help but think how much better I have been understood and accepted in America than in Denmark."

That same year she spoke to another interviewer about *Seven Gothic Tales* with what he reported as embarrassment. It was "too elaborate," she said, and had "too much of the author in it." Last year, Pauline Kael, film critic of *The New Yorker,* took the occasion of the Meryl Streep movie to tell us, with her customary verve and firmness, that Isak Dinesen's "baroque stories are lacquered words and phrases and no insides. Some seem meant to be morality tales, but you never get the moral. . . . *Seven Gothic Tales* are a form of distraction; they read as if she had devised them in the fevered atmosphere of all-night debauches." This verdict echoes the prim censoriousness of the young Danish reviewer Frederick Schyberg, who wrote when the book was new, "There are no normal human beings in *Seven Gothic Tales.* The erotic life which unfolds in the tales is of the most highly peculiar kind . . . There is nothing, the reviewer finds . . . behind [the author's] veil, once it is lifted."

> Like Hemingway, Dinesen urges upon us a certain style of courage, courage whose stoic acceptances are plumed with what the old Cardinal, in the first Gothic Tale, calls "divine swank."
>
> —*John Updike*

Well, as Dorothy Canfield advised half a century ago, "Take a taste, yourself." Enter a deliciously described world of sharply painted, dramatically costumed heroes and heroines posing, with many a spectacular gesture and eloquent aria, in magnificent landscapes maintained by invisible hands as a kind of huge stage set. This operatic Europe, like opera itself, would call us into largeness. One character is "hurt and disappointed because the world wasn't a much greater place than it is," and another says of himself at a moment of crisis, "Too small I have been, too small for the ways of God." Though Isak Dinesen's leisurely and ornate anecdotes, which she furnishes with just enough historical touches to make the stage firm, have

something in them of the visionary and the artificial, they are not escapist. From the sweeping flood of the first story to the casual and savage murder of the last, they face pain and loss with the brisk familiarity of one who has amply known both, and force us to face them, too. Far from hollow and devoid of a moral, the tales insistently strive to inculcate a moral stance; in this her fiction especially suggests that of Hemingway, who thought well enough of her to interrupt his Nobel Prize acceptance speech with a regret that she had not received it. Both authors urge upon us a certain style of courage, courage whose stoic acceptances are plumed with what the old Cardinal, in the first Gothic Tale, calls "divine swank." Dinesen even called this quality *"chic,"* ascribing it to the costumed Masai warriors who, "daring, and wildly fantastical as they seem, are unswervingly true to their own nature, and to an immanent ideal." She also admired, in Africa, the Moslems, whose "moral code consists of hygiene and ideas of honor—for instance they put discretion among their first commandments."

This admiration of the warrior's code surprises us in a woman. She was a feminist, but of an oddly unblaming kind, who includes within her ideal of the energizing sexual transaction what is heedless and even hostile in the male half of the sexual dichotomy. The three men she most loved—her father, her husband, her lover—all conspicuously failed to shelter her, and she took their desertions as a call to her own largeness. This call, which reverberates throughout her tales in all their abrupt and sternly mysterious turnings, was, it would appear, more easily heard and understood in the land of Emerson and Whitman than in tightly inhabited England and Denmark. America played the role of Africa for an older Europe: a place of dangerous freedom, of natural largeness and of *chic,* discreet natives. The discretion in Dinesen's writing, the serene and artful self-concealment even in her memoirs, is an aspect of the personal gallantry which, in the social realm, masked her frightful bouts of pain and debility with the glamorous, heavily made-up, in the end sibylline persona who sought to be entertaining.

The teller of tales would ennoble our emotions and our encounters with divine fatality. Isak Dinesen wrote that we must take "pride in the idea God had, when he made us." She was a theist of a kind (and was much twitted about this by her brother Thomas, a sensible Danish atheist). For there to be "divine swank," after all, there must be a divinity. She placed these Gothic Tales in the Romantic era when God, no longer housed in churches and institutions, was thought to be outdoors, in the mountains and sunsets. But even this evaporated divinity seems in the tale-teller's 20th century too benign to be credible, too unironical a guarantor of our inner sense of honor. In **"The Dreamers,"** the storyteller Mira Jama asserts of God, "To love him truly you must love change, and you must love a joke, these being the true inclinations of his own heart." Such a deity feels pre-Christian—a vitality at the dark heart of things. One of the many magical atmospheric sentences in **"The Poet"** runs, "The stillness and silence of the night was filled with a deep life, as if within a moment the universe would give up its secret." The brand of stoicism which these tales invite us to share is not dispassionately

Roman or of the pleasure-denying Protestant variety; it has Viking intoxication and battle-frenzy in it. Intoxication figures frequently in Isak Dinesen's work, and mercilessness was part of the storyteller's art as she construed it: the story must pursue its end without undue compassion for its characters. Combat lies closer than compassion to the secret of **Seven Gothic Tales,** and its exhilaration is their contagious mood.

Sidonie Smith   (essay date 1992)

SOURCE: "The Other Woman and the Racial Politics of Gender: Isak Dinesen and Beryl Markham in Kenya," in *De/Colonizing the Subject: The Politics of Gender in Women's Autobiography,* edited by Sidonie Smith and Julia Watson, University of Minnesota Press, 1992, pp. 410-35.

[*In the following excerpt from an essay in which she examines Beryl Markham's* West with the Night *(1942) and* Out of Africa, *Smith considers the ways in which Dinesen's autobiographical persona reflects the influence of western colonial and patriarchal power in Africa.*]

Africa meant a variety of things to the Europeans who settled there in the early decades of the twentieth century. For representatives of the British Empire, the land was an outpost of national expansion, a source of natural resources and inexpensive labor necessary for the defense and expansion of the empire. For the average citizen, the land represented the possibility of wealth and privilege unavailable in the home country. For the wealthy who had squandered their inheritance at home, Africa represented a place of new beginnings. For the truly wealthy, Africa represented a new kind of playground, "a winter home for aristocrats," as one Uganda Railroad poster advertised. In its unknown and unmapped expanses, "man" could test himself against the elements, the animals, and time. "Untamed" and "undomesticated," it seemed a frontier of relaxed mores and unimaginable adventures not yet contaminated by bourgeois conventionality and emasculating comforts. The Africans, decentered and disempowered in their own space, watched as they continued to lose ownership of their land, labor, and culture.

Coming to this land, European settlers brought with them the "discursive territory" of Africa. And so, before turning to the autobiographical texts of Isak Dinesen and Beryl Markham, I want to follow one strand of the ideology of blackness that emerged in the nineteenth century as prelude to the great colonializing moment of the early twentieth century. Until it was abolished in the early nineteenth century, the slave trade reflected and effected certain justificatory discursive practices pertaining to black sexuality. Categorized as less civilized, located closer to nature, black Africans were identified with reproductive capacities that serviced the slave economy. Significantly, after the slave trade was abolished and imperialist expansion into the continent gained momentum, Europeans shifted their locus of identification, linking black Africans increasingly to "uncivilized" practices. "When the taint of slavery fused with sensational reports about cannibalism, witchcraft, and apparently shameless sexual customs,"

suggests Patrick Brantlinger, "Africa emerged draped in that pall of darkness that the Victorians themselves accepted as reality" [Brantlinger, "Victorians and Africans: The Genealogy of the Myth of the Dark Continent," in *"Race," Writing, and Difference,* edited by Henry Louis Gates, Jr. (1986)]. In identifying the physical characteristics of black sexuality as markers also of prostitutes (the most sexualized of white women) and in describing the sexual practices of primitive tribes as forms of prostitution, medical anthropologists during the century linked black sexuality and prostitution as two sources of social corruption and disease (syphilis in particular).

European scientists and scholars thus projected onto the native African abnormal sexual appetite, that "dark" force lurking inside "civilized man," threatening the very basis of Western culture. Yet this "Africa" beckoned to Europeans, inviting the adventurer and the missionary into its vast spaces with its promise of illicit pleasure and imperial power. Journey into the jungle in search of treasure became journey into "the heart of darkness," as treasure and pleasure, economic and erotic desires, tangled. The image of Africa constructed by Europeans both invited and justified colonization, on one hand the project of "civilizing" the native Africans, on the other the aggressive expression of the will to power, the desire to dominate, appropriate, and transform. Thus Africa itself became, as did the Orient, a space effectively "feminized" by an imperial Europe.

There are resonances here between colonial ideologies of race and patriarchal ideologies of gender, as well as radical differences. Western discursive practices assigned to woman the potential for a contaminating and disruptive sexuality that it ascribed also to the very body and the body social of the African. Thus both (black) African and (white) woman threatened to lure Western man into some forbidden, unholy, sexually clandestine place. Tellingly, Freud invoked the Victorian phrase describing Africa as "the dark continent" in his twentieth-century metaphor for the inscrutability of female sexuality. Coupling sexuality and Africa in this way, argues Sander Gilman, "Freud ties the image of female sexuality to the image of the colonial black and to the perceived relationship between the female's ascribed sexuality and the Other's exoticism and pathology" [Gilman, "Black Bodies, White Bodies: Toward an Iconography of Female Sexuality in Late Nineteenth-Century Art, Medicine, and Literature," in *"Race," Writing, and Difference*]. This discursive conjunction of the erotic, exotic, and pathologic points to the specular bases upon which the (white, male) subject of Western humanism identifies himself as disembodied. "Masculine disembodiment," argues Judith Butler, "is only possible on the condition that women occupy their bodies as their essential and enslaving identities. . . . From th[e] belief that the body is Other, it is not a far leap to the conclusion that others *are* their bodies, while the masculine 'I' is a noncorporeal soul" [Butler, "Gender Trouble, Feminist Theory, and Psychoanalytical Discourse," in *Feminism/Post-modernism,* edited by Linda J. Nicholson, 1990]. The patriarchal assignment of embodiedness to woman, mapped by Butler, parallels the colonial assignment of primitive sexuality to the African. As a result of in/corporation, woman and African remain other-than-fully human, on the one hand childlike and on the other monstrous. And always, they require some kind of "parental" oversight.

Yet despite or, rather, because of this essentializing gaze, both woman and African remain the potential site of disruption—subjects waiting to speak. As Hélène Cixous warns: "*The Dark Continent is neither dark nor unexplorable. —*It is still unexplored only because we've been made to believe that it was too dark to be explorable. And because they want to make us believe that what interests us is the white continent" ["The Laugh of the Medusa," in *New French Feminisms: An Anthology,* edited by Elaine Marks and Isabelle de Courtivron, 1981]. What interests me here is "the white continent" of autobiography and the way in which two white women living on the frontier of colonial Kenya traversed the discursive borderlands of gender, race, and autobiographical practice. Since canonical Western autobiography functions as one of those discourses that inscribe white male subjectivity, Isak Dinesen and Beryl Markham of necessity engaged the colonial discourses of African otherness as they engaged the androcentricity of Western autobiography.

Isak Dinesen and Beryl Markham knew each other, if casually. They loved the same man at the same time. As white women in colonial Kenya, however, they shared more than a lover. On the one hand, they shared their privileged status vis-à-vis the native Africans, a privileged status manifest throughout their texts in the offhanded assumptions and conventional rhetoric of colonialism. (Of this, I will say more later.) On the other, they shared a marginal positionality in relation to white men, caught as they were in their embodiment; and this embodiment they shared with the Africans, who vis-à-vis Europeans were cast in the essentialism of race as surely as the women were cast in an essentialism of gender. (I do not mean to imply here that they experienced the same degree of marginalization as the Africans. They did not.) Chafing at the confinements of female embodiment, they discovered that residency on the colonial "frontier" provided them an arena of resistance. At the margins of the empire, far from the European center's hold, they could as white women break through the borderland of female embodiment and achieve a mobility of autobiographical script unavailable to them in the "home" country. Thus both Markham and Dinesen claim to be born "out of Africa" to use the phrase as horse trainers such as Markham use it. Attesting to the mystery that for them is "Africa," both represent the space of this mysterious otherness as a territory in which to escape the kind of identity that would have been theirs had they remained in Denmark or England. And yet, while both wrote haunting autobiographical accounts of their African experience, they offer the reader radically divergent readings of subjectivity in and through Africa. I want to read *West with the Night* and **Out of Africa** against one another, and to read them in ways attentive to the textual figure of the indigenous African woman, in order to explore the complications of colonized place, gender, and race in the politics of self-representation. . . .

"In my life at the farm," [Dinesen writes in **Out of Africa**],

"I saw few women, and I got into the habit of sitting, at the end of the day, for a quiet hour with the old woman and the girls in Farah's house." Dinesen figures the Somali women as mothers, wives, and sisters sequestered within patriarchal institutions and systems of meaning, what she elsewhere called "ancient citadels of males." Furthermore, the women are physically enclosed within yards of elaborate clothes, signs of male ownership of and in/vestment in them. Embodied testaments to male privilege, they are "luxuries," commodified in systems of exchange. Yet Dinesen insinuates into this locale of enclosure a politics of agency by foregrounding the other woman's sources of power: her intelligence, her cunning, her sophisticated manipulation of male investments. Most important, she identifies the other woman, as she identifies herself, with Scheherazade, the colonized woman who escapes literal and symbolic death by fabricating bold and imaginative tales. "Sometimes, to entertain me," she writes, "they would relate fairy tales in the style of the Arabian Nights, mostly in the comical genre, which treated love with much frankness." Only apparently passive, the Somali women stake out a locale of female desire, empowerment, subversive laughter: "It was a trait common to all these tales that the heroine, chaste or not, would get the better of the male characters and come out of the tale triumphant."

Dinesen identifies the old Somali mother with a former dispensation characterized by matriarchal rule. A "Sibylline" figure "with a little smile on her face," she is the wise witch, the living trace of an earlier dispensation. "Within this enclosed women's world," she writes,

> I felt the presence of a great ideal, without which the garrison would not have carried on so gallantly; the idea of a Millennium when women were to reign supreme in the world. The old mother at such times would take on a new shape, and sit enthroned as a massive dark symbol of that mighty female deity who had existed in old ages, before the time of the Prophet's God.

The old mother becomes the great mother, to use Erich Neumann's phrase [from *The Great Mother: An Analysis of an Archetype,* 1963], a matriarchal witch-goddess predating the great prophet Mohammed. And her subversive smile signals the residual matrilineal linkage backward in time through this maternal heritage. It also points forward to a fictive Millennium, an already and always deferred possibility, yet an always potential site of laughter's disruption.

While Dinesen elsewhere presents herself as entertainer and her guests as entertained, in this scene the white woman reverses the pattern, presenting herself as the listener who sits at the feet of the other woman. The reversal signals not the subordination of white woman to black woman, but rather membership in a sisterhood of female storytellers, in a community of women who "remember" the time past when the great goddess reigned supreme. For Dinesen too has lost "the forest matriarchy" she figures in her representation of Africa. In 1931, after seventeen years in colonial Kenya, the Danish woman was forced by bankruptcy to return to her family home in Rungstedlund, Denmark, where she would remain the rest of her life. Describing the circumstances in which the *Ngoma* about to be danced in honor of her leaving is canceled, Dinesen writes toward the end of her narrative: "Perhaps they realized at once how completely the Ngoma was off, for the reason that there was no longer anybody to dance to, *since I no longer existed*" (emphasis mine). Abjection, the dispersal of "identity," attended expulsion from the paradisiacal Africa. And so, "out of Africa," Karen Blixen experienced the loss of autobiographical story that comes from returning to the same old story of bourgeois embodiment. Enclosed in her mother's house, she could only dream of the past and in dreaming create the myth of an "African" identity. Like the Somali women, then, she is forced to tell stories to save her very "life," to abandon herself to writing in an elegant dance of loss.

"The discovery of the dark races was to me a magnificent enlargement of all my world," Dinesen writes early in the text. In this expanded universe she claims to have discovered a truer "home" than the one she left in Denmark: "In the highlands you woke up in the morning and thought: Here I am, where I ought to be." Figured as a place of sensual pleasure, a garden of delight profoundly different and distant from the repressive, cold environment of Denmark, this "Africa" invites Dinesen to luxuriate in a rich, thick sensuality—a sensuality whose traces are then deployed throughout the text from the very first pages when she immerses the reader in descriptive passages ranging across the landscape and through the smells, colors, sounds, sights, the very feel of Africa. Sensuality resonates through the music of Africa and the music of the text's voice: "When you have caught the rhythm of Africa, you find that it is the same in all her music." Africa's very air is a sensual medium. Walking in the morning, she writes, "you are not on earth but in dark deep waters, going ahead along the bottom of the sea." Living becomes "swimming" as life takes place inside a global amniotic fluid always washing across the body.

Learning from the Africans how to live "in accordance with [the landscape]" this white woman represents herself as being at one with Africa in a powerful commingling of subjectivity and place: "The grass was me, and the air, the distant invisible mountains were me, the tired oxen were me. I breathed with the slight night-wind in the thorn-trees." Geographically her farm blurs seamlessly into the wild space of Africa. She writes of the adopted Lulu that she "came in from the wild world to show that we were on good terms with it, and she made my house one with the African landscape, so that nobody could tell where the one stopped and the other began." Boundaries between human and animal are likewise blurred. Animals take on attributes of human beings; human beings are identified through animals. And metaphysically good and evil blend into one another. She writes of the Africans that their "assurance, [their] art of swimming, they had, I thought, because they had preserved a knowledge that was lost to us by our first parents; Africa, amongst the continents, will teach it to you: that God and the Devil are one, the majesty coeternal, not two uncreated but one uncreated, and the Natives neither confounded the persons nor divided the substance." In Dinesen's "Africa," human beings, ani-

mals, space, metaphysical forces commingle with one another in revelries and reveries of interdependence and non-differentiation.

"Africa distilled" thus signifies for Dinesen a space outside the menacing borders of a European "enlightenment" that brutally disjoins "self" and "other," a space uncontaminated by patriarchal arrangements and representational repertoires with their self-splitting repressions, an "Eden" uncalibrated by "man's" time and its gendered autobiographical scripts. Identified with animism, sensuality, transport, pleasure, mystery, music, laughter, power, "she" is the great goddess, nourishing "matrix space," locale of union and of jouissance, all that Julia Kristeva ascribes to the semiotic and Dinesen herself to female sexuality ["Women's Time," in *Feminist Theory: A Critique of Ideology,* edited by Nannerl O. Keohane, Michelle Z. Rosaldo, and Barbara C. Gelpi, 1982].

In this space Dinesen positions herself as the great goddess's daughter, recovering from patriarchal representations of female subjectivity through reclamation of the repressed body and enactment of an empowered autobiographical script. "To ride, to shoot arrows, to tell the truth" reads the inscription that opens the text—a manifesto of a mythical Diana, the active, effectual, independent woman, not the enclosed woman of bourgeois domestic scenes. Throughout the narrative "the lioness Blixen" assumes by turns the roles of empress, creatrix, healer, priest, protector, judge, genie (or *jinn,* in Islamic mythology). Figuring herself as honorable, resourceful, courageous, dependable, hardworking, and socially responsible, she identifies herself as a hybrid of "manliness" and "womanliness."

The desire to posit an independent subjectivity suggests why Dinesen says little about her relationship with Denys Finch-Hatton. In fact, the little she presents of the relationship is purposefully cast in an idealized mold as she makes of that relationship one of coequals, based on the classical Greek model of homosexual liaisons. Their hunting experiences, for instances, become metaphors of idealized lovemaking. In the first lion-killing adventure Finch-Hatton lends her his rifle so she can participate actively in the action rather than remain a passive observer. Dinesen describes his gesture as "a declaration of love" and asks: "Should the rifle not then be of the biggest caliber?" The experience of shooting takes on the quality of orgasm: "I stood, panting, in the grass, aglow with the plenipotence that a shot gives you." In the second scene the man and woman meet the male and female lions alone in the moonlight. There, in a gesture of reckless courage ("risk[-ing] our lives unnecessarily";), they enter "the centre of the dance," where two human beings face two animals, male and female together. Life, death, silence, darkness, pleasure, coalesce in a scene of unity: "We did not speak one word. In our hunt we had been a unity and we had nothing to say to one another." Precisely in this imaginative Africa, Dinesen finds the opportunity to contest the Old World arrangements between men and women, to refigure herself against the conventional cultural assignments of gender, and to celebrate a unification that collapses the binary opposition of male and female into silence and elides consciousness and animality.

Like Markham, Dinesen contests conventional gender assignments. Unlike Markham, however, Dinesen situates her empowerment in the recovery of female sensuality. In this text the female body is not the source of evil and contamination; female labor is not alienated but a source of pleasure; woman's body is not what Christine Froula calls "the symbol of patriarchal authority." "No longer divided and no longer inscribed with the designs of an external mastery," body and spirit commingle [Christine Froula, "When Eve Reads Milton: Undoing the Canonical Economy," *Critical Inquiry* 10, December, 1983].

But, of course, this "life" is but a dream, for Dinesen's tale is ultimately the tale of loss. Once again domesticated in Denmark, Dinesen can only revisit in fierce nostalgia and lyrical imagination that "preexilic state of union" and that former dispensation, the reign of the goddess's daughter [see Bella Brodzki, "Mothers, Displacement, and Language in the Autobiographies of Nathalie Sarraute and Christa Wolf," in *Life/Lines: Theorizing Women's Autobiography,* edited by Brodzki and Celeste Schenck, 1988]. Now, this invocation of nostalgia leads me to ask of Dinesen . . . : Does her intervention in traditionally engendered autobiographical scripts imply an intervention in Western ideologies of race and the old arrangements between black and white?

On the one hand, Dinesen, as Susan Hardy Aiken argues, quarrels with the very ideologies of race that stabilized colonial regimes in early twentieth-century Kenya and does so through her narrative practices [see Aiken *Isak Dinesen and the Engendering of Narrative,* 1990]. For instance, she contests the old autobiographical arrangements sexualized in the androcentric ideology of the autonomous individual by deploying her speaking voice fluidly through the "I," the "you," and the "we," especially in the first pages of the text. Opening this way, she signals an alternative autobiographical practice, one that testifies to the ways in which her subjectivity emerges "out of Africa" and the Africans. She describes how the Africans name her "Lioness" Blixen, assigning to her the power identified with the "king" of the beasts. Making of her "a brass serpent," symbol to them of one who bears burdens, *they* elevate her above other Europeans. With this belief in her, she writes home, the natives effectively cast a "spell" on her, constituting her identity as Lucifer, light-giver, rebellious angel [*Letters from Africa*]. They also create her as storyteller by laying their stories before her. Moreover, the African environment intensifies existence, alchemically changing the mundane into the poetic, the mythic. Only here, she seems to suggest, can she bring to light the "dark continent" of her sexuality and the full resources of her hybridized subjectivity.

Recognizing the mutuality of identifications between herself and the native Africans, Dinesen in turn re-creates the mystery of Africa as mythic space, in turn elevates the Africans above the mundane by turning their stories and their land into poetry through a thick web of allusion and compelling prose. And she does so without making a spectacle out of them, without serving a voyeuristic reader. In fact, as Aiken elaborates, she undercuts any voyeurism on the part of narrator and reader by rendering "Africa" narratively unmasterable: "As with Africans, so with the book-as-Africa: no more than the colonists can we finally 'know its real nature' or subject it to hermeneutic mastery." It can never be contained in a Western gaze.

Other narrative practices in *Out of Africa* destabilize colonial gestures of power. Dinesen often directs the focus of her text away from herself to those people inhabiting what Lord Delamare and his fellow colonists would label the "margins" of the "civilized" world—to Kamante Gatura and Kinanjui. Surrounding them with majesty, mystery, and power, she ennobles rather than denigrates Africa and Africans for failing to meet the measures of Western practice, experience, and identity. Honoring the orality of African culture, she "speaks" in the sonorous storytelling voice that resonates with the elegant rhythms and tonal richness of Africa. As her letters indicate, she adopts from Farah Aden, her Somali house servant, the metaphor of life lived underwater. She takes her worldview from the Africans, discovering in their philosophical conjunction of good and evil a compatible orientation to the world and experience. Unwilling to make her narrative the totalizing whole of a unitary self, she joins together bits and pieces of African life, allowing Africa and herself to exist in fragmented, multiple forms, refusing the clear boundedness and certainty of the Western "I." She also multiplies the specificity of native Africans by differentiating the tribes and incorporating the diversity of peoples into her text. Implicitly rejecting European rationalism, she contests the denigrating embodiment of native and of woman by turning the ideology of sexual contamination on its head, ennobling the body—of the African, of woman. Celebrating African culture, she resists the colonizing tendency to stabilize, explain, judge, and hierarchize the other's differences, as if to recognize that to do other/wise would be to suppress the story of the great mother, to oppress the racial other, and ultimately to repress her own subjectivity.

Dinesen's keen consciousness of her own marginality as a woman who sought to "achieve something *as myself*" [*Letters from Africa*] and of the larger cultural politics of gender, and her consequent positioning of herself as an "outsider" in the British colony, encouraged her to embrace native African culture in more sympathetic ways than the British colonials who assumed their privileges and their cultural superiority unquestioningly. Unlike other European settlers, whose racism was reflected in such pronouncements as that of Lord Delamare that "the British race . . . was superior to heterogeneous African races only now emerging from centuries of relative barbarism" [quoted in Elspeth Huxley, *White Man's Country: Lord Delamere and the Making of Kenya,* 2 volumes, 1968], Dinesen expressed what other colonists at the time termed "pronative" sentiments, implemented "pronative" practices. And yet, Dinesen was herself one of the colonizers, a woman who participated in the appropriation of native land, who hoped to profit from native labor, who enjoyed native service and idolization. Thus other of her narrative practices collude in the exploitative agenda of colonialism. The recurrent possessive ("my farm," "my boys"), the generalizations about native tribes, position her as a "European" speaker and reinscribe colonial relationships. By embedding native Africans rhetorically in an intricate web of literary allusions, she textually contains Africans and Africa in Western discursive nets of meaning and reference. Beyond these rhetorical gestures, however, lies a more complex ambiguous colonial practice. Dinesen's nostalgia works to constitute "Africa" as a romanticized territory, inhabited by romanticized "natives" and "animals." "Africa" functions therefore as a kind of "Afro-disiac." The distanced setting ("I had a farm. . ."), the achronological rather than linear time, the elegance and distance of the narrative voice, the "artifice" of a text that constantly insists, through its dazzling display of metaphor, on its imaginative status, all aid and abet Dinesen's romanticism. Certainly it is a different kind of romanticism from Markham's cavalier and stoic brand, but it is a brand nonetheless. And so, without dismissing the very real practices of subversion in the text, I want to pursue certain problematic implications of Dinesen's autobiographical practices.

Since the native Africans name her with the natural aristocratic title of "Lioness Blixen" as replacement for the derived nobility of "Baroness Blixen," Dinesen in turn must maintain their nobility as essential to her own by resisting the conventional racial stereotypes of the white settlers. Thus she privileges a certain alignment of African "difference." Dinesen assigns imagination, bondedness with nature, elegance of style, and sensuality to the native Africans as she pursues her conspiracy of nobility in the face of bourgeois philistinism. She thereby distances native Africans and herself from the repressive, prosaic, paternalistic culture of the white settlers and situates herself as romantic outsider whose bravado and rebellious excess are evident in her identificatory gesture, "I am a Hottentot," a gesture she directs defiantly at white passengers on a ship returning to Africa, not at black Africans. Dinesen invokes the politics of race to engage in her own class resistance because it is within bourgeois institutions that she experiences imaginative, economic, and sexual oppression. But as class disidentification encourages her to align difference along a certain axis, it also leads her to participate in a mystifying essentialism.

Dinesen's positioning of the body in the text reveals the potentially conservative effects of mystification in the midst of colonialism. Pressing the patriarchal myth of Christianity in the crucible of her African experience, Dinesen locates the source of female oppression in male mastery of the female body and promotes the recovery of that body as the beginning of a liberated female subjectivity. Doing so, she celebrates the body and its pleasures, the romanticized identification of woman with nature and the maternal body. Thus when Dinesen identifies herself as a "Hottentot," she invokes a body politics that "extolls" the "shadowy, nocturnal, oneiric domain" of the great goddess as "the interior locus of mystery and creativity" [Domna C. Stanton, "Difference on Trial: A Critique of the Maternal Metaphor in Cixous, Irigaray, and Kristeva," in *The Thinking Muse: Feminism and Modern Philosophy,* edited by Jeffner Allen and Iris Marion Young, 1989]. This return to the body through maternal metaphorization becomes what Domna C. Stanton calls

"a heuristic tool for reworking images and meanings" ["Difference on Trial"]. A strategy of subversion, it works to "countervalorize the traditional antithesis that identifies man with culture and confines woman to instinctual nature" to the primitive and childlike. But the problem is that, in pursuing this "enabling mythology" as "a negation/subversion of paternal hierarchies" ["Difference on Trial"]. Dinesen takes the Africans with her into the textual forest. The African is once again allied with the natural world, nativistic alliance already deployed in the justificatory discourses of racism and colonialism. Thus, in the historically specific context of early twentieth-century colonialism, the assignment of animal names to native Africans as part of her mythography operates racially, not just mythically. It is one thing for a white woman to be positioned metaphorically in the "black continent" of her sexuality and for her to identify herself and other white settlers with animals. It is quite another for the black Africans, no matter how regal and untamed the animals with which they are identified, to be positioned metaphorically where they are already positioned literally and discursively. The material realities of racial politics disrupt the largess of metaphorical politics.

Furthermore, any utopian myth of unification, even if an admittedly failed one, is problematic. In Denmark the exiled Dinesen crafts her imaginative return to Africa as a return to an empowering origin, "the maternal continent," and the effect of that return is the mythification of the mother, the figure Luce Irigaray has called "the dark continent of the dark continent" [Luce Irigaray, *Corps à corps avec la mere,* 1981]. But mythification of a paradigm of maternal origins, warns Bella Brodzki, even as it contests hegemonic myths, potentially betrays the same "inherent dangers of privileging principles" as patriarchal mythification ["Mothers, Displacement and Language"]. There are many motherhoods, not just one reified "motherhood." Mythification, however, wears everything to a patined homogeneity; it universalizes. Dinesen's dream of imaginary at-oneness requires the erasure of multiple and calibrated differences among and between people, races, and classes, between women, between mothers. Thus the textual identification of the narrator and the Somali women, while acknowledging certain realities of female oppression, glosses such complex material realities as their doubled colonization.

She also takes the native Africans into an oneiric realm that, however effectively it disperses coherent and totalizing interpretive possibilities, distances the Africans from history itself. Such "nativism," as Edward Said cautions, "reinforces the distinction [between colonizer and colonized] by revaluating the weaker or subservient partner. And it has often led to compelling but often demagogic assertions about a native past, history, or actuality that seems to stand free not only of the colonizer but of worldly time itself" [Edward W. Said, "Yeats and Decolonization," in *Nationalism, Colonialism, and Literature,* 1990]. There was such a past, certainly, but that past was past long before Dinesen journeyed to Africa. While Said cautions specifically against the excesses of nativist nationalism, his admonition captures my own concern about Dinesen's passionate countervalorization of native culture, which seems to abandon specific countervalorization of native culture, which seems to abandon specific histories in favor of oneiric and aestheticized myth.

Moreover, her powerful evocation of the sense of loss and dispossession that supports her ethics of self-dispersal seems to suggest that only by losing does one gain, an ethics of love as letting go elaborated by Aiken [in *Isak Dinesen*]. Yet this reverence for loss and dispersal leads the narrator to position the native Africans in an irrecoverable past, to identify them with an inevitable loss, to ennoble them certainly but also to contain them. Distilling native Africans through specific axes of identification, she locates them in an exoticized and timeless place, in a nostalgically crystallized past, even as she acknowledges the historical changes being wrought on the land and on native culture through the historical march of colonialism. Positioned in such spaces, they function as passive subjects of history's corrupt and corrupting march into the future. Thus they are positioned as victims of history, not as active agents within vibrant, ongoing, complex histories.

Dinesen's fictive "Africa" becomes an imaginative map on which we see projected a white woman's desire for an irrecoverable past of empowered subjectivity. Mapping can be disruptive; it can be complicit. It is not innocent, as Dinesen herself understood. The romanticized cartography of "Africa distilled" in an expression of an "artistic primitivism" that in its reification of the other reveals certain totalizing investments in an imperialist autobiographical practice. Against what might have been her own best intentions, and certainly in tension with very real and sophisticated contestatory practices, Dinesen's "I" participates in the "imaginative opportunism" that characterizes all manner of imperial projects.

In an essay titled "Changing the Subject" [in *Feminist Studies/Critical Studies*, edited by Teresa de Lauretis, 1982], Nancy K. Miller elaborates a central strand of current feminist practice: "The formula 'the personal is the political' requires a redefinition of the personal to include most immediately an interrogation of ethnocentrism; a poetics of identity that engages with the 'other woman.'" Gayatri Spivak, in "French Feminism in an International Frame" [in *In Other Words: Essays in Cultural Politics*, 1987], argues too for "a simultaneous other focus: not merely who am I? but who is the other woman? How am I naming her? How does she name me?"

The concern for the "other woman" that now weaves throughout feminist theory in the West derives from a profound rethinking of a hypostasized sexual difference, a homogenized "woman." It is a rethinking that problematizes with postmodernism generally the Western notion of a sovereign "self," but also a rethinking insists that historical specificities are the "grounds" outside the text that position us complexly and relationally in consciousness, behavioral practices, and politics. The shift derives also from a rethinking that rejects any simplistic or romanticized notion of "marginality," recognizing instead that positions of marginalities and centralities are nomadic, that each of us, multiply positioned in discursive fields, inhabits margins and centers. Thus the call for reading the other woman requires that we consider the multiplicity of

differences between one woman and another, the multiplicity of differences within each of us. It is an acknowledgment that the other woman troubles Western theories. It is a recognition that the other woman also troubles generic rules that function to govern and discipline identifications, and that she forces us to remap the ideology of identity and the horizons of subjectivity within autobiographical texts.

John Burt Foster, Jr.   (essay date Summer 1995)

SOURCE: "Cultural Multiplicity in Two Modern Autobiographies: Friedländer's *When Memory Comes* and Dinesen's *Out of Africa*," in *Southern Humanities Review,* Vol. XXIX, No. 3, Summer, 1995, pp. 205-18.

[*In the following excerpt from an essay in which he discusses both* Out of Africa *and Saul Friedländer's memoir of the Holocaust,* When Memory Comes *(1978), Foster examines the ways in which Dinesen's autobiographical persona represents an amalgamation of the cultures she experienced: her native Danish culture, the British colonial culture in East Africa, and the native African cultures.*]

The phrase "cultural multiplicity" in my title is a deliberate variation on "multiculturalism," whose core meaning raises issues of curricular choice, educational philosophy, and public policy. "Cultural multiplicity," by contrast and for the purpose of this essay, refers to a more intimately personal cultural site: to the conflicts, the feelings of tension, the revelations of affinity, or the sense of triumph that can come from living among several cultural traditions and to some degree internalizing their diversity. Though this condition of multiplicity is not limited to border regions, states of exile, or diasporas, it is obviously one that has flourished at such points of cross-cultural contact. But multiplicity, I should stress, can only arise when more than two cultures meet at once, so that binary strategies of either polarization or synthesis must yield to more complex processes of negotiation, shifting alliances, and interplay.

Autobiography, and especially modern autobiography, provides fertile ground for exploring the varying ways people experience cultural multiplicity. As we all know, the twentieth century has witnessed a vast number of cultural migrations and displacements. The life story of someone who has undergone such large-scale change, even if seen as just the retrospective account of a personality formed by several cultures, can already reveal a great deal about multiplicity. But such an autobiography should not be read merely for the author's explicit thesis or conclusions. In particular, the writer's delight in transcribing certain memories can lead to a saturation effect, to an excess of detail about the past that can ultimately convey more than the author is willing to state outright.

At the same time, moreover, no autobiography concerns itself solely with the past events that are its ostensible subject matter. Unlike other forms of life-writing, such as letters or a diary, an autobiography has been composed at a certain temporal remove from the events it records, so that the author's present self can deeply influence such elements of the narrative as point of view, choice of events, and style. Some theorists of autobiography even hold that in the last analysis the genre deals with the authorial present more than the remembered past. As a result the texture of the writing can act as a gauge of the author's *current* state of multiplicity, at least to the extent that one's cultural identity is registered in words, as opposed to gestures, clothing, eating habits, and the like. Readers of autobiography thus gain access to a realm suspended between the written past and the writing present, a realm that ambiguously interweaves the story of an experience that the author views as formative with a provisional settling of accounts at the time of writing.

For an example of how saturation and temporal ambiguity can combine to reveal cultural multiplicity, let me turn to Vladimir Nabokov, whose work first alerted me to these issues and thus helped guide my approach to the two books I shall be discussing in this essay, Saul Friedländer's *When Memory Comes* and Isak Dinesen's *Out of Africa.* At one point in his autobiography, *Speak, Memory,* Nabokov recalls the bedtime ritual of his pre-World War I Russian boyhood, which in his multilingual family culminated with prayers recited not in Russian but in English. Then, as the remembered scene sharpens in the telling, and thus becomes "saturated," some pictures come to mind. Nabokov recalls an icon above his bed, then the nearby watercolor of an "eerily dense European beechwood." This memory, in turn, reminds him of the English fairy tale of a boy who actually entered such a picture, and Nabokov rounds off the scene by stating that in time he too visited that enchanted beechwood.

In cultural terms, what is most striking about this passage is the infusion of English elements into a Russian childhood. Beyond this documentary element, Nabokov has located a retrospective basis for his switch in the late thirties from writing in Russian to writing in English, as shown by the very fact that a decade later he composed most of *Speak, Memory* in English. Yet the detail of the European beechwood lingers as a mysterious third term. As the book develops, aspects of this motif will reappear to complicate the Anglo-Russian dualism in several ways. As a beechwood in Vermont, it calls attention to Nabokov's glide from a British to an American sense of English, while as an explicitly European setting it foreshadows his exile in Germany and France in the twenties and thirties. As a visual artifact, finally (and here we should note that in Russian the words for icon and image are the same), it implies that European as well as Russian models have guided Nabokov's interest in image-making throughout his literary career.

The dense textuality of this passage thus conveys both the cultural multiplicity of a certain childhood moment and the even more complex outcome known to the author as he writes. Nabokov's basic attitude in reviewing his life story deserves attention as well. It is emphatically triumphant, with the mature writer now realizing that he has indeed earned the fairy-tale privilege of entering an enchanted picture—one that permits unexpected new developments and rich juxtapositions in the cultural realm. As we turn to Friedländer's and Dinesen's autobiographies, we shall encounter similar experiences of cultural multi-

plicity, which nonetheless contrast with Nabokov's in two key respects. First, Friedländer's dramatic religious odyssey and Dinesen's two decades among the peoples of East Africa involve more drastic cultural challenges than even Nabokov's passage from Russia through western Europe into the English-speaking world. And second, although Nabokov's cultural multiplicity depends upon his being a refugee from Lenin and then Hitler, *When Memory Comes* and *Out of Africa* both grow out of and bear more immediate witness to even harsher historical conflicts—to the Jewish Holocaust and to African colonialism. Still, both books address the reader in ways that recall a major border-crossing built into the very words on the page of *Speak, Memory.* Neither the original French of Friedländer's autobiography nor the English that Dinesen used to compose one version of hers is the language spoken at the time of writing by those authors in their intimate, everyday lives. . . .

Cross-cultural interaction [leads to] complex negotiations in Dinesen, but let me begin by acknowledging a certain falsity to her position in East Africa, where the British colonial regime was then seeking to create an area of exclusive European settlement in the Kenyan highlands. Thus the unintended irony of an ad recently cited in *Public Culture,* under the heading "Out of Africa 1906": "Between the years 1906 and 1939, a trickle, then a light rainfall, then a downpour of Englishmen, Germans, Scots, and some remarkable women began to fall upon the immense gorgeous plateau of East Africa" [*Public Culture,* Vol. 6, No. 1, Fall, 1993]. Such prose raises troubling questions about the popular reception of Dinesen's book, or at least about the movie that borrowed its title. But if the ad undercuts the justification of Dinesen's very presence in Africa as well as some of her romantic attitudes about the landscape, her life story also includes situations whose rich cultural multiplicity points in a very different direction.

In fact, if we bracket the overarching colonial dichotomy which (as her autobiography makes clear) Dinesen herself learned to question, the multiplicity in *Out of Africa* surpasses even the triadic patterns in *Speak, Memory* and *When Memory Comes.* Thus in one key passage Dinesen reviews the great variety of cultures that mingled in East Africa in the 1920s, then concludes that "[a]s far as receptivity of ideas goes, the Native is more a man of the world than the suburban or provincial settler or missionary, who has grown up in a uniform community and with a set of stable ideas". The third of her book's five units, called "Visitors to the Farm," clearly identifies with this East African responsiveness to diversity, for she arranges her experiences in a broad panorama that includes the Kikuyu, the Masai, Asian Indians, Somalis, Scandinavians, and British, to name only the leading groups. And if the progression among these peoples seems to replicate the colonial hierarchy, it should be noted that when this unit closes by evoking the thrill of flying in the early days of aircraft, it circles back to an old Kikuyu, whose skepticism about the enterprise gets the last word.

Perhaps because Dinesen wrote this autobiography some years after the failure of her coffee farm in 1931 forced her back to Denmark, she can imagine herself as "out of Africa" in a sense quite different from that title's main implication of a direct, documentary account. Thus she knows that alongside the colonial order, and never totally displaced by it, there exist the cultural orders of the East African tribes, who have other interpretations for her presence in Kenya. In the unit called "A Shooting Accident on the Farm," in which the Kikuyu request her help in an inquiry into damages, she realizes that she also functions as part of *their* cultural system, in a process she calls "brass-serpenting." "They can turn you into a symbol," she remarks, then concludes, "in spite of all our activities in the land, of the scientific and mechanical progress there, and of Pax Britannica itself, this is the only practical use that the Natives have ever had of us." As this episode continues, however, Dinesen discovers that beyond accepting this passive role in the Kikuyu system of justice, she cannot help taking a more active part as well. Thus a key insight about the dispute flashes on her in Swaheli, and she takes steps which help settle the case. In a book the very existence of which depends upon the author's bilingualism in Danish and English, this further crossing of linguistic boundaries must be seen as a key token of cultural multiplicity.

One might be tempted to simplify Dinesen's East Africa by speaking of three main groups—the Europeans, the Muslims, and the local Africans. Certainly the community which forms on her coffee farm suggests as much, since it consists of Dinesen's British and Scandinavian friends, of her major-domo Farah and his Somali relatives, and of the so-called Kikuyu "squatters," led by their chief Kinanjui. But such a scheme overlooks both some gaps in Dinesen's coverage and the strong tensions *within* two of these groups. Regarding the gaps, though she clearly knew Arab, Indian, and local African Muslims, she gives far more attention to the Somalis, an interest which might repay closer study than is possible here. Such a discussion would have to consider the chapter on Farah in *Shadows on the Grass* (1960), a second African memoir written more than twenty years later.

My purpose, however, is to consider tensions within the European and African groups. The bearing of these tensions on cultural multiplicity can be hard to see, given Dinesen's reticence about herself in *Out of Africa,* which is emphatically *not* an autobiography in the confessional mode. Thus, though she does show conflicts among different groups, she does not explain their personal relevance, except through saturated details whose connection with her personal life remains deeply encoded. This relative silence follows the narrative logic suggested by her portrait of old Knudsen, a fellow Dane who normally told grand stories about himself in the third person, but who only admitted "I am very sick" on the single occasion that he spoke in the first person. As a result, though *Out of Africa* describes the multicultural variety of East Africa with much zest, it obscures how Dinesen identifies with or negotiates among these traditions while coping with personal experiences of isolation, illness, and distress. The route to interpreting her cultural multiplicity, though finally rewarding, is thus a tortuous one.

Dinesen alludes to her problems as a Scandinavian in a British colony at the very end of her narrative. The occasion is the day when everyone in Nairobi avoided her because her lover Denys Finch-Hatton had just died in a plane crash, and she was the only person who did not know. Dinesen gets a nightmarish feeling that "I myself was somehow on the wrong side, and therefore was regarded with distrust and fear by everyone." She explains that this mood recalled her experiences some twenty years before, at the start of World War I, when she was mistakenly considered pro-German.

What she does not say is that her later feeling of separation probably included separation from Denys himself. Her book has already indicated that when visiting her farm he liked to hear her retell the stories she was then writing, thus he acquired a certain responsibility for Dinesen's crucial transition from writing in Danish to writing in English. But subsequently, when her money problems had decisively worsened, he recited a poem that shows his unwillingness to get too closely involved: "You must turn your mournful ditty / To a merry measure, / I will never come for pity, / I will come for pleasure." This is the most explicit trace in the book of what Dinesen's biographer Judith Thurman says probably happened, that Dinesen and Finch-Hatton had ended their affair just before his death [see Thurman, *Isak Dinesen: The Life of a Storyteller*, 1982]. But rather than giving a direct account of their relationship, *Out of Africa* acts this story out on a literary plane: Denys' gift of English in the storytelling sessions ironically turns into the medium for a warning to "come no closer." This revelation of aloofness is then mirrored in the British who avoid Dinesen in Nairobi after her lover's death just as they shunned her in World War I.

A pointed answer to Denys' poem of disengagement appears in a final scene from *Out of Africa,* where Dinesen "cites back" at the British. Her farm has gone bankrupt and she must sell; but then she discovers that the Kikuyu squatters have no legal rights to the land. Not only will they lose their homes, but they will be resettled piecemeal, with no regard for their standing as a community. When she pleads for some compromise (which comes at the last minute, but only as an unprecedented exception to colonial policy), she thinks of Shakespeare. "You can class people according to how they may be imagined behaving to King Lear," she reflects, and, to the officials who cannot understand why the community should be preserved, she inwardly protests, "Oh reason not the need." Yet unlike Lear with his daughters, she suddenly realizes, "the African Native has not handed over his country to the white man in a magnificent gesture." Only when she has lost her own land, and with the added irony that it is the very land she is now disputing on behalf of the Africans, does Dinesen reconsider a vaunted achievement of the English, so that instead of offering an alibi for the civilizing mission of colonialism, she attacks the whole enterprise.

A Scandinavian counterweight to Dinesen's disillusionment with the British appears in the chapter describing the Swede Emmanuelson in "Visitors to the Farm." Dinesen overcomes her dislike for this former waiter at a Nairobi hotel when she learns that he was once a tragic actor and that he plans to walk to Tanganyika, a week-long journey through the harsh lands of the Masai. His passionate love of tragic drama implicitly sets him apart from the emotionally neutral British, and she also admires his affinity with the Masai, with whom he can communicate only by pantomime but who, it turns out, still show him "great kindness and hospitality." In fact, Emmanuelson clearly functions as an alter ego for Dinesen, not just because his isolation amidst a group of Africans echoes her isolation in World War I, but also because one of his favorite tragic texts is Ibsen's *Ghosts*. This saturated detail looks ahead to Dinesen's situation while writing *Out of Africa,* when she learned that the syphilis she had contracted from her womanizing husband had not, as she had once thought, been cured, but had become her fate, thus mirroring Ibsen's Osvald Alving, who similarly returned to Scandinavia after a long period abroad.

Dinesen does not write of her illness or of her husband in *Out of Africa,* but traces of this painful experience do mark her treatment of the two African tribes she knew best. In general she draws distinct contrasts—the proud Masai warriors versus the humbler Kikuyu agriculturalists, the slave takers versus the victims in the Arab slave trade. But despite strong tensions between the tribes in the past, the Masai have begun to intermarry with the Kikuyu, since, as Dinesen puts it, "the Masai women have no children and the prolific young Kikuyu girls are in demand." It is here that Dinesen's personal situation comes closest to the surface. For, as Thurman tells us, the Masai were infertile due to widespread syphilis, and it was from a Masai woman that Dinesen's husband probably got the disease that he then passed on to her. This history, I think, underlies and helps explain the evolution of Dinesen's sympathies for the local Africans, from a rather facile admiration for Masai warriors to a deeper identification with old Kikuyu women.

On the one hand, the young Dinesen was greatly taken with her Swedish husband's noble title. Though he is banished from her book, she nonetheless calls herself "Baroness Blixen" in a key passage, and once even indicated in a letter to her brother that the title was worth a case of syphilis. In her identification with the Africans, she sees this aristocratic mystique embodied in the Masai men. Their "rigid, passive, and insolent bearing" gives them the look of "creatures trained through hard discipline to the height of rapaciousness, greed, and gluttony," and, in a less lurid passage, their sense of freedom is said to be so strong that they cannot survive three months in prison.

However, the older Dinesen, who has lost her land and writes with the knowledge that she suffers from an incurable case of spinal syphilis, prefers to identify with the old Kikuyu women. Early in *Out of Africa* she pays tribute to these women, "who have mixed blood with Fate, and recognize her irony, wherever they meet it, with sympathy, as if it were that of a sister." Read hastily in the context of Dinesen's status as mistress of a coffee plantation, these words may seem condescending; what gives them a deeper resonance is the temporal ambiguity implied by the image of "mixing blood with Fate," which surely reflects

the author's awareness of her illness as she wrote the autobiography in Denmark.

Somewhat later in the book, in a naming scene that contrasts "Baroness Blixen" with another, quite different Dinesen persona, the old women call her "Jambo Jerie." But this phrase, once spoken, will remain an enigma until much later: writing of her departure from Africa, Dinesen explains that "whenever a girl is born to a Kikuyu family a long time after her brothers and sisters, she is named Jerie." Dinesen clearly prizes this acknowledgment of honorary kinship from her elders. Not only did it give her the strength to face the distress of involuntary displacement—one of her last African memories is of an old Kikuyu woman carrying part of her dismantled house on her back—but even now, as she writes, it steels her against the arrival of old age. Her tribute is too long to quote in full, but here are some key phrases: "The old Kikuyu women have had a hard life, and have themselves become flint-hard . . . they were afraid of nothing. They carried loads . . . of three hundred pounds . . . , they worked in the hard ground . . . from the early morning til late in the evening. . . . And they had a stock of energy in them still; they radiated vitality. . . . This strength . . . to me seemed . . . glorious and bewitching." In a set of cross-cultural exchanges that began when her husband consorted with a Masai woman, Dinesen's narrative suppresses this all-too painful personal event only to highlight another symptom of the same situation, the syphilis-enforced intermarriages between the Masai and the Kikuyu. Identifying with both tribes, she thrills at first to the aristocratic warrior ethic of the Masai but settles in the end for the toughness of her self-described sisters, the old Kikuyu women.

Thus in *Out of Africa,* for all its studied reticence, as well as in the more directly confessional *When Memory Comes,* the upheavals of twentieth-century history thrust the autobiographer into situations where it becomes possible to take part in three or more cultures. Saul Friedländer as boy and youth experienced central-European secular, French Catholic, and Israeli Jewish cultures; Isak Dinesen as an adult woman experienced Scandinavian, British, and East African cultures, with East Africa opening up to reveal both the Kikuyu and the Masai. In each case, as the autobiography develops, the author comes to occupy a complex multicultural site where the binary logic of simple biculturalism no longer applies, where even the two-dimensional concept of boundary lines may appear inadequate.

Instead, as the autobiographical persona passes through these worlds, the multicultural vision of external diversity turns inward, leading to what I call cultural multiplicity. In the intimacy of such questions as "Who do I admire?" or "What do I believe?" or "Where do I belong?"— questions which, amid the flux of experience, challenge and sometimes alter or widen one's deepest cultural affiliations—the autobiographer identifies with and assimilates certain specific traits of the multicultural world that he or she portrays. The result is an autobiographical text which projects a polycentric field of cultural forces, forces which interrelate across a spectrum of options from tension to negotiation, from conflict to triumphant resolution. Such an autobiography, moreover, communicates these possibilities to its readers, who as they read learn to share to some extent in the author's multiplicity. At our present moment, with its heightened and often polarized sense of cultural identity, this kind of cultural literacy seems well worth cultivating; for rather than associating identity with certain monolithic, unchanging traits, it acknowledges both the many-sidedness of experience and the capacity of that experience to stir complex sympathies.

FURTHER READING

Criticism

Aiken, Susan Hardy. "The Uses of Duplicity: Isak Dinesen and Questions of Feminist Criticism." *Scandinavian Studies* 57, No. 4 (Autumn 1985): 400-11.
    Examines the short story "The Cardinal's First Tale" from a feminist perspective and addresses the issue of women's selfhood within patriarchal culture.

——. "Writing (in) Exile: Isak Dinesen and the Poetics of Displacement." In *Women's Writing in Exile,* edited by Mary Lynn Broe and Angela Ingram, pp. 113-31. Chapel Hill: The University of North Carolina Press, 1989.
    Discusses the role of "woman as artist and exile" in the short story "The Dreamers."

Arendt, Hannah. "Isak Dinesen: 1885-1963." In her *Men in Dark Times.* pp. 95-109. New York: Harcourt, Brace and World, 1968.
    Discusses Dinesen's development as a writer. The essay, originally published in *The New Yorker* in 1968, is a review of Parmenia Migel's *Titania: A Biography of Isak Dinesen* (1967).

Bjørnvig, Thorkild. "Who Am I? The Story of Isak Dinesen's Identity." *Scandinavian Studies* 57, No. 4 (Autumn 1985): 363-78.
    Explores the theme of identity and its relation to the depiction of animals in a number of Dinesen's works.

Bogan, Louise. "Isak Dinesen." In her *A Poet's Alphabet,* pp. 104-06. New York: McGraw-Hill, 1970.
    Brief overview of Dinesen's main themes in *Seven Gothic Tales, Out of Africa,* and *Winter's Tales.* The essay was originally published in *The New Yorker* in 1943.

Cate, Curtis. "Isak Dinesen." *Atlantic Monthly* 204, No. 6 (December 1959): 151-55.
    Overview of Dinesen's life and literary career which focuses on her work in the short story form.

Davenport, John. "A Noble Pride: The Art of Karen Blixen." *The Twentieth Century* CLIX, No. 949 (March 1956): 264-74.
    Surveys Dinesen's life and works and examines the autobiographical aspects of her writing.

Green, Howard. "Isak Dinesen." *The Hudson Review* XVII, No. 4 (Winter 1964-1965): 517-30.
    Survey essay on Dinesen's main thematic concerns.

Høyrup, Helene. "The Arabesque of Existence: Existential

Focus and Aesthetic Form in Isak Dinesen's 'The Roads Round Pisa.'" *Scandinavica* 24, No. 2 (November 1985): 197-210.
    Examines "The Roads Round Pisa," from *Seven Gothic Tales,* as a philosophical work that reveals Dinesen's "urgent need to interpret existence from the viewpoint of the individual."

Langbaum, Robert. *The Gayety of Vision: A Study of Isak Dinesen's Art.* London: Chatto & Windus, 1964, 305 p.
    Focuses on Dinesen's development as a writer, the tragicomic elements in her work, the theme of identity in *Seven Gothic Tales,* the autobiographical and mythic elements of *Out of Africa,* and examines the themes and literary styles in *Winter's Tales, Last Tales, Anecdotes of Destiny,* and *Ehrengard.*

Lee, Judith. "The Mask of Form in *Out of Africa.*" *Prose Studies* 8, No. 2 (September 1985): 45-59.
    Investigates the extent to which *Out of Africa* can be considered a "hybrid text," both autobiography and fiction.

Lydenberg, Robin. "Against the Law of Gravity: Female Adolescence in Isak Dinesen's *Seven Gothic Tales.*" *Modern Fiction Studies* 24, No. 4 (Winter 1978-1979): 521-32.
    Discusses the ways in which Dinesen's writings celebrate the "freedom and potentiality" in adolescent girls and the "surprising affinity [they share with] the spirited old crones who often dominate her stories."

Mishler, William. "Parents and Children, Brothers and Sisters in Isak Dinesen's 'The Monkey.'" *Scandinavian Studies* 54, No. 4 (Autumn 1985): 412-51.
    Asserts that the short story "The Monkey" is a profound and enigmatic allegory on sexual identity.

Schow, H. Wayne. "*Out of Africa, The White Album,* and the Possibility of Tragic Affirmation." *English Studies* 67, No. 1 (February 1986): 35-50.
    Comparative analysis of Dinesen's *Out of Africa* and Joan Didion's collection of essays, *The White Album* (1979).

Stambaugh, Sara. "Imagery of Entrapment in the Fiction of Isak Dinesen." *Scandinavica* 22, No. 2 (November 1983): 171-93.
    Examines Dinesen's interest in the way nineteenth-century women were required to "mask" their individuality by using socially accepted manners of dress and standards of behavior.

Van Doren, Mark. "The Eighth Gothic Tale." *The Nation,* New York, 146, No. 11 (12 March 1938): 306.
    Favorable assessment of *Out of Africa.*

——. "They Do as They Like." *The Nation,* New York, 138, No. 3589 (18 April, 1939): 449.
    Favorable review of *Seven Gothic Tales.*

Walter, Eugene. "Isak Dinesen." *Paris Review* 4, No. 14 (Autumn 1956): 43-60
    Discusses Dinesen's life and career in light of her works.

Wescott, Glenway. "Isak Dinesen, the Storyteller." In his *Images of Truth: Remembrances and Criticism,* pp.149-63. London: Hamish Hamilton, 1963.
    Examines Dinesen's storytelling ability in *Out of Africa* and *Last Tales.*

Whissen, Thomas. "The Magic Circle: The Role of the Prostitute in Isak Dinesen's Gothic Tales." In *The Image of the Prostitute in Modern Literature,* edited by Pierre L. Horn and Mary Beth Pringle, pp. 43-51. New York: Frederick Ungar, 1984.

> Examines the role of the prostitute in "The Old Chevalier" and "The Monkey," suggesting that "there is more of the geisha than the streetwalker in Dinesen's image of the prostitute. . . . In her obedience to the laws of myth, to the spontaneous appropriateness of her behavior, she comes . . . to symbolize woman at ease with her own mystery and strangely empowered by it."

Additional coverage of Dinesen's life and career is contained in the following sources published by Gale Research: *Contemporary Authors,* Vols. 25-28; *Contemporary Authors New Revision Series,* Vol. 22, 50; *Contemporary Authors Permanent Series,* Vol. 2; *Contemporary Literary Criticism,* Vols. 10, 29; *Major 20th-Century Writers; Short Story Criticism,* Vol. 7; and *Something about the Author,* Vol. 44.

Max Gallo

1932-

(Has also written under pseudonym Max Laugham) French novelist and historian.

The following entry provides an overview of Gallo's career through 1995.

INTRODUCTION

A popular author of historical fiction and nonfiction, Gallo is praised for his detailed and accessible accounts of modern historical events and biographies of European leaders. *La nuit des longs couteaux* (1970; *The Night of Long Knives*), a nonfiction work that examines Adolf Hitler's 1934 assassination of SA leader Ernst Röhm and about one hundred other political opponents within the Nazi party, ably demonstrates his command of complex historical data and his readable journalistic style.

Biographical Information

Born in Nice, France, Gallo was educated at the Lycée du Parc Imperial and at the Faculté des lettres et institut d'études politique of Paris, earning doctorates in contemporary history and letters. While teaching at the Lycée du Parc between 1960 and 1965, Gallo wrote his acclaimed *L'Italie de Mussolini* (1964; *Mussolini's Italy*), after which he became a journalist, television writer, and novelist. A socialist activist during the 1970s and 1980s, Gallo was named to various posts in the French government under François Mitterand.

Major Works

Most of Gallo's works, fiction and nonfiction alike, focus on contemporary historical themes and people. *Mussolini's Italy,* for example, incorporates extensive historical documentation in a biographical exploration of the complex character of Benito Mussolini—tracing the rise and fall of Italy's Fascist dictator during World War II. *Maximilien Robespierre* (1968; *Robespierre the Incorruptible*) examines the character of Robespierre, one of the principle agents of the French Revolution. Subtitled "A Psychobiography," this work incorporates detailed historical information and psychological theory to construct a portrait of Robespierre, showing him to be a lonely man struggling with an inner need for recognition and dignity. In *Histoire de l'Espagne franquiste* (1969; *Spain under Franco*), Gallo examines the life and political career of General Francisco Franco of Spain. Working from extensive primary documentation, Gallo follows Franco's rise to power and explores his dictatorial governing style. Gallo's first novel, *Le cortège des vainqueurs* (1972; *With the Victors*) also takes place in Italy during World War II. The story follows the wartime career of Lieutenant Marco Naldi, who is a press secretary for Mussolini's son-in-law. Motivated by his desire to maintain the values and traditions of his aristocratic Italian upbringing, Naldi lives a sexually promiscuous life in and around some of the major figures and political events that have changed the course of western civilization in the twentieth century. Following the publication of *I manifestinella storia e nel costume* (1973; *The Poster in History*), which traces the history of western poster art from 1789 to 1970, Gallo wrote the *La baie des anges* novel trilogy (1975-1976) and the two-novel sequence *Les hommes naissant tous le même jour: Aurore* (1978) and *Les hommes naissant tous le même jour: Crepuscule* (1979). These novels, according to the author, were designed as imaginative explorations of twentieth-century western society and its people. The plots of the two novels are interconnected, following the same seven people of varying socio-economic backgrounds over a period of forty years. As the stories unfold across Europe, the United States, and South America, the characters grow up and mature amid some of the most decisive events of the twentieth-century. *Le regard des femmes* (1991) tells the story of Lisa and Philippe's disintegrating marriage against the backdrop of contemporary French society. In the novel *La fontaine des innocents* (1992), Anne-Marie Bermont, a divorced career woman, encounters Jonas, a street hoodlum. As the plot unfolds, the lives of Jonas, Anne-Marie, and the tenants of Anne-Marie's Paris apartment building begin to intersect. Eventually, all of the characters get an opportunity to tell their own troubled stories about how they manage to survive in the disintegrating Parisian society of the late twentieth century. Although Gallo's *L'Amour au temps des solitudes* (1993) is set in present-day France, the plot ranges from Nice to Antibes, Italy, and to war-torn Yugoslavia. An aging magazine director, Catherine Vance, and members of her family recall several tragic events in their lives. In order to avoid the painful memories, family members devote themselves to their careers. For example, Catherine is totally occupied with managing her magazine. Eventually, Catherine's daughter Jeanne and Jeanne's husband Vincent are able to rise above their painful pasts and experience a sense of hope and self-acceptance, which is sparked by the rescue of a small child from a burning building in war-torn Croatia.

Critical Reception

Most critics have applauded Gallo's command of contemporary western history in both his nonfiction and fictional works. These critics have also noted his straightforward and conversational journalistic style, and have compared his plot structures and story development with the works of Honore de Balzac. While some commentators have faulted his use of flashbacks and flash forwards in such nonfictional works as *The Night of Long Knives,* other critics, such as Joseph Lee, have contended that Gallo knows how to turn history into "a rattling good yarn." Although some critics have pointed out occasional historical inaccuracies in *Spain under Franco* and have accused Gallo of relying too heavily on personal opinion to flesh out his portraits of Robespierre and Mussolini, other commentators have suggested that his fictional characters are well drawn, such as Marco Naldi in *With the Victors* and Anne-Marie Bermont of *La fontaine des innocents*. Finally, because he is able to present contemporary western history in an engaging manner, commentators have generally agreed that Gallo's nonfiction and fictional works contribute to a deeper understanding of the complexities of the people and history of the twentieth-century.

PRINCIPAL WORKS

L'Italie de Mussolini: Vingt ans d'ere fasciste [*Mussolini's Italy: Twenty Years of the Fascist Era*] (nonfiction) 1964

La grand peur de 1989 [as Max Laugham] (nonfiction) 1966

L'affaire d'Ethiopie (nonfiction) 1967

Gauchisme, réformisme et révolution (nonfiction) 1968

Maximilien Robespierre, histoire d'une solitude [*Robespierre the Incorruptible: A Psychobiography*] (nonfiction) 1968

Histoire de l'Espagne franquiste [*Spain under Franco*] (nonfiction) 1969

La nuit des longs couteaux: 30 juin 1934 [*The Night of Long Knives*] (nonfiction) 1970

Au nom tous les miens [*For Those I Loved*] (nonfiction) 1971

Le cortège des vainqueurs [*With the Victors*] (novel) 1972

La Mafia, mythes et réalitiés (nonfiction) 1972

I manifestinella storia e nel costume [*The Poster in History*] (nonfiction) 1973

L'affiche miroir de l'historie [with Regis Delnay] (nonfiction) 1973

Demain l'Espagne [*Dialogues on Spain*] (nonfiction) 1974

L'oiseau de origines (novel) 1974

La baie des anges, Volume I (novel) 1975

La baie des anges: Le palais des fêtes, Volume II (novel) 1976

La baie des anges: La promenade de des Anglais, Volume III (novel) 1976

Santiago Carillo (nonfiction) 1976

Le pouvoir à vif, despotisme, démocratie et révolution, que sont les siécle pour la mer (novel) 1977

Régis Debray (nonfiction) 1977

Les hommes naissant tous le même jour: Aurore, Volume I (novel) 1978

Les hommes naissant tous le même jour: Crepuscule, Volume II (novel) 1979

Une affaire intime (nonfiction) 1979

Et ce fut l défaite de 40: La cinquième colonne (nonfiction) 1980

France (nonfiction) 1980

La bague magique (novel) 1981

Un crime très ordinaire (novel) 1982

Garibaldi: La force d'un destin (nonfiction) 1982

La demeure des puissants (nonfiction) 1983

Le cinquième colonne (nonfiction) 1984

Le grand Jaurès (nonfiction) 1984

Les idées décident de tout (nonfiction) 1984

La troisième alliance pour un nouvel individualisme (nonfiction) 1984

Le beau rivage (nonfiction) 1985

Belle époque (novel) 1986

Lettre ouverte à Maximilien Robespierre sur les nouveaux muscadins (nonfiction) 1986

La route Napoléon (novel) 1987

Que passe la justice du Roi: Vie, procès et supplice du chevalier de La Barre (nonfiction) 1987

Jules Vallès, ou, la révolte d'une vie (biography) 1988

Manifeste pour une fin de siècle obscure (nonfiction) 1989

La gauche est morte: Vive la gauche! (nonfiction) 1990

Le regard des femmes (novel) 1991

L'Europe contre l'Europe: Entretiens avec Eric Fournet et Olivier Spinelli (nonfiction) 1992

Une femme rebelle: Vie et mort de Rosa Luxemburg (nonfiction) 1992

La fontaine des innocents (novel) 1992

L'amour au temps des solitudes (novel) 1993

La condottiere (novel) 1994

Jè: Histoire modeste et héroïque d'un homme qui croyait aux lendemains qui chantent (novel) 1994

Les rois sans visage (novel) 1994

CRITICISM

John P. Reid (review date 5 May 1972)

SOURCE: A review of *Robespierre the Incorruptible: A Psychobiography*, in *Commonweal*, Vol. XCVI, No. 9, May 5, 1972, pp. 219-20.

[*In the following review, Reid favorably assesses* Robespierre the Incorruptible, *contending that it is a laudable study of the psychological aspects of Robespierre's character.*]

The French Revolution was the first major political upheaval in the entire history of the Western nations to deserve the revolutionary epithet. This distinction says more about the relative inconsequence of centuries of successive and diverse political change and development than it does about the depth and seriousness of the events of 1789 and the years which followed. In desperation, partially at least, historians have examined and analyzed the Revolution in its broadest sweep and most far-reaching implications as well as in its minutest and frequently most trivial details. Burke and deMaistre, no less than Marx and Michelet, bestowed on the largely uninformed reading public accounts of what happened and why, already prefabricated according to selective interpretive canons. More perhaps than any other episode in modern times, the Revolution itself, what in fact took place, its causes and consequences, has scarcely been allowed room in the pages of its chroniclers and critics. The moral is devastatingly clear, however reluctant historians have been to own it as integral to their craft. What is objectively important is, of course, of paramount interest to the observer and commentator, but it is not "what happened," it is what is most appealing, after the fact.

The principal agents in the revolutionary drama, if we are to be guided by the recognized authorities, were mostly Parisians, striking figures, individualists, tireless theoreticians, tiresome propagandists. This is ludicrous, on the face of it, almost equivalent to crediting Herb Klein and Eric Sevareid with making contemporary history. But if history is what historians decide to write about, the men of letters effectively insert themselves between the past and us and we have no choice except to weigh their evidence as carefully as may be. The name of Robespierre is practically synonymous with the French Revolution, yet he spent most of his waking hours, from the fall of the Bastille until his execution in 1794, talking—just that, talking. I have no doubt either that he excelled in interminable speechifying or that he was incapable of doing anything else. I do not like him and I cannot imagine that anyone who knew him found him likable. I will admit, in spite of these feelings, that he made history, which is to say that historians made him.

[In *Robespierre the Incorruptible: A Psychobiography*] Gallo has given us what he calls a psychobiography, something far more ambitious than a slice of conventional history and immensely less reliable. Everyone knows well enough what Robespierre did, in the half-decade during which he survived the Revolution, just as everyone knows what others did to him when they could no longer tolerate his incorruptibility. Gallo approaches his subject armed with Freud and with a lack of subtlety well suited to his topic. Early on the author lays out enough data to convince the most benign skeptic that the Incorruptible-to-be suffered enormous, irreversible emotional deprivation in childhood. From this premise it is a piece of cake to penetrate Robespierre's mind and feelings in every situation, at every crucial turn, whatever the other factors involved. Gallo does his job well enough; he is orderly and thorough and from time to time casts an eye around, to note that France was troubled by more than his hero's agonizing over an unhappy consciousness. The result, inherently a dubious job, is fairly well carried off.

My doubt is pricked by the ambiguity and patent vagueness of the kind of interpretation Gallo has attempted. It may be a generic hazard attached to biography as such, but its risks are more important when the subject is so closely involved in great historic movements. Yet the biographical entry opens upon vistas and perspectives of endless fascination, and Gallo has explored every likely corner of Robespierre's character and personality. The whole adds up to a compelling portrait, of a man hopelessly limited, distorted even, by the legacy of an early life starved of affection and pride of accomplishment and by overweening ambition. Only in his last months, in the late Spring and early Summer before his death, did Robes-

pierre's inner torments escape his rigid self-control. Under threat of deposition and assassination he mounted every available rostrum and poured forth endless vituperation in a self-justifying frenzy that masked as lofty judgment on the betrayers of the revolutionary ideal. Gallo's insights into the man's deepest sentiments and aspirations lift his narrative, finally, to lyrical heights. The end casts its mordant glow back over the five years, almost to the day, since the Paris mob stormed the royal prison. The liturgical symbols with which Gallo clothes the ultimate scenario seem oddly appropriate; one has left the public stage of mass movements and impersonal forces and focused on the altar of a man's soul. The Freudian categories need not be taken at full heuristic value; what matters is the vision of immortality, the glorious prospect of his countrymen's admiration and homage, that shimmered before the spent fanatic's inner gaze.

Gallo's is a study of this man's life-long quest for recognition and a sense of his own worth and dignity. In the midst of turmoil and chaotic events, Robespierre's struggle with his past left him little energy with which to weigh alternatives or preserve balance and moderation. It may be, in Stendhal's words, that his soul was too ardent to content itself with the reality of life. To his adversaries, to posterity, he wanted to bequeath "the terrible truth and death." The truth that stands forth hauntingly in this man's career is the inexorability of death. The flesh is corruptible.

Robert E. O'Brien   (review date 1 August 1972)

SOURCE: A review of *The Night of Long Knives,* in *Best Sellers,* Vol. 32, No. 9, August 1, 1972, pp. 213-14.

[*In the following favorable review of* The Night of Long Knives, *O'Brien discusses Gallo's use of historical documentation as a basis for understanding why Hitler liquidated several powerful allies.*]

"The Führer himself is law and justice." It must be true that the will of the sovereign has the force of law, even if the sovereign is tyrant, or madman, or both. The above quotation is part of the writings of the Nazi jurist, Karl Schmitt, in justification of the wave of murder and assassination by which Hitler broke the power of the SA, *Sturmabteilung,* "Brown Shirts," People's Militia, or whatever one may care to call them. The action took place over the week end of June 30, and July 1 and 2, 1934.

In addition to . . . [*The Night of Long Knives*], Max Gallo is author of *Robespierre, the Incorruptible. Long Knives* was first published in France, and this edition is a translation from the French by Lily Emmet. It is characterized by the author as a historical narrative, source material for it being the Institute of Contemporary History in Munich, trial documents, newspapers, memoirs, historical studies, interviews, and trips to the scenes of the events.

The Brown Shirts were the bully boys who brought Hitler to power by their violent quelling of opposition to the Nazi party. With Hitler Chancellor under Hindenburg, they became an embarrassment, particularly because these ruffianly braggarts worked for a revolution against the conservative elements who controlled Germany: industrialists, monarchists, and aristocrats. The genius of Hitler realized that he could never attain to the power he craved without the support of these conservative elements.

"The seething brew of ambition, intrigue, and rivalry" which surrounded Hitler consisted of the Wehrmacht, the SS, and the Gestapo, in addition to the SA. Representing these elements were four men: Goering of the Wehrmacht, Heydrich of the SS, Himmler of the Gestapo . . . and Ernest Roehm, leader of the SA.

It was not too much of a trick for Himmler to convince Hitler of Roehm's disloyalty. Himmler played up every hint of it, warned Hitler of an apparent SA coup, stressed the notorious homosexuality of Roehm and SA leaders, and thus succeeded in presenting to Hitler the opportunity greatly to consolidate his power. Hitler knew the Army despised the SA. Rumor had it that he had agreed to eliminate Roehm and break the power of the SA in exchange for Army support. Hindenburg was dying. Hitler knew he would have to step into his place or risk falling from power.

The tragedy for Hitler was that Roehm was and always had been Hitler's loyal friend, who had manned the barricades for him. For Hitler to sacrifice Roehm must have meant to everyone who could learn the circumstances that no one could be safe from the danger of Hitler's lust for power. There were five years to go before the march on Poland, and the diplomatic adventuring that led to it. The "Night of Long Knives" had much to do with setting the inexorable course.

The writing is vivid and suspenseful, with background descriptions of the beautiful German countryside. There are eighteen pages of illustrations, appendices of extracts of Hitler's and Roehm's speeches, and bibliography.

Joseph C. Harsch   (review date 23 August 1972)

SOURCE: "Nazi History: The Haphazard Purge," in *Christian Science Monitor*, August 23, 1972, p. 11.

[*Harsch was a journalist, news correspondent, and author of books on contemporary world politics. In the following favorable review of* The Night of Long Knives, *he comments on Gallo's literary style and his utilization of the historical record.*]

Reporters called it "the night of the long knives." It happened in Germany on the night of June 29-30 in 1934 when Adolph Hitler allowed his fascist revolution to devour its own original children.

The devouring was a savage, ruthless, vindictive affair. What was conceived of as a means of purging the Nazi movement of some of its embarrassing elements ended in a careless butchery of anyone on the purge list of one or another of the plotters. Many were killed because they knew too much. One victim was a man who had dared to suggest changes in the text of Hitler's *Mein Kampf.* Some were killed because of mistaken identity. A musician named Schmidt was totally innocent of any connection with Nazism in any form—the Blackshirted execution squad had picked the wrong address from the telephone book.

The records are not complete; to this day no one knows exactly how many died on that dreadful night. The mystery to outsiders was whether there actually had been a plot among the leaders of the Sturmabteilung to kill Hitler and his intimates and establish a Brown Shirt dictatorship under their leader, Ernst Roehm.

Roehm had once been one of Hitler's closest associates. He was among the very few whom Hitler addressed by the familiar German "du" instead of the formal "Sie." But by June of 1934, shortly before President Von Hindenburg died, when Hitler was finally within reach of supreme power in Germany, a coolness had developed between the two. Largely it sprang from the fact that the street thugs, ne'er-do-wells, misfits and failures who made up the ranks of the original Brown Shirt units wanted more from the victory of Nazism than Hitler was allowing them. They wanted jobs. They also hated the old upper classes which dominated all phases of German public and business life. They were revolutionaries who felt that their revolution was unfinished.

[In *The Night of Long Knives,*] Max Gallo has written a dramatic account of the dreadful night and the events which led up to it. The essential details are not new: they appeared in Sir John Wheeler-Bennet's authoritative account of the rise and fall of Hitler's Germany, *Nemesis of Power*. The Gallo book treats the same material in more detail, and in a style perhaps more suited to today's readers.

As retold it puts to rest convincingly the question of whether there was a plot against Hitler. The answer is no. Roehm and his lieutenants were brutish, extremely unattractive as individuals and greedy for their loot.

But there is not the slightest evidence that they seriously intended to kill Hitler and take over the Nazi movement. Trapped in a plot manufactured against themselves, they were totally unaware of what was intended for them. Hitler lent himself to the manufacture of a false plot, and then took part personally in destroying those falsely accused.

It adds up to a dramatic reminder of what truly dreadful things happened in Germany under Adolph Hitler—not so long ago.

Joseph Lee   (review date 28 April 1973)

SOURCE: "Joseph Lee on Interpretations of Hitler, the Man," in *The Spectator*, Vol. 230, No. 7557, April 28, 1973, pp. 523-24.

[*In the following excerpt of a review of several books on Hitler, Lee examines* The Night of Long Knives, *focusing on its literary style and historical credibility.*]

Hitler is much the most fascinating politician of twentieth-century Europe. Stalin, with whom he is frequently compared, faced far fewer problems. Stalin never had to worry about his public. They were already prisoners of a system which Stalin had merely to capture, not to create. Hitler, on the other hand, had to woo a mass electorate, and intrigue for power from outside rather than inside the existing political elite. Once in office, Hitler found the army still a potential obstacle to his plans. Stalin felt sufficiently secure to exterminate his assumed enemies in the officer corps. Hitler had to manipulate his. Hitler set an incredible pace. No politician has ever imposed so many deadlines on himself. It was his constant seizing of initiatives which largely defined the range of options confronting his contemporaries. After making the 'thirties indubitably his decade, he proved an inspiring war leader. The German performance between 1939 and 1945 is the most remarkable in the annals of war, even more remarkable for the resolution displayed in the face of impending defeat than for the stunning early victories. No army in modern history has sustained such a disciplined retreat as the German between the surrender of Stalingrad and final capitulation over two years later. More of the credit for this tenacity must go to Hitler himself than to German military traditions, for long after the common soldiers lost faith in their generals they continued to believe in the Führer, however remorselessly the engulfing tide rolled on. . . .

[Hitler] liked to keep his options open as long as possible. His apparent indecision before the night of the Long Knives, when he had several SA leaders, including his old friend Ernst Roehm, whom he personally arrested, as well as many non-SA men, killed on the pretext of an imminent *putsch* allows Max Gallo . . . to construct gripping accounts of that macabre episode [in *The Night of Long Knives*].

Gallo has won some publicity as Martin Gray's collaborator. "If Gallo were not a professor at the Institut d'Etude Politique," gushes a reviewer cited on the blurb, "he could be mistaken for a Hollywood scriptwriter. . . ." His book is eminently shootable, with bucketfuls of blood brightening up the scene whenever interest threatens to flag. Gallo claims to be writing an historical narrative, but hastens to reassure readers alarmed by such an austere invitation that he intends transcending "the somewhat abstract limits of historical analysis." He succeeds. There are few tedious reflections on the meaning of it all.

The reader who merely wants a rattling good yarn, much of it demonstrably historically accurate, will not be disturbed by the bland assurance that Generals Schleicher and Bredow once counted among Hitler's closest friends, or by the incompatibility between some of the captions and the text, though cognoscenti may be surprised to learn that some Nazis stood so frequently with their legs so wide apart. The eager seeker of knowledge of German weather conditions at the end of June 1934 need search no further for information on where the sun shone, the rain spat or the clouds glowered.

But Hitler himself eludes Gallo's grasp. He remains a shadowy figure, a fly caught in a web woven by Himmler, Goering and Blomberg. This picture does conform to the impression of some observers, who considered Hitler such an evanescent presence during June 1934 that they spoke of virtual abdication. Gallo assumes that Hitler did not decide until June 29 to exterminate the SA leadership and, that immediately on reaching a decision he flew from

Bonn to Munich to arrest them himself, before giving Goering, Himmler and Heydrich in Berlin permission to assassinate several other enemies, private and public. Why did Hitler hesitate to move against his old SA friends? Because of the bonds of friendship? Because he 'really' believed in their demands for a 'socialist' revolution? Because he imagined himself the puppet of the army if he were compelled to decapitate its rival, the SA? Gallo evokes a host of possibilities by skilful use of the flash-back technique as Hitler gropes to a decision, though it is unfortunate that he chooses to take us through June on the two hour flight from Bonn to Munich in the early hours of June 30. Hitler's decision was then already taken. In view of Hitler's reluctance to brood on decisions already reached it seems more likely that his mind was moving ahead to the next stage in the course of the flight rather than lingering on the past.

Gallo's reconstruction could well be true, though only if one assumes that Hitler's political brain was paralysed during most of June. Some rather central questions that might held to establish the *a priori* plausibility of this assumption aren't asked. Did Hitler leave Berlin to attend a wedding reception in Essen on June 28 still undecided on his course of action, or to evade responsibility for the projected murders in Berlin, or to lull suspicious minds? Hitler could conceivably have taken his decision in early June, when he failed to persuade Roehm, in a five hour interview, to moderate his revolutionary tone. Since when had the trip to Essen featured in his schedule? Who selected the victims? . . . More importantly, was Hitler prepared to give a free murdering hand to Goering and Himmler in Berlin while he himself was in Munich? Is it conceivable that they would have killed Schleicher, an ex-chancellor whose death might distress the army, without Hitler's consent? Would they have dared murder Strasser, or even Papen's secretary, without Hitler's knowledge? Had Himmler had a free hand he might well have killed Papen and thus upset the whole scheme by infuriating Hindenburg. It seems highly improbable that Hitler should not have been fully informed of these plans. It is not even impossible that he was feigning reluctance to move against Roehm in order to implicate potential Nazi rivals if anything went wrong. The masterly manner in which he began shifting responsibility on July 1 for the 'excesses' onto Goering and Himmler, while retaining credit for his resolute reaction to the threat to the state, may have reflected something more than instant inspiration. Without further evidence it is impossible to accept as final the verdict that sees Hitler as little more than the tool of Goering and Himmler. I find Richard Hughes portrait of a Hitler retaining ultimate control more convincing. Nevertheless, Gallo would point to one crucial possible oversimplification in Hughes's account. Did Hitler, as the consensus suggests, try to save Roehm by refusing to have him executed with the other S. A. leaders on June 30, before finally consenting under concerted pressure from Himmler and Goering on his return to Berlin? This account, followed by Gallo, claims that Hitler directed that Roehm be given a revolver, with a ten minute deadline to commit suicide, on July 1. Only when he refused this last favour to his solicitous Fuehrer was Roehm executed. Hughes, however, has the revolver placed at Roehm's disposal on June 30, without a deadline, and Himmler, not Hitler, ordering the execution on hearing from Munich the following day that Roehm had failed to oblige. Hitler, according to this interpretation, had decided on Roehm's death on or before June 30. That no deadline should have been set seems inconceivable in the circumstances. But why should Hitler save Roehm? Did he really think he might need him against Himmler and Goering? Did he think the generals would condone Roehm's release, or even imprisonment, when lesser fry had been shot? Was Hitler genuinely distraught about his friend?

Uncertainties like these will probably make a definitive biography of Hitler impossible.

In *The Night of Long Knives,* Gallo claims to be writing an historical narrative, but hastens to reassure the readers that he intends transcending "the somewhat abstract limits of historical analysis." He succeeds.

—*Joseph Lee*

The Times Literary Supplement (review date 13 July 1973)

SOURCE: A review of *The Night of Long Knives,* in *The Times Literary Supplement,* No. 3723, July 13, 1973, p. 817.

[*The following is a mixed review of* The Night of Long Knives.]

The dramatic story of Hitler's purge of the SA on the night of June 29-30, 1934 is told by Max Gallo [in *The Night of Long Knives*] in a detailed "scenario in which time shifts both forward and backward, the past flowing into the present, the present moment containing the past", in an attempt "to recreate events not only in terms of general causes and political mechanisms, but also by evoking the attitudes, thoughts and faces of the various actors and . . . the skies and landscapes which set the scene". His sources are given only in general terms and it is difficult to assess what is vouched for and what imagined in this reconstruction. His presentation is effective, and the events of the June and July days of 1934, when not only Roehm and the other SA leaders but also Schleicher and a number of miscellaneous enemies of the SS were liquidated, are shown in the perspective of Hitler's *Deutschland* pact with the Reichswehr and his subsequent assumption a few weeks later of complete control of the Reich as Hindenburg's successor Head of State. The plates include a number of unusual photographs which illustrate the story excellently, and the translation is smooth, though the historic present which is so convincing in French tends to jar on the English ear. The flash-back, flash-forward technique gives all that is required by a reader coming fresh to the story, but it needs all his con-

centration if he is not to be confused by the almost over-whelming detail of this *Sekundenstil.*

The Times Literary Supplement (review date 2 November 1973)

SOURCE: "The Caudillo: A Strategy for Survival," in *The Times Literary Supplement,* No. 3739, November 2, 1973, p. 1336.

[*In the following review, the critic favorably assesses* Spain under Franco, *applauding its detailed history of Francisco Franco's rise to power but faulting its examination of the inner workings of the Franco government.*]

General Franco has long enjoyed favourable publicity in England. During the Spanish Civil War he was described by conservative and Catholic commentators as a crusader against barbarism, a defender of Western Civilization. In 1937, Douglas Jerrold wrote in his *Georgian Adventure* that Franco was "a supremely good man, a hero possibly; possibly a saint". Virtually the only dissenting voice was that of the Left Book Club, and with its demise the field was left to a new wave of admirers. These were the Cold War mongers who lavished praise on the new-found "sentinel of the West". Of late, there has been a trend towards appreciative biographies of Franco, the elder statesman, guiding Spain's ship of state on its course of order and prosperity. This view, to the ostentatious delight of Francoist propagandists who have courted foreign intellectuals, is becoming an orthodoxy in Anglo-Saxon circles—following from that other orthodoxy which sees Franco's rising in 1936 as an inevitable but reluctant response to left-wing provocation (see *TLS,* March 26, 1971 and March 16, 1973).

Among the more unsatisfying features of this benign "orthodoxy" is the fact that, following Francoist sources, it tends to gloss over the repression upon which the régime is founded and consequently to ignore the extent of opposition to it. This is partly a question of sources—pro-Franco material is conveniently available in Madrid, while the student of the opposition faces a search for clandestine literature scattered throughout Europe and South America. Hence, we are still in a position in which the central question concerning Franco's régime—how has it survived so long?—has neither been properly posed nor adequately answered.

Winston Churchill summed up the problem as the military rebels occupied Madrid in March, 1939: "General Franco's triumph opens to him only a vista of difficulties. He cannot live by terror. Half a nation cannot exterminate or subjugate the other half. He must come to terms with the rest of his fellow-countrymen." Max Gallo's powerful and absorbing book [*Spain under Franco*] gives the most detailed account we have had so far of how Franco proved Churchill wrong and has remained in power to the present day.

This is essentially a political history which has turned a mass of information concerning Spain's diplomacy, economy and society into a most readable narrative. Four main themes stand out: the régime's dominance of its enemies by a heavy repressive apparatus; Franco's skill in tacking to the prevailing diplomatic winds; the weaknesses of the very considerable anti-Francoist opposition and the Caudillo's own blend of nerve and ruthlessness.

In the crucial period when Nationalist power was consolidated after the Civil War, those members of the Left and the working class who did not escape into exile were cowed by a state terror befitting a general who had climbed to power on the backs of Mussolini and Hitler. In the first twelve months after the war, M Gallo tells us, there were one and a half million political prisoners throughout Spain and 100,000 executions in Madrid alone. A police force trained by the Gestapo initiated a cycle of denunciations, arrests and torture.

A more subtle form of repression was, and is, corruption. At its most simple, this consisted of bureaucratic graft and the distribution of monopolies. But the poverty and hunger of the 1940s also spawned a blackmarket and a prostitution network, out of which grew an entire new bourgeoisie beholden to the régime, whose police connived at their existence. Malpractices—ranging from the Argentinian wheat, sent in 1949 to relieve Spain's hunger and sold abroad before it arrived, to the monster Matesa swindle of 1969—have been benevolently overlooked by the régime. The complicity of the corrupt and of those who conducted the day-to-day administration of terror was assured and with it their loyalty.

This is a bleaker picture of Spain than has been previously current in England. Of course, the misdeeds of the 1940s were committed while the world's media were involved elsewhere, those of the 1950s when the Cold War justified everything. Yet it is not an inaccurate picture even when applied to the Spain of the economic "miracle". Workers are still shot—Granada 1970, El Ferrol 1972; torture is still practised—Grimau, the treatment of prisoners after May Day this year; and even as the Matesa scandal died down, there emerged the story of Redondela, the Galician town whose olive oil stocks had been replaced by water.

The control of domestic order has always been complemented by Franco's triumphs in the diplomatic field. Indeed, his survival of his fascist past during the international ostracism of 1944-47 is arguably his greatest achievement. He had regularly declared himself a bitter enemy of liberal democracy and of Bolshevism. When Hitler undertook a war against both, there was no doubt where the Caudillo's sympathies lay. He visited both Hitler and Mussolini—still his only trips abroad—and only economic exhaustion stood in the way of Spain's joining the Axis war effort. His awareness of British control of vital sea lanes also suggested caution. Yet when Belgium and Holland fell, he refused a $100 million credit from the US and in 1941 the British Embassy was attacked by Falangists.

Paradoxically, it was Russia's entry into the war which was to save Franco from his commitment to the Axis, since from the earliest days he had spoken to the Allies of Russia as the common enemy. The Blue Division of Falangist fanatics fighting in Russia enabled him to play down his hatred of democracy and emphasize his continuing crusade against Communism. Thus, he was able to ride the crisis caused by exclusion from the United Nations in 1946 and the UN condemnation of his régime in the following year, for he had struck a chord among the Allies. After Churchill's iron curtain speech at Fulton, it was plain sailing. International anti-Communism converted Franco into a bulwark of Western defence and he was soon happily trading bases for credits.

M Gallo's account of how Franco survived the 1940s goes far to explain the tragedy of the Spanish Left. In fact, his history of the opposition is probably the most original part of his story. Decimated by the Civil War and the slaughter of Francoism's early years, internal opposition was non-existent apart from isolated *guerrilleros*. The exiled Republicans continued the struggle against fascism in the French resistance, confident that their contribution to the Allied cause would be rewarded by the overthrow of Franco. The conservatism of the Allies crushed their hopes. A small invasion force of *maquisards* held out for ten days against a well-equipped army of 45,000 troops. Yet faced by this material superiority of Francoism, the opposition still looked for outside help, and henceforth was condemned to impotence, split into moderates and extremists. The moderates' insistence on their democratic credentials could never be as attractive to the Western powers as Franco's unflinching authoritarianism. The extremists have intermittently tried to start a *guerrilla* for which they have had neither the fire-power nor the popular support. The only group which seems to have escaped the vicious circle is the Basque liberation army, the ETA.

In the 1960s, the growing prosperity of considerable sectors of Spanish society made the prospects of opposition look grim. But the soaring consumption of television sets and cars concealed the imbalance of an economic growth heavily weighted towards tourism. Deflationary attempts to stabilize the economy hit an increasingly militant working class. Waves of strikes and university demonstrations in recent years suggest that the workers' commissions and a vocal student movement embody a real threat to the régime. M Gallo's book was originally published in 1969 and has not been revised to cover subsequent developments. However, his description of the build-up of crisis illuminates the present situation in which the Caudillo is gradually handing over power to his dry-land admiral deputy, Carrero Blanco, who is increasingly reliant on repressive measures.

The picture of Franco himself which emerges is revealing. He sees through crises with incredible *sang-froid* and discards members of his team with a dispassion bordering on brutality. He is still seen here to be the familiar grand arbiter between the power groups in whose interests Spain is run. However, it is underlined that the crucial piece in the game is more than ever the army. In his account of the rise to power of Spain's holy mafia, the Opus Dei, M Gallo shows the army in the background ready to quell any disorder liable to arise from the so called *liberalización*. The overriding impression is summed up in the words of the recently arrived ambassador in London, Manuel Fraga, who told *The Times* some years ago "Whatever happens, the armed forces will continue to stand surety for the situation, and no solution will be possible without their consent".

Elbridge Colby   (review date 1 February 1974)

SOURCE: A review of *Spain under Franco,* in *Best Sellers,* Vol. 33, No. 21, February 1, 1974, pp. 482-83.

[*Colby was an educator, journalist, and author of books about contemporary world politics. In the following review of* Spain under Franco, *he comments on Gallo's journalistic style and his mixing of historical fact with personal opinion.*]

Having recently published a detailed and perceptive volume by this author on Italy under Mussolini, Dutton now comes along with a translation from the French of the same author's history of the Spanish under Franco. (The translation [of **Spain under Franco**] by Jean Stewart is done with all the ease of original writing, with little trace of alien idiom.) Like the work of any master of political studies, and lecturer on them, this book is rich in detail of trends, forces, and influences, with occasional (but not too many) statistics from other fields—agriculture, industry, and education. It touches on the origin of the Opus Dei and upon its intrusion into public affairs.

The tale starts with the appalling conditions in Spain before the Civil War, treats military events always with their political emphasis, and goes right through the rise of Franco, his increase in personal appeal, his leanings on "repression and restriction," his use of the army "to maintain order," his "life and death struggle" to primacy. Then there was the steadiness of the postwar period followed by "grief, bitterness, despair, and flight" for some and terroristic control, with a slowly transforming and settling situation and still "Franco remained in charge." Students demonstrated, strikes began again. Young poets (oft quoted) were "harried," and the Church continued as "a political force," until finally things seemed to settle down with the nation transformed and Franco still "in charge."

The author has written with the same deliberate detail which he showed in his book on Mussolini, and which we praised him for. He has used an impressive bibliography, but also has shown this almost contemporary history in such detail by very frequent use of reference or quotation from contemporary journalism—for instance: *New York Times, New York Herald-Tribune, Washington Times-Herald, United States News, Le Monde, Paris-Match, and L'Illustration,* to name a few. He writes for a daily newspaper in Paris, and has the narrative style of a sober journalist. Certain specific facts which he inserts are curious to note, at least, even if they are not very significant.

He says that "when (F. D.) Roosevelt died, the Falangists felt a real sense of relief and joy" for they thought him not conservative enough. He digs up the fact that Ambassador Carlton Hayes was "demanding" during the war that the Soviet communiques be included in the Spanish newspapers. He says that when V-E day came "few hung out their flags for victory," and the falangists were "embarrassed." He declares that Franco "naturally enjoyed the support of the military men in the Pentagon and this contributed considerably to his strength" in 1963. He strongly alleges that in 1968 "the majority of the Spanish people turned their backs on politics, even of the proletariat." He mixes facts with opinionating and strong judgements.

But perhaps this is merely nit-picking at the usual professorial pertness. The volume well deserves to stand beside the Mussolini volume and is a detailed history of important events of our time: I finish this review on the day of the assassination of the Fascist premier Carrero Blanco, in days dominated by politics and placing front-rank emphasis on the Falangists. I paste the new item in my copy as being in tone and tune with the book.

C. F. Latour   (review date March 1974)

SOURCE: A review of *The Night of Long Knives,* in *American Political Science Review,* Vol. LXVIII, No. 1, March, 1974, pp. 300-01.

[*In the following review, Latour states that despite some faults,* The Night of Long Knives "*is a fine tale of horror for the general reader.*"]

The Night of Long Knives by Max Gallo chronicles the liquidation of Ernst Röhm and associates, the destruction of the *SA* as an element of revolutionary political power in the Nazi state, and the gangland slaying of uncounted victims of political or personal vendettas carried out with great verve on June 29-30, 1934 by men then grasping for ascendancy in Hitler's regime. . . . Mr. Gallo, a French journalist, writes fluently, often grippingly about what Otto Strasser has called "the German St. Bartholomew's," with minimal recourse to research in depth and no scholarly apparatus at all.

As popular history, Mr. Gallo offers a rousing suspense story, featuring as chief plotters Himmler, Heydrich, and Goering, busily manufacturing damning evidence against former comrades-in-arms, and joining an uneasy alliance with military, industrial and conservative political leaders fearful of the *SA*'s radical threat to the *Reichswehr* and to the financial and industrial establishment. Pushed by these factions, himself in an agony of indecision, Hitler forces himself to make a move which, for a variety of reasons, he dreads. The fact remains: the old Field Marshal lies dying. General von Blomberg's offer—for once the "Rubber Lion" meant business—to trade the *SA* for the Reich's presidency, prompts the Führer. The unwary Röhm (though hardly an object for righteous compassion), his followers and protegés, and scores of others quite uninvolved are doomed.

Mr. Gallo's somewhat irritating device of telling his story in a series of hectic flashbacks and shifts of scenery, with impressionistic-pointillist effects, does not really obscure the events, which are described with reasonable accuracy, even though the author relies almost exclusively on memoirs, secondary works, and newspaper accounts. Unfortunately, he gives little weight to the bias of his sources: to accept, for example, Franz von Papen's accounts of his motivations and actions at face value seems downright touching. Odd gaffes in the translation are due to the author's frequent use of German sources in a French edition.

Still, *The Night of Long Knives* is a fine tale of horror for the general reader to curl up with on a lazy afternoon or a long evening.

Kurt J. Frohlich   (review date 6 April 1974)

SOURCE: "The Dream of Empire, Again," in *The Nation*, New York, Vol. 218, No. 14, April 6, 1974, pp. 441-43.

[*In the following review, Frohlich applauds Gallo's command of contemporary history in* Mussolini's Italy.]

When on June 13, 1921, Mussolini, as deputy of the young Fascist Party, rose in the Italian Parliament and declared, "We deny that the history of mankind can be explained by economic determinism," he repudiated his Socialist past and opened the way for his new role. Italy with its colorful history of varied forms of small duchies and city republics had never lacked swashbuckling *condottieri,* and Professor Gallo in his book [*Mussolini's Italy*] explains how a people can fall prey to a system seemingly incompatible with its temperament. And here is the rub: existing forces, not the temperament of a people, determine its political path.

Professor Gallo follows Mussolini's oblique career from his youth to the pinnacle of his power during the Dollfuss crisis in Austria, and thereafter to his ignominious death. It is most strange that his end is so much like that of another usurper of Roman power—Cola di Rienzi.

Filippo Turiati and Anna Kulishova founded a periodical, *Critica Sociale,* in 1891. The two had a strong influence on Mussolini and Gallo cites an interesting observation of Kulishova which may be a clue to Mussolini's apostasy from Left to Right. Kulishova thought of him as a "Non-Marxist, not even a Socialist but an individualist and autocrat." In any case, when Bissolati established the *Avanti* in 1896, Italy had its influential daily Socialist paper, and it eventually joined with *Il Trentino,* edited by Cesare Battisti, in calling for the reunification of the Trentino and Trieste with the Italian fatherland. This movement gave impetus to the interventionists for Italy's entry into World War I, and in its later course was an important element of fascism. Mussolini, who became editor of the *Avanti* in 1912, was one of the most fervent proponents of intervention until October 1915 when he was dismissed from that post. With financial help from big industrialists, Mussolini started his own paper, *Il Popolo D'Italia,* which with his ascendance became the voice of the Fascist Party.

An army which had not learned the lessons of the Western Front entered a fateful war. The Italian defeat at Caporetto in October 1917 marked the ten days that shook Italy to its core and left it with the trauma that later made possible the takeover by the unemployed and rowdy *Avanguardisti,* the returning stormtroopers. Mussolini shed the last vestiges of his Socialist past in dropping the subtitle of his paper, "A Socialist Daily." He replaced it on the masthead with a name that better expressed its policy: "The Newspaper of Fighters and Producers." This in practice meant an alliance between the military and big business.

The 19th-century Italian bourgeoisie, much damaged by World War I, welcomed the opportunity to finance the new capitalism. Gallo is most thorough in exposing the financial rivulets which nourished the Fascist torrent. The year 1922 was one of economic disaster; this was the climate that made the takeover of the government possible. Big industry got its man in power and could rely on suitable legislation and budgets.

The Concordat with the Vatican placated the old members of the Catholic Party. The assassination of Dollfuss in Austria by the German Nazis aroused Mussolini's fear that the Italian frontier at the Brenner Pass might be violated by the upsurge of German irredentism in the new Italian province of Alto Adige (the former South Tyrol). The attacks in the *Popolo D'Italia* on Hitler are unmistakably in Mussolini's personal style. The widespread Italian resentment of the role played by the army during the war, Italy's late entry into that conflict, and the shabby treatment of its representatives during the peace conference had to be compensated for by aggression. Mussolini's frantic desire to gain equal status with the West European great powers led to his attempt to achieve supremacy in the Near East—hence his short-lived invasion of Corfu, and the establishment of a stronghold in the Dodecanese Islands.

The founding of an Empire meant the founding of colonies. October 1935 marked the birthday of the Blitzkrieg, waged with tanks, poison gas and dive bombers against a primitive Abyssinian Army. Their defeat brought no glory to the Italians, only the illusion of grandeur and the title of Emperor to their king—as well as that of Duke of Addis Ababa to Marshal Badoglio, who later would have liked to forget this phase of his career. The civil war in Spain found Mussolini on the side of Franco. (His were not the only Italian forces in the conflict; in the International Brigade, fighting to defend the Republican government, was the Garibaldi Battalion manned by antiFascist exiles, and among them Pietro Nenni, Luigi Longo, Palmiro Togliatti.) Thereafter, the signing of the anti-Comintern pact and the formation of the Rome-Berlin-Tokyo Axis tied Italy's destiny to Germany in return for guarantees not to violate the Brenner frontier. That left Mussolini no choice in his reaction to Hitler's occupation of Austria, in contrast to his stand during the Dollfuss crises.

The days of Munich and the dismemberment of Czechoslovakia are thoroughly covered by the author. World War II found Italy again a latecomer on the side of its ally, and again with an inadequately equipped army. Hitler promised to deliver the necessary supplies and weapons and his promise brought 250,000 Italian soldiers to the gates of Stalingrad and a disastrous retreat. The Allied landing in Sicily, the abandonment by the Italian forces of the island of Pantelleria, the open withdrawal of the Italian industrialists from the sinking Fascist ship are all put in fascinating perspective in Gallo's book. He spotlights the role of King Victor Emmanuel III, who clung to fascism rather than open the door to forces that might threaten the monarchy.

When, faced with complete defeat, the Grand Council of the Fascist Party stripped Mussolini of his military command, it also abrogated the Fascist constitution and restored supreme power to the King. Mussolini was arrested and Marshal Badoglio, Duke of Addis Ababa, appointed Prime Minister. At this point the downhill course of fascism gains momentum, and Max Gallo, the author of **Night of the Long Knives** now turns to events which he narrates with a masterly dramatic sense. Mussolini is dramatically abducted to Munich and later established in the Villa Feltrinelli on Lake Garda, the same luxurious place to which he had exiled Gabriele D'Annunzio in earlier years. Hitler's decision to keep the old dictator around was prompted by his need for a personality to head the puppet government of the new "Socialist Republic" which was created as a counterweight to the monarchy under Badoglio.

Mussolini is now a shell eroded by syphilis, a virtual prisoner of his S.S. supervisors, left with a sham pretorian guard, humiliated by the generals of his German ally. His former comrades and advisers are brought to trial by him, accused of treason, to make common cause with the Badoglio regime. Four of his old hierarchs, his son-in-law Ciano, Farinacci, Marinelli and De Bono are condemned to the firing squad and executed; thirteen others are condemned *in absentia*. This was the last chapter of Mussolini's Italy. A new Italy would try to revive those aspects of the moral and intellectual life of the nation destroyed by twenty-one years of fascism. The ignominious end of Mussolini and his mistress at the hands of partisans is Gallo's final epos. This section is written with a novelist's instinct for the high drama of crime and punishment.

Max Gallo puts before us the facts expertly gathered, documented with the names, locales and incidents which became synonymous with the exploitation of a distorted patriotism. The literature about the rise and fall of fascism in Italy is voluminous. Whereas much of the German record of the same period has been written by Nazi generals and freed war criminals in well-remunerated memoirs, Max Gallo has contributed to the relative objectivity of the Italian story, making sophisticated use in particular of the newspapers and magazines of the time. And while there was an Italy that was heart and soul with the Mussolini regime, there was also an Italy of expatriates who could not publish their writings in their homeland and had to seek refuge in Switzerland and France. It is most gratifying that Max Gallo draws on the testimony of the voices that Mussolini could not still.

> **Max Gallo has contributed to the relative objectivity of the Italian story, making sophisticated use in particular of the newspapers and magazines of the time.**
>
> —*Kurt J. Frohlich*

José M. Sánchez (review date 18 May 1974)

SOURCE: A review of *Spain under Franco*, in *America*, Vol. 130, No. 19, May 18, 1974, pp. 403-04.

[*Sánchez is an educator and author of books about Spanish politics and religion. In the following favorable review of* Spain under Franco, *he applauds Gallo's writing style and use of historical detail while faulting his one-sided view of Francisco Franco.*]

At age 81, Francisco Franco has managed to stay in absolute power in Spain for 35 years, longer than any Spanish executive since Philip V in the early 18th century. He has controlled one of the most politically volatile people in Europe with threats and blandishments, but he has managed to stay on top.

How has he done this? Arthur Whittaker tells the marvelous story that on Franco's desk there are two stacks of paper, one labeled "problems that time will solve," and the other "problems that time has solved." The *Caudillo*'s chief occupation, the story goes, is transferring papers from the first stack to the second. The French historian Max Gallo [in his **Spain under Franco**] sees Franco as having "the ability to change one's line in order to preserve what is essential—power."

Gallo's study is well-written, full of important statistics and facts, chronologically well-developed and comprehensive. But Gallo is so one-sidedly anti-Franco that his interpretation inevitably suffers, and at times the story becomes nothing more than a dreary history of abortive rebellion and political repression. The Civil War is seen in such simplistic terms that it leaves one wondering how the Nationalists won; after all, a sizable number of Spaniards supported Franco, else no amount of German and Italian aid would have helped.

Gallo's handling of the postwar period is much better. He shows how Franco manipulated the other powerful institutions, the Church, the Falange, the Army and the monied interests to perpetuate himself in power. He describes in detail the various crises of the early years: support for the Axis, then neutrality, the condemnation of Spain by the Potsdam conference and then by the United Nations in 1946, and agitation by the monarchists for the return of the Pretender. At the same time, he shows how American aid in the early 1950's was such an important factor in stabilizing Franco's rule. The book, while generally weak on the Church, has an excellent study of Opus Dei's rise to influence. It also includes facts on guerrilla activity against the regime that cannot be found elsewhere. On the economic miracle of the 1960's, Gallo's statistics show that per capita income rose from $281 in 1958 to $637 in 1966, while the cost of living did not even double during the same period.

Naturally, much of the history of recent years is taken up with the problem of succession, both to the Crown and to Franco's own position. Unfortunately, the book was published too late to take into account the recent assassination of Luis Carrero Blanco. In any event, much of the *Caudillo*'s power has been based on a diminishing asset, namely the vivid memory of the Civil War.

Edgar Lustgarten (review date July 1974)

SOURCE: "Demon into Clown," in *Books and Bookmen,* Vol. 19, No. 10, July, 1974, p. 46.

[*Lustgarten is a freelance writer and broadcaster. In the following review of* Mussolini's Italy, *he favorably assesses Gallo's writing style, historical competence, and biographical skill.*]

Was Mussolini a Fascist? Or a Socialist? Or an Anarchist? In fits and starts, by twists and turns, all three. That, at any rate, would appear from the bare record of his political acts, his formal declarations. But [in ***Mussolini's Italy***] Max Gallo's vivid portrait is that of a character less complex, and—in one sense—more consistent. He depicts Mussolini as an opportunist; motivated by ambition, uninhibited by doctrine, pursuing any path and exploiting any instrument which—in his own opinion—at any particular moment might best serve his undeviating purpose. 'Insanely individual,' the author says, 'he was primarily concerned with power, and for himself'.

This judgement is borne out at every stage in Mussolini's life of glory, violence, perfidy, and farce. It was opportunism that made him oppose the war with Turkey over Libya in 1911; that made him support the Red Week strikers in 1914; that made him—as editor of *Avanti*—demand neutrality on the eve of World War One, and that made him—as editor of *il Popolo*—demand intervention less than four months later. It was opportunism that made him—in September 1919—cheer d'Annunzio when he seized Fiume for Italy; and yet made him—in November 1920—approve the Rapallo treaty with Yugoslavia which acknowledged Fiume as an independent state. It was opportunism that made him (revolutionary, anti-clerical, republican) bargain with big business, the Vatican, the Crown. It was opportunism that made him, in 1935, appear to join 'the Stresa front' against aggressive Germany; that made him, in 1938, through the *Manifesto on Race,* import antisemitism into Fascist policy; that made him, in 1940, deliver a token blow at a France which the Wehrmacht already had defeated. A pattern of egocentric cynicism, each. And the list could be indefinitely extended.

The remarkable career of this amoral mountebank has already been reflected in distinguished writing. For instance, Gaetano Salvemini's *Origins of Fascism in Italy.* . . . Salvemini, though, adhering very strictly to his title, dealt with Mussolini only in that context; his book began with an economic survey and ended with the Lateran agreements. Mr Gallo adheres rather less strictly to *his* title, which anyway allows him wider scope and longer span. Beginning with Mussolini's birth and ending with his death, he *supplements* the earlier writer's work by chronological expansion, and *complements* it by a different approach. Salvemini—fundamentally—was writing history, in which Mussolini featured solely as a participant in events. Mr Gallo—fundamentally—was writing biography, in which events featured solely as a setting for his subject. Moreover, Salvemini was a philosophical historian (school of Acton rather than Macaulay). Mr Gallo is a dramatic and intimate biographer (school of Roy Jenkins mixed with that of Lytton Strachey). He presents, as

well as il Duce, Benito Mussolini, the omnivorous lecher of the tiny ante-chambers as well as the national leader of the vast Mappamundo Room.

Some people object to any close inquiry into the private lives of bygone public men. I understand without sharing their objection. The public and private personalities of a man are, like Siamese twins, by nature bound together; disclosures about the latter often cast light upon the former. Mussolini as a youth 'chasing girls and having them on staircases'; as a young man, contracting syphilis, never properly cured (which did not prevent him including 'pestilential syphilitics' in his choice vocabulary of dialectical abuse); as dictator, receiving countless demireps in the Palazzo Venezia 'where he had them on the floor'—I do not regard these as irrelevant scraps of scandal, but as proof that the fascist messiah was a diseased and randy boor.

Admittedly, however, such details are etceteras. But Mr Gallo does not fail us with the main material. He is particularly good on the period past the peak; when Mussolini's luck had turned and the deadly rot set in. Actually long before uninformed observers realised. While any vestige of a stage and an audience remained, Mussolini still acted the part of Superman when he had shrunk to the role of a Nazi gauleiter and lackey of the Fuehrer whom he had once dwarfed and despised. The Axis and the Pact of Steel, in their own time paraded (and accepted by a multitude) as Mussolini triumphs, were in fact early milestones on the road which—via the Fascist Grand Council's revolt, the royal dismissal, the impotent and absurd 'Social Republic' of Salo—led to the Partisans' firing squad at Bonzanigo and the crowds spitting on the corpse dumped in Milan. A bad road for Italy; unrelieved disasters. A worse road for Mussolini: unrelieved humiliations. And none can have been more painful than his performance as a War Lord, evoking derision from friend and foe and neutral, transforming him within three weeks from demon into clown. Westbrook Pegler, on 7 January, 1941, in a piece for the *World Telegram* exactly caught the mood—a piece which, for that reason and its hilarious invective, I cut out and have ever since preserved.

> What a bum that never adequately to be laughed at palooka, Benito Mussolini, turned out to be the minute they rang the bell, yanked the stool from under him and sent him out to fight. History has given us some memorable bums in the ring and some historic stumblebums in command of nations too, but never one like this ludicrous tramp with a silly tassle dangling before his eyes from a trick hat designed to make him look ferocious and scare the world . . . What a bum this Duce is, this colossal phoney who placed himself at the head of a mob of burlesque show generals in lion-tamers uniforms and backed by all the chiselling grafters and posturing fancy dans in Italian suburban society.

That was Mussolini, seen through the eyes of a columnist at the time of his Greek Fiasco. This is Mussolini, seen through the eyes of a historian three decades after he died.

> Without a thought for tactics or strategy, without the faintest knowledge of military problems.

There is, of course, a contrast in style, in idiom. But, on Mussolini's merits as a warrior chief, the conclusions of Gallo and Pegler are the same . . .

One final word about ***Mussolini's Italy*** as a whole. In his Foreword, Mr Gallo announced his aim; to sketch a complete but also a *living* history. That aim he has admirably achieved. I note that he lectures on contemporary history at the Institut d'Etudes Politiques in Paris. If he is half as good on the platform as he is on the page, the House Full notice should be up whenever he appears.

Mr Gallo is a dramatic and intimate biographer.

—Edgar Lustgarten

The Times Literary Supplement (review date 2 August 1974)

SOURCE: A review of *Mussolini's Italy,* in *The Times Literary Supplement,* No. 3778, August 2, 1974, p. 828.

[*In the following review, the critic favorably comments on* Mussolini's Italy, *contending that it is good "popular" history.*]

Max Gallo's book [***Mussolini's Italy***] does not claim to offer a distinctive interpretation of Mussolini and Fascism; it relies almost completely on secondary sources. M Gallo has written an unashamedly "popular" history, and his book should be judged in those terms. It is, in effect, a series of dramatic set-pieces linked by narrative; it ranges from Mussolini's errant and itinerant youth and early manhood, through the March on Rome, the Matteotti affair, the Ethiopian conquest and the Second World War, to the final collapse of Fascism and the humiliation of the dictator's corpse in a Milan garage.

Il Duce himself monopolizes the centre of M Gallo's stage, and the author's fascination with the "human angle" often reduces the impact of what was undoubtedly a turbulent life: "He was Il Duce whom Chamberlain and Hitler had taken by the hand, whom the Pope had received; he was Il Duce, the peer of the greatest, with the kings, the marshals, the heads of states round him, and the crowd like a sea beneath the balcony of Palazzo Venezia; and he was a hunted man in a corner of a foreign truck. . . ." They don't write scenarios like that any more.

Like all good epics, ***Mussolini's Italy*** is overweighted in favour of the dramatic incident. The Fascist system in its maturity during the 1930s receives cursory treatment; M Gallo is thirsting for the next piece of action. Yet despite omissions and lapses into banality, the book works. M Gallo has flashes of genuine intuition, and at his best succeeds in evoking something of the atmosphere and feel of the Fascist era. One paragraph describing the Arditi, for example, brilliantly captures the mood and conduct of those guerrilla units, whose members undertook individu-

al and largely superfluous acts of heroism across enemy lines during the First World War, and found a peacetime outlet for their reckless brutality in the Fascist squads. The final sections, describing Italy's disastrous performance in the Second World War and the disintegration of the regime, also make powerful reading.

Publishers Weekly (review date 19 August 1974)

SOURCE: A review of *With the Victors,* in *Publishers Weekly,* Vol. 206, No. 8, August 19, 1974, p. 74.

[*In the following review, the critic favorably assesses* With the Victors.]

In this sensitive account, history and conjecture are imaginatively interwoven in the story of Marco Naldi, son of an Italian landowner. [***With the Victors***] begins in the fall of 1917 at the time of the Italian defeat at Caporetto. Marco's father is killed in the war and he is gruffly befriended by Ferri, one of his father's contemporaries, who later becomes a prominent Fascist. Marco enlists in the army in his father's place and also makes friends with Alatri, a Communist. In the Post World War I Italian political upheaval Marco feels he should take his place with the aristocracy, which now means Fascism, especially when he is mocked and insulted by the peasants for his wartime bravery. Yet he also feels bound by the principles of *noblesse oblige* which characterized his father, at least in part. And Marco is also prone to the fears and weaknesses of the flesh. Naturally, torment follows in this interesting perspective on the important figures and events of the Mussolini era. By the author of ***Spain under Franco***.

The New York Times Book Review (review date 6 October 1974)

SOURCE: A review of *With the Victors,* in *The New York Times Book Review,* October 6, 1974, p. 40.

[*In the following unfavorable review, the critic assesses Gallo's literary style and development of characters in* With the Victors.]

[In ***With the Victors***] Max Gallo's Marco Naldi is one of those superheroes, like Robert Briffault's Julien Bern or Upton Sinclair's Lanny Budd, who leads a panoramic life on the stage of history. He meets world leaders in person, and makes the scene of big political happenings. Naldi starts as a lieutenant in the Arditi after Caporetto, and joins the fascist movement when the war is over. He becomes an aide to Mussolini's son-in-law, Count Ciano, specializing in press relations. These include Merry Groves, of *The New York Times* ("a very dark young woman with short hair curling over her forehead and a face full of laughter"). Also Maud Kaufman, a Trotskyite journalist married to a Stalinist, by whom Naldi has a son. And Elizabeth Loubet, an undercover media maid, whom our hero finally marries. Meanwhile, Naldi is on the spot wherever big things are happening from Abyssinia to the Russian front.

What is wrong with ***The Victors***? Well, rhetorical questions, for one thing. Marco asks too damn many of them, like:

> Why was there only the connivance of habit between us, after a few drinks in the middle of the night came the time for nondeforming mirrors and confessions, why would I do nothing; why did our bodies, though, skin against skin, go to each other and why did we let them go, without illusions and almost without pleasure?

There are too many apostrophes, too much hot air, too many names without bodies, and just not enough of the detail that simulates human life.

Anne Hollander (review date 30 November 1974)

SOURCE: A review of *The Poster in History,* in *Saturday Review,* Vol. 2, No. 6, November 30, 1974, pp. 20-2, 24-5.

[*Hollander is a lecturer in fine arts and author of the book* Moving Pictures *(1989). In the following excerpt, she reviews* The Poster in History, *contending that the book is a "sloppy treatment" of the subject.*]

Poster art has a separate history, although, as we have seen, serious artists have lent their talents to the genre. *The Poster in History,* by Max Gallo . . . , is authored by a French historian of journalistic, rather than scholarly, accomplishments who has no art-historical background to speak of. The posters illustrating the book date from 1789 to 1970; they are divided into sections corresponding to historical periods that represent successive eras of social change in which poster art reflected prevailing attitudes. The text, translated from the French, describes this process but omits any stylistic commentary on the posters, which is a pity, since the style is an integral part of the poster's message. Some early ones are even obviously incorrectly dated, in view of the evidence of dress and other details in them. These errors are perhaps supposed to be redressed by the inclusion of a diffuse essay by Carlo Arturo Quintavalle on the development of poster art, illustrated mainly by small black-and-white examples of still other posters. This book is a somewhat sloppy treatment of a subject that is much in need of study. One would have liked to have seen it responsibly done.

Virginia Crosby (review date February 1975)

SOURCE: A review of *Le cortège des vainqueurs,* in *French Review,* Vol. XLVIII, No. 3, February, 1975, pp. 664-65.

[*In the following review of* Le cortège des vainqueurs, *Crosby praises the book's detailed historical setting and literary style but faults the poor character development.*]

Sealed off by time from any further physical or moral actions of significance, an old man turns toward the past and to an accumulated sum of events whose finality is an accusing silence. In writing his life for his son Philippe, Marco Naldi is attempting to reach a young man he has never known and, at the same time, to release his spent life from the opacity of appearances.

The bulk of these fictional memoirs spans the rise and defeat of Fascism and Naldi's involvement with its leaders from 1917 to 1945. Naldi's years of moral oscillation are framed by two terms of duty as a soldier. From World War I and his first battle with the Italian army on the Pavie at age seventeen to a decisive moment when, during the long trek back from Russia, he repudiates the double standard in his life, Naldi is caught up in myths: the myth of heritage, of class, and, above all, the myth of history as destiny. Though he eventually sees these forces as meaningless constructs of words without substance, Naldi still allows himself to be swept along by an idealogy he privately refuses.

It is this sense of meaninglessness, mixed with that of the inevitable, that gives Marco Naldi his justification for falling into step with the "cortège des vainqueurs." He moves on special assignments from Rome to Ethiopia, to embassies in Berlin and Paris, never out in the arena, but standing close behind the tribune of the powerful, contemptuous of the leaders, horrified by the acts of brutality performed in history's sacred name, yet allowing moments for overt commitment to slip away. A self-imposed inner code based on a distrust of all *collectivités,* a belief in individualism, and in the concept of a "complicité limitée" permit an equivocal position that unites both faithfulness to duty and occasional clandestine activity.

In Nice, at the very end of the war, Naldi marries a resistance worker—a gesture as belated as his decision for active opposition to Fascism. Two "wrecks of war," he and Elizabeth grow old together, and in silence. In an ending that seems artificially contrived to match the pattern of his life, Naldi's manuscript is stolen unread from his son's car, relegating his past once more to ambiguous obscurity.

Max Gallo, a contributor to *L'Express,* is well-known as an historian of the Fascist and Nazi years. In his *Avertissement,* he expresses his hope for his first novel "[que] comme l'a dit Aragon, 'le menti dans le roman' permette de 'montrer le réel dans sa nudité.' " Max Gallo's knowledge of the period is sure, he is an impeccable craftsman, the possessor of a vigorous and sensual style. Yet, in the long run, [*Le cortège des vainqueurs*] is disappointing. In Naldi's act of testimony, the self, as its own witness, becomes its own alibi—a stance that precludes any ironic distance, creating, instead, an aura of sentimentality that is further accentuated by Naldi's tendency toward exalted feelings and banality of expression: life is hard—or brief; he is a pawn, in a rut, or caught up in a carnival. A certain uniformity in the long look backwards is imposed by the character's near-total recall that carries very little of shifting perspectives in time or in the flux of the personality. In consequence, Naldi's character lacks dimension or mystery; it is dulled, stained by the historical scene, by the massive and somber tones of Fascist black and Nazi brown. The monotonous repetition of the same mistakes, his moral passivity, are neither redeemed nor illuminated by the author's vision, for the language is transparent, without overtones or ambiguities; moral implications regarding conformity and freedom, esthetic implications regarding permanence and change remain implicit. A film could release them. Until such a time, the **Cortège des vainqueurs** is a somewhat long and *triste corbillard*.

Nancy M. O'Connor (review date October 1979)

SOURCE: A review of *Les hommes naissent tous le même jour 1: Aurore,* in *The French Review,* Vol. 53, No. 1, October, 1979, pp. 151-52.

[*In the following review of* Les hommes naissent tous le même jour 1: Aurore, *O'Connor favorably assesses the book's literary style and plot but faults the character development.*]

Max Gallo is a frequent contributor to the book review section of *L'Express,* and is well known as an historian of the Fascist years in Europe. Eight long novels written and published in the course of the last six years also make him a remarkably prolific novelist, and a successful one to judge by the regularity with which his books figure among the best sellers in France. **Les Hommes naissent tous le même jour,** true to form, was on the list for nine weeks during 1978. This is the first of a two-volume sequence; the second volume, **Crépuscule,** appeared in April 1979. As Gallo says in his foreword, he is continuing the "exploration imaginaire du vingtième siècle" which he undertook with **Le Cortège des vainqueurs** and the three-volume **La Baie des anges**. He sees these books as elements in a "fresque romanesque" devoted to this century of progress and upheaval. Each is independent of the others and can be read separately, but they share a common historical background, and in each one finds a minor character from the previous book. Other novels—other elements in the fresco—will follow.

The title **Les Hommes naissent tous le même jour** is to be taken in the figurative sense that all men—and women—resemble each other through a shared common destiny, and in a literal sense as well: the novel traces the lives of seven individuals, four men and three women, all born on 1 January 1900, in various parts of the world and with various socio-economic backgrounds. Gallo follows the seven into their fortieth year, "le milieu de la vie": it is 1939, and Europe is on the brink of World War II. By that time the action has taken us to the United States, France, Germany, Russia, Poland, China, and South America, and we have relived many of the events that mark the first four decades of the century: World War I, the Bolshevik Revolution, the Stalinist purges, the Spanish Civil War. History is inextricably woven into the lives and fates of the seven main characters, and we see its unfolding through their eyes. In some cases it overcomes them; in other, fewer instances it is influenced by them. Allen Roy Gallway, son of a San Francisco laundry woman and a sailor, becomes a famous novelist and journalist (Gallo/Gallway?); the Pole, Sarah Berelovitz, becomes a renowned concert pianist and a secret Communist courier; her life is linked to that of the bureaucrat Serge Cordelier, son of a French scientist. Anna Spasskaia, born of wealthy parents in Saint Petersburg, joins the Bolsheviks. The others are no less interesting, but fewer pages are devoted to them—the Chinese Lee Lou Ching, the Bolivian Dolorès, the German Karl Menninger. These lives are interwoven, and paths cross and re-cross, sometimes unbelievably (unbelievably only *because* this is a novel). Nowhere has it been clearer that Gallo is a strong believer in chance.

Les Hommes naissent tous le même jour is an eminently readable book once one develops an interest in the characters, which always takes a little longer when the author is telling several stories instead of one. Gallo's style is natural, almost conversational, and his ability to convey the atmosphere of different settings and social *milieux* is unerring. But the primary focus is on the characters, and in my estimation he does not succeed in making them live, with the possible exception of Allen Gallway. They hold our attention, but we never really get inside them. Whether this is the author's failing or a built-in drawback of the form the novel takes is hard to determine. I felt mildly irritated by the preview or trailer effect sought (and achieved) in the short final chapter of the book: what will become of these people, Gallo asks? "Qui peut le dire en ce mois de janvier 1939?"

Danielle Chavy Cooper (review date Summer 1993)

SOURCE: A review of *La fontaine des innocents,* in *World Literature Today,* Vol. 67, No. 3, Summer, 1993, pp. 583-84.

[*In the following review of* La fontaine des innocents, *Cooper favorably assesses its plot, themes, and characters.*]

On two levels, both factual and symbolic, the title of Max Gallo's massive new novel [**La fontaine des innocents**]—his nineteenth—solidly anchors the work in today's Paris, intimately allying the traditional and the new, as it is in the Halles district where the eponymous fountain is located. The very structure and development of Gallo's powerful novel as well as its overall theme are closely linked to the famous Renaissance fountain, well known for its Jean Goujon statues of graceful nymphs, erected on the site of a medieval cemetery by the same name, in pious homage to the Holy Innocents of the New Testament slain by Herod. The time span of the novel is two years, from late 1989 to early 1991, with many hang-ups from a recent past. As in other novels by the historian Gallo, contemporary history and fiction convincingly intermingle.

The factual element of the title is present from the start, as the novel opens near the Forum des Halles with two of the main characters from opposite sides of society who are to play a major role throughout the novel and around whom everything revolves. Anne-Marie Bermont, a divorcee and a career woman in the publishing business, has come to do some Christmas shopping. She is assaulted by a hoodlum, later identified as Jonas, whose sinister recurring presence in the novel means only serious trouble for everyone concerned. The reader next becomes acquainted, floor by floor, with the other tenants of Anne-Marie's apartment building and with people she meets at her workplace, with her politician husband Julien Rivière, and with their teenage daughter Isabelle and her teachers and classmates at the Lycée Montaigne, as well as Isabelle's problems when she becomes entangled with the wrong crowd. This approach provides the novelist with a wide range of mushrooming possibilities to explore many different milieux, thus building a new *Comédie humaine* of his own (actually an *Inferno*) of the late twentieth century.

The symbolic importance of the title becomes clear as one progresses through the novel. Indeed, it underlines the unifying theme linking all episodes (sixty-nine untitled chapters) and the many characters from every walk of life whose paths are somehow crossing—all very plausibly intertwining, as is characteristic of Gallo's work. Deterioration of modern society at all levels is the central theme, with a sense of organic decomposition as seen by Parrain, a journalist (*Paris-pourri, Paris-connerie*), and the resurgence of racism, the alarming increase in corruption and violence, and finally the victimization of the unfortunates, whether children, adolescents, or adults, caught in a maelstrom of destruction—i.e., a new Massacre of the Innocents. The most perceptive characters, such "innocents" as Hélène Milner, a language teacher, and François, her husband, who is a police inspector with a degree in Philosophy, or Gilles Duprez, a Don Quixote-like writer working on a *livre-enquête* exposing a former war criminal, all feel that they are seeing the end of an era: "Et qu'ils allaient vivre, qu'ils avaient déjà commencé à vivre . . . des temps troublés."

Gilles Duprez intends to call his book *Scènes de la vie parisienne fin de siècle,* in an update of Balzac. Other Balzacian titles come to mind in relation to **La Fontaine des Innocents** and the milieux depicted by Gallo: *Scènes de la vie politique,* particularly *L'envers de l'histoire contemporaine,* for the world of politics; *Les illusions perdues* for the world of journalism and Paris publishing houses, with the addition of course of big-time television, through the interesting character of Brigitte Georges, an anchorwoman and talk-show hostess in deadly rivalry with her estranged husband, a journalist at *Le Monde.*

Like Balzac studying city maps before writing his novels, Gallo, for authenticity and evocation of a given milieu, gives each of his numerous characters a specific address as well as a definite age and profession. Where a character lives or works is very much part of his or her personality, as are the places familiar to that individual, the cafés or brasseries, bistros or restaurants, squares and streets, subway stations or R.E.R. Paris place-names are richly evocative without a need for description. Such details accurately compartmentalize the different layers of the Paris populace. Thus Paris (with its periphery and *banlieue*) emerges as a major character in Gallo's novel. *La Fontaine des Innocents* is the drama of contemporary Paris, changed from the City of Light to a city of bizarre, shapeless graffiti creeping all over like ivy, *une ville difficile à vivre,* where life, loaded with frustration and anguish, has turned, as for Julien Rivière, into a trompe l'oeil. At the end one realizes how pertinent were the two quotations chosen as epigraphs by the author: one from Balzac's *Père Goriot*—"Paris est un véritable océan. Jetez-y la sonde"—and one from Aragon's *Plus belle que les larmes:* "Paris de nos malheurs . . . Paris plus déchirant qu'un cri de vitrier."

Paris emerges as a major character in Gallo's *La fontaine des innocents*.

—Danielle Chavy Cooper

Danielle Chavy Cooper　(review date Autumn 1993)

SOURCE: A review of *L'amour au temps des solitudes,* in *World Literature Today,* Vol. 67, No. 4, Autumn, 1993, p. 772.

[*In the following favorable review, Cooper comments on the character development and the mixture of history and fiction in* L'amour au temps des solitudes.]

Over the last three decades Max Gallo has enjoyed a nonstop literary career, in both fiction and nonfiction, with some fifty titles to his credit, including best sellers and Livre de Poche reissues. As in his preceding novel, **La Fontaine des Innocents** . . . **L'amour au temps des solitudes** again intertwines contemporary history and fiction. "Tout y est imaginaire," the author declares. "Et donc tout ce qui est écrit ici peut avoir eu lieu."

Through his central character, the aging career woman Catherine Vance (née Kemsky), the novelist concentrates on the tragic aftermath of earlier dramatic events in individual lives and their long-lasting repercussions on younger family members. Catherine has been traumatized for life by her ordeal during World War II in Nice as a Jewish refugee arrested by the militia in 1942, which she somehow survived. The fact that Catherine is the central character of the novel, and the pivot around whom everything revolves, is emphasized by the author's choice of the illustration on the book's cover: a reproduction of Matisse's *Woman by the Window,* a solitary figure seated next to a window opening onto the Promenade des Anglais.

The story ranges from Paris (now and over fifty years ago), to Nice and Antibes, to Italy, and to war-torn Yugoslavia. Thus, well anchored in contemporary European experience, **L'amour au temps des solitudes** once more rings a bell, stirring lifelong memories. The epigraph, borrowed from Pestalozzi, stresses the underlying theme (and the lesson): "You may chase the devil away from your own garden, but he will still be there in the garden of your son." History is made of repetitions through different generations, and such is the case here.

An expert novelist, Gallo varies his narrative approach and supports his story with a superb inner architecture. A cryptic summary of moods or events is provided in filigree by the titles given to each of the nine parts, vague enough to intrigue the reader and maintain suspense.

The novel begins in the first person, *je* being a reporter, Vincent Janovers, just back from Malawi, who brings his work to his boss (Catherine Vance) and unexpectedly meets a mystery woman in the street, who reminds him of a lost love. All the characters are at least glimpsed in the twelve chapters of part 1, entitled "She Was Still Such a Beautiful Woman." The cast is fully set at the very start of a crisis, as in classical tragedy. Its being the only part written in the first person establishes Vincent as a participant as well as a witness, heralding his own importance in the novel as a point of convergence. Part 2, "Nighttime Is for Remembering," concentrates on the mystery woman, Jeanne (Catherine's daughter), whose life is falling apart as she mourns the death of her son Matthew, a recent suicide at sixteen. It is the third and longest part, "Under the Mask," however, that is the actual core of the novel, focusing on the older woman. As Catherine stands at the door of her daughter's apartment, where she used to live as a child, her past is revealed in flashback. In her obstinate will to survive after her imprisonment during the war years, Catherine has been blocking off her feelings and has kept her memories to herself. She has learned to wear a social mask like a second skin, reflexively, in self-defense—this at the expense of her own family but bringing her success in her work as the director of a feminine magazine she founded. Writing has been for her a refuge, to prove to herself that she was still alive and in control, "pour tenter une fois encore de bâtir avec des mots un mur qui la protègerait des souvenirs, du gouffre où ils l'entraînaient." All the characters here wear a "mask" of some sort as self-protection, hiding some weakness, sorrow, remorse, or shame. It is "le temps des solitudes." Only Vincent and Jeanne, perhaps, may learn to accept themselves as they are and unite forces in a newfound love. The child they rescue together from a burning city in Croatia may provide the hope for a new beginning. As to Catherine, she returns alone to Antibes, at peace near the sea, "so close, so tranquil, so deep."

Richard Kopp   (review date October 1993)

SOURCE: A review of *Le regard des femmes,* in *The French Review,* Vol. 67, No. 1, October, 1993, pp. 160-61.

[*Kopp is an educator and author of books about French literature. In the following favorable review, he comments on the plot, themes, and literary style of* Le regard des femmes.]

Max Gallo appears fascinated by the relationship between the public and private elements which make up human existence. He is capable of introducing the public individual and uncovering the hitherto unknown private facts which explain the public persona, but in the same manner he is capable of introducing the private individual and explaining the public facts not known previously by the reader (or seer). In the end, a persona is formed, one which satisfies the viewpoint of everyone who may be interested in the character in question.

In [*Le Regard des femmes,*] the "look of women" or perhaps "the way women look at others" forces the "hero," a diplomat and member of the European commission, to define himself as the result of being caught in an amorous conflict. We have already experienced this manner of observing in Robbe-Grillet, the obvious example being *La Jalousie,* in which we view everything through one pair of eyes and are not always sure of what we see because

the seer may be sifting the information. In *Le Regard des femmes,* the author presents a lengthy passage during which the reader gets to know the wife (Lisa) of the voyeur (Philippe) through the latter's eyes. This may at first seem unexciting, the way that many of the New Novels have a curious dullness about them: little happens but the authors have sufficient style that the reader remains fascinated.

In *Le Regard des femmes* Gallo has succeeded in bringing together literary qualities which, combined, provide pleasurable reading. The plot starts out simply as a tale of the disintegration of a marriage, then grows to depict a social milieu which includes political intrigue, academic interest (Lisa is writing a dissertation on a fifteenth-century adventurer), friendships, lovers—old and new—and a secret from World War II which rises from the past like the hidden treasures on a sunken boat, to affect definitively the principal players in this complicated social game. Gallo brings together all the threads of intrigue in a manner reminiscent of Balzac and Proust. But the final analyses are left to the reader just as they are in a work by Robbe-Grillet, Sarraute, or Duras.

Mature readers may come away convinced that the new world order of the 1990s is as significant as the changes of the fifteenth century when the Ottoman Turks were moving closer to Western Europe. Students, however, may be limited to views of marriages and love affairs in different states of disintegration. The parallels between such personal relationships and the political relationships (past and present) may also require some clarification for any but the most discerning student. The novel may also seem rather slow to students. Gallo's language and style are not complicated, but the lack of action may try their patience; important points in the uncovering of this mystery require several retellings in versions which differ from character to character, none of whom is truly *sympathique.* For the mature reader the work may be seen to reveal an art at least the equal of the New Novel, but with the added attraction of a contemporary intrigue.

FURTHER READING

Criticism

Adams, Phoebe. Review of *The Night of Long Knives,* by Max Gallo. *Atlantic Monthly* 230, No. 2 (August 1972): 92.
    Favorably assesses *The Night of Long Knives.*

Gough, Hugh. "Genocide and the Bicentenary: The French Revolution and the Revenge of the Vendée." *The Historical Journal* 30, No. 4 (December 1987): 977-88.
    Reviews Gallo's *Lettre ouverte á Maximilien Robespierre sur les nouveaux muscadins* and other books, reflecting on the French Revolution in its bicentenary year.

Rosselli, John. "Italian Centaur." *The Listener* 91, No. 2343 (21 February 1974): 247.
    Favorably assesses *Mussolini's Italy.*

Additional coverage of Gallo's life and career is contained in the following source published by Gale Research: *Contemporary Authors,* Vols. 85-88.

Peter Høeg

1957-

Danish novelist and short story writer.

The following entry provides an overview of Høeg's career through 1995.

INTRODUCTION

Høeg is primarily known for his novel *Frøken Smillas fornemmelse for sne* (1992; *Smilla's Sense of Snow*), which has received widespread critical and popular acclaim and has been published in thirteen countries. In his works, Høeg questions the cultural and political values of modern Denmark, particularly as they relate to the struggle between individuality and societal conformity, values which he believes have detrimental effects on the lives of Danish children. Reviewer Nader Mousavizadeh has stated that "Høeg has brought to modern Danish literature an intensity, a worldliness, a love of language and a depth of learning that entirely on their own have raised the standards for contemporary writing in Denmark."

Biographical Information

Born in Denmark in 1957, Høeg worked as a dancer, actor, athlete, and sailor prior to becoming a writer. Reviewer Laura Shapiro quoted Høeg as saying: "I knew all the time, as I was starting other careers, that this was not final, it was a transition, something that would be replaced by something else. I don't have that feeling any longer. One thing that came to me with writing was peace."

Major Works

Høeg's first novel, *Forestilling om det tyvende århundrede* (1988; *The History of Danish Dreams*), covers over four centuries of Danish history through a multi-generational narrative of four families whose descendants are brought together by marriage and chance. In this work, Høeg traces the development of his country from the feudalism of the early 1500s to the post-industrial state of present-day Denmark. *Fortællinger om natten* (1990) is a collection of stories which examine "love and its conditions on the night of March 19, 1929," focusing on the effects of conformity upon love. Høeg's third work and his first to be translated into English, *Smilla's Sense of Snow* is the story of Smilla Qaavigaaq Jaspersen, a half-Dane, half-Greenland Inuit glaciologist whose knowledge of snow leads her to question the death of her neighbor and friend, an Eskimo child named Isaiah, who is believed to have fallen from a rooftop. Smilla's journey is not only an investigation into Isaiah's death but is also an exposé of cultural conflict in Denmark. Høeg's novel *Da måske egnede* (1993; *Borderliners*) chronicles the story of three unrelated orphans named Peter, Katarina, and August, who meet at a boarding school outside of Copenhagen. The school is renowned for its oppressiveness, and Peter and Katarina, who develop an instant attraction to one another, are aided by the wild and uncontrollable August in devising a scheme to upset the regimented routines the headmaster imposes on the students. Peter, who is eventually adopted by a family named Høeg, tells the story in flashback segments which alternate with discourses regarding the nature of time and the effects of social conformity.

Critical Reception

Critical reaction to Høeg's work has been generally positive. While most critics have praised his strong characterizations and suspenseful plotlines, particularly those in *Smilla's Sense of Snow,* others have faulted his works for what they consider an obsessive attention to details and disjointed narratives. Høeg's ability to make contemporary Danish social issues appealing to a wider, international audience prompted Mousavizadeh to state: "[No] contemporary writer has done more to liberate Danish culture from its ennui than Peter Høeg." While his combination of genres, plots, and themes can produce mixed reactions among readers, Julia Glass noted in a review of *Borderliners* that Høeg "is persisting on an uncharted course in fiction, using science to elucidate character and add a new dimension to suspense."

PRINCIPAL WORKS

Forestilling om det tyvende århundrede [*The History of Danish Dreams*] (novel) 1988
Fortællinger om natten (short stories) 1990
Frøken Smillas fornemmelse for sne [*Smilla's Sense of Snow;* also published as *Miss Smilla's Feeling for Snow*] (novel) 1992
Da måske egnede [*Borderliners*] (novel) 1993
Kvinden og aben (novel) 1996

CRITICISM

John Williams (review date 3 September 1993)

SOURCE: "Fire and Ice," in *New Statesman and Society,* Vol. 6, No. 268, September 3, 1993, p. 41.

[*In the following review of* Miss Smilla's Feeling for Snow, *Williams favorably discusses Høeg's protagonist and the novel's setting.*]

Miss Smilla's Feeling for Snow [is] a European literary sensation from Denmark written by Peter Høeg. . . .

Miss Smilla is 400 pages long and has a title that screams "dour Teutonic art movie of the 1970s, probably scripted by Peter Handke". And, sure enough, *Miss Smilla* has its longueurs (not to mention a plot straight out of the Michael Crichton school of scientific conspiracy thrillers). But it is still a very good book indeed.

Its strength lies in the remarkable skill with which Høeg has evoked his heroine and narrator, Smilla Jesperson. Half Dane, half Greenland Eskimo and an underemployed glaciologist, she lives on a bleak, white Copenhagen housing estate, and has frozen herself off from the world.

Then an Eskimo boy, who lives with his alcoholic mother in the flat below, falls to his death and Smilla asks some questions. So a chain of events begins that leads in the end to the warming of Smilla's heart and to a bloody reckoning in eastern Greenland. It's Greenland that gives the novel its strangeness and power as Høeg relieves it of its normal fictional role as empty, hostile territory, there to be conquered, and turns it into a place where people live. And are transported from. . . .

[*Miss Smilla*] is an arctic tale worthy of Conrad.

Laura Shapiro (review date 6 September 1993)

SOURCE: "A Hot Thriller from a Cold Climate," in *Newsweek,* Vol. 122, No. 10, September 6, 1993, p. 54.

[*Shapiro is an American reporter, journalist, and critic. In the following review of* Smilla's Sense of Snow, *she compares Høeg's work to that of John le Carré.*]

Smilla's in another tight spot—a narrow area of open deck, to be specific, on a ship forging through the ice off Greenland in a dark, freezing rain. The man walking toward her wants to throw her overboard, and so does the man coming up behind. This part of the deck is completely isolated, and Smilla's 110 pounds will be easy to toss down to the sea. Even if someone were to hear a scream she isn't likely to get much help; most of the creepy people on board hate her. For a moment she recalls what she knows about drowning. "You hold your breath until you think your lungs are going to burst. That's when you feel pain. Then you exhale and take a deep breath. After that there's only peace." It doesn't appeal to her. Smilla fears the sea, always has. So she grabs hold of an iron rung welded onto the side of the ship, and inches up the rain-soaked ladder as the ship pitches and rolls. When she loses her foothold for a minute, she just has to hang there with her eyes closed, so she won't look down at the water.

Smilla's Sense of Snow is a thriller, but it's a thriller like no other. Maybe a le Carré novel comes closest, with its brainy characters enmeshed in deliciously intricate conundrums fraught with moral, emotional and geopolitical dangers. But le Carré, whose view of women can most charitably be called old-fashioned, could never have created a narrator as daring and self-sufficient as Smilla. Most extraordinary of all is the setting: this novel takes place in the snows of Greenland, the ice floes of the North Atlantic, the endless dark of a Copenhagen winter. The only thing that thaws during this adventure is Smilla's long-frozen heart.

Smilla's mother was a hunter: "She shot and paddled a kayak and dragged meat home like a man." Her father, a Danish physician who went to Greenland to do research, married there but hated the place and left when Smilla was 3. Four years later she was forced to join him in Denmark when her mother died. As a half-Greenlander, she has always felt like a misfit in Denmark, the country that colonized her birthplace. For a while she dabbled in protest politics, but her driving passion is ice. Smilla knows ice and snow the way le Carré's operatives know locks or codes or bombs; there's nobody better. She's a regular on Arctic expeditions, and her publications include such titles as "Mathematical Models for Brine Drainage from Seawater Ice." She hates cooking, loves clothes and was relentlessly independent until a small, neglected boy named Isaiah moved into her apartment building and made himself her friend. Now Isaiah is dead.

It's clear to the police that the little boy fell off the roof of the building—his footprints on the snowy rooftop prove it. But not to Smilla. She knows Isaiah was terrified of heights; what's more, she can read his tracks in the snow. They're footprints made too fast, made in fear, not in play. Somebody was chasing him. When the authorities refuse to investigate—when, in fact, they start investigating Smilla—she sets off on her own. Soon she's joined by another friend of Isaiah's, the quiet mechanic who lives in her building. Their sleuthing partnership doesn't begin very auspiciously—mistaking him for an enemy in the dark, she shoves a bookcase at him and bashes him across the neck with a brass rod—but love manages to bloom. Together they amass clues that reveal widening circles of death, greed and deceit. Finally, Smilla joins the crew of a mysterious shipping expedition and heads out toward the icy straits off Greenland. There she discovers the answers she has been seeking—and an ugly surprise as well.

Smilla's Sense of Snow is such a hugely satisfying novel that it's hard to believe Peter Hoeg never wrote a thriller before. But according to the Danish novelist, he didn't even know this one was a thriller until people started telling him. "I only knew I was writing a book about an enigma," he says. Hoeg, 36, is the author of two previous books—a novel about Danish history, and a collection of love stories—but this is the first of his books to be translated into English (and beautifully, by Tiina Nunnally). He worked as a dancer, an actor, an athlete and a sailor—"on rich people's boats"—before settling down to write. "Ten years ago I was much more restless than I am now," he says. "I knew all the time, as I was starting other careers, that this was not final, it was a transition, something that would be replaced by something else. I don't have that feeling any longer. One thing that came to me with writing was peace."

With his wife, a dancer from Kenya, and their daughter, Hoeg has spent much of his time recently in Africa and Cuba. So how did he happen to write a novel about snow and ice? He can't explain it, but one winter the idea simply came to him. "I had dreams about Greenland," he says—a place he's visited often. A lot of Americans are going to be dreaming about Greenland, too, after they close this wonderful book.

Jim McCue   (review date 17 September 1993)

SOURCE: "Arctic Nights," in *The Times Literary Supplement,* No. 4720, September 17, 1993, p. 20.

[*In the following review of* Miss Smilla's Feeling for Snow, *McCue discusses the style and themes of Høeg's work.*]

Every remove from safety makes us feel more reckless, abandoned. [In ***Miss Smilla's Feeling for Snow,***] Peter Høeg stretches the supply-lines of security so far that there seems no way back for the ice-maiden Smilla Jaspersen. She is a Greenlander, resettled in Denmark, which already makes her feel like a tightrope-walker "misunderstood by the person holding the rope". Forces which neither she nor the reader can fully comprehend propel her out into the arctic night, on an unregistered ship, on an illegal mission, with a press-gang of criminals, several of whom wish to kill her. In trying to find out what is going on, and why a young waif has died, she penetrates a forbidden part of the ship by travelling in a dumbwaiter, in which she is briefly trapped. It's not just bad weather and night-time; it's so bad that one would invite in a stranger, even an enemy, to sit by the fire; even an enemy's dog; even if it bit you. Smilla enjoys nobody's protection, but she will not give up her search for the truth, whatever the extremity of adversity.

The terrors are piled on, but Høeg is oblivious to the dangers to his narrative. For he writes like an escapologist. Smilla is as resourceful in the face of extinction as James Bond, and this story too has implausible, entertaining shifts—of gear, tone, direction, genre—whenever a premature ending has to be avoided. One of Smilla's special talents is her ability to flabbergast businessmen, policemen and hardened killers. When challenged by a mercenary tough, for instance, she hands over her booty. His resistance collapses when this turns out, randomly enough, to be a pair of knickers. The storyteller doesn't have to say exactly what happened next.

Another time, she is hiding in a shower when a naked sailor comes in to urinate in the basin, pursued by an apparently murderous woman,

> holding a belt with the buckle down. When she strikes, she does it with such precision that only the buckle hits him, leaving a long white stripe across one buttock. . . . He takes hold of the sink, bends over, and urges his backside towards her. She strikes again; the buckle hits his other buttock. Romeo and Juliet come to mind. Europe has a long tradition of elegant rendezvous.

Homicide turns out to be sex-play; this moment of tension no more than a knockabout turn.

The tale is packed with such descriptions, a mass of details—those different sorts of ice—which yet never set the shifting scene. Melodrama and slapstick, epic journey and social indictment: the book proudly declines to limit itself.

Early on, Smilla tries to retreat by barricading herself into her flat, with the phone disconnected.

> This is the kind of day when you can't rule out the possibility of someone knocking on your windows. On the fifth floor.
>
> Someone knocks on my window. Outside stands a green man. I open the window.
>
> "I'm the window cleaner. I just wanted to warn you, so you don't go and take off your clothes."
>
> He gives me a big smile. As if he were cleaning the windows by putting one pane at a time into his mouth.
>
> "What the hell do you mean? Are you implying that you don't want to see me nude?"

In a story which generally asks to be taken seriously, these jokes are sprung in the most disconcerting way, as here, where even a train of thought ("the kind of day . . .") can be ambushed. But as events rush on, their significance is unexamined.

An expensive lawyer's office is being described with distaste. It has an extra-wide letter-box, "so that even the largest cheques can get through." For a moment this looks like comically bad translation; but no, the translation is excellent. How well rendered, for instance is Smilla's observation, in one threatening encounter, "of the division of labour between the two men. Verlaine taking care of the physical violence." The thug's pride in the way he breaks people is conveyed in that choice of "taking care"; and yet that is only the secondary, only the *physical* violence.

Selfishness, menace and systematic corruption form the fabric of this mysterious novel. Relationships are all based on suspicion, and love has to be "like a military operation" (one inventive manoeuvre has a particularly Scandinavian explicitness). Survival is for the richest and those with special skills, whether in classifying snow or sounds, in engineering or administering injections. Honed expertise even in violence, makes for a chilling, unreflecting efficiency. There is no such thing as society. Peter Høeg has a remarkable feeling for sinister surprises.

Richard Eder   (review date 26 September 1993)

SOURCE: "They Have 23 Words for It," in *Los Angeles Times Book Review,* September 26, 1993, pp. 3, 11.

[*Eder is an American journalist and critic who won the Pulitzer Prize for Criticism in 1987. In the following review of* Smilla's Sense of Snow, *he discusses the novel's characters.*]

Like John le Carré and Graham Greene before him, Peter Hoeg has given a thriller, ***Smilla's Sense of Snow,*** moral and political resonance. As Smilla pursues the killers of an Eskimo boy through Copenhagen and then into the ice fields of Greenland, this outwardly stiff, inwardly passionate and quite unforgettable protagonist is after something larger than a particular crime. Half-Eskimo herself, she is puzzling out a violence that has malformed her own spirit: the corruption of a traditional culture by the greed and technological prowess of the civilized West.

In some ways, Hoeg, a Dane, shows the very particular influence of George Smiley's creator. His Smilla has something of the latter's torn and complex nature. Like Smiley—curious, the similarity of names—she conceals an affronted disposition to love; only she does it with rage rather than aloofness. As with Le Carré's protagonist, her pain is a tangible character that follows her around and attaches us to her. Northern bleakness prevails with cold, fog, gray streets and a dinginess of the senses. The plot is a densely complex series of concealments and revelations, a continuous unmasking that does not dispel ambiguity but deepens it.

Hoeg makes the sinuous turns of his story deeply engrossing but, unlike Le Carré, he is not quite master of them. The book's only real weakness is an ending that doesn't live up to what has gone before and that fails to satisfy, not our emotional expectations, but our logical ones. It is not a matter of anti-climax—true mysteries are always anticlimactic—but of not quite making sense.

The plot of *Smilla's Sense of Snow* is a densely complex series of concealments and revelations, a continuous unmasking that does not dispel ambiguity but deepens it.

—Richard Eder

Certainly this is a drawback in a thriller, yet the deeper suspense here lies in revelations not of plot but of character. There is Smilla's character and that of half a dozen figures whom she encounters. There is the character of a process that has despoiled her Eskimo culture both of its adeptness and its sense of wonder within its own world, as it had done long before in the industrial world. And in this respect, Hoeg has written an artful and astonishing book.

Smilla is a troubled, unstable and pugnacious woman in her 30s, with some impressive scientific achievements in her narrow field: the structure and properties of ice. She was born in Greenland of an Inuit mother, an Amazon-like figure who hunted with the men and drowned in an encounter with a walrus. Here as elsewhere, Hoeg succeeds in conveying the mythic world of his Greenlanders: a walrus may seem ridiculous to us, but to the Inuit hunters it is more monstrous and dangerous than a bear.

Smilla's father, Moritz, is a Danish doctor who worked in Greenland, fell passionately in love with his Amazon and, upon her death, brought Smilla to Denmark. There, with his capacity for mythic enchantment exhausted, he became famous, rich and self-indulgent. Smilla grew up rebellious and angry. Hoeg succeeds, uniquely, I think, in using her anger, alternately cold and violent, her clumsy impetus, her half-mannish bearing, to make a portrait of a sexy, mysterious and profoundly alluring woman.

The Inuit have a legend of the raven who initially was given a human form and was never easy until he was allowed to be a bird. Smilla lives lost and fierce in her Danish guise—she milks her father, whom she despises, for money and dresses with defiant elegance—until one night coming home she finds that Isaiah, a 6-year-old Eskimo boy who lives with his mother in the same building, has fallen from the roof and is dead. She cannot believe the police version of the accident. Her Inuit knowledge—quite specifically, her sense of snow—tells her that his tracks on the roof, the way the ice crystals are compressed, are not those of a child playing but a child fleeing.

With this and one or two other clues she will begin a pursuit through a violent labyrinth. One of the clues is a pension letter from the mining company that employed Isaiah's father in Greenland, sent after he died in a mysterious accident. It bears an oddly anguished handwritten postscript from the chief bookkeeper. Smilla's search will take her into the company's archives, made available to her by the troubled bookkeeper. It will put her on the trail of two secret expeditions to Greenland, financed through but perhaps not by the company: of other deaths and of the treasure that the expeditions were after—a shameful one that powerful and eminent figures are desperate to conceal.

It will send her up against the authorities, who alternately offer help and threats. It will make her a fugitive. It will get her aboard a freighter, lavishly outfitted for a third expedition with ice-breaking equipment, expensive communications and security devices, laboratories and out-sized, temperature-controlled holds. It will turn her into a clandestine shipboard investigator, give her two or three ambiguous allies, get her manhandled and nearly killed, and finally lead her—once ashore on the Greenland ice—to the expedition's real purpose.

In her rough odyssey, Smilla comes up against a vividly-drawn series of characters. Some help her. There is a pathologist with a greenhouse full of tropical plants, whose sense of medical honor rebels against a cover-up. There is the chief accountant whose note helped set off Smilla's quest. She is an austere, devout woman, torn between her conscience and loyalty to the company that gave her a long and successful career. When she makes her choice, it is a piece of scintillating moral drama.

There are richly ambiguous figures: a lover who seems sometimes to be Smilla's ally and sometimes her enemy, a state investigator whose motives are revealed only partly and only at the end, the tormented captain of the freighter on which Smilla makes her fearful journey. There are the villains whom Hoeg draws distinctively but flatly. He is less interested in evil individuals than in the evil that modern life works through them.

Most memorable of all are Smilla and the Eskimo child she avenges. In our brief glimpses of Isaiah we see the pure directness of his culture. When he is read a children's teddy-bear story, he asks what the bear would taste like. Smilla reads Euclid to him, as well; the geometer stands for another kind of purity. Her battle to find Isaiah's killers is a protest against a defilement that has taken his life, and exploited and destroyed an indigenous culture. Smilla fights it within her own divided self, as well. Hoeg's moving and suggestive book is an anti-colonial thriller.

Robert Nathan   (review date 26 September 1993)

SOURCE: "Irritable, Depressed, Spoiled, and Terrific," in *The New York Times Book Review,* September 26, 1993, p. 12.

[*In the following review of* Smilla's Sense of Snow, *Nathan praises the book, especially for its elements of suspense.*]

Try this for an offer you could easily refuse. How would you like to be locked in a room for a couple of days with an irritable, depressed malcontent who also happens to be imperiously smart, bored and more than a little spoiled? Say no, and you will miss not only a splendid entertainment but also an odd and seductive meditation on the human condition.

With **Smilla's Sense of Snow,** his American debut following two previous books, the Danish novelist Peter Hoeg finds his own uncommon vein in narrative territory worked by writers as varied as Martin Cruz Smith and Graham Greene—the suspense novel as exploration of the heart. Mr. Hoeg's heroine, Smilla Jaspersen, is the daughter of an Eskimo mother who was a nomadic native of Greenland and a wealthy Danish anesthesiologist father, parentage that endows her with the resilience of the frozen north and urban civilization's existential malaise. One day just before Christmas, Smilla arrives at her Copenhagen apartment building to find a neighbor boy, 6-year-old Isaiah Christiansen, sprawled face down in the snow, dead after a fall from the roof of a nearby warehouse.

But did Isaiah fall? Smilla suspects not, based on her accidental enchantment with this adorable and neglected child. Isaiah, also an Eskimo, lived with his alcoholic, welfare-addicted mother, Juliane, who could barely rouse herself to dress him sufficiently, let alone protect and nourish him. Though Smilla cheerfully hates children, she allowed herself to be adopted by Isaiah as his caretaker, giving him baths, sometimes letting him sleep in the same bed with her and reading to him from, of all things, Euclid's *Elements.*

The choice of books is not arbitrary. Mathematics is the first of two reigning metaphors in Smilla's view of the world. "The number system is like human life," she says, with negative numbers "the formalization of the feeling that you are missing something." Perhaps as a result of both casual racism toward Eskimos and her own temperament, Smilla admits she finds numbers easier to cope with than people, a trait that could make her disagreeable. But whether rooted in mathematics or a preference for her own company, Smilla's capacity for observation never fails to charm—or amuse. Playing a Danish Pascal, she tosses off inspired epigrams on any subject at hand—friendship, self-centeredness, children, death.

Her second essential metaphor is the cold, not surprising given her history, and appropriate to a novel set emotionally and literally in winter. Told she courts danger by walking on the frozen Copenhagen harbor, she replies, "I

have a good relationship with ice." When asked how, based solely on seeing Isaiah's footprints, she can be certain someone chased him from the warehouse roof, she replies, "I have a sense of snow." It is a tribute to Mr. Hoeg's skill that such lines do not seem laughable, not least because Smilla's upbringing, divided between Greenland and Denmark, is continuously fascinating and feels unquestionably authentic.

The truth is that aside from her sense of snow, Smilla has stronger reasons to doubt the official story. Honoring a "pact with Isaiah not to leave him in the lurch, never," she sets out to discover who killed him. The journey starts at the local medical examiner's office and ends weeks later, on a ship navigating the ice floes Greenland—a long, potentially lethal road on behalf of a boy who once ingenuously asked, "When you die Smilla, can I have your hide?" Along, the way, Smilla sketches a shrewd and moving portrait of her parents marriage, viciously dissects Denmark's near-colonial treatment of her mother's people and discovers, at the age of 37, how it feels to fall in love.

Any man who dares to write an entire novel from a woman's point of view should be wary. But Mr. Hoeg succeeds. The investigation on which he sends Smilla, however er never quite measures up to the brilliant tone of its telling. Far too often the story takes convoluted turns, some so ill motivated as to seem random. In the adventure's final chapters, a reader may wish Mr. Hoeg had supplied marginal notes to explain precisely what's going on.

This sort of haphazard plotting would sink an ordinary novel; but Smilla makes the trip worthwhile. Her voice, in an engaging translation by Tiina Nunnally, is the nervy, insistent voice of modernity—cynical, angry, desperate for meaning, weary of the state and its intrusions. "I don't like being watched," Smilla says. "I hate punch cards and flex time. . . . I detest passport control and birth certificates . . . the whole rotten monstrosity of government controls and demands." Blithely sardonic, she is always ready with the clever quip. Of Bertrand Russell's dictum that pure mathematics is "the field in which we don't know what we're talking about or to what extent what we say is true or false," Smilla tells us, "That's the way I feel about cooking."

If **Smilla's Sense of Snow** is an indication of what Peter Hoeg has in store for us, he may yet be offered a provisional chair in the corner of literary heaven reserved for great suspense novelists, permanent residency being denied until he forsakes confusion as a plot device. In the meantime; he has created an irresistible heroine. Despite her professed misanthropy Smilla Jaspersen has far more sympathy for human foibles, and for herself, than she can acknowledge. Being locked up with her turns out to be an unexpected pleasure.

Shaun Whiteside   (review date 7 November 1993)

SOURCE:"Telltale Footprints in the Snow," in *Manchester Guardian Weekly,* Vol. 149, No. 19, November 7, 1993, p. 29.

[*In the following mixed review of* Miss Smilla's Feeling for

Snow, *Whiteside declares preference for the first half of the novel.*]

Famously, the Inuit people have an enormous number of words for different kinds of snow. The snow falling on little Isaiah's coffin, as Peter Hoeg's intriguing thriller [*Miss Smilla's Feeling for Snow*] opens, is *qanik*—"big, almost weightless crystals falling in stacks and covering the ground with a layer of pulverised white frost"—and we have encountered many more by the conclusion. Isaiah, a child from Copenhagen's impoverished Greenlandic community, has been found dead, face down in snow after falling from a high building, leaving footprints on the roof that only those initiated into a snow-based culture might be able to read. Solitary Smilla Jaspersen can read them, and she isn't happy about what they say. Smilla is herself from Greenland and, tellingly, a glaciologist by profession.

Isaiah has for some time been Smilla's only companion, since an unpropitious meeting on their prefab stairs: "Piss off," I say. "Don't you like kids?" "I eat kids." Reading to him from Euclid's *Elements* fails to scare him off ("I could have read aloud from the telephone directory"), and Smilla thereafter spends evenings watching him eat boiled mackerel while his mother drinks herself into a stupor elsewhere. So when Isaiah dies, Smilla begins her own inquiries.

Her desire to see Isaiah avenged keeps her own pronounced suicidal tendencies at bay, and she proves a dourly genial companion as her hunt for clues leads her from the Institute of Eskimology, via a blind professor of Inuit linguistics, into a strange netherworld where Danish shipping-brokers rub shoulders with experts on tropical parasitic worms.

> On the way to the great showdown in the polar margins, we learn much in *Miss Smilla's Feeling for Snow* about the names and nature of ice, but more engaging than this are the glimpses into the lives of the Greenlanders themselves.
>
> —*Shaun Whiteside*

The beguiling build-up is slow, strange, and often very funny, with plenty of quirky detail, and some fairly peculiar sex. Then, about two-thirds of the way through the narrative, the tone seems to change, and the novel loses a level of its humanity.

Smilla finds herself on a mysterious ship bound for the Arctic wastes, peopled by junkies, prostitutes and power-freaks and as the Kronos ploughs its way towards the ice-caps, we find ourselves entering the world of the apocalyptic eco-conspiracy thriller. All the passengers are linked in some way to the death of a Greenlandic child in the Co-

penhagen snow. The ending itself will be either spine-chilling or endearingly loopy, according to temperament.

On the way to the great showdown in the polar margins, we learn much about the names and nature of ice, but more engaging than this are the glimpses into the lives of the Greenlanders themselves.

More of this, and less of the overlong Arctic voyage—more Nanook of the North, less Ice Station Zebra—would have been welcome. But for all that, it's an engaging oddity of a book—ably translated by F David—casting a little light on marginal European lives that most of us would never think about. It would be interesting to meet grumpy Miss Smilla again, perhaps under less earth-shattering circumstances.

Michael Meyer (review date 18 November 1993)

SOURCE: "Danger: Thin Ice," in *The New York Review of Books,* Vol XL, No. 19, November 18, 1993, p. 41.

[*In the following review of* Smilla's Sense of Snow, *Meyer, though praising Høeg's descriptions of Greenland, contends that many of the novel's characterizations are too undifferentiated.*]

Smilla's Sense of Snow, by the young and already much acclaimed Danish novelist Peter Hoeg, is a mystery story with heavy scientific undertones. The chief character and narrator is a half-Eskimo, half-Danish woman of thirty-seven, living in Copenhagen, a semi-voluntary exile haunted by her Greenland heritage and her memories of that strange and magical land. She is single, childless, a moody misfit. Her Eskimo mother, whom she adored, died beneath the Greenland ice, and she does not get on with her father, a distinguished Danish medico. She is on the side of the Greenland Eskimos against the Danes who have colonized them.

A six-year-old Eskimo boy whom she knows falls off a roof and is killed. The police dismiss it as an accident, but Smilla thinks he was pushed. Her investigation takes her into confrontation with various high-up Danes and finally, in disguise, on to a villainously crewed ship bound with a mysterious cargo to Greenland. No shortage of plot here, or of attempts at characterization, though these are sometimes sketchy. It is a long book, 453 pages, and almost entirely written in the present tense. "Verlaine moves—with one hand he fumbles at his back."

By far the best things in the book are the frequent evocations of Greenland, expressed through Smilla's memories and reactions:

> No one who falls into the water in Greenland comes up again. The sea is less than 39° F, and at that temperature all the processes of decomposition stop. That's why fermentation of the stomach contents does not occur here. . . .
>
> But they found the remains of her kayak, which led them to conclude that it must have been a walrus. Walruses are unpredictable. They can be hypersensitive and shy. But if they come a little farther south, and if it's autumn, when there are

few fish, they can be transformed into one of the swiftest and most meticulous killers in the great ocean. With their tusks they can stave in the side of a ship made of ferrocement. I once saw hunters holding a cod up to a walrus that they had captured alive. The walrus puckered up his lips as for a kiss and then sucked the meat right off the bones of the fish.

And:

> The most dangerous kind of avalanches are powder snow avalanches. They're set off by extremely small energy disturbances, such as a loud noise. They have a very small mass, but they move at 125 miles per hour, and they leave behind them a deadly vacuum. There are people who have had their lungs sucked out of their bodies by powder snow avalanches.

Vivid passages such as these illuminate the book, and you long for the next one to turn up because they are so much more interesting than the story or the large cast that enacts it. Smilla herself comes across clearly—dogged, irritating, and foul-mouthed, putting everyone's back up and well able to take care of herself in a tight situation despite her tininess, using whatever is to hand such as a surgeon's scalpel to disable her opponents in a variety of nasty ways. And we have some idea of the boy, little Isaiah, who is murdered before the story begins, and of the stolid artisan who becomes Smilla's lover, known to her simply as "the mechanic," with whom she fornicates rather tediously. But, though useful to her (he turns up unexpectedly on the mystery ship too), he is a dull fellow, and the others are a cardboard collection, especially the wicked crew of the ship, on which the final half of the book takes place. Lukas, Hansen, Jakkelsen, Verlaine, Tork, Seidenfaden, Maurice, Urs, Kutzow—none seems any different from the rest, except that one is a junkie, and after a while it becomes impossible to distinguish between them. The plot becomes increasingly obscure, and even after rereading I am still not quite clear what the point of the expedition was, though it is something to do with a long-buried meteorite and enormous parasites which can quickly destroy the human body. Much scientific information, not always easy for the layperson, is offered:

> The growth patterns of stalactites and descriptions of their formations were outlined by Hatakeyama and Nemoto in *Geophysical Magazine,* no. 28, 1958. By Knight in the *Journal of Crystal Growth,* no. 49, 1980. And by Maeno and Takahashi in their article "Studies on Icicles" in *Low Temperature Science,* vol. A., no. 43, 1984. But the most viable configuration to date was proposed by myself and Lasse Makkonen at the Laboratory of Structural Engineering in Espoo, Finland. It demonstrates that a stalactite grows like a reed, a hollow tube of ice that closes around water in its liquid state. That the mass of the stalactite can be simply expressed as:
>
> $M = \pi D^2/4 \; QaL$
>
> where D is the diameter, L is the length, Qa is the density of the ice and π in the numerator of the fraction is, of course, a result of the fact that

we are calculating based on a hemispheric drop with a diameter set at 4.9 mm.

But of course.

The story is left open-ended, after a welter of violent deaths, and I am not clear whether we are supposed to believe that Smilla herself will survive. The trouble is that we do not much care. If only Mr. Hoeg had written a straightforward and unpretentious evocation, at half the length, of the Greenland which he clearly knows so well and of the Inuit Indians who live there. But such a book might not have been sold to thirteen countries, as the publishers assure us this one has been.

Pearl K. Bell   (essay date Winter 1994)

SOURCE: "Fiction Chronicle," in *Partisan Review,* Vol. LXI, No. 1, Winter, 1994, pp. 80-95.

[*In the following excerpt, Bell offers a mixed assessment of* Smilla's Sense of Snow, *praising the characterization of Smilla but lamenting Høeg's loss of focus towards the end of the novel.*]

There are impenetrable mysteries of a very different kind in **Smilla's Sense of Snow** by the young Danish novelist Peter Hoeg. For one thing it's hard to figure out what genre this dense and tantalizing story belongs to—is it a murder mystery, science fiction, morality tale, or an intricately plotted adventure wrapped in a carapace of technical information, a la Tom Clancy? At first reading, it appears to be a manically complicated thriller narrated by a truculent, ferociously opinionated, erudite, disorganized, strangely beguiling woman of thirty-seven named Smilla Qaavigaaq Jaspersen, her mother an Inuit of Greenland, her father a world-renowned Danish anesthesiologist who fell in love with a beautiful bearskin-clothed Eskimo while doing medical research in Greenland.

Nor is her curious parentage the only oddity in Smilla's history and temperament. She has a degree in glaciology and has published papers in various journals, but Smilla is by nature too rebellious and ornery to hold a permanent job, preferring to use her specialized knowledge about ice and snow on occasional scientific expeditions to Greenland. An indomitable loner and outsider, she feels "the same way about solitude as some people feel about the blessing of the church. It's the light of grace for me." And she runs into trouble whenever some arm of Danish authority tries to force her to conform. Though she is half-Danish and lives in Copenhagen, her deep-rooted loathing for the culture and government and moral climate of Denmark—"humiliating, exhausting, monotonous"—erupts with unmediated bitterness throughout the novel. She gives no quarter, thinks of herself as a colonial through and through, and blames her father for her "loss of cultural identity." And she is as antisocial as a polar bear: "I think more highly of snow and ice than love. It's easier for me to be interested in mathematics than to have affection for my fellow human beings."

When Smilla's six-year-old Eskimo neighbor and friend, Isaiah, plunges to his death from the snow-covered roof of their apartment house in Copenhagen, she refuses to accept the police verdict that his fall was an accident. She knows the child was terrified of heights, and when she examines the tracks on the wintry roof, she is convinced that the boy, running in terror, was pushed. Intrepid as her mother, who was a fearless hunter, Smilla is determined to uncover the truth behind Isaiah's murder, and she soon finds herself in lethally hazardous waters. Probing and snooping, she begins to suspect a vast conspiracy of corruption that is ominously connected with a ship equipped for a mysterious scientific project in Greenland. Undeterred by the danger she is exposing herself to, not in the least from the thuggish crew, Smilla signs on as a stewardess. She will unearth the evil truth no matter how terrible the consequences.

As the ship sails from Copenhagen toward the icy caverns off Greenland, Hoeg's story begins to slip ineluctably out of the more or less rational confines of a thriller into the exploitative fantasies of science fiction, complete with mad scientists hunting for supposedly extinct parasites, long preserved in the glacial eternity (along the lines of *Jurrasic Park*). But Hoeg also struggles to ballast his wild abundance of ingenious imaginings with the sober fruits of his voluminous research, and provides us with a dizzying lode of information about glaciers, different kinds of ice, maritime law, cooking, meteorites and asteroids, and a great deal more. It would all become intolerable, for it is certainly more than most of us would ever want to know, were it not for Hoeg's stylistic virtuosity, his prose by turns seductively lyrical, hallucinatory, uncanny in its descriptive magic.

Unfortunately, as the rich stew of mayhem, madness and fantasy comes to a boil in the final third of the novel, the mettlesome heroine we encountered at the start slowly fades away, even as she is being shot at, bludgeoned with marlinspikes, turning black and blue all over. The arresting intensity, the sardonic eccentricity that made Smilla so appealing is overwhelmed by the violent requirements of a "riveting" sci-fi plot. And the end of the story is so murky and impenetrable, so contrivedly opaque and unfathomable, that we long with poignant regret for the opinionated, uncompromising, straight-talking Smilla who beguiled us from the start with her boldly original fix on the world. But she is nowhere to be found. And we are lost in the glacial silence.

Julian Loose   (review date 12 May 1994)

SOURCE: "Cool," in *London Review of Books,* Vol. 16, No. 9, May 12, 1994, p. 27.

[*In the following review of* Miss Smilla's Feeling for Snow, *Loose finds the work to be more than a murder-mystery thriller, declaring it "a remorseless, unforgettable indictment of (the Danish) colonial history (of Greenland)."*]

Thrillers are routinely deemed 'chilling', as though our feelings of fear and cold are in some way interchangeable. Yet outlandishly low temperatures alone cannot account for the tremendous success of Peter Høeg's *Miss Smilla's Feeling for Snow,* even if it does open with a bleak Copenhagen December, and go on to describe a still colder place—Greenland, covered by an icecap up to a mile

thick, with a climate so severe that if you need to drop your trousers to relieve yourself, you must first light a Primus stove under a blanket to prevent instant frost-bite. *Miss Smilla* differs from other chilly bestsellers like *Ice Station Zebra* not least in its celebration of this apparently cruel setting, its infectious sense of 'snow's mysterious warmth'.

Along the way, in a narrative as unrelenting and fiendishly contrived as a toboggan ride, *Miss Smilla* teaches us many things about snow, ice and Greenland. 'Cold' itself depends, not on temperature, but on wind force and air humidity; the most dangerous avalanches consist of powder snow, for they move at 200 kilometres per hour and leave behind a deadly vacuum; floating ice covers a quarter of the earth's oceans, and Greenlandic glaciers calve icebergs which are 40 metres tall and weigh 50,000 tons, yet can be capsized by the vibrations from a single ship's propeller. Within the Arctic Circle, the weather can work breathtaking transformations:

> One October day the temperature drops 30 degrees in four hours, and the sea grows as motionless as a mirror. It's waiting to reflect a wonder of creation. The clouds and the sea now glide together in a curtain of heavy grey silk. The water grows viscous and tinged with pink, like a liqueur of wild berries. A blue fog of frost smoke detaches itself from the surface of the water and drifts across the mirror. Then the water solidifies. Out of the dark sea the cold now pulls up a rose garden, a white blanket of ice blossoms formed from salt and frozen drops of water. They may last for four hours or two days.

Such lyrical yet precise descriptions are characteristic of Høeg's half-Western, half-Inuit protagonist. To paraphrase Wallace Stevens, Smilla has a mind of winter: or, as it states in her Danish police report, 'anybody needing to know anything about ice will benefit by consulting Smilla Jaspersen.' In fact Smilla thinks more highly of snow and ice than of anything, even love: pure mathematics makes her happy, but only because it supplies the equation for the mass of a stalactite, or makes it possible (via complex number systems) to explain the crystal formation of ice. Walking the frozen wastes around her native Thule from a young age, Smilla has developed an uncanny sense of direction that enables her to find her way in the worst blizzard. This special gift is reinforced by an unusually comprehensive knowledge: a student of glacial morphology, she is equally versed in the Inuit gradations of snow, the difference between *qanik* (big weightless crystals) and *pirhuk* (light snow).

Borrowing the conventional form of a murder mystery, the novel opens with Smilla studying the rooftop snow prints of a six-year-old boy who has fallen to his death. The child, a neighbour, is the one person she has allowed herself to grow close to, and grief sharpens her already considerable powers of attention. Examining his tracks, she finds signs which indicate panic rather than play, and is then struck by the police's nervy insistence on a verdict of accidental death. And so she is set in irreversible motion, 'a foreign body skating on top of the ice'. Her momentum takes her on a dangerous collision path with Denmark's rich and powerful, and ultimately carries her onto a boat full of enemies heading towards the West coast of Greenland, and a conspiracy which stretches back to a geological expedition to the Barren Glacier several decades earlier.

'I'm no heroine,' declares Smilla, even though she's fully aware that her Inuit background gives her a certain edge. She knows the tell-tale way frost will retreat at dawn from a suspiciously-parked car, and when in danger senses just how far she can safely walk out on Copenhagen harbour with its various degrees of 'frazil', 'porridge' and 'pancake' ice. But Høeg has made her too individual, too self-aware, to fit into the formulaic mould of her detective sisters. At one point she needs to act like a V.I. Warshawski and approach a group of workmen, knowing that a bold and enterprising detective 'would go right up to them and salute like a girl scout and talk their lingo and pump them for information'. Smilla despairs of such directness, only to discover that the intimidating group are affable middle-aged men, only too eager to chat. It's entirely typical of this elegantly ruminative thriller that Smilla takes from the encounter not only the required information, but also the observation that 'inside even the most paranoid suspicion the sense of humanity and the desire for contact are waiting to emerge.'

Like all the best fictional detectives, Smilla is a misfit with serious problems of her own. Her unloved Danish father is a wealthy scientist who met her mother, an Inuit Eskimo, during field experiments in Greenland. When her mother failed to return one day from a hunting expedition (a walrus staved in her kayak), the seven-year-old Smilla found herself transported against her will to Denmark. Since then she's been thrown out of every academic institution and organisation she's ever joined, including groups protesting Greenlander rights. Stubbornly independent although largely reliant on her father's money, a confirmed loner heading into middle-age yet inordinately vain about her appearance, Smilla is troubled by despair and thoughts of suicide. She lives in the area of Copenhagen where the marginalised Greenlanders congregate, but suspects she has lost her cultural identity along with her command of Greenlandic. Yet however unsure she is about her own objectives, she's quick to perceive the intentions of others.

Much given to philosophical and political musings, Smilla is engagingly quick to deflate her extensive range of reference: 'Bertrand Russell wrote that pure mathematics is the field in which we don't know what we're talking about or to what extent what we say is true or false. That's the way I feel about cooking.' Wit sustains her as it enlivens the story—she even manages to come off best in an exchange with a window cleaner who has an over-large smile ('as if he were cleaning the windows by putting one pane at a time into his mouth'). A police threat of solitary confinement, an unthinkable predicament for a Greenlander, provokes the comment: 'I feel the same way about my spatial freedom as I've noticed men feel about their testicles.' Increasingly battered and isolated, Smilla keeps quipping: when a mean-looking sailor tries to intimidate her with his knife, she asks him why, if his blade is really as sharp as a razor and more pointed than a nail file, he's so unshaven and has such filthy hands. Such brave responses are the very stuff of the detective genre, of course. As the form extends its range to include other voices, it is interesting to see how the recklessly rude rejoinders of a Philip Marlowe are perpetuated and modified. In Smilla's case, her wisecracks signal an obstreperous refusal to disguise her hybrid, outsider status, and draw everyone's attention to the uncomfortable fact that this is 'only a matter of a shitty Greenlander'.

What lifts *Miss Smilla* above the ordinary is Høeg's sense of how mixed motives have grotesquely deformed the unequal relationship of Denmark and Greenland.

—Julian Loose

Høeg is clearly aware of the numerous writers who have adopted the detective mystery form to demonstrate the death of all master-narratives. Like Calvino's *If on a winter's night a traveller* or Eco's *The Name of the Rose,* his novel manages to head remorselessly towards a climax, while assuring us at the same time that there is no such thing as a conclusion. The philosophically-inclined Smilla is certainly wise to all the meta-fictional questions: 'Who am I? Am I the scientist, the observer? Am I the one who has been given the chance to get a glimpse of life from the outside? From a point of view made up of equal parts of loneliness and objectivity? Or am I only pathetic?' But Høeg's ambition extends beyond the literary: he wants to make us see that motives are always complex, that we are all implicated in the desire to understand and coerce the Other. Although Smilla's need to know the truth is a personal imperative, it is not dissimilar to the very conspiracy she is uncovering, or indeed the scientific urge that made exploitation of Greenland possible: 'Deep inside I know that trying to fathom things out leads to blindness, that the desire to understand has a built-in brutality that erases what you seek to comprehend.'

What lifts *Miss Smilla* above the ordinary is Høeg's sense of how mixed motives have grotesquely deformed the unequal relationship of Denmark and Greenland. The uncompromising title of one of Smilla's articles—'Ice Research and the Profit Motive in Denmark in Connection with the Exploitation of Oil Resources in the Arctic Ocean'—says it all (and not surprisingly has resulted in her ejection from the Danish Glaciology Society). Høeg reminds us that Denmark 'incorporated' Greenland as a province in 1953, abandoning its blatant exploitation in the Sixties only to pursue the more subtle approach of educating the 'Northern Danes' (the Inuit) in their 'equal rights'. This teaching took place solely in Danish, and entailed the centralisation of employment in fish factories, depriving many Inuit of their livelihoods, and more of their independence and self-respect. By the end of the Seventies, the suicide rate in Greenland had become the highest in the world, and the homicide rate was comparable to that in a war zone.

Miss Smilla is a remorseless, unforgettable indictment of this colonial history. In this way Høeg expands his chosen form almost beyond recognition, and it seems only appropriate to learn that there is no word for 'thriller' in Danish. Yet Høeg is nothing if not sophisticated, and his deep sense of grievance at the degradation and decline of Greenland informs rather than distorts his perspectives. The annual salary for a Dane is five times that of an Arctic Eskimo, and so to Smilla the entire population of Denmark seems irredeemably middle-class. She goes to a Copenhagen café where elegant ladies drink cocoa and eat *Sachertorte,* and finds there the quintessence of Western civilisation—'the union of exquisitely sophisticated crowning achievements and a nervous senselessly extravagant consumption'. But even that truth is double-edged: Smilla later acknowledges the irony that Danish colonisation has helped Greenland, for in this desperately unforgiving environment there's no longer any starvation, and basic material needs are met. Recognising Denmark's strengths, its integrity and enterprise, Høeg merely discloses the dirty little secret that it is as susceptible as anywhere to the glacial pull of power and money. Høeg, like the Eskimos he describes, 'can live with the tension between irreconcilable contradictions, without sinking into despair and without looking for a simplified solution.'

Richard Eder (review date 6 November 1994)

SOURCE: "Time Never Stops," in *The Los Angeles Times Book Review,* November 6, 1994, p. 3, 11.

[*In the following review of* Borderliners, *Eder describes the novel as "more a philosophic allegory than a story" in which the most evil force is time itself.*]

Ostensibly, the villain of Peter Hoeg's novel about the rebellion of three tormented children at a progressive Danish boarding school is the tyrannically self-righteous headmaster. *Borderliners,* though, is more a philosophic allegory than a story; and its real villain is linear time—time, that is, as an inflexible progress that the powerful misuse to constrain the circular talents and zigzag impulses of human nature.

Hoeg's second book to be translated into English makes an austere contrast to his *Smilla's Sense of Snow,* a novel of suspense about a turbulent Greenland woman who investigates the death of a child and comes up against a vast political-economic-scientific conspiracy. *Smilla* offered a churning narrative excitement, and a vivid and affecting protagonist. In the dryer *Borderliners,* the characters are drawn finely but much more abstractly. At bottom, both are novels of moral and social argument but in *Borderliners* the bottom eddies right up to the top.

Hoeg's pervasive theme in both books is the abuse of children by the means that civilization—especially, perhaps, an enlightened Scandinavian civilization—has used to advance itself. More generally, his children stand for humanity's instinctive and unspoiled possibilities; by making

them the victims, Hoeg is able to distill the passionate rage that gives energy to his writing.

What gives distinctiveness to the rage is the supercooled bleakness with which it is conveyed; the unmodulated grays, the darkness without a penumbra, the light without warmth and the distances that separate the characters even when they are embracing—or brutalizing—each other. Peter, the 14-year-old narrator-protagonist, and the 16-year-old Katarina share a bench and a kiss in the school shed they've managed to escape to; it is a blinding consummation, but more celestial than material. Biehl, the headmaster, shamefully slaps students who break the rules of his Utopian establishment; the pain is not in the blow but in the seconds preceding and following it. It is in the abasement.

Biehl's school is set up, in cooperation with the state authorities, as a model educational experiment, "a workshop of the sun," as he lyrically puts it. With 26 teachers and 200 students, the pedagogical attention is overwhelming; big brothers and sisters continually watch everyone. It is entirely dedicated to the notion of progress; specifically, measurable scientific progress. It is a temple to linear time—year by year not only do the students learn more but they are also advanced to higher floors in the school building—and it is ruled by the bell that signals where everyone is to be, and when.

Laboratory conditions, isolation from the sloppiness of the outside world, and a sterile totalitarianism. Discipline is by restrictions and verbal suasion, in principle, but Biehl has not been able to exclude the germs of human weakness; not even his own. He slaps occasionally, once in a while he hits, and once or twice he has beaten. He keeps a coded record, a secret confessional.

Part of the rigor is justified by a utopian aim: the eventual integration of all students, from the gifted and cooperative to those who have been placed in centers for the disturbed and the delinquent. As a preliminary experiment, three such children are introduced; and they are the three who serve as the novel's protagonists and the vehicles of Hoeg's passionate anti-utopian thesis. Peter is an orphan who has shuttled between reform schools of greater and lesser rigor. Katarina comes from a more privileged class, but her mother has died of cancer and her father, unable to cope, has hanged himself. And finally, an extreme case has been admitted: August, a violently abused child who has killed both his parents.

> ***Borderliners* is more a philosophic allegory than a story; and its real villain is linear time—time, that is, as an inflexible progress that the powerful misuse to constrain the circular talents and zigzag impulses of human nature.**
>
> *—Richard Eder*

Peter tries to conform; to be expelled would be to perish. Katarina questions, and her questioning soon enlists him in a compact to explore and try to understand the system that oppresses them. To test out the constraints, Katarina makes herself deliberately unpunctual. Peter steals school records. Their hesitant experiments take on urgency when August is put under Peter's care. The child's violence—at one point he breaks Peter's finger—and his agony—he sneaks out to the chemistry lab at night to inhale gas so he can sleep—are one single denunciation. Peter and Katarina would escape, but they cannot abandon August: their burning resolve, forged against the institution's chilly experiments, is that a child must never be abandoned.

They rebel, instead, in an act of sabotage that involves a complex disruption of the inviolate schedule—at one point Peter switches the mechanism that regulates the bells—and that ends in tragic disaster. Peter will survive; August won't; Katarina's fate is uncertain. Eventually Peter will get himself adopted by a nurturing family, will grow up, get married and have a child. Human love saves him where social and scientific notions of progress have all but destroyed him.

Borderliners moves back and forth between a part-magical story of childhood rebellion—there are suggestions of such classics as Alain-Fournier's *The Wanderer* and Cocteau's *Les Enfants Terribles*—and a wide-ranging series of speculations by Peter, now an adult and speaking retrospectively. The former is suggestive but often schematic. Neither Peter nor Katarina is particularly distinct as a character—August, the child psychotic, is much more affecting—and Biehl and the teachers are little more than sketches of different kinds of baleful authority.

The speculative asides are awkwardly integrated. They parallel the story and certainly explicate it, but they rarely manage to haunt or enhance it. They have their own strength, however. Though some passages drag on wordily and though Hoeg has a tendency to hammer repetitively at points he has already made, his ideas are, in fact, at the heart of the book, and some have an alluring edge.

There is his discussion of linear versus circular time, for example. If the former is essential to a great part of our practical and intellectual life, he quarrels with what he considers its abuse. He associates such abuse with mathematical and scientific notions of progress; what he objects to is their spread to other fields; notably those of social science and education.

Sometimes the argument is dry; nor does it, in itself, have notable originality. Sometimes, though, an image will transfigure it. Take spider webs. Rarely, Hoeg writes, are they more than two feet across. A spider could not handle more information than a two-foot web brings in. It would destroy its nature. Too much information, too much perfecting, can destroy human nature as well, he argues. Again, it is not the argument that particularly stands up. But Hoeg on spider webs and the dew that hangs on them between two trees on an early morning manages to enhance the notion of limits, and how necessary they are to humanity, in ways beyond argument. He does for spider webs and us what he uncannily did for snow and us in *Smilla.*

David Sacks   (review date 20 November 1994)

SOURCE: "Last Chance, and a Nasty One," in *The New York Times Book Review,* November 20, 1994, p. 31.

[*Sacks is an American educator and critic. In the following review of* Borderliners, *he praises Høeg's descriptive details but notes problems with the novel's plot and philosophical underpinnings.*]

At an elite but monstrously repressive prep school outside Copenhagen, circa 1971, the human spirit is affirmed by three teen-agers, a girl and two boys, who band together subversively. All three are orphans, wards of the state, admitted to the school as part of a national scholarship program for the underprivileged. All three are "borderliners," with social or academic problems. If they can graduate, they will move up to university and the hope of a happy future in Denmark's tightly ordered society. If they break the rules or flunk out, they descend to reform school and the abyss. They have one chance left to build a normal life: "Biehl's Academy was that chance."

How that chance is defiantly thrown away by the three is the moving story of *Borderliners,* the second novel to be published in English by the 37-year-old Danish author Peter Hoeg. Mr. Hoeg soared to prominence here a little over a year ago with an earlier novel, *Smilla's Sense of Snow,* a delightfully fresh detective thriller set in Copenhagen and Greenland. The book spent 11 weeks on the *New York Times* best-seller list, its popularity due in part to its unique yet believable protagonist—the diminutive, female, authority-hating, half-Greenlander, half-Danish, Arctic survival expert, Smilla.

Like *Smilla, Borderliners* deals with social outsiders who deliberately confront an authoritarian evil, but *Borderliners* occupies a smaller canvas. The tale seems autobiographical: its narrator is 14-year-old Peter (who will later, we learn, be adopted by a family named Hoeg). Beaten down by his brutal orphanage childhood, Peter wrestles with inner demons of anxiety and despair that the "absolutely normal pupils" around him can hardly guess at.

In his third year at Biehl's, Peter finds himself drawn to the brilliant, self-destructive older teen-ager, Katarina. Equally, Peter feels compelled to protect a strange new student named August. August wants to succeed but is clearly psychotic; for instance, he tends to break the fingers of anyone trying to touch him.

Why has the school accepted the grotesquely unsuited August? ("He is chaos," Katarina muses in her oracular way. "If their plan is order, why have they taken him?") And how does August's arrival relate to wider changes at the school, such as intensified security and psychological testing, evidently paid for by the Government? To uncover the answers, Peter and Katarina embark on a furtive investigation. Meanwhile a web of surveillance closes around them.

Unfortunately, despite some wonderful details *Border-*

liners suffers from a disjointed, repetitive plot that bogs down under its own philosophical baggage. The author avoids simple storytelling, preferring instead to explore the nature of time. "What is time?" are the book's opening words, and later Mr. Hoeg actually provides brief historical passages on the development of theories of time. In a related device, the novel employs a dreamy, associative narrative, moving back and forth through the years, including flash-forwards to the adult Peter's family life. Early in this process, however, the tale of young Peter loses its urgency for the reader.

The novel does explain well why the borderliners at Biehl's should feel at odds with elitist, linear notions of time. Time might seem destructive or at best cyclical to children who are deprived. But the school—steeped in a "covert Darwinism" that apparently embraces Nazi eugenics as well as Christian piety—views time as a purely progressive force, for improvement, refinement and selection. This belief not only goes to justify the fear and conformity imposed by the school, it also opens onto a demented, messianic view of education. "We wanted to help," the headmaster explains pitifully, after disaster has struck. "We wanted to carry the rest of you along with us."

Borderliners is written from the heart, and its portrait of the embittered survivor Peter is moving. But the eccentric storytelling may disappoint Mr. Hoeg's fans, of whom I am surely one. In this work, the talented novelist seems mainly intent on exorcising certain devils of his past.

Laura Shapiro   (review date 28 November 1994)

SOURCE: "A Gripping Tale out of School," in *Newsweek,* Vol. CXXIV, No. 22, November 28, 1994, p. 68.

[*In the following review of* Borderliners, *Shapiro, though noting the "choking" effect of the narrative voice, offers a positive assessment of Høeg's book.*]

Peter Hoeg has been a popular novelist in his native Denmark for years, but hardly anybody in this country had heard of him until *Smilla's Sense of Snow* appeared here last year. What a calling card! A brainy, witty thriller, *Smilla* caused a sensation; when Hoeg mentioned in interviews that he had finished another novel, his new fans were delighted. "It's very different," he said at the time.

Borderliners is very different—a denser more introspective novel than *Smilla,* with fewer of its easy pleasures. It's set in Biehl's Academy, a boarding school known for its high standards and willingness to take difficult children—like Peter, the narrator. An orphan who has experienced the brutality of Denmark's child-welfare system, he meets still more physical and psychological repression at Biehl's. With his friends Katarina, a strong survivor of childhood horrors, and August, much frailer, Peter sets out to uncover the secret experiment he senses going on behind the school's grim functioning.

Writing in Peter's cool, clipped narrative voice, which remains uninflected whether he is describing his yearning for a family or his escape from a molesting teacher, Hoeg

keeps such tight control of these hefty issues that the novel sometimes feels choked. Yet the well-crafted suspense, the emotions that strike unexpectedly and the intimate portrayal of Peter himself make this a forceful tale. The ending is especially charged. According to the publisher, *Bordeliners* is not autobiographical, but Hoeg appears to have a powerful personal stake in these ideas and events. Just as with *Smilla,* one question hangs in the air when the last page is turned: when do we get his next book?

Michiko Kakutani   (review date 29 November 1994)

SOURCE: "From a Sense of Snow to a Tussle with Time," in *The New York Times,* November 29, 1994, p. C19.

[*Kakutani is a regular reviewer for* The New York Times. *In the following review of* Borderliners, *she assesses the novel as "a willfully elliptical narrative that often tries the reader's patience."*]

Like Peter Hoeg's last novel, the best-selling *Smilla's Sense of Snow, Borderliners* is one of those books that functions on two levels. *Smilla* was both a thriller and a philosophical meditation on the human condition; *Borderliners* is both a harrowing tale of an orphan's ordeals within the Danish child-care system and a philosophical meditation on the nature of time.

The biggest difference between the two novels—and it is a huge one—has to do with language and tone. Whereas *Smilla* boasted a marvelously eccentric narrator, who related her story in wry, impatient prose, *Borderliners* features an evasive and depressed narrator, who cloaks his anxiety in windy, metaphysical asides. The result? *Borderliners* is a willfully elliptical narrative that often tries the reader's patience.

As a reader gradually discovers, *Borderliners* is narrated by a man named Peter, who not only shares the author's first name but also says he was adopted by a family named Hoeg when he was 15. The story Peter relates takes place in the 1960's and early 70's, in the years before his adoption.

The fictional Peter tells us that he spent his early years at a series of institutions for orphans: first a home for infants, then a children's home, a reform school and a school for troubled but academically gifted children. The last was known as Crusty House, Peter says, because of the crusts the students "had to make do with instead of proper bread." After he is nearly raped by a teacher there, Peter is transferred, under a special program, to an elite private school, Biehl's Academy.

The portrait Peter draws of Biehl's makes the school seem like a miniature police state: children are monitored day and night by a strict and unforgiving staff, and transgressions are punished with reprimands, blows and beatings. Peter soon begins to suspect that there is a secret "plan" behind the school's strict regimen, a plan he determines to expose.

In the course of his troubled tenure at Biehl's, Peter manages to make two friends he will treasure for the rest of his life: Katarina, a beautiful girl with whom he promptly falls in love, and August, a psychotic boy whom he adopts as a kind of son. In retrospect, Peter observes, his love for Katarina and August has taught him the meaning of family and responsibility; it has given him hope and the will to live.

With the help of Katarina and August, Peter begins to conduct an investigation of the school. He suggests, in portentous asides to the reader, that some sort of Darwinian experiment is being conducted with the students. As evidence, he cites some disturbing incidents: a student's attempt to cut off his own tongue, the administration of sedatives to August, the concealment of student records.

Although Mr. Hoeg is intermittently able to use such incidents to orchestrate a sense of narrative tension, one later learns that many of them are little more than deliberately placed red herrings, a realization that leaves the reader with a vague sense of dissatisfaction.

To make matters worse, Peter embroiders his story with stilted and pretentious musings about the nature of time. "What is time?" he asks near the beginning of the novel. "I shall have to try to say, but not yet. It is too overwhelming for that. You have to begin more simply. What does it mean—to measure time? What is a timepiece?" And later: "To sense time, to speak about time, you have to sense that something has changed. And you have to sense that within or behind this change there is also something that was present before. The perception of time is the inexplicable union in the consciousness of change and constancy."

These highly abstract soliloquies are apparently meant to add resonance to Peter's story, and to underscore one of the novel's central themes concerning the dehumanizing effects of science and the scientific method. Unfortunately they have another effect entirely: they weigh the story down, turning what might have been a deeply affecting story about a young boy's painful coming of age into a lugubrious and strangely impersonal allegory.

Sarah A. Smith   (review date 6 January 1995)

SOURCE: "Clock and Watch," in *New Statesman and Society,* Vol. 7, No. 334, January 6, 1995, p. 37.

[*In the following review of* Borderliners, *Smith positively assesses the novel and finds that Høeg "writes with a sense of ambiguity that seems appropriate to the voice of the disturbed."*]

Borderliners is Peter Høeg's second novel to appear in English translation. Written with extraordinary intellectual and creative energy, it explores the plight of three children caught within a rigorous and idealistic education system. Although not as accessible as *Miss Smilla's Feeling for Snow,* the sense that Høeg's writing is so passionately felt makes this a compelling and curiously moving work.

The "borderliners" of the title are society's "unaccountable children"—emotionally deprived orphans, abused and abusive infants, some with mental handicaps. At Biehl's Academy in 1971 they are the subject of an experiment to integrate abnormal children into a normal school

(and society), with the hoped-for consequence of a drop in the crime rate and even, the narrator Peter posits, respect for scholarly virtues and world peace.

The school is run with military precision and police-state tactics. Time is the instrument of control. In this colossal plan, even God, associated by the pupils with Biehl, seems to be implicated.

Into this Orwellian world come three orphans of varying hope: Peter, Katarina, and tiny, terrifying August. Their quest is to discover the "plot" they sense behind the school and in so doing to disrupt and destroy it. Høeg's oblique narrative follows their fight with the school and their own experiment to "touch time", which is effected quite simply when they stop the school clock. Moving backwards and forwards through time, he details Peter's final escape and shows us the narrator writing up his researches into the school.

Høeg employs the strategy of the thriller, wrestling the reader into a narrative and psychological grip. Long before he reveals the horror of August's background, we sicken with suspense at the thought of what it might be. He writes with a sense of ambiguity that seems appropriate to the voice of the disturbed, so that for much of the first part the reader is vaguely troubled. What is happening and can this narrator be trusted? Added to this is Høeg's focus on the child. Children can be a powerfully emotive force in literature, and in *Borderliners* the violent, damaged child is almost heart-rendingly so. The quasi-religious imagery that Peter takes from the educationalists—of bringing children from the dark into the light—enforces this sense of tragedy.

In Barbara Haveland's translation Høeg's writing is careful, controlled, and delicately wrought. He records Peter's experiences with wry, black humour and unsettling irony: recalling only the torture practised at one particular children's home, he apologises "One ought to have remembered more. But that was the only thing that had stuck." Høeg's skill only slips in his ponderous meditation on Time in the third section of the book.

His passion sparkles through the translation. One senses that, although *Borderliners* is about a special school and special children, it is also an indictment of all schools as children experience them. The sense of being watched but never listened to, of the need to occupy every minute, of the impossibility of grasping the theory behind certain practices, is familiar to any pupil anywhere.

Borderliners has already had some success in Denmark. Britain's current alarm at rising child crime and childhood mental illness may give Høeg's quietly devastating tale some potency here too.

Nora Underwood   (review date 20 February 1995)

SOURCE: "Prisoners of Time," in *Maclean's,* Vol. 108, No. 8, February 20, 1995, pp. 66-7.

[*In the following review of* Borderliners, *Underwood praises Høeg's storyline but finds his discourse regarding the nature of time an encumbrance to the narrative.*]

When Peter Hoeg's novel *Smilla's Sense of Snow* was released in 1993, it caused a sensation, garnering rave reviews and residing on best-seller lists for months. It deserved the acclaim. The third novel by Danish author Peter Hoeg—and the first to be translated into English—*Smilla* was a gripping thriller that took its intellectual, emotionally cool heroine on a mysterious journey from the wind and snow of Copenhagen to the glaciers off Greenland in search of answers to a six-year-old boy's death. In Hoeg's latest novel, *Borderliners,* the setting is once again Copenhagen. But while snow was the motif that ran through *Smilla,* the new book is permeated with—and at times bogged down by—an inquiry into the nature of time.

The story begins in the early 1970s when the narrator, a young teenager named Peter, is in his 10th institution. Abandoned in infancy, Peter has been shunted from children's homes and reform school to the Royal Orphanage, better known to its students as Crusty House "because of the crusts they had to make do with instead of proper bread." After a teacher tries to rape Peter in a telephone booth, the boy is unaccountably transferred to Biehl's Academy, an elite private school attended mostly by bright children from well-to-do families, but also by a few "borderliners"—marginal cases like Peter. He is so malnourished when he arrives that during his first year at Biehl's he gains 37½ pounds and grows 10 inches.

Inside the oppressive academy, order rules. Teachers monitor the children's every move, and punishment for such crimes as not keeping perfectly still during assembly often takes the form of beatings. Doors between floors are kept locked; children may not even go to the bathroom unaccompanied. During one class, a teacher asks a student to fetch something from a locker. In the locker is the teacher's son, who has tried to cut out his tongue with a razor blade. When the pupil discovers this, she returns to her seat and vomits. "She did it all over the desk, where others might have tried to reach the sink or wastepaper basket," writes Hoeg. "But she never got up without permission."

Into Peter's bleak existence come two other borderliners who inspire his first real feelings of tenderness. One is August, a sickly psychotic boy who has murdered his abusive parents and in whom Peter takes an almost fatherly interest. At one point, when August cannot get to sleep, he slips down to the school kitchen and inhales gas from the stove. Peter, who has followed him, carries the woozy boy back upstairs and puts him safely to bed. Grappling with the horror of what he has just witnessed, Peter tries to justify it. "Unaccountable pain overwhelms," he says. "So one tries to explain it away by means of time. One had to say to oneself that it was because it was hard for him to fall asleep. That in itself was not disturbing; it was just a difficult time of the day for him. Time was the problem, one said to oneself."

Peter's other soul mate is the recently orphaned Katarina. In rare stolen moments alone, they tell each other the stories of their lives. Together, the two come to realize that the borderliners are part of some kind of school experiment involving time—one that ultimately has tragic consequences. "We were held down as tightly as anyone can

be held down by a clock," says Peter, alluding to the institution's extremely rigid schedule. "So hard, in fact, that if your shell was not very thick, then you fell completely or partially to pieces."

Hoeg moves his story back and forth between the narrator's adolescence and the present as Peter, now a husband and father in his late 30s, tries to make sense of it all. The early period ends when Peter, at 15, is adopted by a family named Hoeg, which suggests that the novel is at least partly autobiographical (something which the book's publisher denies). In both the early and presentday passages of the book, the young and the adult Peter are continually ruminating about the nature of time and timepieces. Time, says the older Peter in retrospect, "was at the root of everything. It screwed life down. Like some kind of tool."

As with *Smilla's Sense of Snow,* Hoeg has written *Borderliners* in such a way that the reader feels rivetted to the story yet removed from its horrors. The narrators of both books, like many abused or traumatized people, have adopted an attitude of detachment in order to protect themselves. For different reasons, both books are demanding to read, but the new novel delivers fewer rewards for the effort. Hoeg has obviously devoted himself to the subject of time: the adult Peter muses confidently about the theories of Albert Einstein, Isaac Newton, St. Augustine and Stephen Hawking, among others. But no matter how interesting they may be, the narrator's ramblings often slow down the story, detracting from what is otherwise a chilling tale of an unfortunate boy's trip through adolescence.

Nader Mousavizadeh (review date 3 April 1995)

SOURCE: "Strangers in Paradise," in *The New Republic,* Vol. 212, No. 4185, April 3, 1995, pp. 39-41.

[*In the following review of* Borderliners, *Mousavizadeh discusses the figure of the outsider in Høeg's works.*]

"With the knife of light they would scrape the darkness clean," observes the young narrator of *Borderliners,* who languishes in the private boarding school that is the setting for Peter Høeg's new novel. Barely a teenager, barely sane, he speaks of the zealotry of his superiors, of the cruelty of best intentions, with the weariness of an old man. Høeg's novel is the story of three children whose shattered lives merge at the center of an educational experiment that seeks to socialize the abandoned and the most alone—the story of the real consequences of an unimpeachably enlightened social policy. But the cause of these children is a lost cause. They want no part of a community that wants no part of them; and their unwillingness to abide by rules whose rewards they have never known sets the stage for a reckoning of quiet magnitude—between the child and the adult, between the unique and the uniform, between doubt and certainty.

The author of *Borderliners* is, of course, also the author of *Smilla's Sense of Snow. Smilla,* Høeg's third book, was his first to be translated into English, and introduced him as a brilliant and intriguing writer of thrillers. And so to his English readers, *Borderliners* appears as a departure, though in fact it was *Smilla* that was the detour for Høeg. His stories have generally relied for their power not on suspense, but on a more traditional and demanding standpoint for fiction: the standpoint of the stranger and the outsider. Høeg is a contemporary master of the outsider's perspective.

Høeg arrived on the Danish literary scene in 1988 with *Forestilling om det Tyvende Århundrede* [*A History of Danish Dreams*], or *A Vision of the Twentieth Century,* which introduced a deeply original voice. With his second book *Fortællinger om Natten,* or *Night Stories,* he made clear that the raw originality of his first novel was in no way incompatible with writing of a more subtle and literary kind. Høeg has brought to modern Danish literature an intensity, a worldliness, a love of language and a depth of learning that entirely on their own have raised the standards for contemporary writing in Denmark (and throughout Scandinavia). In a country and a culture whose guiding principle, for good and for bad, is the common denominator, and whose celebration of the mediocre is almost religious, Høeg's voice has been a welcome disturbance. Throughout his career he has sought to alert his readers to the perils of complacency and rectitude, and to the rewards of a world view that embraces nuance and prizes doubt. And those lessons are best learned, he avers, from the lives of those who do not belong.

[*A History of Danish Dreams*] and [*Fortællinger om Natten*] . . . comprise the beginnings of a fractured literary evolution. Høeg's first book is perhaps best described as one long premonition, "a history," as he writes, "of the Danish dreams, an account of what we have feared and dreamt and hoped and expected of the twentieth century." Høeg recounts the last 450 years of Danish history through the lives of a dozen ordinary and extraordinary people. None of them is conventional, and yet they each embody or illustrate a salient aspect of the Danish experience—gradualism, peaceful accommodation, civic prosperity, the struggle for difference and distinction in a crushingly conformist culture.

It was not until Høeg published [*Fortællinger om natten*], though, that it became apparent that the elan of his first book could be harnessed to a greater purpose. These stories are, in many ways, the finest moments of Høeg's writing. Their subject is, quite simply, "love and its conditions on the night of March 19, 1929." Høeg, of course, did not choose an arbitrary date for these stories. He chose the moment in the history of Denmark, and of Europe, when the descent into barbarism was still avoidable, when it could be imagined that Europe's past needn't be Europe's future. Still, Høeg manages to probe the period's resonances without letting its heavy symbolism overwhelm what remain, at heart, love stories. The love in these stories comes in many ages and kinds: between a city and its children, between a young avant garde artist and his provincial lover, between a physicist and her science, between two young dancers at the Royal Ballet in Copenhagen.

These "night stories" are all inquiries into the fate of love as a hostage to convention; and, as in [*A History of Danish Dreams*], their power derives from the way they unveil a crucial pillar of Danish culture or society: the fanaticism

of the Royal Ballet, the worship of science and the protective instincts of the state, the adulation of convention and the ennui of a life of manners. Høeg illuminates the political and the cultural through the prism of small, intimate lives of no apparent consequence, simultaneously elevating and denigrating, mocking the grand and dignifying the petty. Little is left as it seemed.

In Høeg's first two books, so different in style and subject, a central figure did begin to emerge: the figure of the outsider. In [*A History of Danish Dreams*], Danish history is portrayed more often than not through the eyes of the gypsy, the artist, the circus clown. In [*Fortællinger om natten*], Høeg tells more conventional tales, but their conventionality is often set in relief or foiled by the presence of a foreigner, a dissident, or, as in the story **"Hommage à Bournonville,"** a club-footed boy. "I have learned something," says the narrator Jacob:

> "I have learned that it can be necessary to stand outside to see clearly. . . . I've also learned something else. . . . I've stopped feeling regret, I have seen the theater and the girl and Andreas without anger, as if I had been able to experience it all through the eyes of another human being, as if it were still possible to be inside."
>
> "Whose eyes," asked Rumi.
>
> "The clubfoot's," answered Jacob, "and at that moment I forgive them all."

The idea of gaining wisdom through pain, and knowledge through alienation, is hardly a new idea; but Høeg complicates it subtly by implying the tension between the emotional need for inclusion and the truth that is wrested from the absence of such acceptance. We may prefer the ignorance of approval to the wisdom of solitude, Høeg seems to be saying, but we do so at a cost to ourselves and to our world.

Nowhere has Høeg developed this theme more compellingly than in *Smilla's Sense of Snow*. In Smilla, a woman of part Danish, part Inuit descent, he has created a character of singular spirit and poise. With remarkable alacrity, she draws the reader in as an accomplice in her search for a young boy's killers and, ultimately, for a measure of restitution for an Inuit culture that has been direly wounded by Danish colonial rule. We follow Smilla from her first suspicions of deception through her confrontation with the Danish medical and scientific elite, as well as with more personal demons in the characters of her father and her lover. And all along we listen and argue and guide her in our minds, imagining that our indignation at the cruelties that she meets may prove her indignation stronger, more true, perhaps even heroic.

Høeg's great achievement in the creation of this character is that Smilla's struggles are never resolved clearly or complacently. We are left with an unsettling sense of the ineliminable unknown, with a confirmation of the fear that there are questions for which there are no answers and loves for which there are always conditions. As Smilla says at the end of the journey that has left her at the very edge of the arctic glacier, "Tell us, they'll say to me. So we will understand and be able to resolve things. They'll be mistaken. It's only the things you don't understand that you can resolve. There will be no resolution." And no forgiveness, Høeg seems to suggest, no reconciliation between the Inuit and the Dane, between the woman and the men, between Smilla and her demons.

There is in **Borderliners,** as well as in **Smilla's Sense of Snow,** an echo of Conrad's thought that we "live as we dream—alone." If Smilla's loneliness was that of an outsider breaking in, the loneliness of the children in Høeg's new book is that of outsiders on the inside breaking out. These children all seek to break out of the conformity and the social control of an all too well-meaning educational system. Their early lives have been shattered by the loss of their parents and their violent passage through orphanages, reform schools and asylums. Each of them has been abandoned, first by family and later by the state, and by the time they meet, they are bound to nothing but their own damaged souls. They are brought together at Biehl's Academy, a private boarding school whose headmaster, Biehl, acts with the fervor of a missionary among bewildered, malleable converts.

Peter, Katarina and August have been brought into Biehl's orbit as part of an experiment to socialize the wayward by means of strict control and unrelenting discipline. The novel begins as the children are trying their best to adapt to the rules of yet another institution. Soon, though, they begin to fall through those cracks whose existence Biehl's life is dedicated to fill. His is a Manichean world of good and evil, of light and darkness. He is a disciple of N.F.S. Grundtvig, the nineteenth-century Danish writer and philosopher of Christian hope, for whom education was a sacred blessing to be visited on every man, woman and child, and for whom the journey from the darkness of superstition to the light of Christian faith and Enlightenment reason was one of divine ordination. Biehl, too, sees no nuances, no byways in the path from ignorance to enlightenment.

Peter, the narrator of the novel, at first finds a haven at Biehl's. But his sense of security is abruptly cut off when he discovers that here, too, he is viewed merely as a guinea-pig in a greater "plan." He soon finds an ally in the older Katarina, a fellow doubter, and together they begin to challenge the assumptions of a system whose intolerance of borderliners is matched only, in Høeg's metaphor, by the inflexibility of time itself. The dictatorship of the clock becomes a greater, even less forgiving expression of the cruel discipline to which these children are subjected.

Peter has arrived at the school after a series of harrowing experiences at other institutions, where he suffered beatings and near-rapes by male teachers. What he brings with him—all he brings with him—is a conviction that it is the rule of time, and the controls it imposes on the most intimate aspects of childhood, that is the source of all other evil in his little world. In a stunning image of time suspended, Peter describes to Katarina how he and a friend would swing from a tree overlooking a set of railroad tracks, and time it precisely so that they barely passed the engineer's window before the train swept by. In that moment, when meeting the engineer's shell-shocked eyes, they made time stand still, "touched it" as Katarina later

says. Ordinary time, a "barbed wire," is simply too painful—too slow for the days and weeks of horror, too fast for the fleeting moments of lightness and tranquility:

> I know I cannot bring anyone to understand this. How our lives back then were totally saturated by time. . . . I believe we were as far out as anyone can go with time. We were held down as tightly as anyone can be held down by a clock. So hard, in fact, that if your shell was not very thick, then you fell completely or partially to pieces. I have felt that time ran in our veins like blood.

To this tortured bildungsroman, Høeg cannot resist adding the vulnerable figure of an abandoned boy, as he did with Smilla's young friend Isaiah, whose murder sparks her search for restitution, and with the club-footed boy in **"Hommage à Bournonville."** Here the boy is August, a 9-year-old whose primal act of sin was to murder his parents with a shotgun blast from the cupboard drawer in which they kept him. An autistic, psychotic child, he is, as Katarina realizes, chaos itself in Biehl's world of Grundtvigian lucidity. The search for the school's purpose with August leads the three children through a maze of deceptions—both educational and personal—to a violent denouement whose resolution is as empty as it is tragic.

This senselessness is nowhere more apparent than when the children capture Biehl and he pleads with them not for his life but for his cause:

> "We wanted to help," he said. "Not just the children of the light. We wanted to carry the rest of you along with us. From the halls of the dead to the land of the living." . . .

> "What about the darkness inside people," said Katarina.

> "The light will disperse it," said Biehl.

> August brought his face right down to Biehl's ear. They looked like two people exchanging confidences.

> "There's not that much light in the whole world," he whispered.

August's nihilism, premature as it may seem, is not ironic or intellectual; it is the lived nihilism of one for whom there never really was any hope. His hopelessness is authentic. It is, in fact, not nihilism at all, but a kind of bleak realism, in its insistence that there is a darkness which cannot be banished, a place in which no light, no human effort can survive; and this is the realism that has been central to much of Scandinavian art, from Strindberg to Munch and even to Bergman. Høeg is writing in, and brilliantly extending, a tradition. His novel is a coming-of-age story, but in his hands the coming-of-age story is the story of a loss of humanity.

Unfortunately there is more than this story in Høeg's novel. **Borderliners** is marred by the presence within itself of two other stories—a philosophical exploration of the nature of time and a jarring set of first-person references to Høeg in his study with his infant daughter. A passage recounting the events at Biehl's school is followed immediately by a reference to the science of time or to Kant's musings on the Milky Way. And somewhat more sparsely, the narrative is interrupted by what appear to be diary entries: "This is the laboratory. It is next to the bedroom, where the child and woman are sleeping. I am afraid . . . . Order. When the child was about 1 year old she started talking. At first it was just single words, but pretty soon they formed into strings. Into lists."

With *Borderliners,* Høeg has mounted a courageous assault on the compulsive conformity and the shallow inclusiveness of the Danish experiment.

—*Nader Mousavizadeh*

The problem is evident from the very first sentence of the book: "What is time?" This is already a betrayal of Høeg's narrative gifts. He seems insecure about the capacity of the novel, as if philosophical notions can be developed only in philosophical forms. The power of *Smilla* was that her convictions seemed completely believable as expressed in her person. In *Borderliners,* ideas are announced rather than embodied, and so they often seem pompous and even banal.

Høeg's mediations are also not helped by a translation that is only competent and rarely elegant. Ironically, the translation succeeds most in these analytical passages, where the language is more familiar and its resonances less important. The translator most fails Høeg when he is at his most lyrical, as in this passage when Peter discovers Katarina's closeness as an epiphany of belonging:

> We sat there and I knew that this was how it felt
> to be totally accepted. You sit close to another
> person and are understood and nothing is judged
> and you are indispensable.

In Danish, the fullness of the relief of this moment is expressed by the words *"og man kan ikke undværes,"* for "and you are indispensable," which in English sounds rather like something said about a manual or a servant. What it really means is that you cannot be lived without. Wooden as this formulation may be, it evokes the need rather than demeans it. A little less fidelity on the part of the translator would have better conveyed the depth of the bond that is the subject of the passage, the bond that is all that stands between the boy and the abyss.

With *Borderliners,* Høeg has mounted a courageous assault on the compulsive conformity and the shallow inclusiveness of the Danish experiment. He has singled out an essential feature of a society whose successes have blinded it to its soullessness. Its crimes are largely not those of omission—poorly funded schools, single mothers left to fend for themselves, and inner cities in Dickensian decay—but crimes of commission, such as the intrusion into the sacred, the invasion of the private and the failure to abide or to honor difference. This is, to be sure, the

darker side of an otherwise remarkable achievement in fairness and equality; but still it is a story that long has needed telling. For the cultural price of such material equality has been a stifling, almost suffocating sense of ennui. And no contemporary writer has done more to liberate Danish culture from its ennui than Peter Høeg.

John David Morley   (review date 22 October 1995)

SOURCE: "Northern Exposure," in *The New York Times,* October 22, 1995, p. 26.

[*Morley is a British novelist, translator, and critic. In the following positive review of* The History of Danish Dreams, *he compares Høeg's writing to that of such writers as Milan Kundera, Selma Lagerlof, and Hans Christian Andersen.*]

If books could be assigned geometrical shapes (an idea that Smilla, the heroine of *Smilla's Sense of Snow,* with her feeling not only for snow but for higher mathematics, would surely have endorsed), then Peter Hoeg's new novel, actually his first, might be viewed as a pyramid. *The History of Danish Dreams* has a tripartite structure. Part 1, the base, establishes the story of four Danish families over almost exactly four centuries, from 1520 to 1918. The middle is inhabited by two families, descendants of those on whose shoulders they are standing. The already sharply attenuated shape of the pyramid reflects the much briefer interval of time it represents, a mere 20 years between the end of one war and the beginning of the next. At the top live the descendants of the descendants, merged as a single family.

A writer who chooses to make his debut with a novel that opens in the manorial-patriarchal environment of feudalism; that roams on to encompass the nouveau riche ambitions of the rising bourgeoisie in the 19th century; that peers into lost souls whose desolation exercises the Danish evangelical mission at the turn of the century; that evokes the gaudy extravagance of the 1920's and the threadbare existence of the 1930's before dissolving them both in the postindustrial welfare state society of late 20th-century Scandinavia—such a writer will be flailing and panting for breath after 350 pages unless he keeps a tight grip on his subject. It is a mark of the debutant Hoeg's confidence that he makes the attempt and a mark of his skill that for much of the time he succeeds.

In the opening chapters, with their self-conscious epigraphs, "Time that stands still" and "Time that passes," Mr. Hoeg is experimenting with style. At first he seems drawn to the magic realism of a Gabriel Garcia Márquez, but his contrived medieval stage props creak with the brittle sound of pastiche.

Next, he flirts with the conceptual structures of a Milan Kundera, the mode of ironic self-quotation, but conceptualism is not Mr. Hoeg's idiom either. He is a storyteller, and eventually he discovers the local traditions of Selma Lagerlof, Johannes Jensen and Hans Christian Andersen, which serve him best—legends tinged with romantic melancholy, fictitious biographies, tall tales told with zest in bold lines. Mr. Hoeg's contribution to this kind of storytelling is his tongue-in-check humor, notably his lively sense of the absurd. It was these qualities, along with the newness of the Arctic world as a backdrop to modern fiction, that made *Smilla's Sense of Snow* an international best seller.

The dreams of the title—more broadly, the stuff of human hopes and disappointments—are many, both abstract and specific. They range from socialism and evangelical redemption to dreams of the circus, of the Orient, of being thin. Individual characters embody the dreams, but it is an aspect of Mr. Hoeg's storytelling that the dreams manage to come more alive than the characters. The people in the book never fully emerge from the bas-relief story panel in which they figure—they seem to be there to illustrate. The narrator talks about them; they do not project their own existence from the page.

About halfway through the novel Mr. Hoeg hits his stride. Perhaps this is because he is more interesting writing about rich people than poor, about masters rather than their servants, about booming aristocratic eccentrics rather than cowed civil servants or tight-lipped, self-effacing bourgeoisie. At the fast pace at which Mr. Hoeg's prose likes to bound along, and with the high-altitude air his fiction likes to breathe, such people thrive. Thus his portrait, or caricature, of the between-the-wars extravaganza of a marriage between the tycoon Carl Laurids and the anorexic Amelie, who transforms herself into a man-eating whore and dragon of a mother after Carl Laurids absconds, is a very fine piece of imaginative writing. The 90 pages of this section—about one-quarter of *The History of Danish Dreams*—are utterly absorbing.

John Skow   (review date 6 November 1995)

SOURCE: "Old Trunk," in *Time,* Vol. 146, No. 19, November 6, 1995, p. 84.

[*In the following review, Skow offers a mixed assessment of* The History of Danish Dreams, *noting that the novel contains elements of magic realism as well as satire.*]

One of the strong subsurface themes of *Smilla's Sense of Snow,* the fine 1993 thriller by Peter Hoeg, a Danish novelist then new to America, was a slyly expressed contempt for what the author saw as his country's bourgeois self-satisfaction. This much relished contempt and cheerfully malign slyness are the driving forces of Hoeg's first novel, *The History of Danish Dreams,* which has now been issued in the U.S. That said, there's not much similarity between the two novels. *Smilla* has a powerful narrative flow; *Dreams* is a lumpish absurdity that fuddles to a halt after several dozen pages, begins again with new characters and repeats this throat clearing until well past the book's midsection. In these first chapters Hoeg tries something like magic realism, then gives up a promising experiment.

This extreme awkwardness of construction makes *Dreams,* which belabors the smugness and provincialism of Danish society from feudal times to the present, seem far longer than it is. There are passages, not murky but mightily centrifugal, in which the reader's eyes slide off the page. And in something like equal number, or a bit

more, there are set pieces, two or three or several dozen pages long, that are among the funniest satirical sketches seen in years.

In Hoeg's ferocious burlesque, *bürgerlich* awfulness has its own flavor in Denmark. One of his best chapters has a dissolute theology student, who has been drinking, whoring and mocking his professors for several years, sneering as his negligee-clad girlfriend reads him a letter from home. "Your father is dead," she reports. "To hell with him," says he. Just then his mother's portrait falls off the wall to the floor. His shallow rebellion vanishes at this omen. He sinks to his knees, repents and returns home to preach hellfire to amazed and grateful peasants. If *Dreams* is regarded not as a novel but as a marvelous trunkful of loosely related funny bits like this one, it is a great success.

Jim Shepard   (review date 24 December 1995)

SOURCE: "Beauty, Truth and the Danish Way" in *The Los Angeles Times Book Review,* December, 24, 1995, pp. 3, 8.

[*Shepard is an American educator, novelist, and critic. In the following review of* The History of Danish Dreams, *he discusses Høeg's treatment of the self-deluding "dreams," or myths, present in both Danish and Western culture and how they contribute to human suffering.*]

One of the many good things that happens to an author when his third book is acclaimed far and wide is that his first and second books receive renewed attention. (This means that whenever one of our books disappears, we console ourselves with the belief that once we publish our own *All the Pretty Horses,* everything we previously wrote will be appreciated again.)

The History of Danish Dreams, Peter Hoeg's first novel, follows his second, *Borderliners,* into English translation, which followed his third, the universally admired *Smilla's Sense of Snow.* Which means poor Mr. Hoeg will probably have to endure his share of reviews that announce with disappointment that his first novel is different from his third.

And it is different. Hoeg chose for it a familiar model—the multi-generational family saga as social chronicle—torqued in the unfamiliar way the title suggests.

His history of four families who, over the course of generations, merge into one is told as a history of Danish dreams: dreams because both grandiose aspiration and self-delusion are so central to the ways in which families and societies operate; dreams because of the book's pessimism concerning the likelihood of progressive change; and dreams because a history of dreams is, of course, by definition a sly critique of history itself.

The principal dream under assault may be that dream of order, prosperity and goodness that underlies Danish—and by extension, 20th century Western—culture. Though the novel spans four centuries, its main focus is on the confusions of this century, and, along the way, most aspects of modern Danish life—cultural, political, social—take a beating.

Although the novel's cast ranges from tenement dwellers to millionaires, most of the traits exposed for our castigation are essentially bourgeois. From pre-feudal to postindustrial society, the culprit turns out to be Good Middle-Class Common Sense, that peculiar mix of quiescence and complacency and faith that all men want the same things: law and order and a steady job and respect for the eternal truths.

Such convictions are what allow the good citizens of Denmark and the West to keep their heads down and go about their business. This enables them to ignore suffering on the international scene, within their own borders or in their own families without compromising either that dream of themselves as good people or the invincible sense that their culture is progressing smoothly toward an even brighter future.

We're treated to all manner of good and bad Danes—with the latter predominating—from those who die resisting Nazism (our century's ultimate Manichaean test, apparently) to those who help enable it. We witness, too, their penchant for remaining admirably neutral while profiting handsomely from world wars, or their own usually unspoken agreement with the notion that the Nordics do constitute a master race.

A good deal of energy is devoted over the course of the book to the demolition of the virtues of free enterprise and "Hygge, that particular Danish blend of warmth and coziness" that they've been so successful in convincing the world is their principal attribute.

That attribute masks and may contribute to the poverty of their—and our—inner life, the novel insists, even to the extent that our literature and art find themselves accomplices in the tending of such ritualized hypocrisy. ("They walked along the gravel paths, past the whispering trees and the filmy patches that Carsten recognized as the ghosts of Danish writers who had wept, in Frederiksberg Gardens, the Danish writers' lament that says, 'Why can't I have more mistresses? Why can't I have more money?' ")

What inner life that does exist seems to consist primarily of a pinched emotional reticence and lack of generosity, as well as an impressive capacity for luxuriously melancholic self-pity—that standard why-does-nobody-like-me feeling. All of which is bad news for the children these adults are raising, and many of the novel's most compelling passages revolve around the ways families seek, and assert even without seeking, control over their members through and over time.

Over and over again we find gathered around cribs "all the hopes of the poor and the rich and the middle class and those on the nethermost rung" and under "the weight of so many dreams that refuse to amalgamate." It's no wonder that child after child is unable to bear up. With parents who are either indifferent or determined to turn their homes into "barred incubators," and with the rapidity of change in the 20th century ensuring that parents' experiences are not only outdated but possibly dangerous as child-rearing models, the overall effect of the family dy-

namic is to not only keep the children submerged but to ensure that their snorkels never break the surface.

All these damaged children find perhaps their ultimate embodiment, in the third and last section of the novel, in the figure of Carsten, the perfect Dane: serene, uncomplaining, discreet, modest and ambitious, a lawyer to the wealthy so fiercely attentive to the work at hand and inattentive to its larger implications that he all but wraps up a successful prosecution before realizing that the defendant is his wife.

The novel's strategy of building toward Carsten and his children as a culmination has its drawbacks. In the early going we often feel as if we're in the presence of a comic historical pageant of some sort, illuminating and funny in fits and starts but fragmented enough that the narrative takes quite a while to build momentum.

Characters, especially at the beginning, are paraded by at such a pace they're inevitably reduced in the reader's mind (when they stay in the reader's mind at all) to a few key traits, and motivations are accordingly reduced at such times to psychological commonplaces eloquently rendered. ("They reenact the convoluted rituals of middle-class culture, designed to foster that heartfelt, tingling sense of belonging; combined with the realization . . . that at least we here on the inside, we who have come in from the cold, stand united.")

Too many characters are brought a little too smartly into line on the organizing principle of their dreams; most are reduced to emitting a few cheeps and tugging ever so slightly at the leash.

That leash is held by a casually chatty narrator, who intermittently intrudes to guide us on our way ("To me the situation seems symbolic. Looked at from a particular angle, it presents us with the most significant feature of the nature of the Child Welfare Services in 1920s Denmark."); who explains his methodology ("What I, on the other hand, have to look for here is whatever it is that makes the common factors visible"); who coyly insists on the limits of his own power ("It was not long after this that Anna started to clean. This is a historical fact, and, no matter what I do, history is history. Nor do I need to excuse anything over which I have no influence"); and whose omniscience shrinks while we watch as his own stake in things becomes more and more overt. ("Again I have this urge to shout at Amalie, across the expanse of history, 'What the hell do you mean by treating a little boy like that, making him your confidant, using him the way your customers use you—like someone you can pound away at and extract relief from?' ")

The playful artifice of such narration helps mediate for us the ongoing shift in the novel's style as it gradually moves from a kind of pointedly satiric magical realism, more in the style of Danilo Kis than of Gabriel Garcia Marquez, to a more traditional narrative—and narrator—as the book moves into its final section.

What we enjoy throughout are the tall tales spun with verve, intelligence and a highly developed appreciation for the absurd, always with satiric intent in mind. At one point a war profiteer holds a dinner in the gondola of a balloon for others who've "made their fortunes to the distant musical accompaniment of the shellfire," during which are served dishes "devised and derived from large, dangerous animals, as a way of showing everyone that they could relax."

And if the social criticism is at times insistent, or unsubtle, the novel's gathering force—and its persistent return to the specifics of human suffering, particularly the suffering of children—ultimately grants such satire an affecting sadness.

FURTHER READING

Criticism

Frank, Jeffrey. "Prisoners of Time and Chance." *The Wash-ington Post Book World* XXIV, No. 50 (11 December 1994): 9.

> Review of *Borderliners* in which Frank discusses Høeg in comparison to other Danish writers, touches upon the theme of time, and outlines the oddities in the work's English translation.

Glass, Julia. "Peter Høeg's New Tale of Time, Trauma and Character." *Chicago Tribune–Books* (1 January 1995) 3, 7.

> Mixed review of *Borderliners* in which Glass states that Høeg "is persisting on an uncharted course in fiction, using science to elucidate character and add a new dimension to suspense."

Koenig, Rhoda. "In Very Cold Blood." *New York* 26, No. 37 (20 September 1993): 66-7.

> Mixed assessment of *Smilla's Sense of Snow.*

Smiley, Jane. "In Distant Lands of Ice and Sun." *The Wash-ington Post Book World* XXIII, No. 43 (24 October 1993): 1, 11.

> Positive assessment of *Smilla's Sense of Snow* as a thriller with political implications.

R. D. Laing

1927-1989

(Full name Ronald David Laing) Scottish-born English psychiatrist, essayist, poet, and autobiographer.

The following entry presents an overview of Laing's life and career.

INTRODUCTION

Laing was an internationally known Scottish psychiatrist best-known for his controversial interpretation and treatment of schizophrenia. In his first work on the subject, *The Divided Self* (1960), he maintains that schizophrenia is not a pathological disease, that the development of schizophrenic personalities is created and promoted by society and the family, and that present-day psychotherapeutic tactics fail to realistically address the needs of the schizophrenic. Since Laing's psychotherapeutic theories challenged the approach of mainstream psychotherapy, many of his colleagues condemned or ignored his insights.

Biographical Information

Born and raised in Glasgow, Scotland, Laing received his M. D. from the University of Glasgow in 1951 and entered the British Army as a psychiatrist. In 1953 he returned to the University of Glasgow as an instructor in psychological medicine, after which he worked as a psychiatrist at the Glasgow Royal Mental Hospital. Following the publication of *The Divided Self,* he became a family therapist at London's Tavistock Institute of Human Relations and the director of the Langham Clinic for Psychotherapy in 1962. In 1967, he opened a private psychotherapy practice in London, and founded Kingsley Hall, a psychotherapeutic community, while continuing to write and lecture. Laing died in St. Tropez, France, in 1989.

Major Works

Laing proposed a new psychotherapeutic approach to schizophrenia and analyzed the contributions of society and the family in the development of the human psyche. *The Divided Self* sets forth Laing's thesis that schizophrenia is not a pathological disease. He argues that schizophrenics, who use their own system of logic and understanding to deal with the exigencies of their lives, require an experientially-based psychotherapeutic approach in order to help them adjust to their social and familial environments. While *The Self and Others* (1961) focuses more on the role of fantasy and interpersonal relationships in the development of the schizophrenic personality, *Sanity, Madness, and the Family* (1964) examines the lives of eleven families in order to illustrate the ways in which collective insensitivities, pathological fantasies, and anxiety affect the psychological development of family members. In *The Politics of Experience* (1967) Laing details his "phe-

nomenological" psychotherapeutic method, emphasizing the importance of personal experience and scientific training in the assessment of an individual's psychological makeup. *The Politics of the Family, and Other Essays* (1971), on the other hand, is a collection of radio talks and essays that focus on the intervention of the therapist in family crises. This work examines such themes as schizophrenia, victimization, and psychological liberation within the family setting. Among Laing's poetic works are *Knots* (1970) and *Do You Love Me?* (1976), which address such psychological themes as human communications and feelings, and interpersonal, familial, and societal relationships. In *Conversations with Adam and Natasha* (1977) and *Conversations with Children* (1978), Laing uses recordings of his own children as the basis for an examination of the values and ideas of all children. Laing's final work is his autobiography, entitled *Wisdom, Madness and Folly* (1985), which traces his personal, intellectual, and professional development from 1927 to 1957 and the publication of *The Divided Self.*

Critical Reception

Critical reception of Laing's works has generally been

harsh. While most critics agree that his approach to the treatment of schizophrenia is intriguing and original, the majority reject and ignore his theories and his psychotherapeutic insights. Critics are also divided on the value of his poetry; some describe it as "dense and difficult" with "a surface brilliance," while others charge that it is "ugly" and full of "unbearable bathos." Regarding his prose style, many commentators admit that Laing can tell a good story, whether it is about his own life in *Wisdom, Madness and Folly* or about the case histories of schizophrenic patients. However, in the books about his children's conversations, several critics dismiss them as ordinary and unenlightened, but pleasant reading. Finally, several commentators note a significant change in Laing's writing style. Whereas his earlier works, such as *The Divided Self,* employed rigorous research, well-developed ideas, and a disciplined literary style, these elements appear to be lacking in his later works. Nevertheless, while many commentators are loathe to accept all of his ideas, they readily admit that his theories about schizophrenia, society, and the family remain a challenge to the thought and practice of contemporary psychiatry.

PRINCIPAL WORKS

The Divided Self: A Study of Sanity and Madness (essays) 1960

The Self and Others: Further Studies in Sanity and Madness (essays) 1961

Reason and Violence: A Decade of Sartre's Philosophy, 1950-60 [with David G. Cooper] (essays) 1964

Sanity, Madness, and the Family [with A. Esterson] (essays) 1964; also published as *The Families of Schizophrenics*

Interpersonal Perception: A Theory and a Method of Research [with A. R. Lee and H. Phillipson] (essays) 1964

The Politics of Experience (essays, poetry) 1967

Knots (poetry) 1970

The Politics of the Family, and Other Essays (essays) 1971

Do you Love Me? An Entertainment in Conversation and Verse (poetry) 1976

The Facts of Life: An Essay in Feelings, Facts, and Fantasy (essay) 1976

Conversations with Adam and Natasha (nonfiction) 1977

Conversations with Children (nonfiction) 1978

Sonnets (poetry) 1980

The Voice of Experience (essays) 1982

Wisdom, Madness, and Folly: The Making of a Psychiatrist (autobiography) 1985

CRITICISM

Forrest Williams   (review date 6 January 1966)

SOURCE: A review of *Reason and Violence,* in *The Journal of Philosophy,* Vol. LXIII, No. 1, January 6, 1966, pp. 26-8.

[*In the following review of* Reason and Violence, *Williams maintains that, while Laing's summaries of Jean-Paul Sartre's* Saint Genet: Comédien et martyr (Saint Genet: Actor and Martyr; *1952),* Questions de méthode (Search for a Method; *1963), and* Critique de la raison dialectique (Critique of Dialectical Reason; *1960) are accurate and succinct, the book fails to make Sartre's ideas accessible to the reader unfamiliar with his philosophical terminology.*]

Reason and Violence is a résumé of the three major works written by Jean-Paul Sartre in the fifties. In a brief foreword, Sartre himself praises the book of R. D. Laing and D. G. Cooper as "a very clear and faithful exposition." There can be no question, indeed, of the economy and accuracy of their summaries of *Saint Genet, Questions de méthode,* and volume I of *Critique de la raison dialectique,* "Théorie des ensembles pratiques." But precisely because these *are* entirely faithful condensations, one is hard put to conceive the Anglo-American reader to whom the book will be useful. Sartre's philosophic prose is among the most ungrateful in the twentieth century, and a faithfully miniaturized version in English can be of little help to the uninitiated. The two shorter sections, on the Genet essay and on the methodological essay, will be somewhat comprehensible to the noncommunicant of Sartrean philosophy. But certainly the longest section, summarizing the *Critique,* will baffle the very audience the book presumably wishes to reach. Thus, an American or English reader unfamiliar with the *Critique* would probably not be able to make head or tail of the key terms, principles, and argumentation which Laing has faithfully compressed into an 85-page résumé.

The short methodological essay, as Sartre has explained, is a general consideration of dialectical method in relation to Marxist theory, derived from the mammoth *Critique,* and contains much of great interest to all who are concerned with categorical and procedural problems in the study of man and his works. Sartre's study of the celebrated author-criminal, Genet, is a *sine qua non* for psychologists and literary critics as well as philosophers, and is undoubtedly the most readable of the three résumés, because of its comparative concreteness. The *magnum opus,* or *Critique,* is a dialectical theory of the practical dialectic of *"ensembles pratiques,"* or conduct-generated relationships (groupings, collectivities, sociohistorical realities). Though for all the *Critique* says they might never have existed, G. H. Mead and John Dewey are certainly the two American philosophers to whose themes and concerns Sartre is closest in this gigantic rethinking, almost Augustinian in dimensions and aim, of Marxist theory and practice.

To many non-Continentals, Sartre's intricate dialectical speculations will seem, as Stuart Hampshire has averred recently, recidivist and pre-Marxist. Marx supposedly has liberated us from metaphysics and "all that." But in the minds of most intellectuals in Europe, where Marxism is more actively experienced and debated, Marx's concern with changing the world is not tantamount to our hyperempiricism and political pragmatism. Thus, Sartre's theory of "totalizations," "alterity," "serialization," and "analyticoregressive method," is not generally regarded on the Continent as a *vieux jeu* polemic of neo-Hegelian obfuscations, but as an interpretation of Marxism which may well be much closer to Marx than our own narrowly pragmatic, even positivistic versions. The publication of **Reason and Violence** does, for all the difficulty presented by mere résumés, convey some sense of the contemporary relevance of Sartre's *Critique*.

Robert Coles   (review date 13 May 1967)

SOURCE: "Life's Madness," in *The New Republic,* Vol. 156, No. 19, May 13, 1967, pp. 24-8, 30.

[*Coles is an American psychiatrist, educator, nonfiction writer, essayist, and poet whose particular area of interest is the psychological development of children; he is the author of, among other works,* The Spiritual Life of Children *(1990). In the following review of* The Politics of Experience, *he praises Laing's literary skills and the ways in which he articulates his views regarding "the demonic and chaotic in man" and modern psychotherapy's approach to madness.*]

One of the ways psychiatrists have sorted themselves out in recent years has to do with the importance they give to concepts like "the normal," or "maturity" or "mental health." Some are dead serious about letting their patients and the public know what is abnormal or immature. On television they urge me to "fight mental illness," and though I am not exactly sure how to go about doing it, I am certainly left with the idea that there *is* such a thing as mental illness, that there is such a thing as its presumed opposite, mental health.

In contrast stand those psychiatrists who question the entire practice of calling one or another variation in human behavior "sick" or evidence of "disease." Thomas Szasz in this country has made his position quite clear by the title, let alone the content, of his book *The Myth of Mental Illness.* The English psychiatrist R. D. Laing has come to the issue from a somewhat different angle—he is less interested in legal problems than Szasz and is much more the philosopher. In one of his earlier books (**The Divided Self**) he wrote as follows:

> A man who prefers to be dead rather than Red is normal. A man who says he has lost his soul is mad. A man who says he *is* a machine is "depersonalized" in psychiatric jargon. A man who says that Negroes are an inferior race may be widely respected. A man who says his whiteness is a form of cancer is certifiable.

> A little girl of seventeen in a mental hospital told me she was terrified because the Atom Bomb was inside her. That is a delusion. The statesmen of the world who boast and threaten that they

have Doomsday weapons are far more dangerous, and far more estranged from "reality" than many of the people on whom the label "psychotic" is affixed.

For Laing, as for other so-called "existential" analysts, what psychiatrists are busy classifying and labeling is actually a "false self."

—*Robert Coles*

That book and a later one (**The Self and Others**) demonstrated that Laing is a physician and psychoanalyst who can easily come to terms with the complicated thinking of Sartre, Heidegger and Binswanger. He has been trained to place people in psychiatric categories but he finds the practice worse than useless, in fact an insulting and gratuitous way of ignoring both the person, who is called a "patient," and his ideals or convictions, so easily dismissed as "delusions" or "problems." For Laing, as for other so-called "existential" analysts, what psychiatrists are busy classifying and labeling is actually a "false self," presented to the world by a man or woman who has learned from long standing, nerve wracking experience the futility of anything but disguise, deception and escape. In contrast, somewhere in anyone who has managed to survive infancy, there resides what Laing calls the "inner self," the anxious, frightened person's sense of what he "really" is, what he wishes he might more solidly be, what he once thought he could be—alive, whole, secure, trusting, trusted, whatever. (The word is not the issue, and in any event words can only suggest the intricacies and ironies of experience.)

Laing would see the most angry, withdrawn or incomprehensible of psychotics as a person who is struggling to make his thoughts and feelings known to a disbelieving, unreliable and impassive world, more bent on demanding compliance than enabling each man to stumble upon and seek out his own kind of vision or faith. What do we do with the radical doubts of a man who distrusts the words and postures of his fellow men, who uses a different syntax, carries himself in a different way, and finds in the sights and sounds of his private world a bit less of the cruelty and the cant that "we" take in our stride? Laing says we call him "crazy," call him "ill," fall back on our laws, and send him "away," where he stays until he learns to change his ways and abide by ours. ("The psychiatrist, as *ipso facto* sane, shows that the patient is out of contact with him. The fact that he is out of contact with the patient shows that there is something wrong with the patient, but not with the psychiatrist.")

Laing has now published a new book, **The Politics of Experience,** which contains a collection of essays published before in medical or philosophical journals and various quarterlies. As a psychiatrist I once again find his writing quite literally stunning. I am over-powered by the challenges he dares make to what has become a rather conventional profession, very much the property of (and a source of solace to) the upper middle-class American, this century's *civis Romanus*. To Laing, we psychiatrists are something else, too: willing custodians, who for good pay agree to do the bidding of society by keeping tab on various "deviants," and in the clutch "taking care" of them—the double meaning of the verb being exactly to the point.

There seems to be something seriously wrong with Dr. Laing: he doesn't believe that the educated, literate and often enough psychoanalyzed Americans and Englishmen who read his books are without exception alert, vital and honest people. As a matter of fact he asserts that they commonly are the dead rather than the quick, well behaved rather than alive. In a word, they do not experience—"life," one another, the ridiculous and the sublime that the world offers so freely.

Laing's new book is organized around a discussion of "experiences," whether they be called psychotherapeutic, schizophrenic, or transcendental. Even more, he asks the reader to experience this book, to meet rather than understand at a distance the mind of R. D. Laing—a doctor, a writer, a human being trying to live enthusiastically and suffer honorably. What troubles Laing, however, is his conviction that he will fail, that deaf ears and blind eyes are everywhere, particularly among those who declare books "interesting" and those who "treat" what they call "syndromes." Intellectuals, he feels, turn the writer's passion into academic capital, ideas that come and go. Psychiatrists convert the experience of talking with another person, sweating it out with him, into one more icy, abstract "process."

We have, then, a psychiatrist who doesn't seem to distinguish between sanity and madness. On the contrary, he appears to be worried about us, the "well adjusted" men and women that society values so very much. He sees us educating our children "to lose themselves and to become absurd, and thus to be normal." Then he adds: "Normal men have killed perhaps 100,000,000 of their fellow normal men in the last fifty years." As I read the book I kept thinking of Auden's poem *The Unknown Citizen,* where the same painful message is spoken. Step by step, year by year, we make sure a child falls in line, so that when he becomes grown-up we call him "mature," meaning he will follow the leader, who in turn follows the polls. In Auden's words we will be able to say "he worked in a factory and never got fired," and he wasn't "odd in his views," and "our social psychology workers found that he was popular with his mates and liked a drink," and "his reactions to advertisements were normal in every way." Naturally, "when there was peace, he was for peace; when there was war, he went." At the end the poet asks: "Was he free? Was he happy? The question is absurd. Had anything been wrong, we should certainly have heard."

Laing also despairs, and tells why in this book. We are in the same sinking ship, oppressor and victim. Men of success live haunted and frightened by the climb they have made over the minds, bodies and rights of others. What they did to their neighbor can be done to them—and that goes for nations as well as individuals. As for the "failures," they have their "problems" too, everything from

hunger to the sense of worthlessness "we" make sure "they" feel. Laing devotes a whole chapter to "us" and "them," to the ways we cut off others, deny them in desperate spite the humanity we ourselves have lost. He also insists that psychiatrists have allowed themselves to be separated from their patients, to categorize them rather than learn from them and with them, to use "the economic metaphor," so that one hears physicians talk of emotions "invested" and "objects" gained or lost. In sum, because of their emphasis on "function," on getting people "going" or "adjusted" (to what?) Laing views his colleagues as captives of their own amoral pragmatism.

> **Madness is not only confusion and loss, an inner world of ideas, voices, shapes and impulses asserting itself like never before; madness is a radical departure, and Laing sees it as "potentially liberation and renewal."**
>
> —*Robert Coles*

Dr. Laing is no glib and smart-aleck critic, masquerading as a psychiatrist. He has a good deal of clinical research to his credit, much of it done with schizophrenics and their families. (His work is described in two books, each written with a colleague: ***Reason and Violence*** and ***The Families of Schizophrenics.***) He sees schizophrenia as a "special strategy that a person invents in order to live in an unlivable situation." He does not know why some people (rather than others) feel so utterly, decisively thwarted, but he wants insanity understood as an effort to reach out, to break out; and further, he wants it understood as potentially something more, something "transcendental." Madness is not only confusion and loss, an inner world of ideas, voices, shapes and impulses asserting itself like never before; madness is a radical departure, and Laing sees it as "potentially liberation and renewal."

It is refreshing to read his discussion of insanity, even if one does not accept his viewpoint completely. He is not out to blame anyone, or call people thinly disguised (psychiatric) names. He isn't hammering away at the weakness, the morbidity, the deviance of people. Nor does he glorify or romanticize madness; he wants to understand it, to see it for the universal and quite human condition that it is. He knows what many of his colleagues think, how they scan minds for "disorders of thinking" and sign commitment papers, one after another, so that patients—they are sick, sick, sick—will get "treatment." He asks what kind of treatment, and from whom. Will the psychiatrist under the best circumstances be someone highly trained but ultimately condescending, more interested in getting the patient to be like others than in finding out where he himself is going, and would like to go?

Yet, language itself fails us when we try to distinguish the "individual" from others, from the "social." On the first day of life a child begins to find out where and when he was born. The way he is handled, clothed and fed, the nature and amount of food he gets, his mother's moods, worries, fears—all that and more begins to affect him, and urge on him what I suppose could be called "conformity." Then he enters the backyard, and the neighborhood, and later the school—where he learns to accept this and forego that. I know of no society where children are not "indoctrinated," that is "brought up" and in the course of things subjected to some kind of conformist restraint.

Since Dr. Laing realizes all that, the reader must ask why he as a psychiatrist objects so strenuously to what he knows to some extent is inevitable. As a matter of fact the book's real value stands or falls on whether the author makes his criticisms unqualified to the point of irrelevance. Will we hear once again, and from a psychiatrist this time, that children are by nature *only* sensitive, kind or honorable, and destined to remain so were it not for the thieves and cheats who teach them and rule them, let alone bring them into the world? Are we to understand that things have to be pulled inside out, that madness is sanity and sanity the worst kind of madness? Are the murky existentialist words going to replace the dumb psychiatric ones—say "authenticity" for "mental health"? Do we have yet another author who tears down everything around with a certain vindictive relish but has not a damn thing to offer the millions who don't read him, who live outside of his coterie and whom he can only grant the scorn of his pity?

In my opinion, Laing comes off very well on such questions. He acknowledges the demonic and chaotic in man, and he does not try to make a religion out of psychosis. ("Certain transcendental experiences. . . . I am not saying, however, that psychotic experience necessarily contains this element more manifestly than sane experience.") In other words, he holds to the *reality* of madness, but insists upon its integrity—and so emerges as only a man, with precisely that "status," a knowing and searching human being rather than a self-important doctor.

Unquestionably, he is thoroughly dissatisfied with what 20th-century industrial society does to the minds of people; and he is equally unhappy with the way psychiatrists generally manage to avoid facing sticky and controversial problems like that one. He will not have his profession used to "cure" those who dare question social or political absolutes, and even more radically, he is willing to find madness—in some cases—a necessary way station or a point of departure in a spiritual voyage all too few people care or dare to make, particularly since if they do the middle-class world will shun them, mock them and when they make enough "trouble," cart them off.

At the end of the book Laing demonstrates what he means by offering us first a "case-history" and then in a chapter called "The Bird of Paradise," his own flight of fancy and terror. These last pages do not read easily, and at times I could not understand what was before me, which may be the author's point about me, you, and him—that in today's world we barely can hold on to the senses we are still permitted, let alone call them ours or convey their "meaning" to others. In any event the book as a whole

presents an exceptionally courageous psychiatrist who is willing to plumb his own depths and challenge head-on the hypocrisy and duplicity of his own profession and the larger society of which it is so prominent a part. I can only hope that he will be heard and heard respectfully. I can only further hope that those who disagree will spare him and the rest of us those dishonest and contemptible *ad hominem* remarks that some psychiatrists reserve for any and all "opposition." (So-and-so has this kind of problem, Laing has that kind, and they need more analysis, more of a "going over.") Nor do I think Dr. Laing deserves the eager company of the psychoanalytically disenchanted, a growing minority in America today. It seems to me that he is trying to give the essence of Freud's journey (not the dead-end streets that he like all men walked) a particular kind of historical, political and philosophical perspective. I do not think he means to deny the validity of the analytic method; quite the contrary, it has enabled much of his vision. The point anyway is not to pit views against one another, but find whatever coherence possible out of them all—without resort to ideological squabbles. Freud called himself a conquistador, and if the bookkeepers and bureaucrats have now descended upon the psychoanalytic "movement" in droves to claim his mantle, all the more reason for a man like Laing to stand fast as the psychoanalyst he is.

When I finished this unusual and troubling book, I thought of Bob Dylan and the loneliness he has described squeezing at people, the things they do to distract themselves, and the obligation to be compassionate that anyone who would criticize them must feel. I think that Laing shares a similar sense of horror, a similar spirit of generosity, and not always do we find in one man that range of sensibility.

Rollo May (review date 20 May 1967)

SOURCE: "The Frontiers of Being Human," in *Saturday Review*, Vol. L, No. 20, May 20, 1967, pp. 37-9.

[*May was an internationally known American psychiatrist, minister, and educator who wrote many books on psychology for lay readers. Regarded as the father of existential psychotherapy in the United States, May eschewed many of Sigmund Freud's psychoanalytic principals and focused on anxiety and its impact on human behavior. In the following favorable review of* The Politics of Experience, *he applauds Laing's challenge to conventional psychiatric theories and contends that, by emphasizing the importance of life experiences, Laing "humanizes" schizophrenia and takes "important steps toward a science of interpersonal relationship."*]

Arguing in this book that psychotherapy does not need to become a pseudo-esoteric cult, Ronald Laing writes:

> We must continue to struggle through our confusion, to insist on being human. Existence is a flame which constantly melts and recasts our theories. . . . We hope to share the experience of a relationship, but the only honest beginning, or even end, may be to share the experience of its absence.

That the whole field of psychotherapy has been and is now

in confusion no one can doubt. All over the country one is being asked, "Is psychoanalysis dead? Is Freud dead?" Generally the question arises from the same faddist, dogmatizing sort of thinking that led some people to make Freud a god who could do no wrong, and their particular brand of psychotherapy a catechism that was guaranteed to save us from our human agony and struggle. At the same time, different kinds of therapy have continued to appear—family therapy, behavior therapy, marathon group therapy, Gestalt and transactional therapy, etc. However, the studies of the results of therapy seem so often to be based on the externalistic question of how the individual "adjusts" to our alienated society that their "proofs" that therapy does or does not do any good strike one as being curiously irrelevant.

In this confusion everyone tends to forget the real issue: that human beings do change, for good or ill. They are born, live, work, suffer travail, sometimes achieve a measure of love and meaning—and die. Order could come out of the confusion if we kept our minds on the question, what does it mean to be human? The directness and single-minded honesty with which Ronald Laing asked this question in his recent lectures in New York as the Visiting Distinguished Psychoanalyst, under the auspices of the William Alanson White Institute, are what make the present book so refreshing and compelling.

Laing, by training a psychiatrist, represents a creative synthesis of a number of significant streams in the psychotherapeutic field. He is an associate member of the British Psychoanalytic Society and principal investigator of the Schizophrenia and Family Research Unit at the Tavistock Institute of Human Relations in London. Closely associated with American anthropologists like Gregory Bateson and Jules Henry, he is also concerned with contemporary sociology, and has played a central role in the significant recent research on family therapy, reported in a previous book, *The Families of Schizophrenics.* Laing, moreover, is thoroughly grounded in modern existential and phenomenological thought; thus he knows how critically important it is for the therapist to clarify his own philosophical assumptions. And not least important, he is of that rare breed in which the scientist and artist dwell in the same skin: the last fifteen pages of this book consist of a long prose-poem of Laing entitled **"The Bird of Paradise."**

"A revolution is currently going on in relation to sanity and madness, both inside and outside psychiatry," Laing writes as a kind of theme for this book. "The clinical point of view is giving way before a point of view that is both existential and social." We are, he believes, in the midst of a shift in approach no less radical than that three centuries ago from the demonological to the clinical. When mental disturbances were classified as illnesses a concerted endeavor was made to find in schizophrenic behavior certain symptoms and signs of a disease of unknown origin, presumed to be largely genetic-constitutionally determined. What actually happened, by and large, was that the patient was adjudged "psychotic" if he could not adjust to society's requirements.

We are now, Laing states, in the third stage, in which it is seen that schizophrenia is a strategy, a necessary way the person must pick to survive in an alienated world.

> In over 100 cases where we studied the actual circumstances around the social event when one person comes to be regarded as schizophrenic, it seems to us that *without exception* the experience and behavior that gets labeled schizophrenic is *a special strategy that a person invents in order to live in an unlivable situation.*

Psychiatrists and psychologists who maintain that schizophrenia is pathology show much resistance to Laing's position. But he cites the research of Bateson—based on the important double-bind theory—and the new studies of the families of schizophrenics at Yale, at Palo Alto, at the National Institute of Mental Health, as well as his own research. "In all these places, to the best of my knowledge, *no* schizophrenic has been studied whose disturbed pattern of communication has not been shown to be a reflection of, and reaction to, the disturbed and disturbing pattern characterizing his or her family of origin."

What is refreshing and exciting in Laing is not his glorification of the irrational—of which he is sometimes accused by psychiatrists and psychologists who preach adaptation—but his frank challenge: "Adaptation to what? To society? To a mad world?" To Laing the height of irrationality is adjusting to what is called "normal"—to a world of Vietnam, a world in which cities not only poison their citizens physically through air pollution but shrink the individual's consciousness, a world in which "machines are already becoming better at communicating with each other than human beings with human beings. The situation is ironical. More and more concern about communication, less and less to communicate."

Laing's constructive contribution has been to blend the interpersonal theory of Harry Stack Sullivan with an existential, phenomenological foundation. These two go together, asserts Laing: the only way we can understand and deal with human beings is to clarify the "nature of being human"—which is ontology. "Any theory not founded on the nature of being human is a lie and a betrayal of man." And such a theory will have, to the extent the therapist is consistent, inhuman consequences. He believes that a fundamental source of our confusion in psychology and psychiatry is the "failure to realize that there is an ontological discontinuity between human beings and it-beings." Here Laing is in accord with Martin Buber's theory that psychoanalysis always tends to transform the "I" into an "it."

Though Laing appreciates Freud more deeply than many who make a dogma of the master's teachings, he holds that we must frankly face the fact that Freud thought and wrote in an alienated age and to some extent is himself an expression of this alienation. "The metapsychology of Freud, Federn, Rapaport, Hartman, Kris, has no constructs for any social system generated by more than one person at a time. . . . This theory has no category of 'you' . . . no concept of 'me' except as objectified as 'the ego.'" But it is precisely the function of psychotherapy to "remain an obstinate attempt of two people to recover the wholeness of being human through the relationship between them."

We need a form of psychology that does not dwell on behavior to the exclusion of experience or experience without regard for behavior, but centers on the relation between experience and behavior.

In Laing's opinion the severe social disturbance the schizophrenic is enduring provokes the biochemical changes in his body.

—*Rollo May*

Laing is aware of the widespread emphasis in our day, particularly in America, on studying the individual solely in terms of his behavior. Yet to the extent that we do so, we lose the person, for the human being is characterized by both inner experience and outer behavior, and the critical point is the relation between the two. Of this, comments Laing, "natural science knows nothing." A new method is required, one he calls social phenomenology.

> We are a generation of men so estranged from the inner world that many are arguing that it does not exist; and that even if it does exist, it does not matter. . . . Quantify the heart's agony and ecstasy in a world in which when the inner world is first discovered, we are liable to find ourselves bereft and derelict. For without the inner the outer loses its meaning, and without the outer the inner loses its substance.

Laing's own sincerity gives his words a compelling power. Although with his convictions it is natural that he would find himself ranged on a number of battlelines, his chief fight is with the organicists. In Laing's opinion the severe social disturbance the schizophrenic is enduring provokes the biochemical changes in his body. But he discerns no conclusive evidence as yet that there are the organic bases for such "difficulties in living," as Sullivan called them.

Also ranged against the behavior therapists, Laing charges that "behavior therapy is the most extreme example of schizoid theory and practice," proposing "to think and act purely in terms of the other without reference to the self of the therapist or the patient. . . . It is inevitably therefore a technique of nonmeeting, of manipulation and control."

Laing's work is also to be distinguished from the kind of oversimplified humanism, unfortunately shown in the later work of Erich Fromm, that purchases its confidence at the price of denying or blocking off significant aspects of man's predicament such as grief, tragedy, and death. "Man's aim in life," Fromm writes, "is to be attracted by all that is alive and separate himself from all that is dead." And he then must argue, "Sadness is sin." Laing takes a very different approach. Remarking that "love" in our society is often a cover for violence, he states, "We have to

begin by admitting and even accepting our violence, rather than blindly destroying ourselves with it, and therewith we have to realize that we are as deeply afraid to live and to love as we are to die."

I have already implied that I do not agree with a main criticism of Laing—that he glorifies schizophrenia. Rather, he humanizes it. In this humanizing, Laing's words have in them the ring of Blake and Dostoevsky in literature, and of Sullivan in psychiatry.

Nevertheless there remains a real problem in Laing's work. If, with respect to psychic problems, he rejects the concept of "illness," what criteria, what norms does he have as alternatives? What structure does he propose that he, and the rest of us, build upon? His writings, which in this book have a somewhat fragmentary character, may well be misunderstood and misused as a justification for mere "feeling" or anti-intellectualism. Or his work may be taken as indicating that if the truth is not readily at hand by our rational methods, LSD and other drugs will open the magic doors to new truth. (Granted the hysterical preoccupation—both pro and con—with LSD in this country, the publishers do neither the public nor the book a service in promoting it, as they do on the jacket and in ads, as leading the reader "to experience the kind of emotions often linked to the taking of drugs.")

Laing himself is no anti-intellectual; he thinks with dedication and profundity. But the tension in consciousness of holding together such different streams of thought and science—the task that Laing essays—is great indeed. And consequently the tendency to slide into anarchy or go off on disintegrating tangents is also great. Laing has developed a framework in his ontological bases, and taken important steps toward a science of interpersonal relationship. We can hope he will be able to continue building on both, for he has much to give.

The Politics of Experience will excite, even enthrall many readers, and disturb and anger others. But no one who reads the book will remain unaffected.

Marshall Berman   (review date 22 February 1970)

SOURCE: A review of *The Divided Self* and *The Self and Others,* in *The New York Times Book Review,* February 22, 1970, p. 1-2, 44.

[*Berman is an American professor of political science, nonfiction writer, and critic. In the following review of* The Divided Self *and* The Self and Others, *he favorably assesses the development of Laing's theory and method for the treatment of schizophrenia, contrasting it with "the prophetic, evangelical (some would say, messianic) tone" of* The Politics of Experience.]

For a great many Americans, particularly young Americans, the 1960's were a time in which two of the deepest streams of consciousness—self-consciousness and social consciousness—converged. The radical vision and energy of the sixties aimed at a fusion of ideas and experiences which the fifties had found either unrelated or incompatible: political freedom and personal ecstasy, activism and mysticism, voter-registration drives and mind-expanding drugs, sit-ins and love-ins.

This fusion animated much of the most powerful literature of the decade: in the work of Allen Ginsberg, Bob Dylan, Norman Mailer, Eldridge Cleaver, for example, Americans learned to look harder and deeper at once into themselves and into the institutions and environment they lived in. They sought both to expand the self and open it up, and to create a society in which the self could survive.

As self-consciousness and social consciousness flowed together, the critical and speculative thought of the "Freudian Left" suddenly found itself in the mainstream of American culture. The term "Freudian Left" denotes a family of thinkers—Wilhelm Reich, Erich Fromm, Herbert Marcuse, Paul Goodman, Norman O. Brown are among the most prominent—who have tried to synthesize the insights of Marxist historical sociology and those of Freudian psychology, in order to give us a fuller and richer idea of what we are doing and who we are. Although some of these men began their project of synthesis as early as the 1920's, and though much of their work has been brilliantly imaginative, it was only in the sixties that they got the widespread attention and recognition they deserved.

Their theoretical perspectives opened up a whole new dimension in American social thought, a dimension of psychological depth. Their impact on American radicalism was especially striking: they provided a new direction and a new vocabulary for the emerging New Left. The essential trouble with our society, radicals began to say, is that it forces us all to play roles and fulfill functions that cut us off from our deepest feelings and needs: it alienates us from ourselves.

Once the problem was perceived in this way, two crucial questions emerged: How and why does this alienation occur? And what can we do about it? In the last few years an increasing number of people, especially young and radical people, have been turning to the British psychoanalyst R. D. Laing as a man who can answer these questions. The appearance in uniform cloth-bound editions of *The Divided Self* and the new, extensively revised *Self and Others* should be welcomed.

Although Laing's work has been known in America for only a few years, and known only in limited circles—in mental hospitals and medical schools, among students and artists and intellectuals—it has shaken just about everyone and everything it has touched. It has forced people to decide where they stand—and, implicitly, who they want to be. To a new generation of psychiatrists his work is inspiring, liberating; to their supervisors it is irresponsible and mind-destroying. The Living Theatre chants the gnomic last words of Laing's *The Politics of Experience* . . . : "If I could turn you on, if I could only drive you out of your wretched mind, if I could tell you I would let you know"; audiences are unhinged, enraged, they shout out obscenities and shake their fists. The intensity of response which Laing evokes—both favorable and unfavorable—suggests that he really *is* turning people on, he really *is* driving peo-

ple out of their minds, and he is letting more and more people know.

Laing's own radicalism has developed only as he has approached and entered middle age. The facts of the first 30 years of his life sound conventional and bland. He was born in Glasgow in 1927, educated at a grammar (i.e., state, rather than private) school and at Glasgow University (M.D., 1951), worked as a psychiatrist in the British Army, taught and practiced in Glasgow again for awhile. In the late 1950's he went to London, and got psychoanalytic training at the Tavistock Institute, the British center of Freudian orthodoxy.

It was only gradually, in the course of the 1960's, that he emerged from the protective warmth of that orthodoxy. He became an outspoken and trenchant critic of traditional approaches and methods in psychiatry. He began to experiment with the therapeutic use of mescaline and L.S.D. He established in London a therapeutic community, Kingsley Hall, where patients, doctors and staff live and work together democratically, without hierarchy, free of distinctions of rank or role.

Quite early in his career, Laing focused on a human condition which has been acutely embarrassing to psychiatry since Freud's time: the state of mind called schizophrenic. Few have ever broken through into the schizophrenic's closed world, fewer still have been able to make this world even remotely intelligible to the rest of us outside. Laing is one of the few who have got through: he has penetrated and explored this underworld, both in his patients and, increasingly, in himself; and he has come back to tell the tale. This is the source of his charismatic power. Since his first book, *The Divided Self: An Existential Study in Sanity and Madness* (1960; written mostly in 1957), he has been telling us that there is treasure buried there, and showing us maps. We can find this treasure for ourselves, he says, if we only let ourselves take this trip with him, if we follow him down and in.

In *The Divided Self,* the trip begins with one of the classical accounts of schizophrenic behavior. Laing quotes E. Kraeplin's 1905 description of a catatonic 18-year-old boy, who is carried into a medical lecture room, but seemingly pays no attention to his surroundings. He does not answer or even look up when he is spoken to, but talks animatedly to himself in a long monologue which Kraeplin conveys vividly. Kraeplin finds this patient "inaccessible": "His talk was . . . only a series of disconnected sentences having no relation to the general situation." Laing is not so sure. Maybe, he suggests, the patient's talk has all too close a "relation to the general situation," but a relation that the doctor does not want to see.

Laing invites us to look more closely into this supposedly incoherent talk. For example, the patient says: "You want to know that too? I tell you who is being measured and is measured and shall be measured. I know all that, and I could tell you, but I do not want to." With a little empathy and sensitivity, Laing says, we can see that the patient is talking very plainly, and that "he deeply resents this form of interrogation, which is being carried out before a lecture-room of students." This becomes clear if we approach the schizophrenic not as a specimen, but as "a tortured and desperate human being"; if we interpret his weird and frightening behavior not as "signs of a disease," but as "expressive of his existence." Consider the boy: "What is he 'about' in speaking and acting this way? He is objecting to being measured and tested. He wants to be heard."

Laing has listened closely, more closely than anyone before him. He has "decoded" the language of schizophrenics, and transmitted some of what they are trying to tell us. Much of what they are saying, he makes clear, is "existential truth"; and very often it is a truth that we do not want to hear.

How do schizophrenics get that way? In recent years there has been much evidence that it may be essentially genetic and hereditary. Laing neither accepts nor rejects this hypothesis. He believes, however, that if schizophrenia did not biologically exist, our culture would invent it. So many people seem inexorably driven to it, trapped in environments which destroy their sense of identity before it has any chance to develop.

Laing brings to life a great variety of these insulted and injured people. Here we have space enough for only one: Julie, a 26-year-old psychotic girl. In her story Laing's enormous literary gifts unfold; his feeling for a patient's language and imagery, his ability to bring an individual human being concretely to life, the clarity and intensity of his style, pull us irresistibly into her world.

Julie feels "crushed," "smothered," "flooded," "burned up," every moment of her life, by terrible forces that never leave her in peace. The most ordinary circumstances of life constitute a mortal threat to her being. She feels that she is not a real person; she "has nobody because she is nobody." She is empty inside, and yet, somehow, innately destructive: she had better not touch anything, lest she damage it; other people must not touch her, lest they be destroyed. Terrifying images explode inside her: she was "born under a black sun"; she is a "prairie," "a ruined city," a "broken pitcher," a "well run dry"; she is "the ghost of the weed garden." The one thread that runs through everything she says is that somewhere "a child has been murdered"—a child wearing Julie's own clothes.

Laing's attempt to get at the "existential truth" of what his patients are saying leads him to investigate the context in which they are saying it. In *The Divided Self,* and further in *Sanity, Madness and the Family, Volume One: Families of Schizophrenics* (with A. Esterson, 1965 . . .), he focuses on family structures, and analyzes brilliantly the psychic pressures they generate. Thus Julie's family is perplexed: "Julie was always such a good child" until she suddenly, inexplicably went mad. Her goodness, they explain, was manifest virtually from her birth: "she never was a demanding baby." Unlike her older sister, who was always a "bad" child, Julie "never really cried for her feeds. She never sucked vigorously. She never finished a bottle." Her sister was "selfish," "greedy," "voracious," always crying, wanting, demanding. But Julie "was never a trouble." Her mother "had no bother with her. She always did what she was told." The whole family—except

for her bad sister—all recall nostalgically those good old days, "before she got sick."

What is going on here? The crucial thing about Julie's family, Laing says, is that "none of the adults in her world know the difference between existential life and death." Any assertion of feelings or needs, any instinctive energy, any expression of life—from the very beginning of life—is condemned. The basic norm of this system is clear: the only good child is a dead one. Julie has picked up the signals: it is only by playing dead that she can preserve herself; if she tries to live, she will be killed.

Under such pressure, out of total insecurity, the individual constructs a network of defenses, which Laing calls a *false-self system.* The purpose of a false-self system, he explains, is to split the self off from all its activities. Thus the self is "uncoupled" from the body: the body becomes merely one object among other objects in the world, the core of a "false" self; the "true" self is felt as something detached, disembodied, hidden within.

Thus the true self is protected from participation in the life of a world that is set up to destroy it. From now on the self will be purely a spectator; it will observe, judge and criticize whatever the body, that alien object, happens to be experiencing or doing, but it will not get involved. It will leave no fingerprints or footprints in the world. It will be a stranger in a strange land. Divided, the self may be able to stand; united, it will surely fall.

"But the tragic paradox," writes Laing, "is that the more the self is defended in this way, the more it is destroyed. The apparent eventual destruction and dissolution of the self in schizophrenic conditions is accomplished not by external attacks from the enemy (actual or supposed), from without, but by the devastation caused by the inner defensive manoeuvers themselves." If the shut-up self cannot be enriched by outer experience, its whole inner world will become more and more impoverished; it will find even less living space within its citadel than it had outside. Inner life will be felt as empty, cold, dry, impotent, desolate, worthless, dead; the self will suffocate within its own walls. Worse: the false-self system will be felt as a fifth column, a base for the enemy; every move, every breath comes to be controlled and directed by hostile, destructive forces—by a mother or father, by the authorities, by "Them"—that are continually closing in. The self grows desperate to break out. But outside it sees only the malignant power structure that drove it inward in the first place. There is nowhere for the individual to go. So he goes mad.

Laing makes us aware how much of our whole modern sensibility and awareness is rooted in the radical doubt and anxiety that permeates schizophrenics' whole lives.

—Marshall Berman

The Divided Self vibrates with the excitement of discovery, a discovery that resonates far beyond the hospital gates. Laing is steeped in modern literature and existentialist philosophy. He is aware, and he makes us aware, how much of our whole modern sensibility and awareness is rooted in the radical doubt and anxiety that permeates schizophrenics' whole lives; he evokes the alienation they feel with a vividness that strikes a sympathetic chord in all of us. Their dread of nameless threats embedded in everyday life, their sense of aloneness and emptiness, of the precariousness of a person's being—all this is fundamental to our culture. Laing points it out in Baudelaire and Kierkegaard and Dostoevsky, in Kafka and Eliot and Yeats, in Beckett and Genet. (He explores Dostoevsky and Genet lengthily and brilliantly in *Self and Others.*)

Laing knew from the first, then, that he was on to something big. But he did not know at first, in 1957, how big it was. He spent the 1960's trying to discover the meaning of his discovery. The trip which at first led him into schizophrenia and away from "reality" has more recently led him through schizophrenia and back to reality, deeper into it than ever before, with a new vision—a more radical and more political vision—of how schizophrenic our reality really is.

Laing's new perspective is foreshadowed in some of the darkest passages of *The Divided Self.* He intimates, uneasily, tentatively, that perhaps Julie's family is not so "deviant" after all, not so different from all other families. Is not their model of the "good child" a model that we have all grown up with—and still carry around in our heads? In growing up to be good and dead, Julie was fulfilling an ideal that was (and is) quite typical in her society—fulfilling it with a vengeance. Laing's insight into closed family systems gradually opened outward, into the larger systems in which all families are enclosed.

By 1964, in the preface to the Penguin edition of *The Divided Self* (inexcusably left out of the new Pantheon edition), his new radical vision is clearly defined. He asserts boldly that, from its deepest roots, our whole society is mad. Indeed, he suggests, the only difference between his schizophrenic patients and "normal" men is that his patients know that they are mad, while normal men deceive themselves into thinking that they are sane:

> A man who says that men are machines may be a great scientist. A man who says that he is a machine is "depersonalized" in psychiatric jargon. . . . A little girl of seventeen in a mental hospital told me she was terrified because the Atom Bomb was inside her. That is a delusion. The statesmen of the world who boast and threaten that they have Doomsday weapons are far more dangerous, and far more estranged from "reality", than many of the people on whom the label "psychotic" is fixed.

Laing's most recent writing, *The Politics of Experience* (1967) and the new, revised edition of *Self and Others* (1970), focus on the dilemma of psychiatry in a sick society. In *Self and Others* Laing generalizes the conceptual scheme he developed in *The Families of Schizophrenics* all social relationships, it appears, are closed "fantasy systems" whose members are alienated from themselves. Some members of these systems (few? most? all? Laing is very abstract here, and the reader is left to infer the worst) are placed in "untenable positions," in which "it is impossible to leave and impossible to stay." They are psychically up against the wall.

The members of any social fantasy system are taught by "Them," the authorities, to believe that "the box," the system, "is the whole world." It follows from this premise that the only way to get out of the box is to "step off the end of the world"—to go mad; and Laing has shown us how fearful going mad can be. Hopefully, the authorities are wrong. If they are wrong, then there are (in principle) ways for the self to get out of the box and to live sanely and happily in the world. But what if the authorities are right? What if the box *really is* the whole world? Then madness, terrifying as it may be, is the only way for the self to survive. And Laing seems to suggest that everyone should indeed go mad.

Is the self really so totally boxed in? Laing does not make a very good case to back up his drastic indictment: his discussion of our social system is disappointingly abstract, moralistic, derivative, unconvincing; his feeling for ambiguity and contradiction, his sense of tragedy, seem to disappear. Our common sense tells us to dismiss Laing's indictment out of hand, and probably our common sense is right. And yet, having once said this, it is hard not to feel uneasy. Laing's view of society may strike us as paranoid, even schizophrenic; but it is a paranoia that strikes deep, and it creeps imperceptibly into our minds.

"She was such a good child. . . . She always did what she was told." For "child" substitute "student," "worker," "neighbor," "citizen"—any role you like. In all our institutions don't we depend on false-self systems to get us through the day? How else could we adjust ourselves to people and activities that would tear us to pieces if we cared about them? Knowing how to manipulate false-self systems: isn't this the secret of success?

"The observable behavior that is the expression of the false self is often perfectly normal. We see a model child, an ideal husband, an industrious clerk." Or a "liberated" girl who can be so refreshingly casual about her body because, as it turns out, her body has nothing to do with *her.* Or a kept intellectual who, for the same reason, can be equally casual about his mind. It is so much easier to fulfill other people's needs and expectations, we all know, if we have no (possibly conflicting) needs or expectations of our own. It should be clear to us by now that our schizoid character structure, as much as any other power, is what makes our world go round.

Can madness really be a way back into ourselves? We must take very seriously Laing's argument that it can. It can, he says, if we go mad only for awhile, and only under very carefully controlled conditions. Then madness can propel us out of the box, and can liberate all the feelings that the box has kept locked up. Thus "the cracked mind of the schizophrenic may let in light which does not enter the intact minds of many sane people whose minds are closed." Madness may bring to the surface all our repressed fear, rage, hatred, violence and despair; but this opening up can also release all our repressed hope and love and creativity, all our buried feeling for life. We must let go, Laing believes, because only if we lose ourselves can we authentically find ourselves.

The prophetic, evangelical (some would say messianic) tone of Laing's later writings—particularly *The Politics of Experience*—is deliberate. In recent years he has moved from merely interpreting the world to trying actively, in his own way, to change it. His way has been to try to create new kinds of inner space in the interstices of our society. He sees Kingsley Hall as only a beginning, a nuclear community from which others can grow. In these communities, he hopes, doctors, patients, friends, lovers, others, will be able to live and work together for their common health and liberation. Here men will be free to go mad, but free also to go *through* their madness, and to return to the world restored to themselves. As each one of us descends deeper and deeper into the nightmare of his own aloneness, we will be surrounded by friends who have taken such trips into themselves, and who, because they genuinely know the terror we are undergoing, will be able to help us come through.

Laing knows that these projects, even if they are realized, will be small and fragmentary at best. Kingsley Hall will share the fate of many other utopian communities: it may, if it is lucky, insulate itself from society; it will never change society. Still, it already has the distinctive value that utopias have always had.

The life and energy of Laing's vision—in his practice as well as his books—creates a little more open space for the self in the world. It is this that so many respond to. In a time when the open spaces are being closed off fast, Laing can at least give us a start in the direction we need to go. To have made such a start may be, in the end, the best thing the 1960's can leave to the hard times ahead.

James S. Gordon   (review date 13 December 1970)

SOURCE: A review of *Knots,* in *The New York Times Book Review,* December 13, 1970, p. 6.

[*In the following favorable review of* Knots, *Gordon discusses how Laing uses the themes of communication and interpersonal relationships as "patterns . . . of human bondage" in his poetry.*]

At the beginning of his first book, *The Divided Self,* R. D. Laing quoted the French psychiatrist Minkowski: "This is a subjective work which tries with all its might to be objective."

For the last 12 years, in eight books and numerous articles, Laing has, to the dismay of much of orthodox psychiatry, pushed his own subjectivity to its limits. He has returned with observations, insights and formulations which seem quite pertinent to the lives of thousands of devoted readers. Like Freud 40 years ago, Laing is read as psychiatric theoretician, political philosopher and personal guru.

In *Knots,* his most recent book, Laing continues to explore some of the themes that have been prominent in his work since 1958. The emphasis is on disorders of human communications and feelings, their origins in the family, and their tortured, mutually unsatisfactory elaboration in later relationships. But in *Knots,* Laing has abandoned his ordinarily graceful prose for highly condensed poems, the knots of the title. Poetry, the most personal of the literary arts, is used as a medium for highly formal philosophical and psychological descriptions which themselves delineate intensely personal experiences.

The knots are "patterns . . . of human bondage," descriptions of the bonds (or binds) that people—parents and children, lovers, friends, therapists and patients—put each other and themselves in. They are meticulously constructed, often hilariously and painfully recognizable. But they do not yield easily. Several readings—preferably aloud—are sometimes not enough. Each reader, after their initial dizzying resistance is overcome, will probably untie them differently.

There are five chapters or five knots which are themselves composed of smaller, related knots. One can discern an approximate focus in each—love, possessiveness, understanding, fear, the nature of being—but all these themes are echoed in each knot. And through them all the emphasis is on the possibilities for self-deception and mutual mystification.

The book opens with an ironic non-invitation to participation:

> They are playing a game. They are playing at not
> playing a game. If I show them I see they are,
>   I
> shall break the rules and they will punish me.
> I must play their game, of not seeing I see the
>   game.

Though the tone is playful and childlike, the logic is painful and inexorable, and the meaning many leveled. It is a description of a familial process that Laing details in *The Politics of the Family* (which unfortunately has not yet been published in America). But doesn't it also prefigure a game that Laing will be playing with his reader?

A few pages later the knot enlarges and tightens. The verses may be about a child, a patient, about Laing himself, or his reader, or all of these and more:

> There must be something the matter with him
> because he would not be acting as he does
> unless there was
> therefore he is acting as he is
> because there is something the matter with him.

Sometimes the small knots proceed in a developmental sequence. "Jack" who as a child wanted to "devour his mother and be devoured by her" is, as an adult in his relation to Jill

>   . . . devoured
> by his devouring fear of
> being devoured by
> her devouring desire
> for *him* to devour her.

The large knot of which this is a part climaxes in a series of variations on the theme of differentiation between the self and the world, the "me" and "not me," the "mine" and "not mine." The formal logic seems hopelessly complex, its component propositions mutually contradictory. But the impossibility of logical explanation of this earliest stage of human development is in a creative tension with the process itself.

This knot's musical notation—*moderato* at the beginning, *poco a poco accelerando al fine* as the permutations multiply—led me to try to work it out as a composition. A musician friend improvised while I read. What logic could not solve, the rhythms and variations of speech and music seemed to elucidate. The knots demand to be puzzled out, but like other works of art answer most directly to the reader's experience.

The last section of the book moves more deeply into the nature of this experience. The roots of interpersonal relations are seen to dwell in the same soil as religious mysticism. One feels the connection between the infant's struggle to define what is inside his body and what is outside and the mystic's strenuous denial of this separation, but both these pursuits are seen as "webs of *maya*" against a more remote background. Everything that Laing has described, everything that has gone before, as well as what follows, may be illusory:

> Although innumerable beings have been lead to
>   Nirvana
> no being has been led to Nirvana.

Ultimately, descriptions which have delighted the reader and compelled him to mental gymnastics yield to that which cannot be described. The most basic human experiences and all the precise and elegant forms Laing has used to convey them—words, logic, music—have arisen out of formless silence:

> What an interesting finger let me suck it

> It's not an interesting finger take it away

> The statement is pointless
> The finger is speechless.

In his earlier work Laing guided the reader to understanding. In *Knots* he compels him to experience. The surface brilliance of phenomenological description gives way to the vortex of contradictions which make up the unconscious. To grasp this dense and difficult book one must be willing to follow Laing in his spirals of descent. If *Knots* is to yield, one must yield to the knots.

Alan Tyson   (review date 11 February 1971)

SOURCE: "Homage to Catatonia," in *The New York Review of Books,* Vol. XVI, No. 2, February 11, 1971, pp. 3-4, 6.

[*Tyson is a Scottish psychiatrist, musicologist, and author of several studies on Beethoven. In the following review, in which he examines seven of Laing's major works, he discusses such themes as the role of the family and society in the development of an individual's pathologies, the influence of fantasy and spirituality in the development of self-*identity, and Laing's abiding effort "to make madness, and the process of going mad, comprehensible."*]

In theory the publication of a substantially revised edition of R. D. Laing's *The Self and Others,* and the reissue of his first and I suppose still most celebrated book *The Divided Self,* now more than ten years old, should provide as good an occasion as any for a retrospective survey of his work and an attempt at a critical assessment. But in practice this seems both difficult and discouraging.

Why is that? It is not as though *reading* Laing is discouraging or uncongenial. He is an attractive, even seductive writer—a point to which I shall return, since it calls for closer examination. In England *The Divided Self* must be counted as the most widely known of all recent psychiatric writing, popular or specialist; and although paperback psychiatry—I use the phrase as a loose categorization, not as a disparagement—is a much more highly developed genre in the States (where Laing's works have had to complete with the productions of writers as varied as Norman O. Brown, Eric Berne, Erich Fromm, Hannah Green, and Ken Kesey), the recent *Politics of Experience* has probably reached a wider readership than any.

Wider, but not necessarily broader. It seems a rather curious readership. For Laing, as everyone knows, has become a cult figure; and this fact imposes on the reviewer of his books a burden not merely of trying to understand the points that Laing is making, and of testing them against his own judgment and experience, but of attempting to discover the basis of their appeal to people not otherwise apparently interested in psychiatric theory.

Commentators on Laing frequently lump his writings together, as if each book were saying much the same thing, or at any rate as if the basic message were homogeneous. By doing so they indicate that they must have a high tolerance of inconsistency. Perhaps an approach of that kind has advantages; those who are very squeamish about inconsistencies will not expect to get much from Laing, and there are in any case rewards for one's industry in reading right through the canon, in that obscurities in one book are illuminated by discussions in another (the somewhat diffuse and possibly underrated *Self and Others* is helpful in this regard).

But the opposite also happens, so that what one felt one had mastered becomes obscured by later writings—not strangely, perhaps, if one sees Laing's output as representing a personal odyssey—and one is left with a total picture that surprisingly seems *less* than the sum of its parts. In view of these ambiguities it seems a wise plan (though not an easy task) to examine in rough chronological order the way that he has presented some of his central ideas. Let me try to describe, obviously in a very much simplified form, something of the shifts of emphasis.

In all his more formal writing Laing is evidently concerned with the struggle between the core or essential nature of a person and some deforming, inimical forces— inimical at any rate to the continued survival of the core in an undistorted form, though the forces are not perhaps necessarily malevolent. Survival in this struggle ensures a state of "ontological security" in which one will "encounter all the hazards of life, social, ethical, spiritual, biological, from a centrally firm sense of one's own and other people's reality and identity" (*The Divided Self* . . .). Failure to achieve this security results in various concessions having to be made at the expense of one's own sense of well-being, one's identity, one's integrity, or one's sanity: terms, it must be said, that appear to become somewhat blurred when Laing is writing loosely.

Where, then, is the denaturing "enemy" located? In spite of some considerable overlap throughout the books, there does appear to be an increasing "distancing," or removal from the center, in locating this enemy. Thus in *The Divided Self* (1960) the enemy is represented by some unaccepted, possibly unacceptable, parts of the self. (The concept of one part of the self repudiating another part has of course an immensely long intellectual history, besides being central to Freud's thought.) But in *The Self and Others* (1961) there is already a markedly greater concern over interaction with others in producing pathology (cf., for instance, the chapters on "collusion" and on "driving the other crazy," a concept referred to below). This is further developed in the 1964 book on families of schizophrenics, where the "enemy" must, I think, be seen in the pathological communication between parents and children within the family circle. Finally, in *The Politics of Experience* (1967) it is society that attempts to clap a strait jacket of conformity on children at their birth, devastating their potentialities, curdling the milk of human kindness.

Although this scheme is oversimplified, I think that the progression is undeniable; it is even true that up to a point *The Self and Others* is concerned with interaction between two people ("dyadic relationships"), whereas the later book on families (as one might expect) never deals with fewer than three people. The changes of viewpoint are not made very explicit by Laing, except for some comments in the 1964 Preface to the English paperback edition of *The Divided Self*, the tone of which is like much of *The Politics of Experience.* It may be that the omission of this preface from the new American hardcover edition represents some theoretical or ideological back-tracking.

Omitted from the foregoing scheme are two works of collaboration: the examination by Laing and D. G. Cooper, under the title of *Reason and Violence* (1964), of three philosophical works by Sartre, and the development, in conjunction with H. Phillipson and A. R. Lee, of a set of symbols for describing dyadic relationships (*Interpersonal Perception: A Theory and a Method of Research,* 1966). Neither volume would ordinarily be supposed to be about madness—though the former is intermittently concerned with alienation, and the latter with distorted communication and perception. For it is, of course, on his approach to madness, and especially to one puzzling form of it, schizophrenia, that Laing's serious reputation rests.

The basic purpose of *The Divided Self,* not only his first but up to now his best organized book, is "to make madness, and the process of going mad, comprehensible." The work is in three parts, the first being a very necessary theoretical introduction to the second and third that deal respectively with schizoid and with schizophrenic patients.

Laing's approach, as he states at the outset, is "existential" and "phenomenological"—terms whose somewhat individual use he exposes in his discussion of a crucial question: In what language are the inner experiences of people, and particularly mad people, to be discussed? His own dissatisfaction with the psychiatric and psychoanalytic language in which he was himself trained is quite clear:

> The most serious objection to the technical vocabulary currently used to describe psychiatric patients is that it consists of words which split man up verbally in a way which is analogous to the existential splits we have to describe here. But we cannot give an adequate account of the existential splits unless we can begin from the concept of a unitary whole, and no such concept exists, nor can any such concept be expressed within the current language system of psychiatry or psychoanalysis. . . .

> How can we speak in any way adequately of the relationship between me and you in terms of the interaction of one mental apparatus with another? . . . This difficulty faces not only classical Freudian metapsychology but equally any theory that begins with man or a part of man abstracted from his relation with the other in his world. . . . Only existential thought has attempted to match the original experience of oneself in relationship to others in one's world by a term that adequately reflects this totality. [*The Divided Self*]

The terms that Laing subsequently employs to describe his patients—terms such as self (whether true or false, embodied or unembodied, divided or undivided), security and insecurity, self-consciousness, reality and unreality, inner and outer—are for the most part close to popular speech and far removed from psychiatric jargon; but more importantly for him they are the language of *experience*—one of Laing's key words—and not merely of observation, description, classification, or categorization. (In another context he criticizes psychiatrists for seeming to be more concerned with a patient's behaviour than with his experience.) Moreover they are terms of intrapersonal or interpersonal experience rather than of "it-processes." The latter two-thirds of the book—the schizoid and schizophrenic case histories—can be taken as a demonstration of the advantages in using this kind of language when attempting to make the experiences of such patients intelligible.

Within these chosen limits this demonstration is brilliantly successful. The memorable vignettes with which the book is crammed—of James, David, and of Peter, whose complaint was that "there was a constant unpleasant smell coming from him," of the more flamboyantly mad Joan and Julie, self-described as "the ghost of the weed garden"—distinguished the book as something of a landmark in descriptive writing on the fragmented personality, and in any event as an astonishing and admirable performance for a man of twenty-eight.

Particularly moving, perhaps, is the sense of pain that these case histories convey. The defensive maneuver, whereby, as Laing describes it, the self is divided, aims at preserving the "true self" while offering to the world both as ambassador and hostage a compliant persona (the "false self"). But the loss of integration is evidently extremely painful to bear. Most painful of all, it would seem from the case material, is the feeling of being split into a mind and a body, usually involving an identification with the mind and an alienation from the body. It is not perhaps surprising, in view of the widespread distribution of schizoid character traits, that the clinical material of *The Divided Self* evoked a cry of recognition from thousands of readers who felt that the dimensions of their own sense of alienation had been charted for the first time.

There are, of course, hazards in linking the structure of one's theory so closely to the inner experience of going or being mad. Although, as I have hinted, Laing's comments on the difficulties of finding language in which patients are to be discussed are often acute, they appear to be part of a less plausible attack on abstractions in general; he seems to have a horror of any abstraction that is not immediately intelligible in the language of the patient's inner experience. There may indeed be dangers in abstraction or reification, as he suggests, but there are also dangers in anthropomorphizing, as psychoanalytic theoreticians know. In his attempts to make even the apparently most bizarre statements that patients make about themselves meaningful in some way, Laing is led rather dangerously in the direction of saying that their statements are in a certain sense true.

To make this claim outright would be to neglect the extent of phantasy; and it would be a poor theory that went all the way in identifying a patient's phantasies about himself with the truth about himself. It is perhaps not surprising, therefore, that in his next book, *The Self and Others,* Laing begins with an examination of the phenomenon of phantasy: in effect, a critique of a psychoanalytic paper on unconscious phantasy. By this time Laing shows that he has been influenced by some recent but now very well-known work on the interpersonal aspects of the causation of schizophrenic behavior and experience: H. F. Searles's 1959 paper on "The effort to drive the other person crazy," and the work of Gregory Bateson and others (1956) in developing the "double bind" hypothesis. Searles lists six modes of driving someone crazy within the context of a relationship; each of the six techniques (e.g., exposing the other person simultaneously to stimulation and frustration, or to rapidly alternating stimulation and frustration) "tends to undermine the other person's confidence in his own emotional reactions and his own perception of reality."

The thesis of Bateson and his coworkers at Palo Alto is more complex and harder to summarize; but the "double bind" situation involves two or more persons, one of whom is defined as the "victim." The "victim" is caught in a tangle of paradoxical injunctions (instructions) in which he cannot do the right thing. Each of the contradictory injunctions is likely to be backed up by bribes or threats (sometimes of a devastating kind), and to be conveyed to the "victim" by different means and at different levels of communication (e.g., by gestures at variance with words), making a robust repudiation of the trap by its "victim" impossible. Sometimes indeed the injunctions masquerade as attributions (statements by one person as to what another person is, or is like): "You love me, don't forget that." The suggestion of Bateson et al. is that the double bind pattern is highly characteristic of the childhoods of schizophrenics.

Like the double bind, *The Self and Others* is hard to summarize, but much of the book is devoted to classifications, with examples, of ambiguous and incompatible injunctions and attributions. In the second edition (1969), called *Self and Others,* the language has been very much sharpened by an entire rewriting.

The influence of Searles, Bateson, and others is seen even more clearly in what some consider Laing's most accessible and straightforward book, the study of "Families of Schizophrenics," which he wrote with Aaron Esterson in 1964 and which appeared as the first volume of *Sanity, Madness and the Family* (there are to date no further volumes). This presents extended examples of family dialogue and polylogue in eleven families each of which includes a girl diagnosed as schizophrenic.

Laing and Esterson make plain in the Preface that in their view schizophrenia is not a fact but an assumption or hypothesis—though their exact purpose in drawing this distinction is rather less clear. They begin with some definitions, derived ultimately from Sartre's usage:

> Events, occurrences, happenings, may be deeds done by doers, or they may be the outcome of a continuous series of operations that have no agent as their author. In the first case we shall speak of such events as the outcome of praxis; in the second case, as the outcome of process. . . . What happens in a group will be *intelligible* if one can retrace the steps from what is going on (process) to who is doing what (praxis).

The book is a study of family interaction, and this interaction is investigated in a series of interviews with various combinations of family members; most of these interviews were recorded on tape. Each of the eleven families studied contained a woman between the ages of fifteen and forty who had been diagnosed as "schizophrenic" by at least two senior psychiatrists and who was regarded as such by the staff, and whose condition was not complicated by specific factors such as brain injury, epilepsy, subnormality, brain surgery, electrotherapy beyond certain stated limits. The above criteria were applied to the new patients admitted at two hospitals, provided that at least one parent was alive and resident in the United Kingdom. The families studied were the first eleven to satisfy the criteria.

Within the limits set by the size of the book the presentation is exemplary. There is no doubt that for most readers these eleven families, with their stifling atmospheres, their subtle emotional blackmail systems, their killing by kindness, become palpable, so that the deforming pressures to which the daughters were exposed are easy to grasp. And by the end of the book most readers will have gained the impression that Laing and Esterson are offering an explanation of what went wrong: that these parents, through their insensitivities, their pathological phantasy systems, and their anxieties, first drove and then kept their daughters crazy. But is this what Laing and Esterson are saying?

Apparently not; in the Preface to the second edition they state, or restate, that their aim was a much more modest one:

> We set out to illustrate by eleven examples that, if we look at some experience and behavior without reference to family interactions, they may appear comparatively socially senseless, but that if we look at the same experience and behavior in their original family context they are liable to make more sense.

The sense of anticlimax, which I cannot believe I am the only reader to have felt on meeting these words, as well as an unfamiliar note of bluster in the new Preface, suggest that Laing and Esterson have been forced into a partial retreat, possibly from criticisms that there were flaws in their techniques for fostering scientific objectivity (their lack of a control group, for example). The material that they have presented in this highly original study seems at any rate much more fertile than the conclusions that they are prepared to draw from it.

The Politics of Experience was published in 1967, but most of it had already been presented in public in the form of articles or lectures during 1964 and 1965. It is not really organized as a book, being diffuse and somewhat short-winded. Nor is there the development of a continuous argument; rather, it is a series of discussions each linked to a single topic and strung together by the concept of "experience." But even in the individual chapters the treatment tends toward aphorism. The topics range from brief criticisms of schools of psychotherapy and of educational institutions, another attempt to describe the schizophrenic experience, to two chapters dealing implicitly and explicitly with the possible positive values of the psychotic experience. The book ends with an extended prose poem, rich in autobiographical allusion, called **"The Bird of Paradise."** Though it is somewhat surprising to find it in the book, it is undeniably interesting—perhaps rather like finding a lock of some medical author's hair in his textbook on alopecia.

Besides being diffuse it is an intemperate book. No doubt it will be said—as Laing himself says in the Preface—that things have now come to such a pass as to justify the stridency. There is certainly a fashionable element in the denunciations, whether they are addressed to the institutions of society, the "often fibrillating heartland of senescent capitalism," or to the human beings who inhabit it: "we are all murderers and prostitutes." Occasionally the language becomes dithyrambic; here is the voice of the bard in best Messianic-Ossianic vein:

> I am a specialist, God help me, in events in inner space and time, in experiences called thoughts, images, reveries, memories, dreams, visions, hallucinations, dreams of memories, memories of dreams, memories of visions, dreams of hallucinations, refractions of refractions of refractions of that original Alpha and Omega of experience and reality, that Reality on whose repression, denial, splitting, projection, falsification, and general desecration and profanation our civilization as much as on anything is based.

There is not much sustained argument in the book. If indeed the deforming, inimical agents are not to be seen in one's unaccepted, repudiated impulses, or in parental mis-attributions, or in particular mystifying, confusing patterns of family interaction, but are produced by the nature of modern society itself, this is a much harder process to exemplify, illustrate, and indeed to identify, though it is easy enough to roar against. Society, Laing claims, has processed us all on Procrustean beds.

But are these deforming influences of society at large to be found in every family, and in the pressures exerted by every institution? Laing does not really bother to clarify this. He seems indeed to believe that man is born in original innocence but is irremediably maltreated by everything that shapes his growing up. Continuing to live in a society is only a daily renewal of this distortion, deformation, alienation.

He talks rather airily of realizing the extent of our alienation as "the essential springboard for any serious reflection on any aspect of present interhuman life," but—apart indeed from some murmurs against the psychiatric profession, certainly not *wholly* unjustified—he does not say how this is to be done. The family, psychiatry, capitalism are vaguely attacked. There seems to be a confusion of various myths and fables, such as the myth of Primeval Innocence, or an updated version of the Emperor's New Clothes in which Laing, speaking for the innocence of childhood, declares that the Emperor is really wearing a strait jacket.

These and other myths are worth examining for it seems to me that the mythopoeic element in Laing is the source both of his diffuse appeal and of the difficulty that is often experienced in getting him into focus. The views that are implied by the impetus of much of Laing's writing (though I am left in some doubt how far Laing still holds them)— that most psychotic behavior is intelligible and meaningful within the sphere in which the patient has to operate; that a psychotic breakdown can be in itself a means to recovery; that the statements of psychotics about themselves are in a profound way true; that society itself literally traumatizes its children into psychosis, just as in one of his earlier formulations (later abandoned) Freud conceived of fathers as literally seducing their daughters into neurosis: these seem to me to be romantic myths which contain a strong wishful element and have just enough truth in them to prevent that distressing fact from being easily recognized. Some of them are at any rate no worse than their antagonistic positivist myths (e.g., that all "psychiatric" or emotional disorders will be found to have a biochemical cause). I wish however that they had not been confounded in Laing's work with other, more trite, observations and aspirations, such as that life in an industrial society is often frustrating to personal development, or that doctors should treat their patients more humanely, and so forth.

In any case it is often possible to be impressed with a point that Laing is making without the necessity of being stampeded into sharing all his conclusions. He notes, for instance, that in the case of those who are regarded as "long-standing schizophrenics" medical and nursing reports tend to become more stereotyped as time goes on (*Sanity, Madness and the Family* . . .) The insinuation is that the continued institutional treatment of such patients makes them into automata; but the laconic or repetitive reports may also have something to do with the prejudices and laziness of medical personnel who find that new cases claim more of their time and interest them more than old ones.

Similarly, one can be appalled by "the statesmen of the world who boast and threaten that they have doomsday weapons" (*The Divided Self,* Preface to English paperback edition) without accepting a definition of psychosis that would include them but omit many of those now in mental hospitals. What is undeniable is that the temptations and anxieties of high office dull the imagination to an alarming degree and fail to place a check on insensitivity and cruelty. But this has been known since the Pharaohs. To redefine "psychotic" is scarcely going to help those in mental institutions.

As to the direction in which Laing's work is taking him: it is hard to guess. It will be a pity if his impressive but at the same time exasperating gift for aphorism and paradox, and his sense of how to appeal to the *Zeitgeist,* should tempt him to abandon the more tedious tasks of rendering his views clearer and more sharply argued and of resolving some of the ambiguities that undoubtedly lurk in them. For I cannot myself think it entirely coincidental that someone who has written so sensitively about the forcing of people into unacceptable, untenable positions should seem to find himself so often misunderstood by those he is trying to reach; nor would I have thought it a very gratifying position to be acclaimed, as surely Laing is acclaimed, by another, more popular, readership that is unable to render a convincing account of his views.

This wide gap, to which any cult figure is exposed, between his followers and those as yet unconvinced, is unlikely to be bridged by his latest work, though it may put everyone in a better temper. *Knots* (1970) is a series of dialogues between "Jack" and "Jill" (or of meditations on their respective points of view) in which they explore the dilemmas that result from their feelings and their expectations concerning each other.

> JILL   I am frightened
>
> JACK Don't be frightened
>
> JILL   I am frightened to be frightened when you tell me I ought not to feel frightened frightened frightened to be frightened not frightened to be frightened not frightened frightened not to be frightened not frightened to be not frightened

The *vers libre* format and the highly abstract formulations enable certain points to come across: the symmetry or near-symmetry of the emotional patterns, or their circularity which preserves the structure of the emotional clinches and prevents either partner from breaking out:

> JACK Forgive me
>
> JILL   No
>
> JACK I'll never forgive you for not forgiving me

But *Knots* seems to me to be a fairly extravagant way of making a few simple points for which a plain prose style is the natural medium. In the Preface Laing writes rather grandly: "The patterns delineated here have not yet been classified by a Linnaeus of human bondage"; but I suspect that Laing's models for elegant bondage may have been the classic paradoxes of the philosophers ("Zeno," "Achilles and the tortoise," "Epimenides the Cretan," etc.) rather than anything classifiable by Linnaean taxonomy.

I doubt in any case if it contributes much to the greater themes raised in Laing's earlier work. The question of the nature of schizophrenia is still of course unresolved; and I do not imagine that the discovery of some enzyme lesion or genetic defect as a proven etiological factor in schizophrenia would now very much influence the nature of Laing's explorations. No doubt some people will be more impressed by "praxis" as a subject to be investigated while others will be drawn to a study of "process." Although failure of members of the same profession to communicate with each other is naturally worrying, there are many ways in which doctors and others can go about seeking understanding.

Thinking about process and praxis I was reminded of an anecdote in Thurber concerning a man who began to see double and consulted a psychiatrist. The psychiatrist decided that the man's problem lay in his inability to make up his mind as to which of two girls he was in love with. The distracted fellow then called on a great eye-man, who cleared up the condition with certain eye drops. Thurber told the story to S. J. Perelman, who commented: "The story is incomplete. Which girl *was* he in love with?" I think we may take it that in the area that Laing is exploring it will be a long time before the story is complete.

Richard Sennett   (review date 3 October 1971)

SOURCE: A review of *The Politics of the Family, and Other Essays,* in *The New York Times Book Review,* October 3, 1971, pp. 2-3, 40-41

[*Sennett is an American sociologist and educator. In the following unfavorable review of* The Politics of the Family, *he charges that Laing's "thought has disintegrated dramatically" and that he "has lost that capacity to dream which is necessary in any enduring radical vision."*]

In a moment of anger in his new book, R. D. Laing writes, "Our own cities are our own animal factories; families, schools, churches, are the slaughterhouses of our children; colleges and other places are the kitchens. As adults in marriages and business we eat the product." These charges may all be true, but they are tiresome, written in such a way that the reader turns them off. The strongest impression I have after reading **The Politics of the Family and Other Essays** is that Laing has substituted an easy rhetoric of accusation and condemnation for the struggle to understand people's feelings that dignified his earlier work.

In the dullness of his attacks on an inhumane society, Laing is, of course, not alone. Many of those who took fire during the recent years of turbulence are now passing through a moment when a great number of painfully acquired ideas threaten to enter the comfortable landscape of cliché. I don't mean that radical rhetoric is out of date, because the fissures in society stimulating it are still there; I mean rather that something is going wrong with the way we perceive injustice, something is atrophying in the words and ideas to express anger, so that the rhetoric remains true but no longer truly angers. Why this should be so, Laing's new book, in its very weariness, helps make clear.

Lassitude follows periods of upheaval with almost monotonous insistence in history, but an exhaustion of sensitivity usually comes upon a people after they have endured a revolution or great change in their lives. The extravagants of Paris who emerged after the death of Robespierre gloried in precious clothing and precious sentiments, all the while mouthing the old revolutionary slogans; the "empty men" of the Weimar Republic, as Brecht called them, also bore the marks of exhaustion left by a domestic war. But the present loss of sensitivity is different, and puzzling, for when we turn away from the enthusiasm for apocalypse that sets the tone of newspapers and television, we face a society whose wars, poverty, racism and all the rest, are changing slowly if at all. Can it be only that we are tired from listening to so much talk about the need for change?

The writings of R. D. Laing have moved from early books which put forth a complex, painful vision of the human oppression involved in the phenomenon society labels "insanity" to books which replay all the early themes in such a fashion that the reader feels he is in a closed and stuffy room. Laing's thought has disintegrated dramatically in the last four years, but it is unworthy of him simply to itemize that decline. For what has happened to him shows why it is not just a matter of words that makes contemporary words of anger stale.

The Divided Self, his first book, appeared in England in 1960, when Laing was 28. The book's power lay in Laing's ability to catch the rationality behind seemingly irrational behavior, a logic he revealed by making the reader see through the eyes of someone labeled schizophrenic. Laing did not "explain" schizophrenia as a disease; he showed how schizophrenia was a perfectly logical way of coping with impossible, longstanding situations in a person's family or immediate society. Much of this ground was prepared for Laing by the American anthropologist Gregory Bateson—probably one of the greatest and most neglected writers on human behavior in this country.

A few years earlier (1956) Bateson had arrived at a theory of "double binds" to explain the contradictory language people called schizophrenics speak. A double bind is a situation in which a person is issued two contradictory negative commands he or she must follow in order to gain love. A mother tells her daughter to do dishes before math homework if she wants love from Mommy; the father tells the girl she must do math first if she wants *his* love.

When contradictions like this persist, what is the child to do? She wants and needs the love of both parents. It becomes logical for her to obey both parents at once: she may make dishwashing motions while reading her math, or call the dishes she handles plus and minus signs. In this way she comes to appear disconnected and deranged to her teachers or to a social worker, when in fact it is a situation she had no hand in creating that is deranged.

Bateson was concerned with the logic of "illogical" language. What Laing seized on in *The Divided Self* and in books that followed in rapid succession—*Self and Others* (1961), and *Sanity, Madness and the Family* (with A. Esterson in 1964)—was to ask why these contradictory and painfully disorienting situations should come into being.

In the course of these books Laing came to think that parents are no more to blame for posing the child insane demands than is the child for responding insanely. Forces out of their personal control make them hurt the child; few of the people in families of schizophrenics, Laing remarked, ever *want* to create sickness; they *have* to, they are driven souls. Who then is responsible?

Laing came to believe that everyone and no one is. Society makes insanity, he argued; sanity is a condition in which people are willing to obey social rules, even if the commands are inhumane and irrational. The rebels are labeled insane. That little girl is a rebel in her acts because she didn't try to paper over a contradiction; she tried to respond as honestly as she could to the demands made on her, and her show of honesty prompted others to think she was sick.

Here, too, Laing was not alone. Michel Foucault's brilliant first book, *Madness and Civilization* (1961), argued that a long history stands behind the practice of treating the deviant as insane, so that, in his "illness," he doesn't have to be taken seriously. The incarceration of Soviet dissidents in mental hospitals is an overt example today, but Foucault and, later, Laing argued that all of "civilized" society practices this behavior, unaware of its own repression.

By the time Laing wrote *The Politics of Experience* (1967), it seemed logical that he would become a social analyst, a man whose experience as a psychiatrist would give him, and his readers, new insights into how society organized repression. But these insights were not forthcoming. Rather than follow the logic of his own anger and become a social critic, he chose to make his patients, whom he had formerly seen as dignified in their suffering, into heroes. He dealt with society only by clinging to those people who were its victims and whose actions, if not intentions, showed they were fighting back.

This tendency to cling to the victim as hero took hold of Laing in two ways. Everything he saw in his consulting room, all his intellectual associations and allies, made him think that traditional psychiatric logic, positing "rational" standards of behavior, was a sham, was really a tool for keeping dissidence down. If Laing were to become a social critic, if he began to ask why society brought into being these human traumas, wouldn't he run the risk of becoming one of "them," wouldn't his gifts of sensitivity and originality fall prey to the deadness of that sane world? There is a failure of nerve here, a fear of putting himself in enemy territory, but it is complex and humane because it is a fear of losing his own humanity.

Of course the victims of brute power arouse sympathy,

and any victims who show signs of resistance command respect. But the spectator of their plight, free to leave them and go home, engaged in their woes by empathy rather than necessity, always runs the risk of feeling that the victims have something he doesn't, that in their suffering they have transcended the vicious world that the empathetic observer gets along in. He is led by the force of his own sympathy to admire them, to want to be like these rebels, at least to champion them. As a result, society seems ever less real apart from its effect on the lives of its victims, and the sympathizer's own life seems less real too; he orients his own reactions to society by those who are suffering so much more than he is. As their follower, their champion, he feels he too is resisting.

Blacks in the South and the urban ghettoes who were treated this way during the 1960's told their white friends to go home; the blacks felt used. Laing's sympathy for his mentally ill patients is enmeshed in the same contradictions that led to a crisis between black and white civil rights workers, but he has gone a step further. Laing has come to see madness not just as an act of rebellion, but as an act of "liberation," of "waking up," of a "freeing" of the individual from society's constraints. Rebellion and liberation are separated by a simple matter of fact: a liberation ends the causes of the distress that makes people want to rebel. Laing, however, has turned this around, and looks at madness as a liberation in which the individual reorganizes the world on his or her own terms, so that society can be shut out. But why then are mentally ill people usually in great and unending pain?

We do not know much of how Laing's patients feel about their doctor's sympathy. Kingsley Hall, the therapeutic community Laing organized in London, has had some dramatic successes and failures. But I suspect that the patients' relief at finding a professional who does not treat them with condescension must be balanced by the burden Laing places on them as his proxies. Further, we must ask what does the conversion of a victim into an existential hero do to the sympathizer, to the man losing himself in the struggles of others? This tendency is not Laing's alone, it is characteristic of many of his readers, who have learned during the last decade to feel angry by identifying with the victims of our society; the results of this identification are what Laing's latest book has to show.

Sadly, the few passages in *The Politics of the Family* with the old fire are sandwiched between dead prose.

—Richard Sennett

The Politics of the Family and Other Essays has as its main section a rewrite of five radio talks given in 1968 over the Canadian Broadcasting Corporation as the eighth series of Massey Lectures; the three other essays in the book come from a talk given to English social workers during

the same year and two pieces previously published in specialized medical books in England. All the essays are ostensibly concerned with the role of the therapist intervening in family crises.

I should say at once that the reader who was moved by *The Divided Self* will find in these essays of a decade later a few pages with the old force. For example, Laing gives a brilliant analysis of how the famed 19th-century French psychiatrist B. A. Morel drove a patient mad: failing to explore the reality before him seriously, that a young boy hated his father, Morel assumed instead that there was some hidden physical disease to explain this unnatural and impolite feeling; the boy was institutionalized and eventually became no more than a vegetable because the doctor refused to accept the "mad" idea of father-hatred as equal in lucidity to the presumptions of natural filial affection ruling the doctor's own world.

Sadly, the few passages with the old fire are sandwiched between dead prose like the following: "As Sartre would say, the family is united by the reciprocal internalization by each (whose token of membership is precisely this interiorized family) of each other's internalization." Much of the book reads at this level or worse; Laing can no longer write clearly unless he is showing someone being hurt.

Laing cannot talk about the theories and intellectual constructs surrounding mental illness with the same imagination and originality with which he talks about the mentally ill patient because he won't permit himself to. All of Laing's own powers of originality are concentrated on speaking *for* the patient; but the patient, as Laing elsewhere argues so strongly, is not the maker of his own illness. What can Laing use to confront the tormentors? Examples of their practices gone wrong. But there is no way of explaining what has gone wrong other than by using their terms. He sounds like Doctor Laing, pompous and boring, because it is he who made the split between doctor and human being, for fear he would not have the strength to confront the doctors without his patients to hold on to.

Making the victim a proxy for his own anger forces Laing's thoughts about victimization itself into a pedestrian mold. In *The Politics of the Family* he argues that there is a triangle composed of blind authority, the invasion of intimate feelings, and "waking up" through mental illness. From the moment of their birth men are contaminated by others, ultimately by society. Laing draws a "map" of this invasion, but the countryside and the routes of invasion have all been laid out before by Freud, David Rappoport and Alfred Adler—none of whom gets much credit. Laing argues that nuclear war and genocide are connected to schizophrenic feelings without drawing the connections at all. How can this psychiatrist help us if outside the consulting room his great gifts of intelligence go dead, and he mechanically and woodenly repeats the ideas of others? This failure of intellect is especially disturbing since the behavior Laing perceived in his consulting room could not be adequately explained by the older theories.

This invasion from the outer world, Laing says, is blind, unintentional: each person or social group wounds others only hoping to protect itself. I believe this, but I don't understand why. Laing believes it, and doesn't think it matters why, because "why" gets us too far away from the "reality that is the patient."

So when Laing talks of waking up, of liberation, he ends at an impasse. If this is a vicious and insane world what are men to do? How are they to wake up? The analysis of schizophrenia on which Laing's work rests is that people are forced into what society calls insane behavior when they try to take the world seriously; it is the essence of his argument that you do not become insane by some willful act or failure of your own. If you did, we would be back in the world of Morel where patients needed to learn to control themselves better. If I, a sane man, want to wake up, and I can't will myself into mental illness, what am I to do?

Here is the closest Laing comes to an answer:

> I consider many adults (including myself) are or have been, more or less, in a hypnotic trance. . . . Attempts to wake before our time are often punished, especially by those who love us most. Because they, bless them, are asleep. They think anyone who wakes up . . . is going crazy. Anyone in this transitional state is likely to be confused. To indicate this confusion is a sign of illness, is a quick way to create psychosis.

It is an obsessive litany: You will be punished for being mentally ill when you wake up. But how do I get there? There is no therapy in this therapist's writings.

The conversion of his patients into "models" of behavior inhibits Laing from talking about three issues. The first is himself:

> When I was thirteen, I had a very embarrassing experience. I shall not embarrass you by recounting it. . . . The first family to interest me was my own. I still know less about it than I know about many other families. This is typical.

A humanistic psychiatry does not have to bear the burden of autobiography or confession, yet Laing cannot talk about himself openly in the detail he feels entitled to talk about his patients. When he uses "I" in this book, it usually is in terms of putting himself in the place of a suffering patient.

Laing thinks of himself as an existentialist—indeed, one of his best books is a commentary with David Cooper on Sartre called ***Reason and Violence*** (1964), which has just been published for the first time in this country by Pantheon and Vintage Books. But as a writer he has become the worst of existentialists, one of the "spectators" Sartre so detests. How can a writer be an existentialist when he discounts himself?

Secondly, Laing talks about how emotions get twisted, but seldom talks about what emotions there are in the heart to twist. A reader who wants to find out about the range of feeling involved in human trust, in friendship, in sensuous pleasure, will not find it in Laing. ***The Divided Self*** described an idea of "ontological security" in which men felt able to take a wide variety of risks; the books since ***The***

Politics of Experience show a writer who can imagine only one.

This is to say, finally, that Laing has lost that capacity to dream which is necessary in any enduring radical vision. Critics like Marx and Freud did not content themselves with saying justice would reign when the old abuses disappeared. Each of them tried to create a scenario for a just life that was greater than a mirror image of the old. For Marx, socialism ended the abuses of capitalism, but Communism instituted human relationships of a wholly new order. The acts of intelligence Freud called ego strengths were not compromises between the warring factions of instinct and external circumstance; they were creative powers to make new meanings, new satisfactions. Because Laing now has lost the power to dream and make his readers dream and desire, his catalogue of abuses is losing its power to anger.

What has gone sour in Laing is not unique to him, but is representative of the deadening of sentiment in the last few years that has seized us, his contemporaries. His refusal to think about the enemy mirrors our own: white racism, genocide, monopoly capitalism—these are the villains and what more do we need to know about them but that they must be destroyed?

In truth, the resistance each man can mount to repression has to be renewed in his life, not by repeated declarations of will, but by continual doubts about what and why he is fighting. "A revolutionary is motivated by great feelings of love," said Che, but he is also moved by curiosity; I think a man is liberated not by becoming completely absorbed in the fact that he is oppressed, but in exercising his power to understand with a certain grim disinterest the forces impinging on him. Political sensitivity thrives on uncertainty because the possibility to be moved, to revolt, and be moved again, comes only from a deep distrust that at last one has settled what is wrong.

Intellect keeps uncertainty alive, and the failure to use it closes one up in the room where Laing is imprisoned. White, middle-class persons who have come to sense what blackness means to an American black, or warfare to a Vietnamese, now speak of "identifying" with these struggles. Few of us in Laing's generation speak of identifying with the middle class, because we don't like it, and we think we can make change only by orienting our sensibilities around persons or conditions ineradicably different from ourselves. When Laing crossed that barrier and began to live through others, he went dead inside, could not speak of himself as probingly as he could speak for his patients, lost the power to create anger at the world which held them both so harshly in its grip. I wish I knew where it would lead to think out the realities of our lives as persons who are not dramatically suffering, but I do know that until we stop this presumptuous sentimentality, until uncertainty and curiosity about who we are ourselves return, we will become increasingly bored with our own "causes" and tolerant of the society that brings them into being.

David Martin   (essay date 1971)

SOURCE: "R. D. Laing," in *The New Left,* edited by Maurice Cranston, The Library Press, 1971, pp. 179-208.

[In the following excerpt, Martin summarizes Laing's views on society and the family and his theory and method for the treatment of schizophrenia. He also argues that Laing's work is characterized by generalities, exaggerations, and undeveloped ideas, stating: "(Laing is) on the fringes of the irrationalist Left which stigmatizes and condemns all aspects of socialization and civilization as injurious to truth and the individual's being."]

Ronald Laing must be accounted one of the main contributors to the theoretical and rhetorical armoury of the contemporary Left. By the contemporary left is meant that soft variant of the utopian urge which has jettisoned the Marx of *Capital* for the spiritual exploration of alienation, which acknowledges that capitalism 'delivers the goods to an ever increasing part of the population' and therefore concentrates its attention on the salvation of the all-too-common man from what Marcuse calls 'one dimensionality' [see *The Dialectics of Liberation,* edited by D. Cooper, 1968].

With the erosion of a proletarian communism, its confinement to institutional rigidity or its continuing commitment to Stalinoid deformations, one is left with a *salon* communism, whereby the Ortega y Gassets of the Left join forces with their conservative opposite numbers on the other side of high table in a lament for the regrettable tendencies of mass society. It is they who—to take an image of Laing's—are the lonely 'survivors' in a neo-capitalist civilisation which is condemned to swinish contentment; confined to the pleasures of consumption without appropriate refinement of palate. 'Consume more, live less' as one of the slogans has it. So pessimistic is this approach that hope is only thought possible by calling in a Third World to redress the balance of the two old ones.

This is the general and by now familiar picture presented by the 'soft left', and it is the aim of this essay to locate the place of R. D. Laing within its broad syndrome of attitudes. . . .

R. D. Laing was born in 1927 in Glasgow, educated at a grammar school and at Glasgow University. The flyleaves tell us that he graduated as a doctor in 1951 and became a psychiatrist in the Army for two years. He then held various posts at Glasgow Royal Mental Hospital, at the Department of Psychological Medicine at Glasgow University and the Tavistock Clinic (1957-61). He worked for the Tavistock Institute of Human Relations and has been Director first of the Langham Clinic and then of the Kingsley Hall Clinic in London since 1962. At the Tavistock Institute he concentrated initially on research on schizophrenia and the family. From 1961 to 1963 he held a fellowship of the Foundations Fund for Research in Psychiatry. So much for mere external biography.

The main writings of Laing are *The Divided Self* (1960), *The Self and Others* (1961, revised edition 1969) and *The Politics of Experience* (1967), which consists largely of miscellaneous writings from the years 1964-7. He collabo-

rated with his fellow psychiatrist David Cooper in *Reason and Violence* (1964) which examines Sartre's principal writings between 1950 and 1960. He also collaborated with Aaron Esterson in *Sanity, Madness and the Family,* Vol. I, *The Families of Schizophrenics* (1964) and with H. Phillipson and A. R. Lee in *Interpersonal Perception* (1966). Both Laing and David Cooper helped to organise the Congress on the Dialectics of Liberation, at the Round House, Chalk Farm, in 1967, an event which resulted in twenty-three gramophone records and a book of the same name edited by Cooper. Laing contributed to those records and that book a piece entitled **'The Obvious',** and the Introduction by Cooper illustrates how closely linked their thinking is.

A broad although ultimately unreal distinction needs to be made between Laing's work as a psychiatrist, which seems to be best represented in *The Divided Self,* and his politics. It is not a prime concern of the present essay to evaluate his psychiatric work, except insofar as the leading ideas of the psychiatric school he represents are connected with his political attitudes and also insofar as the professional perspectives deriving from psychiatric training of whatever school often seem to lead to sociological and political naïveté. Clearly a discussion of this latter could develop into a full-scale sociological critique of psychiatric perspectives on social processes which is not appropriate here but which is clearly much required. All that can be attempted here is a brief summary of Laing's methodological prescriptions, and some indication of his major substantive ideas as a psychiatrist. That done, we may pass to an analysis of the broad syndrome of attitudes, and especially religious elements, embodied in Laing's work, notably as illustrated in *The Politics of Experience.*

Laing's position is best summarized in his own remark that one does not *have* schizophrenia, in the same way as one has the measles, one *is* schizophrenic.

—David Martin

The main methodological prescriptions of Laing are broadly of a kind with which the present writer is in sympathy. These are mostly and perhaps appropriately addressed to psychoanalysts rather than to social scientists, and are not so much new in psychoanalysis as inadequately disseminated among the general public interested in such issues. One thinker who illustrates these trends is [Ludwig] Binswanger, and he is only one of a number of theorists to whom Laing is indebted. By methodological prescriptions is meant not so much therapeutic techniques as the fundamental therapeutic strategy and personal stance taken up by the analyst in consequence of his basic assumptions about the nature of the human entity and about the status of the notion of 'person'. However, this will clearly have its impact on what one considers therapeutically and *ethically* appropriate techniques.

Perhaps Laing's position is best summarised in his own remark that one does not *have* schizophrenia, in the same way as one has the measles, one *is* schizophrenic. A succinct statement of his position is to be found [in his] Introduction to **Reason and Violence,** in some paragraphs where he is discussing both Sartre's position and his own on the limits of psychoanalysis. Laing argues that at a certain point in the process of explanation some psychoanalysts cease to make their observations within the context of mutual exchange between persons and assume a one-sided superiority of objective external judgment towards the condition of the patient as if he were a mere biological organism. Both the personal relationship and 'the person' disappear.

There are several different points encapsulated here, and some confusion. For example, there is no necessary relation between stepping into an objective role for the purpose of 'judgment' and losing the reciprocity of a relationship. Indeed, there must be *some* assumption of superiority which the analyst will take up in his role as specialist in psychological dynamics, otherwise he is simply interacting with the other person. This need not be the almost absolute assumption characteristically made (say) by a consultant in relation to biological disease, since the patient is always himself experienced in what it is to be a human and often acquires insight comparable in kind if not usually in degree to that possessed by the analyst. The patient may even, in particular instances and in relation to particular aspects, have superior insight.

Presumably Laing is not objecting to the assumption that on the average and at the margin the psychoanalyst is more experienced and in a sense more objective than the patient, and therefore must on occasion step back for a 'review' on the basis of that experience, objectivity and detachment. Moreover, a doctor may recognise how marginal the superiority of his experience and how frail and partial his objectivity while not wanting to trumpet the fact to patients who are often specialists in using such admissions as means of avoiding whatever fragments of the truth the analyst has managed to acquire. He may also legitimately restrict the degree of reciprocity and involvement which he allows himself, since he, too, has to survive.

Yet there are real dangers here to which Laing points, though it is regrettable that some of his criticisms are not more specific. For example, the psychoanalytic profession is not only expert at the game of 'tails I win, heads you lose', not only curiously indifferent to external fact such as perfectly genuine threats and difficulties, not only often oblivious to ongoing social situations, but also protects itself far more than mere personal or professional survival requires in terms of a group of ploys designed to cover the extent of professional failure. These ploys are not anything very much to do with treating people as things or with biological reductionism or anything so grandiosely perverse, but are simply the verbal mechanisms for coping practically with patients, for the reduction of proliferating involvements and for the safeguarding of medical prestige. In a way one feels that Laing prefers to concentrate on the grandiose perversity to the neglect of these unhappy mundane truths. Perhaps the exploration of the personal and

professional defects which psychoanalysts share with the rest of us has less éclat than accusing them of misconceived ontology, and of treating persons as things.

Just as there is no necessary relation between elements of objectivity assumed for purposes of review and the loss of genuine reciprocity, so there is no necessary connection between either of these things and treating persons as biological entities, although there may be a necessary connection in reverse, insofar as those with a biologically and neurologically reductionist approach must find it difficult to achieve a full recognition of the equality involved in person-to-person relationships. Insofar as psychoanalysts do take up biological reductionism, Laing is surely right in pointing out that it explains all and explains nothing:

> It explains all in the sense that . . . ultimately perfected biochemical and neuro-physiological techniques, and carefully delineated instinctive units of behaviour, will account 'correlatively' for every possible 'psychic drive' that can be thought up. Meanwhile the person, his purposes and choices (his 'project') have disappeared: his ongoing mental life has been explained out, stultified with 'fetishised pseudo-irreducibles'.

As Laing says, 'It is only through the discovery of a freedom, a choice of self-functioning in the face of all determinations, conditioning, fatedness, that we can attain the comprehension of a person in his full reality.'

All that is well said, though those of us who are not doctors or psychoanalysts can only wonder that those who are should discover so painfully what the rest of us are not tempted to forget: that people are, after all, people. Most human beings do not require to be reassured that a person is a person by a long détour through the more verbose, pretentious and obscure German philosophers in the existentialist and phenomenological tradition. Maybe such trials are reserved as necessities for those who specialise in the science of persons, since they, it seems, have a special facility (not to say training) in forgetting what the rest of humanity remembers without thinking about it. Yet no doubt we *do* need to think about these matters: to establish as part of a carefully articulated phenomenology and ontology the validity of personal life qua personal life, independent of our unreflective awareness of it or as imparted to us through the partly unspoken assumptions of humanist and religious traditions. A philosophical détour which articulates what one always knew is not a waste of time, and the emphasis achieved by Laing in so doing is important.

Yet it *is* an emphasis, and at times so emphatic and careless as to be absurd. Presumably what he is saying amounts to an assertion that the interpenetration of levels of analysis from physics and chemistry to existential philosophy does not destroy the independent validity of each level in its own terms or render them reducible to each other. Presumably he is also saying that reductionist assumptions lurking in the medical mind lead doctors to resort more frequently than is appropriate to drugs and to physicalist methods of dealing with particular problems, such as pre-frontal surgery and electric treatment. Occasionally he bothers to state this position in a qualified and commonsense form, but at other times the assault on his own profession must seem so extreme as to prevent fellow-doctors hearing what he has to say. Thus: 'Doctors in all ages have made fortunes by killing their patients by means of their cures. The difference in psychiatry is that it is the death of the soul' (*The Dialectics of Liberation*).

Laing's second main point with respect to methodological prescription concerns the relevance of the social context in interpreting individual psychology. This leads in two different directions: one is to establish the relevance of social context in any explanatory model of behaviour and the other involves a philosophical issue insofar as the positivistic abdication from value judgments prevents one seeing how the psychoanalyst is in his whole mode of operation expressing and executing the values of society. The latter point is linked with the issue already mentioned in relation to physicalist methods: an executioner dealing with crime by the rope does not absolve himself by declaring that ethical judgments are not his business. But the analogy is very partial, and in any case methods do not need to be physicalist for the essential point to be made that the psychoanalyst may act as an agent of current values by defining madness within the terms set by his society, thus failing to observe the partial responsibility of the mechanisms and institutions approved by that society for the genesis of mental disorder, overlooking the valid protest lurking behind the supposed abnormality, and assisting the patient to acquiesce again in the mad routines of supposedly normal people. This is an important point, however much overstated.

The point about the relevance of the social context is also genuinely helpful, but it suffers like almost all psychiatric excursions into sociology from excessive universalism. Let us take Laing's wholly acceptable remark about men qua men ultimately being free, choosing as well as 'chosen'. He both asserts this as a universal truth about the human person as such and refers to the nature of capitalist society as being a near-universal social context in which that freedom is deformed. Unless he appeals to contemporary communist society as *not* implicated in such deformations, which seems an unlikely and certainly an unpersuasive recourse, he is saying that developed society as such is a universal context within which freedom is distorted. Indeed, where he appeals to an alternative type of society he actually looks back to periods notorious for their deformation of the possibility of freedom, actually postulating in one instance a decline over the past thousand years. Since he firmly indicates no concrete milieu where deformations do *not* occur, one suspects that his category of society is not limited at all, even when it appears to have special reference to capitalist society: it is society *tout court* in all its historical manifestations hitherto which is at fault. *Vide* Freud. Thus we have two universals, the universality of freedom and the universal repressiveness of society as such.

Now it is worth asking here whether men are more or less free according to the *variations* in their social milieu, within societies as well as between them. It has been suggested, for example, that the British working class is a less 'free' milieu than the middle class because it lacks the dramatur-

gical skills and appropriate 'role distance' (in Goffman's sense) to exercise its freedom. Without endorsing so gross a contrast it remains true, surely, that given milieux (within the overall repressiveness of society as conceived by Laing) do make freedom more or less accessible, so that the experience of a person in the one milieu may lead him or her to have that margin of desire to exercise freedom and therefore climb by beneficent spirals out of a psychological cul-de-sac. Conversely another person may lack just that margin and by parallel vicious spirals reach a point where he is literally without option—where he may say, quite correctly, there is no way out.

Such examples do indicate both the relevance of a milieu *much* more specific and particular than society as such (though clearly this plays its part too as an overall environment) and also the possibility of losing one's freedom, in some cases entering a vicious spiral very early in the process of life such that no human mercy or grace can save one or elicit one's free choice. Personally, I would agree with Laing that freedom is a universal option of humanity, but I would also want to know whether that affirmation, as stated by Laing, takes adequate account of the variation in its availability. At what levels of analysis is it universal, at what levels variable?

There is a subsidiary point which arises here and has some relevance to Laing's politics insofar as those people who are burdened with a metaphysic of freedom frequently ignore or despise the concrete variations in the institutionalisation of liberties. Just as a psychiatrist may proceed with a crude dichotomy of the individual and society which ignores the variable intermediate institutional network from society to society, so philosophers in the pursuit of genuine individual freedom despise the variations in stabilised liberties. British society, no doubt through a concatenation of favourable circumstances, has been relatively successful in the institutionalisation of liberties, yet Laing's criticisms presumably apply to it with equal vigour as to anywhere else, and, since he lives here, with added emotional violence. In short, the denunciatory style of radical psychiatrists touched by existential philosophy is likely to be indiscriminately global, whereas there are, after all, seven circles both in hell and in heaven.

The points just made have been related to the variable cultural context of personal freedom and of institutionalised liberty, but they also can relate to Laing's general attempt to bring the social context into account as contributing to explanation of psychological phenomena. Laing does, of course, speak of the socialisation provided by the family, and very occasionally by the school, as agents of the general socialising process emanating from global society. But he gives almost no impression whatever of the hierarchy of status and class, the processes of aspiration, of mobility and peer-group formation, and all the vastly differentiated milieux in terms of cultural pattern from one area to another, town and country, north and south. He may describe very well a highly generalised social process such as the mechanisms of gossip and scandal by which everybody is caught up in a situation which thereby acquires its own autonomous momentum because each person is primarily concerned about what the other thinks. But while he refers to persons and to groups and to society, there is little particularised social and historical location through which the universal processes have to be channelled if they are to be truly explanatory.

This is perhaps more a complaint about psychiatry as such than about Laing, but it does indicate why the jeremiads and lamentations in which he engages refer so much and so indiscriminately to 'the society', 'the family', 'the school' and so on. Since he seems not personally to have rejected the family, this suggests that some families in certain circumstances are better than others. The question is: which? By always referring to institutions in general, his work is a triumph of masterful evasion.

Moreover, the generality of his work also weakens his remarks about sociology, in that sociology simultaneously aspires to adequate generality and adequate particularisation. Laing's concentration on *the* group or on *the* society leads him to draw conclusions either from reading the social psychology of groups or from very abstract consideration of *the* nature of society. His comments on sociology contain very occasional slanting references to Parsons and Durkheim, but any serious acquaintance with the vast literature on the explanation of all the varied institutional patterns of modern society, or for that matter with the equally enormous literature discussing what are among his major interests—objectivity, internal personal knowledge, etc.—seem entirely lacking. While he rightly criticises Sartre for attacking sociology on the basis of fragments from Lewin (a social psychologist) and Kardiner (a 'cultural' psychoanalyst), Laing is engaged in precisely the same exercise himself [*Reason and Violence*].

This is equally evident in his plea for an evaluative stance and an enveloping 'total' perspective within which social science may operate. Such a plea rests on an objection to positivism, the very word 'positivism' (or 'vulgar positivism') being a 'boo-word' in certain circles. The core of this objection has already been stated above insofar as it relates to the abdication of the social scientist from judgments of value and his silent implication in a supposed consensus. This is a persistent theme to which one may return later. But first let us analyse, by way of example, the statement, 'Much social science deepens the mystification. Violence cannot be seen through the sights of positivism' (*Politics of Experience*). This issue has been discussed in a thousand academic articles, and the proportion of social scientists accepting a crude positivism is very small, whether in denying the relevance of what Polanyi calls 'personal knowledge' or in asserting an unqualified scientific objectivity, whether in dismissing value judgment as merely emotive or in refusing to acknowledge the imperatives that should operate on the scientist qua person as distinct from the special role taken up with respect to problems at a given analytic level. Sociologists are simply determined to assert that it is important at least to note the *distinction* between 'is' and 'ought'. Ethical judgments will be none the less forceful for not being confused with scientific propositions. And similarly scientific propositions will not gain by being worked up and then stuffed as a mediate element in some totalising synthesis, even one continuously constituted and reconstituted. It is one of the major

achievements of social science to loose itself from the bonds of ethical judgments and global metaphysics, *not* in order to reject the importance of ethics or metaphysics but to acquire a necessary (not merely a provisional) autonomy, a fragile but genuine independence for its own particular scientific purposes.

Having discussed certain aspects of Laing's methodological prescriptions one may very briefly note what are his substantive ideas in the field of psychiatry. Indeed, since a great deal of Laing's work has been on schizophrenia, it may be worthwhile utilising a summary indicating his approach from *The Divided Self*. . . . This is perhaps the place to say that his analyses of interpersonal relations, either dyadic ones such as those between husband and wife or within the overall nexus of the family, strike me as rich in insight. Such skill in understanding interpersonal relations does not of course validate his contentions vis-á-vis the geneticist-constitutional school with respect to schizophrenia, except insofar as he may quite rightly insist on the provisional hypothetical character of their approach, nor does such skill validate the naïve set of attitudes informing his political comment.

In schizophrenia the self is 'out of the body' and both wishes and fears to be reintegrated with it. The result is a disembodied self which may be lost in fantasy or engaged in a kind of dry 'observation', or else may regard itself as essentially lost or destroyed. If the self is bent on self-destruction it may do so because what has been destroyed is then eternally safe. Alternatively it may be self-destructive because it has lost any sense of the personal right to be alive, or the ability to operate with a sense of what is due to one, even (say) the right to occupy a chair. The result is an experience of 'chaotic non-entity' whereby verbal expression acquires a quite bizarre and obscure coherence and in which the obscurity is deepened further because the schizophrenic is preserving his being from intrusion. His attempt at mad privacy is an effort to tell without being understood, to inform and communicate without giving anything away. To meet another person and communicate with him is to acknowledge the other's free existence and thus open up the possibility of the other treating one as a mere object. One takes no risks, because one believes that advantage will always be taken, and one may avoid any contact not only by secrecy but by an over-compliance which also expresses the sense of other people's ontological weight poised threateningly against one's own insubstantiality. Yet at the same time one's greatest desire is to be allowed to *be*, and to be understood and accepted. The schizophrenic is knocking obscurely on the walls of the sunken submarine, terrified of the dangers involved in the upward route to safety and conscious of the steady diminution of the possibility of life within.

Now in Laing's view this is a condition, or rather an experience, to be investigated not primarily on an individual basis but within a social context, notably the context of family dynamics, and these constitute a complete pattern of interaction, processes and structure. Sometimes his focus of understanding is the family, though at other times he seems to suggest that one may conceive of a kind of primary network of some twenty to thirty people within which schizophrenia is to be treated. Neither the family nor this group ought to be regarded as a pathological organism, since the problem must be viewed as an intelligible outcome of people's intentions and actions (praxis), however much the resultant processes acquire an autonomy of their own. The schizophrenic within the family and within the wider group exists to conduct its tensions, to take the brunt of its 'unlived living' and bear the weight of its crazy structure for the rest. Perhaps one might even say that 'one dies for the people' in that the rest achieve a kind of corrupt and desperate viability through the sufferings of the chosen one. In David Cooper's words, 'Most people who are called mad and who are socially victimised by virtue of that attribution . . . come from family situations in which there is a desperate need to find some scapegoats, someone . . . to take on the disturbance of each of the others, and, in some sense, suffer for them.'

The basic unit of interaction is dyadic, 'I' and 'You', and what happens in all the possible combinations of 'persons' in the family or beyond it can be partly illustrated in the basic interaction of personal perspectives. These constitute a kind of spiral based on how 'I' look in the view of 'the other'. As Laing puts it, this takes the form of 'I like you; you like me but I do not know that you like me; however I do know that you know I like you; and I do not know that you do know that I do not know that you like me'. This does not necessarily lead to withdrawals, but it is clearly potent with 'mismatched interpretations, expectancies, attributions and counter-attributions' and is particularly relevant to understanding the various circles of misunderstanding, desolation, fear and corrosion into which husband and wife relations frequently fall [*Interpersonal Perception;* see also **'The Spiral of Perspectives'**, with H. Phillipson and A. R. Lee, in *New Society,* 10 November 1966].

These are, if you like, the basic notions: schizophrenia as a problem of personal ontology and threats to the affirmation of personal being; the 'mad' person as essentially 'bearing' the condition of the group; and the 'spiral' of potential misunderstanding informing all interlocking personal relations, but most dramatically of all perhaps, the dyad of husband and wife.

Such a brief account, however inadequate, does allow us to move on to an analysis of the underlying personal attitudes of Laing, since the fact that he sets a particular type of 'abnormal' experience within a social context, coupled with a suspicion of the psychiatrist as representing an undesirable society, allows him to question both the abnormality of the supposedly mentally ill and the normality of the society which is the context of the illness. Indeed it is perhaps central to Laing's position that modern society attempts to turn every child into a conformist and in so doing deprives the child of its potentialities and creativity, devastating its being with the chains we choose to call love. The child has gradually to be converted to a treason against itself by making a pact with the madness of society. And in this process the schizophrenic may be the one who cannot suppress his instincts enough to perform the much-solicited treason. The psychiatrist is not so much the objective representative of health as the corrupt solici-

tor, the secret agent of society whose modus operandi is tainted by precisely the ills he attempts to heal. (Those who do not view patients as persons depersonalise themselves.)

Here one must turn to a group of ideas and attitudes which provide a bridge passage between his psychiatric stance and his politics: they are contained in the notion of the 'mystification of violence'. For Laing, a central element in the broader task of 'demystification' is an attempt to 'demystify' violence, and the essence of this task is to recover access to that direct experience which socialisation so successfully violates and destroys. Socialisation, for him, is the local agent of that canalised institutional violence which is located in central government and which stalks society cloaked in the language and unspoken assumptions of the mass media. Socialisation is the first and primal violence against the person which can only be met by projecting violence on to others, acting violently towards them and justifying oneself by attributing violence to them. *It is this view of socialisation which links the experience of the family to politics, psychiatry to global issues, approaches to upbringing and pedagogical method to Vietnam.*

For people of this mind, all delimitation of issues, all academic division of scholarly labour, and all attempts to view phenomena objectively from a variety of specialised perspectives at different analytic levels, are part of a policy of divide in order to rule. There can be no taking apart of Humpty-Dumpty even in order to put him together again: the question is, as Humpty-Dumpty himself said, 'Who is master?' The appeal of this to the kind of young person looking for quick global answers, impatient with the requirements of careful study, and armed with a drifting paranoid suspicion of all authority, is obvious. The psychology of identifying a malevolent 'Them', which he describes, is usually well developed in his followers.

Global accusation, like libel and rumour, is easy: refutation, like art, is long and difficult. There is no answer to a grain of truth eked out by indiscriminate misrepresentation except a disciplined understanding. It would take too long; but one can at least begin by pointing to the central assumption, derived from Rousseau, that man as man is originally innocent, and civilisation, especially modern civilisation, the focus of original sin. Incidentally, it is interesting that this assumption links Laing with another large success in the field of commercial publishing: the type of egregious ethological speculation represented by *The Human Zoo* and *The Naked Ape* [by Desmond Morris]. In short there are those who see human institutions as dykes canalising a raw, variable, morally ambiguous human potential into the fructifying ways of civilisation, and those who see those institutions as barriers to a flood of inherent generosity, innate humanity and abounding creativity. Laing is of the latter.

That said, it is instructive to look more closely at what appears to be a very confused discussion ([in] *The Politics of Experience*) which Laing conducts concerning socialisation, violence and value judgments. What he says is this. First, socialisation, including moral and political socialisation, is a violence against personal experience because it is socially derived and imposed rather than individually achieved. Now it is not clear how else moral perspectives can be derived in the first instance except from society, and it is even less clear that people do not, as they mature, partly transform what is so derived into a personal and critical perspective. Secondly, Laing argues that to regard animals and humans in a given scientific context as (e.g.) biochemical complexes is equivalent to a denial of their true nature as animals and persons; and such a context prevents those who adopt it from an ethical response when violence against men and animals is perpetrated.

Now there is a tiny grain of truth here, which is that a person specialising at a given level of scientific interest such as biochemistry may become so professionally deformed as to forget that what he studies is also a human being, may indeed refuse to acknowledge that in principle results may need to be reassimilated within a wider view which includes the specifically human. Humpty-Dumpty may lie shattered on the floor. It may even happen that such an attitude enters into a scientist's general moral perspective. But it happens to a certain degree to certain people, and the extent to which it does would require extensive documentation; unfortunately the techniques of the propagandist asserting the primacy of his 'genuine' human experience do not allow so wasteful an expenditure of intellectual energy in the cause of mere verification. It is more economical and more effective to say, 'Meanwhile Vietnam goes on.' And here, of course, one encounters a cheapness of effect which in Laing goes with this kind of intellectual economising. The situation in Vietnam is too appalling, the issues too confused, the murderous intent on both sides too typical of war at almost all times, for it to be used as a catch-all riposte by those too lazy or too frenetic to engage in honourable argument.

In any case, a more appropriate intellectual economy might have been employed, since what is being said is even more simple than appears. Laing is claiming that his value judgments are rooted in his genuine experience as a human being, whereas those who disagree with him are the deluded facsimiles of over-successful socialisation. He has not adequately considered the possibility that—to quote him from a different context—his opponents may be people like himself, dressed differently. They, too, may be human.

With world enough and time, it would be worth while indicating just how grossly Laing exaggerates the pressure of socialisation on the child in the democratic West as compared with almost any other period or type of society. It is in fact so affected by a degree of indecision and by a measure of self-indulgent irresponsibility (backed by fashionable psychologies) about its right to socialise, that it often neglects to give those firm, compassionate guidelines within the family and the school without which the child is a flailing ego. Many children rightly suspect that absence of discipline is absence of love. Our school systems are attempting to achieve a balance between required structures and individuality: if they err it is sometimes in taking the sentimentalities deriving from Rousseau too seriously, in acceding too easily to callow cults of spontaneity. On the contrary, it is the duty of a home or school proudly and exultantly to induct a child into that incredibly rich human achievement called civilisation, and into those social, spiritual and intellectual disciplines on which it is built.

It would also be worth showing that some element of mystification is inherent in every civilised social achievement, including the violence socialised, rationalised and sometimes civilised, in the state. Masked (or 'mystified') violence is often a step forward in a peaceable direction; in certain circumstances men gradually conform to their own peaceful self-portraits and are pressed by opinion to implement their misleading idealisations. Men always partially misrepresent their actions: legitimate and minimum authority can be labelled repressive violence; repression can be labelled the maintenance of civilised order. That is not surprising. Men do attempt to delude themselves and others. There are indeed certain situations where the total truth is the grossest violence and where the question is always: what is the most responsible and compassionate proportion of truth and delusion? That is as true of politics as it is of person-to-person relations. Confronted by one's own humanity and others', there is only one possibility: a relaxed compassion towards oneself and other people.

The logic of Laing's position is ultimately violent and totalitarian in spite of (or because of) its extreme libertarian gloss. Perhaps its possibilities are best illustrated by a passage from John Gerassi in *The Dialectics of Liberation.* Gerassi presents as an alternative to Stalinism something exemplified in Cuba, where 'one way to guarantee that their people are genuinely free is not elections, is not free press, is not all the trappings of the so-called political democracy that we have, but simply to arm their people'. In short, if democracy and a free press are less genuine than they claim, the best answer is to abolish free elections and ban open comment; and the best response to militaristic tendencies is the total militarisation of everybody. It is a curious consummation to the metaphysics of freedom.

This is the framework, these the plausible half and quarter-truths which are major keys to the syndrome of attitudes found in Laing. They are allied to a stress on the need for transcendence, which is in part a range of experience akin to mystical illumination which modern society is held to inhibit and denigrate and which is also an ability to see beyond the confines of one-dimensionality to another mode of social life. Since this is important, any exposition must include some reference to the religious elements found in Laing: our alienation from ecstasy and the problem of an original sin uniquely focused in capitalist society. The best way into such an exposition is to concentrate on these attitudes as illustrated in *The Politics of Experience,* and to preface them with a brief look at Laing's contribution to *The Dialectics of Liberation* entitled, **'The Obvious.'** The crucial point for criticism of Laing is the contrast between his politics of experience and the experience of politics.

It is 'obvious' to Laing that what is 'irrational' in the individual can be understood in the context of the family, and that the irrationality of the family is intelligible within its 'encompassing networks', and so on up to the society itself and the total social world system. Each of the wider systems pervades the smaller sub-systems. There is nothing within which the irrationality of the world may be made intelligible, unless it be God, and perhaps He is mad too. Social salvation is not possible by individual conversion nor by seizing the state apparatus but by working outwards from the middle range of institutions, e.g. factories and schools. Psychiatry is the unwitting agent of a political operation against the individual, and the patients are thrown up and selected by a system of which psychiatrists are the malign solicitors. This violence against the individual is paralleled by violence on the societal scale: while the micro-system selects an individual, the macro-system selects 'them'. 'Them' currently comprise the Third World, the have-nots, the exploited. We are enabled to see the Third World as 'them' by our own misconception of what we wrongly believe to be the western desire for peace and by our faith in its vaunted democracy. We project our own unjust violence on to them, are surprised at their just violence against us, and so feel justified in destroying Vietnam.

So universal is our ignorance of and obedience to this system that the number of those surviving as human beings is minute. Socialisation makes us into unwitting subjects of the system just as psychiatrists are made into its unwitting agents. The normal mode of socialisation, terrorisation into submission by love, repeats an endless spiral back through countless generations to the beginning. This spiral backwards is the precondition of our projecting a world composed of 'us' and 'them' in which the hatefulness of 'them' is ourselves seen in the mirror. The crux of the system is obedience resting on the generation of guilt and on the reflex of believing in the authorities. The state, the church, the government, scholarship and science—authority and authorities—all are partners in such a morass of delusion that almost nothing can be truly known: we can only trust something deeper than ourselves, and it is most obvious that *this* is most hidden.

These basic themes are simply found on a larger scale in *The Politics of Experience*: white western society, its governmental system, its methods of upbringing, its science and its scholarship are part of a tissue of delusion which is responsible for stereotyped divisions into 'us' and 'them', and is to blame for violence and counterviolence. We think 'they' are to blame; not at all, it is we who are to blame in the world. This is a simple diagnosis, easily achieved by standing an equally simple diagnosis on its head. The basic stratagem of this style of thinking is: if you want to know what to believe, find out what is the current consensus and turn it upside down; that way you won't necessarily be right but at least you won't inevitably be wrong. If, in addition, you hope for a hint as to what is right, listen to those whom society stigmatises as abnormal. They've got something.

As one proceeds to document the Laingian position one can hardly help noticing two characteristics in his own work which illustrate his own analysis of what constitutes a fundamentally irrational view of the world. One is the simple stereotyping of 'us' and 'them', encapsulated in vast assertions about what people in western societies think: a grandiose simplification of all issues achieved by

stigmatising whole societies as solidary elements in 'the Enemy'. No evidence is cited, just projections about what people in the disapproved societies are projecting about 'them'. This looks like an unfortunate example of the spiral perspectives in which Laing is himself a specialist. The other characteristic is the repetition on the macro-scale of what he describes as inherent in the experience of schizophrenia on the microscale. All other types of society *except* his own have some kind of ontological root, something which may be admired, some kind of right to exist. Only that which is his own constitutes a kind of delusion, a mass of subhumanity, suffering from ontological weightlessness. There is in Laing's writing not a single word suggesting that any virtue inheres in what is his own inheritance. So total a rejection, so wholehearted a separating out of the self from the body of society, so extraordinary a fear of becoming re-attached to it by fiendish subtleties, looks like a curious analogue of the self hating what is most truly its own. Perhaps the condition could be called macro-schizophrenia.

In *The Politics of Experience* the viewpoint expressed is religious not only in the chapter concerned with 'transcendental experience' but throughout. The word religious is not used figuratively: it happens to be accurate. The more extreme forms of a religious rejection of the world often result in two apparently contradictory responses both illustrated in Laing: the first is a flailing violence towards all mundane structures, all those things which for others may mediate elements of truth and personal being. Roles, institutions and everyday experience are rejected because what they mediate is not *the* Truth, because they partly mask what they partly reveal. This obsessive pilgrimage towards the Absolute may result in a total rejection of all the way-stations where other people have rested on their journey, and in an excoriating contempt for their blindness. They are the blind led by the blind. They 'scurry into roles, statuses, identities, interpersonal relations'. In other words they escape into the boltholes of partial sanity because they cannot bear too much sanity, just as others escape into partial madness because they have an inkling how partial the sanity found in those boltholes really is. Laing's choice of visionary viewpoint is allied to Eliot's 'Mankind cannot bear very much reality', but without his compassion.

The second form taken by this religious rejection of the world is silence, because the search for the Absolute has been attempted and failed. The Truth itself was not available (or only intermittently) and, since all the mediate intervening half-truths have been rejected, nothing can be said. Speech is an impropriety and the structured or prepared speech is a blasphemous attempt at order when no order is possible. This is close to the Quaker experience. One must be silent concerning that which cannot be spoken. As Laing puts it, 'Black on the canvas, silence on the screen, an empty white sheet of paper, are perhaps feasible. There is little conjunction of truth and social "reality".' Stylistically the only mode of expression is unprepared, unstructured, gnomic, enigmatic. There is no truth in mere knowledge, no truth in social forms, no truth in ourselves. 'We are all murderers and prostitutes. . . .' Here the Quaker experience mutates back to the characteristic Calvinist experience: the total reprobation in which man as man is universally implicated. Indeed, in Laing we have constant shifts between four main modes of the religious consciousness: mystical experience of the *coincidentia oppositorum,* intense prophetic violence, withdrawal into silence, into institutional and intellectual dissolution, and total reprobation. And Laing himself, through a residual Presbyterianism, is unwilling to assert that he is one of the Elect—'the survivors'. As he puts it: 'We who are half alive, living in the often fibrillating heartland of a senescent capitalism. . . . Can we do more than sing our sad and bitter songs of disillusion and defeat?' *Super flumina Babylonis* . . . the reference appears to be to capitalism *or* to Babylon: universalised it is the essence of the religious awareness that 'here we have no abiding city'. Whether our civilisation is so hostile to this awareness as he maintains, so relentlessly secular, as compared with others, is open to doubt. The nature of the dissent it is capable of producing may be taken both as its condemnation and its salvation. Laing himself contradicts his own thesis. It is a kind of compliment.

Although religious experience can achieve a general prophetic denunciation of a given social condition it is a poor guide to day-to-day politics. These are inevitably, and *quite properly,* conducted in a dubious half-light of more or less unhappy compromises, and to the extent that they are invaded by religion then either each shifty pragmatic compromise is papered over by religious legitimation or intimations of the New Jerusalem drive *l'homme moyen sensuel* relentlessly and intolerantly towards a predestined goal. Essentially the politics of experience are no adequate guide to the experience of politics; a denunciation is not a viable policy. It is this fact that should be the basis of any critical appraisal of the type of politico-religious awareness found in Laing.

When earlier in this essay I located Ronald Laing on the fringes of the irrationalist Left there was one sense perhaps in which it was untrue. He does not explicitly embrace irrationalism, and indeed he uses the word 'irrational' to stigmatise institutions and activities of which he disapproves. However, in such instances he rarely tells us what he means by 'irrational' and one can only assume he uses the word simply as a stand-in for emotional disapproval. He can certainly be considered an irrationalist in that he finds rational and argued discussion of religious questions uncongenial, and insists that the essence of religion is ecstasy. And while it would be better to regard ecstasy as supra-rational rather than irrational, there is in Laing's whole style a *substitution* of ecstasy for argument and a disinclination to build up a sequence of ordered points, supported by carefully collected evidence, qualified in respect of this issue or that.

His method consists in random accusation and sloganised virulence, which destroys the possibility of genuine discussion. Patient refutation has to build up on a basis of carefully verified evidence, has to define its terms (whereas Laing simply prefers to use them) and eventually to build up a cumulative impression, usually in terms of more or less, of marginally this rather than that. Such a method cannot compete with a rhetorical either/or, with grossly

simplified alternatives, with slogans used as an excuse for not thinking. You cannot talk with a man who throws his sincerity at you and who persistently implies that you and every other person who disagrees with him is a racialist, an anti-semite and a crass authoritarian. It is like a discussion arranged between a Pentecostalist in the pulpit and a Unitarian in the congregation: the convention within which the exchange takes place is set by the enthusiast, not by the enquirer.

Laing will not engage in rational argumentation because that is not the way converts are made. Laing is also an irrationalist in the sense that he proposes no means to achieve his vision, apart from offering vague hints about psychic subversion in the middle-range type of institution, such as the school and the university. He proposes no policies, articulates no alternatives, raises no queries about viability, weighs no costs and advantages, assesses no immediate and remote consequences. For obvious reasons: if he did, the whole visionary edifice would collapse like the baseless fabric of a dream. The old Left at least proposed a method of bringing dreams to fruition: when that method proved a nightmare the Left was reduced to the dream again and to variants of peyote. Not indeed that mankind should or can give up its dreams, but without an articulated machinery for the dream to be brought on stage it remains generalised in proclamations, embedded in rituals and confined to what can be achieved by sympathy and goodwill: in short, it remains religious. Holy Communion—by sharing bread and wine—is a symbol and sometimes also a realisation of a preliminary achievement in brotherhood and a pointer to the need for extending both its fellowship and the presence at the heart of that fellowship: but it cannot substitute for the pragmatic turmoil and administrative grind and cold calculation necessary for political action. Politics cannot simply be a Gospel, or else that Gospel eventually declines not only into ritual but into mere ritual.

So much contemporary protest of the kind that Laing admires seems to consist of precisely these rituals and exhibitions executed by those who have no access to the idea of cost and are therefore unwilling to pay the administrative and personal costs of their gospels. For example, Laing's collaborator David Cooper refers to the schizophrenic as the author of the 'totally gratuitous crazy act' and the once-for-all 'happening' is precisely this: a negative symbol whose only point is its negation and which explodes violently into nothingness. As Laing himself might put it: a 'happening' is the negation of the negation. On the continuum running from pragmatic articulated politics to the gratuitous crazy act Laing and Cooper stand about midway, but their sympathies clearly turn towards the latter end of that continuum. They find it easy to indulge in generalised abuse of politicians, easy to sympathise with the psychotic and to regard him as less 'estranged from reality' than the politician. Yet sympathy for psychotics need not be linked to a modish contempt for politicians.

There is no more important task in defending the disciplines of civilisation against writers such as Laing than the rehabilitation of the political vocation. The abuse of politicians is one of the major forms of contemporary self-indulgence. In the demonology of those who aspire to be *real human beings* (and who so often inflict their humanity indiscriminately on others) politicians are the archetypes of the straw man, drained of all ontological root. They are regarded as the prisoners of themselves and the gaolers of the rest of us. Yet in this competition for ontological supremacy perhaps even the politicians and the bureaucrats have a chance. When one considers the nature and constraints of politics there is perhaps in politicians a kind of heroism. Let us at least nominate them as competitors in the ontological stakes, alongside those traditionally easy winners, the artists and intellectuals.

David Martin   (review date February 1972)

SOURCE: "Me Doctor, You Patient," in *Encounter,* Vol. XXXVIII, No. 2, February, 1972, pp. 71-6.

[*In the following review of* The Politics of the Family, *Martin argues that while Laing's subject matter is fascinating and his style is compelling, he is polemical and defensive regarding his theories about madness and the family/society relationship.*]

This latest collection of Dr Laing's sermons will appeal to all those who follow the publications of the North London Pulpit. The rhetoric [in ***The Politics of the Family***] is brilliant, the expository style persuasive, the content intriguing. Unlike Dr. Cooper, his fellow preacher, Ronald Laing is not so much a prophet of the death of the family as a student of its present reality. Like the preachers of the seventeenth century he provides an analysis of the soul on its way to the Light. His text is the dominical injunction against family piety, "Let the dead bury their dead", and his metaphors are those of awakening and rebirth.

His work is hortatory in style and content. In one sense it is—as I have written before [in "R. D. Laing," *The New Left,* edited by Maurice Cranston, 1971]—gnomic and testamental, but in another it is most cunningly structured in the manner of the conventional sermon. For one thing it makes its impact by slight variations on constantly repeated themes. In the first essay one finds the following. The family consists of relations. It exists in each of its elements and nowhere else. The family is not an introjected object but an introjected set of relations. What is internalised are not objects as such but patterns of relationship by internal operations upon which a person develops an incarnate group structure. Relations are internalised and construed for significance. This family-in-common shared group presence exists in so far as each member has it inside himself. Thus in a mere 11 pages the basic phenomenological doctrine is hammered home: the family is not a *thing* but a more or less internalised pattern of relationships.

Similarly, the sermon technique is evident in the employment of another basic phenomenological mode: the slow preliminary exegesis of the framework of the obvious, the fundamental grammar of relationships. In the manner of Schutz he articulates the structure of the family in space and time: it is either close-knit or scattered in space, married once and now divorced in time. There is a relational grammar of we, me, you, us and them, hers, his and mine.

All are members one of another as men may be members in the Party, the Nation, or the Church.

Again, sermons use analogy and word play. [Laing discusses] "secondary transformations," *i.e.* what happens when one's inner experience has to be denied and when internal reality becomes out of phase with external definition. Wishes and memories are outlawed and excommunicated. Immediately the penal analogy takes over: the psychiatric "mind police" are called in; they take the criminal (patient) into custody (hospitalisation); he confesses by a show of insight and a therapeutic sentence is pronounced. Because his experience has been invalidated he becomes an invalid (word play almost worthy of Lancelot Andrewes or Donne).

A final characteristic of sermonising is vagueness. One moves very slowly and deliberately at the level of personal relationships, spelling it out carefully, repeating, illustrating, and then suddenly one spirals as rapidly as a firework up to a vague outer space comprising "the world" and "society." The mediating levels of all the various interstitial social spheres are traversed by the merest mention, and it is the total system which comes under prophetic judgment. From a discussion of familial rules which one is prevented from acknowledging (and from acknowledging, or even knowing, that one *is* so prevented) the rhetoric roars upward to the "Western conscience" into which we are all supposed to be so tightly knit and knotted together. As he says, in a final exordium, the more we comply with the rules the more we have to break them. He completes the sermon with the proper appeal to Scripture: "our righteousness is as filthy rags."

Consider for a moment another successful series of sermons: the pieces delivered by Edmund Leach under the auspices of that august presbyter, Lord Reith [the Reith lectures for 1967]. Certain points of comparison are worth making. [In *A Runaway World,* 1967] Leach took as his theme the great Abelardian text *"I have said ye are gods"*, and he called on us to awaken to our status as incipient godlings, masters of all we surveyed. It was yet another evangelical call to take full charge of our own destiny. Then, Leach attacked that vehicle of continuity the family, lashed out at those who obediently conformed to parental expectations, and confidently claimed that the family

> with its narrow privacy and tawdry secrets, is
> the source of all our discontents. . . .

By this he meant the competitive pressures of status and economic emulation. He also pointed to changes in the family from an extended kinship network to a primary nucleus. Now, there is little in Laing that suggests either this important *external* history of the family or to indicate that (in another scriptural phrase) "the love of money is the root of all evil." *Homo economicus* does not play any role on the family scene, whereas it is a fact that people *do* have jobs and that the role divisions and status tensions attendant on them *can* be crucial for the analysis of family dynamics. Perhaps Laing thinks so too but he makes almost no reference to the fact.

To be sure Leach and Laing conform to type in attacking

conformity as well as in attacking the family. This much is *de rigueur*. Laing, however, goes further. In the process of attacking conventional wisdom he succeeds in illustrating it. Not everything in Laing is conventional, and some of it is very neglected common sense—neglected at least among psychiatrists—but in certain respects (which I shall indicate below) he repeats the contemporary wisdom about being a Real Genuine, Authentic Person and about the ontological deprivation of the desiccated bureaucrat as if it were revelation. That inverts the normal practice of sermons. In conventional sermons revelation becomes platitude; in *soi-disant* unconventional sermons platitude becomes revelation.

Sermons require a congregation if not a church. The Round House at Chalk Farm (N.W.1), may be regarded as the great Tabernacle of the North London Pulpit. Hither the tribes of Judah come: the graduate proletariat, shifting from unhappy liaison to unhappy liaison, wandering from bed-sitter to bed-sitter. All the young pseudo- and sub-intelligentsia congregate on the small, windy hills of northern London, fleeing their middle-class backgrounds, affecting authentic squalor, leading the messy lives that prove their rejection of achievement and their search for *spontaneous*—and hence real—selfhood. If Laing never refers to *homo economicus* it is not surprising a large part of his congregation is in part-time employment. This sad, voluble, resentful and intermittently employed flotsam is Dr Laing's congregation, for whom the revelation provides a sort of validation of personal disorder by claiming it is the pre-condition of real life and creativity. The saddest thing about these people is the dreary predictability with which his disciples repeat the revelation in the name of the holy spirit of spontaneity Dr Laing has many creative and interesting things to say: the *epigoni* are repetitive bores.

I said above that in a special restricted sense Dr Laing purveys conventional wisdom. The conventional wisdom is the prejudice against rules, roles and relations on the ground that they stultify the expression and achievement of the Real Self. To study the tragedies consequent on rules is not to invalidate the need for rules or the fact that equal and infinitely more numerous tragedies would arise if rules were absent. Dr. Laing somehow sets rules against authenticity, personal experience against external rite, people against a structure of relations—when, in fact, rules and roles and relations are the necessary though not the sufficient condition of any kind of authentic person.

People thrown on the random resources of the unhedged psyche are set on a path where the achievement of authenticity becomes a passion which consumes its capacity to gain its own object—or rather its own subject. Furthermore, one person's pursuit of authenticity is another person's blasted possibility. It only needs one such liberated spirit to leave a trail of other people's broken potentialities behind him.

Over-development of the aspiration towards "the real" devalues the common, repeated, everyday in which the profoundest satisfactions can lie. Thus family life both breeds a sense of quiet desperation and suffocation *and* a common life of steady ritual, renewed confidences, demarcated pri-

vacies and deep familiarities without which people are lost souls. The familial is the familiar: that which defines, orders, and maintains the personal world. People can die within that order; they can barely live without it or without some substitute which is usually more, not less, restrictive. Moreover, many of the processes he describes are general phenomena of life operating as the necessary ground of social existence: *e.g.*, partial reciprocity, focussed and restricted identifications, unacknowledged systems of rules, proffered ranges of distinctions, definitions and options, processes of prescribing not by directions but by attributions and labels. These processes have their costs, which are sometimes heavy and repressive, but they admit an amelioration in the way they operate, and *total* reciprocity, *absolute* openness and lack of demarcation are neither possible nor desirable. All viable culture is a restriction on "world-openness", and that restriction in turn makes possible (though not inevitable) the recovery of some openness to the world. To push for *total* openness is to fall over into an inherent contradiction. Kibbutzim replace the family only by being *more* restrictive; universal communities of love rigorously exclude the outside world; rejection of any Them which is Other ends up by identifying as a sub-human Them all who do not reject that division in the way you do. I'm not sure that Laing himself does not acknowledge as much.

I have previously characterised Dr Laing's condemnation of his own profession as exaggerated to the point where he destroys the likelihood of a favourable reception. Nevertheless, he is quite right about the deficiencies of a great deal of psychiatric practice, particularly the kind of individual therapy which inhibits wider explorations.

Thomas Hardy has a haunting poem where he describes the constant reduplication of "the family face." Laing documents the way in which generation after generation the fallen face of a family is projected down a hall of mirrors. He rightly draws on common observation of the way people recognise this partial re-duplication generation after generation and points out that the way this operates in any given family is often least understood by the participants. People *note* the fact of reduplication without *understanding* the process; and that process is such that it interdicts any recognition of itself. The process is only weakened by slow dilutions and the criss-crossing of one type of process by another, some of these processes being more benevolent than others. Laing does not tell us anything about *benevolent* family systems. For him particular pathology is the key to universal pathology. There is no variable incidence in the structural location of sin, unless maybe in the institutions of non-Western cultures. (When he is not condemning Society as such, the West does tend to be his particular malevolent Other).

Laing is a *social* psychiatrist in that he does understand the structural location of illness in the family and in wider networks. This, again, is a commonsense position which the practice of too many psychiatrists denies. The extraordinary resistance of the psychiatric profession to investigating the whole familial context is remarkable even in institutions dedicated to communal therapy.

Thus, psychiatrists may rely entirely on treatment of the

individual in that they make no provision for altering the context to which the "patient" returns, acknowledge no impact deriving from the real exigencies of social living at the time, and *avoid* alternative sources of evidence from other members of the system in which the patient is implicated. It is not merely, of course, that a parent may need treatment as much as a child but that there is a structure of relationships about which all the relevant perspectives need to be understood. To see the patient as a hall of mirrors apart from current constricting exigencies and without assessing the total distribution of psychic weights in the crazy structures in which he is implicated is, to put it correctly, a form of madness to which only a carefully trained doctor could aspire. Only the "Me Doctor, You Patient" syndrome (to quote Eric Idle) could lead to such monstrous professional deformation. When Laing says that psychiatrists often do little more than operate a few standard myths he tells no more than the truth. No wonder that the prestige of psycho-analytical procedures exists most strongly in the social work field where it acts as a myth of professional legitimation and is uniquely low in the academic world of the social sciences

Yet Laing does not carry his analyses far enough. The additional standard myth which he is proposing cuts off large segments of familial reality. For example, one of his primary modes of analysis is in terms of tragic drama—a Greek tragedy repeated with variations over generations in which the basic meaning is often hidden from the participants. He employs a dramatic image and aspires to study the "scene" as it unfolds in terms of multiple refracting perspectives and the reciprocal mutations of the story proposed by the participants. But even within this dramatic mode a crucial element is lacking: comedy. If one looks at his index there is no entry under "joke"; yet what the anthropologists call "joking relationships" are a very important key to the "politics of the family."

Partly this is because what is joked about is often no laughing matter. People can convey their meaning and their understanding of the situation through the joke when no other means are open. Yet it is also because jokes are based on a sense of incongruity, and it is the disjunction between experience as felt and as defined which is Laing's primary interest. His whole analysis turns on the dire consequences of the Inner not matching the Outer, and a primary mechanism of expressing this lack of fit is the joking relationship. Indeed jokes derive from the Inner not meeting the Outer and are actually part of the richness which can result from that disjunction. One suspects that the crusade against lack of fit is a crusade against comedy. Laing's analyses describe no comedy and contain none. The family is not only a tragedy but also a comedy, and anyone sitting down with a book called *the politics of the family* should be anticipating something pretty ludicrous.

The approach based on the unfolding scene parallels approaches in sociology (*e.g.,* Dalziell Duncan, or ethnomethodology); and like them, it neglects segments of the external. For example, the specific semi-discrete networks of work and status and their semi-autonomous processes are largely absent from Laing's analysis. These impinge on the family, often in quite a crucial manner. I suggested

above that Laing's congregation is in part-time employment, which is why his internal mode of analysis appeals to them. But many of them also know themselves to be the consequences of "objective" external processes in the social system: their joblessness related to the overproduction of graduates, their emotional difficulties related to patterns of educational striving operative in their homes, or to the status tensions reflected in their families. Thus one knows of psychiatrists who on principle avoid not only knowledge of wider networks but any sensitivity to their *specific* sociological character.

Imagine, for example, a working-class family in which the mother retains middle-class connections and therefore practises certain varieties of social withdrawal from neighbourhood ties. Imagine, also, a father deep in work and trade union activities and, to that extent, partly withdrawn from the family. Impose on these a pattern of educational striving and a particular division of roles between son and daughter whereby the son is offered partial autonomy at the price of relative insensitivity.

Thus the psychic burden of family sensitivity falls on a daughter for whom the father does not provide the necessary degree of support and contact. The daughter receives the same cues demanding educational success as the boy, but in an emotionally charged situation which cripples her so that she feels unable to meet the call to daughterly and intellectual perfection. She feels incapable of feeling and becomes immobilised. Now, at this point the "double binds" so brilliantly described by Laing—the rules contradicted by other rules, the rules whose existence is denied, and whose denial is denied—begin to operate so that their incidence falls more on the daughter than the son.

Imagine, in addition, a psychiatrist who treats this all in terms of the father- or mother-aspect of the patient and who insists as a methodological *principle* on not knowing about, let alone understanding, the wider context of class, status, and educational striving. Consider what it must imply for a psychiatrist *not* to understand the role of educational striving in particular groups—and, in addition, to see all relationships in the wider network outside the family as pure extensions of the family images and, therefore, denuded of inherent relevance. Consider what it means if therapy is purely concerned with understanding and does not provide clues about how to cope with the maternal relation *in the future,* how to exist in a milieu likely to contain an unusual concentration of persons in a similar (or worse) condition, and how eventually to "pass that exam" to do the kind of job which would bring genuine interest. Laing partly mends this; it needs mending altogether.

Consider, too, one further point about the impact of Laingian ideas in the kind of milieu indicated of the loosely interlocking, partly employed, intellectually frustrated inhabitants of North London (and not only, of course, of North London). On the one hand, we have psychiatrists whom Laing rightly criticises for opting out of the real task of analysis. On the other hand, we have "patients" for whom the Laingian position comes as (literally) a godsend since they, defined as disturbed, are offered the counter-ideology of defining the world in general as mad. The world becomes defined as a malevolent Them with which no contact ought to be renewed and in which no job ought to be done. Thus unemployment and effortless sensitivity is ideologically legitimated. This separating out from the *body* of society, and the chronic fear of being reattracted to it by fiendish subtleties—this confused, bizarre denunciation of society—is the analogue of schizophrenia, at the social level. Laing essays to cure micro-schizophrenia by inducing macro-schizophrenia. He calls for responsibility by legitimating its opposite. There is nothing more seductive than to see oneself as a "scapegoat" appointed by one's family and the system.

I have said that Laing is a preacher and that his congregation consists of the shaggy prophets of bed-sitterdom. As a preacher he is a heretic, and heresy means choice: he is in fact the apostle of spontaneous choice. His theology is obsessed with the secular location of original sin, tracing its taint from familial generation to generation. Unfortunately, like so many contemporary intellectuals, he believes in original sin *and*—when he permits himself some optimism—Rousseauesque means of social redemption. Now, a secular version of original sin makes the whole world mad by defining man himself as innocent. Like Jeff Nuttall [in his *Bomb Culture,* 1969], another prophet in similar vein, he holds to the Augustinian and Rousseauesque view at the same time and has the two in a state of misconceived relation. The great tradition of the church has been concerned to hold both original sin and the rational possibility open to man in creative relation. The rational possibility must not be denied, but it is made *impossible* if the fact of man's radical deviation from his centre is stood on its head. It is this radical deviation from his centre which not only "infects" all structures but also creates that radical incongruity which is the key to all movement and dynamism.

Laing's fundamental error is that he wishes to cure the "lack of fit" in human affairs and, therefore, attacks the common condition of man and the tragic comedy which legitimately belongs to it.

Robert Boyers   (essay date Winter 1974)

SOURCE: "The Laingian Family," in *Partisan Review,* Vol. XLI, No. 1, Winter, 1974, pp. 109-18.

[*Boyers is an American psychologist and educator whose written works include* Psychological Man: Approaches to an Emergent Social Type *(1974). In the following excerpt, he discusses the influence of Wilhelm Reich on Laing's work and explores the development of Laing's notion that madness is comprehensible and that the family plays a pivotal role in the creation of a schizophrenic personality.*]

The attack on the nuclear family will probably turn out to be the most important development of our period, a phenomenon beside which other militancies, of whatever character, will eventually seem ephemeral and even somewhat parochial. What we confront is the general loss of faith in the efficacy of the family unit to nurture the kind of people most of us apparently think we ought to be. With this particular erosion a whole variety of alternate faiths have been intermittently promoted—faith in the extended family, in the communal mode, faith in the necessary

breakdown of sex-role distinctions and the consequent emergence of unisexual experience, faith in life without children—the list can be indefinitely extended. Most of these alternate faiths have been promoted, bought, and largely forgotten in a spirit of casual abandon the likes of which many of us could not have imagined. Especially where the front men and promoters have been professional intellectuals and psychoanalysts we have been struck by a specious commitment to change for its own sake and to liberations on behalf of liberation which we would not readily have identified with cultivated and thoughtful people.

Obviously, we had no right to be surprised, for the prospect of overcoming everything that may conceivably be overcome has seemed to most intellectuals a delightful prospect at least since the time of Nietzsche, and those who have found much to be stimulated by in *Zarathustra* might certainly have seen where all of it would lead. The spiritual timbre of the counterculture is not often Nietzschean, of course, but the roots are clear enough. Perhaps a more appropriate, and less distant forerunner, is Wilhelm Reich, whose assaults on the family and other established cultural institutions are decidedly more pointed and programmatic than Nietzsche's, if no less eccentric. Reich, to be sure, identified himself with a whole range of liberation to which Nietzsche could not have been less favorably disposed, but both have lately been appropriated by movements whose distinctive coloration neither could have foreseen. That Reich would have felt a good deal more comfortable with recent developments in the counterculture than Nietzsche may be explained at once by the greater proximity of his age to ours and by the superficiality of his thought by comparison with Nietzsche's.

> In his writings after *The Divided Self,*
> Laing came more and more to grow
> restive in the role of alien therapist and
> sensitive observer. The writing became
> consequently more polemical and, in fact,
> insensitive.
>
> —*Robert Boyers*

In his *Character Analysis,* Reich states what for our time has become almost a conventional notion: "The first and most important place of reproduction of the social order is the patriarchal family which creates in children a character structure which makes them amenable to the later influences of an authoritarian order." Or again, in *The Sexual Revolution,* Reich argues that the family "creates the individual who is forever afraid of life and of authority and thus creates again and again the possibility that masses of people can be governed by a handful of individuals." For precise understanding of "the authoritarian order" one must go to sources other than Reich's books, as one will need to look elsewhere for a scrupulous analysis of the character structure to which he refers. What is important, though, is that we have in Reich an unqualified attack on the nuclear family, launched from a perspective that considers both its impact on individuals and on the larger social order that sustains, and is sustained by, those individuals. As such he has given encouragement and direction to a variety of thinkers, whether serious or tritely polemical, who are unhappy about that culture. In Herbert Marcuse or Norman Brown or Ronald Laing, to name only a few of the more serious thinkers, we can find Reich's views writ large, though frequently his influence is obscured by references in their work to more respectable authors.

In Laing, for example, Reich has figured very prominently, though Laing has lately taken some pains to dissociate himself from despoilers of the nuclear family ethic. In his early work, of course, though there were pointers careful readers might have seen, Laing was careful not to draw large conclusions about the nature of families or to deal in abstractions like "the character structure of western man." As anyone knows who has kept abreast of developments in psychotherapy during the last fifteen years or so, Laing was originally part of a very widespread and still growing tendency in mental health circles to focus attention on psychotic patients, people who had in an earlier time been diagnosed as relatively incurable, hopelessly resistant to all forms of therapy, whether Freudian, Jungian, or whatever. Teams of therapists and researchers had worked quietly, roughly since the end of the Second World War, trying to understand the experience of schizophrenic patients and of others diagnosed as generally untreatable. Men like Nathan Ackerman, Theodore Lidz, and Lyman Wynne had hit tentatively upon a number of conclusions regarding the relation between particular individuals labeled schizophrenic and their families of origin. In the fifties and early sixties Laing came to conclusions similar to theirs, and began to publish them in a series of books whose popularity has made familiar even to lay people the dynamics of psychosis and the rationale for family therapy. In a book like *The Divided Self,* Laing worked scrupulously to locate and understand the nexal dynamics of the schizophrenic family. His object was not to assign blame or to discover new worlds but to understand the sources of interpersonal mystification, and to see whether the fiercely consistent perspective of psychotic patients might not have something to teach the rest of us.

In his subsequent writings, though, Laing came more and more to grow restive in the role of alien therapist and sensitive observer. The writing became consequently more polemical and, in fact, insensitive. In a 1962 article entitled **"Series and Nexus in the Family,"** Laing wrote satirically of a fictitious Peter and Paul, members of a nuclear family in which the demand for reciprocity was seen by Laing as coercive and intolerable:

> If Peter is prepared to make sacrifices for Paul, so Paul should be prepared to make sacrifices for Peter, or else he is selfish, ungrateful, callous, ruthless, etc. "Sacrifice" under these circumstances consists in Peter impoverishing himself to do something for Paul. It is the tactic of *enforced debt.*

> One way of putting this is that each person *invests in the other.*

In his essay, "Self, Symptom and Society," Peter Sedgwick responded to the passage as follows:

> The blindness of these passages is unbelievable. For, of course, assumptions of a continuing reciprocity, along with anticipations of a possible limit to the relationship in the event of a nonreturn of affection or action, are very common indeed outside family ghettos and even outside families.

Further,

> To "invest in" another being's anticipated response is seen as literally capitalistic and hence disreputable: the "debt" of a relationship has to be "enforced," a deliberate *tactic.* The converse might be expected to follow: that the sacrifice of one individual for another ought to continue indefinitely even if it remains unacknowledged or despised. But ought we to expect such saintly expenditure of infinite pains in our families?

What we get in Laing, in other words, is a growing conviction that since families generally do not do for their members what we would like them to, and since some at least are the source of severe functional disorders in one or more members, there is something in the nature of the institution itself that makes it unsuitable in the present state of culture. Moreover, since it is assumed that mental disorders like schizophrenia are functional rather than genetic in origin, if mystification patterns are observable in the life of schizophrenic families, it is more than likely that such patterns will characterize so-called normal family communications patterns as well. How do we know? Since, when we are considering so-called normal families, we have no patients to point to, no outrageously disrupted speech patterns or monstrously aggressive behaviors to work from, we need to posit something else as evidence. It is at this point that Laing turns to the social order, and culls from his observation one example after another of "mad" behavior—the bombing of cities, the hideous regimentation of masses of people under the guise of benevolent liberality, and so on—phenomena discussed at length by Marcuse and others. That is to say, from the consideration of severely disturbed people in their family settings, Laing progressively turned his attention to the dynamics of those families or institutions, until he concluded that so much could go wrong in families that they had inevitably to be cast as sources of oppression and mystification, and madness politically certified as perfect sanity. From this it was but a short step to those chapters in *The Politics of Experience* in which Laing proclaims the superior authenticity of madness, at least as a step through which enlightened people will inevitably pass, especially by comparison with those lives of quiet desperation and spiritless normality to which most men are committed.

The attack on the family has been taken up by all manner of therapists, but as yet not many have rallied to the figure of schizophrenic as seer, even as Laing himself has seemed no longer to be taken with the notion in its original crudeness. Even Laing's most ardent disciples, those in a position to follow his lead professionally, have seemed to step back from claims earlier made on behalf of the view that much madness is divinest sense.

Rosemary Dinnage (review date 5 August 1976)

SOURCE: "Over the Edge," in *The New York Review of Books,* Vol. XXIII, No. 13, August 5, 1976, pp. 38-9.

[*In the following excerpt from a review of Laing's* The Facts of Life *and David Reed's* Anna, *Dinnage negatively compares the former book to* The Divided Self.]

Laing's new book [**The Facts of Life**] is more about the factlessness of life than about its facts. It has a chill air of slackness and confusion. Laing begins with a short—too short—autobiographical sketch, which gives us a few devastating glimpses of his early life: the only child of estranged parents, his mother ill after his birth, his care at the hands of a "drunken slut"; he and his mother sleeping in one bedroom of a Glasgow tenement, his father in the other; his mother fainting when, at fifteen, he used the phrase "fuckin' well" without knowing what it meant; and at sixteen, still without any idea of the facts of life—hence the book's title.

He continues, it seems here, to be bewildered, in search of facts and meaning. But whereas in his earlier books, and notably **The Divided Self,** Laing used his acquaintance with ontological borderlands, the mind's cliffs of fall, to reveal the structure of pathological states of consciousness as lucidly as a microscope enlarges a crystal, here he seems lost in those borderlands, all intellectual vitality spent. "Who knows if life is not death and death life?" is the book's epigraph, from Euripides. The question was originally asked in a pattern of purposes and meanings; here it hangs isolated on the page, about as meaningful as an empty nutshell. Who knows? Who is going to make us care?

> Am I dead or alive?
>
> Am I asleep or awake?
>
> How can I be certain this is not a dream?
>
> . . . What are we seeing? We cannot be sure we are seeing what we *suppose* is out there, whatever we suppose. Nor can we be sure even that we see some sort of copy, or picture, of what we suppose is out there. If it comes to that, we cannot be certain that there *is* anything out there apart from what we see. . . .

This is from the chapter "Speculations," which follows the biographical opening.

We know these speculations, they are familiar. When they are formalized and worked with, they are philosophy; when obsessive, they are a psychosis; in the hands of Beckett or Hopkins, they are given artistic life; in the case histories of **The Divided Self** they are set in the dense context of the way an individual constructs, or fails to construct, his sense of identity and of the reality of outside objects. Set down as limply as they are here, platitudinous and insubstantial, they add up to nothing.

In a further chapter of ruminations later in the book, Laing ponders such questions as how he took a walk to buy a jar of honey, unblocked his left nostril in a state of non-egoic consciousness, and sneezed at a party. The vapidity of most of these introspections is only heightened by the style he has adopted, again so different from that of his earlier writing: rhetorical questioning ("Is this not a serious state of affairs?"—"am I single or multiple?"—"Why? And even, is why a proper question?") and the irritating habit of spacing out his lines as if they were poetry:

> Sobbing, and moaning,
> unrestrained
> for two or three minutes
> then over.

A few pages are given over to "field notes"—scraps of observation, overheard conversations: these are sometimes entertaining and percipient, and cut across the solipsistic tension with the voices of real people—even though rather dreadful ones ("Should we try to get in touch with our feelings now, or wait until we graduate?" asks an American student couple). These dialogues apart, and the "speculations" and the morsel of autobiography, the greater part of this miscellany is devoted to two subjects, the critique of psychiatric methods and of scientific assumptions that we expect from Laing, and a new theme—the trauma of birth, and not only birth, but intra-and pre-uterine life as well.

"Many of my contemporaries," he argues,

> *feel* that what has happened from their conception to and through birth has a relevance of some kind to them now as adults. These feeling patterns deserve serious attention. It does not seem to me to be, *a priori,* nonsense, or antecedently impossible, that prenatal patterns may be mapped onto natal and postnatal experience.

He relates (quoting from Rank) a common pattern of myth that could relate to birth experience; cites as relevant experiences of claustrophobia and agoraphobia; accuses modern medicine, as does Leboyer, of traumatically mishandling the birth process; describes the so-called "birthing" sessions given by a New York psychotherapist.

There need be no great difficulty in accepting the idea that birth leaves a formative imprint on the nervous system (although, as far as I know, not even the simplest study has been carried out to match the severity of birth experiences against later development); fifteen or so years ago the possibility of a psychology of the newborn baby was considered farfetched, whereas now it is one of the most interesting and rapidly growing areas for study, and an experimental psychologist can respectably state in print that he considers psychological processes to begin at conception. And rebirth has been one of the great themes of myth, rite, and dreaming. But it has always been approached with seriousness and respect, as part of the imaginative concept of a new beginning; only in this spirit could it have therapeutic energy. Laing's superficiality here, his attribution of his daily need for a drink around 5:15 to the fact that this was his birth hour, his description of the therapeutic "birthings"—fifteen minutes each, twenty in an afternoon—makes nonsense of the scrupulous attention he once paid to the intricate mental processes of his fellows. Shall we get reborn now or wait until after lunch?

Laing has contracted himself, and his intellect and compassion, back into a single cell, a point, a death.

—*Rosemary Dinnage*

Laing's meditations on a uterine theme go back before birth, back to the single cell: to conception, anxious hours in the Fallopian tubes, implantation in the endometrium. All are permanently recorded, he suggests, and form the basis for the problems of the homeless spinster who wanders around department stores (existentially fixated in the tubes), the underground train driver (searching for implantation), the businessman who faints in the bathroom (catastrophic encounter with the endometrium). It is embarrassing to have to pay serious attention to this kind of thing; but if this is anything more than sheer dotiness, it is a kind of angry blotting out of life: there are greater varieties, he says, of prenatal than of postnatal experiences—so much for this postnatal world and its occupants and occupations. Laing has contracted himself, and his intellect and compassion, back into a single cell, a point, a death.

There remain to be mentioned the chapters, one of them originally a lecture, in which he once again attacks the psychiatry practiced in mental hospitals, and in particular ECT treatment. They are more composed than the rest of the book, but do not add much to what he has written in the same vein elsewhere. . . .

H. J. Eysenck   (review date October 1977)

SOURCE: "But Is It Art?," in *Books and Bookmen,* Vol. 23, No. 1, October, 1977, p. 41.

[*Eysenck is a German psychologist, educator, and author of several books, including* Personality and Individual Differences: A Natural Science Approach *(1985). In the following negative review of* Do You Love Me?, *Eysenck charges that the poetry has the characteristics of an "undergraduate joke" and that Laing's "undisciplined verbal ability" has produced "ugly" poetry of "unbearable bathos."*]

Laing's Autobiography, [*Wisdom, Madness and Folly,*] which I reviewed in these pages a few months ago, already departed considerably from his usual style of writing; this book [*Do You Love Me?*] does so even more. The blurb promises much. 'These verses and conversations which go straight to some of our deepest worries, aggressions and puzzles are written in the tradition of the music-hall and cabaret. Reading them is like going to an intimate review. Each scene, each number is complete in itself but compels us to read the next'. It is also claimed that '. . . . the forms of this allusive writing derive from jazz, from nursery rhymes, from popular songs and from writers like Johnny Mercer, Thomas Wyatt, Dorothy Parker and Robert Burns'. We are also told that the book ' . . . is funny, savage and sometimes even scurrilous, but it successfully avoids flippancy, callousness and sentimentality'.

Any book would have difficulties in fulfilling these promises, and sadly I must admit that I found nothing remotely as witty as Dorothy Parker or within light years of Robert Burn's lyricism. To be quite frank the book reminded me of two things.

The first of these was an undergraduate joke played by some students at an Australian University on a Society which was offering a prize for the best modern poem. They sent in a couple of pages from the Melbourne Sanitation Department Report on the Drains, suitably cut up into short lines but otherwise quite unchanged. They won first prize! This has always seemed to me a befitting comment on modern poetry and art in general, eclipsed only by the experience of seeing dirty nappies hung up on the wall as examples of artistic endeavour. However, critics uncertain of the dictates of good taste often object to criticisms of modern writing and modern art in general, saying that surely all new forms of art have encountered hostility in the past, and that we should be careful not to throw out the baby with the bath water. If my reading of history is correct, then most of the great artists were recognised in their lifetime, and thus falsify this belief as a statement of general practice. Shakespeare and Goethe, Milton and Titian, Raphael and Bach, Moliere and Wanger—the list is endless, and it contains almost all the great figures in writing, music and painting. One might also add that of those who were considered to have produced rubbish in their lifetime, 99.999% did in fact produce rubbish. The fact that there were some very occasional exceptions should not blind us to the fact that if we called rubbish what we conceive to be rubbish in our time, the probability of being wrong is less than 0.001%! This may reassure those who do not trust their own good taste.

The other comment which I recall on reading through Laing's new book is one made by Dr Johnson on seeing Angela Rippon dance (or was it hearing a woman preach?); he said it reminded him of a dog walking on its hind legs; it was not so much that it was done well, as that it was done at all. It is the same with this book; it is not done well, but it is surprising that it was done at all. Laing has of course always shown a mild literary talent, sufficient at least to hide the emptiness of his antipsychiatry thoughts behind grandiose verbal formulations. This rather undisciplined verbal ability now seeks new fields to conquer, but poetry is not a good choice, to judge by this small volume. The almost unbearable bathos of much of its content is characteristic of the naturalist school of writing; readers might like to savour an example of Laing's 'art'; here is one:

> she well then?
> he   well then what?
> she you did didn't you?
> he   what are you talking about?
> she you know perfectly well what I am talking
>   about
> he   if you're still on about that I've said all I am
>   going to say
> she you did didn't you?
> he   I've already told you
> she you did didn't you?
> he   I'm not going to be interrogated
> she just tell me the truth

he   I've told you

she   who was it?

he   no one

she   you're such a liar

he   you said you weren't jealous

she   don't change the subject

he   what are you going on about? I've already
      told you

she   I'm not jealous I only have to know

he   why have you such a suspicious mind?

she   I know who it was

he   you've made up your mind. There's nothing
      more I can say

she   you think you're going to get away with it

he   there's nothing to get away with

she   you did I know you did
          (pause)

he   no

she   you might as well admit it

he   there's nothing to admit

she   she told me herself

he   I know you are making that up

she   she came and told me herself

he   why do you have to resort to such lies?

she   I'm not going to let you destroy my sense
      of reality along with everything else

he   you are paranoid

This is indeed very much like the kind of talk you might hear from a rather silly couple of half-educated adolescents, but it does not make good poetry, and it does not make good reading, at least to me. Others might be attracted by it; if that is so then they may find joy and comfort in this book. As for me I would much rather read the report on drains of the Melbourne Department of Sanitation. At least it does not pretend to be other than it is.

I am reminded of Kipling's famous line, in one of his poems: 'It is pretty, but is it art?' This doubt has now reached epidemic proportions, and nowadays we would almost have to rephrase it: 'It is ugly, but is it art?' Laing's verse is certainly ugly, but that alone does not qualify it as art.

Anthony Storr   (review date 12 February 1978)

SOURCE: "From the Mouths of Babes," in *The New York Times Book Review*, February 12, 1978, p. 8.

[*Storr is an English psychiatrist and educator whose written works include* The Dynamics of Creation *(1972),* C. G. Jung *(1973), and* The Art of Psychotherapy *(1980). In the following review of* Conversations with Adam and Natasha, *Storr contends that, while the book's subject matter—transcriptions of conversations between Laing's young children—holds a certain fascination, the work is ultimately insubstantial.*]

Admirers of R. D. Laing will enjoy this book. I liked it better than any book of his that I have read since his first two, *The Divided Self* and *The Self and Others.* Laing is evidently a compulsive writer who, in addition to his regular production of books (and his psychoanalytic practice), keeps a journal. In this, over a period of six years, he has recorded conversations with Adam and Natasha, the two elder children of his second marriage. Adam was born in

September 1967, Natasha in April 1970; but Natasha easily wins out, in that far more of her remarks are recorded than those of Adam. What effect this has had on Adam, we are not told. It may be that, like many fathers, Laing prefers his daughter; but it is equally likely to be the effect of age. The stunning spontaneity of small children tends to decline as they get older, and most of these conversations date from 1973 onward, after Adam had reached his sixth birthday.

Let us have a few examples:

(on a journey)

NATASHA I'm going to run away

JUTTA (her mother) well run away then

NATASHA how can I run away when I don't know where I am?

Lewis Carroll would have liked that one. He would also have appreciated:

Adam is standing looking seriously puzzled

DADDY What is it?

ADAM this staircase wasn't even *here* until they put it here.

That Laing's children talk a good deal about God is not surprising, but some of Laing's disciples may not have expected that the children are recurrently enjoined to say their prayers. Some of their remarks about God have a (slightly sickly) flavor of J. M. Barrie:

NATASHA Do fairies go up to God?

MUMMY I don't know

NATASHA Adam says they do (pause) but they can come down again and see their mummies, and they can go to church, and sing to God: and then they go to their homes underground.

Others are less Victorian in sentiment:

NATASHA Can God kill himself?

MUMMY I don't know

One of Laing's friends, called Monty, presumably an analyst, is told of this last remark. The following conversation ensues, almost the only one recorded between two adults:

MONTY there is an incredibly close relationship between sex and death. I will tell you what the question is saying. She is asking "Does God masturbate?"

RONNIE and that is "Does daddy masturbate?"

MONTY precisely. She wishes to know whether you do it without mummy, whether you need mummy: whether she can do it with you instead of mummy.

RONNIE there you go

MONTY I hope you don't mind me being so direct

RONNIE O not at all

"There you go" indeed! Monty's assumption that God and Ronnie are necessarily equated in a household in which children are taught to say their prayers is not only unsupported, but, if correctly reported, insufferably arrogant: "I will *tell* you what the question is saying"! Laing says of these conversations in his introduction, "So many constructions can be placed on them," but Monty *knows* that he is right and that his is the only truth. I can guess what analytical school he owes allegiance to, but, because not all his colleagues are so dogmatic, I will not name it.

Laing's book reveals him as a predominantly ordinary father: sometimes impatient, sometimes unreasonable. His advantage seems to be his accessibility. Unlike many authors, he seems able to write in the midst of family life with children milling around and interrupting. In the introduction he writes:

> It is just as useful for adults to be in touch with childhood as for children to be in touch with adults. We learn about children only from children. Our understanding of ourselves is enormously impoverished if we are out of touch with childhood. Adults can suffer as much from the deprivation of children in their lives as the other way round.

I am sure he is right here. On the other hand, like many other parents, he overestimates the "cuteness" of his own children's remarks. "Some of the conversations have struck some people as so incredible that I've been asked if I made them up." I think it is only people who are out of touch with children who will be so struck. Many parents could match these conversations if they had taken the trouble to record their children's remarks; and I think that it must be largely because Laing is now world-famous that the publishers agreed to make this into a book. As Natasha said of a previous book, *Do You Love Me*:

> they've printed it very well (turning the pages) There's not much on the paper. Look, there's hardly anything on that page. Or that page. There's the littlest *I've* ever seen.

Laing has, I think, been going through a long fallow period with not very much new to say. Let us hope that his children will inspire him to make his next book more substantial.

Rosemary Dinnage (review date 14 July 1978)

SOURCE: "Knuts," in *New Statesman*, Vol. 96, No. 2469, July 14, 1978, pp. 55-6.

[*In the following review of* Conversations with Children, *Dinnage contends that, while the transcribed conversations between Laing's children are interesting at times, and may in fact raise serious "theoretical considerations," Laing is simply wrong to claim that this kind of material has never before been published.*]

R. D. Laing has protested against being considered a gloomy fellow who sees no hope for the human race, and wants to show that he has another side; also he has a writ-

ing problem ('*Natasha:* why are you feeling sad? . . . *Ronnie:* I want to write things but I don't seem able to. *Natasha:* why are you not able to? *Ronnie:* I don't know'). So he has cribbed from a couple of non-alienated, unmystified human beings and presents, without comment, scraps of conversation he has recorded over six years with his youngest children [in *Conversations with Children*].

Laing is into communication. He has always enjoyed repartee and dialogue, he says, and has spent much of his life studying miscommunication, the deadly nuances of 'this division of hell'; now he wants to reproduce the interlace of dialogue, rather than the knots: 'the free and open space between us where we can play with reality together, where we question and answer, inquire into what is the case and what is not, for the sheer heaven of it'. He could have had a worse idea, though his kids are no cuter than yours or mine. *Conversations with Children* takes about half an hour to read and, on the whole, not much longer to forget, but the only boring thing about it is Laing's claim that it is unprecedentedly significant.

The Laing children say their prayers, are conventionally Oedipal, and show no signs of being paralysed by psychological understanding like most psychiatrists' and psychoanalysts' children. The only really Laingian note is struck by their father ('don't do that again unless I know it isn't you'). Like most children, however, they are natural existentialists: if she is half German and half Scottish, Natasha asks, what is the whole of her? She has an invisible car: that is, she has one wheel, and a car with invisible doors, invisible seats, and invisible engine, and three invisible wheels. Adam also has metaphysical concerns: 'this stairway wasn't even *here,* until they put it here.' They have a rather fine eight-year-old friend who cuts through incipient knots admirably: 'I'm sorry I only allow myself to be kissed by my mummy and other relatives.' The only buffoon is an adult called Monty who comments, on the perfectly reasonable question 'can God kill himself ?', that it means 'does God masturbate?', which means 'does Daddy masturbate?', which means 'can she do it with you instead of Mummy?' I hope Laing included this to show how much children's conversation is often to be preferred to adults'.

He says he deliberately decided, after some thought, not to accompany the dialogues with a theoretical essay, nor to footnote them. I am glad he didn't, though I can think of some of the things he might have said. That children are concerned with where they end and other people begin; with what time means, and how to disentangle it from space; with thereness and not-thereness; that they hate and love ungovernably; have a natural gift for ritual and symbolic action; live with the most abstract and most concrete conceptions side by side. At times they see death everywhere, as matter-of-factly as Laing does when he says:

> such was the richness of their earlier epoch, before the onslaught of language that our pleasure having [*sic*] our children talk to us was tinged with sadness and nostalgia for the subtlety of their music and dance before they spoke. It's sometimes difficult to keep up with one's children: not to mourn, in gaining a girl, a boy, the

> **Laing's plea is that our understanding of schizophrenia, which is one kind of a number of related kinds of human thought and behavior, should be of a piece with our understanding of the rest of human behavior.**
>
> *—Hugo Meynell*

It is difficult to see any good *a priori* reason for denying that the behaviour of some or all of those who are regarded as schizophrenic might be subject to type B rather than type A explanation; that is to say, that such behaviour might become comprehensible once it was shown how the agent understood his situation, and consequently what his motives and purposes were in regard to it. Whether this is or is not the case—whether schizophrenia is to be understood in terms of type A or type B explanation now or in the future—can be determined only by actual research.

It is essential to Laing's position that the behaviour of those classified as schizophrenics is to be understood, and so can best be influenced, in the same general kind of way as the behaviour of other agents. This is as much as to say that, if one wishes to understand the behaviour of a schizophrenic, one must get to know such things as how he envisages his situation, what he hopes to achieve out of it and in what respect he thinks that achievement will be worthwhile. Someone might argue somewhat as follows: 'Granted that the schizophrenic's action is intelligible in some cases in the light of what he deems his situation to be, we cannot assume in his case, as we can in the case of a person who is mistaken in the usual kinds of ways and for the usual kinds of reasons, that his ideas about his present situation are to be understood as due merely to mistaken, but at least intelligible, reflection on the course of his past and present experience. Thus a normal but ignorant person might well refuse to believe that the sun is larger than the earth; though we disagree with him, at least the course of reasoning by which he reached his erroneous conclusions is in principle clear to us. The sun certainly does not look larger than the earth; it takes a great deal of sophisticated reflection before it becomes at all natural to believe that it is in fact so. But in the case of the schizophrenic our disagreement is much more fundamental than this: we do not have the feeling that, if we were a little more stupid or less educated than we are, or if we had had certain experiences without access to certain information, we would say what he says or act as he acts. This is what makes it so plausible to look for explanations in terms of abnormal chemistry of the brain, or something similar.'

But it is precisely Laing's contention, which he supports by a weight of evidence, that the schizophrenic's words and actions *can* be understood as the result of a series of attempts to construe, and to act in relation to, the situation in which he actually is or has been. Here again is a matter which cannot be settled either way *a priori*, but only by consideration of the available evidence.

It seems characteristic of those schizophrenics investigated by Laing that: (a) they have come to experience themselves and their environment in an unusual way, owing to their attempts to cope with certain kinds of difficulty within that environment; (b) they express, in some of their more bizarre utterances, a kind of poetic analogy with what the sympathetic enquirer may eventually find their real situation to be.

It will be convenient to summarise Laing's account of schizophrenia under the following headings:

1 The Family and Interpersonal Background of Schizophrenia.

2 The Schizoid Condition.

3 The Change from the Schizoid Condition to Schizophrenia.

4 Truth expressed in Delusion.

5 The Recovery of Sanity.

1 *The Family and Interpersonal Background of Schizophrenia*

That the future schizophrenic patient may be genetically predisposed is admitted by Laing. It appears that the patients studied, when babies, had difficulty with the expression and implementation of their instinctual needs. But what is remarkable is that all or most of those in the early environment of the patient

> took this very feature as a token of goodness and stamped with approval the absence of self-action. The combination of almost total failure by the baby to achieve self-instinctual gratification, along with the mother's total failure to realise this, can be noted as one of the recurrent themes in the early beginnings of the relation of mother to schizophrenic child.

When it was first guessed that some features in the relationship of mother to child might predispose to schizophrenia in the child, there was a tendency towards a witch hunt for 'schizophrenogenic mothers'. But to admit the importance of the relationship between mother and child in the aetiology of schizophrenia is not to be committed to regarding it as of exclusive importance. All that is at issue is whether there are 'some ways of being a mother that impede rather than facilitate or "reinforce" any genetically determined inborn tendency there may be in the child' to fail to achieve the relatively confident and useful interaction with his fellows which is characteristic of the majority of people. In any case, the evidence goes to suggest that what contributed to schizophrenia in the child is the whole family situation rather than merely the behaviour of the mother. Over and over again, it seems in retrospect that parents have regarded with alarm what the investigators felt to have been normal signs of growing up in the child and adolescent—like engaging in normal domestic activities on its own initiative.

Recurrent in the description of the lives of schizophrenics by their families is a division into three main stages; during the first of which they were exceedingly 'good', until they abruptly became so 'bad' that it was quite a relief to realise

Laing's plea is that our understanding of schizophrenia, which is one kind of a number of related kinds of human thought and behavior, should be of a piece with our understanding of the rest of human behavior.

—Hugo Meynell

It is difficult to see any good *a priori* reason for denying that the behaviour of some or all of those who are regarded as schizophrenic might be subject to type B rather than type A explanation; that is to say, that such behaviour might become comprehensible once it was shown how the agent understood his situation, and consequently what his motives and purposes were in regard to it. Whether this is or is not the case—whether schizophrenia is to be understood in terms of type A or type B explanation now or in the future—can be determined only by actual research.

It is essential to Laing's position that the behaviour of those classified as schizophrenics is to be understood, and so can best be influenced, in the same general kind of way as the behaviour of other agents. This is as much as to say that, if one wishes to understand the behaviour of a schizophrenic, one must get to know such things as how he envisages his situation, what he hopes to achieve out of it and in what respect he thinks that achievement will be worthwhile. Someone might argue somewhat as follows: 'Granted that the schizophrenic's action is intelligible in some cases in the light of what he deems his situation to be, we cannot assume in his case, as we can in the case of a person who is mistaken in the usual kinds of ways and for the usual kinds of reasons, that his ideas about his present situation are to be understood as due merely to mistaken, but at least intelligible, reflection on the course of his past and present experience. Thus a normal but ignorant person might well refuse to believe that the sun is larger than the earth; though we disagree with him, at least the course of reasoning by which he reached his erroneous conclusions is in principle clear to us. The sun certainly does not look larger than the earth; it takes a great deal of sophisticated reflection before it becomes at all natural to believe that it is in fact so. But in the case of the schizophrenic our disagreement is much more fundamental than this: we do not have the feeling that, if we were a little more stupid or less educated than we are, or if we had had certain experiences without access to certain information, we would say what he says or act as he acts. This is what makes it so plausible to look for explanations in terms of abnormal chemistry of the brain, or something similar.'

But it is precisely Laing's contention, which he supports by a weight of evidence, that the schizophrenic's words and actions *can* be understood as the result of a series of attempts to construe, and to act in relation to, the situation in which he actually is or has been. Here again is a matter which cannot be settled either way *a priori*, but only by consideration of the available evidence.

It seems characteristic of those schizophrenics investigated by Laing that: (a) they have come to experience themselves and their environment in an unusual way, owing to their attempts to cope with certain kinds of difficulty within that environment; (b) they express, in some of their more bizarre utterances, a kind of poetic analogy with what the sympathetic enquirer may eventually find their real situation to be.

It will be convenient to summarise Laing's account of schizophrenia under the following headings:

1 The Family and Interpersonal Background of Schizophrenia.

2 The Schizoid Condition.

3 The Change from the Schizoid Condition to Schizophrenia.

4 Truth expressed in Delusion.

5 The Recovery of Sanity.

1 *The Family and Interpersonal Background of Schizophrenia*

That the future schizophrenic patient may be genetically predisposed is admitted by Laing. It appears that the patients studied, when babies, had difficulty with the expression and implementation of their instinctual needs. But what is remarkable is that all or most of those in the early environment of the patient

> took this very feature as a token of goodness and stamped with approval the absence of self-action. The combination of almost total failure by the baby to achieve self-instinctual gratification, along with the mother's total failure to realise this, can be noted as one of the recurrent themes in the early beginnings of the relation of mother to schizophrenic child.

When it was first guessed that some features in the relationship of mother to child might predispose to schizophrenia in the child, there was a tendency towards a witch hunt for 'schizophrenogenic mothers'. But to admit the importance of the relationship between mother and child in the aetiology of schizophrenia is not to be committed to regarding it as of exclusive importance. All that is at issue is whether there are 'some ways of being a mother that impede rather than facilitate or "reinforce" any genetically determined inborn tendency there may be in the child' to fail to achieve the relatively confident and useful interaction with his fellows which is characteristic of the majority of people. In any case, the evidence goes to suggest that what contributed to schizophrenia in the child is the whole family situation rather than merely the behaviour of the mother. Over and over again, it seems in retrospect that parents have regarded with alarm what the investigators felt to have been normal signs of growing up in the child and adolescent—like engaging in normal domestic activities on its own initiative.

Recurrent in the description of the lives of schizophrenics by their families is a division into three main stages; during the first of which they were exceedingly 'good', until they abruptly became so 'bad' that it was quite a relief to realise that they were really 'mad'. Reports of an early model childhood come, after prolonged experience of these cases, to have a rather sinister ring—especially as so often the ideas of 'goodness' and 'normality' held by the families concerned seem applied to what is rather indicative of inner deadness. It is just this deadness, this lack of independent liveliness and initiative, which appears to receive the highest commendation in these families. The effect of the family attitude may be augmented by a remarkable isolation from the human environment at large, which again is characteristic of these families. It tends to be extremely difficult for the future patient to make direct relationships with others outside the family, at an age when most young people would be doing so. For example, in the case of Lucie's contacts with other people, 'the way she saw them, how she thought they saw her, and how she saw herself, were all equally mediated by her father backed up by her mother.' When people do at length break away from their families, often they have been so affected by them that they are unable to make use of their apparent freedom.

The family tends to see the prospective schizophrenic in terms of a stereotype, departures from which are either not acknowledged at all, or stigmatised as bad or mad. They tend to be unable to see things from his point of view, or even to acknowledge that it is 'really' his point of view, whatever he himself may have to say about it. The patient Claire admitted that she had been well provided with material things when she was a child, but complained that she as a person, who had feelings and desires which she tried to express, was completely ignored. Claire's mother insisted that Claire's feelings were just like her own; when occasionally the recognition appeared to be at the point of breaking in upon her that this might not be so, her only response was alarm and puzzlement. One is struck in this case, as in very many similar ones, by 'the imperviousness of the mother to the daughter as a person separate to and different from herself' [*The Families of Schizophrenics*].

Of June in her earliest years, her mother's account never varied; June used to be happy, boisterous, and affectionate. This account seemed quite impervious to June's own statements to the contrary. Whenever the account did not exactly fit June, so far as her mother was concerned there was only one explanation—that she was ill. This 'essentialism' in their view of the prospective patient, this 'Procrustean identity' that they impose upon him, again seems characteristic of these families. In the case of Ruth, her parents *both* denied that Ruth led the kind of life that she, and they on other occasions, said she did lead, *and* attributed that kind of life to 'mad' or 'bad' behaviour on Ruth's part. 'Thus, she is said to drink excessively, while, simultaneously, she is said not to drink at all'. Her mother tells the interviewer, 'She's brought people home—when she's been ill she's brought people home she normally wouldn't tolerate, you know, these beatniks'; Father adds, 'There have been writers and God knows what'. When Ruth asserts herself in any way against the parental view of her real essence, by going where she wants with whom she chooses, or wearing clothes she likes, her parents infer that an attack of her illness is coming on. Hazel, though already an adult, has never once had a boy or girl friend in the house; according to her mother, though not accord-

ing to Hazel, this is what Hazel wants. The wife of David, again, *really* agrees with him. Whenever she does not do so, it is a sign that she is ill. In this case, neither the husband nor the parents of the patient—all of whom, it ought to be added, were devoutly religious—seemed to have any understanding of the patient's point of view, or of the fact that they had no understanding of it.

Not only is the prospective patient very often seen in terms of a stereotype, but the attitudes of his family towards him tend to be confusingly contradictory. Maya said that her parents constantly put difficulties in the way of her reading what she wanted to; they denied this with laughter. When Maya mentioned her Bible reading as an example, her father, still laughing, asked why she wanted to read the Bible anyway when she could find out better about that kind of thing from other books. Again, the father and mother constantly winked at one another when the whole family was interviewed together. The interviewer commented on this after twenty minutes of the interview; at which the parents denied they were doing it, went on doing it, and went on denying that they were doing it.

All of us have a tendency to doubt the validity of our perceptions when other persons do not confirm them; and it is worth reflecting on what might be expected to happen when the reality of states of affairs which we seem to perceive is habitually denied by those who are most intimately involved with us.

2 The Schizoid Condition

Jean, in order to get any real satisfaction out of her life in a very 'Christian' family, had been compelled at an early age to 'split' (as she herself put it) her personality. First, at the age of nine, she had gone to the cinema with a friend and the friend's parents without letting her own parents know. Having got away with this, she went on leading a double life. She wore make-up, went to the cinema and went out with boys—all without telling her family. As a corollary to this she systematically cultivated a split between a true inner self, whose thoughts and desires were in accordance with her secret life, and a false outer self which acted and spoke according to what was felt to be proper within the family circle. Jean felt acutely guilt-ridden as a result of this duplicity. Now of course everyone has sometimes to conceal his feelings from others or at least to fail to reveal them; it is only when the habit of thinking and feeling in one way, and speaking and acting in a way which is wholly other, becomes more or less unremitting owing to inner predisposition or outer circumstances or both, that one may reasonably surmise that the consequences might ultimately be pathological.

The schizoid disconnects his speech and actions from his thoughts and feelings out of motives of fear and hatred; the unpleasant consequences of speaking and acting as he feels are too great for him to bear. But his inner world, since it has no real interaction with the outer, becomes progressively more and more impoverished, futile and empty. Unfortunately such withdrawal from others, in order not to be hurt by others, does not work in the long run, since no one feels more at the mercy of others than the schizoid. He may try to forestall being got at by others by getting at them. As one patient said, 'I emphasise people's faults to regain my self-possession'. A more unequivocal withdrawal seems to be at the basis of the behaviour of a patient who had been severely 'depersonalised' for some years; she described her attitude as due to a desire to play possum—in effect, to feign deadness in order not to be killed. The chronic insecurity of some schizoids will make them compulsive sticklers for neatness. One patient said, 'I don't know how to deal with the unexpected. That's why I like things neat and tidy. Nothing unexpected can happen then.' Genuine and spontaneous interaction with others is what is at once most longed for and most dreaded in such cases. Now everyone sometimes has moods in which life seems to him futile and meaningless; in the case of the schizoid these seem to be particularly frequent and severe. Within the inner world of his fantasy, the schizoid is omnipotent and free; in real projects, he is subject to agonies of humiliation. There are two main obstacles to the individual getting out of his state of isolation: anxiety and guilt.

Schizoid false selves, when they are 'good' rather than absurdly 'bad', as sometimes happens, are very compliant with others; but this compliance tends to caricature. The schizoid is liable to be a model child or husband, or an admirably industrious clerk. But his posture becomes more and more stereotyped, and bizarre features develop. The false self tends to assume more and more of the characteristics of those on whom its compliance is based; as this tendency increases, the underlying hatred becomes more and more evident. (It is to be remarked that this compliance and impersonation may be with and of a fantasy figure rather than a real person.) For instance, the father of James had a habit of asking guests at his table whether they were sure that they had had enough to eat; but James's own solicitations became compulsive and beyond all reasonable bounds, and a general embarrassment and nuisance. James sensed the aggressive implications in his father's habit and, by exaggerating them, exposed them to general ridicule and anger. Thus by his satirical comment he evoked from others feelings which he had about his father, but which he dared not express directly. A compliant daughter, again, may be using her very compliance, with its singular exaggeration, as a means of attack.

The schizoid needs to be seen and recognised by others as he is; but others are at the same time a threat to him. Rose had a way of embarrassing people in order to convince herself that she was real, that she could have a real effect on other people. She herself came to realise that the more she withdrew from other people, the more vulnerable she became. The more she cut herself off from other people, the more she felt threatened by inner disintegration. The result of such desire and fear is that the schizoid is apt to compromise by seeking out company, but never being himself in it. He is inclined to laugh at what he does not think is funny, to make friends with people he does not like, to dress ostentatiously, to speak loudly—and in general to draw attention at once to and away from himself. James's behaviour was due to a compound of resentment of others and contempt for himself, which resulted in a bizarre product of shown and concealed feelings. He had eccentric ideas; he was a theosophist and astrologer, in spite

of his genuine understanding of more orthodox scientific theories. That he could share with others these odd notions of his may be guessed to be one means by which he preserved his sanity. A girl schizoid was fantastically and irrationally unpunctual for interviews with her doctor, and was in general very secretive about herself and what she was doing. Her speech was listless, and she sedulously avoided talking about herself, but would discuss politics and economics instead.

3 The Change from the Schizoid Condition to Schizophrenia

It is not always possible to specify the exact borderline between the sane schizoid individual and the schizophrenic. The psychosis has sometimes an abrupt, sometimes a gradual, apparent onset. It seems that the potential schizophrenic's outer appearance of normality is preserved by more and more desperate means. What was in the first instance a guard or barrier for the self to hide behind becomes a gaol; the person has engaged in 'a deliberate cultivation of a state of death-in-life as a defence against the pain of life'. Once a certain point has been passed, efforts either at further withdrawal or at re-establishment of authentic interaction with the world will lead straight to psychosis—whether the sufferer decides to murder his true self once and for all, or to be honest in spite of everything. In either case, the adaptation to reality of the false self will have seemed to the subject (to judge from what is claimed by many patients) to be a more and more shameful, futile or ridiculous pretence. It seems that when the false self has been externally a pretty normal person, who is not noticeably bizarre in speech or behaviour, that there occurs one of those sudden onsets of insanity which seems totally unprepared in the subject's previous history. A man who was twenty-two years old and previously quite normal by his family's account, put out to sea in a small boat, and when he was picked up said that he had lost God and was trying to find him. A father of a family who was in his fifties, on a picnic and in sight of other picnickers, plunged naked into a river to wash away his sins, saying that he had never loved his wife and children.

The kind of behaviour shown by these two people, for all its prima-facie absurd quality, is only too tragically intelligible, in terms of reaction to a trivial and meaningless life in the first example and, in the second, to guilt at having pretended to have feelings that one should have had but did not have. In other cases, the impossibility of the patient's position in life and the intelligibility of his 'mad' acts and sayings as a response to it, come out quite clearly, at any rate when the circumstances are taken into account. Maya was regularly told by her parents that she felt what she did not feel she felt, and that she was not in the habit of performing actions which she remembered quite vividly that she was in the habit of performing. She accused them of trying to 'obliterate' her mind—a way of speaking which seems to convey very well how deeply and radically confusing their attributions must have been to her. But she had been taught that this view by her of her parents was merely a symptom of illness. So inevitably she sought refuge in her private shell. But *this* was to exhibit the schizophrenic characteristic of being 'withdrawn'. Her denial that she was the subject of her thoughts—'I don't think, the voices think'—appeared to be an effort to evade the barrage of criticism and invalidation by her family of what she said and thought.

Lucie, a chronic schizophrenic, was inclined to wonder seriously about the significance of life, and was rather awkward in the company of those who seemed to her merely to chatter superficially, rather than trying to say what was important and worthwhile. 'She was never sure whether they talked superficially on purpose, or whether they really did not know what they seemed to be denying. With anyone with whom she could genuinely talk, she was not . . . in any way "withdrawn", or "asocial" or "autistic".' Jean had delusions to the effect that her parents and husband were dead, and that her husband was not really her husband. 'Unable to express, and inwardly forbidden to feel, dissatisfaction with, or disappointment in, her husband, she said he was not her husband. Not daring to reject or defy her parents openly, she did so quite clearly but in a way that is "schizophrenic."

4 *Truth expressed in Delusion*

A sympathetic attention to what the schizophrenic is saying, and an attempt to grasp what he is trying to express, may provide a real insight into his state in life. One's understanding of his statements is often analogous to one's grasp of the meaning of an obscure poem. Laing's theories are reminiscent of those of Freud and Jung in that what is at issue is a matter of *interpretation,* of what the patient *means,* rather than of the physical *causes* of his words and actions. A schizophrenic may be subject to the delusion that he is an 'unreal man', or that he is 'made of glass' or 'transparent'. But is it not remarkable that these expressions convey, albeit in a disconcertingly concrete way, feelings that, in a milder form no doubt, no one is altogether a stranger to—feelings of unreality and vanity, and the uncanny conviction that others can read one's thoughts?

Lucie—faced by behaviour on her father's part that the whole of the rest of the family admitted was unreasonable, but that she was not allowed to react to as such, confronted with constant bewildering contradiction between what her mother said and what her mother said she said, and largely bereft of those contacts with the outside world which might to some extent have confirmed her perception of her situation—tried to make some sense of it all as follows:

> I can't trust what I see. It doesn't get backed up. It doesn't get confirmed in any way—just left to drift, you know . . . I know some truth about things, and yet I can't defend it—I don't think I've got a real grasp of my situation. What can I do? How can I get on my feet again? I'm not certain about anything. I'm not certain about what people are saying, or if they're saying anything at all. I don't know what really is wrong, if there is anything wrong.

This was the occasion for her psychiatrist to diagnose 'thought-disorder'; perhaps one may grant to her that there is some difficulty in conceptualising that relation between the acting subject and his world which *no one* has yet succeeded in conceptualising adequately.

The schizophrenic who tells you that he has committed suicide may know perfectly well that he has not cut his own throat or thrown himself into a canal. After all, given the apprehension of the relation between the self and the body which is characteristic of the schizoid, the self and the throat may have a rather tenuous relationship. It is not too difficult to get at the sense that a 'depersonalised' patient is trying to convey when he says that he has murdered himself, or lost himself. He may for instance have deliberately set out to obliterate all feeling from himself as a way of evading the slights and humiliations which he fears at the hands of others. The individual is led to 'kill' his 'self' in this way not only out of anxiety, but out of a crushing sense of guilt. As one patient put it, 'I had to die to keep from dying . . . I guess you had to die emotionally or your feelings would have killed you'.

In many cases, once some kind of rapport has been established between doctor and patient, interpretation of the patient's speech and actions is relatively easy. But in other cases, one has to translate out of 'schizophrenese'. This may be illustrated by the example of a patient who, in the official terminology, was subject to depersonalisation and derealisation, and suffered from autism and nihilistic delusions. Much of what she said is readily intelligible if one starts by trying to understand it rather than regarding it simply as a symptom caused by illness; she felt she was not a person, that she was unreal, that she wanted to become a person, that she was at once empty and powerfully destructive. But beyond this point her communications do seem to be utterly unintelligible. Her accusations against her mother in particular seem wild and far-fetched. When she says, for instance, that her mother is responsible for the murder of a child, she is alone in a world that no one can share. It is at such a point as this that a detailed study of the family background may prove helpful.

It must be admitted, of course, that research into the family history of a schizophrenic is an arduous and chancy business, since it is so difficult to establish who, if anyone, in the family situation is speaking the truth. But one important aspect of the matter appeared in this case from interviews with the patient's family and involved the very minimum of extrapolation or interpretation. All of the really 'significant others' in her life, interviewed at the time of her illness, saw her life in the three stages already mentioned: there was an early one when she was 'good', normal and healthy; but later, 'her behaviour changed so that she acted in terms of what *all* the significant others in her world unanimously agreed was "bad" until, in a short while, she was "mad" '. The nature of the reports of the transition between the two last stages gives a clue to the meaning of her delusions. It was a relief to her family when, instead of saying such wounding and terrible things as that her mother wouldn't let her live, she said instead that her mother had murdered a child. As her mother said, 'I'm glad that it was an illness after all'. The hint thus provided, of a cryptic connection between a sane appraisal of the patient's situation and the content of her delusions, gives a clue to other features of her madness as well, like her insistence that she was a 'tolled bell'. She was or had been a 'belle' who did precisely what she was told, without her heart being in what she did. Another psychotic feature was that she said her name was 'Mrs Taylor'. She was conveying that she was 'tailor-made', a 'tailored maid' cut out to suit other people in all her overt words and actions. This kind of psychotic statement, in its elliptical, punning and parabolic nature, may be quite impossible to decipher without the help of the patient himself. The patient's experience in this case was that her mother, in the areas of conflict between them, had to be right, totally right; but she herself felt that in order for her to be able to exist, to breathe, her mother must admit herself wrong about *some* things. At last she began to convert the way she felt about her relationship to her mother, which she could not and dared not avow, into physical fact; to talk as though her mother had literally murdered a child. It was a relief to her family when they could pity her for being 'mad', and hence no longer felt compelled to vindicate themselves by condemning her as 'bad' or 'wicked'.

5 Recovery of Sanity

It is important to distinguish sharply between mere restoration of the *status quo ante* and genuine therapy. In cases of the first kind, the patient merely gives up the struggle, and plays at being sane by retreating once more into schizoid shut-upness. The recovery of Jean, the member of the deeply religious family, seems to have been just such a return to 'normality'. During her 'breakdown', she had fleetingly, and to be sure somewhat frenetically, expressed her real feelings, while her family prayed, successfully it is to be feared, that she would get 'better'—on their own terms. The means of genuine therapy seems to be to make contact with the original self, which seems to remain a possibility even in the most apparently far-gone cases.

It goes without saying that incomprehensibility is the great barrier in getting to know a schizophrenic. Even when he is *trying* to tell someone about himself, his speech is difficult enough to follow. And he has many motives for not trying: it seems, from what schizophrenics themselves say, that obscurity and complexity are deliberately used as a smokescreen behind which to hide. As one patient explained, the schizophrenic is apt to feel crushed and mangled even by ordinary conversational exchanges. Understanding by another, however much of a relief it may be to him in some respects, constitutes a threat to the defensive system which he has erected. Much of his outward behaviour is analogous to underground passages which appear to lead to the citadel which one is trying to enter, but which in fact lead nowhere. The schizophrenic is apt not to be inclined—why *should* he be?—to reveal himself to any philandering passer-by. Binswanger thus has good reason to advise the therapist not to try to get too near the patient too soon.

The schizophrenic is often deliberately distracting in what he says, but will occasionally throw in something really significant to see whether the doctor has the intelligence and concern to follow it up. When he finds someone who he has any reason to believe can and will help him, there is no more need to resort to distractions. (This throws an interesting light on the remark I once heard from a psychiatrist, that Laing seems never to have met any real schizophrenics.) The first step to cure may actually be when the patient comes to express hatred for the doctor. One might

indeed have expected this, since the doctor will be reopening the patient's wounds in establishing personal contact and so getting inside his defences. Not the least significant of the barriers to real cure, as opposed to mere reestablishment of the *status quo ante,* may be the patient's family. Every step in Mary's achievement of autonomy and maturity—at least as these were seen by Laing and his colleagues—were stigmatised by her parents as so much evidence of selfishness and conceit. Maya thought that her main task in life was to become a person in her own rights, to act on her own initiative and independently of her parents. But any steps she took towards achieving this were and had been consistently regarded with alarm by her family.

> **Laing's theories are reminiscent of those of Freud and Jung in that what is at issue is a matter of *interpretation,* of what the patient *means,* rather than of the physical *causes* of his words and actions.**
>
> —*Hugo Meynell*

Having summarised what I take to be Laing's account of schizophrenia more or less without comment, I shall raise and answer a few objections and add some final comments. It is perhaps worth emphasising that this chapter is in no sense an apologetic for all or most of the views which Laing expresses in his books. Thus objections to any general moral or political doctrines which may be attributed to him, whether such objections are well-founded or not, simply are irrelevant to the point at issue. I am concerned only with Laing's account of schizophrenia as it is found in the two books summarised. I mention this only because of the common practice in controversy of discrediting an author's views on one subject by criticising his treatment of another.

With this preliminary caution, I will consider objections one by one:

(a) 'Why should not the schizophrenic have affected the behaviour of his family, rather than the family that of the schizophrenic, as Laing assumes?' That the effect should be mutual does indeed seem likely on the face of it, and is not in the least inconsistent with Laing's account, which merely emphasises the way in which the family affects the schizophrenic rather than the way in which the schizophrenic affects the family. Certainly, if Laing himself, or someone else who claimed to support his views, were to state or to imply that the schizophrenic's behaviour had no reciprocal effect on his family's treatment of him, he would almost certainly be wrong. As to Laing's emphasis on the one side, one may perhaps plead with Kierkegaard that it is difficult at once to provide a corrective and the corrective of that corrective.

(b) 'It may be that the same genetic factor has influenced the behaviour both of the schizophrenic and of his family.

This is certainly the case with Huntingdon's chorea, which is known *both* to be hereditary *and* to occur in families which are highly eccentric in other respects.' Now it appears to me, from what I know of the evidence—for example Kallmann's research and the discussion which it has provoked—that the existence of a hereditary predisposition to schizophrenia is virtually certain. But Laing himself *admits* the possibility of genetically predisposing factors, which admission is indeed in no way incompatible with his general account.

(c) 'The wide acceptance of Laing's account would put an intolerable strain on the families, and especially the mothers, of schizophrenics. The unhappiness which would arise from their feelings of guilt would be intensified by the witch hunts to which they would be subjected by psychiatrists.' This is certainly a point which ought to be borne in mind when one considers how Laing's theories ought to be implemented, if they are true; but it really has no bearing on the question of whether they are true or not. Those doctors who prescribed thalidomide for the prospective mothers of 'thalidomide babies' must have many feelings of guilt and regret, for which they deserve a great deal of sympathy from those who have the good luck not to be involved; but this has no bearing on the truth of the proposition that the drug which they prescribed had the appalling results usually attributed to it. In any case, Laing's researches provide flimsy grounds at best for those who would argue that the families of schizophrenics are in some absolute sense worse than other families. They merely tend to support the view that dispositions which are surely almost universal, when carried beyond a certain point, and brought to bear on someone who is to a certain degree vulnerable in the relevant respect, tends to result in schizophrenia.

(d) 'Laing's schizophrenics are very untypical cases.' If this is true, there might be several reasons for it; one perhaps being, as Jung suggested long ago, that many schizophrenics stop being at least typically 'schizophrenic' when approached with understanding and respect. And even if it is granted that his cases remain untypical when the attitude of the psychiatrist is taken into account, Laing's theory may still provide a useful avenue of approach to the treatment of *some* schizophrenics. How untypical the cases discussed by Laing are, if they are untypical at all, can be decided only be extensive research into the responses of schizophrenics to different kinds of treatment, and into the normality or abnormality of their family backgrounds.

(e) 'The validity of Laing's account depends on acquisition of information about the schizophrenic's early life, and the history of his relations with his family. But reliable information about these is impossible to get, owing to the subjective bias of all concerned.' Such bias is admittedly difficult to reveal and allow for all at once; but it can all the same progressively be shown up for what it is when a sufficient number of circumstances and other relevant viewpoints are taken into account. The procedure which has to be followed in order that a relatively fair picture may be obtained is rather like that of detective work, as Laing remarks; rather like that of historical research. One

should view an account with increasing suspicion the less self-consistent it is, the less it is corroborated by other circumstances and witnesses, and the more the giver of the account has to gain by his story being accepted. The facts that such information is often difficult to get and to evaluate, and that it cannot be quantified by the procedures usual in the physical sciences, provide no grounds whatever for supposing that it is not relevant to the psychiatrist's purposes.

(f) 'Laing seems intent on blaming the family, and perhaps especially the mother, for the condition of the schizophrenic. But the important question is not who is to blame for the situation, but how it may best be coped with.' But the point of Laing's account is not the assigning of blame as such, but rather an analysis of the nature and causes of schizophrenia, in order not only that patients should in future be more effectively cured, but that they should be prevented so far as possible from falling ill in the first place. Whether blame is appropriate, and to what extent it is so, is another matter.

(g) 'If therapy is to be reliable, it ought to be based so far as possible on scientific psychological theory. Laing's account, whatever its virtues may be in other respects, certainly is not scientific'. This objection has already in principle been dealt with; but something more remains to be said. Let us take as a paradigm case of a scientific psychological theory Skinner's theory of operant conditioning. Now therapy on Laing's account consists, in essentials, in (a) getting to understand the patient's point of view, and (b) finding or creating an environment for him in which, given that point of view, he can interact with his fellows in a way which is fairly satisfying to all parties. It can scarcely be denied that there is a difference of some kind between, on the one hand, getting to understand the patient's point of view and taking it into account in preparing him to re-enter society and society to receive him, and on the other hand, readjusting him to society without taking his point of view into account. Now it is true, as a matter of logic, either that Skinner's theory of operant conditioning is subtle enough to preserve this difference, or that it is not. If it is, well and good: Laing's account is not in essential conflict with Skinner's theories; Laing's stipulations amount merely to the insistence that one kind of operant conditioning rather than another is the most effective in achieving the desired result. If Skinner's theory is not sufficiently subtle to preserve the difference, then Laing's clinical experience is only one among many indications that there is something inadequate in the whole theory of operant conditioning as providing a basis for the explanation of human behaviour.

(h) 'There is reason to think that Laing's methods are the very opposite of therapeutic, since patients, by being encouraged to talk about the delusions which are constitutive of their illness, will have them reinforced.' This objection neglects the very great difference between merely being encouraged to repeat some bizarre statement and being asked to explain or account for it. To be asked to explain or account for what one says or does is by no means necessarily to be encouraged to persist in saying or doing it.

(i) 'It is surely an argument in favour of the biochemical theory of the causation of schizophrenia that states very similar to it can be brought about by means of drugs.' It is perhaps worth bearing in mind the parallel with depression. I understand that it is agreed on all hands that one may be depressed either *about* some situation or other, or *owing to* some organic condition. These forms of explanation are of course not mutually exclusive. One who is organically so predisposed may get depressed for some trivial reason; in such a case, both the reason for the depression, and the physical causes of it, would have to be taken into account if one were to arrive at a complete explanation. It has been pointed out as well that a cutting of the *corpus callosum* between the hemispheres of a person's brain induces signs and symptoms closely analogous to neurotic dissociation and to self-deception; I do not know whether anyone would want to argue from this that cases of self-deception should not be explained as a rule as at least primarily due to a subject's motives for avoiding adverting to some unpleasant fact. I cannot see why this should not also be the case with schizophrenia; that causes of the kind described by Laing and physiological causes should not both contribute in different proportions to different cases. Also it seems not unlikely on the face of it that repeated experience of a certain kind of situation, and of the emotions associated with it, may have long-term effects on the biochemistry of the brain.

Mention of self-deception invites a speculation with which it seems fitting to conclude this chapter; on the relation between Schizophrenia and self-deception by members of the patient's family. It is remarkable how often the 'bad' behaviour of the schizophrenics described by Laing, before it is finally decided that they are 'mad', consists in their drawing attention to oppressive or inconsistent features in the behaviour or discourse of their families, which the families themselves are unable to face. Self-deception certainly seems to be at the root of the so-called 'double-bind', when one person A, typically a parent, puts another B in a situation in which whatever B does will be wrong. The fact that A can always get away with blaming B will save him from making the humiliating discovery of pathologically vindictive elements, for example, in his own character. It has been argued that repetitions of such situations as this are liable to lead ultimately to schizophrenia in B. That we would rather drive our nearest and dearest mad, than acknowledge defects in our own characters, is a reflection on human nature perhaps more melancholy than implausible.

It is worth summarising what is to be learned from Laing, on the general problem with which this book is concerned. Above all he brings out the extraordinary capacity of a certain kind of self-deception in some people to give rise to suffering in others. A restriction of my own effective freedom, through sloth, fear, self-indulgence or self-esteem, may result in a total denial of effective freedom to one or more persons in my environment. A full appreciation of this fact is bound to have a profound effect on one's judgement of what kinds of action are good and bad, and in what degree. Is it not to be plausibly inferred, for example, that one kind of parental behaviour, which is almost universally tolerated and very widely commended, is ob-

jectively worse than many kinds of indicatable crime? Laing's case histories bring out with wonderful lucidity and force a typical pattern of oppression existing between members of families. . . .

David Ingleby   (review date 3 September 1982)

SOURCE: "In Place of the Placenta," in *The Times Literary Supplement,* No. 4144, September 3, 1982, p. 939.

[*In the following mixed review of* The Voice of Experience, *Ingleby examines Laing's theory of the mind and suggests that his thinking has undergone a change, even a "regression," taking up positions he had dismissed in earlier works.*]

No merely human author could have lived up to the legend which R. D. Laing generated in the 1960s: yet this was not the only reason why his recent publications have come as a disappointment to many. One sometimes suspected that the promptings of the publisher had been louder than those of the muse. A burnt-out case? On the evidence of **The Voice of Experience,** far from it; here, finally, is a book both coherent in its design and sustained in its intensity. If, at the end of the day, Laing's argument seems almost to invite its own rejection, we will have lost a few comfortable certainties by the time we get this far.

The kernel of the book is a set of wildly "unscientific" ideas about the human mind, and Laing starts out with a pre-emptive strike against science itself. His concern is with human experience: science has nothing to say about this worth listening to, since

> . . . the methods used to investigate the objective world, applied to us, are blind to our experience, necessarily so, and cannot relate to our experience. Such blind method, applied blindly to us, is liable to destroy us in practice, as it has done in theory.

According to Laing the world of science is created by operations which "exclude immediate experience in all its apparent capriciousness from its order of discourse"; starting with Galileo, scientists have sought to eliminate themselves as experiencing subjects from the picture—and having thus lost sight of themselves, have failed to recognize their own human motives. What are these motives? Science calms our dread:

> It was all a machine yesterday. It is something like a hologram today. Who knows what intellectual rattle we shall be shaking tomorrow . . . ?

"Macho" scientists seek to strip nature naked and dominate her: in the words of one biologist, "we torture Nature's secrets from her". But, Laing asks dourly, is this the best way to get to know a lady?

He is surely right when he says that science is blind to its own motives: for the most part, it shelters behind the comforting positivist notion that it doesn't have any. But something is seriously wrong with the idea that experience has no place in it; after all, appeal to experience is supposed to be the very hallmark of science. In part, the confusion is engendered by the delusion common among scientists, that laboratory operations can somehow replace "personal knowledge"—an idea which doesn't survive any philosophical analysis. But the basic muddle is a conceptual one, and Laing himself seems trapped in the very epistemology he attacks: for his own concepts of "experience" and "objective fact" admit no intercourse between them. "Our experience", he says, "cannot dictate to science on matters of objective fact"; since experience is all we have, "facts" would seem therefore to be unattainable—and if objectivity is for him an illusory goal, it comes as little surprise later on that Laing not only fails to make some of his own claims convincing, but doesn't seem to know how to go about doing so.

This sharp division between experience and fact takes Laing back to a position one thought he had left behind in his early works. There, he challenged the division of experience into "inner" and "outer", and showed how subjective certainty was intersubjectively constructed—or, in those unforgettable "schizophrenogenic" families, destroyed. Now, Laing's universe seems populated by nomads, locked in their private worlds, with no means of communication except perhaps telepathy.

If scientists are blind to the nature of their own "gaze", this failing is all the more treacherous when science turns its gaze on the mind, as it does in psychiatry. Here Laing is back on familiar ground. Twenty-two years ago, in *The Divided Self,* he presented a devastating critique of organic psychiatry, as exemplified by Kraepelin: here, he broadens the attack to include those who claim to operate outside the medical model. We see more clearly now that the critique is essentially a moral one: Laing has an unfailing eye for the callousness, the sheer effrontery of those to whom "patients" become no more than pressed flowers to add to their collection—or, in his more violent image, who "bury them alive and screaming in their tomb of words". Even if they call themselves psychoanalysts or existentialists, Laing shows, what they are best at is blaming their own bizarrely deformed way of relating to people (the "diagnostic look"), on the patients themselves. Their deliberate lack of reciprocity rules out the possibility of true understanding: for one cannot expect to uncover the humanity of another without exposing at least some of one's own.

Having thus blasted off, like a jealous gamekeeper, at the encircling predators, Laing proceeds to set out his fledglings. These turn out to be exotic birds indeed. We might have mistaken his opening chapters for a defence of common sense and ordinary experience: now, it becomes apparent that for Laing, these too have become so adulterated by scientific dogma that they are not to be trusted. Only the mad, and primitive or past cultures, seem to respect the sorts of extraordinary experience he describes here, which are simply incommensurable with both science and common sense. Reliving earlier lives, living out of one's body, casting spells and being spellbound, "hosts of raptures, ecstasies, illuminations, voices, visitations, transportations . . ."—all these are not simply hard to understand within our ordinary frame of reference, but literally impossible: "the stability of a whole world-view is threatened."

Do we really have the right, Laing asks, to consign these experiences to the slop-bucket, to dismiss those who take them seriously as "over the hill"? "Stories of experiences we continue to regard as impossible continue to well up from the very depths of ourselves." Our problem is to judge between these subjectively real happenings and our objective knowledge of their impossibility: "Is there a judge of appeal within ourselves who is not an appellant?" Laing himself gives no verdict: his aim, he says, is merely to "open a space in the discourse"—the space which science has crushed out of existence.

The particular kind of "impossible experience" which interests Laing, as we know from his recent writings, concerns mental life before birth and outside the body. He considers the views of Leboyer, Freud, Rank and Winnicott on the point at which conscious life begins; then produces the startling hypothesis that the primal relationship, which serves as a "template" for all others, may be that between foetus and placenta. The original "tie" is therefore a physical one, the umbilical cord: many people's deep sense of being "cut off" is a quite literal one, stemming from the breaking of this tie, and the partner they yearn for is none other than their placenta. Further back, the implantation of the blastocyst within the endometrium furnishes yet more archaic recollections; and beyond that lies the possibility of previous incarnations.

Laing marshals a formidable collection of data to support these ideas, much of it collected by anthropologists or psychologists. Among the latter, none posited more than a metaphorical relationship between life in the womb and certain myths or mental patterns: Laing, however, argues that a causal relationship is more consistent with the data—preposterous as it may seem. But his arguments are marred by serious deficiencies. There is no analytic approach here to the concepts Laing is using. Knowing what these extraordinary claims mean surely comes before deciding whether they are true. However much he may disagree with their conclusions, Laing surely cannot afford to ignore what philosophers of mind have to say about this. And when it comes to weighing up the claims, he is curiously bad at assembling convincing arguments.

It is here that his problem about connecting the world of subjective experience and objective fact comes to the fore. The "umbilical cord" that is required in this instance is the social activity of negotiating true accounts, and Laing has not much feel for that. Experience can deceive us; yet our very ability to communicate with each other implies (and is implicit in) our ability to know when it is doing so. To convince us that the extra-ordinary experiences he describes are not deceptive. Laing would have to show that there is no satisfactory way of "explaining them away", but he does not have much patience for that. Yet is it so bizarre, for example, that a woman should dream about a baby at the time when she conceives one: or that patients should recount experiences consistent with their therapists' known beliefs? Again, though Laing may feel little in common with the many psychologists who have investigated paranormal experience, this hardly entitles him to ignore their work.

As a therapist, Laing seems to have undergone a kind of

regression, abandoning his earlier emphasis on the social world and reverting to a form of biological reductionism even more severe than that of the organic psychiatrists he despises. For there are many social reasons why people might feel inescapably "cut off "—some of which Laing himself uncovered, though he never got much beyond the immediate family.

To prefer a social explanation is a form of *a priorism*, of course, but we are dealing here in questions of opinion and interpretation, and there are strong reasons for suspecting a willingness to opt for the biological and individual. To attribute our unhappiness to pre-natal life is an explanation as satisfyingly complete as it is profound, and far less disturbing than tackling our relationships. Indeed, every psychology has its own way of explaining away alienation: for Freud, it was first the Oedipus Complex, then the Death Instinct; for Jung, the eternal opposition of male and female; for Lacan, the infant's misrecognition of itself in its own mirror image. All of these, like the doctrine of the Fall, manage to exonerate the social order. In psychotherapy, too, we have learned to be suspicious of the short half-life of theories: a sort of planned obsolescence seems to be built into them, so that last year's "cured patient" has to start all over again when the latest discovery is announced. What is behind the Laingian gaze? He of all people cannot ignore, as many scientists do, the motives and presuppositions underlying his own approach.

Peter Sedgwick   (essay date 1982)

SOURCE: "R. D. Laing: The Radical Trip," in *Psycho Politics: Laing, Foucault, Goffman, Szasz, and the Future of Mass Psychiatry,* Harper & Row, 1982, pp. 66-101.

[*Sedgwick was an English political scientist and translator best known for his socialist critiques of the treatment of the mentally ill. In the following essay, he outlines Laing's early career; the philosophical, psychological, and theological sources for some of his ideas; and the evolution of his theories about schizophrenia, the family, and society.*]

The anti-psychiatry movement required a whole train of concurrent, convergent influences before it could gather force. Some of these factors lay in the changing age structure of Western societies, as the prolongation and intensification of active life span, extending back into the teenyears as well as onward into maturity, encouraged unprecedented strains at the boundaries of dependency, both in youth and old age. The expansion of welfare facilities as part of the price of working-class consensus in all the capitalist democracies had encouraged a flow of expectations, mingled with rising disappointments, in matters affecting the public health—and, within this complex of recently assembled social rights, the standing of psychiatric provision was due for some serious challenge and scrutiny. Mental illness became an urgent source of welfare politics, but at the same time touched on deeper, more intimate political structures: the relations of authority between doctor and patient, between administration and clientele, between parent and child, between woman and man became open to fresh and simultaneous collisions in the post-war boom years, even as the authority relations between employer and worker became continually and centrally challenged in the politics of the factory. The sixties, in most countries of the West, constituted the high-water mark in the assertiveness of the various discontented classes.

But before the swing into counter-revolution which we have experienced since, consciousness was raised, and confidence was still relatively intact. The confidence arose from the strong trading position of a labour force and an electorate able to extract substantial benefits either from employers or from politicians. Consciousness changed partly through diffuse spontaneous changes in ideas refracted from altered circumstance, and partly through the propagation of militant alternatives to the status quo. Militancy in argument, in mood, in manners was the work of groups and leaders who offered, in various models and images, the outline of a logic that could vanquish the hallowed syllogisms of everyday banality. The movement for a critical psychiatry had (and still has) its leaders, its world-historic individuals who gathered the questionings and forged them into questions, who became prophets and sages. And amid the succession of psychiatric prophets who compelled attention through the sixties and early seventies it was R. D. Laing who dominated the scene longest, as arch-seer and prophet-in-chief. 'After Freud and Jung, Now Comes R. D. Laing. Pop-shrink, rebel, yogi, philosopher-king? Latest reincarnation of Aesculapius, maybe?' trilled the headline over *Esquire*'s interview with him in January 1972. On his college lecture tour of America later that year, one university billed him as 'The Controversial Philosopher of Madness', and at another his arrival was greeted with bumper-stickers proclaiming 'I'm Mad About R. D. Laing'. 'Two chicks who dig Coltrane, The Dead and R. D. Laing' advertised for compatible guests to meet them at a party, in a back-page column of the New York *Village Voice* in the previous year: and Laing's assumed connection with the lifestyle of popular music had been earlier instanced in the assertion by a book reviewer (*Library Journal,* 1 June 1969) that he 'is reputed to have treated the Beatles'.

More serious and sustained attention was accorded to Laing by an unusual range of publics and specialists. The paperback editions of his main writings have been reprinted in most years since their first appearance, and the invocation of his name and work by philosophers, creative writers, and co-workers in the field of abnormal psychology was unabated even during periods when the mass media were angling their spotlights towards other celebrities. The reputation and rumour which has surrounded Laing has both eased and impeded his accessibility to intellectual audiences. The hundreds of thousands of young readers who bought and absorbed the scraps of psychedelic autobiography in ***The Politics of Experience*** found, for the first time in their lives, an apparently medical authority who, unlike most doctors and scientists, was not afraid of philosophising, or of quoting or writing poetry, or of expressing powerful and deep emotions that could variously either excite or shock his listeners. Others, from a more established vantage-point, felt outraged: one group of promedical polemicists even queried his right to speak as an accredited member of his profession:

How much more serious he would seem if he gave up his medical identity. . . If Laing wishes to be a guru or a philosopher, there is no doubt a place for him, but young people who are suffering from schizophrenia may prefer to entrust themselves to a doctor who will treat their illness as best as he can. [M. Siegler, H. Osmond, H. Mann, 'Laing's Models of Madness', *British Journal of Psychiatry*, Vol. 115, 1969]

The resistance to Laing's ideas was not simply a matter of professional pique; the very idiom in which he couched his early contributions, a blend of psychoanalytic and existentialist concepts interspersed with close reportage on the inner experience of deranged patients, presented obstacles for those not fully attuned to these rather particular sensibilities. Professor Roger Brown, an experimental social psychologist from the Harvard laboratory, has remarked of *The Divided Self* that 'In the course of several years I read it three times—that is, all the pages passed my eyes, but nothing happened that I would call "understanding"' [in R. Brown and R. J. Herrnstein, *Psychology*, 1975]. The fact that Brown's fourth reading was much more successful, leading him to his choice of Laing's work to round off an introductory undergraduate psychology textbook, and to the conclusion that 'there is a sense in which Laing better than anyone else enables us to "understand" schizophrenia' [*Psychology*, 1975], is a tribute to the power of Laing's ideas to work their way past what were clearly the entrenched methodological defences of a sceptical scientist. This experience of illumination, whether into mental illness or into a more general human situation, was common among those who followed Laing's writings. Equally frequent, though, was a blockage of comprehension like Brown's earlier response, or an irritated rejection either of Laing's own positions or of the manner in which they were being construed and used by his following.

A survey of R. D. Laing's intellectual history has to labour under certain special handicaps which I have tried to overcome without the hope of securing complete success. In the first place, Laing has performed some of his work in collaboration with others. One phase of his most important activity was conducted side by side with two other existential psychiatrists, David Cooper and Aaron Esterson, whose views cannot be assumed to be identical with his or to have remained in tune with the later alignment of his work after he ceased collaboration with them. Esterson has maintained the interest in family networks which he developed in the book [*Sanity, Madness and the Family*] he wrote with Laing and has gone on to produce more detailed sample descriptions of some of the very same families that were the subject of this old joint work. In different ways, Cooper and Esterson have appeared in Laing's biography as the bearers of theoretical concerns which blended for a while with his—radical existentialism in Cooper's case, neo-Freudian family therapy in Esterson's—until the paths of the three began to branch separately. Although both Cooper and Esterson have intensified their 'Laingianism', the one as critic and the other as researcher of family life, Laing himself has moved on independently from them. Our analysis in this and the next chapter will deal with Laing rather than with his coworkers, disciples or camp-followers.

The second difficulty arises from Laing's habit of offering all at once several lines of enquiry which, pushed to any sort of conclusion, would yield obvious inconsistencies. The texts of his works are like the old Egyptian palimpsests, manuscripts with the first draft rubbed away and, while still partly visible, written over by another scribe—in this case Laing himself in a different ideological phase. We shall quote variant glosses from the canon of Laing's works in order to illustrate the way in which he sharpens (or tones down) an ambiguous rendering, much as a poet will re-shape the meaning of a key line through altering one or two of its words. In one particularly expansive phase of his development, roughly from 1964 to 1970, his writings and public activity consorted with a number of vanguard trends in society and politics—marxism, the counter-culture, psychedelic experimentation, romantic-expressionist literature, the critique of the mental institution, the critique of the family, transcendental mediation, Sartrean existentialism, Freudian psychoanalysis—which are normally, for quite good reasons, taken to be to a certain extent divergent or even dissonant. Laing's utterances held these disparate trends in intellectual suspense, counterbalanced in a kind of equilibrium that was bound to collapse once he advanced one particular element or argument to preclude certain others. During his lengthy balancing act he was continually misunderstood by those who saw him as more committed to one item—to marxism, let us say, or to mediation—than he was. The outline of Laing's career that we shall give is in the form of an account of development stages, a progression in which one stance is negated and transcended by a successor position. But Laing has at certain points refused to concede that any such progression took place, denying, for instance, that he had ever been a marxist, or that his involvement in mystical practice has 'represented any major switch of direction or change of any fundamental position. . . . It was simply that what I did with my own time has become a little more publicly noticed than it used to be' [quoted by S. S. Mahan, 'Schizophrenia in Santa Monica', *Los Angeles Free Press*, December 10, 1972].

We may see in Laing's assertion of continuity in his intellectual development more than a convenient forgetfulness for awkward and outgrown phases. His strength, as well as his weakness, has come precisely from the wide span of his identities and from his capacity to entertain opposites as a prelude to marrying them off to each other.

Ronald David Laing (accurately pronounced *'Layng'*, with *a* as in 'angel') was born in October 1927 and raised as the sole child of a family living at the edge of the Gorbals on the south side of Glasgow, in poor, cramped housing. The family, lower-middle-class and strictly Lowlands-Presbyterian in religious outlook, was characterised by the mixture of moral repressiveness and occasional violence between male relatives which is normal among working-class puritans. Laing records that he was never let out to play with other children until he was sent to school, and that a programme of continued mystification and misinformation about sexual matters was conducted by his parents and school authorities until, near the age of 16, he himself was able to find and read a book on venereal disease with an account of the basic 'facts of life'. The solitariness of young Laing's conditioning was fortunately broken by the presence of the great books of religion and rationalism: Darwin, Thomas Huxley, the Bible, Mill, Haeckel and Voltaire. At 14, he says, 'I knew I was really only interested in psychology, philosophy and theology'; he became the initiate of 'a sort of Neoplatonic Christianity'.

Even during adolescence the moral idealism of this Christian outlook competed oddly with a gratuitous egocentricity. In 1972 his acolyte, Peter Mezan, heard Laing admit, while 'sitting on the floor of Suite 608 (of New York's Algonquin Hotel) in a terry-cloth bathrobe', to having been 'very much motivated by the whole fame complex, especially in my teens'. Thus, he decided he would produce his first book by the time he was 30, and stuck to that with the date of publication of *The Divided Self.* He resolved early on that the kind of fame he craved was 'the fame of a wise man', and to this end 'I decided at the age of 13, for instance, that I would make a point of forgetting anything that was painful' [Peter Mezan, 'R. D. Laing: Portrait of a Twentieth-Century Skeptic', in *R. D. Laing: The Man and His Ideas,* edited by R. D. Evans, 1976]. We do not know what sort of intellectual dialogue touched him during his education, with a 'Classical' emphasis on ancient languages, at a state-supported boys' grammar school; but Laing was 18 before he met with astonishment, for the first time in his life, people of his own age 'who had never even opened a Bible'.

Domination by religious questions was shortly succeeded by an exposure to the anguished secular humanism of French postwar literature. In January 1948 he came across a translation, in the magazine *Horizon,* of extracts from Antonin Artaud's vigorous attack on psychiatry and psychiatrists, 'Van Gogh, le suicidé de la société'. This early anti-psychiatric polemic, the product of Artaud's resentment as a confined lunatic in an appalling French asylum and of his strong identification with Van Gogh as a fellow-artist and fellow-victim, came to Laing as 'a revelation' which played a decisive part in his development. Sartre is another noteworthy influence in the same period: it was through *Being and Nothingness* that Laing was introduced to Husserl, Hegel and the European phenomenological tradition that would inform his own psychiatric enquiries.

However, this preliminary involvement in the humanities had to compete with the lengthy rigours of a medical training organised around the empirical natural sciences. The contradiction sensed by Laing between a humane theory based on 'the whole person' as subject and a scientific practice dealing in inert part-objects is a common theme in his work, and partly explains his repeated insistence on the necessary autonomy of a separate 'science of persons' distinct from the medical sciences. His writings are scattered with grisly stories of the pathology he encountered in patients and—more usually—in doctors during his years as a medical student, and he has come to believe that 'at its very best, medical training was bedeviled, and still is, by its own insane theory and insane practice'. The textbook descriptions of schizophrenia struck Laing, when he first read them in these days, as 'a very good description

of much of medicine itself, including psychiatry. The heartlessness, the divorce, the split between head and heart. The fragmentation, indeed disintegration behind all that, and its disavowal and projection' [*The Facts of Life*].

In 1951 Laing took his medical degree, and chose to specialise in psychiatry, like nearly all of his student friends, as a refuge from 'the medico-surgical lunacy all around'. After six months on duty as a junior doctor in a neurosurgical unit, he was conscripted, working immediately as a practising psychiatrist in the British Army's Central Hospital. It was here that he began to develop his renowned capacity to enter into prolonged and meaningful relation with individuals regarded as hopelessly 'mad' by the rest of the world—one of his first such encounters being with a young patient of 18 with delusions of being Julius Caesar and Hamlet, kept in the padded cells of the military hospital where Laing used to go and talk at length with him, sharing his fantasies of robbing the gold from the vaults of the Bank of England.

From this posting, he returned to civilian life as a psychiatrist in the National Health Service, working in the 'female refractory ward' of Glasgow's Royal Mental Hospital. Here he made special efforts to get to know the most neglected and apparently hopeless patients, resuming the padded cell visits in which he could sit and listen to what others had dismissed as ravings, and eventually enticing both patients and staff into the construction of an experimental day-room in which a dozen of the most withdrawn 'chronic schizophrenic' women on the ward could go for occupation and recreation. Laing's approach was still to a large extent formed within a conventional natural-scientific framework: he accepted the current view of his milieu that schizophrenia was the name of a disorder in individuals, possibly genetic or biochemical in origin and manifested as the result of some innate intolerance towards stress. He selected the patients for this study through drawing up detailed 'sociograms' of the ward's relationships, counting the number of times each inmate addressed or paid attention to another. Even a short exposure to the bright humane regimen of the day-room produced encouraging results. The women opened up socially, losing at a stroke the 'withdrawnness' that had been inscribed indelibly in their case-notes for year upon year. Laing, together with members of a research team working in the same ward with a rather more formal psychoanalytic perspective than his, hastened to have the immediate results published in a medical journal. However, it turned out that the progress of the patients was fairly short in duration. All 12 were discharged from the hospital within 18 months; but within another year they were all back inside again.

Such an outcome would nowadays be considered unsurprising by many psychiatrists, since most of the discharged patients would be returned to a family environment in which the other members were much too involved with the patient for anybody's good. The period of innovation in British social psychiatry that had generated the work of Laing and his colleagues in Glasgow was at this very time on its way into a series of researches that would demonstrate, in terms independent from Laing's own orientation, the pathogenic character of the family nexus into which many schizophrenic ex-patients were being discharged. However, at this stage, Laing did not respond with a direct challenge to the reigning orthodoxies on 'the schizophrenia question'. Instead, he worked over some case-material from his Glasgow experience, adding recollection to theoretical reading in a draft that would become the basis for two books, *The Divided Self* and *The Self and Others.* In 1957 he moved to a post at the Tavistock Clinic in London. Here he would discover a particularly close affinity to the psychoanalytic ideas with which he had long been fascinated even when in the toils of physiological medicine. His training analysis was undertaken with a Freudian psychoanalyst attached to the Tavistock, Dr Charles Rycroft; and he was soon to be influenced by the analytically informed services of marriage and family counselling that are undertaken at the same centre. Soon after the move to London he completed his manuscript of *The Divided Self,* offering its preliminary text to several Tavistock colleagues for their comments. It was published in 1960 by Tavistock Publications. By the time it entered a paperback edition, five years later, the New Left had arrived on the British scene, and Laing had progressed into political radicalism and the status of celebrity. In the moment of its first appearance, however, the impact of *The Divided Self* was far from sensational.

Looking at the work now, we can see how hard it was for many of its readers to take bearings on the many intellectual origins that had helped to compose it. Laing's use of existentialist material was most unusual for a writer born and nurtured within the Britain of that time. It is striking that he was able to extract fertile insights into psychotic and allied states of mind not only from clinicians of the European phenomenological school (Binswanger, Minkowski, Boss), but from theologians (Tillich, Bultmann), philosophers (Sartre, Heidegger, even Hegel) and writers (Beckett, Lionel Trilling) who dealt in nonpathological, indeed fundamental situations of human existence. These concepts, in partial conjunction with those of Freudian psychoanalysis, were applied to the knotted thought processes and behaviour of an obscure group of severely disturbed mental patients, who had been hitherto regarded as inaccessible to rational comprehension. One of the most difficult of philosophies was brought to bear on one of the most baffling of mental conditions, in a manner which, somewhat surprisingly, helped to clarify both. Existential philosophy, with its reputation of introverted cloudiness and speculative indiscipline, was here set working in a concrete, practical and socially urgent context—the understanding of the mentally ill. Conversely, a major form of psychosis was elucidated as a mental system possessing lawful shape and sequence, comprehensible in existential terms as the outcome of rational strategies adopted by the patient in the face of an ambiguous and threatening personal environment. The clinical descriptions in *The Divided Self* are set in a vivid, clear style, often with an unobtrusive poetic skill, as with the portrayal of the patient Peter's imaginary smell ('the sooty, gritty, musty smell of a railway waiting-room') or the images of desolation (like 'the ghost of the weed garden' or 'the black sun') which haunt the remnants of personality inside the young hebephrenic Julie.

As we begin *The Divided Self,* Laing informs us that he personally as a psychiatrist finds great difficulty in detecting the 'signs and symptoms' of illness in psychotic patients, since their behaviour actually appears to him as meaningful and appropriate rather than as odd or irrelevant. He then provides us with a stunning demonstration of what it means to understand patients as human beings rather than to classify them as instances of a disease. He gives a long quotation from the nineteenth-century psychiatrist, Emil Kraepelin, who reported a spate of excited talk produced, in front of an audience of students, by a young catatonic patient in response to the doctor's questions. Laing is able to show very convincingly that, through the adoption of only a slightly more sophisticated vantage-point on the patient's behaviour (i.e. by assuming that he is capable of discreetly ridiculing his interrogator), almost all of the young man's utterances, which have struck Kraepelin as the inconsequential ramblings of an organic disease process, can be seen as comprehensible responses to the immediate situation he is in. What is particularly noteworthy about Laing's use of this example is the fact that Kraepelin's interpretation (or rather, noninterpretation) of his patient's behaviour has been on record for decades in several countries as a classical case-note of psychiatry without anybody, apart from Laing in 1960, trying to re-value it.

The final chapter of *The Divided Self,* a 30-page discussion of a single schizophrenic patient named Julie, introduces what will be a characteristic theme of Laing's theorising: an extended analysis of the patient's family background. Julie's relatives have developed a sequence of definitions about her which runs, throughout her lifetime, roughly as follows: as an infant, Julie was a 'good' girl; later, particularly in adolescence, she became a 'bad' girl, negative and rejecting towards her parents; finally, in her present condition, her behaviour has overstepped even the bounds of 'badness' and she is 'mad', mentally ill, a patient. This sequence forms, in a number of ways, a prototype of the analysis of schizophrenia that will be developed by Laing in future works, where the Good-Bad-Mad progression will be seen as the usual pattern for the 'election' of an individual into the role of madness by other members of his or her insidiously demanding family.

However, this first book of Laing's can be distinguished from his later work on at least three counts. There is not a hint of mysticism in it, not the faintest implication that there is any further world of being beyond that described by natural and social science (phenomenology being included in the latter). There are no intimations of an innermost substance or grounding of all things and appearances, lying perhaps in some core of inner personal reality beyond the probings of the clinician. Laing has in fact been at deliberate pains, in his borrowings from the more opaque existentialist writers, to de-mystify their categories. The floating, abstract concepts of Being and Not-Being, the whiff of dread before death and the hints of the supernatural, characteristic of Kierkegaard and Heidegger, are replaced by transparent, empirical usages. 'Ontological insecurity', which is said to lie at the heart of serious mental illness, simply means a profound personal uncertainty about the boundaries between the self and the world, which can be contrasted with the differentiation of ego-boundaries that takes place in normal child development. 'Being-in-the-world' means social interaction between persons, and Kierkegaard's 'Sickness Unto Death' is not the loneliness of the soul before God but the despair of the psychotic. Laing is, in short, naturalising the mystical elements of continental existentialist thought.

The second cardinal feature of *The Divided Self* follows from this. Since there is no super-reality beyond the here and now of actual people, psychotic patients are not seen as the mystics or prophets of this supersensory world. They are not, as in the later Laing, pioneers in the exciting endeavour of exploring 'inner space'. The only inner space that is ever even hinted at in the text amounts simply to the set of private coordinates which map out the fantasies of the psychotic. Material and interpersonal reality is the only one we have got: consequently it forms the only standard against which the schizophrenic's experience can be tested. By this criterion, the schizophrenic has failed, has fallen short of normal, healthy sensory and emotional achievement: we are left in no doubt, in fact, that she or he is in a thoroughly bad way. Laing's reluctance to use the term 'disease' (because of the implication that a 'disease' may have discrete and impersonal 'symptoms') does not imply any refusal to admit the disturbance, disorder and profound alienation of the psychotic state.

Thirdly, this disturbed state is an attribute, at least in large part, of the individual as the patient. The condition called 'schizophrenia' by doctors is, in Laing's terms, still very much like a syndrome, i.e. a set of characteristics attributable to an individual, cohering typically and meaningfully with one another and demarcating this person from other conditions which are given different names (such as 'hysteria' or 'normal development'). These defining, co-existing characteristics are not impersonal or subpersonal attributes of individuals, isolated bits of behaviour like a high temperature or a twitching leg. They are, on the contrary, deeply personal in quality, occurring at the highest level of integration of the individuals' behaviour, and related to their whole fundamental orientation towards the world they perceive and move in. All the same, 'schizophrenia' is still a pattern of responses manifested by individual persons: it has not vanished, as it does in the Laing of five years hence, into the criss-cross of distorted and distorting signals that typifies Laing's description of the patient's family in which no individual is 'ill' or 'schizophrenic' at all. Even the patient Julie of the last chapter of *The Divided Self* (with all its detail of the family cross-press at work upon the patient) is presented unmistakably as a disoriented individual operating with a complex repertoire of psychotic mental gambits. Her 'existence', and the modes in which she construes it, form the basic material of the narrative. By contrast, the schizophrenic women of *Sanity, Madness and the Family* (1964) have no existence separable from that of their relatives: it is not they, but their families as a whole (though it is not always clear whether the women themselves are included) who bear the basic attributes of the syndrome.

Laing has himself recognised this important shift in his thinking, and has even apologised for his earlier concentration on the individual patient. In the preface to the 1965 Pelican edition of *The Divided Self,* he wrote that while the book did entail an understanding of the social context of the patient, 'especially the power situation within the family, today I feel that, *even in focusing upon and attempting to delineate a certain type of schizoid existence,* I was already partially falling into the trap I was seeking to avoid' [italics added]. If 'schizophrenia' is not a name which refers to any kind of a personal condition, then any attempt to describe it, even in very sensitive terms, must be a 'trap'. However, Laing has not gone on to explain how far he still regards as valid the mode of analysis practised in *The Divided Self;* it is doubtful how much of the early Laing could be reconciled with the radical scrutiny of the later books.

Laing leapt ahead of the theoretical framework of his first work very soon after it was published. In 1960 Jean-Paul Sartre issued the 750-page Volume One of *Critique de la Raison Dialectique.* The *Critique* marked a sharp turn in Sartre's philosophy in that it purported to offer a new foundation for a general science of man, an 'anthropology' in the broadest sense which was intended to expose the basic nature of all thinking about society (including both sociological and historical thought), to outline the structural prerequisites for the formation of all social groups, and to state the laws governing the succession of one form of social organisation by another. At this time, from 1958 to 1962, Laing was settling into a research programme at the Tavistock Institute dealing with interaction inside families (both with and without a schizophrenic member). His research now tended to emphasise the interdependence between a subject's outlook on other people and their perception of her or him, especially within a closed social group: the main ideas of the *Critique,* with their emphasis on the formation and bonding of groups, lent themselves to assimilation by this theoretical perspective. Laing's next book *The Self and Others* (1961, revised as *Self and Others,* 1969) was a collection of essays partly reaching into his new preoccupation with family communication patterns, partly developing his earlier analysis of the world-view of the psychotic patient. It owes no debt to Sartre's *Critique,* but in the following year Laing published an article (**'Series and Nexus in the Family'** [in *New Left Review,* May-June, 1962]), which, for its analysis of family interaction, drew on Sartre's newest ideas as well as on the early findings of the Tavistock project.

Laing's work was now becoming closely associated with that of Cooper and Esterson. Cooper had come to London following his medical training in Capetown and was working as a doctor in British public mental hospitals, in one of which he was to supervise a research programme of treatment based on Laing's theory of schizophrenia. In the early sixties he co-operated with Laing on a more literary enterprise, the production of a short book summarising for English readers the gist of Sartre's recent philosophical writing. The fruits of this intense labour of exegesis appeared in 1964 as *Reason and Violence: A Decade of Sartre's Philosophy.* It is a straightforward condensation of Sartre's *Critique* to one-tenth of its original length, so compressed as to be virtually incomprehensible to anyone seeking an introduction to Sartre's thought, and resembling a précis for private study rather than a popularisation for any intellectual audience. (Cooper's chapter in the book on Sartre's *Saint Genet* forms a clear contrast to the rest of the text in its liveliness and clarity.) At any rate, the intellectual collaboration of Laing and Cooper was well under way by the early sixties, and was soon to result in more creative forms of common writing and therapeutic practice.

Esterson has been a shadowier figure, less associated with public occasions (such as the 'Dialectics of Liberation' conference) than the other two. He had graduated in the same year as Laing from the Glasgow medical school, and then became a British general practitioner, a doctor on an Israeli kibbutz and a hospital psychiatrist back in Britain. In 1958 there was published the report of a research collaboration between Laing and Esterson on the effects of 'collusive pairing' among members of a psychotherapeutic group. Through the author's existentially interpretative glosses, the group comes through as an uneasy, abrasive gathering of seven small-time con-men, but the report does offer a foretaste of the later Laing-Esterson work on human ploy and counterploy in small social settings. Esterson joined Laing as a research associate in the Tavistock family project, publishing its main report with him in 1964.

On Laing's thinking in the Tavistock Clinic programme, influences now converged from two widely separated quarters: Paris and Palo Alto, California. Terror and engulfment had defined the schizophrenic's personal desolation in *The Divided Self;* engulfment and terror, exercised overtly or insidiously by the familiars of the mental victim, were now specified as crucial agents of human derangement both in Sartre's essays in psychoanalysis and in the contributions of the Palo Alto school of schizophrenia research headed by Gregory Bateson. (Research groups in the United States led by Theodore Lidz and Lyman Wynne had come to a similar viewpoint on the origins of schizophrenia, but Bateson's approach must be credited with some priority in time as well as a more general influence.) Sartre had produced case studies illustrating his new sensitivity to pathological social pressures for some years before the *Critique:* both the Genet of *Saint Genet* and the main character of the play *Altona,* the war criminal Franz Von Gerlach, are shown as experimenting with mental strategies of self-definition in response to the ignominious labelling which society has affixed on them. Suffocating in a web of competitive, exploiting relationships, Genet and Franz both express and evade their human responsibilities by performing intense mental work (involving a criminal and homosexual career in the former case and a sort of voluntary psychosis in the latter) on the demeaning and degrading social categories ('thief' or 'murderer') which they know to constitute the terms of their appearance in the eyes of others. The omnipotent unconditioned ego of the old Sartre is now an 'alter ego': Self and Others (to crib from Laing's terminology) now mutually and ferociously impinge on the most critical areas of personal choice. The parallelism between the vision of human bestiality given in Franz's death speech at the end of *Altona* and the history of the normal social bond outlined in the *Critique* has often been pointed out: in both, humanity

is a cruel, malignant species lying in wait to thwart and destroy humanity itself. And the *Critique*'s version of human evolution is basically a detailing of this social cannibalism, which is an ineluctable historical imperative in a world of scarcity, accompanying all social transitions and transformations so long as individuals are replaceable by one another in the struggle for scarce resources.

Laing's *New Left Review* article of 1962, **'Series and Nexus in the Family'** makes use of two of Sartre's basic group categories, applying them in the context of family behaviour. The *Critique* visualises an initial, minimal stage of group formation in which the members share a common goal but do not depend on each other for its practical achievement. They may, however, fabricate a crude sort of group identity through their awareness of one another's behaviour, or by being able to name a single target as the subject of their separate hostilities. A bus queue, a bunch of anti-Semites and the world's system of stock exchanges are examples of this type of group, which Sartre terms a *series*. A deeper and more solid form of social unity is attained in the *bonded group,* whose members each take a decision or 'pledge' before the others to join together in linked activity for the achievement of the common group goal: revolutionary cells, football teams and lynch mobs are examples of bonded groups. The basis for this fusion is always *terror,* registered within each individual as the fear of what the other group members will do to the member who secedes or betrays.

Laing describes two family patterns which correspond to Sartre's identification of human groups. There is one domestic situation which is essentially a 'series'; the members of such a family lack any personal concern for one another though they may make a great display of concern for the likely effects of scandal, thereby showing that the basis for their group's existence lies in an anticipation of 'what the neighbours will say' rather than in any shared relationships within the home. Laing also describes a family constellation, termed a 'nexus', which like Sartre's bonded group is held together by fear, anxiety, enforced guilt, moral blackmail and other variants of terror. The nexal family is like a criminal society where mutual protection is only the obverse of mutual intimidation. Another Sartrean distinction which Laing now emphasised in his analysis of families is the difference between 'praxis' and 'process' in the explanation of human action. *Process* refers to events that appear to have originated from no particular person or persons: they just happen or proceed, with no identifiable human decision or wish at the back of them. (Most people perhaps regard every-day politics in this light, as something that just happens to happen, like the weather.) In contrast, *praxis* is action that can be traced to definite decisions undertaken out of definite motives by definite people; social analysis should undertake to show praxis at work where apparently only process exists. That is, social events can be rendered *intelligible* (a term of some importance in the later Sartre and Laing) by showing that they are the outcome of decisions taken in a social field by motivated actors; and Laing is issuing notice of his purpose to seek intelligibility and praxis in quite gross and grotesque forms of human pathology.

Laing had already written, in *The Divided Self,* about the necessity for understanding in the interpretation and treatment of psychotic behaviour. Even before his baptism in Sartre's *Critique,* he was emphasising the potential intelligibility of much that was apparently crazy. But the type of understanding that Laing sought after 1960 was distinct in its concern for the anchoring of explanation in the social setting of the patient. The psychotic 'symptoms' of the schizophrenics in *The Divided Self* can be rendered intelligible (in a broad, non-Sartrean sense) by viewing them as expressions of a fragmented or split Self. They do not have to be converted into forms of 'praxis', i.e. of human communication within a set of people, in order to be understood. In his first book, Laing translates psychotic behaviour into the terms of action, which may include inner or mental action; subsequently he insists on a translation into the terms of *re*action, or of action in the flux of others' actions on the subject.

But the neo-Sartrean framework was only a general specification of the type of understanding which Laing had already begun to accept and seek in the clinical field. The American research groups who were working on the family backgrounds of their schizophrenic patients were also situating the 'process' of psychotic illness within the 'praxis' of communication from parents to their children (even though they did not use the terminology of Sartre in describing their work). In his second book *The Self and Others* Laing drew heavily on the work of these researchers; their concepts become interwoven with those of Sartre in later writings by Laing and his collaborators. Here we will provide only a short composite account of the hypotheses and findings of the American teams.

The pathology of family communication has become one of the great research enterprises of American science. Hundreds of families have trooped into the laboratories of academic institutes and hospitals, there to have their entire verbal output tape-recorded over many sessions, their gestures and eye movements filmed and their biographies unearthed in depth by interdisciplinary panels of doctors, psychologists, sociologists and technicians. The families inhabit this select theatre for a period of hours or more, enacting a kind of real-life TV serial based on their usual domestic interchange, and then depart. They leave behind them a mass of sound-tracks, videotapes, behaviour, checklists, completed test-sheets and other revelatory material, a huge deposit of past praxis which is then worked over for months by the bureau of investigators, and in due course delivered to the interested public as a journal article. The cumulative bibliography of the Schizophrenic Family forms a veritable saga of modern home-life, running in repeated instalments through some half-dozen scholarly channels over about 25 past years, and with no end yet in sight. The origin of the series is usually traced to Bateson's 1956 paper outlining what has become known as the 'double bind' theory of the origins of schizophrenia. The expression 'double bind' refers to a specific pattern of disturbed communications, detectable within pathological families, in which one member is subjected to a pair of conflicting injunctions or 'binds', both of them highly unsettling or traumatic; a third injunction, implicit in the situation, may prevent the threatened party from leaving the

field and so avoiding the conflict. The unfortunate recipient of these messages is lost whatever s/he does, and if the ordeal is repeated tends to opt out of social interaction and to lose confidence in the accuracy of her/his perceptions of other people.

The 'double bind' mechanism, is, however, only one of many modes of violence and fraud which have been seen to operate in disturbed families. A double-bind household constitutes, in the very cast-list of its *dramatis personae,* a group whose principal characters, both separately and together, would bode ill for domestic peace, even independently of the discovery of any specific types of intimidation in their language and behaviour. Mr Doublebind is reported to be a shifty, spineless, passive father, impoverished and rigid in his mental processes and bewildered by tasks involving quite elementary social graces. In the enactment of the family drama, he is constantly upstaged by his spouse, a domineering dragon of a woman who sets unrealisable demands on the life-style of her children and is then insecurely reproachful to them when they fail to live up to her immature stereotypes. The suffocating, spiky embrace of Mrs Doublebind, her tiresome niggling obsession with conventional manners, her intellectual and emotional dishonesty and her incessant moral blackmail are all repeatedly documented in the literature. The Doublebind children are a dependent, weedy brood, mentally unstimulating and mutually disloyal. If they are ever more than bit players in the tribal charade, it is through their role in ganging up, in coalition with their unspeakable parents, against the unlucky fall-guy or -girl of the house: Charles (or Clarissa) Doublebind. It comes as no surprise to note that Charles/Clarissa, a naive and dithering but basically rather sweet personality, has been driven into a spiralling psychosis through this unholy conspiracy of pressures from his/her nearest and purportedly dearest. The Doublebind menage is a blood-besmirched arena for internecine assaults and insults, a telephone network of crossed lines, scrambled messages and hung-up receivers. The research agents who have eavesdropped on Doublebind conversations and painstakingly decoded their obscure content have let us know just what has been going on in this grim parlour. The Doublebind family is duly incriminated as a *pathogenic communications system* or *nexus of mystification.* They are convicted in the fact of their disagreement one with another, for such discordances of outlook are to be taken as attempts to *disconfirm, disqualify* and *invalidate* the autonomous personal experience of the other, especially of the victim Charles/Clarissa. Let them not, on the other hand, try to escape the charge by agreeing with one another: the common assent of the Doublebinds is a *collusion,* and any mannerisms of warmth or co-operativeness should be seen as expressions of *pseudo-mutuality,* a false front of domestic solidarity tricked up for the outside world by this collection of competitive, mutually suspicious individuals. Any counter-move by Charles/Clarissa against this onslaught of mystification is met with a successful counter-counter-move which places him/her in an *untenable position.* (No younger Doublebind has ever been found to be in possession of a tenable position: on this the witnesses are unanimous.)

The climax of this vicious campaign against an offspring is reached when the Doublebind family decides to 'elect' Charles/Clarissa as an insane mental patient, thereby expelling him/her from their totalitarian kingdom. The chorus of false attribution and impossible injunction, orchestrated by the monstrous Mrs Doublebind (who at this stage exercises the wily stratagems of a Goneril or Regan against the combined Lear-Cordelia figure of her child) rises to a crescendo of rejection; at this point orthodox psychiatry affixes the label of 'schizophrenic' upon the family scapegoat, in a degradation ceremonial of hospital admission which inaugurates a lifetime's career as a mental patient.

In the last sentence of this dramatised account of the theory, the incrimination of psychiatric medicine comes from Laing and his London colleagues; the American researchers have in the main refrained from any radical indictment of psychiatry's own collusions. For the American teams tend to regard 'schizophrenia' still as the name of a behavioural and cognitive disorder attributable to individual patients (though caused by their family circumstances); the notion of 'treating' such a disorder by appropriate medical or psychotherapeutic means is not usually queried in their analysis. Laing, on the other hand, is sceptical about the very existence of a schizophrenic malfunction from which the patient can be said to be suffering: 'schizophrenia' means, if anything, the communications disorder of the whole family, so that the language of 'diagnosis' and 'treatment' of somebody called 'a schizophrenic' would simply mask the web of familial connexions which is the real truth of the matter.

The framework outlined above, admittedly in the bold strokes of caricature, but not, I believe, with any essential infidelity to those authors' meaning, takes us from the Laing of *The Divided Self* to the stage his work had reached by 1963-64. *The Self and Others* (1961), *Sanity, Madness and the Family* (1964) and the *New Left Review* article of 1962 are the products of this stage, which still refrains from any celebration of a supersanity achieved by the psychotic in his voyage into inner space. (The first indications of what has been termed Laing's 'psychedelic model' of schizophrenia appear during 1964.) The book *Interpersonal Perception: A Theory and a Method of Research,* written by Laing with two Tavistock team-mates, H. Phillipson and A. Russell Lee, also belongs in the phase under present review (despite its date of actual publication in 1966) since its focus is on the perception of family members by one another.

In *The Divided Self,* the boundaries of Laing's existential analysis have been drawn around the patient: its typical chapter headings run 'Ontological insecurity', 'The embodied and unembodied self ', 'The inner self in the schizoid condition', 'Self-consciousness' and 'The self and false self in the schizophrenic'. The space of the patient's self is not of course uninfluenced by other people, but its topography is mapped as that of a relatively closed system. By contrast, *The Self and Others* is nearly always inside relationships involving at least two persons; its second part deals with those stratagems of small-group action which may 'drive the other person crazy', while its first

section is a *tour de force* which tries to establish the social, interpersonal content of such apparently private modes of experience as masturbation and psychotic depression. The change in Laing's standpoint for the analysis of schizophrenic behaviour becomes quite dramatic. *The Divided Self* had achieved its comprehension of madness by entering the apparently fractured logic of the patient's worldview and supplying the missing terms. When the hebephrenic Julie speaks, in her disjointed way, about 'a told bell', 'the occidental sun' and 'Mrs Taylor', these utterances are rendered meaningful by construing them as puns: Julie is a 'told belle' (a girl told what to do and be); 'accidental son' (because her mother had half-wanted a baby boy); and 'tailor-made by her parents'. But in the 1964 book by Laing and Esterson, interpreting the family patterns around 11 schizophrenic women as variations on the theme of Clarissa Doublebind, none of the patients is ever reported at any point as uttering 'schizophrenese'. There are no word-salads or schizoid puns to be interpreted. At any rate none are transcribed in the text out of nearly 200 hours of recorded interviews with these patients. The symptoms have become totally dissolved in the flux of social praxis. One patient, Lucie, displays what might be thought to be a rather hesitant speech style, with an abundance of rambling qualifications to her remarks, but most of us have come across a fair number of interviewees with the same style and no psychotic diagnosis. The parents of these young women are scarcely less confused and 'thought-disordered', in the quoted transcripts, than their disgraced and labelled offspring. The insane patients of *The Divided Self,* with their dislocated body-images, splintered self-systems and depersonalised fantasies, sound as though they need some kind of specialised and continuous attention; Laing does not object to the provision of this attention under medical auspices. But with the 11 women of the 1964 series, one is at a loss to understand why they were ever sent into hospital at all, unless on the assumption that the medical authorities are in collusion with their rejecting families. For we are given no reason to suppose that anything is actually the matter with Maya, Lucie, Claire, Sarah, Ruby, June, Ruth, Jean, Mary, Hazel or Agnes.

The disappearance of the symptom can be indicated from Laing's changing attitude towards schizophrenic speech. In *The Divided Self* he admits, in effect, that he is unable to understand, or translate for others' benefit, everything that a schizophrenic patient has to say:

> A good deal of schizophrenia is simply nonsense, redherring speech, prolonged filibustering designed to throw dangerous people off the scent, to create boredom and futility in others.

Compare this with the conclusion to the preface of the 1970 edition of *Sanity, Madness and the Family*:

> Surely, if we are wrong, it would be easy to show it by studying a few families and revealing that schizophrenics really are talking nonsense after all.

The pawky sarcasm here comes from a new confidence. Incoherence and confusion will vanish into comprehensibility once the family context is supplied. It is no longer 'simply nonsense', to be explained as the outcome of a deliberate effort to talk nonsense.

At several points during Laing's argument in this period, one could encounter a constant and serious ambiguity over the applicability of his ideas to 'normal' families. It was not even clear whether, within his terms, 'normal' families could be said to exist at all. Part of the uncertainty arose from the way in which Laing took over some of Sartre's descriptions of the social bond in non-pathological groups, and used them to explain developments within what must have been rather severely disturbed family settings. It will be recalled that Sartre accounts for the more intense kinds of group affiliation by positing the internalisation of violence or 'terror' among the membership. Laing's construct of the 'nexal family' outlines a similar process of bonding through terror, but he widens the category of terror so as to include within it virtually any form of concern felt by one member of a family over the effect that another member's actions may have personally on her or him.

> The highest ethic of the nexus, then, is reciprocal concern. Each person is concerned about what the other thinks, feels, does.
>
> My security rests on his or her need for me. My need is for the other's need for me. His or her need is that I need him or her. My need is not simply 'need' to satisfy biological drives. It is my need to be needed by the other. My love is a thirst, not to satisfy my love, but a thirst to be loved. My solitude is not for another, but for another to want me . . . And in the same way, my emptiness is that the other does not require me to fulfill him or her. And, similarly, the other wants to be wanted by me, longs to be longed for by me. Two alienated loves, two self-perpetuating solitudes, an inextricable and timeless misunderstanding—tragic and comic—the soil of endless recrimination.
>
> In such families it is assumed that to be affected by the others' actions or feelings is 'natural'.
>
> . . . If Peter is prepared to make sacrifices for Paul, so Paul should be prepared to make sacrifices for Peter, or else he is selfish, ungrateful, callous, ruthless, etc. 'Sacrifice' under these circumstances consists in Peter impoverishing himself to do something for Paul. It is the tactic of enforced debt.

The blindness of these passages is unbelievable. This is Laing's description of the life-style of families living in a sort of 'family ghetto', involved in a 'reciprocal terrorism' as 'gangsters' caught in a mutual-protection racket. In a knowing tone not free from a certain lofty satire, Laing is attacking any human relationships which have built into them some anticipation of exchange, or some sense of a limit that will be violated if the exchange is unreciprocated. Such assumptions of a continuing reciprocity, along with anticipations of a possible limit to the relationship in the event of a non-return of affection or action, are of course very common outside family ghettoes and even outside families. The agony of unrequited sexual passion; the feeling of 'unwantedness' in infirm parents dependent on

their children; the unease aroused by oblivious guests who overstay their welcome; the unpopularity of the non-union worker who accepts a wage increase won through the activity of organised mates; our disillusionment in fair-weather friends who are on hand for social pleasantries but absent in times of distress—all these, on Laing's analysis in this period, are targets just as eligible for criticism as the nexal family. To 'invest in' another being's anticipated response is seen as literally capitalistic and hence disreputable: the 'debt' of a relationship has to be 'enforced', a deliberate tactic.

But can expectations of reciprocity be dismissed so easily? Are women liberationists simply wrong to rebel against the endless impoverishment of culture and personality which has been women's traditional lot? May not parents ever decide that they have had enough insufferable presumption from their children, or children from their parents? Would not, in short, a little more 'terrorism' in the cause of reciprocal concern be a highly desirable outcome in many homes? And is not recrimination ('comic' or 'tragic' as the case may be) some times a more progressive state of affairs between two partners than the submissiveness of one partner? For it seems inconceivable that new demands for equality in personal relationships could ever be founded without some expectation of the very reciprocity which is so frowned on here by Laing.

The mystery of the 'normal' family becomes more perplexing when we look at the home lives of the schizophrenic women reported in the Laing-Esterson book. The original perspective of *Sanity, Madness and the Family,* on its first publication in 1964, appeared to be straightforwardly comparative: it was subtitled *Volume I: Families of Schizophrenics,* a formula with the clear implication that a Volume Two would follow dealing with families untenanted by a schizophrenic member.

Laing did in fact report that the Tavistock programme was making comparisons with the patterns of communication in non-schizophrenic, 'normal' families. Both elementary scientific method and common curiosity would dictate the choice of a comparative framework for this research; in the absence of a control group drawn from non-schizophrenic households, how could any behaviour of the patients' families be said to explain the origins of schizophrenia? Yet the descriptions of the families in the 1964 study contain remarkably little that might be specifically schizogenic. These are rigid, demanding parents, setting unrealistic, overweening standards which block their children's autonomy; they define the approved behaviour-patterns for their daughters in ways which stifle the women's self-images; and their expectations for the family's future are often contradictory and incoherent. But all this is true nowadays of many households that display feuding between generations, suppression of young personalities—and a complete absence of schizophrenic children. Laing's and Esterson's account of the Abbotts and the Lawsons is striking not because it presents unfamiliar material but because we have seen it or heard about it all before. And the theoretical framework outlined in the introduction is again non-specific to schizophrenia: 'we are interested in what might be called the family *nexus. . . .*

The relationships of persons in a nexus are characterised by enduring and reciprocal influence on each other's experience and behaviour.' The concept of 'nexus' is now used to include not simply the disturbed family but any family at all (or, for that matter, any close and enduring face-to-face group). Laing seems to have resolved the ambiguity of his earlier description of 'the nexal family' by taking a decision that all families must be nexal.

In the later re-issue of **Sanity, Madness and the Family** the effort to sustain a comparative explanation without resorting to a comparative research method appears to have been abandoned. For the work is no longer presented as the first instalment of a series that will deal in turn with schizophrenic and non-schizophrenic families. The sub-heading *Volume I* has been dropped, and it is made clear in the new preface that no comparative data from other kinds of families are ever going to be presented: 'Would a control group help us to answer our questions? After much reflection we came to the conclusion that a control group would contribute nothing to an answer to *our* question.'

Laing and Esterson posed the 'question' that was the topic of the investigation as follows: 'Are the experience and behaviour that psychiatrists take as symptoms and signs of schizophrenia more socially intelligible than has come to be supposed?' They claim that they are not out to test the hypothesis that certain family interaction patterns cause schizophrenia (a project that would indeed, they admit, have required a control group) but simply concerned to show that the patients' experience and behaviour 'are liable to make more sense' when viewed in the family context than outside it. Yet, even if we were to take at its face value the authors' disclaimer of any interest in a causal investigation, it by no means follows that comparative evidence 'would contribute nothing' to illuminating the problem of social intelligibility in schizophrenic behaviour. Supposing it were found, on examining normal families, that these displayed interaction patterns of mystification that were precisely similar to those found in households with a schizophrenic member: would not the vision of schizophrenic behaviour as an intelligible reaction to such mystification become rather more uncertainly founded? Or supposing that we were to analyse the family processes surrounding patients with an acknowledged organic diagnosis of mental disorder (epilepsy, say, or Down's disease) and found that the reactions of the patient 'made more sense' within the domestic context than when taken in isolation from it. We might conclude that there was some general syndrome of interaction within handicapped families, affecting schizophrenic and other diagnoses in roughly parallel ways, where the initial disability and the parents' reaction to it, the child's reaction to the parents' reaction and the child's physiological deficit were deeply intermingled and confused. This would tend to tell against a view of schizophrenia that regarded it as a reactive condition pure and simple, requiring no organic predisposition in the patient. If the demand for 'intelligibility' in the description of human action means more than a preoccupation with telling stories—*any* stories—about the person cast as subject, we must be careful to check the stories that we tell about that person with the stories that might be told just as easily about quite different sorts of people. Laing cannot evade the requirements of comparative method by an appeal to 'intelligibility'.

This lapse is all the stranger because Laing's other published study from the Tavistock Programme (**Interpersonal Perception,** 1966, jointly with H. Phillipson and A. Russell Lee) pays explicit tribute to conventional scientific canons in its use of empirical control material and tests for the statistical significance of comparisons. The Interpersonal Perception Method (or IPM), devised by these three authors on the basis of a hypothesis by Laing on the supposedly greater interpersonal insight displayed by schizophrenic patients vis-à-vis their relatives, is validated in this study by comparing the test scores of couples from disturbed marriages with those produced by relatively trouble-free couples. The assumptions of the book are by and large those of orthodox marital counselling: we do not have here a radical-nihilist critique of the lie at the heart of human relationships, but a liberal-reformist statement that some relationships are discernibly better than others. The better ones, within the terms of the IPM, are those where the parties achieve a close matching in their perceptions (a) of the way in which they are perceived by one another (b) of the fact that their partners perceive them correctly as perceiving something or somebody. Disturbed couples, on the other hand, exhibit constant mismatchings, or disjunctions between what each thinks the other perceives or feels. The postulates of the study could hardly be in greater contrast with the rest of Laing's work. 'Reciprocal concern' (in the case of the untroubled couples) here hardly implies terror, but rather an achieved harmony. The possibility of a mutually benevolent 'nexus' is conceded, and the anticipation of violence as the cause of social bonding is totally absent from the analysis.

Interpersonal Perception does not, however, represent a break or interlude in the development of Laing's thought. Despite its rather kindly inconsistency, its uncharacteristic hint of mellowness in the understanding of intimate relationships, it does follow through his earlier emphasis on the spiral of interlocking perspectives in the transaction between persons. We have suggested that, as Laing's theory progresses, this vision of interlocking others tends to take precedence over any attention of those characteristics of an individual which are not defined in terms of his immediate peers' perception. The 'vanishing of the symptom' is only part of the disappearance of the subject, the displacement of 'the self' from an internally structured space to a group-directed field. The couples who get tested on the IPM are asked about their judgement of their partners purely in relation to those aspects of behaviour which are manifested within the couple itself: other characteristics of the person remain unchallenged. The husband and the wife will rate themselves and each other on such statements as 'He finds fault with me'; 'I take her seriously'; 'He is wrapped up in himself'; and so on. It is out of bounds for them to consider whether one or the other of the pair is a depressive, a spendthrift, hysterical, career-minded or even sexless. In the world of the IPM, marital disharmony depends not on whether Mr Smith is a drunken good-for-nothing but on whether Mrs Smith thinks that he thinks that she is bitter towards him and on whether he actually does think that she is bitter. In the marital case-history provided as an illustration by the authors, the focus on, so to speak, the outer leaves of the onion is remarkable. 'Mrs Jones' is reported to be very unhappy with her husband, largely through her (unfounded) suspicion that he has slept with another woman. The IPM questionnaire sheets completed by the Jones couple establish (a) that she does not love him; (b) that he is conscious of the fact that she does not love him. But these (on the face of it, plausible) indicators of marital rupture need not be taken as definitive, since they are drawn only from the first windings of the perceptual spiral. They matter less than the fact that Mr and Mrs Jones are in considerable agreement at the higher, more indirect levels of attribution: thus, she correctly perceives him as perceiving her as feeling disappointed in him, and so on. The Jones's perspectives on one another may be at odds, but their meta- and meta-meta-perspectives concur: they may be out of love, but *at least they know it.* And on the strength of these disillusioned, bitterly refracted awarenesses, the authors conclude that the unloved Mr Jones and the unloving Mrs Jones have a hopeful marital prognosis, with 'a good capacity to work with and contain their conflicts'. It needed an awful lot of statistics to produce that avuncular twinkle.

Up to the mid-sixties, Laing's conceptual journey had been from Self to Others: it was soon to concentrate once again on the charting of an individual rather than a social space. From 1964 onward he was associated with an interpretation of schizophrenic experience which was not entirely original (Gregory Bateson [in his introduction to *Percival's Narrative: A Patient's Account of His Psychoanalysis,* 1961] had a few years earlier hinted at a similar perspective), but that has since become identified as Laing's personal vantage point on the field; schizophrenia was henceforth to be seen not as a psychiatric disability but as one stage in a natural psychic healing process, containing the possibility of entry into a realm of 'hypersanity' as well as the destructive potential of an existential death. This view was developed in a number of articles and speeches and then in *The Politics of Experience.* Psychiatric medicine offered, at best, a mechanistic bungling which would frustrate the lawful progression of this potentially natural process; at worst, it drove its patients insane with its murderous chemistry, surgery and regimentation. Instead of the 'degradation ceremonials' performed on patients by doctors and nursing staff (a degradation inherent in the very act of diagnosis and examination no less than in the impersonal processing of mental hospital admission), what was needed was a sympathetic 'initiation ceremonial, through which the person will be guided with full social sanction and encouragement into inner space and time, by people who have been there and back again.' Schizophrenic experience was, at any rate in some patients, no more than the first step in a two-way voyage which led back again into 'a new ego' and 'an existential rebirth'. Laing's therapeutic community (Kingsley Hall) was organised between 1965 and 1970 in an attempt to provide just such a sympathetic setting for the completion of the schizophrenic's cyclical voyage; hospitals, with their formalisation of roles and their traditions of interfer-

ence, could not be expected to furnish the conditions for successful 'initiation'.

The novelty of these views, measured against not only orthodox psychiatric theory but also against Laing's own previous writings, should be apparent. Their introduction was both sudden and confident: fully fledged statements of the position appear in lectures and articles presented by Laing in the course of 1964 and 1965, often before a nonmedical public. The Institute of Contemporary Arts, the *Psychedelic Review,* the radical journals *Peace News, Views* and *New Left Review,* the London weekly *New Society,* and an inconsequent jamboree dignified under the name of 'First International Congress of Social Psychiatry' (which met in chaotic conditions in a large London school) were the first recipients of the new message. Laing also presented his case to the writers and artists who were working with him in the 'sigma' project: Kingsley Hall, and to some extent David Cooper's schizophrenia research ward at the Shenley Hospital outside North London, were in this period part of the scene frequented by this wing of the cultural left. Laing's presentations before medical audiences were to continue in the vein of his pre-1964 theorising: he did not usually try to tell doctors and psychoanalysts that their schizophrenic patients were super-sane voyagers into aeonic time, but rather developed (often with impressive skill and clarity) his classifications of misleading family talk and his notations of the psychotic's layered fantasies.

Laing's sharp turn towards the celebration of the schizophrenic condition was accompanied by two developments in his thought whose conjunction appears as something of a paradox: his language becomes at once both *more socially committed* and *more mystical.* The schizophrenic's experience is seen as an indictment of the conventional world's standards of what is sane or insane; and his incarceration and punishment in the mental hospital necessitates a critical appraisal of 'the larger context of the civic order of society—that is, of the political order, of the ways persons exercise control and power over one another'. In his 1965 preface to the Pelican edition of **The Divided Self,** Laing insisted that his critique should be taken as a condemnation not simply of the micro-world of the family but also of the larger social order, the civilisation of 'one-dimensional men' which 'represses not only "the instincts", not only sexuality, but any form of transcendence'. 'The statesmen of the world who boast and threaten that they have Doomsday weapons are far more dangerous, and far more estranged from "reality" than many of the people on whom the label "psychotic" is affixed.' Two years later, in his contribution to the 'Dialectics of Liberation' conference in London (which he sponsored with three other psychiatrists) he again juxtaposed the small-scale assaults of modern psychiatry and the huge lunacies and systematic violence perpetrated by the world system of imperialism.

However, in this period, from 1964 until seven or eight years later, Laing enjoyed a degree of appreciation among the marxist left which was perhaps excessive in relation to his own rather guarded commitment to political radicalism. The British playwright David Mercer, who collaborated with Laing over much of this period (and wrote the scripts of a TV play, *In Two Minds,* and a film, *Family Life,* exhibiting the causation of a psychotic illness in a young woman through 'double-bind' pressures from her parents) has recounted how

> There was one particular instance when he [Laing] gave what was in effect a private lecture to a group of friends, which lasted about four hours, in which he, first of all, declared himself as a marxist and said that he wanted to try to relate the question of Marx and marxism to his ideas in psychiatry; and there's no doubt that for Laing the two are very closely interwoven. [From a BBC *Radio 3* program, *The Politics of the Imagination,* broadcast in March, 1972.]

The impression of a marxist commitment in Laing was reinforced by the appearance of his name among the signatories welcoming the May Day Manifesto, a campaigning pamphlet coauthored for the socialist-humanist New Left in Britain by Stuart Hall, Edward Thompson and Raymond Williams in 1967. This was a militant and developed anti-capitalist statement; it was in the same year that Laing wrote the short introduction to his collection *The Politics of Experience and the Bird of Paradise,* with its somewhat elliptical denunciation of the capitalist system and its acknowledgement of the importance of Marx's work (along with that of Kierkegaard, Nietzsche and assorted other thinkers) in the critique of modern alienation. By 1970 a commentator on the British New Left could assert that 'Ronald Laing must be accounted one of the main contributors to the theoretical and rhetorical armoury of the contemporary left' [David Martin, 'R. D. Laing: Psychiatry and Apocalypse', in *The New Left,* edited by M. Cranston, 1970]. Outside Britain the link between Laing and the far left seemed a strong one in the later sixties. A laudatory reference to *'el trabajo psiquiatrico de R. D. Laing, D. G. Cooper y sus asociados'* appeared in a literary magazine produced in Havana at a time when the Castro regime was still interested in appeasing the intellectuals; and, arriving in the wake of the 1968 'May events', the French translations of Laing's and Cooper's work came at exactly the right moment to detonate an explosion of interest in 'l'antipsychiatrie' among an enlarged and confident left public.

The other and contrary move, towards an apparent celebration of mysticism and the inward-looking delights of the psychedelic 'trip', took place in the same period of left-wing politicisation in Laing. Jeff Nuttall, the chronicler of project 'sigma', has described how, in a room of the large country house where the first conference of the group took place in 1964, 'Laing enacted a catatonic ceremonial, summarily describing its magical function'.

> 'It's a question,' he said, 'of coming down from the surface of things, down to the core of all things, to the central sphere of being in which all things are emanations.' [Jeff Nuttall, *Bomb Culture,* 1968]

> Laing started to talk about this coming down to a place of being where there was no differentiation between separate entities, to a place of being where there was a total unity in the universe . . .

And in doing that he related it to catatonic behaviour by suddenly standing up and walking quietly to the middle of the room, saying 'One might almost only have to do this to maintain one's relationship to existence.' And he turned right towards the window and he looked at the ceiling; and then he returned to his place. [BBC broadcast, *The Politics of the Imagination*]

In Laing's published work from the 1964-67 period a number of pronouncements can be found with a distinctly otherworldly flavour.

> Orientation means to know where the orient is. For inner space, to know the east, the origin or source of our experience.

> There is everything to suggest that man experienced God. . . . It seems likely that far more people in our time neither experience the Presence of God, nor the Presence of his absence, but the absence of his Presence. With the greatest precautions, we may trust in a source that is much deeper than our egos—if we can trust ourselves to have found it, or rather, to have been found by it. It is obvious that it is hidden, but what it is and where it is, is not obvious. [*The Politics of Experience*]

Occasionally we even find an explicit analogy drawn between the role of the psychoanalyst and that of the religious celebrant:

> I believe that if we can begin to understand sanity and madness in existential social terms, we, as priests and physicians, will be enabled to see more clearly the extent to which we confront common problems . . .

> Among physicians and priests there should be some who are guides, who can educt the person from this world and induct him to the other. ['Transcendental Experience in Relation to Religion and Psychosis,' *Psychedelic Review,* No. 6, 1965]

Laing, in short, regarded the psychotic's experience of an alien reality as something akin to a mystical apprehension: it is not 'the effulgence of a pathological process' but the faithful reflection of another actuality which is concealed from us by the blinkers of our mundane civilisation. The lunatic can be 'irradiated with light from other worlds', and partakes of 'those experiences of the divine which are the Living Fount of all religion' ['Transcendental Experience'].

There are moments when Laing appears to approach the thought of Carl Jung in his emphasis on religious archetypes, necessary to the integrity of the personality and deeply embedded in the collective memory of the human race.

—Peter Sedgwick

What is the nature of the apprehension achieved by the mystical lunatic? It appears that the psychotic condition may enable one to overcome a deep rift in the human personality, characteristic of 'normal' people in our type of society. Modern civilisation has created a fissure between the 'inner' and the 'outer' layers of existence, between 'me-here' and 'you-there', between 'mind' and 'body'. These divisions of personality are not inevitable or natural, but the outcome of 'an historically conditioned split'; we can conceive of a point in human existence before this lapse from fusion occurred, an 'original Alpha and Omega of experience and reality' to whose one-ness the mystic and the schizophrenic both manage to return. It is not the psychotic who is 'alienated' or has the 'split personality', in Laing's terms, but the so-called 'normal' person: alienation and splitting are indeed the basic conditions of our repressive normality and its apparatus of anti-human institutions.

Schizophrenic patients, then, are engaged in a lonely voyage back towards the primeval point of one-ness: it appears that they are in some sense re-tracing the steps taken by the whole course of human evolution, and that once they have regressed far enough they will be able (just how or why is not at all clear) to advance back again into the world of common twentieth-century normals. Laing's description of the destination of the backward voyage is picturesque if imprecise: 'in and back and through and beyond into the experience of all mankind, of the primal man, of Adam and perhaps even further into the being of animals, vegetables and minerals'; 'to temporal stand-still . . . to aeonic time . . . back into the womb of all things (prebirth)'. The psychotic return is recommended to all who are able: 'we have a long, long way to go back to contact the reality we have all long lost contact with'; and, 'This process is one, I believe, that all of us need, in one form or another. This process would be at the very heart of a truly sane society' [*The Politics of Experience*].

This perspective on psychosis is, of course, unique in psychiatry. There are moments when Laing appears to approach the thought of Carl Jung in his emphasis on religious archetypes, necessary to the integrity of the personality and deeply embedded in the collective memory of the human race: as when he speaks of 'the emergence of the "inner" archetypal mediators of divine power, and through this death a rebirth, and the eventual reestablishment of a new kind of ego-functioning, the ego now being the servant of the divine, no longer its betrayer' [*The Politics of Experience*]. But neither Freud nor Jung nor any neo-Freudian or neo-Jungian, nor for that matter any other existential analyst has taken the stance that psychosis is a higher form of sanity. Schizophrenia is breakdown, sheer affliction, for virtually all psychiatric schools; only for Laing does it mean also breakthrough and blessing. Both of Laing's movements, towards social criticism as well as towards a mystique of psychosis, are intelligible only as the systematic development of some elements in his earlier perspective on madness. *The Divided Self* had taken the first step of viewing schizophrenic experience in goal-directed terms. Laing went on to extend the area of meaning in the schizophrenic's world-view, which was to be seen now not simply as shot through fitfully with inten-

tion but as a valid vantage point in its entirety. Psychotic reality is in essence a competitor, a rival, a challenge to the reality defined by the normal and the sane. The sane and the normal eliminate their rival by declaring it to be madness, a deviation to be visited with legal and other penalties. Peaceful co-existence between the normal and the psychotic ideologies is impossible, and it follows that any person who accepts the psychotic vision as authentic must at once declare war on the world-view of the normal consensus; at the very least she or he must declare a critical suspension of judgement on the received social values which decree the limits of sanity and insanity. At times Laing seems to be saying that one cognitive system is as good as another, that your 'delusion' is my 'reality' and nothing can adjudicate between us. At other times it looks as if the patient is right in perceiving as he or she does, and the rest of the world is blind or wilfully ignorant. In Laing's celebration of the schizophrenic we sometimes find hints of the traditional literary figure of the Holy Fool, the crazed seer, the Cassandra or Poor Tom whose disjointed prophecies condemn a society ripe for judgement. This is of course only a limited and rhetorical radicalism: it is saying 'How dare a crazy world label me as crazy?' But then, if his movement towards critical social analysis was primarily a consequence of his identification with patients, one would not expect it to develop the intellectual energy of a more committed politics.

The sympathy with mysticism followed naturally from Laing's position of solidarity with the schizophrenic. We may see the growth of his ideas as a sequence of challenges to the whole catalogue of schizoid 'symptoms' which is customarily presented in psychiatric textbooks. Each manifestation of behaviour that in orthodox medicine is offered as a 'sign' of clinical pathology is taken by Laing to be a comprehensible act which, when aligned against its social context, appears as eminently reasonable and sane. Does the schizophrenic utter a 'word-salad'? Well, it isn't quite as mixed-up and incoherent as that: here, here and here it makes rather good sense, with one or two poetic turns of phrase that are pretty striking. Besides, the schizophrenic does start talking stark nonsense every now and then, quite deliberately, just in order to throw the likes of you and me off the scent. Does this patient present 'inappropriate affect', grimacing when he should keep his face still and reacting coldly in situations demanding a show of emotion? Only according to that mother of his, an unreliable and partisan witness; and besides, who wouldn't grimace at that old tyrant? If that patient hears voices inside her head, it is because she lacks the personal confidence that would enable her to claim ownership of her own thought-processes; if she retreats into the waxy automaton passivity of the catatonic state, we can understand her withdrawal from a responsibility and an agency she feels to be impossible.

So far, so good: all the symptoms have been validated as meaningful and even worthy forms of behaviour. But what are we to make of that peculiar syndrome of the dissolution of personality itself, the 'loss of ego-boundaries' characteristic of so many severely deteriorated schizophrenics who literally do not know where they themselves leave off, and a reality exterior to themselves begins? Up to his psychedelic phase, Laing accepted the typical medical and psychoanalytic description of these states of being; his existential accounts of 'depersonalization' and 'boundary-loss' augment rather than contradict the orthodox texts of clinical psychiatry. But if the schizophrenic experience was to become completely validated, to enter the realm of health and normalcy rather than of sickness and handicap, ego-loss and de-realisation had to become positive virtues, or at least viable alternatives to our common sense, interpersonally bonded realism. Laing called this identity-anchored, space-and-time-bound mode of experience, common to most members of society, *egoic experience*. The ego is 'an instrument for living in this world', and as such is scarcely an unmixed blessing. Characteristic of the modern age is an overemphasis on egoic adaptation to exterior realities, a drive to control 'the outer world' at the cost of forgetting 'the inner light' of imagination and fantasy. Laing appears to concur with traditional mystic philosophy in regarding the egoic mode as 'a preliminary illusion, a veil, a film of *maya* . . . a state of sleep, of death, of socially accepted madness, a womb state to which one has to die, from which one has to be born' [*The Politics of Experience*].

Laing's phase of apparent mysticism must be seen as part of his rationale for non-intervention in a schizophrenic's delusions; it sprang from his insistence that all human experience is potentially valid and potentially intelligible.

—Peter Sedgwick

The alternative to downgrading the 'egoic' (which appears to be a synonym for humanity's perception of and activity in the world of nature and society) would have been to admit that the loss of the boundary between 'inner' and 'outer', 'ego' and 'world', was a terrible misfortune; and this Laing could not do if he was to pursue his project of out-and-out solidarity with psychotic experience.

Thus, Laing's phase of apparent mysticism must be seen as part of his rationale for non-intervention in a schizophrenic's delusions; it sprang from his insistence that all human experience is potentially valid and potentially intelligible, that none of it should be shunted off into a garbage heap for incineration by sanitary technicians. The analogy between the psychotic and the psychedelic states, between the schizophrenic's withdrawal and the mystic's other-worldliness, was an inevitable move in his campaign to upgrade the status of the apparently abnormal and insane. It was a crucial move, because if we refuse to follow Laing this far we are left with the position that the schizophrenic is a disabled victim—of precisely what set of circumstances need not be considered here—whose basic perceptions and reactions can only to a limited degree be understood in the terms of 'intelligibility'. Laing could maintain this total suspension of judgement on 'egoic' ra-

tionality only at the cost of losing his own professional and personal identity. His position at the end of the sixties therefore confronted him with the choice of joining some of his patients and followers in a mystical or psychotic 'boundary-loss', or else of moving on, away and back, from anti-psychiatry to psychiatry.

Maurice S. Friedman   (essay date 1984)

SOURCE: "The Politics of Dialogue: Ronald Laing," in *Contemporary Psychology: Revealing and Obscuring the Human,* Duquesne University Press, 1984, pp. 107-16.

[*Friedman is an American educator who has written extensively on philosophy, religion, and psychology, including several books about the Jewish philosopher and theologian Martin Buber. In the following excerpt, he examines Laing's views on the relation of the individual to the "other," comparing them with similar ideas found in the writings of Buber, Rollo May, and other psychologists, philosophers, and theologians.*]

"More significant than the issue between atheist and theological existentialists," I have written in my chapter on "The Existentialist of Dialogue" in *To Deny Our Nothingness,* "is the issue between those existentialists who see existence as grounded in the self and those who see it as grounded in the dialogue between person and person." Existential and humanistic psychotherapists may also be roughly divided along these lines. Except for Kierkegaard, all existentialists recognize the importance of intersubjectivity. There is, nonetheless, an important difference between those existentialists who regard the relations between subjects as an additional dimension of self but see existence primarily in terms of the self, and those who see the relations *between* selves as central to human existence. Among existentialist philosophers, Heidegger, Sartre, Berdyaev, and Tillich might well fit into the former category, with Buber, Marcel, Karl Jaspers, and Albert Camus in the latter. Rollo May and Carl Rogers both emphasize the centered self or becoming, while both recognize the centrality of dialogue in psychotherapy. But there are other existential and humanistic psychotherapists who might properly be considered existentialists of dialogue. Among these are Ludwig Binswanger, Ronald Laing, Viktor von Weizsacker, Hans Trub, Leslie H. Farber, Sidney Jourard, and Erving and Miriam Polster, the last six of whom we shall deal with at length in *Dialogical Perspectives in Psychotherapy.*

Dialogue, or the I-Thou relationship of openness and mutuality between person and person, is not to be confused with interpersonal relations in general. Dialogue includes a reality of over-againstness and separateness quite foreign to Sullivan's definition of the self as entirely interpersonal. Moreover, neither Sullivan nor Mead makes any basic, clear distinction between indirect interpersonal relations in which people know and use each other as subject and object—the I-It relation in Buber's terms—and direct, really mutual interpersonal relations in which the relationship itself is of value and not just a means to some individual satisfaction or goal. This latter relationship Buber calls "the interhuman." In interhuman relationships, the partners are neither two nor one. Rather, they stand in an interaction in which each becomes more deeply his or her self as he or she moves more fully to respond to the other.

Ronald Laing might well have been discussed under the heading of "Phenomenology and Existential Analysis" since, in important respects, he represents a continuation of this trend, particularly as it is represented by Sartre, Merleau-Ponty, and Binswanger. Nonetheless, unlike Sartre and like Binswanger, he recognizes the centrality of meeting, or the I-Thou relationship, and his use of Sartre is very often for the purpose of illustrating the pathology that results from the absence of relationship. What is more, he has gone beyond Binswanger in his direct attempts to use healing through meeting in his work with schizophrenics. In this respect, he represents a continuation of the work of Harry Stack Sullivan and Frieda Fromm-Reichmann. At the same time, he has attempted to construct a theoretical understanding of schizophrenia in *interhuman* and not just *interpersonal* terms, as Sullivan and Fromm-Reichmann have.

In *The Divided Self* Laing criticizes the tendency of psychiatry to take the person in isolation from that person's relation to the other and the world and to substantialize aspects of this isolated entity. Laing proposes instead to found a science of persons on the relationship between I and Thou:

> Mind and body, psyche and soma, psychological and physical, personality, the self, the organism—all these terms are abstracta. Instead of the original bond of *I* and *You,* we take a single man in isolation and conceptualize his various aspects into "the ego," "the superego", and "the id." The other becomes either an internal or external object or a fusion of both. How can we speak in any way adequately of the relationship between me and you in terms of the interaction of one mental apparatus with another? . . . This difficulty faces not only classical Freudian metapsychology but equally any theory that begins with man or a part of man abstracted from his relation with the other in his world. [*The Divided Self: An Existential Study in Sanity and Madness*]

One acts toward an organism entirely differently from the way one acts toward a person. "The science of persons is the study of human beings that begins from a relationship with the other person and proceeds to an account of the other still as person." Laing postulates as fundamental that separateness and relatedness are mutually necessary. "Personal relatedness can exist only between beings who are separate but not isolated." Both our relatedness to others and our separateness are essential aspects of our *being.* Psychotherapy, accordingly, is an activity in which the patient's relatedness to others is used for therapeutic ends. Since relatedness is potentially present in everyone, the therapist "may not be wasting his time in sitting for hours with a silent catatonic who gives every evidence that he does not recognize his existence." "Inclusion," in Buber's sense of the term, is an absolute and obvious prerequisite in working with psychotics:

> One has to be able to orientate oneself as a per-

son in the other's scheme of things rather than only to see the other as an object in one's own world, i.e., within the total system of one's own reference. One must be able to effect this reorientation without prejudging who is right and who is wrong. [*The Divided Self*]

Laing goes even further than Rollo May in his distinction between knowing the person and knowing *about* the person. One can have a thorough knowledge of ego defects, disorders of thought, and hereditary incidence of manic-depressive psychosis without being able to understand one single schizophrenic. In fact, such data are all ways of *not* understanding the person; for seeing the "signs" of schizophrenia as a "disease" and looking and listening to a person simply as a human being are radically different and incompatible ways of knowing. If we do the latter, however, we must have the plasticity to transpose ourselves into another strange and even alien view of the world without forgoing our own sanity. Only thus can we arrive at an understanding of the patient's *existential position*. None of this means that we see the schizophrenic as really just the same as ourselves. "We have to recognize all the time his distinctiveness and differentness, his separateness and loneliness and despair" [*The Divided Self*].

Laing is at his best in his insight into schizophrenia as a deficient mode of relatedness. In order that one may be related as one human being to another, he points out, a firm sense of one's own autonomous identity is required. But this is just what the schizophrenic lacks. Any and every relationship threatens the schizophrenic with the loss of identity, or engulfment. "The individual experiences himself as a man who is only saving himself from drowning by the most constant, strenuous, desperate activity." This main maneuver for this purpose is isolation, as a result of which the schizophrenic substitutes for the polarities of separateness and relatedness of the autonomous individual "the antithesis between complete loss of being by absorption into another person (engulfment) and complete aloneness (isolation)." The schizophrenic does not have the option of a third alternative—a dialogical relationship between two persons each sure of his or her own ground and for this very reason able to "lose himself" in the other.

Although it is lonely and painful to be always misunderstood, this is relatively safe compared to the danger of being understood: "To be understood correctly is to be engulfed, to be enclosed, swallowed up, drowned, eaten up, smothered, stifled in or by another person's supposed all-embracing comprehension." Similarly, all love is intolerable to the schizophrenic for it places him or her under an unsolicited obligation. The last thing therapists should do is to pretend more love and concern for their schizophrenic patients than they have. If their concern for the other is genuinely prepared to "let him be," as opposed to either engulfment or indifference, then there is some hope on the horizon. For the schizophrenic is equally threatened by being turned into a robot, automation, or thing, an it without subjectivity. If one is treated as an "it," "one's own subjectivity drains away from him like the blood from the face"; for "he requires constant confirmation from others of his own existence as a person." Yet such a one cannot sustain a person-to-person relationship and will regard the therapist as a robot, feeling that one can thereby appear to be a "person" in contrast. Thus, one who is frightened of one's own subjectivity being swamped frequently is found trying to swamp or kill the other person's subjectivity. By so doing one becomes in actuality less of a person oneself: "With each denial of the other person's ontological status, one's own ontological security is decreased." One's lack of a sense of autonomy means that one feels one's own being to be bound up in the other or the other in oneself "in a sense that transgresses the actual possibilities within the structure of human relatedness." In the face of this situation Laing sees the task of the psychotherapist as appealing to the freedom of the patient. "A good deal of the skill in psychotherapy lies in the ability to do this effectively" [*The Divided Self*].

One special form in which the schizophrenic accomplishes this desired isolation from others is through divorcing oneself from one's body, which is felt more as an object among other objects than as the core of one's own being. This keeps the self in a pure I-It relation with other persons. Deprived of any direct participation in any aspect of the life of the world, the self becomes pure observer and controller. Such a schizoid individual is trying, in fact, "to be omnipotent by enclosing within his own being, without recourse to a creative relationship with others, modes of relationship that require the effective presence to him of other people and of the outer world." This shut-up self can only lead, of course, to despair, futility, and a progressive impoverishment of the inner world until one comes to feel one is merely a vacuum.

The isolation of the self is the corollary of the need to be in control. The schizoid individual is afraid of letting anything of oneself go, of coming out of oneself or losing oneself in any experience because one imagines one will be depleted, exhausted, emptied, sucked dry. Laing analyzes this schizoid condition of the inner self in terms of a deficiency in I-Thou relatedness: *The reality of the world and of the self are mutually potentiated by the direct relationship between self and other.* But for the schizoid self, a creative relationship with the other in which there is mutual enrichment is impossible. For this I-Thou relationship one substitutes a quasi It-It interaction which may seem to operate efficiently and smoothly for a while but which is sterile and has no life in it. The schizoid "self can relate itself with immediacy to an object which is an object of its own imagination and memory but not to a real person" [*The Divided Self*]. Thus, in the case of the schizophrenic, Sartre's "bad faith," which introduces the structure of intersubjectivity into the intrasubjective, or psyche, is identical to Buber's description, in the second part of *I and Thou,* of the Thou that strikes inward when there is no longer any genuine relationship to any really other Thou.

Laing's *Self and Others* goes beyond *The Divided Self* in its understanding of forms of interpersonal action. Writing in 1961, Laing declared that the most significant theoretical and methodological development in the psychiatry of the previous two decades was the growing dissatisfaction with any theory or study of the individual which isolates him from his context. Our identities are complemen-

tary, Laing points out; for "every relationship implies a definition of self by other and other by self." "A person's 'own' identity cannot be completely abstracted from his identity-for-others." In fact, other people become a sort of identity kit through which one can piece together a picture of *oneself.* This very fact leads to the temptation of seeking confirmation from others by "seeming," Laing asserts, using Buber's categories from *The Knowledge of Man.* It also leads to a collusion between persons in which they shore up each other's false identities. It is essential that the therapist basically frustrate the self's search for a collusive complement for false identity. Put positively, "one basic function of genuinely analytical or existential therapy is the provision of a setting in which as little as possible impedes each person's capacity to discover his own self." Put negatively, "the therapist's intention is not to allow himself to collude with the patients in adopting a position in their phantasy-system and, alternatively, not to use the patients to embody any phantasy of his own" [*The Politics of Experience*].

It is in *The Politics of Experience* (1967) that Laing attains the fullest expression of what we might call his "politics of dialogue." Essential to this politics of dialogue is the recognition that although experience is invisible to the other, it is neither "subjective" nor "objective," "inner" nor "outer," process nor praxis, input nor output, psychic nor somatic, and least of all is it "intrapsychic process." My experience is not in my psyche; my psyche *is* my experience. The relations between persons are not merely the interplay of ongoing intrapsychic processes. There is no thing that is between two people, and the "between" itself is not a thing: "The ground of the being of all beings is the relation between them. This relationship is the 'is,' the being of all things, and the being of all things is itself nothing" [*The Politics of Experience*].

Laing bases his approach to psychotherapy squarely on this ontology of the between:

> We all live on the hope that authentic meeting between human beings can still occur. Psychotherapy consists in the paring away of all that stands between us, the props, masks, roles, lies, defenses, anxieties, projections and introjections, in short, all the carryovers from the past, transference and countertransference, that we use by habit and collusion, wittingly or unwittingly, as our currency for relationships. [*The Politics of Experience*]

But the metapsychology of Freud, Federn, Rapaport, Hartman, and Kris is incompatible with this approach to psychotherapy; for it "has no constructs for any social system generated by more than one person at a time," for social collectivities of experience shared between persons, or a category of "you," such "as there is in the work of Feuerbach, Buber, Parsons."

> It has no way of expressing the meeting of an "I" with "an other," and the impact of one person on another. . . . How two mental apparatuses or psychic structures or systems, each with its own constellation of internal objects, can relate to each other remains unexamined. Within the constructs the theory offers, it is possibly incon-

ceivable. Projection and introjection do not in themselves bridge the gap *between* persons. [*The Politics of Experience*]

Laing criticizes even more severely behavior therapy and, by implication, the psychology of B. F. Skinner as the most extreme example of a schizoid theory and practice that proposes to think and act purely in terms of the other without reference to the self of the therapist or the patient. Behaviorism implies behavior without experience, objects rather than persons. "It is inevitably therefore a technique of nonmeeting, of manipulation and control." He sees it, indeed, as one of a number of theories that, not founded on the nature of being human, betray the inhuman and inevitably lead to inhuman consequences if the therapist is consistent:

> Any technique concerned with the other without the self, with behavior to the exclusion of experience, with the relationship to the neglect of the persons in relation, with the individuals to the exclusion of their relationship, and most of all, with an object-to-be-changed rather than a person-to-be-accepted, simply perpetuates the disease it purports to cure. [*The Politics of Experience*]

In contrast to all these theories, Laing insists that "it is the relations *between* persons that is central in theory and practice." We must, says Laing, continue to struggle through our confusion and persist in being human. "Psychotherapy must remain *an obstinate attempt of two people to recover the wholeness of being human through the relationship between them*" [*The Politics of Experience*]. In the last part of *The Politics of Experience,* Laing loses sight of the "between" that transcends the inner-outer dichotomy in favor of a celebration of the inner, for which he rightly cites Jung as the groundbreaker in psychology. Nonetheless, even there he sees the (sometimes romanticized) schizophrenic voyage as *"as natural way of healing our own appalling state of alienation called normality"* [*The Politics of Experience*].

Following the tradition of the existential analysts, Laing has been more concerned with portraying the negative aspects of the family that obscure the human image than with revealing the avenues toward healing that might bring the human image out of its eclipse.

—*Maurice S. Friedman*

As an outgrowth of his work with schizophrenics, Ronald Laing has been more and more directly concerned with family therapy. Following the tradition of the existential analysts, Laing has been more concerned with portraying the negative aspects of the family that obscure the human image than with revealing the avenues toward healing that might bring the human image out of its eclipse. In *The*

Politics of Experience, Laing defines the family as a "protection racket" in which each person incarnates the nexus of the family and acts in terms of its existence. Since the person is essential to the nexus and the nexus to the person, the danger to each person is the dissolution or dispersion of "the family." As a result, each member of the family may act on each other member "to coerce him (by sympathy, blackmail, indebtedness, guilt, gratitude, or naked violence) into maintaining his interiorization of the group unchanged." Any defection from the nexus is accordingly punished, with the worst punishment being exile or excommunication: group death. In numerous studies of families of schizophrenics in England and America, "*no schizophrenic has been studied whose disturbed pattern of communication has not been shown to be a reflection of, and reaction to, the disturbed and disturbing pattern characterizing his or her family of origin*" [*The Politics of Experience*].

In *The Politics of the Family,* Laing offers a somewhat subtler analysis of the families of schizophrenics. What is internalized in the individual, he points out, is not the individual members of the family but the sets of relations between them, the *family as a system*. Since "each family member incarnates a structure derived from relations between members," each person's identity rests on a shared "family" inside the others who, by that token, are themselves in the same family. A crisis occurs if any member of the family wishes to leave by dissolving the "family" in himself or herself since the "family" may be felt as the whole world and the destruction of it as worse than murder and more selfish than suicide. This leads to an acute dilemma for the person who feels himself or herself threatened by the family: "If I do not destroy the 'family,' the 'family' will destroy me. I cannot destroy the 'family' in myself without destroying 'it' in them. Feeling themselves endangered, will they destroy me?"

It is not surprising that the "family" comes to serve as a bulwark against total collapse, disintegration, emptiness, despair, and guilt. It is this understanding of the family that leads Laing to his insight into "knots," to which he devotes a whole book and which he himself makes still knottier with his choice of language: "Each person's relations to himself is mediated through the relations between the relations that comprise the set of relations he has with others." Laing's family scenarios are full of inductions, attributions, and double binds.

> What they tell him he *is,* is *induction,* far more potent than what they tell him to do. Thus through the attribution: 'You are naughty,' they are effectively telling him *not to do* what they are ostensibly telling him to do. [*The Politics of the Family, and Other Essays*].

Despite this grim picture of the family, Laing's approach to family therapy is still that of healing through meeting. To Laing, diagnosis and therapy cannot be separated. "Diagnosis *begins* as soon as one encounters a particular situation, and never ends." Diagnosis means *seeing through the social scene,* and the way one sees through the situation changes the situation. In contrast to the nonreciprocal static model used by the doctor and the still predominantly medically oriented psychiatrist, Laing offers a reciprocal and dynamic model of therapy: "As soon as we interplay with the situation, we have already begun to intervene willy-nilly. Moreover, our intervention is already beginning to change *us,* as well as the situation. *A reciprocal relationship has begun*" [**Politics of the Family**].

In contrast to Sartre, then, Laing does not rule out fully mutual and reciprocal relationships a priori, and he uses Sartre, as we have seen, for illustrations of negative, pathological relationships. On the other hand, Laing is like Sartre in that he is at his most brilliant in describing the negative, while he has great difficulty in articulating the nature of trusting and positive interhuman relationships. The one example of the positive that I remember, in fact, is Laing's emphasis on what it means really to give someone a cup of tea!

Peter Barham   (review date 4 July 1985)

SOURCE: "Two Ronnies," in *London Review of Books,* Vol. 7, No. 12, July 4, 1985, p. 12.

[*In the following review of* Wisdom, Madness and Folly, *Barham disputes many of Laing's assertions about his work and the state of modern psychiatry. He also negatively assesses the quality of the writing in this and much of Laing's later work.*]

Schizophrenia is now held to be one of the major illnesses of mankind, but its recognition as a clinical syndrome is of relatively recent origin. There is something very odd about the sudden arrival of the chronic schizophrenic on the stage of history at the end of the 19th century. One hypothesis which has been canvassed recently is that schizophrenia was a novel condition, unknown before the end of the 18th century, which spread as a slow, possibly viral epidemic across Europe and the United States in the 19th century, contributing in large measure to the vast increase in the population of asylums, and culminating in its recognition, under the name dementia praecox, as a definite syndrome by Emil Kraepelin in 1899. But a more historically-minded reading delivers a rather different interpretation of the coincidence between the identification of the chronic schizophrenic as a progressively deteriorating type and the transformation of the asylum into a custodial institution for the socially unproductive. On this view, the formulation of schizophrenia as a chronic condition was deeply implicated in a field of social forces in which people who suffered from mental tribulation came to be represented as lacking any semblance of social value.

To argue in this way is to espouse the kind of dynamic nominalism which Ian Hacking proposes as a way of understanding the dilemmas of the human sciences. 'Categories of people,' Hacking suggests, 'come into existence at the same time as kinds of people come into being to fit those categories, and there is a two-way interaction between these processes.' So, for example, the writings of Michel Foucault are to be understood as 'in part stories about the connection between certain kinds of description coming into being or going out of existence, and certain kinds of people coming into being or going out of existence'. On this reading, the category of schizophrenia, and

the authoritative description of the schizophrenic, came into being at a time when different kinds of people became available for diagnosis as chronic types and scientific operators stood prepared to identify them as such. What was offered was not an innocent reporting: under the institutionalised conditions of observation afforded by the asylum the chronic schizophrenic came more closely to resemble what others in any case already took him to be.

Recent studies of schizophrenic lives across the years of this century have lent a good deal of plausibility to arguments of this kind and demonstrated, among other things, the crucial role played by the individual's sense of his own value—his assessment of his relation to moral community—in the outcome of schizophrenic illness. The lives of schizophrenics are certainly not devoid of causal properties, but the extraction of these from their historical context is a hazardous affair, and over the past century our understanding of schizophrenic predicaments has been greatly impeded by intellectual frameworks which have sought to disclaim the historical constitution both of schizophrenic lives and of the categories in which we attempt to describe schizophrenics.

Within this difficult, and often bewildering, territory the voice of Dr R. D. Laing has been heard—and in equal measure celebrated and scorned—for more than a quarter of a century. The historical sensibility of Western psychiatry, particularly in its British manifestation, has been very limited and that Laing's writings received such startling acclaim—well beyond any reasoned evaluation of their contribution to our understanding of schizophrenia—is in no small part a tribute to the intellectual ineptitude of a good number of his colleagues and to the widespread suspicion that the proclamations of psychiatry have failed to measure up to the important issues. What has motivated Laing all along has been the belief that psychiatry has tended to put schizophrenic patients beyond the human bond and to denude them of any form of value, and his aim has in part been to devise accounts which restore a sense of dignity and human connection to schizophrenic lives. 'Some enhanced understanding of what is going on between psychiatrist and patient,' he says in the present volume, 'does not preclude a scientific explanation of what is going on in the patient alone, and such a scientific explanation does not need to be a way to cut off a cut-off person from the possibility of human reunion, communion and renewal.' However, there are different strands in Laing's writing which compete and conflict with one another and it must be admitted that the present work displays relatively few of the strengths of his earliest and all of the weaknesses of his later writings.

Wisdom, Madness and Folly is an account of Laing's personal, intellectual and professional development over the first thirty years of his life—the period that culminated in the writing of ***The Divided Self,*** his first and best book—together with a lengthy diatribe on what he takes to be contemporary psychiatry. One cannot but be appalled and angered by much of what is said here. 'No facts,' Laing tells us in the introduction, 'are in dispute': rather his endeavour is to describe these 'facts' from a different point of view. Yet in numerous instances he reveals a stunning disregard both for the detail of what others have said and for what can demonstrably be seen to be happening to psychiatric patients. He asserts that 'according to orthodox psychiatry' ('orthodox' and 'mainstream' are favoured words in Laing's vocabulary, used to distance himself from almost everybody), 'over one in ten of us is a schizophrenic.' No one to my knowledge has ventured such a claim: in this country, for example, the lifetime incidence rate for schizophrenia is between 0.8 and 0.9 per cent, or about one in every 125 of the population. Similarly, in the chapter entitled 'Psychiatry Today', there is nothing about such 'facts' of our contemporary existence as the run-down and closure of mental hospitals (a movement in which one might have expected Laing to take an interest), or about the vicissitudes of ex-mental patients in the community. Instead we are told that the preliminary psychiatric examination of a person 'may, and often does, inaugurate a period of weeks, months or years during which that person is kept imprisoned—that is, in involuntary custody, and there drugged, regimented, reconditioned, brain given electric lavages, bits possibly taken out by knife or laser, and anything else the psychiatrist decides to try out'.

The account of his childhood (the trials of 'wee Ronnie' in negotiating, and attempting to make sense of, his family situation), and of his early professional development, has its moments, but, in the main, two things come through: a laziness in the writing, an unwillingness to follow a line of argument to its completion, a constant shifting from one anecdote to another; and a sharp contrast, as displayed in the writing itself, between the Laing of today and the intense self-discipline of Laing in his twenties, a discipline that is most evident in the text of *The Divided Self.* Those parts of the present volume which work best are the ones where Laing permits himself to re-engage with the institutional contexts of his youth, the Army psychiatric unit at Netley, the Gartnavel Royal Mental Hospital in Glasgow, and the Department of Psychological Medicine at Glasgow University. Concerned to mitigate the worst excesses of institutional environments and to engender more hopeful possibilities in his relations with his patients, Laing emerges as a dedicated and perceptive practitioner, for whom the institutional framework provides at one and the same time the limitations against which he struggles and the condition of a notable empirical rigour.

Wisdom, Madness and Folly displays relatively few of the strengths of his earliest and all of the weaknesses of his later writings.

—Peter Barham

The strength of *The Divided Self* was that it enabled us to expand our sense of human community to include the realities of schizophrenic predicaments. If it was not possible to identify the schizophrenic as a social agent, he was nonetheless a social agent whose life had run into serious

trouble. There was nothing to suggest that (to quote from the present book) he was one of a 'motley crew of geniuses, psychotics and sages' who have awakened from the socially 'induced fiction in which we are all enmeshed'. If we ask the question 'what is the schizophrenic doing?' then, contrary to the traditional view of him as 'talking nonsense' or 'displaying his symptoms', it may be helpful to propose the answer: 'he is trying to sort out his relation within community or within the story of which he is part.' Such a frame can help suggest the forms of vocabulary that are appropriate to coping with schizophrenic people as fellow citizens (if that is what we are minded to do) rather than exclusively as objects of clinical investigation. But it cannot give us an exclusive purchase on what schizophrenics are doing, neither can it disclose anything 'deep' about the world-views of schizophrenics. If in one important aspect Laing's aim has been to show that, contrary to what others have said about them, schizophrenics, for all their peculiarities and confusions, are viable human beings, the besetting weakness in his writings has been the tendency to develop extravagant claims around his observations: most notoriously, the claim that the utterances and performances of schizophrenics can be rendered 'socially intelligible' when viewed in the light of their family circumstances. If late 19th-century psychiatrists, and some of their 20th-century counterparts, proclaimed a privileged view of the schizophrenic as a form of degenerate, then Laing has proclaimed an equally privileged insight into the lives and circumstances of schizophrenics. It is indeed an index of Laing's sense of his own privilege that he can so easily abjure the writings of others in this field, notably the work of Manfred Bleuler from the Burghölzli Hospital in Zurich, whose study *The Schizophrenic Disorders* is not only the most thoroughgoing account of the life-histories of schizophrenics available, but also the most perceptive discussion of the dilemmas of the social scientist in the study of schizophrenia.

To confront Laing's later writings with the criterion of scholarly rectitude is perhaps the wrong way to read him. We might do better to see him, not as an investigator of empirical histories, but as a sectarian preacher inveighing against a generalised failing of modern life. What we are given is an insistent highlighting of the worst case as a means to sustain the general vision.

The key word, which serves to identify this failing, and to specify the longing for a pre-modern condition of community, is 'camaraderie'. Psychiatry 'was, and is', he tells us, 'one interface in the socio-economic-political structure of our community where camaraderie, solidarity, companionship, communion is almost impossible, or completely impossible'. The absence of camaraderie between doctor and patient was borne upon him when he was 'in the British Army, a psychiatrist sitting in padded cells in my own ward with completely psychotic patients, doomed to deep insulin and electric shocks in the middle of the night. For the first time it dawned upon me that it was almost impossible for a patient to be a pal or for a patient to have a snowball's chance in hell of finding a comrade in me.'

The restrictions on community in contemporary society are certainly an impediment to the well-being of schizophrenics, but those who are attempting to take current policies of community care seriously, and to treat them with less cynicism than the present government, will want something more than lamentations of this kind. At his best Laing serves to remind us (as did the Quakers in previous centuries) of a capability—a form of response and relation—which has to a considerable extent disappeared from our dealings with the mentally ill. The rationalisations of the last century helped to mitigate the more brutal features of the 18th-century's treatment of the insane, but what they also brought about was a vast increase in the population of the insane and the reduction of large numbers of people to a condition of chronic demoralisation. The degree of self-understanding displayed by psychiatry in this affair has not always been encouraging, but if we are to attempt to negotiate new understandings of (and new prospects for) schizophrenic lives then we shall need something a good deal humbler than what Laing has to offer. The present volume of reminiscences ends in 1957. We must hope that we will be spared further volumes covering the subsequent decades.

Carol Tavris (review date 8 September 1985)

SOURCE: "Things We Don't Talk About," in *The New York Times Book Review,* September 8, 1985, p. 9.

[*Tavris is an American psychologist. In the following review of* Wisdom, Madness and Folly, *she contends that the book is an appealing account of the first part of Laing's career.*]

The second sweetest set of three words in English is "I don't know," and it is to R. D. Laing's credit that he uses it often. For psychiatry really does not know much about madness. It cannot explain why an American catatonic schizophrenic, crouched in apparently mindless rigidity in front of a television set for a month, can later recite every detail of the World Series he has seen. It cannot explain why Scottish catatonic schizophrenics "come out" on New Year's Eve to smile, laugh, shake hands, and dance, only to revert to apathy the next day. "If any drug had this effect," Dr. Laing says, "for a few hours, even minutes, it would be world famous," hailed as a medico-psychiatric, biochemical, scientific breakthrough of the first order.

This appealing book is Dr. Laing's account of his first 30 years, from 1927 to 1957: his childhood, education, early training in psychiatry, the observations and decisions that led him to break from traditional psychiatry. The reader unacquainted with Dr. Laing's work and writings will have no inkling that he was the charismatic leader of the English "antipsychiatry" movement (a term he disclaims); that his 1960 book, *The Divided Self,* launched his fame as a counterculture rebel, mentor and mystic; or that he once celebrated schizophrenic thinking as a comprehensive, even superior, mentality. The reader acquainted with Dr. Laing will not learn here why he became disenchanted with his earlier ideas and abandoned the politics of madness, why his own methods of treating schizophrenics failed, or what he now believes about mental illness.

"I am not trying to justify myself, or prove that I am right," Dr. Laing begins, and, *mirabile dictu* for an autobiography, this is absolutely true. Only once does he defend himself against charges that he idealizes mental suffering, romanticizes despair, or denies the existence of painful emotional disorder. He understands, he says, that society must do something with people who are too disruptive or too crazy. "If a violinist in an orchestra is out of tune and does not hear it, and does not believe it, and will not retire, and insists on taking his seat and playing at all rehearsals and concerts and ruining the music, what can be done?"

In trying to answer that question, Dr. Laing came to three realizations: first, that much of the unalleviated misery he saw in his patients was manufactured by psychiatry itself; second, that he would not like to be treated the way his own patients were treated; and third, that no one had the foggiest idea of how to treat people who were severely disturbed. "What does one do, when one does not know what to do?" Dr. Laing asks. The answer must weigh the patient's pain against the psychiatrist's power. "I am still more frightened by the fearless power in the eyes of my fellow psychiatrists," he writes, "than by the powerless fear in the eyes of their patients."

These observations about psychiatry and the power of psychiatrists are not new, nor are they limited to Britain. (Jonas Robitscher's brilliant analysis of the American system, *The Powers of Psychiatry,* made the same points several years ago.) Some of the treatments that horrified Dr. Laing—insulin-induced convulsions and coma, lobotomies, electroconvulsive shock, straitjackets—were supplanted by drugs in the late 50's. Yet the issues of treatment, control and care of patients remain exactly the same. The "snake pit" is not ancient history in some hospitals. Drugs have not been universally helpful (indeed, that is one reason why modified electroshock treatments have returned). The war between somatic and psychological interpretations of mental disorder rages as noisily as ever, with each side making tragic errors of diagnosis and treatment.

Moreover, then as now, many psychiatrists fail to *talk* to patients, much less listen to them. A patient of Dr. Laing's complained of deafness and pain in his ear, although no neurological damage could be found. No one had asked the man, until Dr. Laing, whether he had any idea what was causing the pain in his ear, which led Dr. Laing to a psychological answer. Another ward patient in a British Army hospital had the same "delusion" of being dragged out of bed at night and beaten up by men in army uniforms. A second patient had the same delusion. So did a third and fourth. Dr. Laing listened, and the result was a court-martial of two men responsible for abusing patients. Does this seem unusual? A psychiatrist told me recently that at a recent conference members of his panel and the audience debated endlessly about possible physical and chemical interventions in treating a chronically depressed man. "No one," he said, "had thought to ask the man what he was depressed *about.*"

Dr. Laing's account of his upbringing and family life consists of impressionistic dabs on a canvas; the reader must construct the picture. Some dabs convey aloof, punitive parents—the kind of mother who burned a 3-year-old's toy horse because he was becoming too fond of it, the kind of father who slapped him for using "the wrong tone of voice." Particularly subtle dabs suggest a bizarre story of his mother's manipulations to break the friendship between her husband and his female piano accompanist, a story told as vaguely as it must have seemed to a little boy. " 'Ronald [she would have said], we never talk about that sort of thing.' Hence I became fascinated by all those sorts of things we don't talk about."

Dr. Laing's account of his upbringing and family life consists of impressionistic dabs on a canvas; the reader must construct the picture.

—Carol Tavris

Sometimes Dr. Laing offers his own connections between experiences. Asthma, he suggests, was the price he paid for his sense of suffocation and his policy of keeping out of trouble for the sake of a quiet life. "I just had to live with the most unpleasant queasy sense of corruption," he writes. "It is terrible to feel you have to pretend you love someone when you do not."

Other experiences do not connect. Dr. Laing grew up in a world of pervasive anti-Semitism, hearing that Jews have different germs from us and what was happening to Jews in Germany was their own fault. Yet he and a friend were the only medical students in a class of 200 to feel sickened and outraged by "training" films of Nazi experiments on Jews, and later he found a "spiritual father" as well as a medical and intellectual mentor in a Jewish neurosurgeon, Joe Schorstein. Did he lose his anti-Semitism easily, like baby teeth, or did it have to be extracted, like an impacted molar? Or did the remarkable empathy he was later to bring to talking with patients prevent him from sharing his family's anti-Semitism in the first place? He doesn't say.

Dr. Laing's doubts about psychiatry began early. "It looked the same as the rest of medicine, but it was different," he recalls. "I was puzzled, and uneasy. Hardly any of my psychiatric colleagues seemed puzzled or uneasy. This made me even more puzzled and uneasy." Fortunately for psychiatry and for his patients, Dr. Laing has retained his uneasiness. It is a good quality to have in approaching the "breakthroughs" that appear every so often in the treatment of mental disorder. A few years later, after some successes and many failures, excitement subsides; Dr. Laing's own method had the same fate. But this book reminds us of what psychiatry, ultimately, is for. "How can we entice these ghosts to life, across *their* oceanic abyss, across *our* rivers of fear?" I don't know, he says, but I'll try.

David Ingleby   (review date 11 October 1985)

SOURCE: "Precocious and Alone," in *The Times Literary Supplement,* No. 4306, October 11, 1985, p. 1130.

[*In the following review of* Wisdom, Madness and Folly, *Ingleby contends that, while Laing's autobiography "is absorbing and enjoyable as a story," it fails as a document of his intellectual development because of its exclusive presentation of his own point of view: his life "is presented as a solitary journey, and we hear little . . . about the fellowship that must surely have sustained it."*]

As everybody knows, R. D. Laing is a psychiatrist who sees things very differently from his colleagues, many of whom indeed believe him to be crazy. How did he get that way? Here [in *Wisdom, Madness and Folly*] he sets out to answer this question, by telling us about some of his experiences up to the point when, as a thirty-year-old Senior Registrar, he left Glasgow for London to embark on his controversial career.

Laing begins by recapitulating what his views on psychiatry are—and what, despite the exaggerations put about by his colleagues, they are not. Yes, of course some people are mentally very deranged—perhaps even brain-diseased; no, they don't usually enjoy this. Yes, they may be impossible for their nearest and dearest to put up with; and if psychiatrists didn't take them off our hands, somebody else would probably have to—not necessarily with better consequences. Yet for all that, the degree of power which psychiatrists routinely exercise is frightening and unique. Moreover, "psychiatrists never tire of telling us that there is an unbridgeable gulf between some people and the rest of us", but they are unwilling to recognize that this gulf is very largely of their own construction, and unable to devise ways of reaching out across it. In brief, Laing seems to want to get back to the conception of madness attributed by Foucault to medieval Europe, when it was recognized as such but seen, nevertheless, as an experience endured by fellow human beings. But it took Laing many years to formulate this ambition, and to overcome the fear of being regarded as mad himself for having it.

Long before he went to medical school, however, Laing seems to have been used to being an outsider. His account of his early family life reads like one of his own later case-studies: the double-binds and mystifications, the crushing burden of shame and guilt (Presbyterian variety) and the inevitable (perhaps *too* inevitable) suffocating mother. His father, however, appears as a sympathetic, albeit relatively powerless, figure: sensitive, humorous, never likely to leave wee Ronnie in the lurch. Like his father, Laing found solace in music and (later) in voracious reading.

Yet the compulsion to do well—or rather, to avoid the shame of failure—seems to have followed him even here. On the back of the book's jacket is a photo of Laing as a student wining a cross-country race for Glasgow University—lungs bursting, face contorted with agony. The image sticks in the reader's mind: whatever he was doing, it seems that Laing always had to come in first. The theme of precocity occurs over and over again: music diplomas, fluent Greek and Latin, senior registrarship, first book— even this autobiography, perhaps; all are achieved at an astonishingly early age. Undoubtedly Laing was, and is, extremely talented: but one doesn't have to be an analyst to suspect that this need to prove how "good" he was had something to do with having been made to feel very, very "bad". There are, however, more unfortunate hang-ups.

Laing treats the characters from his past—including himself—with wry affection: above all, he is a gifted raconteur, and knows how to grip his audience with a good story.

—David Ingleby

His family also bequeathed him certain enduring preoccupations: the things people don't talk about, and the power they wield over each other—the power to make others believe they are a certain way, so that, like hypnotic subjects, they become that way. Hypnosis, indeed, later became one of Laing's specialities—one of his recurring themes (nightmares?) is that maybe we have all been hypnotized to forget or deny certain things, including the fact that we are forgetting or denying them. Despite the black comedy of family and school (where, after all, "none of the masters were *serious* sadists"!), the adolescent Laing could still contemplate the world with serenity, sitting in front of the fire each evening before going to bed. It was in such moments that he asked himself what had gone wrong with the human race.

> What the hell was the matter with us? Why did we not join the rest of creation, and all have a great time on this glorious jewel of a planet together? No. Nothing remotely like it. Why not? In God's name why not?

Why was love so readily betrayed, and simple human solidarity and companionship so hard to find? No one could doubt their power: as Laing discovered as a psychiatrist, the spirit of "Auld Lang Syne" was capable of transforming a back ward full of chronic schizophrenics into smiling, laughing revellers—for a few moments each New Year. "If any drug had this effect, for a few hours, even minutes, it would be world famous."

Indeed, the most potent residue from Laing's early life can best be described as a profound religiosity—all the stronger for being a reaction against the narrow-minded puritanism of his environment. The world was an absurd and terrible place, yet it had to be taken seriously: somehow it had to be made to yield up its truth. "What was the trouble? What was the matter? What the hell was going on?" Like many others, Laing felt that becoming a doctor would help resolve some of these mysteries. Like them, too, he found that coming face to face with the appalling senselessness of some people's suffering only intensified the mystery. Worse still, the ethical blindness of science (exemplified by the professor who could see nothing wrong with using Nazi doctors' X-ray films as teaching material) invalidated any answers coming from that quarter. Yet the relationship between brain and mind proved an irresistible fascination for Laing, and it was on neurosurgery that he now focused his ambition.

It was there that he met "a master of the European tradition to which I was beginning to be mature enough to pre-

sume to belong": his friend and mentor, Joe Schorstein, "one of the most tormented human beings I have ever met". Schorstein, moreover, was a Jew—and thus a symbol, in the Glasgow of Laing's youth, of everything strange and sinister. Although Laing struggled for many years to avoid a "divorce" between neurology and his philosophical interests, by the time he became an Army psychiatrist at the age of twenty-four his mind was in a "theoretical ferment" over dialectics, existentialism, phenomenology and hermeneutics: traditions, in short, for which mainstream Anglo-American psychiatry has no use, except as a source of case-studies in psychopathology. Already, one can see, a divorce was on the cards.

Chiefly, however, his misgivings about psychiatry were acquired first-hand. In the British Army Psychiatric Unit at Netley, he witnessed gross and primitive methods of physical treatment, and "a régime of misery, absurdity and humiliation". More than witnessed—he helped to administer it: gradually, however, he "lost any sense of desire or duty to force on people treatment that I would not want forced on me". It was here that he dared to break the sacred rule of not talking to patients (which, as his teachers had tried to impress on him, can only make them worse), and (worse still) tried to befriend them—even taking one "case" home with him for the weekend. Yet the "Auld Lang Syne" ambience of solidarity and companionship was not so easy to conjure up: "For the first time it dawned on me that it was almost impossible for a patient to be a pal or for a patient to have a snowball's chance in hell of finding a comrade in me."

It was only when Laing left the Army in 1953 and took up a hospital appointment at Gartnavel that he started to deal with chronic, hospitalized, "hopeless" cases. Here he undertook his first experiment in group living, with eleven schizophrenic patients. Soon, the women were baking cakes for tea: but when these were offered round among the doctors, few of the latter were "brave, or reckless, enough to eat a bun baked by a chronic schizophrenic". "Who was crazier," asks Laing, "staff or patients?" In his next post, in Glasgow, he delved more intensively into the histories and private experiences of his patients, developing the phenomenological approach written up in that truly precocious book, *The Divided Self.* At the end of this memoir, Laing is thirty years old and only just embarking on his London career: but the foundations of his viewpoint had already been firmly laid.

Apart from the insights it provides into that viewpoint, this book is absorbing and enjoyable as a story in itself. However harsh life felt at the time, Laing treats the characters from his past—including himself—with wry affection: above all, he is a gifted raconteur, and knows how to grip his audience with a good story.

But precisely because the story is such a good one, it is easy to forget that the data Laing provides are highly selective and described from only one point of view—his own. His intellectual development is presented as a solitary journey, and we hear little, with one exception, about the fellowship that must surely have sustained it. Nor is there a hint that anyone else in the profession shared his misgivings about psychiatry: everything came, apparently, from within. This highly individualistic attitude became the hallmark of British "alternative psychiatry", providing the basis of its approach to mental illness, and also—inevitably—the reason for its failure: for despite all the 1960s-style political rhetoric, it could not recognize itself in a movement calling for a wide range of reforms, in the way that Italian "democratic psychiatry" did. Laing is most definitely not to be blamed for the fact that British psychiatry trundles on as if he had never existed; but he is not the person to ask for an explanation of it.

FURTHER READING

Criticism

Bettelheim, Bruno. Review of *The Facts of Life,* by R. D. Laing. *The New York Times Book Review* (30 May 1976): 5, 12.
    Compares the psychotherapeutic methodologies pres-ented in Laing's *The Facts of Life* with those of Thomas Szasz in his book *Heresies (1976)*.

Cioffi, Frank. "Honours for Craziness." *London Review of Books* (17-30 June 1982): 10-11.
    Discusses *The Voice of Experience* and Peter Sedgwick's *Psycho Politics (1982)*.

Raksin, Alex. Review of *Wisdom, Madness and Folly: The Making of a Psychiatrist,* by R. D. Laing. *Los Angeles Times Book Review* (14 December 1986): 10.
    Comments on Laing's psychotherapeutic approach to the doctor-patient relationship as it is presented in *Wisdom, Madness and Folly.*

Solotaroff, Theodore. "The Uses of Madness." *Washington Post Book Week* (9 July 1967): 3, 12.
    Mixed review of *The Politics of Experience.*

Warren, Neil. "Freudians & Laingians: The Naturalisation of False Consciousness." *Encounter* 1, No. 3 (March 1978): 56-63.
    Compares the psychotherapeutic approaches of Sigmund Freud and R. D. Laing, discussing their influence on contemporary psychiatric theory and practice.

Additional coverage of Laing's life and career is contained in the following sources published by Gale Research: *Contemporary Authors,* **Vols. 107, 129 (obituary);** *Contemporary Authors New Revision Series,* **Vol. 34; and** *Major 20th-Century Writers.*

Armistead Maupin

1944-

American journalist and novelist.

The following entry presents an overview of Maupin's life and career.

INTRODUCTION

Maupin's novels are noted for their witty, realistic dialogue, bizarre plot twists, memorable characters, and the presentation of gay life as an integral part of the broader social milieu. His critically acclaimed six-novel *Tales of the City* series is set in San Francisco during the 1970s, 80s, and 90s, and follows the lives of numerous characters. Maupin's main themes include homosexuality, alienation and discrimination, religion, sex and drugs, and love and romance. Critics have noted that with the advent of the AIDS crisis, his later works have taken a more serious and somber tone.

Biographical Information

Born and raised in North Carolina, Maupin graduated from the University of North Carolina in 1966. He became a highly decorated soldier during the Vietnam War and was honored by the president of the United States. In the early 1970s he formally disclosed his homosexuality and moved from North Carolina to San Francisco, where he pursued a career in journalism. While writing for the *San Francisco Chronicle* he created the popular "Tales of the City" newspaper serial about people and life in the Bay Area; the characters became the protagonists of the six novels that comprise the *Tales of the City* series. Maupin has also written for the stage and screen and, in 1992, published *Maybe the Moon,* which is a departure from the *Tales* series.

Major Works

The *Tales of the City* series—*Tales of the City* (1978), *More Tales of the City* (1980), *Further Tales of the City* (1982), *Babycakes* (1984), *Significant Others* (1987), and *Sure of You* (1989)—are set in San Francisco and follow the lives of Mary Ann Singleton, Michael ("Mouse") Tolliver, Brian Hawkins, Mona, Dede, Jonathan, Mr. Halcyon, and the mysterious Anna Madrigal, who oversees the lives of her tenant "family" at 28 Barbary Lane. In *Tales of the City* Mary Ann leaves the midwest to make a new life for herself in San Francisco during the 1970s; Michael, a gay neighbor who is currently between lovers, befriends her. Mrs. Madrigal, the landlord, becomes very protective of Mary Ann and all her tenants. Eventually, Michael falls in love with Jonathan, a young doctor and Dede Halcyon's gynecologist. Mrs. Madrigal also takes particular interest in Mona, a new tenant and friend of Michael. *More Tales of the City* follows Mary Ann and Michael in their

search for love on a Mexican cruise ship. Back in San Francisco, Mary Ann and Michael also become embroiled in a bizarre series of circumstances, which involve an amnesia victim and lead to the discovery of a secret Christian cannibal cult that is operating out of Grace Cathedral. As the story draws to a close, Michael and Jonathan permanently get together, and Mrs. Madrigal reveals two very important secrets. In *Babycakes,* which begins with Queen Elizabeth II's royal visit to San Francisco, Mary Ann has become a successful TV reporter and has married. The mood of *Babycakes* is decidedly somber, as the AIDS issue is introduced into Michael's life and the rest of the characters at 28 Barbary Lane. As *Significant Others* begins, Jonathan has died from AIDS, Michael has AIDS, and Mary Ann has become a very popular local talk show hostess; Dede Halcyon, her twin Eurasian children, and her lover Dorothea spend a week at Camp Wimminwood, a summer music camp for lesbians. Meanwhile, Brian, Michael, and Booter are up-river at the Bohemian Grove, which is a summer camp for heterosexual men. In *Sure of You,* the last novel of the *Tales* series, 28 Barbary Lane has closed. Mrs. Madrigal goes off to Greece with Mona, but career-minded Mary Ann decides to leave San Francisco, her husband and child, and go to New York City. *Maybe the*

Moon (1992) is a departure from the *Tales* series and is a first-person narrative about the life of a heterosexual dwarf actress who lives in Los Angeles and pursues a career in films.

Critical Reception

Most commentators on the *Tales of the City* novels have applauded Maupin as a chronicler and satirist of contemporary American culture and have praised the realism and flow of his dialogue and the way he handles homosexual themes. Furthermore, many have commented favorably on his use of short chapters, outrageous plot twists, and his ability to interweave complicated subplots. Some critics, however, have faulted *Maybe the Moon* for its weak presentation of the themes of discrimination and alienation, and for its stereotypical portrayal of Los Angeles and the film industry.

PRINCIPAL WORKS

*Tales of the City (novel) 1978
*More Tales of the City (novel) 1980
*Further Tales of the City (novel) 1982
*Babycakes (novel) 1984
*Significant Others (novel) 1987
*Sure of You (novel) 1989
†28 Barbary Lane: A Tales of the City Omnibus (novels) 1990
‡Back to Barbary Lane: The Final Tales of the City Omnibus (novels) 1992
Maybe the Moon (novel) 1992

*These works comprise the *Tales of the City* series.

†This collection contains *Tales of the City, More Tales of the City,* and *Further Tales of the City.*

‡This collection contains *Babycakes, Significant Others,* and *Sure of You.*

CRITICISM

Publishers Weekly (review date 1 February 1980)

SOURCE: A review of *More Tales of the City,* in *Publishers Weekly,* Vol. 217, No. 4, February 1, 1980, p. 106.

[*In the following review, the critic provides brief synopses of the story lines in* More Tales of the City.]

[In *More Tales of the City,*] things are hopping once again at Anna Madrigal's San Francisco rooming house, and Maupin fills us in on the latest crises in the lives of the Barbary Lane crew. Anna finally reveals that she is not the man she once was, which comes as quite a shock to several of her boarders (one of whom turns out to be her daugh-

ter). Mary Ann and Michael set out to find the loves of their lives on a cruise to Mexico. She takes up with an amnesia victim who—as the two eventually discover—lost his memory after becoming involved with an Episcopal cannibal cult. And it looks as though Michael's future will be rosy when he meets Jon, a kind gynecologist. Mona and Brian, two of Anna's more frustrated tenants, find solace in each other at the end of this entertaining, highly dramatic saga, which takes well-aimed pokes at just about every imaginable human lifestyle and personality.

Stephen Harvey   (review date 31 August 1982)

SOURCE: A review of *Further Tales of the City,* in *The Village Voice,* August 31, 1982, p. 40.

[*Harvey was an American film curator and critic. In the following review, he focuses on the characters and plot of* Further Tales of the City.]

According to Michael, the *Tales of the City* trilogy's gay-clone Candide, there are two kinds of people in this world—or at least in San Francisco, which in Armistead Maupin's oeuvre amounts to the same thing. Either you are a Tony, one of those benighted souls who think the city's theme song is the Bennett rendition of "I Left My Heart in San Francisco," or a Jeanette, an aficionado of the blithe and gallant Miss MacDonald's anthem, "San Francisco," from the movie of the same name. Michael, *ca va sans dire,* is a Jeanette; his best female chum Mary Ann, a budding local TV personality, is one by osmosis, although when she first arrived on the scene fresh from Cleveland at the start of book one, she was indisputably a Tony. Their landlady Mrs. Madrigal (father—don't ask—of Mona, who is getting her head together in Seattle) probably thinks she *is* Jeanette, especially when she has partaken of the leaves pruned from Miss Barbara Stanwyck, the most potent marijuana plant in her herb garden. Hillsborough matron Franny Halcyon just can't help being a Tony. But then Franny's endured so many traumas in the past—having lost her husband from bum kidneys, her closety son-in-law in an auto wreck, and daughter Dede Halcyon Day to that mess in Guyana—that one can hardly begrudge her her foibles, which also include an unfortunate predilection for mixing Quaaludes with her Mai Tais.

New York could never inspire a chronicle quite like Maupin's. It requires a burg which, for all its cosmopolite airs, is sufficiently insular to allow for such unexpected incestuous connections. Still, vicarious Jeanettes everywhere (plus the besotted Franny herself) should be pleased to learn that on the other side of the Embarcadero, Dede and her half-Chinese twins have rematerialized in **Further Tales of the City,** more or less unscathed by their ordeal. They'll likewise be relieved to discover that Maupin's quill is as ruefully bitchy as ever. He nimbly skewers those local social butterflies whose idea of an urgent civic project is an upscale Madame Tussaud's to enshrine the effigies of such notables as Nan Kempner and Ann Getty. When it comes to what is euphemistically called the gay subculture, Maupin is, in the words of Margo Channing, as trustworthy as *The World Almanac.*

The passages devoted to Michael's irony-tinged interlude with middle-aged movie idol ———(the one who used to make those sex comedies co-starring———before reportedly exchanging matrimonial vows with TV rube———), are only surpassed by his mirthsome account of his hero's trip to a gay rodeo, during which Michael becomes blissfully lost in the arms of a construction worker from Salome, Arizona, who, best of all, has never even heard of Oscar Wilde. At a rustic whoop-up of the San Francisco Gay Men's Chorus, "there were so many different plaids . . . that it looked like a gathering of the clans"; in his favorite bar, Michael muses that someday "the homoerotic cave drawings in San Francisco's gay bars would be afforded the same sort of reverence that is currently heaped upon WPA murals and deco apartment house lobbies." Maupin indisputably gives great punch line, and he's pretty adroit at sallies of flippant sentiment to cap off the book's more tranquil chapters.

Presumably because both first saw the light as serials in the popular press, Maupin's sagas have been likened by some to Dickens's treatments of Victorian London—a comparison best left unfathomed. Maupin's deftness is in direct proportion to the parochial nature of his observations; his half-hearted attempt to give *Further Tales* broader contemporary resonance turns out to be a queasy misfire. The book climaxes with a wild loon chase to Alaska by Mary Ann and Dede, in quest of a man who may or may not turn out to be Jim Jones incarnate. But Maupin's etching of this figure is too glib for horror, and its subject too disquieting and tangible a memory to comfortably suit as the red-herring gimmick in a camp melodrama plot. (The fanciful cult of Episcopal cannibals that graced *More Tales* was rather more like it.)

Here's hoping Maupin stays faithful to the dizzy mundanities of his characters' slapstick soap-opera lives in the next installment. Will Mary Ann's new spouse, the lackadaisical ex-activist Brian, be able to cope with her ascent to media celebrity? Will Michael contract GRID and his sporadic lover, Dr. Jon, come up with the cure? Who's willing to bet that the transplanted Mona just happened to take a camping trip in the shadow of Mount St. Helens moments before the big bang, and will return to the hearth on Barbary Lane, slightly ashen but sardonic as ever? I can hardly wait to find out.

Jacqueline Austin   (review date 18 November 1984)

SOURCE: A review of *Babycakes,* in *The New York Times Book Review,* November 18, 1984, p. 32.

[*In the following review, Austin favorably assesses* Babycakes, *predicting that the book will win over some of Maupin's critics.*]

Queen Elizabeth has arrived in San Francisco; just as Mary Ann Singleton, television reporter, goes to cover the scene, one of the Queen's officers jumps ship. Mary Ann's husband, Brian, doesn't know that he's infertile, but Mary Ann does, so she decides to. . . . Thus begins *Babycakes,* and the fourth installment of Armistead Maupin's San Francisco saga careens beautifully on. People who haven't read his *Tales of the City, More Tales of the City* and *Fur-*

ther Tales of the City might initially be confused by the plethora of characters, but they should continue. *Babycakes,* unlike the *Tales,* preserves a sense of irony while making paramount the values of warmth and love. Almost a decade into their promiscuous but caring friendships, the characters are tempered by age and wisdom, though still layered in reflecting, intermittently revealing levels of absurdity. Gestures have a life of their own—an "Elizabethan" wave of the hand, for example, belongs first to the Queen, then to a socialite, then to Mona, a mail-order lesbian bride, making equal the essentially unequal. If British high life and low life don't come across as different from San Francisco's, who cares? Credit, as Mr. Maupin does, "the global village," or suspend disbelief and concentrate on the mostly deft twists and turns of plot. *Babycakes* seethes with pleasantly nasty topical references and has been likened by the over-enthusiastic to Dickens's Victorian melodramas and to Wodehouse's cheerful fables. Mr. Maupin's style, though, with all its near-perfect ear ("crumbling umber castle"), is still too alienated and grotesque for many, and Babycakes herself—Mary Ann—isn't central enough to function as a proper picaresque heroine. But this book will probably win over some of Mr. Maupin's critics while delighting those who enjoy his continuing satire on the San Francisco milieu.

Tom Spain   (essay date 20 March 1987)

SOURCE: "A Talk with Armistead Maupin," in *Publishers Weekly,* Vol. 231, No. 11, March 20, 1987, pp. 53-4.

[*In the following excerpted essay, which is based on a conversation with Maupin, Spain discusses Maupin's homosexual themes and attitudes, the AIDS crisis and its effect on his writing, his method for creating characters and plots, and his wide appeal among both heterosexuals and homosexuals.*]

It's the Friday before a long holiday weekend in San Francisco, and many of the city's residents are preparing to escape to the country for some time away from their day-to-day concerns. The readers of the *San Francisco Examiner,* however, will take at least one daily concern away with them—namely, a worried curiosity about what Monday will bring for the cast of characters whose lives *Tales of the City* author Armistead Maupin outlines daily in the *Examiner* serial *Significant Others.* . . .

San Franciscans are accustomed to the suspense. Maupin has been serializing the adventures of a cross-section of Bay Area characters off and on since 1976, when the original series first appeared in the *San Francisco Chronicle.* Readers elsewhere have followed these tales in four editions, beginning with *Tales of the City* in 1978, followed by *More Tales* . . . (1980), *Further Tales* . . . (1982) and 1984's *Babycakes;* together they have sold over 200,000 copies. . . .

While the latest serial lacks the *Tales of the City* label—lost when Maupin jumped from the *Chronicle* to the *Examiner*—the same, familiar characters are there, along with Maupin's trademark tone, which blends humor, melodrama and deadly accurate social satire. Its three main story lines follow in the tradition of bucolic comedy, in which city dwellers escape to the proverbial forest for a weekend of romantic misadventure, set against the backdrop of the Bohemian Grove men's retreat, a women's music festival and the predominantly gay Russian River resort. But the story that San Franciscans were left to ponder on the holiday weekend in question has an immediate relevance that separates it from its predecessors, and perhaps from anything else that is currently being published. For at Maupin's Russian River retreat, the character Brian Hawkins, who has blazed a trail of heterosexual promiscuity through all four books, awaits the results of a test that will reveal whether or not the illness, fatigue and sudden weight loss that have afflicted him the past few weeks—weeks through which *Examiner* readers suffered with him day after day—are indeed the undeniable signs of Acquired Immune Deficiency Syndrome.

The result is a portrait of the devastating effects of the AIDS epidemic that achieves an intimacy that could scarcely be duplicated in any other format. Whether they read the newspaper series or the book, readers are faced with the prospect that someone they've "known" for 10 years may be dying before their eyes. While this hardly sounds like material for romantic comedy—miraculously, it is—the AIDS issue reflects Maupin's sensitivity to the responsibilities he takes upon himself as a homosexual, a novelist and a member of the press—responsibilities that became clearer in 1985 when he emerged as a de facto spokesperson on gay matters surrounding his friend Rock Hudson's death.

Significant Others, like its predecessors, offers Maupin a welcome opportunity to extend his social commentary to a broader audience than the subject matter might usually attract. "I'm lucky, because my books cross over," he says. "I constantly fight the premise that because I'm gay my books are only for gay people." The crossover element is central to Maupin's mission. Maupin sees his work in the tradition of the 19th century serialists, whose fiction brought social issues to life for the masses; *Significant Others* even aspires to evoke those historical serials graphically, with decorative chapter headings and an elaborate frontispiece. But the key to that crossover, and to Maupin's most important affinity to his 19th century influences, has nothing to do with his stories' look or content. Rather, it's the way they draw in any reader, gay or straight, from San Francisco or beyond. For shaping his every plot twist or satirical barb is a set of three simple rules of serial fiction handed down from Dickens's contemporary, Wilkie Collins: "Make 'em cry, make 'em laugh, make 'em wait."

When *PW* [*Publishers Weekly*] visited Maupin, San Francisco had just received the 80th installment of the series, and Maupin was completing #86, with 41 left to go. "That's actually pretty far ahead for me," he confessed. "My Achilles heel is that I'm very late getting copy in. I'm both a perfectionist and a procrastinator—a deadly combination." While his one-step-ahead strategy may unnerve his editor, it gives him the opportunity to respond to the reaction of a city full of readers. "I'm writing my first draft in public," he says. "It's nerve-racking, but I get marvelous feedback."

Even on his "first draft," though, Maupin is working from a blueprint. "When I sit down to start, I have a rough idea of the journey ahead with little idea of the side trips," he explains. "I map out the overall theme, some sort of emotional resolution that I want for all of the characters. But there's enough room to surprise myself in the process."

At the same time that he's writing the serial, he's thinking about how it will work as a novel as well. "I'm programmed to write for both," he says. "I've learned how to do that over the course of four books. I know that some of the seams can be stitched together later." It wasn't always this way, however. A former reporter, Maupin launched the original series as an ongoing column with no plans for turning it into a book. Then Harper & Row senior editor Harvey Ginsberg spotted it in the paper while vacationing in the area and the first deal was struck. While the original daily installments had to be "severely reworked" in the process of becoming *Tales* and *More Tales,* the third and fourth books were "more structured for novels" from the outset.

Significant Others marks the first time that Maupin signed a book contract before he wrote the serial—one reason that he left the *Chronicle,* which refused to deal with his book agent, Jed Mattes. Even in serial form, it reads more like a novel than the previous books. "This time, I'm deliberately lessening the number of twists and turns in the plot to give the reader a sense of character studies," Maupin acknowledges. "Some readers object that there aren't as many cliff-hangers as there used to be. But when I have a novel in mind, I can't have that herky-jerky rhythm anymore. Now I tone down the cliff-hanger endings for the novel."

The story is "a different creature" in the different formats, he says, and both have their advantages. "The daily form lets air in," he explains. "People have 24 hours to speculate on what's going to happen, so they remember it in a different way. It becomes part of their own experience." The transition to novel form, on the other hand, allows the author to correct mistakes—such as a few inaccurate details in the Bohemian Grove pageant scene in *Significant Others*—which pleases the reporter in him. "I like to maintain some basis in fact," he says.

And the facts, when you're talking about the people Maupin's writing about, include sex, of which there is much more in the books than in the newspaper. While *Examiner* publisher Will Hearst did allow Maupin to include some fairly "mature" situations in the "family newspaper," many of the scenes will be racier in the book, Maupin reports. "Will Hearst is a child of the '60s, and he gives me free reign," he says. "Still, there are whole passages I'm going to embellish that simply couldn't be handled in newspaper form."

Sex and sexuality are central issues in all of Maupin's books, but are especially prominent in *Significant Others.* In addition to the AIDS-test vigil, the story offers the adventures of an adulterous Bohemian Grove member who ensconces his mistress at a cabin near the all-male jamboree; a pair of lesbians with conflicting responses to an all-female festival; and a gay man contemplating his first affair since his lover Jon, a character in earlier books, died of AIDS. Of course, all of the action occurs in the same general vicinity, and the various story lines inevitably end up overlapping and knotting up before the end. "I'm interested in the juxtaposition of characters—who's forced to meet whom and how they deal with it—the meeting of different worlds, through fate."

Significant Others' premise takes off from the "fairly natural instinct for the sexes to want to spend some time away from each other," explains Maupin. "The humor arises when they try to be rigid about it. It's not really a natural state to live with just one gender." He sees that as a relevant message for his San Francisco gay audience in particular. "Here is a town known for being all-male," he says, and while that attracts some of the transplants who come to live there (Maupin himself was raised in Raleigh, N.C.), it can result in an unhealthy degree of "male exclusivity."

A variation on that exclusivity is something that Maupin has carefully avoided in his fiction. "A lot of gay writers," he says, "lose their effectiveness by writing only about gay people," which can result in a "rarefied" atmosphere "that sends me running and screaming. I would like to see myself as part of the world at large." So, too, his characters: "The books show gay people in context. They give their relationships the blessing of heterosexual friends, and make them more real, I hope."

"The bottom line—the message—is acceptance, love and understanding," he continues. "I try to celebrate difference through the books, the way 19th century writers did, to show all the classes, the richness of humankind." That effort is directed in part at heterosexual readers, to assuage their fears or hostilities toward homosexuals. "The reader is besieged by so many combinations that you just see them as relationships." But he also feels that his gay readers have to be reminded that they need not be at odds with the straight world, and he finds himself in an "advocacy position of urging other gay people to be honest about who they are. There's still a lot of improvement needed in that department."

AIDS, he says, could be a valuable catalyst in the elimination of homophobia. "It's taken a thing like AIDS to jar people into discussing the one thing they want most to avoid." Writing about it in the context of his serial is not without its risks. "People stop me in the street and say, 'Don't you dare kill that sweet boy,'" he says. "I got into enough trouble killing Jon [the above-mentioned character died 'off-camera' between *More Tales* and *Babycakes*]." And while some may criticize his humorous treatment of the matter, Maupin defends it. "A lot of people have taken an unctuous approach to AIDS," he says. "Their solemnity is frightening—almost as much as the disease." His tone, he says, is "one step up from the tedium of real life. At the same time, interwoven in there, I'm trying to confront issues that people are having to deal with now."

Maupin is outspoken on the need to confront those issues, and on the responsibility of homosexuals with influence to apply that influence toward constructive ends—namely, communication. "The problem lies with the homosexuals in power who lead lives of deceit and through their secrecy imply that it's something to be ashamed of," he says. "I travel all over the country speaking to gay groups, but I spend very little time decrying the Jerry Falwells of the world. I point the finger at the closet, at the people who are making life hell for the rest of us. They hold a lot of people in their hands, because the degree to which people have been kept ignorant about homosexuality is directly responsible for our government's failure to take action on AIDS research."

Nevertheless, Maupin is encouraged by the dialogue about homosexuality that the events of recent years have engendered. "I don't see that anything but good can come from the stories about AIDS that have been in the press in the last year," he says. "The degree to which the subject of homosexuality has been opened for discussion is enormous. It has been demystified—it's less scary now. My goal is the day it becomes boring—the day it's just people and relationships, and we just leave it at that. That's what it comes down to, anyway."

Harry Baldwin   (review date 19 July 1987)

SOURCE: A review of *Significant Others,* in *Los Angeles Times Book Review,* July 19, 1987, p. 15.

[*In the following favorable review, Baldwin discusses the development of character and theme in* Significant Others.]

First, up popped *Tales of the City* in 1978, a collection of his serialized newspaper columns chronicling the hopelessly, comically tangled lives of selected fictional soul mates from widely disparate sexual, geographic and social orientations—and all this in a charmed, anything-possible San Francisco. There followed *More Tales of, Further Tales,* and *Babycakes* (a communal nickname). Now, almost 10 years later, Armistead Maupin's spool of labyrinthine plot, barbed-wire dialogue (that doesn't really sting long), and playful trend-skewering is winding its way unflaggingly on. Well, almost unflaggingly.

If you've been tracking and giggling over Maupin's jolly crew all along, no explanation is necessary; if however you come to *Significant Others* like a virgin, some explanation is possible. The first Maupin one comes upon is usually the funniest; still, this one strikes me as his most skillful balancing act yet in a self-limiting genre, especially one additionally limited by current events.

Most of the same crew reports in: the sweet gay hero, Michael (Mouse) Tolliver, the once-naive Mary Ann, now Oprah-Winfrying it on local TV; her house-husband and Michael's best straight friend, Brian (with a new *Angst* to grind); DeDe and D'orothea, rich lesbian lovers, and mother and step-mother respectively of Eurasian twins (see *More Tales*), DeDe's even richer stepfather, Booter Manigault, bastion of the San Francisco Bohemian Club (where white Republican males go to escape from characters like these), and Anna Madrigal, everybody's favorite enigmatic landlady, still dispensing sinsemilla and sympathy, if this time only on the fringe of the plot.

But what a plot. Let me clue you, Babycakes, this one has more converging lines than *Intolerance* and more curves than Lombard Street on a drug trip. Maupin, like a chess champion, moves DeDe and D'or one summer week to Wimminwood, a lesbian music festival (no men over 10 allowed) on the Russian River, Booter upriver to Bohemian Grove (no women allowed) for his annual reactionary hootenanny, and Brian, Michael, and an instant friend of Michael's to points in-between. Also along is Wren Douglas, overweight, beautiful, detoured to the river from a book tour by none other than Booter to be his temporary mistress. When drunken Booter drifts downstream toward Wimminwood while the lesbian security guards rumble, and while Brian falls on the ample breasts of Wren. . . . Well, you had to be there (if only in spirit) to track this bucolic chessboard that comes to resemble the landscape beyond Alice's looking-glass.

But, as in all midsummer night's dreams, the unsolvable dilemmas are solved, people are bedded, unbefuddled, and sorted out, each to his and her own significant other ("Your spouse and/or lover and/or best buddy"). I was anticipating a Thurberian battle of the sexes/orientations between Wimminwood and Bohemian Grove; Maupin concentrates instead on smaller, tamer clashes to educate his characters on the significance each holds for the other. Michael sums it up: "That's all anybody wants, isn't it? The feeling of being safe with somebody."

Maupin can then confront his biggest problem: How can he continue his comic saga about the sexual peccadillos of San Francisco gays and straights in this age of AIDS anxiety? The author like the larger society previously tip-toed around it (a lover of Michael's died in between books); can't do that anymore, dear, as Anna Madrigal might put it.

His partial solution is to reassign the sex (and the fun or the guilt of it) to the medically safe lesbians. (Michael ruefully comments early on: "If gay men could no longer snort and paw the ground in fits of purple passion, it seemed only fitting that gay women could. *Somebody* had to keep the spirit alive.") And the plot moving. A big chunk of the sex is provided by straight, promiscuous Wren Douglas. Is that why she seems less a fabulous new character than a large, obstructive plot device who doesn't pull her weight nearly as amusingly as, for example, Mabel, the hard-drinking gay Gabby Hayes at Wimminwood? (Mabel's scenes with Booter hold for me some of the book's comic and sentimental high points.) Poor, sweet Michael, who had already tested positive, rejects porno and safe-sex orgies for love; Brian, (after a hetero exposure) suffers agonies of fear waiting for his test results throughout the book, but finds his way back to Mary Ann's arms. You were expecting maybe "As Is?"

Oh well, Maupin isn't trying for Swift, or even Waugh; he's after affectionate fun-poking, not black comedy; skillful soap-opera farcist that he is, he knows that the deftest of souffles will flatten from too much of reality's acid. Let's give him credit for showing that AIDS is now an unfunny part—but part, not all—of his character's still laughable every-day lives and for solving, somewhat, the problem in his own sweet and sour way.

Adam Mars-Jones   (review date 8-14 April 1988)

SOURCE: "Crisis in the Beloved City," in *The Times Literary Supplement,* No. 4436, April 8-14, 1988, p. 384.

[*In the following review of* Significant Others, *Mars-Jones contends that the story lacks the "inventiveness" and "high camp" of Maupin's earlier pre-AIDS novels.*]

Significant Others is the fifth in Armistead Maupin's endearing *Tales of the City* series of sagas, about high and low life (but never depressingly low life) in San Francisco. In each book, Maupin plants a new generation of plot and character-seedlings, re-pots some mature blooms and thins out some others. He has the literary equivalent, in his wry, easy-going prose, of green fingers. He knows exactly when to be sharp and when sentimental.

If there is a break in the sequence, it is between volume three (*Further Tales of the City*) and four (*Babycakes*). The cause of the break can be stated very simply: AIDS. It's not just that the early books assume a high level of sexual exchangeability, without consequences, among the characters, though that is enough to give those volumes a period flavour. The first book of the series, *Tales of the City,* was only published in book form in 1978 (all the volumes were originally serialized in San Francisco papers), but reading it today is to feel like a Scott Fitzgerald character, contemplating the Jazz Age from after the Wall Street Crash with an unwanted wisdom.

More to the point, Maupin's technique depends on switching smoothly between stories. It is a technique that thrives on irony and contrast, but breaks down almost at once if one story-line begins to outweigh the others. A kaleidoscope can only contain so much black and still glitter.

Babycakes accommodated AIDS, but only in the past tense, with Michael "Mouse" Tolliver, the nearest thing the saga has to a hero, mourning the death of his doctor lover Jon Fielding. Maupin was adapting to changing reality. But there was relief to be felt as well as sorrow, since he was also writing off a liability: Jon was never quite believable as a character, and had to be taken on trust as Michael's soulmate.

In *Significant Others* the health crisis has made further inroads. Michael has learned he is HIV-positive, though he remains asymptomatic, and his best friend Brian finds that a woman with whom he has had an affair has come down with the syndrome. Brian, moreover, has swollen glands and a low fever; he takes the HIV test in fear and trembling, and waits the two weeks for the results.

Again, Maupin is doing all he can to be true to what is happening to his beloved City. If he leaves AIDS out, he must abandon the precious basis in reportage of his inventions; but if he lets AIDS too far in, his chosen tone of worldly sweetness cannot survive. It becomes obvious before the event that Brian will test negative, since only fear followed by relief can maintain the balance of the series.

So, too, when Michael contemplates his own health and the predicament of his city, Maupin produces some of his least convincing modulations. He starts on a powerful note: "It wasn't just an epidemic anymore; it was a famine, a starvation of the spirit . . . ." But soon he is cracking jokes about pornography (it "wore out" but "reactivated itself if you looked at it upside down"). He closes off the issue on a note that even the most besotted City-dweller must find inadequate: "The worst of times in San Francisco was still better than the best of times anywhere else." At moments like this, Maupin is clearly out of his depth—unless it is the genre that lets him down.

Babycakes had a sombre feeling to it, and although the mood of *Significant Others* is much brighter, Maupin's inventiveness has not returned to pre-*Babycakes* levels. The first three volumes have bravura plotlines that aren't afraid of melodrama or high camp: the first book features transsexual secrets and child pornography, the second a mysterious sect based in Grace Cathedral, the third (most memorably) a return from the dead of the Reverend Jim Jones. Since then the peaks and troughs have been levelled out, whether from depression or an honourable sort of self-censorship: a resolve on Maupin's part that since he can only let a little reality into his fiction, he will try to keep the fantasy similarly constrained, so as not to offer false comfort.

As a result, *Significant Others* has a narrowness of range that makes it seem almost parochial. Much of the book describes goings-on at two contrasting festivals, The Bohemian Grove, a holiday camp that returns grown men if not to the womb then at least to the security of a college fraternity, and Wimminwood, a jamboree of heavy-duty feminism. The adventures are only moderately amusing. The book is a relatively sober romp, a decaffeinated brew compared to the heady espressos of the past.

Andrew Lumsden   (review date 15 April 1988)

SOURCE: "If You Go Down to the Woods Today," in *New Statesman*, Vol. 115, No. 2977, April 15, 1988, p. 42.

[*In the following review of* Significant Others, *Lumsden describes Maupin's writing as "urbane" and notes his propensity for humorous assessments of both hetero- and homosexuals.*]

As I write this review [of *Significant Others*] I am babysitting—actually, he's nine—while Zak's straight parents go off to court.

And that means that I'm inside the world that Maupin has made peculiarly his own. Listen: at breakfast, just half an hour ago, young Zak gazed at me earnestly—for we haven't met in a couple of years—and said without the least animosity, "God had to make it a man and a woman in the Garden of Eden, didn't he? If he'd made two men, we'd all be dead, wouldn't we?"

Great Heaven, I thought to myself, as every other adult around the table looked at the ceiling, the child's acknowledging a memory of having very properly been told that I am gay. Or is the kid giving me gay paranoia at 8.30 a. m.? "Very true," I said gravely back to him. And wondered whether it was through school or home or TV that his echo of the old moral majority "joke" about "Adam and Steve" had drifted into his upbringing by sensible English straight parents. How do sensible straight parents ex-

plain the existence of lesbians or gays to children who now see or hear the words, sprawled across the headlines of papers or on government publicity, from their first dawning of consciousness? How do gays and straights muddle along together?

Significant others are the emotional partners for life, or for the time being, whom we choose to nominate when words like husband or wife won't do, as in the real world they so very often won't. The book of the title is the fifth adaptation (the first of them was *Tales of the City*) of a column Maupin wrote for the San Francisco *Chronicle* from the 1970s and now writes for the same city's Hearst owned *Examiner*.

Like a Peter Simple who is grown up, an enthusiast for human beings' strivings rather than an opponent of them, he has an imaginary cast of characters, inhabitants of the imaginary 28 Barbary Lane, San Francisco, who reflect the fads and the fun and the pains of pursuing that un-English obligation of America's Bill of Rights, the pursuit of happiness.

On this occasion, Maupin's cast of straight and lesbian and gay Americans are all off, for wildly different reasons and with ludicrous resulting contretemps, to the redwood forests, as if Londoners should depart for Epping Forest. There are male separatists in one redneck of the woods (right wing straight Republicans in luxurious summer camp) and there are lesbians at quite another encampment, Wimminwood; and others who float unattached, getting involved with both camps, all at last fleeing back to the city. Nobody escapes Maupin's affection, even the absurd and of course dangerously powerful Republicans. Or his dry sendups of all humanity's propensity to try to be more than human: "Edgar" (a little boy brought by his lesbian parents to Wimminwood) "had acclimated instantly . . . when his NCQ (Non-Competitive Quotient) was measured he had beaten the socks off all the other kids in the compound."

Maupin, our gay columnist, loves gays—whom he symbolises in the "mischief and sweetness of expression" of his perennial hero, Michael Tolliver—without disliking or failing to include in his, their, our world the sexualities and ups-and-downs of straights. This is *urbane* writing, to a degree quite unknown or acceptable to the English prints that might be thought equivalent to the *Examiner*. Go for it.

Walter Kendrick   (essay date October 1989)

SOURCE: "Serial Thriller," in *The Village Voice Literary Supplement*, No. 79, October, 1989, p. 13.

[*An American educator and critic, Kendrick is the author of* The Novel-Machine: The Theory and Fiction of Anthony Trollope *(1980). In the following essay, he focuses on the development of the characters and themes in Maupin's* Tales of the City *novels.*]

Eleven years and 2000 pages later, Mary Ann Singleton has finally arrived. Way back when, at the beginning of Armistead Maupin's *Tales of the City* (1978), she was a naive Clevelander who'd come to San Francisco for a week's vacation and decided not to go home. Now, at the end of the sixth and final installment, *Sure of You,* she's moved to New York, where she hosts a nationally syndicated talk show, *Mary Ann in the Morning. People* calls her "the new Mary Hart."

"The who?" asks Mrs. Madrigal (Mary Ann's ex-landlady) when Brian Hawkins (Mary Ann's ex-husband) tells her that bit of news.

"Just this woman on *Entertainment Tonight.*"

"Oh."

"I'll bring you the article."

"Don't go to any trouble, dear."

He smiled a little.

It's a seemingly casual exchange, typical of Maupin's colloquial style, but if you've been following his characters through their six volumes, you know it means the end of Mary Ann. Mrs. Madrigal doesn't care about her anymore, and when Mrs. Madrigal drops you, you'd be better off dead.

Not that Mary Ann didn't have it coming: there was something a little dubious about her from the start. In *Tales of the City,* she was the sole witness of Norman Williams's drunken tumble off a cliff into the Pacific. Granted, she didn't push him, and he'd been a child pornographer as well as a private detective spying on Mrs. Madrigal—but Mary Ann never reported the death, and she told the full story only to Michael Tolliver, her best friend.

In *Further Tales of the City* (1982), she helped DeDe Halcyon Day bury Jim Jones's corpse under the azaleas in Frannie Halcyon's garden. Granted, Mary Ann didn't kill him (Emma, Frannie's maid, shot him between the eyes), and nobody would wish Jim Jones resurrected a second time. But that made two secret deaths to Mary Ann's discredit.

Things worsened in *Babycakes* (1984), when she tried to get pregnant by Simon Bardill, former officer aboard the royal yacht *Britannia.* Simon's physical resemblance to Brian (whom Mary Ann had married at the end of *Further Tales*) would enable her, she thought, to pass off the baby as Brian's. She knew, you see, that Brian, the flaming heterosexual, was sterile; she'd had his sperm tested, secretly, and never told him the results. What she didn't know was that Simon, at his nanny's suggestion, had had a vasectomy.

Her scam came to nothing, but at the 11th hour a messenger arrived with Connie Bradshaw's baby, whom the dying Connie had instructed him to hand over to Mary Ann and Brian. Now, Connie was a high school friend of Mary Ann's she'd roomed with during her first days as a San Franciscan. Brian had once picked Connie up at the Come Clean laundromat; she was so terminally tacky she owned a Pet Rock, and . . .

Do I digress? I sound like a contestant in the *Days of Our Lives* summarizing contest. You had to be there—rather, you have to read it, all 1500 pages. *Sure of You* is being advertised, correctly, as a self-contained novel. The story

is touching, funny, all the things it's supposed to be, and all on its own. But if you've read its five predecessors, you feel a special warmth at moments like that exchange between Brian and Mrs. Madrigal. You feel it resonate across a decade.

Anyhow, it's impossible not to digress when you talk about Maupin's tales: he deploys his characters so skillfully, intertwining their lives in such surprising ways, that none of their stories can be understood without taking everybody else's into account. Mary Ann isn't the saga's central character (it doesn't have one), but her sojourn in San Francisco, from 1976 to 1989, defines Maupin's chosen tract of history. And her departure doesn't just mark the end of Maupin's tales. It means that, for him, an era has ended.

Mary Ann really hit the skids in *Significant Others* (1987). Sometime since *Babycakes,* she'd landed her own local talk-show—no crime in itself. However, in keeping with her new "lifestyle" (Mary Ann's word), she'd made Brian and little Shawna (Connie named her) move into a 23rd-floor apartment in The Summit, a glitzy high-rise atop Russian Hill. Of course, they couldn't conveniently bring the kid up at 28 Barbary Lane, where they used to live with Mrs. Madrigal, Michael, and a shifting assortment of extras; as late as 1987, it was still easy to make excuses for Mary Ann. Yet the two buildings had become symbolic of contradictory values, and Mary Ann chose the shabby ones.

From the start of the *Tales of the City* series, Maupin has sought to portray a microcosm in which every sexual bent— homo-, hetero-, bi-, trans-, and undecided—coexists amid comprehensive love and respect.

—*Walter Kendrick*

Her treachery in *Sure of You* stems directly from that move to the 23rd floor. The proximate cause is Burke Andrew, who appeared in *More Tales of the City* (1980) as a sexy amnesiac bent on filling in the three-month gap in his recent past (it turned out to involve an Episcopal cannibal cult, but that's another story). Now he's a hotshot New York producer, and Mary Ann secretly sells out to him. She dumps husband, child, friends, past, everything, for the sake of showing her face on national TV and lying to millions through her ivory teeth. The last we see of her, she's helping designer Russell Rand (who came on to Michael at a party) perpetuate the loathsome fiction that he's straight.

"You're one coldhearted bitch, you know that?" Brian snarls when he confronts her with his knowledge of her scheming. And so she is—now. Foreshadowings aside, she wasn't always that way. Not too many years ago, she fit in perfectly at 28 Barbary Lane. She laughed and cried with Brian and Michael, smoked Mrs. Madrigal's home-grown sinsemilla, and thumbed her nose at conventionality like the rest of them. But she changed with the times.

In *Significant Others,* Michael described her to his new-found love, Thack Sweeney:

> "Perky. Sweet. Ambitious. Too serious about the eighties."
>
> "Oh"
>
> "It doesn't bother me. She was just as serious about the seventies."
>
> "Are you friends with her?"
>
> ""Oh, sure," said Michael. "Not as much as I used to be, but . . .'"

For Maupin, it seems, taking the '80s seriously means turning into a coldhearted bitch. And at least as far as these old friends are concerned, he's given up on the '90s in advance.

Not only Mary Ann changed, of course. DeDe Halcyon and Mona Ramsey both came out as lesbians. DeDe still lives at Halcyon Hill with D'orothea, who used to be black, and DeDe's twins by the Japanese grocery boy; in *Sure of You,* the women have opened a restaurant in the newly fashionable Tenderloin. Mona, meanwhile, remains in England, still Lady Roughton, still tending the moldy splendors of Easley House; Teddy, Lord Roughton, drives a San Francisco taxi and frequents JO parties. In *Sure of You,* Mona and Mrs. Madrigal vacation on the Isle of Lesbos, where Mrs. Madrigal has a fling with a local man and Mona meets several lesbians. Mona, by the way, still thinks Mrs. Madrigal is her father. You see . . .

These characters—and Michael and Brian, all the good guys—have changed, grown, and suffered, too, but they haven't junked the past. And they never forget their friends, who mean more to them than family. At the whimpering end of the '80s, they linger a bit forlornly, perhaps, in a world captured by the likes of Mary Ann; at least since *Significant Others,* their best days have seemed to lie behind them. Nevertheless, they hold on to their embattled virtues, and they look forward. Even Michael does—though during the same dire years that transformed Mary Ann, he lost the love of his life to AIDS and tested HIV-positive himself.

Until Maupin supposedly crossed over with *Significant Others,* he had been categorized as a "gay writer." This amphibious species is said to write chiefly about gay life, for like-minded readers. Maupin's tales, however, have never been so narrowly focused. From the start, he has sought to portray a microcosm in which every sexual bent—homo-, hetero-, bi-, trans-, and undecided—coexists amid comprehensive love and respect. In the '70s, when gay fiction (maybe gay life, too) was full of all-night discos and pining for love, Michael danced in a Jockey-short contest; now he attends memorials and pops AZT. But Michael's is only one career among many. If Maupin's sparkle has dimmed, AIDS and the tarnishing of the gay dream can be held only partly responsible. He started by celebrating a generation's goofy, reckless freedom; 11 years later, he sees us all, gay or straight, going into the dark.

The easiest way of summing up Maupin's tales is to call them imaginative history: They show how some typical characters lived in a real place during a span of real years. Future historians, if there are any, will revere his books, both for the quaint attitudes they portray and for the ephemera they put on record. Maupin's era—mine, too—is the first in human history that defined itself by what it loved for an instant, then threw out. Future readers (if there are any) may require footnotes. Even now, I can hardly recall what a Pet Rock signified in 1976.

In this, I'm not so different from the despicable Mary Ann. When she digs Connie's Pet Rock out of the closet, late in *Sure of You,* she gives us on explaining it to five-year-old Shawna: "Well . . . people used to have these" is the best she can manage. I'm no coldhearted bitch, but I couldn't do better. So it goes with modern milestones. The plus side is that, very soon, the whole world may join Mrs. Madrigal in drawing a blank at the name Mary Hart.

The down side is that Maupin, who has tallied a decade's parade of trivia, risks being pigeonholed as merely the chronicler of late 20th century fads and foibles. Despite some evident limitations, he's done better than that. His scope is narrow: All but a few of his major characters are white, middle-class, college-educated men and women, between 35 and 45 years old in 1989; they spend little time on politics, indeed on ideas of any kind; if you called them airheads, you'd be unkind, not wrong. Yet it's a rare airhead who gets caught up in the labyrinthine intrigues that snare Maupin's characters every time the phone rings.

His characters may be shallow, but their stories spin like bedroom farces on a grand, sometimes global scale. Each volume sets up three or four plots and leapfrogs from one to another in a series of short chapters; suspense builds, until you're getting a cliffhanger every couple of pages. The plots range from improbable to bizarre, but Maupin lays them out beautifully. Just seeing how he ties up his loose ends (as, with one exception, he never fails to do) can make you dizzy with delight.

It's an old-fashioned pleasure, too; there's been nothing like it since the heyday of the serial novel 100 years ago. To savor the fun at full strength, I suppose you had to read the tales as they originally appeared, a chapter a week, in the *San Francisco Chronicle* and later the *Examiner.* (*Sure of You* is the only volume written to be published as a unit.) But tearing through them one after the other, as I did, allows instant gratification; it also lets you appreciate how masterfully they're constructed. No matter what Maupin writes next, he can look back on the rare achievement of having built a little world and made it run.

So eat shit and die, if I may say so, Mary Ann. I'll miss Brian, Michael, DeDe, and the rest; my only regret is that I'll never know why Mrs. Madrigal didn't tell Mona she wasn't really her mother. Father. Whatever.

David Feinberg (review date 22 October 1989)

SOURCE: "Goodnight, Mrs. Madrigal," in *The New York Times Book Review,* October 22, 1989, p. 26.

[*An American novelist, essayist, and critic, Feinberg was a member of the AIDS Coalition to Unleash Power (ACT UP). His final work,* Queer and Loathing: Rants and Raves of a Raging AIDS Clone, *was published near the time of his death in 1994. In the following review of* Sure of You, *Feinberg examines the influence of the AIDS crisis on the novel's characters and plot.*]

Farewell to 28 Barbary Lane. **Sure of You** is the sixth and final volume in Armistead Maupin's remarkable *Tales of the City* series, an extended love letter to a magical San Francisco. The first five volumes were serialized in San Francisco newspapers. A master of compression, Mr. Maupin crams information into short, delectable, addictive chapters ideal for post-Vonnegut attention spans. I know I'm not the only one who was up until 2 in the morning with the latest installment, promising myself to stop after just one more chapter.

Mr. Maupin juggles plots adeptly. In past volumes he has written lurid subplots including cannibal cults and child pornographers with clip-on ties. Along the way we've learned some of the mysteries of Mrs. Madrigal, the transsexual hophead landlady of 28 Barbary Lane; we've watched Mary Ann Singleton's climb to success from small-town secretary to successful television talk show host; we've seen her husband, Brian Hawkins, change from a promiscuous bachelor to a doting father; and we've followed Michael (Mouse) Tolliver from sexual escapades and Jockey-short contests to coping with his HIV-positive antibody status while in a new relationship with Thack Sweeney.

John Updike's Rabbit novels are time capsules of Middle America of the past three decades; Mr. Maupin's series is a set of sociological snapshots of contemporary San Francisco with a gay slant. There is a veritable potpourri of pop references in the current installment, covering freeze-dried pets, Freddy Krueger of *A Nightmare on Elm Street, The Singing Detective,* safe sex for lesbians, bare-chest contests at the Eagle bar, AIDS deaths disguised as liver cancer on the obit page, Madonna and Sandra Bernhard talking about the Cubby Hole (a gay bar) with David Letterman, Act Up, Pee-wee Herman and Jessica Rabbit. But Mr. Maupin writes for everyone: gay, straight, single, married, hip or square. His most subversive act is to write in such a matter-of-fact manner about his gay characters. There is nothing exceptional or lurid about them: acceptance is a given. By focusing on Mrs. Madrigal's extended family of tenants on Barbary Lane, Mr. Maupin is able to capture the foibles of modern living through a variety of viewpoints. His writing is light as a soufflé, whimsical, cozy and charmingly innocent.

At the start of **Sure of You,** the main characters have left 28 Barbary Lane; Mrs. Madrigal's "family" is breaking up. Michael lives with Thack in a house above the Castro, the gay section of San Francisco; Brian and Mary Ann live on the 23rd floor of a luxury high-rise. Mary Ann is of-fered a job in New York by the sophisticated Burke Andrew, a former lover.

"Burke, after all, was a practicing New Yorker, and the breed had a nasty way of regarding San Francisco as one giant bed-and-breakfast inn—cute but really of no consequence."

Through Burke she meets the Rands, a celebrated designer and his wife. She envies their evident style and questions the adequacy of her marriage with Brian. Without telling her husband, Mary Ann mentions the television offer to Michael and confides her doubts about her relationship. Michael, trying to remain neutral, is caught between Mary Ann and Brian. Meanwhile Mrs. Madrigal goes to Greece on her first vacation in years, with her daughter Mona.

Mary Ann and Michael have always been at the center of the *Tales.* I will admit that I have always been partial to Mouse. Still, I was amazed at how much I worried about him. Michael is taking AZT at four-hour intervals in this volume. When he forgets to call Anna before her departure to Greece, I was beside myself with concern. When he discovers the inevitable bruise on his calf, I bit my tongue. AIDS pervades the book. The mood is rawer, tenser, sadder than earlier books in the series, with an undercurrent of anger.

An author can take certain liberties in the final volume of a series. When the writer is no longer constrained by what may follow, anything can happen. Thus my agony was acute as I read **Sure of You,** knowing something irrevocable must happen. I can only say that Mr. Maupin does not cheat the reader, and Michael finally learns who his real friends are. Although **Sure of You** stands on its own, I urge readers to follow the inhabitants of Barbary Lane through the entire series: *Tales of the City, More Tales of the City, Further Tales of the City, Babycakes, Significant Others.*

I have no plans of leaving Manhattan for San Francisco, but I have to confess that I left my heart with Michael Tolliver. Thanks for the journey, Armistead Maupin.

Tony Clifton (review date 30 October 1989)

SOURCE: "Mainstreaming a Cult Classic," in *Newsweek,* Vol. 114, No. 18, October 30, 1989, p. 77.

[*In the review below, Clifton describes* Sure of You *as a dark finale to the* Tales *series set "in a city now haunted by AIDS."*]

Armistead Maupin is a jovial fellow, a witty gay writer who can even make wry jokes about AIDS—which he does in his latest book, **Sure of You.** . . . There is only one subject that annoys him, irritates the hell out of him, *enrages* him, in fact. It is the subject of The Closet, and the cowards and traitors still cowering in its darkness.

Sure of You is the sixth—and Maupin says the last—novel in his famous series chronicling the lives of characters who, like Maupin himself, were drawn to San Francisco from all over America. The first five books, starting with the frothy *Tales of the City* in 1978, were based on his daily newspaper columns, which described San Francisco social life through a fictional parade of people. The books became cult classics; the *Times* of London called them "the funniest series of novels currently in progress." The new novel is the first that Maupin has written from scratch. It is a much darker, tougher book, about the breakdown of relationships among his familiar characters in a city now haunted by AIDS. With the first printing of 50,000 sold out before the official publication date, *Sure of You* is likely to promote Maupin once and for all from underground humorist to mainstream satirist.

The new book introduces a character as close to villainous as could be found in Maupin's usually comic universe: Russell Rand, an immensely successful gay fashion designer, married for camouflage to a beautiful woman. The Rands represent the kind of New York glamour and wealth that finally entices the series's heroine, Mary Ann Singleton, into leaving her husband and child to become a TV talk-show anchor in the East. Maupin's alter ego, Michael Tolliver, berates Rand for staying in the closet, calling him a money-grubbing hypocrite: "You're just greedy. Keeping up a front while your friends drop dead . . . You could've shown people that gay people are everywhere, and that we're no different."

"That designer is not just my creation," Maupin said in a recent interview; he based the character on one of America's fashion leaders. "He's a hypocrite, and there're a lot more like him," says the author, naming a long list of Hollywood stars, sportsmen and entrepreneurs both male and female, who pretend they are heterosexual. "I really despise them for the way they cover up. What I'm trying to say is that being gay is normal for people like me, and a lot of other Americans. Just as it's no news if I say Robert Redford is a heterosexual, it shouldn't be news if I say a male star is gay. But it isn't like that."

Maupin (pronounced Moppin), a rangy 45-year-old with a bushy mustache, is quick to proclaim his own homosexuality, although he comes from a conservative family in Raleigh, N.C., who rather wish he wouldn't. By the age of 13, he knew he was gay; because nobody in his circle would ever have admitted such a thing, he grew up feeling completely alone. But he could, if he chose, pass as an upper-crust good ole boy. His résumé is perfect: he served in the Navy in Vietnam, worked for Jesse Helms at a radio station in Helms's pre-Senate days and was awarded a Presidential Commendation by Richard Nixon for his work with refugees in Southeast Asia. He was working as a journalist in San Francisco when he decided to come out of the closet. "A magazine wanted to include me in their list of the 10 sexiest men in San Francisco," he recalls. "They assumed I was straight, and I thought how ridiculous it had become. I said they could include me as long as they said I was gay."

Maupin first introduced his cast of whimsical characters when his newspaper audience was still living out the hedonism of the '60s. In his earlier books, boy meets girl, girl meets girl, boy meets boy: they make sure that their astrological signs are in synch and off they go, usually for not much more than a night. They smoke dope, snort some coke, go on to the next partner—and the next, and the next. For the gays, there is no sense of the terrible times to come; life is at its most promiscuous in the bathhouse capital of the world.

The characters live in San Francisco but travel all over the world, from the blue-blooded all-male Bohemian Club romps in the California redwoods to elegant English manor houses to a women-only camp on a Greek island (Lesbos, of course). There's a lot of Maupin himself in the books, and when Michael, in *More Tales of the City,* writes to his mother to tell her he is gay, it was Maupin's own way of telling his parents the same thing.

"I knew they would read it, because they were reading the serial in the *San Francisco Chronicle* at the time," he recalls. "My father later said that he suspected I was gay, and my mother knew because a girlfriend of mine had told her. They reacted the same way to the letter: my mother wrote to say it was killing my father, and my father wrote to say it was killing my mother." His mother is now dead, and he and his father "respect each other," says the author. But his father has remarried, and his stepmother, close to his own age, won't let Maupin and his lover, Terry Anderson, stay in the family house.

Anderson, 30, who runs a bookshop in San Francisco, has tested positive for AIDS (Maupin remains negative). They live together in a penthouse in the Mission district, which is filled with flowers grown from seeds sent them by a friend just before he died of AIDS. The disease is very much a part of their lives, but they will not let it overwhelm them. "It's very hard to tell you how it feels to be in love with someone who might be dead in six months," says Maupin. "But the knowledge makes love infinitely more exquisite."

Adam Block (review date November 1989)

SOURCE: "Out on the Town," in *Mother Jones,* Vol. 14, No. 9, November, 1989, p. 54.

[*In the following review, Block describes the tone of* Sure of You *as serious, noting the novel's concern with such themes as the AIDS crisis and homosexuality.*]

"The thing of calling something a 'black' or a 'gay' or a 'women's' novel: it sounds like some medicine that you've got to take," writer Armistead Maupin says, smiling almost wearily. "And that does a terrible disservice to those of us who are simply trying to tell stories about the real world, simply trying to include the people into the real world where they belong."

There is still a hint of North Carolina to the author's accent: a reminder of the world he was born into, and its distance from the one he inhabits and writes about in his witty *Tales of the City* novels. A young protégé of Jesse Helms, campus conservative at Chapel Hill, and unapologetic Vietnam vet in the sixties, Maupin, now forty-five, has emerged as an armchair anarchist who dedicated his latest book to his male lover in San Francisco and to his sister back in Raleigh. "I helped a lot of debutantes come out," says Maupin, "but Jane was the only one who ever returned the favor."

The transformation can be traced back to 1977, when Maupin began serializing his fiction in the *San Francisco Chronicle,* coming out quite publicly in the process. What began as a city sketch pad, offering comical cliff-hangers set amid the sexual and social diversity of San Francisco, evolved into a series of six novels chronicling an endearing, ecumenical cast of characters through tumultuous times.

Sure of You, the sixth and final installment of the series, focuses on the toll that yuppie ambition can take on friendship and marriage; on the way people live, matter-of-factly, with AIDS today; and on the overwhelming sexual hypocrisy that is widely accepted as the price of success. When it came time to write this book, Maupin explains, "I realized that I had never had my characters speak as strongly as I do, in interviews and my private life." He adds, "I felt that it was time for them to catch up with me.

"What bothers me most is the way that so many liberals still make apologies for famous people in the closet. 'That's his private life,' they'll tell you. This merely perpetuates the notion that homosexuality is some dirty little secret that sophisticated people are gracious enough not to mention. So, I created this character, Russell Rand— roughly inspired by a famous New Yorker whose homosexuality is so well known that this charade, played out by everyone from *Vanity Fair* to the *Today* show, is like a case of the emperor's new clothes.

"I wanted to address what I see as a new gay radicalism that has emerged as a result of AIDS: an impatience, a very natural impatience that emerges from the sheer day-to-day grind of living with an ax over your head. . . . That is why you're seeing this impatience with closet cases . . . people who got sustenance and support from gay culture in the seventies, who now have run for cover and expect *us* to be grateful when they show up at AIDS benefits with their wives in tow."

Maupin is brilliant at restoring the human dimension to worlds that have been concealed and demonized, yet he realizes he hasn't achieved the level of mainstream recognition that being openly gay is supposed to preclude. He has yet to prove the Russell Rands of the world wrong.

That may be about to change.

This spring, the musical *Hearts Desire* (starring Patti Lu-Pone, with Peter Gallagher, the cad in *sex, lies, and video-tape*) is slated to open on Broadway. Maupin is one of four writers who collaborated with composer Glen Roven on the anthology musical. . . . Caedmon Records plans to release abridged dramatizations of all six books, and Working Title Films (the British company responsible for *My Beautiful Laundrette*) has put in a bid for the entire series with plans to produce six two-hour films for release on British and U.S. TV. "The British have a much better track record," says Maupin, "when it comes to reflecting the rich variations of modern life. I think American audiences are hungry for the same fare."

Charles Solomon (review date 5 November 1989)

SOURCE: A review of *Tales of the City, More Tales of the City, Further Tales of the City, Babycakes,* and *Significant Others,* in *Los Angeles Times Book Review,* November 5, 1989, p. 20.

[*In the following review, Solomon remarks favorably on the* Tales *series.*]

Bedtime stories for Baby Boomers. Armistead Maupin's continuing saga of life in San Francisco began as a serial in the *Chronicle* in 1976, and his tongue-in-cheek depiction of the late '70s sex-and drugs singles scene seems as remote today as the misadventures of the Pickwickians.

Although the search for love and security in an increasingly uncertain world remains at the heart of this popular series, the tone has darkened. The three earlier books played relatively down-to-earth characters against such extravagantly silly plot twists as the discovery of the Episcopal Cannibal Cult in *More Tales.* But as the liberated '70s gave way to the grayer, grimmer '80s, Maupin grew more serious. He began to confront the AIDS crisis in *Babycakes,* which features his most sensitive writing; the threat of the pandemic and the responses it engenders dominate *Significant Others.*

Maupin also has lost interest in Mary Ann Singleton: The sweetly bewildered ingenue from Cleveland who was the main character of the first books has become a materialistic, upscale yuppie. The focus of the story has shifted to her husband, Brian Hawkins (once the archetypal stud on the prowl, now a doting father), and to her gay confidant, Michael Tolliver, who struggles to cope with the death of his lover and his own HIV+status.

Maupin's clean, readable style, broad sense of humor and flair for dialogue that rings absolutely true make these novels as difficult to put down as a dish of pistachios. The reader starts playing the old childhood game of "Just one more chapter and I'll turn out the light," only to look up and discover it's after midnight.

Harriet Waugh (review date 10 February 1990)

SOURCE: "City of the Plain and Not So Plain," in *Spectator,* Vol. 264, No. 8431, February 10, 1990, pp. 31-2.

[*Waugh, the daughter of English novelist Evelyn Waugh, is an English editor, critic, and novelist whose works include* Kate's House *(1983). In the following review, she examines the* Tales *novels, focusing on character and theme.*]

Armistead Maupin started his fictional—and mainly homosexual—saga of life and times in San Francisco in the Seventies and Eighties as a contemporary serial in the *San Francisco Chronicle.* In all, there are six novels chronicling the sexual connections and life-styles of the original cast of characters and their friends. Now, the last of these, *Sure of You,* and the first three, in an omnibus volume, have been published [in Great Britain]. For those who become insatiable fans, the other two are also available (*Significant Others* from Chatto & Windus, and *Babycakes* from Black Swan). The novels span the first gay (in the traditional sense) ardour of the sexually permissive Seventies, when San Francisco became the fun place to be if you were homosexual, to the gloom of the middle-aged, Aids-responsible citizenry of the late Eighties. Because it has been written as things happened, there is the added, slightly voyeuristic interest of witnessing social history in the making, which gives a depth to the colourful flutterings of the characters that might not otherwise be there.

As is often the case, the opening novel, *Tales of the City,* is the best. It follows the fortunes of Mary Ann, a Cleveland girl, on her arrival in San Francisco looking for a new, independent life away from her family. She is lucky to fall into the clutches of a mysterious, eccentric landlady, Mrs Madrigal, who owns and runs an apartment house at 28 Barbary Lane. Mrs Madrigal, who takes a maternal interest in her lodgers and tapes home-grown, neatly-rolled joints to their doors, has a past, and a dark secret. At the start I imagined that her secret might be that she was a lesbian, as her interest in her female lodgers seemed rather over-signalled, but it turned out to be more bizarre than that.

28 Barbary Lane acts as the domestic hearth for the characters as they forage in the exotic highways and seedy byways of San Francisco, looking for their individual nirvana. The hero is Michael Tolliver, known as 'Mouse', whose lighthearted attempts to find romance in the supermarkets, bath-houses, pick-up bars and 'gay night' skating-rinks mostly end sadly. He soon becomes best friends with Mary Ann after she makes the mistake of trying to pick up his boyfriend in a supermarket, and takes a kindly interest in her passage through the convoluted and over-relaxed mores of the city.

However, whereas Michael remains the same enjoyable, witty, sentimental fellow to the end, Mary Ann, setting out as she does in *Tales of the City* as Miss Goody Two-shoes with a heart of gold and an innocent attraction to bisexual shits, paedophiliac nutcases and amnesiac cannibals, develops, by the last novel, into a media monster trying to dislodge her gloomy husband, Brian, and adopted child from her star-spangled coat tails. At the start of the saga Brian is a low-life heterosexual on the look out for any kind of uninvolving sex. This culminates hilariously in a fixation on a woman whom he spies through binoculars spying on him through binoculars from a high-rise block across town, whose windows face his. A relationship gradually develops in which at ten o'clock every evening they do a striptease for each other, and more.

Bizarre events pile up on bizarre events. Michael Tolliver's brushes with death, which allow for a number of affecting hospital scenes (one of his main boyfriends is a gynecologist), do seem to suggest that Armistead Maupin intends his saga to be read as no more than an entertaining soap. Perhaps it is not particularly surprising that Mr Maupin has a cult following. There is considerable pleasure and addiction to be had from soaps, and the novels, although a bit cloying when read in bulk (rather like being force-fed chocolates), are very entertaining. No chapter is more than two pages long and things happen at great speed, though narrative tension is somewhat limited by this kaleidoscopic style of plotting.

By the last novel, however, the action has slowed down somewhat. A glum domesticity seems to reign, and the humour is overlaid with sentiment. What should be moving fails because the writing is not quite good enough, or possibly because Mr Maupin has a strong sentimental streak in his make-up which over the years has come to dominate his humour. But then he has lived through these times. Some of the characters die of Aids. Michael ends up HIV positive, and being homosexual in San Francisco acquires a socio-political dimension. Standing up to be counted matters, and you can't get glummer than that—or at least not in Armistead Maupin.

Nicci Gerrard   (review date 2 March 1990)

SOURCE: "Soap without Suds," in *New Statesman and Society,* Vol. 3, No. 90, March 2, 1990, pp. 36, 38.

[*In the following review of* Sure of You, *Gerrard praises the story as a "bright, funny, engaging and loquacious soap."*]

Writers—like Dickens or even Fay Weldon—have written newspaper serials which have then appeared in novel from; others—like Trollope, Anthony Powell, Catherine Cookson—have written novel series. Armistead Maupin has combined both, and become a cult. It is easy to see why. *Sure of You,* the sixth and final novel in his *Tales of the City* sequence—written in installments over the years—has a narrative as easy to pick up as *The Archers* after a long holiday, and as hard to put down as any good potboiler.

Set in San Francisco, *Sure of You* is about the contemporary life of the city as much as any of its inhabitants. Each vignette—the dinner parties in chintzy condos, the gay nightclubs, the AZT bleepers uniting strangers in bars, the celebrity gatherings where West Coast personalities feel like hicks beside their New York colleagues, the triangular trellis round which one character grows pink flowers (symbol of gay liberation), the journey that a mother and daughter make to Lesbos—fills in our picture of San Francisco. The novel is littered with specific contemporary references: the latest fads (like a realistic model of Jeff Stryker's Cock and Balls', clitoris jewelry, pamphlets about G-spot delights, or designer wedding rings); the latest changes to hilly street names; the newly fashionable venues.

Armistead Maupin follows the fortunes of its main characters through their unashamedly episodic crises. There is the TV chat show hostess, oh so sweet Mary Ann Singleton, with cute clothes, swizzly eyes and a greedy ambition that makes her—by the end of the novel—leave husband, unworldly Brian the lawyer turned nurseryman, and daughter Shawna for New York's bigger pond. Then there's Michael, HIV positive and in love with life; his lover Thack, proud to be gay, mordant and witty; engaging Mrs Madrigal (Mary Ann's landlady from previous novels) who wears her hair in spikes and grabs pleasure where she can; Mrs Madrigal's daughter Mona, married to a lord in Gloucestershire but looking for sisterly love among the tents at Lesbos.

Each chapter brings two or more characters together—

very often to discuss the others. For such a fast-paced and garrulous novel, there is actually very little plot. Apart from the frisky sub-plot in Lesbos, **Sure of You** is the opposite of picaresque: when Mary Ann moves to New York she can only re-enter the novel on the TV screen in a San Francisco flat.

The threat of Aids shadows the central characters' lives: Michael's former lover Jon (a ghost from other *Tales of the City* novels) has died of Aids; Michael's bleeper punctuates the episodes like a kind of narrative time-keeper. But in spite of its political messages and sense of life lived on the edge of tragedy, **Sure of You** is a bright, funny, engaging and loquacious soap. It is light entertainment, but never quite frothy. It is happy, but pulls back, in its final episodes, from any suggestion of the everafter. And, unlike so many other soaps, is never boring. Which is why, of course, it has run and run, but never dribbled away.

Tania Glyde   (review date 9-15 March 1990)

SOURCE: "From Bath-House to Bleeper," in *The Times Literary Supplement*, No. 4536, March 9-15, 1990, p. 258.

[*In the following review, Glyde favorably assesses the* Tales *novels, discussing the difference in tone of the first three volumes with that of the last three.*]

The daily column in the form of a story (no rumination allowed): it worked for Dickens, and Armistead Maupin, writing for the *San Francisco Chronicle*, quickly saw an advantage in the agonizing hurry to get each instalment out on time. Current events and absurdities could be skinned and fictionalized immediately. What Maupin calls "defenders of serious journalism" complained, but to no avail. In this landscape, there are no expanses of contemplative and plot-wasting sky. Everything connects tightly and tantalisingly. There is much for lovers of fiction (and soaps): love, despair (but not for long), idiosyncrasy and the death of the really bad, carefully mixed with the preoccupations of real-life readers.

From cock-rings to cruets, from *The Karmic Anchovy* to *thirtysomething,* Maupin has described thirteen years in the life of a city and its people. *Tales of the City* begins in 1976, when the bath-houses of San Francisco still thrummed with the fearless frothings of the happy. Heads or tails, you might say, are the choices where sex and dope are the forces of life, followed, at a distance, by money. San Francisco also seems to be full of escapees from duller parts of the United States. Maupin's cycle intertwines the lives of the newcomers and their landlady, Mary Ann, Mrs. Madrigal, Michael and Dede, with the rich and established of the A-list.

Flirting with the sentimental, the stories are full of companionship, support and love, as if the heart of San Francisco were a kind of up-to-date paradise where hypocrisy, and drug raids, are unknown. This feeling is set against the occasional grey missive from Michael's parents, archetypal Christian bigots from the sticks. A story-book morality is definitely at work here. A child pornographer falls off a cliff. A really unpleasant character burns to death when his car overturns. But reality intrudes as San Francisco

changes, over the years, from the Big Dildo into the Big Bleeper. Film showings are interrupted by a four-hourly shower of electronic alarms that remind the HIV-positive to take their AZT. "In this town", thinks Michael, "the Love That Dare Not Speak Its Name almost never shuts up." His words have a sadder ring after he tests positive himself.

The first three books, *Tales of the City, More Tales of the City* and *Further Tales of the City,* run to 1981, indulging decadeist reflections on what was and can never be regained. Then follow two more, **Babycakes** and **Significant Others,** before **Sure of You,** the last in the series, which takes us up to 1989. By the final book, Maupin's style has mellowed into longer conversations, in which careers are more than just diversions. The atmosphere is far more domestic, with no more providential deaths and outrageous undercurrents. The story rests on the up-to-the-moment dilemma of Mary Ann. By now a successful local television chat show host and married to an ex-Barbary Lane housemate, she is offered the syndicated big time in New York. She takes it, leaving husband and adopted daughter behind. She barely struggles, with herself at any rate, to cast off the last twelve years, cutting loose from the seat of all her experience much as she left Cleveland as a young innocent desperate to see the world. **Sure of You** is less exciting than the earlier books but fittingly so, as the heroes fight, whine, laugh and hug their way into middle age.

The dialogue, which carries nearly everything, is witty but not self-consciously comic, and a far cry from the nebulous verbalizing of so much contemporary fiction. Cameos abound: Michael slow dancing with a construction worker in Reno, the mailboy sacked for xeroxing his genitals and two lonely people's binocular relationship through their apartment windows. Maupin also knows the important trick of using brand names for social comment, though to the uninitiated many of them are meaningless. Although Maupin had to make some revisions when putting his columns into novel from, the idea, in the first three books, of printing them in their daily chunks with titles works brilliantly. The story moves quickly back and forth, creating suspense by forcing us to wait six or seven installments before returning to the nail-biting truth. We are looking at a country which could cut the sound of Dustin Hoffman and his son peeing in the television showing of *Kramer vs Kramer,* but allows Freddy Krueger, the child-molester of the *Nightmare on Elm Street* series, to romp freely in the imaginations—and pockets—of every one of its children. Bizarre dualities of all kinds keep life going at 28 Barbary Lane. It is not coy to refuse to divulge the *Tales'* many plots. The surprises give such pleasure that it would be sadistic to take it away.

Charles Solomon   (review date 14 October 1990)

SOURCE: A review of *Sure of You*, in *Los Angeles Times Book Review*, October 14, 1990, p. 14.

[*In the review below, Solomon remarks favorably on* Sure of You.]

The seventh installment in the popular *Tales of the City* series continues Armistead Maupin's chronicle of contemporary life in a romanticized San Francisco. Part soap opera, part *roman a clef* and part ably written contemporary novel, **Sure of You** is as entertaining as Maupin's earlier books. While Michael Tolliver confronts the permanent terrors of his HIV-positive status, Mary Ann Singleton, who began as the heroine of the books, succumbs to an insidious disease within her soul. She's turned into an uncaring, status-hungry yuppie. Even Anna Madrigal, the ethereal, stoned den mother who presides over 28 Barbary Lane, has given up on her. Like the earlier **Significant Others, Sure of You** is really about Brian Hawkins, Mary Ann's beleaguered husband. Originally a singles barfly, Brian has developed into an increasingly sympathetic figure, an intelligent baby-boomer grappling with the problems of growing older and growing up. Maupin has said **Sure of You** is the final volume in the series, but that decision is probably reversible: His characters, like his readers, may demand that he continue the story.

James Levin   (essay date 1991)

SOURCE: "Politics, Power and Pride," in *The Gay Novel in America,* Garland Publishing, 1991, pp. 288-89.

[*The author of* The Gay Novel: The Male Homosexual Image in America *(1983), Levin is an American educator, biographer, and nonfiction writer. In the following excerpt, he contends that* Tales of the City *presents homosexuality as "a single facet of the human persona" and an ordinary part of the social milieu.*]

Armistead Maupin's **Tales of the City** consists of interrelated vignettes that were originally printed as a column in the *San Francisco Chronicle.* (The work was so commercially successful that it led to six sequels.) Despite the humble newspaper origins, the tales offer pleasant diversions mixed with insight—more so than works with more prestigious aims. The short escapades describe the lives of young San Franciscans, most of whom are single; a few older characters and married couples complete the picture. About half are lesbians and gay men and most of the tales revolve around their efforts to find a genuine lasting relationship. Often this quest merely leads to sex. The married characters try to improve their relationships or supply what they feel is missing through extramarital activity. Some of the humor results from the bizarre intermingling of the characters.

Some of the ambience appears that gives San Francisco its cosmopolitan reputation, especially about sexuality and drugs. However, Maupin also has fun mocking the foibles of both heterosexual and homosexual elites. A marvelous description occurs of an upper-class ladies' meeting at which rape is the subject of discussion. Another clever scene is an elegant gay male dinner

> "So," said William Devereux Hill, III, passing the braised endive to Edward Paxton Stoker, Jr. "Tony and I checked the St. Louis Social Register, and they are NOT in it. Neither one of them. . . . And let's face it, honey. In St. Louis, it's not that difficult."

Maupin has an ear for contemporary dialogue and captures the distinction of gay San Francisco. He excels at finding particular status symbols by which Americans rate each other. By describing a piece of furniture, some clothing or a hair style, he manages to deflate some pretensions. No group or social class escapes this gentle satire, and many of the peculiarities of gay men are spoofed in the book.

Maupin's gay characters cover the range of professions from doctors to hangers-on. In terms of personality, they are often genuine, thoughtful, and wise; or phony, exploitive, and stupid; or varied combinations. The book admirably demonstrates that homosexually oriented men have a normal range of good and bad characteristics. While Maupin's work avoids the direct political advocacy of [Potricia Nell] Warren [*The Beauty Queen* (1978)] or [N.A.] Diaman [*Ed Dean Is Queer* (1978)]. it effectively shows that homosexuality is only a single facet of the human persona. Sexual orientation does not alter other parts of one's personality. By showing this truth, Maupin makes his own contribution to a more understanding view of homosexuality.

Micheline Hagan   (review date Fall 1992)

SOURCE: "Out of the Fog," in *San Francisco Review of Books,* Vol. 17, No. 2, Fall, 1992, pp. 5-6.

[*In the following review, Hagan compares the themes of* Maybe the Moon *with those of the* Tales *novels.*]

It's an airy spacious place, a penthouse cresting a Noe Valley hill, that Armistead Maupin calls home. Even on a cloudy San Francisco summer day, the living room glows with light from the expanse of windows looking out over the city—Maupin's home of twenty years. As an avid reader of *Tales of the City,* I arrived with a bounty of questions regarding his latest novel, in which he strays from his familiar San Francisco cast and setting and moves to contemporary Los Angeles to explore the trials of a 31-inch tall Jewish woman in Tinseltown. I had read the new book, had been assured that Maupin was still Maupin, and was anxious to discuss this new display of familiar Maupin themes. But first I wanted to know why L.A? —why a dwarf?

"I had a friend [Tammy De Treaux] who was 31 inches tall. I met her on a cruise, at a cocktail party, and we hit it off instantly. I was like anybody else—thrown at first and in love in about twenty minutes. The best way to describe her is as a sort of condensed Bette Midler: enormous personality obviously developed to compensate for her size, with a great loving heart and a terrific sense of humor."

Seeing Tammy's constant struggle to be recognized in a world none too receptive to her, Maupin found a parallel to his own experience as a gay man, and the inspiration for Cadence Roth, the main character of **Maybe the Moon.** He was well aware that people would be skeptical about the ostensibly bizarre subject matter, and that many would open **Maybe the Moon** in search of the familiar and beloved *Tales* cast. But he was ready for fresh material, something perhaps less "white bread" than the *Tales* series, a challenging new range for his voice. "I think in many ways the messages are identical," he says rightfully, ending with a light laugh. "I'm not sure I *could* turn a corner and come back as Dennis Cooper."

"I get a tremendous kick out of recording the flavor of the times and I didn't think it should pass unnoticed that there were hookers on Hollywood Boulevard wearing desert camouflage tube tops." And certainly one printable quality of Maupin's writing is his ability to deliver social message through intuitive, timely portraits.

"I thought, if nothing else, in years to come people will pick the book up and read it and realize that there were some people in this country who thought that it was barbaric for us to go over and bomb 200,000 people to no end except to protect the interests of an oilman president. Hopefully people will read *Maybe the Moon* and realize that being ridiculous lies not in being 31 inches tall, or gay, or a nonwhite American, but in hanging yellow ribbons from mailboxes to commemorate a massacre."

There's no denying that the book carries an agenda, or that Maupin always writes with an agenda, but he does so without obscuring the humanistic, empathetic intentions of his work. His agenda is one of feeling the constants in human nature, seeing the differences, and celebrating both. "The real message of *Maybe the Moon* is that the only true stars are the people who present themselves to the world exactly the way they are, and that should be the only true goal of any full-fledged human being. So many people spend a lifetime trying to be normal and end up tragically becoming that way. They succeed and it's the worst thing that could possibly happen to them."

While Cadence struggles against the Hollywood norm for stardom as actress and singer rather than freak-show attraction and costume stuffer, her gay friend Jeff finds himself playing mistress to Callum, a closet gay. "When he's lamenting the fact that stars won't come out [of the closet] she remembers that her mother used to wait for Paul Newman to declare himself as a Jew and was never rewarded in that regard. These are simply people trying to be themselves in a world that doesn't ask that of them." These are minorities in America struggling against their relegated closet roles.

"There may be people who think that my hatred of the closet comes through too loud, but I really don't care because I haven't seen that position taken in novels ever. Because there are a lot of gay writers out there, but very few of them are really attacking the web of secrecy that I feel keeps us enslaved. . . . To be against the closet is to have to stand up against very powerful gay people, and I think that's probably slowed my career to a certain degree, because a lot of people in Hollywood would have been much more receptive to *Tales of the City* if I hadn't been so openly contemptuous of their own secret lives. But I'm convinced, after nearly twenty years of being out of the closet, that the problem remains our unwillingness to declare ourselves and get on with our lives."

Since he completed *Maybe the Moon* in May, Maupin has been enjoying his post-writing period of respite, preparing for book tours in America and Britain and taking care of business, or rather, he says with a laugh, watching his lover Terry Anderson take care of business. He excitedly recounted the details of a production deal with Working Title Films of London. He and Terry recently lead British producers around San Francisco on the "Tales Tour"—a group of landmarks featured in the first novel. In Fall of 1993 the first of the *Tales* books will be aired as a limited series in six one-hour episodes on Channel Four in Britain. Richard Kramer, the head writer for *Thirtysomething,* is adapting the book for television and, as Maupin relayed with obvious excitement, "He's being extremely faithful to the text. . . . To see one's words become truly three-dimensional—it's an exhilarating experience."

So why not in America? "They're scared to death of it in this country, especially in Hollywood, because it treats homosexuality in such a matter of fact and innocent way. They don't mind producing movies for television in which tortured teenagers or tortured grownups are dealing with this terrible secret, because that falls right in line with their notion of homosexuality as the last taboo. They're tremendously wary of communicating the idea that same-sex relationships have strong parallels with opposite-sex relationships . . . But its actually a relief there's no Hollywood money involved because that means there will be no Hollywood censorship." Still, he is hopeful that the success of this series will help prod American producers out of their squeamish, adolescent treatment of sexuality, and there'll be takers after all.

Maupin isn't sure where his writing will take him next. "Terry and I bought a farmhouse in New Zealand. When we go this year it'll be our third New Zealand summer, which is during our winter . . . it's perfect. The weather's identical to Northern California but its flipflop so you get a nice San Francisco summer all year round." (Looking out to the fogshrouded city, he falls into laughter). "I've become so intrigued by the experience of being a gay couple living in this small rural New Zealand community that it *may* just show up in the next novel. I'm not really positive at this point. I like to let things percolate for a while."

Nora Johnson   (review date 29 November 1992)

SOURCE: "Everybody's Beautiful," in *New York Times Book Review,* November 29, 1992, p. 24.

[*Johnson is an American novelist and critic. In the following review of* Maybe the Moon, *she centers on the theme of discrimination and the protagonist Cady Roth.*]

Cadence (Cady) Roth longs to be a real movie star. But she cannot get away from her most famous role, as Mr. Woods, an E.T.- or Yoda-like character—in an electronically controlled rubber suit—in a hit science fiction movie. That this otherwise intelligent person does not understand why other offers are not rolling in is soon apparent to readers of Armistead Maupin's novel *Maybe the Moon.* Cady is a 31-inch-tall, fat dwarf.

Cady lives in Studio City, near Hollywood, with her airhead friend Renee, who is unaccountably happy to pay the entire rent, rub lotion on Cady's legs and lift her up onto chairs. Their dialogue is as snappy as that in a situation comedy, and like sitcom characters they live in a timeless world where nothing much matters but who had sex and who is auditioning for what, and there are long afternoons to hang out at the mall.

Though there are hints that the novel is a feminist parable, Cady identifies more with her many gay male friends than with other women. Intimately involved in their love lives, she describes herself as "the biggest fag hag this side of Susan Sarandon" and is more casually knowledgeable about S & M devices than one would expect of a woman who has to be lifted in and out of cars. "You look good together. I knew you would," she says after a successful matchmaking. She is less a woman at heart than one of the boys, everybody's tiny raunch confidant.

Cady represents not only a gay man, but all who must fight for acceptance—a mixed metaphor for the downtrodden. The most moving words in the novel are those that gay men would speak: "You spend your life accommodating the sensibilities of 'normal' people. You learn to bury your feelings and honor theirs in the hope that they'll meet you halfway. It becomes your job, and yours alone, to explain, to ignore, to forgive—over and over again."

In *Maybe the Moon,* Mr. Maupin's first novel since he completed his Tales of the City series, myths are the enemy. When Cady meets the handsome and incredibly kind Neil, who becomes her lover, she tells herself, "Don't objectify this guy. The black man as superstud is a dehumanizing myth." Nor should Neil objectify *her.* In case he hasn't heard, she tells him, "some black people see little people as . . . sort of enchanted. Like a good luck charm or something." Neil denies having ever heard *this* dehumanizing myth (Cady tells him Norwegians believe it too) and denies being affected in any way by her odd size.

The affair ends when Neil fails the blindness test; by not telling his young son the true nature of his relationship with Cady, he proves unable to rise above the reality of her appearance—which, annoyingly, is never really described. Cady "grosses me out," the child says, confirming what we hoped was not so—that Cady is no pretty little doll but a misshapen monster. When she mentions that *some* of her parts are normally sized, we are drawn into unpleasant prurience.

Cady's megalomaniacal ambition is to play herself in a movie about herself. Toward this end, Mr. Maupin includes directions to the set designer and, at the end, letters from a fictitious director and screenwriter who propose to turn these pages, written as Cady's diary, into a film (posthumously, for Cady dies shortly after a prank that she hopes will free her from her movie image forever). Both heap praise on the story, and the screenwriter makes sanitizing suggestions, such as removing interracial sex, dwarf sex and so on.

The screenwriter describes Cady as "this tiny, ambitious, infuriating, lovable woman who is both enslaved and ennobled by an icon of popular culture." But this theme is less striking than the one that lies everywhere between the lines: the challenge to all of us to see one other stripped of all racial and sexual myths and associations. Dwarf and gay, black and female are all equal under the sun.

This all may be ethically admirable, but as we strain to ignore appearance, as we struggle to rid our minds of all associations about groups of people and see them only in their plain, pure humanness, at the same time we wash away all their marvelous variety and consign all mankind to the dullness of perfect justice. It is the assumption that life is supposed to be fair that keeps Mr. Maupin's story on the level of situation comedy.

David L. Ulin   (review date 1 December 1992)

SOURCE: "Size Matters," in *The Village Voice,* Vol. 37, No. 48, December 1, 1992, p. 58.

[*In the following review of* Maybe the Moon, *Ulin contends that the characters are stereotypical and the story fails to mirror real life.*]

Back in the late '70's, Armistead Maupin came up with a truly brilliant idea: to write a serial novel, a comedy of manners that would unfold day to day in the pages of a major metropolitan newspaper. It was a very 19th century concept—Dickensian, even—but Maupin's approach seemed completely here-and-now. His intention was to take America's shifting cultural landscape and reflect it in a work that would feature a wide cross-section of characters—gay and straight, male and female, rich and poor—all residents of Maupin's beloved San Francisco. The result, *Tales of the City,* grew over the next decade from a local Bay Area phenomenon into a six-volume national bestseller and, ultimately, assured its author's place among the most inventive and light-hearted social satirists of his era.

Now Maupin has completed his first post-*Tales* effort, *Maybe the Moon,* a novel that takes on the myth and reality of Hollywood, where secrets are regularly guarded under the guise of "movie magic." That's the situation Cadence (Cady) Roth—31 inches tall and a former "World's Shortest Mobile Adult Human"—finds herself in. Having briefly flirted with fame, or at least notoriety, in the early '80s, Cady is forbidden by directorial decree to tell the public that she was the actor inside Mr. Woods, an E.T.-like elf who once took the motion picture world by storm. To further complicate matters, her best friend, Jeff, falls in love with Callum Duff, the former child star of *Mr. Woods,* who, at 21, is a lonely, closeted man, playing a cop in a *Basic Instinct*-type psychokiller film that has the gay community up in arms.

It's a set-up that's pure Maupin, full of delicious ironies and ripe for the tweaking. As usual, the author's portrayals of his characters' tangled motivations, their longings and desires, are right on the mark, especially in moments between Cady and Jeff, or Cady and her valley-girl roommate, Renee. And when Cady meets Neil Riccarton, a piano player who becomes her accompanist and eventually her lover, Maupin almost makes sparks fly off the page. Their lovemaking scenes in particular are handled deftly, with an easy humor that avoids the more obvious pratfalls which come to mind when we try to visualize a full-size man and a two-and-a-half-foot-tall woman having sex.

Despite its inspirational flashes, *Maybe the Moon* doesn't

take shape as successfully as *Tales of the City* did. Perhaps that's because Maupin has a less detailed knowledge of Hollywood, of its dirty secrets and hidden charms, than he did of San Francisco, a city where he's lived for over 20 years. Possibly he lacks confidence in this new territory, a literary landscape he's just learning to explore. Whatever the reason, his accounts of the movie business are often too stereotypical to ring true. It's a little tired, for instance, that Cady's agent never returns her calls unless he wants something, or that Philip Blenheim, the Spielbergesque director of *Mr. Woods,* acts like an overgrown child playing with expensive toys. Such images develop into black-and-white pictures of a world that Maupin has, up to now, always portrayed in subtle and luxurious shades of gray.

Then there's the problem of topicality, of **Maybe the Moon**'s relationship to the headlines we all know so well. Similar impulses, of course, were at work in **Tales of the City,** which, running in a daily paper, had no choice but to keep up with the news. *Tales* used front-page stories—such as the saga of Jim Jones and the Peoples Temple—to maintain its characters and plot lines within a recognizable universe, but those elements hardly ever got in the way of the narrative.

In **Maybe the Moon,** however, nearly every page brings a new political commonplace: Cady takes on Operation Desert Storm, "that nifty little Super Bowl of a war [we] all just watched on television"; she talks "about the scary new coup in Russia, about Peewee, about the white man's black man Bush wants on the Supreme Court." Even though I'm sympathetic to Maupin's politics, all the editorializing tends to trivialize his story, turning it into a snapshot rather than a reflection of the times.

That's too bad, because fiction functions best as a mirror, as something we can use to show us how we live. Such was the beauty of **Tales of the City.** Maupin clearly aims for the same universal quality in **Maybe the Moon** but, unfortunately, gets stuck on the launching pad.

Edmund White   (review date 5 February 1993)

SOURCE: "Larger Than Life," in *The Times Literary Supplement,* No. 4688, February 5, 1993, p. 19.

[*The author of* States of Desire: Travels in Gay America *(1980), White is an American educator, novelist, essayist, and critic. In the following review, he describes Maupin's dialogue in* Maybe the Moon *as "crisp" and discusses the development of both the major and minor characters.*]

In the 1960s, it was fashionable to define a work of art as a machine for creating sensations. If so, **Maybe the Moon** (a deliberately corny title invented by a Hollywood producer in the novel) is an extremely efficient machine for producing sensations of pleasure, suspense, pathos and a highly critical kind of irony.

Armistead Maupin is a consummate entertainer who has made a generation laugh with his six-volume San Francisco saga, *Tales of the City.* If this time out he's more cutting, the change in tone may be ascribed to his change of venue, from San Francisco to the much more dynamic, violent and hypocritical Los Angeles of the movies.

The heroine is Cadence Roth, a former Guinness record-holder as the world's smallest woman, whose greatest role was one in which she was entirely invisible and anonymous. She animated the styrofoam body of a lovable elf, Mr Woods, in a top-grossing film epic of the *ET* variety.

The text we are reading is Cady's diary, in which she evokes: her airhead, affectionate room-mate Renee; her best friend, a gay militant named Jeff; her Hollywood agent, the fast-talking Leonard; her black lover, the considerate Neil; and, finally, her co-star in *Mr Woods,* the eternal juvenile Callum. The tone is relentlessly up-to-date, full of snappy one-liners and *shtick,* Hollywood name-dropping, bitchy come-backs and celebrity gossip—exactly the tone out-of-work actors adopt to assure themselves they're still in the "business". The "diary" is also funny and intelligent:

> I found a copy of Rumpelstiltskin at Book City. I've been looking for a good one for ages, since it would make a fabulous movie and I'd be just right to play him. I wouldn't mind cross-dressing one more time, as long as my face remained visible. In this new version of the fable, which I read tonight, while I drank my Cher shake, Rumpelstiltskin is delicately described as "a little man" rather than as an evil dwarf. Such liberal revisionism is progress only if one prefers complete invisibility to outright scorn; I'm not sure I do.

Cady's vantage on the film industry is highly peculiar, since she is an anonymous star and, as a little person, is treated as a freak, even though her passions and needs and ambitions are larger than life. She finds her real place only in her inner circle. Within that circle a great deal of love circulates. It is Maupin's Dickensian gift to be able to render love convincingly.

Maupin is openly gay, but he cannot be defined as a "gay writer". In **Maybe the Moon** there are three gay characters, and the theme of being in the closet is a critical one, but the sympathetic gay character is absorbed into a circle of straight friends, and closetedness is seen as just one more form of hypocrisy in an industry ruled by greed and fear. Yet Maupin's experience as a gay man is everywhere apparent, in his humanizing treatment of marginal characters, his understanding of duplicity and his appreciation of the liberating power of honesty.

Sometimes the book veers towards a brassy mawkishness, but the sentimentality is always held in check by crisp dialogue, which serves to deflate everything exaggerated. Nabokov once said that he knew at first glance if a book was rubbish by checking to see if it was mainly dialogue. Reliable as his method usually is, it would have deprived him of the novels of Ivy Compton-Burnett, Ronald Firbank, Henry Green—and of Armistead Maupin, all novelists who work their dialogue with jeweller's precision and a playwright's deployment of dramatic irony. When people speak, they are usually either deceiving others or fooling themselves, and this grim little truth has not escaped Maupin's attention.

With a raffishness worthy of his improbable name, Maupin has created a funny, memorable character in Cadence Roth. Fiercely independent, unapologetic about her pint size and gallons of desire, combative, quick-witted, she is a person readers will recall long after all the topical references in this novel have faded.

It's no longer popular to criticize Hollywood. There's something priggish and dated about it, as though one were an uncomprehending member of the Frankfurt School who simply can't get with the charms of mass culture. What this novel demonstrates is eccentric America where the masses are made up of nothing but weirdos. The close of *Maybe the Moon* reveals how Hollywood inevitably banalizes its subjects. The miracle is that Maupin's demonstration is itself far more polished and amusing than the narrative he satirizes.

Adam Mars-Jones (review date 25 March 1993)

SOURCE: "Tweak My Nipple," in *London Review of Books,* Vol. 15, No. 6, March 25, 1993, pp. 21-2.

[*In the following review of* Maybe the Moon, *Mars-Jones charges that the story is poorly paced, the characterizations are lackluster, and the themes lack consistently serious treatment.*]

Armistead Maupin's *Tales of the City,* which started appearing as a newspaper serial in the mid-Seventies, and in volume form a few years later, are little classics of light literature: in their lightness they outweigh any number of more earnest enterprises. Maupin's San Francisco is a carousel lightly disguised as a city, a continuous party where everyone is welcome without any tedious obligation to fit in, and even the hangovers are fun.

To gay readers these books offered an extraordinary experience, of having their difference neither denied nor insisted on, but dissolved for the duration—far less of an existential branding in this jaunty utopia than, say, coming from Cleveland. Maupin was always a pragmatist rather than an ideologue (he waited until after his probationary period with the newspaper that was publishing the serial was safely over before introducing a gay character), or perhaps it would be more accurate to say that he was a pragmatic ideologue. With his deft braiding of characters and story-lines, he won an enormous and diverse audience. With the advent, though, of Aids, Maupin faced a greater problem even than most writers with a tacit commitment to chronicling their times, in however breezy a fashion. Aids attacked the central principle of soap opera, the democracy of problems, the approximate interchangeability of crises. What could possibly act as a counterweight to a virus that was not only fatal in its operations, but apparently discriminatory in its targets?

Maupin's solution, in the later, Aids-era books of the series (**Babycakes, Significant Others, Sure of You**), was to slow the carousel down. The earlier volumes had gone in for almost impudently assured dramatic plotting, featuring, for instance, transsexualism, child pornography, strange cults and the return to San Francisco of a Jim Jones reprieved from death. Now Maupin cut back on

lurid invention, and his focus became more domestic. But his work had always been defined by its airy momentum, and lost a lot of its distinctiveness when the ride slowed down, the bunting flown at half-mast. It began to seem that Aids was something that Maupin could neither responsibly leave out nor satisfactorily represent, but then the literary response to something so abruptly devastating can only be assessed by degrees of failure.

Now, with *Maybe the Moon,* Maupin has reformulated his fictional universe, choosing a first-person protagonist who is heterosexual, female and lives in Los Angeles. Of these innovations, the most crucial turns out to be the change of city. San Francisco, compact and well-served by public transport, provided much convenient infrastructure for the narrative counterpoint of the earlier series: the bars, neighbourhood shops, parks and launderettes where disparate characters could collide without too much contrivance. Los Angeles by contrast is a town of meetings and unlisted numbers, and above all—if you are a struggling actress—of waiting for the phone to ring. With ten times the area of San Francisco, it offers far less promiscuous mutual mingling of lives, particularly for someone who for a specific technical reason (being, at 31 inches tall, the world's smallest mobile adult human) lacks access to personal transportation.

Cadence Roth, known as Cady, is a dwarf whose showbusiness aspirations were both fulfilled and strangled at birth, ten years before the action of the book, by a starring but paradoxical role in a classic film for children of all ages, *Mr Woods.* She played an elf who transforms the life of a shy 11-year-old boy living in the suburbs, but she was enclosed in a suffocating rubber suit at the time. Not only that, but afterwards she was under strong pressure from the film's director, Philip Blenheim, not to reveal that she was anything more than an operator of special effects. Publicising her human contribution would spoil the magic of the film, you see, and he was bound to be against that.

The echoes of *ET* are pretty deafening here, though Maupin is careful to give Blenheim a physical description incompatible with Spielberg's, and indeed to refer to actual Spielberg once in a while, so as to establish that the fictional Blenheim cannot be any sort of intended representation of the *wunderkind* that was. All the same, the book's relatively modest disclaimer of fictiveness, unusual in both acknowledging and disavowing a connection with fact ('Although it was inspired by a real person, it is entirely a product of the author's imagination') and also its dedication ('For Tamara De Treaux/1959-90/Tammy phone home'), reinforce the suggestion of a link with *ET.* The film itself gets no mention in the book.

Perhaps Maupin can identify with his heroine's resentment of a great success that stifled her. The early *Tales of the City* made his reputation, but he can't go on writing in that vein, not because he has changed but because he hasn't, while the times have—and so has the City. Part of Maupin certainly gets to work establishing the reality of his heroine's history and predicament, but another part can't so easily let go of his own preoccupations. It's not just that Cady's best friend, Jeff, is gay and politically aware, so that he can chip in authoritatively from time to time on subjects that matter to Maupin, but that Cady's own construction of her position in the world is patterned on a gay original as if it was an ideological equivalent of a back-formation in language.

The analogy is explicitly made early on: 'Little people can turn up anywhere, just like redheads and queers.' (Cady is an insider confident enough to use words like 'queer' and 'homo' without fear of being misunderstood.) It's plausible that Cady should like the company of gay men, who never make her feel 'Martian'—whose sexual rejection of her, to put it another way, is reassuringly undiscriminating. It's a little less plausible that the should be so quietly up-to-the-minute about gay life, to the point where she never puts a foot wrong. Even her sex-play, when some comes her way, is gay-informed. She has learned from Jeff that some men like to have their nipples tweaked at intimate moments, and takes a chance on this exotic manoeuvre. It's a great success.

Some passages, though, read as if gay politics were being not so much absorbed by an intuitive fellow-traveller as projected onto his character by a writer straying a little nervously from his patch. When Cady wonders whether the rare man who fancies her is merely being kinky, this shows her how thoroughly she's been 'victimised by the semantics of the larger world'. When she finds a denatured edition of *Rumpelstiltskin,* in which the evil dwarf becomes no more than a 'little man', she comes to a resoundingly ideological conclusion: 'Such liberal revisionism is progress only if one prefers complete invisibility to outright scorn.'

'Invisibility' is a watchword in gay politics because it is in fact possible to conceal or deny one's sexual orientation, and so the absence from the media of a range of homosexual representations encourages self-oppressive silence. But dwarfism is a rather different condition, visible to excess, impossible to disavow (the book contains a closet midget, a full-grown actor who plays a child, but dwarfs don't have that option). It strikes a false note that Cady should articulate her feelings in a register more off-the-peg than made to measure for her. Her analysis of her situation is simply too slick to convince, coming from someone who gains no meaningful help from the one organisation that sets itself up as a support group, the LPA—Little People of America.

Sometimes it seems that dwarfism is analogous not simply to being gay but to living with Aids: 'When you're a walking bag of organs like *moi,* you just can't help wondering how much time you've got left.' Cady misses at one particular point in the story Jeff's dead lover Ned: 'In the last months of his life we spent hours together, playing cards and putzing in his garden and enjoying the unspoken irony that fate had made us equals of a sort. Ned and I treasured each other's company all the more, I think, because we both knew what it felt like to be living on a deadline.' Aids, the subject that so troubled the progress of the later *Tales of the City*—impossible either to accommodate or to exclude—here puts in an equally troubling return. The tone darkens uncomfortably, with the first mention of Cady's likely short span of life.

Many elements of the book in fact have the same property, of seeming both too serious and not serious enough—like Cady's silence-equals-death badge, in pink rhinestone. The tone of the novel is often rather unsettled, with a characteristic dilute spikiness, as of someone with a talent for bitchy observation taking care to rein it in. Cady's love-interest, who is also a co-worker (they put on entertainment at children's parties), has a living room 'that had almost certainly been furnished on a single Saturday morning at Pier One Imports'.

A later description, of a long-married couple, conveys the same impression of acidity brought artificially down to a more neutral pH: 'You could tell at a glance they were one of those couples who do everything together. I just knew they owned matching nylon windbreakers.' Artificial fibres in fiction always betray authorial judgment.

This is a couple whose daughter has just killed herself, an act about which Cady, who was making a film with her just before the suicide, feels both guilt and a queasy self-exoneration. But the funeral becomes a romantic excursion, and the death that occasioned it is rapidly forgotten.

The vital ingredient of Maupin's style at its best is pace. He has never gone in for pages or paragraphs that readers are likely to read again and again or get by heart, but specialises in a spry contrapuntal forward movement. In the absence of such momentum, which the single-strand plotting of *Maybe the Moon* more or less precludes, none of his effects quite comes off. Take a paragraph like this one, which ends a chapter: 'Like I've always said, love wouldn't be blind if the braille weren't so damned much fun.' With a brisk narrative breeze blowing through the book, no reader would dwell on this epigram *manqué.* But without a strong urge to move on to the next chapter, the eye is bound to linger that fraction too long, and the mind to do a double take. 'Hold on. *Love* wouldn't be *blind* if . . .' Such pedantic hesitations are fatal to the Maupin magic.

The experienced Maupin reader can even pinpoint the moment in *Maybe the Moon* when on past form he would change up a gear, or thicken the brew with a new and wholly unexpected ingredient. Cady is in unfamiliar territory, having a pee in the house of Neil, the co-worker to whom she is attracted, and who has just made her an impromptu and all the more satisfying dinner. The mood of the passage is mutedly lyrical, but then so it should be for maximum effect—or so says the part of a reader's mind that loves to be manipulated, that glories in its own susceptibility. Cady scans the pictures on the bathroom wall, drawings by Neil's son Danny, photos of Neil, family and friends. In the *Tales of the City* series, Maupin created characters who were not the gender they seemed, who were not the *race* they seemed. What surprise can he be working now?

No surprise. The passage continues with Cady reflecting: 'I felt such a part of him suddenly, such a perfectly natural adjunct to his life. I wouldn't make a big deal out of that, I promised myself; it was enough just to know it was there.' The reader is left feeling not 'Aaaah' but, thanks to a slight sloppiness of phrasing, '*What* was *where?*' The mood is sustained without surprises, and the section fizzles out. It's as if Maupin is writing Cady with his left hand, as an exercise (left-handers, reverse the polarity). He's an accomplished enough craftsman that he warms to it all the same, and produces scenes of considerable poignancy, but then something he reads in the papers fires him up, and then that restless, practised right hand of his gets in on the act. So he manages to bring off a scene of his heroine having foreplay in a swimming-pool, without undue coyness: she even breaks free of gay-derived technique, and uses her foot in a way that just doesn't work for couples of equal size. But only a few pages later, along comes something much closer to home for the author, and a real issue swamps these invented lives.

The issue is the film *Basic Instinct,* transparently fictionalised as *Gut Reaction,* a homophobic shocker that Jeff's new lover, a young movie actor very much in the closet, accepts a big part in. As the gay ideologue and the closet case confront each other, a novel that has put a low priority on tension briefly crackles with it. Cady's role in the confrontation is to keep the peace ('For all I knew, he had a valid point, but he'd picked a crummy time to make it'), but the book's centre of gravity has certainly moved away, for the duration of the scene, from its narrator.

The underlying conceit of **Maybe the Moon** is that Cady writes a diary, at the instigation of her roommate Renee, with a view to starring in the movie version of her life. The book then ends with an exchange of letters between Philip Blenheim and Dianne Hartwig, director and screenwriter respectively of *Mr Woods,* in which they plan to make a very different film from this raw material, one in which Cady's life is thoroughly sweetened and trivialised. (Rather perversely on Maupin's part, they consider disguising the elf, in their fictionalised film, as an extraterrestrial.)

This sort of final ironising twist isn't really in Armistead Maupin's line, and perhaps wouldn't have occurred to him if Cady's story had properly taken off. But the mixture has never quite jelled. There's more of the reality-principle here than the genre can hold, a mortal sigh inside the soap-bubble. At first, for instance, Cady is a great success at children's parties, but when her novelty has worn off her grotesqueness remains (Maupin doesn't take the easy way out of having a heroine who is a midget rather than a dwarf) and makes people uncomfortable.

Escapism is a precarious business, since we are doomed to carry with us, no matter where, those things from which we want to escape. The subject of Aids is what Armistead Maupin is trying to get away from with his new heroine and new city, but though the epidemic is barely present in the book it still seems to inhibit his loss of himself in his story, like the speck of yolk that makes it impossible to beat egg whites to full fluffiness. There is a heart-heaviness about **Maybe the Moon** that makes this colourful balloon hug the ground.

Armistead Maupin   (essay date 8-14 January 1994)

SOURCE: "A Tale of the '70s," in *TV Guide* Magazine, Vol. 42, No. 2, January 8-14, 1994, pp. 26-8.

[*In the following essay, Maupin discusses the creation and development of the* Tales of the City *series from newspaper serial to novel to television miniseries.*]

PBS—famous for such British-made epic dramas as *Upstairs, Downstairs; Brideshead Revisited;* and *The Jewel in the Crown*—will broadcast yet another this week: *Armistead Maupin's Tales of the City,* a sweeping period saga whose literary origins can be traced directly to the vegetable department of a San Francisco supermarket.

Let me back up a little.

It was 1974. I'd come to the local Safeway as a reporter for a weekly paper to follow up on a tip I'd received. According to my source, hordes of "swinging singles"—as we once so quaintly called them—descended upon the store every Wednesday night in search of romance.

Sure enough, the place was overflowing with dudes in puka shells and eager young women in rhinestone-studded, brushed-denim pantsuits. The veggie section seemed particularly active, so I headed there, full of probing questions: When did this all begin? What's the best pickup line? Why Wednesday night? For some reason, no one would talk to me.

I settled on a fictional shopper to explain the phenomenon to my readers. I named her Mary Ann Singleton (as in "single town") and made her a reluctant but hopeful participant in the Safeway mating ritual. After several grim encounters, she meets the man of her dreams by the snow peas—only to discover that he's there with the man of *his* dreams.

The story was a hit. It struck such a nerve with single women, in fact, that I was asked to submit more episodes, following Ms. Singleton on her various adventures as a new girl in town. When the paper folded five weeks later, the most vocal protests came from readers wondering what had happened to Mary Ann.

Encouraged by this response, I eventually pitched the idea of a daily serial to the editors of the *San Francisco Chronicle.* To my amazement, they accepted, so in 1976 *Tales of the City* was launched, and I was faced with the daunting prospect of writing 800 words a day.

I brought back Mary Ann, of course, and found her a nice place to live: a rambling old wooden apartment house with a partial view of the bay. Her landlady, Mrs. Madrigal, was a motherly middleaged free spirit with a cloudy past and a fondness for naming the marijuana plants she grew in her garden.

The other tenants at 28 Barbary Lane were Mona Ramsey, a bright, Brillo-haired cynic learning to lower her expectations: Brian Hawkins, an amiable but amoral lawyer-turned-waiter who picks up women in laundromats; and Norman Neal Williams, an awkward, fortyish outsider partial to clip-on ties. Six weeks into the series they were joined by Michael "Mouse" Tolliver—a sentimental young Southerner who is unapologetically gay. His arrival was a source of grave concern at the newspaper. Expecting a backlash from suburban subscribers, my editors held their breath, mumbling dire warnings about "the limits of tolerance."

> **When I collected *Tales of the City* into a novel of the same name in 1978, I found people all over the world who could relate to my characters.**
>
> **—*Armistead Maupin***

They were dead wrong. In fact, when Michael met a handsome gynecologist at a roller rink and brought him home to Barbary Lane, suburban housewives actually wrote me to say how much they wanted the romance to succeed.

As the series progressed, my characters took on minds of their own. I was almost as surprised as my readers when Mrs. Madrigal herself, normally such a homebody, embarked on a tender love affair with a most unlikely suitor.

Tales succeeded in a way I'd never dreamed. Reading installments aloud became a watercooler ritual, and readers whose newspapers had been mangled by a neighborhood dog or drenched in a downpour wrote to tell me how frantic they'd been to find a replacement.

For a long time I attributed all this madness to local chauvinism, but I was happily mistaken. When I collected *Tales of the City* into a novel of the same name in 1978 (with five more to follow in the '80s), I found people all over the world who could relate to my characters. Fans at book signings in Sydney or Edinburgh or Iowa City would introduce their friends to me as "my Mary Ann" or "my Brian" or "our Mrs. Madrigal." The novels had become a kind of shorthand for explaining the dynamics of their own free-form urban families.

When Warner Bros. took an option on *Tales* in 1979, I celebrated by having a T-shirt made that said "Soon To Be A Major Motion Picture"—a hugely premature act, if ever there was one. Within days studio executives began to let me know that "certain minor adjustments" would be required before the property could be offered to the American public.

Michael Tolliver, for instance, was OK for a campy walk-on but could never be shown in an intimate moment with another man. Furthermore, Mrs. Madrigal's friendly practice of taping joints to her tenants' doors might have been acceptable on the printed page but would not do on the screen. In other words, they wanted my intricate plotlines but not the non-judgmental spirit that had rendered them interesting in the first place.

I met with similar squeamishness when HBO acquired the property in the early '80s. By then, Reaganism was in full bloom and the onset of the AIDS epidemic had created an ugly backlash in Hollywood against anything regarded as remotely gay. After several excruciating attempts at "updating" the material, *Tales* was eventually shelved. Over

the next decade, the property was rejected by every major network and studio in Hollywood. I finally resigned myself to the notion that my work would never be translated into film.

Then, in the early '90s, only weeks after I'd ended the series, help arrived from a most unlikely source. Channel 4, the British network that commissioned the films *Howards End* and *The Crying Game* agreed to fully fund a six-hour miniseries. Even more miraculously, the story would be filmed exactly as written, with its loopy '70s spirit intact in an eloquent and poignantly funny script by Richard Kramer of *thirtysomething* fame. Filming took place last spring in Los Angeles and San Francisco with a remarkable American cast headed by Olympia Dukakis as Mrs. Madrigal. *Tales* was broadcast in Britain last fall to critical and popular acclaim, prompting PBS's *American Playhouse* to obtain the U.S. rights.

Looking back on these past two decades of false starts, I realize there was never a better time than the present for *Tales* to reach television The '70s, after all, are back in a big way. Teenagers have embraced the era's garish clothes and music and its live-and-let-live doctrines as if they'd been invented yesterday. And some adults who once trashed the '70s with a vengeance have begun to admit to a growing nostalgia for a time when status wasn't everything and sex wasn't potentially fatal.

So, *Tales of the City,* once so relentlessly "now," finally found its niche as a costume drama about a simpler time, an extended joy ride into the past.

If you'd like to come along, I'll meet you in the vegetable department.

FURTHER READING

Biography

Gillespie, Elgy. "Armistead Maupin at Tale's End." *San Francisco Review of Books* 14, No. 3 (Winter 1989-1990): 18-20.
   Discusses Maupin's early life, his military career and work as a reporter, the evolution of the stories that became the *Tales of the City,* and his views on homosexuality.

Criticism

Barker, Michael. Review of *Tales of the City,* by Armistead Maupin. *Books and Bookmen,* No. 35 (August 1984): 22.
   Favorable review of *Tales of the City.*

Biemiller, Lawrence. "Memoirs of a Midget." *Book World—The Washington Post* (22 November 1992): 11.
   Mixed assessment of *Maybe the Moon,* focusing on character development and themes.

Degnan, James P. "Cowboy and Crazies: The American West, Then and Now." *The Hudson Review* XXXIII, No. 1 (Spring 1980): 146-50.
   Reviews several books about California, including Maupin's *Tales of the City.* Degnan contends that

Maupin's themes of alienation and nonconformism are "tiresome."

Olson, Ray. Review of *Significant Others,* by Armistead Maupin. *Booklist* 84, No. 1 (1 September 1987): 28.

Describes the plot and characters of *Significant Others* as engaging, warm and witty, with believable dialogue.

————. Review of *28 Barbary Lane: A Tales of the City Omnibus* and *Back to Barbary Lane: The Final Tales of the City Omnibus,* by Armistead Maupin. *American Libraries* 23, No. 6 (June 1992): 536.

Favorable assessment of the complete *Tales* series.

Review of *28 Barbary Lane: A Tales of the City Omnibus,* by Armistead Maupin. *Virginia Review Quarterly* 67, No. 2 (Spring 1991): 67.

Overview of *28 Barbary Lane.*

House Made of Dawn

N. Scott Momaday

(Full name Navarre Scott Momaday; also rendered as Navarro and Novarro) American novelist, poet, autobiographer, nonfiction writer, editor, and artist.

The following entry presents criticism on Momaday's novel *House Made of Dawn* (1968). For further information on his life and works, see *CLC,* Volumes 2, 19, and 85.

INTRODUCTION

Of Kiowa descent, Momaday is widely recognized as one of the most successful contemporary Native American literary figures. Considered a major influence by numerous Native writers, he has garnered critical acclaim for his focus on Kiowa traditions, customs, and beliefs, and the role of Amerindians in contemporary society. Although highly regarded for *House Made of Dawn* (1968), Momaday considers himself primarily a poet. All of his writings, however, are greatly influenced by the oral tradition and typically concern the nature and origins of Native American myths. *House Made of Dawn* received the Pulitzer Prize for fiction in 1969. It was the first novel written by an American Indian author to be so recognized, and its publication along with the award initiated what has come to be called a Native American Renaissance of literature.

Plot and Major Characters

The action of *House Made of Dawn* takes place between July 20, 1945, and February 28, 1952. The narration comprises an undated prologue and four dated portions set in the Jemez pueblo of Walatowa, New Mexico (the prologue and sections one and four take place here) and the Los Angeles area (sections two and three). After the brief prologue which describes a young man running, the story proper opens on July 20, 1945, when a young man named Abel, an orphan raised by his traditionalist grandfather, Francisco, returns to Walatowa after serving in the second world war. Alienated and disorganized by war experiences (and also, it is suggested, by the early loss of his mother and brother and previous bouts of malaise), Abel is unable to make a meaningful reintegration into the life of the village. He takes a temporary job cutting wood for Angela St. John, a troubled, sensuous visitor to the area, and has an affair with her. He participates in a village festival and is singled out by a strange, ominous-appearing albino man. Meanwhile, the omniscient narration follows a parallel line with the village priest, Father Olguin, as he studies the diary of his predecessor, Fray Nicolas. On August 1, Abel stabs the albino to death in a cornfield. This section of the story ends the next day with Abel's grandfather Francisco, again alone, hoeing his fields.

The two parts of the second section are dated January 27

and 28, 1952. This section takes place in Los Angeles and centers on the character of Tosamah, a Kiowa storefront preacher and believer in the divine properties of peyote, a hallucinogenic drug. The January 27 section contains the first of two sermons by Tosamah, a long discourse on a verse from the Gospel of John: "In the beginning was the Word." Tosamah maintains that language has been debased by white people and its power lost or corrupted. At the time that Tosamah is giving this sermon, Abel appears to be lying miles away, barely conscious after having suffered a terrible beating that has disabled his hands. The omniscient narrator moves back and forth in time presenting fragments of Abel's past: filling out forms in prison or afterwards; meetings with an earnest social worker, Milly, with whom he has an affair; life in prison; and testimony at his trial by Father Olguin and by a friend of his from the army. This section also contains a depiction of a peyote ceremony and introduces Ben Benally, who will play a significant part in Abel's eventual apparent rehabilitation. The January 28 section is composed almost entirely of Tosamah's second sermon, a passage in which Momaday meditates on his Kiowa grandmother's life and the history and passing of the magnificent Kiowa culture. (This piece was previously published as an essay in *Ramparts* magazine and was later incorporated into Momaday's autobiographical work, *The Way To Rainy Mountain* [1969].)

The third section is dated February 20, 1952, and is narrated by Benally. His rambling narration includes references to more of Abel's life in Los Angeles: his job at a box-stapling factory, his encounters with a sadistic policeman named Martinez, his participation in peyote services, and their occasional socializing with Milly. Benally also recollects the recent encounter with Angela St. John, who visited Abel in the hospital as he was recovering from the beating that left his hands broken; Angela, now the mother of a son, told Abel a story with a heroic theme, intimating that he reminded her of the hero. Benally also recollects going with Abel to a party in the hills outside the city on the night before Abel was to leave; Benally recalls that at this time he sang traditional songs from Navajo healing ceremonies, including the verses beginning the actual Navajo song called "House Made of Dawn."

The fourth section of the novel is very brief, comprising two sections dated February 27 and February 28, 1952. Abel returns to Walatowa in time to perform the appropriate burial rituals for his grandfather. Having seen to this duty, he begins to run into the dawn. The novel has moved in a circle, returning to the event depicted in the prologue.

Major Themes

House Made of Dawn takes its title from a translation of a Navajo song which is part of an extensive religious ceremony. The text of the translation is included in the novel as a song sung by Benally. The house referred to in has been identified as one of the prehistoric cliff dwellings along the upper Rio Grande, and the song alludes to it as the home of the semi-divine personification of the dawn. Throughout the novel, important events and insights occur at dawn or sunrise. Also, throughout the novel Momaday incorporates ceremonial, mythical, and anthropological material from three different American Indian nations—Jemez Pueblo, Kiowa, and Navajo—into the texture of the contemporary story of psychological disintegration and renewal. *House Made of Dawn* is narratively complex, constructed on a principle of fragmentation and reconstitution somewhat like the modernist poems of Ezra Pound and T. S. Eliot, which Momaday studied with noted American poet and critic Yvor Winters while in college and graduate school. The story has a circular rather than linear or strictly chronological structure: the prologue that begins it actually depicts the closing event of the book, and within each section linear time is reshaped through the wandering thought patterns of the narrators and central consciousness. Moreover, within the story are inserted various non-narrative verbal forms: besides the translated poem text mentioned above, there is another translated poem, fragments purporting to be the diary of a priest, pieces of bureaucratic/legal documents and testimony, and folk tales and legends. The reader's attention is repeatedly drawn away from the story and toward the author's literary devices.

Critical Reception

Consistently praised for his exploration of Kiowa concerns and traditions, Momaday is a seminal figure in both mainstream American and Native literature. *House Made of Dawn* is frequently taught in literature courses, and critics note that all his works are of great importance to Native and non-Native students alike. Momaday's blending of ancient and traditional material with contemporary and modernist techniques has reminded many critics of James Joyce, who combined Catholic religious and Irish political contexts with parallels to classical Greek mythology in such works as *A Portrait of the Artist as a Young Man* (1916) and *Ulysses* (1922). Also, Momaday's use in *House Made of Dawn* of a fragmented, stream-of-consciousness narrative style, multiple narrative voices, and flashbacks have earned him favorable comparisons with American novelist William Faulkner. Alan R. Velie has observed: "Momaday's achievement in *House Made of Dawn* is significant. He was able to employ the rhythms and imagery of his verse in creating a prose style that is both lyrical and powerful. It is no mean achievement to make the self-destructive, alcoholic Abel a sympathetic and complex character, or to portray the dusty pueblo of Jemez as a beautiful and exotic place. . . . *House Made of Dawn*, Momaday's first literary success, is also his masterpiece."

PRINCIPAL WORKS

The Complete Poems of Frederick Goddard Tuckerman [editor] (poetry) 1965
The Journey of Tai-me (folktales) 1967
House Made of Dawn (novel) 1968
The Way to Rainy Mountain (autobiography) 1969
Colorado: Summer, Fall, Winter, Spring (nonfiction) 1973
Angle of Geese, and Other Poems (poetry) 1974
The Gourd Dancer (poetry) 1976
The Names: A Memoir (autobiography) 1976
The Ancient Child (novel) 1989
In the Presence of the Sun: Stories and Poems, 1961-1991 (stories and poems) 1993

CRITICISM

John Z. Bennett (review date Spring 1970)

SOURCE: A review of *House Made of Dawn*, in *Western American Literature*, Vol. V, No. 1, Spring, 1970, p. 69.

[*In the following review, Bennett praises the literary and sociological aspects of* House Made of Dawn.]

In academe, where there is a growing tendency to employ literary works as casebooks for social protest or ethnic studies, **House Made of Dawn** may encounter a curious fate. Because it deals with an interesting variation of the old alienation-theme, namely, the Southwest Indians' conflict with twentieth century America, Momaday's novel may be valued as a social statement rather than as a substantial artistic achievement.

The sociological bias, of course, is insidious insomuch as it tends to reduce the literary work to its thematic clichés: in this case, the Indian hero's ruinous journeys into the white man's world, to war, to prison, to the monolithic city, Los Angeles, and his evident redemption in a return to the old ways; the inevitable "civilized" woman, Angela St. John, who discovers the primordial life-force in Indian ceremonials and in the wilderness; and the grandparents who are the last links to the old varieties.

These are the commonplaces of the alienation-theme; but the fact is that the novel clearly transcends them. Through a remarkable synthesis of poetic mode and profound emotional and intellectual insight into the Indians' perduring human status, Momaday's novel becomes at last the very act it is dramatizing, an artistic act, a "creation-hymn."

Yet even where social consciousness is significant in the novel, Momaday is far from being simplistic or unilateral, as a didactic reading might require. On the contrary, his polarities—animism and the machine—comprehend very complex and intricate human values. For example, the white man's world, as Benally the Navaho tells us, is not without its charm and joy, could one but learn how to join it; and alienation from his own Indian culture is a function of Abel's struggle for affiliation. In fact, Momaday's sophisticated understanding of the Indian world's potential for evil produces one of the most intriguing themes of the book.

House Made of Dawn is a mature and complex work, and therefore, if it must dwindle into a textbook of social protest, one might at least hope that its students will perceive not only its "sociology" and its "relevance" but also something of the art by which it rises above such narrow categories.

Marion Willard Hylton   (essay date 1972)

SOURCE: "On a Trail of Pollen: Momaday's *House Made of Dawn*," in *Critique*, Vol. XIV, No. 2, 1972, pp. 60-9.

[*In the following essay, Hylton presents a thematic analysis of* House Made of Dawn, *relating "the tragic odyssey of a man forcibly removed from* [*the Native American*] *psychic environment and placed within a culture light-years away from the attitudes, values, and goals of his former life."*]

Abel was the land and he was of the land; he was a long-hair and from that single fact stemmed the fearsome modern dilemma explored by N. Scott Momaday in *House Made of Dawn*. Abel is an Indian of the American Southwest, a member of a culture for whom Nature is the one great reality to which men's lives are pegged, the only verity upon which men may rely. Within this massive concept lie all the religion, all the mores and ethics, all the spiritual truth any man may require. To shatter the concept is to shatter the man. Momaday describes the tragic odyssey of a man forcibly removed from this psychic environment

and placed within a culture light-years away from the attitudes, values, and goals of his former life. His anguished ordeal, heightened by his encounter with a white woman, endows him at last with courage and wisdom; he comes to know who he is and what he must do to maintain that identity.

In the Indian view, the universe or Nature is a great cosmological unity characterized by a harmony and oneness of all living things. Religion is not a thing apart from life, it is life itself. Oral communication is minimal; words are not needed between people sharing a common culture whose limitations and capabilities are known to all. Abel growing up in this timeless tradition is endowed with an understanding that transcends the ordinary limits of the word: "the boy could sense his grandfather's age, just as he knew somehow that his mother was soon going to die of her illness. It was nothing he was told, but he knew it anyway and without understanding, as he knew already the motion of the sun and the seasons."

After four centuries of Christianity, the essential way of life is unchanged. The people still pray to the old deities in their own language. They have assumed the names and some of the habits of their enemies but have kept their own souls and their own secrets: "in this there is a resistance and an overcoming, a long outwaiting." Evil spirits as well as good are a part of the pantheon, and Momaday uses both in the unfolding of his remarkable novel. Slowly, by means of fragmentary glimpses into the lives of Abel, Ben, Francisco, and others, Momaday leads to an understanding not only of the Indian's dilemma in the modern world, but of Abel's particular torment and what brought it about.

Francisco, Abel's grandfather, has lived all his life on the reservation, within and a part of this culture. The important events of his life are totally alien to outsiders: the ritual killing of the bear to symbolize the coming of age, the marks of pollen made above the eyes of the bear, the arduous period of instruction preliminary to his participation in a sacred ceremony, and the healing powers he later acquires as a result of his growing "understanding." In many ways, Abel and his grandfather are much alike and only a very careful reading of some passages will make clear which of them is being referred to.

One is reminded that the diminutive of Abel, "Abelito", is much like "Abuelito", the affectionate term for grandfather. The resemblance is not accidental, of course; in a sense, his close attachment to his grandfather and the old ways is the burden Abel must struggle with during the course of the novel.

Abel is not a superficial human being. His suffering is profound and moving, as is the catharsis wrought by that suffering. In a striking passage describing the shoes Abel wears when he leaves the reservation, Momaday points up the differences in attitude: "they squeaked when he walked. In the only frame of reference he had ever known, they called attention to themselves, simply, honestly . . . but now and beyond his former frame of reference, the shoes called attention to Abel. They were brown and white and they were conspicuously new and too large . . . they shone; they clattered and creaked . . . and they were nailed to his feet. There were enemies all around, and he knew that he was ridiculous in their eyes." Years later, after a stint in the army, he returns, reeling drunkenly from the steps of the noisy bus into the arms of his weeping grandfather: "everything in advance of his going—he could remember whole and in detail. It was the recent past, the intervention of days and years without meaning, of awful calm and collision, time always immediate and confused, that he could not put together in his mind." Fully twenty-four hours elapse before Abel begins to realize where he is, both geographically and culturally. Not until he walks out, just before dawn, to a high and distant hill where he sees the vast beauty of the valleys and remembers incidents from his youth, does a kind of peace come to him. But it does not last. Less than two weeks later, during the feast of Santiago, an evil spirit reveals himself to Abel, who, acting entirely within the Indian tradition, kills him.

The albino or, significantly, the white man, has been seen earlier as a figure of evil when Francisco heard whisperings from the corn and was afraid; after he left, the albino emerged or rather seemed to materialize from the green leaves. Since corn is life itself to the Indian, to hear an evil spirit breathing in the corn is a dangerous thing. A snake, or *culebra*, is likewise a symbol of evil, and when the albino threatens to turn into a snake, Abel's course is clear. Significantly, after his years in prison his attitude is unchanged. "They must know," Ben says, "that he would kill the white man again, if he had the chance . . . for he would know what the white man was, and he would kill him if he could. A man kills such an enemy if he can."

Abel's real suffering and purgation begin after he leaves prison and wanders to Los Angeles. There he meets Ben, Milly, and Tosamah. Ben, like Abel, has been raised on the reservation but has managed to make an adjustment of sorts. Ben can compromise; he is willing to overlook evil or unkindness and is able to see good in most situations: "You know, you have to change. That's the only way you can live in a place like this. You have to forget about the way it was, how you grew up and all . . . You wonder how you can get yourself into the swing of it, you know? . . . And you want to do it, because you can see how good it is . . . it's money and clothes and having plans and going someplace fast." Because Ben wants to be a part of it, he is willing to live on the fringe of white society, like a child outside a candy store window. When he speaks, one can clearly hear the voice of a lonely man: "this place is always cold and kind of empty when it rains," "you never have to be alone. You go downtown and there are a lot of people all around and they're having a good time." Ben has not yet admitted to himself that he is only an outsider; he feels the American Dream is his, too, and he is committed to pursuing it. "I could find someplace with a private bathroom if I wanted to, easy. A man with a good job can do just about anything he wants."

Tosamah (John Big Bluff Tosamah) is a very different sort of man. Like Ben he acknowledges his heritage but is not chained to it like Abel. "Priest of the Sun" is a key section for understanding the Indian concept of "The Word" as opposed to the Christian. Tosamah begins by stating in Latin, "In Principio erat Verbum." Caught up in the mystery of the words, he continues, "in the darkness . . . the smallest seed of sound . . . took hold of the darkness and there was light; it took hold out of the stillness and there was motion forever . . . it scarcely was; but it was and everything began." But at this point, his voice and attitude abruptly switch from that of a priest to that of a huckster, as he tells how this mystery was corrupted by a Christian interpretation: "But it was more than the Truth. The Truth was overgrown with fat; the fat was John's god and God stood between John and the Truth . . . and he said, 'In the Beginning was the Word . . .' and man, right then and there he should have stopped . . . Old John was a white man and the white man builds upon [the word], he adds and divides and multiplies the Word and in all of this he subtracts the Truth." Tosamah's bitterness can be heard in his parting words to his "parishoners": "Good night and get yours."

Tosamah, the Priest of the Sun, is as much an outsider in white society as Father Olguin is in Indian society. The dry, mechanical Mass which Father Olguin conducts contrasts interestingly with the peyote ritual at which Tosamah presides, where the mysticism each participant comes to feel is translated into a moving and spontaneous prayer without the embarrassment of spoken prayer; it is part of the old tradition. The tears of one of the participants are not despised, they are accepted; weeping is no disgrace if the occasion calls for weeping. The Mass has the bread, the wine, the incense, the bell; the peyote ritual has the peyote buttons, the prayer sticks, the "makings," and the drummer. The Indian's ritual marking is with pollen, and the priest's with ashes. Tosamah reverts to a caricature of American speech in explaining the impact of peyote: "that little old woolly booger turns you on like a light, man. Daddy peyote is the vegetal representation of the sun," recalling the transformation of the bread and wine into the body and blood of Christ.

Where the Indian view is at one with Nature, one might say the Catholic view, as typified by Father Olguin and Angela Grace St. John, exists in spite of Nature; the basic difference would seem to doom in advance any hope of accord. Reflecting the missionary zeal which is characteristic of his faith, Father Olguin tries over the years to enlarge his small flock and to urge his parishoners away from the old ways. In the end, he comes to recognize tacitly that some old and final cleavage still exists which he can never bridge. He tries, however, to make the legal authorities understand, as best he can, what prompted Abel to kill the albino. Once again we see the clash of the two cultures: "I believe that this man was moved to do what he did by an act of imagination so compelling as to be inconceivable to us. . . . Yes, yes, yes. But these are the facts: he killed a man—took the life of another human being. . . . Homicide is a legal term, but the law is not my context; and certainly it isn't his. . . . Murder is a moral term. Death is a universal human term."

Both the parole officer and the Relocation people attempt to keep Abel out of trouble, but his problems only deepen. "They have a lot of words," as Ben says, "and you know they mean something but you don't know what . . . Everything is different and you don't know how to get used to it." Ben understands Abel's plight, and is compassionate. Tosamah understands and is contemptuous.

Ben and Milly literally keep Abel alive in his darkest hours. Where he has understanding based on knowledge, she has understanding based on love. "She was a lot like Ben. She believed in Honor, Industry, the Second Chance, the Brotherhood of Man, the American Dream and him— Abel; she believed in him." She also loved him; she gave him money, a place to stay, and ministered to his needs out of love. On a few rare occasions, she could even make him laugh. But Milly is gentle and vulnerable. And Abel is possessed by an evil spirit. They are drawn together by their awful loneliness, but it is not enough. All her experience had been a getting away from the land where his had been a returning. At the height of his suffering, her name echoes through his mind; only her name, and a question mark. Sadly, the name is remembered, but not the identity.

Abel sinks ever deeper in the white world's web. One night, too drunk and helpless to answer Tosamah's taunts, he sets out to seek some kind of release, to kill the evil spirit, the culebra, that has brought about his misery. Instead of exorcising the evil, he undergoes a mortal combat (presumably at the hands of Martinze, the sadistic cop) that leaves him broken and near death. "He had lost his place. He had long ago been at the center, had known where he was, had lost his way, had wandered to the end of the earth, was even now reeling on the edge of the void . . . The sea reached and waned, licked after him and withdrew, falling off forever in the abyss."

Abel, badly beaten and lying on the beach, is unable to see because of his swollen eyes. We remember that Father Olguin's vision is also poor and that the albino masks his weak sight with small dark glasses. All, in one way or another, "see" with difficulty. The albino's vision is clouded by evil, Father Olguin's by his Christian beliefs, and Abel's by not accepting his birthright. If Abel's suffering suggests that of Oedipus, then we might say that the grunion form a chorus, and it is no mean comparison. Momaday's evocation of the grunion metaphor seems singularly appropriate for the situation. They, like Abel, belong to the natural order of things; they respond from the tradition of centuries, only to fall victim to the wanton ways of the white man. Abel, too, has been beaten by an evil spirit of the white world and must somehow get back to his own environment in order to survive. "His body was mangled and racked with pain. His body, like his mind, had turned on him; it was his enemy." He has tried to do what seemed to him must be done: extirpate evil. But he has failed; in the white man's world, right and wrong are not the same, and the old values somehow do not apply. He remembers seeing, in his youth, the old men running after evil. Here, it is not the same. He knows at last that he must survive beyond his pain, and return to the life he understands.

Abel has indeed, "lost his place." A reason for his particular suffering lies in the ancient Indian belief that all secrets, even those of sorcery and evil, are divulged during sexual intercourse. Abel had lain with a woman, Angela Grace St. John, and both were altered by the experience.

When Angela comes to live at Los Ojos (The Eyes), she is a distant, disturbed woman. Her attitudes are as far as possible from the Indian's. She keeps herself coldly apart from human contact and "would have her bath and read from the lives of the saints." She despises her body and the child growing within her: "She could think of nothing more vile and obscene than the raw flesh and blood of her body, the ravelled veins and gore upon her bones. And now the monstrous fetal form, the blue, blind, great headed thing growing within and feeding upon her . . . at odd moments she wished with all her heart to die by fire, fire of such intense heat that her body should dissolve in it all at once." To the suggestion of disharmony is added the hint of evil: Abel would not bargain, hence, "it remained for her to bring about a vengeance."

Their coming together is an epiphany for each of them; she draws from him a kind of vision she has never experienced before, a "knowingness" of who she is, and of her relationship to other living things and to life itself. But the evil spirit which has hitherto clouded her days now descends upon him. "Angela put her white hands to his body. Abel put his hands to her white body."

Father Olguin is the first to sense the change in her. He has seen her as an ally with whom he can share his world of words; a fellow outsider in the Indian world. But "she listened through him to the sound of thunder and of rain that fell upon the mountains miles away, . . . she had a craving for the rain . . . 'Oh, my God' she said, laughing, 'I am heartily sorry . . . for having offended Thee.' " Her laughter horrifies him almost as much as her confession.

When the sky darkens and the storm breaks, Angela no longer fears nor shrinks from Nature: she "stood transfixed in the open door and breathed deep into her lungs the purest electric scent of the air. She closed her eyes, and the clear aftervision of the rain, which she could still hear and feel so perfectly as to conceive of nothing else, obliterated all the mean and myriad fears that had laid hold of her in the past." From that moment on, evil stalks Abel's steps; the disharmony and alienation that had characterized Angela's life now infects his.

Not until years later, when she visits Abel in the hospital and, in effect, releases him, does the evil finally begin to ebb. As she speaks of her son, Peter, and the Indian tales he loves to hear, Ben remembers the stories told by his grandfather who spoke from the legends of his heritage. Abel understands; he does not speak, nor refer to her visit afterwards. Hearing Angela and seeing how she has changed has at last made clear to him just how and why he has lost his way.

House Made of Dawn is an intricately structured novel, and difficult to analyze. Time, for the Indian, is conceived not as a rigidly divided set of days, months, and years, but as experience and wisdom and knowledge, occurring today or yesterday or many yesterdays ago. Memory is the only immortality. Through memory history is transmitted from generation to generation. Memory, too, presents the novel; events from Francisco's past, or from Abel's, Ben's, or Tosamah's, are juxtaposed with events of the present moment, giving the reader a dimensional montage of thought and attitude.

Few of us suffer from our pasts as Abel must suffer. The Abel who comes back to the reservation to tend his dying grandfather is broken in body but healed in spirit. Wordlessly, he attends the last hours until death, then dresses the body according to the ancient ways. Summoned at night, the priest, significantly, is indignant over the time: "Good Heavens, couldn't you have waited until—Do you know what time it is?" By then, Abel indeed knows what time it is as far as his life is concerned, and he knows, too, that the particular hour of the day or night is of no consequence. Father Olguin, for all his good intentions, understands the Indian no better than his late nineteenth-century predecessor, Fray Nicholas, who, we learn from the old journal, was called on a similar occasion only after the Indian rites had been performed on a body.

After a long and bitter odyssey and much suffering, Abel has come home. He knows at last where he belongs in the scheme of things. During the long vigil before Francisco's death, he begins once again to feel a peace and a kinship with his heritage: "it was the room in which he was born, in which his mother and his brother died. Just then, and for moments and hours and days, he had no memory of being outside of it." When Abel leaves the mission, rubs himself with ashes, and goes on to join the other dawn runners, he is not only assuming his role as male survivor of his family, but also completing the final phase of his own spiritual healing. As he runs, as he becomes a part of the orderly continuum of interrelated events that constitute the Indian universe, Abel is the land, and he is of the land once more.

Carole Oleson   (essay date Spring 1973)

SOURCE: "The Remembered Earth: Momaday's *House Made of Dawn,*" in *South Dakota Review,* Vol. 11, No. 1, Spring, 1973, pp. 59-78.

[*In the following essay, Oleson analyzes the structure and symbolism of* House Made of Dawn, *paying close attention to the symbol of the earth.*]

> Once in his life a man ought to concentrate his mind upon the remembered earth, I believe. He ought to give himself up to a particular landscape in his experience, to look at it from as many angles as he can, to wonder about it, to dwell upon it. He ought to imagine the creatures there and all the faintest motions of the wind. He ought to recollect the glare of noon and all the colors of the dawn and dusk.

The landscape is of central importance, holy in itself, and closely associated with Momaday's theme in *House Made of Dawn,* as it is in *The Way to Rainy Mountain,* from which the above quotation was taken. The two books are complementary; taken together they each contribute to the meaning of the other. The leisurely contemplation that Momaday asks a man to give to the earth, he asks his reader to give to *House Made of Dawn.* A single reading of a book as richly layered in meaning, as intricately struc-

tured, as forcefully compressed through the poetic device of abrupt juxtaposition without transition as this one is, leaves one with a vague impression of emptiness. One must look for a long time to appreciate fully the subtleties of its form.

Some of Momaday's reviewers have commented on the lack of plot line, the indistinctness of the characters, the mistiness of the novel as a whole. Plot and character development are insignificant compared to the wealth of patterns woven into the narrative, the power of the meaning carried in the unifying symbol of the everlasting earth. It is appropriate to judge the book by the conventional standards of plot and character development only if in fact it is a novel in the conventional sense. The difficulty is in classification; *House Made of Dawn* is not a short novel about Abel, but a long prose poem about the earth, about the people who have long known how to love it, and who can survive as a people if they will cling to that knowledge. This can be made more clear through a detailed examination of the structure and use of symbolism in each section.

In the prologue the book begins where it ends, with Abel on February 28, 1952, naked to the waist and smeared with ashes, running in the annual long race of the black men at dawn. The prologue is thus a flash-forward to the final scene of the book. All that Momaday will tell us of the human condition is summarized on that one page of prologue, but we must go on to the beginning of the story and curve around to the end, then read again the prologue in order to understand what he is saying here. More exactly, there is neither beginning nor end, for like the circle of the horizon on the open plain, the narrative moves around without break as the reader turns naturally from [the last page back to the beginning] and the eye begins a second sweep of the horizon, this time with more awareness of what it sees.

At first we view from a distance the large expanse of land under the light of dawn. "Still and strong" are key words striking the theme that will be repeated and developed throughout the book of the everlastingness of the earth, the strength that comes precisely from changeless change, the unending repetition of the seasonal cycle.

Then, we move in closer to focus on Abel running, also a key symbol. Here we have not only the cycle of seasons (the traditional race is annual on the day when the sun rises from the "saddle" of the mesa), but also the cycle of generations, for the most important event of Abel's grandfather's life was his victory over Mariano in this race in 1889. Continuity with a culture 25,000 years old is precariously maintained as each generation teaches the following one the old way. Abel, running as Francisco ran, does not break the chain of his fathers, a chain which is his strength, not his bond.

Finally, Momaday deals more explicitly with the themes of hope and despair implied in such symbols as dawn, land, and the running figure, now small in the distance.

> For a time the sun was whole beneath the cloud; then it rose into eclipse, and a dark and certain shadow came upon the land.

When the sun is hidden by a cloud, Abel becomes at first

glance a pitiable figure running through vastness that makes it seem as if he were making no progress out of the shadow, seeming "very little and alone." Yet a cloud is not so big compared to the whole sky; nor will it cover the sun forever.

This is no "heartbreaking novel" as the blurb on the paperback cover states; its major symbols are dawn, everlasting earth, and runners *able* to outlast their pain—all symbols of hope which contain a prophecy of the Indian culture's prevailing ultimately. Nor is it the proud natives who are strangers in their land, but the latecomers who have never known it intimately.

The seven chapters of Part 1 are the first of several groups of seven. Seven is a sacred number: the four directions plus the two of the vertical axis (up and down) plus the center. Its repetition makes a pattern, particularly in the similarity and spacing of Abel's reveries in the second chapter and Francisco's in the second from the last chapter. Such precision reminds one of the geometric design woven into cloth.

Part 1's title, "The Longhair," refers to the reservation Indian; the term is used pejoratively by Tosamah chiding Abel for his reluctance to adapt to urban industrial life. Momaday plays with the word in Part 1 by means of a snare made from a long horse hair attached to a bent reed in the river. The bird snare is introduced in the first chapter as Francisco checks it to see if he has caught a brightly colored bird for his prayer plume. "The Longhair" closes with a short chapter in which Francisco, riding out to his fields, mourns Abel's arrest. By habit, he looks for the bird snare as he drives his mares by the river; it is sprung. Through position in the story, the snare becomes a symbol of the trap set for Abel. Abel has killed the albino because he almost mystically perceived him as an enemy. The context of his thought and action here is "longhair," for Abel refuses to recognize the Euro-American legal structure in which killing such an enemy is not encouraged. To act upon the traditional values is to suffer at the hands of the invader.

Enclosed between the two references to the snare which are about equidistant from the beginning and ending of Part 1 are, among other things, (1) Abel's reminiscences, (2) the story of Abel's affair with a bored young matron, Angela St. Martin, (3) a perceptive picture of the priest, and through an old journal, of his predecessor, (4) the drama of Abel and the albino, and (5) the clearest and most complete statement of the theme in the book. I will briefly discuss each part in that order, although (2), (3), and (4) are interwoven in the narrative.

(1) Abel's memories give us essential details about his life that help us understand how he feels about his family, the traditions of his people, the land and the creatures upon it. Particularly significant are the related tales of the Bahkyush people and Abel's mercy killing of an eagle.

About a century before, twenty Bahkyush survivors of persecution and plague had joined their distant kin, bringing with them four sacred and ceremonial objects which helped them remember that they were a people. Those Euro-Americans who think of Native Americans as an anachronistic people who belong nostalgically and safely to the past will probably take this tale as mere sentimentality—the heartbreak of being a proud stranger in one's own land again. But, taken in context with other portions of the book, the message is clear: Native Americans must cherish the concept of being a people, cherish the ageless traditions. Pride and faith in their heritage will bring a destitute people out of misery into a better age. A parallel scarcely needs to be drawn between the Bahkyush and all other tribes threatened with cultural extinction by the European invaders.

The Eagle Watchers Society, the principal ceremonial organization of the Bahkyush, takes Abel on an eagle hunt. When Abel strangles a captive eagle, we sense with a jolt the unacceptable difference to him between the mighty bird in flight (described in one of the most beautiful passages in the book) and the "drab," "shapeless," "ungainly" bird in the sack.

> The sight of it filled him with shame and disgust.
> He took hold of its throat in the darkness and
> cut off its breath.

Those two abrupt sentences may give us some insight into the high suicide rate among young Native Americans today and also why we are never given more than a flickering image from Abel's memory of the six years he spent in prison. The years of his captivity are evidently almost cut off from his consciousness.

(2) As ironic as Abel's encounter with obtuseness and brutality in The City of the Angels is the name of the adulterous Angela St. Martin, containing both angel and saint. She is in the early stages of sacred motherhood, piously attends mass, and reads the lives of the saints. Yet there is no sting in the irony, for Momaday draws her with sympathetic, if slightly amused, understanding. Though certainly no intellectual—her reading is apparently limited to the lives of the saints—she has the gift of poetic vision.

> He leaned into the swing and drove; the blade
> flashed and struck, and the wood gaped open.
> Angela caught her breath and said, "I see."

The episode with Angela is an exquisitely-drawn picture of war between the sexes, and also between the races, in which no one really loses anything worth keeping, unless the reader interjects a moralism that is not in the narrative. Angela's loss of face is only funny, not dramatic or pathetic, because she had planned to amuse herself at his expense and was caught, defeated by his patience, his long waiting without concession. There is probably a lesson behind the fun which corresponds to that in other more edifying examples of perseverance.

(3) Father Olguin fits no simple stereotype; he can neither be admired as a blessing to the people he serves—though he sincerely tries to be good to them—nor condemned as a curse, though he fails to appreciate the value of their culture. Because Father Olguin identifies with Fray Nicolás, we may assume that he shares the former priest's attitudes revealed in such journal entries as the following:

> Tomacita Fragua died this late morning & again
> I was not called to it. But the son-in-law Diego

came in the afternoon & gave me leave to make the burial. I saw they had finished with her according to their dark custom & there was blue & yellow meal about on the floor.

and in a letter:

> [Francisco] is evil. . . . He is one of them & goes often in the kiva & puts on their horns & hides & does worship that Serpent which even is the One our most ancient enemy. Yet he is unashamed to make one of my sacristans & brother I am most fearful to forbid it . . . Where is the Most Holy Spirit that he is not struck down at that moment? I have some expectations of it always & am disappointed. Why am I betrayed who cannot desire to betray? I am not deceived that he has been with Porcingula Pecos a vile one I assure you & she is already swoln up with it & likely diseased too God grant it.

Neither priest is conscious of the unholy spite and narrow prejudice in his attitude toward the people of Walatowa. The priests are more pitiable than reprehensible, for they are outsiders in the village, feeling rebuff but never understanding it, humiliated by the small role they play in the village life, hurt and bewildered by the people's unwillingness to reject their own religion in order to embrace Christianity more completely. The priests see themselves as models for the heathen, but the villagers relegate to them only a part of their religious traditions, adding Catholic mass to their ceremonial life while subtracting nothing of their own.

Father Olguin is also humorously out of touch with reality in his relationship with Angela. Proud of his ability to resist her strong attraction, he is reduced to childish fury when he realizes how easily she resists him. His celibacy is an almost-safe retreat like the safety of his bargain with the world to make a little place for himself in the Indian mission. Father Olguin is only half-blind, but then only half-seeing.

(4) If there is a mistiness in ***House Made of Dawn,*** the albino Indian is surely the center of the mist. Momaday refers to him as "the white man" in small letters, as if he were an ordinary, if striking, character. But there are signs that he stands for White Man: he is large, powerful, very skillful and brutal in contest; there is something unnatural about him, something repulsive to the point of horror in his huge face and lax lips. He wears dark-colored glasses as if his eyes were weak. An albino often has poor vision, making this an apt choice as symbol for hordes of white men who poured over the land, proving themselves insensitive and unseeing even when they were trying to be fair, which was not often. A sentence like:

> Abel was not used to the game, and the white man was too strong and quick for him.

is heavy with double and even triple meaning, alluding possibly in a large historic sense to the land grab game played for centuries and still being played; or in a more immediate sense, perhaps to the game of making one's way in twentieth century America which Abel will play and lose in Walatowa, then in Los Angeles.

Mystery completely envelops the white man when in the first darkness of evening on July 28 he appears in the corn field, ominously watching Francisco finish a long day's hoeing. Francisco doesn't quite hear him, but he senses an "alien presence" which has been there a long time, recognized as evil.

(5) The chapter labeled July 28 begins with one of those passages of description that the hurried reader skips in his impatience to get on with the plot and character development. Yet nothing in the book is more vital to its theme than this passage. Momaday contrasts the wild animals that "have tenure in the land" and the "late-coming things"—the domestic animals. There is an implied analogy with Native Americans and Euro-Americans. . . . Domestic animals have a "poverty of vision and instinct" like Father Olguin's blind eye and the white man's weak eyes. They are "estranged from the wild land" like Milly's father (Part 3) in his war with the land he has come to hate.

The paragraph beginning, "Man came down the ladder" could serve as a thesis statement for the book. It says in part:

> . . . as if the prehistoric civilization has gone out among the hills for a little while and would return; and then everything would be restored to an older age, and time would have returned upon itself and a bad dream of invasion and change would have been dissolved in an hour before the dawn. For man, too, has tenure in the land; he dwelt upon the land twenty-five thousand years ago, and his gods before him.

Four hundred years is to twenty-five thousand years as a single cloud over the sun is to the vast dome of the sky. It will pass; the sun will shine through again. Momaday makes his intention clear in the next paragraph when he points out that the people of Walatowa have chosen carefully what they wanted to borrow from their conquerors, but haven't forgotten that they are enemies:

> They have assumed the names and gestures of their enemies, but have held on to their own, secret souls; and in this there is a resistance and an overcoming, a long outwaiting.

The theme is made still more concrete as Abel sheds the stress of his sojourn in the white man's world and once again finds himself attuned to his own. This harmonious state will soon be broken by the prison term, but he is destined to regain it in the last pages of the book.

Of the four parts, Part 2, "The Priest of the Sun" is the most like poetry in structure, requiring the reader's patience with a train of seemingly unrelated elements. For instance, it opens with a description of small fish having no first-level connection with the action of the book. The reader is forced to go to second level to understand what those fish have to do with what was a relatively straightforward narrative. If not already unbalanced, the reader will surely lose his footing when he comes to the sentence:

> They hurl themselves upon the land and writhe in the light of the moon, the moon, the moon; they writhe in the light of the moon.

There is no precedent in the book for a comic rhythm like that; it is a freak even in its own paragraph in which the other sentences are as factual as a biology text. There *is* a precedent for the rhythm of that sentence, however, in our English heritage of nursery rhymes: the owl and the pussycat "dance by the light of the moon, the moon, the moon; they dance by the light of the moon." . . .

[The] fish reappear as suddenly as they were dropped, this time explained as a thought occurring to Abel. Abel's thoughts do not enlighten the reader at this point, however, for he is just regaining consciousness and we must wait for bits of information about where he is and what has happened to him as he gets things sorted out in his pain-crazed mind. Once we understand that he is lying on a beach with both hands broken, then we can see that the fish symbolize Abel, for "they are among the most helpless creatures on the face of the earth." Abel at the moment is in the very posture of the fish who spawn upon the beach; he is prone on the dark, foggy beach with hands as useless to him as fins on land. Unable at first to stand up, he is defenseless and surrounded by enemies, the city dwellers who, except for two friends, range from indifference to savage hostility.

It may not be until after Part 3 that we fully understand the symbol in its larger sense. When Abel, or any other "longhair," leaves the reservation and migrates to the city, he is leaving his element to venture into a hostile environment very much as the fish leave their home in the sea to flop awkwardly on the beach, easy prey for anyone. With this in mind, the nursery rhyme sentence changes its comic quality to irony; those are Native Americans writhing in Anglo rhythms, but they are not mindless like the fish; they understand what is being done to them, therefore suffering more.

Structurally, this section, and indeed all of this chapter, is within the boundaries of poetry, outside the usual requirements of fiction. Its elements are juxtaposed like the blocks of a dry wall, without transitional mortar. Superficially there seems to be no connection at all between one passage and the next, but from a deeper perspective, there is nothing random about the order. This chapter has the power that can be compressed into two- or three-level poetry through vibrations created by the interaction of images jammed together as in (1) the fish, (2) Tosamah on the Word and (3) Abel lying unconscious, lost in a world of strange words. Another example is . . . where this poetic structure allows Momaday to get "He was afraid," and "He was not afraid, no, sir," close enough together to set up ironic vibrations.

The chapter is not merely a string of images that act upon each other, however; its unity comes from a theme of conflict between the Native and European Americans and from a pattern of repetition. The fish, the moon, the sea, and the Word run through the chapter like threads holding it together.

Abel's mental condition after being first inebriated and then severely beaten justifies the apparent fragmentation of the information, but I am inclined to believe that Momaday selected the time of Abel's regaining consciousness because it provided a rationale for hurling the assorted vignettes together, freed from the logic of fiction, bound by the very different and perhaps more demanding logic of poetry.

When the Priest of the Sun is introduced suddenly, he has no yet-known relationship to the characters we have met in Part 1. As in a symbolic poem, we must hold the elements in mind and wait for the whole of the poem to reveal the connections. The names are fascinating: John Big Bluff with its double reference to topography and deception, and Cristóbal Cruz with its pun on crystal ball, containing also the Spanish spelling of Christ and of cross. The two men make an entrance rather like the Duke and Prince of *Huckleberry Finn* with their shabby theatricals.

And yet the sermon on the Word is beautifully, powerfully, and for the most part, earnestly done. In character with the opposing elements bouncing off each other within Tosamah, the sermon goes from the drama of

> It rose up in the darkness, little and still, almost nothing in itself—like a single soft breath, like the wind arising; yes, like the whisper of the wind rising slowly and going out into the early morning.

to the comedy of

> Gracious me, I see lots of new faces out there tonight. *Gracious me!* May the Great Spirit—can we knock off that talking in the back there? —be with you always.

to the informality of

> Now, brothers and sisters, old John was a white man, and the white man has his ways. Oh gracious me, he has his ways. He talks about the Word. He talks through it and around it. He builds upon it with syllables, prefixes and suffixes, and hyphens and accents. He adds and divides and multiplies the Word. And in all of this he subtracts the Truth. And, brothers and sisters, you have come here to live in the white man's world. Now the white man deals in words and he deals easily, with grace and sleight of hand. And in his presence, here on his ground, you are as children, mere babes in the woods.

Here we have the connection between the Word, Abel, and the fish. The Native American's respect for the sacredness of language—as Tosamah explains next with the tale of his grandmother—is so unlike the Euro-American's adroit manipulation of language (exactly like their contrasting attitudes toward land), that the Native American in the city is at the mercy of the Euro-American, as the fish on the beach are at the mercy of passersby. Much later, in Part 3, Ben will dovetail into this presentation of the Word when he discusses the newly relocated Indian's sense of loss at discovering:

> They have a lot of *words,* and you know they mean something, but you don't know what, and your own words are no good because they're not the same; they're different, and they're the only words you've got.

Again, the sermon on the Word is echoed in the passage describing Abel's trial six years before:

> When he had told his story once, simply, Abel refused to speak. . . . Word by word by word these men were disposing of him in language, *their* language, and they were making a bad job of it.

Powerless in a world of someone else's words, someone else's rule, Abel's holy vision comes to him as he lies delirious on the beach. He sees himself getting down to his knees to put his ear on the ground and listen to the mystic race of the "old men running after evil."

> The runners after evil ran as water runs, deep in the channel, in the way of least resistance, no resistance. His skin crawled with excitement; he was overcome with longing and loneliness, for suddenly he saw the crucial sense in their going, of old men in white leggings running after evil in the night. They were whole and indispensable in what they did; everything in creation referred to them. Because of them, perspective, proportion, design in the universe. Meaning because of them. They ran with great dignity and calm, not in the hope of anything, but hopelessly; neither in fear nor hatred nor despair of evil, but simply in recognition and with respect. Evil was. Evil was abroad in the night; they must venture out to the confrontation; they must reckon dues and divide the world.

Momaday uses this vision to exhort the people to remain faithful to the old ways and outlast invaders' temporary dominance, saying here that one must recognize evil, not pretend that evil is either neutral or good (as Ben does), but one cannot clear the world of it. One must give way to its power as water gives way to force, but never lose a sense of the difference between good and evil. And outlast evil.

Abel is on the edge of this awareness that will make him spiritually whole and strong again. But in the meantime he is also "on the edge of the void." He has lost "perspective, proportion, design in the universe"; he has lost meaning, dignity and calm; "the world [is] open at his back." Described earlier as an alien world, the sea is here the void, not a passive void waiting disinterestedly for him to fall into it, but an active void seeking to pull him in.

In Part 2 basic information is sparingly slipped in through seemingly insignificant statements; consequently, the reader is quite likely to feel disoriented throughout "The Priest of the Sun" the first time through. Most readers have to wait until Part 3 to get relationships straightened out. For instance, with jarring poetic juxtaposition, Milly's questionnaire is inserted as if in a word association test. Abel thinks of the sea, the abyss, the helpless fish and the prying social workers in one logical train of thought. But the reader does not know that it is Milly's questionnaire yet, or even suspect the existence of Milly at this point. Later, she herself is thrown into the story via Abel's erratic memory. First we learn that she is an Idealist and then we learn that Abel made love to her. We must accustom ourselves to the flight pattern of a mosquito as one paragraph ends with a remembered sexual orgasm and the next begins with an awareness of the sea and his pain as Abel comes around again.

Perhaps the most significant part of the peyote prayer service inserted in Part 2 is Ben Benally's vision of blue and purple horses and a house made of dawn. Also tending toward hope for the restoration of meaningful existence is Tosamah's going out into the street to blow the eagle whistle in the four directions, serving notice "that something holy was going on in the universe."

Another significant passage in this part is Milly's story of her childhood. Because Milly's father is presented through the eyes of a loving daughter, he is handled with compassion and understanding. Yet he stands in stark contrast to Francisco to the disadvantage of the former.

> The earth where we lived was hard and dry and brick red . . . and at last Daddy began to hate the land, began to think of it as some kind of enemy, his own very personal and deadly enemy.

He expressed his love for Milly by going out daily to fight the barren land and by giving everything he had to get her away from it even at the cost of being separated from her. Francisco, on the other hand, taught his grandsons to study and revere the land. He did not consider himself pitted against it, but in partnership with it. He laid a blessing on the corn as he left in the evening; he lived by the great organic calendar. Without rancor or unfair method, Momaday illustrates these contrasting attitudes in a way that indicates the superiority of the Native American's relationship with earth and the pathetic state of the Euro-American, alienated from earth.

The last of this long, difficult chapter is the story of Abel's torturous journey back to Ben's apartment, although, of course, we do not know at this point his destination or whether or not he makes it. Moon, beach, and the fish back in the depths of the sea are the final image.

The second chapter of "The Priest of the Sun" is much more simply structured and needs little analysis for my purposes. The entire chapter is a quoted sermon by Tosamah which, while valuable to our understanding of Kiowa thought, is not difficult to follow; we can see clearly the philosophy of man's sacred bond to the land, his place in the pattern of the universe that includes the other creatures and establishes his kinship even with the stars of the sky. Interestingly, this chapter appears as the introduction of *The Way to Rainy Mountain.* Different as the two books are in structure, they meet in this chapter which they share.

In summary, "The Priest of the Sun" is a title charged with the positive force associated with the source of all life and yet this is the section which depicts Abel at his most sunless moment. Literally, his chances of ever seeing another sunrise are very slight. Figuratively, he is at his low point physically, mentally, emotionally. Nevertheless, a new dawn is coming.

But before the dawn runner, the night chanter. The Night Chant, a major Navajo ceremony of nine days' duration, is performed only after the first killing frost. Abel's spirit has been severely "frostbitten" twice since coming to Los

Angeles: the humiliation suffered at the hands of Tosamah and that inflicted by Martinez in Abel's first encounter with him. But the second encounter with Martinez is the killing frost leaving him broken in body and soul, the life drawn back into the roots of his being for safekeeping until the warmth of spring lets him live again. The Night Chant is a healing ceremony, arranged and paid for by the friends and family of the person who is ill.

Part 3, "The Night Chanter" is one long chapter, broken several times by Ben's interior monologues, the three lengthier ones in second person as if he were talking to himself. The rest of the chapter is Ben speaking directly to the readers, blessing us with details which clear up the confusion of Part 2.

Ben is the night chanter, the Singer, in the sense that he sings the sacred songs to Abel and interprets their meaning to him, thus performing in his modest way the function of priest, preserver of the sacred ceremonials. Ben as priest or Singer contrasts sharply with both Tosamah and Father Olguin (and Fray Nicolás). In the sermons quoted, Momaday gives Tosamah credit for his own fine artistry and even loans him his own grandmother, yet Tosamah as a character is not entirely admirable. He enjoys verbally tormenting his flock. Abel needs help, but the Priest of the Sun is among the pack nipping at his heels. Father Olguin probably does less harm and also less good than Tosamah because the priest does not understand Abel's situation well enough either to help or hurt him. Tosamah knows how to explain the religious dilemma of the twentieth century Native American as well as he knows how to "get under the skin" of a relocated reservation Indian. He does both. Ben, on the other hand, does not have claim to the titles and honors of the priesthood. Because he is concerned about his distant kin and best friend, Abel as a person, he shares with him the comforts of their ancient religion as naturally as he shares his home, food, and overcoat.

He is not an intellectual like Tosamah; he does not think about how Navajo or Kiowa philosophy can speak to industrial civilization. Instead, he tries not to think about it because it mixes him up. It is Ben who has the vision at the peyote ceremony; he lives his religion on a level deeper than the intellect, the level of spirit and emotion. And in the spiritual poverty of the City of the Angels, Abel's need for the precious traditions and songs is great. Ben apparently has made his place in the white man's world in the white man's way—by keeping his religion tightly locked up in its compartment, away from his work-a-day life:

> And you *want* to do it [get yourself into the swing of city life] because you can see how good it is. It's better than anything you've ever had; it's money and clothes and having plans and going someplace fast. . . . You go up there on the hill and you hear the singing and the talk and you think about going home. But the next day you know it's no use; you know that if you went home there would be nothing there, just the empty land and a lot of old people, going no place and dying off.

and again:

> It's a good place; you could fix it up real nice. There are a lot of good places around here. I could find someplace with a private bathroom if I wanted to, easy. A man with a good job can do just about anything he wants.

and yet again he lectures himself:

> It's a good place to live. There's always a lot going on, a lot of things to do and see once you find your way around. Once you find your way around and get used to everything, you wonder how you ever got along out there where you came from. There's nothing there, you know, just the land, and the land is empty and dead. Everything is here, everything you could ever want.

Sensitive to the feelings and needs of others as he is, responsive as he is to the rhythms and images of the old songs, Ben deadens his mind and violates his soul trying so desperately to convince himself that the material values of industrial society are worth dedicating one's life to. His rewards for industry and dependability are an airless room, an occasional escape in alcohol from the meaninglessness of being a replaceable bolt in a huge machine, and police protection in the person of Martinez, who can rob or beat him for amusement whenever he likes; he can watch other people having fun if he gets lonely; he can pretend that his longings are only a sensible desire for things that he can buy on credit; he can tell himself over and over that the sacred land is dead and the old way gone forever. Momaday, on the other hand, has been saying that the old way is not dead, but sleeping, and soon it will emerge to continue its development.

The prayer song, "House made of dawn" is another key to our understanding of the theme of the book, but a key that is probably in the hands of only its Navajo readers. The rest of us can do some speculating, keeping in mind that our errors may be gross. The song is a prayer to a male deity for recovery from a "spell" which would seem to be anxiety, depression, mental pain. It has on the believer who sings it roughly the effect that the twenty-third psalm has on the devout Christian:

> I fear no evil; / for thou art with me,
> Thy rod and thy staff, / they comfort me.
>
> You have taken it away for me;
> Happily I recover.
> Happily my interior becomes cool.

Surely the song loses much of the subtle turn of language in translation, but still it carries something of the feeling for order in its pattern of repetition and variation that may be the model for Momaday in his use of repeated phrases.

"Happily my interior becomes cool. . . . May it be beautiful all around me. / In beauty it is finished." Abel is at the low point of his illness, but close now to recovery; his memories are of home. He will begin again on the land that goes on forever, where nothing really changes.

The first chapter of Part 4 is largely devoted to the six memories of Francisco as his mind clears each dawn. In the first we may get some help with the difficult concept of a house made of dawn. Rather than dismissing it with a snort as a "broken-backed title" [as William James Smith did in *Commonweal* LXXXVIII (20 September 1968)] we can begin with the skyline of the black mesa as the house of the sun. From there it is easy to see the sun's house as made of dawn when the sun rises over the mesa's edge, as made of evening light, dark cloud, male rain, dark mist, female rain, pollen, and grasshoppers at appropriate times. The associations of each word would greatly increase our understanding of the symbolism, but that kind of analysis should be done by a Navajo scholar, or at least by a student of Navajo culture. There is, I believe, an entire level of the book that remains unseen by those of us who do not know the languages and legends of the people depicted. Mr. Momaday has given us some help in both his books, but much more is needed before outsiders can fully appreciate all the subtleties of *House Made of Dawn.* We can find the symbols by the emphasis given them, but we cannot read all the levels of their meaning once we have found them.

The importance of the house of the sun is indicated as Francisco tells the little boys to learn the contour of the mesa as they know the shape of their hands:

> . . . and they must live according to the sun appearing, for only then could they reckon where they were, where all things were, in time. . . .

> But his grandsons knew already; not the names or the strict position of the sun each day in relation to its house, but the larger motion and meaning of the great organic calendar itself, the emergency of dawn and dusk, summer and winter, the very cycle of the sun and of all the suns that were and were to come.

House Made of Dawn is a story of human thought, action and emotion placed in the organic patterns of the earth, sun, and moon. Man is not a self-contained whole whom the universe serves, but a part of a larger whole. He finds himself only by relating to the universal scheme. He loses himself by boxing himself up in the city ("The Kiowas reckoned their stature by the distance they could see, and they were bent and blind in the wilderness.") and dedicating his life to obtaining things. A luxury apartment and an executive position are but a larger-scale version of Ben's pitiable existence.

In the second memory, the story of Francisco's (and the colt's and half-grown bear's) coming of age illustrates the sacredness of man's proper relationship to earth's creatures.

> And he did not want to break the stillness of the night, for it was holy and profound; it was rest and restoration, the hunter's offering of death and the sad watch of the hunted, waiting somewhere away in the cold darkness and breathing easily of its life, brooding around at last to forgiveness and consent; the silence was essential to them both, and it lay out like a bond between them, ancient and inviolable.

There is a vast difference between this "ancient and inviolable bond" and the impersonal relationship between the man behind the air hammer and his hundreds of victims each day in the assembly line of the slaughter house.

In the third memory, the strangeness of Porcingula and her mother, Nicolás *teah-whau,* is compounded by the enigma of their names. Porcingula is also the name of the wooden statue of Maria de los Angeles, patroness of the Bahkyush; Nicolás is also the name of the priest of the mission at the time of Francisco's youth. The fourth memory is of the mystic race of the dead that Francisco takes his grandsons to hear. In the fifth memory, Francisco becomes a respected member of the clan as he plays the drums well. As the dancers move out they are so attuned to each other and the beat that there is a perfect chain of motion. When Francisco changes drums, there is no minute loss of timing. Both are demonstrations of the values of cooperation and harmony.

The sixth memory, of Francisco's moment of glory in the race, is Momaday's primary symbol after dawn itself, related to it since the race is run at dawn. Francisco has made a misjudgment which should have finished him, but instead of collapsing, he runs "beyond his pain" to win.

The final chapter is a packed three pages. Francisco dies just before the seventh dawn. There is a vague likeness between God's creating the world in six days and resting on the seventh and Francisco's articulating the high points of his life for six dawns and expiring on the seventh.

Our last glimpse of Father Olguin is of his "peering out into the darkness" shouting, "I understand! Oh God! I understand—I understand!" And he really tried.

The climax of the book is a paragraph of incomparable beauty, beginning without emotion in very simple language, ending in the poetry of sound, color and motion that gives form and meaning to life.

> He came among them, and they huddled in the cold together, waiting, and the pale light before the dawn rose up in the valley. A single cloud lay over the world, heavy and still. It lay out upon the black mesa, smudging out the margin and spilling over the lee. But at the saddle there was nothing. There was only the clear pool of eternity. They held their eyes upon it, waiting, and, too slow and various to see, the void began to deepen and to change: pumice, and pearl, and mother-of-pearl, and the pale and brilliant blush of orange and of rose. And then the deep hanging rim ran with fire and the sudden cold flare of the dawn struck upon the arc, and the runners sprang away.

In the last long paragraph Abel re-enacts Francisco's race, running in spite of soreness from the near-fatal beating not quite a month before. Derivatives of "run" appear more than a dozen times in the passage, giving the sense of an endless drum beat, an eternal continuum of ash-blackened men running, rather than a single act with a beginning and end. Singing under his breath, "he went running on the rise of the song." *House Made of Dawn* is a book of courage, faith, and hope for a "new world coming" which will be a dynamic, not static, continuation of an old world's wisdom and order. "In beauty it is finished."

Harold S. McAllister   (essay date Winter 1974-75)

SOURCE: "Incarnate Grace and the Paths of Salvation in *House Made of Dawn,*" in *South Dakota Review,* Vol. 12, No. 4, Winter, 1974-75, pp. 115-25.

[*In the following essay, McAllister provides a character sketch of Angela Grace St. John and examines religious themes, images, and allusions in* House Made of Dawn.]

Angela Grace St. John is one of the most intriguing characters in Scott Momaday's novel, *House Made of Dawn.* It seems as if Momaday intended for her to have more thematic importance than is immediately apparent. Her thoughts are one of the centers of "The Longhair," and her affair with Abel suggests that she will have some influence on his future. Yet the major action of the novel, the murder of the albino, has no direct relation to Angela, and after confessing her adultery she disappears almost entirely except for two brief appearances in "The Night Chanter." With her Laurentian lust for dark flesh, she is sufficiently stereotyped to offend some female readers. If Angela is no more than a stereotype, she is a flaw in the novel, and if her significance does not extend beyond her brief but suggestive appearances on the forestage, then the novel is less well structured than a fine piece of fiction should be. There are many clues throughout *House Made of Dawn* which indicate that Angela is indeed more important than she seems and which connect her to the central theme of the novel, the way of salvation. Many of these clues relate to her Catholicism; some of them even indicate a symbolic identity with the Virgin Mary.

House Made of Dawn is filled with arcana, some of it coherent, some either incoherent or primarily of private significance to Momaday. There seems to be no strictly literary significance, for instance, to the very suggestive fact that Abel's age at the end of the novel is approximately the same as Momaday's when he finished it or that February 27th, 1952, one of the last dates in the novel, is Momaday's eighteenth birthday. One of Tosamah's sermons, delivered on January 26 and 27, 1952, had been published by Momaday as a personal reminiscence in the January 26, 1967 issue of *The Reporter.* A string of details, including the names of Angela St. John, Juan Reyes Fragua, and John Big Bluff Tosamah, links St. John the Evangelist to the novel. Tosamah's sermon on "The Gospel According to St. John" is delivered on the feastday of St. Polycarp, John's beloved disciple, and the "Rainy Mountain" sermon occurs on the feastday of St. John the Eloquent, author of the eighty-eight homilies on the Gospel of St. John. Dates and their significance form another set of "coincidences": July 20, the first day of the novel, is the anniversary of a cultural crisis for each of the three Indian nations most important in the novel; Kiowa, Navaho, and Jemez Pueblo. Twice Momaday mentions the day of the week; in each case his matching of day and date is correct, and February 27, 1952, was Ash Wednesday. The dates of the communications from Father Nicolas form a pattern based on the sanctoral cycle and the Feast of the Sacred Heart, and that pattern is a commentary on Nicolas's character.

Lending coherence to these apparently disjointed facts is not my present purpose; some of them may be immediately illuminating to readers of the novel, others much less so. What is surely clear, however, is that Momaday's novel is very carefully constructed and that Catholicism plays a much greater role in it than a first reading might suggest. Even disregarding such obvious items as the presence of two priests, four church services, and two fiestas, or the selection of names like Abel and Angela Grace St. John or Francisco and Porcingula, there remain details that illustrate Momaday's concern with making Christianity and, more particularly, Catholicism part of the fictive world of *House Made of Dawn.* Angela assists at a mass which is "a feast of Martyrs," with "scarlet chasuble." Waiting for Abel, she reads "from the lives of the saints." In at least three cases, Father Nicolas quotes the appropriate Gospel for the day's Mass at the beginning of his journal entry (November 22, December 25, January 5) and once he quotes a very pertinent section of the Credo.

This information suggests that *House Made of Dawn* may be a Christian morality play; its subject is spiritual redemption in a squalid, hellish temporal world. The Christianity of the novel is unorthodox, like the Catholicism practiced at the pueblos of New Mexico. It shares the chthonic, carnal nature of Pueblo Catholicism illustrated so well by Margot Astrov's description of a Christmas Mass at San Felipe:

> When I reached the sanctuario to give my little offering, I set eyes on the most unexpected sight of my life. Maria and Jose were lying in a bed on the altar, offerings of bread piled at their heads. The Indian in front of me was just lifting the bedcover gently. . . . and then kissing Maria, lightly, but with great devotion.

Abel requires reconciliation with his death, reunion with his culture; the spiritual redemption he ultimately finds through a return to his own place, his own center, at Walatowa. Angela comes to a similar peace with her own culture; she is saved through her affair with Abel and her contact with the Pueblo Indians, who teach her to accept her body and its needs. She shows Abel the path of salvation, serving as the mediatrix between his lost soul and the culture he is seeking to rejoin. Like the Virgin, she is not a savior but a model of salvation.

Among the structures of the book is a system of analogies between Angela and the Virgin Mary; the system begins with her name: since Mary was given to St. John's safekeeping after the death of Jesus, Angela's last name is appropriate, and her middle name may remind us of "Hail, Mary, Full of Grace." It is her first name that carries the most complex references. She is Angela because Our Lady of the Angels is the patroness of both her home, Los Angeles, and Walatowa. Her first name serves the double purpose of underlining her place of origin and hinting at some connection with the Virgin. Further analogies occur in the text; the last major one develops a thematic center of the book.

When she comes to visit Abel in the hospital, she recounts to him the story she likes to tell her son

> . . . about a young Indian brave. He was born of a bear and a maiden, she said, and he was

noble and wise. He had many adventures, and
he became a great leader and saved his people.
It was the story Peter liked best of all, and she
always thought of *him,* Abel, when she told it.

Though Ben, who recounts the incident, recognizes that
the story is "secret and important to her," he misunder-
stands the reference to Abel; he thinks Abel is the son in
the story, but he is the father. In their love scene, Angela
imagines Abel as a "great Bear." Though she is pregnant
by her white husband, she fears and hates the fetus. Her
story is the myth of Peter's birth, and Ben's Navaho version of a similar myth makes it clearer. Ben is reminded
of the Mountain Chant story, of two girls who are seduced
by a bear and a snake. The snake does not impregnate his
lover, but the bear has a child by his and begins a generation of bearmen. If Abel is the bear, then Martin St. John,
Angela's husband, should somehow be a snake. The witch
of "The Longhair" was a "white man" and a snake, and
Abel's assailant in "The Priest of the Sun" was a white
man named Martinez and nicknamed *"culebra"* or rattle-
snake. These parallels establish a clear connection between these two characters and Martin St. John; the implications of these correspondences is that Peter's white father is spiritually sterile, like the sterile snake of the Navaho story, and Peter's spiritual father is Abel. In Angela's
mythmaking, her son becomes the savior Christ. Like
Christ, Peter has dubious parentage; like Christ, he has a
physical father and a spiritual father; and like Christ, he
is to "save his people." That Peter's "people" are white
adds an ironic overtone to this complex system of meanings and associations. But Abel's role in Angela's myth of
her own transfiguration is clear. The great bear is a new
agent of divine impregnation when it mounts her in the
body of Abel.

Smaller, less important, but provocative contact points between Angela and the Virgin occur in the early part of the
novel. She first appears on July 21, the feast of two
Marys—the Virgin because it is Saturday, Mary Magdalene because the latter's regular feast falls on Sunday the
twenty-second and hence must be celebrated on Saturday.
Angela's appearance in the novel is immediately preceded
by the ringing of the Angelus, a hymn of the Virgin. Later
Momaday reveals rather circuitously the exact date of her
arrival at Walatowa. Of July 25 and the Benavides house
he says:

> It was no longer the chance place of her visita-
> tion, or the tenth day, but now the dominion of
> her next day and the day after, as far ahead as
> she cared to see.

"Visitation" is the key word, referring to the visitation of
a priest and to Mary's visit to Elizabeth, the mother of
John the Baptist. "Dominion" is also a key word, with its
religious connotations. But the strange fact is the selection
of days. If July 25th was the tenth day, then Angela arrived on the feast of Our Lady of Mt. Carmel, July 16th.
And the day on which this information is revealed is July
26th (it is after midnight), the feast of St. Anne, the mother of Mary.

One's immediate reaction to this data might be that Angela is a blasphemous caricature of Mary, but in fact she rep-

resents a revision of the orthodox mother of God, and the
form of that revision suggests the form of Abel's salvation.
Angela's physical appearance changes to dramatize the revision: when she first arrives at Walatowa, Father Olguin
is attracted to her because she seems a proper type of the
Virgin. She is beautiful but not sensual; her beauty is of
the spiritual or ascetic sort. She is all black and white, with
black hair and pale skin, pale nails, pale lipstick. She is
thin though not unattractively so. She is, in fact, a-sensual,
a hater of flesh and disgusted with the workings of her own
body, which she speaks of in terms drawn from the anatomical and physiological preoccupations of a doctor, like
her white husband:

> She could think of nothing more vile and ob-
> scene than the raw flesh and blood of her body,
> the raveled veins and the gore upon her
> bones . . . She did not fear death, only the
> body's implication in it. And at odd moments
> she wished with all her heart to die by fire, fire
> of such intense heat that her body would dis-
> solve in it all at once. There must be no popping
> of fat or any burning on of the bones. Above all
> she must give off no stench of death.

Her affair with Abel changes her attitudes, Olguin's attitude toward her, and even her appearance. When she re-
enters the novel, near the end, she is no longer black and
white but "golden," "silver," and "copper." Her child is
no longer a "monstrous fetal form . . . feeding upon her,"
but an object of almost religious adoration. And when she
confesses to Olguin, immediately after making love to
Abel, her confession is "far from desperate, underlain with
perfect presence"; she confesses as a way of informing Olguin and of deflating his pretensions of understanding the
Indians, rather than from a sense of sin. While Olguin is
with her and after he departs in a rage, she communes
with the rain, craving its touch and listening to it instead
of him:

> She closed her eyes, and the clear aftervision of
> the rain, which she could still hear and feel so
> perfectly as to conceive of nothing else, obliterat-
> ed all the mean and myriad fears that had laid
> hold of her in the past.

Through the agency of her affair with Abel, Angela
achieves the reconciliation of flesh and spirit which, ironically, Abel is seeking. The new savior is born of a sensual
mating with a bear, not through the chaste agency of a
dove. The virgin is not a virgin but adulteress, since Angela's spiritual lover is a sensate being. This integration of
flesh and spirit is represented by Angela's transformation
into a chthonic mother in the latter part of the novel, and
her return to her own roots, to Los Angeles, points the
way of Abel's salvation. Angela accepts the real world into
which she must fit, and Abel must return to Walatowa for
the same spiritual peace. Angela sustains her life with a
self-fulfilling myth, the "lie" of Peter's paternity, and Abel
must, in his fashion, create or adopt a myth to sustain himself.

Bleak and painful though the conclusion may be, clearly
the implication of the final pages of the novel is that, for
Abel, to live in holy poverty is better than to subsist in Los
Angeles. Ben Benally, a Navaho who has "made it" in the

big city, illustrates the hollow merits of low income living. He protests that in the Indian Southwest, "the land is empty and dead" and full of "a lot of old people, going no place and dying off," a view explicitly contradicted by the narrator. Ben talks of opportunity in Los Angeles, of getting "money and clothes" and "going someplace fast." Yet he has one Goodwill coat, which he gives away in a futile gesture of Christian charity; he lives in a flat with cobwebs and soggy floor. In this surreal environment, "it's dark all the time, even at noon, and the lights are always on. But at night when it rains the lights are everywhere." Even his wages are at the mercy of a sadistic policeman's whims. He sits alone in his room for some fifty pages of text, yet says of his town, "You never have to be alone," adding that you can always go downtown and mingle with the crowds of white shoppers—though they are people whose talk "you can't understand." Even Ben's sexual aesthetics are distorted by his environment. The beautiful women of Momaday's Southwest are characterized by slimness and grace, girls iike Francisco's Porcingula, Abel's Angela, and even Ben's girl Pony. But in Los Angeles Ben says of Manygoats' girl, "She was goodlooking, that girl—you know, great big breasts" and he wonders at Abel's interest in Angela because "she was goodlooking, all right, but she wasn't young or big anywhere and I couldn't see anything to get excited about."

In spite of the consolations of peyote and sing-parties, even an enterprising go-getter like Ben leads a bleak, barren, and dehumanizing life in Los Angeles. Through the entire "Night Chanter" runs a thread of defensiveness and homesickness. In rainy Los Angeles, one can have money if he pays the price, as Ben does, but perhaps money without spiritual sustenance is as worthless as rain falling on asphalt streets. Water is wealth in New Mexico; rain is the greatest blessing of God in Indian country. But in the white world, as represented by Los Angeles, the rain is wasted; it ruins floors, ceilings, beds, and it fertilizes nothing.

It might appear that Milly, Abel's white girlfriend in the city, represents a way of coming to terms with the white world. But Milly offers a merely temporal assistance. As a social worker, her primary concern is with Abel's secular well-being. She offers the same stagnant life that Ben is trapped in:

> . . . Milly believed in tests, questions and answers, words on paper. She was a lot like Ben. She believed in Honor, Industry, the Second Chance, the Brotherhood of Man, the American Dream . . .

Milly offers no more than the illusion of an escape; there is nothing she can do for Abel's soul, because she doesn't understand his spiritual needs. She can't even share her own heritage with him, because she comes from a childhood more painful, more barren, than his own. She, like Angela, has a myth of her motherhood, but hers is founded on the terrible, nihilistically final death of her daughter Carrie. Neither Milly nor Angela can offer Abel any relief from his physical situation. To stay with Milly means to become another Ben, cut off from all but the most meager spiritual benefits, living in too much rain, with enough money to stay drunk but not enough to escape a private, one-room ghetto, talking about getting ahead but running in place, a victim like the helpless grunions Abel imagines on the seashore. Not even Angela can intervene to save him. No real relationship is possible between her and Abel, since for Angela their relationship is not real or social, but mythic, something she has created from the raw material of her experience with him, and the myth can only be sustained in his absence. Her salvation is parallel to, rather than equal to, his; Abel must learn to live in his native world, just as Angela learns to function in her world.

Angela has learned to let her mind and body move evenly together; she alone of all the women is a successful mother, and aside from Tosamah's grandmother, Aho, only she can create nurturing myth and recognize its value. Milly, Porcingula, Abel's mother, all in some way fail their children. Of the three young men in the novel—Ben, Abel, and Tosamah—only Tosamah has achieved a significant melding of flesh and spirit and "seen to the center of the world's being." He attributes his good fortune to the teaching of Aho. Angela's role as analogue of the Virgin is not to provide salvation, but to aid and comfort Abel as he seeks it. By re-creating for him the myth of their affair, she demonstrates for him the sustaining power of mythic perspective, the redeeming strength of sacramental vision.

In her wholeness of flesh and spirit, Angela can survive in her own world; but the tragedy of Abel, and, by extension, of the Indian in white America, is that he must choose between spiritual and physical poverty, between the dehumanizing and spiritually sterile white world and the material poverty of the pueblo. Any romantic heroism in Abel's final choice is undercut by the fact that the decision is practically made for him. He does not so much choose to go back as permit himself to be driven back by circumstances beyond his control. [The critic adds in a footnote: "If Momaday had simply had Abel pack his bag and go back, surely he would be open to charges of romanticizing his hero. From a sociological viewpoint, his return to Walatowa is a defeat."] Nevertheless, his return is the proper end; he could never find peace—or prosperity—in the land's end hell of Los Angeles.

Bleak and ambiguous though Abel's return and the final moments of the novel are, Momaday loads his concluding pages with suggestions of potential, perhaps even imminent triumph. Francisco and Angela are the two models for Abel's redemption; these two, the "longhairs" of the first part of the novel, point a path to him from their different perspectives. In a deathbed dream, Francisco recalls the sacramental killing of a bear in his youth, his initiation into manhood, and the rite is in a sense Abel's initiation, the sacrament of Abel's atonement. After this rite, Abel can truly be the bear and feel its medicinal power. As Francisco and the bear act out their drama, they demonstrate that death is natural and not to be feared; Francisco sees death in a sacred manner, and the bear feels no fear, not even any hurt as Francisco shoots it, only sadness. Abel's inability to see the rightness of the death of creatures is part of the wound in his soul that must be healed.

In a white man's way, he sees the empirical reality of things—a shot goose, a huddled captive eagle—instead of their transcendent, sacramental forms. After his experiences in Los Angeles, his skirmish with death, Abel has lost his paralyzing horror of mortality and learned, as Francisco has always known, that evil is abroad in the night and must be faced,

> not in the hope of anything, but hopelessly; neither in fear nor hatred nor despair of evil, but simply in recognition and respect.

This vision of the dignity in dancing over the abyss, recalled by Francisco in his last delirium, is the motive for Abel's dawn run; this vision opens onto the path of salvation.

Angela adds one further undertone to these final moments of the novel, for she is in the background of February 28th, that last dawn, giving one last Catholic association to the theme of Abel's salvation. In 1952, the feastday of Angela of Foligno, the spiritual child of St. Francis of Assisi and the author of a book on the way of salvation, fell on February 28th, the day after Ash Wednesday. Described in Butler's *Lives* as one of the three great medieval mystics, her final vision closely parallels the last moments of the novel and sums up the theme of spiritual and temporal well-being: she saw an "abyss of light in which the truth of God was spread out like a road . . ." and the Lord said "Follow my footsteps from the cross on earth to this light." When Abel begins to run in the gathering light, pursuing the strong and healthy runners outdistancing him, running like Francisco after the shadows ahead, running beyond his pain, it is the morning after Ash Wednesday. When he joins the runners that morning, the day signifies not a resurrection, not a completed assimilation into his culture, but the beginning of forty days of penance. Abel's first act of penance, running in the rain, dusted with ashes, gives him back the words of Ben's song about the generative pollen, the rising sun; then gives him back his own language. The dawn is not a salvation but the beginning of salvation, the forty days in the wilderness from which Abel could return in triumph.

Joseph F. Trimmer   (essay date Autumn 1975)

SOURCE: "Native Americans and the American Mix: N. Scott Momaday's *House Made of Dawn,*" in *The Indiana Social Studies Quarterly,* Vol. XXVIII, No. 2, Autumn, 1975, pp. 75-91.

[*Trimmer is an American nonfiction writer, editor, and educator. In the following essay, he provides an overview of the themes and structure of* House Made of Dawn, *and discusses whether the book meets the Pulitzer Prize's criterion of recognizing works which support "the wholesomeness of culture."*]

At the beginning of this century when Joseph Pulitzer was composing the citations for the literary awards to be given in his name [in recognition "for the American novel published during the year which shall best present the wholesome atmosphere of American life and the highest standard of American manners and manhood"], he could not

have foreseen that in 1969 the fiction prize would be given to a Kiowa Indian, N. Scott Momaday, for a novel, *House Made of Dawn,* that would reveal why the wholesome American way could not assimilate and sustain everyone on the American continent. Even in our own time, the savants of contemporary literature did not foresee that this first novel by an unknown author would be singled out by the Pulitzer judges. It produced no extensive commentary when it was published—perhaps, as [William James Smith mused in a review of the work in *Commonweal* LXXXVIII (20 September 1968)] because "it seems slightly un-American to criticize an American Indian's novel"—and its subject matter and theme did not seem to conform to the prescription above. W. J. Stuckey has demonstrated [in *The Pulitzer Prize Novels: A Critical Backward Look* (1966)] that throughout the controversial history of the Pulitzer competition, the judges have usually adhered to the original prescription by selecting books that express a very traditional or conservative view of American culture. The major tenet of this view is that the ideal of rugged individualism, as it was formed on the frontier and codified in the American dream of success, remains the most reliable way of characterizing the mainstream of "American manners and manhood." Perhaps the Pulitzer judges saw the novel as dealing with a different form of the frontier experience or appreciated its affirmation of the conservative values of continuity and tradition. But *House Made of Dawn* would be better characterized as offering a view of American culture that is absolutely alien to the Pulitzer prescription. Indeed, because it reveals the deficiencies of American culture and affirms the values of Indian culture, the novel illustrates Leslie Fiedler's contention [in the 1968 *The Return of the Vanishing American*] that the Indian is the "utter stranger . . . [who] in his ultimate otherness has teased and baffled the imagination of generation after generation" of Americans.

To say that *House Made of Dawn* describes a different culture is not to say that it describes an indecipherable one. Early reviewers [such as Marshall Sprague in his "Anglos and Indians," *New York Times Book Review* (9 June 1968)] complained that the novel contained "plenty of haze" but suggested that perhaps this was inevitable in rendering "the mysteries of cultures different from our own." And those few critics [such as Carole Oleson in her "The Remembered Earth: Momaday's *House Made of Dawn,*" *South Dakota Review* II (Spring 1973)] who have given the novel extended analysis acknowledge that much more explanation is needed "before outsiders can fully appreciate all the subtleties of *House Made of Dawn.*" Because much of our contemporary fiction has been written by authors from America's various ethnic minorities, some spokesmen for these ethnic groups have challenged the right of disinterested critics to interpret "minority" literature. But the recognition of cultural differences should not prevent outsiders from attempting to discover the meanings amidst the apparent haze. To suggest that the novel's cultural differences make it incomprehensible to the non-Indian reader not only limits the universality of its theme, but also denies it its rightful place in the history of American literature, a history that has always been distinguished by the achievements of artists who have written out of their individual ethnic or regional experience rather than some vague notion of an homogenous American experience.

It is true that *House Made of Dawn,* like many modern American novels, presents some initial problems for the uninitiated. The characters seem flat and enigmatic because their motivation is not detailed with clinical precision; the plot seems, on occasion, fragmented and confusing because the transitions are not signaled by elaborate exposition; and the style seems unnecessarily compressed and cryptic because it is punctuated with a variety of oblique images. But given his subject, Momaday's use of these characteristic features of the modern novel seems appropriate: the world of the Indian in modern America appears to be a world with an eroding center, a world of fragments in danger of losing whatever cultural coherence it still retains; it is also a world dominated by the enormity of the physical landscape and the immediacy of sensory perceptions, a world diminished rather than explained by extensive use of "the word." Yet the world of the novel, like the world it describes, operates in accord with laws that confer perspective, design, and meaning. And like the novel's major character Abel, the reader will be able to find his place in this world once he learns to understand and accept these laws.

The Prologue that opens the novel depicts Abel, naked to the waist and smeared with ashes, running in the annual race for good hunting and harvest. As Carole Oleson points out, "all that Momaday will tell us of the human condition is summarized on that one page of prologue, but we must go on to the beginning of the story and curve around to the end, then read again the prologue in order to understand what he is saying here." The first paragraph describes the "old and everlasting" land: it is immense, multicolored, and seems to abide forever in the cycle of the seasons. The second paragraph describes Abel as he runs alone across this landscape, and his running, as we shall see in more detail later, functions as a multiple symbol: it is a ceremonial designation of the dawning of a new season, it marks the continuation of a cultural tradition into the next generation, and it embodies the essential wisdom Abel gains about his purpose and place in the world. Later in the novel, Abel will have a vision of men running: "they were whole and indispensable in what they did; everything in creation referred to them. Because of them, perspective, proportion, design in the universe. Meaning because of them." But here in the Prologue, the image of the running man carries no such significance. The reader is certainly not aware of the meanings that will eventually accrue to this simple act, and Abel does not *see,* at least not in a symbolic sense, the ultimate importance of his act, a fact suggested by his inability to see around the curve in the road and through the bank of rain. Once the reader reaches the end of the novel, however, he, like Abel, will understand the significance of the race, will understand that the end is in the beginning.

The novel proper is divided into four sections each marked by titles that seemingly refer to the major character developed in that section: "The Longhair" (Abel); "The Priest of the Sun" (Tosamah); "The Night Chanter" (Benally); and "The Dawn Runner" (Francisco). This identification

is not nearly as neat as it would appear, however, because Abel is the center of consciousness for much of section 2, the major subject of section 3, and the major actor in section 4. Equally important stories, such as Angela's, Father Olguin's, Fray Nicolas's, Milly's, and old Carlozini's, are also mixed into sections 1, 2, and 3. More significantly, the identities of Abel and Francisco are intentionally blurred in sections 1 and 4 to reinforce the theme of generational continuity: Francisco, who begins, appears intermittently throughout, and ends section 1, is as surely a "longhair" as Abel, whose memories and actions dominate the section and who is labeled a longhair in section 3; similarly, although Francisco's deathbed memories dominate section 4, Abel begins the section and ends the novel when he becomes "the dawn runner" in the race that was once the major event in his grandfather's life.

The design and sequence of the four sections are also important to the themes of the novel. The first and last take place in the expansive sunlit landscape of Walatowa and the middle sections take place in the claustrophobic darkness of Los Angeles. The journey to and from Los Angeles, reinforced as it is by the onset of night and the return of day, suggests not only the cyclical pattern already mentioned but also the sense of dawning awareness experienced by both Abel and the reader. On first reading, section 1 appears almost incomprehensible. Abel's fragmented memories are elliptical and confusing, and the inscrutable tribal ceremonies in which he participates are only partially explained by the "outside" commentator, Father Olguin. When we move away from the sunlight of the reservation to the neon of the city in section 2, we feel momentarily enlightened by the elaborate analysis of the historical-cultural condition of the Indian offered by The Right Reverend John Big Bluff Tosamah, Pastor of the Los Angeles Holiness Pan-Indian Rescue Mission and Priest of the Sun. And in section 3, we feel even more enlightened by Benally's sympathetic interpretation of why Abel, the unlucky longhair, failed to make it in Los Angeles. But this linear movement from mystery to meaning is misleading because neither Tosamah nor Benally really sees the significance of Abel's experience. In this context, it should be noted that Momaday uses a variety of sight images throughout the novel to symbolize degrees of knowledge and insight. Once we read section 4, we *see,* and perhaps in a different sense Abel also *sees,* that the seductive glitter of the white world has corrupted Tosamah's and Benally's vision. They may see Abel's return to the reservation as a return to darkness and defeat, but it is they who remain unenlightened (literally, in the dark) about the meaning of Abel's assumption of his foreordained place. Thus, as certain traditions are clarified and passed on to Abel in section 4, the reader is educated about the meaning of the mysterious events in section 1—again, the novel recycles to the beginning.

One final comment needs to be made about the overall design and structure of the novel before moving on to an analysis of its individual sections. Each of the four sections is subdivided into smaller chapters designated by dates: section 1 contains seven such chapters identified by seven dates between July 20 and August 2, 1945; section 2 contains two chapters, January 26 and 27, 1952; section 3, one, February 20, 1952; and section 4, two, February 27 and 28, 1952. Once we piece together the major events in Abel's life—his service in the army, his return to the reservation, his imprisonment for killing the Albino, and his abortive stay in Los Angeles—these dates present themselves as a meaningful seven-year sequence. They are as important to Abel's growth into manhood as the date of Francisco's victory in the dawn race is to his, a date that Francisco commemorates with a pencil drawing of a running man inscribed with the legend "1889." But like the headings for the major sections, the dates for these chapters only nominally control content. The chronological unity of each chapter is fractured by the personal recollections of characters and by the more extensive historical context provided Fray Nicolas's journals and the prehistoric accounts of the epic migration of the Kiowas out of the forested mountains, the tragic journey of the Bahkyush in search of a home, and the legendary descent of man from the caves down the ladder of the canyon to the plains. This constant mixing of contemporary experience with historical, and even mythical, experiences suggests that the novel renders time more as a repetitive cycle than a linear sequence. Certainly, the reader is more aware of time evolving within the cycle of a single season, from February (Prologue) to February (Section 4), than time advancing along a continuum from 1945 to 1952. In fact, time, like vision, is a major motif in the novel: Abel must see, must understand, must know what time it is, if he is to be able to find his place in the world. In section 4, Francisco explains the "long journey of the sun on the black mesa . . . the larger motion and meaning of the great organic calendar," and suddenly everything falls into place. We see that the dates of the chapters mark not only the major events in Abel's life but also the important ceremonial days of a culture. Like the sun's journey along the mesa, Abel's journey can thus be understood as a sequence within a cycle: the end of all his journeying is to return to the place where he began; once there, his race, like his grandfather's, will commemorate the dawn of a new beginning.

The seven chapters of "The Longhair" make it the largest and most complex of the novel's four sections. Repeating the pattern of the Prologue, the section opens with a description that organizes the landscape and evokes the orderly cycle of the seasons. We next see an old man, Francisco, stopping his wagon near the river to inspect a snare he has constructed to trap a bird for a prayer plume; he hopes to catch a bird with bright feathers, like a bluebird or tanager, but when to his disappointment he finds only a sparrow in his trap, he resets the snare and drives on. This small episode contains images and themes that reappear everywhere in the novel. The theme of disappointment is a constant, emerging with particular poignancy in the Los Angeles sections, but of more significance is the theme of entrapment. The trapping and killing of a variety of birds throughout the novel represents metaphorically the sense of imprisonment Abel feels whenever he is forced out of the world he knows and is enmeshed in the confusion of an alien culture: for example, at the end of section 1, he will be trapped in the embrace of the mysterious Albino, and in Los Angeles, he will be cornered in an alley by the equally ominous Martinez.

The first chapter concludes with two brief episodes. As Francisco continues his journey along the ancient road, he remembers the details of his victorious run in 1889. Invading this environment is the "strange sound" of the bus as it brings Abel home from the army. The bus stops, "the door swung open and Abel stepped heavily to the ground and reeled. He was drunk and he fell against his grandfather and did not know him." In contrast to his grandfather, who knows the place of the snare and whose running has earned him a place in the tribe, Abel is here portrayed as having lost his place. His experiences in the white world have disturbed his balance, blurred his vision, and infected him with "bad medicine."

It is to exorcise the influence of these experiences and to restore his sense of place that on the next day Abel climbs high above the valley to watch the coming of dawn. As he sits above this familiar landscape, Abel tries to "remember" the fragments of his shattered life. Each of the memories in this biographical sequence of seven touches on the themes of confusion, disappointment, and estrangement. The first three, which deal with Abel's early boyhood, underscore his sense of his difference from others, the foreboding mystery of the landscape, and the impermanence of life. We learn, for example, that his father, a Navajo who has deserted the family, was considered an "Isleta, an outsider . . . which made him and his mother and Vidal somehow foreign and strange." And we learn that Abel lives in dread of the moaning wind because "it would be for him the particular sound of anguish," a sound he connects with the unintelligible curses of the witch woman Nicolas, and the deaths of his mother and brother, Vidal. The fourth memory details Abel's initiation into manhood and acceptance by the community, but even though he kills a doe and returns with it for a triumphant ceremonial dance, he is disappointed in the evening's lovemaking with one of Medina's daughters. When he wants her a second time, she runs and then stands at some distance laughing at his drunken attempts to follow her.

The fifth memory, Abel's experiences with the Eagle Watchers Society, contains information vital to our understanding of Abel's final decision at the end of the novel. Outsiders often assume that Indian culture is a single entity, but this episode and others throughout the novel suggest that Indian culture, like American culture, is quite diverse. The twenty Bahkyush survivors of persecution and plague demonstrate not only the essential pluralism of Indian culture, but also those qualities that insure their survival within the dominant culture of their hospitable kinsmen. In fact, the Bahkyush did more than survive. By maintaining an allegiance to the traditions and ceremonies central to their faith, they became an important and even a superior society within their new tribe: "It was as if, conscious of having come close to extinction, they had got a keener sense of pride. . . . They had acquired a tragic sense, which gave to them as a race so much dignity and bearing." Abel's vision of the exalted sport of a pair of eagles in the sky above Valle Grande qualifies him to join these medicine men on their November hunt. But he feels "something like remorse or disappointment" when he has to kill rabbits for bait, and he experiences "shame and disgust" once he sees the noble eagle he has captured reduced to a "drab," "shapeless," "ungainly" bird in a sack. The eagle, unlike the society that bears its name, cannot survive with dignity in a different environment. Abel, who will eventually find himself caught in a similar situation in the alien environment of Los Angeles, responds sympathetically to the eagle's plight when he holds its "throat in the darkness and cut[s] off its breath."

Abel's final two memories concern his initial departure into the anomalous world of the white man. Both memories concern the nightmarish movements of a machine. The bus that takes him away to the army represents a new and strange form of imprisonment: he feels trapped behind its glass windows, estranged from his environment, as he experiences "the jar of the engine and the first hard motion of the wheels, . . . the lurch and loss of momentum." Abel's single recollection of the war focuses on a monstrous tank that appears dramatically in his vision as it climbs over a ridge and blots out the sun. As it passes him, "a wind arose and ran along the slope, scattering leaves."

This allusion to the wind reminds us that Abel's war experience is only one of many that have contributed to his alienation: he has never felt at home in the world. His actions throughout section 1 suggest, however, that his return to Walatowa signals the beginning of an attempt to find his place within the orderly traditions of his people. But before we examine his participation in these activities, it would be best to consider two other characters who suffer from the torments of alienation.

Like Abel, Angela St. John (the white woman who has come to the Benevides house, Los Ojos, searching for a vision of the good life) has lost her sense of place. Her pregnancy has caused her to feel vaguely dissatisfied and trapped. Her doctor-husband has sent her to Walatowa for the cure, but as she paces throughout the house it is clear that her daily baths and reading from the lives of the saints will not provide her with the perspective she desires. She senses in the Indian ceremonies and in Abel's expressionless face "some reality that she did not know, or even suspect. . . . Somewhere, if only she should see it, there was neither nothing or anything. And there, just there, *that* was the lost reality." She searches for this exotic other-reality in her relationship with Abel; she even compares their love-making to a totemic vision she has had about touching the wet, black snout of a bear. Her position between the white and Indian worlds is indicated by her names: *Angela* ties her to Los Angeles (the scene of Abel's abortive relocation) and the Catholic tradition but also to Maria de Los Angeles, Porcingula, and Our Lady of the Angels, interchangeable names for the patroness of the Bahkyush, the old witch-woman Francisco loves, and the totem at the center of the ceremony of the little house and the bull; similarly, *St. John* ties her to the Catholic tradition but also to Tosamah's sermon at the Pan-Indian Rescue Mission in section 2. By the conclusion of section 1, Angela has learned to *see* the value of these multiple traditions and no longer feels lost: she sees no need to confess to Father Olguin, and despite the onset of a horrifying storm, she does not feel threatened by the environment. In section 3, back in her place in the suburbs of Westwood,

she will demonstrate that she has learned something from her experiences in Walatowa.

Like his predecessor Fray Nicolas, Father Olguin feels trapped in the confusing world of the Indian. Both men want to educate and sanctify those poor souls still bewitched by "dark custom," but neither has had much impact on the culture around him. Fray Nicolas's poor health and Father Olguin's limited vision suggest that their religious tradition can neither thrive nor bring enlightenment to the Indian community. Fray Nicolas's journal indicates that he was "not called" to attend the death of Tomacita Fraqua until it was time for burial, and in section 4 Father Olguin will not be called to attend the death of Francisco, one of Fray Nicolas's sacristans, until Abel has finished preparing his grandfather for burial. As Oleson points out, "the priests see themselves as models for the heathen, but the villagers relegate them only a part of their religious traditions, adding Catholic mass to their ceremonial life while subtracting nothing of their own."

Because Father Olguin is half-blind, it is ironic that he should *explain* the meaning of the first of the two major ceremonial occasions in section 1. According to his narrative, the rooster race commemorates Santiago's successes in the games at the royal city and his gifts of animals and harvest to the Pueblo people. By tradition, Santiago (St. James) is said to have brought Christianity to the primitive culture of Spain. In Father Olguin's version of the story, Santiago appears disguised as a peon in the American Southwest, is given hospitality by an old couple who sacrifice their only possession of value, a rooster, to provide him a meal, is victorious in the royal games and thus wins the king's daughter ("a girl with almond-shaped eyes and long black hair"), avoids the king's treachery when the rooster he had previously eaten is miraculously restored to warn him and to provide him with a sword to slay the king's guard, and insures the wealth of the Pueblos forever by sacrificing the rooster and his horse. The ceremony that Father Olguin and Angela observe contains many of the details from this legend, but their precise identification and meaning remain obscure, and the results of the ceremony seem enigmatic indeed. The rooster race is a game; Angela, whose "hair is long and very dark," can be seen as the prize for victory; and Abel, who has only recently exchanged his army uniform for his old clothes might conceivably be seen as enacting the role of one of the king's guard. The Albino, whose name, Juan Reyes, is perhaps meant as a symbolic allusion to John, brother of James, triumphs at the game and holds the rooster high above his head as he reins his horse to a stop in front of Angela. Abel, astride "his grandfather's roan black horse," is then singled out, trapped, and beaten with the rooster. The Albino, who is larger and more powerful than the other contestants and whose poor eyes are covered by black glasses shaped like pennies, is clearly a figure of mystery. But unlike the legendary Santiago, the Albino's victory does not seem to portend success for the Indian culture. His brutality and destructiveness seem impulsive, somehow not part of the normal ceremony: "there was something out of place, some flaw in proportion or design, some unnatural thing." The white man plays the game but does so with a malice that seems to reverse rather than exemplify the theme of the Santiago legend. In fact, his un-natural whiteness and insatiable cruelty seem to tie him symbolically to the white culture that brutalized and de-stroyed the wealth of the Indian culture. Whatever the Al-bino's exact identity, Francisco and Abel seem justified in identifying him as an alien and evil force.

The second major ceremony contains a similar cast of symbolic characters and is enacted to celebrate the "re-turn of weather, of trade and reunion," of wealth to the town. At the center of the ritual is Porcingula, Our Lady of Angels, who serves as both the shrine at the center of the Catholic Mass and the patroness of the Bahkyush. The two other characters in this ritual, the bull and the little horse, are also part of the tradition of the Bahkyush. The little horse, with its spotted hide, "black hat and black mask," is reminiscent of the little horse that Abel rode in the rooster race, and the bull, with its black costume "painted with numerous white rings" and its eyes repre-sented with black metal buttons, evokes the image of the Albino, particularly since the bull also has the "look of evil." But this ceremony reverses the results of the first: the bull is made an object of ridicule and revelry as the children, dressed as black-faced clowns, chase it through the streets and the little horse not only leads the lovely Lady through the streets but also is given prayers, plumes, pollen, and meal by the medicine men.

For the outsider, the ultimate meaning of each detail in these ceremonies remains inscrutable. And significantly, the white outsider (Father Olguin) who attempted to ex-plain the first ceremony in which the Albino is triumphant is excluded from this second ceremony when he is trapped in his car and, like the bull, ridiculed by the children. But for Francisco, this montage of rituals forms a unified tra-dition that gives design and meaning to existence. Con-fronting and exorcising evil as well as bestowing wealth are the inescapable conditions of the yearly cycle: he has sensed the presence of an evil force (the Albino) amidst the rows of corn awaiting harvest and he has even played the bull several times in the annual harvest ceremony. But he acknowledges that it is difficult to understand these things "now that the men of the town had relaxed their hold upon the ancient ways, had grown soft and dubious." Abel too recognizes the deeper significance of these ceremonies. When, after a long day of harvest celebration, he is trapped by the embrace of the Albino, he kills him. Later, at his trial, he will say that he killed an "evil spirit": "He had killed the white man. It was not a complicated thing after all, it was very simple. It was the most natural thing in the world. . . . . A man kills such an enemy if he can."

The white judge is not satisfied with this explanation, how-ever, and so condemns Abel to jail for committing "a bru-tal and premeditated act." Thus, while Abel has symboli-cally slain Cain, Abel remains Cain's victim. His experi-ences in the white man's jail, like his experiences in the white man's army, produce bewilderment. When he serves his seven-year term and is relocated in Los Angeles, he can recall from his prison experience only the vague shape of the walls of his cell. Los Angeles proves even more disori-enting. As Oleson points out, Abel resembles the small

silversided fish he sees spawning on the California beach: "they hurl themselves upon the land and writhe in the light of the moon, the moon; they writhe in the light of the moon. They are among the most helpless creatures on the face of the earth." Like the fish who once thrived in the sea, Abel is floundering on the beach: "He had lost his place. He had been long ago at the center, had known where he was, had lost his way, had wandered to the end of the earth, was even now reeling on the edge of the void." This is the situation for all the Indians who gather at the bar called The Silver Dollar or who attend the peyote cere-monies at the Pan-Indian Rescue Mission. But like Father Olguin, who continues to celebrate the Mass in the primi-tive culture of Walatowa, these Indians continue to try to find a place in urban America.

"The Priest of the Sun," section 2, is centered in Abel's consciousness as he lies drunk and beaten on a California beach. The memories that form in his mind are more dis-jointed and garbled than the more orderly sequence he re-called in section 1, but his loss of intelligibility is indicative of both his immediate situation and his experiences ever since he came to Los Angeles. Those experiences are given an historical context by The Priest of the Sun, John Big Bluff Tosamah, whose sermon on "The Gospel According to John" appears as a coherent unit amidst Abel's incoher-ent reveries. He begins by fashioning a vision of creation for his audience to illustrate that "in the beginning was the world." But then, like the John in his text, John Tosa-mah's vision fails him and he must go on to explain what the Truth meant: "He tried to make it bigger and better than it was, but instead he demeaned and encumbered it." According to Tosamah

> . . . old John was a white man, and the white man has his ways. Oh gracious me, he has his ways. He talks about the Word. He talks through it and around it. He builds upon it with syllables, with prefixes and suffixes, and hyphens and accents. He adds and divides and multiplies the Word. And in all this he subtracts the Truth. And, brothers and sisters, you have come here to live in the white man's world. Now the white man deals in words, and he deals easily, with grace and sleight of hand. And in his presence, here on his own ground, you are as children, mere babes in the woods.

In the long history of the Indian's relationship to white America, he has often been betrayed and deceived by the word. And certainly Abel feels, at his trial, in prison, and in Los Angeles that the white man's *words*—especially as they are characterized by the endless questionnaires he is given by prison officials and social workers—have no di-rect relationship to his life. Indeed, the white man has for-gotten that words, in Emerson's terminology, are signs of natural facts: the white man's words no longer connect with the physical world. And because his words abstract, dilute, and attenuate experience, the white man has be-come sated and insensitive to the world around him. His fascination for the prolification of paper and the enclo-sures of cement and steel protects him from confronting either himself or nature.

Certainly this alienation from nature helps explain the history of Milly, the white social worker Abel lives with in Los Angeles. Like Abel, Milly is a refugee in Los Angeles. Her father was a farmer, but unlike Francisco, who reveres the land he cultivates even though it is often cracked and dry, "Daddy began to hate the land, began to think of it as some kind of enemy, his own personal and deadly enemy." His counsel to his daughter is to leave the place, but her arrival in the city of lights brings only tragedy and death: her husband deserts her and her child dies of a burning fever. Like Angela before her, Milly gives herself to Abel out of a vague sense of her own incompleteness. She may provide for Abel by bringing him food and finding him jobs, but it is Abel who sustains Milly by providing her with a symbolic link to the land she has left and lost.

In a slightly different sense, Tosamah is also a refugee. He may possess all the sophistication of white culture, but in his second sermon, "The Way to Rainy Mountain," he acknowledges that he too has lost something. It is because he wishes to understand his grandmother's culture that he reenacts the epic journey of the Kiowa tribe. Originally, the tribe lived in the high wall of woods in the mountains, but "the Kiowas reckoned their stature by the distance they could see, and they were bent and blind in the wilderness." They migrated to the open plains where they confronted the immensity of the landscape and the constant illumination of the sun. It was only natural that the sun became their god, but the tribe lost contact with their god when the white man killed the buffalo and forbade the sun dance, "the essential act of their faith." Thus, unlike the Bahkyush, the Kiowas were denied their sense of cultural identity. Without such an identity, Tosamah finds it difficult to understand his place in the world. Of course, Tosamah continues to serve as a "priest of the sun," but he enacts this role with a mixture of "conviction, caricature, callousness." The sun he worships is merely a red and yellow decorative symbol in the dark basement of a Los Angeles tenement. Symbolically, he is as bent and blind within the walls of cement as his ancestors were in the wilderness; he sees the dawn only in the fire of the peyote ceremony, a ceremony that is surely a parody of the way "the ol' people . . . tol' us to do it" and about as meaningful in Los Angeles as the Mass is in Walatowa. In fact, the names of John Big Bluff Tosamah and his disciple Cristabal Cruz suggest that both men may be more interested in conning than serving the Indian community.

Milly's memory of the world her father never loved has turned to nostalgia and Tosamah's understanding of the world his grandmother revered has turned to cynicism, but Abel's experiences in Los Angeles reaffirm his commitment to the old way. He is ridiculed by the urbanized Indians at The Silver Dollar for being a "longhair"; he is dismissed from his job because he fails to adapt to the dulling regimen of time clocks and to maintain the mindless, machine-like perfection required of workers on the line; and he is humiliated and beaten by the powerful Martinez, a representative of the white man's law whom the Indians correctly identify as a *culebra*. Of course, this last experience is not dissimilar to the humiliating beating Abel received from the malevolent Albino, but in Walatowa the culture provided a way to understand and respond to the

evil in the world. As Abel lies beaten on the beach, he sees through his swollen eyes a vision of "the old men in white leggings running after evil in the night. . . . They ran with great dignity and calm, not in the hope of anything, but hopelessly; neither in fear nor hatred nor despair of evil, but simply in recognition and with respect. Evil was. Evil was abroad in the night; they must venture out to the confrontation; they must reckon dues and divide the world." It is the sense of coherence and continuity communicated by this vision that convinces Abel to return to his place in the old culture, to give up the rat race and become a dawn runner.

Benally, Abel's healer and ally, narrates the third section of the novel, "The Night Chanter." The occasion is Abel's departure for the reservation, and as he returns from the train station through the misting rain and blurry neon to his dark apartment, Benally is disturbed by what he takes to be his friend's failure: "He was unlucky. . . . He was a longhair, like Tosamah said. You know, you have to change. That's the only way you can live in a place like this. You have to forget about the way it was, how you grew up and all." Unlike the recalcitrant longhair, Benally is able to change, mainly because he recognizes that "there's nothing else. And you *want* to do it, because you see how good it is. It's better than anything you've ever had; it's money and clothes and having plans and going someplace fast." But as he sits alone in his apartment watching a befuddled pigeon attempt to find its way amidst the maze of dark buildings, it is clear that Benally too has lost his way. He spends his days working on the line and his evenings searching for some momentary human contact. His plight is not unlike that of his neighbor old Carlozini, who shuts herself up in her apartment and shuts her pet guinea pig Vincenzo up in a box: they will all die trapped and alone. Thus, despite his insistence that life can be good in the land of plenty, Benally unknowingly reveals the truth of Tosamah's cynical carping about "Relocation and Welfare and Termination."

Although Benally dismisses the old way—"there's nothing there, you know, just the land, and the land is empty and dead"—he spends a good deal of time thinking about the way it was. His three chants, to the dawn, to his horse, and to beauty, all end with a reckoning of perspective—before, behind, below, above, all around—that suggests the way his culture once made him feel "right there in the center of everything." And his memories of his Navajo grandfather, the cycle of the seasons, and the changeless land suggest that Benally may still wish to be a longhair. In fact, as he recalls riding across the land at dawn on a black horse to dance with the girl named Pony at Cornfields, Benally's memories seem to fuse with Abel's memories of Medina's daughter in section 1. But Benally is finally different from Abel: he has been away to school and he has learned to trade successfully with the white man. He went to the dance at Cornfield once, but he never sees the girl named Pony again. Like the other Los Angeles refugees, he has become trapped on the American treadmill.

At the end of Benally's narrative he tells us that Angela visited Abel when he was in the hospital. Before Abel killed the Albino, "she was going to help him get a job and go away from the reservation." At the hospital, Angela tells Abel that she has thought about him a great deal and that she has passed on to her son "a story about a young Indian brave. He was born of a bear and a maiden . . . and he was noble and wise. He had many adventures, and he became a great leader and saved his people. . . . and she always thought of *him,* Abel, when she told it." This allusion to the bear and the maiden returns us to Angela's totemic vision in section 1 and suggests that Angela has grasped some intimation of that other-reality. For rather than assisting Abel to stay away from the reservation, her story about the young Indian brave confirms his decision to return to his people. Benally responds to Angela's story by saying that it reminds him of a story his grandfather passed on to him about the bear and the snake, the theme of which is the recurrent nature of experience: the bear fathers a child who in turn gives birth to two children, one of whom was carried away by an owl but then escaped to the east where he became a medicine man and fathered an illegitimate child who was found by the bear. This story serves as an appropriate conclusion to Abel's relocation experience because it reinforces the pattern of Abel's return east, to the house of dawn, to the scene of his new beginning.

The scene for much of section 4, "The Dawn Runner," is Francisco's hut. Although the landscape looks bleak and gray, winter is coming to an end. But so is Francisco. Abel sits entrapped in the dark of his grandfather's house for six days while Francisco dies. As he did at the deaths of his mother and brother, Abel feels a sense of despair, a sense of betrayal and abandonment. But Francisco's deathbed memories suggest the continuity rather than the end of a tradition. His memories parallel Abel's memories in section 1, thus suggesting not only the eternal repetition of experience, but also the appropriateness of Abel as an heir to his grandfather's place within the culture. Significantly, Francisco's first memory concerns his attempt to explain the meaning of the "great organic calendar" to his grandsons. Each time the sun dawns along the ridge of the black mesa, it marks the beginning of an important day in the life of their culture: "They must know the long journey of the sun on the black mesa, how it rode in the seasons and the years, and they must live according to the sun appearing, for only then could they reckon where they were, where all things were, in time." Because the events Francisco uses to illustrate the working of this calendar are the major ceremonial occasions in the novel, the reader now understands the schedule of the mysterious rituals in section 1; more importantly, he understands why the novel's title, *House Made of Dawn,* directs and controls the life of the novel.

Francisco's remaining memories concern his own participation in the cycle of events marked by the "house of dawn." He remembers his solitary hunt for the bear along the black mesa, the hunt that marked his initiation into manhood. He first visits the caves of his ancestors where, among the things of the dead, he sees a "great swooping bird" kill a small rodent. Then he tracks the bear along the mesa and finally kills it, marking the bear's eyes with yellow streaks of pollen, disemboweling the bear, and eating quickly of the bear's liver. When he returns to the vil-

lage with the bear, "the men came out to meet him. . . . The men and women were jubilant and all around, and he rode stone-faced in their midst, looking straight ahead." In contrast with this triumphant victory, Francisco remembers his love relationship with Porcingula which, like Abel's love relationship with Angela, produces nothing. But Francisco's dead child is symbolically reborn in Abel who will continue the tradition, just as Francisco remembers that he continued the tradition when the old man passed the drum to him—"and nothing was lost, nothing." Francisco's last memory concerns his discovery that he can no longer go on in the dawn race; this memory comes before the seventh dawn of his dying and marks his death. But Abel emerges on the seventh dawn, smeared with symbolic ashes, to assume his grandfather's place. He falls once, but he gets up and runs on. His running marks the death of winter and his grandfather and the return of life to the land, the day, and his soul: the end is in the beginning.

Just as section 4 returns us to the beginning of the novel, so this conclusion will consider again some of the issues raised at the beginning of this essay. Clearly, the judges were in error if they thought *House Made of Dawn* extended the long tradition of Pulitzer novels which "presented the wholesome atmosphere of American life." In fact, the novel warns native Americans that they may lose more than they gain if they assimilate into the American mix. That culture—represented in the novel by the army, the legal system, the social agency, and the factory—is revealed as distempered, impersonal, moribund, productive of frantic motion and useless objects, but no true life. To believe that this manic activity is not only wholesome, but also productive of "the highest standard of American manners and manhood" is to be willfully deceived by the most pernicious of American fantasies. Tosamah and Benally may continue to pursue this deadly dream, but Abel chooses the Indian culture because its rituals, traditions, and ways of perceiving offer a more wholesome and sustaining vision of manners and manhood. Yet the novel does not prophesy that Abel will actually save his people from cultural disintegration or that his people will save America from its own malignancies. Momaday is realistic enough to agree with Tosamah about the outcome of "What's His Name v. United States." Besides, Momaday is a novelist, not a social leader. He wants to evoke, to make us *see,* as he says in *The Way to Rainy Mountain,* "a landscape that is incomparable, a time that is gone forever, and the human spirit, which endures."

Because Momaday's novel makes us *see,* it confirms, in a rather ironic way, the appropriateness of its selection for the Pulitzer. Such a selection may indicate that we are neither too indifferent to the complexities of Indian culture nor too presumptuous about the superiority of American culture. Certainly, from one perspective, the wholesomeness of American culture depends on its ability to tolerate and learn from those diverse groups in its midst that offer an absolutely alien version of the American experience. Momaday has said that "the Indian is a man from whom a great deal can be learned, for the Indian has always known who and what he is; he has a great capacity for wonder, delight, belief and for communion with the natural world contradictory to the destruction rampant in 'civilization'." Perhaps by the end of *House Made of Dawn* the reader, like Father Olguin, has glimpsed some of what the Indian has to teach:

> Father Olguin shivered with cold and peered out into the darkness. "I can understand," he said. "I understand, do you hear?" And he began to shout "I understand! *Oh God! I understand—I understand!*"

Baine Kerr   (essay date Spring 1978)

SOURCE: "The Novel as Sacred Text: N. Scott Momaday's Myth-Making Ethic," in *Southwest Review,* Vol. 63, No. 2, Spring, 1978, pp. 172-79.

[*In the following essay, Kerr examines Momaday's ability to render Native American culture and beliefs within the Western literary construct of the novel.*]

Recently I sat through a noisy, irreconcilable argument between two Anglos about Indians. An Irish lawyer for the Navajos from Chinle, Arizona, accused an anthropologist friend of blind sacrilege in the Southwest. The anthropologist, who was not present, was defended as an ally of Indians and preserver of culture. The specific issue concerned the unearthing of Anasazi pueblos and especially gravesites in New Mexico's Chaco Canyon, and the withering fear of the Navajo crews once within the Old Ones' middens. The most unholy of trespasses, the lawyer called it, and one likely to bring charges that the crew were *brujos.* Help the Indians, he said, but don't transgress the sacred charnel.

The larger issue, of course, is the dilemma not only of anthropologists but of any investigator, interpreter, even traveler, and perhaps especially writer, dealing with another people. To what degree is it possible to shed one's civilization and descend (to use William Carlos Williams's phrase, applied to Sam Houston) into a different culture? To what degree is it possible to bring forth honestly and intact the findings of the descent? Should the transcultural leap be attempted at all? Is it sacrilege, another form of feckless Anglo plunder? Can the imagination ever really presume to transcend cultural borders?

Near the end of N. Scott Momaday's *House Made of Dawn* the old man, Francisco, in the fever of dying, recalls a solitary bear hunt from his youth. A preliminary and, it seems, self-imposed ritual to the hunt was a visit to a cave of the Old Ones. He climbed the face of a cliff where the "ancient handholds were worn away to shadows . . . pressing with no force at all his whole mind and weight upon the sheer ascent." He entered a cave, stood among mounded dead embers, earthen bowls, a black metate, charred corn cobs. An eagle rushed across the mouth of the cave, struck a rodent, and rose, and Francisco, we assume, went on. The bear hunt which follows is a central tale in the novel, in the same way that Francisco, the protagonist's grandfather, is a central cohering character. The hunt was an occasion of great, self-conscious manliness, carried off through conscientious application of racial skills and virtues, and accorded, in the pueblo, well-earned

esteem. But most interesting, I think, is the quiet trespass in the Anasazi cave—a terrifying sin of commission, according to the lawyer. A sacrilege, and therefore the height of bravery.

Francisco works as a structuring principle in *House Made of Dawn.* His lime-twig trap, his hope to snare the sacred, frames the eighty pages and thirteen days of Part One. His inexpressible grief sets the tone that broods behind every page. Until the last part, Francisco is inarticulate and peripheral, a still point against whom the story's violence brushes and whom it then leaves alone. But in this book peripheries are profound, delineating limbuses. Francisco—heroic, crippled, resonant with the old ways, impotent in the new—acts as a lodestone to the novel's conflicting energies. His incantatory dying delirium in Spanish fixes Momaday's symbolic compass: Porcingula, the white devil, the black runners. The commotions of the narrative gather and cool around the old man, and around his dying the book shapes its proportions. Francisco becomes at the end the lens for the single sharp image the novel has been struggling to focus on: Abel's convalescent, redemptive participation in the running. The direction, the structure of *House Made of Dawn* is toward proportion, toward a falling into place. The novel resolves into Francisco's recollections and is driven by tensions revealed to be his: sacrilege and sacredness, fear and courage.

It is a brave book. Momaday's ambition is enormous and untried; he is attempting to transliterate Indian culture, myth, and sensibility into an alien art form, without loss. He may in fact be seeking to make the modern Anglo novel a vehicle for a sacred text.

In the effort massive obstacles are met by author and reader, and one should perhaps catalog Momaday's literary offenses. Style must be attended to, as it demands attention. The first paragraph—six quite short sentences—is a composite of quiet, weak constructions: only one active verb (grazed), eight uses of the verb *to be* (primarily in the verbals *there was* or *it was*), *and* repeated nine times. Repetition, polysyndeton, and *there* as subject continue to deaden the narrative's force well into the book. Happily, the style crisps a good deal after the first twenty-eight pages, when the story finally begins. But what are we to do with, for example, "There is a town and there are ruins of other towns," or "The rooms were small and bare, and the walls were bare and clean and white"? The reader (this reader, at any rate) is tempted to shelve the book instantly; it seems spackled with pretentious, demipoetic cheap shots intended to solemnify, without justification, simple declarative statements.

The language in the first part vacillates between lugubrious flatness of this sort and fascinating thought, as in "the eagle ranges far and wide over the land, farther than any other creature, and all things there are related simply by having existence in the perfect vision of a bird," or precision of imagery:

> She could see only the flashes of lightning and the awful grey slant of the flood, pale and impenetrable, splintering upon itself and cleaving her vision like pain. The first fast wave of the storm passed with scarcely any abatement of sound;

the troughs at the eaves filled and flowed, and
the thick ropes of water hung down among the
hollyhocks and mint and ate away at the earth
at their roots; the glaze of rainwater rose up
among the clean white stones and ran in panels
on the road; and across the road the rumble and
rush of the river.

But, whether fascinating or irritating, the language, especially in Part One, *is* disconcerting. We have all been told that when language distracts from character or story or sense the author is sliding into unforgivable error. It is the sin of poets writing fiction, and unacceptable in a conventional novel.

Even more blameworthy, or brave, is Momaday's mutilation of narrative. The story does not begin until page 29, when Abel meets Angela Grace St. John (a rather heavy-handedly significant series of names). No writer, we feel, can expect his audience to dally undirected that long. Moreover, once the story begins, it diffuses, delays, fades in and out. We muddle back and forth from ceremony, through seemingly arbitrarily introduced material such as an antique diary; to beautifully evoked place information and history; to ceremony again; through powerful but incompletely explained passion in the priest and white Angela; to Abel's surreal and inscrutable murder of the albino; then back to the old man, his lime-twig, and his inchoate loneliness. And that is Part One—a staggeringly difficult interrupted narrative.

But the fact is that it works. Something is going on here. Momaday, one realizes, is adhering to the perception of one of his characters, Father Olguin, of "an instinctive demand upon all histories to be fabulous." Halfway through the novel one forgets aggravations and begins to hope that he can pull it off.

The plot of **House Made of Dawn** actually seems propelled by withheld information, that besetting literary error. We know virtually nothing of Abel's brother Vidal until a flashback on page 109, and never learn about his death, clearly a crucial tragedy for the family. The critical character of Francisco builds only in slow accretions, not complete until a few pages before the end when we discover that he was "sired by the old consumptive priest." That bit of suppressed information cannot be excused. We cannot be expected to recognize the meaning of the old priest's diary, 138 pages back, only then. And the revelation of Francisco's cross-cultural mestizo blood, his sacrilegious parturition, is too vital to have been procrastinated.

But Momaday very effectively adumbrates the identity of Porcingula. She is characterized partially, vaguely, and as different figures in different places; she emerges as a fleshed-out, dramatic character only at the end—here again providing a gloss to the old priest's diary. But the author is not confused or contemptuously confusing us with this masquerade. Porcingula *is* many things: the totem of the Bahkyush; a Christian saint (Maria de los Angeles); a whore; Francisco's lover; and, in remote yet richly possible connections, Pony, Angela, and most importantly Tai-me, Momaday's heartfelt creation deity. Porcingula is a spirit drifting through the book, and, by

its end, credible in any guise. The same holds for the novel's figures of evil. Not conventional three dimensional villains, they remain shadowy and unknown—as evil is to Indians—and should not be expounded. We don't need to know who the albino was or what became of Martinez the *culebra,* the bad cop. In this sense of the art's springing from within Indian experience, the distractions of language are likewise appropriate. Image *can be* more important than story or sense because in Momaday's, the Pueblos', the Kiowas' social reality, image *is*.

But Momaday has to give a little. Part One—the story of Abel's return from the war, his brief affair with Angela St. John, his weird murder of the ophidian albino—might stand alone as a portrait of reservation life and anxiety, but as narrative it remains a farrago riddled with half-developed possibilities. Consequently the book is structured in form, not function, as is Nabokov's *Pale Fire:* introductory poetics followed by commentary. Parts Two, Three, and Four are each dominated by a new voice supplanting Momaday's coy omniscience in Part One, supplying fact and context which the novel could not have done without.

The first of these voices is "Big Bluff" Tosamah, the prolix, brilliant "Priest of the Sun." Tosamah, in his two magnificent "sermons," is really an incarnation of the author, Momaday's mouthpiece, giving us what we've been denied: interpretation of Indian consciousness, expatiation on themes. In the first sermon, "The Gospel According to St. John," Tosamah perceives the Book of John as an overwrought creation myth, applies the lightning bolt concept of the Word to the Kiowa myth of Tai-me, and apotheosizes the Indian gift of the human need for a felt awe of creation: "There was only the dark infinity in which nothing was. And something happened. At the distance of a star something happened, and everything began. The Word did not come into being, but *it was*. It did not break up the silence, but *it was older than the silence and the silence was made of it.*"

At the same time the sermon precisely elucidates aspects of Part One. St. John refers specifically back to Angela St. John, her half-understood awareness of the need "To see nothing, slowly and by degrees." Angela, like John, did glimpse *it,* "the last reality," but, we may assume, also like John "had to account for it . . . not in terms of his imagination but only in terms of his prejudice." Tosamah is providing an exegesis of Part One, formulating what Angela's and Anglos' limitations are, what Abel and Indians are losing, and buttressing Momaday's themes of the importance of myth ("the oldest and best idea man has of himself ") and mystical vision.

The point is that Momaday had to root his story in sense and significance here, had to help us mystified Anglos out. Tosamah is an intriguing, well-crafted interlocutor, but also a slightly caricatured self-portrait—like Momaday a Kiowa, a man of words, an interpreter of Indian sensibility. "He doesn't understand," we are informed later through Ben Benally, "he's educated." It is as if, by speaking through the voluble megaphone of Tosamah, Momaday is apologizing for having to stoop to *words* to convey the obvious. To be sure, it is an oblique approach to a necessary literary office—the clear explication of mythic and intellectual context—but right on the mark.

Tosamah's next sermon leaves the web of the novel entirely and expands a personal journey into an elegiac history of the Kiowa. This is so much the author speaking, and speaking, he must have felt, correctly, so well, that Momaday lifted this chapter straight (except for a few inexplicable alterations and deletions) into his next book, titled, as is the sermon, *The Way to Rainy Mountain.* This monumental instance of self-plagiarism illustrates, I suppose, that Momaday fears no literary taboo. Unfortunately, *The Way to Rainy Mountain* does not much profit from a reworking and distension of Tosamah's sermon and Tai-me story.

The book recounts the Kiowa's pilgrimage in a conversation of sorts between three distinct voices seriatim: a teller of legends, a historian/anthropologist, and the first-person author connecting memory to myth. Each of the three interpreters is a representative facet of Momaday's imagination, and their counterpoint is a self-conscious exercise in salvaging both the letter and spirit of the Kiowa's epic quest. Momaday is indulging his ethic of myth-making, is gunning for the sacred text. He was more on target in *House Made of Dawn.*

Both books develop from within the culture, but the perspective of *The Way to Rainy Mountain* is wholly locked inside Indian sensibility, focusing on itself. The novelist's hand is not in evidence contriving character or tale. It appears that the more successful *House Made of Dawn* owes its strength partly to the distancing and emotional content that a novel can bear. Momaday's ambition—the transfiguration of culture through art—seems to require a fictional imagination.

Ben Benally, the interpretative voice following Tosamah in *House Made of Dawn,* was, like Tosamah, pressed again into service in *The Way to Rainy Mountain,* though not identified by name. Here Benally's conversational argot records antique times and tales: "You know, everything had to begin, and this is how it was." In *House Made of Dawn,* however, Benally complements Tosamah's exposition of history, myth, and theme by setting forth contemporary Indian ways. For example, speaking directly to the reader, he explains, "You know, you have to change. That's the only way you can live in a place like this [Los Angeles]." Once more Momaday is responding to the need to inform, to keep us with him, and the response is excellent. Benally's sane, quiet voice applies a leavening perspective to the book's turbid events. With him Momaday has begun fashioning the proportions vented in the voice of the third and last interpreter to speak—Francisco.

Abel's grandfather acts as the alembic that transmutes the novel's confusions; his retrospection marks off the book's boundaries, points of reference, and focal themes: the great organic calendar of the black mesa—the house of the sun (which locates the title)—as a central Rosetta stone integrating the ceremonies rendered in Part One, and the source place by which Abel and Vidal could "reckon where they were, where all things were, in time." The summoning of the highest of Indian graces and abilities in Francisco's initiatory bear hunt. His passion for the wild witch spirit Porcingula; his fear and loss with their still-born child. His participation in ritual, "his perfect act" in drumming for the dancers, which determined his stature and enabled him to heal. Then, his running "beyond pain" in the race of the dead.

The dawn runners, the runners after evil, compose the central, framing image of the novel: "They were whole and indispensible in what they did; everything in creation referred to them. Because of them, perspective, proportion, design in the universe." Similarly, the method of the last part, "The Dawn Runner," is to arrange perspective, proportion, design in the novel. Francisco's voice, which had "failed each day only to rise up again in the dawn," parallels the running. His memories, "whole and clear and growing like the dawn," infuse the book with sense and order. And his death urges Abel's stumbling regeneration through joining the race at dawn.

In Los Angeles Benally and Abel dreamt of a "plan" to go home together and ride out to the hills alone: "We were going to get drunk for the last time, and we were going to sing the old songs." Their plan, in other words, was to hold a valedictory for their heritage. But Momaday eschews this highly exploitable scene and leaves us with Abel running, an image that argues perfectly against a valediction for the Indians. "All of his [Abel's] being was concentrated in the sheer motion of running on, and he was past caring about the pain . . . he could see at last without having to think." In this ability is Abel's survival and that of his people.

The novel concerns survival, not salvation, enduring rather than Faulkner's sense of prevailing. The dawn runners physically manifest *the* Indian strength—they abide, "and in this there is a resistance and an overcoming, a long out-waiting." And Momaday is proposing not only a qualified hope for cultural continuity, but a holy endurance. The running is a sacred rite and an act of courage, thus a warding off of fear and evil, the specters (consolidated in such demons as Martinez and wine) that gnaw at Indian probity throughout the book. The race at dawn is additionally a sacrament of creation. As such it outlines the novel's purpose and achievement.

House *Made* of *Dawn.* Its subject is creation myth, the antithesis of Benally's "plan." The book's metaphysics build from a sequence of creation schemata: the diaspora of the Bahkyush, the feast of Santiago, St. John's Word, Tai-me, Benally's songs, his grandfather's story of the Bear Maiden. The book *is* a creation myth—rife with fabulous imagery, ending with Abel's rebirth in the old ways at the old man's death—but an ironic one, suffused with violence and telling a story of culture loss. Sacrilege repeatedly undercuts sacredness. Father Olguin constantly faces the corruption of his faith, from Angela's mockery, from the perverse vision of a Pueblo Christ child. The vitality of ceremony is juxtaposed to the helplessness of drunks. The peyote service is sullied, almost bathetic. But sacrilege impels sacredness here, as fear does courage, and loss survival. The series of myths, each variously imperfect, each with common corruptions and shared strengths, overlap, blend, and fuse as this novel.

The word *Zei-dl-bei* or "frightful," Momaday tells us in **The Way to Rainy Mountain,** was his grandmother's response to evil. "It was not an exclamation so much, I think, as it was a warding off, an exertion of language upon ignorance and disorder." Language, then, can be a fundamental cultural defense. And as the expression of the imagination, language defines culture. Culture, Momaday writes, "has old and essential being in language." A people come of age by "daring to imagine who they are." Such mythifying, "peculiarly the right and responsibility of the imagination," is clearly Momaday's literary ethic and the one process on which he places a sort of moral value. The imagination that transfigures reality is the source of cultural identity.

Momaday has ur-Anglo Angela St. John compose a creation myth honoring Abel, her Indian lover. It is her son's favorite story—a young Indian brave, noble and wise, born of a bear and a maiden. Her tale astounds Ben Benally: Angela has become a myth-maker, has transcended cultural boundaries with her imagination, has preserved what was holy in Abel. Likewise Momaday is a preserver of holiness in **House Made of Dawn.** He has transported his heritage across the border; in a narrative and style true to their own laws, he has mythified Indian consciousness into a modern novel.

Marilyn Nelson Waniek   (essay date 1980)

SOURCE: "The Power of Language in N. Scott Momaday's *House Made of Dawn*," in *Minority Voices*, Vol. 4, No. 1, 1980, pp. 23-8.

[*Waniek is an American poet, translator, and essayist. In the following essay, she analyzes the role of language as a source of power in* House Made of Dawn.]

In 1969, one year after the publication of his novel **House Made of Dawn,** N. Scott Momaday, in an article entitled **"The Story of the Arrowmaker,"** interpreted the Kiowa legend of the arrowmaker as a story essentially about the power of language. For the arrowmaker, says Momaday, "language is the repository of his whole knowledge and experience, and it represents the only chance he has for survival." The legend depicts "the man made of words." Other writers have pointed out the native American's belief in the power of language; Margot Astrov, in her introduction to *American Indian Prose and Poetry,* writes, "The word, indeed, is power. It is life, substance, reality. The word lived before earth, sun, or moon came into existence." In their anthology [entitled *Literature of the American Indian*], Thomas E. Sanders and Walter W. Peek say this about the power:

> Whether it existed before Wah'kon-tah, simultaneously, or shortly after, the word is vital to the Great Mystery, being perhaps the greatest mystery, for it has power to cause medicine to work, to lure game into range, to cause plants to grow, to allow man to address, be heard by, and join with the Great Mystery. As such, language itself is sacred . . .

The belief in such powers of language is not peculiar to the American Indian; Ernst Cassirer and Bronislaw Malinowski, among others, discuss the power of the word in various societies. Cassirer, writing of the bond between the linguistic consciousness and the mythical-religious consciousness [in his *Language and Myth*] tells us that, "the Word, in fact, becomes a sort of primary force, in which all being and doing originate. In all mythical cosmogonies, as far back as they can be traced, this supreme position of the Word is found." [In an essay appearing in Max Black's 1962 *The Importance of Language*] Malinowski links this supreme position of the word to the development of language in every individual. He writes, "we realize that all language in its earliest function within the context of infantile helplessness is protomagical and pragmatic." The writings of N. Scott Momaday, himself a Kiowa, show him to be aware of the creative and healing power of the word in this broad understanding, and the power of language is an important theme in **House Made of Dawn.**

The prologue of the novel begins where the hero ends, running in the race of the black men at dawn. Later in the novel we learn the significance of this race; it is the race

> of old men in white leggings running after evil in the night. They were whole and indispensable in what they did; everything in creation referred to them. Because of them, perspective, proportion, design in the universe. Meaning because of them. They ran with great dignity and calm, not in the hope of anything, but hopelessly; neither in fear nor hatred nor despair of evil, but simply in recognition and with respect. Evil was. Evil was abroad in the night; they must venture out to the confrontation; they must reckon dues and divide the world.

The race, then, is man's confrontation with his universe; his division of the world into good and evil; his creation of meaning. The prologue begins with a prayer, the Navajo Night Chant—or more properly a song from the Night Chant—through which the singer restores order in the world through his reverence for the words of the song and the influence of his voice. The prologue demonstrates the dual function of language to create and to heal, and represents in capsule form the primary concerns of the novel.

Abel is drunk when we first meet him, and the flashbacks of the second chapter serve to explain that his drunkenness is the result of his long isolation, his dislocation, the anguish of his life. Through his sight and capture of an eagle he is linked to the Eagle Watchers Society, the principal ceremonial organization of the Bahkyush, a small group of survivors of an otherwise extinct people, who "in their uttermost peril long ago . . . had been fashioned into seers and soothsayers." Yet Abel has not been fashioned into a seer and soothsayer, one who has "consummate being in language." He thinks, one week after his return to Los Ojos from the Army, that his return has been a failure.

> He had tried in the days that followed to speak to his grandfather, but he could not say the things he wanted; he had tried to pray, to sing, to enter into the old rhythm of the tongue, but he was no longer attuned to it. And yet it was

there still, like memory, in the reach of his hearing, as if Francisco or his mother or Vidal had spoken out of the past and the words had taken hold of the moment and made it eternal. Had he been able to say it, anything of his own language—even the commonplace formula of greeting "Where are you going"—which had no being beyond sound, no visible substance, would once again have shown him whole to himself; but he was dumb. Not dumb—silence was the older and better part of custom still—but *inarticulate.*

This early in the novel, Abel can use the creative and healing power of his own language neither to communicate with his grandfather nor to pray: ". . . he wanted to make a song out of the colored canyon, the way the women of Torreon made songs upon their looms out of colored yarn, but he had not got the right words together." This early inarticulateness seems to be the result of Abel's experience in the war. Yet, when after the Festival of Santiago he is able to use the power of the word to identify the evil of the albino, Abel faces the white man's understanding of the word and loses the power. During the trial Father Olguin tries to explain Abel's motivation to the court: "I believe that this man was moved to do what he did by an act of imagination so compelling as to be inconceivable to us." The ensuing discussion centers on the definition of Abel's act: "Homicide is a legal term . . . Murder is a moral term. Death is a universal human term." Abel thinks, "Word by word by word these men are disposing of him in language, *their* language. . . ." Thus caught between two conflicting uses of the power of language to define his act, Abel again becomes inarticulate. He is sent to prison, paroled, and finally he rediscovers the power at the end of the novel.

The five other major characters of the novel represent in varying degrees the power of language. Father Olguin shares Abel's isolation from the world. Indeed, his isolation stems to a large degree from his literal and symbolic blindness. Blind in one eye, he is also blind to the mysteries of the Indian's spiritual life because of his pride and the prejudices of his religion. Like the earlier priest, Fray Nicolas, whose journals he reads as something of a saint's life, he is unable to articulate his concern for his parishioners. He sees them variously as "degenerate squaws . . . sullen bucks . . ." and "wizened keepers of an old and sacred alliance." He fails in his attempt to explain the motivation of Abel's killing the albino, and his suffering for Abel embarrasses and humiliates Abel. When Abel comes to tell him of Francisco's death the priest tries to express sympathy, but fails again. His position is best described in his own words: "That safety—that exclusive silence—was the sense of all his vows, certainly; it has been brought about by his own design, *his* act of renunciation, not the town's."

Similarly isolated is Angela Grace St. John, a white woman who comes to Los Ojos to rest and await the birth of her child. She frequently demonstrates a profound sensitivity to the mythical potential of appearances, as when she thinks of Abel as a badger or a bear, or when, watching him cut wood, she says, "I see," and is "aware of some useless agony that was spent upon the wood, some hurt

she could not have imagined until now," but her concern early in the novel is to escape that power of her imagination, "to see nothing at all, nothing in the absolute." Her seduction of Abel is a battle for power which Abel wins, and which leads Angela to reject the Church in favor of the power of the individual imagination to name and create reality. Years later Abel calls for her in pain from his hospital bed, and she comes to him, not as a lover, but as one who has accepted the ability to name the mystery of their affair. She has transformed their affair into a myth of a maiden and a bear and told her son that myth. Ben Benally says about her story:

> Peter always asked her about the Indians, she said, and she used to tell him a story about a young Indian brave. He was born of a bear and a maiden, and he was noble and wise. He had many adventures, and he became a great leader and saved his people. It was the story Peter liked best of all, and she always thought of *him,* Abel, when she told it. It was real nice the way she said it, like she thought a whole lot of him, and I could tell that story was kind of secret and important to her, you know. . . .

Ben is struck with wonder by Angela's story, and compares it to the legends told him by his grandfather years ago. The significance of these legends is explained in Tosamah's sermon about the Gospel According to St. John (which may be a hint as to the significance of Tosamah's first and Angela's last name):

> My grandmother was a storyteller; she knew her way around words. She never learned to read and write, but somehow she knew the good of reading and writing; she had learned how to listen and delight. She had learned that in words and in language, and there only, she could have whole and consummate being. She told stories, and she taught me how to listen . . . When she told me those old stories, something strange and good and powerful was going on. I was a child, and that old woman was asking me to come directly into the presence of her mind and spirit; she was taking hold of my imagination, giving me to share in the great fortune of her wonder and delight. She was asking me to go with her to the confrontation of something that was sacred and eternal.

Section two of the novel, which bears Tosamah's name, consists of slices of sermons delivered by him and of Abel's thoughts. Yet this section is unified by the theme of the power of the word. Abel cannot at first understand the experiences he remembers, yet immediately after his vision of the old men running after evil in the night, who, he understands, create an order in the universe, he realizes what has long been his problem: "Now, here, the world was open at his back. He had lost his place. He had been long ago at the center, had known where he was, had lost his way, had wandered to the end of the earth, was even now reeling on the edge of the void." And he begins to understand that this has happened because he has lost "the power to name and assimilate" the world. He remembers the powerlessness of being disposed of in language during his trial, the meaningless questionnaires according to which the individual is defined in white society, the blank emptiness of his prison cell, the way his fellow soldiers referred to him as "the chief" and talked about him as if he were not there. Juxtaposed to these memories are those of the wonder of the natural world, in which Abel remembers himself as being articulate. The one passage in the novel in which Abel is fully capable of describing the world around him is the one in which he describes his hunting wild geese with his brother. Abel's memories are clarified by Tosamah's sermons, and this second section of the novel serves to explain the resolution approached through Angela, Milly, Ben, and Francisco in the next sections.

Milly, a white social worker, and the Navajo Ben Benally become Abel's mistress and friend in Los Angeles after his parole from prison. Though Milly believes in the power of language, her belief is "in tests, questions and answers, words on paper . . . She believed in Honor, Industry, the Second Chance, the Brotherhood of Man, the American Dream, and him. . . ." When she first enters Abel's world, it is as a social worker who is, according to Ben, "always asking him about the reservation and the army and prison and all . . . at first she used to bring a lot of questionnaires and read them to us, a lot of silly questions about education and health and the kind of work we were doing and all. . . ." After Milly stops bringing these questionnaires, she begins to talk about her life to Abel, and it is her story rather than her physical love which enables Abel for the first time to share his memories of his own life. Though she does not understand the power of the word, their relationship thus starts Abel on the way toward realizing that he can talk, and toward regaining the power of the word.

Ben Benally also shares with Abel the stories of his life, but his belief in language, unlike that of Milly, is in the power of prayer, song, and legend to heal and create. It is from Ben that Abel learns the Night Chant, the healing prayer which he sings in the final section of the novel. Indeed, the third section of the novel, called appropriately the "Night Chanter," is primarily about Abel's learning the power of prayer from Ben. Ben, like Angela and the old grandmother of Tosamah, draws Abel again and again into the presence of his spirit to confront the truth; Ben says:

> "House made of dawn." I used to tell him about those old ways, the stories and the sings, Beautyway and Night Chant. I sang some of those things, and I told him what they meant, what I thought they were about.

Ben understands the way life in white society strips the reservation Indian—and has stripped Abel—of his language:

> . . . they can't help you because you don't know how to talk to them. They have a lot of *words,* and you know they mean something, but you don't know what, and your own words are no good because they're not the same, they're different, and they're the only words you've got.

And Ben understands both the fear which drove Abel to kill the albino and the act of the imagination by which the evil of the albino was identified:

> That, you know, being so scared of something like that—that's what Tosamah doesn't understand. He's educated, and he doesn't believe in being scared like that. But he doesn't come from the reservation. He doesn't know how it is when you grow up out there someplace. You grow up out there, you know, someplace like Kayenta or Lukachukai. You grow up in the night, and there are a lot of funny things going on, things you don't know how to talk about. A baby dies, or a good horse. You get sick, or the corn dries up for no good reason. Then you remember something that happened the week before, something that wasn't right. You heard an owl, maybe, or you saw a funny kind of whirlwind; somebody looked at you sideways and a moment too long. And then you know . . . You just know, and you can't help being scared. It was like that with him, I guess.

Although Ben has chosen to remain in the city, his memories of life on the reservation show his reverence for the traditional Navajo way of life, and his belief in the efficacy of prayer and storytelling link him to the old man Francisco, Abel's grandfather.

Francisco is the only character who is able early in the novel to articulate his relation to the world, yet he is divided between the traditional ceremonialism of his tribe and that of the Catholic Church. This division is represented literally by his being the son of the old priest, Fray Nicolas. He has tried to teach Abel the old ways, but we are told several times by Abel that his grandfather does not understand him. At the end of the novel, however, in the "Dawn Runner" section, Abel has learned to understand Francisco. As Francisco lies on his death bed, he speaks six times on six successive dawns, in what seems to be a last attempt to tell Abel what it is to be a man. Francisco, like the teller of the legend of the arrowmaker, takes and has taken the risk of passing a heritage on to his grandsons through his words:

> These things he told to his grandsons carefully, slowly and at length, because they were old and true, and they could be lost forever as easily as one generation is lost to the next, as easily as one old man might lose his voice, having spoken not enough or not at all.

Here is the risk of the oral tradition, always "one generation removed from extinction." And here is the creative and healing power of all stories told by one individual to another, the risk of entrusting one's being to another, the risk of "consummate being in language." Francisco places the stories of his young manhood, his tragic love, and the race of the black men at dawn into Abel's hands. It becomes Abel's responsibility to grasp these stories, to respect their power, and to pass them on.

Francisco dies, but Abel has learned from him and from the several other characters of the novel the power of language to create and to heal. When he continues the tradition of the race of the black men at dawn he is joining the tradition of naming the world, he is saying to the universe that the word of the ancients has survived. Running alone behind the other men whose bodies are painted black with ashes, Abel begins under his breath to sing, to pray the Navajo prayer taught to him by Ben Benally. We are told that, "he had no voice; he had only the words of a song. And he went running on the rise of the song." Of the arrowmaker Momaday writes that, "the arrowmaker has more nearly perfect being than other men have, and a more nearly perfect right to be. We can imagine him as he imagines himself, whole and vital, going on into the unknown darkness and beyond. This last aspect of his being is primordial and profound." So it is with Abel.

In *House Made of Dawn* as in Cassirer's *Language and Myth* there is a distinction between the language of logic and the language of myth. In the novel the language of logic belongs to the white man, and has no magic or religious properties. It names, it fixes the world, but it does not go beyond itself. The language of myth belongs to the Indian, and it is this language which has the power to confront the truth, to create, and to heal. Cassirer writes of the language of myth that, ". . . Whatever has been fixed by a name, henceforth is not only real, but is Reality." This is the understanding which is so crucial to *House Made of Dawn.*

Momaday on the role of language in *House Made of Dawn*:

I believe that as soon as Abel leaves his traditional ground, his language begins to deteriorate. He is bombarded and threatened by the language around him. He is threatened by the currency of the English language, and so he is isolated in his own language, and finds that it does not operate for him outside its context. And so little by little, as this is driven home to him, he falls silent. In the court scene, where everybody is not only talking in something other than his language but talking in a language that is even more highly artificial than languages in general—legalese—at that point he's just done in. Language becomes his enemy. It has turned on him, and he understands that there's nothing he can do about that. So he turns his back and remains silent. And that's the loss of his language—the loss of his voice. What could be more devastating? In the scene where Abel wants to say something and can't, he is reduced to something almost subhuman. He's very nearly lost his life at that point.

N. Scott Momaday, in an interview with Charles L. Woodward in his Ancestral Voice: Conversations with N. Scott Momaday, *1989.*

R. S. Sharma (essay date January 1982)

SOURCE: "Vision and Form in N. Scott Momaday's *House Made of Dawn,*" in *Indian Journal of American Studies,* Vol. 12, No. 1, January, 1982, pp. 69-79.

[*In the following essay, Sharma explores Momaday's focus on spirituality and depiction of the Native vision of the world in* House Made of Dawn.]

Though initially received with cautious condescension, N. Scott Momaday's *House Made of Dawn* has now come to be regarded as a major statement by a major American Indian writer. Confused by the novel's "rapidly shifting and sometimes ambiguous chronological frame of reference," earlier reviewers and critics found the novel nothing but "an interesting variation of the old alienation theme"; "a social statement rather than . . . a substantial artistic achievement"; "a memorable failure," "a reflection, not a novel in the comprehensive sense of the word" with "awkward dialogue and affected description"; "a batch of dazzling fragments" which made one critic "itch for a blue pencil to knock out all the interstitial words that maintain the sophoric flow." They criticised its lack of a proper narrative continuity, its haziness, its ethereal characters, its indistinct plot line and its language on the rather unacceptable ground that "American Indians do not write novels and poetry as a rule or teach English in top ranking universities either," referring obviously to the author as a professor of English. Now, there is a greater recognition of Momaday's fictional art and critics have come to recognise its unique achievement as a novel which succeeds in "interpolating and translating" one for another culture. Despite a qualified reception the novel had succeeded in making its impact even on earlier critics though they were not sure of their own responses. They found it "a story of considerable power and beauty," "strong in imaginative imagery," creating a "world of wonder and exhilarating vastness." In more recent criticism there are signs of greater clarity of understanding of Momaday's achievement. In his review [appearing in *Western American Literature* 5 (Spring 1970)], John Z. Bennett had pointed out how through "a remarkable synthesis of poetic mode and profound emotional and intellectual insight into the Indians' perduring human status Momaday's novel becomes at last the very act it is dramatizing, an artistic act, a 'creation hymn.'" In ["The Novel as Sacred Text: N. Scott Momaday's Myth-Making Ethic," *Southwest Review* 63 (Spring 1978)] Baine Kerr has elaborated this point to suggest that Momaday has used "the modern Anglo novel [as] a vehicle for a sacred text," that in it he is "attempting to transliterate Indian culture, myth, and sensibility into an alien art form, without loss."

That the novel is an embodiment of the American Indian's vision and his deepest spiritual yearnings is beyond doubt. How this vision has been translated into the language of fiction remains yet to be examined. In this paper, I intend to examine how Momaday translates the Indian's "eye and action" view of the world in fictional terms. A proper understanding of Momaday's vision of the American Indian is, therefore, an essential prerequisite for a grasp of the novel's complexity.

The novel, a blend of many techniques, achieves its synthesis through the "eye" which is peculiar to the Indian. In an essay called **"A Vision beyond Time and Space"** [appearing in *Life* 71 (2 July 1971)] Momaday provides us many insights into the Indian's vision of life. Wonder, according to him, is the principal part of the Indian's vision.

His active life is nothing but "an affirmation of the wonder and regard, a testament to the realization of a quest for vision." "This native vision, this gift of seeing truly, with wonder and delight into the natural world" according to him "is informed by a certain attitude of reverence and self-respect. It is a matter of extrasensory as well as sensory perception. . . . In addition to the eye, it involves the intelligence, the instinct and the imagination. It is the perception not only of objects and forms, but also of essences and ideals." To quote him, "Most Indian people are able to see in these terms." This vision is "peculiarly native and distinct, and it determines who and what they are to a great extent." It is indeed "the basis upon which they identify themselves as individuals and as a race." It is the "very nucleus" of their self residing in their blood. Thus, in Momaday's world view the Indian is identified in his ability to see differently. Commenting on the "cultural nearsightedness" of contemporary Americans, he says: "our eyes, it may be, have been trained too long upon the superficial, and artificial, aspects of our environment . . . and consequently we fail to see into the nature and meaning of our own humanity." He emphasizes the need "to enter upon a vision quest of our own, that is, a quest after vision itself" and feels that the American Indian was "perhaps the most culturally secure of all Americans" because he was gifted with a vision: "In the integrity of his vision he is wholly in possession of himself and of the world around him; he is quintessentially alive."

The "equations" that constitute this vision are "a sense of heritage, of a vital community in terms of origin and destiny, a profound investment of the mind and spirit in the oral traditions of literature, philosophy and religion." *House Made of Dawn* is essentially a realisation of these equations. It is about vision, about perception, articulation, repossession and reenactment of this vision. It is Genesis and Apocalypse at the same time. The fusion of vision and form in this novel which [Marshall Sprague writes in "Anglos and Indians," *New York Times Book Review* 63 (9 June 1968)] is "as subtly brought out as a piece of Navajo silverware" is a unique achievement in contemporary fiction; it has [according to Baine] "mythified Indian consciousness into a modern novel." The novel demands of the reader an intuitive grasp of the Indian vision. Momaday himself defines this vision in terms of a song [in **"I am Alive,"** in Jules B. Billard's 1974 *The World of the American Indian*]:

> You see, I am alive,
> You see, I stand in good relation to the earth,
> You see, I stand in good relation to the Gods,
> You see, I stand in good relation to all that is
>   beautiful,
> You see, I stand in good relation to you,
> You see, I am alive, I am alive.

Thus, "a sense of place, of the sacred, of the beautiful, of humanity" are essential components of the Indian vision which is at once spiritual, moral and esthetic. It is woven in the very fabric of Indian life. For the Indian, every creative act is an act of "blood recollection, . . . a whole and inevocable act of the imagination." It is a "synthesis," not a general experience and in this "there is an evocation of tribal intelligence, an exposition of racial memory." Indi-

an art, according to Momaday "is the essence of abstraction, and the abstraction of essences" and this understanding "of order, and spatial relationships, proportion and design," is most fully realized in language, in the oral tradition. "The oral tradition of Indian," says Momaday "even more than his plastic arts, is vast and various." In its stories and songs, its legends and love and prayers, it is not only "exceptionally rich and imaginative," it also reflects "an understanding of, and belief in, the power and beauty of language" that is lost on those "who have, by and large, have only the experience of a written tradition." This vision is one of "great moment and beauty" but it "has certainly to be believed in order to be seen." We can see *House Made of Dawn* only if we believe in this vision. The key to this vision apparently lies in an understanding of the oral tradition that Momaday seeks to translate in terms of fiction.

The novel begins and ends with fragments of a traditional song as Abel, the protagonist and symbolic carrier of this tradition, joins the dawn runners in a ritual enactment of a primitive ceremony after the death of his grandfather Francisco. Thus, Abel and Francisco are the two major characters of the novel, linking the past, present and future. In their polar lives, the two re-enact the "quintessential life of the Indian."

The novel begins as Abel comes home after his shattering experience in the war in a "truck," while Francisco is going to receive him in his "wagon." It ends while Francisco is going to join the spirits of the dead and Abel goes with the dawn runners in quest of the vision of the race. The novel is about this "quest" for vision. It begins where it ends, producing the notion of a circularity that is interminable. There are points in it which give us an impression of terminality but there is no termination, each ending is a new kind of beginning. The novel is about a series of beginnings and a series of endings which keep turning on each other. It therefore does not offer us a plot but only fragments of a vision, the totality of which we can arrive at only if we read it "creatively" recreating the entire experience as it is enacted in racial memory. That way alone can we see its unity and its meaning, for there is a unity between the four sections "The Long Hair," "The Priest of the Sun," "The Night Chanter," and "The Dawn Runner," which are aspects of the same reality, the same experience, the same tradition. Though primarily concerned with Abel's quest for identity the novel is also about Francisco who, as Baine Kerr points out, "works as a structuring principle" in the novel and "acts as the lodestone to the novel's conflicting energies." Abel's tragedy lies in the fact that he does not have the vision which will enable him to see his own destiny. More specifically it lies in his failure to connect himself with the vision of his race available in the oral tradition. He must recover this vision before he can recover his self. The seemingly confused and hazy narrative suggests Able's incapacity to see properly his own place in the universe.

The novel begins during the "relocation" years, the most inglorious period in the history of the American Indian, but the choice of the period seems to be suggestive of the fact that before people "relocate" him, Abel and his people must "relocate" themselves, must find their proper place and destiny. Abel returns from the war totally disoriented, a long hair, and the novel records his progression towards the House Made of Dawn. He must recover the vision which he has lost and which alone will help him to become the dawn runner. He must "relocate" himself by repossessing what he has lost, his vision, his sense of place. Abel initially appears as one who has lost his sense of land. He cannot relate himself to any place. He is out of place everywhere. We cannot appreciate his predicament without taking into account the fact that away from the land he is like fish out of water, suggested in the beginning of the section "The Priest of the Sun." Cut off from their land, the Indians are like fish out of water that "writhe in the light of the moon, the moon, the moon," "the most helpless creatures on the face of the earth." This land-and-man equation is crucial to the understanding of the novel. To quote Momaday [from **"I am Alive"**],

> the Indian conceives of himself in terms of the land. His imagination of himself is also and at once an imagination of the physical world from which he proceeds and to which he returns in the journey of his life. The landscape is his natural element; it is the only dimension in which his life is possible. The notion that he is independent of the earth, that he can be severed from it and remain whole, does not occur to him. . . .
>
> In his view the earth is sacred. . . .
>
> It is a living entity, in which living entities have origin and destiny. The Indian does not lose sight of it, even; he is bound to the earth forever in his spirit.

Abel's tragedy is that he is alienated from the land and in the process alienated from his true self. This connection between man and land is suggested repeatedly in the novel by reference to land and landscapes. The House Made of Dawn is rooted in a land "still and strong" "beautiful and around." This philosophy of landscape is most explicit wherever there are references to the sacred complex of the Indian society. Participating in the ceremony of eagle watching, Abel gets a sense of the "spatial majesty of the sky" and discovers a strange and brilliant light "that lies" upon the world, in which "all the objects in the landscape" are "washed clean and set away in the distance." In the landscape he also discovers a divinity, for

> Such vastness makes for illusion, a kind of illusion that comprehends reality, and where it exists there is always wonder and exhilaration.

When Abel returns he discovers his loneliness, as if he were already miles and months away "from everything he knew and had always known." The land-life equation is more explicit in the section "July 28." Here life in form and motion seems to be emerging from the land itself. Each form of life has only a "tenure in land." Abel discovers his lost connection only when he is able to relate himself to the land sacred to his forefathers. The violence that man has done to nature is revealed in "an old copper mine" that is "a ghost," with its "black face" and its "gray wooden frame."

The way alienation from land cripples Abel's faculties is revealed in his incapacity to see and articulate. Abel discovers his lost sacrality and his place by participating in the rituals and ceremonies of the tribe that lead him to a greater and greater clarity of vision. He discovers his sense of place by perceiving "the culturally imposed symbolic order" inherited from his grandfather. In the beginning he is insecure, and inarticulate. He is cut off from his roots and consequently he has lost his voice. "One of the most tragic things about Abel," Momaday says [in an interview in *Sun Tracks: An American Indian Literary Magazine* 2 (1976)], "is his inability to express himself. He is in some ways a man without a voice. . . . So I think of him as having been removed from oral tradition." In the novel itself, Momaday refers to Abel's initial inability to speak. After his return from the town, he had tried "to speak to his grandfather," but "he could not say the things he wanted; he had tried to pray, to sing, to enter into the old rhythms of the tongue, but he was no longer attuned to it." The words are there "like memory, in the reach of hearing," words that could take hold "of the moment and make it eternal." He could get back his wholeness, "Had he been able to say . . . anything of his language which had no being beyond sound, no visible substance." He is dumb, not just silent but "inarticulate." He needs words and language to discover himself. When he is in the valley where "nothing lay between the object and the eye," he wants to make a song "out of the coloured canyon," but "he had not the right words together." He wants to write a creation song "of the first world, of fire and flood, and of the emergence of dawn from the hills." He is able to sing that song only when he becomes the dawn runner, when he is able "to see at last without having to think." As he discovers his vision, he runs and begins to sing, "There was no sound, and he had no voice; he had only the words of a song." He at last discovers the words that he needs to be a dawn runner but that comes only after he cuts his way through the Babel that surrounds him.

This philosophy of the soundless word is beautifully adumbrated in the sermons of Tosamah, the Priest of the Sun. In his sermons, reinterpreting the Biblical *"Principio Verbum,"* Tosamah offers a severe indictment of a dominantly verbal culture. Abel's final song is thematically linked with Tosamah's Genesis story:

> It was almost nothing in itself, the smallest seed of sound—but it took hold of the stillness and there was motion forever; it took hold of the silence and there was sound and everything began.

The indictment of a purely verbal culture comes sharply in Tosamah's indictment of the Anglo love for words:

> Now, brothers and sisters, old John was a white man and the white man has his ways. Oh gracious me, he has his ways. He talks about the word. He talks through it and around it. He builds upon it with syllables, with prefixes, and suffixes and hyphens and accents. He adds and divides and multiplies the word. And in all this he subtracts the truth.

This indictment is followed by criticism of a culture based on the manipulation of mere words:

> The white man takes such things as words and

literatures for granted, as indeed he must, for nothing in his world is so commonplace. On every side of him there are words by the millions. . . . He has diluted and multiplied the word, and words have begun to close in upon him. . . . It may be that he will perish by the word.

Abel's final triumph comes, therefore, not in a verbal triumph, but in a formal movement, a ritual that relates him at once to his forefathers and to a spirituality of motion and movement. The race is a manifestation of a newly earned knowledge that is power. Momaday comments on the significance of the race [in his essay **"The Morality of Indian Hating"**]:

> It is a long race, and it is neither won nor lost. It is an expression of the soul in the ancient terms of sheer physical exertion. To watch these runners is to know that they draw with every step some elementary power which resides at the core of the earth and which, for all our civilized ways, is lost upon us who have lost the art of going in the flow of things. In the tempo of that race there is time to ponder morality and demoralization, hungry wolves and falling stars.

His novel is not only about the recovery of this vision but it is also about the way it is recovered. It is not only about seeing, it is also about doing. The illusion of mist and haziness that Momaday creates initially is related to Abel's incapacity to see. He recovers his vision and with that his other faculties only gradually by participating in the collective heritage, which is mythic and historical at the same time. It comes to have through the discovery of the sacrality of life, another major equation of the Indian vision. Abel repossesses his sense of the sacred by participating in the ceremonies and rituals of the race. In them he is "restored as a man and as a race." Through his narrative Momaday wants his readers also to participate in this sacred ritual of recovery. The novel, therefore, assumes the nature of a sacred text in which the ethos and mythos of the Indian are embodied in a manner that is peculiar to the Indian mind.

Momaday, therefore, narrates the story not in the conventional manner but rather in the Indian manner, the manner of the oral tradition. It is [according to Momaday] a fictional transfer of a memory "that persists in the blood and there only," a memory that remains "beyond evolutionary distances." It is "a blood recollection," "an intricate image" indeed, composed of innumerable details "vivid and immediate." That the novel seeks to recapture the rhythms of the oral narrative is suggested not only in the story of Abel but also in those of Tosamah, The Priest of the Sun and Francisco, The Night Chanter. The narrative validates the oral tradition which helps Abel recover his identity finally, and operates through a series of powerful images which leave an overwhelming impact on our consciousness. Those images are seen through the consciousness of Abel and that is why they come in fragments, but through them and with Abel we see the "sense of beauty of proportion and design" that is the essential qualification of the dawn runners. The section "The Long Hair" is a series of such "intricate images" which leave us dis-

turbed, looking for order, for patience, for connection, imposing upon us the need for a vision, a vision where all things "are related simply by having existence in the perfect vision of a bird."

The visual impact of the Indian eye can be felt in the narrative skills of Momaday. It is most powerfully felt in the scene depicting the flight of the golden eagles in the air, in the narration of the feast of Santiago, and in the bear hunt. They give us a vision which is peculiarly Indian, revealing his sense of form and beauty. For in all their inchoateness they have a unity that transcends all. The insects, birds and animals that populate the novel are part of the Indian's consciousness; he sees himself and the divine and the sacred through them. Francisco, who is snaring the sacred in the bird initially, discovers it finally in the bear. This sense of the sacred, which is peculiar to the Indian, can be seen in all that Francisco does. In and through him Abel relates himself to his heritage. In the section "The Long Hair," Abel returns to his grandfather physically; his final return to him is rituo-symbolic.

Abel has a mixed heritage, a heritage in which the racial line between the Red and the White is totally blurred—the Indian is distinguished not by his colour but by his vision. His genealogy is confused, "He did not know who his father was. His father was a Navajo, they said, or a Sia or an Isleta, an outsider anyway," which makes him an archetypal Indian, representing all Indians. On the other hand, through his grandfather he inherits an ancestry which links him with the white Christian race. Through Francisco he is at once connected with Father Fray Nicholas and Porcingula Pecos. The historic identity of Fray Nicholas is established through the concrete device of Diary and Letters, but Porcingula remains enigmatic, the archetypal mother in her various aspects. She is, as Kerr puts it "many things; the totem of Bahkyush; a Christian saint (Maria de los Angeles); a whore; Francisco's lover; and in remote yet richly possible connections Pony, Angela, and most importantly Tai-me, Momaday's heartfelt creation deity." Through her, Abel participates in the diaspora of Bahkyush, the feast of Santiago, the holy rites and rituals of regeneration and reawakening. From Fray Nicholas he also inherits a legacy of sin and guilt, which he keeps confronting again and again. It relates him not only to the eagle hunters but also to the "marauding bands of buffalo hunters and thieves." It reminds him of a long lost war, which impinges on his consciousness again in the image of the tank and disorients him for the time-being.

The novel is about his reorientation, the most crucial aspect of which is his understanding of evil. Momaday's treatment of evil is subtle, complex and profound; for him evil is what the Indian is not. In his treatment of evil Momaday again shows [what he terms] the humanity of the Indian's perception, "a moral regard for the beings, animate and inanimate, among which man must live his life." Consequently, the novel is free from the kind of racial violence that characterizes the fiction of some of the black writers. Evil does not have a specific identity in the novel though [Alan R. Velie has pointed out in his "Cain and Abel in N. Scott Momaday's *House Made of Dawn*," *Journal of the West* 17 (April 1978)] that by making Abel an

Indian, Momaday has indirectly led many [to] reexamine the identity of Cain. It is definitely associated with whiteness, but by making it a matter of chance in the case of the Albino, Momaday seems to imply that pigmentation is only accidental: "Whiteness has an ambiguity that is creative in the Albino—the white man, the Albino, that equation whatever it is." It is "in the Melvillian sense," as Velie put it "the intensifying agent in things most appalling to mankind." What the novel succeeds in communicating is the fact that despite repeated betrayal the Indian continues to be the carrier of the seed of life, a source of renewal and regeneration. The other characters of evil in the novel are similarly vague and shadowy, almost spectral. They are evil presences like the Albino, who follows the movements of Francisco and whom we vaguely identify through the "coloured glass." The evil figures appear as those who seek to deprive Abel of his sacred heritage or of his mobility, most characteristically expressed in his manual movements. It is significant that Martinez, the culebra, seeks to destroy Abel by destroying his hands, "And his hands were broken; they were broken all over." The characters of evil disappear as soon as they appear, never to be heard of again. By universalizing evil and by reducing whiteness to a metaphysical and ambiguous dimension, Momaday strikes a positive note in Red-White relationship.

This brings us to the consideration of the most controversial incident in the novel, the murder of the Albino. There is no "explicit explanation of motives" and the reader is left wondering about the exact nature of the entire episode. There is a strong element in the novel to suggest that Abel does not think of the Albino as a human presence. The narrative suggests him to be a kind of "presence" for when Abel and the Albino speak to each other, they say something so low "as if the meaning of what they said was strange and infallible." The Albino is constantly described as a "white man" whose laughter ends "in a strange, inhuman cry" and it "issued only from the tongue and teeth of the great evil mouth, and it fell away from the blue lips and there was nothing left of it." The language clearly suggests the image of a snake here and it is obvious that Abel sees the Albino as a snake. The narration of the murder also indicates that the Albino tries to kill Abel in a mortal coil, a fatal embrace, which has homosexual overtones. That Abel sees the Albino as a snake is again emphasized when he tells in the court, "Well, your honours, it was this way, see? I cut up a little snake meat out there in the sand." Father Olguin suggests it to be "An evil spirit," attributing it to a "psychology about which we know very little." For him it was "an act of imagination so compelling as to be inconceivable to us." Even otherwise it is indicated that Abel sees the Albino as a witch or sawah, for Abel's inexplicable behaviour in the war is also suggestive of his capacity to visualize evil in terms of his own psyche. It is obvious from the narrative that he responds to the tank not as a machine but as an evil presence, which so disorients him that he temporarily loses his sense of identity and his connection with land, "He reached for something, but he had no notion of what it was; his hand closed upon earth and the cold, wet leaves." Later in his delirium, he challenges it in the instinctive manner with a war dance, "And there he was, hopping around with his finger up in the air and giving it to that tank in Sioux or Algonquin or something." These incidents clearly refer to the instinctive self of Abel which is liberated from the white presence.

The snake-albino-whiteman-evil connection is too complicated to lead to any clear explanation, but it is apparent that Abel is striving to get rid of something not natural to his self. Earlier, he kills the young eagle to liberate it of its anguish, symbolically liberating himself from the hood that deprives him of his vision. It is quite possible that Abel kills the Albino, "as a frustrated response to the whiteman and Christianity," or in him he kills "the whiteman in the Indian" or "a part of himself and his culture which he can no longer recognize and control" [Lawrence J. Evers, "Words and Place: A Reading of *House Made of Dawn*," *Western American Literature* 11 (Winter 1977)]. Abel's responses after the incident are like that of a person bitten by a snake and Tosamah describes his case as that of a "snakebite."

Abel's reemergence is like a therapeutic process, a kind of exorcism, a process of healing in which the ritual of the sexual act has a tremendous significance. In the Indian world-view the act of sexual union is a sacred act in which all secrets, even those of sorcery and evil, are revealed to the participants. This is suggested by Momaday's detailed narration of the sexual act and its impact on the participants, whose natures are altered by the experience. Sex in the novel is a fertility rite which leads to healing and restoration of self. It is almost a rite of initiation through which the sacred enters into the human like the bear that Angela St. John thinks to have conceived. These episodes are thematically connected with the quest of the life-seed that Abel is looking for. The two most crucial of these rites are the ones between Angela and Abel and Porcingula and Francisco which initiate them into their heroic quests. The two episodes have a symbolic function, for, the union of Francisco and Porcingula is reenacted in the union of Abel and Angela St. John, who, identifying Abel with the bear, connects him with the bear that offers Francisco the secret of eternity and makes him the seer and medicine man of his people. In the two, myth and history become social reality. It is obvious that throughout the novel, Momaday's stress is not on race but on a vision and a participation mystique peculiar to a race. Abel overcomes all onslaughts on his self by discovering this vision which enables him to participate in a tradition that goes back to a mythic past. Momaday's art lies in his ability to give us glimpses of this lost world in a world now full of hatred, violence and bloodshed. In him vision and form become one and the same.

Alan R. Velie (essay date 1982)

SOURCE: "*House Made of Dawn:* Nobody's Protest Novel," in *Four American Indian Literary Masters: N. Scott Momaday, James Welch, Leslie Marmon Silko, and Gerald Vizenor,* University of Oklahoma Press, 1982, pp. 52-64.

[*Velie is an American nonfiction writer, editor, and educator. In the following essay, he presents a thematic overview in which he discusses the dangers of viewing* House Made of Dawn *as a protest novel, then maintains that the work is about the protagonist's search for acceptance of his identity and heritage.*]

House Made of Dawn is Momaday's masterpiece. In fact, I do not think it is excessive praise to say that it is one of the best American novels of the last decade. The book received the Pulitzer Prize for literature in 1969, an indication that its merits have not been lost on the critics. Although it has been thoroughly praised, it has been less thoroughly understood.

House Made of Dawn is the story of Abel (we never learn his last name), an illegitimate son of a Tanoan mother and an unknown father, probably a Navajo. The story begins with Abel's return from World War II to his village of Walatowa, a fictionalized version of the Jemez Pueblo where Momaday grew up. Abel is so drunk when he arrives that he fails to recognize his grandfather, who has come to pick him up. Abel feels lost on his return, and obviously his problem is largely that he has lost his cultural identity.

On the Festival of Santiago, Abel enters a ceremonial game in which men on horseback attempt to pull a rooster out of the ground. The rider who accomplishes this feat is then entitled to beat another of the participants with the rooster. The winner, an albino Tanoan named Fragua, chooses to beat Abel, who is unnerved and humiliated. Several days later Abel kills the albino in a knife fight outside a bar and is sent to jail for seven years.

When Abel gets out of jail he is "relocated" in Los Angeles, where he works diligently at his job for a short period. But he is harassed by a sadistic policeman named Martinez and taunted by a Kiowa named Tosamah, who considers Abel an ignorant savage. Eventually Abel turns to drink and loses his job. In his drunkenness Abel attacks Martinez, and Martinez gives him a beating that is almost fatal. After a long, slow recovery, Abel returns to Walatowa as his grandfather is dying. When his grandfather dies, Abel performs the traditional preburial rituals and then prepares to enter a traditional Tanoan race for good hunting and harvests that his grandfather had won years before. The book ends with Abel running, singing the words to a Navajo prayer. Apparently he has found a sort of peace of mind by joining in the cultural life of the Tanoan community.

Knowing about Momaday's experiences as a Kiowa growing up among the Navajo and Jemez is very important if we are to understand Momaday's treatment of Abel. There are also recognizable literary influences: Momaday owes a debt to writers like Faulkner for his use of stream of consciousness and limited point of view—for instance, in the scene in which Abel lies half dead on the beach after Martinez beats him. Also apparent is the influence of Melville's symbolism in the significance Momaday makes of the whiteness of the albino.

The result of these influences is a masterfully complex novel. Unfortunately, the tendency of most white American readers (at least if my students of the past ten years are any indication) is to read the book simplistically, as a protest novel. According to this reading, Abel, the Indian protagonist, is a noble red victim of the barbaric forces of white America. The impression is based on several things. First, because Momaday is himself an Indian, readers often expect him to blame Abel's failure on racial injustice. Second, Abel's name is an obvious allusion to the Bible's first victim. When I ask my students who is the Cain that destroys Abel, they always answer that it is white society. Last, if not least, there is the inevitable comparison with Ira Hayes, the Pima Indian who helped raise the flag on Iwo Jima, an act memorialized in the famous Marine Corps statue. When Hayes returned to his reservation after the war, he became an alcoholic and one evening, out of doors, he passed out and died from exposure. His death received a good deal of attention from the press, and Hayes's story served as the basis of the film *The Outsider.* Tony Curtis played Hayes in accordance with the Hollywood stereotype of the Indian as victim. The point of the movie was that Indians can die for their country but cannot live in it with dignity.

Whatever the reasons for the reader to believe that Abel is simply a victim of white society, the conclusion is incorrect—far too simplistic. Momaday presents a highly-complex portrait of Abel and does not rely on Hollywood clichés or on those of students.

First of all, although there is a general similarity in the situation of Abel and Ira Hayes—both are Indian veterans from the Southwest who cannot readjust to their role in postwar America, and so turn to alcohol—the resemblance may simply be coincidental. Momaday has said that his chief models in creating Abel were Indians he knew at Jemez. In an interview in November, 1974, Momaday told Charles Woodard, "I knew an Abel at Jemez who was a close neighbor. . . . I was thinking of him; he's one of the people who adds to the composite Abel."

No doubt Momaday was familiar with Hayes's story, and it may have been somewhat in his mind when he created the character of Abel, but there is an enormous difference between Momaday's complex character and the stereotype into which Hollywood turned Hayes. To those who read press accounts of Hayes's death or saw *The Outsider,* Hayes was a hero during the war and a victim of white injustice afterwards. In the normal way these terms are used, Abel was neither. In a very curious, ambiguous sense, he may have been both, but in ways so different from Hayes that there is really no basis for comparison.

The only glimpse we get of Abel's combat experience is a curious scene in which Abel gives an enemy tank the finger. His fellow soldiers find this bizarre, not heroic. The gesture, totally inexplicable in terms of modern warfare, seems a rough equivalent of the old plains Indian custom of counting coups. Plains warriors considered it more glorious to ride up to an armed enemy and touch him harmlessly with a stick they called a coupstick, than to shoot him from a distance. Counting coups, which insulted the enemy by showing him that you scorned his ability to harm you, seems to be what Abel has in mind, though Momaday never says so. This is not to imply that Abel, a Navajo/Tanoan, would have known about or have consciously thought about coups; nevertheless, he is displaying the same attitude toward the enemy. Momaday, a Kiowa, would certainly know about counting coups.

The matter of Abel as victim of white injustice brings us to the next point, the significance of his name. Momaday told Woodard, "I know about Abel and the Bible and that certainly was in my mind, but I don't think I chose the name on that account." This seems a slight evasion. Momaday may have chosen the name because he knew an Abel, but he does not give Abel a surname, and a man as sensitive to symbolic meanings as Momaday could not have failed to realize that his readers would have imagined a link between a character named simply Abel and the Bible's first victim. The question is, victim of what? In these secular times, even in the Bible Belt, where I teach, students have forgotten the Bible. Cain was Abel's brother, not some hostile outsider. In *House Made of Dawn* two of the men who do the worst damage to Abel are his brother Indians, John Tosamah, the Kiowa "Priest of the Sun," who ridicules Abel until he drives him to drink (admittedly a short haul) and Juan Reyes Fragua, the Tanoan albino who humiliates Abel, and whom Abel murders, as a result spending seven years in jail. Abel's third tormentor, the sadistic policeman Martinez, is either a Chicano or an Indian with a Spanish surname—at any rate, he is not an Anglo-American. He appears to be a free-lance grafter, and not in any very direct sense a representative of the white society the students have indicted.

The albino is a very curious figure. From Fray Nicolas's letter of January 5, 1875, we know that at the time Fragua and Abel participate in the Festival of Santiago, Fragua is seventy years old, although apparently still remarkably athletic. In some mysterious way the albino is evil. In the scene in which the albino watches, or spies on, Abel's grandfather Francisco, Francisco senses the presence of evil, although he sees no one. The scene is ambiguous, but it is evident that Momaday wants the reader to apprehend the albino as evil and possibly to recognize him as a witch (Indians use the term for men and women both). [In "Incarnate Grace and the Paths of Salvation in *House Made of Dawn*," *American Indian Quarterly* 2, No. 1 (1975)] H. S. McAllister argues that the albino is linked through witchcraft and possession with Fray Nicolas and the Bahkyush witch Nicolas *teah-whau*. The three are, in McAllister's words, "three manifestations of a single person." I find this thesis far-fetched, or at least in excess of the evidence McAllister has marshaled, but according to Momaday himself, the albino is a witch. Momaday told Woodard about the passage in question: "He [the albino] is manifesting the evil of his presence. Witchcraft and the excitement of it is part of that too." Abel is aware that the albino is evil, but his decision to kill him seems to spring from a specific incident, his beating at the Festival of Santiago.

When the albino pulls the rooster out of the ground and chooses Abel to beat, Abel is infuriated by the humiliation and determines to kill the albino. Momaday refers to this gory ritual as a game, and it is a game in the sense that it is an activity done for entertainment and governed by a well-defined set of arbitrary rules. If Abel decides to play the game, he should be aware of the risks and willing to

suffer the consequences. His anger and decision to kill the albino exceed the rules of the game, and indicate a mind out of touch with its cultural context. It is as if a black halfback, considering it a racial incident when he is tackled by a white linebacker, wants to fight him. A man who does not want to be knocked down should not play football, and a man who does not want to be beaten with a rooster should avoid participating in rituals in which that is the practice. Nonetheless, Abel does not see it that way. He kills the albino.

In understanding the albino we must recognize the symbolic dimension to his character. The conjunction of whiteness and evil inevitably suggests Melville's *Moby Dick*. In chapter 42, "The Whiteness of the Whale," Melville describes how white not only symbolizes purity and goodness to men but also transmits the spectral qualities of terror and evil. As Melville puts it, white is "the intensifying agent in things the most appalling to mankind." Melville particularly mentions the albino man who "so particularly repels and often shocks the eye, as that sometimes he is loathed by his own kith and kin." Momaday told Woodard of his special interest in Melville, whom he teaches in his course on antiromantic American literature. In his interview with Woodard he confirms the influence of Melville in the depiction of the albino.

One of the most interesting things about the albino is that throughout *House Made of Dawn,* Momaday refers to him as the "white man." We must remember that we are dealing with symbolism here, not allegory. Momaday's albino does not stand for Caucasian Americans in the way that Bunyan's Mr. Wordly Wiseman stands for earthly knowledge. Primarily, Juan Reyes Fragua is a Tanoan Indian who interacts with other characters on a purely realistic level. There is an additional symbolic and ironic sense, however, in which the "white man" represents white society. Perhaps this is most strongly apparent in the scene in which Abel murders the albino. Although Momaday is describing a stabbing, the terms he uses are obviously sexual:

> The white man raised his arms, as if to embrace him. . . . Then he closed his hands on Abel and drew him close. Abel heard the strange excitement of the white man's breath, and the quick, uneven blowing in his ear, and felt the blue shivering lips upon him, felt even the scales of the lips and hot slippery point of the tongue, writhing.

What is happening here, on a literal level, is that Abel is killing the albino while, on a symbolic level, the white man is raping Abel. What exactly this means in symbolic terms is impossible to put neatly into words. Momaday has told Woodard about Fragua: "There is a kind of ambiguity that is creative in the albino—the white man, the albino, that equation, whatever it is."

Abel's other "brother" is Tosamah, the enigmatic Priest of the Sun who resembles Momaday in a number of respects. First of all, Tosamah is the only Kiowa in *House Made of Dawn.* Second, Momaday's description of Tosamah—"big, lithe as a cat, narrow eyed"—fits Momaday himself. More important, Momaday has Tosamah express some of his most deeply felt ideas about the sacred nature of the word and the power of language in the sermon Tosamah delivers to his parishoners. Finally, and most remarkably, when Tosamah tells his life story, it is the story of Momaday's life. The chapter headed "January 27" in the "Priest of the Sun" section of *House Made of Dawn* is also the introduction to *The Way to Rainy Mountain.*

If Tosamah is the character in *House Made of Dawn* who most closely resembles Momaday, how do we account for the way Tosamah despises Abel? Tosamah says of Abel that the whites

> deloused him and gave him a lot of free haircuts and let him fight on their side. But was he grateful? Hell, no, man. He was too damn dumb to be civilized. . . . He turned out to be a real primitive sonuvabitch, and the first time he got hold of a knife he killed a man. That must have embarrassed the hell out of them.

Obviously Tosamah is being ironic about the generosity of the whites—"they let him fight on their side"—but he means what he says about Abel—that he is "too damn dumb to be civilized," and "a real primitive sonuvabitch." Tosamah does not see anything noble in Abel's savagery. He is ashamed that Abel, a member of the same ethnic group, has made a spectacle of himself. Abel has "embarrassed the hell out of" Tosamah by fulfilling the white stereotype of the Indian—primitive, violent, superstitious, backward, and, significantly, dumb—inarticulate.

Tosamah is so scornful of Abel that he baits him until he breaks Abel's spirit. After Tosamah's taunts, Abel gets violently drunk and loses his job; with it go his hopes for a new life in California. Tosamah never shows any compassion or understanding of Abel; to Tosamah, Abel is simply an object of derision. Momaday's attitude toward Abel is obviously more sympathetic than Tosamah's, but it is hard to avoid the conclusion that Tosamah reflects one side of Momaday.

Recall that, during Momaday's youth, although he too was an Indian, he was an outsider among the Navajo and Jemez Indians. In his fantasy world he often saw himself as white and Indians as hostile. This side of Momaday is reflected in Tosamah.

But Tosamah is only one side of Momaday, and he is a caricature at that. Momaday gives him the middle name of Big Bluff, and Tosamah, in fact, sounds very much like the Kiowa word for "woman of the house," *to•so•a•mah.* Momaday says Tosamah has the voice of a "great dog," and there are deflating, comic touches in his sermon. "May the Great Spirit—can we knock off the talking back there—be with you always." In short, Tosamah reflects Momaday's self-irony, and he is clearly more of a caricature than a self-portrait of the artist. If Momaday is like Tosamah, however, he is also like Abel: both are outsiders. Although Momaday got along well with the Jemez, his accounts of early life at Jemez Pueblo make it clear that he felt he was different from the local Indians.

Abel's problems, in fact, seem to stem chiefly from the intolerance of other Indians. I do not mean just a few individuals like Tosamah and the albino, but the whole Tanoan community of Walatowa. Abel's mother and grandfather Francisco were Tanoans, but Abel was considered an outsider because of his illegitimacy: "He did not know who his father was. His father was a Navajo, they said, or a Sia, or an Isleta, an outsider anyway, which made him and his mother and Vidal somehow foreign and strange."

Abel's mother and brother die during his childhood, and Abel is alone in a hostile world save for his grandfather. Obviously Abel is not living successfully within the Indian cultural tradition before he goes to live in the white world, although this is the impression given on the cover of the New American Library edition—the one the students use: "His name was Abel, and he lived in two worlds. One was that of his fathers, wedding him to the rhythm of the seasons, the harsh beauty of the land, the ecstasy of the drug called peyote. The other was the world of the twentieth century, goading him into a compulsive cycle of sexual exploits, dissipation, and disgust." Abel's chief problem, both before he goes to war and immediately after he returns, is that he is *not* living in the world of his fathers. He does not know who his father is, nor does he know who he is himself.

Abel's problem is most acute just after his return from the war. He finds that he is totally alienated from his grandfather. He is frustrated because he is completely inarticulate. Language, the power of the word, is extremely important to Momaday, and he makes it clear that, because he cannot express himself, Abel is emotionally stifled and repressed, and so potentially violent.

> His return to the town had been a failure, for all his looking forward. He had tried in the days that followed to speak to his grandfather, but he could not say the things he wanted; he had tried to pray, to sing, to enter the old rhythm of the tongue, but he was no longer attuned to it. . . . Had he been able to say . . . anything of his own language . . . [it] would have once again shown him whole to himself; but he was dumb.

A short time later Momaday describes Abel's walk into the hills:

> He was alone, and he wanted to make a song out of the colored canyon, the way the women of Torreón made songs upon their looms out of colored yarn, but he had not got the right words together. It would have been a creation song; he would have sung slowly of the first world, of fire and flood, and of the emergence of dawn from the hills.

The song Abel is looking for is the Navajo hymn "House Made of Dawn," which he later learns from his friend Benally.

Abel remains inarticulate and emotionally repressed throughout his years in jail and during his relocation in Los Angeles, where, as Momaday points out symbolically with a scene that includes grunions, he is like a fish out of water. Abel achieves emotional release with the death of his grandfather. When Francisco dies, Abel buries him in the prescribed Tanoan fashion. For the first time since his disastrous participation in the rooster ceremony, Abel takes part in a Tanoan ritual. The act symbolizes his entry into the culture of his fathers. Immediately after preparing his grandfather for burial, Abel participates in the traditional race for good hunting and harvests. His grandfather had won this contest more than half a century earlier, in what had been the climactic point of his life: "Some years afterward, when he was no longer young and his leg had been stiffened by disease, he made a pencil drawing on the first page of a ledger book which he kept with his store of prayer feathers in the rafters of his room. It was the likeness of a straight black man running in the snow." One cannot help thinking of the contrast between him and A. E. Housman's runner ("To an Athlete Dying Young"), who dies shortly after winning his race. Francisco survives to join the "rout / Of lads that wore their honors out, / Runners whom renown outran."

As the novel ends, Abel smears his arms and chest with ashes, as the ritual prescribes, and joins the runners, though unlike Francisco he runs behind them. As he runs, he sings the song he had longed to sing: "House made of pollen, house made of dawn."

This is a happy ending, or as happy an ending as the novel will allow. Abel has entered into the ceremonial life of his people, and he has regained his voice. His running is symbolic of his emotional and spiritual health, even though his legs buckle and he falls. For him to win the race would be impossibly corny—a totally discordant note of contrived cheerfulness.

Abel does not win this race, nor does Momaday imply that he will win in the future. Yet by the simple act of entering the race Abel establishes that, despite the onslaughts of the Cains who have attacked him, he has survived. Abel survives because he is able to integrate himself into Tanoan culture. But this is not to say that he has rejected white culture and returned to an Indian culture. There is no such thing as a pure culture.

The culture of Walatowa is particularly complex. It was originally a Tanoan Pueblo settlement. When the Conquistadores conquered the Pueblos, they introduced the Spanish language and Catholicism; with the Mexican War, Walatowa became part of America, and a new language and culture were superimposed on the other two. For centuries the Walatoans practiced both Christianity and their native religion, but slowly the religions merged, and by the time of the novel's central action the people of Walatowa have their own peculiar brand of Pueblo Christianity, with its own rituals and mythology. Momaday explicitly chronicles the shift. Fray Nicolas, the nineteenth-century priest who keeps a diary, reveals his horror that his sacristan Francisco (Abel's grandfather) participates in the traditional Tanoan ceremonies by dancing in the Kiva, the sacred dugout of the Pueblos. Fray Nicolas believes that practicing traditional Indian rituals is sinful and disgusting, and he expects the Holy Spirit to strike Francisco down when the boy assists at mass. By 1945 the attitude of the church apparently had changed, because the current priest, Father Olguin, proudly shows Angela St. John the ceremonial dancing and other rituals that take place on the Feast of Santiago.

In fact, the whole myth and ceremony of Santiago is an illustration of the merging of the cultures. Santiago is Momaday's name for San Diego (both are Spanish names for Saint James), the saint whose day was celebrated in Jemez on November 12. The Tanoans celebrate the holiday in the novel by going to mass and then carrying an effigy of Porcingula, Our Lady of the Angels—a saint they inherited from the Bahkyush—through the streets to her position next to the kiva where

> The Lady would stand all day in her shrine, and the governor and his officials would sit in attendance at her feet, and one by one the dancers of the squash and turquoise clans would appear on top of the kiva, coming out upon the sky in their rich ceremonial dress, descend the high ladder to the earth, and kneel before her.

Momaday's myth of Santiago also shows the blending of the cultures, as it combines the Christian genre of the saints tale, with its miracles, and the Indian myth of origin that features the trickster as culture hero. Santiago, who escapes the evil king by the miracle of the rooster and horses (which is as much trickster prank as Christian miracle), ends by providing plants and animals for the Pueblo people, the standard task of the culture-hero trickster.

Like Joyce's *Finnegans Wake*, **House Made of Dawn** ends as it begins. Abel is running and, as he runs, he sings. It is important to notice *what* he sings: the Navajo prayer song, **House Made of Dawn.** Abel has found himself in his own culture, a blend of Tanoan, Spanish, and American influences, and he is singing a Navajo song, appropriate in light of his own mixed ancestry.

Bernard A. Hirsch   (essay date Winter 1983)

SOURCE: "Self-Hatred and Spiritual Corruption in *House Made of Dawn*," in *Western American Literature*, Vol. XVII, No. 4, Winter, 1983, pp. 307-20.

[*In the following essay, Hirsch analyzes the characters of Martinez, Tosamaah, and Benally and their relationships with the protagonist, noting that for these characters Abel is a symbol of contempt and a reminder of their Native selves.*]

N. Scott Momaday, referring to his protagonist Abel, has said, "None but an Indian, I think, knows so much what it is like to have existence in two worlds and security in neither." True as this is of Abel in **House Made of Dawn,** it is truer still of Martinez, Tosamah, and Benally because they, unlike Abel, try earnestly to conform to Euro-American social values. Indeed, the strong responses Abel generates in each of these characters indicate their perception of something unyielding and incorruptible in him, something which throws into stark relief the humiliating spiritual compromises they have felt compelled to make. In his suffering Abel is both a sorry example and stinging rebuke to them, a warning and a goad, someone both to fear and reverence, for he reminds them of who and what they are—of what they find most contemptible in themselves and most holy. Martinez, Tosamah, and Benally have been spiritually corrupted to varying degrees by the white world, and to the extent that they have, they make

Abel their scapegoat and regard him as an evil to be exorcised.

This scapegoating is most apparent in the case of Martinez who, Ben tells us, is "a cop and a bad one." [The critic adds in a footnote: "Most readers assume that Martinez is white, but given his name and the fact that a number of the novel's Indian characters have Spanish names and/or surnames, it seems more likely that he is at least part Indian or Chicano—if the latter, his situation would nonetheless parallel to a significant extent that of the urban Indians. Moreover, to regard Martinez as white is to reduce him to an overworked stereotype—the sadistic white cop—of the sort that Momaday, in his portrayal of every other white character in the novel, has scrupulously avoided."] He derives his sense of self from the power and authority vested in him by white society. That power, in his eyes, makes him superior to his "brothers" in the street by enabling him to identify with the oppressor and victimize them at will. He acts out his own version of the American Dream with every Indian he extorts, yet his violent response to Abel's slight resistance suggests that he has paid a price for the power he enjoys.

Martinez emerges, appropriately enough, from a dark alley as Ben and Abel are returning home from Henry's bar. Ben meekly complies with Martinez' order to hold out his hands, and he recalls that his hands "were shaking bad and I couldn't hold them still." He had just been paid and he gives Martinez "all I had left." Martinez then notices Abel:

> Martinez told him to hold out his hands, and he did, slowly, like maybe he wasn't going to at first, with the palms up. I could see his hands in the light and they were open and almost steady. "Turn them over," Martinez said, and he was looking at them and they were almost steady.

Enraged, Martinez smashes Abel's hands with his nightstick, but Abel "didn't cry out or make a sound." From Benally's description, we can see that it is Abel's attitude rather than his actions that engenders Martinez' wrath. Martinez could not help but notice the contrast between Ben's involuntary shaking and Abel's relative steadiness, and this implied slight to his authority threatens him. His response to it indicates just how precarious his sense of self is, and the extreme viciousness of his later beating of Abel further reveals the self-hatred that is the price of the Anglo authority he covets.

By his mere presence Abel threatens the protective illusions so necessary to Martinez' emotional and psychological survival, and he poses the same threat to Tosamah and Benally. Martha Scott Trimble maintains [in her 1973 *N. Scott Momaday*] that "the suffering of the urban Indians is . . . rendered painful to watch because of their reluctance to admit to themselves that they suffer." They are so reluctant because they have been conditioned by the dominant white culture to regard their very suffering as evidence of their own inferiority. Their suffering is at least as productive of guilt as of rage and therefore they have devised what Trimble calls "strategies" to avoid acknowledging that suffering to themselves. By means of these strategies, they seek not only to adapt to white society but

to retain while doing so a sense of themselves as free agents making intelligent decisions. They have chosen, in Ben's words, to "go along with it" not out of fear or because they have been seduced by the false promise of the white world, but because, they would believe, it makes sense. And as regards Tosamah and Benally, it is indeed painful to watch them disparage that which they most love and most need—their Indianness.

Tosamah, for instance, tries to better his situation by assuming a superior posture toward it—as is apparent in his use of language. In his first sermon, "The Gospel According to John," Tosamah tries to convince both himself and his congregation that he understands the white man by telling them how the white man conceives of and manipulates language. He says that "the white man deals in words, and he deals easily, with grace and sleight of hand. And in his presence, here on his own ground, you are as children. . . ." Tosamah knows what he is talking about; his assertions are verified by Abel's experience in Los Angeles and Benally's explanation of Abel's language problems. But ironically, Tosamah uses language much as the white man does, and to much the same purpose. In fact, he uses it as Martinez uses fear and violence. Like Martinez, he has carved out a little fiefdom of sorts in the Los Angeles ghetto, and language is his means of controlling it.

By manipulating a variety of verbal styles in "The Gospel According to John," Tosamah keeps his parishioners off balance, dazzling as much as enlightening them. Through an ever-shifting combination of biblical oratory, street talk, exposition, and the simple, direct narrative style of the storyteller, Tosamah tries to relate to his audience on several levels simultaneously, to establish at once his oneness with and superiority to them. He wants to be perceived as a follow Indian sharing a similar culture and values, as a ghetto brother sharing the hardship of the streets, and as a teacher in both the shamanistic and professorial senses. The sermon is full of insight, but it is a masterpiece of verbal gymnastics as well.

Tosamah is perceptive enough to know that the agonizing conflict within himself also exists to varying degrees in the other urban Indians, and he exploits their insecurity and self-doubt to shore up his own tenuous conception of self. Indeed, his need continually to assert himself over the others is one indication of his sense of inadequacy. Like them, he both loves and fears his Indianness, and this entails a roughly similar ambivalence toward the white man. Tosamah sees through the white man to a significant extent and pointedly ridicules his blindness, but like Martinez he also feels a troubling yet insistent need to identify with his oppressor. This need underlies his use of language to intimidate and manipulate the other urban Indians. But he also feels the same need with regard to his heritage and his people. When Tosamah speaks so lovingly, so evocatively in his second sermon, "The Way to Rainy Mountain," of his journey to rediscover his Indian self, we cannot doubt his sincerity. This sermon is longer than his first, and it is free of the verbal gamesmanship that characterizes much of "The Gospel." Still, he needs to be a winner. He sees in his parishioners, and even more clearly in Abel, the fate of Indians in a white world, and he cannot accept such a density. If white society has consigned him, despite his education, intelligence, and talent, to a small, severely limited space, it has at least taught him how to control that space. Like Martinez, he has learned to exalt himself by undermining others. Oppressed, he becomes an oppressor victimizing, as Martinez does, the only people he can—his own.

As Martinez batters Abel's body, so Tosamah batters his spirit, and Momaday, through his use of narrative structure, stresses the parallel between them. The novel's second chapter, "The Priest of the Sun," in effect begins and ends with a sermon by Tosamah. These sermons frame a badly beaten, semiconscious Abel whose murder trial and life in Los Angeles pass in fragments before him. Ironically, Tosamah's second sermon, which recounts his journey to the land of his people, the Kiowa, to visit his grandmother's grave, reveals the path to salvation for Abel, tells how he might be made whole again. But Abel is not there to hear the sermon. Indeed, as we later learn from Benally, it was after Tosamah had earlier humiliated Abel that, in Ben's words, "He went downhill pretty fast . . . ," decided "to get even with" Martinez, and was beaten half to death by him. Tosamah calls himself "Priest of the Sun," and he is sufficiently imaginative, sensitive, understanding, and articulate to be that. But he lives his day-to-day life as Coyote, the trickster who is both culture hero and buffoon. Like Coyote, Tosamah has the capacity to bring spiritual gifts to his people, to be a savior of sorts, but his actions are generally self-centered and done in ignorance—in Tosamah's case, a self-imposed ignorance—of their consequences for the world, his people, and himself. Tosamah is quick to take advantage of others to satisfy his own needs, but because he is himself a slave to those needs (emotional and psychological needs as opposed to Coyote's purely physical ones), he is at times the victim of his own tricks. Coyote is a master of self-deception and, as his own ambivalence toward and treatment of Abel indicates, so is John Big Bluff Tosamah.

Despite his awareness of the beauty and value of his native culture, despite his profound understanding of the nearly overwhelming spiritual problems modern America has created for his people, Tosamah is himself tormented by his Indianness. Abel, in his view, is the incarnation of that Indianness, and as such he fills Tosamah with shame and guilt and reverence. Tosamah, for all his insight into its workings, has been conditioned by the white world and by himself in response to that world to see with two pairs of eyes and the result, at least as regards Abel, is a mélange of contradictory impressions and impulses. For example, Ben remembers Tosamah's warning him about Abel: "He was going to get us all in trouble, Tosamah said. Tosamah sized him up right away. . . ." Perceptive as he is, Tosamah can sense in Abel the unyielding integrity that will make him especially vulnerable in urban Los Angeles, that will keep him from "fitting in"; and that integrity implicitly confronts Tosamah with his own compromising and compromised self.

When Tosamah speaks of Abel's trial, he is both ironic and envious. True, the white society that is puzzled by

Abel is the target of his irony, and he ostensibly mocks its view of Abel as "a real primitive sonuvabitch" and a "poor degenerate Indian"; but his own view of Abel, as his warning to Benally and his later psychological attack on Abel make clear, parallels to some extent that of the society he ridicules. Consider in this regard his impression of how Abel's testimony must have sounded to the court:

> " 'Well, you honors, it was this way, see? I cut me up a little snake meat out there in the sand.' Christ, man, that must have been our finest hour, better than Little Bighorn. That little no-count cat must have had the whole Jesus scheme right in the palm of his hand."

Tosamah's tone conveys both embarrassment and admiration here, but alone with Ben in the privacy of Ben's apartment he lets his admiration show. Of the court's verdict, he says:

> "They put that cat away, man. They *had* to. It's part of the Jesus scheme. *They,* man. They put all of us renegades, us diehards, away sooner or later. . . . Listen here, Benally, one of these nights there's going to be a full red moon, a hunter's moon, and we're going to find us a wagon train full of women and children. Now you won't believe this, but I drink to that now and then."

If Ben "won't believe this" it is because the sentiments Tosamah here expresses hardly parallel his actions, and Tosamah knows it. He seeks to identify with Abel, referring to "us renegades, us diehards," and to the white man as "they," but merely to wish now and again for vengeance is an empty gesture. No doubt Tosamah's desire to avenge himself on those who have poisoned his spirit is sincere, but the courage, the spirit of defiance he recognizes in Abel, lies dormant within his own heart. Ben, as he does throughout the novel, undercuts Tosamah's pretentiousness, telling us that "He's always going on like that, Tosamah, talking crazy and showing off. . . ."

Seeing Abel through white eyes, Tosamah finds him embarrassing. Though Tosamah ridicules Anglo cultural arrogance and the stereotypes that feed it, Abel—alcoholic, at times violent, and inarticulate—seems to him to lend credence to the stereotypes; thus Tosamah, educated and articulate as he is, feels misrepresented, degraded by association. This is the "trouble" of which he warns Benally. Seeing Abel through Indian eyes, Tosamah cannot help but admire him as a kind of modern-day warrior who refuses to give in meekly to the torment and tribulations of urban Indian life. But if Tosamah as an Indian is vicariously elevated by Abel's integrity, he is at the same time humbled by the lack of his own. Viewed from either perspective, then, white or Indian, Abel engenders in Tosamah self-contempt so strong that it is beyond enduring; he is anathema to the illusory conception of his own superiority that is Tosamah's primary means of emotional and psychological survival. Therefore, because of the guilt he feels, a guilt stemming from a profound sense of his own inadequacy, he projects upon Abel his own diminished sense of self.

Tosamah needs to tear Abel down and one evening, during

a poker game at his place, the opportunity presents itself. In a seemingly expansive mood Tosamah, Ben tells us, was "going on about everything . . . and talking big." Ben, seeing that this talk bothers Abel, wants to leave, but Abel, already drunk and becoming more so, ignores him. Ben recalls,

> I guess Tosamah knew what he was thinking too, because pretty soon he started in on him, not directly, you know, but he started talking about *longhairs* and the reservation and all. I kept wishing he would shut up, and I guess the others did, too . . . because right away they got quiet and just started looking down at their hands, you know—like they were trying to decide what to do. I knew that something bad was going to happen.

Abel, too drunk to seriously threaten Tosamah, lunges impotently toward him, and the others, to relieve their own discomfort, laugh at his futility.

Ben tells us that the laughter "seemed to take all the fight out of him. It was like he had to give up when they laughed; it was like all of a sudden he didn't care about anything anymore." Abel's response to the laughter indicates that, though perhaps not consciously aware of it, he attacked Tosamah not merely to avenge a personal insult but to avenge all the Indians at the table and back home, to avenge the honor of his people. Tosamah, who "doesn't come from the reservation" himself, has made the others ashamed of what they are, and when they try to dispel their shame by projecting it onto Abel, Abel's rage loses its foundation and he feels empty and alone. Ben remembers "that he was hurt by what had happened; he was hurt inside somehow, and pretty bad." Tosamah, the Priest of the Sun of the Holiness Pan-Indian Rescue Mission, has lost sight of the needs of his people in pursuit of his own isolated ends and in so doing, as his attack on Abel symbolically suggests, he has violated the very essence of his own Indianness. By shaming his people he has done the white man's work.

Unlike Tosamah, Benally is compassionate towards Abel; he is, from the time of their first meeting, instinctively protective of him. He trains Abel for his new job, introduces him around, and though he has very little himself, readily shares his home, his food, and his clothing. Most important of all, he shares with Abel, and Abel alone, his dearest possession—his native religion. It is Ben's honest, profound spirituality that sets him apart from the other urban Indians. As has often been noted, Ben is the one who has the vision during the peyote ceremony, and whereas Tosamah's understanding of his native culture seems at times largely intellectual, Ben "lives his religion on a level deeper than the intellect, the level of spirit and emotion" [Carole Oleson, "The Remembered Earth: Momaday's *House Made of Dawn*," *South Dakota Review* II, No. 1 (Spring 1973)]. Yet there are definite similarities between Ben and Tosamah as well, and to ignore them is to obscure considerably the scope and horror of the spiritual compromises white society, for its own material and psychological convenience, requires of Indians.

Sincere as his religious beliefs are and sensitive as he is, Be-

nally has compromised himself almost as severely as Tosamah has, and this is most apparent from the contradictions in his narrative. Ben is trying earnestly to sell himself on the American Dream in a vain effort to convince himself that the life he feels compelled to live is in fact better and ultimately more fulfilling than the life he knew on the reservation. His pathetic monologue on the wonders of Los Angeles is a case in point:

> It's a good place to live. . . . Once you find your way around and get used to everything, you wonder how you ever got along out there where you came from. There's nothing there, you know, but the land, and the land is empty and dead. Everything is here, everything you could ever want. You never have to be alone.

But for all practical purposes Ben, until Abel comes, is alone. He has drinking buddies, true, but no one with whom he can share what is most important to him. Moreover, the "radios and cars and clothes and big houses" which, Ben says, "you'd be crazy not to want" and which are "so easy to have" have managed to elude him. He lives in a leaky, dilapidated slum tenement, gets his clothes second-hand, and is a cipher in the plant where he works. He willfully mistakes the racist ridicule of his co-workers for good-natured kidding and the pseudo-amiable hustle of the salespeople in the stores for friendliness. The extent and cost of his self-deception, however, are most painfully revealed in his comments about the land.

Ben's narrative is punctuated at several points by contrapuntal remembrances which rise unbidden in his mind, memories of growing up on the reservation, on "the land south of Wide Ruins where I come from," on the land he still loves. These recollections are full of precise, beautiful, and evocative details which belie his remark that "the land is empty and dead." The land he recalls is rich with vitality and meaning; it is the sacred center of all life and being. He remembers childhood on the land:

> *And you were little and right there in the center of everything, the sacred mountains, the snow-covered mountains and the hills, the gullies and the flats, the sundown and the night, everything—where you were little, where you were and had to be.*

The vision of the land inherent in his memories is that which contemporary America requires him to abandon, and he tries to do just that. After all, "That's the only way you can live in a place like this [Los Angeles]. You have to forget about the way it was, how you grew up and all." The need to "go along with it" is a recurrent motif in Ben's narrative, and all that gives his life meaning must be subordinated to it:

> If you come from the reservation, you don't talk about it much; I don't know why. I guess you figure that it won't do you much good, so you just forget about it. You think about it sometimes, you can't help it, but then you just try to put it out of your mind . . . it mixes you up sometimes. . . .

But Abel does not let Ben "forget about it." He is to Ben what he is to Tosamah, the incarnation of all that is Indian within him, and Ben intuitively apprehends this. He remarks,

> We were kind of alike, though, him and me. After a while he told me where he was from, and right away I knew we were going to be friends. We're related somehow, I think.

Abel's mere presence evokes his memories of home, and the first of Ben's "flashbacks" occurs as he recalls their first real conversation. Ben's history resembles Abel's in certain respects, and his memories [according to Lawrence J. Evers in his "Words and Place: A Reading of *House Made of Dawn*," *Western American Literature* XI, No. 4 (February 1977)] "reveal a sense of place very like that Abel groped for on his return to Walatowa." What is especially sad about these memories is that they convey a sense of wholeness and security that contrasts sharply with the fragmented, fear-ridden, tenuous existence Ben now endures. He appears to regain a modicum of that sense with Abel, however; Ben knows that his most precious treasures are safe with him:

> "House made of dawn." I used to tell him about those old ways, the stories and the signs, Beautyway and Night Chant. I sang some of those things and told him what they meant, what I thought they were about.

Abel is wonderfully receptive, as Ben knew he would be, and "would want me to sing like that."

And Abel, Ben fears, is the only one who would. Just as Tosamah finds "longhairs" like Abel an embarrassment to him in the white world, so is Benally, within the context of that world, embarrassed by his own best impulses—and that world includes the other urban Indians. He tells of a night when he and Abel, along with the others, are drinking and having fun on a hill overlooking the city:

> . . . I started to sing all by myself. The others were singing, too, but it was the wrong kind of thing, and I wanted to pray. I didn't want them to hear me, because they were having a good time, and I was ashamed, I guess. I kept down because I didn't want anybody but him to hear.

Only with Abel does Benally feel good about being an Indian; only with Abel can he free his spirit in song and prayer, and see past and future merge into an all-inclusive present. When Abel is in the hospital recovering from his beating, Ben, to comfort him, makes up a plan about going home, about "going out into the hills on horses and alone. It was going to be early in the morning, and we were going to see the sun coming up." There, they would "sing the old songs," sing "about the way it used to be, how there was nothing all around but the hills and the sunrise and the clouds." Ben at first did not take his plan seriously, but Abel "believed in it" and "I guess I started to believe in it, too." Dream and waking reality come together for Ben in Abel's presence, albeit briefly, and the deepest impulses of his spirit are vindicated in Abel's existence. In that respect Abel is truly a blessing for Benally. But they live in a world uncongenial to these impulses, a world contemptuous of vision and song, and in that world Abel also becomes an agonizing problem for Ben.

Ben's Indianness can find expression only through his religion and his friendship with Abel, and in a world hostile to Indians both, Ben feels, must be sheltered and protected. This is one reason why he tries to shepherd Abel as he does at the factory and why he takes him into his home. That Ben truly believes he is acting in Abel's best interest is undeniable, and in a very real sense he is. Abel sorely needs the kind of support Ben provides, and if Tosamah's attempt to isolate Abel is a denial of his own Indianness, Ben's generous inclusion of Abel in his own life is a wonderfully rich expression of his. Moreover, by telling Abel of the old traditions and teaching him the old songs, Ben not only provides him with necessary spiritual sustenance in a world unresponsive to spiritual need, but prepares him for his return to Walatowa to try again, this time more successfully, to find himself in the life of his people. But Ben's concern for Abel is motivated by fear as well as by compassion. Tosamah feared that Abel "was going to get us all in trouble," and so does Ben. He speaks to Abel of things Indian, for, as we have seen, his own spirit requires as much, but throughout his narrative he emphasizes repeatedly Abel's inability to "get along." He understands why Abel has difficulty adjusting and implies that he himself has faced similar obstacles, but he never questions the need to accommodate oneself to the white man's world, and that is why he eventually loses patience with Abel. Abel's problems, in Ben's view, go beyond those which confront every relocated Indian, severe as these problems may be. What Tosamah recognizes as Abel's unyielding integrity Benally sees as sheer obstinacy; or rather, the sustaining illusion he has constructed about the "good life" in Los Angeles demands that he see it as such. After all, Abel has a steady job, a place to live, drinking buddies—everything he needs, Ben would believe, to make it in urban America. Yet despite these advantages, he persists in being a trial to those who care for him.

Abel scares Ben. He scares him when he subtly defies Martinez in the alley and he scares him during Tosamah's harangue about "longhairs and the reservation." In both instances his actions threaten to undermine Ben's illusions by confronting him with the truth that life in urban America is incompatible with his identity as an Indian. Benally, as Carole Oleson has said, has whitened himself considerably by removing his religion from his daily life. He retains the songs and traditions within himself, and that is good, but he also compromises the old religion by confining it like a retarded child whom the family loves but of whom they are ashamed. Like Angela St. John, whose affair with Abel in Walatowa puts her in touch, if only temporarily, with her body's potential for joy and wonder, he turns off his own light, as it were, denies his own intuitive wisdom in a futile attempt to avoid emotional and psychological conflicts which might prove irreconcilable. And like Father Olguin, Benally also preaches the white man's religion—not in the form of Christianity, as Olguin does, but in its true aspects of materialism and conformity; like both Olguin and his predecessor, Fray Nicolás, he would convert the Indian to a new and alien faith for, like them, he needs converts to vindicate his own. Thus it is that when Abel ultimately proves "unregenerate," the usually mild Benally, possessed by anger but more by fear, loses patience:

He wouldn't let anybody help him, and I guess I got mad, too, and one day we had a fight . . . he was just sitting there and saying the worst thing he could think of, over and over. I didn't like to hear that kind of talk, you know; it made me kind of scared, and I told him to cut it out. I guess I was more scared than mad; anyway I had had about all I could take.

As with Martinez and Tosamah earlier, Ben knew "something bad was going to happen and . . . didn't want any part of it." At this point Abel goes to look for Martinez, but even after he is gone and Ben cools off, Ben nonetheless maintains that "It had to stop, you know; something had to happen."

Benally, then, like Tosamah, is a priest whose saving message, because he has divorced his religion from his everyday life, has an ironic as well as a revelatory dimension. It is especially ironic that despite his deeper, more sincere spirituality, Ben lacks Tosamah's awareness of the redemptive potential of the old ways of seeing and knowing. As the "Night Chanter," Ben, as we have seen, is essential to any hope Abel has for recovery, but Ben himself does not see the sharing of himself and his religion in this way. The road to recovery he consciously charts, as we have also seen, involves passively assimilating the values and accommodating oneself to the demands of white America, even at the cost of one's heritage and identity. Thus the role of "Night Chanter" assumes a second, and contrary, meaning. Though with the best intentions, Benally also, and quite unknowingly, chants the dark night of the soul, the tortured, fragmented, solipsistic state of being that Los Angeles comes to symbolize in the novel. Through the distorting lens of his own desperate need for some sense of meaning to his life, Ben sees an urban paradise, and it is this vision that he consciously advances as salvation.

Though it exists to differing degrees in each of them and, given their enormously diverse natures, manifests itself in various ways, Martinez, Tosamah, and Benally all share a single quality: self-contempt. Each is ashamed of being what he is, of being an Indian, and that is why Abel, when he is relocated in Los Angeles, becomes a kind of sacrifice to their fear and desperation. A "longhair" from the reservation, he is, among other things, a constant reminder to them of how they are perceived by the dominant culture and of that which has made them wretched. They have been made to feel, against all logic and common sense, that their suffering is somehow deserved because of what they are; thus each of them projects his own diminished sense of self upon Abel and responds to that self in his own way. Martinez tries to obliterate it through violence, Tosamah tries to disassociate himself from it, and Benally tries to remake it to fit the white world he inhabits. The issue is agonizingly complicated, however, because the very Indianness within them which they have been taught to hate is that which they intuitively love. Tosamah and Benally especially know in their very depths that fulfillment and wholeness lie in the realization and free expression of their Indian selves. Tosamah has made a long journey to the land of his people to rediscover his Indianness, and Ben hoards the old songs like treasure within his heart. Therefore, their self-contempt is further intensified by a pro-

found sense of guilt stemming from their perceived inability to live their Indianness, by what they themselves see as a personal betrayal of their heritage and of themselves. However, though it saddens him, Momaday does not condemn the urban Indians for feeling as they do. Their self-hatred is in fact his most telling indictment of a modern America which relentlessly tries to compel its native peoples to barter dignity and self-respect for material, emotional, and psychological survival.

Michael W. Raymond (essay date Spring 1983)

SOURCE: "Tai-me, Christ, and the Machine: Affirmation through Mythic Pluralism in *House Made of Dawn*," in *Studies in American Fiction,* Vol. 11, No. 1, Spring, 1983, pp. 61-71.

[*Raymond is an author, critic, and educator. In the following essay, he discusses the role of technology, Christianity, and the Kiowa Tai-me in* House Made of Dawn.]

Many critics interpret N. Scott Momaday's *House Made of Dawn* as depicting disharmony, alienation, and the need for spiritual redemption in a squalid, hellish, temporal world. Martha Scott Trimble, for example, sees it [in her 1973 *N. Scott Momaday*] as a story of how differences in "language and culture tend through their own territorial imperatives to encompass one, sometimes to a point of isolation." Even those critics not advocating themes of alienation see *House Made of Dawn* as an insider's novel. To them, it portrays "the orderly continuum of interrelated events that constitute the Indian universe" and "warns native Americans that they may lose more than they gain if they assimilate into the American mix." With its alternative to Christianity and to a modern civilization based on secular, technological structures, *House Made of Dawn*'s optimism has to be inappropriate for an outsider.

Neither of these approaches accounts for the full richness of Momaday's Pulitzer Prize-winning novel. Rather than denying the possibility of affirmation or suggesting that affirmation can come only through a monolithic cultural identity, *House Made of Dawn* focuses on the pluralism of ordinary contemporary life and the possibility of finding meaning in it. Depicting a pervasive cultural diversity in even remote, seemingly culturally isolated areas, the novel suggests that meaning in contemporary life comes when one finds his sense of place by recognizing and living within that large and diverse context.

At the end of *House Made of Dawn,* Abel is "running on the rise of the song." By seeing and going among the runners, Abel unmistakably associates himself with the dawn runners of eternity:

They were whole and indispensable in what they did; everything in creation referred to them. Because of them, perspective, proportion, design in the universe. Meaning because of them. They ran with great dignity and calm, not in the hope of anything, but hopelessly; neither in fear nor hatred nor despair of evil, but simply in recognition and with respect. Evil was. Evil was abroad in the night; they must venture out to the confrontation; they must reckon dues and divide the world.

Abel saves himself when he identifies with the dawn runners, sees them as a part of the whole, becomes a part of them, and feels significant. But Abel's path to the beginnings of salvation is not easy. Abel's story is one of a journey through and from placelessness. It is a sordid and seemingly chaotic journey through a self-conscious and reflective uninvolvement, an alienation from people and places, homelessness, a sense of the unreality of the world and of not belonging. Abel's choices and their outcome are neither simple nor clear-cut. It is more than just the matter of returning to the fulfilling pueblo from the nasty white man's world. Abel's tribulations involve all the complexities inherent in contemporary life. He is forced to face the army, the legal system, and the social service agencies of a society almost totally alien to him. He must deal with such personal tragedies as the deaths of his mother and brother and his own alcoholism. He is torn between personal pride and the necessity for survival in a hostile environment. Swirling around him are the complicated and often obscure promises of value systems inherent in at least three Native American cultures, in Christianity, and in modern technology.

Clearly this journey through placelessness is not restricted to the white man's army, city, or values. He experiences the twentieth-century sense of alienation before ever leaving the pueblo. At Walatowa, Abel's father was an outsider of an undetermined tribe. His family is considered foreign and strange. As an adolescent, Abel unexplainably strangles an eagle he captures during a ceremonial Eagle Watchers Society hunt. On his return to Walatowa in 1945, Abel is drunk and does not recognize his grandfather. At the rooster pull, he is awkward and uncomfortable. Unattuned to the old rhythm of the pueblo, he is unable to sing a creation song. In Los Angeles, Abel is no more attuned to the white man's world. The Kiowa priest Tosamah labels him a longhair, a primitive, a What's-His-Name, and a renegade. Abel himself acknowledges that his own body and mind had turned on him and had become his enemy.

Showing that Abel's problems transcend simplistic red-white, rural-urban, primitive-modern conflicts, that not all of his villains are external, and that his problems are not unique to him or to being a Native American, *House Made of Dawn* exposes more fully the complexities of Abel's story. Furthermore, it becomes apparent then that Abel's salvation is not wholly due to his return to the ceremonial life of the pueblo and that salvation does not occur in an entirely Native American place as Marion Willard Hylton, Lawrence J. Evers, Alan R. Veile, and Joseph Trimmer suggest.

[In his 1977 *In Time and Place: Some Origins of American Fiction*] Floyd C. Watkins finds *House Made of Dawn* "made almost incomprehensible by a profusion of elaborate cultural, mythical, and ritualistic detail." Indeed, Momaday includes in his narrative materials from the Jemez pueblo, the Pecos pueblo, the Navajo, the Kiowa, and Christian cultures. Set in Walatowa and Los Angeles, and narrated in multiple points of view that move freely back and forth in time, the novel provides a wide range of experiences within these many cultures. Frequently old and current rituals are alluded to or described in detail. Characters from all conditions of life and faith are a part of Abel's struggle. *House Made of Dawn* easily creates a sense of Abel's confusion, self-consciousness, and alienation.

As just three of the many cultural influences in *House Made of Dawn,* technology, Christianity, and Tai-me represent but a sample of the divergent and apparently conflicting values in the novel. Their clashing seems ubiquitous. At first glance, technology appears as the usual nightmarish movements of a machine. The novel seems structured on the archetypal conflict between the treadmill of the pursuit of the American Dream and the salvation of the natural order, between the urban industrialized life and the rural Native American sense of place, between Los Angeles and Walatowa. One has no difficulty recognizing the distinctions between the two places which represent these conflicting ideals. Los Angeles is a warehouse for A. A. Kaul Office Supply Company, a place much like a basement that is "cold and dreary, dimly illuminated by two 40-watt bulbs which were screwed into the side walls above the dais. . . . The walls were bare and gray and streaked with water. The only windows were small, rectangular openings near the ceiling at ground level; the panes were covered with a thick film of coal oil and dust, and spider webs clung to the frames or floated out like smoke across the room. The room was heavy and stale." As a location, Walatowa is the house made of dawn, a place where

> the river lies in the valley of hills and fields. The north end of the valley is narrow, and the river runs down from the mountains through a canyon. The sun strikes the canyon floor only a few hours each day, and in winter the snow remains for a long time in the crevices of the walls. There is a town in the valley, and there are ruins of other towns in the canyon. In three directions from the town there are cultivated fields. Most of them lie to the west, across the river, on the slope of the plain. Now and then in winter, great angles of geese fly through the valley, and then the sky and the geese are the same color and the air is hard and damp and smoke rises from the houses of the town. The seasons lie hard upon the land. In summer the valley is hot, and birds come to the tamarack on the river. The feathers of blue and yellow birds are prized by the townsmen.

All of Abel's problems connect apparently to modern technology and its machines. His first departure from the pueblo is by a bus that jars, creaks, and lurches Abel into alienation and estrangement. At war, he dances on a leaf-covered, wooded hill around a black, massive enemy tank that "seemed apart from the land." After the war, Abel returns by bus to Walatowa drunk, a shame to his grandfather, and inarticulate in his own culture. In Los Angeles, Abel is a longhair "too damn dumb to be civilized." He refuses to adapt to the Jesus scheme, to the bright lights and cacophony, to the assembly-line job, and to the modern social system of prison, questionnaires, and brutal cops. All bring him down. Psychologically and physically, Abel is mangled and racked with pain. Significantly, as he attempts to revive himself from a near-fatal beating presumably administered by Martinez, his feeble efforts take place near a heavy wire-mesh fence, tractor trailers, and an industrial loading dock. As Abel tries to move, retches, and wants to die, he hears "sounds of the city at night, ticking on like a clock," foghorns, and ships. The nightmare of the modern technologically created Los Angeles apparently offers Abel only danger, chaos, and exposure.

Abel is not the only one who apparently suffers from the machine. In general, the Native Americans "do not hanker after progress" and consider the white man with his beasts of burden and trade as an enemy invader. With their changes, their unending succession of things, and their attempts to make everything bigger and better, the invaders dilute and multiply all into commonplaces. But the whites also suffer. Milly bears physical scars from barbed wire and psychological scars from her daughter's death in the hospital. Old Carlozini lives silently, alone, and afraid in a smelly, dark city apartment. The only time she comes out or speaks is to lament the death of her only friend, a black and white guinea pig. Even Angela St. John, wife of a successful doctor and a shopper in the affluent Westwood section of Los Angeles, needs to escape to Walatowa. Uncertain who she is and disgusted with her pregnant body, she seeks a vision of "some reality that she did not know, or even suspect."

Christianity is apparently as ineffectual as technology is threatening. The Jesus scheme is personified by Father Olguin and the Right Reverend John Big Bluff Tosamah. Father Olguin is a prematurely old, blind-in-one-eye Catholic priest at the pueblo mission. A native of Mexico, he had dreams of becoming "an example in the town." However, he seems obtuse and insensitive. His services are routine and formulaic. His knowledge of his parishioners' culture seems memorized rather than understood. His attraction to Angela St. John is hardly spiritual. That Father Olguin finds comfort in Fray Nicolas's ethnocentric and misanthropic journal seems incongruous with his supposed purpose for being at the mission. His return to town after Angela's mocking rejection is symptomatic of his Christianity and its effect. Driving his car through the pueblo's narrow, dusty streets which are filled with his flock, Father Olguin bears down upon the people, leans on the car horn, and nearly hits them. While the Catholic priest is torn between revulsion, fear, and despair in his stopped car, the children laugh at him and mock him with "a shrill and incessant chant: 'Padre! Padre! Padre!'"

With the versatile abilities of an experienced confidence man, the Kiowa Reverend J. B. B. Tosamah does not seem much more effective than the pueblo priest. Pastor and Priest of the Sun, he personifies the seemingly irreconcilable conflict between white and Native American religious cultures. On Saturday, he preaches "The Gospel According to John"; on Sunday, "The Way to Rainy Mountain." Preaching in the cold, dreary basement of the A. A. Kaul Office Supply Company, Tosamah wavers between agony and arrogance, between the voice of a dog and the virtuosity of a scholar. In his three performances during the sec-

ond section of *House Made of Dawn,* he goes back and forth among conviction, caricature, and callousness. He is dressed in black cleric clothes for the first sermon. Tosamah begins his traditional Christian sermon about the Word, God, and Truth with Latin and Genesis. Then he attacks the white man's assault on truth and ends with the paradoxical advice to listen and to learn from the white man. The peyote ceremony is as paradoxical. Ceremonially painted, Tosamah clinically describes the chemical ingredients and the psychological effects of peyote. Then he uses street slang to describe it and finally announces the Kiowa idea of peyote as "the vegetal representation of the sun." Sunday's sermon is the most personal and straightforward. Tosamah, however, cannot resist inserting into his story of his grandmother and his pilgrimage to Rainy Mountain an account of the Christians' destruction of the Kiowa deity.

Tosamah mocks both the longhairs and the Jesus scheme. His rule is "get yours." Very little seems sacred. Apparently, he does not believe in being reverent; becoming civilized is learning how to exploit the dominant culture or social system. He preaches assimilation into white society but has no respect for the white man. As a result, Tosamah's congregation is made up of Ben Benallys who consider the pastor-priest a bad drunk, a show-off, a madman, and an insensitive outsider.

Compared to the seemingly threatening technology and the apparently ineffectual Christianity, the Native American Tai-me would appear to be the only viable solution available to Abel and the twentieth century. In fact, because *House Made of Dawn* contains innumerable references to the sun as well as Tosamah's explicit commentaries, it would seem that Tai-me, the sun dance god, would be the most accessible, comprehensible, and affirmative myth in the novel. Tosamah's sincerely reverent account of his grandmother's memories of Tai-me is a history of the Kiowa sun dance culture. This most sacred and most powerful fetish represented the transformation of the Kiowa culture from a nation of slaves struggling for survival to one of divinity with the sun. Tai-me provided a sense of destiny, the attributes of courage and pride, and the fulfillment of an old prophecy. It led to the golden age of a "lordly and dangerous society of fighters and thieves, hunters and priests of the sun."

The attributes and effects ascribed to Tai-me seem congruent with every description of the sun in *House Made of Dawn.* From the novel's title to Tosamah's sermons, from the dawn running to the dance rituals, from Francisco's accounts of the organic calendar to the light images associated with Angela St. John, the sun seems to be a symbol of life, growth, and knowledge. The sun seems to be the unifying symbol of affirmation. The inclination is to link these sun references unilaterally to Tai-me. However, this would simplify inappropriately intricate but certainly more satisfying systems of cultural complexity in *House Made of Dawn.* This inclination is much like those critics who contribute to the reductive approaches to *House Made of Dawn* as just an ethnic novel in which only the vanishing breed can win or—as is more often the case—no one can win. *House Made of Dawn* does not sustain or deserve a reduction of itself into simplistic conflicts. The novel eschews dire warnings of ethnic apocalypse or strident calls for ethnic isolationism by emphasizing the complexities inherent in interpreting Tai-me and, therefore, in contemporary culture. One cannot eliminate or isolate any single myth or culture when it is inextricably mixed in with a score of other myths or cultures. One cannot reduce the struggles of contemporary life into an "us vs. them" conflict when one has difficulty discriminating between "us" and "them."

Not all references to the sun are in a Native American context. Furthermore, those references that are in such a context certainly do not allude only to the Kiowa sun dance fetish Tai-me. The title *House Made of Dawn* comes from Ben Benally's Navajo Night Chant; Francisco's dawn running emanates from the pueblo culture; the sun as a center for the organic calendar represents an archetype for even the whites in Los Angeles. Another reason for eschewing any simplified cultural conflict is that even those rituals, legends, and ceremonies directly connected to Tai-me are clearly depicted as neither pure Kiowa nor pure Native American. Tosamah's sermon on the way to Rainy Mountain indicates the influence of several cultures on Tai-me. As he indicates, the chief symbol of the Kiowa worship was given to the migrating tribe by the Crows in the late seventeenth century. Using an old hide rather than a buffalo, the last sun dance was in 1887. In 1890, the U. S. Cavalry stopped an attempted revival of the ceremony. By the time of the novel, the vestiges of Tai-me are entirely oral, relayed by Christian Kiowas, and in languages lost to the newer generations. Just from the evidence presented in *House Made of Dawn,* Tai-me was not indigenous to the Kiowa culture and was not left unchanged by the peoples and forces of history. Also, one should be careful to note that the blending with Tai-me was not depicted entirely as destructive dilution. The Crows provided the migrating hunters with a sense of destiny. Although a Christian in later years, Tosamah's grandmother was able to transmit with ancient awe and holy regard the sacredness of this memory to her grandson.

The blending of cultural materials indicated in the presentation of Tai-me is characteristic of how cultures are presented throughout *House Made of Dawn.* Momaday repeatedly emphasizes the blending of the pueblo, Kiowa, Navajo, Christian, and technological cultures and indicates the mixed blessings resulting from the blending. For example, the festival of Santiago and the feast for Porcingula dominate the "Longhair" section. The "halting talk of old fellowship" is in Tanoan, Athapascan, English, and Spanish. The participating characters are the Catholic Father Olguin, the sacristan and holy medicine man Francisco, the albino witch Juan Teyes Fragua, and the recently returned army veteran Abel. The observers include the shy Navajo children, the Jemez pueblo people, the Bahkyush descendants, and the white doctor's wife Angela St. John. The myth behind the festival is a curious adaptation of St. James' bringing Christianity to Spain into Santiago's founding of the pueblo culture. The rooster-pull or gallo is the featured event. As Watkins and Trimmer indicate, the gallo observed in *House Made of Dawn* is a more profane ceremony than the original, with the emphasis on the white albino-red Abel conflict and the presence of the uncomprehending Angela St. John. The feast for Porcingula mingles the worship of Catholic Virgin Mary with the adoration of the Bahkyush patroness; a procession following mass and communion leads to the dance with the Pecos masks of the bull and the horse. In the dance before the kiva, Francisco notes "the bull was a sad and unlikely thing, a crude and makeshift totem of revelry and delight . . . no holiness to it. . . ." However, regardless of the sense that the hold had been relaxed upon the ancient ways, both ceremonies remain sacred. The townswomen finish the gallo by throwing water in sacrifice on the rooster remains; the Porcingula procession leaves as the cacique prays and sprinkles ceremonial meal on the Pecos horse.

In "The Priest of the Sun" section, the peyote ceremony conducted by Tosamah in the dreary Los Angeles basement is another example of cultural blending. While the ceremony follows in detail the traditional Kiowa peyote rite, the prayers of four participants reflect values besides those of the Kiowa. Cristobal Cruz ends his prayer with "in Jesus' name. Amen"; Napoleon Kills-in-the-Timber prays to the Great Spirit for help in being "frens with white mans" [sic]; Ben Benally sees a Navajo house made of dawn. The ceremony itself ends as brassy jukebox music and street sounds filter into the basement and as Tosamah strides into the street blasting his eagle-bone whistle to signify "that something holy was going on in the universe."

In "The Night Chanter" section Ben Benally recalls the old Navajo ways of the Beautyway and Night Chant, of the squaw dance, and of the Bear and the Snake story. His recollections come as he goes into the hills above Los Angeles to forget about everything. As with the ceremonies in Walatowa and in the supply company basement, Benally's ceremonies have been changed. The chants are shortened; the prayers are done quietly because Ben is ashamed. Once for the Navajo a three-day ceremony of healing, the squaw dance is now primarily a social event. Even the Bear and the Snake story—one that moves from fear to affirmation—is not initiated by Ben. The Navajo legend is Ben's response to Angela's own story in the hospital of a bear and a maiden. Each of these Navajo customs reflects Ben's empathy with Los Angeles and what it stands for. Ben (and his practice of the Navajo ways) exhibits emotional and behavioral participation in a culture of which he is not a full member. His involvement with Milly, his acquiescence to the "bright and clean" city lifestyle, and his efforts to convert Abel indicate how Ben's practice of his native ways has been affected by the cultural forces around him.

Abel's situation among such varied cultural forces as Tai-me, Christianity, and technology is difficult to pin down specifically. Each affects him but how, to what degree, and to what result are uncertain. However, what seems certain is that Abel is not the only character affected by confusion, self-consciousness, and alienation. From the sketches of the individual and collective influences of just these three cultural forces, one notes that everyone experiences some sense of placelessness. Francisco and Milly belong to and identify with their particular place as natives, but each suffers: Francisco through the changes to the pueblo and the particular absence of Abel; Milly through the separation from her father, the desertion of her husband, and the death of her daughter. Angela St. John and Ben Benally participate in other cultures, but they are not full members. She reacts physically and emotionally to the pueblo activities and rituals and senses the spiritual vision but finds it all strange and incomprehensible. Although Ben repeatedly says he is devoted to the city, there is little doubt that he envies Abel's return home. The practice of Father Olguin's and Tosamah's professed callings as priests reveals two men who engage in the activities of two cultures but remain dispassionate observers.

What also seems certain is that the others who suffer from the same sort of placelessness as Abel do not suffer as much as Abel. They seem to have either overcome the sense of not belonging or at least come to grips with it. To a degree, Angela, Milly, and Father Olguin come to their sense of place in the novel. Francisco, Ben, and Tosamah are there already. A character's acceptance of or adjustment to the many cultures around him marks that character's discovery of his sense of place. Native American or white, each seems to balance the various demands, promises, and perspectives inherent in the complexities of so many cultures. The sense of place does not come as one culture overcomes another; over and over again it is shown that conquerors are conquered by "a long outwaiting." Generally, the cultures are not depicted as absolutely hostile, absolutely evil, or absolutely good. They are parts of a larger context.

As *House Made of Dawn* moves to its conclusion with Abel symbolically running in the culture apparently more appropriate for him, three scenes signify Abel's coming to his sense of place and show how he accomplished it. These three concluding scenes also show in the background other characters achieving a similar blending of cultures.

The first scene involves the aftermath of Abel's brutal beating in Los Angeles by the policeman Martinez, which precipitates Abel's return to Walatowa. Benally finds Abel almost dead, "all broken and torn and covered with blood" in the darkened hallway. But Abel is saved by the ambulance, the hospital, and Angela St. John. The city's technology heals his body, and the white woman's stories about a young brave born of a bear and a maiden allow him to turn away and to return home.

The second is Father Olguin's next-to-last appearance in the novel at the beginning of "The Dawn Runner." The Catholic priest sits passively in his rectory. The long passage describes him as having "grown calm with duty and design" with the "hectic fire of his spirit" burned low. Composed and at peace,

> he had come to terms with the town, and that, after all, had been his aim. To be sure, there was the matter of some old and final cleavage, of certain exclusion, the whole and subtle politics of estrangement, but that was easily put aside. . . . The fair price of his safe and sacred

> solitude. . . . He had done well by the town, after all. He had set an example of piety. . . .

The scene ends with an allusion to Fray Nicolas' journal and Father Olguin's mild spiritual exercise for faith and humility.

The third takes place following the death of Francisco. After seven days remembering the rituals, the hunting, his marriage, his teaching, and his running, Abel's grandfather dies. Abel prepares the body by using some traditional ceremonies and disregarding others. Not calling in the singers, he wets and winds the hair; dresses and wraps the body; sprinkles meal and places corn, feathers, and pollen beside him. Abel then takes the body to Father Olguin at the mission. As the generator kicks on to power the lights, the bewildered priest comes to the door. Abel leaves the body and goes to run and to sing in the house made of dawn.

In these three concluding scenes, seemingly disparate cultures are seen together. In each scene, someone has arrived at some sense of place. The Navajo Ben Benally, the white Angela St. John, and the city hospital's technology restore Abel's body and spirit. Ben and Angela demonstrate through their instinctive reliance on technology, their invocation of Native American legend, and their apparently effortless return to daily life an unconscious sense of place that Abel must leave Los Angeles to find. Father Olguin—with his Christianity and his technology—senses the rhythm of life in the pueblo and accepts "a holiness more intrinsic than any he could ever have imagined." Finally, Abel, having employed Jemez and Catholic customs for burial, runs in a pueblo tradition, sings a Navajo prayer, and affirms himself within a community larger than one culture.

Thus, Momaday asserts that everyone has tenure in the land. Like Abel, everyone can come to accept cultural diversity and learn the necessity of finding one's place within the larger context. Using seemingly isolated or conflicting cultures, such as those surrounding Tai-me, Christ, and the machine, Momaday shows characters such as Abel, Ben Benally, Angela St. John, J. B. B. Tosamah, and Father Olguin finding a sense of place or significance. Originating from a primary culture that seems insufficient for dealing with complex, contemporary life, each character settles into his respective world by accepting the existence of a basic pluralism in cultures.

While not denying the efficacy or integrity of individual myths and cultures, *House Made of Dawn* continually and artistically suggests that myths or the people that make up a pluralistic society are rarely independent, insular units. By advocating compatibility in cultural pluralism and the authenticity of individual identity within that pluralism, Momaday emphasizes the potential for the individual to find a sense of place in contemporary life.

Linda Hogan (essay date 1983)

SOURCE: "Who Puts Together," in *Studies in American*

An excerpt from *House Made of Dawn*

He had killed the white man. It was not a complicated thing, after all; it was very simple. It was the most natural thing in the world. Surely they could see that, these men who meant to dispose of him in words. They must know that he would kill the white man again, if he had the chance, that there could be no hesitation whatsoever. For he would know what the white man was, and he would kill him if he could. A man kills such an enemy if he can.

He awoke coughing; there was blood in his throat and mouth. He was shuddering with cold and pain. He had been moaning softly until he choked; now he was gasping for breath. There was a faint vibration under him. *Be quiet!* He had to be quiet; something was going on. He peered into the night: all around the black land against the star-bright, moon-bright sky. So far had his vision reached that the owl, when he saw it, seemed to fly in his face and break apart, torrential, ghostly, silent as a dream. He was delirious now and gasping for breath; he hurried on in his mind, holding the owl away in the corner of his eye. The owl watched him without meaning, and something was going on. There was the faintest tremor at his feet. The night was infinite and serene, and there was an owl in the darkness and a tremor in the earth. He got down on his knees and put his ear to the ground. Men were running toward him. He left the road and hid away in the brush, and soon he could see them in the distance, the old men running after evil, their white leggings holding in motion like smoke above the ground. They passed in the night, full of tranquillity, certitude. There was no sound of breathing or sign of effort about them. They ran as water runs.

There was a burning at his eyes.

The runners after evil ran as water runs, deep in the channel, in the way of least resistance, no resistance. His skin crawled with excitement; he was overcome with longing and loneliness, for suddenly he saw the crucial sense in their going, of old men in white leggings running after evil in the night. They were whole and indispensable in what they did; everything in creation referred to them. Because of them, perspective, proportion, design in the universe. Meaning because of them. They ran with great dignity and calm, not in the hope of anything, but hopelessly; neither in fear nor hatred nor despair of evil, but simply in recognition and with respect. Evil was. Evil was abroad in the night; they must venture out to the confrontation; they must reckon dues and divide the world.

Now, here, the world was open at his back. He had lost his place. He had been long ago at the center, had known where he was, had lost his way, had wandered to the end of the earth, was even now reeling on the edge of the void. The sea reached and leaned, licked after him and withdrew, falling off forever in the abyss. And the fishes . . .

N. Scott Momaday, in his House Made of Dawn, *Harper & Row, 1968.*

Indian Literature: Critical Essays and Course Designs, edited by Paula Gunn Allen, Modern Language Association of America, 1983, pp. 169-77.

[*Hogan is a Chickasaw poet, short story writer, novelist, playwright, and essayist. In the following essay, she relates Momaday's focus on healing and his incorporation of Native American chants in* House Made of Dawn.]

N. Scott Momaday, in his novel ***House Made of Dawn,*** draws on the American Indian oral tradition in which words function as part of the poetic processes of creation, transformation, and restoration. Much of the material in the novel derives from the Navajo Night Chant ceremony and its oral use of poetic language as a healing power. The author, like the oral poet/singer, is "he who puts together" a disconnected life through a step-by-step process of visualization. This visualization, this seeing, enables both the reader and Abel, the main character, to understand the dynamic interrelatedness in which all things exist and which heals. By combining the form of the Navajo healing ceremony with Abel's experience, Momaday creates harmony out of alienation and chaos, linking the world into one fluid working system.

Momaday is able to achieve this harmony because of his awareness of the language and poesis used in Navajo Chantway practice. The Night Chant is a complex ceremony for healing patients who are out of balance with the world. Its purpose is to cure blindness, paralysis, deafness, and mental disorders by restoring the patient to a balance with the universe, through symbolic actions and through language in the form of song or prayer. Words used to paint images and symbols in the minds of participants evoke visual and imaginative responses from and in the hearer. By multiplying, through speech, the number of visual images in the mind of the hearer, the ceremony builds momentum. Language takes on the power of generation. Various forms of verbal repetition intensify the rhythm, and as description and rhythm build, words become a form of internal energy for the listener.

With knowledge of how language and creative visualization work, a capable singer or writer is able to intensify and channel this energy that derives from words. Sound, rhythm, imagery, and symbolic action all combine so that the language builds and releases, creating stability and equilibrium. [In his 1974 *Four Masterworks of American Indian Literature*] John Bierhorst regards this buildup and release of tension as a form of charged energy: words are positively and negatively charged and resemble electricity. The plus and minus charges allow a transmission of force: "Their ceremonial method is twofold; on one hand the ritual repulses 'evil,' on the other it attracts 'holiness.' Accordingly, each of its separate rites may be categorized as either repulsive or attractive, as either purgative or additory."

This verbal and symbolic accumulation and exorcism have a parallel effect on the body. The mind produces sympathetic responses within the organism. In *The Seamless Web,* Stanley Burnshaw discusses the physiological effects of language. He claims that "the sources of an artist's vision involve aspects of biological responses and processes of accumulation and release to which no investigation has yet found access." Although Burnshaw is concerned more with the creative act as a release, he finds that the biological organism responds to the suggestion of words and images. In this way, healing can occur as a result of the proper use of language—language as a vehicle for vision, as a means of imagination.

Momaday makes use of accumulation and release in various sections of *House Made of Dawn.* Before Abel can be returned to balance, he is undone in many ways by language. In the exorcistic sections, Abel is broken down by language, his own as well as that of others. We see him taken apart by the words of those who rely on the destructive rather than on the creative capabilities of language: "Word by word by word these men were disposing of him in language, *their* language."

The word stands for what it signifies. It has both the power of creation and the power of destruction. For those who do not understand this potential of language, words lack power. Words degraded and overused are capable of destruction. Using language without knowledge of its functions diminishes its creative power. And there is a difference between the understanding that Navajos and other Indian people have of language and the way in which white people use language:

> The white man takes such things as words and literatures for granted . . . . He has diluted and multiplied the word, and words have begun to close in upon him. He is sated and insensitive; his regard for language—for the Word itself—as an instrument of creation has nearly diminished to the point of no return. It may be that he will perish by the Word.

Abel's muteness is a form of paralysis. He is unable to put the past together in his mind, to make use of his own language to make himself whole:

> He had tried in the days that followed to speak to his grandfather, but he could not say the things he wanted; he had tried to pray, to sing, to enter into the old rhythm of the tongue, but he was no longer attuned to it. And yet it was there still, like memory, in the reach of his hearing. . . . Had he been able to say it, anything of his own language—even the commonplace formula of greeting "Where are you going"—which had no being beyond sound, no visible substance, would once again have shown him whole to himself; but he was dumb. Not dumb—silence was the older and better part of the custom still—but inarticulate.

Abel's inability to articulate, to form a song or prayer, keeps him from achieving wholeness. Without language, his own or that of others, he is unable to visualize. Remembering imprisonment, he realizes the need for imaginative vision and knows that his own lack of seeing narrows the world even more than did the walls of his cell: "After a while he could not imagine anything beyond the walls except the yard outside, the lavatory, and the dining hall—or even the walls really." But after he gains a full awareness of language, vision opens up to him. In "The Priest of the Sun" section, Abel recalls several incidents

that reveal the importance of language. He remembers Tosamah's sermon on the Word, Benally's recitation of the Night Chant, Francisco's chanting and praying, and Olguin's discussion of "acts of the imagination" and legal terminology. After this awareness, this memory of language, occurs, Abel's vision takes place. It descends on him like a miracle of health. He sees the runners, "the crucial sense in their going, of old men in white leggings running after evil in the night. They were whole and indispensable in what they did; everything in creation referred to them. . . ." And Abel, at this turning point where memories begin to piece together, sees the division and loss of balance that have affected him:

> Now, here, the world was open at his back. He had lost his place. He had been long ago at the center, had known where he was, had lost his way, had wandered to the end of the earth, was even now reeling on the edge of the void.

Imagination and vision follow language. Description allows seeing. The potential of language to heal and restore lies in its ability to open the mind and to make the world visible, uniting all things into wholeness just as the runners are whole and indispensable.

That Abel is divided is obvious. He is a person incapable of speech, one who "could not put together in his mind," or imagine. Momaday, in his essay **"The Man Made of Words,"** addresses this contemporary division of self from the world and the problem of how the inability to visualize, to imagine, keeps us from harmony with the rest of creation:

> We have become disoriented, I believe; we have suffered a kind of psychic dislocation of ourselves in time and space. . . . I doubt that any of us knows where he is in relation to the stars and to the solstices. Our sense of the natural order has become dull and unreliable. Like the wilderness itself, our sphere of instinct has diminished in proportion as we have failed to imagine truly what it is.

The imaginative experience, inspired by the images and symbols of language, becomes a form of salvation. Just as language takes apart and distances, it can also put together. When this crisis of imagination is healed, restoration takes place. Those who understand the potential of words as accumulated energy, as visualization of the physical, can find balance and wholeness. Words used properly and in context, whether in written prose or in the oral form of prayer and incantation, return us to ourselves and to our place in the world. They unify the inner and outer. In this respect, for Abel and for the reader, *House Made of Dawn* works much like the Night Chant. It focuses the imagination, creates a one-pointedness of mind through concrete images. It breaks down and then builds momentum, using the two forces to restore balance.

Language as accumulation is a means of intensifying the power of words. This accumulation combined with the exorcistic, or release, sections of the book takes Abel on a journey of healing, a return to the sacred and to the traditional. When words take on these powers, one is careful with them, careful not to dilute and diminish their meanings as white people have done. Each word needs to carry weight, and this is central to Momaday's understanding of language as a distillation where meaning is intensified by careful use of words. When Tosamah speaks of his grandmother, he shows an understanding of both the healing function of condensed language and the importance of the imaginative journey, guided by words:

> She was asking me to go with her to the confron-
> tation of something that was sacred and eternal.
> It was a timeless, *timeless* thing. . . . You see,
> for her words were medicine; they were magic
> and invisible. . . . And she never threw words
> away.

Tosamah is able through language to reach some "strange potential of Himself." The ability to say, in poetic form, that which is unspeakable, to create and hold an image in the mind, gives language its power. What is spoken is seen. Words draw images and symbols out of the mind. They take hold of the moment and make it eternal. Tosamah, who in a sense speaks for Momaday, reaches that "strange potential" by experiencing the language he has spoken. He speaks as an inspired poet. As mythically the word created the earth, Tosamah's language creates vision. He is inspired by the language that speaks through him and by its capacity to recover, mentally, the world from which people have become divided. As Octavio Paz says of the poet, [in *Alternating Current*], "Through the word we may regain the lost kingdom and recover powers we possessed in the far-distant past. These powers are not ours. The man inspired, the man who really speaks, does not say anything personal; language speaks through his mouth."

Language, speaking through Tosamah, restores him to unity with the world. After his speech, he steps back from the lectern, and "In his mind the earth was spinning and the stars rattled around in the heavens. The sun shone, and the moon." He recognizes that a single star is enough to fill the mind and that the value of language lies in its ability to operate on the mind.

Abel also realizes his potential through language, through Benally's recitation of the Night Chant and through Francisco's memories that are "whole." As in the Night Chant, order is achieved through an imaginative journey: Benally takes Abel through this step-by-step process of visualization, singing parts of the Night Chant ceremony. Understanding the power words hold and the sacred action they contain, he sings quietly:

> Restore my feet for me;
> Restore my legs for me,
> Restore my body for me,
> Restore my mind for me,
> Restore my voice for me.

This excerpt from the Night Chant allows the hearer to visualize each part of the body being healed, from the feet up to the voice. The purpose of describing health is to obtain health. This purpose is furthered by taking the patient on an imaginative journey and returning him, restored to himself. Sam Gill, talking about the nature of Navajo ceremonials [in his "Prayer as Person," *History of Religions* 17, No. 2 (1977)], points out that "The semantic structure of the prayer is identical to the effect the prayer seeks, the

restoration of health." Benally continues, and his singing returns Abel home to his grandfather, Francisco:

> Happily I go forth.
> My interior feeling cool, may I walk.
> No longer sore, may I walk.
> Impervious to pain, may I walk.
> With lively feelings, may I walk.
> As it used to be long ago, may I walk.
> Happily may I walk.

Francisco's dying memories continue the journey, completing the ceremony for Abel. The memories are similar to those Abel experiences in the first section of the book, and they symbolically connect the two men, using identification, which is also an important function of the language in the Night Chant, where the patient and singer identify with the holy ones. Because "the voice of his memory was whole and clear and growing like the dawn," Francisco's words finally restore Abel. Abel, running, at the end of the book, is finally able to sing, and the words he hears are from the Night Chant: "House made of pollen, house made of dawn."

Momaday's use of the journey derives from oral tradition, in which the journey is used as a symbolic act that takes the hearer out of his or her body. The journey is an "act of the imagination" fired by language. In *The Way to Rainy Mountain,* Momaday defines the psychic potential of the mental, or symbolic, journey as a miracle of imagination made up of mythology and legend, an idea in itself:

> It is a whole journey, intricate with motion and
> meaning; and it is made with the whole memory,
> that experience of the mind which is legendary
> as well as historical, personal as well as cultural.

He says that the imaginative recalling of the journey reveals the way in which "these traditions are conceived, developed, and interfused in the mind." It is this interfusion with which we are concerned. The interfusion of things in the mind acts as a catalyst, merging myth, history, and personal experience into one shape, to reassemble the divisions of the self.

Healers and singers from other nations or tribes are also familiar with this traditional use of language as journey, as interfusion. The Mazatec Indians in Mexico use a similar oral technique to cure disease. [Henry Munn notes in his "The Mushrooms of Language," an essay appearing in Michael Harner's 1973 *Hallucinogens and Shamanism* that a] medicine woman says of the patient, "Let us go searching for the tracks of her feet to encounter the sickness that she is suffering from." And the healer goes, imaginatively, out of her own body:

> She is going on a journey, for there is distancia-
> tion and going there, somewhere without her
> even moving from the spot where she sits and
> speaks . . . and the pulsation of her being like the
> rhythm of walking.

The healer follows the footprints of the patient, looking for clues to the cause of disease in order to return the patient to balance.

Just as the symbolic journey in the Night Chant and the journey in *House Made of Dawn* have their physiological components, so the Mazatec healing ritual [according to Munn] has an organic, biological parallel: "it is as if the system were projected before one into a vision of the heart, the liver, lungs, genitals and stomach." Through seeing, through visualizing, the words interact with the nervous system. In traditional oral literature as well as in *House Made of Dawn,* speaking is healing.

Momaday's imaginative, visual creation and fusion of myth and history with the present returns us to the idea of positively and negatively charged language. For what takes place within the mind, acted on by language, also takes place within the body. Language conceived as accumulation and release is language that can pass the reader/hearer across a threshold into equilibrium. Burnshaw, in a discussion of creativity, focuses on the transformational qualities of words used in this capacity:

> . . . a creative artist inhales the surrounding world and exhales it. Whatever is taken in is given back in altered condition or transformed into matter, action, feeling, thought. And in the cases of creative persons, an additional exhalation: in the form of words or sounds or shapes capable of acting upon others with the force of an object alive in their surrounding worlds.
>
> Such an object arises out of characteristic cycles of accumulation and release. . . .

A singer, writer, or healer is able to unite the internal with the external. This unity of word with the force of an object is the theoretical framework for *House Made of Dawn.* The structure of the book replicates the progression of the Night Chant, making use of mythology, history, symbolism, and creation to stimulate response in the reader. Just as the Night Chant ceremony seeks to duplicate the universe in the mind of the hearer, Momaday creates a model of the universe in the book. Each section contains repetitions of images and symbols of the universe that are fragmented and need to be united again into one dynamic system.

These repetitions are important in channeling the energy of language. In Navajo Chantway practice, according to Gladys Reichard, the more often something is repeated, the more power it has to concentrate the mind and focus attention. Through this concentration, through a balance brought about by accumulation and release, the union of time, space, and object takes place within the imagination. The words of prose or poetry function like an opening of the self into the universe and the reciprocal funneling of the universe into the self.

This repetition and the replication of the universe assist seeing, or vision. [According to Elizabeth Sewell in her 1971 *The Orphic Voice,* language] in this poetic function, which resembles the oral traditions, "provides a double system of images and forms for the body and mind to work with in seeking to understand one system by another." It is as though two universes, or systems, one internal and the other external, act simultaneously upon the hearer and fuse together. Inner and outer merge and become the same. Words are linked with the objects they designate. Past and present merge. This comes about through the circular organization of the book, the expansion and contrac-

tion and the order that give the book its sense of poetic presence and immediacy.

These methods are characteristic of oral tradition, in which the word and the object are equal and in which all things are united and in flux. The distinctions between inner and outer break down. Momaday, making use of these oral techniques in his poetic language, returns Abel, along with the reader, to an earlier time "before an abyss had opened between things and their names" [Octavio Paz, *The Bow and the Lyre,* 1973].

This return gives to words a new substance and power not unlike that of oral ritual. The life of the word and the fusion of word and object, by means of the visual imagination, return the participant or reader to an original source that is mythic, where something spoken stands for what is spoken about and there is [according to Momaday in his **"Man Made of Words"**] "no difference between the telling and that which is told." It is a form of dynamic equilibrium in which all things are assembled into wholeness and integrated and in which persons can "name and assimilate."

Speaking or hearing becomes a form of action. Reichard comments [in her 1944 *Prayer: The Compulsive Word*], "The Navajo believe, in common with many American Indians, that thought is the same or has the same potentiality as word. To thought and words they add deed, so that there is no use trying to differentiate." Words are actions that have the ability to align and heal. This concept is the basis for the Night Chant, in which the patient identifies with the gods, goes on a symbolic journey, and is made holy. By the patient's visualizing the action, the action takes place and the patient is restored. [According to Gill, the] ceremony consists of "words the utterance of which is actually the doing of an action." Abel's ability to see, to concentrate his being, at the end of the book is the result of language.

Words, therefore, are a materialization of consciousness. And deeds are the manifestation of words. By evoking in the hearer or reader a one-pointedness of mind, the poem, song, or prayer becomes more than just expression. It is a form of divine utterance that moves us to action, that is action itself. It is an extension of the internal into the external.

Language used in this way becomes a form of dynamic energy, able to generate and regenerate. Attention, focused by language, has the power to give existence to something imagined. Words, sung or written, cast off their ordinary use and become charged with a luminous new energy. They accumulate the power to return us to a unity of word and being, linking the internal with the external. As in the Orphic tradition, language creates the world and lets the world return through the song or the word.

The song or word in oral tradition is responsible for all things, all actions. According to Navajo accounts, the universe was created by the word. According to Reichard, the Navajo say that in prehuman times the original state of the universe was one word. Tosamah, a Kiowa, also acknowledges this creative ability of the word and understands that through this creation (which was the word) all things begin and are ordered:

> Do you see? There, far off in the darkness, something happened. Do you see? Far, far away, in the nothingness something happened. There was a voice, a sound, a word, and everything began.

Language perceived as creation and as a unity of word and being has the power to heal. Combining the oral elements of word energy created by accumulation and release, imaginative journey and visualization, Momaday restores Abel to his place within the equilibrium of the universe. Momaday assumes the traditional role of speaker as healer by permitting Abel and the reader to see the order of the universe. He speaks as a poet, combining the verbal and the visual. Language restores the poet to this role as the primordial speaker "whose power of language undergirds the word, thus to provide man with a dwelling place." [Gerald L. Bruns, *Modern Poetry and the Idea of Language: A Critical and Historical Study,* 1974]. When the world is engaged and all things are seen and understood as one great working system, balance and healing take place, and this is beyond language.

The ability of the word to control visualization and therefore unite all things is the concept behind **House Made of Dawn** and the Navajo Night Chant. [According to Sam Gill, in his "The Trees Stood Rooted," *Parabola* 2, No. 2 (1977) the] speaker understands that the "Magic of the Word lies in the fact that it is capable through image and symbol of placing the speaker in communion with his own language and with the entire world." The healing that takes place beyond language comes of the resonance, the after-image of speech in the imagination. The visual energy remains, having been sparked by words. In literature, whether oral or written, it is that which allows us to "put together" in the mind. Restoration follows language and results from the figurative aspects of words and their ability to open out the imagination and thereby affect the physiological. As energy, language contains the potential to restore us to a unity with earth and the rest of the universe. Accumulation, repetition, and resonance all unite to tie us, seamlessly, to the world.

Matthias Schubnell　(essay date 1985)

SOURCE: "The Crisis of Identity: *House Made of Dawn*," in *N. Scott Momaday: The Cultural and Literary Background,* University of Oklahoma Press, 1985, pp. 101-39.

[In the following excerpt, Schubnell discusses Abel's search for belonging and identity in House Made of Dawn.*]*

My reading of **House Made of Dawn** focuses on the novel's thematic center: the problem of identity. First I deal with Abel's early years of harmony and the gradual emergence of conflicts which lead to his departure from the community. Next I examine Abel's attempts to resolve his confusion after his return from a war which has further undermined his sense of belonging. In fact, Abel has become a man between two cultures, unable to cope with either. In the last section of this reading I argue that Abel's eventual return to his native culture takes the course of a

rite of passage. The interpretation is based on a close analysis of the novel's symbolism against the background of Mircea Eliade's studies of initiation ceremonies and religious patterns.

By way of introduction to the tragic effects of identity conflicts among American Indians as Momaday witnessed them at Jemez, it may be best to quote from one of his letters. I have deleted the names of the victims to protect their privacy and that of their families:

> Abel is a composite of the boys I knew at Jemez. I wanted to say something about them. An appalling number of them are dead; they died young, and they died violent deaths. One of them was drunk and run over. Another was drunk and froze to death. (He was the best runner I ever knew). One man was murdered, butchered by a kinsman under a telegraph pole just east of San Ysidro. And yet another committed suicide. A good many who have survived this long are living under the Relocation Program in Los Angeles, Chicago, Detroit, etc. They're a sad lot of people.

This statement spells out the disastrous violence, suffering, and despair which frequently accompanies cultural change. While Abel's conflicts are aggravated by a particularly unsettling historical period, his difficulties in reconciling his tribal origin with the presence of a modern world are a latent and potentially disruptive problem for every generation of American Indians.

Abel is struggling to find an identity within his own tribe long before he comes into direct contact with the culture of modern America. From a developmental point of view his experience is universal: it is the struggle of a young man to establish a stable position in his community. From a historical perspective his crisis reflects a crisis of his culture which denies its young tribal members accommodation to changing conditions.

Abel's problem grows out of a generation conflict within a tribal community in which the ancient traditions tend to lose their meanings for young Indians in their confrontation with the cultural tradition of modern America. The old generation of traditionalists tends to exert pressure on young tribal members in order to assure the perpetuation of the old ways. This can lead to a conflict between communal obligations and the search for a new Indian identity which must include the benefits of modern society.

Abel cannot simply adopt the traditional customs of his tribe as would have been natural in a community unaffected by the encroachment of an alien culture. He turns his back on the Indian world and enters modern America. Here, under the influence of an unsympathetic environment, Abel's conflict is aggravated. He shows all the symptoms of identity confusion: estrangement from both the tribal and the Anglo-American cultures, sexual and emotional disturbance in his personal relationships, and an inability to channel his aggression appropriately.

His return to the native community suggests that Indian cultures are capable of overcoming such crises, not by isolating themselves but through an adherence to basic traditional values and by the selective acceptance of new elements from other cultures. This strategy, which has been a strength of American Indian societies throughout the period of contact with other cultural groups, must be continued. In giving an account of the developmental crisis in the protagonist's life history Momaday makes a statement about Indian life in a period of increasing cultural and economic pressures. *House Made of Dawn,* then, is a novel about an individual and a communal search for identity.

The Indian community in which Abel grows up belongs to the Rio Grande Pueblo villages in New Mexico. Momaday opens the first chapter with the place name "Walatowa, Canyon de San Diego." Walatowa literally means "the people in the canyon." It is the native name of Jemez. As a result of their geographical isolation and their cultural conservatism the Rio Grande Pueblos have succeeded in keeping their languages, religions, and traditional customs relatively intact despite the pressures of Spanish and Anglo-American cultural encroachment. This is how Momaday portrays life in the village:

> The people of the town have little need. They do not hanker after progress and have never changed their essential way of life. Their invaders were a long time in conquering them; and now, after four centuries of Christianity, they still pray in Tanoan to the old deities of the earth and sky and make their living from the things that are and have always been within their reach; while in the discrimination of pride they acquire from their conquerors only the luxury of example. They have assumed the names and gestures of their enemies, but have held on to their own, secret souls; and in this there is a resistance and an overcoming, a long outwaiting.

Abel grows up in a world where the preservation of old values counts more than progress. Even today Pueblo life revolves around a complex system of religious ceremonials based on a solar calendar, whose keeper is the cacique, the Pueblo medicine man. According to his observation of the course of the sun, the cacique determines all the essential events of tribal life, the planting, harvesting, and the religious ceremonies.

In *House Made of Dawn* the old man Francisco functions as the teacher and guardian of the traditional Pueblo way of life. He represents the old generation of the tribe which possesses the cultural heritage and strives to preserve it by handing it down to the next generation. Francisco teaches his grandsons, Abel and Vidal, to observe the sun. He tells them that "they must know the long journey of the sun on the black mesa, how it rode in the seasons and the years, and they must live according to the sun appearing, for only then could they reckon where they were, where all things were, in time." In revealing the connection between the sun, the landscape, and the rhythms of Indian life, Francisco roots the two boys in the old ways of the tribe. Francisco's teachings are central to their development as well as the perpetuation of Jemez tradition.

Under the guidance of old man Francisco, Abel is raised according to the tribal patterns of his people and acquires a deep feeling for his environment. Typical of Abel's consciousness is his natural attitude toward death: ". . . he

knew somehow that his mother was soon going to die of her illness. It was nothing he was told, but he knew it anyway and without understanding, as he knew already the motion of the sun and the seasons." Abel is at the center of Indian life. He herds sheep, takes part in a deer hunt, and participates in the ceremonial activities of his tribe.

Despite this seeming harmony with the tribal world, however, Abel somehow remains a stranger within his community. Not only during his time away from the reservation but also while growing up among his own people, he lives in a state of isolation. He was born into his position as an outsider: "He did not know who his father was. His father was a Navajo, they said, or a Sia, or an Isleta, an outsider anyway, which made him and his mother and Vidal somehow foreign and strange." Tribal communities are not necessarily homogenous entities as they are often perceived by outsiders; within the tribe subgroups may exist which do not meet the full acceptance of the majority. The early deaths of his mother and brother increase Abel's isolation. He is left with his grandfather, Francisco, as his only other relation.

Preoccupied with Abel's conforming to the tribal tradition, Francisco monopolizes his education. He forbids him to find a substitute mother in Josie, one of the women in the village. The lack of family ties prevents Abel's full integration into the native community. As Abel approaches adolescence he finds it increasingly difficult to accept tribal patterns and the domineering authority of his grandfather.

It is common for young people at this stage of personal development to question the way of life which adults in their families or communities expect them to adopt. Momaday shows in his novel the severity of the conflict between a budding individual and a rigid tribal pattern which depends for its perpetuation on the absence of individual awareness. He reveals how the crisis in Abel's personal development reflects a crisis in Pueblo culture.

Pueblo traditionalists maintain that in an age of growing pressure from outside the tribal culture can only survive in isolation. Even though technical attainments of Anglo-American culture have been adopted for their obvious usefulness, Pueblo communities are very reluctant to allow any interference that could dilute traditional tribal life. This inevitably leads to tremendous pressures in the educational processes of young Indians. A culture which depends for its survival on the adoption of age-old patterns by the next generation not only shelters against influences from the outside but also ignores or even suppresses the individual needs of its members. Thus a generation conflict is almost unavoidable. . . .

Abel's decision to leave the Pueblo community grows out of the realization that he cannot find an identity simply by adopting the teachings of his grandfather. Momaday shows by means of a few central events that Abel has no choice but to step out of the limiting realm of his native village in order to remain true to himself.

A most significant experience during Abel's adolescence is his vision of an eagle which carries a snake in its talons: "He had seen a strange thing, an eagle overhead with its talons closed upon a snake. It was an awful, holy sight, full of magic and meaning." Both eagle and snake have deeply religious meanings for the Indians of the Southwest. The snake is associated with the coming of water and is worshiped in ceremonies such as the famous snake dance of the Hopis. The eagle is believed to attain supernatural powers on its flights and is revered in the eagle dance. The appearance of the eagle and snake together is of particular religious importance, just as the plumed serpent is a major mythological figure.

For Abel the eagle is a symbol of freedom, beauty, and life: "They were golden eagles, a male and a female, in their mating flight. They were cavorting, spinning and spiraling on the cold, clear columns of air, and they were beautiful." When Abel first sees the two birds, he is "on the rim of the Valle Grande, a great volcanic crater that lay high up on the western slope of the range. It was the right eye of the earth, held open to the sun. Of all places that he knew, this valley alone could reflect the great spatial majesty of the sky." Standing high above the plateau he has a view of the whole extent of his world and observes the eagles as they fly across and beyond the land, disappearing in the endless sky. Perhaps it is in this vision that Abel realizes the limitations of his life under the rules of his tribal community.

His observation of the eagles and the snake gains him the permission of the Eagle Watcher Society to take part in an eagle hunt. Again he sees the two eagles and eventually succeeds in catching the female bird. He returns to the other hunters in the plain who celebrate him in much the same way as Francisco was celebrated after his successful bear hunt. Abel, however, cannot enjoy this honor. He does not understand or cannot accept that his respect for the animal can be reconciled with his act of depriving it of its freedom for the benefit of the community. Eagle feathers are highly valued as indispensable requisites for ceremonials. The closeness of the captive eagle's spirit to the village is regarded as a beneficial influence on the life at Jemez.

When his peers allow the less attractive male eagle to return to the sky, Abel is overcome by a feeling of longing, as if he wanted to follow the bird:

> It leveled off and sailed. Then it was gone from sight, but he looked after it for a time. He could see it still in the mind's eye and hear in his memory the awful whisper of its flight on the wind. It filled him with longing. He felt the great weight of the bird which he held in the sack. The dusk was fading quickly into night, and the others could not see that his eyes were filled with tears.

Instead of feeling victorious about the hunt, in keeping with tribal tradition, Abel is sad and disgusted. He decides to kill the bird rather than allow it to live in captivity in the village. This killing is not a ritual act, as one critic assumed, but an act of rebellion against a tribal custom Abel cannot comprehend. This interpretation is corroborated by the absence of any ritual preparation and by Abel's psychological state when he acts.

There are a number of other scenes in the novel which show Abel in similar emotional states in response to animal life. After the rabbit hunt he feels "something like remorse or disappointment" about the killing of animals. Similarly, he shows a strange affection for the small fish along the coast of California: ". . . small silversided fishes spawned mindlessly in correlation to the phase of the moon and the rise and fall of the tides. The thought of it made him sad, filled him with sad, unnamable longing and wonder."

These emotional reactions reflect a deep respect for the well-being of other life forms, an attitude common among American Indian peoples. However, Abel fails to see the wider implications of the man-animal relationship in his tribal religion. The hunting and killing of animals does not constitute a breach of the spiritual bond between man and animal if it is performed in the appropriate traditional way. . . .

Momaday dramatized this concept in Francisco's bear hunt. Francisco proceeds strictly according to the code of honor which regulates the hunt:

> And he did not want to break the stillness of the night, for it was holy and profound; it was rest and restoration, the hunter's offering of death and the sad watch of the hunted, waiting somewhere away in the cold darkness and breathing easily of its life, brooding around at last to forgiveness and consent; the silence was essential to them both, and it lay out like a bond between them, ancient and inviolable.

The bear's knowledge of Francisco's approach, the absence of fear and hurry, and Francisco's following "in the bear's tracks" suggest an old intimacy between the hunter and the hunted. The ritual blessing of the bear with pollen is an expression of gratitude and respect, a plea for propitiation.

Without the knowledge of these ancient practices Abel reacts emotionally rather than ritualistically. His shame and disgust are inappropriate responses within the framework of traditional Indian thought and reflective of his estrangement from his tribal heritage. Abel's failure to perceive or accept the intricacies of tribal tradition is also at the center of his conflict with Francisco. The young Indian not only is unable to comprehend certain aspects of his native tradition but also has lost respect for his grandfather as the representative of the ancient ways. Abel is "almost a grown man" when he has a riding accident: " . . . for days afterward there was a sharp, recurrent pain in the small of his back. Francisco chanted and prayed; the old man applied herbs and powders and potions and salves, and nothing worked." This incident may well have contributed to Abel's loss of faith in his grandfather and his native culture.

His inability to adhere to the rules of tradition brings about the final break between Francisco and Abel: "You ought to do this and that, his grandfather said. But the old man had not understood, would not understand, only wept, and Abel left him alone. It was time to go, and the old man was away in the fields." Abel's decision to leave is the final rejection of authority, grown out of the conviction that in the rigidness of his tribal environment he will be unable to find fulfillment and an identity. His leaving is a departure in dread, accompanied by fear of an unknown future in an unknown world.

Momaday stresses the young Indian's position between two cultures by means of Abel's shoes. The shoes are typical of the white man's fashion in the city and therefore conspicuous to traditional Indians. In some Pueblo communities tribal rules demand that shoes or boots can be worn only if the heel is cut off, to avoid injury to the sacred earth on which the community's existence depends. Abel, however, does not share this orthodox view; to him the shoes are simply objects of good craftsmanship, admirable in their own right, like "the work of a good potter or painter or silversmith." As Abel steps out of his native community, he is wearing these shoes, having waited "a long time for the occasion to wear them." In this situation they signify the world he is about to enter, and as Abel realizes this he grows anxious and afraid:

> But now and beyond his former frame of reference, the shoes called attention to Abel. They were brown and white; they were conspicuously new and too large; they shone; they clattered and creaked. And they were nailed to his feet. There were enemies all around, and he knew that he was ridiculous in their eyes.

Despite Abel's fears of what awaits him in the alien world of modern America, his departure is a necessary step toward his understanding of himself.

Abel's withdrawal from the tribe is the result of a disturbed communication between the old and the young generation. Anxious to preserve the ancient tribal ways, the old members of the pueblo have grown blind to the needs of the young. In the following section I examine Abel's struggle for an identity in the context of the tension between modern American and tribal cultures.

When Abel returns to his grandfather after having served in the U.S. Army in World War II, he is drunk. His flight into alcohol indicates his inability to cope with the horror and turmoil of his recent past. Abel is confused. His drunken state reflects a lack of inner stability as a result of his bicultural situation. Alcoholism, in part a reaction to being cut adrift from native cultures and being unable to come to terms with the mainstream of American society, is a widespread problem among the American Indian population.

During the two weeks Abel spends in his grandfather's house, he tries to halt his mental and physical disintegration and find his way back to the center of Indian life. He struggles to become attuned to the culture he left as an adolescent, and he tries to rid himself of the destructive influences of a war in an alien world.

On the morning after his return Abel climbs the hill outside the village. In the growing light of the new day, he looks out over the pueblo and the land. As he is standing there, a number of episodes from his boyhood and the war come to his mind. The series of flashbacks must be seen not merely as a technical device Momaday employs to make the reader familiar with the protagonist's past. In reliving central episodes of his childhood and adolescence,

Abel tries to reintegrate himself into his environment, to imagine himself into an existence he can understand and with which he can identify. He re-creates previous experiences in his mind, trying to come to grips with his confused state. His recollections become a psychological process of searching for the roots of his confusion.

While Abel is very capable of comprehending the memories of his Indian boyhood, he is unable to come to terms with the months and years he spent away from the pueblo: "This—everything in advance of his going—he could remember whole and in detail. It was the recent past, the intervention of days and years without meaning, of awful calm and collision, time always immediate and confused, that he could not put together in his mind."

The shock of war is the determining factor in Abel's early manhood, as the vision of the eagles' flight was a central event in his adolescence. In the alien world he becomes subject to a dehumanizing military conflict. The dehumanization comes across forcefully in his recollection of his war experience through the recurrent reference to the tank as "the machine." The tank symbolizes the deadening force of an aggressive, technological society. The atmosphere of death and destruction is reinforced by another recurrent image pattern; damp, matted, wet, cold, and falling leaves intensify the scene's implications of decay and annihilation:

> Then through the falling leaves, he saw the machine. It rose up behind the hill, black and massive, looming there in front of the sun. He saw it swell, deepen, and take shape on the skyline, as if it were some upheaval of the earth, the eruption of stone and eclipse, and all about it the glare, the cold perimeter of light, throbbing with leaves. For a moment it seemed apart from the land; its great iron hull lay out against the timber and the sky, and the center of its weight hung away from the ridge. Then it came crashing down to the grade, slow as a waterfall, thunderous, surpassing impact, *nestling* almost into the splash and boil of debris. He was shaking violently, and the machine bore down upon him, came close, and passed him by. A wind rose and ran along the slope, scattering the leaves.

The image of the machine as the embodiment of destruction and denial of life stands in sharp contrast to the crucial experience in Abel's youth when the eagles appeared to him as symbols of life and freedom.

It has already been pointed out that Abel had no stable identity when he left the pueblo; indeed, he entered the world of modern America because the restrictive environment of his home impeded his growth toward personal identity. During his absence from the Indian village his inner stability does not grow but is further disturbed by the traumatic events of the war. As an Indian among white soldiers he is denied a personal identity by his comrades. He is the "chief" who is "giving it to the tank in Sioux or Algonquin or something." This statement by one of Abel's war companions shows why Abel is prevented from becoming assimilated. The dominant Anglocentric environment has stereotyped him as an Indian without regard for his individuality. In pressing him into this misconceived role, his peers not only shut him out from their culture but also deny his identity as a Jemez man.

Abel returns to the reservation in a state of identity confusion which is typical of adolescence. Even though Abel is approximately twenty-five years old, he is devoid of the sense of wholeness which is the basis for maturation into adulthood. [In his *Identity: Youth and Crisis*] Erik Erikson wrote that "the young person, in order to experience wholeness, must feel a progressive continuity between that which he had come to be during the long years of childhood and that which he promises to become in the anticipated future: between that which he conceives himself to be and that which he perceives others to see in him and expect of him."

For Abel progressive continuity is disrupted by his inability to accept tribal rules and by the damaging impact of his life outside the native community. The break from his culture and the effects of the war lead Abel into a state of confusion, isolation, and estrangement. With regard to such a crisis Erikson pointed out that "youth which is eager for, yet unable to find access to, the dominant techniques of society, will not only feel estranged from society, but also upset in sexuality, and most of all unable to apply aggression constructively." Abel shows all these symptoms of identity confusion in his estrangement from the ritual and ceremonial practices of his tribe, in his relationship with Angela, and in his outburst of aggression which leads to the killing of the albino.

First Abel tries to reattune himself to the land and the culture of his tribe by searching for a sign in his environment: "He stood for a long time, the land yielding to the light. He stood without thinking, nor did he move; only his eyes roved after something." Abel is feeling his way back to a center which has been lost to him. Only by relating himself to this center can he reestablish order and overcome his inner chaos. His search is informed with religious meaning, as it aims at a communion with the land which is sacred to his people. This search for a sign, as Mircea Eliade pointed out [in *The Sacred and the Profane*], is a universal religious impulse in a state of disequilibrium: "A *sign* is asked, to put an end to the tension and anxiety caused by relativity and disorientation—in short, to reveal an absolute point of support."

When a little later Abel sees his grandfather and some of the other Indians working in the fields, he acquires for a moment the old familiar sense of unity with his homeland: "The breeze was very faint, and it bore a scent of earth and grain; and for a moment everything was all right with him. He was at home." But even as Abel recognizes that he has not entirely lost the ties to his native environment, he soon finds himself unable to enter the ceremonial life of his tribe.

Five days after Abel's return, the people of Jemez celebrate the game of the Chicken Pull. This activity was introduced by the Spaniards and adopted by many of the southwestern tribes. The Rio Grande Pueblos view the insertion of the rooster into the ground and its subsequent removal as a symbolic representation of planting and reaping. The scattering of the rooster's feathers and blood are representative of rain and are believed to increase the fertility of the land and the success of the harvest.

Abel's participation in this ancient ceremony offers him an opportunity for reconciliation with his tribal culture: "For the first time since coming home he had done away with his uniform. He had put on his old clothes." His effort in the game, however, proves to be a failure: "When it came Abel's turn, he made a poor showing, full of caution and gesture." And when the albino as the victorious rider turns against Abel and starts beating him with the rooster in accordance with the rules of the game, he is unable to cope with the situation: "Abel was not used to the game, and the white man was too strong and quick for him." He is estranged from the old traditions and consequently fails to integrate himself into the cultural context of his community.

Another Pueblo ceremonial which could have been of help to Abel is the Pecos Bull Dance, which the Jemez people perform on August 1. Momaday witnessed the ceremony as a child. He described it thus [in ***The Names***]:

> On the first of August, at dusk, the Pecos Bull ran through the streets of Jemez, taunted by the children, chased by young boys who were dressed in outlandish costumes, most in a manner which parodied the curious white Americans who came frequently to see the rich sights of Jemez on feast days. This "bull" was a man who wore a mask, a wooden framework on his back covered with black cloth and resembling roughly a bull, the head of which was a crude thing made of horns, a sheepskin, and a red cloth tongue which wagged about. It ran around madly, lunging at the children.

Alfonso Ortiz noted [in *New Perspectives on the Pueblos*] that one purpose of burlesque and mock violence in Pueblo ritual drama is catharsis, the "purgation of individuals or community of rebellious tendencies so that they behave during the rest of the year." The ceremony could have offered Abel a chance to vent his aggression against white Americans in a ritual way rather than in the hostile manner he later employs against the albino. . . .

Abel's reluctance to take part in the Bull Dance arises from his lack of identification with tribal rituals and perhaps also from his disbelief in their effectiveness. His loss of confidence after the Chicken Pull is a further obstacle to his participation in the event: "It was a hard thing to be the bull, for there was a primitive agony to it, and it was a kind of victim, an object of ridicule and hatred; and harder now that the men of the town had relaxed their hold upon the ancient ways, had grown soft and dubious. Or they had merely grown old." Momaday indicates in this context the increasing difficulty of adhering to the old traditions, which is a major problem, particularly for the young Indian generation represented by Abel. The ancient traditions tend to lose their meaning for young tribal members in their confrontation with mainstream America. This crisis in the Indian cultures adds to the identity problem exemplified in the figure of Abel.

A further indication of Abel's failure to reenter the Indian world of his childhood is his loss of articulation. His inability to find the proper words to acquire wholeness and communion with his culture and his homeland makes him aware that his return to the town has failed:

> Abel walked into the canyon. His return to the town had been a failure, for all his looking forward. He had tried in the days that followed to speak to his grandfather, but he could not say the things he wanted; he had tried to pray, to sing, to enter into the old rhythm of the tongue, but he was no longer attuned to it. And yet it was there still, like memory, in the reach of his hearing, as if Francisco or his mother or Vidal had spoken out of the past and the words had taken hold of the moment and made it eternal. Had he been able to say it, anything in his own language—even the most commonplace formula of greeting "Where are you going"—which had no being beyond sound, no visible substance, would once again have shown him whole to himself; but he was dumb. Not dumb—silence was the older and better part of custom still—but *inarticulate.*

Some sense of the old harmony still remains, but Abel lacks the active power to reestablish harmony. This power is the power of the word. . . .

The word links the Indian to his religious and mythological heritage. Indian culture is based on an oral tradition and maintained through the creative power of the word. If the word is lost, culture and identity are forfeited, as wholeness can only be established by the word. The following passage shows that Abel has indeed lost the power of words:

> He began almost to be at peace, as if he had drunk a little of warm, sweet wine, for a time no longer centered upon himself. He was alone, and he wanted to make a song out of the colored canyon, the way the women of Torreón made songs upon their looms out of colored yarn, but he had not got the right words together. It would have been a creation song; he would have sung lowly of the first world, of fire and flood, and of the emergence of dawn from the hills.

As his imaginative re-creation of his childhood and adolescence was an attempt to understand his problematic situation, his effort to make a song is an endeavor to restore harmony between himself and the universe. Abel's creation song would have been a bid for the creative power that heals, restores harmony, and provides wholeness. However, he "has not the right words" and thus remains isolated. It is not until his recital of the Night Chant at the end of the book that he regains his voice.

The second symptom of identity confusion, according to Erikson, the upset in sexuality, becomes apparent in the relationship between Abel and Angela St. John. After his failed attempts to find access to the tribal rituals and ceremonies, Abel tries to acquire some kind of stability in an intimate relationship with the white woman. This second endeavor proves to be as unsuccessful as the first. The insecurity Abel exposes in both his dealing with tribal roles and his relationship with Angela is a symptom of his confused identity. Erikson described the crisis of intimacy as

the first postadolescent identity crisis. He pointed out that without a well-developed identity formation true intimacy cannot be achieved. "Where a youth," he continued, "does not accomplish such intimate relationships with others—and . . . with his own inner resources—in late adolescence or in early adulthood, he may settle for highly stereotyped interpersonal relations and come to retain a deep *sense of isolation.*"

Abel's inability to achieve true intimacy, then, can be seen as the result of the absence of meaningful relationships in his formative years. He grew up fatherless, lost his mother and brother in early boyhood, and never fully achieved an intimacy with the tribal community. There was also a possibly decisive, unsuccessful encounter with a young Indian girl during his adolescence. Abel's behavior toward Angela seems to indicate that this incident is still somewhere in the back of his mind. He tenaciously avoids exposing himself to humiliation and chooses to remain in the shell of his own self: "He would give her no clear way to be contemptuous of him."

Abel is portrayed as the stereotype of the mute Indian. He avoids talking at any length and frequently does not react at all to Angela's questions. His fear of getting hurt and his inability to communicate his feelings are typical of his behavior: "His face darkened, but he hung on, dumb and immutable. He would not allow himself to be provoked. It was easy, natural for him to stand aside, hang on." His lack of articulation, which earlier in the novel prevented him from bringing forth a creation song, is now the main obstacle to an intimate relationship with Angela. She grows aware of a kind of powerlessness in Abel: "There he stood, dumb and docile at her pleasure, not knowing, she supposed, how even to take his leave."

Abel's failure to establish a relationship with Angela seems to be the result of his incomplete identity formation. Throughout the novel he appears as a loner on a quest for a secure place, for a stability which he cannot find in an intimate relationship because he has not found himself. This dilemma accompanies Abel on his odyssey between Indian and modern American culture.

The third characteristic of identity confusion, the inability to vent aggression appropriately, leads to the climax of the first chapter, Abel's killing of the albino. This act of violence reflects Abel's inability to cope with the confusion he is subject to in his personal and cultural isolation. American culture has estranged him from his home: his endeavor to enter into the ceremonial life of his tribe has been unsuccessful; his attempt to establish an identity in an intimate relationship with Angela has failed. The resulting frustration is one source of the aggression Abel directs against the albino. Another is the deeply rooted fear which has dwelt in him since his early childhood—the fear that evil forces in the universe may exert their influence in him. This anxiety is common among Indian tribes. Abel's inability to comprehend the intricate nature of witchcraft leads to his individual and violent reaction against the albino, which could have been avoided through ritual.

The figure of the albino is a complex image of Abel's schizoid state of mind: his outburst of violence is an act of revenge against the "white man's world" and is at the same time the execution of an evil spirit. . . .

Abel's first encounter with the albino takes place during the Chicken Pull: "The appearance of one of the men was striking. He was large, lithe, and white-skinned; he wore little round colored glasses and rode a fine black horse of good blood." The albino turns out to be the winner in the game, even though Angela observes that in his movements "there was something out of place, some flaw in proportion or design, some unnatural thing." This is the first indication, apart from the physical otherness of the white man, that there is something strange about him. In the course of the game Abel finds himself confronted with the albino and loses out because of his alienation from tribal customs.

Although the albino is an Indian, he carries the stigma of an outsider and, in Abel's mind, seems partly associated with the evils of the white world. In the community he is believed to be a witch. Old man Francisco has a vague notion of his presence when working in the fields: ". . . he was suddenly conscious of some alien presence close at hand. . . . He was too old to be afraid. His acknowledgment of the unknown was nothing more than a dull, intrinsic sadness, a vague desire to weep, for evil had long since found him out and knew who he was." Francisco can accept the existence of evil embodied in the albino. He has an understanding of the presence of sinister forces in the universe. Abel, however, cannot rationalize the inevitability of evil at this stage. It is not until his vision of the runners after evil later in the novel that he comprehends this idea.

Abel's latent fear of witchcraft is awakened by his encounter with the albino. Perhaps he is reminded of his childhood experience with the ill-reputed old woman Nicolás teah-whau.

The fear of witchcraft is Abel's conscious motive for killing the albino, which makes his action an act of self-defense. The problem, however, is more complex, for Abel's action cannot be seen simply in terms of the tribal context which allows the execution of witches. Abel's act of violence grows out of his frustration about his cultural estrangement and his feeling of inadequacy. It is possible that Abel recognizes himself in the figure of the albino, a mixture of Indian and white. Viewed in this light, Abel's act of destruction is an attempt to annihilate his own confused self. In doing so by culturally sanctioned means he is trying to find his way back to his tribal background. The albino, then, serves as a scapegoat. The cultural ambiguity of the albino figure is highlighted in this scene:

> Then he [the white man] closed his hands upon Abel and drew him close. Abel heard the strange excitement of the white man's breath, and the quick, uneven blowing at his ear, and he felt the blue quivering lips upon him, felt even the scales of the lips and the hot, slippery point of the tongue, writhing. He was sick with terror and revulsion, and he tried to fling himself away, but the white man held him close. The white immensity of flesh lay over and smothered him. He

withdrew the knife and thrust again, lower, deep into the groin.

Abel's destruction of the "white immensity" which threatens to crush him appears not only as an act of self-defense against an assault by a witch but also against the corrupting forces of Anglo-American culture. This latter interpretation is reinforced by the scene's sexual implications—"the white man raised his arms as if to embrace him . . . , the blue, quivering lips . . . the hot, slippery point of the tongue, writhing"—all of which suggest a homosexual assault.

Questioned on the ambiguity of this scene, Momaday accepted an interviewer's suggestion that Abel's motif for stabbing the albino is left "entirely open to interpretation." He explained his deliberately ambiguous presentation of the incident by saying that there is "an ineffable aspect to the killing so you simply point to it." One critic pointed to the snake symbolism—"the scales of the lips"—and concluded that it is indicative of Abel's conception of the albino in traditional Christian terms of evil. He judged the killing [according to Lawrence J. Evers] as "more in accordance with Anglo tradition than Indian tradition." There is, however, strong evidence to suggest that Abel is involved in the ritualistic killing of an incarnation of evil which is consistent with the laws of his tribal culture. Abel's statements at the trial that the killing was "the most natural thing in the world" and that "a man kills such an enemy if he can" give credence to such a reading. Moreover, the cruelty and messiness of the slaying are typical of witch executions. . . .

The killing of the albino is a symbolic representation of the cultural conflict which Abel is trying to resolve. In the context of his native culture his act is justified and necessary. Momaday himself said that "not a person at Jemez would have held Abel liable." Nevertheless, Abel's subsequent recognition of the ritual defenses against evil forces and his realization that evil can only be contained, but not eradicated, are fundamental steps to the resolution of his dilemma and his eventual understanding of his tribal tradition.

Many critics of **House Made of Dawn** have dealt with the albino figure from an anthropological point of view. Only a few have realized that the albino reflects not only Momaday's knowledge of the Indian world of the American Southwest but also his indebtedness to American literature. Charles Woodard was the first critic to point out that the whiteness of the albino owes something to the whiteness of the whale in Melville's *Moby-Dick*. A closer look at Melville's writings, however, reveals that *Moby-Dick* is only a minor influence on **House Made of Dawn**. Momaday's novel shows a more obvious similarity to *Billy Budd, Sailor*. This is by no means surprising—Billy Budd was one of Momaday's great favorites as a graduate student. Claggart, the albino's counterpart in Melville's story has "an evil nature," is referred to as a "snake," and has a "pallid" complexion as the outer manifestation of his depraved character. Moreover, the story is permeated with homosexual innuendo. Both Billy and Abel are inarticulate, both react violently in their respective crisis, and both are victimized. . . .

The "Priest of the Sun" chapter is the most puzzling and haunting section of *House Made of Dawn.* The narrative voice is centered in Abel's consciousness as he is lying, delirious from alcohol and the brutal beating he received from Martinez, a violent and corrupt police officer, on the beach outside Los Angeles. Through multiple flashbacks Momaday reveals the psychological situation of a man who is lost between two worlds, torn apart culturally and spiritually, and drifting toward death. Abel is "reeling on the edge of the void," but he does not fall. The very moment when Abel seems to have exhausted all the possibilities of finding redemption holds the seed to his ultimate recovery. In the extremity of his situation Abel gains insights into the core of his native culture which lead him to a new understanding of his place in the scheme of things.

A gap of about six and a half years lies between the end of the opening chapter and the beginning of the next, "The Priest of the Sun." During this time Abel served his prison sentence for killing the albino and, after his release, settled in Los Angeles. However, the burden of the past proves too heavy and the pressure of life in the city too great to allow him integration into his new environment.

In this second chapter Momaday abandons a continuous plot line and operates instead with a device resembling the cutting technique employed in film. Whereas the series of flashbacks in the opening chapter showed a certain continuity by following Abel's growth, this characteristic is now absent. Without any apparent logical connections, fragmentary scenes from Abel's past alternate with blurred perceptions of his immediate environment. The flashbacks encompass scenes from Abel's childhood—Josie, Francisco, Vidal, and his departure from the village—from the trial and his stay in prison, and finally from his relationships with Milly and Angela.

The trial scene is of particular significance, for it is here that the issue of cultural relativism is addressed most explicitly. Abel registers the proceedings with detachment and a keen awareness that his case lies beyond his judges' frame of reference: "Word by word these men were disposing of him in language, *their* language, and they were making a bad job of it. They were strangely uneasy, full of hesitation, reluctance. He wanted to help them." Father Olguin, the Catholic priest in the pueblo, tries to explain Abel's perception of his victim as an evil spirit, admitting that the motivation behind and execution of the killing must ultimately resist comprehension by anyone outside the Jemez world. The nature of Abel's act is such that it cannot be assessed in terms of American law.

Abel states his own feelings on the issues with the conviction of someone who believes himself to be in accordance with the relevant law:

> He had killed a white man. It was not a complicated thing, after all; it was very simple. It was the most natural thing in the world. Surely they could see that, these men who meant to dispose of him in words. They must know that he would kill the white man again, if he had the chance, that there would be no hesitation whatsoever. For he would know what the white man was,

and he would kill him if he could. A man kills such an enemy if he can.

The tragedy is that Abel's law and the law of his judges are incompatible, resting on different cultural assumptions, and that it is in accordance with his judges' law that he is sentenced and sent to prison.

This passage of *House Made of Dawn* is reminiscent of the trial scene in Albert Camus's *The Outsider.* In fact, Momaday declared that he had Camus in mind when he wrote about Abel's trial. Although for different reasons—philosophical rather than cultural in nature—Meursault in *The Outsider* is unrepentant of his killing. He too experiences his case with a profound sense of detachment and isolation. Like Abel he "wasn't to have any say," and "his fate was to be decided out of hand." Yet he too feels the need to help his judges: "Quite often, interested as I was in what they had to say, I was tempted to put in a word, myself." In the end neither Abel nor Meursault can make himself understood.

The sequence of sense perceptions and flashbacks in "The Priest of the Sun" is connected by an underlying image pattern. The intensity of these images, the apparent disjunction of time elements, and the surface illogic—all typical of dreams and hallucinations—account for the haunting, nightmarish effect of this chapter. The reader gets only fragmentary impressions of the conflicts which contributed to Abel's decline. Most of the fragments remain obscure until Ben Benally's first-person narrative in "The Night Chanter" chapter, which gives a coherent account of Abel's life in the city. But in allowing the reader to enter Abel's consciousness in the final stage of his decline Momaday conveys not only the protagonist's confusion but also the possibility that social and cultural barriers are the sources of Abel's disintegration. On the symbolic level Abel's isolation is evoked by the image of the fence: "There was a fence on the bank before him; at his back there was a broad rocky beach, tilting to the sea. The fence was made of heavy wire mesh. . . . There were cans and bits of paper and broken glass against the fence; . . . he could almost touch it. He raised himself to reach for the fence and the pain struck him again." Abel's inability to reach let alone overcome the fence is symbolic of his failure to break through the barriers between him and the mainstream of society. After realizing the source of his dilemma during his vision of the men running after evil, Abel finds the strength to reach the fence. It is with its help that he manages to raise himself. Thus the fence symbolism stresses the theme of cultural segregation and at the same time emphasizes Abel's vision as the turning point of the novel.

It is not only the fragmentary structure which precludes any easy interpretation of this crucial chapter. Equally complex is Momaday's use of imagery; only when the seemingly unrelated symbols are combined in a coherent pattern does the full meaning of the beach scene surface. I have argued above that Abel has been suffering from the lack of stable identity, as evidenced by his position as an outsider in the community, his inability to identify with tribal rituals and ceremonies, and his failure to relate on a level of intimacy to his female partners. The process of degeneration resulting from this lack of stability reaches its climax in Abel's struggle with the murderous police officer and subsequently with death itself. The symbols which surround these events suggest that what is actually happening in this powerfully conceived scene is a rite of passage in which Abel progresses from lack of understanding to knowledge, from chaos through ritual death to rebirth.

The scene's setting is in itself suggestive. Abel is "lying in a shallow depression in which there were weeds and small white stones and tufts of long grey grass." It is a common feature of initiation ceremonies that the initiate is placed into a shallow grave from which he eventually rises as a new being. Moreover, the scene happens at night. Darkness, according to Eliade, signifies in such rituals "the beyond, the 'infernal regions.'" The beating Abel receives results from his attempt to get even with Martinez, who has tyrannized him. On the symbolic level this beating represents the initiatory mutilations which are frequent features of rites of passage. Abel's injuries are numerous: "His hands were broken, and he could not move them. Some of his fingers were stuck together with blood, and the blood was dry and black; . . . there was blood in his throat and mouth." These injuries point to his symbolic death, and it can hardly be a coincidence that amputations of fingers and the knocking out of teeth are common initiatory tortures.

That Abel is lying on the beach, close to water, is of further importance in this context; although there is no suggestion that he actually comes into contact with the sea, he is closely associated with it and the small, silver-sided fish which dwell off the California coast. Water is traditionally a symbol of potential life, of creation and fertility, the element from which all cosmic manifestations emerge and to which they return. Water creates and dissolves. According to Eliade:

> Immersion in water symbolizes a return to the pre-formal, a total regeneration, a new birth, for immersion means a dissolution of forms, a reintegration into the formlessness of pre-existence; and emerging from the water is a repetition of the act of creation in which form was first expressed. Every contact with water implies regeneration: first, because dissolution is succeeded by a "new birth," and then because immersion fertilizes, increases the potential of life and of creation. In initiation rituals, water confers a "new birth."

Abel's proximity to and association with water, then, suggest the dissolution of his state of estrangement and the potential for rebirth into his tribal culture.

Abel's connection with the fish reinforces the meaning of his transformation:

> There is a small silversided fish that is found along the coast of southern California. In the spring and summer it spawns on the beach during the first three hours after each of the three high tides following the highest tide. These fish come by the hundreds from the sea. They hurl themselves upon the land and writhe in the light of the moon, the moon, the moon; they writhe in the light of the moon. They are among the most helpless creatures on the face of the earth.

The meaning of this seemingly unimportant descriptive passage becomes gradually apparent through the affiliation of Abel with the fish. Like them he is lying on the beach. He too is a helpless creature removed from the natural element of his native culture. In his delirious state Abel's thoughts constantly return to the fish, "His mind boggled and withdrew . . . and it came around again to the fishes." He feels a kind of sympathy for the "small silversided fishes spawned mindlessly in correlation to the phase of the moon and the rise and fall of the tides. The thought of it made him sad, filled him with sad, unnamable longing and wonder." Finally Abel is directly identified with the fish, "He had the sense that his whole body was shaking violently, tossing and whipping, flopping like a fish."

The fish imagery not only reflects Abel's suffering but also indicates the upward movement in his development after he has become aware of his situation. When Abel raises the energy to fight against and eventually escape the drift towards death, the fish too have found their way back to safety in the depth of the sea, as Abel will eventually return home to his tribal community: "And far out in the night where nothing else was, the fishes lay out on the black water, holding still against all the force and motion of the sea; or close to the surface, darting and rolling and spinning like lures, they played in the track of the moon."

The most complex symbol Momaday employs in this chapter is that of the moon. The common denominator in a number of scenes throughout the novel, it brings the various episodes together in Abel's and the reader's minds. The moon, of course, is also associated with the sea and the initiation ritual. Most important, however, it is Abel's realization of the cosmic significance of the moon which brings about his new understanding of a universal order. To appreciate the subtlety of this image pattern, we need to scrutinize in detail its various functions.

The connection of the moon with initiation rituals has already been mentioned. The moon's reappearance after her three-day "death" has traditionally been read as a symbol of rebirth. The Juan Capistrano Indians of California, according to James Frazer [as quoted by Eliade], declared, "As the moon dieth and cometh to life again, so we also, having to die, will again rise." In a number of shamanistic initiation rites the novice is "broken in pieces" in analogy to the phases of the moon. Among the Plains Indians it was customary to focus one's eyes on the moon in order to secure help in a moment of distress. The Pueblo medicine-water chief implored the moon to give him power to see disease. With this information the prominence of the moon image in Abel's consciousness becomes more readily intelligible.

However, it is not just the meanings of regeneration, spiritual assistance, and clearer vision which make the moon such a revealing image of Abel's struggle for recovery. His rise to a securer mode of being is effected above all by his growing awareness of the moon as a unifying and controlling force in the universe. Eliade pointed out [in *Patterns on Comparative Religion*] that "the myths of 'quest' and of 'initiation trials' reveal, in artistic or dramatic form, the actual act by which the mind gets beyond a conditioned, piecemeal universe, swinging between opposites, to return to the fundamental oneness that existed before creation." An important step towards Abel's understanding of cosmic unity lies in his realization that the moon controls the sea as well as the land: "Why should Abel think of the fishes? He could not understand the sea; it was not of his world. It was an enchanted thing, *too,* for it lay under the spell of the moon. It bent to the moon, and the moon made a bright, shimmering course upon it" (italics added). This recognition of the moon's universal power to order and control the universe reflects Abel's growing reattunement to American Indian thought.

In the Southwest, as elsewhere among tribal peoples, the moon functions together with the sun as the measure of the yearly cycle in the life of the community. The Santa Clara Pueblos believe that "the function of the sun, the moon, stars, the Milky Way, and other such features, is to make the earth inhabitable for human beings" [Edgar L. Hewett and Bertha P. Dutton, *The Pueblo Indian World*, 1945]. This idea has practical consequences for everyday Indian life. The belief, for instance, that the moon exerts a strong influence on the growth of plants has immediate impact on the process of sowing and reaping. At the beginning of **House Made of Dawn,** Momaday refers to the moon's influence on the communal work in the fields: "The townsmen work all summer in the fields. When the moon is full, they work at night with ancient, handmade plows and hoes." The holiness attributed to the moon by American Indians is alluded to in the "red and yellow symbols of the sun and the moon" which decorate the lectern in the Indian church in Los Angeles. Eliade noted that "the moon shows man his true human condition; that in a sense man looks at himself, and finds himself anew in the life of the moon." If one subscribes to this idea, then Abel's rediscovery of his native heritage appears to be a result of his reattunement to a lunar rhythm.

Abel's understanding of the secrets of lunar control of the universe also arises from recollections and reinterpretations of some of his earlier hunting experiences. The image of the moon functions as an associative link to other scenes where animal imagery mirrors Abel's distress. One of these instances, the parallel between him and the fish, has already been discussed. The eagle hunt is another example: "Bound and helpless, his eagle seemed drab and shapeless in the moonlight, too large and ungainly for flight." A third event of this kind occurs in one of Abel's recollections of his childhood. It is the hunting scene in which he recovers a shot water bird:

> He took it up in his hands and it was heavy and warm and the feathers about its keel were hot and sticky with blood. He carried it out into the moonlight, and its bright black eyes, in which no terror was, were wide of him, wide of the river and the land, level and hard upon the ring of the moon in the southern sky.

The depiction of the dying bird strikingly resembles the description of Abel's own suffering in the face of death: "He awoke coughing; there was blood in his throat and mouth. He was shuddering with cold and pain. . . . He peered into the night: all around the black land against the star-bright, moon-bright sky."

In these instances the moon imagery connects Abel's present and past experiences. In recollecting the dying water bird, with its fearless black eyes, Abel can establish a link between his own desperate state and the reaction of the animal. The bird is part of the complexity of nature and is by nature without the fear of death. Abel too had a natural attitude towards death when, as a boy, he was still close to the Indian understanding of the universe. His loss of identification with his heritage has led him away from this natural view of death and contributed to the intense fears which are haunting him now.

The moon, then, is strongly suggestive of a hope for rebirth. This is an entirely new perspective for Abel. If one recalls the scene in which he destroys the eagle because he felt pity and shame, it is obvious that Abel did not share in the traditional belief of many hunting communities that the spirit of the animal survives and returns in a new physical manifestation. If he had been attuned to the rituals of the hunters, as old man Francisco was on his bear hunt, he could have killed the eagle in the appropriate ritual way, with a sense of gratitude and appreciation rather than remorse.

Momaday uses a number of devices to reinforce further the connection between Abel and the moon. In two instances the course of the moonlight on the water functions as a bridge, and in the following passage a flock of birds serves as a link: "Then they [the birds] were away, and he had seen how they craned their long slender necks to the moon, ascending slowly into the far reaches of the winter night. They made a dark angle on the sky, acute, perfect; and for one moment they lay out like an omen on the bright fringe of a cloud."

Abel's recognition of the moon as a vital influence shows that he is beginning to return to the traditional Indian concept of the universe. The following passage, which comprises the three images of sea, moon, and fish, unites bird and fish imagery and thus widens the scope of Abel's vision to a universal dimension:

> And somewhere beyond the cold and the fog and the pain there was the black and infinite sea, bending to the moon, and there was the cold white track of the moon on the water. And far out in the night where nothing else was, the fishes lay out in the black waters, holding still against all the force and motion of the sea; . . . And far away inland there were great gray geese riding under the moon.

Land and sea, man and animal are related in their connection with the moon. This notion coincides with the general idea of the interrelatedness of all elements in the Indian universe. By growing aware of this idea Abel discovers that he too is tied up in the totality of creation and has a legitimate place in it.

Another major step towards restoration and initiation into his tribal culture is Abel's vision of the runners after evil. Dreams and visions have always been of utmost significance in the lives of American Indian peoples. John Skinner commented on the religious nature of dreams in the Indian world: "Man succeeds first in his dreams. . . . man becomes in dreams and words before he becomes in deeds. A man becomes his successful dream, not his successful deed" ["On Indian Poetry and Religion," *Little Square Review,* Nos. 5-6 (1968)]. Abel's experience must be seen in the light of this statement. In his vision he catches, for the first time, a glimpse of the meaning of tribal ritual as he becomes aware of its importance for the relationship between the individual and the universe:

> The runners after evil ran as water runs, deep in the channel, in the way of least resistance, no resistance. His skin crawled with excitement; he was overcome with longing and loneliness, for suddenly he saw the crucial sense in their going, of old men in white leggings running after evil in the night. They were whole and indispensable in what they did; everything in creation referred to them. Because of them, perspective, proportion, design in the universe. Meaning because of them. They ran with great dignity and calm, not in the hope of anything, but hopelessly; neither in fear nor hatred nor despair of evil, but simply in recognition and with respect. Evil was. Evil was abroad in the night; they must venture out to the confrontation; they must reckon dues and divide the world.

The vision confronts Abel with the ritualistic practices the elders of the tribe employ to maintain control over the supernatural. The race is connected with the ceremony of clearing the irrigation ditches in the spring. It is an imitation of water running through the channels, a magic bid for the vital supply of rain, and a ritual act to prevent the harvest from being influenced by evil powers. This vision modifies Abel's view of his own actions in the past; he realizes that, although his destruction of the albino as a source of evil was in accordance with tribally sanctioned practices, Pueblo religion offers nonviolent ways of controlling supernatural powers. The ritualistic expression of human creativity through words in songs and prayers and through motion in dance and ceremonial races is the central instrument by which the Indian maintains a balance between himself and the universe.

Abel's growing understanding of the cosmic order in terms of his tribal heritage leads him to the recognition that his estrangement from the center of Indian life has been the cause of his dilemma. This diagnosis of the source of his "disease" puts him on the road to recovery. Abel's previous inability to make sense of his situation is indicated in a flashback to his departure from the village, which is the continuation of the corresponding passage in the opening chapter: "He tried to think where the trouble had begun, what the trouble was. There was trouble; he could admit that to himself, but he had no real insight into his own situation. Maybe, certainly, *that* was the trouble; but he had no way of knowing."

Now in his hallucinatory state the insight for which he had searched so long suddenly comes to him: "He had lost his place. he had been long ago at the center, had known where he was, had lost his way, had wandered to the end of the earth, was even now reeling on the edge of the void."

This recognition epitomizes the entire development of the novel up to this point. Abel realizes that the Indian world of his boyhood is the only place where he can find a meaningful existence and an identity. As in a vision quest Abel receives a sign which shows him the way to personal wholeness.

Once Abel has by means of his subconscious gained insight into the meaning of ritual and the controlling forces in the universe, he is ready to establish a formal union with his tribal heritage through the ceremony of the Night Chant which Ben Benally conducts for him. The changes he undergoes as a result of his vision enable him to make the "spiritual commitment" of submitting himself to the healing powers of the Night Chant. In doing so, he shows his newfound trust in the effectiveness of Indian ceremonials. In the Night Chant ceremony Abel, as the "patient," remains passive yet, but it is the first step toward his own conduction of a ceremony—the funeral rite after the death of his grandfather—and toward his participation in the ceremonial race that ends the novel.

The result of the Night Chant is the restoration of the wholeness Abel had lost in his crisis of identity and through his exposure to the disruptive forces of incompatible cultural patterns. American Indian ritual and song aim at the preservation of order and at the integration of the individual into the larger context of his environment. [In her "The Sacred Hoop: A Contemporary Perspective on American Indian Literature," an essay appearing in Abraham Chapman's *Literature of the American Indians*] Paula Allan remarked that through ceremonial practices "the isolated individualistic personality is shed and the person is restored to conscious harmony with the universe." The Night Chant, then, reestablishes Abel's inner balance and equilibrium with the world around him. In order to achieve this harmony Abel must regain his physical and mental wholeness and his power of the word.

Physical disintegration is the outward sign of Abel's inner conflict: "He had loved his body. It had been hard and quick and beautiful; it had been useful, quickly and surely responsive to his mind and will; . . . [now] his body was mangled and racked with pain. His body, like his mind, had turned on him; it was his enemy." The line "restore my body for me" in the chant is directed at the return of Abel's physical strength and his control over his body. The line "restore my mind for me" aims at the restitution of Abel's mental wholeness and the coordination between his body and spirit.

Abel's lack of articulation stood at the center of his personal and cultural isolation. It was a syndrome of his estrangement from the oral tradition without which he remained cut off from his tribal heritage. Gladys A. Reichard stressed the fact that "the 'word' . . . is of great ritualistic value, and in order to be complete, man must control language. The better his control and the more extensive his knowledge, the greater his well-being." The desire to regain power over the word finds expression in the request "restore my voice for me."

Finally, it is necessary to bring back the power of motion Abel lost in the course of his decline. Reichard pointed out the importance of the power of motion for the Navajos: "Man may breathe and speak, his organs may function well, but without the power of motion he is incomplete, useless." The lines "Restore my feet for me, / Restore my legs for me, / Restore my body for me, / . . . Happily I recover. / . . . Happily I go forth. / . . . Being as it used to be long ago, may I walk" call for the return of Abel's power of motion. The race at the end of the novel shows that the request has been granted.

Abel's return to the Jemez world proceeds from a visionary, subconscious level through a ritualistic to a rational level. His recovery, which originates in his hallucinatory visions and is furthered through Ben's performance of the Night Chant, continues after his return to the pueblo. There he finds Francisco dying. For six days the old medicine man struggles against death, uttering memories of his life during the hours of dawn. Abel listens to his voice but initially fails to understand the meaning of his words. And yet the "voice of his memory was whole and clear and growing like the dawn." It reminds Abel of the secrets of the solar calendar which his grandfather had taught him many years ago, of the ceremonial races and festivities of Jemez, and, in the story of Francisco's bear hunt, of the traditional hunting ways and rituals. Francisco's final recollections seem to refresh Abel's knowledge of the ancient ways of his people; in the end they begin to make sense and carry meaning, for on the morning of the seventh day Abel for the first time conducts a ceremony: ". . . he knew what had to be done." Strictly adhering to the timeless practices of his tribe, he prepares Francisco for the funeral. In doing so he takes over the role of the dead medicine man.

Significantly, Abel's return to his tribal tradition takes place only a short time before dawn. This event is part of a coherent pattern of dawn images which permeate the novel. The book opens and closes with Abel running across the land at dawn. When Abel is lying on the beach after his fight with Martinez, struggling against death, he can hear the "sound of the city at night, ticking like a clock toward the dawn." If one takes the symbol of dawn to stand for rebirth, a new beginning, and creation, the reference to dawn at this point anticipates Abel's resurrection.

The connection between the symbol of dawn and the idea of creation is suggested in the following passage about Abel's attempt to bring forth a creation song: "He would have sung lowly of the first world, of fire and flood, and of the emergence of dawn from the hills." The first world, fire, and flood are references to the creation myths of many southwestern Indian tribes, such as the Hopi, Zuni, and Navajos. They hold in common the belief that they emerged to their present land after a migration through several underground worlds, in which they encountered floods or fire. Dawn marks the moment of emergence from the underworld, the beginning of tribal life, and the creation of tribal culture. Every new morning "is the moment of invigoration, when new life awakens and all creation is astir—it is creation itself, an 'in the beginning.' . . . From the dawn comes generation and birth" [Hartley Burr Al-

exander, *The World's Rim: Great Mysteries of the North American Indians*].

At the center of the dawn image pattern stands the following passage, which encompasses the historical migration of a tribe, its cultural crisis, and its potential regeneration:

> Man came down the ladder to the plain a long time ago. It was a slow migration, though he came only from the caves in the canyons and the tops of the mesas nearby. There are low, broken walls on the tabletops and smoke-blackened caves in the cliffs, where still there are metates and broken bowls and ancient ears of corn, as if the prehistoric civilization had gone out among the hills for a little while and would return; and then everything would be restored to an older age, and time would have returned upon itself and a bad dream of invasion and change would have been dissolved in an hour before the dawn.

This short passage [from *The Way to Rainy Mountain*] encapsulates the essence of *House Made of Dawn*: the novel shows how a traditional Indian community which is threatened in its cultural survival by an encroaching alien world is struggling to defend itself against this influence. The demand for strict adherence to traditional practices leads to pressure within the tribe and thus aggravates the crisis. This pressure may result, as in Abel's case, in identity conflicts among young Indians, who, though rooted in their cultural background, cannot ignore the reality of a modern age brought about by an alien culture. Their need to develop their individuality within the tribal community must find the support of their elders.

In the passage quoted above Momaday puts a cultural crisis in its wider historical and mythological context. He points out that the archaeological remnants of previous Indian generations only seem to indicate the extinction of an ancient civilization, because Pueblo culture has survived to the present. In referring to the cyclical concept of time Momaday demonstrates his belief in the inherent potential of American Indian cultures to survive historical crises. That the new rise of the old culture should take place an hour before the dawn seems unimportant in the narrow context of this passage. In the larger context of the novel, however, it becomes most significant: Abel's celebration of the funeral rites for his grandfather "a while . . . before the dawn" is not only the moment when he finds his way back to his tribe but also, from a historical perspective, the point where Jemez culture gains new impetus in its struggle to survive a period of cultural encroachment and oppression. Like the Bahkyush people who had once journeyed along the edge of oblivion and recovered to become eagle hunters and rainmakers, Abel, who is associated with this group as an eagle hunter, also returned from the edge of the void to become a dawn runner. As the Kiowas' migration from the north of the American continent to the south and east was "a journey toward the dawn" which "led to a golden age," the positive outcome of Abel's migration between two worlds can be seen as a hopeful beginning of a new period of Pueblo culture.

In much the same way as the reference to the cyclical concept of time indicates the potentially positive resolution of the historical crisis in Indian culture, the cyclical structure of the novel justifies a hopeful reading of Abel's future. At the close of the book Abel returns to the personal wholeness and harmony with the universe which were his main strengths at its beginning. Indeed the cyclical concept of tribal history and the cyclical movement of Abel's personal history interconnect at the end. Abel, whose dilemma is the product of historical crisis in Indian culture, overcomes his identity conflict and symbolically resolves the communal crisis of his tribe. Momaday's own comment on *House Made of Dawn* points in this direction: "I see the novel as a circle. It ends where it begins and it's informed with a kind of thread that runs through it and holds everything together" ["An Interview with N. Scott Momaday," *Puerto del Sol* 12, No. 1 (1973)] This race, then, is a race for identity, both personal and communal. It finds its final resolution in the ceremonial race which shows Abel reconciled with his native culture and the Indian universe.

Many alienated characters in recent American fiction—Ralph Ellison's *Invisible Man,* Faulkner's Joe Christmas in *Light in August,* and John Updike's Rabbit Angstrom in *Rabbit Run*—are running away from something and have no viable alternative to which they can turn. Abel is unique in that his running manifests an act of integration, not a symbol of estrangement. Momaday himself suggested this reading of the symbol by referring to its cultural context: "The man running is fitting himself into the basic motion of the universe. . . . That is simply a symbolism which prevails in the southwestern Indian world." In ["The Morality of Indian Hating"] Momaday explained this ceremonial race which is "run at dawn before the spring cleaning of the Jemez irrigation ditches":

> It is a stick race: the runners imitate the Cloud People who fill the arroyos with life-giving rain, and keep in motion, with only their feet, a "stick-ball" which represents the moving drift of the water's edge. The first race each year comes in February, and then the dawn is clear and cold, and the runners breathe steam. It is a long race, and it is neither won nor lost. It is an expression of the soul in the ancient terms of sheer physical exertion. To watch those runners is to know that they draw with every step some elemental power which resides at the core of the earth and which, for all our civilized ways, is lost upon us who have lost the art of going in the flow of things.

Abel's running at dawn, singing the words of the Night Chant, marks the end of his struggle for identity. He has finally returned to his place in the house made of dawn. He has found the right words to articulate himself and he has a vision of the appropriate path to wholeness. The novel's final scene is charged with mythological overtones: according to a Pueblo emergence myth, Iatik, the corn mother, after creating the present world, called on the people to emerge from the previous world underground. As they entered their new environment they were blind. Then, the story [as related by Richard Erdoes in *The Rain Dance People*] goes on to explain, "Iatik lined them up in a row facing east and made the sun come up for the first time in this new world to shine upon them. And when its rays shone upon the eyes of the people, they were opened and they could see."

In the primordial setting of dawn over the Jemez Valley, Abel too "could see at last without having to think. He could see the canyons and the mountains and the sky. He could see the rain and the river and the fields beyond. He could see the dark hills at dawn." His new vision and voice are expressions of his communion with his native tradition and raise the hope that he may become the living link between the ancient past and a promising future for his tribal culture.

Momaday on the character Abel:

Abel is commonplace in the sense that he is a kind of, a kind of—I can't think of the word I want—he represents a great many people of his generation, the Indian who returns from the war, the Second World War. He is an important figure in the whole history of the American experience in this country. It represents such a dislocation of the psyche in our time. Almost no Indian of my generation or of Abel's generation escaped that dislocation, that sense of having to deal immediately with, not only with the traditional world, but with the other world which was placed over the traditional world so abruptly and with great violence. Abel's generation is a good one to write about, simply because it's a tragic generation. It is not the same, the generation after Abel did not have the same experience, nor the one before. So it is, in some sense, the logical one to deal with in literature.

N. Scott Momaday, in an interview with Laura Coltelli, in her Winged Words: American Indian Writers Speak, *1990.*

N. Scott Momaday with Dagmar Weiler   (interview date April 1986)

SOURCE: "N. Scott Momaday: Story Teller," in *The Journal of Ethnic Studies,* Vol. 16, No. 1, Spring, 1988, pp. 118-26.

[*In the following excerpt from an interview conducted in April, 1986, Weiler and Momaday discuss various aspects of* House Made of Dawn.]

[*Weiler*]: *I'd like to talk very briefly about your position as an Indian writer. Last semester, I took an undergraduate class in which we read Leslie Silko's* Ceremony *and Storyteller, and I remember that some of the students had problems with those works. We also read House Made of Dawn, which I think was the last novel, and they found difficulty there, too. They asked the question: "Where is the message [in* House Made of Dawn] *comparable to that of an angry woman like Leslie Silko, or that found in some of the poems by Joy Harjo and what enables them to take a stand?" The students seemed to be missing this. I remember two years ago in an interview you said that you didn't make social comments. In connection with this "Indian" issue, how do you see yourself?*

[Momaday]: I don't see myself as an Indian writer. I don't know what that means. I am an Indian, and I am a writer, but I don't just want to say "Indian writer" or to talk about Indian literature. I don't know what that means, exactly, and I don't identify with it at all.

You did a review of several books in 1971. You talked then about Vine DeLoria and other Indian writers. I had the impression you criticized them somewhat for stressing their Indian stand. Let me quote this. You said: "As far as I can see, the Indians who are giving the best account of themselves at present are doing so without any particular regard to movement as such or to the ways in which they are accounted for by the others." So you would say that first of all you are a storyteller, a writer who happens to be an Indian?

Or I'm an Indian who happens to be a storyteller. I don't order those things in any particular way. I am an Indian and a writer, but I'm a lot of other things as well. They are all very important to me.

It just struck me that you have had many discussions with these young people. They were looking, especially in the early 70s, to Red Power, and these young students were expecting something out of, for example, **House Made of Dawn.** *You know, what the Indian should do, and they didn't find it there. Maybe they missed something. They immediately realized or thought that the Albino was the symbol for the White man. It was easier with an angry woman like Silko. It was much more out in the open: the social, political, and economic problems. You stress the fact that you are a poet, but I would like to talk about the prose.* **"The Way to Rainy Mountain":** *it appeared as an essay; it has been anthologized.*

Yes, the introduction.

The introduction appeared as an essay: you published it as a book together with short Kiowa tales, and later the priest Tosamah uses it in **House Made of Dawn.** *Is there a difference between the three forms? Would you say the impact is different?*

Well, yes. I would say that it functions as the introduction to **The Way to Rainy Mountain.** In **House Made of Dawn,** it functions in a different way because it tells us something about one of the characters in the novel. It is the delineation of Tosoma's character, among other things, so it's completely different.

That is one thing that I had problems with—that Tosamah was telling the story. **House Made of Dawn** *fascinates me. It is disturbing—*

Good!

—mainly because there are many beautiful voices. Let's talk about Father Olguin and Angela, or maybe not so much about Father Olguin but Frey Nicolas. How did Nicolas appear in **House Made of Dawn?** *Did you rely on old manuscripts? Is he right out of old missionary ledgers?*

I didn't research the book at all. It just came right out of my imagination. I don't know how I happened to get the idea of the character of Nicolas. He's very much in place because he's a missionary, and the missionaries, especially the Catholic missionaries in pueblos, are very important. I think they have, in over four hundred years, made a

great difference—. Well, I'm not sure I want to say that. I don't know if they have made a difference or not, but they have become a kind of institution in the pueblos over that period of time, and they are interesting, you know, the priests and the pueblos. I got to thinking about their lives and what they must feel, being the representatives of the Catholic church to what in the past certainly had been a pagan society. They must have felt very isolated, and I wanted a character that would represent that sort of dichotomy in pueblo life. Frey Nicolas was the answer for me. He could occupy that position of an intermediary in the pueblo and articulate some of the conflicts that informed the pueblo world. In a sense, Father Olguin comes as a later representative of that same conflict; Angela comes as a later representative of that conflict. So it seemed that such a character would be interesting and, indeed, I enjoyed working with both Frey Nicolas and Father Olguin.

I think many of us find it fascinating that all the voices are distinctive. Nicolas, for example, in the first entry: the voice is that of [a] missionary who is still in concert with his belief. It's "They will, Lord" and "Have mercy" and "I pray." And later he falls apart. There is also this beautiful scene— "Dear Lord," I think he is talking about Francisco. He remembers watching this boy, and what fascinated me is that, by the time you tell this story, this man is dead. But still, through your style, you make him come alive. We can hear him.

Yes.

And that is why it seems as if you opened a ledger and copied it.

Well, that's wonderful. I'm glad that you have that sense of it because that was my intention.

You mentioned Angela. I have a problem there. Angela seems to me to be the only one whose voice is not convincing. What is Angela's role?

Angela's role is to be a kind of foil to Abel. She represents the antithesis of the pueblo world. Yet, she and Abel are able to relate to one another on one level although they are so diametrically opposed in most of their cultural attitudes. So she enables us, I think, to see the pueblo world and Abel in a particular way, a way in which you would not otherwise be able to see him in his traditional context.

I think my criticism may derive from a comparison of Angela and Milly. Later in the book we hear Milly talk. It is a wonderful, almost Faulknerian passage as she remembers her life on the farm. It is printed in italics, but we hear her talk. Her voice is "listening"; she has her own style. Angela's is somewhat weird, a blurring sound, a compulsive cycle of sexual exploits; Angela is there, and then she vanishes. What about Milly? Would you say that while Angela is disturbing Abel, Milly has a human touch? I noticed that Milly is almost the only one Abel is communicating with. He hardly speaks throughout the whole book, except to Milly.

Yes, I would say that. I think that Milly is much more selfless than Angela. Angela is motivated by things that are deep within her that we don't know much about and she is strange, a stranger, as you suggest. Milly is not that. She is concerned about Abel and she, I think it is fair to say, wants to help him. He's certainly aware of that. He's able to perceive that she means him well, so he responds to her in a very sympathetic way. And, you know, Angela's something else. It's a sexual relationship, and I think that Angela does not mean him well, and he understands that, so he is wary of her. In a way, he plays the game with Angela. He understands that she requires a certain response on his part and he makes it. He's willing to make it; he's willing to go that far. But with Milly, I think, the feelings are much more genuine and deeper.

The priest of the sun is one character who deals explicitly with the problem of language. He uses the introduction to "Rainy Mountain." I think he accuses other people of taking the word and convoluting it, overusing it.

He says, in effect, that this is what the White man does. This is the Western tradition as far as language is concerned. They overdo it. They go too far. He talks about this in the sermon "According to John." He lets us know it's important.

To exaggerate a bit, it is Tosamah whose speech seems to be a little convoluted.

Of course. He's a trickster figure.

This is a wonderful irony.

Thank you. I agree.

There is this hipster language, such as you hear in caricatures of almost all Black preachers.

Yes. He's a trickster and he takes advantage of language in the situation and he's bright. Much of what he says, I think, is provocative and true. I think of his sermon as being a wonderful kind of commentary on language, even in his own ironic terms. What he says is thoughtful and makes sense.

What is his position in the Indian world as created in the story we have been discussing?

What is Tosamah's position? Well, I think of Tosamah as being uprooted and lost. He and Abel are poised somewhere apart from their traditional world. They are also apart from the other world, but they have fashioned an existence in that no man's land. And Tosamah has done it better than most people have because he's shrewd and a cynic and he takes advantage. He exists. He wears masks. He knows how to take a bad situation and make the best of it.

Tosamah's voice seems to be the one that will be out there, the one person who will be heard by the White man as well as by uprooted Indians in the city.

Well, perhaps that's true. Tosamah speaks the White man's language. He is able to turn the tables, as it were. He takes, after all, one of the great, classic doctrines of the Western world, *The Gospel According to St. John,* and he twists it around so that he condemns the whole White culture. It's a wonderful thing to do. It's a tour de force. In a way, it's fair to say that the White man, if he listens to any of these characters, will hear Tosamah. The Indian,

if he hears any of these characters, will probably be most receptive to Ben Benally. When Ben Benally talks of bone craft to the traditional world and sees the sunrise on the red mesas, that's the reality of the Indian. Tosamah does both things. He speaks for both worlds, and he does it eloquently, you know. But you never know quite where he is in relation to the reality of any given moment. He wears masks.

That's right. I found him one of the most disturbing figures, and that's one of the reasons why I asked about him. The first time I read it, I thought of the story in **Rainy Mountain** *and Tosamah's voice. It's not right. After his ranting, there is that mythical voice, and I thought, why this man? Earlier you mentioned the traditional form of the novel.*

I did?

Yes, today!

Today? I don't remember. What did I say?

I'm thinking of the plot, the straight story line, the main protagonist. Although Abel may be at the center of **House Made of Dawn.** *I don't think it is really Abel's story. All the characters have their own stories, even if they appear only once briefly, like Milly. But they are evocative, even the dead man because he is so articulate and because he has his own voice. You can imagine his whole story. In the structure of the novel and the prologue we see Abel running—does the ritual of running have a healing effect on Abel?*

Well, yes!

He runs again at the end.

I think in the novel it says rather explicitly that his running provides him some of the rehabilitation. He is coming to terms again with his traditional world in the act of running. The question of whether or not he makes it, is open. I mean a lot of people want to know what happens after the last page, and I don't know. I don't know what happens to Abel finally, and I don't want to know.

Paula Gunn Allen   (essay date 1987)

SOURCE: "Bringing Home the Fact: Tradition and Continuity in the Imagination," in *Recovering the Word: Essays on Native American Literature,* edited by Brian Swann and Arnold Krupat, University of California Press, 1987, pp. 570-78.

[*Allen is a Pueblo Laguna and Sioux poet, critic, essayist, novelist, and editor. In the following excerpt, she discusses the inclusion of Navajo and Pueblo beliefs in* House Made of Dawn, *arguing that Momaday's focus in the novel is sickness, healing, and harmony.*]

As familiarity with the Bible makes Western culture accessible to the understanding, the basic texts of the Pueblo or the Navajo make their cultures, especially their literature, accessible to scholarly interpretation. It is a nearly hopeless task to explicate *House Made of Dawn* without such a familiarity, though an understanding of historical processes in the Southwest and of Western attitudes and lore is also important to this task. The basic meanings important to these American Indian systems are carried over into the book. To be unaware of the meanings of these symbols and their accompanying structures is to miss the greater part of the significance of the novel.

It is not impossible to read this novel when one is not conversant with the underlying symbolic structure, but the reading will result in confusion and distortion of what the writer was up to. It will also probably result in political distortions that will have an ultimately disastrous effect socially, for such is the power of the imagination over our more conscious activities. The symbols are there; the deep meanings are there. It is necessary to bring these factors into consciousness when studying the novel in order for them to have the ultimate curative or restorative effect which is the basic purpose of that book. For if elements improperly understood are imagined with sufficient care, a distortion will occur in our relationships with those misimagined persons. If *House Made of Dawn* is seen only as the chronicle of a man "fallen between two chairs," the impact on Indian men and women will continue to be that of victimization. For as we perceive, so we behave; and as we behave, so we create.

In order to imagine Abel as he is, the symbol-structure of the novel must be carefully examined. The underlying assumptions about the nature of reality and of the human being's place within it must be imagined truly; for Abel is not so much a man caught between two cultures and two orientations to reality as he is a medicine person who does not understand the nature of his being or of his proper function. The novel, in its structure and in its symbolic content, carefully makes this clear, though the meaning of Abel's experience is not evident unless the beliefs of the Pueblo and Navajo are taken into account. Momaday makes this point through the eyes of Angela St. John, through the eyes of Benally, and through the peculiar character of Tosamah as it contrasts with that of Abel. The identity of the protagonist is drawn through the author's personal history, through the history of the Bahkyush and through the journals of Fray Nicolás; it is apparent in the peculiar interweaving of names and places and, especially, in the sequence of events as they occur in the novel.

House Made of Dawn is an act of the imagination designed to heal; it is about the relationship between good and evil, and the proper place of a certain human being within that relationship. It is not about redemption, for redemption is not a Pueblo (indeed, not an American Indian) notion; it is not about a fall from grace. It is about sickness and disharmony, and about health and harmony. The title is the clue: "House Made of Dawn" is the first line of the chant sung on the third day of the Navajo healing ceremony called the Night Chant. It is the first prayer of the third morning ritual; the third day is designated the Day of the West. The prayer appears in the third chapter of the novel. Narrated by the Navajo friend of Abel, Ben Benally, this chapter is concerned with Abel's sojourn in Los Angeles, the major relocation center for southwestern Indians on the west coast. The prayer is sung in the Night Chant as part of the Purification section of the ceremony, and is accompanied by a rite in which a set of eight prayer

offerings "sacred to gods of the shrine known as the House Made of Dawn (in the distant canyon of *Tségihi*)" are used to bless or purify the patient and are then sacrificed or offered to the sun. Tségihi is an ancient Pueblo ruin, and the controlling metaphor of the book can be said to be the relationship of the sun to Abel. The sun forms the central issue of life at Walatowa. It is the race which is performed each year at spring equinox as an offering of the strength of the people to the sun and as a source of strength and power among them for the coming planting season which frames the book. The peyote ceremony in Los Angeles is a sun rite, and so is one of the purification rituals which Abel must go through. It is also significant that a patient participating in a Night Chant offers himself on the last morning of his healing to the rising sun, singing these words:

> Thus will it be beautiful.
> Thus walk in beauty, my grandchild.

As these words are sung, the patient faces east and breathes in the breath of dawn.

In addition to these clues, Momaday has structured his novel in ways that are directly analogous to the major Chantway structure. The events of twelve days are chronicled, and each of these is divided into subsections that consist of flashbacks, events of that day in the past, and events surrounding the main action on that day.

According to Leland C. Wyman [in his 1975 *Beautyway: A Navajo Ceremonial*], there are ten or twelve more-or-less standard rituals within a major Chantway. These can vary with circumstances and the particular Chantway selected for healing the particular illness troubling the patient. The major variants which appear in *House Made of Dawn* include the consecration of the hogan (which does not appear in the novel until Abel returns home), a short singing, a setting-out of prayer offerings, a purification, an offering ceremony (to attract the Holy People), a cleansing, an all-night singing, a shock rite, blackening and ash-blowing, and the final dawn procedure. A feature of a healing is that various ceremonies may be tried experimentally; it seems that this may be the case with Abel. Another practice of note is the fact that the completion of a ceremonial healing may be delayed for years. Not surprisingly within a Native American framework seven years pass as Abel seeks his appropriate ceremonial and is finally healed.

In addition to the ceremonial structure, there is a layer-structure that is Pueblo at the deepest layer, Christian at the next layer, and modern Anglo at the topmost layer. Or, to phrase it another way, the book at its most superficial layer is about a displaced Indian caught between the old and the new; it is, in that sense, a sociological novel. In its middle layer it is concerned with religious conflict, that conflict which began with the first Franciscan missionaries in the Southwest and continues on to the present in the person of John Big Bluff Tosamah, missionary and Priest of the Sun. Its deepest layer is Indian: the tradition, the knowledge, the deep values of the Indian on a continent whose land and creatures are also Indian, but whose surface has been overlaid with a thin epidermis of European society. In its branching and circularity, the novel operates structurally in a way similar to the Navajo Chantway system, and in its careful divisioning it follows the number structure of 4-7-6 and 12, which are the major ceremonial numbers of the American Indian and are the classic divisions of a major chantway. . . .

As the mythic structure of *Moby Dick* is the Bible, so the mythic structure of *House Made of Dawn* is Beautyway and Night Chant. As there are departures from the source in the former, so there are departures from the text in the latter. This is the nature of continuity: to bring those structures and symbols which retain their essential meaning forward into a changed context in such a way that the metaphysical point remains true, in spite of apparently changed circumstances. It is, perhaps, a manifestation of that law which demands that literature have a quality that appeals to humankind universally: Surely there is no more universal a theme than that of the play between good and evil, and no more universal a plot than the part humanity plays in the balance between them. There are those laws of our being which are always true; there are those processes common to humankind which always occur. It is this fact of commonality which allows a Kiowa to read and understand *Moby Dick,* given appropriate references, and which allows a New Englander, also appropriately guided, to read and understand *House Made of Dawn.*

The exchange between good and evil is not to be understood in the context of *House Made of Dawn* as it is understood in the context of Christian cosmology. It is the understanding that evil is an unavoidable aspect of the universe which finally allows Abel to begin his return to wholeness and to his proper place in things. It is the way of the Christian to oppose evil, and this Abel attempts to do. But it wounds him, like the arms of the dying witch, "only in proportion as Abel resisted."

Abel had thought that he could leave the pueblo and get a job, but he did not reckon with universal processes. Angela St. John was to help him get a job, but then, according to what he'd told Benally, "he got himself in trouble." The dream of the modern world was not for Abel, for it was his part to be Monster Slayer and, in his own time, to bring the people to a new world. The story, in its mythic dimension, began with Francisco—perhaps it began before Francisco, with the coming of the Bahkyush to Walatowa. Perhaps it began with the European invasion. But it was Francisco who slept with the daughter of a witch, and who abandoned her after their child was still-born. And because of his perfidy and fear, Porcingula's mother (the old Pecos *bruja*) cursed Abel. In the pueblo, witches traditionally transform themselves into snakes (or snakes turn themselves into humans for the purpose of witchcraft), and after the little boy is cursed by the Bahkyush bruja known as Nicolás *teah-qhau,* and runs, he hears a certain sound: the wind whistling around a snake hole, "and it filled him with dread. For the rest of his life it would be for him the particular sound of anguish." Indeed, for the rest of his life, as it is known to us through the novel, he would bear that curse; he would kill a snake and in turn be mortally wounded by another, the *culebra* Martinez in Los Angeles. Yet, had it not been for the curse and for his encounters with evil, had it not been that within his own person, perhaps because of that curse, he contained the

contrary principles of light and darkness, Abel could not have made that final run and delivered that final blessing to himself and his people. Abel, like his grandfather Francisco, is a *brujo* himself, and so he recognizes evil. He is Snake Man and he is Bear Man. At some level, he is also Monster Slayer, prototypical hero of the Navajo. He is, like his grandfather, kin to those spirits who must run forever, keeping evil in its place. In order to do this he must first come to terms with the enormity of the thing; he must, like his grandfather, acknowledge that "evil had long since found him out and knew who he was."

The idea embodied here is perhaps strange to the Westerner. It is presumed that the forces of good are separate from the forces of evil, and the universe is conceived as a dualistic structure forever at war with itself. And so Abel perceives it, or tries to, and Tosamah perceives it so as well. But the point that is being made is that such a concept is not so: The old priest learns this, and through his journals, so does Father Olguin, who considers Fray Nicolás a saint—perhaps because the old priest was more like Francisco than like those with pious fantasies of sanctity being that condition untainted by any form of sin or evil.

The interplay between the dual forces of good and evil in this system must be recognized. It is not for human beings to attempt to annihilate either force; it might be said that it is our destiny to be forever manifesting one or the other, until we can locate the balance between them. This balance is located for Pueblos in the House of the Sun, at the mid-point of the northern and southern poles of its journey. "Just there at the saddle, where the sky is lower and brighter than elsewhere on the high black land" is the position that signals the time to clear the ditches and the "long race of the black men at dawn." The House of the Sun, which is a feature of every pueblo, is the calendar which allows the people to locate their own equilibrium in the continuous interplay of the forces of the universe; it is the ceremonial timepiece which allows a person to know "who and what and *that* they are."

The essential nature of pueblo life is its mysteriousness. The central issue of pueblo belief is growth and transformation; the belief in spirit is strong among them, and their life is a matter of locating the mortal being in spirit. This is not a factor of historicity, nor is it a matter of linear chronology. There is, for each individual, a perfect moment when the balance of mortal and spirit is achieved, though this moment occurs at a different point in the life of each person. Francisco achieved his perfect moment when he was a young man. He played the drum during the clan dance for the first time; he changed drums without missing a beat: "there had been nothing of time lost, no miss in the motion or the mind . . . and it was perfect." Afterward, the women came out and distributed food among the assembled people "in celebration of his perfect act. And from then on he had a voice in the clan, and the next year he healed a child who had been sick from birth."

In some sense, all the stories of the pueblo are about the ways in which that perfect act is achieved. The ways are different as the individuals are different; in that sense, *House Made of Dawn* is in the long tradition of the people, for it is a story about how a modern Indian locates his being within the center of all things, and achieves that equilibrium which is beyond words and thought.

But Abel is sick, disequilibrated; in order for him to discover himself balanced in the universe of being, he must be healed. The Navajo elements of the story are the healing elements, and the events which Abel experiences are analogous to those commonly experienced by those who have been wounded or cursed as they make their journey toward wholeness. For wholeness is the essential nature of healing: One who is whole is healed; one who is whole is holy.

Abel's trials are in the nature of the testing which the protagonist of the Chantway undergoes. Abel is subjected to at least eight such tests, and . . . he disobeys prohibitions established by the Holy People and gets himself into trouble. But, by this disobedience, Abel, like the Chantway protagonists, is taught the ceremonial which will be brought back to the people item by item.

What penetrates Abel's consciousness during those final brutal weeks in Los Angeles is the song Benally sings. For him, thoughts of home, the music, the stories, are the only comfort he finds; not even Milly can reach across the barriers of his isolation after he has been wounded by Tosamah, and by Martinez. Benally narrates his account: "House made of dawn. I used to tell him about those old ways, the stories and the sings, Beautyway and Night Chant. I sang some of those things, and I told him what they meant, what I thought they were about."

The prime feature of Navajo life is the healing. Singers devote many years to learning one Chantway perfectly. The ceremonies are handed down in the traditional way, but must be learned and paid for by the apprentice before he can practice independently. The Navajo may be the finest healers in the world; certainly, their Chantway system is one of the more complex metaphysical systems, made even more so by its relationship to Pueblo ceremonialism. The two are related, vaguely, as are Abel and Benally, who says "We're related somehow, I think. The Navajos have a clan they call by the name of that place." This relationship is an old one. It goes way back in time, beyond the coming of the Spaniards, and is as complicated in its interworkings as the Chantway system itself. The relationship is important, for clansmen have a tighter bond than might be supposed, and this bond is of more Spirit than of earth. For clanspeople derive from the same mythic, the same archetypal source; their power and their consciousness are more closely attuned, because of their common source, than are those of many blood relatives. Then, too, Benally is a deeply traditional person himself; he'd have to be since he is able to sing parts of the Chantways and talk about what they mean. Benally is not a singer, but he is as much of one as Abel is of a priest when they meet—he is as much of one as many modern Indians will ever be, and it is enough. For through the power of his song, Abel survives the worst beating Benally has ever seen and returns to Walatowa to spend the seven days of Francisco's dying with him. After preparing the old man for burial, Abel takes up his place; running into the dawn, he performs his own perfect act of pure balance, and learns the true meaning of the songs:

He was alone and running on. All of his being was concentrated in the sheer motion of running on, and he was past caring about the pain. Pure exhaustion laid hold of his mind, and he could see at last without having to think. . . . He was running, and under his breath he began to sing. There was no sound, and he had no voice; he had only the words of a song. And he went running on the rise of the song. *House made of pollen, house made of dawn.*

So Abel finds himself healed, and in the recovery of his primal completeness he sings the chant to the sun, in the dawn light, which is sung by one who is healed.

The ceremonial is the means of achieving wholeness of being; it is the vehicle of the imagination which allows the human being to imagine himself fully—outside the bounds of social concerns, and beyond the constraints of physical imperatives. It is that part or function of consciousness where the Spirit and the Human meet and merge and become one, and it is beyond history or time as it is far from the narrow confines of pure reason. . . . The narrative concerning his journey toward the center of his being is analogous to the narratives connected to the Chantways and the ceremonial narratives of the Pueblo, in which the significance of events is embodied and transmitted. It is this process of working events into meaning which makes them true—more true, perhaps, than they would have been otherwise.

FURTHER READING

Biography

Trimble, Martha Scott. "N. Scott Momaday (1934-)." In *Fifty Western Writers: A Bio-Bibliographical Sourcebook,* edited by Fred Erisman and Richard W. Etulain, pp. 313-24. Westport, Conn.: Greenwood Press, 1982.

> Provides an overview of Momaday's life, a discussion of the major themes of his works, critical reception of his writings, and a listing of primary and secondary sources.

Criticism

Antell, Judith A. "Momaday, Welch, and Silko: Expressing the Feminine Principle through Male Alienation." *The American Indian Quarterly* XII, No. 3 (Summer 1988): 213-20.

> Examines Momaday's *House Made of Dawn,* James Welch's *The Death of Jim Loney,* and Leslie Marmon Silko's *Ceremony,* arguing that their treatment of the alienated Native American male underscores the role and power of Native American women in tribal communities.

Lincoln, Kenneth. "Comic Accommodations: Momaday and Norman." In his *Indi'n Humor: Bicultural Play in Native America,* pp. 280-308. New York: Oxford University Press, 1993.

> Discusses Momaday's use of humor, irony, caricature, and the Trickster figure in *House Made of Dawn.* This chapter also includes an examination of these and simi-

lar elements in Howard Norman's novel *The Northern Lights.*

Scarberry-García, Susan. *Landmarks of Healing: A Study of "House Made of Dawn."* Albuquerque: University of New Mexico Press, 1990, 208 p.

Provides essays on the motif of the twin, animal imagery, Native myths, and the theme of healing as presented in *House Made of Dawn.* The critic notes: "This study attempts to interpret the dialectical relationship between the text and the cultural worlds that engendered the text by examining the ethnographic record as it pertains to Navajo, Pueblo, and Kiowa events in the novel."

Additional coverage of Momaday's life and career is contained in the following sources published by Gale Research: *Authors & Artists for Young Adults,* **Vol. 11;** *Contemporary Authors,* **Vols. 25-28 (rev. ed.);** *Contemporary Authors New Revisions Series,* **Vols. 14, 34;** *Contemporary Literary Criticism,* **Vols. 2, 19, 85;** *DISCovering Authors; Major 20th-Century Writers; Native North American Literature;* **and** *Something about the Author,* **Vols. 30, 48.**

Alice Munro

1931-

(Born Alice Laidlaw) Canadian short story writer and essayist.

The following entry provides an overview of Munro's career from 1980-1995. For further information on her life and works, see *CLC,* Volumes 6, 10, 19, and 50.

INTRODUCTION

Munro is one of Canada's most critically acclaimed contemporary authors. Often referred to as a regional writer because her fiction frequently centers on the culture of rural Ontario, Munro credits the short story writers of the American South, particularly Eudora Welty and Flannery O'Connor, with shaping her fictional perspective. In Munro's works the mundane is juxtaposed with the fantastic, and she often relies on paradox and irony to expose meanings that lie beneath the surface of commonplace occurrences. Munro acknowledges the autobiographical influences on many of her stories, which are most often framed as episodic recollections that chronicle the emotional development of adolescent and adult female characters. Although some critics regard her collections as loosely structured novels, Munro insists they are short stories. Munro's first collection, *Dance of the Happy Shades* (1968), as well as two subsequent collections, *Who Do You Think You Are?* (1978) and *The Progress of Love* (1986), won Governor General's Literary Awards. It was her second book, however, *Lives of Girls and Women* (1971), that established her as a prominent figure in contemporary Canadian literature.

Biographical Information

Munro grew up on the outskirts of Wingham, Ontario, where her family struggled to maintain a decent living from her father's silver fox farm. She characterizes this locale as belonging neither to the town nor the outlying rural communities, and critics note that Munro sets many of her stories in similarly ambiguous areas. Munro was a diligent student and earned a scholarship to the University of Western Ontario in 1949. Married two years later, she moved with her husband to British Columbia where she concentrated on raising a family. Motivated by what she calls a personal selfishness and toughness, she compiled the stories that constitute *Dance of the Happy Shades* over a twelve-year period. In the early 1970s after her marriage had dissolved, Munro accepted a position as writer-in-residence at the University of Western Ontario and a few years later moved to Clinton, Ontario, a few miles from her childhood home of Wingham, with her second husband. That same year some of her stories were accepted by *The New Yorker,* beginning her long association with the magazine as a regular contributor. Between 1979 and 1982 Munro toured extensively in Australia, China, and

Scandinavia. In 1986 she received the first Marian Engel Award, given to a woman writer for an outstanding body of work, and in 1990 she won the Canada Council Molson prize for her "outstanding lifetime contribution to the cultural and intellectual life of Canada."

Major Works

The fifteen stories in Munro's first book, *Dance of the Happy Shades,* explore the personal isolation that fear, ridicule, and the inability to communicate often impose. Critics note that Munro's consistent focus on social and personal divisions provides the collection with an ironic thematic unity. In several stories Munro examines the segregation of a town's misfits. She often creates characters who initially seem certain of their identities but who gradually begin to question the basic assumptions under which they live. The title story, "Dance of the Happy Shades," for instance, centers on an annual piano recital in which a group of retarded children are silently feared and ridiculed by mothers of the "normal" students. The story ends with an exceptional performance by a retarded girl that leaves the mothers stunned and uncomfortably impressed by her talent. In this piece, as in many of her short stories, Munro explores the sources of social inhibitions and exposes the insecurities of self-righteous and self-centered characters. Other stories in the collection are "coming-of-age" tales. In "Images," a young girl and her father meet an axe-wielding recluse in the woods. The girl establishes a bond with her father when she agrees not to tell anyone about the stranger's axe. In the end, however, she realizes that she too is "[like] the children in fairy stories who have seen their parents make pacts with terrifying strangers, who have discovered that our fears are based on nothing but the truth. . . ." The stories in *Lives of Girls and Women* and *Who Do You Think You Are?* are similar in their depictions of the development of their central characters, and for this reason are often referred to as "open-form" novels. In the former, Munro focuses on specific experiences that affect protagonist Del Jordan's perceptions of her changing environment. Critics have compared *Lives of Girls and Women* to James Joyce's *künstlerroman Portrait of the Artist as a Young Man* (1916), for Munro's portrayal of Del as an alienated and misunderstood artist is akin to Joyce's portrait of Stephen Dedalus. In this work's opening piece, "The Flats Road," Munro compares Del's adolescent perception of reality to that of her Uncle Benny, whose vision of life is overly influenced by the irrational ideals of his childhood. Although Del is young, she recognizes that her Uncle's behavior is abnormal, and she gradually becomes aware that his freedom and playfulness are fragile, sensing that they are continually threatened by the workings of everyday reality. By the story's end, Del attempts to write about her experiences and hometown but feels that her understanding has been limited by the entrapping and demanding nature of adult life. Like *Lives of Girls and Women, Who Do You Think You Are?* focuses on moments of confrontation in the protagonist's life. Although many commentators treat the work as a novel, Munro refers to it as a collection of "linked stories" that deal with the maturation of the central character, Rose. Critics note the prevailing depressive quality of the stories in *Who Do You Think You Are?* and comment on Munro's harsh depictions of Rose's relationships with men. While the abrupt time shifts and overlapping experiences in this work provide a multifaceted characterization of Rose, some critics have suggested that the cool objectivity of the third person narrative undermines the authenticity of the characters. Munro's other collections have also received widespread critical attention. *Something I've Been Meaning to Tell You* (1974), *The Moons of Jupiter* (1982), *The Progress of Love,* and *Friend of My Youth* (1990), focus on the lives of mature characters and deal primarily with adult themes. Again in these collections Munro uses irony to create an overriding sense of uncertainty and insecurity in her characters. While some critics claim that these collections lack the vitality of her earlier works, others praise Munro's ability to reveal the subtleties and dynamics of adult relationships.

Critical Reception

Many critics echo the sentiments of Catherine Sheldrick who states that the stories of Alice Munro present "ordinary experiences so that they appear extraordinary, invested with a kind of magic." It is this emphasis on the seemingly mundane progression of female lives that prompted Ted Solataroff to call Munro a "great stylist of 1920's realism, a Katherine Anne Porter brought up to date." Similarly, Joyce Carol Oates finds "the evocation of emotions, ranging from bitter hatred to love, from bewilderment and resentment to awe . . . [in] an effortless, almost conversational tone" evidence that "we are in the presence of an art that works to conceal itself, in order to celebrate its subject." Occasionally faulted for limiting herself to a narrow thematic range, Munro is, nevertheless, widely regarded as a gifted short story writer whose strength lies in her ability to present the texture of everyday life with both compassion and unyielding precision.

PRINCIPAL WORKS

Dance of the Happy Shades   (short stories)   1968
Lives of Girls and Women   (short stories)   1971
Something I've Been Meaning to Tell You: Thirteen Stories
    (short stories)   1974
Who Do You Think You Are?   (short stories)   1978; also
    published as *The Beggar Maid: Stories of Flo and
    Rose,* 1979
The Moons of Jupiter   (short stories)   1982
The Progress of Love   (short stories)   1986
Friend of My Youth   (short stories)   1990
Open Secrets   (short stories)   1994

CRITICISM

Helen Hoy   (essay date Spring 1980)

SOURCE: " 'Dull, Simple, Amazing and Unfathomable': Paradox and Double Vision in Alice Munro's Fiction," in *Studies in Canadian Literature,* Vol. 5, No. 1, Spring, 1980, pp. 100-15.

[*In the following essay, Hoy discusses the paradoxical elements of Munro's fiction.*]

> *Royal Beating*. That was Flo's promise. You are going to get one Royal Beating.
>
> The word Royal lolled on Flo's tongue, took on trappings. Rose had a need to picture things, to pursue absurdities, that was stronger than the need to stay out of trouble, and instead of taking this threat to heart she pondered: how is a beating royal?

In this delight in language and exuberant pursuit of absurdities despite ensuing complications, Rose reveals herself, in Alice Munro's latest work *Who Do You Think You Are?,* to be very much a child of the author herself. Munro's own sensitivity to individual words and images, her spare lucid style, and command of detail have given her fiction a precision which is one of her most distinctive accomplishments. What an examination of the texture of her prose reveals, in particular, is the centrality of paradox and the ironic juxtaposition of apparently incompatible terms or judgements: "ironic and serious at the same time," "mottoes of godliness and honor and flaming bigotry," "special, useless knowledge," "tones of shrill and happy outrage," "the bad taste, the heartlessness, the joy of it." This stylistic characteristic is closely related to the juxtaposition, in the action, of the fantastic and the ordinary, her use of each to undercut the other. So, sensational revelations of evil in pulp newspapers which leave young Del Jordan reeling, bloated, and giddy must give way to the pale chipped brick, hanging washtubs, and brown-spotted lilac bush of her home, while, by contrast, an unwelcome, retarded cousin, Mary Agnes, is revealed, in her enigmatic, daring and composed touching of a dead cow's eye, to have unexpected mystery and secrets of her own. The linking of incongruities in language or action, however, is more than a stylistic technique or fictional quirk. It reflects Munro's larger vision, one which underlies all her fiction and which emerges as a central theme in *Lives of Girls and Women* and in several of the short stories in *Dance of the Happy Shades* and *Something I've Been Meaning To Tell You*. Paradox helps sustain Munro's thematic insistence on the doubleness of reality, the illusoriness of either the prosaic or the marvellous in isolation.

The freshness of language and image, which is Munro's great strength, she herself explains in an interview with Graeme Gibson: "I'm not an intellectual writer. I'm very, very excited by what you might call the surface of life, and it must be that this seems to me very meaningful in a way I can't analyze or describe. . . . It seems to me very important to be able to get at the exact tone or texture of how things are." This impulse she, of course, embodies in *Lives of Girls and Women* in Del Jordan who, as a maturing writer, attempts to pin her town to paper and realizes,

> "no list could hold what I wanted, for what I wanted was every last thing, every layer of speech and thought, stroke of light on bark or walls, every smell, pothole, pain, crack, delusion, held still and held together—radiant, everlasting.

The last words hold the clue to Del's, and Munro's obsession with external realities: it is an obsession which Munro, in her interview with Gibson, says can best be compared to a religious feeling about the world. So too when another interviewer John Metcalf asks perceptively whether she glories in surfaces because she feels them not to be surfaces, she agrees, adding, "It's just a feeling about the intensity of what is *there*." In the struggle to capture this intensity about very ordinary things, paradox not surprisingly becomes one of Munro's most important tools.

Sometimes this persistent "balance or reconcilement of opposites or discordant qualities" (to echo Coleridge's celebrated definition of the imagination) occurs almost in passing as an unobtrusive feature of Munro's style, in her description, for instance, of the way children whimper monotonously "to *celebrate* a hurt" (italics mine). Often, though, the inherent contradictions in people and situations are more explicitly confronted. Paradox becomes Munro's means of capturing complex human characteris-

tics whether wittily as in the description of successful academics as "such brilliant, such talented incapable men" or more seriously, gropingly as in Del's discussion of an egotism women feel in men, something "tender, swollen, tyrannical, absurd". In an attempt, in **"Dance of the Happy Shades,"** to convey the reality of the Marsalles sisters, "sexless, wild and gentle creatures, bizarre yet domestic," Munro extends paradox into physical description itself, characterizing both as having kindly, grotesque faces, and eyes which are at the same time tiny, red, short-sighted, and sweet-tempered. The same incongruities multiply in the world encompassing Munro's characters. A housewife and writer finds herself sheltered and encumbered, warmed and bound by her home; a growing girl is both absolved and dismissed by her father's causal acceptance of her moment of rebellion; the struggle of wills between an amateur hypnotist and a stubborn old woman ends with her "dead, and what was more, victorious"; a teenage girl feels that her mother's concern creates for her an oppressive obligation to be happy, as another feels that her mother loves her but is also her enemy; a maiden aunt, stumbling on her niece and a lover naked and passionate, perceives them as strange and familiar, both more and less than themselves. A character's feelings for her relatives are described as "irritable . . . bonds of sympathy," a writer's techniques as "Lovely tricks, honest tricks". In these examples as in many, Munro employs not an elaborated paradoxical statement but a more concentrated phrase, an oxymoron, most often in the form of two parallel but incompatible verbs or adjectives. The startling fusion of warring terms gives to her style at its best a denseness and precision characteristic of poetry.

Paradox is most prominent in the fiction's portrayal of human character and emotional reaction. At times this is simply a means of suggesting inconsistencies, variations over time, as in Del's discovery (in contrast with her youthful belief in the absolute finality of some quarrels) that people can feel murderous disillusionment and hate, then go on to love again. More often, Munro explores the emotional contradictions persisting side by side in time. A character in **"Tell Me Yes or No"** not only expects her lover, like a knight, to be capable alternately of "acts of outmoded self-sacrifice and also of marvellous brutality," she also goes on to describe him as *simultaneously* mild and inflexible. Paradox, therefore, is frequently an admirable means of conveying the intense emotional ambivalence of adolescence: in response to an example of purely decorative femininity, for example, Del reveals, "I thought she was an idiot, and yet I frantically admired her". She finds the idea of sex totally funny and totally revolting, hopes and fears she will be overheard shouting the forbidden word "bugger," and later is both relieved and desolate at the loss of her lover Gamet. In the same way, of other adolescent girls, we are told that "any title with the word popularity in it could both chill and compel me," that "she was quivering . . . with pride, shame, boldness, and exhilaration" (note how "shame" here is even flanked by two differing contraries), and that the pregnancy and marriage of a friend "made me both envious and appalled". (In the last example, the friend herself is concomitantly characterized as "abashed and proud.") Lest we conclude, however, that Munro is mainly recording the confusions of youth, we might note that almost the same formula is applied to an adult woman, in her response to some men's invulnerability: "I envy and despise". Rose's friend Clifford argues that his marital dissatisfaction is not simply a change of heart over time, informing his wife, "I wanted to be married to you and I want to be married to you and I couldn't stand being married to you and I can't stand being married to you. It's a static contradiction".

In fact, the matter-of-fact union of incompatible tendencies is Munro's means of bringing life, precision, and complexity to her depiction of emotions generally. Occasionally, as in the example just given, she actually acknowledges and spells out the paradoxical nature of such feelings: "They [Del's aunts] respected men's work beyond anything; they also laughed at it. This was strange; they could believe absolutely in its importance and at the same time convey their judgement that it was, from one point of view, frivolous, non-essential". (Compare this incidentally with a later character's mingling of "flattery and a delicate sort of contempt" in her conversation with a man). Similarly the reader is deliberately drawn into a contemplation of the paradoxical quality of Milton Homer's unsocialized behaviour in *Who Do You Think You Are?* as the narrator, describing his goggling, leering expressions as both boldly calculating and helpless, involuntary, asks if such a thing is possible. More often, we simply have subtle touches in the portrayal of characters, even minor characters—a landlord with an "affable, predatory expression," an aunt "flashing malice and kindness," a grandmother whose renunciation of love is a "self-glorifying dangerous self-denying passion," the same grandmother predicting problems with "annoyance and satisfaction," an unhappy lover bound by rules "meaningless and absolute." The same duality is found on a larger scale with more central characters too, like the pathetic heroine of **"Thanks for the Ride,"** whose combination of defiance and need, scorn and acquiescence is summed up in the final sound of her voice, "abusive and forlorn".

At one point in *Lives of Girls and Women,* Del somewhat ironically characterizes the Anglican liturgy as presenting "lively emotion *safely* contained in the most *elegant* channels of language" (italics mine). In contrast to this, Munro's own technique, rather than using language to defuse emotion, creates a resonance or current, releases an intensity through the juxtaposition of oppositely charged words or ideas. The effect is not a wild splattering of emotion—in the careful precision of Munro's language, and a certain intellectual detachment as well, there is some of the control attributed here to the liturgical ritual—but it is controlled *energy,* a galvanic interaction between the poles of the paradox rather than a safe elegance. Through the originality not of craziness but of unexpected revelation, Munro's oxymorons have something of the same vitality as the bizarre childhood rhyme about fried Vancouvers and pickled arseholes, which so pleases Rose for what she calls "The tumble of reason; the spark and spit of craziness".

So positive emotions are unexpectedly qualified—"heartless applause," "smiling angrily," "hungry laughter," "accusing vulnerability," "aggressive bright spirits";

negative ones are similarly—"tender pain," "semitolerant contempt," "happy outrage," "terrible tender revenge"; and even an epithet like absurd, which might seem sweeping and inarguably dismissive, must coexist with its opposite: Del's mother in her youthful enthusiasm is "absurd and unassailable," Del, naked, feels "absurd and dazzling," and a boy reassures a drunken girl, with "a very stupid, half-sick, absurd and alarming expression." While such pairings can sometimes become automatic or mechanical in Munro's writing, most often the originality of the details produces a slight, revelatory wrenching of assumptions and perspective.

We should note that the effect of paradox in Munro is never to invalidate, rarely even to diminish either of the contradictory impulses. Characteristically, in fact, she employs the unifying conjunction "and," disregarding for her purposes conjunctions of limitation or concession. As Cleanth Brooks says of the technique in poetry, the ironic or paradoxical union of opposites "is not that of a prudent splitting of the difference between antithetical overemphases." So, Del in ignoring her aunts' dreams feels "that kind of tender remorse which has as its other side a brutal, *unblemished* satisfaction," quotes sentimental poetry "with absolute sincerity, absolute irony," and comments explicitly about her youthful curiosity over sex, "Disgust did not rule out enjoyment, in my thoughts; indeed they were inseparable" (italics mine). The contradictory emotions retain their individual intensity.

In her examination of human inconsistency, Munro presents the contradictions not only within emotions but also between emotion and behaviour. Again there is often little attempt to reduce the inconsistency or explain why actions defy their motivations; the two conflicting realities are simply juxtaposed—"The thought of intimacies with Jerry Storey was offensive in itself. Which did not mean that they did not, occasionally, take place," "The ritual of walking up and down the street to show ourselves off we thought crude and ridiculous, though we could not resist it," "not bothering to shake off our enmity, nor thinking how the one thing could give way to the other, we kissed'. At times, in fact, Munro actually uses human perverseness itself as the explanation for behaviour, in identifying the "aphrodisiac prickles of disgust" in the appeal of the idiotic saintly whore or the perversely appealing lack of handsomeness of the lecherous minister Rose encounters. Faced with an invitation to sneak away to a dance, Del feels paradoxically, "I had no choice but to do this . . . because I truly hated and feared the Gay-la Dance Hall."

The unexpected challenge to common assumptions which is the source of such paradoxes' power need not always be spelled out. The same shock of recognition, Coleridge's union of "the sense of novelty and freshness, with old and familiar objects," is achieved when, for instance, Del's mother's radical defence of women's independence is described unexpectedly as innocent in its assumption of women's damageability, when Del comments on the concealed jubilation and eagerness to cause pain in parents' revelations of unpleasant realities, when the narrator of **"Shining Houses"** makes a matter-of-fact, parenthetical reference to the way people admire each other for being drunk, or when Rose reveals that outspoken hostility does not pose the threat to one of her friendships which genteel tact would. The freshness of perception which Alice Munro brings to very familiar situations lends itself to the creation of observations such as these which remain startling, although the underlying paradox is never articulated.

Indeed Munro sometimes even seems to go through an initial process of making the strange familiar so that she can then go on paradoxically to justify the originally familiar (but now strange) as also possible. An interesting example of this occurs in *Who Do You Think You Are?* in Rose's analysis of her reconciliation with Patrick, her fiancé. Disregarding any immediate, popular explanations like romantic love (and through silence apparently dismissing them as naïve), Munro accustoms the reader to more sophisticated, sceptical analysis by consideration of such similarly complex motivations as comradely compassion, emotional greed, economic cowardice, and vanity (with only subtle hints of glibness). Only then, ironically, does she reveal Rose's secret explanation, which Rose has never confided and which she cannot justify, namely that she may have been motivated, oddly enough, by a vision of happiness. The paradoxical revelation of unacknowledged, even denied, but recognizable aspects of human behaviour has, in the context of worldly characters and readers, been taken a step further here and turned on itself. Having directed attention towards less obvious explanations of behaviour, Munro then revitalizes from a new perspective a vision of innocence and good will which has paradoxically become unexpected.

Verbal paradox, however, particularly cryptic oxymoron, remains a more distinctive feature of Munro's style, and, as many of the examples already cited suggest, functions particularly as a means of definition, of zeroing in on the individual qualities of an emotion or moment. More than evocativeness, it is precision which she seeks in the description of "a great unemotional happiness," "sophisticated prudery," or a character "kind but not compassionate." In light of Munro's love for clear images and her insistence on her inability to put characters in a room without describing all the furniture, it is interesting that many of these paradoxes involve abstract not concrete language (an aspect of her style easily overlooked). It is the exactness and poetic explosiveness of the internal contradiction which give them their vividness. Admiring the discontinuities of modern experimental prose, Munro has complained that her writing tends "to fill everything in, to be pretty wordy." As this discussion suggests, however, while within a traditional narrative form and concerned with articulating rather than simply suggesting, her use of language generally is not discursive or rambling, but tight, economical, exact.

Paradox for Alice Munro, at the same time, is more than simply a means of definition and a stylistic tool for clarity; it reflects her vision of the complexity of human emotion, as we have seen, and of the human situation more generally. Munro defines writing itself as "a straining of something immense and varied, a whole dense vision of the world, into whatever confines the writer has learned to

make for it." In the short story, **"Something I've Been Meaning to Tell You,"** the protagonist Et is disgruntled to discover that her sister, bad-tempered and hot amid the steam and commotion of washday, is at the same time classically beautiful, "that the qualities of legend were real, that they surfaced where and when you least expected". Et's disgruntlement, we are told, occurs because she dislikes contradictions or things out of place; the implication is that she is rejecting reality, which Munro characterizes as inherently contradictory. Among the contradictions of existence, one of the most fundamental in the author's eyes is that of the coexistence of the ordinary and the mysterious, seen in this example and spelled out in some of Munro's oxymorons. So the fiction speaks of the "open and secret pattern" of the town Jubilee, the smoky colour of a sweater "so ordinary, reticent, and mysterious," and the "terrible ordinary cities" of Uncle Benny's experience. (Compare, incidentally, a similar insistence on "the poetry and wonder which might reveal themselves in the dunghill, and. . . . the dunghill that lurks in poetry and wonder" in the work of Robertson Davies, an insistence I have discussed elsewhere. The comparison is illustrative. Although Davies takes care in his fiction to root the marvellous in the commonplace, he nevertheless suggests a romantic world of good and evil found within and yet transcending everyday reality. For Munro, on the other hand, everyday existence reveals nothing beyond itself but is simply marvellous in itself. Notice in the interview with Metcalf, cited above, Munro's conclusion that, for her, surfaces are not surfaces; this formulation avoids the dualistic argument that surfaces are not *merely* surfaces.) The exploration of the prosaic and the marvellous runs through Munro's fiction, is developed most extensively in *Lives of Girls and Women,* and becomes more complex and ambiguous in *Who Do You Think You Are?*

Among the contradiction of existence, one of the most fundamental in the author's eyes is that of the coexistence of the ordinary and the mysterious.

—Helen Hoy

Not surprisingly in light of Munro's fascination with tangible reality, discussed above, her fiction challenges romanticism which ignores the commonplace. A character warns, "Life is not like the dim ironic stories I like to read, it is like a daytime serial on television. The banality will make you weep as much as anything else", while another, introduced to her mother's childhood home, experiences the disappointment of confronting "this source of legends, the unsatisfactory, apologetic and persistent reality". In *Who Do You Think You Are?* the reality of harmless, malicious, eccentric Becky Tyde contradicts her extravagant role in town tales of beatings, incest, infanticide, and Rose from her own experience challenges male fictional versions of the idiotic saintly whore for their omission of drooling, protruding teeth, and phlegmy breathing. This is not a reductive elimination of imagination, but a re-establishment of balance, as are the contrasting revelations of fantastic elements, like the mystery of Et's sister's beauty, in apparently ordinary experiences. In the fiction, the extravagant and the unimaginative stand in relation to each other in much the same way as do incompatible social realities in *Who Do You Think You Are?*: "What Dr. Henshaw's house and Flo's house did best, in Rose's opinion, was discredit each other. In Dr. Henshaw's charming rooms there was always for Rose the raw knowledge of home, an indigestible lump, and at home, now, her sense of order and modulation elsewhere exposed such embarrassing sad poverty". The ultimate reality revealed is a paradoxical mixture of both. As Alva concludes at the end of **"Sunday Afternoon,"** when she discovers a new excitement and power but also a new mysterious humiliation in her sexual attractiveness to her employers' friends, "things always came together".

The basic thrust of the short story **"Dance of the Happy Shades,"** for example, is the confrontation, through the exquisite piano-playing of a retarded girl, between the pragmatism of "people who live in the world" and the casual acceptance of miracles of a pathetic old piano teacher, Miss Marsalles. Although the emphasis of the story, narrated from a commonsense viewpoint, is on the momentary revelation provided by this "one communiqué from the other country where [Miss Marsalles] lives," neither vision triumphs. Rather, we are told that as soon as the child has finished playing, "it is plain that she is just the same as before, a girl from Greenhill School. Yet the music was not imaginary. The facts are not to be reconciled". Similarly, the portrayal of the music teacher Miss Farris in *Lives of Girls and Women,* which begins with her doll-house home apparently containing no secrets or contradictions, ends with two conflicting pictures of her, one of her absurdly naïve flamboyance around town, the other of her apparent suicide by drowning: "Though there is no plausible way of hanging those pictures together—if the last one is true then must it not alter the others? —they are going to have to stay together now". In **"Walker Brothers Cowboy,"** a child's introduction to a secret love in her father's past causes her to compare his life to an enchanted landscape, ordinary and familiar while it is observed but changing mysteriously immediately afterwards. And the short story **"Images"** is actually structured on an easy movement away from and back to unexceptional everyday existence, as a young girl is introduced to a bizarre and frightening acquaintance of her father's. Suggesting both the reality of an ever-present mythic or nightmare world and the absorption of the marvellous into daily experience, it concludes by comparing the heroine to "the children in fairy stories who have seen their parents make pacts with terrifying strangers, who have discovered that our fears are based on nothing but the truth, but who come back fresh from marvellous escapes and take up their knives and forks, with humility and good manners".

Lives of Girls and Women sets out, even more directly, to investigate the nature of reality; *Real Life,* in fact, was the original title for the book. Del Jordan's growth, besides being an examination of contrasting options available to women, is an exploration of the realities of evil, death, religion, sex, and art. In this process, a series of self-contained, often mutually exclusive worlds, both communal and individual, are played against each other and against Del's uncertain sense of "real life": the world of bizarre and inventive evil of the tabloids; Uncle Benny's helpless vision of an unpredictable and unmanageable universe; the anarchical world of boys' mysterious brutality; the sealed-off country of Aunts Elspeth and Grace with its intricate formalities and private language, set against Del's mother's world of "lumps in the mashed potatoes and unsettling ideas"; Uncle Craig's world of facts and public events; the comforting created worlds of books; the solid ground of spelling bees and arithmetic problems, and the fanciful world of the school operetta, each challenging and temporarily cancelling the other; the hothouse atmosphere of winter, encouraging daydreams, and the ordinary geography of springtime; Owen's world of intense play, pityingly contrasted by Del to her own real one; the cool ordinary light of commercial classes and unreality of more academic studies; Jerry Storey's world of science and mental gymnastics; and Naomi's "normal life" of showers, hope chests, gossip, and sexual diplomacy, contrasted with a romanticized nineteenth-century life of rectitude and maidenhood. Munro is doing more here than simply identifying differences in life-styles. These visions, internally coherent and explicitly identified as independent worlds, in most cases vie with each other for the exclusive right to define experience. In the end none has ultimate authority; each is clearly presented as *one* reality in the context of others.

The insufficiency of many of these worlds lies in their disregard for life's complexity, their allegiance to either romanticism or empiricism at the expense of the other. Del's own tendency towards undiscriminating romanticism is presented ironically, or undercut by insistent everyday realities. She is mocked for her expectation of a pure depravity in the town prostitutes, "a foul shimmer of corruption," and for her insistence on seeing the ordinary details of their lives (the newspaper, dotted curtains, geraniums in tin cans) as merely "tantalizing deception—the skin of everyday appearances stretched over such shamelessness, such consuming explosions of lust." Her night-time fantasies of Frank Wales are followed by real dreams "never so kind, but full of gritty small problems, lost socks, not being able to find the Grade Eight classroom." Irony appears even in Del's final position after ending her sexual involvement with Garnet: "Now at last without fantasies or self-deception, cut off from the mistakes and confusion of the past, grave and simple, carrying a small suitcase, getting on a bus, like girls in movies leaving home, convents, lovers, I supposed I would get started on my real life." Romanticism, though far more subtle, persists here, for her litany of alternatives, "*Garnet French. Garnet French. Garnet French./Real Life,*" involves a disregard (in one sense, at least) for the reality of her own past experience. (This concern becomes explicit in **"Forgiveness in Families"** when a character muses that everyday routines are dismissed as mere preparation for life until the fact of death gives them value.)

Again though, while romanticism is challenged, ordinary

reality is shown to contain its own mystery. Uncle Craig, in his disposable, vacated condition after death, is presented as the conductor of dangerous unknown forces which could flare up in the midst of the funeral rituals. Although the simple rowdiness of the Catholic children and shabbiness of their church fail to cohere with the sensational legends of their exotic and dangerous faith, and although Del's pursuit of a dramatic religious revelation must accommodate her need to go on living as usual with her family and her fear of literally bumping into things with her eyes closed, a spiritual reality is not discounted. Del finally asks, *"Could there be a God not contained in the churches' net . . . God real,* and really in the world, and alien and unacceptable as death? Could there be God amazing, *indifferent, beyond faith?"* (roman type mine). Munro uses Del to mock sentimental fictional accounts of sex which employ symbolism, of a train blasting through a tunnel, for instance, to evade the reality; certainly her own account of Del's loss of virginity demythologizes sexuality through a clear-eyed unromantic emphasis on the numerous factual details of painful belt buckles, aching arches, indiscreetly visible bare buttocks, and entangled underpants. Nevertheless she does not strip sex of its power and wonder, showing Del also experiencing miraculous revelations which make even the term "pleasure" explosive, and crossing over "into a country where there was perfect security, no move that would not bring delight . . . a floating feeling, feeling of being languid and protected and at the same time possessing unlimited power."

Just as death, religion, and sex reveal themselves ironically to be both more prosaic and more fantastic than at first appears, so do human beings. Del's experience of Mr. Chamberlain's masturbation undermines her expectant belief in a mad dreamlike plunge through decent appearance into absolute impersonal depravity and pure passion, revealing that "people take along a good deal—flesh that is not overcome but has to be thumped into ecstasy." Here, too, though, among the realities people take along are "all the stubborn puzzle and dark turns of themselves." Del goes through the same process, on a more sophisticated level, with Garnet. In his attempt to baptize her and force her into the mould of his world, we have a conflict between the legendary and the real, with Del realizing that she has wanted to keep him sewn up in his golden lover's skin, not wanted him out of the context of their magical game of sex, not wanted the real Garnet. Even here, however, the reality of Garnet which she must now acknowledge includes his secrets; complexities, mysteries persist even in prosaic existence.

Because the everyday world has marvels of its own, they need not be artificially imported into it. This paradoxical insistence that the truest mysteries are to be found not beyond but within the most uninspired facts, Munro underlines in the novel's final vignette, of the Sherriff family. Del's black gothic tale, her extravagant fictionalized portrayal of mad Bobby Sherriff and his sister Marion, a suicide victim, collapses in the face of the ordinariness of their home, the wicker chairs and souvenir vase, Bobby's deferential offer of cake and matter-of-fact discussion of vitamin deficiencies: "It is a shock, when you have dealt so cunningly, powerfully, with reality, to come back and find it still there." And yet that insistent reality includes the mystery of Marion's act of suicide, unillumined by the school portrait of her stubborn unrevealing face. It includes too (in place of the spectacular revelations of madness Del has been naïvely desiring) Bobby's final enigmatic gesture, a letter in an unknown alphabet, when with private amusement he rises on his toes like a plump ballerina in wishing Del luck. It is such persistent, unfanciful, yet mysterious facts which inspire Munro's most explicit formulation of the work's theme and her own paradoxical vision (a formulation, incidentally, which in the concreteness of its imagery emphasizes the power of the *ordinary*): "People's lives, in Jubilee as elsewhere, were dull, simple, amazing and unfathomable—deep caves paved with kitchen linoleum."

With *Who Do You Think You Are?,* a new ambiguity enters Munro's dialectic of the ordinary and the marvellous. The work continues the usual discounting of unenlivened empiricism: Flo's mockery of people's pretensions and diversions, her delight in seeing people brought down to earth, and her quite literal flaunting of dirty laundry are shown to be deficient, in her aggressive blindness, for instance, to the splendour as well as the inadequacy of glossy, indolent, over-weight Cora, Rose's childhood idol. Irony plays too over conventions (of Hanratty's "living link with the past" or of the saintly whore) and fantasies (Rose's childhood idol. Irony plays too of angora sweaters or vision of long-suffering care for her belligerent, aging step-mother) for their ignoring of reality. Munro continues furthermore to reveal the true sublimity of the mundane: Flo's generous performance of a difficult calisthenic feat at a moment of family tension takes on some of the luminosity of a fabulous American airship whose existence has just been discredited. (At times a darker note, found also in the earlier works, colours such revelations, as in Rose's discovery when beaten by her father that familiar witnesses, the linoleum, the kitchen calendar, the pots and pans, can participate in this grotesque act, that *"treachery* is the other side of dailiness" [italics mine].)

At the same time, distinctions between the illusory and the real have become less confident and straightforward in this work, and the focus of objections to the visionary has changed somewhat. Rose is discomfited to discover the relative accuracy of her step-mother's lurid warnings about lechers disguised as ministers; what Rose and the reader reject at first glance as evident "nonsense" becomes difficult to differentiate from actual occurrence. Rose's own dream of someone falling instantly and helplessly in love with her is discredited not because it is fanciful and impossible but because, as she discovers with Patrick, the idea of worship is preferable to the reality: "It was a miracle; it was a mistake. It was what she had dreamed of; it was not what she wanted." The incompatibility of dream and reality has become more complex, no longer simply a matter of mutually exclusive spheres. Rose's romantic involvement with Clifford alters her morning kitchen with stained coffee pot and jar of marmalade into a dazzling scene, "exploding with joy and possibility and danger." Is this an illusion or an actual transformation of reality? Irony colours her expectation of a glittering secret or a conflagration of adultery, the affair does fizzle out anticlimactically, Rose is tempted to condemn her suffering as the self-inflicted pain of ridiculed fantasy, and, in retrospect, she prefers to focus instead on "small views of lost daily life" like her daughter's yellow slicker. Yet we receive no final verdict on the substantiality of that past passion and grief, and even the narrator's tone has become more noncommittal.

The ambiguity intensifies in the depiction of Rose's encounter with Simon; although this story culminates in a familiar synthesis of the marvellous and the commonplace, the same absence of certainty in identifying idle fancy and arid materialism continues. Some of Rose's predictions about the future of this friendship—that she will persist in the "foolishness" of a miserable obsession because of intermittent "green and springlike reveries," that a return to her job will bring the shock and yet comfort of "the real world"—designate the involvement as a delusion. Its ultimate rejection though (like the rejection of Patrick's worship) is not a pragmatic if reluctant concession to probability. Fleeing involvement with Simon, Rose realizes she has been fleeing the realization of her dreams of love as much as disappointment and the collapse of dreams; whether successful or unhappy, love she believes removes the world for you. The choice seems to be between a particular material reality, represented here by the comforting solidity of thick, glass, restaurant ice-cream dishes, and another, still possible reality. Rose requires "everything to be there for her, thick and plain as ice-cream dishes" and feels that love robs you of "a private balance wheel, a little dry kernel of probity" making this awareness possible. The weight of the narration seems to come down on the side of mundane reality (lacking here, significantly, the everlasting radiance Del eventually perceives in all the small physical details of her world). This triumph of uninspired but adequate tangible reality over the marvellous which can invade but also distort the real world is not, however, the definitive conclusion of the episode. Rose's appraisal of the limiting effects of love ends with the ambiguous phrase, "So she though." Rose has fled "the celebration and shock of love, the dazzling alteration"; her subsequent startled discovery of Simon's death from cancer reveals the susceptibility even of this matter-of-fact existence to "disarrangements which . . . throw the windows open on inappropriate unforgettable scenery." Like *Lives of Girls and Women* then, *Who Do You Think You Are?* does disclose not only the importance but also the mystery of the ordinary. At the same time, the narrator here displays a greater unwillingness, even in retrospect, to make assertions about the nature of specific events, an unwillingness reflected in Rose's lingering uneasiness that in her acting and in her life, she may have been "paying attention to the wrong things, reporting antics, when there was always something further, a tone, a depth, a light, that she couldn't get."

Like her heroine Rose, caught between Patrick's contempt for her artistic friends and her friends' contempt for her reactionary husband, Munro demonstrates what is ruefully described as an ability to "see too many sides of things;" it is this complexity of vision which informs both themes and style in her fiction.

Alice Munro   (essay date September 1982)

SOURCE: "What Is Real?," in *The Canadian Forum*, Vol. LXII, No. 721, September, 1982, pp. 5, 36.

[*In the following essay, Munro explains how she writes and how reality figures into her work.*]

Whenever people get an opportunity to ask me questions about my writing, I can be sure that some of the questions asked will be these:

"Do you write about real people?"

"Did those things really happen?"

"When you write about a small town are you really writing about Wingham?" (Wingham is the small town in Ontario where I was born and grew up, and it has often been assumed, by people who should know better, that I have simply "fictionalized" this place in my work. Indeed, the local newspaper has taken me to task for making it the "butt of a soured and cruel introspection.")

The usual thing, for writers, is to regard these either as very naive questions, asked by people who really don't understand the difference between autobiography and fiction, who can't recognize the device of the first-person narrator, or else as catch-you-out questions posed by journalists who hope to stir up exactly the sort of dreary (and to outsiders, slightly comic) indignation voiced by my hometown paper. Writers answer such questions patiently or crossly according to temperament and the mood they're in. They say, no, you must understand, my characters are composites; no, those things didn't happen the way I wrote about them; of course not, that isn't Wingham (or whatever other place it may be that has had the queer unsought-after distinction of hatching a writer). Or the writer may, riskily, ask the questioners what is real, anyway? None of this seems to be very satisfactory, people go on asking these same questions because the subject really does interest and bewilder them. It would seem to be quite true that they don't know what fiction is.

And how could they know, when it is, is changing all the time, and we differ among ourselves, and we don't really try to explain because it is too difficult?

What I would like to do here is what I can't do in two or three sentences at the end of a reading. I won't try to explain what fiction is, and what short stories are (assuming, which we can't, that there is any fixed thing that it is and they are), but what short stories are to me, and how I write them, and how I use things that are "real." I will start by explaining how I read stories written by other people. For one thing, I can start reading them anywhere; from beginning to end, from end to beginning, from any point in between in either direction. So obviously I don't take up a story and follow it as if it were a road, taking me somewhere, with views and neat diversions along the way. I go into it, and move back and forth and settle here and there, and stay in it for a while. It's more like a house. Everybody knows what a house does, how it encloses space and makes connections between one enclosed space and another and presents what is outside in a new way. This is the nearest

I can come to explaining what a story does for me, and what I want my stories to do for other people.

So when I write a story I want to make a certain kind of structure, and I know the feeling I want to get from being inside that structure. This is the hard part of the explanation, where I have to use a word like "feeling," which is not very precise, because if I attempt to be more intellectually respectable I will have to be dishonest. "Feeling" will have to do.

There is no blueprint for the structure. It's not a question of, "I'll make this kind of house because if I do it right it will have this effect." I've got to make, I've got to build up, a house, a story, to fit around the indescribable "feeling" that is like the soul of the story, and which I must insist upon in a dogged, embarrassed way, as being no more definable than that. And I don't know where it comes from. It seems to be already there, and some unlikely clue, such as a shop window or a bit of conversation, makes me aware of it. Then I start accumulating the material and putting it together. Some of the material I may have lying around already, in memories and observations, and some I invent, and some I have to go diligently looking for (factual details), while some is dumped in my lap (anecdotes, bits of speech). I see how this material might go together to make the shape I need, and I try it. I keep trying and seeing where I went wrong and trying again.

> **Everybody knows what a house does, how it encloses space and makes connections between one enclosed space and another and presents what is outside in a new way. This is the nearest I can come to explaining what a story does for me.**
>
> —*Alice Munro*

I suppose this is the place where I should talk about technical problems and how I solve them. The main reason I can't is that I'm never sure I do solve anything. Even when I say that I see where I went wrong, I'm being misleading. I never figure out how I'm going to change things, I never say to myself, "That page is heavy going, that paragraph's clumsy, I need some dialogue and shorter sentences." I feel a part that's wrong, like a soggy weight; then I pay attention to the story, as if it were really happening somewhere, not just in my head, and in its own way, not mine. As a result, the sentences may indeed get shorter, there may be more dialogue, and so on. But though I've tried to pay attention to the story, I may not have got it right; those shorter sentences may be an evasion, a mistake. Every final draft, every published story, is still only an attempt, an approach, to the story.

I did promise to talk about using reality. "Why, if Jubilee isn't Wingham, has it got Shuter Street in it?" people want to know. Why have I described somebody's real ceramic elephant sitting on the mantelpiece? I could say I get mo-

mentum from doing things like this. The fictional room, town, world, needs a bit of starter dough from the real world. It's a device to help the writer—at least it helps me—but it arouses a certain baulked fury in the people who really do live on Shuter Street and the lady who owns the ceramic elephant. "Why do you put in something true and then go on and tell lies?" they say, and anybody who has been on the receiving end of this kind of thing knows how they feel.

"I do it for the sake of my art and to make this structure which encloses the soul of my story, that I've been telling you about," says the writer. "That is more important than anything."

Not to everybody, it isn't.

So I can see there might be a case, once you've written the story and got the momentum, for going back and changing the elephant to a camel (though there's always a chance the lady might complain that you made a nasty camel out of a beautiful elephant), and changing Shutter Street to Blank Street. But what about the big chunks of reality, without which your story can't exist? In the story **"Royal Beatings,"** I use a big chunk of reality: the story of the butcher, and of the young men who may have been egged on to "get" him. This is a story out of an old newspaper; it really did happen in a town I know. There is no legal difficulty about using it because it has been printed in a newspaper, and besides, the people who figure in it are all long dead. But there is a difficulty about offending people in that town who would feel that use of this story is a deliberate exposure, taunt and insult. Other people who have no connection with the real happening would say, "Why write about anything so hideous?" And lest you think that such an objection could only be raised by simple folk who read nothing but Harlequin Romances, let me tell you that one of the questions most frequently asked at universities is, "Why do you write about things that are so depressing?" People can accept almost any amount of ugliness if it is contained in a familiar formula, as it is on television, but when they come closer to their own place, their own lives, they are much offended by a lack of editing.

There are ways I can defend myself against such objections. I can say, "I do it in the interests of historical reality. That is what the old days were really like." Or, "I do it to show the dark side of human nature, the beast let loose, the evil we can run up against in communities and families." In certain countries I could say, "I do it to show how bad things were under the old system when there were prosperous butchers and young fellows hanging around livery stables and nobody thought about building a new society." But the fact is, the minute I say *to show* I am telling a lie. I don't do it to show anything. I put this story at the heart of my story because I need it there and it belongs there. It is the black room at the centre of the house with all other rooms leading to and away from it. That is all. A strange defence. Who told me to write his story? Who feels any need of it before it is written? I do. I do, so that I might grab off this piece of horrid reality and install it where I see fit, even if Hat Nettleton and his friends are still around to make me sorry.

The answer seems to be as confusing as ever. Lots of true answers are. Yes and no. Yes, I use bits of what is real, in the sense of being really there and really happening, in the world, as most people see it, and I transform it into something that is really there and really happening, in my story. No, I am not concerned with using what is real to make any sort of record or prove any sort of point, and I am not concerned with any methods of selection but my own, which I can't fully explain. This is quite presumptuous, and if writers are not allowed to be so—and quite often, in many places, they are not—I see no point in the writing of fiction.

Lorraine M. York   (essay date 1983)

SOURCE: " 'The Other Side of Dailiness': The Paradox of Photography in Alice Munro's Fiction," in *Studies in Canadian Literature,* Vol. 8, No. 1, 1983, pp. 49-60.

[*York is a Canadian educator and critic. In the following essay, she discusses the postmodernist elements of Munro's fiction and relates how her work incorporates several theories of photography.*]

> But o, photography! as no art is,
> Faithful and disappointing! that records
> Dull days as dull, and hold-it smiles as frauds,
> And will not censor blemishes
> Like washing-lines and Hall's Distemper
>   Boards . . .
>
> —Philip Larkin, "Lines on a Young
>   Lady's Photograph Album"

In various writings and interviews, Alice Munro has often expressed interest in photography and photographic realism. In an **"Open Letter"** to a small Wingham, Ontario journal, *Jubilee,* Munro summarized her feeling about the emotional power of local detail by referring to an Edward Hopper painting. This canvas, entitled "The Barber Shop," is a fairly static, symmetrically-composed, sunlight-flooded interior scene; yet for Munro it becomes "full of a distant, murmuring, almost tender foreboding, full of mystery like the looming trees." This Conradian phrase, so akin to Marlow's concept of "the truth disclosed in a moment of illusion," [Joseph Conrad, *Lord Jim,* 1958] reveals precisely that which characterizes the vision of Munro and the photographic realists—paradox. In fact, it was while reading Susan Sontag's *On Photography,* a searching commentary on the art which is couched in paradoxical terms, that I realized that Munro's fiction reveals those very same paradoxes and syntheses. Although studies have been written outlining the use and frequency of paradox in Munro's fiction (most notably Helen Hoy's "Paradox and Double Vision in Alice Munro's Fiction,") there has been no satisfactory answer as to why paradox is so congenial to her particular way of "fictionalizing" experience.

Munro's fiction, like the Edward Hopper painting and like the work of photographic "realists" from the 1920's on, centres on the paradox of the familiar and the exotic. What Victor Shklovsky termed "defamiliarization" (*ostraneniye*), the making strange of common experience, is precisely what the German *Neue Sachlichkeit* (New Ob-

jectivity) group and Americans like Paul Strand and Edward Weston wished to accomplish in their photography. Weston, with his close attention to surface textures, took the most prosaic and humble of objects—a paprika—and transformed it into a lusciously-textured object resembling a sitting nude. Closer to Munro's own concerns, however, is the work of a journalist-photographer team to which she makes fleeting reference in an interview with John Metcalf—that of James Agee and Walker Evans. *Let Us Now Praise Famous Men* takes the humblest of human subjects—Alabama tenant farmers in the 1930's—and combines literary and visual images to turn them into hauntingly strange visions of both nobility and despair.

To return to one of the central paradoxes of the photographic vision, one discovers that characters in Munro's fiction witness both the familiar and prosaic becoming unfamiliar, even threatening and the reverse process as well. In **"The Ottawa Valley"** it is the foreboding sense of sickness and loss which turns the most familiar of presences—the mother—into something dark and remote:

> She went on as if she had not heard, her familiar bulk ahead of me turning strange, indifferent. She withdrew, she darkened in front of me, though all she did in fact was keep on walking along the path that she and Aunt Dodie had made when they were girls . . . It was still there

This remarkably compressed passage contrasts the vulnerable present with the comforts to be found in memory (unshifting as it is) and in physical objects.

Objects, however, as many of Munro's characters realize with profound amazement, have a mysterious inner layer as well; they possess the hidden potential to turn treacherous or supremely indifferent. As the young protagonist in **"Day of the Butterfly"** witnesses the future of an unpopular schoolmate "turn shadowy, turn dark" in the hospital ward, she also has a new vision of the schoolgirls' hypocritical gifts as "guilt-tinged offerings." She muses that "they were no longer innocent objects to be touched, exchanged, accepted without danger." In the last event, then, she avoids the danger that is human sympathy; Myra's parting gift to her is indifferently shrugged off as "the thing."

In **Who Do You Think You Are?** the source of this threat is an objective nature which is simply indifferent to human sentiment. As Rose gradually foresees her argument with Flo reach its malicious climax, she fixes her eyes upon the shoddy linoleum tiles. At this moment she sees with frightening clarity that even familiar objects are not man's familiars:

> Those things aren't going to help her, none of them can rescue her. They turn black and useless, even unfriendly. Pots can show malice, the pattern of linoleum can leer up at you, treachery is the other side of dailiness.

Distortion of the commonplace becomes specifically identified with art—photographic art, in fact—in the epilogue to *Lives of Girls and Women,* entitled **"The Photographer."** Like Del's fictional treatment of Marion Sheriff, the art of her photographer has the frightening power to create grotesqueness from surface innocence:

> The pictures he took turned out to be unusual, even frightening. People saw that in his pictures they had aged twenty or thirty years. Middle-aged people saw in their own features the terrible, growing, inescapable likeness of their dead parents . . . Brides looked pregnant, children adenoidal. So he was not a popular photographer . . .

Munro applied this theory of the dual nature of art—both creative and parasitic—to her own writing in a manifesto statement which echoes Rose's musings about the other side of dailiness: "There is a sort of treachery to innocent objects—to houses, chairs, dresses, dishes and to roads, fields, landscapes—which a writer removes from their natural, dignified obscurity and sets down in print." Such visual paradox, then, underlines the more morally troubling paradox of the writer who "murders to create" by representing yet altering elements of the experienced world.

Perhaps more bewildering for Munro's protagonists is the experience of the inverse paradox—the exotic becoming familiar. Del Jordan, after her sexual flights of fancy with a black negligé as stage prop, reflects after Mr. Chamberlain's sexual theatrics, "I could not get him back to his old role, I could not make him play the single-minded, simple-minded, vigorous, obliging lecher of my daydreams. My faith in simple depravity had weakened." Earlier, this faith in depravity had been slightly shaken by the shabby ordinariness of the newspapers and potted geraniums of the local whorehouse; by "the skin of everyday experiences stretched over such shamelessness, such consuming explosions of lust." Such bathetic transformations of the exotic into the merely prosaic fill the writings of other Canadian postmodernists, most notably Margaret Atwood's *Lady Oracle.* When the Royal Porcupine is diminished to the point of becoming ordinary Chuck Brewster, Joan Foster becomes alarmed and disillusioned: "But I didn't want him to spoil things, I didn't want him to become gray and multi-dimensional and complicated like everyone else. Was every Heathcliff a Linton in disguise?" [*Lady Oracle,* 1976.]

The frequent appearance of clearly "odd" characters has often been noted by reviewers of Munro's work, but to characterize these figures as belonging to some aberrant "other world" is, I believe, another example of making distinctions when syntheses are more in order. As in the photographs of Diane Arbus, the grotesque makes its appearance in Munro's stories in order to make us reform our Gestalt—our conceptions of what is "odd" and "normal." The eccentric hermit Joe Phippen, whom Ben Jordan takes his daughter to meet in **"Images,"** is not so much a creature from a competing world as an additional scrap of knowledge which Del must synthesize in order to construct an "image" of her father:

> Like the children in fairy stories who have seen their parents make pacts with terrible strangers, who have discovered that our fears are based on nothing but the truth, but who come back fresh from marvellous escapes and take up their

knives and forks . . . like them, dazed and powerful with secrets, I never said a word.

Unlike Sherwood Anderson, to whose work Munro's has often been compared, Munro would never say (as Anderson did of *Winesburg, Ohio*) that "All the men and women the writer had ever known had become grotesque." Rather, oddity is another element in the synthesis of life in the fictional small town. "It is not true," Munro once commented, "that such a place will not allow eccentricity. Oddity is necessary as sin is . . . Within these firm definitions . . . live bewildered and complicated people."

In *Who Do You Think You Are?* this bewildering reconciliation of truth and illusion becomes the dominant theme of the collection. I agree with Helen Hoy that Munro passes into a subtler "dialectic of the ordinary and the marvellous" but not merely in terms of the recognized illusoriness of Rose's adventures. Rather, it is a self-aware dialectic of an artistic nature especially which reaches a synthesis that is typically postmodern. It is no accident, for example, that the final, title story of the volume begins with the "comic" figure of Milton Homer and ends with the "tragic" figure of Ralph Gillespie. In the description of the town parade—an event which mixes theatricality (socially-sanctioned "showing off") and "real" identities— Milton Homer accentuates this blurring of fantasy and fact: "Nobody looked askance at Milton in a parade; everybody was used to him." This overlapping of fiction and fact, wherein oddities become acceptable, is evidenced in his epic-serious name and is beautifully captured in the episode in which young Ralph Gillespie changes the title of Keats's sonnet to "On First Looking Into Milton Homer"! In fact, this subtle bridging of these two figures becomes even more significant at the end of the story, when Ralph Gillespie, *imitator* of Milton Homer, becomes a "fiction" which Rose is unable to read:

> The thing she was ashamed of, in acting, was that she might have been paying attention to the wrong things, reporting antics, when there was always something further, a tone, a depth, a light, that she couldn't get and wouldn't get. And it wasn't just about acting she suspected this . . . She had never felt this more strongly than when she was talking to Ralph Gillespie.

Instead of prodding Ralph about his talent for mimicry, much as she might do in a public interview, Rose realizes that she might have delved further, beyond the surface fiction to the essential story of one man's life. This synthesis is completed only after Ralph's death which leaves Rose with the knowledge that "she felt his life, close, closer than the lives of men she'd loved, one slot over from her own." Thus, the blurring of the distinctions between fact and fiction which lies at the basis of postmodernist fiction develops with increasing intensity in Munro's art, as the "Photographer" as artist and Del as experiencer fully merge in Rose—the artist of experience.

If the photograph is the meeting place of the known and the unknown, it is no less the meeting place of motion and stillness in human experience. The photograph is the static moment snatched out of the *perpetuum mobile* of time— what French photographer Cartier-Bresson described in a now-famous utterance as the "decisive moment." As such, it has been seized upon by postmodernists as a contemporary example of what T. S. Eliot called "the still point of the turning world"—the breathless moment of intersection between the time-driven and the timeless. In architecture, we witness the continuum of flowing water in a curiously static setting (the home) in Frank Lloyd Wright's Bear Run House. In the visual arts, David Hockney's tiger is arrested in midpounce with the following admonition printed above its ferocious head: "No, this is not in motion"!

In their very form, Alice Munro's interconnected short story collections, *Lives of Girls and Women* and *Who Do You Think You Are?* function on the same borderline between motion and stasis; each self-contained story is an image in itself, linked to the larger continuum by the main character and a roughly chronological progression. To those who wrongly approach these series of linked images as a traditional novel, however, gaps are bound to appear. This is no shortcoming but a conscious choice on Munro's part, for this imagistic effect closely resembles the very texture and process of memory.

On a more minute level, Munro uses this photographic stillness in motion consciously and overtly to create her "decisive moments." One such moment occurs at the end of *Lives of Girls and Women* with the spontaneous act granted by Bobby Sheriff to Del Jordan. His sudden rising upon his toes Del as artist interprets, in a self-conscious fashion, as having "a concise meaning, a stylized meaning—to be a letter, or a whole word, in an alphabet I did not know." The alphabet which Del is just beginning to learn is the flux and flow of human life, and the letter or word—those special, mysterious acts of men and women—are the keys to the code. Munro uses the same linguistic analogy, never forgetting the vital link between literary device and human experience, in *Who Do You Think You Are?*. In "Spelling," Rose visits a home for the aged, soon to be the home of her stepmother, Flo, and observes an old woman whose only participation in life is to spell out loud words supplied by others. Rose (and Munro) choose words charged with vitality which become curiously static:

> Forest F-O-R-E-S-T . . .

> Celebrate. C-E-L-E-B-R-A-T-E.

This contrast between the isolated, lifeless linguistic fragments and the lush vitality of the concepts which they suggest when experienced in continuity speaks volumes about the aridity of the home, and of solitary aging itself. It is intriguing, indeed, that Susan Sontag should refer to photography on exactly this dual level, as "a grammar and, even more importantly, an ethics of seeing."

Munro even incorporates this contrast between motion and stasis into her imagery: in **"A Spanish Lady,"** a woman's self-contained musings about her own troubles are jarred by the sudden death cry of an old man in a train station. She becomes transfixed in more senses than one:

> It seems as if I should not leave, as if the cry of the man dying, now dead, is still demanding something of me, but I cannot think what it

is . . . What we say and feel no longer rings true, it is slightly beside the point. As if we were all wound up a long time ago and were spinning out of control, whirring, making noises, but at a touch could stop, and see each other for the first time, harmless and still.

The implicit image of the spinning top, its vibrant colours never perceptible until we timidly stretch out a finger to interfere, to participate, is the perfect image of our everyday experience and of our all too characteristic reticence.

Here, as elsewhere, Munro is at one with her self-conscious contemporaries. Michael Ondaatje, in *Coming Through Slaughter,* overtly uses the photograph of jazz master Buddy Bolden as a symbol of the meeting of stillness and fluidity in art—and experience. There is a constant melting and blurring of the lines separating subject and object, experience and fiction, as, for example, when the narrator or researcher of Bolden's story reflects, "When he went mad he was the same age as I am now. The photograph moves and becomes a mirror." Again, the static fact becomes fluid fiction, as the members of the group photograph (their names typographically set on the page in the position they assume in the photo at one point by Ondaatje) melt into voices giving testimony, telling their own stories along with that of Buddy Bolden. In all editions of the novel this interaction between print and image is preserved through the prominent displaying of the actual photograph on or inside the cover.

This photographic seizing of the moment becomes an overt model for Munro as well in the collection which includes **"The Spanish Lady"**—*Something I've Been Meaning to Tell You.* On the very last page, the photograph becomes the act of writing, of capturing and thus exorcising experience. The narrator tells us, first of all, that if she had been making a "proper story" out of her experiences, she would have altered certain details. This affirmation of fidelity to experience then assumes a visual form: "Now I look at what I have done and it is like a series of snapshots, like the brownish snapshots with fancy borders that my parents' old camera used to take." Referring to her fictional creation as a journey, she claims to have undertaken it with the sole purpose of capturing for all time her mother—"To mark her off, to describe, to illumine, to celebrate, to get rid of her," but all in vain, for her edges "melt and flow." Thus, as Eliot reflects, we are left with "the intolerable wrestle with words and meanings" for "Only through time is time conquered."

As this comparison suggests, Munro moves to explore the further paradox of art as both power and vulnerable helplessness. In other Canadian postmodernist novels, most notably Leonard Cohen's *Beautiful Losers* and Hubert Aquin's *Blackout,* the association of fiction-making and power is set in an intensely sexual and political frame of reference. In the case of Aquin, though, this attempt at mastery—of one's experience, one's own national identity—is continually frustrated, for the novel, like the land which lies behind it, is the constant object of a power-struggle among several controlling powers. Is this attempt to gain power over the threat of extinction really so different from the power which Del Jordan learns to exercise over her dominating lover, Garnet, and eventually over the recalcitrant details of experience? Earlier in her development, after the death of Uncle Craig, this power over extinction is sought by Del through the mastery of knowledge:

> I followed her [Del's mother] around the house, scowling, persistent, repeating my questions. I wanted to know. There is no protection unless it is in knowing. I wanted death pinned down and isolated behind a wall of particular facts and circumstances, not floating around loose ignored but powerful, waiting to get in anywhere.

This wish for power, for security, becomes tied to a sexual theme as Del fights both a literal and metaphorical battle against being submerged by her lover in **"Baptizing."** "I felt amazement," she marvels, "not that I was fighting with Garnet but that anybody could have made such a mistake, to think he had real power over me." Finally, the theme of artistic power over chaos is established in the epilogue, with the actual physical presentation of the lists of prosaic details which Del compiles and orders with sacred devotion:

> And no list could hold what I wanted, for what I wanted was every last thing, every layer of speech and thought, stroke of light on bark or walls, every smell, pothole, pain, crack, delusion, held still and held together—radiant, everlasting.

Interestingly, this drive to control through representation of concrete objects, besides reaching back to Neolithic cave paintings, turns up in a surprisingly parallel passage in *Let Us Now Praise Famous Men:* "If I could do it," writes Agee, "I'd do no writing here at all. It would be photographs; the rest would be fragments of cloth, bits of cotton, lumps of earth, records of speech, pieces of wood and iron, phials of odors, plates of food and excrement . . . ." This consideration of the power that photography and fiction hold, to bind together disparate chunks of the world, links Munro's work to the very impulses of mimesis in man.

At the same time, however, the other half of the paradox is completed with the realization that fiction and photography reveal to man the utter hopelessness of ever ordering the chaos of the outer world or the inner landscape. Both outer and inner chaos break forth, for example, in Margaret Atwood's poem, "Camera," in which the lover's insistence that both scenario and woman become immobilized for his "organized instant" is frustrated by the emotional wreckage of the scene. As though through a "zoom" lens, we are taken beyond the imagined chaos of dispersed leaves and coats flapping from tree-tops to the true eye of the storm:

> travelling towards the horizon
> there has been a hurricane
> that small black speck
> travelling towards the horizon
> at almost the speed of light
> is me

As in "Progressive Insanities of a Pioneer" or *The Journals of Susanna Moodie,* this imposition of order and stasis (comparable in spirit to the fixity of the camera's view) is cynically rejected as untenable and even sadistic. Indeed, as in Ondaatje's novel, one senses the same grinding tension between photographic image and flowing experience—a tension which is ultimately darker than Munro's energetic study of paradox.

Nevertheless, in *Lives of Girls and Women,* we note a similar, though milder, process of undercutting as in the Atwood poem, after Del's brash description of her lists, with her disheartening comment, "The hope of accuracy we bring to such tasks is crazy, heartbreaking," This artistic hoarding of detail is tellingly associated with Del's saving of her own life in **"Baptizing,"** for the simple reason that writing, for Munro, is the constant "hedge" against the chaos that is death. She observed to Graeme Gibson that writing "has something to do with the fight against death, the feeling that we lose everything every day, and writing is a way of convincing yourself perhaps that you're doing something about this." How fascinating it is, then, to see that Munro's work, like that of Aquin, displays the curious paradox which Robert Alter notes of the self-conscious novel in our century; that while it is a celebration of generation, it more often than not proves to be "a long meditation on death" [Robert Alter, *Partial Magic: The Novel as Self-Conscious Genre,* 1975].

The reason for such an abundance of paradox in contemporary literature lies in the age-old conflict between Romantic and Classical impulses—those of sympathetic identification and aesthetic detachment. Munro's work, representative of the twentieth-century hybrid, often reveals both conflicting tendencies. In **"The Office,"** for example, the writer's final mental portrait of her persecutor, Mr. Malley, poses delicately and painfully this question of sympathy and distance:

> Mr. Malley with his rags and brushes and a pail of soapy water, scrubbing in his clumsy way . . . at the toilet walls . . . arranging in his mind the bizarre but somehow never quite satisfactory narrative of yet another betrayal of trust. While I arrange words, and think it is my right to be rid of him.

Like the plants and teapot which Malley forces on the young writer, the "gifts" which experiences bestow on their authors have their own price, their own nagging demands which cannot be ignored. This, in effect, is the same realization which Rose reaches in *Who Do You Think You Are?.* While she is prevented from turning a letter from Flo into a public storytelling exhibition by "a fresh and overwhelming realization" of the "gulf" which lies between her and her past, she nevertheless comes to recognize through Ralph Gillespie that the gulf is also a living link. In terms of the photographer's art, Susan Sontag sums up these, and many of the other conflicting tendencies already noted in Munro's art, with characteristic insight:

> Photography, which has so many narcissistic uses, is also a powerful instrument for depersonalizing our relation to the world; and the two uses are complementary. Like a pair of binoculars with no right or wrong end, the camera

makes exotic things near, intimate; and familiar things small, abstract, strange, much further away. It offers, in one easy, habit-forming activity, both participation and alienation in our own lives and in those of others.

Like the photographer, then, who establishes distance through a selective rectangular frame, writing is both a selection and a distancing. Nevertheless, as Cartier-Bresson observed of his art, "in order to 'give a meaning' to the world, one has to feel involved in what he frames through the viewfinder." This precept should be remembered by critics who deplore the constraint and morbidity of Munro's "town," for Munro affirms her link to her created world in characteristically paradoxical terms: "Solitary and meshed these lives are, buried and celebrated."

Like her postmodernist contemporaries, Alice Munro is intensely fascinated by the burials and celebrations, links and gulfs, fictions and nonfictions of the world around her. By fusing these disparate elements into the synthesis which is paradox, Munro accomplishes what a recent reviewer observed of Cartier-Bresson: "He has brought his intuition to the surface of his skin and he has kept it there, bonding into single entity photographer, camera, time, and the objective world." In fact, like all sensitive men and women in a disconcerting, exhilarating age, Alice Munro is "coolly obsessed with humanity."

George Woodcock   (essay date Summer 1986)

SOURCE: "The Plots of Life: The Realism of Alice Munro," in *Queen's Quarterly,* Vol. 93, No. 2, Summer, 1986, pp. 235-50.

[*Woodcock was a Canadian educator, editor, author, and critic. In the following essay, he explores realism in Munro's writing, particularly as it relates to her younger female characters.*]

> But the development of events on that Saturday night; that fascinated me; I felt that I had had a glimpse of the shameless, marvellous, shattering absurdity with which the plots of life, though not of fiction, are improvized. (Alice Munro, ***Dance of the Happy Shades***)

There is a challenging ambivalence in Alice Munro's stories and her open-ended episodic novels, a glimmering fluctuation between actuality and fictional reality, or, if one prefers it, a tension between autobiography and invention which she manipulates so superbly that both elements are used to the full and in the process enrich each other.

The paperback edition of Munro's second novel, ***Who Do You Think You Are?,*** bears on its cover the reproduction of a neo-realist painting by Ken Danby, called "The Sunbather." It has no illustrative function; none of the episodes that make up the novel concerns or even mentions sunbathing. Yet it is hard to think of a painting that could have been better chosen to convey the special tone and flavour of Munro's writing.

A girl sits naked on a partly shaded patch of grass, her knees drawn up, her arms resting on them, her cheek resting on a wrist. Everything is rendered with the meticulous exactitude that only tempera, as a medium, makes possible—the tones of the gently tanning skin perfectly caught, the grass blades spiky yet pliable in the darkening green of high summer; the girl's face shows neither joy nor discontent, but a kind of indrawn pensiveness. Yet the realism, precise and particular as it may be, is much more than mimetic. The artist is not merely representing life, not merely recording how a particular girl with rather greasy hair and a largish bottom looked when she sat on the grass on a certain day in July. He is creating an image, outside time and place, that stands in our minds not merely as a painted surface, but as an epitome, a focussing of several generalities that come together in its eternal moment—generalities like youth and girlishness and the benison of sunlight and the suggestion of fertility that we sense in the girl's broad hips and at the same time in the springing green of the grass and weed leaves among which she sits.

And this, except that she is using words rather than paint to impress her images on the mind, is very near to what Alice Munro tries to do. Just as magic realist painters create a kind of super-reality by the impeccable presentation of details in a preternaturally clear light, and in this way isolate their images from actuality, so Munro has combined documentary methods with a style as clear as the tempera medium in painting. In this essay I propose to discuss the methods in the hope of illuminating the ends.

Alice Munro has been rightly reluctant to offer theoretical explanations of her methods, for she is quite obviously an anti-dogmatic, the kind of writer who works with feeling ahead of theory. But even on the theoretical level she is shrewd in defining the perimeters of her approach, perhaps negatively rather than positively. She once, for example, in an essay written for John Metcalf's *The Narrative Voice,* entitled **"The Colonel's Hash Resettled,"** cautioned against attempts to read symbolism excessively into her stories. And she was right, for essentially her stories are what they say, offering their meaning with often stark directness, and gaining their effect from their intense visuality, so that they are always vivid in the mind's eye, which is another way of saying that she has learnt the power of the image and how to turn it to the purposes of prose.

Her visuality is not merely a matter of rendering the surface, the realm of mere perception, for she has understood that one of the great advantages of any effective imagist technique is that the image not merely presents itself. It reverberates with the power of its associations, and even with the intensity of its own isolated and illuminated presence. Munro herself conveyed something of this when John Metcalf, remarking on the fact that she seemed to "*glory* in the surfaces and textures," asked whether she did not in fact feel " 'surfaces' not to be surfaces," and she answered that there was "a kind of magic . . . about everything," "a feeling about the intensity of what is *there*."

When Alice Munro first began to write, her work tended to be undervalued, except by a few exceptionally percipient readers like Robert Weaver, because her tales of Ontario small-town life were taken to be those of a rather conventional realist with a certain flair for local colour. And realism at that time, following its decline in the visual arts, was going into a somewhat lesser eclipse in literature. Canada was becoming aware of modernism, and this meant that for a time at least writers were concerned with thematic and symbolic fiction rather than with anything that savoured of the mimetic.

Alice Munro has always been one of those fortunate and self-sufficient writers who never really become involved in movements or in literary fashions. From her start she had her own view of life, largely as she had lived it herself, and her aim was to express it in a fiction distinguished by craftsmanship and clear vision rather than by self-conscious artifice. It was a curiously paradoxical method of self-cultivation and self-effacement that she followed, for she has always written best when her stories or the episodes in her novels were close to her own experience in a world she knew, yet at the same time she cultivated a prose from which authorly mannerisms were so absent that it seemed as though the stories had their own voices. In the process Alice Munro became, next to Marian Engel, perhaps Canada's best prose stylist.

But linked to the pellucid clarity of that voice, or voices, there was always the intense vision—and in this context I mean vision as a power of visualizing. The comparison with magic realist painters that I made early in this essay is not merely an analogical one, for Munro is always deeply concerned with describing, with establishing scenes and people clearly in the mind's eye, and as in real life, so in her stories, we establish our conception of the character of people first by recognizing what they look like and how they speak, and then, such familiarity established, proceeding inward to minds and feelings. The photographic element in her presentation of scenes and characters as visualizable images is an essential factor in her writing.

The camera, of course, does not always lie, but through the photographer's conscious selectiveness and even more through the tendency of the lens to isolate the image from the chaos of actuality, it does offer us a different reality from that which we normally perceive. In an interesting essay entitled "Alice Munro and the American South," J.R. (Tim) Struthers discussed the influence on Munro of writers like Eudora Welty and James Agee, and in doing so he talked of the way in which both these writers were fascinated by the possibilities of photography as a medium and its relationship to the kind of realistic writing which they carried on. They saw the special literalness of the photograph not as a usurpation of the role of imaginative perception but as a means of enhancing it. In this sense Struthers talks of Munro as having a "visual or photographic imagination," and as an example he cites the ending of a harrowing little story of the scalding death of a baby, **"The Time of Death,"** which appears in her first volume of short stories, ***Dance of the Happy Shades***. The story drifts away into its intended anticlimax as the little shabby neighbourhood absorbs the minor tragedy and then, at the very end, the narrator steps backward out of the stunted lives of the characters and stands like a photographer taking a middle-distance shot of the setting:

> There was this house, and the other wooden houses that had never been painted, with their steep patched roofs and their narrow, slanting

porches, the wood-smoke coming out of their chimneys and dim children's faces pressed against their windows. Behind them there was the strip of earth, ploughed in some cases, run to grass in others, full of stones, and behind this the pine trees, not very tall. In front were the yards, the dead gardens, the grey highway running out from town. The snow came, falling slowly, evenly, between the highway and the houses and the pine trees, falling in big flakes at first and then in smaller and smaller flakes that did not melt on the hard furrows, the rock of the earth.

This paragraph, which terminates the story, is not only a good example of Munro's ability to create sharply visual images, still shots, that stir our feelings, in this case pitying despair. It also, by an echo many readers must have recognized, establishes her links with an earlier strain of realism, that of the James Joyce of *Dubliners*. The Joyce story I mean, of course, is "The Dead"; though the title of the story is reminiscent of Munro's, the main action of the story is quite different from hers, but in the end there is the final paragraph in which, as in **"The Time of Death,"** the idea of death and the image of snow are brought together:

> Yes, the newspapers were right: snow was general all over Ireland. It was falling on every part of the dark central plain, on the treeless hills, falling softly into the Bog of Allen, and, farther westward, softly falling over the dark mutinous Shannon waves. It was falling, too, upon every part of the lonely churchyard on the hill where Michael Furey lay buried. It lay thickly drifted on the crooked crosses and headstones, on the spears of the little gate, on the barren thorns. His soul swooned slowly as he heard the snow falling faintly through the universe and faintly falling, like the descent of their last end, upon all the living and the dead.

The resemblance is tenuous but haunting, and the echo is quite clear. I am not suggesting that there is a conscious borrowing here, for, as all writers know, recollections of their reading can lodge in recesses of the mind until they are called up to fit into the *bricolage* that the imagination makes out of the resources of memory, conscious and unconscious alike. More important, perhaps, is the general resemblance between the kind of realism that Alice Munro developed during the 1950s and that of the early days of modernism, the kind of realism one finds not only in the early Joyce and—more lyrically expressed—in the early Lawrence, but also in their continental European contemporaries like Thomas Mann and Italo Svevo. There is the same tendency towards the *Bildungsroman,* whether manifest in a novel or disguised in a cluster of related stories; the sense of a society observed with oppressive closeness from within by someone who wants to escape; the concern for the appalling insecurities created by what was then called social climbing, and now is called upward mobility; the agonized awareness of the perils of moving through the transitions of life, from childhood to adolescence, from adulthood to age.

While Alice Munro's approach has a great deal in common with this European realism of the early part of the century that trembled on the edge of modernism, without herself going forward—as some of the modernists like Joyce and Wyndham Lewis did—from realism to the extremes of formalism, it has little in common with the kind of prairie writing that represented realism for Canadians during the decades between the great wars. Writers such as Robert Stead, Martha Ostenso and Frederick Philip Grove were concerned with the pioneer farmers and their struggle with the frontier lands of the great plains. Alice Munro was dealing with a society that had long passed out of the pioneer stage, and represented a decaying established culture rather than a frontier one. The problem of those who inhabited it was not, as it had been with Grove's characters, to conquer the wilderness without being destroyed in the process, but to escape before one had been dragged down into the mental stagnation and physical decay of the marginal farmlands of Ontario.

Alice Munro herself grew up in this background, and much of the content of her stories and novels, if it is not strictly autobiographical, does echo the experiences of her youth. Like Del Jordan in *Lives of Girls and Women,* she was brought up on a farm where her father bred silver foxes without ever prospering greatly; her mother, like Del's, was a bright, frustrated woman, whose iconoclastic cast of mind contradicted her social ambition, and who died of Parkinson's disease. Again like more than one of her heroines, Munro married and moved west to British Columbia, which gave her another terrain for her stories; also like them, she stepped out of a disintegrating marriage and returned to Ontario. In other words, she wrote of what she knew best, and while each of her stories lives within its own complete world and is not a mere mirroring of the writer's life, it is inevitable that the fictions she drew out of the intensely remembered country of her childhood should be more convincing than those she conceived in British Columbia, where she was never completely at home.

Turning to the books themselves, there are three collections of short stories, *Dance of the Happy Shades, Something I've Been Meaning to Tell You* and *The Moons of Jupiter,* and two novels, *Lives of Girls and Women* and *Who Do You Think You Are?* They have appeared at fairly symmetrical intervals, between three and four years from one book to the other, and up to now they have alternated in form, a novel of related episodes following a collection of miscellaneous stories.

Dance of the Happy Shades appeared in 1968. It was a late date in terms of Munro's writing life, for she had been publishing stories sporadically since the early 1950s, and I remember when I met her round about 1955 I did so with pleased recognition, since I had already read and admired some of her stories. I am sure I became aware of them through Robert Weaver, who more than anyone else "discovered" her, broadcasting her stories on various CBC programmes he ran, publishing them in *Tamarack Review* when it began in 1956, and including them in his Oxford anthologies, *Canadian Stories,* of which the first appeared in 1960.

Munro's experience was not unique; it was that of almost all Canadian writers of fiction, who during the 1950s and 1960s had to face a reaction against the short story on the part of both book publishers and popular magazines in Canada. It was only in the later 1960s, largely because of the success with which Weaver had introduced stories to radio audiences, that publishers once again began accepting collections and finding that willing readerships existed.

Once Munro's *Dance of the Happy Shades* appeared in 1968, her acceptance by Canadian readers was assured, and her later volumes were successful not only in Canada, but also in the United States, where the marginal agrarian communities she portrayed were recognized as familiar, and where reviewers, ignorant of other Canadian writers, almost automatically compared her with American analogues like John Cheever and Joyce Carol Oates. In fact, like Al Purdy with his poetic rendering of the "degenerate Loyalist" heritage of Ameliasburgh and thereabouts, Munro offers the portrait of a distinctively Canadian society and does it in a distinctively Canadian way. Her sense of the interplay of setting and tradition is impeccable, so that there are really two ways of reading Munro, the exoteric one of the reader who knows a good story when he comes upon it, and reads it with enjoyment and not too much concern for authenticity, and the esoteric one of the Canadian who is likely to read it with a special sense of its truth or otherwise to the life and land he knows.

Perhaps because, unlike the later collections of stories, it is gathered from the writings of a relatively long period—at least fifteen years as against three or four—*The Dance of the Happy Shades* is more varied and tentatively venturesome than the later volumes. It shows the author trying out different modes and approaches. There are stories, like **"The Office,"** that rather self-consciously explore the problems of women setting out as writers in an unsympathetic environment. There are others, like **"The Shining Houses,"** a study of the callousness young property owners can show in defending their "values" (i.e. the selling prices of their homes), that are as ambivalently suburban as anything by John Cheever. **"Sunday Afternoon"** is a little social study, highly class-conscious for a Canadian writer, of the relations between a country girl hired to serve in a rich middle-class home and her brittle-brainless employers. And in **"Thanks for the Ride"** Munro makes a rare foray across the sex line and tells in the voice of an adolescent boy the story of his first lay; in fact, the point of view is deceptive, since the real interest of the story lies in the portrait of his partner Lois, a fragile yet tough working-class girl, much used by men and yet—in her coarse independence—strangely inviolate.

Most of the remaining stories fall into a group of which the main theme is childhood and growing up in the Ontario countryside, with action centred sometimes on the farm operated by the father of the central character and sometimes in the nearby town where the mother at times lives separately and where the girl attends school. The father-dominated farm represents the world of nature and feeling, a world devoid of ambition. The mother-dominated house in town represents the world of social and intellectual ambition, just as the school is the setting where the heroine establishes her relationship with her peers among the small-town children but also develops her desire to escape into a broader world. In some of the stories the mother, living or remembered, is shown advancing into the illness—Parkinson's disease—that will accentuate the oddity which most of her neighbours have already mocked in her.

The three stories of childhood, **"Walker Brothers Cowboy,"** **"Image"** and **"Boys and Girls,"** are perhaps the most important of this group, both for their vivid evocation of the decaying rural life a century after the pioneers of Upper Canada, and for their delineation of the relationships between parents and children in hard times.

"Walker Brothers Cowboy," the opening story of the book, takes us to a time when the silver fox farm has failed and Ben Jordan has taken up peddling the patent medicines, spices and food flavourings distributed by Walker Brothers. The story, told by his daughter who does not name herself, begins by relating this time of stress and need to the slightly better past on the farm. The girl's mother, also unnamed, tries desperately to maintain self-respect in a situation she sees as a demeaning loss of social standing, even though she lives physically better in the town than on the farm.

> Fate has flung us onto a street of poor people (it does not matter that we were poor before, that was a different kind of poverty), and the only way to take this, as she sees it, is with dignity, with bitterness, with no reconciliation. No bathroom with claw-footed tub and a flush toilet is going to comfort her, nor water on tap and sidewalks past the house and milk in bottles, nor even the two movie theatres and the Venus Restaurant and Woolworths so marvellous it has live birds singing in its fan-cooled corners and fish as tiny as finger-nails, as bright as moons, swimming in its green tanks. My mother does not care.

The father, more self-contained, more ironic, finds ways to live with Depression conditions and salvage his pride. As the story opens we see him walking with his daughter beside Lake Huron and telling her how the Great Lakes were gouged out of the earth by the ice coming down in great probing fingers from the north. Clearly the girl prefers her father's company to her mother's:

> She walks serenely like a lady shopping, like a *lady* shopping, past the housewives in loose beltless dresses torn under the arms. With me her creation, wretched curls and flaunting hair bow, scrubbed knees and white socks—all I do not want to be. I loathe even my name when she says it in public, in a voice so high, proud and ringing, deliberately different from the voice of any other mother on the street.

Travelling his route of the desperate dusty farmlands, Ben Jordan makes fun of his situation by improvising as he rides a kind of endless ballad of his adventures on the road, and this becomes a kind of *leitmotiv* one day when he sets out with the girl and her brother and, leaving his Walker Brothers territory, takes them to a farmhouse where a woman who was once his sweetheart is living. The clean

bare farmhouse with Catholic emblems on the walls and an old woman dozing in a corner becomes a kind of stage on which is revealed to the girl that people we know may have dimensions to their lives of which to this point we have been unaware. The sense of something theatrical and unreal and different from ordinary life is given by the fact that Ben Jordan and his old sweetheart Nora Cronin name each other, but nobody else in the story is named. The strangeness of the hitherto unknown past is framed within the nameless ordinariness of the present.

In **"Image"** a different kind of framing takes place. The story begins with the girl, again unnamed and again mainly a spectator, remembering the coarse cousin, Mary McQuade, who comes in to act as a kind of nurse in family crises and who is now filling the house with her overbearing presence because the mother is ill. The father—once again Ben Jordan but now an unspecified farmer—runs a trapline down by the river, and one day he and the girl go down to harvest the muskrats. On their way they encounter a crazy recluse, Joe Phippen, who patrols the river bank with an axe in search of imagined enemies. They go to the cellar where Joe has been living since his house burnt down; for the girl it seems like an underground playhouse, except for its sinister smells and a mad cat the hermit feeds whisky. As they leave the cellar Ben Jordan cautions the girl when she gets back to tell nobody in the house about the axe. At table with Mary McQuade he relates the story of Joe and his drunken cat, and Mary is filled with indignation.

> "A man that'd do a thing like that ought to be locked up."
>
> "Maybe so," my father said. "Just the same I hope they don't get him for a while yet. Old Joe."
>
> "Eat your supper," Mary said, bending over me. I did not for some time realize that I was no longer afraid of her. "Look at her," she said. "Her eyes dropping out of her head, all she's been and seen. Was he feeding whisky to her too?"
>
> "Not a drop," said my father, and looked steadily down the table at me. Like the children in fairy stories who have seen their parents make pacts with terrifying strangers, who have discovered that our fears are based on nothing but the truth, but who come back from marvellous escapes and take up their knives and forks, with humility and good manners, prepared to live happily ever after—like them, dazed and powerful with secrets, I never said a word.

In this story the filial link is complete. The father puts his trust in his daughter, and she keeps it in a kind of complicity to protect the strange and eccentric and unpopular in human behaviour—a complicity that will re-emerge in Munro's fiction.

But in **"Boys and Girls"** the trust between father and daughter is broken, and that is one of the complex aspects of growing up, involving as it does the girl's gradual realization of the difference between the sexes that in the end, and no matter what Freud may have said, makes fathers see sons as their successors and makes men stand together.

The action of this story takes place entirely on the fox farm. In a passage of admirably clear and restrained description Munro creates the feeling of the place and details the daily tasks the girl performs as she helps her father, keeping the pens supplied with water and spreading grass over them to prevent the foxes' pelts from being darkened by sunlight. Her little brother also helps, but she jealously guards the main tasks for herself, and resents her mother's attempts to trap her into household tasks. The curiously detached centre of all this activity is formed by the foxes which, despite generations of captivity, have not ceased to be wild animals, hostile and intractable:

> Naming them did not make pets out of them, or anything like it. Nobody but my father ever went into the pens, and he had twice had blood-poisoning from bites. When I was bringing them their water they prowled up and down on the paths they had made inside their pens, barking seldom—they saved that for nighttime, when they might get up a chorus of community frenzy—but always watching me, their eyes burning, clear gold, in their pointed malevolent faces. They were beautiful for their delicate legs and heavy, aristocratic tails and the bright fur sprinkled on dark down their backs—which gave them their name—but especially for their faces, drawn exquisitely sharp in pure hostility, and their golden eyes.

One has the sense that although loyalty to her father would never let her admit the thought, these wild captive creatures have earned the girl's sympathy, and what happens shortly afterwards seems to confirm this. She begins all at once to realize that her cherished position in the little world of the farm has become insecure:

> This winter also I began to hear a great deal more on the theme my mother had sounded when she had been talking in front of the barn. I no longer felt safe. It seemed that in the minds of the people around me there was a steady undercurrent of thought, not to be deflected, on this one subject. The word *girl* had formerly seemed to me innocent and unburdened, like the word *child;* now it appeared that it was no such thing. A girl was not, as I had supposed, simply what I was; it was what I had to become. It was a definition, always touched with emphasis, with reproach and disappointment. Also it was a joke on me. . . .

The critical point comes shortly afterwards, when her loyalties are all at once tested, and her response is as astonishing to her as it is to anyone else. Her father buys superannuated horses to slaughter for fox food; occasionally there will be a perfectly healthy animal among them for which in these days of increasing mechanization a farmer no longer has any use. A mare of this kind, whom they call Flora, is bought and kept over winter. She is a nervous animal, in some ways almost as proud and intractable as the foxes, and on the day she is being taken out to be shot she breaks away into a meadow where a gate has been left open. The girl and her brother are sent to close it.

> The gate was heavy. I lifted it out of the gravel and carried it across the roadway. I had it half-

way across when she came into sight, galloping straight towards me. There was just time to get the chain on. Laird came scrambling through the ditch to help me.

> Instead of shutting the gate, I opened it as wide as I could. I did not make any decision to do this, it was just what I did. Flora never slowed down; she galloped straight past me, and Laird jumped up and down, yelling, "Shut it, shut it" even when it was too late. . . .

The mare, of course, is eventually caught and killed. And then, at mid-day dinner, her brother Laird tells on the girl:

> My father made a curt sound of disgust. "What did you do that for?"

> I did not answer. I put down my fork and waited to be sent from the table, still not looking up.

> But this did not happen. For some time nobody said anything, then Laird said matter-of-factly, "She's crying."

> "Never mind," my father said. He spoke with resignation, even good humour, the words that absolved and dismissed me for good. "She's only a girl," he said.

> I didn't protest that, even in my heart. Maybe it was true.

Two themes that will recur in Munro's later writing have been introduced; the burden of femininity, and the need to break free. They take on increased importance in her first novel, *Lives of Girls and Women*. This appears to have begun as another collection of stories that had enough of a common strain for the publisher to suggest she might turn them into a novel; its origin survives in the episodic and rather discontinuous structure of the work.

Lives of Girls and Women really completes the three stories I have just been discussing. The inconsistencies that existed between them are ironed out. Ben Jordan is still the father and he runs a fox farm. The other characters are now all named, the girl becoming Della (or Del), the mother Ida, the brother changing to Owen, and with this naming everything seems to become more precise in intent. Even the locality is named, for the farm is on Flats Road in the disreputable outskirts of the town of Jubilee, and the action alternates between the farm and the town, where Ida takes a house where she and Del live except in the summer months.

The eight parts (significantly they are named but not numbered, so that they seem as much stories as chapters) really serve two functions. Each is an exemplary episode, self-contained even though its characters spill over into the other episodes, so that it can stand on its own. Yet, in the classic manner of the *Bildungsroman,* each episode builds on the last, revealing another side of Del's education in life, and as the progression is generally chronological, the continuity becomes that of a rather conventional novel, which begins in the heroine's childhood and ends when, as a young woman who has just allowed a love affair to divert her from winning a scholarship, she turns to the world of art and begins her first book.

The general inclination of *Lives of Girls and Women* is indeed that of a portrait of the artist, and the first-person voice in which it is told is appropriate. It looks back to the final and title story of *Dance of the Happy Shades,* which tells of the last party of an old music teacher who astonishes and annoys her middle-class pupils and their parents by producing a girl from a school for the retarded who is clearly, whatever her intelligence, something near to a musical genius:

> Miss Marsalles sits beside the piano and smiles at everybody in her usual way. Her smile is not triumphant, or modest. She does not look like a magician who is watching people's faces to see the effect of a rather original revelation; nothing like that. You would think, now that at the very end of her life she has found someone she can teach—whom she must teach—to play the piano, she would light up with the importance of this discovery. But it seems that the girl's playing like this is something she always expected, and she finds it natural and satisfying; people who believe in miracles do not make much fuss when they actually encounter one. Nor does it seem that she regards this girl with any more wonder than the other children from Greenhill School, who love her, or the rest of us, who do not. To her no gift is unexpected, no celebration will come as a surprise.

The sense of art as a miracle, and the sense also of some special kind of intelligence that recognizes it recurs in Munro's books, and it is linked with the idea that there are levels of access to truth which have nothing to do with what in the world passes for wisdom or intelligence.

This is shown quite clearly in the first chapter—or story—of *Lives of Girls and Women,* **"The Flats Road,"** where the central character is an eccentric, Uncle Benny, who lives in a house full of junk on the edge of the bush and works as a hired man on Ben Jordan's fox farm:

> Probably the reason he kept on working for my father, though he had never worked steadily at any other job, was that my father raised silver foxes, and there was in such a business something precarious and some glamorous and ghostly, never realized, hope of fortune.

It is through Uncle Benny that Del and her brother begin to learn the perilous wonders of the natural world, represented by the great bog with its ravenous quicksands that stretches beyond his home; it is through him that they begin to recognize the inexpressible strangeness of human relations, represented by his disastrous adventure with a mail-order wife:

> So lying alongside our world was Uncle Benny's world like a troubling reflection, the same, but never at all the same. In that world people could go down in quicksand, be vanquished by ghosts or terrible ordinary cities; luck and wickedness were gigantic and unpredictable; nothing was deserved, anything might happen; defeats were met with crazy satisfaction. It was his triumph, that he couldn't know about, to make us see.

Through the remaining chapters of *Lives of Girls and Women* runs the recurrent theme of people who, whether they intend or know it, "make us see." In **"Heirs of the Living Body"** it is the old great-aunts preserving a model of the idealized Victorian Ontario farm life as they provide for their brother, Uncle Craig, who spends his time writing a vast prosaic chronicle of the history of his district. When he dies, his sisters give Del his manuscript, remarking: "He had the gift. He could get everything in and still make it read smooth." And ironically, though Del rejects Uncle Craig's manuscript by losing it, this is what her narrative seeks to do, to get everything in that is of importance, and to "make it read smooth"—the realist's ambition.

In other chapters her mother's intellectual restlessness, her own search for a faith that seems to meet her poetic expectations of religion, and the frenetic dedication to a parody of art which inspires the hysterically flamboyant teacher Miss Farris who produces the school operetta every year (and having lived to the limit of her own style commits suicide), are all stages on the path to self-realization and to realization of the true nature of the world along which Del is proceeding. So in the strangely poised title chapter, **"Lives of Girls and Women,"** Del's sexual fantasies about middle-aged Mr Chamberlain come to a climax in more ways than one when he takes her out to the country and masturbates in her presence. It could have been a shocking and traumatic experience, but Del takes it in her ironic stride, already at heart the observer-writer to whom everything is grist to the mill. This comes out at the end of the chapter, when her mother makes the statement that gives chapter and book their common title:

> There is a change coming I think in the lives of girls and women. Yes. But it is up to us to make it come. All women have had up till now has been their connection with men. All we have had. No more lives of our own, really, than domestic animals. . . .

It sounds like a good feminist statement until, talking of "self-respect," Ida Jordan makes it clear—at least in Del's mind—that she is talking about the caution and calculation which "being female" must impose on women,

> Whereas men were supposed to be able to go out and take on all kinds of experiences and shuck off what they didn't want and come back proud. Without even thinking about it, I had decided to do the same.

And this is precisely what Del attempts, becoming involved in a love affair with a fervent young Baptist, being so submerged emotionally as to lose the scholarship her brilliance at school has led her to expect, but retaining enough of a will to reject finally his desire to overpower her mentally as well as sexually; resisting his attempt to baptize her forcibly, she brings their relationship to an end.

Her love burnt out, her scholarly ambitions abandoned, Del turns to the writing she has dabbled with over the years, and sets about composing a highly Gothic novel about a Jubilee family all of whose children have ended tragically, in suicide or madness. And then, by chance, she meets one of the sons, recently released from his mental home, and finds how false her perceptions have been, like the distortions of a bad photographer. Writing, she decides, must be true to the spirit of what it portrays, to its often unsensational reality. And it is in this realization, we are free to assume, though Munro never says it directly, that Del has written the book we have just read.

If one reads it in connection with the earlier stories to which it is so closely linked, *Lives of Girls and Women* is a remarkable achievement both in human understanding and in technical prowess, presenting a psychologically and emotionally convincing episodic narrative of a questing child's development into a young woman on the edge of artistic achievement, and using a quasidocumentary form so effectively that we are always aware of the imagination shaping and illuminating the gifts of an obviously vivid memory.

The second novel, *Who Do You Think You Are?*, is a much less convincing book than *Lives of Girls and Women*, in both emotional and aesthetic terms. It too is a *Bildungsroman*, extending well beyond childhood into the darker times of middle age with its failed marriages, humiliating love affairs and mundane careers. The story of Rose, her upbringing in the rural slum of West Hanratty, and her subsequent and doomed marriage to a rich fellow student, develops the theme of social climbing and its perils that is already present in *Lives of Girls and Women*. The novel, again a series of loosely connected episodes, is written in the third person, and this shift in point of view accompanies—perhaps even creates—a notable change in tone from the earlier book. In *Lives of Girls and Women* the sense of familiar authenticity was sustained by the fact that the aspirant writer as central character was assumed to be both participant and observer. In *Who Do You Think You Are?* the participant is observed, and there is a kind of hard objectivity to the book with its relentless social documentation of low life in West Hanratty at the end of the Thirties. Though Munro does make a largely successful attempt to project the inner life of her principal character, the other leading figures in the novel, like Rose's crotchety stepmother Flo, her violent father and her snobbish husband, are shallow projections, almost caricatures, portrayed with none of the feeling and understanding that characterized the presentation of the father and mother, Ben and Ida Jordan, in the earlier novel.

Yet, though the general tone of *Who Do You Think You Are?* is at once harsher and more brittle than that of *Lives of Girls and Women*, there is a variation of quality within the book, and the first four chapters, which deal with childhood in Ontario, are the most effective. When the action moves into other places, notably the alien realm of British Columbia, the documentary background becomes more uncertain, and as Munro deals with the problems of adults living out their erotic fantasies she seems too near her subject for the special kind of luminous objectivity that characterizes the stories of childhood and adolescence to develop.

A similar criticism applies to the later stories contained in *Something I've Been Meaning to Tell You* and *The Moons of Jupiter*. Reading them, one becomes aware how little Munro has changed as a writer since the early period of the 1950s and the 1960s when she first attracted the attention of readers. She is still at her best as the magic realist. She has not moved, like so many of her contemporaries, into fantasy, or into an experimental use of memory like that of Margaret Laurence, while the episodic and open-ended form of her so-called novels arises not from any deconstructionist intent, but, I suggest, from the kind of perception that sees life discontinuously, episode by episode.

An excerpt from "The Jack Randa Hotel," in *Open Secrets*

After Will went away, it seemed to Gail that her shop was filling up with women. Not necessarily buying clothes. She didn't mind this. It was like the long-ago days, before Will. Women were sitting around in ancient armchairs beside Gail's ironing board and cutting table, behind the faded batik curtains, drinking coffee. Gail started grinding the coffee beans herself, as she used to do. The dressmaker's dummy was soon draped with beads and had a scattering of scandalous graffiti. Stories were told about men, usually about men who had left. Lies and injustices and confrontations. Betrayals so horrific—yet so trite—that you could only rock with laughter when you heard them. Men made fatuous speeches (*I am sorry, but I no longer feel committed to this marriage*). They offered to sell back to the wives cars and furniture that the wives themselves had paid for. They capered about in self-satisfaction because they had managed to impregnate some dewy dollop of womanhood younger than their own children. They were fiendish and childish. What could you do but give up on them? In all honor, in pride, and for your own protection?

Gail's enjoyment of all this palled rather quickly. Too much coffee could make your skin look livery. An underground quarrel developed among the women when it turned out that one of them had placed an ad in the Personal Column. Gail shifted from coffee with friends to drinks with Cleata, Will's mother. As she did this, oddly enough her spirits grew more sober. Some giddiness still showed in the notes she pinned to her door so that she could get away early on summer afternoons. (Her clerk, Donalda, was on her holidays, and it was too much trouble to hire anybody else.)

Gone to the Opera.

Gone to the Funny Farm.

Gone to stock up on the Sackcloth and Ashes.

Actually these were not her own inventions, but things Will used to write out and tape on her door in the early days when they wanted to go upstairs. She heard that such flippancy was not appreciated by people who had driven some distance to buy a dress for a wedding, or girls on an expedition to buy clothes for college. She did not care.

Alice Munro, in her Open Secrets, *Random House, 1994.*

In making these remarks I do not mean to suggest that the later stories are unimpressive. They are always skillful in their presentation of human situations, and the prose never falters. There is not a sloppily written piece among them. As studies of generational distancing, some of the stories seen from the viewpoint of old people, like **"Walking on Water"** and **"Marrakesh,"** are entirely convincing, while here and there are still marvelously lucid evocations of childhood and adolescence like **"The Found Boat"** and **"The Turkey Season."** Much less satisfying are the stories of middle-aged women with elusive lovers, and here the very impeccability of the writing seems to emphasize the psychological hollowness. At times, in recent years, one feels that Munro has fallen into the trap of virtuosity. She is so good at the kind of story she has always written that she seems never to have felt the need to try anything different. The result has been a certain leaching of character from her writing; some of her later stories are so well made that they seem anonymous, like those *New Yorker* stories which might have been written by any one of a number of North American virtuosi; indeed, the Munro stories of which this seems especially true, like **"Dulse"** and **"Labour Day Dinner"** in *The Moons of Jupiter,* in fact appeared in the *New Yorker.*

I am conscious, remembering what I expected of Munro when I first read her early stories and *Lives of Girls and Women,* of a disappointment with her career seen as a whole. Most of her early stories and some of the later ones are among the best ever written in Canada. But those whom we think of as major writers, while they do not necessarily evolve in the sense of becoming always better, do tend to metamorphose and so indefinitely to enlarge their scope, as poets like Earle Birney and Dorothy Livesay and novelists like Robertson Davies and Timothy Findley have done. In this respect Alice Munro has remained fundamentally unchanged, applying the same realist techniques with the same impeccable skill and merely varying the human situations. Her potentialities have always been major; her achievements have never quite matched them because she has never mastered those transformations of form with which major writers handle the great climactic shifts of life. She has written of all the ages as she first wrote of childhood, and that is why her lives of girls are so much more convincing than her lives of women.

Lorraine York   (essay date Winter 1987)

SOURCE: " 'Gulfs' and 'Connections': The Fiction of Alice Munro," in *Essays on Canadian Writing,* No. 35, Winter, 1987, pp. 135-46.

[*In the following essay, York discusses the theme of connection in Munro's work, primarily in* Lives of Girls and Woman *and* The Moons of Jupiter.]

"Connection," muses the young narrator of the story section bearing the same title in *The Moons of Jupiter,* "That was what it was all about." The same claim could well be made for Alice Munro's fiction. Although she is often praised for her creation of fictional places—Jubilee, Hanratty, Logan—it is also true that Munro has defined a lin-

guistic area no less peculiar to herself. That area is, of course, partly defined by her spirited use of the oxymoron (amply discussed by Helen Hoy and Lorraine McMullen), but even individual words may be trademarks of Munro's sensibility. My own list of "Munro words" includes: "humiliation," "familiar," "shameful," "hopeful," "amazing," and especially "connection." More than any other term, "connection" sums up the fundamental vision of Alice Munro's fiction.

This emphasis on connections and connectedness—whether religious, sexual, historical, or aesthetic—has become increasingly marked in Munro's works, starting with *Lives of Girls and Women.* In her first collection of short stories, *Dance of the Happy Shades,* "connection" is not a key term at all; it rarely, if ever, appears in any of the fifteen stories. Fourteen years later, however, in *The Moons of Jupiter,* "connection" has become a frequent verbal touchstone, the title of the first section of the very first story (**"Chaddeleys and Flemings"**), and a fundamental organizing motif, drawing together the entire collection of stories.

Appropriately, connections first become of interest to Munro in her first book of interconnected stories: *Lives of Girls and Women.* Connections fascinate Munro profoundly in this work because they are precisely the substance and aim of Del Jordan's search: connections between herself and the external world, and between religious, sexual, and artistic experiences. Indeed, the whole collection chronicles a young female artist's drive to perceive connections between her inner and outer worlds.

Del's search—and ours as readers—begins with an investigation of the connections sought by two characters—Uncles Benny and Craig. (Interestingly, the men also represent two kinds of connection to Del—one is her "false" uncle and one is her uncle by blood.) Uncle Benny, though not a blood connection, has ultimately more to teach Del about connections than does her legal relative. Although Benny is mystified by the workings of the outer world—the connections between Jubilee and the metropolises of Kitchener and Toronto, for instance—he represents a subtler, more mysterious connection for the young Del. "So alongside our world was Uncle Benny's world like a troubling distorted reflection, the same but never at all the same." When Del attempts to express Benny's connections with the universe by writing out in Joycean fashion his cosmic address (*"Mr. Benjamin Thomas Poole, The Flats Road, Jubilee, Wawanash County, Ontario, Canada, North America, The Western Hemisphere, The World, The Solar System, The Universe"*), Benny does indeed become a troubling, distorting "Poole": "Where is that in relation to Heaven?" he persists. Through Benny, Del glimpses a whole array of connections which defy or "lie alongside" rational thought—superstitious, intuitive, or religious connections which she will investigate further in *Lives of Girls and Women.*

Benny's pulp newspapers have, of course, provided Del with a connection to the world of depravity and violence, but Benny's life, his "troubling distorted reflection," has also brought before her eyes the inescapable interconnectedness of human lives. She muses on her parents near the end of **"The Flats Road"** section: "they did not look at each other. But they were connected, and this connection was as plain as a fence, it was between us and Uncle Benny, us and the Flats Road, it would stay between us and anything." *Lives of Girls and Women* is, to a great extent, a dramatization of this idea of connections.

Uncle Craig, on the other hand, is a character who has his connections with the outside world, his place in the cosmos, neatly sorted out: "He saw a simple connection between himself, handling the affairs of the township, troublesome as they often were, and the prime minister in Ottawa handling the affairs of the country." Craig has devoted himself to chronicling the social connections of the pioneers of Wawanash County, and the microcosmic domestic connections of the Jordan family: "And to Uncle Craig it seemed necessary that the names of all these people, their connections with each other, the three large dates of birth and marriage and death . . . be discovered . . . and written down here, in order, in his own large careful handwriting." Although Craig is a fanatical devotee of connections, he lacks both the connection with the abstract or mysterious and the sense of human connectedness which Del has associated with Uncle Benny; his connections are mere data, and his work cuts him off from other human beings, as he sits doggedly typing in his office, significantly locking out the laughter of Aunt Elspeth and Auntie Grace.

Del, then, has had an opportunity to study two modes of connection—one which involves superstition and chaos and one which involves their opposites, calculation and order; her task in *Lives of Girls and Women* will be to find a way of uniting the two. At this early stage, though, Del suffers more often than not from acute feelings of unconnectedness. When she is tickled and tormented by her cousin Mary Agnes she reflects, "I was amazed as people must be who are seized and kidnapped, and who realize that in the strange world of their captors they have a value absolutely unconnected with anything they know about themselves." Understandably, Del reacts to this sense of unconnectedness by trying to gain the upper hand, by trying to sever her connection with the "strange world" of other human beings: she bites Mary Agnes. "When I bit Mary Agnes," she confesses, "I thought I was biting myself off from everything. I thought I was putting myself outside, where no punishment would ever be enough."

Following Uncle Benny's lead, Del initially looks to "Heaven" for a sense of connectedness. Indeed, she seeks a higher connection, an assurance that "all those atoms, galaxies of atoms, were safe all the time, whirling away in God's mind." Soon, though, Del discovers that these connections are, for her, imposed and unsatisfactory; they do not bear any relation to her own experience. "The idea of God," she confesses, "did not connect for me with any idea of being good, which is perhaps odd." Later, during the Good Friday service at the Anglican church, she perceives that Christ himself, because he was partly mortal, may have experienced the same split between divine plan and individual experience when he was on the cross: *"My God, my God, why hast thou forsaken me?* Briefly, the minister said, oh very briefly, Jesus had lost touch with

God . . . He had lost the connection. . . . But this too was part of the plan." Del, however, entertains the thought that this was "the last true cry of Christ"—his final testimony to the unconnected nature of the universe.

Closely related to this concept of religious connection in *Lives of Girls and Women* is the concept of sexual connection. When Del is riding with Mr. Chamberlain through the countryside prior to their sexual "encounter," she recalls that "In some moods, some days, I could feel for a clump of grass, a rail fence, a stone pile, such pure unbounded emotion as I used to hope for, and have inklings of, in connection with God." Now, though, she can only reflect in both excitement and dismay that the landscape has become "debased, maddeningly erotic." Sex, we soon see, can no more give Del the sense of connectedness than could religion; it cannot even rival her former religious feeling. Ironically, her first sexually charged meeting with Garnet French takes place during a revival meeting—a strong indication that this sexual connection, too, will prove as fleeting and unsatisfactory to her as her earlier flirtation with religious belief.

As a child, then as an adolescent, Del tends to see sexuality as a purely physical rather than spiritual connection. When her Uncle Bill and Aunt Nile visit the Jordans, Del never imagines that her aunt and uncle might indulge in sexual relations: "decent adults," she thinks, "made their unlikely connection only for the purpose of creating a child." Later, this mechanistic view of sex is fostered in Del and her friend Naomi by their covert readings of Naomi's mother's sex manuals: *"Care should be taken during the initial connection. . . ."*

In spite of her adolescent fascination with the physical aspects of sexual connection, Del ultimately desires a spiritual connection as well. "It was the stage of transition, bridge between what was possible, known and moral behavior, and the magical, bestial act, that I could not imagine," she confesses. "Nothing about that was in Naomi's mother's book," she adds. Because Del does yearn for a spiritual or "magical" connection in her sexual life, she is particularly upset when she reads a New York psychiatrist's theory that women's mental connections are purely physical; that when a boy and a girl look at the moon, "The boy thinks of the universe, its immensity and mystery; the girl thinks, 'I must wash my hair.'" Ironically, in Del's relationship with Garnet, these stereotypes are completely reversed; Del desires physical *and* intellectual enlightenment in sex and Garnet mistrusts everything beyond the literal: "Any attempt at this kind of general conversation, any attempt to make him think in this way, to theorize, make systems, brought a blank, very slightly offended, and superior look into his face. He hated people using big words, talking about things outside of their own lives. He hated people trying to tie things together." In Garnet, Del, the seeker of connections, finds her natural enemy: a man who is entirely anti-connection.

When Del turns from sex to art as a means of making connections, she is unwittingly illustrating her mother Addie's words, "There is a change coming I think in the lives of girls and women. Yes. But it is up to us to make it come. All women have had up till now has been their connection with men." Even though Del disparages her mother's advice, she breaks the old male-female power connection in **"Baptizing"** and decides finally that it is up to her to make her own connections with the external world. "Unconnected to the life of love, uncolored by love," she dazedly realizes, "the world resumes its own, its natural and callous importance." In her art, Del discovers that it is the physical world, in all its rich and diverse detail, to which she must seek connection. When she meets Bobby Sherriff in **"Epilogue: The Photographer,"** she realizes how she has let this crucial connection lapse in the novel she has been writing: "I hardly connected him with my mad Halloway brother" she confesses. Just as a younger Del discovered that she could not make a connection with spiritual forces by wandering about with her eyes shut, because she was afraid "of bumping into something," the Del of the epilogue discovers that the physical world provides the artist with the only connection to the transcendent that she needs.

In *Something I've Been Meaning to Tell You,* Munro focuses on a particular element of this connection between the artist and the world: the vital connection between self and others. **"Material,"** for instance, is a story concerned with the way artists use and transform human relationships in their work. The narrator sees that Hugo has used the "harlot-in-residence," Dotty, for the purposes of his fiction, and she also sees that *"This is not enough"* because she alone maintained a personal connection with Dotty while they were living in the same building with her. (Hugo's turning off the water pump which services Dotty's basement apartment is a striking example of his tendency to sever human connections.) On the other hand, the narrator's present husband, Gabriel, though he shares with Hugo the knowledge of "what to do" with material (Gabriel is an engineer), at least has what Hugo lacks—a sense of human connection. It is Gabriel who persuades the narrator to buy the book containing Hugo's story for her daughter Clea: "He is interested in Hugo's career as he would be interested in the career of a magician or popular singer or politician with whom he had, through me, a plausible connection, a proof of reality."

Often, in *Something I've Been Meaning to Tell You,* characters lament the absence of these human connections in their lives. In **"Walking on Water,"** Mr. Lougheed's glimpse of the animalistic sexual connection of the flower children, Rex and Calla, increases his own sense of alienation from this younger generation. Although the couple's "essential connection" is abruptly broken when they see Lougheed, "their voices joined . . . in laughter that seemed" to the Mr. Sammler-like Lougheed "not only unashamed but full of derision." Interestingly, this episode is later echoed in **"Marrakesh,"** when Dorothy unwittingly stumbles upon the lovemaking of her granddaughter, Jeannette, and Blair King. She, too, has experienced the lack of connection that Lougheed and many other Munro characters share: "She believed then . . . that Jeannette was in some important way a continuation of herself. This was not apparent any longer; the connection had either broken or gone invisible." Instead, the body of her granddaughter basking in the sun becomes a "hieroglyph" to

Dorothy, a visual sign of the human connection that can never fully be recovered.

In **"Winter Wind,"** Munro argues explicitly and eloquently that the artist, in particular, must not lose faith in these human connections, frail and elusive though they may be. The mature narrator interrupts her story about her grandmother's life to ask herself how much of this story is based on her knowledge of fact and how much her intuition and imagination. Finally, she decides that the latter qualities may yield a truth far superior to that deduced from Uncle Craig-like fact: "Without any proof I believe it, and so I must believe that we get messages another way, that we have connections that cannot be investigated, but have to be relied on."

Munro does investigate these human connections, but her investigations are neither purely rational nor scientific; they are fictional and intuitive. In *Who Do You Think You Are?,* for instance, she examines a character whose sense of unconnectedness is far more acute than that of Del Jordan. Rose suffers from a chronic sense of disjunction: her father is both a secretive reciter of poetry and a hate-filled child beater; West Hanratty, her home, is divided by a river (and by economic conditions and opportunities) from Hanratty proper. Even when Rose is older and more prosperous, this sense of unconnectedness continues to plague her; she senses that "the barriers between people were still strong and reliable; between arty people and business people; between men and women." Rose has a glimpse of other barriers between humans when she tries to read one of her stepmother Flo's letters to an assembled company and suddenly feels a "fresh and overwhelming realization" of "the gulf that lay behind her." This unconnectedness to one's past—to one's Hanratty, Jubilee, or Logan—becomes a major concern in Munro's work, especially in her next collection, *The Moons of Jupiter*.

In *Who Do You Think You Are?,* Rose tries in various ways to attain a sense of connectedness, some more successful than others. Her attempts to forge sexual connections are disastrous, mostly because she expects to derive her essential identity from them. She marries Patrick because he will worship her, make her his "White Goddess," his "Beggar Maid," and she later grasps at Simon because he is "the man for my life." "Without this connection to a man," the narrator observes, "she might have seen herself as an uncertain and pathetic person; that connection held her new life in place." Only dimly, by the end of the collection, does Rose suspect that the only person for her life is herself, and that the important connections to discover are those between herself and her past.

The latter realization, in particular, comes slowly to Rose, for her past seems, from the vantage point of the present, bizarre; it seems to be material for shocking, dramatic stories to be told at cocktail parties. Even as a young girl she reflects that "Present time and past, the shady melodramatic past of Flo's stories, were quite separate." "Town oddity" Becky Tyde, like Bobby Sherriff, seems cut off from her legendary role; "only a formal connection could be made," muses Rose. Eventually, Rose reaches beyond this merely formal connection with her past when she returns to Flo and Hanratty in **"Spelling."** Like Helen in

"The Peace of Utrecht," Rose discovers scraps of her old writing—in this case, old letters she sent to Flo from Vancouver—"False messengers; false connections, with a lost period of her life." Although these scraps of writing do not awaken the texture and feeling of the past, as do Helen's notes about the Peace of Utrecht, they do, at least, force Rose to acknowledge that her connections with the past have been false, and that she must forge honest ones in the future.

Ironically, at the end of *Who Do You Think You Are?,* Rose attempts to forge honest connections with a man she has not seen for forty years—Ralph Gillespie. For Rose, trying to understand Ralph is akin to trying to understand herself; both are mimics, imitators whose imitations of life have become stale, even dangerous. Here, at last, Rose finds the most honest connection of her life: "What could she say about herself and Ralph Gillespie, except that she felt his life, close, closer than the lives of men she'd loved, one slot over from her own?"

The subtitle of Alice Munro's *The Moons of Jupiter* could very well be "Connections," for here she studies the problem in greater depth than in any previous work. Here, too, she gives voice most strongly to the idea that art may be the most reliable means of forging an honest connection with the past.

Family connections, and the guilt or pride they may instil in us, are a central concern of both sections of the first story—sections which are closely interconnected. In the first, "Connection," the narrator claims that her maternal cousins provided "A connection with the real, and prodigal, and dangerous, world." Years later, when one of those cousins, Iris, visits the narrator and her husband in their pretentious Vancouver-area home, it becomes apparent that this connection has vanished; Iris is now out of place, uneasy in an unfamiliar suburban world. Nevertheless, the narrator's act of throwing a lemon meringue pie at her husband when he openly deplores her vulgar connection reveals more emphatically than any words could the persistence of an essential connection with the cousins. It reveals, more specifically, a connection with the cousins' world of jokes and hilarity (throwing a pie is, of course, a stock comic routine). For all of the cousins' pride in their supposedly aristocratic connections in the Old World, this brash exuberance is their true legacy and birthright. (A comic but macabre version of this family pride appears in **"Accident,"** where Frances' sister-in-law Adelaide flaunts her "connection" with an "undertaker . . . in another town" [he is her uncle] by using the latest mortuary terminology.)

Guilt aroused by family connections is the corresponding motif of the second section, "The Stone in the Field." The sight of even an eccentric non-relative, Poppy Cullender, in the family parlour humiliates the narrator: "I disliked his connection with us so much. . . ." Later, she likens one of her paternal aunts to Poppy, and claims that she "couldn't really think of her as my aunt; the connection seemed impossible." Whereas the maternal cousins thrive on connection (they sing interconnected rounds, and they never return to Dalgleish after one cousin's death because, as Iris sadly writes, "the circle was broken"), the paternal aunts are completely unconnected to the outside world. Not only do they have no telephone connections, they spurn physical connection: "No embraces, no touch of hands or laying together of cheeks" in that household, the narrator recalls. And yet, mysteriously, their circle remains unbroken; the sisters remain secluded with each other for the rest of their lives, occasionally sending Christmas cards to the narrator which arouse in her not nostalgia but "bewilderment and unexplainable guilt."

Fiction and story-telling are prime means of creating connections out of an experience which is often choppy and chaotic.

—Lorraine York

Largely as a result of this unexplainable guilt, the narrator, like Rose, makes a concerted effort to return to her childhood town, to forge those forgotten or disparaged connections with her past. Ironically, though, the object of the narrator's search is not a living connection at all; it is a huge stone which marked the grave of a mysterious hermit who was rumoured to be an admirer of one of the paternal aunts. The narrator's failure to find this unmarked gravestone, and her discovery of an up-to-date, businesslike farm in its place give ample testimony to the elusive nature of connections. These are the connections which cannot be "investigated," tracked down, and pinpointed, but which must remain as mysterious and as unlocatable as the stone in the field.

In *The Moons of Jupiter,* Munro elaborates upon the idea that art can be the stone in the field, the marker of our connections with the past. Characters often come across scraps of history while working on a writing project; the narrator of **"The Stone in the Field"** finds the newspaper notice about the hermit's death while reading microfilm "in connection with a documentary script I was working on, for television." The narrator of **"Bardon Bus"** is working in Australia "in connection with" a "book of family history which some rich people are paying me to write." (Ironically, this writer who is investigating family connections which are entirely *un*connected to her forms a false ménage with a man referred to as "X.") Work and life are continually connected, interwoven.

More specifically, fiction and story-telling are prime means of creating connections out of an experience which is often choppy and chaotic. In **"Visitors,"** Mildred compares the storytelling techniques of the two brothers Albert and Wilfred. Whereas Albert baldly presents the facts as separate and unrelated particles, Wilfred is a weaver of connections: "In Wilfred's stories you could always be sure that the gloomy parts would give way to something better, and if somebody behaved in a peculiar way there was an explanation for it." Connections, then, are more pleasing to ponder aesthetically and emotionally. Nevertheless, Munro also reveals the dangers inherent in insisting that connections always be made. At the end of **"The Stone in the Field,"** the narrator admits that "If I had been younger, I would have figured out a story" about the hermit and her aunts, a story which would have featured "a horrible, plausible connection" between the hermit's silence and his death. Connections, when drawn so neatly in life or in fiction, Munro suggests, can hinder imagination and understanding instead of promoting both, as they are supposed to do. Maturity, for the narrator and for the writer, involves a refusal to "believe that people's secrets are defined and communicable, or their feelings full-blown and easy to recognize."

In *The Moons of Jupiter,* Munro follows her own advice; she presents not the final, immutable connections in people's lives but, more frequently, their desperate attempts to find connections. Many characters suffer an acute lack of connection between their inner experience and the world around them: Lydia, in **"Dulse,"** who in the wake of her lover's rejection "could not make the connection between herself and things outside herself"; the narrator in **"The Turkey Season"** whose feelings about the mystery of the universe cannot "be connected with anything in real life"; and the woman in the story Kay tells in **"Bardon Bus,"** who sees her old lover and "can't connect the real man any more with the person she loves, in her head." Maturity for these characters, too, often means accepting that connections may not always be possible or even necessary; as Mildred realizes in **"Visitors,"** the reason Wilfred once gave for his weeping at night is probably "only distantly connected with the real reason. But maybe it was as close as he could get."

In *The Moons of Jupiter,* therefore, the process of working towards connections is more valuable than the product—the connections themselves. The best illustration of this maxim appears in the title story. The narrator's father, awaiting a heart operation in a Toronto hospital, is a man who takes pride in his ability to perceive connections, even if he cannot always understand how he has arrived at them: "I ask my mind a question. The answer's there, but I can't see all the connections my mind's making to get it. Like a computer." Nevertheless, he believes that there can be an answer (the names of the moons of Jupiter, for instance) and he believes that he can attain it through connections. His daughter, on the other hand, finds her faith in such processes seriously diminished. She discovers that sometimes answers are relative; for instance, when she attends the planetarium show she learns that all of the information about the planets which she had learned as a child has been updated, curiously transformed. Similarly, she finds that she cannot make the separate elements of her life connect; it is as though they were moons orbiting a planet. In particular, she sees that her children will follow paths of their own. In the last scene, this new acceptance is signalled by her refusal to go back to the museum to see "the relief carvings, the stone pictures." Like the past, the stone reliefs will always be there; she needn't see them and master the idea of them, in order to affirm their existence, just as the narrator of **"The Stone in the Field"** needn't find the stone in order to assert her connection with the past. Connections in Munro are of central impor-

tance, they are "what it was all about," as the narrator of **"Connection"** says, and yet they needn't be pursued, for they are all around us and deep inside us.

Judith Timson   (essay date 7 May 1990)

SOURCE: "Merciful Light," in *Maclean's,* Vol. 103, No. 19, May 7, 1990, pp. 66-7.

[*In the following essay, based on an interview with Munro following the publication of* Friend of My Youth, *Timson relates the importance and discipline of writing in Munro's life.*]

After a writer has been ranked with Chekhov, accused of perfection and called one of the greatest short-story writers in the world, it can be an intimidating task to write again. But, for Alice Munro, apparently nothing has changed. "I write the way I always have," she says. "I sit in a corner of the chesterfield and stare at the wall, and I keep getting it, and *getting* it, and when I've got it enough in my mind, I start to write. And then, of course, I don't really have it at all." Munro's fans, and the growing recognition and superlatives that her work receives internationally, belie such modesty, bred in the bone of the small-town Ontario native. The publication this spring of her newest collection, *Friend of My Youth,* was an instant literary event not only in Canada but also in the United States, where the writer and her work have garnered rave reviews. Prominent American author Cynthia Ozick hit the high note on the new book's dust jacket, declaring, "She is our Chekhov." But Munro tempers that praise by noting, "*Entertainment Today* called it 'Sex lives of Canadians.' "

Munro's stories, most of them intensely personal accounts of the lives of women of her generation, born in the 1930s and 1940s, have captivated readers around the world. There is now an identifiable Munro country, powerfully mapped out by such earlier collections as *Lives of Girls and Women, The Moons of Jupiter* and *The Progress of Love* (which won Munro her third Governor General's Award, in 1986). For 13 years, her work has appeared regularly in *The New Yorker,* and her editor there, Daniel Menaker, describes her as "a kind of trailblazer, structurally and esthetically." An Alice Munro story zooms effortlessly through time zones, spans generations and offers up more detail and description than do many full-length contemporary novels. It also offers a kind of emotional honesty, said Menaker, which suggests that "the author, along with her characters, has gone through a very painful and disciplined examination of self."

On a recent visit to Toronto to launch her seventh book, Munro appeared to be flourishing as much as her reputation, wearing a pink top with a long scarf of pinks and reds. At 58, she is a writer who is still exploring new ways to do what she does so well, and still surprising even herself with the results. In a story called **"Meneseteung,"** she tells the tale of Almeda Roth, a Victorian-age poet in small-town Ontario, an unmarried woman who, through her flowery poetry, tries to deny the primitive quality of the life around her. It is a tricky work because parts of it, including excerpts from Roth's book of poetry and her obituary, suggest that she was a real person, brought to life from some dusty newspaper clippings. But, in fact, the whole thing, including the poetry, is out of Alice Munro via the chesterfield. And the author recalled that, when she finished the story, "I was excited—I thought it was *good*."

The remark was followed by a whooping laugh—self-congratulation was practically a capital offence in south-western Ontario, where Munro grew up and where many of her stories are set. "The worst thing you could ever do was to make a fool of yourself," she said, "and any kind of self-promotion or self-exposure runs this risk."

By now, Munro has become used to the risks of self-exposure, and she has no need of self-promotion. She adamantly refused to do the usually requisite cross-country book tour, and instead would submit to only five media interviews. In an age in which even celebrated authors have to peddle themselves and their work as talk-show curiosities, Munro's decision to firmly close the door on a certain kind of literary celebrity is notable. She describes her last book tour as "too physically debilitating—I never slept." It was not that she hated the attention. "It's a terrific ego trip and it really gets me high," she said. "But I get used to shooting my mouth off and then I go home and how do I get into that other life, that other person? I feel that whatever it is that is the private person gets drowned."

The private person lives quietly in Clinton, Ont., 35 km from Wingham, where she was the first of three children born to turkey and fox farmer Robert Laidlaw and his wife, Anne. Munro shares a modest house with her second husband, Gerald Fremlin, a retired cartographer. In an earlier life, while living on the West Coast with her bookseller husband James Munro, she raised three daughters.

She recalls that she had to learn how to write short stories between getting apple juice, answering the phone and letting the cat in. "It nearly drove me crazy," she admitted. Munro expresses no regrets about how she brought up her children—"I loved being a mother, I wasn't a monster to them." But one of her most persistent fantasies, she said, is to return to early motherhood "and just enjoy it," free from what her publisher and longtime friend, Douglas Gibson of McClelland and Stewart, describes as "an almost puritanical discipline surrounding her work." Now, she preserves her writing time and energy "with a great deal of guilt and misery," she said.

Munro's guilt illuminates the difference between male and female writers of a certain age: it centres on the personal obligations that have gone unfulfilled. "From the age of 11, art was my religion," she said. "Nothing in my life seemed more important to me." She worries about not having been there when certain people needed her: "This question comes up, especially for a woman of my age. It's spending time with people when I know it would make a difference to them. It's writing the letter, making the hospital visit." She added: "This is what women have always done. They've kept the human warmth of life going. Well, twice in my life I had a chance to do something, to nurse my mother and my mother-in-law, but I didn't give myself over to it because I wanted to write. Of course, no male

writer in middle age would even have considered doing it."

It is possible to read an Alice Munro story and never quite know why a simple observation, or an unassuming sentence, placed at a certain point, adds up to genius and revelation. It simply does.

—*Judith Timson*

Munro's regrets, however, have nothing to do with the demands of the outside world. In contrast to other high-profile writers, including Margaret Atwood and Pierre Berton, who spearhead political causes and act on behalf of the writing community, she easily turns down almost all requests to do so. "I can slough off that duty quite easily," she said. "These people are asking me to do something because I am a writer. If I do it, I will no longer be a writer."

It is possible to read an Alice Munro story and never quite know why a simple observation, or an unassuming sentence, placed at a certain point, adds up to genius and revelation. It simply does. In the title story of her new book, the narrator examines her feelings for her dead mother while telling the tale of two sisters who love the same man. She describes an old farmhouse in the Ottawa Valley, "a torrent of unmerciful light pouring through the window." But the light that Alice Munro sheds on her characters is more forgiving, filled with compassion and humor. In the story **"Wigtime,"** her central character, Margot, is almost pathetic as she dresses up in a wig and dark sunglasses and goes off in a rented van to catch her husband in the throes of a weekend liaison with their teenage babysitter. The point of the story, however, is more than dread and betrayal. It is getting what you want: Margot not only manages to keep her husband in the marriage, but blackmails him into buying her the house of her dreams, complete with an almond-colored kitchen and "swooping pale green figured curtains." Said Munro: "Everyone has such contempt for the suburban housewife and her acquisitions, but I wanted to glorify her."

Munro's characters are, for the most part, ordinary small-town people—schoolteachers, housewives, appliance-store salesmen, retired ministers—who circle back relentlessly to various pivotal events in their lives, as if to finally learn their lessons. Most of them have some sort of subversive quality about them. Half the stories in *Friend of My Youth* deal with adultery, and few writers portray the female adulterer better than Munro. "This might be a problem in Huron County," said the author, recalling at least one editorial directed against her in *The Wingham Advance-Times*. She captures her female protagonists, like Brenda in the story **"Five Points,"** wearing tight white pants and too much perfume, poised to sin. Brenda, walking down a country road to meet her lover, is wearing high heels "just for this walk, just for this moment of crossing the road with his eyes on her, that extra bit of pelvic movement and leg length they give her."

Munro acknowledges that she has a fascination with adultery and the "double life it creates, especially for a married wife and mother who is expected to live her life for other people. Instead, she can be living this secret, exploratory life." Her female characters often use adultery as a way to escape their lives and are unabashedly, in the way they view men, part of an earlier generation. "I don't understand the emotional lives of women under 35," said Munro. She questioned the impact that AIDS is having on the pursuit of romance. "Surely," she said, "it's an interesting thing if passion, which all through literature has been celebrated as a thing that cannot be gainsaid, can be changed through fear of illness and death. I feel, as a writer, I should know about this."

Friend of My Youth is more sombre than Munro's previous books, and her heroines are not as full of high hopes and the certainty that their lives will be transformed by fame and passion. Munro acknowledged that the buoyancy "may have gone down a bit," but she does not link the change in mood to her age or her feelings about her own life. "I think I'm an extraordinarily lucky person," she said. "I was born poor in what is perceived to be a backwater. I don't have a lot of strength of character. To be able to do what I want has been extraordinary luck. I just feel something in my life has gone terribly right."

Munro had originally planned to make *Friend of My Youth* her last collection of short stories, after which she would write an autobiography. "That hasn't worked out—yet," she said. "I can't seem to control what interests me." What interests Munro still is stories, and more stories. And, if she remains true to her pattern, in four years there will be another collection—another torrent of merciful light.

Mary Jo Salter   (review date 14 May 1990)

SOURCE: "In Praise of Accidents," in *The New Republic*, Vol. 202, No. 3930, May 14, 1990, pp. 50-3.

[*Salter is an American poet and critic. In the following review, she praises Munro's portrayal of imperfect women in several of the stories from* Friend of My Youth, *but questions the author's range.*]

Choosing a favorite among Alice Munro's stories is no easy task, but for me one of them would be **"Accident,"** from ***The Moons of Jupiter,*** her collection published in 1983. Frances is a music teacher at the high school where her married lover, Ted, teaches science. They are groping stark naked in Ted's supply room when the school secretary (who, like most people in the Ontario town of Hanratty, knows about the affair but has politely, up until now, kept that knowledge from the lovers themselves) bangs on the door to tell Ted that his son, Bobby, has died in a car accident.

The lovers soon learn that Bobby has not died—though he will, some hours later—and while they wait in separate places for news, Ted realizes that he has an opportunity

to make a superstitious bargain with God: save Bobby, and I'll give up Frances. But Ted, an atheist (or, you might say, a believer in Accident), rejects his own superstition even before Bobby dies, and vows to keep Frances regardless. He even refuses his son a church service, in a selfish rebellion against his wife's family. Nor does he seem terribly sorry for his wife when, in the aftermath of their only son's death, she finally learns about Frances. In fact, in a sudden, cold, thorough upheaval of his life, Ted proposes to Frances, and she accepts—but not before understanding that Ted is not what she hoped he was, and that she never knew much about him or wanted to, apart from sex.

In themselves these events would make quite a story. Instead, cut to thirty years later (a common, but unpredictably varied, Munro device). We are at the funeral of Adelaide, a sadistically pious character who would not be out of place in a Flannery O'Connor story, and who on the day of the accident had asked Frances, as if out of innocent curiosity, whether she thought God was "paying back for" the affair.

Well, Adelaide is now "paid back" for her bad manners and her morbidity, the reader might ungenerously reflect. That's one reason Munro locates us at Adelaide's funeral. Another is to bring Frances back to Hanratty, which she and Ted had left on their marriage, so that she may reencounter the blameless man whose car had been the vehicle, so to speak, of her life's transformation. "If he had not gone out in the snow that day to take a baby carriage across town," Frances thinks (and note the tactfully unelaborated symbol of the baby carriage), she

> would not live in Ottawa now, she would not
> have her two children, she would not have her
> life, not the same life. That is true. She is sure
> of it, but it is too ugly to think about. The angle
> from which she has to see that can never be admitted to; it would seem monstrous.

Here, again, is a chilling potential conclusion to the story. Another writer as skilled and honest and knowing as Munro—and there cannot be many—might well have wrapped it up at this moment. But then a peculiar phrase pops into her character's head:

> *What difference,* thinks Frances. She doesn't
> know where that thought comes from or what
> it means, for of course there is a difference, anybody can see that, a life's difference. She's had
> her love, her scandal, her man, her children . .

But it doesn't matter. Not only because she is still "the same Frances," as she uncomfortably realizes, but because people don't matter. For all the intensity of their relations (which Munro conveys early on with the sexy scramble in the supply room), for all the grief a child's death should occasion, and the disgust we may feel in seeing a parent not deepened by that death but merely deflected to another course, people are not terribly distinctive or important; and we all end up, like Bobby and Adelaide, in a casket.

This is a vision of life customarily reserved for poets, with their penchant for looking down on humanity from a great and generalizing height. But in the heart of the best fiction writer, who is more keen on telling stories about people than on displaying narrative or descriptive technique, has to be a belief that people are unique; that a story about Frances in particular, say, is worth telling. What moves and unnerves me each time I look at **"Accident"** is the simultaneous impression Munro gives that we are all both irreplaceable and dispensable. The story's title in a single word offers a further paradox: every link in the plot's chain derives from the accident, but an accident is, after all, only random.

Another of Munro's most distinguished stories, **"Miles City, Montana"** (from her 1986 collection *The Progress of Love*), also concerns the accidental death of a child. The unnamed woman narrator frames her tale with a childhood memory of the drowning of a neglected boy, Steve Gauley. The main story (also a memory) now begins: the narrator, her priggish but somewhat loved husband, Andrew, and their two young daughters, Cynthia and Meg, are on a car trip from Vancouver to Ontario. The mother loves the "shedding" of her domestic life; at home, besieged by neighbors and the telephone, she has wanted "to hide so that I could get busy at my real work, which was" (and here we might fill in something useful, something respectful toward an otherwise unfulfilled female character, like "graphic design"; but Munro continues) "a sort of wooing of distant parts of myself." We know precisely, are delighted and pained by, what she means: How often does life allow us this wooing?

She goes on:

> I could be talking to Andrew, talking to the children and looking at whatever they wanted me to look at—a pig on sign, a pony in a field, a Volkswagen on a revolving stand—and pouring lemonade into plastic cups, and all the time these bits and pieces would be flying together inside me. The essential composition would be achieved. This made me hopeful and lighthearted. It was being a watcher that did it. A watcher, not a keeper.

In a few pages, it is this mother's very joy in being a watcher, not a keeper that will nearly kill her child. Having stopped to allow the children a swim in a lifeguarded pool (but the lifeguard is kissing her boyfriend at the critical moment), the narrator is absently eyeing a popsicle stick gummed to her heel, philosophizing about the "singleness and precise location" of objects, when it occurs to her: *"Where are the children?"* Three-year-old Meg, that single, singular object, is located at the bottom of the pool; and by a miracle, she is fished out and returned just in time to life.

But the "accident," in the largest sense, isn't over: these parents will again fail their children. Earlier, the narrator's general account of her marital arguments (which might be continuing to this very day, as far as we knew) had concluded with this all-inclusive, single-sentence, lacerating paragraph: "I haven't seen Andrew for years, don't know if he is still thin, has gone completely gray, insists on lettuce, tells the truth, or is hearty and disappointed." And one day, when the children who have so trustingly returned to the back seat of the car achieve some dis-

tance from their parents—parents who wanted to believe themselves more attentive than poor Steve Gauley's—they will have to learn to forgive "whatever was flippant, arbitrary, careless, callous—all our natural, and particular, mistakes."

Not surprisingly, and yet with unforeseeable twists, more revelations about accidents occur in Munro's new collection, *Friend of My Youth*. In the marvelously wide and deep **"Oh, What Avails,"** a three-part story spanning decades in the lives of Joan (who will derail a successful marriage for a mostly happy series of affairs) and her brother Morris (who loses the use of an eye at age four, when he steps on a rake), both protagonists are half-blind, agreeable victims of external chance and their own internal limitations.

That's partly the legacy of their cheerful, feckless mother, who never even thought to take the unfortunate boy to an eye specialist: "Couldn't she have gone to the Lions Club and asked them to help her, as they sometimes did help poor people in an emergency? No. No, she couldn't," Munro amusingly offers, by way of something just short of an explanation. Every problem in this beautifully plotted story falls short of solution—a technique suited to carry the mature Joan's intimations of mortality:

> [She] is aware of a new danger, a threat that she could not have imagined when she was younger. . . . And it's hard to describe. The threat is of a change, but it's not the sort of change one has been warned about. It's just this—that suddenly, without warning, Joan is apt to think: *Rubble.* Rubble. You can look down a street, and you can see the shadows, the light, the brick walls . . . —you can see all these things in their temporary separateness, all connected underneath in such a troubling, satisfying, necessary, indescribable way. Or you can see rubble. Passing states, a useless variety of passing states. Rubble.

No conscious-seeming "style" adorns these sentences. Indeed, if ever there was a writer whose sentences both ornate and plain are essentially invisible, each a well-washed window through which we may see life as she does, it is Munro. Those who do want to remind themselves of the windowpane of style between writer and reader might consider how that unlovely word "rubble" is repeated enough times that the sound alone acquires an intended meaninglessness.

If ever there was a writer whose sentences both ornate and plain are essentially invisible, each a well-washed window through which we may see life as she does, it is Munro.

—*Mary Jo Salter*

Munro shouldn't be mistaken for an absurdist, however; the discourse on rubble doesn't end where I have lopped it off. A new paragraph begins with hope, however feeble or possibly ill-fated: "Joan wants to keep this idea of rubble at bay. She pays attention now to all the ways in which people seem to do that." In another story here, **"Differently,"** the randomness and rubble of life are themselves a source of hope for Georgia, who after remembering the marriage she smashed up and the friendship she allowed to die is grateful for a transcendent moment of forgetfulness, an "accidental clarity."

But the most haunting lines in **"Differently"** appear earlier, where Georgia wonders whether her sons keep pictures of her ex-husband in their homes. "Perhaps they put the pictures away when she comes to visit," she thinks. "Perhaps they think of protecting these images from one who did him hurt." Or, Munro invites us to speculate, they think of shielding the malefactor herself. Protectiveness isn't lavished on the innocent only; we want also to shield the guilty from too piercing a recollection of their crimes. And why? Perhaps as insurance against guilt for our own crimes, committed in the past or waiting in the future. Munro doesn't say; she respects our intelligence, our right to sift on our own the cruel world she shows us.

Cruel and bizarre things do happen in this book, as in all of Munro's collections; and although that staple of modern fiction, sexual betrayal, crops up repeatedly, its power to surprise us is in itself unexpected. Munro's stories often strike us, like life itself, as "stranger than fiction"—that's why we trust them. In the title story, the member of an obscure and punitive religious sect gets his fiancée's sister pregnant and marries her instead; years later he passes over the long-suffering former fiancée again to marry another woman—his dead wife's hateful, tarty nurse. In **"Five Points,"** an Eastern European girl, ugly and fat, pays all the boys in town for sex, until she has emptied the till of her parents' store and they are forced in shame and financial ruin to close it. The not particularly passionate wife in **"Oranges and Apples,"** whose cynicism is "automatic and irritating," takes up her worshipful, jealous husband's tacit invitation to sleep with the friend he found spying on her with binoculars.

There's a tonal harshness, too, which we welcome: the immediate revisions and reappraisals by which Munro strips away illusions that she had at first offered us. In **"Friend of My Youth,"** for example—a many-tiered story about deceit, punishment, forgiveness, death, romantic love, and the love of parents and children—the narrator, remembering her mother, writes:

> I felt a great fog of platitudes and pieties lurking, an incontestable crippled-mother power, which could capture and choke me. There would be no end to it. I had to keep myself sharp-tongued and cynical, arguing and deflating. Eventually I gave up even that recognition and opposed her in silence.

> This is a fancy way of saying that I was no comfort and poor company to her when she had almost nowhere else to turn.

That final sentence is heart-breaking, but it represents, however bitterly, an attempt to laugh. A similar, if lighter, mixture occurs in **"Differently,"** where Georgia's friend has an affair with a man who deserts her in a hotel, after which "she developed frightful chest pains, appropriate to a broken heart. What she really had was a gall-bladder attack." Ever accommodating, her husband comes to take her to the hospital, and then on vacation in Mexico! Or in **"Goodness and Mercy,"** where a daughter escorts her fatally ill mother on a cruise to Europe and then to the hospital in Edinburgh; after all her solicitude, her nearly continuous attendance by land and sea, she is not there when her mother dies but "a couple of blocks away, eating a baked potato from a takeout shop." That the daughter is rather plump, not very much in need of a baked potato, makes the moment more maddening and poignant and, yes, funny.

The recurrence of daughters attached to dying mothers in **"Friend of My Youth"** and **"Goodness and Mercy"**—a subject also addressed superbly in the early novel-in-short-story-form *The Beggar Maid*—raises the interesting question of authorial range. Nearly every major character in this book, as in Munro's others, is a woman; most are adulterers; most are seen over a span of some years; most are perceptive and articulate about their own longings and failings; and every story except for **"Friend of My Youth"** is recounted in the third person. Such a clustering of similarities is often the sign of a limited writer, and, probably, an autobiographical writer (not necessarily, of course, the same thing).

Yet although Munro strikes me as exactly the sort of person I would care to know, I don't at all have the feeling that I do. Like the machinery of her sentences, she is in some important way admirably invisible. Munro writes of certain attributes—selfishness or carelessness, for example—with the authority of one who has "been there"; but she is remarkably selfless in her presentation of material that may, in this way or that, be autobiographical. And given other similarities among her stories—their rueful but not lugubrious tone, the acute sense her characters suffer of the ineffability of life's lessons—the mutations Munro achieves in characterization and plotting are even more impressive. Finally, though, it is the largeness of Munro's wisdom that confirms her range. When, at the end of the intricately designed mansion of a story **"Hold Me Fast, Don't Let Me Pass,"** Munro's woman protagonist wonders, "Meanwhile, what makes a man happy?" and can only speculate, "It must be something quite different," this is no abdication of authorial responsibility; it is a door boldly opened into another room.

One of the things we discover in that mysterious annex that Munro opens up, in story after story, is that all of us have been telling stories too. Many of Munro's characters (novelists, poets, actors, editors, teachers, journalists) are themselves employed as makers or interpreters of tales, but so is the housewife in **"Miles City, Montana"** who sees the "wooing of distant parts" of herself as her "real work." When she hopes that "the essential composition would be achieved," she is speaking of her life; but Munro is also speaking through her of the composition of this story, whose self-reflexiveness reminds us that we can never leave ourselves out of any truth, or truths, we apprehend.

Munro is not merely rehashing the fiction writer's commonplace that all points of view are subjective and relative; she is giving us credit for attempting, nonetheless, now and then, an impossible overview of our lives.

A rage to consider everything simultaneously—not just the "distant parts" of the self but of other selves and, indeed, of a universe of objective fact—is the frustrated, mystical longing at the heart of nearly every story Munro has written. The "distant" is conceived not only in space but in time—hence those perspectives, clairvoyantly convincing, that Munro gives us of thirty years after, twenty years before. The short story has rarely been used (successfully) for so long-reaching a purpose. "Too many things," as the creative writing instructor in **"Differently"** chides his student; "Too many things going on at the same time; also too many people. Think, he told her. What is the important thing? What do you want us to pay attention to? Think."

Good advice, perhaps, to the writer of average talents, but it would not interest Almeda Joynt Roth, the nineteenth-century poet Munro invents in the most ambitious story in this volume, **"Meneseteung."** In a sort of grand, clear-headed delirium, and one of the most inspired moments in any of these extraordinary stories, Almeda demands of herself a God-like vision, a fusion of poetry's timeless themes and fiction's time-specific, place-specific raggedness:

> Isn't that the idea—one very great poem that will contain everything and, oh, that will make all the other poems, the poems she has written, inconsequential, mere trial and error, mere rags? Stars and flowers and birds and trees and angels in the snow and dead children at twilight—that is not the half of it. You have to get in the obscene racket on Pearl Street and the polished toe of Jarvis Poulter's boot and the plucked-chicken haunch with its blue-black flower . . .

Alice Munro knows that you must get all of that in—the bits and pieces of accident flying together into the deliberate whole of art—and once again, in *Friend of My Youth,* she has done it.

Reamy Jansen   (essay date Winter 1989-90)

SOURCE: "Being Lonely—Dimensions of the Short Story," in *Cross Currents,* Vol. XXXIX, No. 4, Winter, 1989-90, pp. 399-401, 419.

[In the following excerpt from a longer essay discussing several writers, Jansen analyzes the roles of male characters and the theme of loneliness in Munro's fiction, especially in the story "Wood."]

Loneliness in [Raymond] Carver often conveys the sense of leaping into a well, followed by a desperate attempt to break the fall. Loneliness in the work of Alice Munro occurs in a broader context and is more the consequence of a darkly deterministic worldview. The flat, featureless landscapes of her Southern Ontario towns are mirrored in the lives of her depleted but idiosyncratic characters. The spectral and alien lives of the men who inhabit this world

appear to her female protagonists as riddles incapable of solution. Married or not, her men are outsiders. With varying degrees of distance, husbands haunt the outskirts of domestic arrangements as if their humanity was beyond the pale.

Munro's women appear to take the measure of their own unhappiness from the depth and distance of male isolation. In her earliest stories, Munro's pattern for men is already in place. The recluse, who dominates the consciousness of Munro's younger female characters, demarcates the extreme of social distance. Reclusive isolation attracts Munro's women as an image of freedom from the world of domesticity and repels them as evidence of the seemingly unbreachable psychic and affective distance between men and women.

Generally, though, Munro's men situate themselves in the world between the home and the "no man's land" of the bush. Frequently, we find the Munro husband doing his work in an outbuilding. He rarely involves himself with the town. There is often a feral quality to such work—a number of fathers are fox farmers or trappers. Del Jordan's father in *Lives of Girls and Women* raises silver foxes, an enterprise Del sees as "precarious and unusual . . . glamorous and ghostly". Rose's father, in *The Beggar Maid,* another collection of related stories, whose furniture-repair business makes him seem superficially more civilized than the other fathers and husbands, is the king of Munro's eccentric males. An isolate, nameless throughout most of the volume, he works in a shed behind the house, his unfathomable interior life hinted at by private and fragmentary mutterings that Rose occasionally overhears—"Macaroni, pepperoni, Botticelli, beans." Once, she catches a fugitive line from *The Tempest,* "The cloud-capped towers, the gorgeous palaces," suggesting that men live entirely in the mythic realms of their own romantic imaginings. To Rose such kingdoms are obviously superior to the mundane worlds women inhabit.

We never entirely understand what propels Munro's men to the backs of yards, to sheds and cages, to the shadow lands beyond the hearth. Yet their inchoate, inarticulate, primitive wildness fascinates Munro women before marriage, although its attraction fades after mating, when the men are sent, or migrate, from the house. The dynamic suggests a grim and implacable biological determinism.

Men's inexplicableness—their attraction, their impulse towards separateness—is what Munro has begun to explore in her more recent work. A turning point in her examination occurs in the story, **"Wood",** her most sustained look into male loneliness and the way out. In a rare departure from her usual narrative methods, Roy Fowler's story is unmediated by a female observer; we see Roy as he is. **"Wood"** tells of a wood-cutter attracted to the bush, and unfolds with fable-like simplicity. Roy Fowler has married into his wife's extended family of Voles, Pooles, and Devlins. A tribal group, his wife's family has a "limited interest in people like Roy." Partly as a consequence of this exclusion, Roy finds himself more and more drawn from his regular business of sign painting, an activity carried on, not surprisingly, in a "shed behind the house". He increasingly feels the pull of his "other interest, which is private but not secret; that is, everybody knows about it but nobody knows how much he thinks about it or how important it has become to him: wood-cutting." This drift worries his wife, but her concern doesn't lessen his desire to journey more often into the bush. Indeed, his thoughts about wood are becoming "covetous and nearly obsessive."

Munro gives this tale of isolation greater force by including two related themes that she has been developing since her first stories in *Dance of the Happy Shades*: the encroachment on nature by greedy, commercial impulses, and the human capacity for self-deception. Encroachers, as Munro portrays them, do not simply clear land and set down tract housing and shopping malls. What disturbs her most are the distortions of reality and rationalizations that serve this domination: everywhere there is denial of what is being done and false romanticizing of the commonplace and the everyday.

In Munro's later stories, encroachment becomes an ironic emblem of the complacent and egotistic illusions of civilization, and her isolates are its most profound, if not most articulate, critics. The motif of encroachment often resonates another Munro concern—self-deception. Here is the closest she has come to connecting a theory of fiction with a theory of life:

> Self-deception seems almost like something that's a mistake, that we should learn not to do. But I'm not sure if we can. Everybody's doing their own novel of their lives. The novel changes—at first we have a romance, a very satisfying novel that has a rather simple technique, and then we grow out of that and we end up with a very discontinuous, discordant, very contemporary kind of novel. I think that what happens to a lot of us in middle age is that we can't really hang on to our fiction anymore.

If Roy Fowler is trying to compose a "romance" in the bush (the metaphoric stance of most Munro males), too much of his action is determined by others' fictions. He seeks loneliness journeying down the path of self deception. Many of Roy's signs depict the pastoral illusions that local farmers still cling to:

> They always want a background of rolling farmland . . . even though the pigs and turkeys . . . never see daylight, and the cattle are often fattened in feedlots.

Perhaps part of the attraction of real trees in the bush is that they seem to be free of this distortion.

It may be our fate, though, to come full circle to the things we wish to avoid. Roy falls in the woods because he is in the grip of another fiction, a story of a rival woodcutter in his domain (and the lovingly Miltonic catalog of "his" trees is clearly a correlative of "The cloud-capped towers, the gorgeous palaces" declaimed by Rose's reclusive father). This tale is told to Roy by Percy Marshall, a Munro solitary who has declassed himself, a farmer turned eccentric scavenger, with an ear for rumors of deals and money matters. Percy is a disturbing vision of what Roy fears becoming, and Roy accepts Percy's story of "a fellow . . .

under contract to the River Inn to get them all the wood they need for the winter." Percy later embellishes the "fellow" into a "housepainter." Readers will recognize what Roy does not, that Percy is speaking of Roy, who once sold wood to the River Inn. The inn is another symbol of encroachment, "a resort hotel built on the ruins of an old mill" where the wood they burn, "they just burn it for the looks." Roy is so anxiously turning this story over in his mind that he cannot see through the romance of what Percy has told him. Instead, he worries, foolishly goes alone to the bush, and almost immediately injures himself on the snowy ground, whose white covering disguises the ruts that trip him. The injury is so severe that he must crawl back, and during this time of rebirth Roy deconstructs the embellished fiction he has hitherto believed:

> The truth is that the paperhanger, the decorator, the housepainter . . . is Roy himself. . . . Everything connected with the River Inn turns into some big fable. . . . Around here any set of facts get turned into a story.

While unraveling the tale, Roy has made it back to the truck, and Munro concludes **"Wood"** with Roy's achieving a "decent sense of victory." The story's final word is "safe": the woods are still safe for Roy, he is safe from the River Inn and the fictions that emanate from it, and he may be safer, more secure within himself. He may even be able to return to the women in his life.

Munro offers no easy answers, but she gives us the most sustained view of a decent man's drift into the isolation of a grotesque world, and then of Roy's "long, successful crawl" to a less fictive view of life. Certainly, one gets the sense from Munro that much of the resigned and saddened loneliness of her women is contingent upon the illusory isolation of the men. If men like Roy can live closer to themselves, they will be able to live closer to home.

Of course, one can't leave this Munro story without noting that "safe" may also promise a host of treacherous ironies. It may be that we need to add another characteristic of the short story to those we've enumerated: it doesn't console. The short story examines loneliness but does not solve it. If it gives no direct answers, it has communicated the feel of loneliness and especially male loneliness. It is a feeling as irreducible as a nail in the heart. As long as the cultural body remains anemically post-modern, short stories will illumine the solitary corners of our lives.

Carol Shields   (review date 7 February 1991)

SOURCE: "In Ontario," in *London Review of Books,* February 7, 1991, pp. 22-3.

[*Shields is a Pulitzer-prize winning novelist, poet, and critic who has lived in and written about Canada. In the following review, she favorably reviews* Friend of My Youth, *calling it a book on which every page contains "particular satisfactions of prose that is supple, tart and spare."*]

The Canadian writer Alice Munro once likened a good short story to a commodious house whose every room possesses an exterior door. So accommodating a house, she wrote, is capable of admitting visitors through any number of openings, just as a story can be entered by way of its separate sections or paragraphs or even its individual sentences or words. The rewards for the reader, she suggests, have to do with language rather than with the sequence of narrative, the rhythm and surprise of linguistic persuasion overriding the fortunes of those who populate the pages of novels—what these characters want and what they eventually get.

It is a pleasure, then, to open Alice Munro's new collection of short stories, *Friend of My Youth,* and find on every page the particular satisfactions of prose that is supple, tart and spare, yet elegant and complex. A typical Munro sentence, with its exact and loving syntax, gestures toward worldliness, toward literary sophistication and art, while at the same time guarding, by means of her unpredictable cadences and spirited vocabulary, the particular salt and twang of rural Ontario—the corner of the universe that Alice Munro calls home. Her voice is unmistakably her own. Artlessness collides with erudition in almost every paragraph, but in Munro's hands these contradictions seem natural, just one more manifestation of a planet whose parts are unbalanced, mismatched, puzzling and random.

Friend of My Youth is Alice Munro's seventh book. Readers familiar with her work are often taken with the lovely fresh suddenness of her titles. *Dance of the Happy Shades,* her first book (1968), finds its name in a young child's piano piece, a name brimming in the title story with the kind of minor-key paradox that spills out into the whole of the book. *Something I've Been Meaning to Tell You* (1974) pays tribute to a favourite theme, the accidental or unintentional gaps in communication that crown us with misery or misunderstanding or, very occasionally, with salvation. *Who Do You Think You Are?* (1978, published in England under the title *The Beggar Maid*) picks up as a running thread that familiar rebuke to those who have the audacity to reach beyond the expectations of others. Munro's new book takes as its reference the flowery, scented phrases once used, twenty or thirty or forty years ago, in the salutations of letters. 'My dearest Mary, my darling Ruth', 'My dear little Joanne', 'My dear old friend Cleta', 'My lovely Margaret', 'Friend of my youth'.

Such beseeching endearments are scorned by the woman who is the narrator of the book's title story. 'My dearest Mary, my darling Ruth'—these are the terms used by the narrator's mother when writing letters to her old school friends; they represent, to the daughter's mind, self-conscious pleas for attention, powdery, pathetic appeals for love, for validation. She is enraged that her mother, who is dying slowly of a paralysing disease, can find the energy to pick up a pen and enter into a conspiracy with falsehood. " 'I have friends all over the country," she would say defiantly. "I have dear, dear friends.' "

In fact, the mother clings to a skewed remnant of memory. As a young woman ('a young woman with a soft, mischievous face and shiny, opaque stockings on her plump legs'), she went off to the Ottawa Valley to teach in a one-room country school, and there she boarded with a local family, the Grieves sisters, one of them married, the other not. This eccentric household—they are members of the strict

Cameronian religious sect—enacts before the young woman's eyes a drama bubbling with melodrama and farce. The teacher lives with them through a season of death, passion and betrayal, taking everything in, but maintaining a curious and giddy detachment; she is young, after all, and engaged to be married, her tenure with the Grieves family is short, she can afford dispassion, even a measure of generosity.

Years later, though, she looks back and romanticises the experience. If only she were a writer, she tells her grown-up daughter, she would put it all in a novel and title it *The Maiden Lady.* Her memory is prepared to sift and resettle actual events, touching up certain episodes, assigning blame and reward, and bringing the story to rich, ripe resolution. The daughter is offended by her mother's cheap and easy distortions. She herself, given a chance, would tell the story differently, bringing hardness to its turnings, bearing down on its erotic suggestiveness. The gulf between mother and daughter widens, and this is where Alice Munro, having brought us this far, overturns our expectations. We are ready to be reassured, to be told that the daughter will come to an understanding of her mother, that we are on the cusp of one of those slightly embarrassing but nevertheless satisfying archetypal reconciliations.

It is not to be. The mother stands by her account, refusing revision or compromise and announcing to her daughter, by means of a mocking smile, her claim to a kind of exalted loneliness. The story, in fact—and it is the finest in the collection—makes a powerful and positive statement for the integrity of the self which is preserved by a steadfast resistance to the notions of others. To be understood, Munro suggests in the radiant, divergent final paragraph, is to be invaded or colonised: hanging on to your own life may mean the excommunication of *all* others.

Relying on the complexity of its narrative threading, on detail, voice and perspective, the story offers one further aesthetic surprise: a range of sympathy capable of embracing both the mother's brave self-delusion and the daughter's stubborn rejection of romanticism. The forces of grace and blame are assigned with a cool eye, with an even hand, and this willingness to allow for contradiction blows across Alice Munro's fiction like a gust of oxygen.

The enchantment to be found in Munro's books lies in the countless, vivid shocks of recognition between reader and writer. The stories deal with the rewards and punishments of erotic love, with girls becoming women, and sometimes, particularly in the early books, with how women make compromises in order to remain human. She writes, too, about how people survive the lives they're born into, their moments of shame, displacement and illumination. Many of the stories are cunningly hinged to moments in time: these stories draw breath from narrowly avoided accidents, the mock suicide, the almost-tragedy, the near brush with happiness.

Details of place are strikingly, almost photographically evoked. Once, speaking about a book she loved as a child—it happened to be Lucy Maud Montgomery's *Emily of New Moon*—Munro admitted to having been drawn in by what was 'going on behind, or beyond, the proper story . . . life spreading out behind the story, the book's life'. In the same way, her own work owes its vividness to the attention she pays to atmosphere, the listed contents of parlours and kitchens, handbags and pockets. She is wonderful describing faces, gestures, a pitch of voice, an article of clothing, the private clamour of an object or thought that drifts out of the past and forms a connection with the present.

In a superb story, **'Miles City, Montana',** from an earlier book, the narrator, a young married woman, describes what she calls her 'real work'. This work is not just looking after her husband and house and children, but, as she says, the 'wooing of distant parts of myself'. These distant parts, these concealed layers of existence, excavating them and holding them up to the light of day—that is what forms the substance of Munro's fiction.

After her first book of short stories in 1968, her publisher, and her readers too, waited eagerly for her to produce a novel. It has not happened, though *Lives of Girls and Women* (1971), with its linked stories and common protagonist, is sometimes thought of as a novel. She is, it has turned out, a writer more at home with shorter structures. Always concerned with the authenticity of material, it may be that she believes that the episodes that make up our lives conform to the hummocky shape of the short story rather than to the slow rising action of the conventional novel, with its final rewards and resolutions, obstacles overcome and goals realised—a pattern that has not proved all that useful to the experience of women.

Munro has gone a long way toward reshaping the short story for her purposes, or rather unshaping it. Strange bits of the world go into her work: digressions of every sort, family histories, notes on cultural artefacts (she has an eye for such notations), newspaper articles, old letters, and, very often, seemingly random anecdotes beaded on a thin string of narrative. It is as though the disorderly men and women who inhabit her pages require extra elbow room; wonderful new openings are for ever appearing—into the past, the future, into a joke or a dream or a flight of fancy. Some stories come out as one long sigh, but others are broken into segments or even, as in the story **'Oh, what avails',** into miniature chapters with their own titles. The meaning of a Munro story emerges from this complex patterning rather than from the tidiness of a problem/solution set-up or the troublesome little restraints of beginnings, middles and ends.

The time line moves all over the place. Sometimes she will stop a story and say, 'I forgot to tell you that—' Sometimes, as in **'Oh, what avails',** she fast-forwards into the future, presenting a scene in which a woman imagines how her husband will welcome her home after a weekend of adultery. Yet another story, **'Differently',** concludes by shifting into an old time-frame, a woman revisiting not the scenes of high drama and conflict in her life, but a rare buried moment of peace and reflection. Munro is good at handling long windy stretches of time, whole lifetimes or generations, and the stories here seem even bolder in this respect.

Occasionally, as in the story **'Five Points',** she will take two apparently separate stories and turn them, one against the other, eliciting sparks of reference and discord. The story-within-a-story, that staple of Victorian fiction, turns up in **'Goodness and Mercy';** other stories work along a strand of loosely related incidents, one opening into the next like a set of rooms; this discursiveness, this willingness to ramble and remark and wonder, resembles nothing so much as the way women, sitting over a mug of tea, tell each other stories, of confession and consolation, stories that seem dredged from some cosmic lost-and-found bureau or pieced together out of shared scraps.

Underlying the fluidity of structure is a formal complexity; the trace of deliberation is lightly drawn on even the most sprawling and diffuse material. Munro is a writer who cares deeply about the shape her books take. A few years ago, shortly before the publication of one of her collections, she realised that the arrangement of the text had gone awry, that certain stories did not belong together; it was a writer's nightmare; locked into a contract, she would have to live with the flawed book or else assume the not inconsiderable cost of printing new galleys. She made the second choice, and ended up with the book she wanted.

Her new book contains one story, **'Meneseteung',** that is about fiction, the materials that go into a narrative, the how of a story rather than the what. Little flags from the past—newspaper reports, scraps of verse and gravestone inscriptions—play against the 'I' of the narrator and the 'she' of the narration. This may sound like a bowl of postmod bubble soup, but the story charms; it also disturbs. Its subject, the genteel lady poet, Almeda Roth, yearns for the substance of authentic love.

> One thing she has noticed about married women, and this is how many of them go about creating their husbands. They have to start ascribing preferences, opinions, dictatorial ways. Oh, yes, they say, my husband is very particular. He won't touch turnips. He won't eat fried meat. He can't stand organ music. He would kill me if I took one puff of tobacco. This way, bewildered, sidelong-looking men are made over, made into husbands, heads of households. Almeda Roth cannot imagine herself doing that. She wants a man who doesn't have to be made, who is firm already and determined and mysterious to her.

A man appears in the role of rescuer, a widower named Jarvis Poulter, and for a brief moment it seems he may be the one to save her. But the narrative turns out to rest on a micro-circuitry of lost opportunities, missed connections.

Munro seldom offers accounts of her work; she claims she would rather not let her left hand know what her right hand is doing. But a credo of sorts can be located in an earlier story, **'The Stone in the Field'.** The stone in question marks the grave of a mysterious farm labourer, a Mr Black, the illicit lover of one of the farmer's daughters—or so legend suggests. The narrator, hungry for legends of her own, visits the field and finds that the stone has been removed. A kind of relief sweeps over her, for she has grown suspicious of the desperation that drives people to make stories of mere stones. And she knows that the manufactured stories can never match the potency of the real; the connections are too easily arrived at, too pat, too consoling, and too selfishly derived. 'I no longer believe that people's secrets are defined and communicable,' she says, 'or their feelings full-blown and easy to recognise. I don't believe so.'

Occasionally one of Munro's stories remains enigmatic, even after several readings. For years I've puzzled over a story called **'Fits'**, while delighting in its texture, and I am baffled now over one of the stories in this new book, an absorbing, sharply detailed story called **'Hold me fast, don't let me pass'**, which is (I think) about the porous nature of history, how much of it simply drains away to nothing. All the elements of the story seem in place, and yet it refuses, in its wider sense, to open up for me. Nevertheless, I'm sure the key is there if I can only find it.

Munro is careful about leaving keys. A reader can almost always find in the closing pages of a Munro piece a little silver ingot of compaction, an insight that throws light on the story. These sentences are often her most graceful, and they are skilfully embedded in the text, cushioned by the colloquialism and ease that define her writing. In **'Pictures of the Ice'**, for example, a retired clergyman and his young housekeeper cherish their secrets but find redemption in complicity. We require, it seems, in our moments of courage or shame, at least one witness. 'No matter how alone you are,' the housekeeper thinks, 'and how tricky and determined, don't you need one person to know?' Georgia, the main character in **'Differently'**, buffeted by time, disappointed by love and friendship, thinks: 'People make momentous shifts, but not the changes they imagine.' There is something old-fashioned and solid about these statements, generously, even humbly offered.

Katherine J. Mayberry (essay date Fall 1992)

SOURCE: " 'Every Last Thing . . . Everlasting': Alice Munro and the Limits of Narrative," in *Studies in Short Fiction*, Vol. 29, No. 4, Fall, 1992, pp. 531-41.

[*In the following essay, Mayberry explores "the relationship between truth and narrative, between knowing and telling" within Munro's stories and characters.*]

Storytelling is the central activity of the characters of Alice Munro's fiction. It is of course the principal task of Munro's narrators—those characters who organize and focalize the events and reflections constituting the short stories; and it is also the frequent activity of a large group of secondary characters whose storytelling is narrated by the chief narrators and thus recessed within the main narrative. Whether seeking or evading truth, all of these characters enlist narrative as the central weapon in their dogged and usually inconclusive struggle with the disturbances born at the intersection of their pasts and their presents. All are impelled to manage their pain, ignorance, and occasional glimpses of knowledge by telling. Some are more successful than others in their struggles, but success, when it occasionally comes, seems more a matter of luck than desert, and is rarely a direct dividend of the narrative act.

Eventually, most of Munro's narrators, both primary and secondary, come to recognize, if only dimly, the imperfection and inadequacy of their medium. In most cases, this inadequacy is a function of the essential incongruence between experience itself and the narrative that would render it, an incongruence complicated by the necessary mediation of memory. The uneasy relationship between language and experience is a recurring concern of Munro's work—one that she neither solves nor despairs of solving. It is stated as early as *Lives of Girls and Women,* where a more experienced Del judges as "crazy, heartbreaking" her earlier project of fitting "every last thing . . . radiant everlasting" within the narratives she would write. And with somewhat different implications, it dominates a late work like **"Friend of My Youth,"** where the problem of narrative fidelity is confounded still further by the issue of proprietorship. As legatee of her mother's stories about her youth, the narrator insists on reshaping them into stories that will better suit her own version of the person she needs her mother to have been: "I saw through my mother's story and put in what she left out."

The 1977 volume *Moons of Jupiter* is one of Munro's most intensely focused examinations of the capabilities and limitations of narrative. A collection of disturbing stories about middle-aged people—mostly women—facing often humiliating uncertainties, *Moons* has been called "a menopausal progression" [Beverly J. Rasporich in *Dance of the Sexes: Art and Gender in the Fiction of Alice Munro,* University of Alberta Press, 1990], a look at "the persistent psychological puzzle of women's masochistic complicity in their own humiliation" [Ildiko de Papp Carrington, *Controlling the Uncontrollable: The Fiction of Alice Munro,* Northern Illinois University Press, 1989], and (by Munro herself) an examination of "what men and women want of each other." But *Moons* is also a work about what stories can do, about the relationship between truth and narrative, between knowing and telling. Confused and uncertain, the women of this volume are groping for knowledge of an unknowable male other: Lydia in **"Dulse"** telling a psychiatrist about her abusive relationship with Duncan; the narrator in **"Bardon Bus"** talking her way through a broken affair; Mrs. Cross in **"Mrs. Cross and Mrs. Kidd"** trying to devise a story about the speechless Jack. Repeatedly, it is through stories, through placing themselves and these others within narrative, that these women seek knowledge, a resolution of their confusion. To tell, they hope, is to know. While some of these characters are temporarily relieved of the pressures of uncertainty, it is not, for the most part, the narrative process that affords this relief. Countless factors conspire against the composition of narrative truth—the failure of memory, the failure of nerve, the discontinuity between past and present, the alienation of language from experience. The stories these women tell must remain incomplete and finally barren of the truths they are seeking.

"Hard-Luck Stories," the tenth story in *Moons of Jupiter,* is the most direct treatment of the problem of narrative in the volume. Its principal characters storytellers and its principal dramatic action their storytelling, **"Hard-Luck Stories"** is a supremely meta-narrative work. The story-telling characters, Julie and the unnamed narrator, are not merely accessing the past through their narrative, not merely remembering, but creating, respectively, "entertaining" and "interesting" stories for an audience of one—the silent and predatory Douglas. These characters are self-conscious storytellers, whose divergent management of the activity of telling affords a deep look into Munro's understanding of the narrative act. Through the stories of Julie and the narrator, Munro probes the impulses, varieties, capacities, and limitations of narrative, insisting once more on the uneasy, discontinuous relationship between narrative and experience, and identifying the various versions of lies and uncertainties that no narrative can escape.

Like all of Munro's work, **"Hard-Luck Stories"** virtually defies plot summary. The story opens in the present tense, with the narrator meeting her friend Julie for lunch. Cryptically, they refer to a day two months earlier when they had been given a ride home from a conference by Douglas Reider, a previous acquaintance of the narrator. The narrative then moves back in time to the day referred to in the first section—the afternoon of the drive. While this afternoon, which includes the drive and a lunch shared by the three, is the principal setting of the story, we are taken back still further in time by three stories told by the two women as they eat lunch with Douglas. Their stories, two by Julie and one by the narrator, relate events occurring at different points in the women's pasts; their common subject is the deceits and stratagems that men practice on women. The telling of these hard-luck stories, which is rendered in direct, quoted speech, constitutes the main action of the work.

In their confessional rendering of sexual confusion and psychological disequilibrium, Julie's stories appear to be concerned with representing difficult personal truths. As a preface to the first story, she admits to having been bulimic at the time:

> I was one of those people who gorge, then purge. I used to make cream puffs and eat them all one after the other, or make fudge and eat a whole panful, then take mustard and water to vomit or else massive doses of epsom salts to wash it through. Terrible. The guilt. I was compelled. It must have had something to do with sex. They say now it does, don't they?

And she refers to her condition at the time of the second story as "Miserable [and] mixed-up." In each story, Julie represents herself as a credulous victim of the deceits of disturbed men—the first a mental patient pretending to be a graduate student, the second Julie's group therapist, pretending a passionate interest in Julie while sleeping with several other group members.

While the content of Julie's stories seems to be the stuff of wrenching confession, their manner is anything but pained. As the narrator recognizes, Julie's self-exposure is measured and self-conscious: she "set herself up to be preposterously frank. There was something willed and coquettish . . . about this." Julie's words have little to do with the past that they would seem to represent; they mark instead a virtual severance of past and present, experience and language. Her narrative cuts her off from the experi-

ence it is ostensibly representing. We see evidence of this in the quality of her confession about bulimia quoted above, in the yawning gap between the bulimia itself—this powerful but speechless register of miserable protest—and the spare, businesslike language with which Julie renders it. Whatever pain expressed itself in that eloquent body language of bulimia is nowhere evident within Julie's recounting of the experience. And we see the gap between language and experience again in her reference to the condition of her inmate almost-lover. When the narrator exclaims upon hearing from Julie that "He'd tried to cut his throat," Julie answers, "It wasn't that bad. He was recovering."

Julie's language here and throughout her two stories is in a dialect common to a number of Munro characters—characters whose stories, with their controlled language and tone, operate at a considerable remove from the original events. The narrative of these characters exploits the inevitable discontinuity between language and experience; for them, narrative functions as a virtual false counter, standing for something, surely, but not for the lived experience their narratives pretend to render. Though variously motivated, the narrative modes of these characters are strikingly similar, marked by flat, sparse, spare language and linear chronology. For these characters, language behaves, protecting its users from the vitality and pain that might be uncaged by a less provident use of the medium. This is the narrative method used by Prue, the title character in another story in the *Moons* volume, whose "anecdotes" pry the told impossibly far apart from its lived antecedent.

> She presents her life in anecdotes, and though it is the point of most of her anecdotes that hopes are dashed, dreams ridiculed, things never turn out as expected, everything is altered in a bizarre way and there is no explanation ever, people always feel cheered up after listening to her; they say of her that it is a relief to meet somebody who doesn't take herself too seriously, who is so unintense, and civilized, and never makes any real demands or complaints.

This is also the method of Wilfred, the younger brother in **"Visitors,"** whose repertoire of stories is predictable and repetitious. As his wife recognizes,

> In Wilfred's stories you could always be sure that the gloomy parts would give way to something better, and if somebody behaved in a peculiar way there was an explanation for it. If Wilfred figured in his own stories, as he usually did, there was always a stroke of luck for him somewhere, a good meal or a bottle of whiskey or some money.

While the careful stories of characters like Prue and Wilfred may temporarily keep deep troubles at bay by depriving them of vivid language, these troubles insist on expression, ingeniously finding translation into a different discourse. Prue's mute rage at Gordon expresses itself in her petty thefts of his belongings ("She just takes something, every now and then"), and Wilfred's unutterable sadness surfaces in crying fits deep in the night.

Given their context of psychic disequilibrium ("I felt I wasn't too far from being loony myself "), Julie's cool and breezy narratives must share some of the protective, distancing motivations impelling Pure and Wilfred. But another agenda also drives her: her stories, with their blithe and studied self-exposure, have the practical effect of attracting Douglas. Her confession to Douglas seeks neither expiation nor representation, but seduction. It is a trick of language and time that converts one thing into another (a painful experience into a "ridiculous" story), just as Julie herself can exchange her earlier "hiking boots and . . . denim jacket" for a pink dress and flowered hat. Her preposterous frankness, her insistent insertion of sexuality into conversation with a man she has just met, is a not-so-thinly-disguised "come-hither" strategy that meets with complete success: Douglas is attracted to her, and, as we learn from the opening of the story, they become lovers. Julie's stories do, in a sense, authorize or empower her, in that their intentions are realized.

But we cannot be sanguine for her chances for happiness, for her hopes of finding "the one kind [of love] nobody wants to think they've missed out on." For as we learn from the narrator's story, which recounts the ending of her earlier relationship with Douglas, like the inmate and the therapist, Douglas is another man who deceives and uses women. The practical effect of Julie's narrative calls into question Gayle Greene's claim that "all narrative is concerned with change . . . [that] there is something in the impulse to narrative that is related to the impulse to liberation." For Julie's story merely delivers her into another round of the same cycle, into an affair with a hard and voyeuristic man, about whom the best that can be said is, he "is better than crumbs."

While Munro is not being harsh or moralistic about characters like Julie and Prue, their disinclination to revive their pasts through their narratives surely disqualifies them from the ranks of her heroines. As a writer of narratives whose recurring subject is the past and the use we make of it, who stubbornly insists on a thing called truth while repeatedly despairing of our ability to reach it, Munro appears not to endorse such an ultimately barren and repetitious narrative strategy, valorizing instead those narrative strategies (like the one practiced by the narrator of **"Hard-Luck Stories"**) more dedicated to, if not more capable of, approximating truth. And while she doesn't always reward those characters who work this way, she *does* present the Julie's and Prue's as trapped in the ignorance constructed by their stories, condemned to reenact rather than to understand their past.

Like Julie's stories, the narrator's single story in **"Hard-Luck Stories"** is about a man's manipulation of a vulnerable woman. But subject matter is the only common feature of the women's stories; the narrator's motives, methods, and intents are vastly different from Julie's. For the narrator, as for Del in *Lives,* words are consequential and vital, with physical properties of their own that, combined with the proliferation of associative logic set in motion by their use, are capable of sensuous, rich, sometimes uncontrollable signification. For Julie, the statement "He'd tried to cut his throat" is a cool, dry factual statement that can be easily contained and qualified by "It wasn't that bad. He was recovering." For the narrator, the statement associates itself with "suicide," a word with an almost unbearably physical reality: "Mention of suicide is like innards pushing through an incision; you have to push it back and clap some pads on, quickly." The narrator's story demonstrates repeatedly the connection between language and physical experience, the ability of a word to call up, not shut down, a reality beyond the context of its present use. We see her acceptance of this connection in her account of an earlier conversation with Douglas:

> I asked him on the way up what Keith and Caroline were like, and he said they were rich. I said that wasn't much of a description. He said it was Caroline's money, her daddy owned a brewery. He told me which one. There was something about the way he said "her daddy" that made me see the money on her, the way he saw it, like long lashes or a bosom—like a luxuriant physical thing.

This somaticizing of language is necessary to any narrator who seeks to resuscitate experience through language, through stories about the past. Unlike Julie, Prue, and Wilfred, the narrator's use of language invigorates rather than vitiates her narrative. Thus it continues the experiment initiated by Del in *Lives*—that insistence on the physical properties of both sides of the signifying transaction—the visual, oral properties of written and spoken language and the sensuality of its referents.

We can't know, of course, how close the narrator's story comes to the events it narrates. This is a comparison quite impossible for Munro or any writer to make, as the original experience—if indeed it existed at all—is unpresentable. But all the evidence suggests that the narrator's story is a far more faithful account than Julie's stories were. Whereas Julie's stories are compact summaries of her experiences, with little attempt made to recreate conversations or the effect the events had on her, the narrator remembers the language of the conversations she had that evening, recounts carefully her reaction to the evening's events—not, as far as we can tell, her reaction as mediated by the intervening time or the present, but her reaction at the time.

> Then she [the hostess] said in her wispy voice how much she loved the way it was in the winter with the snow deep outside and the white rugs and the white furniture. Keith seemed rather embarrassed by her and said it was like a squash court, no depth perception. I felt sympathetic because she seemed just on the verge of making some sort of fool of herself. . . . the man I was with got very brusque with her, and I thought that was mean. I thought, even if she's faking, it shows she wants to feel something, doesn't it, oughtn't decent people to help her?

The most crucial difference between the stories of Julie and the narrator lies in what they are seeking. Julie's stories, though accounts of past events, are concerned with what they can effect in the present and the future; they demonstrate little concern with understanding the painful past that she rather cheerfully recounts. But the narrator does not tell her story as she would don a new dress—in order to achieve a certain effect. She is after something quite different, as she suggests when she distinguishes the effect of her story from Julie's: "It may not be very entertaining. . . . But it is interesting." The different roots of the two words are revealing: *tenir,* to hold, in the first; *esse,* to be, in the second. The narrator's story will have something to do with being, with essence, with experience; Julie's holds that essence back.

Not until the narrator has finished her story do we realize that the "man I was in love with" was Douglas himself, that a member of her audience is a principal character in the story she tells. It is this fact that helps us realize what she is after in giving this account: she is after no less than the actual experience itself *as it was,* a perfect retrieval of the past through narrative. Such a retrieval is only possible if the narrator can replace not just herself, but Douglas as well into the past. To gain Douglas's participation in the narrative would be to collapse present into past, to negate somehow the time that has elapsed between the original event and her story. If the recalcitrant present will cooperate, if Douglas will agree to be put back in the experience, the narrator stands a chance of understanding this troubling experience. And it is this desire for understanding that drives her narrative; she tells so that she may know, so that she may understand the role of the other (Douglas).

The narrator's project is more coincident with Del's ambitions than with the reminiscences of later narrators in *The Progress of Love* or *Friend of My Youth.* Neither Del nor this narrator seeks to recover a past event by demonstrating its messy amalgamation with experience intervening between past and present; both would re-create experience by excising it, perfect and whole, from the matrix of the past. But in **"Hard-Luck Stories,"** this tactic fails; time will not be collapsed, Douglas will not fill in the blanks, knowledge cannot be achieved. Douglas neither confirms nor denies the narrator's account; he remains the other that won't be contained, re-placed, understood. His recalcitrance leads the narrator to recognize the futility of her story, its inability to freeze time by replicating the past and yielding the knowledge she seeks: "I could be always bent on knowing, and always in the dark, about what was important to him, and what was not."

While the narrator's narrative project closely resembles Del's in *Lives,* the stakes to be won by its achievement have increased considerably. In perfectly retrieving the past, the narrator not only could gain understanding of that past, but also could realize the virtual identity between the concepts of inclusiveness ("every last thing") and timelessness ("everlasting"). Her attempt to revive the past is also an attempt to stop time altogether, to fend off the changes overtaking her. She shares this ambition with a number of other characters in the volume—with Lydia, in **"Dulse,"** and the narrator in **"Bardon Bus,"** both desperately trying to understand failed relationships, and with Albert in **"Visitors,"** stubbornly insisting on the truth of his narrative about Lloyd Sallows—"It's not a story. It's something that happened." All middle-aged, these characters are concerned with change and death; in

trying to suspend the past in narrative, they are trying to stop time, to ward off the death coming nearer to all of them. But as the abrupt insertion of the graveyard at the end of **"Stories"** reminds us, death will not be stopped by a trick of language or by any other contrivance. As the narrator realizes, language and story-telling are mocked by the obdurate fact of death: "I heard the silly sound of my own voice against the truth of the lives laid down here."

However pessimistic **"Hard-Luck Stories"** may be about narrative—about its ability to retrieve the past, yield understanding, challenge the flux of time—it does not leave its struggling characters utterly hopeless. For the narrator, Julie, and Douglas (and indeed many of the characters in this and other volumes) do find solace, though not where they were seeking it, not in the stories they tell. As if to point up the inefficacy of narrative, Munro often offers its opposite as a source of comfort. Repeatedly, it is within the unmediated, unprocessed image and act that her characters find at least temporary peace. The three characters in **"Hard-Luck Stories"** are granted a moment of grace through the form of a trillium stitched on a footstool in a country church:

> I was pleased with this homely emblem. . . . I think I became rather boisterous, from then on. In fact all three of us did, as if we had each one, secretly, come upon an unacknowledged spring of hopefulness.

The source of their pleasure in the trillium goes unidentified, the connection between the emblem and the comfort it casts remains uninterpreted, and hence, Munro seems to insist, the image is particularly powerful. A similar moment comes at the end of **"Dulse,"** when Lydia, after desperately seeking shelter in the stories she tells her psychiatrist and her new telephone worker friends, finds relief in the seaweed left her by Vincent: "Yet look how this present slyly warmed her, from a distance." Though Munro must present these moments within narrative, they remain the most immediate, unmediated, uninterpreted moments in the stories. It is as if she is saying that peace, truth, knowledge are unavailable through discourse, intellection; that they are accessible only within the unlocked, untranslated, silent image that, like Keats's "silent form dost tease us out of thought."

Munro's understanding of the function of narrative is mordantly paradoxical. Throughout her career, she has insisted on the existence of pre-linguistic experience, of a truth that originates outside of, independent of language. This truth is wholly experiential and wholly personal, never going beyond the bounds of individual perception. Particular and circumscribed, it would seem a simple truth, though as Munro's vision matures, its constitution grows increasingly intricate, its excision from the surrounding web of falsehoods, uncertainties, silence, and alternative perceptions increasingly difficult. But simple or complex, this truth admits little access. The approaches attempted by most of Munro's characters are memory and narrative—virtually equivalent faculties in that they both order past experience, re-collect lived moments within a chronological frame. These characters attempt to understand their experience by going through it again, and only language allows this review. But as **"Hard-Luck Stories"** demonstrates, to go through it again is to change it utterly; there can be no coincidence between the experience itself and the language that would render it. Narrative is finally not the province of truth; to tell is at best to revise, but never to perfectly revive. The narrator's position at the end of **"Hard-Luck Stories"** is, for Munro, the predicament of all narrators who seek understanding through language—the predicament of being "always bent on knowing, and always in the dark."

Josephine Humphreys   (review date 11 September 1994)

SOURCE: "Mysteries Near at Hand," in *The New York Times Book Review,* September 11, 1994, pp. 1, 36-7.

[*Humphreys is an American novelist whose book on the disintegration of family life,* Dreams of Sleep, *won PEN's Ernest Hemingway Prize in 1985. In the following review, she praises* Open Secrets *as a collection of stories that "dazzles with its faith in language and in life."*]

On a winter night in 1919, in a hotel dining room in Carstairs, Ontario, a librarian who's had a few drinks begins to tell her darkest secrets to a salesman she barely knows. "It's a lesson, this story," the librarian says. "It's a lesson in what fools women can make of themselves."

The story, aptly entitled **"Carried Away,"** is the first in Alice Munro's new collection, *Open Secrets,* her eighth work of fiction. And in fact, all the stories in *Open Secrets* are lessons. Ms. Munro's work has always been ambitious and risky precisely because it dares to teach, and by the hardest, best method: without giving answers.

Sometimes even the characters themselves have only a fuzzy notion of what their own stories mean. **"Carried Away"** isn't really about women making fools of themselves. And none of these eight stories are easy to predict. Just when meaning seems almost revealed, the story changes, veers, steps off a cliff.

The librarian, for instance, tells of the soldier who wooed her by mail during World War I, then came home and married another girl. After she confesses the details to the salesman and asks, "Do you think it was all a joke on me? Do you think a man could be so diabolical?" the salesman says, "No, no. Don't you think such a thing. Far more likely he was sincere. He got a little carried away. It's all just the way it looks on the surface." Then the salesman seduces her.

For many writers, that would be enough. The story, already 20 pages long, would indeed show how women make fools of themselves. But trust Ms. Munro never to be satisfied with a premature ending. Some five years later, an accident occurs in the sawmill at the local piano factory, "a particularly ghastly and tragic accident" in which the librarian's soldier "had the misfortune to have his sleeve caught by a setscrew. . . . His head in consequence was brought in contact with the circular saw. . . . In an instant the unfortunate young man's head was separated from his body."

Few writers would dare such a move, and fewer still could make it work. But Ms. Munro does. The narrative fabric into which this horrible event is woven is tight with a sense of time and place, a solid realism that allows even the bizarre to appear normal. And, as it turns out, decapitation isn't the final twist in the story, or even the most bizarre. Two more follow, a marriage and a vision, and the story concludes with a flashback that proves what we may by now have suspected: Ms. Munro's fiction is out to seize—to apprehend—the mystery of existence within time, "the unforeseen intervention," the unique quality of a person's fate.

Human apprehension of mystery has to start with language, our technique for rehashing and examining experience for any traces of meaning. So in *Open Secrets* people are continually telling and hearing stories—sometimes more than one at a time—in confessions, letters, rumors, ballads, conversations, newspapers. But some parts of life aren't quickly apprehendable through language. Puzzles of love, time, death, spirit—these are the open secrets, near-at-hand mysteries that can't readily be talked or written into clarity, but that nevertheless can be relentlessly turned and poked and studied until, with some luck, they yield something—a lesson that's partial and ambiguous but likely also to be momentous.

Every story in the collection contains some sort of startling leap, whether it's a huge jump forward in time (more than 100 years in **"A Wilderness Station"**), a geographical change (as in **"The Jack Randa Hotel,"** when a woman follows her runaway husband to Australia to spy on him) or a sudden switch in viewpoint that changes the whole nature of the story. Mishaps and accidents twist through like killer tornadoes, throwing everybody off course. By thus expanding—you might even say *exploding*—the fictional context, Ms. Munro reaches toward difficult truths.

Perhaps the most exploded story in the collection is **"The Albanian Virgin,"** which begins with the exotic narrative of a Canadian woman held captive in a remote Albanian village during the 1920's. But after five pages there is an interruption: "I heard this story in the old St. Joseph's Hospital in Victoria from Charlotte, who was the sort of friend I had in my early days there."

The narrator is a young woman of the 1960's who has fled both a marriage and a love affair on the other side of the continent. And *her* narrative is interrupted from time to time by a return to the Albanian adventure. The result is a bold assault on the assumptions and expectations of traditional fiction, with remarkable success.

Generally, we think of fiction as a process of gradual revelation. But what if a story can do the opposite—and still succeed? Just after the librarian in **"Carried Away"** arrives in Carstairs, she looks out at the bare winter trees: "She had never been here when the leaves were on the trees. It must make a great difference. So much that lay open now would be concealed." Gradually, time and experience obscure the easy lessons. Our lives leaf out. What we once thought true may be lost under the ongoing and always surprising accumulation of event and perception.

It's no coincidence that almost every story in *Open Se-*

crets has as its time frame the span of an entire life, for these stories draw upon the complexity of a mature, long-vigilant sensibility. And lifelong learning isn't easy. In **"Vandals,"** a woman perseveres in a troubled marriage: "She learned, she changed. Age was a help to her. Drink also."

The only real guard against despair, against the "devouring muddle" and a life of "arbitrary days," is to make a narrative of the self, constantly reinterpreting the accumulated life. People whose lives have not panned out, like Millicent in **"A Real Life,"** who talks her friend Dorrie into marrying a stranger, can thus achieve a compensatory wisdom, limited but powerful, and vaguely mystical.

In the title story, Maureen Stephens's supposedly lucky marriage has taken a sexually horrifying turn. And when a local girl disappears from a hiking trip, the lost girl reminds Maureen of how girlhood itself vanishes. She remembers her own secret recklessness. "To be careless, dauntless, to create havoc—that was the lost hope of girls." She experiences odd hallucinatory moments when she sees things that "seem to be part of another life that she is leading," as if she were "looking into an open secret, something not startling until you think of trying to tell it."

Fiction is the telling that startles, the telling that teaches. In **Open Secrets,** Alice Munro has written stories of tremendous strength, stories resembling the factory women she describes in **"Spaceships Have Landed"**: "They came jostling and joking down the stairs and burst out onto the street. They yelled at cars in which there were people they knew, and people they didn't know. They spread disorder as if they had every right." Heedless of convention, hazarding everything, firmly convincing us of the unseen good despite acknowledging our fears and harrowing experiences, **Open Secrets** is a book that dazzles with its faith in language and in life.

Ann Hulbert (review date 22 December 1994)

SOURCE: "Writer without Borders," in *The New York Review of Books,* Vol. XLI, No. 21, December 22, 1994, pp. 59-60.

[*Hulbert is an American editor and critic. In the following review, she favorably analyzes the stories in* Open Secrets, *commenting on the provincial setting of Carstairs, Ontario, and the unremarkable, quiet lives of its inhabitants.*]

Alice Munro is the latest and best proof that a provincial literary imagination can be the most expansive kind of imagination there is. Fixated on lives in out-of-the-way Canadian places and dedicated to the short story rather than to what she has called "the mainstream big novel," she finds pioneering energy in the "feeling of being on the margins": it inspires the desire and the power to remake boundaries. For Munro, marginality has nothing to do with isolation, and everything to do with "connection. That was what it was all about," she writes in *The Moons of Jupiter* (1983). In seven collections of stories and one novel, she has shown fate, and also fiction, to be a rather miraculous matter of unexpected linkages and leaps.

"When you live in a small town you hear more things,

about all sorts of people," Munro once explained. "In a city you mainly hear stories about your own sort of people." And when those towns abut on farms, which are edged by woods, you have very different worlds constantly colliding, within and between families. In Munro's unillusioned vision, the contrasts don't harmonize bucolically. They are jarring, and her vigorously supple style registers the prosaic details and the poetic depths of the jumble. "Stars and flowers and birds and trees and angels in the snow and dead children at twilight—that is not the half of it," a small-town poet realizes in **"Meneseteung,"** a story in Munro's previous collection, *Friend of My Youth* (1990). "You have to get in the obscene racket on Pearl Street and the polished toe of Jarvis Poulter's boot and the plucked-chicken haunch with its blue-black flower."

The models for Munro's brand of regional consciousness have been, she has said, the writers of the American South. Especially the women among them—Flannery O'Connor, Eudora Welty, Carson McCullers—have helped to embolden her to claim the far corners of her rural enclaves as literary territory, to elevate "the freakish, the marginal" as major figures in her fictional universe. And the Southerners have also plainly helped to confirm Munro's conviction that such remoteness from the ever more deracinated, commercial commotion of this century offers a special vantage on it. She betrays no trace of the defensive insecurity about her region's place on the map that Margaret Atwood has called "the great Canadian victim complex." On the contrary, the particular, peripheral sense of place that inspires her fiction gives her the assurance to matter-of-factly take up an especially large theme, the disorienting power of time.

In her stories, many of which have the geographical density and the historical sweep of novels, the plots again and again turn on the ways the past has of unsettling the present. Her characters—like their author—are forever trying to find some pattern, however tenuous, in the choices and accidents, the continuities and rebellions, of their lives. They privately set great store by those moments when, as a character in a story from *The Progress of Love* (1986) puts it, life's "bits and pieces would be flying together inside me. The essential composition would be achieved." But they don't expect the compositions to be seamless by any means, or to hold firm.

And they aren't inclined to broadcast their narrative efforts, for shyness is rampant in Munro's rural Canada. ("I can tell you," the protagonist's mother says in *Lives of Girls and Women,* 1971, "there are members of your father's family who would not open their mouths in public to say their house was burning down.") Up north the yarn-spinning tradition lacks the Southern-style public flair, which complicates the writer's role as eavesdropper. To rescue the "essential compositions" is itself a feat of capturing and extrapolating from bits and pieces of unobtrusive tale-telling. "Even in that close-mouthed place, stories were being made," Munro writes in *Something I've Been Meaning to Tell You* (1974). "People carried their stories around with them."

> **In Munro's stories, many of which have the geographical density and the historical sweep of novels, the plots again and again turn on the ways the past has of unsettling the present.**
>
> —*Ann Hulbert*

From the start, Munro's fiction has invoked the classic provincial odyssey of escape, with the important revision that the main figures in the drama are girls and women: the imaginative and proudly intrepid daughter, or wife, or ex-wife, or spinster struggles to move beyond her poor and proudly introverted family and region. Escape means, among other things (such as love and sex, often adulterous), the chance to tell a story about the struggle. But Munro has always specialized, and never more daringly than in her new collection, **Open Secrets,** in exploding the odyssey's conventions as she assembles those stories. The journey from narrow country past to more spacious cosmopolitan future, though it beckons as liberation, is almost always revealed as a disconcerting illusion. The true path turns out to be a much more capricious trail from one shifting territory to another.

The Ontario town of Carstairs, in or near where all but two of the stories in **Open Secrets** mostly take place, is the familiar Munro country of the past. Yet this time she draws attention to just how unfamiliar this vanished world is, where before she often resurrected it with fond (though never softly nostalgic) immediacy through the artistic retrospections of her provincial escapees. "Now that she was sure of getting away," Munro writes of her heroine, Rose, in **The Beggar Maid,** "a layer of loyalty and protectiveness was hardening around every memory she had, around the store and the town, the flat, somewhat scrubby, unremarkable countryside."

In the new collection, Munro's "borderline cases," as she once described her main characters, aren't budding creative interpreters, and they don't escape in the traditional sense. They're odder specimens, and their less self-consciously rendered versions of the place have an indigenous, rough-hewn quality. In Carstairs—more joltingly than in its predecessors Jubilee, Hanratty, Dalgleish—Munro is preoccupied with disconnections and unpredictable, implausible reconnections between then and now, between here in town and there beyond it. In turn, the jaggedness of the juxtapositions doesn't feel predictably postmodern; more than a sense of relativist muddle, there is a sense of miracle in the transformations that have taken place.

"A Real Life" is a good introduction to the physical and social landscape that grounds Munro's world, and to her provincial saga, which she here stands on its head. In her three main characters she deftly maps her typical prewar rural territory, with its well-defined social intersections, which are not conventional class stratifications. "In her

reasonable eccentricity, her manageable loneliness," Dorrie Beck lives on the edge of farmland, happiest when out trapping in the woods, like a grownup child or a trusted animal. ("A man in the area," Munro comments in her fondly comic vein, "had named a horse after her.") Millicent, once a schoolteacher, is now a farmer's wife who keeps a shipshape farming household, and just slightly offbeat friends, since the proper town ladies don't invite her to tea: along with Dorrie (whose house is on her land), Millicent depends on the company of Muriel Snow, the rather scandalous, unmarried music teacher, forever on the lookout for a man.

But this social geography does not turn out to dictate destiny in any formulaic way. Instead Munro unfolds a kind of counter-legend of liberation. Muriel, the classic candidate for leaving town in a cloud of dust, hitches up with a censorious minister. It's Dorrie, the character most rooted in "a life of custom, of seasons," who escapes in an outlandish fashion, married off to an Australian briefly visiting in town. And it's well-settled Millicent who cagily sees to it, when Dorrie balks at the last minute, that her departure actually comes to pass. Yet mixed in with the triumph, Munro admits a hint of melancholy in the way things work out in the long run. Dorrie's innocent independence in Carstairs retains an allure that her adventures in exotic places (she dies climbing a volcano in New Zealand) somehow can't match. And Millicent's great pride in having helped to fulfill a fantasy is shadowed by disappointment in reality.

Social geography and destiny are even more unsettled, not surprisingly, when Munro turns to the more distant past of Carstairs. Her interest is more explicitly historical than ever before in **"A Wilderness Station,"** which opens with the town's original clearing in the mid-nineteenth century, and in **"Carried Away,"** which begins in the disarray of the homefront during World War I. These formative moments of the past serve as a stage for a rather different and earlier provincial saga, which for Munro has always hovered not far behind the mid-twentieth-century drama of frustration and escape: the frontier story of adventurous arrival.

In the two stories the provincial present is revealed to rest on foundations of the most fortuitous kind. Reversing the rural-town-insider-becomes-worldly-outsider story, Munro here relates how the least likely outsiders become the anchors of the town, thanks to completely implausible and violent twists of fate. In **"Carried Away"** a traveling librarian stays in Carstairs, only to see the soldier she'd hoped to marry (having corresponded with him, but never having met him) decapitated in a freak accident at the local piano factory. She ends up marrying his boss and, now a member of the foremost commercial family in town, eventually runs the factory herself. **"A Wilderness Station"** is a variation on the same theme. An orphan recruited by mail to marry a homesteader discovers after her husband has been killed in the woods that the cause is his axewielding brother (not a falling branch, as claimed), but she keeps the secret. The strain of the deception turns her into an eccentric, while her brother-in-law goes on to join a thriving clan that boasts among its descendants a prominent Canadian politician.

It's not easy to convey the texture of these stories, which are epistolary (**"A Wilderness Station"** entirely, **"Carried Away"** in part) and full of stories within stories and multiple perspectives. Here Munro's narrative audaciousness—she routinely includes more plot turns and more angles of vision than most other short story writers would dare—calls special attention to itself. The effect is precisely the disequilibrium she has in mind. We're drawn in by the immediacy of the letters, and yet simultaneously distanced by their fragmentariness, by the elusiveness of the voices in them; the documents are pieces of unreliable second-hand evidence which are meant to do the work that, in Munro's earlier fiction, confident memory has often done. The stories close, tellingly, with glimpses of the erstwhile librarian and orphan, now ancient ladies, struggling to make their memories conform to an utterly transformed world.

"Changing your perceptions of what is possible, of what has happened—not just what *can* happen, but what really *has* happened": that feat of imagination and memory, Munro has said, has come to seem ever more pressing as she has gotten older (she is now in her sixties). The truly momentous journey isn't so much a matter of emerging from cramped provincial home into the wide world as of making it from "that time" to "now," through all kinds of "disconnected realities." It was a challenge that struck an old man back in *Something I've Been Meaning to Tell You* as nearly overwhelming:

> Nobody could get from one such time to another, and how had he done it? . . . It was sensible perhaps to stop noticing, to believe that this was still the same world they were living in, with some dreadful but curable aberrations, never to understand how the whole arrangement had altered.

More recently, a character in *Friend of My Youth* worried over the fragility of any effort to find coherence in life's fragments: you can see them "in their temporary separateness, all connected underneath in such a troubling, satisfying, necessary, indescribable way. Or you can see rubble. Passing states, a useless variety of passing states. Rubble."

Munro in *Open Secrets* doesn't hesitate to dig yet more deeply into time's rubble, insisting on the *useful* variety of passing states, not only within Carstairs but beyond it. She is a regional writer without borders, as she proves in the most unusual of the eight stories in the collection. In it she leaps across one of the historically least passable of all boundaries, Albania's.

"The Albanian Virgin," a story within a story, is a hybrid of extremes: "one such time" is made alien, "now" is thoroughly unmoored, and the links between them almost baffle belief. The plight of the narrator of the framing story, who is nameless throughout, is familiar from Munro's preceding books, especially *Friend of My Youth*. A shaky newcomer to Victoria, British Columbia, from London, Ontario, where she has left a betrayed husband and a lover, she is the provincial astray: one of Munro's women adrift in the changing city of the Sixties, marriages behind them, the drama of their country childhoods crowded out of mind by more recent loneliness and guilt. Like her predecessors, this woman, cut off from friends and family, sets up a half-baked commercial enterprise (in this case, a bookstore), less to make money than to find some solace among strangers.

The narrator establishes a curious bond, "both intimate and uncertain," with the strangest of the strangers, a velvet-cloaked older woman named Charlotte and her husband, Gjurdhi, shabby in his equally peculiar costume and yet also somehow ferocious. Munro manages to make the narrator's odd friendship with these ragged creatures seem outlandish and yet also completely and prosaically real, a vivid piece of Victoria life during a transitional period; they're in a sense hippies before their time, except that the narrator retrospectively appreciates "the risky authenticity that marked them off from all these later imitations."

Just how jarringly, surreally authentic they are only gradually becomes clear as Charlotte, who falls ill and goes to the hospital, spins out the story within the story to the narrator who sits at her bedside. Ostensibly the saga is Charlotte's idea for a movie—an eccentric old woman's scheme for cashing in on the market for fantasy, and the perfect way to bore a captive hospital visitor. The story is theatrical—about a young Canadian woman visiting the Dalmatian Coast in the Twenties who gets abducted into an Albanian tribe and is rescued by a fierce-looking, gruffly protective Franciscan priest of the region. And yet it mocks precisely the Hollywood "historical epic" that jumps from one fabricated climax to another. For Charlotte's tale has a kind of mundane marvelousness that would drag quaintly on the screen but is mesmerizing on the page.

And as the pieces of that far-away fable fall together, the story subtly links up with the trio in Victoria. The narrator isn't quite sure what to make of what she hears. But she like the reader, is gradually drawn to feel that the tale is, as Charlotte mumbles late into it, "from life"—that it really *has* happened, as it could have, the reader realizes with amazement: forty years earlier, in remotest Albania, Charlotte would have been a young woman and everything would have been undreamably different. The narrator's numbness in the wake of her own peregrinations fades as it dawns on her what far-flung realms have been traveled by this wandering pair.

The story works its uncanny effect on another level as well, and marks it as not only (only!) a radical innovation for Munro but also a kind of symbolic culmination. In venturing so far from her traditional landscape, Munro has stumbled on a place in which her peculiar and powerful version of the provincial story meets a ritualized reflection of itself. The young Charlotte is taken prisoner because she boldly sets off alone on her European tour, one of those Munro heroines who reject their small world's assumption for women that "a certain amount of carefulness and solemn fuss and self-protection were called for." The irony of Charlotte's fate is that she is trapped all over again in a clannish, isolated culture, where gender less demurely but just as absolutely divides life: "Women were with women and men were with men, except at times in the night (women teased about such times were full of shame and denial, and sometimes there would be a slapping)."

The salvation from the narrowness of this mirror world lies in a tribal rite of marginalization: Charlotte, now known as Lottar, is anointed a "Virgin" by the clan, an outsider status that entails an androgynous identity and a ruggedly independent existence far from the village. Like Munro's more familiar rite of passage for rebellious girls, which it exotically parallels, Lottar's rescue is liberating, but only provisional; there will be yet another escape. As so often in Munro, the search for a new balance almost always means the discovery of new ambivalence. This precarious predicament, far off in Albania, has become in Munro's hands "shockingly like, and unlike, home." Such jolts of recognition amid strangeness, and of strangeness amid the familiar, inspire the most haunting—and exhilarating—kind of disorientation. It is the restless provincial's spiritual staple, and Munro's seemingly boundless imaginative subject.

Joan London   (review date 1995)

SOURCE: "Never Ending Story," in *Meanjin,* Vol. 54, No. 2, 1995, pp. 233-40.

[*In the following review, London praises* Open Secrets *as a mature work of Munro's that contains "stories of formidable urgency and integrity."*]

Alice Munro has established an international readership based solely on the short story (in Australia we would use Frank Moorhouse's term and call her two novels 'discontinuous narratives'), an achievement which at this moment, in English, is rivalled only by that of Raymond Carver.

Her publishing life spans two decades of exceptional experimentation in the short story form, from postmodern metafiction to 'dirty' realism, from such writers as Barthelme, Barth and Carver in North America, Cower, Moorhouse and Garner in Australia. In the early eighties it reached a peak of critical approval and apparent popularity, which has now receded. In its single defining feature—brevity—the short story has always served as a vehicle for 'having a go', for the 'one-off', for starting out in fiction, or taking a break from longer work. Perhaps this is what keeps the form healthy, edgy, pluralistic: some of the best short stories have come into being this way. But to persist with the short story, collection after collection, to pursue its development over a long period, amounts to a vision as expressed through the form.

From the first, Alice Munro wrote her own sort of story. The form seemed integral to her voice and approach and it developed within her work as indistinguishable from the growth of her own experience and thought. In her practice the short story seems to have come alive, continually expanding its possibilities and range. Along the way she has created a following, and influenced a generation of short story writers.

It is probably always the case with major writers who are widely read by their contemporaries, that the particular story they have to tell is the one their generation is waiting to hear. Although the heartland of her fiction is rural Ontario, and her most direct antecedents are Eudora Welty, Flannery O'Connor and Carson McCullers, Alice Munro's more contemporary version of rural life has foregrounded the experience of women. The central consciousness of her earliest stories was that of a very young, angry, ambitious woman in a country town, like Del Jordan in *Lives of Girls and Women* (1971) who walks the streets of Jubilee "like an exile or a spy, not sure from which direction fame would strike, or when, only convinced from my bones out that it had to." The desire for escape and fulfilment and the issues this raised—such as the life and death struggle with the mother—exactly coincided with the flowering of the women's movement in the seventies, and with the determined reclamation of female experience in the writing of the era. And in the no-nonsense, righteous, Scottish/Irish conservatism of Alice Munro's country folk in town after fictional town, it was possible to identify the forces that a young woman of spirit was up against. Growing up in Jubilee or Hanratty or Dalgleish in the forties was not so different from growing up in suburban Australia a generation later.

Dislocation, it seems to me, is what usually makes a writer first break into a sustained work. Dislocation in time or place, dislocation from a former sense of self. This is mirrored in Alice Munro's earlier fiction: the escape from the provinces is usually achieved through marriage, which is sudden, surprising, dreamlike and entrapping. The young wife finds herself cut off from her ambitions, her class and the country roots which turn out to be after all her emotional touchstone. That is the first dislocation. The second is divorce, in which the eyes are set free to examine marriage and adultery and all the subsequent sexual relationships of the unattached woman. No other writer I can think of has explored so widely the centrality of sex within her cast of characters, or brought into such piercing focus the nuances of the couple, endlessly recast and replayed. And once again this preoccupation was in tune with contemporary experience and women's interest in defining themselves within it.

Dislocation is also a source of the texture of her work, the density of reference to the physical world, the attempt to capture the spirit of a place or person or feeling, of what Virginia Woolf called 'the thing in itself'. At the end of *Lives of Girls and Women,* Del Jordan says:

> It did not occur to me then that one day I would be so greedy for Jubilee . . . I would want to write things down . . . I would try to make lists . . . And no list could hold what I wanted, for what I wanted was every last thing, every layer of speech and thought, stroke of light on bark and walls, every smell, pothole, pain, crack, delusion, held still and held together—radiant, everlasting.

Open Secrets, Alice Munro's most recent book, has dismayed some of her readers. For such a sturdy realist to introduce a ghost, a spaceship, portentous visions, dreams and coincidences, not to mention a love pursuit in disguise which ends up in Brisbane and risks a musichall farfetchedness, is perhaps to court disquiet in the readership she has set up.

Yet she has been signalling these changes for some time now. Increasingly in her later work there has been a sense of challenge to closure, to the constraints of the form, an attempt to draw ever closer to the unyielding rawness of life. Some stories from her last two books would not be out of place here. One of the pleasures for me in this book was to sense both the connection with former work and the step forward, the exhilaration of breakthrough.

These stories are longer. Collection by collection her stories have lengthened, loosened, and as their scope has widened, the juxtapositions of their composition have become more extreme. She has always written of the past, the recent past or that of a generation earlier, but in *Open Secrets* her compass swings wider, goes back further—one of the stories is located in the pioneering past of 150 years ago—and then swings forward, bringing her characters' lives and those of their descendants into modernity, following them through to their effective end. The historical detail, the rendering of the tone, mores, decorum of the period, often through letters, is wonderfully achieved.

All but one of the stories is set in, or sets off from, Carstairs, another version of Munro's country town. But if the earlier stories were about dislocation, these stories hinge about return. Return to a former site where a drama has occurred, or to a relationship which at the time seemed to be definitive, or to an aspect of experience which is only now seen to be definitive. The return to the home town, the meeting between the one who stayed and the one who got away, or between ex-lovers or spouses: this is familiar Munro territory. But over the years the meditative framework has changed. 'Great writers', said Chekhov, 'not only find a truth, but wrap it up and take it somewhere.' In *Open Secrets,* the emotions of these experiences are not only defined, they are given their retrospective place in the passage of the life. The transforming medium is that of time.

There is a sense of an overview, of pieces being put into place in the puzzle: a sense too of pieces which don't fit and the gaps that are left. Louisa in **'Carried Away'**, at the end of her life says: "It was anarchy she was up against—a devouring muddle. Sudden holes and impromptu tricks and radiant vanishing consolations."

Within this vision, the connections made between lives may seem startling, may reach across continents and generations, or across the surface skin of what we accept as real: the ghost, the spaceship, the warning dream, while never 'proved', are shown as real forces in the life in which they occur. The endings, rather than homing in, may be jokily flat, or open out, situate in mystery, linger in feeling like "the darkness collecting, rising among the trees, like cold smoke coming off the snow."

There is an awareness of darkness in these stories, of dark forces which can only be sensed or felt. At the core of each there is a death, or imminent death, or an act of violence, often unsolved, unable to be explained. In *Open Secrets,* Munro takes a long look at unknowing, leaves some ends daringly untied, and for a story-teller this is risky. And yet

every element in the stories seems meaningful. Traced through time, the mysteries are part of a widening acceptance of the eternal, 'radiant' opacity of life.

Sex and death: the source of the drama, and in these stories the two forces are intimately linked. But in counterpoise to this is a state of rest, from what she calls "a din, a battering, a sound of hammers in the street," the wrenching disturbance of sexual relationship. Some stories are set at the moment of cross-over.

'The Albanian Virgin' is the story which has attracted the most attention, not only because it is the first of Munro's stories to have an 'exotic' setting outside Canada (unless you count Brisbane), but because the figure of the Virgin, the woman who is allowed a life of independence provided she gives up sex, is such a resonant symbol for women, and one which recurs throughout this book. It is almost impossible not to read the story of Lottar's capture and escape in the Albanian mountains as allegory. In fact it can be read as a sort of mythical version of the provincial journey undertaken by the young women in Munro's earlier stories: the desire for adventure, the rebellious setting-off, the entrapment within a community of women-as-carers, the unwitting bride, and then the brief sojourn as a Virgin alone on the mountainside, discovering her own resourcefulness.

But the Franciscan priest who rescues Lottar falls in love with her, a realization as they part that takes "the breath out of her body, as she knew too late." Her fate has been decided. Like Dorrie in **'A Real Life'**, like Louisa in **'Carried Away'**, she is 'carried away' by a transforming force, chooses to leave the Virgin state for sexual love.

This is not, however, a romantic vision. Forty years on, the Franciscan priest is her husband, Gjurdhi, an obsessive peddlar, "a mangy but urgent old tiger." The narrator of **'The Albanian Virgin'**, one of Munro's confused young women who has left her husband (it is the early 60s), who, in an episode which parallels Lottar's escape is claimed by her lover Nelson, disguised in fedora and trenchcoat, says of her subsequent married life with Nelson:

> We have been very happy.
>
> I have often felt completely alone.
>
> There is always in this life something to discover.
>
> The days and years have gone by in sort of blur.
>
> On the whole I am satisfied.

This could be offered as a version of her life by any of the long-married women in this book: ordinary women whose lives have been formed by accommodation (as perhaps have the husbands' too: one character talks of "chubby husbands . . . bent on a lifelong course of appeasement"), but also by what can be seen as extraordinary moments, so that this list of truisms is both confirmed and challenged.

Fedora and trenchcoat: the notion of disguise in the love quest has long fascinated Munro. It is the theme of the story **'Wigtime'** in *Friend of My Youth* (1990). It was first mentioned in her definitive meditation on obsessive love, set in Brisbane, **'Bardon Bus'** (*Moons of Jupiter,* 1982). In **'The Jack Randa Hotel'**, Munro returns to Brisbane, and the story of the pursuit from Canada of Will by Gail, in disguise, the hair-dye dripping down her neck in the Australian heat, takes the quest to painstaking, absurd lengths. Perhaps for Australian readers, observed as others see us, even the setting is a little surreal, "this country of non-stop blooming and impudent bird life," of men rowdily drinking beer beneath dazzling jacaranda blossoms, of women with "dim, soft, freckly, blinking faces." It's as if the whole action of the story surreally enacts the caperings, the antics, the pain that people put themselves through for love. And get through. Gail watches an unpleasant old man in a wheelchair who lives in her apartment building with a young male carer. She catches the young man crying one night outside at the rubbish bins and, in a moment of identification with him, realizes he is the old man's lover. Gail's identity is revealed to Will from an ambulance just as the old man, who has collapsed and is clutching her hand, the hand of a stranger, dies. When Will comes after her, calling to her through her keyhole, she finds that "Words most wished for can change . . . Love—need—forgive. Love—need—forever . . . hammers in the street." This time death is the transforming force. She runs away from Will, from the mad game of her quest, and flies home. From there, playfully, bountifully, like a god tossing up a 'shower of gold', she relents to life again, and throws the ball in his court.

Unaccountable forces create a field of energy in the story **'Spaceships Have Landed'**. Rhea, in 1953, drunk, kisses her boyfriend Billy Doud's friend, Wayne, also drunk, at the back door of the local bootlegger's house. Just before she passes out, she hears him say "I'd like to fuck you if you weren't so ugly." The next day she summons him and confronts him about this comment, sitting on the porch of her father's house, while, in typical Munro detail, she cleans eggs with a piece of steel wool. Suddenly, momentously, they run away together, marry, have three children and 'five times as many lovers', grow old together. His comment is never explained. But it has been the galvanizing force for the subsequent course of Rhea's life. It connects with the subtle sexual unease, an unspoken misogyny at the bootlegger's house, and in her sessions parked in the car with Billy Doud. It creates "the clear space in her head with the light buzz around it" that she experiences on the porch as she cleans eggs. And this, imagistically, connects with the empty space of the old fairgrounds in the river flats, where that very same night, a neighbour Eunie Morgan was taken to a luminous spaceship, and her life too was forever changed.

Moments of insight, glimpses of a more stringent, unknowable reality, have always been hallmarks of Alice Munro's fiction. But in **Open Secrets,** this reality is drawn in as a player, is enacted in the narrative itself.

It is a mature vision. Alice Munro is in her sixties now, and sometimes in the sense of risk, of ease, of playfulness, of mischievous disregard for the conventions, these stories reminded me of the late work of Patrick White, or of Elizabeth Jolley. There is more than a whiff of mortality, a

deepening resonance about them, as in all the greatest short stories. I would rate **Open Secrets** as the best, so far, of her later work as I rate *Lives of Girls and Women* the best of the early work and *The Moons of Jupiter* of the middle period. Harold Bloom elects her to the canon with ***Something I've Been Meaning To Tell You.***

Is she still writing the story we want to hear? It is always difficult to judge the contemporary climate, but ours, I think, is or has been an intellectual era in literary endeavour, both in its writing and reception. There is a consciousness of finding a position. Its origin may be emotional but its location, its field of reference, is intellectual. It has yielded some bright treasures and broken some complacent patterns, but in fiction, especially the short story, it's a little as if, in John Updike's phrase, we 'hug the shore', don't quite trust where the open sea will take us. Alice Munro reminds us that there is such a thing as thinking fictionally, in which the focus, the ultimately cold eye of the writer's imagination holds so closely to the given, to the particularity of character, to 'the thing in itself' that its revelation resists self-consciousness, resists orthodoxy, and resides in the experience of the lives she has so deeply explored. And at this stage in her career, in the last years of the twentieth century, the accumulation of experience, story after story, is almost cosmic in its vision.

It can be harder, I think, to read a collection of short stories than a longer form. So many beginnings and endings. One life after another at its moment of intensity. So many little worlds set up which then have to justify their own meaning and sense of closure. Not subject to an overriding narrative project, the short story arises from a very direct response to experience. Its intensity can only be sustained by feeling. Above all, it cannot afford complacency, staleness, or the blunting of feeling.

Alice Munro continues to write stories of formidable urgency and integrity. She does it every time. She does it again and again.

FURTHER READING

Criticism

Baum, Rosalie Murphy. "Artist and Woman: Young Lives in Laurence and Munro." *North Dakota Quarterly* 52, No. 3 (Summer 1984): 196-211.
> Compares Munro's *Lives of Girls and Women* to Margaret Laurence's *A Bird in the House,* both portrayals of a young female artist's coming of age.

Boston, Anne. "Hidden Reasons." *New Statesmen and Society* 3, No. 1233 (19 October 1990): 32-3.
> Lauds *Friend of My Youth* as a "small masterpiece."

Boyce, Plenke, and Smith, Ron. "A National Treasure." *Meanjin* 54, No. 2 (1995): 222-32.
> Interview in which Munro discusses the purpose of her fiction.

Carrington, Ildikó de Papp. "What's in a Title: Alice

Munro's 'Carried Away'." *Studies in Short Fiction* 30, No. 4 (Fall 1993): 555-64.

Explores how the title "Carried Away" reflects the story's structure and action.

DeMott, Benjamin. "Domestic Stories." *The New York Times Book Review* (20 March 1983): 1, 26.

Praises *The Moons of Jupiter* for its sympathetic female characters, its structure, and its craft.

Fowler, Rowena. "The Art of Alice Munro: *The Beggar Maid* and *Lives of Girls and Women.*" *Critique* 25, No. 4 (Summer 1984): 189-98.

Compares the heroines of *The Beggar Maid* and *Lives of Women and Children* and discusses Munro's writing process.

Gorjup, Branko. Review of *Open Secrets,* by Alice Munro. *World Literature Today* 69, No. 2 (Spring 1995): 363.

Brief, laudatory review of *Open Secrets.*

Harris, Gale. "Radiant, Vanishing, Consolations." *Belles Lettres* 10, No. 2 (Spring 1995): 10, 14.

Positive review of *Open Secrets.*

Haviland, Beverly. "Missed Connections." *Partisan Review* LVI, No. 1 (Winter 1989): 151-57.

Favorable review of *The Progress of Love.*

Houston, Pam. "A Hopeful Sign: The Making of Metonymic Meaning in Munro's 'Menesetung.' " *North Dakota Quarterly* 52, No. 3 (Fall 1992): 79-92.

Uses Munro's short story "Menesetung" as a basis for a discussion of metaphor versus metonymy.

Hoy, Helen. " 'Rose and Janet,' Alice Munro's Metafiction." *Canadian Literature,* No. 121 (Summer 1989): 59-83.

Detailed discourse on the evolution and publishing history of the book that became *Who Do You Think You Are?*

Kakutani, Michiko. "Love, Found and Lost, Amid Sharp Turns of Fate." *The New York Times* (6 September 1994): C17.

Compares Munro's *Lives of Girls and Women* to Margaret Laurence's *A Bird in the House.*

O'Faolain, Julia. "In the Territory of Dreams." *The Times Literary Supplement,* No. 4776 (14 October 1994): 24.

Laudatory review of *Open Secrets.*

Smythe, Karen. "Sad Stories: The Ethics of Epiphany in Munrovian Elegy." *The University of Toronto Quarterly* 60, No. 4 (Summer 1991): 493-506.

Essay explores the meanings of melancholy and realism in Munro's fiction.

Solotaroff, Ted. "Life Stories." *The Nation* 237, No. 18 (28 November 1994): 665-68.

Proposes that *Open Secrets* is an example of "maximalist" fiction.

Thomas, Sue. "Reading Female Sexual Desire in Alice Munro's *Lives of Girls and Women.*" *Critique* XXXVI, No. 2 (Winter 1995): 106-20.

Feminist discussion of Del's sexuality in *Lives of Girls and Women.*

Warkwick, Susan J. "Growing Up: The Novels of Alice Munro." *Essays on Canadian Writing,* No. 29 (Summer 1984): 204-25.

Discusses issues of communication and maturation in respect to Del in *Lives of Girls and Women* and Rose in *Who Do You Think You Are?*

Weinhouse, Linda. "Alice Munro: Hard-Luck Stories or There Is No Sexual Relation." *Critique* XXXVI, No. 2 (Winter 1995): 121-29.

Analyzes "Hard Luck Stories" in terms of the theories of Jacques Lacan.

Woodcock, George. "The Rival Bards." *Canadian Literature* No. 112 (Spring 1987): 211-16.

Detailed review of *Lives of Girls and Women,* comparing it to Victorian poetry.

———. "The Secrets of Her Success." *Quill & Quire* 60, No. 8 (August 1994): 25.

Positive review of *Open Secrets.*

Additional coverage of Munro's life and career is contained in the following sources published by Gale Research: *Contemporary Authors,* **Vol. 33-36R;** *Contemporary Authors: New Revision Series,* **Vol. 33;** *Dictionary of Literary Biography,* **Vol. 53;** *Major Twentieth-Century Writers;* **and** *Short Story Criticism,* **Vol. 3.**

The Brothers Quay

1947-

(Born Stephen Quay and Timothy Quay; also spelled Quaij) American-born English filmmakers.

The following entry provides an overview of the Quays' career through 1996.

INTRODUCTION

The Brothers Quay are best known for short "stop-motion" animated films in which puppets, broken dolls, rusted screws, old tools, and other "found" objects participate in highly metaphorical and psychosexually-charged vignettes that both depict and evoke feelings of angst and wonder. Frequently described as Kafkaesque and surreal, the Quays' work is inspired by nineteenth- and early twentieth-century European literature—including the works of Franz Kafka, Bruno Schulz, Robert Walser, and Michel de Ghelderode—and by the work of Eastern European and Russian avant-garde filmmakers—notably Alexander Alexeieff, Ladislaw Starewicz, Jan Lenica, Walerian Borowczyk, Jan Švankmajer, and Yuri Norstein. To an even greater degree than many of their literary influences, the Quays eschew linear storytelling for the evocation of intense psychological states by means of oneiric and obliquely sinister images accompanied by provocative sounds and music. For these reasons, their films tend to polarize critical opinion. The brothers have stated: "Our aim is to create a state of suspension where the effect, if it works for an audience, is not unlike dreaming, albeit dreaming uneasily."

Biographical Information

The Quays were born in Norristown, Pennsylvania, a working-class suburb of Philadelphia. Their father was, in their words, "a second class machinist for Philadelphia Electric" and their mother "was a figure skater before marriage." Their grandfathers, immigrants from Eastern Europe, were skilled tailors, cabinetmakers, and carpenters. With their artisanal heritage and a love of obscure literature—cultivated during long hours spent in Philadelphia's large public library—the brothers developed an early interest in art and design and enrolled in the Philadelphia College of Art. There they discovered the works of Eastern European poster artists and typographers, and the music of composers Gustav Mahler, Jean Sibelius, and—most importantly for their future work—Leoš Janáček. After graduating in 1969, they entered the Royal College of Art in London, England, where they were introduced to the work of Švankmajer, the Czechoslovakian film animator based in Prague whose surrealist and allegorical films remain touchstones within the community of puppet animators. Other abiding influences first encountered in their college days include: filmmaker Luis Buñuel; novelist Louis-Ferdinand Céline; Schulz, a Polish short

story writer and artist executed by the Nazis in 1942 whose semi-autobiographical and wildly imaginative works—primarily *Sklepy cynamonowe* (1934; translated as both *The Street of Crocodiles* and *Cinnamon Shops, and Other Stories*) and *Sanatorium pod klepsydrą* (1937; *Sanatorium under the Sign of the Hourglass*)—are reminiscent of the works of both Kafka and Marcel Proust; Walser, a Swiss novelist and short story writer whose work was greatly admired by Kafka and who spent the last years of his life in a mental institution; and Ghelderode, a Flemish playwright. After graduating from the Royal College of Art in 1972, the brothers returned to the United States, holding various jobs before traveling to Amsterdam where they sold several book cover designs. Frustrated with the limitations of a static, two-dimensional art form, they became increasingly interested in film animation as a means of expressing their visions. In 1977 they set up their own studio in London and began producing animated films when the British Film Institute (BFI) accepted their proposal for *Nocturna Artificialia* (1979). Keith Griffiths, who brought the Brothers Quay to the attention of the BFI, soon became their producer and the third partner in "Atelier Koninck"—the name of their studio and production company. Many of their early works borrowed heavily from the dark, fantastical images that other animators had begun to explore in the years following World War II; they cite Polish animators Borowczyk and Lenica, as well as Russian animator Norstein, as primary influences. In addition to their film work, the brothers have also designed sets for stage productions and operas by Richard Jones.

Major Works

Nocturna Artificialia, the first major work by the Brothers Quay, is a twenty-two minute black-and-white film comprised of diverse visual and aural materials. J. D. Mc-Clatchy described the film as evoking "a decaying metropolis haunted by both a nameless present menace and a nostalgia for shabby remnants of old-world culture. Organ music, tapestry swatches, cathedral views mingle in this dream with peepholes and sudden disappearances." *Leoš Janáček* (1983) is a putative biography of the last years in the life of the Czech composer. The soundtrack presents excerpts from Janáček's late works and last diary entries while a puppet—whose head is an old, faded photograph of Janáček—explores his autumnally-lighted house and meets creatures from his imagination, delicate puppets suggesting a moth and a deer. *The Cabinet of Jan Švankmajer* (1984)—the title recalls Robert Wiene's German-Expressionist silent film *Das Kabinett des Dr. Caligari* (1920; *The Cabinet of Dr. Caligari*)—was originally intended by producers at the British Broadcasting Corporation (BBC) to be a traditional documentary film about the Czech animator. The project was reconceived, however, when Švankmajer refused to be interviewed on camera. Representing him as a puppet whose head is a book, the film takes place in a fantastical room where a young child has his head emptied and lovingly refilled with secrets from his master's workshop. *This Unnameable Little Broom* (1985) is based on the second portion of the ancient Sumerian poem cycle *The Epic of Gilgamesh* (c. 7th century BC), and was to have been part of an adaption of the entire cycle; the BBC withdrew its funding of the project after reviewing this film. *This Unnameable Little Broom* corresponds to the part of the *Epic* in which Gilgamesh—the historical king of Uruk, a city-state of the early third millennium BC in what is now Iraq—sends a prostitute to seduce Enkidu—the uncivilized "wildman" of the forest intended by the gods to be a companion to Gilgamesh, who, in this part of the story, hates and fears him. The Quays render Gilgamesh as a vicious tricycle-riding puppet with a distorted head; Enkidu as a grotesque bird-like creature. The action takes place in a three-sided white box, sparsely decorated, beyond which is only blackness. Mc-Clatchy described the action this way: "The wicked child [Gilgamesh] sets a devious trap for the creature [Enkidu]—a gobbet of raw flesh to lure him, and then a mechanical trapdoor in the shape of a vulva. Once caught, Enkidu is wrapped in silk and beaten with a thorny club, and his wings are scissored off." *Street of Crocodiles* (1987), the title of which comes from a short story by Schulz, is based on themes and images from Schulz's autobiographical oeuvre rather than a direct adaptation of the story itself. The film opens with an old man, a caretaker of some kind, entering a decrepit room, possibly a museum. He approaches a kinetoscope—one of the first motion picture devices—and lets a gob of spit fall into the machine. This brief introductory scene is filmed in a kind of pixillated live-action: while an actor and an actual set are employed, there is a jerkiness to the representation of motion that imparts a sense of unreality to the scene. The camera then descends into the machine as it stirs to life. Gears turn, string travels along a vast network of pulleys, and the main "character" appears, a puppet with a face that is both frightened and sinister. As this figure explores the surroundings, which resemble the cluttered old shops and warehouses of Schulz's stories, other figures appear, objects move of their own accord, and scenes are enacted that make more or less direct reference to Schulz's writings. Whereas the space represented in *Street of Crocodiles* is essentially realistic and conforms to the laws of perspective and three-dimensionality—even though "impossible" things occur within it—the scene of most of the action in *The Comb* (1991) is an "impossible" dream-space, an Escher-like box in which vast landscapes exist alongside claustrophobia-inducing staircases that twist and turn in disregard of the laws of gravity. As in *Street of Crocodiles, The Comb* begins with a "live-action" scene; here a woman is shown sleeping fitfully. The camera appears to enter the box spring of her bed and, thus, enter her dream. Inside, a frightened, decaying puppet attempts to climb a ladder but is besieged by rapidly growing vines, fluttering disembodied hands that behave like insects, and an apparently unstable set of physical laws governing dimensionality, perspective, and gravity. The film occasionally cuts back to the sleeping woman and may draw visual parallels

between the two scenes of action. The film ends when the woman wakes up, the doll falls apart, and she begins combing her hair. The brothers' first live-action and feature-length film, *Institute Benjamenta* (1996), is adapted from Walser's novel *Jakob von Gunten* (1909). The story concerns a training school for butlers where the headmaster and his sister teach submission and humiliation to their students. Shot in black-and-white, the film pays equal attention to actors and objects, scenes and setting. The decor and lighting mirror Jakob's growing suspicion that his teacher and her brother are embroiled in an incestuous relationship. The nature of their relationship, however, is never fully explained.

Critical Reception

The films of the Brothers Quay have tended to elicit either passionately favorable responses from critics or more or less dismissive confusion. For example, Michael Atkinson wrote that even the "smallest moment in their films can make us feel as if we've never known the true and quiet force of film before." On the other hand, Vincent Canby felt that while on "occasion the images are beautiful," the films tend to "blur to the point where they begin to look like one long roll of bizarre, animated wallpaper." Because the Quays' films are short and do not follow conventional narrative logic, and because their adaptations of literary works are oblique and impressionistic rather than "faithful" in the traditional sense, they possess few of the qualities of mainstream cinema. Nevertheless, some of their works—particularly the *Stille Nacht* pieces that appeared on MTV—have proven to be popular with younger audiences and have influenced the appearance of many music videos. As McClatchy concluded: "The root word behind the word 'animation'—*anima,* soul—comes vividly to mind, for what we are watching [in their films] is a state of soul, oppressed, fantastic, haunting."

---

*PRINCIPAL WORKS

Il Duetto (film) 1970
Der Loop der Loop (film) 1970
Palais en Flammes (film) 1970
Nocturna Artificialia: Those Who Desire without End (film) 1979
Punch and Judy: Tragical Comedy or Comical Tragedy (film) 1980
Ein Brudermord/A Fratricide [adaptors; based on the short story by Franz Kafka] (film) 1981
The Eternal Day of Michel de Ghelderode 1898-1962 (film) 1981
Igor—The Paris Years Chez Pleyel (film) 1983
†*Leoš Janáček: Intimate Excursions* (film) 1983
†*The Cabinet of Jan Švankmajer—Prague's Alchemist of Film* (film) 1984
†*Little Songs of the Chief Officer of Hunar Louse, or This Unnameable Little Broom (Being a Largely Disguised Reduction of the Epic of Gilgamesh) Tableau II* [adaptors; based on the poem cycle *The Epic of Gil-*

gamesh (film) 1985; also known as *This Unnameable Little Broom* and *The Epic of Gilgamesh*

†*Street of Crocodiles* [adaptors; based on various writings by Bruno Schulz] (film) 1987

Rehearsals for Extinct Anatomies (film) 1988

Stille Nacht (film) 1988

The Pond (film) 1989

De Artificiali Perspectiva or Anamorphosis (film) 1991; also known as *Anamorphosis*

The Comb: From the Museums of Sleep, Fairytale Dramolet to Scenes and Texts by Robert Walser (film) 1991; also known as *The Comb*

Ex Voto (film) 1991

‡*Stille Nacht II* (film) 1992

§*Long Way Down (Look What the Cat Drug In)* (film) 1993

‖*Stille Nacht IIIA: Tales from the Vienna Woods* (film) 1993

Stille Nacht IV (film) 1993

Institute Benjamenta, or This Dream Which People Call Human Life [adaptors; based on the novel *Jakob von Gunten* by Robert Walser] (film) 1996

---

*In addition to the works listed above, the Brothers Quay have designed sets and stages for opera productions; these include *The Love for Three Oranges* (1988), *A Flea in Her Ear* (1989), *Mazeppa* (1991), and *Le bourgeois gentilhomme* (1992).

†These works are included in the compilation film *The Brothers Quay* (1987).

‡This short film was produced for the musical group His Name Is Alive to accompany the song "Are We Still Married?"

§This short film was produced for musician Michael Penn to accompany his song "Look What the Cat Drug In."

‖This short film was produced for the musical group His Name Is Alive to accompany the song "Can't Go Wrong without You."

CRITICISM

Mark Le Fanu (essay date Spring 1984)

SOURCE: "Modern Eccentrism: The Austere Art of Atelier Koninck," in *Sight and Sound*, Vol. 53, No. 2, Spring, 1984, pp. 135-38.

[*In the following essay, Le Fanu discusses the early career of the Brothers Quay, examining the marginalized status of animated filmmaking and the rise of Atelier Koninck, the name given to the Quays' collaborative partnership with producer Keith Griffiths.*]

If the image of independent British cinema given to the world is that of a rather downbeat, grey-edged, political artform, sustained by its virtues of modesty and integrity, it is sometimes necessary to be reminded that fantasy and extravagance are no less a part of our inheritance. The films of Powell and Pressburger are nothing if not baroque. Our theatrical traditions, feeding into cinema, include the artificial as well as the realist. From the point of view of painting, the set designers at Pinewood and El-

stree include some of the finest fantasy craftsmen in the world. In addition to this, there has been the recent runaway success (success against the odds, so to speak) of Peter Greenaway's *The Draughtsman's Contract*. No need to mention Monty Python. Thus fantasy in one form or another is alive and flourishing. Against this background the work of the Brothers Quaij [in a footnote, Le Fanu adds that their name is pronounced "and alternatively spelt 'Quay' "]—severe and difficult surrealist ventures combining puppets, mime, costume and music, written by Keith Griffiths and animated by the Quaijs—begins, perhaps, to take on a less forbidding, a more welcoming air. Plainly their work is cosmopolitan and avant-garde. But it is also, I would hope to demonstrate, humorous, witty and accessible.

Of the two sides of the collaboration, the first thing to point out is that the Quaijs themselves, twins Stephen and Timothy, are not in fact British but American. Born in 1947, they were brought up on the East Coast, near Philadelphia. The European admiration for things American in matters of popular culture—a widespread phenomenon in the wake of the Second World War—tends to obscure an interesting consideration, that Americans themselves, when they are sensitive and intelligent, are sometimes critical and cautious about their patrimony. While Europeans looked westward towards the United States in the 1960s, the Quaijs looked passionately towards Europe. A chance exhibition of Polish posters seen at the Philadelphia College of Art (where they went in 1965) kindled in them a feel for Surrealism. More or less at the same time, Tarkovsky's *Ivan's Childhood* and Paradjanov's *Shadows of Our Forgotten Ancestors* opened their eyes to the possibilities of grand, operatic, art-based European cinema.

Europe, then, was the goal from the start. A stepping-stone to Europe is England. Their main interest being in animation and illustration, it was into this latter department of the Royal College of Art that they enrolled in 1969. As so often in art school, however, they were left pretty much to their own devices. Unencumbered with the care of their professors, the interest of the Quaijs gradually drifted towards film; and before gaining their diploma in 1972 they succeeded on their own initiative in making three shorts. Two of these I have seen. **Der Loop Der Loop** has a couple of acrobats tossing each other backwards and forwards under the big top, until the disintegration of the limbs of one causes the proceedings to halt abruptly. In **Il Duetto,** slighter and more sinuous of line, a cellist and a lady opera singer slug out a trial by combat to the modernist music of Xenakis. Both films—pugnacious, clever, a touch sinister—share the economy and elegance that is the wit of the born cartoonist.

Their next film, **Nocturna Artificialia: Those Who Desire Without End,** wasn't to be made for another six years; but since the evolution of our film-makers is interesting in its own right I ought to say a word or two about the interim. Upon graduation they returned to America to set about earning their living—odd jobs waitering and cab-driving mixed with more congenial activity, such as poster work and book-jacket design, where they could find it. The goal not to be lost sight of, in the lean years, was a continual self-education. Waiting for their chance to arrive, the Quaijs immersed themselves in Arabic music and in the writings of Kafka and Céline, pushed their acquaintance further and deeper with the art of the Polish and East European surrealists, Borowczyk, Lenica, Cieslewicz, Trnka, Skolimowski. Marvellous short trips to Poland, financed by their labours, put them in touch momentarily with the living tradition (or its remnants) at first hand.

In early 1977 a grant of $3,000 from the National Endowment Fund for the purpose of studying Celtic mythology allowed the brothers to return to Europe. (The name Quaij, incidentally, is Manx: like everyone else, they were partly in search of their origins.) A short, by all accounts disastrous, trip round Wales and Scotland used up the bulk of the money. Moving to Holland and Belgium, they spent the rest of 1977 exposed to the melancholy atmosphere of the Low Countries, whose Spanish inheritance, with its residual flamboyance (observable in the architecture and carnivals), compounds so strangely with the haunted, misty, introverted spiritualism of Northern Europe. It was here, in contact with the paintings of Ensor and Bosch, and more especially with the Toone Marionette Theatre in Brussels, that they discovered the sinister beauty of masks, later to be put into effect in films like *Punch and Judy* and *The Eternal Day of Michel de Ghelderode.* And it was from Holland, that year, that they were recalled by a telegram from Keith Griffiths, deputy head of the British Film Institute's Production Department, telling them that an application for money to make a film in England had been successful.

Keith Griffiths now comes into the story. I should say something about him too, since his partnership and support, first as producer and later as full artistic collaborator, has been crucial to the success of 'Atelier Koninck', the name given to their collaborative enterprise. In fact Griffiths and the Quaijs were contemporaries at the Royal College, but in different departments, so that their acquaintance, though real, had always been at a distance. In the mid-1960s at Leicester College of Art, where he was studying industrial design, Griffiths had run an experimental theatre, putting on plays by the very Michel de Ghelderode ('forgotten' Flemish dramatist of the inter-war years) whose works the Quaij brothers discovered for themselves during their short stay in Belgium and Holland.

Restless and energetic, Griffiths had during the 70s been assimilating the skills of an administrator. First at Lincoln as films and arts officer, subsequently as film officer for Greater London Arts, and then as Peter Sainsbury's deputy at the BFI [British Film Institute] Production Department, he addressed himself to the business of bargaining and compromise, the in-fighting of contemporary arts politics. It was a characteristic piece of opportunism—in fact, the pigeonholing of money left over from Chris Petit's *Radio On*—that finally secured BFI funding for the Quaijs. From his distant perch he had been keeping a paternalistic eye on them. Without ado they accepted, and came to England to set up *Nocturna Artificialia.*

A puppet film, dense and cosmopolitan, *Nocturna Artificialia* extracts a strange lyricism from memories of the damp cobblestones of Brussels and Lodz, their haunted and ghostly churches, the clanking of their city trams. An elegant essay in alienation. Success of a sort—it won prizes in Finland—paved the way for their next film, *Punch and Judy* (1980), a freewheeling account of the assimilation of the Italian puppets into English folklore. The film benefited from the structure and order brought by the writer Griffiths. For the first time the collaborators mixed their elements: mime, masque, painting, archive footage, finally (most ingeniously) opera—puppet highlights of a one-act drama by Harrison Birtwistle, first put on at Aldeburgh in 1968. 'Punch and Judy', then, as history lesson—but for adults rather than children. (It won the prize for the best foreign film at Annecy.) In *A Fratricide/Ein Brudermord* (1981) the Quaijs dramatised a short story by Kafka. The humans of the original become scorpion-like puppets in a whirling five-minute battle—obvious comparison with Buñuel: the same entomological calmness and dispassionate scientific observation.

Next, in *The Eternal Day of Michel de Ghelderode* (1982), the collaborators succeeded in bringing out a rich and sardonic humour lurking at the edge of the playwright's macabre, death-obsessed imagination. The monotony that occasionally attaches to avant-grade theatre is avoided by the deft compression of the extracts from de Ghelderode's plays, the aim throughout being allusive homage rather than literal transcription. Poetic archive footage of high quality was incorporated, showing the artist in old age walking the streets of his 'quartier' in Brussels, pausing to talk to craftsmen in their workshop; finally, sitting brooding in his object-crammed study. In the evening of his life, the gaunt ironic face of a bourgeois recluse—rather like Burroughs or Duchamp. Brilliant work of archaeology and excavation.

Two recent films bring the tally up to date: *Igor Stravinsky: The Paris Years Chez Pleyel* (1983), a mixture of puppet and live animation; and *Leos Janacek: Intimate Excursions,* in tone and spirit something of a new departure. The sinister and exuberant here give way to gentle meditation, the voice of the narrator Witold Shejbal, reading from the diaries of the composer, infusing this film, it seems to me, with an unmistakable and commemorative humanism.

Igor Stravinsky and *Leos Janacek* were financed by Channel 4, indispensable patron and increasing rescuer of independent and small-scale film-making in Britain. But the slight awkwardness of the relationship is evident when one sees on television, as one did last August, a film such as *Janacek.* Television is an electronic medium, whereas the films of Atelier Koninck are geared, as it were, by love and conviction, to a tradition of artisan craftsmanship. They look backwards into the immediate past, rather than forward into the computer-based future. Koninck films have an almost aggressive need to be shown and appreciated 'traditionally'. And yet, given the current state of cinema distribution—given the current state of public taste—what cinemas in their senses would offer these films as their wares? Animation, as everyone knows, is a ghetto. That is its perennial difficulty. How much easier for its practitioners to accept the bribe of commercialism, putting themselves wholeheartedly at the service of advertising, where at least their talents will be paid for. Craftsmanship of the sort I am talking about is tolerated in Western Europe provided that it remains anonymous, or accessory to a conventional commercial project (as in the Special Effects departments at Pinewood).

None the less its autonomous claims should occasionally be restated without recourse to special pleading. Animation's claim to attention (for convenience I include both puppet and line-drawing under the same general heading) lies, of course, in the freedom it gives to the imagination. Beneath the sober rationalism of one's everyday behaviour there lurks in all of us a seething, kinetic substratum of fantasy—vivid, amoral, anarchic and colourfully allusive. More than any other art form one can think of (a true invention of the twentieth century), animation manages to lock into this secret hidden life, bodying it forth in formal exuberance. Dreaming, eventually, is a moral as well as an aesthetic freedom: another way of saying that it is too important not to become a subject for art. Film is the oneiric medium par excellence. And animation, as it were, doubly so.

Why then is it so underestimated? One would be tempted to be amazed at the formal solemnity with which critics probe the psychoanalytic depths of selected feature films, while ignoring altogether the much more obvious affinity to the Unconscious that lies in the art of the animated film-maker. Perhaps this is the answer one is looking for. The wit of the cartoon dispenses with the need to interpret it. In a radical sense, one can never tell, with these works of puppet and line, how far they are shallow or profound. While an avant-garde feature film will *speak* of Desire, the animator will exuberantly exemplify it.

A few examples seem called for. Among the British contingent at last year's London Film Festival, the films most truly the work of an artist were to be found, in my opinion, in the section set aside for animation. Why did one find them so pleasing? They were witty, they were short, they were unpretentious. Among other qualities, their sophistication about culture was striking—especially the culture of painting. Brigitte Hartley, of the London College of Printing, had a small film called *Dada* that seemed to my (admittedly inexpert) eye to capture with genius the light-hearted anarchism, the sheer liberated exaltation, of the extraordinary moment early in the century when it was impossible to tell whether painting was reborn or destroyed. Similarly, in *Taking a Line for a Walk: Homage to the Work of Paul Klee,* by Lesley Keen and Donald Holwill, the homage is genuine in direct relation to its playfulness, and its freedom from academic pomposity. The unfreezing of the static line into the movement it had always seemed to crave says more about Klee's essential wit and purpose than pages of Tate Gallery catalogues. A similar carefreeness, mixed with evident understanding of the subject, is apparent in *New Frontier,* a superior rock promo by Rocky Morton and Annabel Jankel, whose homage to Picasso's 'Musicians' (1934) consists in animating the jagged edges of its figures and filling its silence with music. All three examples miraculously get modernism right. They grasp it, that is to say, as style, and remain

ironical and sceptical about its loftier philosophic ambitions.

Igor Stravinsky: The Paris Years Chez Pleyel has the same *désinvolture*. The respect paid by Griffiths and the Quaij brothers to the revered composer of *Le Sacre du Printemps* is achieved by mischievous irony—shared equally between Stravinsky himself and his companions of the cast, Cocteau and Mayakovsky. Mayakovsky, in particular, is a splendid creation of fantasy. Kitted out in a costume of newspaper headlines, and booming his telegraphic poems through a megaphone, he stands in the film as supreme grotesque example of the poet as attitudinising rebel. One had to wait to see Mayakovsky portrayed as a puppet to appreciate the extent to which modernism itself, in the heroic inter-war period, was a profoundly 'mechanical' phenomenon.

Animation itself, a more important point, comes out of the aesthetic of modern art, and should therefore be well placed to comment on it. Cubism, vorticism, futurism were all in their essence, it seems to me, movements of satire, seeking provocatively to deny the superiority of the human species to other forms of animal enterprise. The obvious way to do this was to insist that man *was* an animal—and if not an animal, an automaton. Hence, in Stravinsky, the passion for precision (symbolised in the Pleyel film by the use of mechanical piano). The unearthly syncopations of his music for ballet were designed to encroach on the dancer's freedom of interpretation, thus to imply that real freedom lies in submission to determinism. The masks of de Ghelderode, similarly, can be seen as so many ruses put on to avoid assuming the responsibility of an individual fate (and with it the certainty of extinction). To become a mere mechanism is to escape from the laws of mortality. Escape into what, one might ask. The piercing, mocking dissonances of the modern operatic score (in composers like Penderecki and Birtwistle) have the effect of dislodging the harmony of song from its attachment to the human voice, pushing it over instead towards the twittering of animals and birds. In its essence, one concludes, it is a world of automatic compulsion that reigns in the films of the Quaij brothers. The twitchings of love become indistinguishably fused with the stabs of the murderer, and the lunges of beasts of prey. The gestures of humans are 'placed', in the last resort, by a similarity to the gestures of animals.

It is this vigour in the films of Atelier Koninck that strikes one as their impressive characteristic. ***Punch and Judy*** takes the ancient puppets and, as it were, shudders them back into life: shakes them with the frenzied single-mindedness that Punch himself, in the days of his prime, was accustomed to mete out on his victims. 'New life in old bones' might be the motto of this film about death. 'They have pulled out my Italian teeth one by one—fed me on saccharine to sweeten my homicide.' The film rummages in the origins of the myth to uncover, once more, the bitterness of its anti-bourgeois satire. As, in sweat-filled sleep, there is no hard and fast dividing line between the register of a dream and the register of nightmare, but the one turns imperceptibly into the other, so the object of the film seems to have been to take the unexceptionable, anodyne, daylight gestures of Punch and infuse them with their old night-time horror. Two horrific murders, with quill and syringe, effect the translation from seaside cabinet booth to the cabinet of Freud or Caligari. And along with Punch—struggling, protesting and snarling—the whole party of dogs, wives, crocodiles, devils and hangmen.

On the other hand, it is not quite so easy. Any serious knowledge of animals (such knowledge as the artist is forced to pick up in order to render their movements with accuracy) exposes the researcher to the fact of their character and humour. Punch was always humorous—and happily will continue to remain so. It is not for nothing that so many books for children are illustrated by animal precepts. Great poets know instinctively, and demonstrate soundly, that a knowledge of animals—and of birds and insects—is the child's education in tenderness. I don't want to force Griffiths and the Quaijs into a humanist mould uncongenial to their character—on the contrary, I hope the collaboration retains its darkness and 'bite', as a mysterious and private quality beyond the reach of an intruding critical exegesis—but I can't forbear to point to a final ambiguity that lies in the midst of their enterprise.

Just as the crawling caterpillar turns into the iridescent butterfly, beauty and tenderness, unbidden and unexpected, hover at the edges of satire. Satire is incomplete unless it is infused with a countervailing sense of the wonderful. Londoners were privileged last year to see at special exhibitions the work of two great poet animators, predecessors to Atelier Koninck. In the films of Ladislaw Starevicz (1882-1965) one glimpsed precisely this vital dual perspective about the operation of animals and puppets. On the one hand his scurrying ants and beetles, with their absurd epic battles and adulterous love affairs, are a mockery of bourgeois human enterprise. On the other hand . . . on the other hand, marvellous to turn it all round and see in these films not the disparagement of the human heart, but the extension of the human heart to cover and comprehend all forms of creation, in their joys and sorrows and catastrophes.

A similarly delicate universalism informed the work of the other great animator on show, the Russian artist Yuri Norstein. Even more than Starevicz, perhaps, he is interested in finding and establishing the true and ancient affections that link the animal and human worlds in bonds of obligation and friendship. The recognition of this mutual interdependence, it seems to me, is the acme of wisdom; how pleasing to see it exemplified in the 'intimate excursions' of *Janacek.* Leaf-winged dragonflies, in this latest film, hover gently round the body of the sleeping composer. Foxes and grasshoppers flit to and fro in his dreams, summoned by memory from the forests of his native Moravia. Harmony reigns in the spheres.

For the rest, then, one looks forward to future work from Atelier Koninck, in which the highest standards of artisan craftsmanship mix penetrating satirical realism with older, gentler douceurs.

> We're totally ignorant and/or naïve about split personalities, inward-turning natures of our relationship, or wishing to work independently of each other. These aren't, and have never been, issues in the remotest sense, and it shows how fantasy-bound others are about twins.
>
> —*The Brothers Quay, in a letter to J. D. McClatchy, in "Movie Magic: The Quay Brothers, the Toast of Eight Film Festivals," in*Connoisseur,*April, 1989.*

Tony Rayns   (review date June 1986)

SOURCE: A review of *Street of Crocodiles,* in *Monthly Film Bulletin,* Vol. 53, No. 629, June, 1986, p. 163.

[*In the following positive review of* Street of Crocodiles, *Rayns examines various literary and cinematic influences on the film and on the Quays' general aesthetic approach, including the writings of Bruno Schulz and the avant-garde film by Luis Buñuel and Salvador Dali,* Un chien andalou *(1928).*]

A somewhat decrepit caretaker enters an equally decrepit museum and (by accident or design) lets a gobbet of his saliva fall into a Kinetoscope machine. Inside the machine, mechanisms begin to turn over, wires run around pulleys, and flaps and hatches open. The puppet figure of a man is conjured into motion. The man severs the wires from which he hangs and begins an exploration of the "Street of Crocodiles", a suite of near-derelict rooms in which screws turn of their own volition at his approach. He observes robotic figures in a strange workshop, is harassed by a mischievous boy (who may be his own younger self), and eventually finds himself dissected, remodelled and reclothed in the inner recesses of a dubious tailoring establishment.

The Quay brothers must be the most dedicated revivalists in present-day cinema. Not content with a stream of impressively sustained—not to say obsessive—homages to the European avant-gardes of the 1920s and 1930s, they have consistently sought to turn their films into the nearest thing possible to forgeries from the period. They lovingly reproduce the textures of pre-war monochrome, and festoon their films with barely decipherable textual graphics in Polish, Czech, German and French; they even took to signing themselves as "Quaij" for a time. Their fetishes were already clinically diagnosable in their student films (made at the RCA), which lived and breathed the cruel, absurdist spirit that first darkbloomed in Germanic expressionism.

In line with the facts of economic life for animators, most of their films since then have been commissioned 'documentaries' on artists (Ghelderode, Janáček, Stravinsky, et al.), but they have almost always succeeded in subsuming the traits of their subjects into their own chiaroscuro vision. And it seems that the more obscure by-ways of the East European tradition with which they align themselves—post-Kafka surrealism with Victorian Gothic spasms?—are sufficiently plentiful to keep them supplied with raw materials for reinvention for the indefinite future. Their films clearly belong in the line that began with Alexandre Alexeieff and Ladislaw Starewicz and continued (most famously) in the early work of Lenica and Borowczyk, and they have obvious shared interests with contemporaries like the Czech Jan Švankmajer and the Russian Yuri Norstein. But the Quays are unique in so resolutely turning their backs on the present. For them, the past is indeed another country, but one in which they have no trouble about residency permits (as opposed to their real-life difficulties with the British Home Office).

Street of Crocodiles is a case in point. It is rooted in the writings and drawings of the almost forgotten Polish artist Bruno Schulz (1892-1942), a small-town contemporary of Witkiewicz and Gombrowicz who published a volume of short stories under the title *Ulica Krokodyli* in 1934. (His death came at the hands of the Nazis in the Drohobycz ghetto.) Without access to Schulz's original story and/or drawings, it's impossible to guess how much of the imagery comes from him and how much from the repertoire of Quay fetishes, but the film certainly conforms to the pattern set by the Quays in earlier films like *Nocturna Artificialia* and *Ein Brudermord.* It uses a gnomic, fragmentary and repetitive narrative to explore a mood of terminal frustration and compulsion, and it wilfully restricts itself to terms of reference from the 1920s and 1930s. As an exercise in retro styling, in fact, it's the Quays' most sumptuous and accomplished 'forgery' yet. The irony is that the film-makers are simultaneously retrieving Schulz from the oblivion of literary history *and* entombing him afresh in the expressionist detritus of his period.

Street of Crocodiles uses gnomic, fragmentary and repetitive narrative to explore a mood of terminal frustration and compulsion, and it wilfully restricts itself to terms of reference from the 1920s and 1930s.

—Tony Rayns

As the extremely tentative synopsis above tries to suggest, the film almost entirely resists analysis at a narrative level. It's a measure of its deliberate inconclusiveness that the live-action opening (the caretaker entering a museum cluttered with objects like a bowlful of screws that will be echoed in the main body of the film) is overlaid with a caption—"Prelude: The Wooden Oesophagus"—that turns out *not* to herald any of the further chapter headings that it undoubtedly implies. A closing quotation from Schulz—spoken in the original Polish and printed in surprisingly legible English—helps to get the film's sense of

incompleteness into perspective: "In that city of cheap human material, no instincts can flourish, no dark or unusual passions can be aroused. The Street of Crocodiles was a concession of our city to modernity and metropolitan corruption. The misfortune of that area is that nothing ever succeeds there, nothing can ever reach a definite conclusion. Obviously, we were unable to afford anything better than a cardboard imitation, a photo-montage cut out from last year's mouldering newspaper". It seems clear from this that Schulz was aiming at a satire on civic bureaucracy, imagining the creation of a kind of cut-rate licensed quarter in which every act of *coitus* was doomed to be *interruptus*. But the Quays leave the element of satire to one side, and focus instead on more palpable images of impotence, paranoia and despair; they even appropriate Schulz's penultimate phrase as a parting shot ("Obviously, we were unable to afford anything better"), turning it into an apologia for their film's supposed inadequacy.

Whether it's a "cardboard imitation" of something better or not, *Street of Crocodiles* offers considerable pleasures to anyone who shares the Quays' absorption in the expressionist and surrealist traditions. A number of old friends make reappearances here. The puppet protagonist is a dead ringer for the young Conrad Veidt, and the film could well be taken as Cesare the Somnambulist's fruitless search for sexual gratification. He carries with him the striped box from *Un chien andalou,* now containing not a striped collar and a severed hand but an equally phallic giant screw, which has equally disturbing effects when removed to the base of a tailor's dummy. There is even an ironic reverse of a motif from Kenneth Anger's early psychodrama *Fireworks* (yet another quest through the dark night, fuelled by Desire), when slabs of all-too-real meat and offal appear amid the props and dummies. This is the Quays' first film in 35 mm., and they have risen to the gain in picture clarity with an astonishing display of sensual and visceral textures: moulds, thick dust, the peeling silvering on mirrors, oily, knotted wires and patinas of cracked glaze. They also have a wonderful score from Leszek Jankowski, somewhere between Schoenberg and a crazed impromptu for the musical saw, apparently composed for the film before a frame was shot, and hence used to shape and structure many of the visual rhythms.

The Brothers Quay with Chris Petit (interview date June 1986)

SOURCE: "Picked-up Pieces," in *Monthly Film Bulletin,* Vol. 53, No. 629, June, 1986, pp. 164-65.

[*In the following excerpt from an interview, the Quays discuss puppet animation, its tradition as an art form, and its significance to their films. Note that the interviewer's questions were deleted in the original publication.*]

In an interview with Chris Petit, the Quay brothers (Steve & Tim, b. 1947), dark twins of the puppet film, open up unknown worlds . . .

PRESERVING THE SPIRIT

[Brothers Quay]: Puppet animation is a footnote to cinema, so we invariably find ourselves drawn to literary and musical figures outside the mainstream in our search for source material. What worries us most in the early stages of any work is that the puppets will become tamed by the weight of the text. You must remember there is a strong spirit of anarchy in puppet history. At the same time, we have to ask ourselves constantly if we're forcing the puppets to carry something they can't manage. After all, in substance they are quite fragile, however strong in spirit.

For us, puppet animation both stems from and breaks with the old marionette tradition. We prefer, like marionette theatre, to deal in myth rather than conventional narrative, not least because it enhances some kind of magic the puppets have. There is something truly magical about actually seeing the strings at work on, say, the Salzburg marionettes. Puppet animation removes that visible evidence of manipulation, cuts a knife right through it, so one has to find a different magic.

Nocturna Artificialia and *Street of Crocodiles,* where we use dolls' forms and comparatively realistic faces, attempt to blur the distinction between what might be called artificiality and artificial reality. Our aim is to create a state of suspension where the effect, if it works for an audience, is not unlike dreaming, albeit dreaming uneasily. By contrast, the style of *This Unnameable Little Broom,* which acknowledges the marionette tradition, had to be deliberately graphic and involved no sleight of hand. Had it been too human, then the reference to marionettes and mythology would have been lost.

Rather in the way that a poster has to convey the whole impression of a film or an opera, working on a puppet scale requires the same kind of immense shorthand. It also requires patience. In live-action cinema, one usually shoots on location and the results are more or less immediate. We, on the other hand, have to find and make everything ourselves. It takes a lot of glue. Feature films are glued together only during the final stages in editing. Ours are being stuck together from the start, they're built with glue. This work requires painstaking conviction. It cannot be achieved by short cuts. Only by trying to make everything believable (however unreal), can we hope to draw the audience into complicity.

At worst we think of ourselves as merely rummaging for lost or obscure footnotes in half-forgotten alleys of music and literature. Our work involves a lot of scavenging. We arrange our lives so that we have the opportunity to snoop around libraries, tips, wherever: most of the elements in our films are found in the sense that they cost next to nothing. Our work is systematic only in its randomness and much is the result of chance. In a curious way, this haphazard process of discovery—which with luck can lead to strange unearthings—is one of the few sanctities left. We are always on the hunt.

In Poland, we found images that, had we invented them, would be called surreal, but there they are part of the ordinary everyday. We saw tram pylons like weird crucifixes, caught up in fantastic congestions of wires. They heightened for us the whole idea of pathological symbolism and drew our attention to anonymous architecture, to the forgotten details of any city.

Looking at the Polish films of Polanski or Skolimowski one thinks, what fantastic imagination, but it's still all there. In Warsaw, we saw things which we used in our work with very little reshaping, like the naive designs in shop windows—proud, neat arrangements of shoe heels in a cobbler's, or a display of old irons in a pressing shop, little pieces of art direction at once utterly banal and striking. Our response has nothing to do with nostalgia, more to do with the realisation that these East European countries (and perhaps Belgium too) have a timeless quality, in part because they are not yet caught up in the consumer rush, also because they are not yet afraid to live with their pasts unlike, say, West Germany.

[As children in the Philadelphia library] we came across the word 'Kafkaesque'. The configuration of letters alone caused us great excitement, although we had no idea what it meant.

—Brothers Quay

LOOKING FOR KAFKA

We grew up in a small town in the U.S. near Philadelphia, which had a tram system and a large European immigrant population. The city is arranged on the typical North American grid pattern so you always know exactly where you are: in one direction the streets are numbered, in the other named after trees. Inside this very obvious grid, we discovered a smaller, more secret one. The layout of the Philadelphia library is similarly crosshatched and apparently just as impossible to get lost in. But in this deceptively simple layout, we discovered books which opened up unknown worlds to us. Nevertheless, the possibilities there were limited. We came across the word 'Kafkaesque'. The configuration of letters alone caused us great excitement, although we had no idea what it meant. So we asked a librarian who, in all seriousness, referred us to a dictionary.

Later, on a chance recommendation, we came to London to study at the Royal College of Art, and so avoided the army draft. Until then, our main nourishment had been a small diet of Czech cinema and Buñuel. In London, we started to drink coffee and wine (rather than Coke and milk), and discovered a city that was like some hugely stocked reference library waiting for us to lose ourselves in. Cinema, opera, ballet and dance, all hitherto remote or hard to find, were suddenly available on an enormous scale.

When the course ended and our money ran out, we returned to Philadelphia, where we waited on tables, washed dishes and waited to return. On the suggestion of a Dutch friend, we went to Holland where we peddled our portfolio around and landed some bookcover designs. Our first was for a novel by Céline. We drafted *Nocturna* in an Amsterdam hotel room where the trams cast their shadows across the ceiling as they passed below, an image that has been an inspiration ever since. We moved on to the Hague and waited there (and washed more dishes) until we heard that Keith Griffiths (whom we'd met at the RCA and is now our constant collaborator) had got us a grant from the BFI to make the film.

FOLLOWING THE MUSIC

We are exiles here but we find that London still possesses that nineteenth-century quality—perhaps now not as much as Paris—of being a city of exiles. It is tolerant towards a certain kind of independent enquiry.

Occasionally we have to counter charges that our work is obscure, particularly in England. This is probably because it is inspired by European literature and cinema. (We seem to alternate between what Bruno Schulz calls a degraded reality and the more graphic and operatic German traditions.) Perhaps the English find the absence of the familiar unsettling in our films. English cinema is usually about identification of character, just as in English art the dominant mode is portrait painting. People look at English cinema the way they look at English paintings, for moral judgments, which we don't feel qualified to make. European art deals more in mythology—landscape, the relation of people to cities, the things that interest us.

One reason why our work doesn't deal in narrative is that the form doesn't lend itself readily to character and dialogue in the usual sense. Puppet animation is much closer to dance and music, which are our biggest sources of inspiration. Music has its own laws which narrative could never begin to shape itself towards. The approach to narrative, the obscurity of narrative you can carry off in music and dance, the relationship of movement to music, the range of music in dance, all these propel our work far more than conventional cinema. Certainly in **Street of Crocodiles,** the music shaped powerfully the directions we took.

Sometimes it shocks us how few references people have to the literature and music that has driven us for fifteen years. It makes us feel élitist by default, which is not what we intend. We would rather our films were treated like department stores—admittedly somewhat manic department stores—in which one can take a lift to whatever level one wants.

Animation, unless one works in mainstream special effects, is a marginal business. One learns to live with the lack of reaction. At least we have each other to rebound off. Alone it would be the most hellish business, the sheer effort makes everything painfully slow. In the end, we travel on instinct, quite happy most of the time to be left alone mapping out our obsessions, working towards something even if we don't quite know what.

Julian Petley   (review date June 1986)

SOURCE: A review of *The Cabinet of Jan Švankmajer—Prague's Alchemist of Film,* in *Monthly Film Bulletin,* Vol. 53, No. 629, June, 1986, pp. 188-89.

[*In the following review, Petley outlines the nine interlinked sections that comprise* The Cabinet of Jan Švankmajer, *an animated tribute to and analysis of the work of Czech surrealist puppet filmmaker Jan Švankmajer.*]

Along with Jan Lenica and Walerian Borowczyk, the Czech Jan Švankmajer is one of the key animators to have emerged in Eastern Europe since the war. Like his Polish contemporaries, his work owes a good deal to Dada and Surrealism, and also carries more contemporary resonances of the Theatre of the Absurd. In Švankmajer's case, the link with Surrealism is particularly strong, since Prague, where he lives and works, was one of the capitals of European Surrealism. But whatever the influences, Švankmajer's vision is uniquely his own, and he has produced some of the most savage and disturbing work of any contemporary film-maker in this field.

In June 1984, Channel 4's innovative film programme, *Visions,* devoted a whole programme to Švankmajer's work, made up of interviews, extracts, the complete *Dimensions of Dialogue,* and a series of animated sequences by the Quay brothers and Keith Griffiths showing a puppet Švankmajer at work. These little vignettes imaginatively visualised various ideas suggested by the interviewees, thus analysing and elucidating Švankmajer's work without recourse to verbal abstractions. **The Cabinet of Jan Švankmajer** is made up of Atelier Koninck's contributions alone, and has become a self-contained work consisting of nine interlinked sections.

In the first, "Pins for Loose Geographies", various objects pinpoint Prague as Švankmajer's home and establish its relationship with Paris. Next, in "The Atelier of Švankmajer—XVIth and XXth Centuries Simultaneously: An Unexpected Visitor", the puppet Švankmajer, whose head is literally stuffed with books and whose arms are graphic instruments, receives a visitor, a young boy, whose head he literally empties of rubbish. In "Pursuit of the Object", Švankmajer rummages about in a room which is completely lined with drawers, all full of highly Švankmajeresque objects which seem to have a bizarre life of their own. In "The Wunderkammer", the child enters this inner sanctum, and then ("The Child's Divining of the Object") reveals a whole series of drawers within drawers. As the search continues, it is as if the universe is imploding: the walls move in and even the Prague marker on the opening map starts to disappear into the paper. Eventually the 'object' is found deep in an inner recess. We then move to "The Migration of Forms": Švankmajer takes scraps of coloured paper from one drawer, and they reappear as brightly coloured birds from another. The pins from the opening section reappear dancing with a lump of sugar in "Metaphysical Playroom: A Tactile Experiment", in which objects continue to defy the laws of gravity and the child conceals a large spider in a box, asking Švankmajer to guess the nature of the object simply by touching it. He mistakes it first for a fox fur and then a fir tree. In "Tarantella: The Child Receives a Lesson in 1/24 of a Second", the boy learns how and why the objects can behave in such strange ways, and finally, in "For a New Dawn", he leaves Švankmajer's studio, but not before the hole in his head has been filled with a new eye and a book.

These little scenes refer variously to the importance of objects in Švankmajer's work, their transformation and bizarre combination through specifically cinematic techniques, the extraordinary power of the camera to 'make strange', the influence of Surrealism on Švankmajer's work, the subversive and radical role of humour. Taken out of the context of the original *Visions* programme, and passing as they do in fairly rapid succession, these nine vignettes might at first sight seem a trifle bewildering. They ideally need to be viewed more than once before they begin to work effectively as quirky introductions to the Švankmajer universe. Then, however, they emerge as surprisingly charming and delightful excursions into this astonishing (and often deeply disturbing) director's work.

Raymond Durgnat   (review date June 1986)

SOURCE: A review of *Igor—The Paris Years Chez Pleyel*, in *Monthly Film Bulletin*, Vol. 53, No. 629, June, 1986, pp. 189-90.

[*Durgnat is an English film professor and critic whose books on the cinema include* Luis Buñuel *(1968),* The Strange Case of Alfred Hitchcock *(1974), and* King Vidor, American *(1988). In the following positive review of* Igor—The Paris Years Chez Pleyel, *he summarizes the events depicted in the film and argues that puppet animation of this kind has "momentous" consequences for film theory.*]

On his first visit to Paris, Mayakovsky (who always bellows through a megaphone) describes the rich diversity of artists overflowing its café terraces and spinning off into their own orbits. He visits Stravinsky in his apartment above a player-piano repair shop at 22 rue Rochechouart. Stravinsky has accepted a contract to transcribe his works on to piano rolls, thus preventing future distortions of his music. He plans multi-pianola compositions, and explains the machine's workings, with its paper roll and pneumatic motor (cut-in shots show pianolist Rex Lawson playing the instrument). When Jean Cocteau calls, Mayakovsky rhapsodises about the pianola mechanising music, and images of its chains and cogs evoke a staid *'ballet mécanique'*. But Cocteau insists on showing Mayakovsky Paris by night. They all speed off in Stravinsky's bullet-shaped sportster, passing neon signs which flash the names of avant-garde movements as if they were cabarets. Mayakovsky having fallen out of the car, the other two ascend the Eiffel Tower for a picnic. But from afar, Mayakovsky harangues Stravinsky to forsake Parisian "perfumes and powders" and assume the leadership of the progressive avant-gardes. Their night out ends in a pissoir, where Cocteau picks up a handsome, but doll-size, working man. Back home, Stravinsky dreams a version of *Petroushka*, with Cocteau, like a one-legged hybrid between a bouquet and a ballerina, being courted by the composer in blue, and Mayakovsky in red toting a scimitar. Mayakovsky, now amidst Russian street signs, exhorts both the Eiffel Tower and Stravinsky to come to the U.S.S.R. ("I'll get you a visa!"). But the Bolshevik's call to "March!" is softened to Stravinsky's quiet "Right . . . left . . ." as his hands work the pianola's phrasing controls. The film's [*Igor—The Paris Years Chez Pleyel*] penultimate images stress the solemn pianolist's treadmill pedalling and quiescent hands.

The Quay brothers/Keith Griffiths oeuvre makes a fine 'show reel' for the resources of animation, and therefore the nature of film form. Theorists commonly pass over the puppet film, and animation generally, as a ghetto of exceptions to 'real' movies, which are supposedly rooted in photography and realism. Yet photo-realism is no part of film form, and merely a practical convenience for achieving it. By ostentatiously parading that indifference to realism in which all the arts rejoice, animation might be the 'royal road' to understanding what film form concretely is. One can't say that puppetry's anti-realism is avant-garde or subversive, for it's as basic and ever-accessible a form as, say, the fairy-story. Its enduring popularity, amply attested to by George Pal and Jiří Trnka, has been emphatically reasserted by *Sesame Street,* the Muppets and *Spitting Image.*

But puppetry knows so many (and such heterogeneous) syntheses of realistic and non-realistic elements as to blur all possible boundaries between them. The consequences for film theory are momentous, and catastrophic for certain 'radical' notions of bourgeois realism and illusionism. Notably, puppet films accentuate film's self-contradictory space (with 3-D forms on 2-D; while movements and angle changes generate a 2½-D space). And other issues abound: 1. Most puppet shows (*Igor* included) rely on looks that directly address the spectator. 2. The puppet figure is one long 'alienation effect'. 3. Narratives like *Igor*'s only make sense given highly stylised figures, thus upsetting notions of prespecified narrative logic and structure. 4. The puppet figure is a *description* of a character, so that film form resides in description not in narrative.

If *Igor* is a minor piece, its very simplicity intensifies the structural paradoxes that make animation not the eccentric Uncle, but the Queen of film. The faces of these *dramatis personae* are cut-out photographs—flat, but folded to suggest the shape of a head. (Some near-profile views involve marvellously pixillated perspectives.) These photo-heads are attached to sculpturally fantasticated little bodies which, unlike the faces, move 'internally' (and with other kinds of 'non-realism'). A 'speeding' car is surrounded by a conspicuously static, decorative, frame; its solid wheels turn slowly, while flat foregrounds flash backwards at super speed. The car's toy form evokes Charles and Ray Eames' crucial distinction between the toy (a bourgeois form: unrealistic, but with imagination lovingly built in) and the model (a 'scientific' form, and 'merely' correct). Again, sensitive live action with hands preludes the film's visual transformation of the piano roll into flat, abstract, 'visual music'. Thus the film's visual texture is a wonderful tissue of contradictions, which spur (or charm) our imaginations into action. The Quays' detailing here is sparer than usual—as befits this little fable—but no less poignant. For this relative minimalism catches that "Punch and Judy" pathos which so often underlies avant-garde extremisms. It also generates a strange symbiosis of detail, scale and space. Indeed, the small screen can't do this film justice (ironically for a Channel 4 production); the big, cinema screen is its rightful environment.

Puppetry is especially appropriate for the nostalgic-fetishistic poetics of pianolas; for the pathos of aspirations to the mechanisation of art; and even for the machine-reflex quality often noted in Stravinsky's 'primitivist' rhythms. Moreover, puppet stylisation deftly distinguishes these 'real', very complex artists from their roles within this morality play. Though Stravinsky did turn out piano rolls (and collaborated with Cocteau, of course), and though Mayakovsky, Stravinsky and Cocteau did all meet in Paris, the action here is quite apocryphal. These exchanges may owe less to the 20s than to the art-and-revolution student moralisms which followed the 60s within the filmmakers' own era. If each of their heroes pays the price of his choice, perhaps Stravinsky epitomises their own, by meticulously sticking to his last. Mayakovsky's booming rigidity foreshadows his double pathos: suicide, and the recuperation of his work by Stalinism.

As a sort of Aesop's Fable about commitment, this little essay belongs with certain live-action movies: notably, Ken Russell's Symbolical freewheelings around artists' lives, which often take on a doll-like quality, and Syberberg's *Ludwig,* another stiff, 'toy theatre' essay in aestheticism. Coprogramming puppet and live-action studies of similar themes is important, for the segregation and relegation of puppet films to animation programmes minimises the richness of puppetry as a figure of style, i.e., as meaning.

The final privilege of puppet form is a certain free-floating of reference. Here are such icons as a bowler hat madly spinning on its peg, like a quick burst of Dada, and Stravinsky's blue-and-red flat, like a joint effort by Picasso, Chagall and Caligari. The last, live-action, images of the pianolist, bushy-bearded and solemnly pedalling away, seem touched with Vigo's wand, from *Zéro de conduite.* The little sequence of Stravinsky falling awkwardly asleep, lulled by the melancholy sounds of a passing tram, eerily invokes Carné-Prévert's populism. Puppetry and 'poetic realism' can indeed bear *rapprochement,* for the latter's atmospheric 'tone-row' was very much a collective poetic, shared with Cocteau.

Yet, and at the same time, it's beguiling to link Keith Griffiths and the Brothers Quay, as Royal College of Art alumni, with some 'RCA School' of exquisite pictorialism, whose other members would include Ridley Scott and Cerith Wyn Evans. Ultimately, perhaps, the Quay-Griffiths tandem (a threeseater!) belongs, with Borowczyk, on the *chosiste* side of Surrealist Street. But in spirit, as in medium, Atelier Koninck's position, at the intersection of categories conventionally kept apart, attests to the passionate and controlled dialectic underlying this quite non-fetishistic, and always delightful, little gem.

Michael O'Pray   (review date June 1986)

SOURCE: A review of *Little Songs of the Chief Officer of Hunar Louse, or This Unnameable Little Broom,* in *Monthly Film Bulletin,* Vol. 53, No. 629, June, 1986, p. 191.

[*In the following review of* This Unnameable Little Broom, *O'Pray describes the film's action and discusses its relationship to the works of painter Max Ernst and to the ancient*

Sumerian poem cycle The Epic of Gilgamesh (c. *7th century* BC) *on which the film is based.*]

The tricycle man goes about a three-walled room testing vicious mechanical traps and devices. He puts something in a table drawer, melts a block of ice on the table top, then disappears under the table through a trap door when a bell sounds. A winged insect creature enters, cautiously approaches the table, and through an eyepiece spies a morsel of flesh swinging in the innards of a female torso. Beneath the table, the tricycle man waits. Inside the drawer, the insect creature sees a small palpitating organ resembling the female vagina. When the creature embraces the organ on the table, a spring ejects him into the overhead wires which seem to decapitate him. The tricycle man emerges to eye his victim, takes from the drawer a black insect which he eventually hurls out of the room, puts his arm through an aperture in the wall and falls asleep. He awakes to pull a length of golden cloth through the aperture, in which he wraps the insect creature before beating him with a stick and cutting off his wings. Outside in the forest, a winged creature is glimpsed. Inside the room, the tricycle man rides furiously around the table under which the insect creature is imprisoned. Outside a siren can be heard.

This Unnameable Little Broom was made for Channel 4 as the pilot for a series of six short films entitled *Sleeping Cars to Eternity.* The series was never made, and ***This Unnameable Little Broom*** remains, in more ways than one, something of an oddity. Its full title betrays its mock-esotericism: ***Little Songs of the Chief Officer of Hunar Louse, or This Unnameable Little Broom (Being a Largely Disguised Reduction of the Epic of Gilgamesh) Tableau II.*** A self-contained, if rather obscure film, it is outstandingly skilled and imaginative. As the title implies ("largely disguised"), to try to locate the *Epic of Gilgamesh* in the film is fruitless and to miss the point of this surrealist titling. Nevertheless, the epic is a genuine source, involving Gilgamesh of Uruk, an oppressive and tyrannical king (the bizarre cyclist in the film) and Enkidu, a wild man created by the gods (the insect creature to equal Gilgamesh). The epic itself was a series of stone tablets from ancient Mesopotamia bearing fragments of a poem.

This Unnameable Little Broom transforms the story into a macabre tale told with grotesque models and a theatrical *mise en scène* in which savage, vindictive machines whirr, slice, decapitate and imprison the unwary. The pace is fast, a rhythmic montage of sound and image, and the editing is a mechanism not only of construction and narrative transition but of sensory shock. The Quay brothers' ability to play with both theatrical conventions (the high shots of the three-walled stage in which the action takes place) and 'realist' ones (the strange garden outside the chamber of torture and desire) resists any facile reading of the film. It is Central European in feeling, in its use of music, and in the child-like quality of its surreal logic and macabre imagery (the *Merry Stories and Funny Pictures* of Heinrich Hoffman come to mind). It has the cold articulation of malignancy and evil commonly associated with the horrific fantasies of children's stories and games.

At the heart of the film is the table-trap, a piece of furniture which contains an image of a woman's naked body for its surface and which, when perceived through a lens, becomes the erotic bait. In the table drawer is an organ which resembles female genitalia and which later becomes a black, evil-looking insect. The character on a tricycle races about the room setting up the trap for Enkidu, who appears as a winged insect (Max Ernst's famous collage series *Une semaine de bonté* comes to mind, with its sexually marauding birdmen, its sense of infernal machines as traps, the duplicity of objects, and above all, perhaps, the innocence of evil).

Mounting the female torso in the preliminary act of copulation, Enkidu is suddenly ejected into the taut wires running across the top of the room; at the end of the film, he is locked into the table. The horror of vaginal castration, the anxiety of sexual coupling, and the power of desire are made flesh here in "repulsive monsters, symbols of mindless power, unchecked brutality and sheer unreason" (to quote Uwe Schneede's book on Max Ernst). This is centred paradoxically (except for the surrealist) on the reason of the machine, the rationality of technology, the exquisite delight of invention in the service of sex, death and torture. The Quays have not located this savage morbidity in the realm of the intellect and high culture, but more effectively in that other world of folk tales, ancient myths and nursery rhymes, where Punch and Judy mercilessly beat each other, where Alice, heroine of that most perverse of erotic tales, reads of the Jabberwocky, and where the red-legged scissor-man servers the thumbs of little boys.

Peter Greenaway   (review date Summer 1986)

SOURCE: A review of *Street of Crocodiles,* in *Sight and Sound,* Vol. 55, No. 3, Summer, 1986, pp. 182-83.

[*Greenaway is an English screenwriter and director whose film* A Zed and Two Noughts *(1985) was inspired in part by the Brothers Quay. In the following positive review of* Street of Crocodiles, *he discusses the aesthetic affinities between the Quays and Bruno Schulz, the Polish short story writer upon whose work the film is based.*]

The Quay Brothers' film *Street of Crocodiles* begins with a glob of spit. It falls from the mouth of an aged museum curator into the ambiguous mechanical parts of what used to be called a philosophical toy—one of those numerous, patented, primitive viewing-machines, precursors of the early cinema. This gift of human saliva, performing the same function as the finger of Michelangelo's God on Adam, animates a universe—a largely monochromatic universe—full of that intermittent stop and start, frenzy and frozen moment that takes you from Marey and Muybridge to Méliès, the three Ms of the cinema's poetic beginnings.

A neatly self-reflexive metaphor for the Quays to choose. And their Adam is a puppet somewhere between a single portrait of their double-selves and a portrait of—in this case—their own animator, Bruno Schulz, who, according to his English translator, was unattractive and sickly with a thin, angular body and deep-set eyes in a pale triangular face. This puppet has the sort of hair that reminds you of the sensation of bare knees on coconut matting and the

sort of shabby black clothes associated with classroom chalk and ink. All very tactile and associative. Rust and dust, grime and slime, oil and blood. It irritates the nasal passages, dries out the natural oil of your palms, makes you want to cut your fingernails, sneeze and spit.

After considerable wandering amongst some of the more recherché heroes and idols of early twentieth century Belgium and Czechoslovakia, the Brothers Quay have alighted in ideal territory—Drohobycz according to Schulz—a city of dark streets, ambiguous rites, abandoned stages, long nocturnal perspectives, creaking machines of dubious purpose, panic, boredom and melancholia.

Schulz wrote about his Polish birthplace in the 1930s in a way that Italo Calvino wrote about Venice in *Invisible Cities*—infinite fictional variations on a favourite city. Both authors could hardly be said to have written short stories with a narrative, more like descriptions with some narrative content. And so it is with the Quay Brothers' film. To ask for anything in the way of a neatly packaged story is to ask for the wrong thing.

Bruno Schulz wrote some twenty-six stories in some ten years, before being shot dead in the street by a Gestapo officer in 1942, an event that apparently terminated a feud fuelled by the ownership of some of Schulz's drawings. For Schulz was a draughtsman. He taught drawing in a boys' secondary school; his drawings reminding you sometimes of Beckmann, even of Sendak. His figures have large heads with the eyes straining up to look at you from under even larger foreheads.

The Street of Crocodiles is marked on the map of Drohobycz as a white space, reluctantly acknowledged, scratched in with a few lines, a place of some equivocation, of dubious purposes, of storerooms of books and photographs of unanticipated licentiousness, of tailors that will dress you at the front of the shop and undress you at the back, of shabby facades where the inhabitants are quite proud of an odour of corruption. It doesn't sound a million miles from Soho, where you can often see the Quay Brothers, nonchalantly dressed to look alike to confuse certain recognition, riding swift, black, skeletal bicycles. Maybe the Street of Crocodiles is the Quay synonym for Soho. Although there is no talk of film in Schulz's Drohobycz, there is much talk of puppets and dolls, paper-thin cutouts, animated pictures, oakum and *papier-mâché* and an extended treatise on the Life and Thoughts of Tailors' Dummies.

The Quays' animated hero gains his freedom at the snip of a pair of crocodile-jawed scissors somewhere near Rathbone Street and Charlotte Street and, going south, tremulously explores the night-time back streets. He finds empty theatres in Wardour Street, witnesses the Dance of the Screws in St Anne's Court and an urchin trapping light in Dean Street. Carrying a black and white diagonally striped box that he must have stolen from *Un Chien Andalou,* he finds a tailor's shop near Shaftesbury Avenue and is a one-man audience to a dance of tailor's dolls. Scalped and eerily lit from above so that their eye-sockets gleam blindly, they entertain and then they remove his head, wrapping it neatly in tailor's tissue. There are moments of nicely ambiguous eroticism involving kidneys and steel pins, wet liver wrapped in tissue-paper, stray hands stroking black serge and moments of shock when brilliant colour floods unexpectedly into a black and white world.

The Quays know Schulz well. It is often possible to see how they have picked out a phrase, an evocative sentence here and an evocative sentence there and have elaborated upon them. It is an analogous method to Schulz himself, who takes a single fact or proposition and extends and elaborates it, building a complex system of metaphors without strain which takes you far from the original starting point. For the Quays, one phrase from Schulz, ' . . . a light grey vegetation of fluffy weeds', is a cue for a fall of dandelion seeds; or maybe it's thistledown which drifts on to the set which beforehand is exclusively man-made. The vegetation decays before our eyes, moulds, festers and becomes covered in wet dust and made part of the ambiguous grime of the city.

In the seven years since the BFI-funded *Nocturna Artificialia,* the Quay Brothers' skill and imagination at handling and binding together the various animation processes suggests maybe that they ought to embark on a larger canvas and a more completely original work. It would be good to see them scale up their world and bring their dramatic lighting, their use of colour, their creation of atmosphere, their unsettling eye and rich delight in the texture of 'stuff' and 'matter'—another Schulz preoccupation—to full human scale.

Their talents could be yoked to the use of actors and free them from the drudgery of the time-lapse animation camera. The prospect of the patience and labour required by such animation processes is daunting at anything longer than ten minutes. They, of course, might find this presumptuous or unnecessary when so many contemporary visual products demand and insist that humans should behave like automatons and robots and puppets. Read the book and see the film.

Richard Combs   (review date July 1986)

SOURCE: A review of *Ein Brudermord,* in *Monthly Film Bulletin,* Vol. 53, No. 630, July, 1986, pp. 219-20.

[*In the following review of* Ein Brudermord, *which is based on the short story "Ein Brudermord" (1917) by Franz Kafka, Combs argues that "puppet films are probably best qualified to give clear and accurate meaning to the notoriously generalised concept of the 'Kafkaesque.'"*]

One night about nine o'clock, Schmar takes up his position with a knife at the corner where Wese, his intended victim, will turn from the street where he works into the street where he lives. Schmar passes the time whetting his knife and practising his thrust, observed by a neighbour, Pallas, who does nothing to prevent the crime. Mrs. Wese looks out for her husband, who is working uncommonly late, but at last the sound of a door bell announces his exit into the street. At the corner, he pauses to contemplate the night sky, then unknowingly advances to meet Schmar's knife. Exultant, triumphant, Schmar stabs his victim to death, then throws away his weapon, experiencing disappointment even in this ecstasy.

All roads, not just for the Quays, but for the European puppet film, might lead through Kafka. First of all, puppet films are probably best qualified to give clear and accurate meaning to the notoriously generalised concept of the 'Kafkaesque'. With their concrete abstractions, their metaphors endowed with a startlingly literal life, they come close to the Kafka method. And that paranoiac vision which sees life as an endless, impenetrable, infernal bureaucracy is most nicely rendered in the 'found' materials of puppetry, a world of arbitrary bits and pieces where the tawdry, the pathetic, the strange and the intimidating freely intermingle. Finally, there is, in the topsy-turvy business of animating that which is clearly not animate, some analogue to the topsy-turvy world of *The Trial* and *The Castle,* where the animate is being made inanimate, where human thought, reason and order has institutionalised its own life away.

There are certain common features of the puppeteers themselves, of a social and biographical nature, which also lead back to Kafka. That resident of Prague, who wrote in German ("a kind of officially subsidised language", according to one Kafka biographer, "dry and artificial, a foreign element"), is kin of sorts to all puppeteers, who are bound to work with a foreign element, taking Frankensteinian short cuts between life and not-life, between the familiar and the strange. Hence the puppeteer himself is inevitably a foreign element, the practitioner of an exile's cinema. The Quays, willing exiles themselves (see last month's interview [Chris Petit, "Picked-up Pieces," *Monthly Film Bulletin,* Vol. 53, No. 629, June, 1986]), have preserved Kafka's alienness in *Ein Brudermord* in their German credit titles, and in the voice-over, drawn from Kafka's story and read as a kind of radio commentary by a heavily accented Lutz Becker. Another resident of Prague (and past Quay subject) is Jan Švankmajer, while the Russian animator, Ladislaw Starewicz, to whom this film is in part dedicated, was born in Moscow to a Polish family, and was originally a scientist who reputedly took to animation when real-life beetles wouldn't perform for a nature-study film (shades of "The Metamorphosis"). The lineage might even take in other writers in the 'alienated' mode, like Kafka's literary model Heinrich von Kleist, who penned an essay "On the Puppet Theatre".

The first thing to say about the Quays' *Brudermord* is that it looks less Kafkaesque in the accepted, or general, sense than, say, *Street of Crocodiles,* which comes up with very concrete images for Kafka's soulless, placeless bureaucracy (but none the less particularly East European limbo). Here the street corner where Schmar waits for his victim is allowed to exist almost on its own—the set is like a casually littered but rather empty lumber-room, its details hardly even urban (the criss-crossing lines that suggest the architecture of the street look more like a ship's rigging). No sense of a city, or even of the streets stretching away from the corner, is evoked; the corner exists in malignant isolation, everything hinges here (at one point, instead of a camera movement, the set pivots to reveal another view). The starkness, strangeness and compacted mystery of this tale don't really lend themselves to the familiar interpretations of Kafka. Which may be because it belongs to a different category of Kafka.

In *The Terror of Art,* Martin Greenberg distinguishes between Kafka's "dream narratives", which represent the major part of his work, and which would give us **Street of Crocodiles,** and what he calls "thought-stories" which "have virtually ceased to be narratives at all and have become a kind of thinking in images, imaginative reasonings in which an image is not represented or delineated in the usual way . . . but, as it were, excogitated". In its original form, "Ein Brudermord" may have actually been more of a dream narrative, or at least a mixture of the two forms. But the Quays' adaptation has stripped away its narrative even more (although in treating the three-page story as a five-minute film, they may have fairly approximated the time it takes to read it). They have truncated the part of Pallas, the onlooker who fails to intervene; deleted Schmar's cry as he attacks Wese ("You will never see Julia again!") which hints at a motive; and dropped the ending in which Schmar "fighting down with difficulty the last of his nausea, pressed his mouth against the shoulder of the policeman who, stepping lightly, led him away".

In this last sentence is encapsulated the collapse of so many Kafka 'heroes' into the arms of the law, delivering themselves to any patriarchal authority in fear of, or in reaction to, the fulfilment of their own innermost wishes. What these might be Kafka's "Brudermord" hints at in dream form—with its clues to matters sexual and Oedipal, supplied by the Kafka who was an ambivalent follower of Freud ("To hell with psychology!" he once declared) and an obsessive diarist of his own mental states. What the Quays' **Brudermord** gives us is the compacted thought-story of a man who has to kill himself in order to be himself. The 'brother murder' is the slaying of Kafka the insurance company clerk (Wese, "the industrious night-worker" who has a wife and a normal family life waiting for him) by the Kafka who longed for all these things but saw his own commitment to his art as being ineluctably, even self-destructively, opposed to them. Martin Greenberg: "He had to die as a human being to live as a writer, to lose in order to win".

Roger Noake (review date July 1986)

SOURCE: A review of *The Eternal Day of Michel De Ghelderode 1898-1962,* in *Monthly Film Bulletin,* Vol. 53, No. 630, July, 1986, p. 221.

[*In the following review of* The Eternal Day of Michel De Ghelderode 1898-1962, *Noake examines the ways in which the Quays use "the framework of the bio-pic to explore and develop formal elements of* mise-en-scène *in live theatre and puppet productions."*]

Maps of fifteenth-century Flanders and present-day Belgium are juxtaposed, while the voice of Michel De Ghelderode announces that he is not a Belgium writer but a man who writes in a room. An eye appears at a peep-hole, and the first of six extracts adapted from Ghelderode's work begins. The eccentric cavalier from the play *Cavalier Bizarre* rides through sinister scenery of wind-

mills and gibbets; another figure in a cart or tumbril spins past, trembling in terror as it is transported into a landscape of towering pylons and gloomy cathedral facades. The peep-hole is suddenly closed and a curtain drawn by a clown. The clown puts on a half-mask and the second extract, from *La Mort du Docteur Faust,* is played out. Faust is presented as a figure marooned outside time: he cannot enter history and thus he can only passively observe the world (which is represented by a spinning top). Finally, he is seen looking in through a window at the world of dead but immortal objects. Michel De Ghelderode is shown entering a theatre; he states that he is the central masked figure of his plays and introduces (in the third extract) the explorer Christopher Columbus, who sits beneath a huge hat made of newspapers, blowing bubbles while he is interviewed by a reporter. In his study, Ghelderode pronounces on the ritualistic nature of theatre and the importance of carnival and procession: images from Bosch and Ensor illustrate the visual roots of his work. In the fourth extract, from *Hop, Signor!,* two dwarfs on stilts and crutches stage a mock fight while Signor Juréal bemoans his crumbling body; the Executioner and Margaret, Juréal's wife, appear and the Executioner (who takes the form of a Swiss army knife) extols the virtues of hanging. Ghelderode arrives at the puppet theatre of Toon in Brussels, for which he wrote five marionette plays, and talks to the puppeteers. In the fifth extract, from *Fastes d'Enfer (Chronicles of Hell),* Jan In Eremo, Bishop of Lapideopolis, who has been poisoned by his own priests, stands over his empty coffin unable truly to die. He struggles with and overpowers one priest, and his mother lays him finally to rest in his coffin, "dead twice dead". In the final extract, from *Masques Ostendais,* the characters from the previous extracts are reintroduced. Two figures with brooms sweep up paper which the clown throws with fake jollity; a puppet is tossed into the air by the dwarfs. The puppet of the Grim Reaper informs us that "We are living in an age lacking in the marvellous".

It was Jean-Louis Barrault's production of *Chronicles of Hell* in 1949 that placed the long-neglected Michel De Ghelderode—his work largely written before 1947—alongside Alfred Jarry and Antonin Artaud as artists who had given voice once more to the primal scream. **The Eternal Day of Michel De Ghelderode,** which incorporates archival material of Ghelderode's life, was a transitional work for the Koninck studio team, using the framework of the bio-pic to explore and develop formal elements of *mise en scène* in live theatre and puppet productions. It is subtitled "Synthesis, Mask, Spectacle", and these are the areas with which it seeks to engage: concepts of total theatre, the uses of archaic ritual, and finally spectacle as the antithesis of naturalism—all central concerns of avant-garde theatre.

In his own pursuit of total theatre, Ghelderode had turned to the marvellous rather than to the fantastic, to a world of alchemy and the visionary images of Flemish painting, rather than the area of the repressed unconscious. The marvellous is full of potential for many forms of animation: the omnipresent voice of the teller of dark tales is paralleled in animation by the ever-present hand of the artist/manipulator. The Quay brothers' animation makes full use of the characteristic jerky action of marionettes to emphasise their manipulations (in *Hop, Signor!,* the hands of the puppeteer are shown working the strings). The extract from *Fastes d'Enfer* (1937), with its gloomy, surprisingly massive Gothic interior, conjures a world of caskets, drawers, half-hidden objects against which the insubstantial puppets flutter and struggle, trapped in their tale, to be returned to their boxes when their usefulness is at an end. This stylisation also suggests the function and power of the mask: to invest the wearer with a role which can be repeated as an endless ritual.

But the attempt to integrate puppets with live performers through the use of mask and gesture produces an unfortunate mimicry where the puppets have the advantage. The extracts staged as tableaux by The Cherub Company reduce the marvellous to whimsy: instead of swallowing up the actors as they should, the masks only make them self-conscious. It is in the use of the documentary archive material that a real synthesis is achieved. Here some of the more simplistic notions of film realism, which would put animation and documentary at opposite ends of the scale, are brought into question. This material is taken from a documentary on the life of Ghelderode made for Radio Télévision Belge, and shows the author as a hunched and overcoated figure—his expressionless face resembling a mask from a Noh play—determinedly hiding himself away at the centre of his own fiction.

The Quay brothers are masters of bricolage, both in their use of found material for making their puppets and in their selection of subject matter and style. They do not work the highways of the European folk-tale, as did Disney, but the more marginal and obscure provinces. This in itself can make their narratives uncomfortable for audiences with other expectations of puppet films. *The Eternal Day of Michel De Ghelderode* represents a move away from the Kafkaesque pessimism of their earlier films, and from their dependence on the stylistic devices, obsessive and fatalistic, of the Polish schools, towards something closer to Artaud's concept of the essential cruelty of spectacle. In *This Unnameable Little Broom* (1985), this comes most fully to fruition.

Vincent Canby   (review date 29 April 1987)

SOURCE: A review of *The Brothers Quay,* in *The New York Times,* April 29, 1987, p. C19.

[*Long associated with* The New York Times, *Canby is one of the most distinguished American film and theater critics. In the following mixed review of the four films that comprise* The Brothers Quay, *he argues that, while the films contain beautiful images, they "don't vary much in style" and begin to "blur" together after awhile.*]

The Brothers Quay is the umbrella title for the four animated Surrealist films (in which miniature objects are photographed in stop-motion) that make up the program opening today at the Film Forum I. The Brothers Quay are, in fact, the American-born, London-based film makers, Timothy and Stephen (identical twins). The Quays, who started out as graphics designers, are now specialists

in clever cinematic nightmares inspired by the fears, frights and longings of others.

The individual films are *Street of Crocodiles* (1986), based on material by Bruno Schulz, a Polish Surrealist writer shot in the street by a Gestapo officer in 1942; *Leos Janacek: Intimate Excursions* (1983), which attempts to find visual references in the correspondence of Leos Janacek, the Czechoslovak composer; *The Cabinet of Jan Svankmajer* (1984), a tribute to the Czechoslovak film animator, and *The Epic of Gilgamesh* (1985), inspired by the Babylonian myth.

Surrealist films aren't meant to be interpreted in the systematic manner of a foreign language. One reads into them what one will, and, in this case, if one has any knowledge of the source material, what one can. The Quay films have the initial impact of monstrous, extremely personal visions of disorder, set in a pocket-sized universe where effects have little to do with causes.

On occasion the images are beautiful. They're always strikingly vivid. Hell looks like a 19th-century steel mill as imagined by Rube Goldberg. Pins can dance. Screws unscrew themselves to screw themselves into a host-substance at a different location. Moths and grasshoppers are the size of 747 jumbo jets. An opera diva has a wire body and the head of a pigeon. The mostly monochromatic backgrounds have the delicacy of old etchings.

No matter what the source material of the particular film, the images don't vary much in style—or in the associations they evoke—from one film to the next. Thus each film might be more effective if seen separately, and in contrast to something more conventional in manner and content. Seen in a group, as these are being presented by the Film Forum, they blur to the point where they begin to look like one long roll of bizarre, animated wallpaper.

David Edelstein   (review date 5 May 1987)

SOURCE: "Double Your Pleasure," in *The Village Voice,* Vol. XXXII, No. 18, May 5, 1987, p. 66.

[*In the following positive review of* The Brothers Quay, *Edelstein describes scenes from the four films and comments on the theme of decay, a common element in several of the works.*]

The Brothers Quay are 39-year-old American twins who live in London and make the damnedest little movies with puppets, primitive machines, and the occasional animal organ. For only a week, the Film Forum will introduce New York audiences to four of their films—74 intense, hypnotic minutes' worth. Their camera floats among wires, rickety scaffolding, Expressionist scenery; artifice is frankly acknowledged, even celebrated. The movements of the puppets are slightly jerky, as in the early work of Méliès or *King Kong*; elsewhere, the textures are squishy and pulsating. The Quays like decay. It's the combination of unreality and ultrareality that gets under your skin; you feel as if you're drifting through the bloodstream of a living theater—a vivarium.

That theater, I'd venture, is like the imagination itself, the place where humans make contact with a universe in frightening, inexorable flux. But that sounds abstract, and the Quay's films are tactile, grounded—they're Surrealists. The 21-minute *Street of Crocodiles,* perhaps their most ambitious work, is launched by a glob of saliva, the spew of a caretaker who enters a parallel universe and watches screws twist out of the grimy floor, dance, and screw themselves down again elsewhere. The world unravels, decomposes, shifts; dust clings to ancient, useless machines; and humans are literally worn down, their heads removed by tailors with the eyeless faces of porcelain baby-dolls, who also thrust steel pins into a large, wet liver. If it's Doomsday, this must be Eastern Europe.

The Quays' work proceeds from a fascination with hidden patterns, shadows, doppelgangers, transplanted to the dark, Expressionist universe of Poland and Czechoslovakia—the paranoid tales of Franz Kafka and Bruno Schulz, the folk operas of Janácek, the alchemical animation of Jan Svankmajer. The search for patterns and the dread of death inform *Leos Janácek: Intimate Excursions,* a 30-minute meditation on the great composer's work. Here, Janácek himself (the puppet affixed with a black-and-white portrait) leads us through excerpts from the operas, explaining somewhat grandiosely his reliance on Moravian folk ballads, dialects, and speech patterns, through which "I can feel—or rather hear—my inner sorrow."

The Quays' work proceeds from a fascination with hidden patterns, shadows, doppelgangers, transplanted to the dark, Expressionist Universe of Poland and Czechoslovakia—the paranoid tales of Franz Kafka and Bruno Schulz, the folk operas of Janácek, the alchemical animation of Jan Svankmajer.

—David Edelstein

This is how the Quays work, too, with found objects; they borrow, probe, manipulate, spinning the specific into the universal. In *Janácek,* their camera wanders through red and green forests, often glimpsing the composer through the trees; creatures from his operas materialize and dematerialize, peering through the windows of his cramped little room. In the most exquisite sequence, set to *The Cunning Little Vixen,* a moth beats its wings above the composer's sleeping head while violins flutter; a locust gazes in sympathy through his long antennae; foxes (fashioned from wood) hover over him, a wedding veil appearing on the cunning little vixen. These creatures—harbingers of Janácek's mortality—reappear for the finale, when the composer explains he has been searching for "a sort of resounding string that vibrates and binds us together, as proof against everything in the world."

The flutter of those wings is in itself mesmerizing, and the Quays use the motif repeatedly. In the excerpt from Janá-

cek's *The Makropulos Affair,* the 300-year-old heroine beats at the air like an insect before she dies, in a furious exertion of will. And in *Street of Crocodiles,* a cobwebbed monkey doll smashes its cymbals together in a blur—mocking, under the layers of dust, the very idea of nonmechanical energy. Machines, even rusted, bring destruction. In their reduction of *The Epic of Gilgamesh,* a tricyclist who looks like a Punch (of Punch and Judy) out of Picasso sets a trap for a virile insect creature. Through a hole in a table, the creature spies a human vagina; when he mounts the table, he's shot into a pair of overhead wires, then tied up in gold cloth and shorn of his wings by the imperturbable tricyclist. This short, part of a series (never completed) for England's Channel 4, presents cruelty at its most basic and childlike; one marvels at the torturer's ingenuity—and ingenuousness.

In a cottony forest outside the tricyclist's lair, an insect decays rapidly through time-lapse photography; that image, along with a broken tennis racket that hangs from the lethal wires, reemerges in *Street of Crocodiles,* the Quay's astonishing adaptation of Bruno Schulz's short story. Schulz (who was shot by a Gestapo officer on the street in 1942) portrayed individuals as subsumed in the primal urban ooze—broken, dehumanized. The curator—papier mâché, with a wizened, mottled face and shock of white hair—finds no release amid the rot, the malignant tailors, the mangled machines (ineffectual attempts to impose order in a universe whose patterns are unknowable). The film concludes with a passage from Schulz, about this city "of cheap human material where no instincts can flourish." It could be Poland—it could be here.

The Quays dress alike and keep their first names to themselves. Seeing their movies, I finally understood the impulse behind Peter Greenaway's *A Zed and Two Noughts,* which features a pair of identical twins (inspired by the Quays, and heavy on the symmetry) obsessed with finding order in decay. (They film animals rotting; through time-lapse photography, maggots devour carcasses in waves that Busby Berkeley would envy.) In his introduction to the published version of that script, Greenaway (who has written brilliantly on *Street of Crocodiles* in *Sight and Sound* [Vol. 55, No. 3, Summer, 1986]) likens the very process by which the Quays work to time-lapse photography of corpses decomposing. What he's suggesting, I think, is that unexpected patterns emerge in the Quays' finished films—patterns that wouldn't be apparent in real time.

Think of it: The Quays improvise while they work and use each other as springboards. Each clearly operates on the assumption that a parallel universe exists—and, of course, in this particular case, each is right. Their films are the product of dual universes, alike and yet separate, and the magic blooms from the tension as well as the harmony—from the give and take, the ebb and flow. The results, as you'll see, are singular.

Amos Vogel (review date May-June 1987)

SOURCE: "Two Iconoclastic Originals," in *Film Comment,* Vol. 23, No. 3, May-June, 1987, pp. 6, 8.

[*Vogel is an American film critic and educator who has long been a champion of American avant-garde cinema. His extensive writings on film include the book* Film as a Subversive Art *(1974). In the following excerpt from a review in which he discusses* Street of Crocodiles *and Masahi Yamamoto's* Robinson's Garden *(1987), he presents an overview of the film and the Quays' career.*]

Radical contents and an aggressive honesty are . . . found in the works of writer Bruno Schulz and the Quay brothers. A young Polish Jew, Schulz was killed by the Gestapo in 1942, aborting a career that might have ranked with Kafka's. In 1986, two American-born twins, the Quay brothers, working in England, transformed Schulz' most famous story, **The Street of Crocodiles** (in Philip Roth's *Writers from the Other Europe* Penguin Series), into a film that must rank among the most illustrious of international animated art.

When a blob of spit drops into the eye-piece of an ancient peep-show kinetoscope, nightmare-ridden mannequins move through a series of bizarre events in ambiguous, shadowy sets that barely define themselves. We may be in Schulz' dubious tailor shop, where sex mingles with fittings; some customers are handed erotic volumes for perusal, while others are fitted in the front and simultaneously undressed in the back. A near-replica of Dr. Caligari's somnambulist encounters threatening situations and transformations: raw meat in a mechanized world evokes erotic response, and objects resemble body parts. The mannequins are dissected and remodeled amidst clouds of dust. Monochrome textures are disrupted by color flashes. Moldy debris and decaying mirrors witness the oblique mechanisms that pop into spasmodic action for no apparent purpose.

Each shot, however brief, is held long enough to display its inexplicability, yet the Quays' entire work is permeated with a whiff of 20th-century terrors lurking at the borders of the narrative. The repetitive, modernist, semi-abstract score by Leszek Jankowski and the camera's strong movements, tracking shots, and pans evoke a universe beyond understanding, an ice-cold world devoid of love.

The Quays' animation is three-dimensional. It utilizes puppets, but puppets for adults that are meant to disturb; they are ominous misfits, cherubic beings with concave cavities where brains should be, fat-faced child mannequins with transfixed eyes that seem blinded by nameless horrors. They may now inflict them, in turn, upon new victims.

The Quay brothers evolved from Philadelphia art students to taciturn, masterful conjurers of a specifically East European sensibility shaped by surrealism and Kafka. Their somber, sealed-off, bizarre works—forever hovering between horror and black humor—are powerful objects manqué. With harrowing techniques of expressionism and surrealism, they capture the echo of Central Europe's wars and revolutions, and the suffocating provincialism of entrenched ruling classes. In the whirrings of peculiar mechanisms, in the cruel transformations of puppets, and in the shadowy incomprehensible events, one senses Europe—the world—at the brink.

The Quay brothers thus become heirs to an illustrious procession of such kindred animators as Ladislav Starevich, whose puppets, once seen, cannot be eradicated from memory; Walerian Borowczyk and Jan Lenica, who as part of the Polish avant-garde of the late Fifties created *Dom,* which featured an upsettingly alive strand of red hair; and the Czech genius Jan Svankmajer, about whom the Quay Brothers have made a wonderful film tribute. Kudos are due the Museum of Modern Art and Film Forum for introducing the Quay brothers to the U.S.A. *The Street of Crocodiles* will premiere nationally, July 20 on PBS.

The Brothers Quay on the influence of their family background:

What if we said we [were] born of a heavily tainted family, neurasthenic, microcephalic, each with one atrophied testicle, a sly liking for geese, chickens, etc., pigtails in pillowcases, suffer from dry tongues, overly predisposed towards music and abandoned organ lofts, blah, blah, blah. No, we grew up sweating with obedience. Our Father was a 2nd class machinist for Philadelphia Electric, our mother your impeccable housewife (who was a figure skater before marriage). On our Father's side there were two grandfathers: one a tailor from Berlin who had a shop in South Philly and the other, who was apparently a cabinetmaker and we were told that the 5th floor of Lit Brothers [department store] in Philly has cabinets by the Quays. (Now we lived in Philly for some five years and never made that tiny little expedition to confirm it.) Our Mother's father was excellent at carpentry and was also a chauffeur when Philly only had 5 automobiles to its name. So! In terms of puppetry it's surprisingly all there—carpentry, mechanisms and tailoring and figure skating to music to score any of our aberrant tracking shots. Big deal, will this help you dear fellow?

The Brothers Quay, in a letter to J. D. McClatchy, in "Movie Magic: The Quay Brothers, the Toast of Eight Film Festivals," in Connoisseur, *April, 1989.*

Terrence Rafferty   (essay date June 1987)

SOURCE: "Twin Cinema: The Animated Art of the Brothers Quay," in *The Atlantic Monthly,* Vol. 259, No. 6, June, 1987, pp. 74-6.

[*In the following essay, Rafferty presents a stylistic and thematic overview of the Quays' body of work.*]

They bill themselves as the Brothers Quay, which has an archaic and faintly ridiculous ring, as if they were a vaudeville comedy act or a family of acrobats. Photographs of Timothy and Stephen Quay, who are identical twins, look like trick shots from the early days of cinema, products of the cheap camera magic that makes a single actor double and allows him, before our eyes, to talk to himself. In interviews the comments of one brother are never distinguished from those of the other: they speak as if with one voice.

The Quays, born in Philadelphia, have lived and worked together for all of their forty years, most recently in London, where since 1978 they have absorbed themselves in the absurd and intricate form of play known as puppet animation—that naively mechanistic genre of film art that preserves, a frame at a time, the memories of a childish delight in small effigies of ourselves, our wonder when at a human touch the dolls begin to move, and our vague horror as we watch their manipulated forms reflect and parody the actions of our own bodies.

Puppet animation is, as the Quays themselves admit, a freakish, marginal art: it can be as trivial as the singing, dancing raisins of American television advertising, or as ponderously symbolic as some of the Eastern European political allegories that turn up with alarming frequency on film-festival programs. But the Quays' puppets seem, like the mysterious twins who make them, to have found in their own marginality an eerier and more suggestive kind of life, a shadowy, feverish half existence in which their movements are like the choreography of dreams. These puppets have the quality, unique in the genre, of appearing to be aware of their secondhand status, conscious that they're the crude doubles of beings once or still alive. And the films—with their sinuous camera movements through rooms full of dust and clutter and dirty glass, the interiors of a playhouse decrepit from overuse—are informed by the philosophical melancholy of their creators, whose art is perhaps the product of an endless and unresolvable obsession, who make puppets perhaps because each of them has spent every day of his life looking at and talking to a moving, three-dimensional, terrifyingly exact copy of himself.

There is, of course, something fanciful about the notion that the Quays' art is a complex ritual of twinhood. It makes the Quays out to be characters in a Romantic horror story—artists haunted by their creations, men looking over their shoulders for the doubles they know (or imagine) are following them, denizens of the unsettling mirror worlds of Hoffmann and Kafka, Poe and Borges. If we see them this way, it's because the films themselves encourage us to. Just as there are dreams so intense, so cryptic, that they hold our imagination for days, even years, the Quays' short movies have the power of the truly uncanny: we sense, without knowing why, that there's something *necessary* in their mastery of this arcane craft, that they're not so much telling stories with puppets as they are searching for the human ghosts in their wood-and-cloth machines. The intimacy of the Quays' relation to their dolls is creepy. Watching these films, we feel like Hoffman characters ourselves, enchanted into an uneasy self-consciousness by arts so overwhelming that they verge on the demonic. We seem, somehow, to have been twinned—dancers mesmerized by the strange reflections of our own movements in the mirror beyond the barre.

The metaphysical theater of the Brothers Quay—whose work until now has been visible only on British television, in European film festivals, and in a film series called *Alchemists of the Surreal,* which has toured English art cinemas since last fall—has taken its show on the road in the United States this year, on a characteristically small scale. In January the United States Film Festival in Utah showed a program of four Quay films: *Leoš Janáček: Intimate Excursions* (which runs for twenty-seven minutes), *The Cabinet of Jan Švankmajer* (fourteen minutes), *Little Songs of the Chief Officer of Hunar Louse, or This Unnameable Little Broom* (eleven minutes), and *Street of Crocodiles* (twenty minutes), their most recent film, and their first in 35mm. This same program has had a week's run at New York's Film Forum, and *Street of Crocodiles* has been screened at the San Francisco Film Festival. There's talk of taking the program on tour to other cities and of showing one or more of the films on public television, but nothing is definite. Right now these films are obscure, sneaking in and out of theaters furtively, which seems oddly appropriate: they're such unlikely objects, and flash past our eyes so quickly, that they leave us dazed, unsure whether we've really seen their images or merely hallucinated them.

Even at their most straightforward, as in the Janáček film, the Quays are disorienting. The brothers, along with their longtime collaborator, the producer Keith Griffiths, have often worked in the portrait-of-the-artist genre, partly because television is always eager to supply funds for such "educational" films: they've also done a biography of the Belgian playwright Michel de Ghelderode, which was mostly documentary and the jazzy, hilarious puppet film *Igor—The Paris Years Chez Pleyel,* about Stravinsky, with Jean Cocteau (who at one point appears in a tutu, dancing to a pianola score of *Petrushka*) and Vladimir Mayakovsky (whose body is an origami nightmare of revolutionary posters) hovering at the edges.

But the Quays' biographical films are like no one else's. In *Janáček,* as in the Stravinsky film, the artist-doll is a startlingly poignant composite—a puppet's three-dimensional body supporting a cutout photograph, slightly oversized, of the great man's head. This technique isn't simply a way of avoiding caricature. Janáček's head, monochromatic and 2-D, has the shocking gravity of many old photos: it's the visual equivalent of the ghostly scraps of the composer's diaries and correspondence that are read to us in voice-over. ("When someone speaks to me, I listen to the tonal modulations in their voice, more than to what they are actually saying. . . . I can feel or rather hear my hidden sorrow.") The tenuous relationship between head and body makes the Quays' Janáček seem, poetically, all mind, and as animated tableaux of the composer's work pass before us, we can't help feeling that we're seeing and hearing this music the way Janáček must have dreamed it. This illusion, almost too fragile to sustain, derives its force and beauty from the rhythms of the Quays' camera, moving in mysterious concord with the stately tempos of the music itself. The camera circles the extraordinary sets—a forest of leafless trees, Janáček's bare room, a deserted gymnasium with grillwork windows, a prison, a ruined church—catching glimpses of spindly, insect-like puppet figures through the trees and the bars of windows, images as fugitive as those that appear and disappear, flickering in the mind's eye, as we listen to a piece of music. At Janáček's death all the phantoms of the composer's imagination—the frail puppets from his works, including *Diary of One Who Vanished, The Cunning Little Vixen,* and *The*

Makropulos Case, among others—gather around him for a moment in the forest, which has moved, somehow, into his stark room, the trunks' dark vertical forms merging with the shadows of the windows' grills, echoing the cathedral's pillars and the prison's bars, filling the space around his fading features with a tangle of lines, like a passionately scribbled score. The delicate calligraphy of a musician's mind has never been represented more beautifully.

The Cabinet of Jan Švankmajer and *This Unnameable Little Broom* (as its impossible title is usually abbreviated) are, though brilliant, perhaps the Quays' most difficult and off-putting films. These two shorts are harder-edged and less lyrical than the Janáček film, and depend more heavily on the Eastern European puppet-film tradition: there's a hint of didacticism in them, even though we're never quite sure what we're meant to be learning. The Švankmajer film is in fact a tribute to a Czech animator whose work has influenced the Quays. It's structured as a series of little lessons in perception, taught by a puppet with an open book for hair, to a doll with a hollowed-out head, in finely detailed settings that evoke the style of encyclopedia illustration (as well as, at various points, Ernst, de Chirico, and the Mannerist painter Arcimboldo). For the viewer, the movie is a short course in the principles of animation, conducted as if the art of Švankmajer and the Quays were a lost discipline of the Renaissance, an ancient form of anatomical drawing.

This Unnameable Little Broom, which is, according to the filmmakers, a portion of "a largely disguised reduction of the *Epic of Gilgamesh*," is a swift, savage, and largely baffling movie about a tricycle-riding monster who traps a strange winged creature in his lair. The camera whips back and forth in slashing, aggressive gestures, and the effect is stunning, but the battle is abrupt and not quite so satisfying. We have no context for what we're seeing—the film is actually a fragment, a single episode from a planned full version of *Gilgamesh*—so the whole encounter, inventively choreographed as it is, seems too starkly mythic.

But *Street of Crocodiles,* the Quays' very free adaptation of Bruno Schulz's dreamlike memoir of Poland between the wars, is a fully articulated vision. Schulz's hallucinatory prose, which renders the world as a fantastic construction whose laws seem always on the tantalizing verge of our understanding, is perfect for the Quays. Schulz writes, in the voice of his narrator's deranged father:

> Figures in a waxwork museum, . . . must not be treated lightly. . . . Can you imagine the pain, the dull imprisoned suffering, hewn into the matter of that dummy which does not know why it must be what it is, why it must remain in that forcibly imposed form which is no more than a parody? . . . You give a head of canvas and oakum an expression of anger and leave it with it, with the convulsion, the tension enclosed once and for all, with a blind fury for which there is no outlet. . . .

> Have you heard at night the terrible howling of these wax figures, shut in the fair-booths; the pitiful chorus of those forms of wood or porcelain, banging their fists against the walls of their prisons?

The Quays, clearly, have heard these sounds. The puppet-hero of *Street of Crocodiles*—who, as we learn in a black-and-white live-action prologue, is part of an elaborate contraption locked away in a provincial museum—looks around him in something like terror when the thread connecting him to his unseen manipulator is snipped, and then, with a haunted, stricken stare, begins to explore. His environment is ominous, a decaying city inside a box, with an inscrutable system of threads and pulleys running along the ground, screws that pull free of floorboards and dance in the dust, shop windows full of blank mannequins and mechanical monkeys beating their cymbals furiously when a light shines on them, and dolls rotating shoulders whose joints are disturbingly exposed. Everything in this world seems to hint at obscure connections—the screws' threads are somehow related to the wires from which the hero has been disengaged, and also to the filaments of the light bulbs in the shops—and everything is a reflection of the weathered materials of which this abandoned puppet is made. It's no wonder he looks anxious as he wanders timidly through this labyrinth of wood and glass, no wonder the camera seems to be skulking with him, moving carefully, as if afraid of what it will find around the next corner. The Quays' *Street of Crocodiles* is a puppet film that, in its self-consciousness, transcends itself. It's about the chill of discovering, through play, what we're made of—about gazing on an aging world and seeing our own fragile anatomies reflected there.

Georgia Brown (review date 2 April 1991)

SOURCE: "Seeing Double," in *The Village Voice,* Vol. XXXVI, No. 14, April 2, 1991, p. 52.

[*In the following excerpt from a review of* Rehearsals for Extinct Anatomies *and Patrick Bokanowski's* L'Ange *(1982), Brown examines the sexual imagery in the Quays' film.*]

Those waiting patiently for *Gödel, Escher, Bach* the movie probably should catch what looks like a made-for-each-other double bill at the Film Forum: Patrick Bokanowski's *L'Ange* and *Rehearsals for Extinct Anatomies* by the Brothers Quay. This may be where the cinema of science-surrealism-music stands today. The Pennsylvania-born, British-based Quay twins have built a cult following here—meeting even the dopey pretentions of *Connoisseur*—whereas the French Bokanowski is virtually unknown in the U.S. Unlike the Quays, he isn't strictly an animator—and he's undoubtedly more esoteric—but the sensibility of all three harks back to early atmospheric, poetic cinema: to Méliès, the Germans of the '20s, and the dreamscapes of Buñuel and Cocteau. One hallucinatory image—a black-and-white striped, heavily patterned Vuillardian room—pops up in both *L'Ange* and *Rehearsals.* (It should be noted that Bokanowski's film was finished in 1982; *Rehearsals* appeared six years later.) Both of these wordless, meticulously crafted works rely heavily on scores for strings—*L'Ange*'s is by Michele Bokanowski and *Rehearsals*'s by Polish composer Leszek Jankowski. And thematically, both seem to have rape on the brain. . . .

Compulsion and obsession are venerable, even intrinsic film subjects. They're the source of crime. With his figures invariably caught inside ritualistic actions, Bokanowski manages to suggest crime—murder, theft, rape—without ever producing a corpse. *L'Ange* is more interested in the semantics of mystery than in solutions.

Kinkier is the Quays' claustrophobic 14-minute *Rehearsals for Extinct Anatomies*—a cerebral cloak with a pubic fur lining. Personally, it reminds me of an illustrated manual on sublimation or the masturbatory origins of intellectual activity. In interviews, the brothers locate the project's initial inspiration in an engraving after Fragonard's *Le Verrou* (*The Bolt*)—that sinister painting showing a rake in white stretching toward a window lock, either before or after he's raped the woman lying on the bed. During research and development, however, the brothers got sidetracked by the "other" Fragonard, the painter's nephew, a meticulous anatomist. Not that source material here prepares you for what you see.

Rehearsals's mad impresario or conductor, plucking at the strings of a bar code, is a puppet with body of bent metal and a wildly spinning cyclopean eye, who pauses only to agitatedly finger a growth on his head. This activity links him to one of the two puppets locked together inside a fetid little room where a fan whirs, a weary-looking figure propped against the door compulsively stroking a sore—or is it a sweet spot?—in the middle of his forehead. Later we catch him scrubbing frantically at a stain on his clothes. As Lytton Strachey is reported to have queried, apropos of a spot on the young Virginia Woolf's skirt: *Semen*?

The significant Other—genders here are difficult to distinguish—palely loiters on a rumpled bed. Surrounding their hermetic box of a room, like the outside world, is a vastly sterile white space with Escher-like staircases and calligraphy graffiti. The relation of the two interior/exterior spaces seems to make a crucial point, though I'm hard pressed to tell you what it is. The climax comes when the standing puppet lends a hand to the masturbating bedridden one. Or is he operating? (Is this *Dead Ringers*?) And it's not really a hand but something that looks like a pendulum or even an inverted metronome. Well, I've only seen the film once.

Instruments for reluctant mechanisms? "Extinct anatomies" may refer to our limited human anatomies, our poor flawed bodies—as if (I'm extrapolating) privileged twinship offers more evolved, less capricious forms of being in the world. Like the twin zoologists in Peter Greenaway's *A Zed and Two Naughts*—inspired, says Greenaway, by a magazine photo of the Quays—the fashionably hermetic filmmakers conduct abstruse experiments in decomposition, decay, and desiccation. In any case, two figures, hardly distinguishable, locked in a junk-filled studio, surely points to an autobiographical component. The hubris of twins notwithstanding, it's tempting to hear *Rehearsals* sending off muffled cries of "help."

Jonathan Romney (essay date March 1992)

SOURCE: "The Same Dark Drift," in *Sight and Sound*, Vol. 1, No. 11, March, 1992, pp. 24-7.

[*In the following essay, Romney presents an overview of the Quays' career focusing on the technical processes they use to create their films. He also discusses* Institute Benjamenta.]

It can be an uncanny experience at the best of times, interviewing the Brothers Quay as they sit at opposite sides of a table, superficially identical in every respect except for the cut of their overalls. It's all the more uncanny when the interview is watched over by a battered doll on a platform, one incongruously flirtatious eye glaring down from under a veiled hat. A baby body with an adult dummy head grafted on, she holds in one hand a mirror or a painted bat, and with the other lifts her skirt to reveal a ragged bush of straw pubic hair, at which an equally ragged rabbit, hugging her ankles, gazes with lovelorn curiosity.

These are the leads in the Quays' latest animation film, a three-minute rock promo for 'Are We Still Married' by the group His Name Is Alive. The Quays call the film *Stille Nacht 2;* they see it as a sequel to a 1988 short they made for MTV's *Art Break* slot which featured a doll, a set of spoons and a forest of magnetised iron filings. What's the connection? "Just the same dark drift", they explain, "basically inscrutable. It's gently mysterious".

Lately there seems to have been little room for inscrutability in animation. Last year, animation hit the public imagination in a big way with Nick Park's Oscar-winning *Creature Comforts* (1989) and the subsequent success of the Aardman Studios video. The coming wave of computer-generated imagery is just beginning to break, with American prodigy John Lasseter scoring a major success in *Knick-Knack* (1989), and animators like France's Pascal Vuong (*Blind Love,* 1991) exploring similar avenues of electronic alchemy. In their different ways, the Claymation and computer schools are technically and imaginatively admirable, but they tend to do pretty much what animation has always done—amaze, amuse and bring life to inanimate matter. Above all—and this is surely the key to their success—they anthropomorphise ruthlessly.

The more mainstream attention such work gets, the more it reminds us of the crucially *marginal* importance of the Brothers Quay, animators whose work is marked by a meticulous eschewal of soft anthropomorphism and of the narrative gag. The Quays have described animation as a ghetto; with their methods and aesthetic, they have wilfully created their own ghetto within a ghetto. Yet the more marginal the Quays appear, the more their work can be seen to be absolutely central to the *question* of animation. With its increasingly fine, even neurotic scrutiny, the Quays' work is nothing less than inquiry into the founding paradoxes of the form.

To bring their puppets to 'life', the brothers work painstakingly through frame after frame of static postures, building them up into the semblance of motion. This is the paradox that underlies all film, one that live action hides and that animation, at its truest, unearths. All animation, of course, is based on this paradox, but the Quays address it directly. Paul Hammond has called their pixillation technique "nudged *nature morte*"—and the play on *nature morte* and its equivalent *still life* is never far from these films' surface.

The Quays do not so much animate *dead matter* as dramatise the *deadness of matter*. The figures in their films—broken dolls, the flotsam of nurseries and curiosity shops, botched-up chimeras of dead bone and wing and tissue and vegetable—are things that have died and been recomposed, re-animated, like miniature mummies. They are ghosts, living uncannily beyond their 'natural' lives, and inhabiting the equally ghostly landscapes that the Quays build in little boxes—the cities, theatres, labyrinths, forests of Eastern European literary myth. Quay puppets are not alive but *undead;* they don't have lives but after-lives.

What makes these little *danses macabres* so haunting is the way they dramatise the viewer's role. In Quay films, the eye—or its surrogate, the camera—is the central character. The puppets themselves incarnate this obsessive opticality. A major discovery for the Brothers—in *Street of Crocodiles* (1986)—was the glass doll's-eye, which by its presence or absence implicates the viewer in the films' scopic dramas. The petrified glare of that film's desiccated doll-hero is parodically returned by the tailor dolls he encounters, whose china heads have empty sockets illuminated from within. The myth of the eye as window to the soul could hardly be more remorselessly defused.

"For us", the Brothers have said, "the camera is the third puppet in a sense, the motivator". Since their 1985 film *This Unnameable Little Broom,* the vagaries of the lens have played an increasingly important role in their work. The camera tracks in, tilts, then tracks back; the image fades out, fades in again; but the film never delivers the revelatory vision it seems to promise. In the micronarratives of perception that fill the Quays' work, there is never any pay-off.

These stories of the eye have recently been refined to an extreme. *Rehearsals for Extinct Anatomies* is built entirely around avatars of the *line*—the lines that compose a Fragonard engraving; a computer bar code that drifts in and out of focus; the strings that cross the screen, twanging imperceptibly; even the strings on the soundtrack; above all, the line of sight. In *The Comb* (1990), a dream narrative in shades of forest red, the narrative is almost entirely composed of shifting focus and field of vision—we are never sure what we are seeing, forever denied a stable vision. Ironically, the Brothers' most clear-cut film, *De Artificiali Perspectiva or Anamorphosis* (1990), explores the elusiveness of sight.

Born in 1947 in Philadelphia, Stephen and Timothy Quay came to Britain in the late 60s, studying illustration at the Royal College of Art. There they met their producer, Keith Griffiths, who set up their first BFI-funded project, *Nocturna Artificialia,* in 1979 and founded with them the production company Koninck Studios (the name was taken from a Belgian beermat). Atelier Koninck is the Quays' South London studio. It occupies a modern industrial unit, but with its prodigal clutter of books, bric-à-

brac and arcane detritus resembles an alchemical stockroom of the 1830s.

Currently, the centrepiece is a scaled-down set for a National Theatre production of Molière's *Le Bourgeois Gentilhomme,* a luminous white construction limned with colour-photocopied ink swirls and chandeliers formed from the baroque calligraphy that is a Quays' leitmotif. This is their latest work with director Richard Jones, for whom they designed sets for Tchaikovsky's *Mazeppa,* Feydeau's *A Flea in her Ear* at the Old Vic, and Prokofiev's *A Love for Three Oranges* at the ENO. This last is their most celebrated work in the public domain, though they have also worked extensively in advertisements—their "pact with the devil", as they call it—including ones for Honeywell Computers, Walkers Crisps, and an essay in grain and veneer for ICI Woodcare. Recently, they made three idents for BBC2, which together tell a story of a paper man, his pen and a flotilla of small feathers.

The Quays have also made two sorties into pop video. The first was as part of a team with various Aardman animators, working on Peter Gabriel's *Sledgehammer* (1986) clip. This was not a happy experience, since they were talked into shuffling fruit and veg in the style of the Baroque *trompe l'oeil* master Arcimboldo—a cheap shot, they felt, and not their style.

Stille Nacht 2 is far more in their line, and 4AD Records, who commissioned it, famously share the Quay penchant for baroque imagery (the affinities become apparent if you look at any Pixies LP sleeve). The film largely disregards the song's stately lugubriousness, working at frenzied speed as a ping-pong ball shoots dementedly around the set and the rabbit's ears flutter in what is probably the only concession to cuteness in the Brothers' entire output. Shot in thirty days on a £12,000 budget, it's a perfect example of the Brothers' hands-on—some would say deliberately archaic—approach. They avoid taking measurements and the luxury of Go-Motion computer control, having learnt with time to do it all by eye.

"There are people out there doing it so perfectly that you say, fuck, I'd like it to be really primitive. For us it's important that physically we do it all, that we don't have assistants. We have a tracking shot on the doll's feet that would be almost impossible in live action—to put that camera on the ground and have a focus puller on his hands and knees".

The Quays now have two scripts in development, both breaking new ground for them. The first, provisionally entitled *Sleepwalkers of Daylight,* is a music project for BBC2 about the German master of the literary fantastic, E. T. A. Hoffmann, and the composers Anton Bruckner and Hugo Wolf. The Brothers have already made two short music films, on Stravinsky and Janacek—imaginative flights that in no way resemble documentaries. The seventy-minute *Sleepwalkers* will mix live action, animation and marionettes, and demand an estimated budget of £600,000. One more investor is needed, but Austrian television has agreed to foot the bill for the recording of the orchestral music. *Sleepwalkers,* the script explains, "aims to depict an imagined world in which both the banal and the commonplace are infused with the exotic and the incomprehensible"—a fair description of Hoffmann's warped, proto-Freudian world.

"It's basically about the notion of Romanticism", the Brothers explain. "Hoffmann was one of the great night figures. We went for the musician in him—he did write music, but having failed at it, he subverted it into his writing. Hence a lot of the writing is based around musical themes and images. That's the side that interested us. We have him fantasising about two musicians into the future, Anton Bruckner the symphonist and Hugo Wolf the miniaturist. It's as though Hoffmann could have imagined two extremes in the Romantic trajectory".

Haunted spaces appeal to the Brothers, especially those that are redolent of a dilapidated Europe swimming in the cultural debris of its own history.

—Jonathan Romney

The other project is a total departure—the Quays' first live-action feature, provisionally entitled *Institute Benjamenta, or This Dream Which People Call Human Life.* It's based on *Jakob von Gunten,* a novel by Robert Walser (1878-1956), a Swiss writer who influenced Kafka and who spent the last twenty years of his life in mental institutions. Walser ranks high in the Quays' idiosyncratic literary canon; they had a dry run with him in *The Comb* which drew on his rewritings of fairy tales. The tales again find their way into *Institute Benjamenta,* set in a school for servants, where pupils learn to abnegate their personalities in the name of good service. Little of this is evident in the script—by the Brothers in collaboration with Alain Passes—which evokes something like the nightmare mood of the animation, with camera movements and shifts of light minutely detailed. It contains little dialogue: the film is dominated by images, and what the Brothers will look for in their cast is a sense of the physical. "Meyerhold talked about the power of the puppet and the mask, the immovability. That's one thing we want to maintain with the actors. It's not that you're treating people *like* puppets, it's just that the actor should conceive of his face as the internalisation of a mask."

As it stands, the script is also fluid, open to influence by matters outside the text. One such factor is the music, by the Brother's longtime Polish collaborator Leszek Jankowski. "We have almost an hour's worth of music that Leszek wrote that will in a sense have provoked a great deal of it. With *Rehearsals* and *The Comb,* Leszek wrote the music first and we very much have it write the scenario. The rhythms he set up were allowed to establish the trajectory of the script—which comes a lot closer to what a dancer would do choreographing Stravinsky. You never ask a ballet to be that clear—you can afford narrative ellipses, sudden changes much cinema doesn't tolerate."

The other factor that will shape the film is the space it is shot in, which—partly for reasons of economy—the Brothers insist should be a found space, an old school or a gym. "A certain approach to a corridor, or a certain set of steps would tell you to rewrite the script a certain way. The space provokes the response. We want to build on accidents". In this sense, the brothers are firm believers in serendipity, and although they rail against the appellation 'Surrealist', one thing they do share with the classic school of Breton and Aragon is this faith in the possibility of encountering the perfect space at the perfect moment. "To catch a glimpse of a church through a mirror, to sense there's a forbidden room there", they enthuse, remembering a visit to Kafka's room in Prague, one window of which offers an unimpeded peephole view into a nearby church.

Such haunted spaces appeal to the Brothers, especially those that are redolent of a dilapidated Europe swimming in the cultural debris of its own history. *Institute Benjamenta* is informed by a fascination for the covered galleries and arcades of the nineteenth century, spaces that also shaped the world of *Crocodiles.* That film is set within a mechanical peepshow or "wooden oesophagus", in which its hero wanders a mirror gallery that alludes to the haunted shopping galleries of Bruno Schulz's fiction. Shot by the Nazis in 1942, Schulz lived and died in Drohobycz in Galicia, an area that's disappeared into a fold on the map of Europe.

A sense of vanished time and space has always haunted the Quays. Schulz is their totem writer, his fiction crammed with passages that read like descriptions of their own aesthetic and their "passion for coloured tissue, for *papier mâché,* for distemper, for oakum and sawdust". "That part of Galicia", they have said, "the borderlines have changed so often, you feel at home being lost in it, rather than within perfectly ordered boundaries . . . That apocryphal thirteenth month, those tracks that lead off into time suspended, it's ideal for animation".

Hence, their canon of arcane or *maudit* writers—Schulz, Walser, Céline, the Flemish playwright Michel de Ghelderode. Their affinities also lie in Eastern Europe, their masters names like Starewycz and Trnka; Yuri Norstein, the Russian maker of *Tale of Tales;* Walerian Borowczyk, who before his career as an art-porn auteur successfully moved from animation to live action with *Goto, Island of Love* (1968), one of the Quays' favourites; and, of course, Jan Svankmajer.

These days, however, the Brothers tend to play down the Svankmajer connection, which has become something of a millstone. Some critics still regard the Brothers as dogged acolytes of the Czech, although they're clearly in a different mould. The connection came about when the Quays and Keith Griffiths discovered Svankmajer's work in Prague and decided to make a homage to him in *The Cabinet of Jan Svankmajer* (1984). However, they feel their bent is closer to Norstein, and point out that Svankmajer is very much a militant Surrealist (practically a card-carrying one, in fact, as a member of the Prague Surrealist group).

With their planned move into live action, the Quays' individuality should be all the more apparent. Of course they worry about giving up the security of their hermetic Atelier to work outside with other people, though their stage designs have already prepared them to some extent for that.

The one thing certain not to change is the uncanny nature of their space and the unsettling narrative style it carries. "Narrative for us", they say, "is always tangential, it just filters in from the side and creates this climate. In the end you feel this conspiratorial climate that makes you think, 'I'm at the centre of something and I don't know what it is'. You come out the other end still looking in the rear view mirror and thinking, 'I haven't arrived yet' ".

Jonathan Romney   (review date May 1992)

SOURCE: A review of *The Comb*, in *Sight and Sound*, Vol. 2, No. 1, May, 1992, p. 64.

[*In the following positive review of* The Comb, *Romney examines the film's sexual imagery and suggests that the Quays purposefully thwart the viewer's attempt to find conventional narrative meaning.*]

As a woman sleeps, a doll on the edge of a forest attempts to climb a ladder out of a hole, while watched over by a figure with a twitching finger. When the woman wakes, the ladder collapses and the doll falls apart. The woman combs her hair.

The Comb carries no less than three subtitles—"From the Museums of Sleep", "Fairytale Dramolet", and "To Scenes and Texts of Robert Walser". The latter is a Swiss writer whose narratives inform the film, particularly his rewriting of fairy-tales, but the film is set *to* his work, rather than derived *from* it—so much so that the extracts from his texts, balefully whispered and muttered in several languages simply become part of the soundtrack, along with various drips, owl hoots, and strident orchestrations of string and wood by the Brothers' regular collaborator Leszek Jankowski.

Of all the Quays' films, this is the one most explicitly concerned with dream, yet it cannot be reduced to the closed schema of the traditional dream narrative; this despite the contrast between the (mainly) colour animation and the black-and-white live-action framing narrative. There is in fact a blurring between the two levels. The live action is less than it appears—the anamorphically stretched figure of the dreamer is itself animated, shot at 6 frames a second. And there are several equivalences between the dreamer and the figures dreamt—the climbing doll which itself falls into a sleep-like state; the menacing figure whose finger, doubled by the dreamer's own nervous digit, seems to propel the narrative; and a more explicit figure of the dreamer within the dream, a supine doll in lace who is literally pierced by a ladder rising out of her.

This is also, then, the film in which the Quays' sexual thematics are most visible. According to the Quays, the story is simple, a variant on the folk tale of the Prince trying to reach his Sleeping Beauty. The Prince would then be as much a projection of the dreamer as the sleeper-princess

within the dream. But for a female dream, the images might seem incongruously phallic. The ladder itself sways deliriously, but immediately after the intertitle, "Suddenly the air grew hard . . .", the puppet that holds it falls limp, as if in a kind of *petite mort*. Yet after this detumescent moment, desire itself seems to become autonomous, as the hands leave the body and themselves control the ladder. Later, they guide the ladder as it moves through the sleeping doll's flesh, and rub it with masturbatory zeal as it sprouts the leafy extensions that (very nearly) allow the Prince to reach his goal.

This is perhaps a faithful representation of the dream state, in which the body can fragment into its separately desiring parts; and puppet animation is surely the form most able to convey it. The phallic elements are in any case subverted by a constant breakdown of linearity. After the penetration of the body, the camera cranes up to reveal a vertiginous dome filled with ladders, in a Piranesi-like perspective. There is no room in this world for an unimpeded penetrating gaze—neither in the red wood *trompe l'oeil* landscape we first see, nor in the constantly changing dimensions of the theatre/toybox in which the action seems to take place.

As usual, the Quays refuse any narrative pay-off. After the dream falls apart, there is no reason to imagine that anything has been resolved, or even revealed. The dream can repeat itself, and indeed the film's visual obscurity demands several viewings one after another. The idea of the Sleeping Beauty narrative may be a useful frame to make the film more readable; but the cutting, the lighting, the shifts of focus and field of vision confound that readability at every stage. This is a film to make uneasy sleepers of us all.

Denise Tilles   (essay date January 1993)

SOURCE: "Degraded Reality: Designing with the Brothers Quay," in *TCI: The Business of Entertainment Technology and Design*, Vol. 27, No. 1, January, 1993, pp. 44-5.

[*In the following essay, which is based on an interview with the Quays, Tilles discusses the brothers' collaboration with theater and opera director Richard Jones.*]

"We sort of rub people's faces in some dirt." Thus speak the Brothers Quay, filmmakers and stage designers. "That's our natural preponderance, towards dirt and especially detail and texture." So sums up the design aesthetic of this artistic team, twin brothers Timothy and Stephen Quay, 45. Although the two have been creating sophisticated and intricately designed puppet animation films for the past 13 years, they have one foot in the theatre and opera worlds as well; since 1988, they have designed scenery for two theatre pieces and two operas exclusively for director Richard Jones.

Their most recent production was *Le Bourgeois Gentilhomme* at London's Royal National Theatre. Reviews were mixed, with one reviewer proclaiming that "An outfit calling themselves the Brothers Quay (why?) have come up with a crudely painted toy-theatre design . . . you feel queasy just looking at the stage." At the other end of the gamut, another critic stated, "The settings, by the Brothers Quay, are inspired. The opening scene is full of wonderfully theatrical touches. The set is a striking black and white jeu d'esprit." It is this kind of absolute disagreement often provoked by the Quays.

Finding that sensibility in the theatre was a bit daunting when they embarked on their first project for Jones. The director had seen one of their puppet animation films, *Leos Janácek: Intimate Excursions* (1983), and was intrigued by their staging of an opera sequence, replete with puppets singing. The Quays think that Jones was not convinced to use them until he saw another film, 1987's *Street of Crocodiles.* Even then, securing the permission of opera producers to use puppet filmmakers as designers was another challenge, they recall: "[Jones] had to convince the opera people that we could go from puppets to live action. Well, in fact there's no difference, because you're still doing a model box. And our model box, was, in fact, slightly larger than a traditional model box. And really, the puppets are the same as actors."

This first opera with Jones was Prokofiev's *The Love for Three Oranges,* a co-production of Opera North and English National Opera in 1988: "We felt a bit intimidated at first. But once we got the actual framing device, which was the slabs going back, it was easy to inject what we wanted. More or less, he gave us certain things to aim for. And then it's up to us to choreograph the whole conception. So, yeah, we were terrified."

The result of their nervous efforts was successful: the set had a controlled filthiness to it, with smudgy wood-slat walls, and billowing and twisted fabric lining the ceiling. Along with Sue Blane's over-the-top costumes, *Oranges* made a definitive visual statement. Clearly it's a look Jones favors, as the Quays have done three productions for the director since then.

Their next two works with Jones, *A Flea in Her Ear* (1989) at London's Old Vic and *Mazeppa* (1991) for the Bregenz Festival/Netherlands Opera demonstrated that similar sense of dark, downtrodden reality that the Quays favor so much. However, even after four theatre productions, both designers insist that they're still in awe of the entire theatrical process: "We don't conceive in theatrical terms. Cinema asks for a different language. So it's hard for us to come to terms with a theatre language, when Richard says 'Can we have a quick change here?' and we say 'How?' and he says 'We'll just drop the curtain.' And we say, 'Yeah, right. That's simple. That's great.' "

The two work together in a manner in which they do not elucidate. After working together since their college days, their collaboration is instinctive: "We start out by talking it out between ourselves. We sort of improvise, each in a different aspect, and vaguely work towards the middle. One of us will pick one piece of the furniture, and the other will start on, for instance, the walls. Then one will sort of inspire the other." The twins feel that if one person has a strength, Stephen is more mechanical-minded (he builds the puppet armatures in their films), while Timothy's strength lies in typography—creating the flowing, calligraphic titles in their films.

The designers' collaboration began in 1972, when they graduated from the Royal College of Art and returned to the United States to pursue a career in designing book covers. They recall that period as "treading water," with little success, and they moved back to Europe in 1977, living in London and Amsterdam. Finally, after submitting a film proposal to the British Film Institute in 1978, the project, *Nocturna Artificialia,* was accepted and the Quays moved back to London permanently. Besides their films, the designers have created several music videos, including Peter Gabriel's award-winning "Sledgehammer," which they designed with Aardman Animators, under the aegis of director Stephen Johnson. The brothers recently completed a video for singer Michael Penn.

> Although *Mazeppa* and *The Love for Three Oranges* had their elegance at times, our natural preponderance is toward dirt, and especially detail and texture. We tend to like degraded reality.
>
> —*Brothers Quay*

There are no plans in the immediate future for more theatre work, however. The designers have only worked with director Jones, and have no real desire to work with anyone else: "We trust implicitly someone like Richard, only because he knows our work. And anybody who came along now and said 'Oh yeah, let's use the twins,' it's because they've only seen this production [*Le Bourgeois Gentilhomme*] and they don't know the cinema background. We respect Richard, because he's the only one who took a chance on someone coming from animation, which would be unheard of."

The Quays seem to be one of several sets of designers Jones calls on to fulfill different needs, among them Richard Hudson, for that distinctive skewed-perspective look. The Quays see their niche this way: "Although *Mazeppa* and *The Love For Three Oranges* had their elegance at times, our natural preponderance is towards dirt, and especially detail and texture. That's not our forte, all this beauty. We tend to like degraded reality."

Michael Atkinson   (essay date September-October 1994)

SOURCE: "The Night Countries of the Brothers Quay," in *Film Comment,* Vol. 30, No. 5, September-October, 1994, pp. 36-8, 40-4.

[*In the following essay, Atkinson presents an overview of the Quays' career and discusses various influences on their approach to puppetry and film animation.*]

To watch, indeed to enter, the impossible, haunted night of a Quay Brothers film is to become complicit in one of the most perverse and obsessive acts of cinema. We're suspended in our own need to see (as we were meant to be at, say, Cocteau's falling chimney) as random, tiny, decaying objects and relationships are fetishized beyond the point of simple imagery and into alchemy. *Street of Crocodiles, The Cabinet of Jan Svankmajer, Nocturna Artificialia, The Unnameable Little Broom, Rehearsals for Extinct Anatomies, The Comb from the Museum of Sleep,* and the *Stille Nacht* pieces are all ferociously hermetic films whose interface with everyday culture is both undeniable and nearly impossible to articulate. Nowhere else has film so leanly and effortlessly rippled the dark subconscious waters ebbing under the surface of our collective experience. Flamboyantly ambiguous, retroactively archaic, obeying only the natural forces of a purely occult consciousness, Quay films are secret, individuated knowledge for each and every viewer. (Try and discuss them with other enthusiasts—the conversation is usually reduced to thoughtful nodding.) To immerse oneself in their chthonic cadences, their sacred sense of the hidden lives of dust, shadow, and broken toys, is to glimpse the infinite within the finite, the ghost in the machine.

A headful of horse feathers, you may be thinking, but Quay films inspire fanatical allegiance and intense superlatives, due in no small measure to the strangely private connections they make with attentive viewers. (It wouldn't matter if every man, woman, and child on Earth saw *Street of Crocodiles.* Only I would truly understand it—which is not to say I literally understand it at all.) Any attempt to invoke and articulate the experience of a Quay film becomes a mad wandering through a dense forest of metaphor, an effort that is inevitably doomed: they're all sublimely textural, possessed of an arcane inner law that is, in the end, unknowable. We become dazzled agnostics. We surrender to ignorant awe.

Much has been made of their evocative choices of thematic imagery—the pervasive lint, insect wings, rusted screws, threadbare fabrics, moldy dolls, antiquated typography, a veritable curiosity shop of self-entwining string, meat watches, stray wire, and the household scraps of a buried yesteryear. But just as vital to the films' creepy mystery is the Quays' protean mise-en-scène, which no sooner confronts a spatial impossibility within the confines of an animated film than it surmounts it. Their arsenal of visual tropes is in fact what clearly differentiates a Quay piece from seemingly countless imitators (MTV is fairly awash with Quayesque apes, most shamelessly Fred Stuhr's videos for Tool's "Sober" and "Prison Sex"). Look carefully at the later films' use of camera movement: the juxtaposition of slow dollies (often *around* moving figures) with sudden, vision-straining sweeps, the point of view moving through its miniature universe like the sightline of a cat hearing a floorboard creak, often finally focusing on a minuscule detail of random movement shot within a microscopic depth of field.

That the film image is animated millimeter by millimeter along with its content reflects an obsessive degree of creative authority that rhymes with the films' subcellar ambience. Thus the "subject" of a Quay film—characteristically, a weathered puppet constructed from common, discarded materials—shares its frame-by-frame life-movement with the "object"—namely, the frame, the

film, the camera itself (referred to by the Quays as "the third puppet"). The seamless animated manipulation of the camera's position, *and* its focal setting, is perhaps the Quays' trump card, a degree of fanatical precision no other animator would, or could, sanely coopt. Like a gifted magician, a Quay film often prompts us to wonder how in hell certain images are achieved, all of them completely in camera—the reconstitution (natural collapse printed backwards) of a dissipated dandelion, shot in looming closeup and within a *moving* focal plane, and the blurred frenzy of the toy monkey in the same frame as ordinarily animated figures, in *Street of Crocodiles;* the nervous mid-air suspension (and focal flux) of the pearls in *Rehearsals for Extinct Anatomies;* the ping-pong ball in *Stille Nacht II;* the fired bullet in *Stille Nacht III.* A Quay film is the closest anyone has come to authentically gnostic cinema. It fascinates and confounds in equal measure on every level, narratively, thematically, technically, even authorially: the mythic image of the reclusive twins secretively tinkering like deranged watchmakers with the subconscious detritus of forgotten Euroculture is one the brothers have never tried to dispel.

> **The mythic image of the reclusive twins secretively tinkering like deranged watchmakers with the subconscious detritus of forgotten Euroculture is one the brothers have never tried to dispel.**
>
> **—Michael Atkinson**

Indeed, though Timothy and Stephen Quay were born and raised in Philadelphia's suburban working class, they have come to seem positively exotic, as if their twinness (they commonly finish each other's sentences and sign collective correspondence "Q."), expatriation, and hobbyists-gone-monastically-insane working methods become an inevitable subtext for their films—a circumstance they are quite conscious of. Think of them as the squared cinematic equivalent to Walter Benjamin with his paperweight, or Swiss author Robert Walser on a semisurreal stroll. (The Quays' first feature, *The Institute Benjamenta,* currently in production, is a live-action take on Walser's first novel, *Jakob Von Gunten.*) Check out a bio excerpted from a letter to poet J. D. McClatchy for a connoisseur profile:

> What if we said we [were] born of a heavily tainted family, neurasthenic, microcephalic, each with one atrophied testicle, a sly liking for geese, chickens, etc., pigtails in pillow cases . . . No, we grew up sweating with obedience. Our Father was a 2nd class machinist for Philadelphia Electric, our Mother your impeccable housewife . . . On our Father's side there were two grandfathers, one a tailor from Berlin who had a shop in South Philly, and the other, who was apparently a cabinetmaker and we were told that the 5th floor of Lit Brothers [department store] in Philly has cabinets by the Quays. Our Moth-

er's father was excellent at carpentry and was also a chauffeur when Philly only had 5 automobiles to its name. So! In terms of puppetry it's surprisingly all there—carpentry, mechanisms and tailoring and figure skating to music to score any of our aberrant tracking shots. Big deal, will this help you dear fellow? [see J. D. McClatchy, "Movie Magic: The Quay Brothers, the Toast of Eight Film Festivals," *Connoisseur,* April, 1989]

There's little extracinematic oddness we can imagine about the Quays that they don't seem happy to confirm, with the exception of parental dementia à la Bruno Schulz, whose father conversed with tailors' dummies. Here's another typical flush of correspondence, in answer to my question about their short *Stille Nacht* Pieces:

> They're all linked by the common thread of Black & White and the belief in oblique salesmanship. *Stille Nacht I* was selling steel wool. *Stille Nacht II* was selling ping pong balls or socks with one vocation in life. *Stille Nacht III* was trying to sell pre-anamorphisized reindeer dining tables with a bullet already fixed in one testicle (which even more accurately & obliquely explains the deformed antlers) (documentary hyperbole). Of course none of all this is really apparent, but it gives us the sublime belief that no one is ever looking. And it's the premise we're most comfortable in starting from.

They're a striking enough public persona to have inspired the twin mortomanic zoologists in Peter Greenaway's *A Zed and Two Noughts,* and it's hard to feel as a viewer of their films that you're not trudging around in their shared cortex, their co-created Hotel Subterranea, where the corridors are piled high with moldering, century-old trash and where a submerged, animistic life-force throbs within the walls, under the floorboards, and inside every morsel of inanimate dross. It is, after all, the secondhand, rust-never-sleeps iconography of their films that grips the imagination most acutely, and while Quay films all often seem closed up in their own independent dimension dynamically, their textural interface with modernist history is palpable and evocative, "adapting" the work or sometimes simply the aura of Kafka, Schulz, Walser, Arcimboldo, Fragonard, Lewis Carroll, Janaček, and Stravinsky, and indirectly invoking the spirits of Bosch, Munch, Ernst, Bacon, Escher, Beckett, Borges, the original Surrealists, Joseph Cornell, Arthur Rackham, Lorenz Stoer, Karl Korab, and countless others.

More than that, Quay films are largely unspoken sleepwalks through environments crushed by the torque of industrial progress, and as such reference the central material drama of the last century—the abandonment of a society constructed around manual labor, around the power of the simple man, a crucial drama that mirrors, not incidentally, the history of movies. (Though Quay films, if they take place anywhere, take place in a fever-dream vision of Mitteleuropa, their blanket of uncomfortably indefinable dead-factory dust is just as appropriate for Philadelphia and the Ohio valley, where empty industries litter the landscape like churches during the Renaissance.) Scarcely proletariat in any other way, films like *Street of*

Crocodiles are dramas of lostness, of man dumbly wandering the dusty cloisters of his own wrecked sense of self.

Films like *Street of Crocodiles* are dramas of lostness, of man dumbly wandering the dusty cloisters of his own wrecked sense of self.

—Michael Atkinson

Most of what is normally thought of as Quayesque is epitomized in *Street of Crocodiles,* the first of their films to be shot in 35mm; the ubiquitous decrepitude and proto-totalitarian menace, the Schulzian characterization of Poland as a moth-eaten stage for existentialist dread, the rusty, perambulating screws and gears, the multiplaned images and bottomless shadows, the amber-mud hues, the pointless contraptions performing rote activities on the verge of entropic breakdown, the spindly, shabbily suited protagonist stalking through the soft machinery of a psychic warehouse in a startled state of paranoid anxiety. *Crocodiles* is arguably still their crowning achievement, the film in which they surpassed contemporaries like Czech animator Jan Švankmajer in creating a curious and original visual syntax, and the film in which that syntax was best expressive of a cultural mood. The design of the film's central figurine exemplifies this: pallid, desiccated, hyperaware of his surroundings yet lost in delirious shock at some unexplained horror, he's the perfect modernist hero, a version of Beckett's Lost Ones, Kafka's Der Verschollene—the Disappearance Man—as well as Bartleby, Gogol's Akaky, and the Underground Man. That he belongs to Schulz, possibly the saddest literary loss to Nazism, imbues him with an added poignancy. His eyes haunted by hopeless fear, the puppet's wary lurch and puzzled regard for the film's shopworn décor bring both Groucho Marx and Caligari's somnambulist to mind, all the while being nakedly a contraption cobbled together from scraps. Like most of the Quay figures, he is a ball-and-socket construction à la Ray Harryhausen, and sometimes the joints show—the Quays never try to disguise the scale or makeshift nature of their films, down to building characters out of drafting compasses, wire tangles, and tattered stuffed animals. This is as much an aesthetic of *detournement* as it is economic necessity. The brothers tell of British animator Barry Purves's puppet armature for his film *Next* costing £5,000, compared with the *Crocodiles* model, which cost a few pounds for the metal hardware underneath the desultory surface.

All Quay films celebrate their own exploding miniatureness in similar fashion, by locating within their tabletop cosmos unsounded depths of image, allusion, and atmosphere. The hallways of *Street of Crocodiles* go on forever, though we never see to where, and we know on the right side of our brain that it's a matter of inches to the table edge. It's endless in the sense of a Borgesian maze, removed from Borges' cool ironies by the autumnal rot and post-Great War era melancholia. In one fabulous scene the scarecrowish hero is led to a small window (not unlike a projection booth port—*Crocodiles* is rife with cinephilic symbols) by a gaggle of half-headed dolls, and through it he observes a plastic infant sitting alone behind dirty glass, playing with a giant lightbulb and watching a stream of antlike screws dislodge themselves from the crud-covered floor and scramble away, all accompanied by the morose dead-soul-of-Europe strings of Quay composer Leszek Jankowski.

Only a handful of cinematic moments match for me this scene's visceral, enigmatic woe: the husband's underwater search for the image of his lost wife in *L'Atalante;* the quiet raft ride up the nighttime Beatrix Potter river in *The Night of the Hunter,* the final self-fetalizing in the rain and in the middle of the road, after three lifetimes' worth of trauma, of the little boy searching for a father who doesn't exist in *Landscape in the Mist.* The Quays' camera seems to be on a perpetual hunt for tableaux and textures that pierce the skin of an ancestral unconscious bruised by failure and fear—at one point, and quite incidentally, one among many screws busy unthreading themselves from the floor suddenly pauses and rotates the other way, back into the floor, for a moment, as if it's unsure of where it's going, unsure of freedom and purpose. Watching *Street of Crocodiles,* you could easily miss it, but in a world assembled frame by frame, there are no accidents. Even the screws are plagued with lostness.

Of course, the implementation of such common and therefore meaning-loaded objects could lend Quay films an overt Freudianness that they neither deserve nor altogether deny. *Crocodiles* even has a few outright genital representations formed from organ meats and gloves, and indeed all Quay films bear undeniable kinship to surrealist impulses, and therefore, technically, to dreams. But saying they're dreamlike is not the same as saying they're Freudian, as the filmmakers rather peevishly pointed out in another letter re: the dreamer and the dream in *The Comb*:

> For us it was *more* a "troubled sleep" (based on a Walser short story) and as in all troubled sleeps it was a restless half-wakened state which produces the possibility of dream material, and a dream syntax, but to say that anything relating to dream is therefore Freudianizing seems a bit too glib and would disqualify a great amount of film . . . We wanted to keep the live action scenes resolutely separate from the animation *and yet* integrated in the overall flow and at hopefully an uncanny level, and this was done thru analogic gestures and cutting.

Clearly, Freud is a troublesome figure, because little of the Quays' dreamish imagery pertains to wish-fulfillment at any rate, but all of it seems scooped from a dark cultural id. Insofar as the Quays have also managed to make so much mundaneness virtually archetypal, the films seem caught somewhere between Freud and Jung, all the while tripping down their own cryptic yet endlessly signifying paths.

This tension is not nearly so much an issue in their earlier, relatively less cunning 16mm films—*Nocturna Artifi-cialia, The Unnameable Little Broom, The Cabinet of Jan Svankmajer,* and, presumably (because unavailable, even from the Quays), *Michel de Ghelderode, Igor: The Paris Years chez Pleyel,* and *Leoš Janaček: Intimate Excursions*—which are all more overt about their parabolic narratives and more Arcimboldoesque about their designs. But nowhere is the tension between psychological translation of any stripe and the Quays' ferocious hermeticism more tangible than in *Rehearsals for Extinct Anatomies,* their starkest and most oblique film, free as it is of any (discernible) relationship with outside source material—a surprising move, coming on the heels of the attention-getting *Crocodiles.* Of all Quays, it's a film governed by superego, albeit a superego twisted into knots by disease and technology. It trades in the previous films' antiquey gloom for the clear lines of bar codes gone berserk and a cool black-&-white biohorror that could make David Cronenberg sweat in his sleep.

The central Cyclopean figure aside, not much in it looks handmade, and this time even the milieu is a neurotic puzzle. By way of explanation, a typically Quayesque title card appears: "These décors have been engraved with great modesty and dedicated to London Underground as part of its present evangelical rampage, and to an anonymous anatomical specimen—to the single still dreaming hair in his head with its desire to disturb the wallpaper. O Inevitable Fatum." Actually the set design is an enlarged etching detail based on Fragonard, which the roaming bar codes mesh with seamlessly, and the film can be read as an abstracted meditation on AIDS, with its physiologically devastated central figure, the shadowed sickbed it presides over, and the occasional glimpse of hypodermics amid the refuse. Sterile and gruesome both, *Rehearsals* chills like a sick ward, and is the only one of their films truly scented with apocalypse. Formally, it's repetitious and cyclical and directionless (by virtue of going in every direction)—it's the Quays' *Last of England,* their *Weekend.*

In terms of set-pieces, it's also the only wholly "modern" film in the Quay corpus inasmuch as it dwells not within a rotten past but in a rotting present. In sharp contrast, *The Comb from the Museum of Sleep* explores new tonal territory while further expanding the brothers' visual patois. After the washed-out linearity of *Rehearsals, The Comb* positively glows with fairy-tale peaches and salmon, resembling a Bosch painting where the sun's come out. If *Crocodiles* is the Quays' journey to the end of night—literally and allusively—then this is their Grimm Brothers morning, complete with sun-saturated hills and trees (albeit with cartographic lettering). Intercut with an anonymous woman's "troubled sleep," a blistered doll journeys through a skyless, uterine-red maze/forest by way of a ladder, which often leaves him in a narcoleptic daze and carries on itself, the doll's detached hands fluttering around it like gnats.

Freud would have had a field day. Essentially a drama of frustrated desire, *The Comb* is not merely a dream but the portrait of a (semi)subconscious moment—which is still several steps further toward understandable daylight than the Quays have ever been before. In this they may have been subject to the same serendipity as Dali and Buñuel, who worked hard at making *Un Chien andalou* incomprehensible but ended up filling it with easily deciphered Freudian symbols all the same. What's more interesting about *The Comb* is its place in the Quay style trajectory, which graduates from tarnished existentialism to gray technodread to auroral phantasia. Certainly Quay films seem on the verge of breaking out of the inner sanctum altogether, an evolutionary urge inherent in the decision to use live action for *The Institute Benjamenta.*

The *Stille Nacht* shorts are purposefully incidental in this process, affording the brothers the opportunity to explore possibly neglected backstreets of imagery within a commercial context—one of the myriad of ways the Quays fund their work and themselves, in addition to shooting commercials, documentaries, and TV trailers and designing book jackets and theater sets. Whatever else the Quays themselves say, these shorts seem to function as working junk drawers, using up whatever the brothers couldn't squeeze into their larger films. (By most reports the Quays' studio in London is stacked floor to ceiling with moldy tea bags, fish bones, and other sundry garbage waiting to be included in a future film.) *Stille Nacht I* was a 60-second MTV "art break" predominated by metal filings and the weathered homunculus later used in *The Comb. Stille Nacht II* is an appropriately quizzical video for "Are We Still Married?" by His Name Is Alive, a Brit pop group whose dirgey melodies play like nursery rhymes on warped vinyl. *Stille Nacht IIIA,* subtitled *Tales of the Vienna Woods,* follows the meanderings of a pair of severed hands and a single bullet through an environment that suggests the monochromatic mildew of *Eraserhead. Stille Nacht IV* is the video for His Name Is Alive's "Can't Go Wrong Without You," and may be one of the Quays' most disturbing pieces, a bizarre Easter suite with the resourceful stuffed rabbit from *Stille Nacht II* battling the forces of evil (a pixilated human in horns and skullface) for the possession of an egg. Like all Quays, plot synopsis is seriously deficient in capturing the film's thrust, and leaves out its extraordinary ashlike visual texture and soundtrack song, which is a childish and creepy nightmare of distorted guitar wails. (In fact, Quay soundtracks, most often engineered by Larry Sider, are their own masterpieces of muffled background noise and suggestive portents.)

Like all artists working in "found," nontraditional imagery, the Quays have too often been dubbed surrealists (most often by people who have little idea what that means). True, they have been compared most often to quasi-mentor Švankmajer's, self-regarded as a "card-carrying militant surrealist," but films like *Alice,* Švankmajer's Lewis Carroll feature, rely too little on audience and too much on gastrointestinal distress for the comparison to hold. From *Crocodiles* on, what distinguishes the Quays is their carefully wrought sense of otherworldliness, of relationships ruled by incomprehensible needs (Švankmajer and most serious surrealists are too busy politicizing [*The Death of Stalinism in Bohemia*], burlesquing traditional forms [*Punch and Judy*], or using outrageous imagery for social commentary, or often, for the imagery's own sake [*Dimensions in Dialogue, Food*]).

The Quays cross paths with the world outside their films in a much more sophisticated manner, opening the forgotten corners of existence to the strangest, quietest, most unpredictable traffic—they have us questioning the meanings things have for each other every 1/27 of a second, which all film would do if we were to look at it more closely. Whereas traditional surrealism regards reality as a weapon best used to beat itself, the Quays summon a latent breed of audiovisual cabala, a new hoodoo way of understanding space, gravity, connectedness. An old saw says that when a butterfly in China beats its wings, it rains in Cleveland. For the Quays a butterfly means rain even, or especially, if they're inches apart.

In this the Quays are the quintessential animators: their films embody the enigma of cinematic cause and effect, of visual persistence, of filmic movement itself. If all animation creates these mysteries by its very nature, then only one tangential arm of the genre—light years away from cartooning à la Disney, the deathless pope king of animation as most people know it—acknowledges it: a heritage of Soviet, Polish, and Czech animators the Quays invoke as often as they're asked about "influences" by interviewers.

Perhaps the most eccentric of all cinematic "secret histories," the lineage that leads up to *Street of Crocodiles* (and, more popularly, *Tim Burton's The Nightmare Before Christmas*) is firmly planted in traditions of puppeteering that go back to the Middle Ages (note the Punch and Judy motifs running through many of the Quays' films, including *The Unnameable Little Broom*), having crept alongside popular cinema and animation virtually since the first kinetoscope. For independent animators (as opposed to the studio assembly lines), making a film is akin to transcribing the Bible longhand—it's an intensely private, laborious, uncommercial act, and such films often reek of hermited obsession, going back to Ladislaw Starewicz, who as early as 1912 began making stop-motion films using the rewired bodies of insects.

The first of the trash-excavating puppet mavens, Starewicz was a true obsessive: his entomological minidramas—*The Revenge of the Kinematograph Cameraman, The Insect's Christmas, The Dragonfly and the Ant, Frogland, The Mascot, The Lily of Belgium*—often played out domestic comedy and Aesopian fables with the creatures of the titles. (His first attempted film was of a live stag beetle fight; when the beetles failed to provide enough action, he began moving them himself.) That his creatures were only barely anthropomorphized—insofar as they might wear hats and carry violins—is Starewicz's lingering legacy. They're still dead beetles (black jaws permanently opened to the sky), dead grasshoppers (folded wings passing as dinner jackets), and dead frogs (standing on their hind legs, their faces pointing forever upward). No matter how lighthearted the scenarios, his films play like ghoulish pantomimes for entomophobes.

Perhaps we can count on Starewicz having been largely unaware of the gulf between his Mother Goose narrative sensibility and his bug corpses. Other animators, the variety seeking the sort of dark poetry the Quays have attained a Baudelairean fluency with, have proved just as important as influences often despite their use of entirely different mediums. Alexander Alexeieff (grandfather, incidentally, of the director Alexandre Rockwell) and his wife Claire Parker have explored the netherworld between 2-D and 3-D animation since the early Thirties with their pinboard films comprised of images formed of shadows cast within a surface made of thousands of movable pins. You may remember Alexeieff's pinboard work from the opening sequence of Welles' *The Trial,* but better he be defined in the annals of "experimental" animation by *Night on Bald Mountain,* a moody black mass that features premorphing transformations and 3-D models, and preceded Disney's version of Mussorgsky by seven years; *Pictures at an Exhibition,* which utilizes two pinboards simultaneously; and *The Nose,* a Magritte-ish adaptation of Gogol that must've made an impact on the Quays, what with its shifting perspectives, hapless Everyman hero, and perpetual East European night.

Of course, most animators have been trapped in the nursery ghetto, including Alexander Ptushko, a Ukrainian animator whose 1935 *The New Gulliver* is considered the world's first puppet feature. Notably, the Quays have never suggested that George Pal's Puppetoons were an influence; Pal's Hungarian roots and the films' stark landscapes and fluid, often startling movements simply could not surmount the Hollywood cartoon taint of the things. Jiří Trnka, on the other hand, is seen as a mentor despite the fact that Pal's films were much more widely available to American audiences years earlier. Trnka was, after all, still a Czech and still trucking in Czech puppeteering traditions, even when satirizing American genres in wonders like *Song of the Prairie.* That film, with its hilarious Georgian figures and elaborate mise-en-scène, is a high-spirited lark compared to the epic *A Midsummer Night's Dream,* a massive and ravishing feature shot in CinemaScope. Trnka's puppet operas, and the equally fanciful work of fellow Czechs Břetislav Pojar and Karel Zeman (whose everything-and-the-kitchen-sink version of *Baron Munchausen* is still the best), broke technical ground without providing the Quays, or us, with much thematic grist. (Even Starewicz's Walpurgisnacht sequence in *The Mascot* reveals a more modernist sensibility.)

Rather, the Polish animators Walerian Borowczyk and Jan Lenica have had, the Quays maintain, the most significant impact on their work, despite the fact that most of the Poles' films are not puppet animation—or even a hybrid à la Alexeieff, though pixilated live action is common. It's easy to see what was so galvanizing: films like *Labyrinth, Renaissance, Dom, A, Le Dictionnaire de Joachim, Le Théâtre de Monsieur et Madame Kabal,* and *Les Jeux des anges* create self-consciously 2-D worlds ruled by dislocating strangeness, horrific savagery, and Theatre of Cruelty surrealism. (In fact, Lenica went on to adapt Jarry in *Ubu and the Great Gidouille.*) In Lenica's *Labyrinth,* a Magritte-style Icarus descends to a city populated by all manner of self-cannibalizing mutant life: a dinosaur skeleton baying at the moon, trenchcoated lizardmen hunting down young girls, etc.; once the dapper witness's inappropriateness is recognized, he's torn to pieces by a flock of vultures. In Borowczyk's *Les Jeux des anges,* a metropolis of hapless angels spends most of its time butchering itself,

rivers of blue blood flowing from the severed heads and wings.

Beautiful and appalling at the same time, the films of Lenica and Borowczyk were perhaps the first of their kind, the animated equivalents to Maldoror, Sade, and Artaud. Seen through the scrim of Quayness, the Polish films represent a liberation of vision, of access to modernist despair otherwise alien to animated films. The means to the vision was new, too: in Borowczyk's *Renaissance,* decimated objects meticulously reenact their own destruction backwards by reassembling themselves, establishing a relational paradox between things the Quays have been exploring ever since. On top of that, Borowczyk moved from animations into live-action feature with no discernible textual or thematic compromise—a shift the Quays are aiming for with their feature (although, they've said in regards to funding difficulties, "we could probably animate the entire thing just as easily").

In terms of the Quays' poetic syntax—their associative whorl of mystic relationships and lyrical disquiet—their closest kin (as the Quays themselves admit in a Norwegian interview) is Youri Norstein, a Russian animator whose *Tale of Tales* remains something of a Holy Grail for animation fans in America. (It can only be seen on a Japanese laserdisc, unavailable here.) Graphically halfway between Gustave Doré and Maurice Sendak, *Tale of Tales* is a folk-artish tapestry littered with elliptical connections and startling images. My favorite, amid the fog-blanketed forests and apples in the snow, is of a lonesome, rather Sendakian wolf huddled over a fire in a dark roadside ditch, the headlights of passing cars falling over him and the surrounding trees like a lighthouse beam. What's felt in scenes like this is what's vital to the film, and what significance each sequence bears to another is difficult to discern with certainty; Norstein's children's book characters leave us unprepared for a degree of meditative mystery on a par with **Rehearsals for Extinct Anatomies.**

The Quays themselves are ironically pragmatic about the whole issue of ancestry: "Our own vision has been crucially marked by these masters who as it conveniently seems will never be known and so the dupery continues and no one will ever know." They're half-right: few will ever realize because most of the animators they extol as vital to the history of the art form are still largely unseen on these shores. (Starewicz, Alexeieff, and Trnka are available on tape in limited quantities.) But as for the dupery, the Quays seem sui generis even to the most jaded viewers, and that may be their largest achievement. The smallest moment in their films can make us feel as if we've never known the true and quiet force of film before: the string twisting up on itself from just a touch of the protagonist's desiccated finger in **Street of Crocodiles;** the camera waiting for the bullet to pass through a particularly troublesome pine cone before continuing along its path in **Stille Nacht III;** the ladder, caressed by disembodied hands, suddenly sprouting leaves out of the focal plane in **The Comb.** As wholes, Quay films are carefully considered answers to the question of how many angels can dance on the head of a pin—and we realize the question is fruitless: It doesn't even matter. What matters is the dance itself.

The Brothers Quay with Ryan Deussing (interview date 9 February 1996)

SOURCE: An interview with the Brothers Quay, in *ThingReviews,* February 9, 1996. http://www.thing. net/ttreview/febrev.02.html (17 April 1996).

[In the following interview, which was originally published on the Internet, the Quays discuss Institute Benjamenta *and their transition to live-action filmmaking.]*

[Deussing]: You both went to Art School—first in Philadelphia and then in England—and wound up working as animators. Is that what you planned on all along?

[Brothers Quay]: We started off as illustrators, drawers, and it was because we became frustrated by the stillness of that image, the lack of sound, of depth, of music, we figured there had to be another way to go. We managed in school to do some 2D, cut-out animation shorts, but we were frustrated by that as well—we wanted the third dimension.

Had you begun to experiment with animation before you arrived in London?

No, we came to animation at about the age of thirty-two. At least puppet animation, the kind of work we've become known for.

What draws you to the literary sources which serve as inspiration for your films? They all seem to be drawn from the eastern European/Germanic vein, such as Ödon von Horvärth, from whom the title Tales from the Vienna Woods *is borrowed, or Bruno Schulz, whose writings were your starting point for* Street of Crocodiles, *and of course Robert Walser, whose novel* Jakob Von Gunten *inspired your latest film,* Institute Benjamenta.

For one the whole universe of the puppet is an eastern European art form, one which really doesn't exist in America, and once we became aware of the region in which European puppetry was developed and refined, we were attracted to the literature which surrounded it. This process led us of course to central European literature and music, although that's not to say it's our only obsession. But the real turning point for us was coming across the diaries of Franz Kafka, because what he left out of the stories, we found in his diary: these half-fragments, things that were unbelievably evocative, so that Kafka really led us in to central Europe. And of course Kafka adored Walser's writing.

Your films are also reminiscent of early German silent cinema. Is it safe to assume that German Expressionist and Weimar film has had a big influence on your style?

I know why people are prone to say that, because our animation draws heavily on a very sophisticated visual language—a certain quality of lighting and decor, of stylized movement—which has a lot to do with Expressionism. But at the same time one could talk Keaton, or early Swedish or Danish cinema, all of which are crucial for us. The essential influence is that of a visual aesthetic which doesn't rely upon dialogue.

This aesthetic seems to me to be a sort of "stylized Germa-

nia", *for lack of a better term, which reminded me immediately of Guy madden's* Careful.

Well Walser's book, which was our foundation, is actually not an expressionist work, it has nothing to do with it, and the relation to *Careful* is purely fortuitous. We had never seen the film when we got started shooting, and he had never read the book. Somehow we do share the same iconography, however. We know Guy and have written each other various letters, but he's got a sense of humor compared to us.

You mentioned music as another thing you culled from central Europe. It plays a big role in all of your animation, and **Benjamenta** *is no exception. Do you begin working with a score already at hand?*

Absolutely. Only once in our life have we had the music done in post-production, for a commercial. We rely on music to propose certain things we would have never foreseen. For us music is the bloodstream and like any choreographer we compose our visual narrative through music—it almost co-writes the scenario. We'd like to achieve a musicalization of space, and would prefer our work to follow musical law rather than a dramaturgical one.

You've described your move from stop-motion animation to live action filmmaking as analogous to a composer moving from chamber pieces to a symphony.

Well it was a giant step for us, but we felt we were quite ready. I mean Christ, we're forty-eight years old. Bertolucci shot his first feature when he was twenty-one or so, which makes us appear slightly retarded. In a sense we've got to make up for lost time.

What is it about the term "surreal" that you object to, when used in reference to your films?

Our fear is that the term is misused. Of course we are familiar with surrealism, we know its history and its place, but the term can too often be used in a cavalier way, without acknowledgement of its real meaning. Like, "Oh, that's cool, that's surreal." When it's used cautiously and intelligently it can be a very descriptive term, but we're weary of it's over-use. At this rate every housewife is a surrealist.

You've said that you are "Europeans by choice", although you were born in Philadelphia. Do you think it would be possible for you to make your kind of films in America?

It would be totally impossible for us to have done what we've done in America. American companies might buy our films, but we work on commission, and the European commissioning bodies are much more open and receptive of our ideas. Our puppetry may well be relegated to the perimeter, but at least it's allowed to exist. Channel Four goes so far as to treat animation as an artform and to set aside a whole budget for it's production. Sadly I don't think that could ever happen here.

I was surprised to find that you were participating in the Digitale festival last year in Cologne, which focuses on digital media and celebrates computer-aided filmmaking.

Your work is very much of the old-school, even if you did use a bit of digital tomfoolery in **Benjamenta.**

Well, the man who runs Digitale is a friend of ours, and I think the reason we were included in the program at the last minute was because he's interested in the alchemical quality of our films. We were sort of a counterweight to the rest of the festival, because our films contain a form of combustion that lies right beyond the realm of digital effects. It was as if to say, "You can work wonders with a computer, but can you do this?"

I'm sure people are always asking you about your decision to work together. It's uncommon for twins to stick by each others side, much less for them to work together in the same field.

For us it's invisible, we don't even notice it. You're only reminded that you're a twin when you walk down the street together and people stare at you. Actually, we passed two old women today, identical twins, probably in their seventies, and immediately we thought "Jesus, will we look that bad when we get old?", "Why don't they just part?", and we had to admit that they were slightly freaks. People of course expect us, as well, to eventually part and to become normal people, to have an individual life, but we find that being twins insulates us quite nicely from the demands of reality.

Stephen Holden   (review date 13 March 1996)

SOURCE: "ABC's of Self-Negation for Aspiring Butlers," in *The New York Times,* March 13, 1996, p. B3.

[*In the following mixed review of* Institute Benjamenta, *Holden praises the visual style of the film but criticizes its overall effect as "vaporous" and "tediously precious."*]

Since most movies portray people struggling to get ahead, it takes a certain kind of nerve to make a film about a man who attends a special school to study self-negation.

The Institute Benjamenta, the imaginary academy that is the setting of the Quay Brothers' first live-action feature film [*Institute Benjamenta*], is a decrepit training ground for butlers situated deep in a misty forest somewhere in central Europe. It is here that Jakob von Gunten (Mark Rylance), an aspiring butler, enrolls for instruction in "the divine duty of servants." Once ensconced, he joins less than a dozen other dedicated students in repeating the same absurd, monkish rituals over and over under the stern tutelage of the school's founder, Herr Benjamenta (Gottfried John), and his sister, Lisa (Alice Krige).

Day after day, the students are drilled in the school's catechism: "None of us will amount to much. Later in life we will all be something very small and subordinate." At moments like these, this solemn pokerfaced comedy dares to crack a smile.

Institute Benjamenta, which opens today, might be described as a Kafkaesque fairy tale with a surreal sense of humor. On entering the school, Jakob is shown around by a chimpanzee and forced to undergo a humiliating physical in which he is yanked by the ears, his teeth and gums inspected with brutally probing fingers, and his head is measured.

As the film goes along, it turns into an elliptical gothic fable. Jakob finds himself the center of a strange romantic triangle in which Herr Benjamenta and his sister confide their loneliness and compete for his loyalty. Hints are dropped that the brother and sister have a tormented incestuous relationship and that Herr Benjamenta might have a sadomasochistic yen for Jakob, but in this film, which sustains a mood of harsh psychological repression, they remain only hints.

Somewhere along the way, Jakob wonders if he is a prince living a fairy tale. But in the film's perverse, downbeat scenario, instead of rescuing the somnambulant princess from the haunted castle, she dies and the dream world he has entered falls apart.

Or so it seems. *Institute Benjamenta,* which was adapted from a novella by Robert Walser, is a purposely ambiguous allegory crammed with symbols—pine cones, deer heads, severed forks, a mysterious goldfish bowl—that can be read any number of ways. Mixing quasi-religious symbolism with a mood of gothic horror, the film could be taken as everything from a spoof of German horror movies to a mock Christian allegory.

The Quay Brothers, American-born identical twins who live in England, have distinguished themselves with exquisitely eerie short films like *Street of Crocodiles,* in which puppets lurch and bob through a rustcovered claustrophobic environment. Handsomely photographed, *Institute Benjamenta,* has a similarly visual fixation on eccentric details and small objects illuminated to lend to them mystical symbolic resonance.

Quasi-mystical may be more like it. For all its dazzling visual chicanery, this vaporous film eventually runs out of ideas. There is a fine line between the deliciously mysterious and the tediously precious, and *Institute Benjamenta* loses sight of it.

The movie is unrated.

J. Hoberman   (review date 19 March 1996)

SOURCE: "Class Action," in *The Village Voice,* Vol. XLI, No. 12, March 19, 1996, p. 65.

[*Hoberman is an American film critic and educator who writes on a wide variety of topics in contemporary and historical cinema; his books include* Midnight Movies *(1983; with Jonathan Rosenbaum),* Bridge of Light: Yiddish Film between Two Worlds *(1991), and* Vulgar Modernism: Writing on Movies and Other Media *(1991). In the following excerpt from a review of* Institute Benjamenta *and Ken Loach's* Land and Freedom *(1996), he describes the Quays' film as "a triumph of atmosphere" but adds that it "may strike some as an Homage to Catatonia."*]

Institute Benjamenta, the first live-action feature by the erudite twin animators known as the Brothers Quay, provides its protagonist with [a] sort of European education. . . . [I]t's a course in obedience. Drawn mainly from the novel *Jakob von Gunten* by Robert Walser (1878-1956), the Swiss writer whose mordant, miniaturist whimsies influenced Kafka, ***Institute Benjamenta*** is set in a school for butlers, which doubles as Quayland—a slice of moldy *Mitteleuropa* petrified as if beneath a bell jar.

Walser's novel, previously filmed in 1971 by Peter Lilienthal with Hanna Schygulla as the Institute's headmistress, was parodied by Guy Maddin in *Careful.* The Quays, however, are never more serious than when they're making fun. Rendering the Walser text even more hermetic by restricting it to the eponymous Institute, they accentuate the book's deadpan masochism by dropping most of the new student Jakob's comical first-person chatter. Mark Rylance (who has a similar, stranger-in-a-strange-land role in *Angels & Insects*) plays Jakob with an obsequious, dry-mouthed quaver and body language so galvanized even his hair seems to twitch.

A triumph of atmospherics, the movie is as rigidly controlled as any of the Quays' early animations. Jakob and his grotesque fellow students study a text called *The Divine Duty of Servants,* endlessly repeating the single lesson taught by the sternly beautiful Lisa Benjamenta (Alice Krige). As the Quays treat their actors like puppets, so does the haughty Fraulein Lisa. The movie's central mystery is the incestuous relationship between the increasingly distracted Lisa and her overbearing brother, known only as Herr Benjamenta. (He's played by the outsized Gottfried John, whose sensual pugilist face made him a favorite Fassbinder heavy.)

Jakob alone ponders the meaning of the Institute: "What was the Institute before it was the Institute?" That the school has a natural history is suggested by the stag antlers the Quays affix to every available surface—even the fascinating Lisa uses a slender cloven-hoofed cane as a pointer. Still, there is nothing in this movie that does not proclaim itself Culture. Shot in pearly black and white, ***Institute Benjamenta*** is a work in which artfully indistinct shadows abet a range of calculated spacial tricks. Nudging for attention, the score ranges from choral shrillness to jazzy noodling to a hurdy-gurdy buzz.

The Quays are often linked to Jan Svankmajer, but where the Czech animator is cheerfully vulgar (sometimes even disgusting) in his gross textural juxtapositions, the Brothers are fastidiously ethereal. Their movie scarcely lacks for creepiness but, a good 20 minutes longer than its preciosity can sustain, ***Institute Benjamenta*** may strike some as an Homage to Catatonia. The ban against oxygen that preserves the Quays' rarefied world is something of a Pyrrhic victory. As Fraulein Lisa loses control, the Institute sinks into an agitated somnolence that mirrored the state experienced by this viewer.

FURTHER READING

Criticism

Canby, Vincent. "The Beauty of the Silents." *The New York Times* (11 October 1991): C10.
    Brief review of *The Comb,* which Canby describes as "hermetic" and "tactile."

Christie, Ian. Review of *Nocturna Artificialia (Those Who Desire without End),* by The Brothers Quay. *Monthly Film Bulletin* 46, No. 550 (November 1979): 242.
    Brief review in which Christie notes the film's Eastern European influences and calls the Brothers Quay "promising newcomers."

Durgnat, Raymond. Review of *Leoš Janáček: Intimate Excursions,* by The Brothers Quay. *Monthly Film Bulletin* 53, No. 629 (June 1986): 190-91.
    Positive review.

Maslin, Janet. "The Pitcher of Spilled Milk as Featured Player." *The New York Times* (27 March 1991): C15.
    Brief, positive review of *Rehearsals for Extinct Anatomies.*

McClatchy, J. D. "Movie Magic: The Quay Brothers, the Toast of Eight Film Festivals." *Connoisseur* (April 1989): 91-5.
    Laudatory overview and analysis of the Quays' work.

Quay, The Brothers. "Five Letters from the Brothers Quay and Stills from *The Comb.*" *The Review of Contemporary Fiction* XII, No. 1 (Spring 1992): 57-61.
    Correspondence from the filmmakers to acquaintances regarding translations of Robert Walser's writings, which served as the basis for the film *The Comb.*

Rafferty, Diane. "Brothers from Another Planet." *The New Yorker* LXXII, No. 4 (18 March 1996): 40
    Brief report on the party following the New York premier of *Institute Benjamenta.*

Rubin, Mike. "Re: Animators." *The Village Voice* XLI, No. 12 (19 March 1996): 74, 76.
    Briefly surveys Quays' career.

Taylor, Paul. Review of *Punch and Judy: Comedy or Comical Tragedy,* by The Brothers Quay. *Monthly Film Bulletin* 47, No. 563 (December 1980): 240-41.
    Short review of the film.

Michel Tournier

1924-

(Full name Michel Edouard Tournier) French novelist, short story writer, author of children's literature, and essayist.

The following entry offers an overview of Tournier's career through 1989. For further information about his life and works, see *CLC*, Volumes 6, 23, and 36.

INTRODUCTION

One of the most popular novelists in France, Tournier writes provocative fiction that blends myth and symbolism with realistic depictions of character and setting. Noted as one of the first major French novelists to eschew the stylistic complexity characteristic of the post-war *nouveau roman*, Tournier often updates or adapts old myths and legends to modern circumstances. Due to his examination of Nazism in *Le roi des aulnes* (1970; *The Ogre*), and his articulation of such themes as initiation, innocence, and identity through representations of sexual deviance and grotesquerie, Tournier's work has generated considerable debate both in France and abroad. Nevertheless, he was honored by the Académie Française—the highly prestigious French cultural institution established in the 1600s by Cardinal Richelieu for the perfection and preservation of the French language—with the Grand Prix du Roman for his first novel, *Vendredi; ou, Les Limbes du Pacifique* (1967; *Friday*). *The Ogre,* his controversial second novel, received the prestigious Prix Goncourt.

Biographical Information

Tournier was born in Paris to educated, middle-class parents. His father, Alphonse, founder and director of a music copyright company, instilled in his son an abiding love of music. By his own admission, the most decisive event of his childhood was the anaesthesia-less tonsillectomy he endured at the age of four. Tournier views this procedure as a kind of primitive initiation rite, and, consequently, "initiation" is a major theme in many of his works. A sickly child, Tournier favored solitary endeavors and was an inattentive student except in those subjects he enjoyed, namely theology and German. During the Nazi occupation of France in World War II—which Tournier admits he found perversely exciting as an adolescent—his family was forced to billet German soldiers in their house. Eventually conscripted to serve in a labor camp, Tournier was spared by the Allied liberation of France. After the war, from 1946 to 1950, he studied philosophy in French-occupied Germany; he also occasionally returned to France to attend classes in structural anthropology taught by Claude Lévi-Strauss. Tournier abandoned his plans for a teaching career when he failed his "agrégation de philosophie," the equivalent of his doctoral dissertation. While working intermittently on various unfinished writing proj-

ects, Tournier supported himself first as a translator at the Plon publishing company in Paris, translating into French the original German works of Erich Maria Remarque and other German authors; he then worked as a scriptwriter, announcer, and host for French radio and television broadcasts. After serving as senior literary editor at Plon from 1958 to 1968, he published his first novel, *Friday,* and has devoted his full time to writing. Appearing frequently on French television talk shows, Tournier is a popular public personality and lectures widely in France and Africa.

Major Works

Friday is a recasting of the story that inspired Daniel Defoe's novel *The Life and Strange Surprising Adventures of Robinson Crusoe, of York, Mariner* (1719; popularly known as simply *Robinson Crusoe*). Strongly influenced by the anthropological theories of Lévi-Strauss, which, in part, stress the complexity and cultural fecundity of so-called primitive societies, the novel reverses Defoe's hierarchy by depicting Friday—the island native—acting as savior and teacher of Crusoe. The main character in *The Ogre,* a French auto mechanic named Abel Tiffauges, is—

with his enormous size, poor eyesight, and deceptively malevolent interest in children—a twentieth century version of the ogres of European fairy tales; foremost among the many literary and historical allusions Tournier attaches to Tiffauges is the ogre depicted by Johann Wolfgang von Goethe in his poem "Erlkönig" ("The Elf King," which in French is *le roi des aulnes*)—a creature invisible to adults that first terrorizes a young boy, trying to lure him away from his father with fanciful promises, only to finally "take [his soul] by storm," killing him. The story is set in France and Germany prior to and during World War II. Tiffauges, whose supreme pleasure is what he calls "la phorie," the act of carrying a child on his shoulders, is wrongly accused of sexual molestation and is sentenced to prison; the outbreak of war and the need for soldiers, however, enables him to be placed in an army unit. Captured by the Nazis and interned in a prisoner of war camp, Tiffauges soon realizes he loves Nazi Germany, identifying particularly with its obsessive worship of youth. When he is released from prison, Tiffauges collaborates with the Nazis by traveling the northern German countryside—much like Goethe's Elf King—recruiting young boys for an SS officer-training school. Near the end of the war, a Jewish child forces Tiffauges to realize the implications of what he has been doing, and both die in the attempt to escape. Tournier's fourth novel, *Les Météores* (1975; *Gemini*), employs varying narrative perspectives and examines the themes of twinship, homosexuality, and the need to make order out of chaos. The protagonists, Jean and Paul, are twins who look so much alike they are often referred to as one person. Conflict ensues when Jean wishes to break from the tight grip of his brother; Paul is determined to maintain their obsessive bond, however, one which he believes makes them a perfect "couple." Tournier's first collection of short stories, *Le Coq de bruyere* (1978: *The Fetishist, and Other Stories*) carries on the themes of order, obsessiveness, and sexual ambiguity. Several of the stories, including "Amandine ou les deux jardins" ("Amandine, or The Two Gardens"), "La Fugue du Petit Poucet" ("Tom Thumb's Escape") and "Tupic" ("Prikli") are meant to speak to children about the difficulties of growing up and dealing with the emotional and physical changes that accompany the transition to the adult world. Although raised Roman Catholic, Tournier broke with the Church because he felt it did not meet the needs of modern man. *Gaspard, Melchior et Balthazar* (1982; *The Four Wise Men*) was his first novel based on a Christian theme, retelling the story of the Magi's journey to Jesus Christ's birthplace. Tournier, however, adds a fourth wise man to the original trio. Tournier continued using religious and mythical themes with *Gilles et Jeanne* (1983; *Gilles and Jeanne*), in which he chronicles the relationship of Gilles de Retz and Jeanne d'Arc. *La Goutte d'or* (1985; *The Golden Droplet*) focuses on Idriss, a shepherd boy in the North African desert who leaves his home for France to regain his identity—which he believes he lost when a Frenchman took his picture. In *Le Medianoche Amoureux* (1989; *The Midnight Love Feast*), Tournier describes an unhappy couple who throw a party for their friends to announce their separation. The friends then recount nineteen stories which lead the couple to reconcile.

Critical Reception

Sven Birkirts asserted: "From one book to the next, [Tournier] has been developing and extending a set of themes that are radically at odds with the common views of Western society. . . . This is his crime. In another age he would have been burned at the stake." Indeed, Tournier has been scorned by some in France's intellectual literary circles. His reputation is somewhat better internationally, however. Roger Shattuck noted: "Tournier is a writer of superb gifts and major achievements from whom we shall be hearing more." His children's stories are particularly acclaimed, and unlike his adult novels, use themes that teach the importance of human values, of retaining a sense of wonder in the adult world, and how one may live peacefully in a chaotic world. Certainly, his adult fiction is lauded by some as visionary, and shunned by others as perverse, fascist, and immoral. Most critics, however, recognize Tournier's gifts as a prose stylist.

PRINCIPAL WORKS

Vendredi; ou, Les Limbes du Pacifique [*Friday; or, The Other Island*] (novel) 1967

Le Roi des aulnes [*The Ogre*] (novel) 1970

Vendredi; ou, La Vie Sauvage [*Friday and Robinson: Life on Esperanza Island*] (juvenilia) 1971

Arroyo (portraits) 1974

Les Météores [*Gemini*] (novel) 1975

Amandine ou Les Deux Jardins (juvenilia) 1977

Canada: Journal du voyage [with Edouard Boubat] (nonfiction) 1977

La Famille des enfants (prose and photos) 1977

Le Vent paraclet [*The Wind Spirit: An Autobiography*] (autobiography) 1977

Le Coq de bruyere [*The Fetishist, and Other Stories*] (drama and short stories) 1978

Des clefs et des serrures [with Georges Lemoine] (essays) 1979

Le Fugue du Petit Poucet (juvenilia) 1979

Pierrot ou les secrets de la nuit (juvenilia) 1979

Barbedor (juvenilia) 1980

Le Vol du Vampire (essays) 1981

Vues de dos (prose and photos) 1981

L'Aire du muguet (juvenilia) 1982

Gaspard, Melchior et Balthazar [*The Four Wise Men*] (novel) 1982

Francois Mitterand [with Konrad R. Mueller] (biography) 1983

Gilles et Jeanne [*Gilles and Jeanne*] (novel) 1983

Les Rois Mages (juvenilia) 1983

Sept contes (juvenilia) 1984

Le Vagabond immobile [with Jean-Max Toubeau] (nonfiction) 1984

A Garden at Hammamet [*Un Jardin a Hammamet*] (novel) 1985

Marseille, or Le Present incertain (prose and photos) 1985

La Goutte d'or [*The Golden Droplet*] (novel) 1986

Le Medianoche Amoureux [*The Midnight Love Feast*]
(novel)　1989

Le Tabor et le Sinai: Essais sur l'art contemporain　(essays)　1989

CRITICISM

William Cloonan　(essay date Autumn-Winter 1983-1984)

SOURCE: "The Spiritual Order of Michel Tournier," in *Renascence*, Vol. XXXVI, Nos. 1 and 2, Autumn-Winter, 1983-1984, pp. 77-87.

[In the following essay, Cloonan traces Tournier's religious development through the characters in his first four published novels.]

> "The whole world is nothing but a stack of keys and a collection of locks."
>
> [*Des Clefs et des serrures*]

Michel Tournier is a controversial Christian. His religious beliefs frequently appear multiple and contradictory. In an interview accorded to the Australian journal, *Meanjin,* Tournier insisted that "God had an undoubted place in my life because I am a Spinozist. That is, I believe that I participate in creation and in the divine spirit when I write and understand" [*Meanjin,* Vol. XXXVIII, May, 1978]. However, Tournier went on to express surprise that his characters do not share his convictions: ". . . this belief is not theirs. My novels are rather atheistic." Critical reaction to Tournier's works has often reflected an uneasiness at the seeming disparity between the author's professed beliefs and what occurs in his fiction. To cite but one example, in a review of *Les Météores,* Robert Poulet claims that,

> . . . the work of Michel Tournier is immoral. Perhaps one should say anti-moral, because of a cunningly aggressive tendency which attempts not so much to erase the distinction between good and evil. . . . as to insidiously reverse moral values so that evil can be taken for good, and vice versa.
>
> [Poulet, "Tournier, romancier hors de série," *Ecrits de Paris,* september, 1975]

Yet, in the same article, Poulet manages to assure his readers that Tournier's ideas " . . . remain open to a kind of abstract and theoretical spiritualism, which he perhaps considers to be a fantasy in his brain." In this climate of confusion and possible annoyance, Pierre Maury's caution, "One must study with great care Michel Tournier's relationship to both God and religion," is well worth heeding [see "Tournier, ou la perversion du mythe," *Revue Générale,* Bruxelles, janvier, 1977].

The publication in 1980 of Tournier's *Gaspard, Melchior et Balthazar,* coupled with the author's statement that this book marks his attempt to write "a Christian novel," have fostered the belief that Tournier has recently converted to some form of orthodox Christianity. This is not the case. Michel Tournier is no latter-day Saul/Paul, and in fact no writer is more a stranger to abrupt transitions than he. Despite the variety of his characters, fictional settings and philosophical enquiries, consistency has accompanied every step of Tournier's artistic and religious development. The key that unlocks the secrets of Tournier's universe is found as early as the opening pages of his first novel, *Vendredi, ou les Limbes du Pacifique* (1967). Captain Pieter Van Deyssel is reading Robinson's fortune from the Tarot deck. The card Robinson chooses is the buffoon:

> . . . this means that there is an organizer in you who struggles against a universe in disorder that he attempts to dominate with the tools provided by fortune. He seems to succeed, but let's not forget that this demiurge is also a buffoon: both his creation and its ordering are illusory. But unfortunately, he doesn't know this. Skepticism is not his strong suit.

The struggle for all of Tournier's heroes is to wrest order out of chaos. This is what prompts Abel Tiffauges in *Le Roi des Aulnes* (1970) to fabricate his miniature and terrifying version of the Third Reich; it leads Paul to chase his brother Jean in *Les Météores* (1975) around the world in a futile effort to restore the harmony of perfect twinship. To take but two examples from *Le Coq de Bruyère* (1978), what makes a radio star of the ridiculous M. Robinet in **"Tristan Vox"** is his melancholy voice, which somehow manages to reassure an army of lonely listeners; the hero of **"Le Fétischiste"** protects himself against life's uncertainties by collecting ladies' underwear. Troubling personal contradictions set three kings on the road to Bethlehem in *Gaspard, Melchior et Balthazar,* and, lest we forget, the autobiographical essay, *Le Vent Paraclet* (1977), informs us that the perfection of the ontological argument first turned Michel Tournier toward the consolations of philosophy.

The problem for Tournier's characters, a problem already mentioned by Captain Van Deyssel, is that too often they are content with false or superficial orderings. During the early years on his island, Robinson can only survive by creating an elaborate and complicated series of laws by which he governs his non-existent kingdom; even at the novel's end Robinson must remain on his aptly named island, Speranza, if he hopes to maintain his fragile victory over chaos. Abel Tiffauges constructs an elaborate and obfuscating mythology replete with "signs" and cipher stencils that prevent this myopic giant from seeing the real cause of the torment within him: a sexual identity that eludes the traditional categories of homosexual or heterosexual. That dangerous notion, *sublimation,* is the final word in *Les Météores,* a word that the mutilated Paul proclaims as a cry of victory, but which is nothing other than the ultimate indication of his rapidly encroaching insanity. In **"Tupic"** (*Le Coq de Bruyère*), which is Tournier's ghastliest example of a false harmony, a young boy, jealous of the privileges he associates with femininity, cuts off his phallus in an attempt to become a girl.

Alexandre Surin is, according to his creator, a secondary

character in *Les Météores*. Yet if readers frequently think otherwise, it is not just because of Alexandre's flamboyance. In a novel flawed by the murkiness of Paul's philosophic ramblings, Alexandre is a figure of clarity, and, within the limits of his own beliefs, of good sense. He is the lone character in Tournier's fiction before *Gaspard* who both experiences the need for order and appreciates that any order he creates will necessarily be artificial. An atheist without guilt, he does the only thing an inhabitant of a Godless, meaningless universe can do: he invents a coherent, totally contrived world which is the perfect expression of his fantasies:

> . . . I have constructed my own universe: maybe it's a bit crazy, but at least it's coherent and it bears a strong resemblance to me. Just like certain molluscs that secrete around their bodies an outlandish but perfectly tailored shell.

Alexandre Surin is Tournier's metaphysician, whose ideas, like his actions, do not hesitate before extremes: "The idea is more than the thing itself, and the idea of the idea is more than the idea." In a world deprived of objective meaning, where all orderings are contrived, the more artificial a structuring of experience is, the closer it will be to the way things really are. All meanings are make-believe, man-made fabrications (Alexandre dislikes women) whose cleverness and complicated illusions protect us from despair.

Without the artificiality that Alexandre champions, there is only what Tournier in *Le Vent Paraclet* calls *le rire blanc* which is what results from taking an honest examination of human experience to its logical limits. It is the experience of the *rire blanc* which leads Alexandre Surin, "a dandy of the manure piles," and apostle of all that is artificial and transient, to a suicidal encounter on a dock in Casablanca. There is, however, another possible effect that ensues when exhausted human reason finally yields to the *rire blanc:* "You experience *le rire blanc* when you touch on something fundamental, when you meet God" [Jean Prasteav, "Tournier et l'ogre de Romiten," *Figaro Littéraire,* 28 Septembre, 1970]. In *Les Météores,* Thomas Koussek, who has also experienced the *rire blanc,* plays theologian to Alexandre Surin's metaphysician. Tournier had originally projected Koussek as a main character in this novel, as a "prophet of the Holy Spirit," but the task proved too difficult and eventually Thomas became, like Alexandre, a secondary personage. Nonetheless, Thomas Koussek represents an important stage in Tournier's religious development. In *Les Météores* Koussek adumbrates a theology of the Holy Spirit which lies at the center of Tournier's religious thought but which does not reach its full development until *Gaspard*.

Thomas Koussek describes his spiritual growth to Alexandre Surin in an early section of *Les Météores*. What stands out from the beginning is that Thomas, unlike other Tournier characters, was seeking a means of ordering experience that stems from something other than his personal fantasies, although fantasies he certainly had. As a young man he rather easily reconciled his homosexuality and love for Jesus by sleeping with a life-size statue of the crucified Christ. Later, after becoming a Catholic priest,

Thomas realized that this particular way of ordering experience was inadequate because it was at once too fantastic and too literal—too fantastic because it was excessively controlled by his sexual reveries, and too literal because it paid too much attention to the figure of Christ. Thomas's reflections took him beyond Christ and toward *l'Esprit* whose original manifestation was a sacred wind, the *ruah,* which, " . . . indicates something vast, large and open, but also the idea of odor, or perfume. Sometimes it is also a light contact, a gentle caress, or even a feeling of well being."

In the Christian era the *ruah* achieved its highest expression in *l'Esprit,* a word that has traditionally been given a too ethereal definition. For Koussek *l'Esprit* never loses its concreteness; it is " . . . wind, storm, breath, it has a meteorological dimension." Later he speaks of *l'Esprit* as "loaded with seed and moods." When Tournier has Koussek say that in relation to *l'Esprit,* " . . . meteors are sacred," the author is referring to Aristotle's understanding of meteors: " . . . their providence is everything that happens naturally, but with regularity" [*Meteorologica,* translated by H.D.P. Lee, 1962]. *L'Esprit* passes over and through all aspects of experience and sanctifies everything it touches. *L'Esprit* proclaims that life's fearful complexity is nothing other than the expression of its richness, and in doing so, renders the majority of distinctions that human beings make otiose. Principal among these distinctions is the one between clock time (*temps de l'horloge*) and meteoric time (*temps des météores*). Tournier's characters can be divided according to whether they adhere to clock time or meteoric time. Clock time bespeaks control at any price; those who espouse it tend to be sedentary. Robinson, fearful of leaving his island; Paul, attached literally and emotionally to his birthplace in Britanny; and Abel, to the extent he is imprisoned by his myths, are all sedentaries. Those who respond to meteoric time are wanderers: Alexandre in constant pursuit of *l'idée de l'idée,* and Jean in flight from his brother, are governed by meteoric time. However, their meteors are not Aristotle's. Meteoric time for Tournier's characters most often means a rejection of one form of control for what amounts to chaos. Alexandre essentially kills himself and Jean disappears from the face of the earth. Deprived of a knowledge of *l'Esprit,* they are victims, as are the sedentaries, of a false dichotomy.

An awareness of *l'Esprit* helps explain the significance Tournier ascribes to the myth of twinship that figures in all his novels. In **"La Famille Adam,"** the first story in *Le Coq de Bruyère* and a Christian version of Plato's *Symposium,* Tournier suggests that all human beings were originally androgynous. As such, they were made in the image of God: "Jehovah is neither a man nor a woman. He is both at the same time. The first man was therefore also a woman." One day God explained to Adam that his nature, human nature, was two-fold: " . . . there are contained within you both sedentary and nomadic elements." Shortly thereafter, in a decision which Tournier implies God might have had cause to regret, He made Eve out of Adam. The problem was not that there was now a man and a woman, but that each creature opted for one role or the other. Eve took the sedentary and Adam the nomadic, but neither God nor Tournier ever said that was the intention. Indeed, the only explanation God gives for his action is quite different: "From now on, when you want to make love, go find Eve."

For Michel Tournier, the conflict between Adam and Eve, between the nomad and the sedentary, is contrived, the product of humans' fear of their own complexity, reinforced by historical events and puritanical religions. The misunderstanding of what constitutes a human being, coupled with individuals' demands for order, has led to the formation of a political and moral universe replete with false distinctions: male roles versus female roles, heterosexuality versus homosexuality, and all forms of racism. Nevertheless, according to Tournier, the myth of twinship, the reconciliation of opposite but not contradictory tendencies, has lingered in the human psyche. Its theological expression is *l'Esprit,* which promises the union of idea and act, word and flesh.

It is tempting to see Thomas Koussek, whose radical theology in **Les Météores** appears to constitute a voice crying out in the wilderness, as Tournier's John the Baptist—tempting, but misleading. Thomas can be no John the Baptist since the fidelity to *l'Esprit* that he preaches involves going beyond Christ. In Michel Tournier's latest novel, his personal version of the Journey of the Magi, Christ never really appears. The novel manages to be deeply religious while eschewing theological discussion; yet, at the same time, it reflects most clearly what Tournier understands by the word "Christian." **Gaspard, Melchior et Balthazar** deals with four men's efforts to discover what they are, and then, (the more difficult task) to accept what they find.

As is typical with Tournier's characters, false contradictions plague each of the Magi. "I am black, but I am a king," are Gaspard's words to open the novel. Melchior's problem is that "I am a king, but I am poor." Most complex of the three is Balthazar, an aging esthete whose love of physical beauty puts him at odds with his nation's religious leaders, who abhor the flesh and graven images of any sort. The journey of the kings is a quest to resolve these contradictions.

In Bethlehem the kings discover that their contradictions are merely apparent. Gaspard's racial shame dissolves as he gazes at the child in the manger—who is black. This is the only physical description of Christ in the novel. Melchior learns that there are kingdoms to be had that require no earthly riches; this leads him to renounce his temporal ambitions and choose the life of an anchorite. Balthazar perceives that earthly beauty is an emanation of God's ineffable beauty. Thus, to love what the world offers and artists produce, is a means of worshipping the Divine Creator of all. Yet aside from each king's personal revelation, the fundamental illumination of Bethlehem is that the Godhead, the Supreme Ordering, is an assemblage of seemingly insoluble contradictions: " . . . this Heir to the kingdom combines incompatible attributes, the gigantic and the infinitesimal, power and innocence, wealth and poverty."

For Michel Tournier, the complexity of God's creation frightens as much as it fascinates; too often human problems emerge from a refusal to accept the richness and variety of the universe. What the Magi learn is not to live with contradiction, but to acknowledge instead that frequently the dichotomies people invent are forms of self-torture that have no existence outside of their own imaginings; they are products of human beings' inability to accept and delight in themselves and the world they inhabit. What provokes the Slaughter of the Innocents and damns Herod is not what the old king thinks: "I am a king, . . . but I am dying." His error, which is typical of Tournier's characters, is to want life to conform to the narrow categories he has constructed. Herod cannot accept human destiny and understand that transience is part of the Eternal Plan.

The story of the Three Kings is the culmination of the reflections on the ordering of experience and the role of contradiction that have marked Tournier's writings from the beginning. There is, however, a fourth king:

> I had been working . . . for a year on my Kings . . . One day, by chance, I heard a program on a German radio station during which the writer Edward Schaper mentions a fourth King, the one who left too late, who did not get to Bethelem on time . . . On that day, I had found the subject of my novel.

Taor is a king who likes candy. Specifically, a concoction called *rahat loukoum.* His voyage is, in a sense, the reverse of that of his fellow kings. He departs in a state of perfect harmony to plunge into a world of contradiction. His quest for a sweet leads him from his sun-filled land into the darkened city of the Sodomites where, although by nature a hedonist, he consents to assume the place of a poor convict and spends 33 years at forced labor in a salt mine. If the other kings had to struggle to accept what they were, Taor had to learn that what he was at the outset, an indolent, pampered heir to a throne, was not the limit of what he could be. The Magi started and stopped before he did; for them the revelation of Christ was sufficient. For Taor, like Thomas Koussek, Christ would not be enough. In fact, Taor would never see Him.

The rumor of the sweet that surpasses all understanding inspired the sedentary Taor to become a nomad. In prison he is once again sedentary, but it is here that his true wandering begins. From a fellow prisoner he learns the secret of *rahat loukoum,* but this knowledge can no longer satisfy him. The thirst that plagues him constantly in the mine cannot be quenched by anything purely physical. What Taor comes to seek is something beyond the physical, but this "something beyond" does not conform to the traditional understanding of the word "spiritual." For Tournier, "physical versus spiritual" is one more false dichotomy. The beauty of the Incarnation was in its union of Word and Flesh, and Taor's voyage of self-discovery, replete as it is with temporary denials of the body, leads not to the rejection of the physical, but to its transformation. Another prisoner tells Taor of Christ's miracles, and when, as an old, broken man, Taor is finally released from the mine, he sets out to find the Savior in Jerusalem. He arrives too late for the Last Supper. Christ has already departed, but He is no longer what Taor needs. All the famished man wants is what he sees before him on a table: some bread and wine. Taor partakes of these seemingly modest foods, and for the first time in his life he is truly sated:

> The two angels, who had been watching over him since his liberation, gathered him in their large wings and . . . transported the man who, after having been the one who was perpetually late for everything, would become the first to receive the eucharist.

The Eucharist, the transformation of the physical into the divine without the loss of physicality, represents for Michel Tournier the essential insight of Christianity:

> . . . I think I've understood the meaning of the sacred . . . I live in the realm of the absolute, in a totally vertical world in which each being, like a tree, plunges its roots deeply into the mud while, at the same time, it rises on the other end to ethereal heights. ["Tournier répond aux critiques: *Les Météores,* chef d'oeuvre ou provocation?," *Figaro Littéraire,* 19 décembre, 1975]

Tournier altered the story of the Last Supper by making Taor the first communicant, and kept Christ in the background throughout the novel, because what interests him is not the particular facts and dogmatic niceties of Christianity. What Tournier discovered in transubstantiation was the confirmation of his belief in transformation: that everything which exists, be it as humble as bread or wine, has the potential to become sacred, a process which occurs when people learn to perceive themselves and the objects which surround them as sources of comfort, beauty and joy. Michel Tournier was not fooling when he said that *Gaspard, Melchior et Balthazar* "will be my Salammbô" [see Xavier Delcourt, "Tournier, dans le mythe se conjuguent roman et philosophie," *Quinzaine Litteraire,* 1 mars, 1977]. While the differences between these two novels are easily ascertained, what they share, and what Tournier's comment alludes to, is a celebration of the lushness and wonder of the universe.

Tournier's Christianity calls to mind the pantheism of the philosopher he claims to follow, Spinoza. Throughout his career Tournier has insisted upon his philosophical orientation ("One must not forget that I was trained as a philosopher") [see Alain Poirson, "Une logique contre vents et marées: entretien avec Michel Tournier," *La Norvelle Critique,* juin-juillet, 1977], and in *Le Vent Paraclet* he mentions that Spinoza's *l'Ethique* " . . . is the most important book that exists after the gospels." What separates Tournier from the pantheism that Spinoza espoused, is that the former's position is not as rigorously developed as the latter's. Tournier, the philosopher of the sacred, tends to yield to Tournier the novelist, who becomes ill at ease when the elaboration of abstract principles moves him too far from the concrete: "I am unable to disincarnate the sacred and to isolate it in the world of the abstract" [*Figaro Littéraire,* 19 décembre, 1975]. It may be useful to recall here that Tournier's *Esprit,* which traverses the world, transforming and sanctifying all it touches, is eternally "loaded with seeds."

If the world is, as Tournier says, filled with keys and keyholes, it remains nonetheless important not to try to force the locks. Tournier is no more a true decadent than he is a consistent Spinozist, although any reader of his autobiography and fiction can find numerous reasons to place him within the decadent tradition. Certainly, an artist who tells us that he lives in a former rectory, who delights in arcane knowledge, who puzzles over the differences—real or imagined—between the natural and the unnatural realms, and whose religious references tend to emphasize the aesthetic dimension, particularly of Roman Catholicism ("Gold, incense and the organ reflect our heartfelt need for jubilation"), would appear to be something of a contemporary *Des Esseintes.* Also, the shadow of Gilles de Rais, which hovers over Abel Tiffauges in *Le Roi des Aulnes* conjures up memories of Huysman's *Là-bas.* Finally, Tournier does share with the decadents the notion that a conscious violation of a Christian dictum can serve as a paradoxical testament of faith: "If I have a taste for blasphemy, at least that proves that I have faith" [*Figaro Littéraire,* 19 décembre, 1975].

There is, nevertheless, an important practical difference between Tournier and the decadents, and it concerns the precise nature of faith. Most important French writers normally associated with decadence, artists like Verlaine, Huysmans, Baudelaire and even Rimbaud, have made some sort of peace with Roman Catholicism. They have used Catholicism for various aesthetic purposes and then usually managed to die within the fold. Tournier does more than play with the rites and beauty of this religion. He evolves a heretical, albeit consistent, theology that separates him from the Church's thinking, and then bluntly distances himself from the Church's practice:

> The Church . . . serving only the institution of bourgeois society and claiming to teach the Gospel while in fact teaching the opposite . . . the Church teaches the respect for property, hatred of the flesh and the respect for existing power (the Gospel despises money, loves the flesh and is revolutionary). We are approaching the only solution . . . a Church restricted to true Christians. Instead of ten million Catholics in France, there will be perhaps only five thousand true Christians.

> [*Meanjin,* Vol. XXXVIII, May, 1978]

The revolutionary, flesh-loving Christian Church that Tournier envisions is not a decadent fantasy and does not have its seat in Rome. As an institution it exists nowhere and perhaps never will. Its text, the Bible, and especially the Gospels, has too radical a message. No institution, no hierarchy, no power structure can be comfortable with it. Francis of Assisi discovered that centuries ago when he first tried to have his new order chartered from Rome. Michel Tournier is no Francis of Assisi, but he does participate in the saint's tradition-shattering belief that the Good News of the Gospel was intended not to alter people's conceptions of heaven, but their understanding of, and love for, God's earth.

Joseph H. McMahon   (essay date 1985)

SOURCE: "Michel Tournier's Texts for Children," in *Children's Literature,* Vol. 13, 1985, pp. 154-68.

[*In the following essay, McMahon examines the themes of Tournier's novels for children and discusses their differences from his adult works.*]

> I think that a child's readings constitute for him an intangible mine, an unattackable base on which are built, more than his literary culture and judgments, his personal sensitivity and mythology.

> *—Le Vent Paraclet*

The texts Michel Tournier—who is thought by some to be France's outstanding living novelist—has written for children are for the most part strikingly different from those he has written for adults. In the latter, he has purposefully played with his readers in an effort to force them to ask themselves questions about the attitudes they bring to reading. He has found other ways of being provocative by enunciating in *Le Vent Paraclet,* where he writes mainly about his own works, elaborate defenses of forms of human behavior which many believe to be aberrant. It is as though he wants, through strident notes, to force his readers to hear a subtler tone.

The same is not true of the works he has written for children, where his purposes are, on the whole, clear; there he often defends the kinds of values he ridicules in the works he has addressed to an adult audience, in which, as he himself has said, "I find myself pawing the ground of taboos" [See Escoffier-Lambiotte, "L'Ecrivain et la société," *Le Monde,* October 8-9, 1978]. The different narrative stances produce a situation in which the texts for children can be used to illuminate those written for grownups. The stances may also be related to some sharp distinctions he draws in *Le Vent Paraclet* about the intentions which lurk behind particular literary forms. Literature has power to influence the ways in which individuals see the world about them. They never shake off the influence of those works which have shaped their views at an early age. That assertion is of great pertinence to his interest in writing for children; it sheds light on the way in which he writes for adults. Implicit in his discussion of reading is a contradiction. On the one hand, he seems to be saying that there comes a moment when one no longer reads as a child does, for various kinds of distances are eventually created between texts and readers, who become wary. On the other hand, much of what Tournier writes seems to suggest his belief that today's readers are willing to look at and even believe almost anything; and, in that sense, they have never ceased being children.

That apparent contradiction may help to explain Tournier's two manners of writing and suggests that, whatever it is he is trying to do in writing for children, what he is doing when he writes for adults is trying to make them read as grownups. He would not put it that way, for he claims, "I never deliberately write children's books but sometimes I write so well that what I've written can also be read by children. When I'm less lucky, what I come up with is only good enough for adults" [Mary Blume, "A Laughing Provocateur Is Launched in Britain," *Herald-Tribune* (Paris), December 30, 1983]. Earlier, in 1979, he had told an interviewer from *Le Monde* that "a work can be addressed to a young public only when it is perfect.

Every weakness reduces it to the level of adults alone. The writer who takes up his pen with that high aim in mind is obeying an immeasurable ambition" ["Comment écrire pour les enfants," *Le Monde,* December 21, 1979].

Those sentiments, as we shall see in one case, do not conform to Tournier's own practice. His first work for children was a revision of a novel published for adults; he has announced his intention of rewriting for a younger public, when he finds the time, two of his other novels. What Tournier seems to espy is a complex situation: children, up to a certain time, bring to their reading a limited amount of experience and many look upon reading as a way of understanding *and adding to* that experience. What adults bring to reading is an indefinable attitude which in many cases may make reading an act *adjacent* to their experience, with the consequence that it may or may not become part of their experience. Those different degrees of susceptibility may demand the use of deliberate, alternate strategies on the part of the writer, strategies designed to give him the chance of having the greatest amount of impact on each of the two audiences he addresses.

Obviously, when he is writing for children, Tournier is under several influences. One is the memory of his own childhood, which he says was miserable, and that may perhaps help to determine the subjects he chooses to explore. Another is his appreciation of what he sees as the needs of today's young reader in the industrialized world. In a number of articles and interviews, he has discussed the rebelliousness and boredom of today's youth and its historical causes.

> If the child is the favorite prey of that gloomy void, of that bleak anguish, of that nothingness colored in dust, it is doubtless the result of a lack of roots in the course of things, the result of an excess of availability. It is in the nature of his age to await the unexpected arrival of something or someone extraordinary who is going to renew everything, overturn everything, even if that entails a planetary catastrophe.

> [*Des clefs et des serrures*]

Complicating that condition is the absence, in the life of the adolescent, of clearly identified, permissible ways of orienting his affectivity and sexuality. Today, Tournier says,

> they continue, in official circles at least, to consider that the absolute evil for the child is his sexuality. . . . If I say that eroticism has never done any harm to anyone, and especially not to children, and that there is no reason why one shouldn't show pornographic films on television on Wednesday afternoons, I am expressing something that is evident; but it runs up against a wall.

> [*Le Monde,* October 8-9, 1978]

A third influence on Tournier's intentions is a desire to get away from his own solitude through contact with readers.

A final influence on his intentions is his own experience with children. Though he has never married and has no children, Tournier has been intimately involved in the rearing of at least two youngsters. He told Theodore Zeldin:

> The ideal companion for me is a boy because I can do things with him that I cannot do alone: go to the zoo, walk in the woods, light a fire, read books with him, rediscover literature: we are both initiators and initiated to each other. It could equally be a girl, except parents don't trust little girls with bachelors. I do not have sexual relations with my boys. But I like to hold a child in my arms, I like to serve a child, to give him food, to wash him, to put him to bed. It's my maternal side. . . .
>
> When I look at a man of 20, and think of the boy of 10 he used to be, I feel a lump in my throat: it's like a death. I prefer to have not my own children, but all the children of the world.
>
> ["The Prophet of Unisex," *The Observer*
> (London), January 30, 1983]

In the context of the intentions I am discussing, those final observations, which recall some of the judgments made by the narrator of André Gide's *L'Immoraliste* as well as many made by the narrator of **Le Roi des Aulnes,** cause problems mainly because they suggest a futile exploitation of children: one takes them through initiatory procedures over the years only to produce, it seems, a condition of being one does not like. A further suggestion is that there is no remedy; accession to adulthood can only be calibrated in losses; to become an adult is to live as a defeated child, unless one associates with youngsters in order to repeat with them the games and other adventures of one's own disappeared childhood. That is the situation which confronts Robinson Crusoe at the conclusion of **Vendredi ou la vie sauvage**.

Initially, the children's version follows closely the story of the adult version, as its story follows closely the story-line of Defoe's novel. Robinson is shipwrecked and finds himself alone on a deserted, verdant island. Gradually, he overcomes his desolation, resists his temptation to wallow in the parental comfort he claims to find in the mud; he makes a commitment to work and eventually recreates on his island a solid bourgeois world. He names it Speranza and writes a constitution for its governance. After the first intrusion on what he considers his space by Indians, who use the island for their sacrificial rites, he begins to fortify it. All these events, and the pattern of life they create, reinforce in the child who reads about them the value of the deeds brought about through resolve and resoluteness.

In the adult version, those events are interlarded with excerpts from Robinson's Logbook where he meditates about and comes to appreciate some of the basic values of the West and where he also explores the relationship between sexuality and death. Indeed, after assuming a fetal position in one of the island's coombs, he initiates a sexual and fecund union with one of her flowers. Tournier excises that last event from the children's version in much the same way he says society bans sex from the eyes of the young.

Friday's arrival on the island is the occasion of another discrepancy between the two versions, apparently to spare children what they might find to be unsettling behavior by Robinson. In the adult version it is his intention to kill the fleeing Friday in order to avoid the eventual wrath of his pursuers; in the children's version, he aims his gun at one of the pursuers. In both texts, Friday's ensuing time on the island is spent being submitted to the ways of Robinson's civilization. As in Defoe's novel, he is sometimes recalcitrant; but in both of Tournier's texts his obduracy leads to disaster, for, fearful of being discovered smoking Robinson's treasured pipe, Friday tosses it behind him. It lands in the powder magazine; the resultant explosions bring down everything Robinson has constructed on the island and also cause his dog to die of fright.

From this point on, though the basic story remains the same in both, the two versions begin to differ in profoundly significant ways. In the original, Robinson's temptation not to start all over again is at first presented in a vocabulary which suggests that to succumb would be retrogression; he would thereby rid himself of the burden of an administered life and island. Gradually, however, Robinson's decision to embrace Friday's way of life becomes a transformation, a purgation, rather than a retrogression; it is not a question of having exchanged a laboriously established civilized life for a savage condition, but rather of having acceded to a higher perception of and participation in the universe, more particularly in the reign of the sun.

In the derivative version, Robinson makes the decision immediately and confesses that he is happy to be rid of a routine which at bottom bored him; once the decision has been made, he asserts that they are now free and moves on to become an attentive witness of Friday's existence. The subtitles clearly point to this difference; the "limbos" of the first version imply that Robinson has moved beyond civilization, the "savage life" of the second that he has reverted to a precivilized state. That variation in ideological tone continues until the very end of the book. Yet both texts invite the reader to consider a form of existence that is better than the repugnant ways characteristic of civilization; it is a condition which, when internalized, leads Robinson to stay on the island.

Friday's decision to abandon the island, without telling Robinson beforehand, is shattering in several ways. In the original text, no explanation is given for it, probably because it raises questions that are too unsettling. In the second version, Robinson says that Friday has seen the frigate, which could have carried both of them back to England, as a novel, irresistible toy, thereby using a child's instinctive reaction to the enchantingly new to explain a catastrophic event. In both texts, its arrival causes Robinson to think about moving swiftly to his death. But, in the first version, before doing so, he ruminates at length over the several stages of his existence on Speranza; death becomes the path to follow only when he finds he has neither the emotional nor psychological strength to pursue some other recourse. Oddly, he never raises, as many readers must, the matter of the *meaning* of Friday's decision to abandon him and thus to become a part of the civilized world. The child reader is given a cause, if not a reason; the adult reader is given nothing, and so is left to his own speculations. That is a challenge Tournier will repeat more than once in later texts.

The final event in the story, Robinson's discovery of the ship's cabin boy who has sought refuge on the island from his unhappy maritime existence, is presented in remarkably different ways in the two texts. In the children's version, Robinson is extraordinarily happy:

> He now had this little brother whose hair—as red as his own—was beginning to blaze in the sun. They would invent new games, new adventures, new victories. A new life was going to begin, as beautiful as the island which was waking up in the mist at their feet.

Since Friday's life consisted of more than games, adventures, and victories, one can reasonably say that Robinson's vision of the future is the second step in his retrogression. Because the cabin boy has never seen him in the role of an adult, Robinson can recreate daily with the youth a child's world. Growing and aging will, until debility sets in, have no meaning. One can say that the child's version of his novel represents Tournier's description of a world in which the differences between children and adults no longer matter. We are not told what the cabin boy thinks about a life devoted to devising new games.

The original text offers a much more unsettling ending, unsettling because it is really a beginning whose outcome we cannot reliably predict. When Robinson sees the child he has an epiphany: the boy is a postulant from the solar realm, sent to allow Robinson to initiate him into the ways of that form of existence. In the face of that challenge, he feels himself assuming gigantic proportions. The scene is not unlike that of Bacchus arriving on Ariadne's island. Robinson tells the boy, "Henceforth, you will be called Thursday. That is Jupiter's day, the god of the Heaven. It is also the children's Sunday." That announcement is fraught with meaning. For years, Thursday was a half-holiday for French schoolchildren, and many of them devoted it to receiving religious instruction, overwhelmingly in Christian religions. Robinson is thereby announcing a new dispensation and incorporating the boy into it by baptizing him with a new name, chosen for him by Robinson. The lessons contained in Friday's departure no longer count now that Robinson can play the role of God. One of the ways in which that role can be carried out is described in Tournier's next novel, *Le Roi des Aulnes,* where the protagonist, moved by a belief that he is called to serve children, ends up witlessly participating in the slaughter of some of them.

Tournier's later and shorter works for young readers are more directly related to the experience of children and are presented through their eyes. In **"La Fugue du petit Poucet"** (Tom Thumb's Escape) [in *Le Coq de bruyère*], we follow the adventures of a young Parisian boy who is disturbed by his father's desire to be thoroughly abreast of modern ways of living; the father is an advocate of shopping malls, car parks, and tall buildings. Indeed, as head of the tree-cutters of Paris, he makes a steady contribution to the creation of those spaces and is proud of his participation. When he announces his intention of moving his family to the twenty-third floor of a building whose cli-

mate is completely controlled and where the family can profit from the joys of color television, Pierre rebels, gathers his rabbits together, and runs away from the family abode in the direction of some milieu better suited to his vague aspirations. Warmed by wine he receives from a truckdriver, who has given him a lift out of the city, the boy finds himself in a forest where he is soon surrounded by enchanting young girls.

They lead him off to their home, where he finds a world quite different from that enjoyed by his father. Here he finds a place of marvels, where the father stays home and the mother goes to work; here he sees a poster on the wall which urges its viewers to make love instead of war; here he meets the girls' father, Logre, who turns out to be a more genial ogre than others in some of Tournier's works. Indeed, unlike Robinson, and unlike the main character of *Le Roi des Aulnes,* he acts as a source of counsel for the young rather than serving as the provider of diversions and dangers. From him, Pierre learns that the grand curse of men is that "they have left the vegetable kingdom. They have fallen into the animal kingdom. . . . What you find there is hunting, violence, murder, fear. In the vegetable kingdom . . . you find the calm growth in the union between the earth and the sun." The idea recalls some of Robinson's thoughts in *Vendredi,* especially in the version for adults. Logre goes on to say that a good example of that union is a tree: it needs sunlight in order to grow and raise its branches toward the heavens, but it also needs to be ever more deeply rooted in the earth in order to remain sturdy. He derives a counsel from the tree's example: "The more you want to raise yourself up, the more is it necessary to have your feet on the ground. Every tree tells you that."

The authorities do not approve of such sentiments; they approve even less of trying to indoctrinate young, impressionable children with them; and so they come to charge Logre with corruption of youth and to take him off to jail. Before being carried off, he tells Pierre to take a gift from the house. The boy chooses a pair of oversized boots like those his father had promised but failed to give him. Obliged to return to his parents' newfound high-rise flat, Pierre is not completely discouraged, for he has learned, as did Rousseau two centuries earlier, to have recourse to his imagination. While his parents watch television in an adjacent room, he stretches out on his bed, his newly acquired boots close by him; and there he dreams of being an immense tree and also, probably, of growing tall enough to fit into those boots.

"La Fugue du petit Poucet" recalls Tournier's detestation of his own childhood years in Paris, his belief that Paris is not a city for children, and his suggestion that a history of cities would be also the history of the possibilities of growth they have made available to the young, and of the good and the harm they have done.

Tournier's next tale, *Amandine ou les deux jardins* (Amandine, or the Two Gardens) has a similar didactic cast. As its subtitle indicates, it is meant to be a story about initiation, one of Tournier's recurrent preoccupations in those interviews where he has discussed the formation of children; it is such, though, only by way of absence. Initiations suggest rites and ceremonies, carefully prepared by someone, so that their intent will be known and eventually assumed by those being initiated. What happens to Amandine is that she makes a series of discoveries and undergoes a few events which lead her toward evidence of another world from that she has known—a world she must try to put together on the basis of the new data she has acquired. In the absence of established initiation procedures, she must assume the initiative in putting things together.

She lives comfortably enough in the two realms represented by her parents. Her mother's world is inside, in the house she keeps; her father's is outside, in the garden he patiently tends. In her diary, where she writes entries only on Sundays and Wednesdays, Amandine inserts descriptions of novel events in her life. Her cat has kittens. Amandine is able to give the male kittens away, but no one wants the sole female. The mother cat begins to show a certain distance from the girl; the remaining kitten is indifferent to Amandine as it goes about exploring the precincts. The child eventually perceives that the kitten's explorations lead it away from Amandine's sphere and into stretches she has never examined; she concludes that the kitten is living in two worlds, the domesticated world of Amandine's home and the wild world found in the other garden.

When Amandine finally climbs over the wall, she finds a space entirely the opposite of the one her father tends—it is a virgin forest, no garden at all, really. On her return to her garden, she exclaims: "How clear and well-ordered everything is here!" Some hours later, having cried long and hard over nothing, she discovers some drops of blood on her leg; when she looks into the mirror, she notices that she no longer looks like the young ten-year-old she had been. In the entry for the following Wednesday, she tells us that she has discovered that her kitten has become a full-fledged cat and is expecting a litter of its own.

Tournier's points are all clear enough; they profit from being stated mutely, by which I mean that he presents the phenomena of the onset of puberty in ways which would not upset those who had not made Amandine's observations and which might help those who had, but who had been baffled by their meaning. Even the implicit criticism of an order which tends its homes and gardens better than its children is presented indirectly. In a way, that criticism is not present until the reader makes it and derives some wisdom from it, which may lead to more attentive ways of helping children understand more clearly what they see all around them.

"La Mère Noel" (Mother Christmas) [in *Le Coq de bruyère*] is little more than an anecdote with ambition. It tells of the Christmas-time rivalry between secular and religious forces in a small French village who conduct competing ceremonies at the same time. For years the local curé has been celebrating a vigil Mass at 6 p. m. on Christmas Eve; its highlight is a live Nativity scene. For years, at the same time, the local schoolteacher has been impersonating Father Christmas and distributing gifts to the schoolchildren. When the teacher retires and is replaced by a divorced woman with two children, the villagers begin to wonder if the longstanding rivalry will now come to an end. It does not. The woman announces her inten-

tion to continue the tradition and to take the part of Father Christmas. She also agrees to have her baby play the role of the Christ Child in the Nativity scene. There is some perplexity in the village over the situation, and there is consternation when the baby begins to cry, as the Mass gets underway, and cannot be satisfied except by the arrival of his mother, summoned from her distribution of gifts in order to nurse her hungry child and thereby to add another vital element to the live tableau. With the hindsight provided by one of his later novels [*Gaspard, Melchior et Balthazar*], one can discern larger reaches in this brief tale, for the infant's need of his mother and the instant response on the part of both congregation and mother to that need point to the power of a child to effect harmonies and perhaps to remind rivals of what the coming of Christ was for a long time taken to mean: the establishment of peace on earth as an ideal worthy of being pursued by human beings.

Tournier's next book, *Pierrot ou les secrets de la nuit* (Pierrot, or the Secrets of the Night), is, he says, his favorite book, and one which he worked on for six or seven years. . . . He says it is an example of what he would have liked to do had he continued with his early career in philosophy. "I would have liked to teach philosophy to children of 10, and that is what I am now trying to do in my books for children." [Zeldin, "The Prophet of Unisex"]. He told another interviewer that the teaching of philosophy to the young "is not done and that's a shame. My little book *Pierrot ou les secrets de la nuit* is metaphysics for 10-year-olds" [Blume, "A Laughing Provocateur"].

What is often made deliberately obscure or ambiguous in Tournier's writings for adults is presented straightforwardly here as a matter of choices and values. The story is also an extension of the concerns expressed in *Amandine,* for here it is a question of how couples are formed in social partnerships and of the information which guides the decisions by which those partnerships are set up.

Tournier's story deals with a Pierrot who succeeds, not only in drawing Columbine back from Harlequin and vagabondage, but also in bringing about a victory for his own stable and domestic values. When he writes to the absent Columbine in his effort to win her back, he tries to explain the meaning of the colors of his world in order to allay her belief that they are sinister hues.

Columbine inspires Pierrot to create a lifesized brioche in her image, which reveals to her other dimensions of her being. Before 1979, Tournier had not written anything so forthright in defense of the values and continuities of the domestic order. In fact his *Météores,* published four years earlier in 1975, had raised serious questions about the attractiveness and viability of that order. Yet this apparent defense of the domestic life—of the washing of linen and the baking of bread—does not go as far as the reader might have expected—though it may go further. We do not read at the end of a marriage between Pierrot and Columbine. Instead we have what appears to be a reconciliation of all the opposed elements in the story. Harlequin returns to ask for the warmth and the hospitality of Pierrot's hearth; his request is honored; the two men watch with fascination as Columbine touches the breasts of the brioche portrait of herself and then invites them to join her in tasting and eating the good Columbine. The text tells us at its conclusion: "They are happy. They would like to laugh, but how can you do that with your cheeks swollen with brioche?"

Tournier is settling a number of matters in this tale which he has not settled as assuredly in his adult texts: the pacification of the nomad as a result of admiration for the security and strength of the sedentary baker, the celebration of the domestic and admiration for the maternal, the union of opposites which is often expressed in the difference between night and day, the absorption of cannibal instincts, whether physical or psychological, in eucharistic ceremony. But he sidesteps one of the main problems he has seen to be of central importance in the world of his readers—their initiation into sexual understanding and performance. What does a young reader make of this conclusion, which either suggests a union of the three or leaves unresolved Harlequin's more distant future? There is something of Marie Antoinette's alleged indifference to the people's hunger in a conclusion which suggests that youthful sexual rivalries can be satisfied by proximity to hot ovens and by the joyous consumption of tasty brioche. In Plato's world, one was encouraged to move from image to form; the same can be said of the world of sex; and Tournier chooses to remain silent about how that passage will occur and whether what it leads to will last.

What Tournier is trying to do in *Barbedor* (Goldenbeard) his recent book for children, puzzles me, though, as we shall see, it has some direct ties to the conclusion of the adult version of *Vendredi*. It is an oriental tale about a not too earnest king who sports a luxuriant golden beard, which each day is brushed and waved by a woman barber; male barbers have been excluded from service because their manner of care involves trimming and cutting. One day the king discovers a single silver whisker in his beard; it is a sign of his age which reminds him that, after two infertile marriages, there is no heir to his throne, and that he has not paid adequate attention to that matter. He thinks of adopting a little heir "who will look strikingly like me . . . like a little twin brother." During his siesta, he feels something like a bite and, on awakening from his nap, discovers that his silver hair has been plucked. The same event happens day after day, reducing the richness of his beard and serving to remind him that his life is passing by. Eventually, he discovers that a bird is the ravisher of his beard. When the last hair has been taken, the bird leaves behind a feather from its plumage; it turns out to have the properties of a compass and leads Barbedor to the nest the bird has made from his beard. There he finds a beautiful gilded egg which he takes from the nest with the intention of bringing it back to the seat of his kingdom. He is stopped by one of his own foresters, who accuses him of a form of poaching. Barbedor discovers at that moment that he has become quite little and is easily able to elude his accuser. He continues on his journey and, as he nears the city, takes note of a great funeral procession in an outlying cemetery. When he arrives at the gates of the city he finds them closed. As he stands before them, the egg begins to open, and a white bird flies out, singing: "Long live the king! Long live our new king!" The transformed Bar-

bedor thus becomes his own successor and repeats fully the events of his earlier reign, even in the matter of marrying the two barren women. At the point in his second reign where his golden beard begins to sprout, he forgets the history of the boy before the gates, the bird flying up from the egg, and the ensuing cry of "Long live the king!"

There were traces of that kind of longing in Robinson's aspiration to become part of the solar reign, to introduce the cabin boy to it, and thus to find a line leading toward immortality. A similar hankering led Paul, one of the narrators of *Les Météores*, to spin out extravagant theories in an attempt to project himself as an integral part of meteorological events. Here Tournier is going even further in his description of the process whereby an undeserving man is visited by renewal and restoration; here he allows for the possibility of a cyclical return of youth. He does not at the same time resolve the problem of how youth can move on to a purposeful, energetic adult life. One ought not to push that reading too far. Perhaps one should assume that what Tournier wanted was something simpler: to turn his hand to the creation of a magical, languorous world where troubling events become marvels, even for those who have not taken full advantage of their own promise and who have not wholly met their responsibilities.

There is a progression discernible in Tournier's works for children and an ever more visible commitment to particular values which are not as certainly appreciated in his writings for adults: sane integration into the natural world, the reconciliation of adversaries who need not be in conflict, the celebration of routines and rituals which enrich understanding of the worth of a serene life, an appreciation of enchantment as opposed to insanity. When Tournier writes about children, rather than for them, he depicts a world in which such values are absent or have been set seriously askew. Fortunately, one has the children's works as the assurance of Tournier's belief that those absences and dislocations are the results of abuses and that the child's world does not have to be a place of suffering and confusion, especially if adults attend to their obligations and writers attend to filling in whatever gaps may be created by negligence of those duties.

Michel Tournier with Maura A. Daly   (interview date 1985)

SOURCE: "An Interview with Michel Tournier," in *Partisan Review*, Vol. LII, No. 4, 1985, pp. 407-13.

[*In the following interview, Daly questions Tournier about his novel* Gaspard, Melchior et Balthazar, *as well as about the function of myth in his work.*]

The following interview with Tournier took place on a sunny summer day in Paris, in the offices of his publisher, Gallimard, after he had just published his seventh major fictional work, *Gaspard, Melchior and Balthazar* (*The Four Wise Men*).

[*Daly*]: *Why did you choose the three Magi as the subject for* **Gaspard, Melchior and Balthazar**?

[Tournier]: I always wanted to do something with my Christian background which is very important to me because I was brought up in Christian schools. Consequently, it was one of the things I wanted to talk about. I think that the choice of the three wise men was a particularly appropriate subject for me. First of all, no one had ever talked about it; second, on the contrary, there is an immense iconographical wealth concerning the three kings. The paintings are wonderful, aren't they?

In **The Four Wise Men,** *did you try to relate the Christian philosophical system to any other philosophical system?*

No. There is only one thing that is very modern in **The Four Wise Men;** it is the idea of image and likeness which is Balthazar's problem. As you know, I am preoccupied with photography; I am very interested it. That's very modern and is, at the same time, biblical because the question of image and likeness is in the beginning of the Bible. The political problem of Melchior is also very modern; in the problem of Herod's tyranny, there are characteristics that bring Stalin to mind: the idea of killing anyone however little he may be suspected. The person is destroyed, that's Stalin. The idea of telling the story of one's life at the end of a meal during the last courses—that was Hitler—he did it all the time. The portraits [in **The Four Wise Men**] are of rather modern tyrants, but there isn't any philosophy.

Nonetheless, concerning what you said, I think that perhaps one can make a connection between **The Four Wise Men** *and Heidegger's essay "Das Ding" ["The Thing"] which speaks of pouring oneself out in order to attain a sort of immortality, to attain a fully human status. Couldn't one make an analogy between that idea and the life of Taor, the fourth king in* **The Four Wise Men?**

I agree completely, but I didn't make the analogy; however, I think that you have the right—completely—to do it. At the moment, I have just submitted to Mercure de France [a French publisher] an anthology of literary studies with a preface about reading. It will come out at the end of the year and will be entitled *Le Vol du Vampire.* I think that it would interest you because it is literature once removed. For the same reason it won't interest many people. You will see that I defend the idea of a reading as an act of possession, so the reader is also the author, a co-author. There is still something that I would like to say about the Magi. There are two things that I like about them. The first is that they are foreigners: they are people who came from far away who are not part of the "family"; I like that very much; they are travelers who arrive, who learn things that they didn't know; who make grotesque errors, for example, as does the one who arrives with his *rahat loukoum* [a pistachio-flavored dessert found in Arabic countries that is the *raison d'etre* of the quest of the fourth wise man]. The second thing is wealth, because the wise men are rich. In Christianity there is a sort of heretical idealization of poverty that I detest because Jesus always defended himself against misconceptions concerning poverty; for example, when Mary Magdalene poured out a very, very expensive perfume on his feet, the disciples were indignant and said, "But that's idiotic, with all that money we could have done . . ." etcetera, and He said, "So then, I have no right to precious ointment? I like nard!" Then, there is the parable of the talents which is

a banking parable. . . . There is also the Transfiguration on Mount Tabor where Christ's beauty was resplendent—a divine beauty. It was not a humble beauty; it was shattering, awe-inspiring: He very much resembled the sun. That is how I conceive of Christianity; I envision a solar Christ, not a mendicant Christ.

Why then does Christ appear only in an oblique fashion in **The Four Wise Men?** *Was it a political question?*

No. It was simply a matter of my inability as a novelist. You know that depicting Christ is overwhelming. It is terribly difficult. . . . Who can allow himself to do it? First of all, I have a model—Flaubert's *Herodiade*—Christ is in it too . . . but He is far off—on the horizon—you know? Everything goes on more or less behind His back.

You employ myths very often in your novels. For you, what is the importance of myth in twentieth-century literature, not only in your works, but in literature in general?

Well, I'll tell you, that doesn't really interest me very much. What interests me a lot is the role of myth in the daily life of people. For example, if you watch advertisements on television, you see myths appear: the myth of purity, everything that concerns cleanliness, etcetera . . . the myth of nature; the myth of Robinson Crusoe who appears everywhere—doesn't he? The desert island, the Club Med, vacations, tans, fixing things—all that is summarized by Robinson Crusoe.

In the history and the literature of the twentieth century one sees a sort of progressive atomization (perhaps related to the discovery of the atomic structure itself). Novels have moved from the interior monologue to those displaying a totally fragmented psyche. Don't you think that myth attempts to put man back into a sort of unified framework and by means of myth man is able to unify his experiences? That view is, however, from a critical perspective.

That seems a very, very good idea to me, because there are unifying myths. In general, however, myths are rather destructive. I mean, myth is almost always the exaltation of an antisocial hero—on the order of Don Juan. Don Juan is antisocial; Tristan is antisocial. Nonetheless, you can still have unifying myths: in France, that of Joan of Arc. So, the national myth, the national hero, which are unifying, those belong to another category. As for me, I am struck by the antisocial function of myth. I have the impression that everything in society tends toward order and that myth is a means for the individual to escape from an order that suffocates him, by means of a hero who is revolting against the established order. For example, the wife who cheats on her husband can think of Isolde. *Tristan and Isolde* is a story of a woman who deceives her husband, isn't it?

That is the question that Denis de Rougemont deals with in Love and the Occident.

Yes, exactly. So, the woman feels exalted because she experiences passion [of mythic proportions]. She can do nothing against it. She is consumed by passion for someone besides her husband; she is even exalted because of it. As for her husband, he doesn't understand—he is King Mark [Isolde's cuckolded husband].

He is overwhelmed by the events.

Exactly.

How do you see the literary hero of the twentieth century?

He doesn't really interest me enormously. I'm interested in the mythological hero. There is a big difference. The mythological hero exceeds the work and is more famous than his author. Don Juan, for example, is more famous than Tirso da Molina; Robinson Crusoe is more famous than Daniel Defoe, whereas the literary hero remains a prisoner of the work. That is the case of Balzac's Vautrin [in *Le Pere Goriot*] or Proust's Charlus [in *Remembrance of Things Past*]. The hero must not dominate the literary work, but he must have an organic place; in the last analysis, I conceive of the novel as a hero. My novel develops, it resembles a tree, and I am nothing but the gardener; I water it; I take care of it; I hope that it will grow—and it grows a little bit outside of me. For example, the three Magi who had been sleeping for years in my drawer suddenly sprang to life. I can explain it a little, but in the end, it is still bizarre. I'm explaining it after the fact—you know?

Was your conception of myth influenced by the structuralism of Levi-Strauss?

Yes, I was a student of Levi-Strauss's.

At the College de France?

No, at the Museum of Man. I was at the Museum of Man during the years 1950-1952 and I had Levi-Strauss as a professor.

Did you study the works of the great ethnologists, for example, Boas, Malinowski, and Durkheim?

As for Malinowski, yes. When I was at the Museum of Man, Levi-Strauss told me, "Listen, since you read German, there is a gentleman whose name is Guisinde, a German who has devoted his whole life to a tribe of Fuegians, the Selknams. You are going to study that and then give an oral report about it." Consequently, I became the "Selknam man." Malinowski is a marvel. The Trobriand Islands—an archipelago—are fabulous. The Trobrianders are extraordinary. They do not make the connection between intercourse and the birth of a child—that's wonderful. Nine months separate the two events—there is no relationship between them. It is the rain that makes the woman fertile. The gentleman who sleeps with her is not the father, but the uncle—he's a lover and a friend. It is a magnificent social structure, much more attractive than ours. It is the mother's brother who lives with the children, who brings them up . . . etcetera.

You use fairy tales as well as myths in your works. What is the difference between the fairy tale and the myth?

The fairy tale—you will see in *Le Vol du Vampire*—I have a chapter on fairy tales—for me, they are broken and diminished myths—little myths. Fairy tales have an effect on us because we do not recognize the myth, but it is there. . . . For example, Charles Perrault's *Bluebeard* is full of unlikely events, and we accept these events because underneath there is a great myth, but we don't recognize

it. Bluebeard leaves, saying to his wife, "I'm leaving on a trip, here are the keys to the house. You can use all the keys except the one that opens this chamber. If you open it, you will die." It is a crazy way to act. He is courting disaster, but he does it anyway, and we accept it. Why do we accept it? Because we recognize, without realizing it—it is a matter of remembering—Yaweh's saying to Adam and Eve, "You can eat of all the fruits of Paradise except that one, and if you eat from it, you will die." And Yaweh goes away. It is that memory that is at work—that explains why we accept Bluebeard's pronouncement. Naturally, the wife opens the chamber door and drops the key on the ground. The key is stained and she cannot get the stain out. In that respect too, the myth of the indelible spot is very much established, very profound—the anguish of the small stain and then besmirched honor, and then virginity. . . . There is a whole mythology of the indelible spot which makes us accept this story but which doesn't hold up apart from it. For me, that is what a story is, but not necessarily a fairy tale.

Which of your novels do you prefer, and why?

I prefer **Gemini**. Simply because it is the most my novel . . . it is the one that (but these are purely personal considerations) is based on nothing. **Vendredi** is based upon Daniel Defoe's *Robinson Crusoe*; **The Four Wise Men** is based upon the Scriptures; **The Ogre,** although it is less obvious, is based upon Nazism; there is the war, etcetera. . . . These are ways of treating, of retreating those things, whereas with **Gemini** there is nothing. It is a thick book based upon nothing. It is I.

A personal invention?

Yes, that's right—and then, it is also the one that is the most ambitious.

How would you describe your literary style?

I was watching a television show the other day—a literary show, *Apostrophes* with Bernard Pivot. Alain Robbe-Grillet, Michel Déon, and Robert Kanters were on. There were two novelists with opposing points of view: Robbe-Grillet and Michel Déon, and two literary critics: Kanters and Poirot-Delpech. They were arguing about how one should write, etcetera. If I had been there and somebody had asked me: "And you, where do you stand in all of this?" I would have said, "Me, I'm not part of all that, I don't understand anything about everything you are saying because I"—what I am going to say is horrible—I wouldn't have told them, but I'll tell you—"I have something to *say!*" For example, in **The Four Wise Men,** I have Christianity, all of Christianity to discuss, you know? So, I am not going to ask myself questions about rhetoric. I have a huge subject matter, a tremendous amount of work to do, and I choose the literary form that is the easiest, the most obvious for me, and the closest to the Scriptures since I have a model. I would have told them, "You have questions that you ask yourselves about construction, all the problems of the *nouveau roman*." As for me, in the last analysis, I am not really literary. I don't have much of a literary bent, I think.

If you were a critic, what would be the aspect of your work that would fascinate you the most?

First, I want to say that there are things that I would criticize. For example, in **The Ogre,** I am sorry that there is only one character who dominates the whole. In my opinion, that isn't a novel. In a novel, there have to be several characters—all of them important and all different from the author. But there is only one of him. Then, there is much too much philosophy.

In **The Ogre***?*

Not in **The Ogre,** but in **Vendredi.** It crops up everywhere.

If you'll permit me to say so, I think that **Vendredi** *is a great success in the line of Flaubert's* Bouvard and Pécuchet. **Vendredi** *is a totally abstract work, but you have succeeded in putting enormous charm, lyricism, and a certain exotic spirit into it.*

Thank you. Something that I prefer, perhaps over **Gemini,** is **Pierrot ou les secrets de la nuit,** because there, really, I succeeded in infusing the story with the maximum amount of philosophy, ontology, Bachelard, matter, color, solidity, smell, biological mechanisms, and nonetheless, it remains a story for children.

Yes, it is a lovely story; that is irrefutable. Now that you have published several very successful books, do you still see your work as an author the same way?

Let's say that formerly I had material concerns which I no longer have, and I also had worries about a public that I don't have anymore. So, now I can really say what I want to—no matter to whom, even to the Pope or to the President of the Republic; they would hesitate to throw me out the door!

Finally, the next-to-last question: in which philosophical current would you place yourself?

In what philosophical current would I place myself? But I abandoned philosophy twenty-five years ago! I no longer have a philosophical leaning.

The last question: Sartre, in his autobiography, The Words, *says that for him language is a kind of absolute. Do you agree?*

He is right. A novel is a thing that is produced with words, and words have a value in themselves. Absolute means cut off from the rest, doesn't it? And it is a verbal construction.

I would say that for Sartre it is not absolutely true, but that language acquires a transcendent aspect.

You are right. It is much truer of other writers; it is actually less true of Sartre.

John Updike (essay date 10 July 1989)

SOURCE: "Michel Tournier," in *The New Yorker,* Vol. LXV, No. 21, July 10, 1989, pp. 92-6.

[*Updike is an esteemed American novelist, short story writer, essayist, and critic whose best-known works include* Rabbit, Run *(1960),* Picked-up Pieces *(1975), and* Roger's Version *(1986). In the following essay, he presents an overview of Tournier's life and career and discusses* The Wind Spirit, Gilles & Jeanne, *and* The Golden Droplet.]

At around the time, in the sixties, when the intellectual innovations of Roland Barthes and Claude Lévi-Strauss and Fernand Braudel began to achieve international influence, French fiction ceased to export well. Alain Robbe-Grillet and his *nouveau roman* suddenly seemed just another idea, and a superficial one at that, producing novels as depthless as movies but on a much smaller screen; simultaneously, it began to appear that Francoise Sagan was not quite another Colette. Though the French literary industry has kept humming away, pining prizes on itself and generating fodder for the wildly popular book chat show "Apostrophes," the reverberations carry but feebly across the Atlantic. Perhaps, having so heavily imported the ideas of Braudel and Michel Foucault and Jacques Derrida, we have no spare change for the light goods of fiction. It is symptomatic of a depressed market, in any case, that Michel Tournier, arguably France's foremost living novelist ("France has produced no novelist of real importance in twenty years, except Michel Tournier," quoth Raymond Sokolov in the *Wall Street Journal*), has come to be published so marginally here. The English version of his autobiography, **The Wind Spirit,** has been brought out by Boston's little Unitarian publishing house, Beacon Press (translated from the French by Arthur Goldhammer), and Grove Press has performed a very skittish dance with Alan Sheridan's English translation of a 1983 novella, **Gilles & Jeanne,** which appeared in England in 1987: Grove sent bound galleys to prospective American reviewers, then cancelled publication, on the ground that the translation was riddled with errors, and now announces that a revised text will be issued in 1990. *Quelle tournure!*

The Wind Spirit, prettily printed, and jacketed with a nineteenth-century German painting of a little shepherd lying on a dune stargazing, would be a good book for the stranger to Tournier to start with. In six lively, digressive, aphoristic chapters, the author presents his life mostly in terms of his opinions and inspirations; only in the first chapter, which sketches his origins and childhood, do biographical facts dominate. This chapter is titled "Born Under a Lucky Star," Mr. Goldhammer's rendition of "L'Enfant Coiffé"; he explains that *coiffé* means to be born with a caul, a piece of luck equivalent to being born with a silver spoon in one's mouth, and that the word ties into the epigraph, by Saint-John Perse, which runs, "When you stop grooming me / I'll stop hating you." Throughout, the translator has added explanatory footnotes to the footnotes provided by Tournier, intensifying the somewhat stern pedagogic atmosphere of **The Wind Spirit**. It appeared in France in 1977, when Tournier was fifty-three years old. The curious but widespread autobiographical impulse in men still enjoying middle age possibly stems from a desire to set the record straight before senility muddles it, and a hope of lightening the ballast for the homeward leg of life's voyage.

Tournier was born in 1924 in Paris, in the comfortable upper reaches of the bourgeoisie. His father was "the upper reaches of the bourgeoisie. His father was "the founder and director of something called the BIEM," the Bureau International des Éditions Musico-Mécaniques, which "orchestrated the complexities of rights and contracts pertaining to recorded music sold outside the rightholder's country of origin." The business was lucrative and complex, involving branches in many countries and feeding with many spare records a small boy's phonograph. Well-off, immersed in music, and further blessed with "an old-fashioned apothecary" for a grandfather, in the friendly village of Bligny-sur-Ouche, the little boy gathered a surprisingly grim impression of life:

> Stripped from his mother's womb like a fox cub from its lair, the child finds tenuous and temporary shelter in his mother's arms, nourished by capricious and parsimonious breasts. Subsequently he must abandon this refuge as well, after which he will be allowed only a few minutes a day in that last haven, his mother's bed, a vast ship, white and shadowy, in which for the briefest of intervals his body again clings to the body from which it sprang. Then comes the final expulsion. Grown "too big," the child can no longer "decently" lie in its parents' bed. Thereupon begins a long trek across a vast and terrifying desert.

At the age of four, Michel was "an extremely nervous child, subject to convulsions, hypersensitive, and perpetually ill." One morning, two white-coated strangers burst into his room and pulled out his tonsils, a bloody deed he has never forgiven: "During the last war prepubescent girls were raped by soldiers. I maintain that they were less traumatized than I was by having my throat slit at the age of four." The doctor became "the only man in the world whom I have ever hated without reservation, because he did me incalculable harm, having branded my heart at the most tender age with an incurable distrust of my fellow human beings, even those nearest and dearest to me." By the age of six, Michel had become "a child with an enormous head upon a sparrowlike body, and I neither slept nor ate." Nor was his physical frailty made up in mental brilliance: "I was an execrable student, and rarely did I finish a school year in the same institution in which I began . . . I read little and late." And yet at some point in his resisted education he took a shine to the rarefied "Monadology" of Leibniz and to Anselm's ontological proof of God's existence: "From earliest childhood I had a yen for the constructs of the mind, for subtle proofs, for a rare and technical vocabulary."

The other unusual yen in Tournier's developing mind was his *Germanistik,* a fascination with German culture inherited from both parents: "My father and mother met at the Sorbonne when he was studying for a doctorate in German and she for a master's." His father's qualifying exam had been scheduled for August, 1914, and he went to war against the Germans instead, incurring serious facial wounds. But Tournier's mother—whose uncle, a priest, taught German—"kept faith with her family tradition, and we grew up with one foot in Germany." As a child, Tournier went on Black Forest vacations with his family. As an adolescent, he improved his German while living with twenty-two German soldiers in his parents' occupied

house in Saint-Germain—"I will never forget the smell of the Wehrmacht, a compound of tobacco and boot polish. For me this was the fragrance of happiness." As a young postgraduate student, he studied for four years (1946-50) at the University of Tübingen, in the French Occupied Zone of what is now West Germany. At the age of twenty, he translated Erich Maria Remarque's novel *All Quiet on the Western Front,* and did not scruple to improve passages of it. Remarque, meeting him, said, "This is the first time that I have been able to converse in my own language with any of my translators. The others . . . spoke German as though it were a dead language, like Latin or Greek." Tournier's enthusiasm for things German is, of course, the animating passion behind his best-known novel, *The Ogre* (1970), which tells the tale of a French automobile mechanic who finds fulfillment and doom as a German prisoner of war in East Prussia. In his own persona Tournier can seem an alarmingly fervid Germanophile:

> Dream a little: had there been no Nazi madness, no war and no defeat, Germany and its outposts in Vienna, Zurich, and Prague would have formed an economic and cultural unit comparable in power and influence to France in the seventeenth or England in the nineteenth century. With the barbarians of the East and West held at bay, the world would have continued to be European, and it would have been German. . . . Because the Americans had won the war, it was their language that one had to speak to become a hotel porter or an airline pilot. But we were not really cheated, for the twentieth century was still built upon a German foundation, or at any rate upon works written in the German language. . . . There are few places where one can scratch the earth without coming upon the soil of old Germany. . . . "Old Germany, mother of us all!"

One could almost resent being called a barbarian while the perpetrators of Buchenwald are so lovingly extolled.

Tournier's chapter on *The Ogre* is the second and longest, and in the four remaining chapters he discusses his early professional years as translator and radio broadcaster; his growing determination to write apparently naturalistic stories that "would secretly be set in motion by ontology and logic"; his belief that humor and celebration are essential to literature; his first published novel, *Friday* (1967), "into which I hoped to pour the essence of what I had learned while employed at the Musée de l'Homme, especially under the tutelage of Claude Lévi-Strauss"; his novel *Les Météores* (1975; translated into English as *Gemini*), a tangled tale "inspired by a fascination with the super-flesh of twins" and crowned by the formula "twinship untwinned = ubiquity"; and the topic of wisdom itself. These connected autobiographical essays are brilliant and possibly wise, though a certain dark and teasingly perverse streak beclouds the even illumination we expect from wisdom. We cannot ignore the saturnine personality projecting itself in such epithets as "that whining female monster, the crowd," such epigrams as "ontology when tossed into the crucible of fiction undergoes a partial metamorphosis into scatology," and such assertions as the one that circumcision keratinizes the glans and makes fellatio "so laborious that it loses all its charm."

Like Pangloss and Candide, Tournier ends up cultivating his garden, which he describes in grand terms:

> Every summer morning, as I toast my bread and steep my tea by an open window through which I can smell the grass and hear the wind in the linden branches, I suddenly become aware that time has been compressed, that space has shrunk to those few square feet enclosed by a stone wall, and that a single living thing—my garden—flourishes in the exorbitant immobility of the absolute. . . . The present lingers on eternally in a divine improvidence and amnesia.

There is no chasing all the hares that Tournier's energetic mind starts during the survey of his personal garden. His theories have a glittering laciness alongside which any actual creative production must look coarsely woven. He works slowly, he tells us, devoting four or more years to a book, and lets the work in progress send him upon mysterious errands of research. "The writer who labors on a book for four years becomes that book and assimilates all its alien elements, which add up to a structure far more impressive, vast, complex, and learned than their author. . . . The work produces itself and the author is only its byproduct." The author and his work exist within a matrix of large and ancient forces: "Man is nothing but a mythical animal. He becomes man—he acquires a human being's sexuality and heart and imagination—only by virtue of the murmur of stories and kaleidoscope of images that surround him in the cradle and accompany him all the way to the grave. . . . That being the case, it becomes easy to describe the social—one might even say biological—function of the creative artist. The artist's ambition is to add to or at any rate modify the 'murmur' of myth that surrounds the child, the pool of images in which his contemporaries move—in short, the oxygen of the soul."

After formulations so spacious and humane, the actual work risks seeming minor. A glance at Tournier's recent fiction does suggest the limits of determined mythicization, of ontology and logic as prime aesthetic movers. *Gilles & Jeanne* sets itself to construct a connection between the two apparently diverse aspects of Gilles de Rais's fame: as the devoted comrade-in-arms and royally appointed protector of the saintly Joan of Arc, and as the Black Mass orgiast and sodomizing slaughterer of children whom legend has transmuted into Bluebeard, slaughterer of wives. A premise of structuralist thought is that opposites (black-white, good-bad, up-down) share the identity of the conceptual structure that holds them and hence are basically aspects of the same thing. It is, for the adroit and learned Tournier, a matter of little more than a hundred pages to demonstrate that Gilles, possessed by the vision of simple goodness embodied in Joan and revolted by her body's horrible end at the stake in Rouen, logically seeks her and the absolute in satanism. As Joan, burning at the stake for witchcraft, cries out *"Jesus! Jesus! Jesus!,"* so Gilles, burning for sorcery nine years later, calls out, "Jeanne! Jeanne! Jeanne!"

This stylized equation—Jeanne / Jesus = Gilles / Jeanne—forms the bare bones of the novel. What is its meat? The era and its cosmology offer many convenient ambiguities: Joan's voices might be angels or devils, Satan is "the image of God," a town square contains "a statue that was in such a sorry state that it would have been difficult to tell whether it was a Virgin or a Venus," alchemical experiments are conducted on "the fundamental ambiguity of fire, which is both life and death, purity and passion, sanctity and damnation." The book's alchemist, the Tuscan abbé Francesco Prelati (a historical figure, de Rais's assistant in his diabolical dabblings), construes his master's psychology in terms of "inversions." Prelati testifies to the court that a "malign inversion" occurred when Joan was captured and condemned, and then a satanist antidote: "To drive the Sire de Rais to the blackest edge of wickedness, then, by the igneous operation, to subject him to a benign inversion, like the one that transmutes ignoble lead into gold. He was becoming a saint of life!" Prelati's fancy thinking and talking rather sap Gilles and Jeanne's tale of human interest. The little novel becomes, atrocious as the facts behind it are, bloodless, with nothing in its arch paradoxes as visceral and memorable as Lucifer's blunt pentameters in *Paradise Lost*:

> So farewell hope, and with hope farewell
>   fear,
> Farewell remorse: all good to me is lost;
> Evil be thou my Good.

Along with Milton's epic of elected sin, the English language holds a play, Shaw's *Saint Joan,* that juggles ideas at the fifteenth-century crossroads with an impudent facility that makes Tournier seem relatively hard breathing. Shaw's drama includes, amid its abundance of historical sidelights, a small part for Gilles de Rais, whom he calls Bluebeard and decorates to suit the name. He characterizes him thus: *"Gilles de Rais, a young man of 25, very smart and self-possessed, and sporting the extravagance of a little curled beard dyed blue at a clean-shaven court, comes in. He is determined to make himself agreeable, but lacks natural joyousness, and is not really pleasant."* The mild suggestion, regarding this legendary sadist, that he lacked "natural joyousness" brings us closer to the mass murderer than Tournier's schematic religious pathology. But as a cultural critic the French author can be dazzling. Here, for instance, is what perspective in drawing and painting meant to a French priest travelling for the first time in Italy:

> It seemed to him that the flat, edifying, worthy image of his pious childhood was suddenly exploding under the impetus of some magic force, was being undermined, distorted, thrown beyond its own limits, as if possessed by some evil spirit. When he stood in front of certain frescoes or pored over certain engravings, he thought he could see opening up in front of his eyes a vertiginous depth that was sucking him in, an imaginary abyss into which he felt a terrifying temptation to dive, headfirst.

Our modern abyss, as experienced by another unfortified sensibility, is the subject of Tournier's *The Golden Droplet* (translated from the French by Barbara Wright). Published in France two years later than *Gilles & Jeanne,* it tells of Idris, a fifteen-year-old Berber dwelling in the Algerian oasis of Tabelbala, who is one day suddenly photographed by a scantily dressed blonde who leaps out of a desert-cruising Land Rover. In pursuit of the photograph, Idris travels to Paris. If psychological structuralism shaped *Gilles & Jeanne,* semiology is the name of the game here. On all sides Idris is confronted by images and signs—which are not, it develops, the same thing. Images—"the opium of the Occident"—bind us to the world, and signs release us from it:

> These Moslem adolescents, submerged in the big occidental city, were subjected to all the assaults of the effigy, the idol, and the figure. Three words to designate the same servitude. The effigy is a door bolt, the idol a prison, the figure a lock. Only one key can remove these chains: the sign. . . . The sign is spirit, the image is matter. Calligraphy is the algebra of the soul craved by the most spiritualized organ of the body, its right hand. It is the celebration of the invisible by the visible. The arabesque manifests the presence of the desert in the mosque. Through the arabesque, the infinite is deployed in the finite. For the desert is pure space, freed from the vicissitudes of time. It is God without man.

Calligraphy lessons form the happy ending of *The Golden Droplet:* the child of the desert, lost in the evil land of images, of cinema and advertising and hair dyed blond, reclaims his semiotic heritage of pure emptiness. A complicated fable of the "Blond Queen," whereby a bewitching human portrait is reduced to a salutary pattern of calligraphed quotations, cinches the moral, which would seem to be that words are better than things.

The Golden Droplet has a denser texture than *Gilles & Jeanne:* the oasis, the trip north through progressively larger and more Westernized cities to Oran, the boat trip to Marseilles, the African quarter of Marseilles, and then the Maghrebi worker environment in Paris are all conscientiously presented. So conscientiously, indeed, that each chapter feels like a discrete essay. In a postscript the author acknowledges his many sources, from Dominique Champault's study *Tabelbala*—"a model of what the ethnological monograph should be"—to Hassan Massoudy, the author of *Calligraphie Arabe Vivante* and a "master calligrapher. .. who enabled me to approach a traditional art whose beauty is indistinguishable from truth and wisdom." It is edifying and pleasing, of course, to be guided by Tournier from one oasis of research to the next, and to view, on our tour, sights that range from a traditional Berber wedding, complete with "a troupe of dancers and musicians from the High Atlas Mountains," to the grisly, exotic insides of a Parisian sex shop, peepshow, pinball palace, mannequin factory, and abattoir. As so often on an educational tour, though, the sights pile up but do not accumulate into an adventure. Idris, our Berber Candide, remains innocent and blank throughout—himself a mere sign, with a significance special to France, where a long involvement with North Africa and a large immigrant population of North Africans form a hot, recurrent issue. Like William Styron's *Confessions of Nat Turner,* Tournier's book is a bold attempt to empathize with an under-

class, but it is carried out (unlike Styron's) behind an impervious screen of intellectual play.

There are, in the stretches of description and sociology, few events in the sense of happenings that invite suspense and pose an outcome that can grieve or gratify us—few moments when the narrative acquires a mind of its own. In one of them, Idris's nomad friend Ibrahim abruptly falls into an old well, which collapses and buries him alive: this sudden nonacademic development startles us, and breaks Idris's last emotional link with his desert life. In another, Idris, having fallen under the spell of the filmmaking magus Achille Mage, is stuck with a camel used in a television commercial for a beverage called Palm Grove, and wanders Paris with the signal creature. In the fashionable districts, people pretend not to see him; only the lower classes allow themselves to express curiosity—"Once again, as the tissue of social relationships became less compact, the camel had become visible." The animal finally, to the reader's considerable relief, finds a haven in the zoo, a collection of living emblems, where it is greeted by a female of its species ("Their morose, disdainful heads met very high up in the sky, and their big, pendulous lips touched") and is outfitted for children's rides by "adolescents dressed as Turks." In general, however, even mild emotional involvement is forestalled by the bristle of forked signifiers, and Tournier's pageant of incidents seems not so much a novel as a cunningly wrought image of one—calligraphy aping portraiture aping appearances.

These books made out of other books—are they what the future holds? To "read up" on an area of geography or history and then be clever and cool about it—is this all the postmodern novelist can do? Italo Calvino managed to include something of himself in the intricate package, a self that in his last novel, *Mr. Palomar,* became poignant, almost pleading. But of Michel Tournier, or of Patrick Süskind, the author of the much admired *Perfume,* or of Julian Barnes, the concocter of such elegancies as *Flaubert's Parrot* and *Staring at the Sun,* we can guess a little but have, as it were, nothing. Joyce and Mann did their research also, but left a palpable weight of personal impulse if not confession in their constructions, whether as elaborate as *Finnegans Wake* or as limpid and light as *Royal Highness.* Their fictions have a presence and voice that are humbly human; their books give off the warmth of a proximate body. To be fair, Tournier did show warmth in such earlier novels as *Friday,* his anticolonialist gloss on the Robinson Crusoe story, and *The Ogre,* generally considered his masterpiece and hailed in these pages by L. E. Sissman, in 1972, as "quite simply, a great novel." *The Ogre* is a thick outpouring of arcane facts and involved feelings, a complex but sensual fable of loneliness and desire and perception which seems, as Roland Barthes said of classic literature, "replete"—a book saturated in its own completely fulfilled tendencies. Like *Gilles & Jeanne,* it is concerned with inversion and pedophilia; like *The Golden Droplet,* it equates purity with nothingness and points out that "the human soul is made of paper." Unlike both these flimsy fictions, it compels interest and arouses dread and pity. But how much of its engaging warmth, I wonder, derives from the entwinement of its intricate parable (a gloss of Goethe's poem "The Erl-

King") with its fascinating facts about the Second World War? This war, at least for Europeans and North Americans, has become the century's central myth, a vast imaging of a primal time when good and evil contended for the planet, a tale of Troy whose angles are infinite and whose central figures never fail to amaze us with their size, their theatricality, their sweep. Göring's sybaritic hunting lodge in *The Ogre,* and the four hundred child-warriors martyred to Hitler's fanaticism, and the East Prussian mud that the Ogre treads belong to an epic we never weary of hearing. Tournier's peculiarly intense mental inhabitation of both France and Germany enabled his matter, for once, to make an equal contest with his mind. The trouble with the French love of pure thought is that thought must operate upon *something*—the world as it impurely exists, an apparently ill-thought-out congeries of contradictory indications and arbitrary facts. The novelist must be thoughtless, to some degree, in submitting to the world's facts: he must be naïve enough, as it were, to let the facts flow through him and unreflectingly quicken recognition and emotion in his readers. And this the French find difficult to do.

Michael Sheringham   (essay date 11-17 August 1989)

SOURCE: "Story as Therapy," in *The Times Literary Supplement,* No. 4506, August 11-17, 1989, p. 879.

[*In the following review, Sheringham examines three works by Tournier*—The Wind Spirit, Le Tabor et le Sinaï, *and* Le Médianoche amoureux—*and two books about his work, Colin Davis's* Michel Tournier: Philosophy and Fiction *and Françoise Merllié's* Michel Tournier.]

Paul Klee talked of "taking a line for a walk": Michel Tournier does something similar with themes, playing brilliant variations on the idea of "carrying" ("la phorie") or of twinhood, and exploiting the revelatory energies of those oppositions—nomad and sedentary, image and sign, instruction and initiation—which he calls "clefs binaires". In *The Wind Spirit,* an intellectual autobiography originally published as *Le Vent paraclet* . . . , Tournier applies some of these keys to himself.

The account of his childhood is dominated by meditation on a quality it for the most part lacked, the sense of initiation which, since the Enlightenment, has been progressively banished from education, along with physical contact and any sense of ritual. Metaphysics, into which he was initiated by an inspiring *prof de philo,* opened up vistas he has ardently surveyed ever since; philosophical systems, those of Spinoza, Leibniz, Sartre, have long held more interest for him than the "comic-strip" efforts of most *littérateurs.* Tournier was slow to find his *métier* as a novelist, but when he did, after a spell in post-war Germany that fuelled his enthusiasm for its cultural heritage, his ambition was to blend the abstract harmonies of the metaphysical systems he so admired with the forward thrust and dynamism of the pre-modernist novel. The basis of this alliance would be myths, those fundamental stories amid whose murmurs we spend our lives. The novelist's task, Tournier decided, was to contribute to this mythological "bruissement", and much of *The Wind Spir-*

it is concerned with the ways he has set about it: rewriting *Robinson Crusoe* as a fable about identity; fusing the most abstruse details about the Third Reich with a welter of public and private myths in *Le Roi des Aulnes;* combining lore culled from psychology, meteorology, sexual pathology, and the socio-politics of waste-disposal in such a way as to make *Les Météores* a novel about fate and destiny, heredity and environment, knowledge and reality.

All this makes excellent reading and stands up well in an able translation, though British readers may be taken aback by some of the Americanisms, for example the description of Hitler as "the man with the bangs [for "la mèche"] and the little mustache," or the choice of "the SOB's" for Sartre's "les salauds". Like one of his own characters Tournier is flamboyantly opinionated, proudly eccentric and doughtily at odds with the orthodoxies of his society; what is more, this theorist of "le rire blanc", a metaphysical laughter he identifies in the noblest products of the human spirit, writes with an amusing verve which sometimes verges on facetiousness. But where the novels are ironically multi-layered, and refuse to privilege a single narrative voice, *The Wind Spirit* brashly lays down the law, piniing fictional incident to anecdotal antecedent, blurring the distinction between the thematic obsessions of the writer and the hobby-horses of the man in the street. Oddly, though, the overall effect is less reductive than one might expect. If Tournier's readers and critics cannot sidestep this authorized version, its whole tone and manner encourage one to question many of its more dogmatic assertions.

Accordingly, throughout his fresh and stimulating study of Tournier's novels [*Michel Tournier: Philosophy and Fiction,* 1989] Colin Davis argues that they are less reassuringly traditional than the author of *The Wind Spirit* tends to imply. Furthermore, it is from the tension between a traditional metaphysics and a generally unacknowledged sympathy for a post-Nietzschean acceptance of fragmentation, difference and the lack of absolute truths, that Tournier's fictions derive much of their energy. Each major novel features a protagonist who tries to impose coherence on his world, creating "self-legitimating spirals of interpretation which seek to exclude the human possibility of doubt". In *Le Roi des Aulnes* Tiffauges's seductively cranky delusions thrive on the hermeneutic zeal with which he greets each day's fresh crop of signs. By imposing a grid on what he sees, Tournier's mild-mannered ogre, gluttonous for meaning, blinds himself to what is really happening. His complicity with the terrible violence of the Nazi regime, which surprises and engulfs him at the end, stems from his unshakeable belief in an absolute order revealed by symbols. Davis justly sees the novel as a cautionary allegory of interpretation. This does tend, however, to reduce its scale and to play down the text's moral ambiguity and its post-modern (intertextual scrambling of fact and fiction) as against its modernist aspects.

In an amusing passage in *The Wind Spirit* Tournier wryly alludes to "the danger of letting loose flamboyant homosexual geniuses in novels". Like Vautrin and Charlus, Alexandre in *Les Météores* slipped the author's leash and took on an unanticipated importance. Appropriately,

Davis devotes considerable attention to this "gay deconstructor" whose caustic strictures on heterosexuality, gender roles, and indeed any fixity in the sphere of identity, constitute a disruptive force in the novel, albeit one which is repeatedly subject to containment, as more traditional ideas, regarding women for instance, reassert themselves.

Since *Les Météores* (1975) Tournier has largely abandoned the full-scale novel for other forms. In treating this period thematically, concentrating on Tournier's attitudes to meaning, language and art, Davis somewhat exaggerates the novelist's concern for purely philosophical questions. The chapter on "Art and Truth" works best, no doubt because the metaphysics of vision, and the visual arts generally, have come to play a commanding role in Tournier's fiction. These concerns dominated his last novel, *La Goutte d'or,* where the pure sign, associated with Islamic calligraphy, was set against the imaginary plentitude with which the Christian, and now the commercialized, West has invested its images. And they are also prominent in *Le Tabor et le Sinaï* (the Biblical mountains reproducing the same opposition), a collection of brief texts on contemporary artists, written mainly for exhibition catalogues, where we can see Tournier elaborating ideas he will use in his fiction.

In a very different vein from Davis, Françoise Merlié's *Michel Tournier* provides an up-to-date, enthusiastic, not to say hagiographic, presentation of the novelist's accomplishments. A lengthy essay, which lays the pop psychoanalysis on a bit thick but ranges fluently across the canon, is followed by copious bibliographical and biographical supplements, and by a concluding essay on Tournier's conception of "le métier d'écrivain". It is interesting to learn that President Mitterrand now pays Tournier an annual visit, usually in August.

Tournier's latest fictional work, *Le Médianoche amoureux,* is a collection of "contes et nouvelles". The distinction is important. A few years ago, in an essay on Perrault's "Barbe-bleu", Tournier situated the *conte* half-way between the opaque realism of the short story, which resists the liberating quality of philosophical speculation, and the crystalline transparency of the *fable,* which allows ideas a ready, and thus altogether hollow, triumph. In the best stories of *Le Coq de bruyère* (1978), an earlier collection, Tournier scored some notable successes in this mode. By comparison the new book, while containing much to admire, succeeds less well. One explanation is perhaps an excess of self-consciousness on the part of one whose self-image as a writer has come to be that of a *conteur*. In *Le Médianoche amoureux* the ethos of the *conte* actually becomes a protagonist in a narrative which frames the very diverse stories in the book.

Yves and Nadège are an unhappy couple: they don't talk any more. Having made up their minds to separate they lay on a great feast at which they plan to announce the sad news to their friends. But in the course of this "médianoche" each of the friends, as in the Decameron, tells a story, and it is these stories which make up the book. Some are *nouvelles* and these, we are told, aggravate the couple's discord. But some are *contes* and these prove so therapeutic that they are reunited.

It is easier to credit the divisive quality of the former than the epithalamic properties of the latter. States of affective isolation and the sometimes bizarre and inventive ways in which the solitary individual seeks to break out of them, have long been a dominant theme of Tournier's and *The Wind Spirit* had some profound reflections on the curse of solitude. The *nouvelles* in *Le Médianoche* are monopolized by the voices of first-person narrators whose own solitude is often reflected in the stories they tell. One story features a consmopolitan business man who revisits his childhood village on impulse and, after catching up with the (usually dreadful) news of his contemporaries from an old school buddy, botches an attempt to buy a house in the neighbourhood. Two stories involve people who devote their entire lives to complicated and rather pathetic acts of vengeance. Another is about a teacher whose own memory of childhood trauma helps her to understand children's needs, but who loses this gift when circumstances force her to undergo psychotherapy: restored to psychic "health" she becomes "une femme sans ombre".

If the symbolic realm is in bad shape in the *nouvelles,* the *contes* amply make up the deficit; here vengeance is sumptuous, commemoration—a central theme of the book—is enriching, colours and shadows abound. What is more, where the *nouvelles,* in spite of the fulsome tones Tournier lends most of his narrators, have the authentic thinness of the *fait divers,* the *contes* are enhanced by the stereophonic effects provided by intertextuality. "Angus" rewrites an episode from Hugo's *La Légende des siècles;* "Pierrot ou les secrets de la nuit" (originally published as a children's book) explores the narrative potential (such as it is) of the words to "Au clair de la lune"; "Les deux banquets ou la commémoration", like the two very fine *contes* interpolated in *La Goutte d'or,* is pure Arabian Nights.

Glad as one is to see Nadège and Yves reunited, it is hard not to have some reservations about these rather whimsical performances. In the days of *The Wind Spirit* Tournier used to extol the virtues of myths: "stories everyone knows". The message now, it seems, is that stories *tout court* can restore us to the amniotic environment from which we are severed by our solitary lives. This is certainly worth thinking about, but it would be worrying to feel that henceforth the main concern of this often controversial writer is to do us good. Perhaps it is a sign of decadence to crave provocation, but Tournier has in the past ensured that we expect nothing less of him.

Susan Petit   (essay date 1990)

SOURCE: "Psychological, Sensual, and Religious Initiation in Tournier's *Pierrot ou les secrets de la nuit,*" in *Children's Literature,* Vol. 18, 1990, pp. 87-100.

[*In the following essay, Petit surveys the themes and techniques used by Tournier in his literature for children.*]

Michel Tournier frequently writes for children, although he is best known for his adult works, which have received some of the most prestigious French literary prizes, including the *Grand Prix du Roman* of the French Academy in 1967 for *Vendredi ou les limbes du Pacifique (Friday)* and the *Prix Goncourt* in 1970 for *Le Roi des aulnes (The*

Ogre). The French public has accepted enthusiastically both his adult and his children's fiction: his novels always make the best-seller lists, and *Vendredi ou la vie sauvage (Friday and Robinson: Life on Speranza Island),* a short version of *Vendredi ou les limbes du Pacifique,* seems to have become a staple in French elementary schools. Although success has been slower to come in America, ever since Roger Shattuck called Tournier "the most exciting novelist now writing in French" ["Why Not the Best?" *The New York Review of Books,* April, 1983], American critics have begun to give Tournier's adult works the attention they deserve. However, his children's fiction is still largely neglected by American and French critics, mirroring the initial difficulty Tournier had publishing it in France, a problem he attributes to conservatism on the part of children's editors. Now, however, his juvenile works have sold so well that Gallimard publishes them in several formats, including tape cassettes on which Tournier himself reads the stories.

Despite the greater acclaim his adult fiction has received, Tournier's fiction for children is no sideline. The greatest literature, he contends, is that which both children and adults can enjoy; therefore, he refuses to divide his work into adult and juvenile fiction. When he is "tired, lazy, not visited by the Holy Spirit, [he writes] books which unfortunately only adults can read" [Sandra Joxe, "Michel Tournier: 'Je Suis un Monstre qui a réussi,'" *Autre Journal,* November, 1985], but when he is inspired, he writes books accessible to all. Given Tournier's desire to write such fiction, it is perhaps not surprising that he says he "would exchange all [his] other work" for a short tale he first published in 1979, *Pierrot ou les secrets de la nuit* (Pierrot, or The Secrets of the Night), which he says is "the best thing [he has] ever written" ["**Writing for Children Is No Child's Play,**" *UNESCO Courier,* June, 1982]. Although much of his juvenile fiction is based on his adult novels, he wrote this brief story in a very accessible form to begin with, and though it contains his essential moral and philosophical ideas, it can be understood even by very young children.

Tournier writes to promote his ideas, many of which are unconventional enough to have provoked a few critics into calling certain of his books subversive [Robert Poulet, "Michel Tournier, romancier hors série," *Ecrits de Paris,* September, 1975], obscene [Robert Kanters, "Creux et plein d'ordures," *Figaro Littéraire,* April 5, 1975], and even fascistic [Saul Friedländer, *Reflections of Nazism: An Essay on Kitsch and Death,* 1984]. His children's fiction, having more overt "commitment to particular values" than his adult works, has encountered less resistance, but Tournier has told me that conservative magazines regularly accuse him of "perverting" youth because he writes about children doing things society disapproves of. For example, in **"La Fugue du petit Poucet" ("Tom Thumb Runs Away")** a little boy drinks, smokes marijuana, and shares a bed with some little girls. Tournier added, "I never said that I recommended doing that. But I talk about it. And one doesn't have a right to do that in children's literature" [Petit adds in an endnote that "these and all other undocumented statements by Tournier come from an unpublished interview he gave me on July 11, 1987"]. More im-

portant than such criticism is the difficulty Tournier has had in finding a publisher outside of France for his children's fiction. *The Fetishist* (the translation of *Le Coq de bruyère*) includes six of Tournier's children's stories, and this journal published *Pierrot, or The Secrets of the Night.* But *Friday and Robinson* is the only one of Tournier's books for children published in English in a juvenile format, and it did not sell well in America, despite its great success in France. Tournier says his children's books have not found a market abroad partly because each country imposes its own type of conformity on children's literature (the United States insisting on a "Walt Disney conformity"), whereas publishers everywhere welcome nonconformist adult fiction.

Tournier's fiction for children is far from conformist. As he explained in *Le Vent paraclet* (*The Wind Spirit: An Autobiography*), when he gave up preparing for a career as a professional philosopher, he turned to literature as a substitute, wanting to write stories "set in motion by ontology and logic." Because Tournier is interested in ethics, his fiction shows how one should live; because he loves metaphysics, his fiction explores the ultimate nature of life. A major ethical concern for him is always sexuality, which he believes should include all sensual aspects of life—except perhaps genital sexuality itself, which usually leads to disaster in his fiction. He says that we must "escape from the sinister alternative of procreation-abortion" by "inventing new erotic paths, cerebral, no longer genital but genial" ["**Lewis Carroll au pays des petites Filles,**" *Point,* January, 1976]. This view explains his criticism of the Freudian theory that sexuality underlies physical attachment to the mother: Tournier believes the opposite, that love "prepares the way for sexuality" (*Wind*) and that something is deeply wrong with Western society because it is anti-sensual, "without smell, without taste, without physical contact" [Guitta Pessis Pasternak, "Tournier le sensuel," *Monde,* August, 1984]. As to the metaphysical, it is virtually fused to the physical in his thinking, for since his childhood he has found in both religion and metaphysics "concrete speculation inextricably intertwined with powerful and brilliant imagery" (*Wind*). The imagery of Christianity remains powerful for him, but he has come to believe that true Christianity must center on the Holy Spirit, representing divine inspiration, rather than Christ, whom Tournier associates with suffering and death.

In his juvenile as well as his adult fiction, Tournier develops unconventional ideas through traditional fictional forms. Whereas most modern children's fiction in France is realistic, Tournier's stories take their inspiration from fairy tales and myths, the form used by Charles Perrault in his *Contes de ma mère l'oie.* Even when Tournier modernizes, localizes, and rationalizes fairy-tale elements, he imitates Perrault. And like characters in fairy tales and myths—but unlike the protagonists of most children's literature—Tournier's main characters are not necessarily children, nor do they generally confront "realistic" problems of everyday modern life. Instead, his young protagonists often find themselves at the threshold of maturity, coping with archetypal problems. Tournier uses the fairy-tale form because he believes children should be initiated into adulthood through a "moral, emotional, indeed magical" education using techniques of myth that appeal to a child's "heart and sensibility" rather than through modern formal education, which he says aims merely at providing a child with information (**Wind**). Through his fiction for children, Tournier hopes to initiate them into his view of the world by awakening their sensibilities with concrete symbols.

To understand Tournier's approach one must know how myths and fairy tales work for children. According to Bruno Bettelheim, the heroes of myth help develop a child's superego, whereas the ordinary, unheroic people in fairy tales help children find full ego integration [Bettelheim, *The Uses of Enchantment: The Meaning and Importance of Fairy Tales,* 1976]. The characters in Tournier's children's fiction fulfill both functions, falling somewhere between the anonymous fairy-tale figures whom Bettelheim calls "people very much like us" and the "obviously superhuman" heroes of myth, but the characters in **Pierrot** are most like those in fairy tales in their quest for ego integration. Bettelheim insists that the message of a fairy tale will not be effective unless the child receives it unconsciously, and Tournier conceives the tale similarly; he believes that it should neither reflect everyday life in a realistic way nor provide too explicit a moral, comparing the tale to a "translucent medium . . . in which the reader sees figures appear which he can never entirely comprehend," a story with a meaning "which touches and enriches us but does not enlighten us" [**"Barbe-Bleue ou le secret du conte,"** in *Le vol du vampire*]. Despite these warnings that we should not try to understand everything, **Pierrot ou les secrets de la nuit** gives an excellent picture of what Tournier wants children to feel.

All the key elements of his children's fiction—strong plot, simple characters, whimsical humor, psychological complexity, and a religious theme—are present in this short tale. Like nearly all of Tournier's fiction, it has a literary ancestor: the first stanza of a song all French children know, "Au clair de la lune," in which Harlequin (Arlequin in French) asks to borrow Pierrot's pen in the middle of the night, saying that his candle is dead and his fire has gone out. Once Tournier realized that Harlequin and Pierrot both came from the Italian *commedia dell' arte,* he could develop the song into a narrative by adding a third character from the same source, Columbine, to create a "perfect adventure-story, with a powerful metaphysical foundation" (**"Writing"**).

Tournier's characteristic whimsy leavens a simple plot. Pierrot and Columbine, a baker and a laundress, have grown up together in the Breton town of Powdersnap (Pouldreuzic). Everyone expects that they will marry, but their occupations keep them apart, for Pierrot works at night to have bread ready in the morning, and Columbine does her washing in the day to bleach and dry it in the sun. These different actions reflect different attitudes to life, for Columbine fears the basement where Pierrot bakes bread and the night when he works. She loves the sun, but he loves the moon, and he can express his emotions only at night, when he walks about the sleeping town while his dough rises, becoming the "watchman of the village, the guardian of Columbine." In the course of the story, Col-

umbine runs away with Harlequin, an itinerant house-painter; then, when winter comes and their love fades, she returns to Pierrot. To celebrate her return, he shapes some of his brioche dough into Columbine's form, and at the story's end the reunited pair share the freshly baked loaf with Harlequin, who has returned to Powdersnap searching for Columbine. Near the end of the story, Harlequin sings "Au clair de la lune" at Pierrot's door.

Like a fairy tale or myth, the story lends itself to a number of symbolic readings. If it is read as a psychological parable designed to help children integrate their personalities, Pierrot and Columbine can be seen as two parts of a single personality, a common pattern in fairy tales about two siblings, such as Hansel and Gretel [see Bettelheim; and Julius E. Heuscher, *A Psychiatric Study of Myths and Fairy Tales: Their Origin, Meaning and Usefulness,* 2nd. ed., 1974]. Although Pierrot and Columbine are not brother and sister, the closeness of their relationship is shown by the fact that they grew up together and wear similar floating white clothes. They represent complementary desires in the same personality: Columbine the desire for summer and light, joy and rationality, and Pierrot the desire for winter and night, peace and emotionality. Only when Columbine begins to realize that night is not black but blue and that Pierrot's oven glows with golden fire can she accept the Pierrot side of herself—the hidden, secret, emotional part.

If Columbine and Pierrot complement each other, Harlequin and Pierrot are opposites. Harlequin represents pleasure based on appearance (as suggested by his multicolored outfit which fades with exposure to the sun); Pierrot stands for inner qualities hidden by an unprepossessing appearance. Harlequin's housepainting merely covers the outside; Pierrot's baked goods comfort the inner self. Harlequin is a nomad; Pierrot is sedentary. Harlequin acts; Pierrot waits. Harlequin loves to speak; Pierrot expresses himself best in writing, particularly in letters to Columbine which he does not dare send. At the end, Pierrot apparently wins: when Harlequin asks for Pierrot's pen and eats Pierrot's bread, his requests imply the baker's superiority to the painter and the writer's superiority to the speaker. But the fact that Columbine becomes for a while a female Harlequin, a **"Harlequinette,"** shows that the choice between the two is not absolute. By welcoming Harlequin into his bakery and gladly sharing the Columbine-loaf with him, Pierrot reconciles the seemingly irreconcilable. Life includes speech and writing, painting and baking, just as it includes Columbine's sunshine and Pierrot's moonlight. Similarly, although Columbine has returned to Pierrot, she does not reject Harlequin, for she invites him to share the bread shaped in her form.

Given this reconciliation, one can read all three characters, and not just Columbine and Pierrot, as representing complementary parts of the same personality. In a Freudian view the dutiful, serious Pierrot would represent the superego, the pleasure-loving Harlequin the id, and the changeable, immature, flighty Columbine the ego, perhaps an unstable adolescent one. Read this way, the story, like some fairy tales, shows a successful personality integration when Columbine, or the ego, symbolically reconciles the superego with the id by sharing the bread with both men.

More interesting, in a Jungian reading, the three figures again represent parts of an entire self, but Pierrot assumes the central role. Despite his association with night and the basement, he is called "the clear consciousness of the village" [in an endnote, Petit adds: "This is my translation of 'la conscience claire du village.' Margaret Higonnet translates *conscience* as the English 'conscience,' but I believe that the passage stresses Pierrot's awareness, or consciousness, rather than his moral values"] and may be taken as the conscious self, or ego, but one which is at first unaware of the other elements of the Jungian self, the shadow and the anima. In Jung's theory the shadow, a same-sex figure in the personal unconscious, carries the "dark aspects of the personality" and is represented here by Harlequin [see Carl G. Jung, *Aion: Researches into the Phenomenology of the Self,* 2nd. ed., translated by R.F.C. Hull, 1970]. Representing the dark side of the self by a character associated with sunlight is the sort of inversion Tournier delights in, but this inversion goes further: he makes us see that Harlequin's day is dreary, if not actually dark, in contrast to Pierrot's night, which "shimmers with thousands and thousands of silvery scales" and "sparkles with stars," while the moon looks down like a smiling face. Pierrot's night is luminous; Harlequin's day is merely bright. As one would expect of a Jungian shadow, Harlequin is an inverted Pierrot, the contrast being mainly to Pierrot's advantage. Pierrot is repelled by the chemical colors in Harlequin's housepaints, which he says "are toxic, smell bad, and peel," unlike the gold of his own glowing oven and of his fresh-baked bread and the "living blue" of his night. In his role as Jungian shadow, vigorous, demanding, nomadic Harlequin incorporates all the repressed sides of shy, gentle, sedentary Pierrot, who would like to chase Columbine but does not dare. Significantly, Jung describes the shadow as having emotional qualities and thus an "obsessive or, better, possessive quality"—a description that fits Harlequin exactly.

In this same Jungian reading, Columbine is the anima, a projection of the female side of the self which Jung calls both "the solace for all the bitterness of life" and "the great illusionist, the seductress." The anima, a "spontaneous product of the unconscious" of a man, is personified as a woman and represents the "feminine element" in a man (Jung). (Jung says a woman has not an anima but an animus, which has a different though related function.) Unlike Harlequin, who represents a rejected, unconscious side of the self of which Pierrot is the conscious ego, Columbine embodies feminine elements which Pierrot admires and desires, even as he unconsciously projects them onto the anima. Like any anima, Columbine includes elements of mother, child, and lover. She shows her maternal side in feeding the men from the "soft gold of her neck"— really, that of the brioche-figure that represents her. She acts like a child when she returns, exhausted, to Powdersnap and falls asleep in the bakery. And, obviously, she is both the lover of Harlequin and the beloved of Pierrot.

The self is unified when consciousness, or Pierrot, inspired by the anima, feeds the shadow. Pierrot first has to accept Columbine, whom he welcomes as soon as she reappears at his bakery; this act represents accepting the anima by dissolving the projection that is its common form and recognizing it as a part of the self. Accepting Harlequin is harder, for, as Jung says, "no one can become conscious of the shadow without considerable moral effort" because to do so means accepting the hidden side as "present and real"; nevertheless, accepting the shadow is essential to arriving at self-knowledge. Pierrot's suffering earlier in the story when he was abandoned has given him the strength to accept his shadow. So both Freudian and Jungian readings find psychological wholeness at the story's conclusion.

Related to the theme of psychological wholeness is the story's presentation of sexuality. Conventional sexuality helps motivate Columbine's flight with Harlequin, but Pierrot's sexuality is more mystical; he imagines the full moon as a woman revealing through the mist the roundness of "a cheek, a breast, or even better, a bottom." More symbolic is Pierrot's occupation as a baker; kneading bread is deeply sensual to Tournier, who says that in our antiseptic and deodorized society, of all shops "only the bakery still has smells" (Pasternak). In Tournier's first novel, Robinson Crusoe remembers that as a child he had been fascinated by a baker's boy kneading dough, *"that headless body of warm and sensuous matter submitting to the plunging caresses of a half-naked man"* (**Friday**; italics in original), and much the same equation applies to Pierrot, another *mitron* or baker's boy: his "hands would like to caress the sleeping girl, of course, but it is almost as much fun to pat and make a Columbine out of dough," and the finished bread has "her round cheeks, her pouterpigeon chest, and her cute little round bottom." This sort of sensual writing is unusual in children's fiction, but it could be a welcome "challenge [to] our conceptions of children's self-image" [Margaret R. Higonnert, "Marguerite Yourcenar and Michel Tournier: The Arts of the Heart," in *Triumphs of the Spirit in Children's Literature,* edited by Francelia Butter and Richard Robert, 1986].

Still, as sensual as the writing is, it is not sexual in the usual sense. The three characters' happiness in sharing the just-backed bread surpasses any sexual pleasure Columbine and Harlequin could have found together, and the trio of friends has replaced the exclusive couple. Tournier calls **Pierrot** a "hymn to physical contact" (Pasternak), but it is contact in which "genial" sexuality (represented by the baker's craft shown in the Columbine-loaf) has replaced "genital" sexuality (the relations between Harlequin and Columbine). Readers may not prefer "genial" over "genital" sexuality, and some may even charge Tournier with "sidestepping" the issue of sexuality by presenting it so indirectly, but this theme is a constant in his fiction [see Joseph H. McMahon, "Michel Tournier's Texts for children," in *Children's Literature* 13, 1985].

Bread, however, is not only sensual; as Tournier's Crusoe also knows, it is *"food of the soul, according to the Christian tradition"* (**Friday**; italics in original); that is how Tournier can consider **Pierrot** "a treatise on ontology" as well as on "morality, and a lesson in loving" (Pasternak). **Pierrot** owes its "powerful metaphysical foundation"

("**Writing**") to being a "reflection on the idea of dough, of substance. Bread has a color, a softness, a smell: that's ontology" (Joxe). Like C. S. Lewis's *The Lion, the Witch, and the Wardrobe,* this story is a religious parable; it reflects Tournier's heterodox version of Christianity and suggests his ideal church, which he has called "sumptuous, subtle, and erotic" (**Wind**). To make the parable work, he uses the same device that he finds in Perrault's "Bluebeard": an "archetypal mechanism," a symbolism which the reader may not see consciously (**"Barbe-Bleue"**). Perrault uses Adam's fall in "Bluebeard," and Tournier uses the Last Supper in **Pierrot**.

As Jean-Bernard Vray has pointed out [in "L'Habit d'Arlequin," *Sud,* 1980], the Eucharist is suggested when Columbine says, "come taste, eat this good Columbine! Eat me!" The bread representing her body corresponds to the Host, the bread of the Last Supper which is Jesus' body (Matthew 26:26). Catholics consider the Host "an antidote whereby we may be freed from daily faults and preserved from deadly sin" ("Holy Communion"). Similarly, it is through sharing the Columbine-brioche that the three characters symbolize their reconciliation and mutual forgiveness. In this reading, Columbine stands for one of the three persons of the Trinity. She is not Christ, as one might expect from the fact that the bread represents (or is) her body; other elements in the story make it clear that she must be the Holy Spirit. The most obvious indication is her name: "everyone called her Columbine the White Dove"—*colombe* meaning "dove," the usual symbol for the Holy Spirit (Matthew 3:16).

To understand why Tournier associates communion with the Holy Spirit and to discover what Pierrot and Harlequin represent in this reading, we need to know Tournier's view of the Trinity, which he presents in greatest detail in **Les Météores** (**Gemini**). In that novel, the central theological argument is made by a heterodox Catholic priest called Thomas Koussek, whose ideas, Tournier says, he originally intended to make central to the book (**Wind**). Koussek insists that to be saved "*Christ has to be superseded*" by the Holy Spirit (italics in original). He describes Christ as having "died on the cross, mutilated and despairing," and concludes that a Christ-centered religion is necessarily a "religion of suffering, of agony and death"; by contrast, the true church will center on the Holy Spirit. Although Koussek identifies the Holy Spirit, quite orthodoxy, with a divine wind—the *ruach* mentioned in the Old Testament—he draws the heretical conclusion that Christ is unnecessary for salvation, and he decries the doctrine of *Filioque,* which assert that the Holy Spirit proceeds from the Son as well as from the Father. For Koussek, Christ's incarnation, crucifixion, and resurrection serve primarily to provide a "certain depth of color, warmth, and grief" without which we would lack religious art, forbidden by the Mosaic law; they are otherwise not important.

Although one cannot always ascribe the views of a fictional character to the author, the working out of the plot of **Les Météores** justifies Koussek's theology, for Paul Surin, theoretically the book's main character, finds happiness through post-Christian revelation, whereas his uncle Al-exandre, a much more interesting character, suffers because the Catholic beliefs he rebels against dominate and constrain him. Besides the evidence in **Les Météores,** it is clear that Tournier agrees at least in part with what Koussek says, for he has often attacked Catholicism in much the same way. Not only did he name his spiritual autobiography for the *ruach* when he called it **Le Vent paraclet** (literally, *The Paraclete Wind*), but he too wants to banish the crucifix from the church (**Wind**). He has said that a "morbid taste for suffering" fuels the cult of the crucifix [**Des Clefs et des serrures**], that Christ on the cross was "deserted by the Word" to the benefit of the Holy Spirit and the apostles (**Clefs**), and that Catholicism in France was "a false Church serving only the institution of bourgeois society" (Hueston).

Keeping in mind Tournier's conception of Christ, we see that the brightly dressed Harlequin, like Alexandre in **Les Météores,** provides the story's "color, warmth, and grief"—the qualities that Koussek associates with Christ (**Gemini**). Like Koussek's version of Christ, who figuratively brings "color" to the world, Harlequin literally brings colors. Not only does he repaint Columbine's house in bright tones, but the story says whimsically that colored linens have invaded the white goods market only since Harlequin inspired Columbine to be not just a laundress (in French, a *blanchisseuse,* literally a woman who bleaches), but a dyer also: Harlequin's romance with Columbine has brightened the whole world. And in token of the idea that Christianity abrogated Mosaic law and thus permitted representational art, a theme Tournier has treated most fully in **Gaspard, Melchior et Balthazar** (**The Four Wise Men**), Harlequin paints a life-size portrait of Columbine on the facade of her building. If Harlequin, then, represents Christ, Pierrot represents God the Father. Not only does he give the town its daily bread, but his creating of a Columbine from dough imitates God's molding of Adam from clay, a theme Tournier has often returned to, most recently in his novel of the magi (**Four Wise Men**). Significantly, Pierrot and Columbine are present from the start, like God the Father and the Holy Spirit (in the form of the *ruach*) in the Old Testament; the absence of Harlequin implicitly denies *Filioque,* the doctrine that the Holy Spirit proceeds from the Son as well as from the Father.

The importance of the Holy Spirit to Tournier's theology explains why the bread represents Columbine, who stands for the Holy Spirit, rather than Harlequin, the Christ figure. Tournier had previously suggested communion with the Holy Spirit in **Le Roi des aulnes** when Abel Tiffauges, a *colombophile* or pigeon fancier, believed that he fed "his soul through intimate communion" with three of his pigeons when he ate them (**Ogre**). Although that act is perverse—Tiffauges eats his beloved pigeons to satisfy the ogre side of his personality—it does anticipate Tiffagues's ultimate salvation, which is sealed in part by his eating a Seder with a Jewish refugee from Auschwitz. Another Seder, the Last Supper, is crucial to **Gaspard, Melchior et Balthazar**. The main character, Taor, arrives late at the Last Supper, but he eats the crumbs and drinks the leftover wine, thus becoming the first communicant (**Four Wise Men**). Because angels carry him to heaven immediately thereafter, he is saved before (and therefore not by)

Christ's death on the cross; it must be the Holy Spirit that has saved him. Tournier's association of communion with the Holy Spirit underscores the centrality of the Holy Spirit in his theology, just as Columbine's role as savior explains why she is a laundress: to Tournier, it is the Holy Spirit that washes away sins.

Pierrot ou les Secrets de la nuit seems simple, but its psychological and religious subtexts give it the depth of the best fairy tales. Tournier could have summarized it much as he did his story **"Le Coq de bruyère"** (**"The Woodcock"**): "A gentleman and a lady . . . fight, and reconcile, which makes children yawn with boredom. Me too, in fact. But I take the subject as a challenge" [Jean-Jacques Brochier, "Dix-huit questions à Michel Tournier," *Magazine Littéraire,* June, 1978]. Rising to this challenge in *Pierrot,* Tournier has written a story of psychic unification and non-genital sexuality. Also, by bringing together sensual and religious meanings in the communion scene, Tournier anticipated a major theme of *Gaspard, Melchior et Balthazar,* the relationship between food and Christianity. *Pierrot* represents a major stage in the development of Tournier's fiction, not only reflecting ideas from *Vendredi ou les limbes du Pacifique, Le Roi des aulnes,* and *Les Météores* but preparing for the concerns of *Gaspard, Melchior et Balthazar*. It is also a major step in his stylistic development, for his subsequent fiction shows greater simplicity and limpidity and a reduction in authorial comment: Tournier increasingly lets plot, character, and symbol present his ideas. *La Goutte d'or (The Golden Droplet),* his most recent novel, is a major breakthrough for Tournier, for it is a long book which both young people and adults can read and enjoy. Tournier achieved this goal first, and perhaps best, in the very short *Pierrot ou les secrets de la nuit.*

Marina Warner   (review date 15 February 1991)

SOURCE: "Happiness and the Daily Round," in *The Times Literary Supplement,* No. 4585, February 15, 1991, p. 19.

[Warner is an English novelist, nonfiction writer, and critic whose scholarly works include Joan of Arc: The Image of Female Heroism *(1981). In the following, she unfavorably reviews* The Midnight Love Feast.*]*

The lovers sculpted out of sand in the beach below Mont St Michel are lapped by the tide and eventually overwhelmed; their creator dances to the sweet unheard music of the "salty tongues" of the sea and exclaims at the beauty of the French word *volubile*. Nature abhors silence, he declares, and as they engulf his art, the waves represent new life, "a baby burbling in its cradle". [In *The Midnight Love Feast*] Yves and Nadège, who come across the sculptor on the shore, are long married and afflicted with silence; they feel the time has come to separate, and they decide to hold a farewell symposium for all their friends, at which everyone will tell a story. This "Midnight Love Feast", this rising tide of language, does not sweep them away, but unexpectedly restores them to happiness. "Literature as a panacea for couples in distress", comments Nadège on the happy outcome.

The controlled cleverness of this schema encloses many Tournier themes: the rivalry between nature and artifice for the golden apple labelled "for the most beautiful", the power of story to shape reality in its image, the decadent raptures over destruction and life-in-death. The main theme belongs to fairy-tales, of course, though in *The Arabian Nights* Scheherazade invents her stories to save herself, and in Basile's *Lo cunto de li cunti,* the narrators uncover, detective-style, a culprit in their midst. By contrast, Tournier's protagonists are passive recipients of their guests' nineteen healing parables, and the shift reflects the author's perception of literature as liturgy and himself as a modern hierophant in an ancient storytelling freemasonry. The formulae he uses are Christian: Yves's last supper of fish gathered by himself and one or two others, the Mass, the vigil, the eucharistic sharing of food. Reconciled, Nadège explicitly invests Yves with sacerdotal powers in the high-flown language that Tournier affects: "You shall be the high priest of my kitchens and the guardian of the culinary and manducatory rites that invest a meal with its spiritual dimension."

The imagery may be sacramental, the desire to instruct, to perform miracles and uphold the power of the Word may be all of a piece with a Christian outlook, but Tournier's content famously does not conform to traditional piety, stories in *The Midnight Love Feast* would make Don Giovanni falter on his way to a tryst; far from reaffirming a marriage, they might help convince a suicide she was in her right mind. The realist *nouvelles* are filled with ugly acts of greed, pandering, revenge, in the lurid tradition of Maupassant or even Sue; some of the concise "legends" or fables that follow introduce a new, sunnier, charming tone more congruent with a happy ending, but they are distressingly feeble: an arch little conceit on the names of French perfumes, a winsome just-so story about the invention of *petits-pains au chocolat,* a plot to explain the nursery rhyme "Au clair de la lune". Not a single marked female voice enters the chorus, though two male narrators remember how women lured and trapped them, while another uncovers a squalid story of a wartime collaborator and her public degradation. A memory lapse on Tournier's part is perhaps significant: when someone mentions Ulysses' descent into the underworld, he says that Ulysses' mother did not dare drink the sacrificial blood that would enable her to speak to her son. In Tournier, mothers do not give voice; though in Homer, Anticleia drinks and speaks to Ulysses, at some length.

Tournier's message seems to be that the daily round, ceremonially performed, holds the secret of happiness, and his final parable, the most satisfying in the collection, teaches that by repetition, daily tasks are ritualized into art—the tired married couple can become the superb lovers on the beach. (In the photograph on the dust-jacket, of an actual sculpture by Patricio Lagos, who is a real-life sand artist, the bodies are in point of fact male.)

Tournier's highly wrought prose suffers seriously in translation. Michael Sheringham, reviewing the French version *Le Médianoche amoureux (TLS* August 11-17, 1989), described the style as "fulsome". Whoever is speaking, the tone is equally lofty, learned, and richly classical; "halieutic", "gangue", "olfactory", "manducatory" and even, "paludal mucosae" fall from the lips of storytellers of every condition. In French this has a quality of the seventeenth-century *précieux* about it, and doesn't become outlandish. In English, however, it veers dangerously into the wind of ridicule, all show-off airs and graces and mock portentousness. Barbara Wright's method is to forge ahead, ignoring the silly sniggerers in the congregation, and to stay with the nearest English phonetic equivalent; she also does this, less understandably, with common words, keeping "lamentable", "mutism", or even "puerile" (giving the odd "my puerile madonna" instead of "my child madonna"); she sometimes prefers not to translate at all, as with *Numéro 5,* when Chanel Number 5 must be one of the most familiar things French this side of the Channel, unlike Tournier's quotidian epiphany of halieutic comestibles: the fishy fare of the daily round made plain.

Nancy L. Easterlin   (essay date Spring 1991)

SOURCE: "Initation and Counter-Initiation: Progress Toward Adulthood in the Stories of Michel Tournier," in *Studies in Short Fiction,* Vol. 28, No. 2, Spring, 1991, pp. 151-68.

[*In the following essay, Easterlin discusses and praises Tournier's technique of inititating the protagonists of his children's stories—and his young readers—into adulthood.*]

In "Michel Tournier's Texts for Children," an article that appeared a few years ago in *Children's Literature* [No. 13, 1985], Joseph McMahon analyzes some of the differences between Tournier's approach to child and adult audiences. Basing his statements both on Tournier's own remarks about audience and on readings of the fictions, McMahon says:

> What Tournier seems to espy is a complex situation: children, up to a certain time, bring to their reading a limited amount of experience and many look upon reading as a way of understanding *and adding to* that experience. What adults bring to reading is an indefinable attitude which in many cases may make reading an act *adjacent* to their experience, with the consequence that it may or may not become part of their experience. Those different degrees of susceptibility may demand the use of deliberate, alternate strategies on the part of the writer, strategies designed to give him the chance of having the greatest amount of impact on each of the above audiences he addresses.

Since several of Tournier's stories blur the boundary of audience appeal between child and adult, McMahon's definition, although helpful and essentially accurate, is a little too general. It seems to me that a useful way of testing McMahon's definition is to look at a few of Tournier's stories *about* children and to determine how his technique varies depending on the audience he is addressing. While some stories have been reordered between *Le Coq de bruyère,* the French edition of the stories, and its English equivalent, *The Fetishist,* it is perhaps not a coincidence that the

three stories about children—"**Amandine, or The Two Gardens**"; "**Tom Thumb Runs Away**"; and "**Prikli**"—are grouped in that sequence and placed in the early part of both texts. McMahon identifies the first two of these as childrens' stories, for so Tournier intended them; but I know at least one adult who finds them well worth reading. Like "**Prikli,**" a tale clearly not to be recommended for the impressionable young mind, "**Tom Thumb**" and "**Amandine**" focus on the children's efforts to form suitable responses as they discover aspects of their own sexuality or psychology against the conflicting, or indifferent, or imponderable restrictions of the adult, world. "**Amandine**" is subtitled "An initiatory story," and "**Tom Thumb**" "A Christmas Story," but insofar as both stories gently dramatize an aspect of the experience of growing up and offer advice on how to cope with it, they are both, to some extent, initiatory stories. Prikli's tale, by contrast, is one of gruesome counter-initiation. The adults in his life perpetuate a sentimental romanticism that dichotomizes sexual identities, representing woman as an idealized object and man as a debased physical brute. For a small boy of aesthetic sensitivities, the inevitable self-identification with masculinity is traumatic and, once subjected to the vagaries of childish logic, ultimately tragic: Prikli tries to correct the injustice of his sexual fate by self-castration. Hence, for Prikli, formative experiences that should result in psychological and social adaption become the vehicle for regression to primitive mental conceptualization and behavior.

Tournier himself, often ironically evasive, is quite explicit about the child's need for guidance via initiation in his or her "transition from a biological state to a social status" [*The Wind Spirit*]:

> Education in the broad sense of the word prepares a child to enter society and to occupy his place in it. In all times and places it appears to come in two forms, one moral, emotional, indeed magical, the other purely intellectual and rational. The first is called initiation, the second instruction. We have this equation:
>
> *education = initiation + instruction.*
>
> Of course these two components of education assume many guises, and their importance varies. My view is quite simply that, historically, the relative importance of initiation has been diminishing compared with that of instruction and that for some time now this has passed the point of being harmful.
>
> (*W*)

To some extent, then, Tournier certainly strives to correct the deficiency of contemporary education through fiction writing. Thus, while the stories are initiatory in their focus on the maturation of young child-characters, they are initiatory in another sense, too, for as Tournier initiates his characters, he simultaneously initiates his readers. In the first two tales, he shows his readers (whether children or adults), how maturation can be a means of self-discovery and a progress through new experiences, an occasion for joy and even wonder at life; in "**Prikli,**" he initiates his readers into the literally and permanently dehumanizing result of outmoded sexual attitudes and of general insensitivity to the child's developmental experience. **"Prikli"** is additionally horrifying to the reader who has read the stories in sequence, invited at first to read **"Amandine"** and **"Tom Thumb"** as McMahon says the child reads, by incorporating them into his own experience and thus reawakening with Amandine and Tom to the ineluctable mystery of life. After this, the damaging nightmare that is realized in Prikli's self-mutilation is all the more perverse and shocking.

Probably Tournier expects his adult readers, whether they have the experience of reading the stories sequentially or not, to note the contrasting treatments of child-characters. As Roger Shattuck, who admires Tournier and deplores his neglect by American critics, nonetheless notes, "Tournier is an incorrigible pedagogue and, having decided not to innovate or experiment with the traditional form of the novel and to maintain the advantages of clear language, falls occasionally into excessive didacticism" ["Locating Michel Tournier," in *The Innocent Eye,* 1986]. The lessons Tournier teaches stand out dramatically in the short stories, which center on well-defined themes and unfold with great economy. But I think Tournier earns his didacticism in these stories for two reasons. First, Tournier sympathizes with childhood experience without sentimentalizing it, thus demonstrating his genuine concern for children as well as his psychological insight into developing human consciousness. If *ignorance* and *innocence* are the standard terms for defining the child's mental state, they are clearly inadequate to the fundamentally dynamic nature of childhood experience as Tournier delineates it. By portraying the child's effort to process information and thus come to grips with the bewildering world around him or her, Tournier implicitly defines the child, given his or her physical and emotional immaturity and lack of logical and analytical skills, as *dependent* even while striving for self-reliance. Again, Tournier's insistence that the child's emotional and physical dependence on adults not be neglected is hardly whimsical, but stems from an informed psychological perspective; in *The Wind Spirit,* he points out that:

> Freudian psychoanalysis has long persisted in viewing the need for physical contact simply as a libidinal impulse given concrete form by the desire of the newborn for its mother's breast or, later, by genital sexuality. But recently several psychologists have more or less simultaneously proposed a new idea, which, though seemingly of modest import, nevertheless profoundly alters the very foundations of psychoanalysis, namely, the idea of *attachment* as a primary and irreducible drive.

For Tournier, in short, the adult's obligation to the child is not simply the result of social convention or convenience, but rather stems from a biological imperative. Finally, in addition to the psychological understanding that partially justifies Tournier's pedagogical agenda, his literary artistry makes these stories a success. In all three, he eschews dogmatism, focusing instead on literary technique. Throughout the stories, Tournier manipulates a variety of materials, including: narrative tone; representa-

tion of the adult world; man's relation to the animal world; and the destructive and creative potential of myth and ritual.

Of the three stories, **"Amandine"** is written in the first person and is hence the closest to the child's experience. Told in the form of a ten-year-old's entries into her diary, the story relates Amandine's observations of her cat, Claude, and her curiosity about the mysterious arrival of four kittens. Over a period of several months, the growth of one of the kittens, Kamikat, parallels Amandine's own tentative sexual awakening.

Since it is told in the first person, the story is not only free of adult self-consciousness, but also perhaps of the self-consciousness of the child who knows she has an audience. Amandine sometimes takes up the role of storyteller, but she tends to collapse her own constructions as quickly as she creates them. For instance, she begins like this:

> *Sunday* I have blue eyes, cherry red lips, plump pink cheeks, and wavy blond hair. My name is Amandine. When I look at myself in the mirror, I think I look a little girl of ten. Which isn't surprising. I *am* a little girl, and I *am* ten.

From the beginning, the chattering, spontaneous little girl overtakes the more orderly one, who is more interested in factual information than exploration and speculation. In the second paragraph, Amandine dutifully announces, "I have a papa, a mama, a doll called Amanda, and also a cat." But her interest immediately moves away from what are the conventionally appropriate high-priority beings in her life, a mama and a papa, to those that interest her, Claude and the kittens. Catalogued along with her doll and then dropped, Amandine's parents are quickly reduced in status in accordance with her reigning passion.

That Amandine's inattention to her parents may be motivated by more than childish impetuosity, however, becomes evident a little further into the tale. After another few weeks, Amandine describes the world of her parents:

> *Wednesday* I like Mama's house and Papa's garden. In the house, it's always the same temperature, summer and winter alike. And no matter what the season, the lawns are always green and well kept. You might think that Mama in her house, and Papa in his garden, are having a competition to see who can be the neatest and tidiest . . . I think they're right. Things are more reassuring like that. But sometimes they're also a little bit boring.

Amandine accepts the ordered world of her parents, beginning her diary entry by conferring approval to their domain. In addition, after describing her parents' world, she iterates the propriety of the manicured and static house and garden. As a result, her admission that this order fails to hold her constant interest is thus slightly tinged with guilt, even though Amandine is not apologizing for her own failure of enthusiasm. Yet despite Amandine's personal conflict between tolerance for and boredom with the well-regulated adult world, what is most striking about her parents is their pervasive absence from the story, which attests to their rather negligible participation in her life. As McMahon has noted, Tournier's "implicit criticism of an order which tends its homes and gardens better than its children is presented indirectly"; and it is perhaps Amandine's current absorption in her cats that relegates her parents to a very secondary existence yet, to the adult reader, they seem unaccountably absent. But at the same time, the absence of the parents from the story contributes to its initiatory function for the *child reader:* in both this story and **"Tom Thumb,"** with parents only vaguely in evidence, the child characters' resourcefulness and self-discovery are positively emphasized. Thus, the absence of parents functions as a social criticism for adult readers while it simultaneously—if somewhat contradictorily—reinforces the self-esteem of the child reader who is invited to participate in the thoughts and actions of a strong, independent child character.

With her parents in the background—either because that is where Amandine leaves them or that is where they choose to be—Amandine must find other beings on whom to focus her inquisitive mind and to serve as the initiators into her sexual self-awareness. Luckily, Amandine is attuned to the animal world, as she indicates when she explains the relationship between the night animals and the day animals:

> The owl is in a hurry to go home before the sun comes up and dazzles her, and she brushes up against the blackbird that's just coming out of the lilac tree. The hedgehog rolls itself up in a ball in the depths of the heather just at the moment when the squirrel pokes its head out of the hole in the old oak tree to see what sort of a day it is.

The world Amandine describes is the reverse of her parents' predictably ordered house and garden: between the night animals and the day animals, the natural world is continually in motion, whereas the world of Amandine's parents is static and actually ceases to exist when they are asleep. In the absence of her parents, then, Amandine turns her attention to the dynamism of nature, which both reflects and complements her own curiosity.

Amandine's cats, tied to the natural order that so enthralls her, thus become the agents of her initiation into puberty. The mystery of sexual identity, symbolized in the cats' androgynous names, Claude and Kamikat, intrigues Amandine from the beginning of the story, when she discovers the kittens around Claude. The end of the story mirrors this beginning, as Amandine watches Kamikat grow plumper and guesses that "he" is a female, but the conclusion also marks the progress of her sexual knowledge. In the beginning she says of Claude, as though such a proposition is entirely ridiculous, "anyone might think the four little kittens had been shut up in [Claude's stomach] and just got out!" By the end of the story she understands that Kamikat is pregnant before she sees kittens, partly because she has learned from Claude but also because she has experienced for the first time, with the onset of menstruation, the meaning of her own sexuality.

Because this is a story for children, Tournier presents sexual realities indirectly and emphasizes the pleasure and knowledge the child can glean from observing nature. For instance, Amandine's first menstrual period is described thus:

> I go upstairs to my little room. I cry for a long time, very hard, for no reason, just like that. And then I sleep for a while. When I wake up, I look at myself in the mirror. My clothes aren't dirty. There's nothing wrong with me. Oh yes there is, though, there's a little blood. A trickle of blood along my leg. That's odd, I don't have any scratches anywhere. Why, then? Never mind. I go over to the mirror and examine my face from really close up.

Only a child who is emotionally prepared to read the clues in this paragraph will do so; in this way, Tournier carefully avoids alarming his small reader. Likewise, the positive representation of the natural world is intended to offer the adult guidance that the author generally finds wanting in contemporary society. Once again, though, Tournier is elsewhere quite pointed about the insufficiency of this kind of instruction:

> Everyone says that young children like to play with dolls and teddy bears, and sometimes they are permitted to play with small animals. It is also commonly said, however, that dogs like bones. The truth is that dogs gnaw on bones when they have nothing else, but you can take my world for it, they would prefer a good cut of steak or a nice veal cutlet. As for children, it is quite simply a dreadful thing that we toss them dolls and animals in order to assuage their need for a warm, loving body. Of course sailors on long voyages sometimes avail themselves of inflatable rubber females, and lonely shepherds in the mountains have been known to mount a lamb or goat. But children are neither sailors nor shepherds and do not lack for human company. Their distress is the invention of a fiercely antiphysical society, of a mutilating, castrating culture, and there is no question that many character disorders, violent outbursts, and cases of juvenile drug addiction are consequences of the physical desert into which the child and adolescent are customarily banished in our society.

> (***W***)

If, then, the child reader has been encouraged to open his or her eyes to nature by **"Amandine,"** perhaps the adult reader has been asked to consider whether Amandine's initiation, its charm notwithstanding, is as complete as it should be by the end of the story. It seems unlikely that she understands her own menstruation, much less makes the connection between this phenomenon and pregnancy. Her realization that the kittens are inside Kamikat is, happily, a correct intuition, but it is not the accurate biological knowledge that, at this point, she might have.

"Amandine" is the most realistic of these three stories, and as such does not make much use of mythic materials. The overrun garden stands in obvious contrast to the ordered garden of Amandine's parents, and consequently Amandine's adventure there symbolizes her confrontation with a new and mysterious aspect of herself. Likewise, the statue of Cupid, the boy-messenger of love, is a kind of double for her, as she attempts to overreach her still-childish interpretations of experience in the effort to confront adult sexuality. **"Tom Thumb Runs Away,"** as its title suggests, is less realistic than **"Amandine,"** incorporating motifs, plot devices, and a narrative tone borrowed from fairy tale into the life of an apparently average young boy. In this story, Tom's father, the captain of the Paris woodcutters, moves his wife and child from a small villa to a Paris highrise. Tom decides to run away, and during his brief adventure in the woods he meets the magical Mr. Ogre and his daughters. He returns home with the pair of "dream boots" given him by Mr. Ogre.

Even though the tale is told by a third-person narrator who employs more elevated diction than Amandine in her diary, Tournier once again draws a sympathetic child-hero. Like Amandine, Tom is a take-charge sort of child, one that any reader little or big is invited to identify with. Even when Tournier directs irony at his hero, as he does just before Tom runs away, he only makes Tom more attractive. And in this particular instance, Barbara Wright contributes another deft touch, exploiting the phonetic similarity between "o" and "u" in English to underscore the keen but intermittent logic of the child's mind:

> They'll say my writing's still babyish, thought Tom in some mortification, reading over his farewell note. What about the spelling? There's nothing like one really stupid, big mistake to rob even a pathetic message of all its dignity. Boots. Should it be *u*, like in "brutes"? Or does it really have two o's? Yes, it must, because there're two boots.

> ["Ils vont encore dire que j'ai une écriture de bébé", pense Pierre avec dépit, en relisant son billet d'adieu. Et l'orthographe? Rien de tel qu'une grosse faute bien ridicule pour enlever toute dignité à un message, fût-il pathétique. Bottes. Cela prend-il bien deux *t?* Oui sans doute puisqu'il y a deux bottes.]

Tom's logic is amusing and of course the reader is invited to laugh at him for a moment but, however faulty, his reasoning *does* lead him to the right conclusion. Moreover, Tom's concern for expressing himself correctly, his desire to carry out what he realizes is a modest task with dignity, makes him more endearing than his lack of knowledge makes him foolish.

Irony, besides, is an extraordinary relative technique, and it is in comparison to the representations of Tom's parents that the irony directed against him loses any edge of serious criticism. The parent world is more fully dramatized in this story than in **"Amandine,"** but the purpose of dramatizing it seems to be to expose its ridiculousness and thus discount it. The exaggerated portrait of Tom's father as a self-important incompetent once again obliquely contributes to the instructive function of the story by strengthening the child reader's identification with Tom. In his or her identification with the story's unequivocal hero, the child reader imaginatively experiences Tom's temporary independence, and thus anticipates his or her own eventual self-reliance.

Just before Tom's struggle with spelling during the composition of his farewell note, Tom's father has shown himself to be an indubitable boob. Thumb explains the value of a walled-up modern life:

> " . . . anyway, as the President of the Republic himself said: 'Paris must adapt itself to the motorcar, even at the expense of a certain aestheticism.' "

> " 'A certain aestheticism'—what's that?" asked Tom.

> Thumb ran his short fingers through his black, close-cropped hair. These kids, eh—always asking stupid questions!

> "Aestheticism, aestheticism . . . er, um . . . well, it's trees!" he finally came out with, to his relief. " 'Even at the expense of'—that means that they have to be cut down. . . ."

Whereas anyone can sympathize with Tom's effort to penetrate the perplexing rules of orthography, his father's glib disregard for logic exposes him as a know-nothing. Thumb digs a nice hole for himself, first using words he does not understand and then grossly misinterpreting them to suit his purpose. In addition, the narrator certainly helps to tip the scale in Tom's favor with the remark about "stupid questions": obviously, the question here is not at all stupid—only the answer is. As in **"Amandine,"** Thumb's dismissiveness should suggest to the adult reader that a child's questions deserve complete, accurate answers, even while it gives the child reader a much-needed opportunity to laugh at a silly adult.

Tom's father proves himself insensitive as well as ignorant when Tom asks if he will still be getting his boots for Christmas. "Here, I'll make you an offer," says his father. "Instead of boots, I'll buy you a color television." First of all, a television is a rather incongruous substitute for a pair of boots, and secondly, Thumb's "offer" seems rather selfish upon later reflection. At the end of the story, Captain and Mrs. Thumb watch Christmas Eve festivities on "their color television set" in their new apartment. Is this the set they bought for Tom? Whether it is or not, Tom evidently does not need the mass-produced fantasies available there: Ogre's boots, outwardly of more limited value and use than a TV, have for him a power far more significant than the prepackaged fantasies of television programs.

The Paris highrise apartment where Thumb moves his family parallels the perfect order of Amandine's parents' house and lawn in its artificiality and sterility and, like Amandine, Tom has the good sense to know a life closer to nature is more meaningful and lots more fun. Amandine can conveniently ignore the adult world, while Tom must run away from it. Just as Amandine's cats assist her in her discovery of sexuality, Tom's pet rabbits prove immediately useful. While Tom is on the run, a truck driver stops, and "the rabbits [have] a brilliant idea. One after the other, they [poke] their heads out of the hamper. Do you take live rabbits in a hamper with you if you're running away? The driver [is] reassured." Tournier's assumption of a rabbit consciousness commensurate with human consciousness implies a tacit conspiracy between the boy and his pets, as though the animals know Tom is in a quandary and purposely reveal themselves to deceive the driver. A little later, when he is tired and lies down under a tree, the rabbits "[nuzzle] up to Tom, poking their little noses into his clothes." Out in the woods with no shelter, Tom finds a warmth and comfort with his rabbits that does not exist in the Mercury Tower apartment. And again, after he meets Mr. Ogre's daughters and goes to their home, he repeats the experience of being in "a live burrow." The scene of the eight children stripping off their clothes and jumping into bed mirrors the nuzzling rabbits, and in so doing illustrates a positive similarity between the human and animal worlds, the comforting and pleasurable nature of physical contact. In **"Tom Thumb,"** the primary need for attachment of which Tournier writes in *The Wind Spirit* is met with nearly ideal, if only temporary, fulfillment; whereas Amandine's affection is concentrated solely upon her cats, Tom finds love among both animals and humans. Only his parents are missing.

The Grimm's tale "Little Thumb" ("Tom Thumb" in some English versions) is the obvious analogue to which Tournier alludes. Like his namesake, Tournier's Tom is ever-resourceful, outwitting wicked adults despite the handicap of his age and size; but unlike the doltish father and seemingly nonexistent mother of the new tale, the parents in the Grimm's tale dote on their precious son. His adventure also takes place in the countryside. But beyond this, there are no strong parallels between the tales; rather, the familiar names become amusing when they are applied to contemporary settings and attitudes, and imply that what we conventionally consider long ago and make-believe may in fact be very real and present.

Tournier undoubtedly wishes to stress the interrelatedness of myth and reality, and the necessary and continuous rethinking of both that their inseparability requires. William Cloonan points out that, in pondering Christian myth,

> What Tournier discovered in transubstantiation was the confirmation of his belief in transformation: that everything which exists, be it as humble as bread or wine, has the potential to become sacred, a process which occurs when people learn to perceive themselves and the objects which surround them as sources of comfort, beauty and joy.
>
> [see *Michel Tournier,* 1985, and "The Spiritual Order of Michel Tournier," in *Renascense,* Vol. 36, Nos. 1-2, 1983-1984]

In **"Tom Thumb,"** Ogre's retelling of the Fall of Man constitutes another use, clearly quite different from that of the Grimm's tale, of mythic materials. Not entirely dissimilar to Tom's father, Ogre is quite glib in his revisionist telling of the myth:

> "Encouraged by Eve, Adam makes up his mind. He bites into the fruit. And he doesn't die. On the contrary, his eyes open, and he knows good and evil. So Jehovah had lied. It was the serpent that had told the truth."

In this case, Tournier has taken sacred myth, the most difficult sort to attempt to revise, and made the deity into a hardly very admirable character. The new version of the Eden myth is not offensive, however, in part because it is

so extreme, but also because it is Ogre's version. And although he is more credible than Captain Thumb (largely because he is simply kind to the children), Ogre's explanations seem almost as idiosyncratic. Part of the reason for this is that Ogre's own beliefs, which constitute yet another mythic dimension to the tale, conflict with acceptance of traditional Christian myth. He is the follower of an older religion, tree worship.

> "Listen to me," he said. "What is a tree? In the first place, a tree consists in a certain balance between aerial foliage and underground roots. This purely mechanical balance contains a whole philosophy in itself. For it is clear that it is impossible for the foliage to spread, to expand, to embrace an ever-increasing portion of the sky if the roots do not at the same time plunge deeper. . . . So you see, the higher you want to rise, the more you must have your feet on the ground. Every tree tells you so."

Ogre's lengthy philosophical explanation for the tree as the perfect example of balance between inner and outer, restriction and freedom, earth and sky is somewhat overly scientific and overstated. But in contrast to Thumb's assertion that trees have only aesthetic value, Ogre's discourse is symbolically significant. What his speech stresses is not so much the sacredness of trees but the importance of balance and harmony with nature. Tom certainly understands the symbolical nature of the lesson, for it is his ability to incorporate Ogre's speech into his imagination that enables him to experience tree-like balance. At the end of the story, all the mythic elements combine in Tom's transcendent moment when he puts on the boots Ogre has given him: unable to escape physically from the sterile environment of the apartment, his feet are nonetheless symbolically on the ground; he becomes his own savior (this is, after all, "A Christmas Story") and escapes spiritually, retaining his connection to nature and hence his wholeness through his imagination.

Both **"Amandine"** and **"Tom Thumb,"** then, have numerous similarities—the narrator's close identification with a strong, central child character; the delineation of a sterile, insensitive parent world that is, however, escapable; the beneficial relationship between the child and the animal world; the representation of myth as a dynamic aspect of current reality—that enable the reader to identify closely with the child-hero. The tales, in effect, invite the reader to share, on whatever conscious or subconscious level is suited to his or her age or experience, in Amandine's initiation into puberty and Tom's initiation into the regenerative power of the imagination. In **"Prikli,"** conversely, Tournier reveals exaggerated and even opposite attitudes toward some of the same phenomena of the children's tales, with a result that stresses the seriousness of the child's life and the adult's responsibility to him.

"Prikli" is told in the third person, but the relatively elevated language and consequently formal tone of the prose makes the narrative voice quite distinct from that of **"Tom Thumb."** The fluent and ordered descriptions of Prikli's perceptions stand in rather striking contrast to the information related, as in this early passage:

The beautiful apartment that Prikli and his family lived in on the rue des Sablons would have had few resources to offer to the child's reveries had it not been for a huge old painting in the Pre-Raphaelite style which had been hung, to get it out of the way, in the narrow corridor leading from the living room to the bedrooms at the back. . . . This painting depicted the Last Judgment. . . . The damned were sinking down into an underground passage made of granite, while the chosen, singing and carrying palms, were ascending to heaven up a great staircase made of pink clouds. Now, what the child found particularly striking was the anatomy of each category. For whereas the damned had brown skin and black hair, and their nudity revealed formidable muscles, the chosen were pale and slim, and their white tunics concealed frail, delicate limbs.

The objective tone in which Tournier delineates a typically overwrought piece of Pre-Raphaelite art is humorous, because it implies a reaction to a clearly outrageous object that is equivalent to the reception of mundane actuality. As it exposes the discrepancy between perception and reality such irony is always amusing; in **"Prikli,"** however, it is at the same time rather terrifying. This is, after all, the child's point of view, and phrases like "what the child found particularly striking" combined with logical coordinators like "for whereas" dramatize Prikli's attempt to form a rational understanding of the painting. While the reader can identify with the child's struggle to form an adult response, the fact that the painting is the sole subject of Prikli's reveries, combined with the excessive seriousness of those musings, indicates that something is askew. Through careful control of his irony, Tournier establishes a difficult position for the reader: Prikli, mystified by the adult world, engages sympathy, but he is simultaneously held at a distance by his foreboding tendency to literalize absurd attitudes.

While Amandine's and Tom Thumb's parents offer their children sterile, uninteresting environments but are nevertheless unthreatening in their distance from the child's world, Prikli's parents are another matter. It is safe to say that their abode, graced by the phantasmagoria of a Pre-Raphaelite Last Judgment, is hardly sterile. Rather, it is governed and shaped by a couple who confuse romantic fictions with reality, and are therefore unable to respond to the natural needs of their child. On the one hand, Prikli's father as an adult male represents everything repulsive; on the other, his mother personifies eternally mysterious femininity:

> After her lemon tea, which she took alone in her bedroom, she shut herself up in the bathroom for an hour and a half. And when she came out, still dressed in a chiffon negligee, she was already a goddess, the goddess of the morning, as fresh as a rose, anointed with lanolin, very different, it's true, from the great black goddess of the evening, the one who leaned over Prikli's bed, her face half hidden behind a little veil, and who told him: "Don't kiss me, you'll wreck my hair."

While the pathos of a child whose parent denies him affection need hardly be glossed, the idealized image of woman that Prikli is encouraged to adopt adds another dimension to his mother's maternal deficiencies. Perceived as "the goddess" in one of her many transformations, Prikli's mother takes on for her child the unbearable value of the feminine ideal realized, yet still unattainable. When Prikli begs to sleep with her gloves, he is granted contact with the symbol instead of the actual person of his mother. Thus, the substitution of symbol for reality is established early in the story, and implies a perverse method of interpreting the world that in the end becomes explicit.

Like Amandine's and Tom's parents, Prikli's have a tendency to take him for granted; but above and beyond this, their refusal to take their child's experience seriously manifests itself in some rather sadistic remarks. Although he has expressed displeasure at his nickname, it (quite literally) sticks, and he is told:

> "But you know, baby hedgehogs don't have prickles—just very soft, very clean down. It's only later. Later, when they grow up. When they become men . . . ."

Prikli may only be a child, but he knows that hedgehogs don't "become men" and hence sees that his mother's remark refers to his own human masculinity. In taunting her child and therefore failing to take him seriously, the mother burdens him with a distorted and disturbing vision of his own future.

Prikli's adventures are limited to the gossamer realm of his goddess-mother and to the garden of the ironically named Desbordes-Valmore Square—places that stand as suggestive images of romantic extremes. If the world of his mother is the interior of a lingering decadence, the square enshrines the spirit of Marceline Desbordes-Valmore, whose poetry waxes rhapsodic on such subjects as lost children, deceased mothers, spent youth, and aestheticized nature. At the same time, the square is incongruously decorated with statues representing Greek mythic heroes. Thus overladen with mythical and romantic resonances, the square is clearly no corrective to the home environment and, unlike Amandine and Tom, Prikli has no opportunity to explore nature in its unsentimental reality. As a result, his only impression of the animal world is that which he receives from the adults around him, to whom animals are dirty and barbaric and fatally associated with masculine sexuality. Prikli imagines a hedgehog as "a miniature pig covered with bristles swarming with vermin," a vision entirely antithetical to Amandine's poetic description of the hedgehog going to sleep. The connection between animals and masculinity is moreover reinforced when Prikli overhears Mamouse, the attendant for the restroom in the square, railing against men as "lechers, wild boars, [and] debauchees," a screed he probably little understands beyond the yoking of male and animal in a highly negative context. And later, Prikli's abortive imitation of canine behavior leads him to the inconvenient conclusion that urination itself is an animal, and therefore despicable, act. Unfortunately for Prikli, he is smart, and the accumulated disgust he feels toward anything animal progresses from the perception that men are like animals to the conclusion that men are equivalent to animals.

Finally, Tournier's treatment of myth in **"Prikli"** reinforces the tensions he has established through distance in narrative tone; rigidly opposed concepts of masculine and feminine, as embodied in the parents; and identification of the natural, animal world with vulgarity and masculinity. Whereas **"Tom Thumb"** exhibits the playful blending of many myths and asserts the flexibility of all, **"Prikli"** dramatizes the destructive potential in literalized misinterpretations of myth. On a general level, Prikli's perception of his mother as a goddess, and the underlying assumption that living humans can be goddesses, is an example of this. On a more specific level, when Miss Campbell, the governess of another young child who visits the square, gives Prikli her seemingly half-hearted explanations of the centaur and the minotaur statues, she unwittingly embellishes Prikli's conviction that the keys to reality reside in phantasmagoria. Because she cannot explain, for instance, why Theseus wears "a skirt," Prikli concludes that Theseus is female and the Minotaur male. The irony of this of course is that the mythic Theseus, the preeminent Attic hero who conquered the Minotaur and led the war against the centaurs, was in fact something of a philanderer, while the Minotaur was an imaginary beast without sexual distinction. But there is more to Prikli's mythic misperception:

> Miss Campbell had given Prikli quite a long lecture, from which he had vaguely gathered that the man-horse—a scent-tar [*sent-fort*]—was obliged, in order to marry, to abduct a woman by main force, precisely because of his bad smell, to which he owed his name. Remembering his father's smell, Prikli had been satisfied with this explanation.

Miss Campbell's creative abilities notwithstanding, her freedom at inventing what she does not know is another example of the unwitting negligence of the adults surrounding Prikli. Like Prikli's mother, she betrays the child's utter faith in the adult's word. Could she have known that her interpretation was precisely the wrong one to give Prikli? In the statue of the centaur, Prikli sees an embodiment of what he has already learned to link, the animal and the masculine, and Miss Campbell's free definition of "scent-tar" reinforces the connection. And while the degree of misinterpretation is certainly no help to Prikli's weird cogitations, the simple fact that neither Marie, Prikli's family's maid, nor Miss Campbell explain that the centaur is a fictional being perpetuates Prikli's tendency to see real men as monsters of mythic proportions. An explanation that pointed out the once-upon-a-time aspect of the myth, placing it back in the days when men wore "skirts," would have suggested to Prikli the difference between artistic representation and reality, and allowed him to avoid his dangerous logic. Instead, it is the disastrous connection that Prikli makes between these "facts" and the revelation that "man" and "animal" are only different terms for the same thing that leads him ultimately to the formulation that "the link between the brown meat of the man in the urinal and Mamouse's saucepan [of giblet broth], was forged by Theseus' sword."

In the end, Prikli's drastic act of self-mutilation displays the total sum of a child's efforts to weave some fabric of reality from many mismatched threads. Through his fear

of the unavoidable bestiality that he sees as the primary characteristic of adult masculinity, he regresses to a psychologically primitive state. In *The Golden Bough,* Frazer recounts several instances of ritual castration, and hypothesizes that, according to the superstitions of some primitive tribes, self-castration constituted a transfer of power:

> [Some] Asiatic goddesses of fertility were served . . . by eunuch priests. These feminine deities required to receive from their male ministers, who personated the divine lovers, the means of discharging their beneficent functions: they had themselves to be impregnated by the life-giving energy before they could transmit it to the world.

In a world where all beauty resides in the femininity that has been denied him, Prikli wants nothing to do with brute strength, and sacrifices his masculinity to the goddess-image of his mother. The disconcerting parallels between his behavior and primitive ritual castration underscore the barbarism that lies just beneath the perverse myths the adults around him continually enact in the name of high civilization. Thus, Prikli's self-castration registers not only his own psychological disturbance, but that of his whole culture; with this counter-initiation, it is as though much that holds itself up as civilization is lost.

Tournier's essay about his visits to French schools, **"Writer Devoured by Children"** [translated by Margaret Higonnet in *Children's Literature* 13, 1985], attests to his enormous sensitivity to the experience of childhood. As always, he tells the tale of his conversations with the children with gentle irony:

> We pass from animals to nature, to ecology, to the quality of life, and then, quite simply, to happiness. Children are not afraid of the big questions. In fact they do not order problems hierarchically. What do you eat for breakfast? Or, How can one be happy? They throw out such questions without making any distinction. One must know how to answer. We may skip breakfast. But what about happiness? "Happiness? Very simple. There is only one condition, but it is absolutely essential: you must passionately love something or someone."

At the same time that he is delighted by the spontaneity of the children's questions, Tournier acknowledges that the adult is not free to exercise the same spontaneity: "One must know how to answer." Prikli's case is an extreme example of the failure to fulfill what for Tournier is the imperative responsibility of adults, guiding the child so that he or she can learn to discriminate and evolve personal possibilities of order. Tom and Amandine are lucky enough to learn this mostly on their own, with the help of their animal friends and, in Tom's case, Ogre. And I think, finally, that Tournier shows what children can give adults as well as vice versa: all three stories suggest that the child's capacity for wonder need never be lost in the adult, but instead can ameliorate the series of initiations into maturity, and thus provide the enthusiasm and self-assurance to "passionately love something."

Karen D. Levy (essay date Winter 1992)

SOURCE: "Tournier's Ultimate Perversion: The Historical Manipulation of _Gilles et Jeanne_," in _Papers on Language and Literature,_ Vol. 28, No. 1, Winter, 1992, pp. 72-88.

[_In the following essay, Levy discusses Tournier's alteration of historical fact in_ Gilles et Jeanne, _comparing the novel's portrayal of the main characters with scholarly accounts of the historical figures upon which they are based._]

The contemporary French novelist and short story writer Michel Tournier has on numerous occasions stressed the various ways in which his works appropriate material from earlier literary texts, both those of others and his own, and from the multi-layered stories he describes as myth. He radically alters the configurations of his borrowings and incorporates them into what both he and many critics describe as perverted re-tellings that depict his own evolving obsessions and reveal the scope of his originality. Beginning with the Robinson Crusoe story, which acts as a springboard for his first novel, _Vendredi ou les limbes du Pacifique,_ up to the final jubilatory tale of festive commemoration in his latest anthology, _Le Médianoche amoureux,_ Tournier constructs an elaborate verbal network of intertextual resonances that disorient us as readers and challenge our imaginations.

Nowhere is the process of textual appropriation and perversion more intricate and more disconcerting than in Tournier's tale, _Gilles et Jeanne,_ in which we encounter for the first time historical figures whose activities can be documented. Tournier recounts the grizzly tale of Gilles de Rais, fifteenth-century wealthy landowner, and Maréchal de France, who fought for a time beside Joan of Arc, and nine years after her martyrdom, was himself executed for having molested and grotesquely murdered numerous children, disposing of the evidence by burning their corpses in the giant fireplaces of his preferred castles of Machecoul and Tiffauges.

Tournier's literary sources for _Gilles et Jeanne_ include Joris-Karl Huysmans's late nineteenth-century description of Gilles's experience in his novel _Là-Bas;_ German expressionist Georg Kaiser, whose work gave Tournier the title for his own text; and more recently Georges Bataille's essay detailing the simultaneous exhibitionistic and tragic aspects of Gilles's drama [see Bataille, _Le Procès de Gilles de Rais,_ 1965]. Bataille's essay provides the background for Tournier's version, which concentrates on the double-sided erotic and mystical fascination he envisions Gilles experiencing for the Maid of Orléans. Even more important than literary transformation, however, which Tournier has been practicing throughout his career, is the way in which he exploits the recorded historical data pertaining to Gilles's situation. He weaves a simultaneously outrageous and bewildering tale, which has polarized critical reaction perhaps more intensely than any of his other writings and become the subject of heated debate. The specific historical manipulation that Tournier undertakes reveals itself only when we unmask the elements which constitute the text's provocativeness and determine their specific function.

The structural simplicity and temporal condensation of Tournier's text suggest what Susan Petit has described as its fairy tale dimension. In her thoughtful study of the work, she argues that "because of its style and subject matter, _Gilles et Jeanne_ may be viewed as Tournier's long-promised children's version of his earlier novel _Le Roi des aulnes._" Using Bruno Bettleheim's analysis of the structure of fairy tales and their importance in children's psychological development, Petit notes that "everywhere there is simplification" [see Petit, "_Gilles et Jeanne:_ Tournier's _Le Roi des aulnes_ Revisited," _Romanic Review_ 76, 1985]. All that was either multidimensional or ambiguous in _Le Roi des aulnes_—point of view, chronology, character presentation and motivation—has been distilled to make the text acceptable for a young and vulnerable audience.

The narrator takes complete control of the material. He filters the historical information concerning Gilles's prolonged, eight-year massacre of innocents and specifies that Gilles was motivated, not by the desire to do evil, but rather by his fidelity to Joan of Arc—his promise to follow her to the depths of hell if necessary. He was, as the narrator stresses, "un brave garcon de son temps, ni pire ni meilleur d'un autre" 'a fine young man of his times, neither worse nor better than any other,' whose personality disintegrated when he witnessed the death of his idol and lost all ability to distinguish the so often finely delineated line separating good from evil. Gilles's ritual murders are never directly depicted in the text itself. The details of his sadism are presented only in excerpts from the testimony of witnesses at his trial in October 1440. Parents sketch the scenarios of their children's disappearances; and his co-defendants describe what occurred in the vaulted rooms and fireplaces of Gilles's forbidding castles in southern Brittany and the Vendée. In reading Tournier's tale the reader "is being protected, as a child is when his parents assure him that there are no dragons any more." Faced with excommunication, Gilles publicly repents and dies invoking Joan's name, suggesting the traditional happy endings of fairy tales (Petit).

As appealing and reassuring as this interpretation may be, it poses some serious problems for the reader—for Tournier's work resolves nothing, even in a fairy tale context, and the tidy reconciliation of contraries it appears to depict is a lure whose seductiveness must be resisted. The apparent simplicity of the text, which proposes to explain Gilles's transformation through Tournier's familiar phenomenon of the double-sided "inversion maligne / bénigne" 'evil / benign inversion' (first explored in _Le Roi des aulnes_) is a screen which masks the complexity of its rhetorical strategies. In his lucid and highly innovative analysis of _Gilles et Jeanne_ Colin Davis points out the way in which Tournier tries to entrap and compromise his reader. He argues that the text serves as "a parable of writing," which depicts the author's double-sided attitude toward his work and his public [see Davis, _Michel Tournier: Philosophy and Fiction,_ 1988]. Tournier seeks to control his reader while simultaneously insisting that he must interpret a work by himself, nourishing it with his own blood to make it come to life and suppressing the author in the process. The aggression implied in such a relationship leaves both writer and reader frustrated and alienated because, as Davis further notes, "the uncontrollable always resides somewhere *other* than where the author attempts to isolate it."

While *Gilles et Jeanne* may be treated as a parable for the writer / reader relationship, it is also parable perverted for a deliberately distorted purpose. Its function is not, as one might traditionally expect from a parable, to impart meaning or provide a moral lesson, but rather to expose some of the textual strategies by which a reassuring illusion of meaning is produced and consumed by the characters, only to be contested by the reader. Tournier exploits in particular the fact, as Rice and Schofer note, that "irony is not semantically marked . . . there is no incompatability between the microcontext and the macrocontext" [Donald Rice and Peter Schofer, *Rhetorical Poetics,* 1983]. Tournier uses irony to expose the way in which the text contests its own authority. The easily assimilated coherence which appeared to exist is called into question when, as Rice and Schofer note, "the 'voice' of the narration talks against itself by presenting signifiers which undermine the apparent signified." This process of undermining occurs in two intertwining contexts in *Gilles et Jeanne,* revealing the unacknowledged gap between historical referentiality and Tournier's invention, which in turn highlights the division that exists between the specifically fictional situations of the two protagonists. The text produces a complex counterpoint of self-deconstructing discourses, which abrogate the seeming legitimacy of its argumentation. It thereby enables us to understand more clearly the verbal maneuvering which seeks to excuse atrocity so that the menace it poses can be confronted more directly and its seductive power displaced.

This textual undermining centers around Gilles's identification with Joan. Gilles seizes upon Joan's image, first as a guide and then eventually as justification for his own disintegration, singling out the qualities that would gradually be highlighted in Joan's five-century rehabilitation as patriotic savior, innocent child, androgyne, sacrificed saint, and angel. The moment Gilles first notices Joan in the reception hall at the castle of Chinon in late February 1429 he sees what the narrator describes as "tout ce qu'il aime, tout ce qu'il attend depuis toujours: un jeune garçon, une femme et de surcroît une sainte . . ." 'everything he loves, everything he has always been waiting for: a young boy, a woman, and moreover a saint.' A little further on in the course of this initial meeting, Gilles himself adds, "Ne voyez-vous pas la pureté qui rayonne de son visage . . . une innocence enfantine . . . une lumière qui n'est pas de cette terre . . . Du ciel, parfaitement. Si Jeanne n'est ni une fille, ni un garçon, c'est parce qu'elle est ange" 'Don't you see the purity that shines from her face . . . a childlike innocence . . . a light which is not of this earth . . . from heaven, absolutely. If Joan is neither a girl nor a boy, it is because she is an angel.' The narrator condenses into a few concise pages the complexity of her historical reality, repeatedly stressing her purity, gentle candor, and fidelity to the voices which counseled her to be a good child. The voices had nothing to do with the devil. Gilles discovers in Joan "l'enivrante et dangereuse fusion de la sainteté et la guerre" 'the intoxicating and dangerous fusion of saint-

liness and war.' He seeks to follow her example in order to exorcise his own evil tendencies, becoming thereby the saint he already perceives her to be. And any hesitation he might feel stems, not from Joan's status, but rather from the ambivalence of his own inclinations.

Despite the enthusiasm of Gilles's commitment to Joan, his loyalty is extremely short-lived. Through the spring and summer of 1429, he serves beside her at Orléans and at Patay and accompanies her in glory to Reims for the coronation of Charles VII, but he abandons her as soon as her royal favor begins to wane. After the ill-fated attempt to capture Paris in September 1429 "Gilles disparaît mystérieusement" 'Gilles disappears mysteriously,' and from this point on the "voice" of Tournier's narration begins to expose the gap between words and meaning. When Joan is captured at Compiègne on 24 May 1430, one of many dates whose citation seems to indicate a concern for historical accuracy, the text stresses that Gilles tries to plead her case with Yolande d'Anjou, regent of that province and the king's mother-in-law, who had initially supported Joan's cause. Historically, there is no evidence that Gilles ever attempted to intercede with d'Anjou or ever tried to rescue Joan from prison. The king's mother-in-law and Gilles were vicious political enemies. We know that Gilles was actually plotting her death with the help of Charles VII's current favorite counsellor, Georges de la Trémouille. In Tournier's tale, Gilles does not move precipitously to help Joan; references both to Rouen and to Joan's trial date Gilles's attempt to intervene sometime in the winter or early spring of the following year. She was kept at the castle of Beaurevoir near Arras until December 1430 and depositions for her trial were not given until 13 January 1431. She was first summoned before her judges on 21 February. Hence Tournier's Gilles waits at least seven months after Joan's capture before interceding on her behalf. Furthermore, even Gilles's bold project to rescue Joan from her Rouen dungeon in the spring of 1431 is proposed by someone else. After his unsuccessful audience with the Queen Mother, Tournier's text notes that Gilles is ready to retreat once again to one of his many estates when La Hire, a former battle companion, proposes "Allons-y [à Rouen] ensemble. Jeanne ne sera pas surprise de voir arriver son compagnon Gilles et son vieux La Hire" 'Let's go there [to Rouen] together. Joan won't be surprised to see her companion Gilles and her old La Hire arrive.' Only at the latter's suggestion does Gilles consider a rescue attempt, and it is with troops loyal to La Hire that they undertake their expedition.

Tournier's work clearly indicates that as soon as Joan begins to lose political support, Gilles equates this fall from royal favor with a moral and spiritual defeat. "Or depuis l'échec devant Paris, il semble qu'a pris fin l'état de grâce où vivait Jeanne et qu'elle lui avait fait partager" 'Thus, since her defeat at Paris, it seems that the state of grace in which Joan was living and which she enabled him to share came to an end.' This initial reaction on his part seems to be confirmed by her trial, mentioned only cursorily, and her subsequent execution, which Tournier describes in all of its macabre detail, making it the focal point of Gilles's transformation. By situating Gilles in the crowd—"Perdu dans la foule, il assiste, le coeur crêvé de haine et de chagrins aux préparatifs du supplice" 'Lost in the crowd, his heart broken by hatred and sorrow, he witnesses the preparations for torture'—the text once again undermines its authority, since historically, Gilles was not present. Furthermore, Tournier's work does not acknowledge that throughout her trial Joan continually emphasized her loyalty to the voices she heard, which instructed her only to do *good* and her "unshakable conviction in . . . the rectitude of all her motives, her passions, and her enterprises" [Marina Warner, *Joan of Arc: The Image of Female Heroism,* 1981]. It likewise ignores the fact that Joan heard Mass and received communion on the day she was to be burned. As Warner stresses, "Her judges failed to prove even to themselves that their victim was the thing of reviled pollution they had hoped. She died with the body of her maker inside her." Hence, even according to the ecclesiastical authority that condemns her, Joan died in the state of grace and therefore escapes hell.

When he witnesses Joan's execution, Gilles both confuses condemnation to death by an ecclesiastical court with personal damnation, and carries the process of appropriation to the lowest level of the abject. When Gilles witnesses Joan's death, he confronts the horror of her strictly physical destruction imposed on her by others, "une charogne à demi calcinée, un oeil éclaté qui s'incline sur un torse boursouflé" ("a half burned corpse, one eye burst open, hanging down over a bloated torso") and seizes upon it as emblem and justification for the final stages of his "métamorphose maligne . . ." ("evil metamorphosis.") In a double move he shifts the level of Joan's disintegration to that of the spiritual, implying her condemnation to hell, while simultaneously internalizing the image of her bodily suffering. He becomes an agent of the physical destruction she had endured as victim and, for the next eight years, he imposes on numerous others tortures even more grotesque than those to which the authorities had subjected Joan.

Once Joan is executed and Gilles's metamorphosis into 'infernal angel' is completed, which takes place in the first third of Tournier's work, the scope of the text's undermining process broadens and becomes more radical in its implications. As in the depiction of the initial stages of Gilles's transformation, careful attention is paid to the overall chronological accuracy of events, as well as to the precise identity of the individuals who played significant roles in the last period of Gilles's life (c. 1432-40), namely the priest Eustache Blanchet, the Italian alchemist and conjuror Francesco Prelati, and the various henchmen who assisted Gilles in carrying out his bloody rituals. Tournier manipulates the historical data, however, and widens the gap between the text's words and their meaning, between the signifiers and the signified.

The role of Eustache Blanchet in Tournier's plot is a typical revision. According to documents pertaining to Gilles's trial, Blanchet was in Florence on business in autumn 1438, when he met Prelati, who was eager to share his alchemic secrets with any French patron who might wish to engage his services. Blanchet had been commissioned by Gilles for several years to search out alchemists and conjurors whose skills could hopefully replenish his dissipated fortune; he proposed that Prelati accompany him

back to Tiffauges, where they arrived on Ascension Day in 1439. In the following months Blanchet gradually came to realize the extent of Gilles's and Prelati's involvement with demons. He heard more and more disturbing rumors about Gilles's human sacrifices, and was forced to seek at least temporary refuge elsewhere when he tried to warn Gilles of the consequences of his scandalous behavior. Despite his discoveries, however, Blanchet remained in Gilles's service up to the time the arresting authorities arrived in September 1440, although he was never a member of the latter's inner circle (Bataille).

Tournier presents Blanchet as childlike and naïve in his beliefs, and enlarges his role in Gilles's life. At least from the time Gilles established an ecclesiastical school for young boys on his estate at Machecoul in March 1435, Blanchet was his personal confessor and heard firsthand Gilles's admission of the pleasure he experienced at seeing children suffer: "C'est si beau un petit corps ensanglanté, soulevé par les soupirs et les râles de l'agonie" 'A small blood-covered body, racked by the moans and groans of its death agony is so beautiful.' There is no indication in Tournier that Blanchet was commisioned to engage alchemists and conjurors for Gilles's experiments. But the priest's knowledge of Gilles's predilections was both more extensive and long-standing than historical evidence indicates, and his personal complicity greater. Awakened to the potential for violence in Gilles's remarks and further alerted by descriptions of a dark-cloaked horseman galloping over the fields with kidnapped children in the folds of his mantle, Blanchet does nothing. Ostensibly, he does not want to violate the sacred seal of confession; but his own cowardice and unwillingness to accept responsibility are equally strong motives. Tournier admits that the truth of the rumors floating up from the surrounding villages would have required "de lui des décisions si boulversantes qu'il préférait aussi longtemps que possible—mais pour combien de jours encore? —Se replier frileusement sur son ministère d'aumônier et de chapelain" 'such overwhelming decisions from him that he preferred as long as possible—but for how many days more? —to withdraw timidly into his role of personal priest and chaplain.' Only much later, when he can no longer dismiss the "odeur de chair carbonisée . . . cette puanteur de charogne carbonisée" 'odor of carbonized flesh . . . this stench of corpses reduced to ashes,' does Blanchet admit the desperateness of Gilles's situation and take action. He leaves Gilles to continue his sacrifices while he sets out for Florence to find someone capable of exorcising his charge's demons.

Once in Florence, however, Tournier's provincial Blanchet is unable to cope with the extremes of opulence and corruption he encounters in the city. He immediately falls prey to the charms of the elegant Prelati, who first saves him from a band of thieves and then proceeds to seduce him with arguments that poverty is the source of all vice, opened cadavers should be used to explore the anatomical secrets, and that one must necessarily descend to the depths of the diabolical to discover the unknown. Although he greatly fears Prelati's outrageous assertions, Blanchet nevertheless decides, without looking further, that only Prelati can help Gilles—"il ne voyait plus de ressource qu'en lui" 'he saw no possibility other than him.'

Prelati proceeds to seduce Gilles with the same eloquence that so captivated Blanchet. Historical data indicates that he was both alchemist and conjuror, and was easily able to convince the acutely superstitious Gilles that, if he followed Prelati's directions, he would amass the wealth and power he desired without jeopardizing his life or his soul. After a number of unsuccessful attempts to make Prelati's private demon Barron appear, the Italian even managed to persuade Gilles to offer one of his victims in a diabolical sacrifice. Although Gilles feared the spiritual consequences of such an offering, he was sufficiently desperate about his financial situation to do anything to protect the assets he still possessed and eventually attain the level of financial omnipotence he so eagerly sought.

In Tournier's text Prelati is even more insidiously manipulative. Unfortunately, he does not live up to the image Mireille Rosello paints of him as a disinterested, truth seeking man of science whose gaze reveals "l'acuité froide d'un observateur, d'un sociologue extérieur aux phénomènes qu'il tente de comprendre" 'the coolheaded sharpness of an observer, of a sociologist detached from the phenomena he is trying to understand.' Prelati tells Gilles exactly what the latter wants to hear, equating, as did Gilles, Joan's political defeat with moral transgression and maintaining that since she was condemned by the Inquisition, she automatically went to hell—"au fond du gouffre ardent" 'to the depths of the burning chasm.' At the same time, in another manipulation of theology, Tournier's Prelati purports to offer Gilles a way to rise from the depths of his degradation through the purifying role of the very fire Joan experienced and to which he is subjecting his tortured victims. "Le pécheur plongé dans les abîmes de l'enfer pouvait en rejaillir revêtu d'innocence pourvu qu'il n'ait pas perdu la foi" 'The sinner, plunged into the abyss of hell, could reemerge, once again clothed in childlike innocence, provided he hadn't lost his faith.' Like Joan, whom Prelati cleverly assures Gilles "serait réhabilitée . . . elle connaitraît la béatification, qui sait même peut-être la canonisation" 'would be rehabilitated . . . she would undergo beatification, who knows, perhaps even canonization,' he too will be able to rise glorious and transfigured from the abyss of his abjection, provided he descends far enough.

Despite Prelati's eloquence he does not exorcise his patron's demons; instead, he encourages his continued massacre of innocents by stressing that the end justifies the means and radicalizing the situation by urging him to offer his sacrifices to Prelati's private demon: "Réussissez pour Barron le sacrifice d'Isaac. Offrez-lui la chair des enfants que vous immolez" 'Carry out for Barron Isaac's sacrifice. Offer him the flesh of the children you are immolating.' In keeping with the evidence of the trial testimony, Tournier has Prelati channel Gilles's narcissistic sacrifices in another direction; but his promise of transmutation, alchemically or morally, is part of his charade. Prelati's final prayer to Barron, after Gilles socially disgraces himself by viciously kidnapping the priest Jean de Fréron during Mass in the church adjoining the castle of Saint-Étienne-de-Mermorte, reveals Prelati's intentions:

> "je n'ai rien négligé pour élever cet homme jusqu'à ton seuil sublime . . . pour venir con-
> vertir sa violence en ferveur et ses bas appétits en élans vers ta face auguste. . . . Et sans doute y étais-je parvenu . . . ne sacrifiait-il pas désormais les enfants, non par basse volupté, mais à seule fin de t'offrir leurs dépouilles en holocauste!"

> [I neglected nothing to raise this man to your sublime threshold . . . to succeed in converting his violence into fervor and his base appetites into passion for your noble countenance. . . . And undoubtedly I had succeeded in doing so . . . wasn't he henceforth sacrificing children, not out of base pleasure, but with the sole intention of offering you their remains as a holocaust!]

Serving Barron is not merely a stage in Prelati's cleverly argued plan, but rather his ultimate goal. He condemns only the puerile violence of Gilles's assault on Jean de Fréron because he had been forced to sell the property to the priest's brother Geoffrey for a pittance. Further, he was outraged when the new owner exacted the back taxes he himself had not collected from the peasants.

The final pages of Tournier's work concentrate on Gilles's trial and execution. They present excerpts from his testimony and that of Prelati; lengthy remarks by Gilles's most intimate and long-serving henchmen, Henriet Griart and Étienne Corrilaut, called Poitou, who describe specific crimes; and brief statements from some of the parents whose children disappeared. The transcript of Prelati's testimony details his experiments with alchemy and conjuring during the sixteen months of his service with Gilles. Prelati is careful, however, to blame Gilles for both the sacrificial offering of the child and the pact made with the devil (Bataille). Prelati invoked the devil purely for material gain, to rebuild Gilles's dissipated personal fortune and to reestablish his political dominance.

In Tournier's version the trial is presented more dramatically—consisting largely of dialogue between Prelati and his judges—and provocatively. It depicts Prelati in the most difficult role of his career, before a hostile and highly skilled audience. The tribunal is as adept as Prelati in manipulating arguments, which makes his triumph all the more dazzling. Prelati succeeds not only in saving his life, which at first seems beyond hope—"aucun calcul, aucune momerie, aucune bassesse ne pourrait sauver une cause aussi compromise que la sienne" 'no calculating, no mummery, no servility could save a cause as compromised as his'—but also in completely silencing all possible opposition. In a clearly calculated move, Prelati decides to push the defiant insolence of his "sourire ironique" 'ironic smile' further than ever before, daring his nonplussed judges to do anything about it and beating them at their own game. He turns the tribunal members' own objections against them in a mounting sequence of outrageous statements, noting God the Father's passion for bloody sacrifices, quoting with "une déférence ironique" 'an ironic deference' Christ's statement urging the children to come to him, stressing with "une douceur affectée" 'an affected gentleness' the essential resemblance between Satan and God, and eventually subdues them completely with the illusion of meaning he offers in his discourse on the parallelism between Gilles's situation and that of Joan of Arc. As the narrator indicates, "Malgré eux, tous ces théologi-ciens, grands amateurs de fines disputes, dressent l'oreille. Pierre de l'Hospital fait signe de laisser parler Prelati" 'In spite of themselves, all these theologians, great enthusiasts for subtle disputes, prick up their ears. Pierre de l'Hospital makes a sign to let Prelati speak.'

The same display of self-serving histrionics likewise char-acterizes Gilles's testimony. Tournier lifts a number of statements directly from the trial transcript and adheres to the chronological accuracy of Gilles's appearances. Consistantly, Tournier again revises historical data to highlight the contradictions in his protagonist's position and to reveal more precisely the differences between his situation and Joan's. In the transcript Gilles at first ap-peared as a defiant accuser, refusing to acknowledge the charges against him and attacking his judges as "si-moniaques et des ribauds" traffickers in holy offices and thieves' (Bataille). Scandalized by Gilles's conduct, the tri-bunal in turn immediately excommunicated him, closing the session and scheduling his next appearance in two days. When Gilles resumed his testimony, he had changed from belligerent accuser to docile penitent. Confronted with the reality of excommunication, he tearfully con-fessed his crimes, "se mettant à genoux et exprimant la contrition par de grands soupirs, douloureusement et dans les larmes, sollicita d'être humblement absous . . . de la sentence d'excommunication" 'getting down on his knees and expressing his contrition with great sighs, he humbly begged to be absolved of the sentence of excommunica-tion' (Bataille). This attitude persisted throughout the rest of the proceedings, and Gilles went to his death reconciled with the power of the ecclesiastical authorities and fully reinstated in the Church.

Tournier begins the trial testimony by changing the se-quence of events, complicating the situation and revealing both the extent of Gilles's own ability to overwhelm his judges and the level of their vanity. The trial transcript re-ports that Gilles was excommunicated on 13 October. When the next session opened, he appeared an effusive penitent. In Tournier's work the initial meeting ends with Gilles's attack on his judges as vengeful debtors, who are jealous of his family's influence: "Non, vous n'êtes pas des juges: vous êtes des débiteurs. Je ne suis pas un accusé: je suis un créancier" 'No, you are not judges: you are debt-ors. I am not the accused: I am a creditor.' Through the power of his own social position, he forces them mutely out of the trial hall: "atterés, ils sortirent piteusement, les uns après les autres . . ." 'shattered, they left pitifully, one after the other.' When the next session opens on Saturday, 15 October, Gilles is equally aggressive, asserting that he is as good a Christian as any one else. He insists that since he confessed to Blanchet, he is "blanc et pur comme l'agneau qui vient de naître" 'as white and pure as the lamb which has just been born' and, like Prelati, dares the court to attack him. In the interim, however, the judges recovered from their humiliation of the last session and unanimously excommunicated him. In keeping with the reaction noted in the trial transcript, Tournier's Gilles is thunderstruck: "L'excommunication est pire que la mort, puisqu'elle débouche sur la damnation éternelle" 'Excom-munication is worse than death because it leads to eternal

damnation.' This statement is significant for the light it sheds on Gilles's much flaunted fidelity to Joan; the text separates for Gilles the issue of condemnation to death and damnation, which it had failed to do for Joan. Fur-thermore, despite his repeated assertions about being will-ing to follow Joan to hell, Gilles does everything possible during his trial to avoid going to hell and experiencing the fire which Joan had suffered during her execution and to which he had subjected his victims.

Descending into hell for Gilles is only a metaphor, another rhetorical strategy used to mask his duplicity. When the tribunal makes his damnation a reality, his reversal is in-stantaneous. The speed of this transformation could be said to correspond to the overnight reversal indicated in the trial documents; but in yet another revision of history, Tournier reinstates Gilles in the Church before he ac-knowledges any crimes. The excommunication order is re-scinded as soon as he begs forgiveness for having insulted the judges, playing up to their own egoism: "Je leur de-mande humblement pardon pour les injures et les paroles blessantes que j'ai proférées" 'I humbly ask their pardon for the insults and offensive words I spoke.' Only when the decree is lifted does he admit culpability, but even then his arrogance stands out as clearly as ever, and his expressions of guilt overwhelm his judges even more profoundly than his earlier vituperative outbursts: "[ils] se sentaient humi-liés plus encore que sous les injures" '[they] felt themselves more humiliated than by insults.' There is no indication at this point that either Gilles or his judges is treating the situation any more honestly and forthrightly than they had earlier. Each manipulates the other in a desperate struggle for power. Only the means have changed, from insults and threats to excessive *mea culpas* and conde-scending pardons.

The process of historical manipulation and textual subver-sion culminates in the scene of Gilles's execution. As indi-cated by the trial documents, Gilles goes to his death rec-onciled with the Church, exhorting his two companions to welcome the death that awaits them, for then "ils se re-verraient dans la gloire, avec Dieu dans le paradis" 'they would see one another in glory, with God in paradise' (Bataille). Tournier's depiction carefully maintains chro-nological and geographical accuracy; it emphasizes Gil-les's public repentance as he proclaims to Henriet Griart and Poitou, "Suivez-moi dans mon salut comme vous m'avez suivi dans mes crimes" 'Follow me in my salvation as you followed me in my crimes.' Once again, however, Tournier's treatment raises troubling questions and re-veals dramatically how the signified slips ever further be-neath the signifier to prevent the production of meaning. Along with seeking to describe Gilles's execution in terms of Christ's crucifixion, with Gilles being paraded through the streets of Nantes to die on "un étrange golgotha" 'a strange golgotha,' Tournier's work attempts one last time to make Gilles's image converge with that of his idol by stressing the parallels between their execution scenes. However, this strategy will not work, for although Gilles and Joan were both executed, they did not, as Tournier's work emphasizes, die in the same way. Joan was burned alive on the Place du Vieux Marché in Rouen, and her ashes were thrown into the Seine (Warner). Out of mercy,

Gilles, the still privileged nobleman, was hanged and died before the fire was lighted. His body was also removed from the pyre "avant que son corps ne fût ouvert" 'before his body burst open' and was then entombed in the Carmelite church in Nantes (Bataille; Nettlebeck). Only Gilles's two servant accomplices were destroyed by fire "de telle sorte qu'ils furent réduits en poudre" 'so that they were reduced to ashes' but after they too had already died by hanging (Bataille).

Despite the frenzied invocation of Joan's name which Tournier's Gilles makes as an "appel céleste" 'celestial appeal' before the crowd at his execution, the images do not converge in either a historical or a fictional context. They cannot even be made to reflect one another as the inverted mirror images that haunt so many of Tournier's writings. Gilles's reaffirmation of Joan's short-lived apotheosis as sainted warrior and her subsequent condemnation by the Inquisition just before his own death merely repeats his earlier declarations and offers no new insight into the differences separating them. And in one final, and perhaps its most splendidly ironic move of all, Tournier passes over in silence the one essential and historically verifiable parallel that does exist between Gilles's situation and Joan's—namely that they *both* died reconciled with the Church. His work denies Joan the official reconciliation it so dramatically grants the master of Tiffauges. Gilles's last comments leave Joan still condemned as a witch, awaiting future rehabilitation, while he prepares to ascend directly "vers la porte du ciel" 'to the gate of heaven.'

Tournier leaves his readers poised on the edge of the abyss his text creates, struggling to find our footing amidst "un réseau de contradictions" 'a network of contradictions.' However, as the ironic "voice" of Tournier's narration exposes the gap between Gilles and the one he appropriated as his idol, it creates the essential space in which our own questioning and contesting can be formulated. It is precisely this ongoing activity on our part which the text itself so vigorously encourages. Tournier's work seeks not to entrap us, but rather to provide us with the means to avoid being "définitivement compromis" 'definitively compromised.' The echoes of Gilles's last dramatic invocation, reinforced by the chanting of the crowd and the roar of the storm, continue to resonate in history and fiction down through the centuries, and the stench from his private holocaust continues to pollute the atmosphere. These signs marking Gilles's spectacular cruelty reached the ultimate level of horror in our era in the Nazi apocalypse, a phenomenon Tournier explores in his earlier work **Le Roi des aulnes,** which creates the fictional experience of his twentieth-century ogre Abel Tiffauges, revealing how acutely urgent it has become for us to be able to decipher the strategies that nourish and sanction atrocity. Only then can the tirades of a Gilles be silenced and the air cleared. More intensely and directly than any of Tournier's other writings, *Gilles et Jeanne* enables us to participate in this process of displacement.

FURTHER READING

Criticism

Apter, Emily. "Fore-skin and After-image: Photographic Fetishism in Tournier's Fiction." *L'Esprit Créateur* XXIX, No. 1 (Spring 1989): 72-82.
    Examines the role of fetishism in Tournier's works.

Birkirts, Sven. "Michel Tournier." In his *An Artificial Wilderness: Essays on 20th Century Literature,* pp. 171-78. New York: William Morrow and Company, Inc., 1985.
    Praises Tournier's daring and innovation.

Cloonan, William. "*Le Roi des aulnes:* Myth as Fiction, Fiction as Myth." *Romance Languages* 3 (1991): 32-6.
    Studies the role of myth in *The Ogre,* drawing on Roland Barthes' definition of myth.

Davis, Colin. "Art and the Refusal of Mourning: The Aesthetics of Michel Tournier." *Paragraph* 10 (October 1987): 29-44.
    Discusses Tournier's use of artistic themes.

———. "Michel Tournier's *Vendredi; ou, Les Limbes du Pacifique*: A Novel of Beginnings." *Neophilologues* LXXIII, No. 3 (July 1989): 373-82.
    Studies Tournier's themes and literary style.

Edwards, Rachel. "Myth, Allegory and Michel Tournier." *Journal of European Studies* XIX, No. 74, part 2 (June 1989): 99-121.
    Provides an in-depth study of Tournier's many definitions and uses of myth and allegory.

Higonnet, Margaret R. "Marguerite Yourcenar and Michel Tournier: The Arts of the Heart." In *Triumphs of the Spirit in Children's Literature,* edited by Francelia Butler and Richard Rotert, pp. 151-58. Hamden: Library Professionals Publication, 1986.
    Praises the thematic portrayals in Tournier's literature for children.

Hueston, Penny. "An Interview with Michel Tournier." *Meanjin* 38, No. 3 (September 1979): 400-05.
    Interview in which Tournier discusses what he considers the most important French novels of the twentieth century.

Ladimer, Bethany. "Overcoming Original Difference: Sexuality in the Work of Michel Tournier." *Modern Language Studies* XXI, No. 2 (Spring 1991): 76-91.
    Discusses the roles that sexuality and perversion play in Tournier's fiction.

Levy, Karen D. "*Le Grand Meaulnes* and *Le Roi des aulnes*: Counterpointed Echoes from a Distant Past." *Romance Notes* XXIX, No. 2 (Winter 1988): 107-18.
    Discusses intertexuality in Tournier's novels. Compares *Le Roi des aulnes* with Alain-Fournier's *Le Grand Meaulnes* (1913).

———. "The Fatal Temptation of the Image: Specular Fascination in Tournier's *Le Roi des aulnes.*" *The International Fiction Review* 19, No. 2 (1992): 76-87.
    Focuses on Tournier's use of signs and images in his fiction.

Maclean, Mairi. "Michel Tournier as Misogynist (or Not?): An Assessment of the Author's View of Femininity." *The Modern Language Review* 83, No. 2 (April 1988): 322-31.

Discusses Tournier's representation of women and the hostility his male characters have for them.

Petit, Susan. "Sexualite Alimentaire or Elementaire: Michel Tournier's Answer to Freud." *Mosaic: A Journal for the Interdisciplinary Study of Literature* 24, Nos. 3-4 (Summer/Fall 1991): 163-77.

Focuses on the sexual themes in *Friday* and *The Ogre.*

Platten, David. "Terms of Reference: Michel Tournier's *Le Roi des aulnes.*" *Journal of European Studies* 21, No. 84 (December 1991): 281-302.

Offers an in-depth study of *The Ogre.*

Quinones, Ricardo J. "Twinning the Twain." In his *The Changes of Cain: Violence and the Lost Brother in Cain and Abel Literature,* pp. 229-37. Princeton: Princeton University Press, 1991.

Examines the Cain and Abel themes in Tournier's *Le Roi des aulnes* and *Les Météores.*

Robinson, Christopher. "Philosophical Dilemmas." In his *French Literature in the Twentieth Century,* pp. 170-77. London: David & Charles, 1980.

Discusses the role of myth in Tournier's first three published novels.

Rushdie, Salman. "Michel Tournier." In *Imaginary Homelands: Essays and Criticism, 1981-1991*, pp. 249-253. London: Granta Books, 1991.

Praises *Gemini,* stating that Tournier "weaves banalities into wonders."

Sankey, Margaret. "Parody, History and Myth in *Le Roi des aulnes.*" *Australian Journal of French Studies* XXVII, No. 1 (January-April 1990): 73-82.

Defends Tournier's use of myth and intertexuality in *Le Roi des aulnes.*

Schehr, Lawrence R. "Tournier's Theoretical Pretext Works Like a Charm." *Studies in Twentieth-century Literature* 12, No. 2 (Spring 1988): 221-38.

Reviews *La Goutte d'or* and discusses the use of the photograph theme throughout the text.

Shattuck, Roger. "Locating Michel Tournier." In his *The Innocent Eye on Modern Literature and the Arts,* pp. 205-18. New York: Farrar, Strauss, Giroux, 1984.

Examines Tournier's status among twentieth-century French novelists.

Shryock, Richard. "Reading Models: Embedded Narrative and Ideology in *La goutte d'or.*" *Modern Language Studies* XXI, No. 3 (Summer 1991): 65-75.

Focuses on the narrative techniques in *La goutte d'or,* examining the ways in which they influence the development of the protagonist and affect the novel's ideological and pedagogical content.

Strauss, Walter A. "Tournier's Quest for Sophia." In *Literature as Philosophy, Philosophy as Literature,* edited by Donald G. Marshall, pp. 306-16. Iowa City: University of Iowa Press, 1987.

Lauds Tournier's depiction of the pursuit of wisdom in his novels.

Worton, Michael J. "Myth-Reference in *Le Roi des aulnes.*" *Stanford French Review* VI, Nos. 2-3 (Fall-Winter 1982): 299-310.

Examines the function of myth in Tournier's *Le Roi des aulnes.*

————. "Use and Abuse of Metaphor in Tournier's *Le Vol du Vampire.*" *Paragraph* 10 (October 1987): 13-28.

Examines the function of the vampire metaphor as it relates to the text-reader relationship in Tournier's fiction.

York, R. A. "Thematic Construction in *Le Roi des aulnes.*" *Orbis Litterarum* 36, No. 1 (1981): 76-91.

Focuses on the thematic progression of obsession, possessiveness, service, sacrifice, and apocalyptic triumph in *Le Roi des aulnes.*

Additional coverage of Tournier's life and career is contained in the following sources published by Gale Research: *Contemporary Authors,* Vols. 49-52; *Contemporary Authors New Revision Series,* Vols. 3, 36; *Contemporary Literary Criticism,* Vols. 6, 23, 36; *Dictionary of Literary Biography,* Vol. 83; *Major 20th-Century Writers;* and *Something about the Author,* Vol. 23.

☐ Contemporary Literary Criticism

Indexes

Literary Criticism Series
Cumulative Author Index
Cumulative Topic Index
Cumulative Nationality Index
Title Index, Volume 95

How to Use This Index

The main references

```
Camus, Albert
    1913-1960 . . . . CLC 1, 2, 4, 9, 11, 14,
    32, 69; DA; DAB; DAC; DC 2; SSC 9;
                                      WLC
```

list all author entries in the following Gale Literary Criticism series:

BLC = *Black Literature Criticism*
CLC = *Contemporary Literary Criticism*
CLR = *Children's Literature Review*
CMLC = *Classical and Medieval Literature Criticism*
DA = *DISCovering Authors*
DAB = *DISCovering Authors: British*
DAC = *DISCovering Authors: Canadian*
DC = *Drama Criticism*
HLC = *Hispanic Literature Criticism*
LC = *Literature Criticism from 1400 to 1800*
NCLC = *Nineteenth-Century Literature Criticism*
PC = *Poetry Criticism*
SSC = *Short Story Criticism*
TCLC = *Twentieth-Century Literary Criticism*
WLC = *World Literature Criticism, 1500 to the Present*

The cross-references

```
See also CA 89-92; DAM DRAM, MST,
    NOV; DLB 72; MTCW
```

list all author entries in the following Gale biographical and literary sources:

AAYA = *Authors & Artists for Young Adults*
AITN = *Authors in the News*
BEST = *Bestsellers*
BW = *Black Writers*
CA = *Contemporary Authors*
CAAS = *Contemporary Authors Autobiography Series*
CABS = *Contemporary Authors Bibliographical Series*
CANR = *Contemporary Authors New Revision Series*
CAP = *Contemporary Authors Permanent Series*
CDALB = *Concise Dictionary of American Literary Biography*
CDBLB = *Concise Dictionary of British Literary Biography*
DAM = *DISCovering Authors Modules*
  DRAM = *dramatists*; *MST* = *most-studied*

authors; *MULT* = *multicultural authors*; *NOV* = *novelists*; *POET* = *poets*; *POP* = *popular/genre writers*
DLB = *Dictionary of Literary Biography*
DLBD = *Dictionary of Literary Biography Documentary Series*
DLBY = *Dictionary of Literary Biography Yearbook*
HW = *Hispanic Writers*
JRDA = *Junior DISCovering Authors*
MAICYA = *Major Authors and Illustrators for Children and Young Adults*
MTCW = *Major 20th-Century Writers*
NNAL = *Native North American Literature*
SAAS = *Something about the Author Autobiography Series*
SATA = *Something about the Author*
YABC = *Yesterday's Authors of Books for Children*

Andrade, Mario de 1893-1945 . . . . . **TCLC 43**

Andreae, Johann V(alentin)
1586-1654 . . . . **LC 32**
See also DLB 164

Andreas-Salome, Lou 1861-1937 . . . **TCLC 56**
See also DLB 66

Andrewes, Lancelot 1555-1626 . . . . . . **LC 5**
See also DLB 151

Andrews, Cicily Fairfield
See West, Rebecca

Andrews, Elton V.
See Pohl, Frederik

Andreyev, Leonid (Nikolaevich)
1871-1919 . . . . **TCLC 3**
See also CA 104

Andric, Ivo 1892-1975 . . . . **CLC 8**
See also CA 81-84; 57-60; CANR 43;
DLB 147; MTCW

Angelique, Pierre
See Bataille, Georges

Angell, Roger 1920- . . . . **CLC 26**
See also CA 57-60; CANR 13, 44

Angelou, Maya
1928- . . . . **CLC 12, 35, 64, 77; BLC; DA;
DAB; DAC**
See also AAYA 7; BW 2; CA 65-68;
CANR 19, 42; DAM MST, MULT,
POET, POP; DLB 38; MTCW; SATA 49

Annensky, Innokenty Fyodorovich
1856-1909 . . . . **TCLC 14**
See also CA 110

Anon, Charles Robert
See Pessoa, Fernando (Antonio Nogueira)

Anouilh, Jean (Marie Lucien Pierre)
1910-1987 . . . . . . **CLC 1, 3, 8, 13, 40, 50**
See also CA 17-20R; 123; CANR 32;
DAM DRAM; MTCW

Anthony, Florence
See Ai

Anthony, John
See Ciardi, John (Anthony)

Anthony, Peter
See Shaffer, Anthony (Joshua); Shaffer,
Peter (Levin)

Anthony, Piers 1934- . . . . **CLC 35**
See also AAYA 11; CA 21-24R; CANR 28;
DAM POP; DLB 8; MTCW; SAAS 22;
SATA 84

Antoine, Marc
See Proust, (Valentin-Louis-George-Eugene-)
Marcel

Antoninus, Brother
See Everson, William (Oliver)

Antonioni, Michelangelo 1912- . . . . . **CLC 20**
See also CA 73-76; CANR 45

Antschel, Paul 1920-1970
See Celan, Paul
See also CA 85-88; CANR 33; MTCW

Anwar, Chairil 1922-1949 . . . . **TCLC 22**
See also CA 121

Apollinaire, Guillaume . . **TCLC 3, 8, 51; PC 7**
See also Kostrowitzki, Wilhelm Apollinaris
de
See also DAM POET

Appelfeld, Aharon 1932- . . . . **CLC 23, 47**
See also CA 112; 133

Apple, Max (Isaac) 1941- . . . . **CLC 9, 33**
See also CA 81-84; CANR 19; DLB 130

Appleman, Philip (Dean) 1926- . . . . . **CLC 51**
See also CA 13-16R; CAAS 18; CANR 6,
29

Appleton, Lawrence
See Lovecraft, H(oward) P(hillips)

Apteryx
See Eliot, T(homas) S(tearns)

Apuleius, (Lucius Madaurensis)
125(?)-175(?) . . . . **CMLC 1**

Aquin, Hubert 1929-1977 . . . . **CLC 15**
See also CA 105; DLB 53

Aragon, Louis 1897-1982 . . . . **CLC 3, 22**
See also CA 69-72; 108; CANR 28;
DAM NOV, POET; DLB 72; MTCW

Arany, Janos 1817-1882 . . . . **NCLC 34**

Arbuthnot, John 1667-1735 . . . . **LC 1**
See also DLB 101

Archer, Herbert Winslow
See Mencken, H(enry) L(ouis)

Archer, Jeffrey (Howard) 1940- . . . . **CLC 28**
See also AAYA 16; BEST 89:3; CA 77-80;
CANR 22, 52; DAM POP;
INT CANR-22

Archer, Jules 1915- . . . . **CLC 12**
See also CA 9-12R; CANR 6; SAAS 5;
SATA 4, 85

Archer, Lee
See Ellison, Harlan (Jay)

Arden, John 1930- . . . . **CLC 6, 13, 15**
See also CA 13-16R; CAAS 4; CANR 31;
DAM DRAM; DLB 13; MTCW

Arenas, Reinaldo
1943-1990 . . . . **CLC 41; HLC**
See also CA 124; 128; 133; DAM MULT;
DLB 145; HW

Arendt, Hannah 1906-1975 . . . . **CLC 66**
See also CA 17-20R; 61-64; CANR 26;
MTCW

Aretino, Pietro 1492-1556 . . . . **LC 12**

Arghezi, Tudor . . . . **CLC 80**
See also Theodorescu, Ion N.

Arguedas, Jose Maria
1911-1969 . . . . **CLC 10, 18**
See also CA 89-92; DLB 113; HW

Argueta, Manlio 1936- . . . . **CLC 31**
See also CA 131; DLB 145; HW

Ariosto, Ludovico 1474-1533 . . . . **LC 6**

Aristides
See Epstein, Joseph

Aristophanes
450B.C.-385B.C. . . . . **CMLC 4; DA;
DAB; DAC; DC 2**
See also DAM DRAM, MST

Arlt, Roberto (Godofredo Christophersen)
1900-1942 . . . . **TCLC 29; HLC**
See also CA 123; 131; DAM MULT; HW

Armah, Ayi Kwei 1939- . . . . **CLC 5, 33; BLC**
See also BW 1; CA 61-64; CANR 21;
DAM MULT, POET; DLB 117; MTCW

Armatrading, Joan 1950- . . . . **CLC 17**
See also CA 114

Arnette, Robert
See Silverberg, Robert

**Arnim, Achim von (Ludwig Joachim von
Arnim)** 1781-1831 . . . . **NCLC 5**
See also DLB 90

Arnim, Bettina von 1785-1859 . . . . **NCLC 38**
See also DLB 90

Arnold, Matthew
1822-1888 . . . . . **NCLC 6, 29; DA; DAB;
DAC; PC 5; WLC**
See also CDBLB 1832-1890; DAM MST,
POET; DLB 32, 57

Arnold, Thomas 1795-1842 . . . . . . **NCLC 18**
See also DLB 55

Arnow, Harriette (Louisa) Simpson
1908-1986 . . . . **CLC 2, 7, 18**
See also CA 9-12R; 118; CANR 14; DLB 6;
MTCW; SATA 42; SATA-Obit 47

Arp, Hans
See Arp, Jean

Arp, Jean 1887-1966. . . . . **CLC 5**
See also CA 81-84; 25-28R; CANR 42

Arrabal
See Arrabal, Fernando

Arrabal, Fernando 1932- . . . **CLC 2, 9, 18, 58**
See also CA 9-12R; CANR 15

Arrick, Fran. **CLC 30**
See also Gaberman, Judie Angell

Artaud, Antonin (Marie Joseph)
1896-1948 . . . . **TCLC 3, 36**
See also CA 104; 149; DAM DRAM

Arthur, Ruth M(abel) 1905-1979 . . . . **CLC 12**
See also CA 9-12R; 85-88; CANR 4;
SATA 7, 26

Artsybashev, Mikhail (Petrovich)
1878-1927 . . . . **TCLC 31**

Arundel, Honor (Morfydd)
1919-1973 . . . . **CLC 17**
See also CA 21-22; 41-44R; CAP 2;
CLR 35; SATA 4; SATA-Obit 24

Asch, Sholem 1880-1957 . . . . **TCLC 3**
See also CA 105

Ash, Shalom
See Asch, Sholem

Ashbery, John (Lawrence)
1927- . . . . . . **CLC 2, 3, 4, 6, 9, 13, 15, 25,
41, 77**
See also CA 5-8R; CANR 9, 37;
DAM POET; DLB 5, 165; DLBY 81;
INT CANR-9; MTCW

Ashdown, Clifford
See Freeman, R(ichard) Austin

Ashe, Gordon
See Creasey, John

Ashton-Warner, Sylvia (Constance)
1908-1984 . . . . **CLC 19**
See also CA 69-72; 112; CANR 29; MTCW

Benet, Juan 1927-............. **CLC 28**
  See also CA 143

Benet, Stephen Vincent
    1898-1943 .... **TCLC 7; SSC 10**
  See also CA 104; DAM POET; DLB 4, 48,
    102; YABC 1

Benet, William Rose 1886-1950 ... **TCLC 28**
  See also CA 118; DAM POET; DLB 45

Benford, Gregory (Albert) 1941-.... **CLC 52**
  See also CA 69-72; CANR 12, 24, 49;
    DLBY 82

Bengtsson, Frans (Gunnar)
    1894-1954 .... **TCLC 48**

Benjamin, David
  See Slavitt, David R(ytman)

Benjamin, Lois
  See Gould, Lois

Benjamin, Walter 1892-1940..... **TCLC 39**

Benn, Gottfried 1886-1956........ **TCLC 3**
  See also CA 106; DLB 56

Bennett, Alan 1934-..... **CLC 45, 77; DAB**
  See also CA 103; CANR 35; DAM MST;
    MTCW

Bennett, (Enoch) Arnold
    1867-1931 .... **TCLC 5, 20**
  See also CA 106; CDBLB 1890-1914;
    DLB 10, 34, 98, 135

Bennett, Elizabeth
  See Mitchell, Margaret (Munnerlyn)

Bennett, George Harold 1930-
  See Bennett, Hal
  See also BW 1; CA 97-100

Bennett, Hal .... **CLC 5**
  See also Bennett, George Harold
  See also DLB 33

Bennett, Jay 1912-............... **CLC 35**
  See also AAYA 10; CA 69-72; CANR 11,
    42; JRDA; SAAS 4; SATA 41, 87;
    SATA-Brief 27

Bennett, Louise (Simone)
    1919-................... **CLC 28; BLC**
  See also BW 2; CA 151; DAM MULT;
    DLB 117

Benson, E(dward) F(rederic)
    1867-1940 .... **TCLC 27**
  See also CA 114; DLB 135, 153

Benson, Jackson J. 1930-......... **CLC 34**
  See also CA 25-28R; DLB 111

Benson, Sally 1900-1972 .... **CLC 17**
  See also CA 19-20; 37-40R; CAP 1;
    SATA 1, 35; SATA-Obit 27

Benson, Stella 1892-1933........ **TCLC 17**
  See also CA 117; DLB 36, 162

Bentham, Jeremy 1748-1832 ..... **NCLC 38**
  See also DLB 107, 158

Bentley, E(dmund) C(lerihew)
    1875-1956 .... **TCLC 12**
  See also CA 108; DLB 70

Bentley, Eric (Russell) 1916-....... **CLC 24**
  See also CA 5-8R; CANR 6; INT CANR-6

Beranger, Pierre Jean de
    1780-1857 .... **NCLC 34**

Berendt, John (Lawrence) 1939-.... **CLC 86**
  See also CA 146

Berger, Colonel
  See Malraux, (Georges-)Andre

Berger, John (Peter) 1926- ...... **CLC 2, 19**
  See also CA 81-84; CANR 51; DLB 14

Berger, Melvin H. 1927-.......... **CLC 12**
  See also CA 5-8R; CANR 4; CLR 32;
    SAAS 2; SATA 5, 88

Berger, Thomas (Louis)
    1924- .... **CLC 3, 5, 8, 11, 18, 38**
  See also CA 1-4R; CANR 5, 28, 51;
    DAM NOV; DLB 2; DLBY 80;
    INT CANR-28; MTCW

Bergman, (Ernst) Ingmar
    1918-..................... **CLC 16, 72**
  See also CA 81-84; CANR 33

Bergson, Henri 1859-1941........ **TCLC 32**

Bergstein, Eleanor 1938-........... **CLC 4**
  See also CA 53-56; CANR 5

Berkoff, Steven 1937-............. **CLC 56**
  See also CA 104

Bermant, Chaim (Icyk) 1929- ...... **CLC 40**
  See also CA 57-60; CANR 6, 31

Bern, Victoria
  See Fisher, M(ary) F(rances) K(ennedy)

Bernanos, (Paul Louis) Georges
    1888-1948 .... **TCLC 3**
  See also CA 104; 130; DLB 72

Bernard, April 1956- .... **CLC 59**
  See also CA 131

Berne, Victoria
  See Fisher, M(ary) F(rances) K(ennedy)

Bernhard, Thomas
    1931-1989 .... **CLC 3, 32, 61**
  See also CA 85-88; 127; CANR 32;
    DLB 85, 124; MTCW

Berriault, Gina 1926-............. **CLC 54**
  See also CA 116; 129; DLB 130

Berrigan, Daniel 1921-............. **CLC 4**
  See also CA 33-36R; CAAS 1; CANR 11,
    43; DLB 5

Berrigan, Edmund Joseph Michael, Jr.
    1934-1983
  See Berrigan, Ted
  See also CA 61-64; 110; CANR 14

Berrigan, Ted...................... **CLC 37**
  See also Berrigan, Edmund Joseph Michael,
    Jr.
  See also DLB 5

Berry, Charles Edward Anderson 1931-
  See Berry, Chuck
  See also CA 115

Berry, Chuck..................... **CLC 17**
  See also Berry, Charles Edward Anderson

Berry, Jonas
  See Ashbery, John (Lawrence)

Berry, Wendell (Erdman)
    1934- .... **CLC 4, 6, 8, 27, 46**
  See also AITN 1; CA 73-76; CANR 50;
    DAM POET; DLB 5, 6

Berryman, John
    1914-1972 ..... **CLC 1, 2, 3, 4, 6, 8, 10,**
               13, 25, 62
  See also CA 13-16; 33-36R; CABS 2;
    CANR 35; CAP 1; CDALB 1941-1968;
    DAM POET; DLB 48; MTCW

Bertolucci, Bernardo 1940- .... **CLC 16**
  See also CA 106

Bertrand, Aloysius 1807-1841 .... **NCLC 31**

Bertran de Born c. 1140-1215 ..... **CMLC 5**

Besant, Annie (Wood) 1847-1933 ... **TCLC 9**
  See also CA 105

Bessie, Alvah 1904-1985.......... **CLC 23**
  See also CA 5-8R; 116; CANR 2; DLB 26

Bethlen, T. D.
  See Silverberg, Robert

Beti, Mongo................. **CLC 27; BLC**
  See also Biyidi, Alexandre
  See also DAM MULT

Betjeman, John
    1906-1984 ... **CLC 2, 6, 10, 34, 43; DAB**
  See also CA 9-12R; 112; CANR 33;
    CDBLB 1945-1960; DAM MST, POET;
    DLB 20; DLBY 84; MTCW

Bettelheim, Bruno 1903-1990 ...... **CLC 79**
  See also CA 81-84; 131; CANR 23; MTCW

Betti, Ugo 1892-1953 .... **TCLC 5**
  See also CA 104

Betts, Doris (Waugh) 1932-.... **CLC 3, 6, 28**
  See also CA 13-16R; CANR 9; DLBY 82;
    INT CANR-9

Bevan, Alistair
  See Roberts, Keith (John Kingston)

Bialik, Chaim Nachman
    1873-1934 .... **TCLC 25**

Bickerstaff, Isaac
  See Swift, Jonathan

Bidart, Frank 1939-.............. **CLC 33**
  See also CA 140

Bienek, Horst 1930-............. **CLC 7, 11**
  See also CA 73-76; DLB 75

Bierce, Ambrose (Gwinett)
    1842-1914(?) .... **TCLC 1, 7, 44; DA;**
               DAC; SSC 9; WLC
  See also CA 104; 139; CDALB 1865-1917;
    DAM MST; DLB 11, 12, 23, 71, 74

Biggers, Earl Derr 1884-1933 ..... **TCLC 65**
  See also CA 108

Billings, Josh
  See Shaw, Henry Wheeler

Billington, (Lady) Rachel (Mary)
    1942-..................... **CLC 43**
  See also AITN 2; CA 33-36R; CANR 44

Binyon, T(imothy) J(ohn) 1936- .... **CLC 34**
  See also CA 111; CANR 28

Bioy Casares, Adolfo
    1914-.... **CLC 4, 8, 13, 88; HLC; SSC 17**
  See also CA 29-32R; CANR 19, 43;
    DAM MULT; DLB 113; HW; MTCW

Bird, Cordwainer
  See Ellison, Harlan (Jay)

Bird, Robert Montgomery
    1806-1854 .... **NCLC 1**

Birney, (Alfred) Earle
    1904- .... **CLC 1, 4, 6, 11; DAC**
  See also CA 1-4R; CANR 5, 20;
    DAM MST, POET; DLB 88; MTCW

Bishop, Elizabeth
1911-1979 ...... **CLC 1, 4, 9, 13, 15, 32;**
DA; DAC; PC 3
See also CA 5-8R; 89-92; CABS 2;
CANR 26; CDALB 1968-1988;
DAM MST, POET; DLB 5; MTCW;
SATA-Obit 24

Bishop, John 1935- .... **CLC 10**
See also CA 105

Bissett, Bill 1939- .... **CLC 18; PC 14**
See also CA 69-72; CAAS 19; CANR 15;
DLB 53; MTCW

Bitov, Andrei (Georgievich) 1937-... **CLC 57**
See also CA 142

Biyidi, Alexandre 1932-
See Beti, Mongo
See also BW 1; CA 114; 124; MTCW

Bjarme, Brynjolf
See Ibsen, Henrik (Johan)

Bjornson, Bjornstjerne (Martinius)
1832-1910 .... **TCLC 7, 37**
See also CA 104

Black, Robert
See Holdstock, Robert P.

Blackburn, Paul 1926-1971 ...... **CLC 9, 43**
See also CA 81-84; 33-36R; CANR 34;
DLB 16; DLBY 81

Black Elk 1863-1950 .... **TCLC 33**
See also CA 144; DAM MULT; NNAL

Black Hobart
See Sanders, (James) Ed(ward)

Blacklin, Malcolm
See Chambers, Aidan

Blackmore, R(ichard) D(oddridge)
1825-1900 .... **TCLC 27**
See also CA 120; DLB 18

Blackmur, R(ichard) P(almer)
1904-1965 .... **CLC 2, 24**
See also CA 11-12; 25-28R; CAP 1; DLB 63

Black Tarantula, The
See Acker, Kathy

Blackwood, Algernon (Henry)
1869-1951 .... **TCLC 5**
See also CA 105; 150; DLB 153, 156

Blackwood, Caroline 1931-1996 ... **CLC 6, 9**
See also CA 85-88; 151; CANR 32;
DLB 14; MTCW

Blade, Alexander
See Hamilton, Edmond; Silverberg, Robert

Blaga, Lucian 1895-1961 .... **CLC 75**

Blair, Eric (Arthur) 1903-1950
See Orwell, George
See also CA 104; 132; DA; DAB; DAC;
DAM MST, NOV; MTCW; SATA 29

Blais, Marie-Claire
1939- .... **CLC 2, 4, 6, 13, 22; DAC**
See also CA 21-24R; CAAS 4; CANR 38;
DAM MST; DLB 53; MTCW

Blaise, Clark 1940- .... **CLC 29**
See also AITN 2; CA 53-56; CAAS 3;
CANR 5; DLB 53

Blake, Nicholas
See Day Lewis, C(ecil)
See also DLB 77

Blake, William
1757-1827 .... **NCLC 13, 37, 57; DA;**
DAB; DAC; PC 12; WLC
See also CDBLB 1789-1832; DAM MST,
POET; DLB 93, 163; MAICYA;
SATA 30

Blake, William J(ames) 1894-1969 ... **PC 12**
See also CA 5-8R; 25-28R

Blasco Ibanez, Vicente
1867-1928 .... **TCLC 12**
See also CA 110; 131; DAM NOV; HW;
MTCW

Blatty, William Peter 1928- .... **CLC 2**
See also CA 5-8R; CANR 9; DAM POP

Bleeck, Oliver
See Thomas, Ross (Elmore)

Blessing, Lee 1949- .... **CLC 54**

Blish, James (Benjamin)
1921-1975 .... **CLC 14**
See also CA 1-4R; 57-60; CANR 3; DLB 8;
MTCW; SATA 66

Bliss, Reginald
See Wells, H(erbert) G(eorge)

Blixen, Karen (Christentze Dinesen)
1885-1962
See Dinesen, Isak
See also CA 25-28; CANR 22, 50; CAP 2;
MTCW; SATA 44

Bloch, Robert (Albert) 1917-1994 ... **CLC 33**
See also CA 5-8R; 146; CAAS 20; CANR 5;
DLB 44; INT CANR-5; SATA 12;
SATA-Obit 82

Blok, Alexander (Alexandrovich)
1880-1921 .... **TCLC 5**
See also CA 104

Blom, Jan
See Breytenbach, Breyten

Bloom, Harold 1930- .... **CLC 24**
See also CA 13-16R; CANR 39; DLB 67

Bloomfield, Aurelius
See Bourne, Randolph S(illiman)

Blount, Roy (Alton), Jr. 1941- ..... **CLC 38**
See also CA 53-56; CANR 10, 28;
INT CANR-28; MTCW

Bloy, Leon 1846-1917 .... **TCLC 22**
See also CA 121; DLB 123

Blume, Judy (Sussman) 1938-... **CLC 12, 30**
See also AAYA 3; CA 29-32R; CANR 13,
37; CLR 2, 15; DAM NOV, POP;
DLB 52; JRDA; MAICYA; MTCW;
SATA 2, 31, 79

Blunden, Edmund (Charles)
1896-1974 .... **CLC 2, 56**
See also CA 17-18; 45-48; CAP 2; DLB 20,
100, 155; MTCW

Bly, Robert (Elwood)
1926- .... **CLC 1, 2, 5, 10, 15, 38**
See also CA 5-8R; CANR 41; DAM POET;
DLB 5; MTCW

Boas, Franz 1858-1942 .... **TCLC 56**
See also CA 115

Bobette
See Simenon, Georges (Jacques Christian)

Boccaccio, Giovanni
1313-1375 .... **CMLC 13; SSC 10**

Bochco, Steven 1943- .... **CLC 35**
See also AAYA 11; CA 124; 138

Bodenheim, Maxwell 1892-1954 ... **TCLC 44**
See also CA 110; DLB 9, 45

Bodker, Cecil 1927- .... **CLC 21**
See also CA 73-76; CANR 13, 44; CLR 23;
MAICYA; SATA 14

Boell, Heinrich (Theodor)
1917-1985 .... **CLC 2, 3, 6, 9, 11, 15, 27,**
32, 72; DA; DAB; DAC; SSC 23; WLC
See also CA 21-24R; 116; CANR 24;
DAM MST, NOV; DLB 69; DLBY 85;
MTCW

Boerne, Alfred
See Doeblin, Alfred

Boethius 480(?)-524(?) .... **CMLC 15**
See also DLB 115

Bogan, Louise
1897-1970 .... **CLC 4, 39, 46, 93; PC 12**
See also CA 73-76; 25-28R; CANR 33;
DAM POET; DLB 45; MTCW

Bogarde, Dirk .... **CLC 19**
See also Van Den Bogarde, Derek Jules
Gaspard Ulric Niven
See also DLB 14

Bogosian, Eric 1953- .... **CLC 45**
See also CA 138

Bograd, Larry 1953- .... **CLC 35**
See also CA 93-96; SAAS 21; SATA 33

Boiardo, Matteo Maria 1441-1494 .... **LC 6**

Boileau-Despreaux, Nicolas
1636-1711 .... **LC 3**

Bojer, Johan 1872-1959 .... **TCLC 64**

Boland, Eavan (Aisling) 1944-... **CLC 40, 67**
See also CA 143; DAM POET; DLB 40

Bolt, Lee
See Faust, Frederick (Schiller)

Bolt, Robert (Oxton) 1924-1995 .... **CLC 14**
See also CA 17-20R; 147; CANR 35;
DAM DRAM; DLB 13; MTCW

Bombet, Louis-Alexandre-Cesar
See Stendhal

Bomkauf
See Kaufman, Bob (Garnell)

Bonaventura .... **NCLC 35**
See also DLB 90

Bond, Edward 1934- .... **CLC 4, 6, 13, 23**
See also CA 25-28R; CANR 38;
DAM DRAM; DLB 13; MTCW

Bonham, Frank 1914-1989 .... **CLC 12**
See also AAYA 1; CA 9-12R; CANR 4, 36;
JRDA; MAICYA; SAAS 3; SATA 1, 49;
SATA-Obit 62

Bonnefoy, Yves 1923- .... **CLC 9, 15, 58**
See also CA 85-88; CANR 33; DAM MST,
POET; MTCW

Bontemps, Arna(ud Wendell)
1902-1973 .... **CLC 1, 18; BLC**
See also BW 1; CA 1-4R; 41-44R; CANR 4,
35; CLR 6; DAM MULT, NOV, POET;
DLB 48, 51; JRDA; MAICYA; MTCW;
SATA 2, 44; SATA-Obit 24

Booth, Martin 1944- .... **CLC 13**
See also CA 93-96; CAAS 2

Booth, Philip 1925-. . . . . **CLC 23**
See also CA 5-8R; CANR 5; DLBY 82

Booth, Wayne C(layson) 1921- . . . . . **CLC 24**
See also CA 1-4R; CAAS 5; CANR 3, 43;
DLB 67

Borchert, Wolfgang 1921-1947 . . . . . **TCLC 5**
See also CA 104; DLB 69, 124

Borel, Petrus 1809-1859. . . . . **NCLC 41**

Borges, Jorge Luis
1899-1986 . . . **CLC 1, 2, 3, 4, 6, 8, 9, 10,
13, 19, 44, 48, 83; DA; DAB; DAC;
HLC; SSC 4; WLC**
See also CA 21-24R; CANR 19, 33;
DAM MST, MULT; DLB 113; DLBY 86;
HW; MTCW

Borowski, Tadeusz 1922-1951. . . . . . **TCLC 9**
See also CA 106

Borrow, George (Henry)
1803-1881 . . . . **NCLC 9**
See also DLB 21, 55, 166

Bosman, Herman Charles
1905-1951 . . . . **TCLC 49**

Bosschere, Jean de 1878(?)-1953. . . **TCLC 19**
See also CA 115

Boswell, James
1740-1795 . . . . . . **LC 4; DA; DAB; DAC;
WLC**
See also CDBLB 1660-1789; DAM MST;
DLB 104, 142

Bottoms, David 1949-. . . . . **CLC 53**
See also CA 105; CANR 22; DLB 120;
DLBY 83

Boucicault, Dion 1820-1890. . . . . . **NCLC 41**

Boucolon, Maryse 1937(?)-
See Conde, Maryse
See also CA 110; CANR 30, 53

Bourget, Paul (Charles Joseph)
1852-1935 . . . . **TCLC 12**
See also CA 107; DLB 123

Bourjaily, Vance (Nye) 1922- . . . . **CLC 8, 62**
See also CA 1-4R; CAAS 1; CANR 2;
DLB 2, 143

Bourne, Randolph S(illiman)
1886-1918 . . . . **TCLC 16**
See also CA 117; DLB 63

Bova, Ben(jamin William) 1932-. . . . **CLC 45**
See also AAYA 16; CA 5-8R; CAAS 18;
CANR 11; CLR 3; DLBY 81;
INT CANR-11; MAICYA; MTCW;
SATA 6, 68

Bowen, Elizabeth (Dorothea Cole)
1899-1973 . . . . . . **CLC 1, 3, 6, 11, 15, 22;
SSC 3**
See also CA 17-18; 41-44R; CANR 35;
CAP 2; CDBLB 1945-1960; DAM NOV;
DLB 15, 162; MTCW

Bowering, George 1935-. . . . . **CLC 15, 47**
See also CA 21-24R; CAAS 16; CANR 10;
DLB 53

Bowering, Marilyn R(uthe) 1949-. . . **CLC 32**
See also CA 101; CANR 49

Bowers, Edgar 1924- . . . . **CLC 9**
See also CA 5-8R; CANR 24; DLB 5

Bowie, David. . . . . **CLC 17**
See also Jones, David Robert

Bowles, Jane (Sydney)
1917-1973 . . . . **CLC 3, 68**
See also CA 19-20; 41-44R; CAP 2

Bowles, Paul (Frederick)
1910- . . . . **CLC 1, 2, 19, 53; SSC 3**
See also CA 1-4R; CAAS 1; CANR 1, 19,
50; DLB 5, 6; MTCW

Box, Edgar
See Vidal, Gore

Boyd, Nancy
See Millay, Edna St. Vincent

Boyd, William 1952-. . . . . **CLC 28, 53, 70**
See also CA 114; 120; CANR 51

Boyle, Kay
1902-1992 . . . . . **CLC 1, 5, 19, 58; SSC 5**
See also CA 13-16R; 140; CAAS 1;
CANR 29; DLB 4, 9, 48, 86; DLBY 93;
MTCW

Boyle, Mark
See Kienzle, William X(avier)

Boyle, Patrick 1905-1982. . . . . **CLC 19**
See also CA 127

Boyle, T. C. 1948-
See Boyle, T(homas) Coraghessan

Boyle, T(homas) Coraghessan
1948- . . . . **CLC 36, 55, 90; SSC 16**
See also BEST 90:4; CA 120; CANR 44;
DAM POP; DLBY 86

Boz
See Dickens, Charles (John Huffam)

Brackenridge, Hugh Henry
1748-1816 . . . . **NCLC 7**
See also DLB 11, 37

Bradbury, Edward P.
See Moorcock, Michael (John)

Bradbury, Malcolm (Stanley)
1932- . . . . **CLC 32, 61**
See also CA 1-4R; CANR 1, 33;
DAM NOV; DLB 14; MTCW

Bradbury, Ray (Douglas)
1920- . . . . **CLC 1, 3, 10, 15, 42; DA;
DAB; DAC; WLC**
See also AAYA 15; AITN 1, 2; CA 1-4R;
CANR 2, 30; CDALB 1968-1988;
DAM MST, NOV, POP; DLB 2, 8;
INT CANR-30; MTCW; SATA 11, 64

Bradford, Gamaliel 1863-1932. . . . . **TCLC 36**
See also DLB 17

Bradley, David (Henry, Jr.)
1950- . . . . **CLC 23; BLC**
See also BW 1; CA 104; CANR 26;
DAM MULT; DLB 33

Bradley, John Ed(mund, Jr.)
1958- . . . . **CLC 55**
See also CA 139

Bradley, Marion Zimmer 1930-. . . . . **CLC 30**
See also AAYA 9; CA 57-60; CAAS 10;
CANR 7, 31, 51; DAM POP; DLB 8;
MTCW

Bradstreet, Anne
1612(?)-1672 . . . . . . **LC 4, 30; DA; DAC;
PC 10**
See also CDALB 1640-1865; DAM MST,
POET; DLB 24

Brady, Joan 1939- . . . . **CLC 86**
See also CA 141

Bragg, Melvyn 1939-. . . . . **CLC 10**
See also BEST 89:3; CA 57-60; CANR 10,
48; DLB 14

Braine, John (Gerard)
1922-1986 . . . . **CLC 1, 3, 41**
See also CA 1-4R; 120; CANR 1, 33;
CDBLB 1945-1960; DLB 15; DLBY 86;
MTCW

Brammer, William 1930(?)-1978 . . . . **CLC 31**
See also CA 77-80

Brancati, Vitaliano 1907-1954. . . . . **TCLC 12**
See also CA 109

Brancato, Robin F(idler) 1936-. . . . . **CLC 35**
See also AAYA 9; CA 69-72; CANR 11,
45; CLR 32; JRDA; SAAS 9; SATA 23

Brand, Max
See Faust, Frederick (Schiller)

Brand, Millen 1906-1980. . . . . **CLC 7**
See also CA 21-24R; 97-100

Branden, Barbara . . . . **CLC 44**
See also CA 148

Brandes, Georg (Morris Cohen)
1842-1927 . . . . **TCLC 10**
See also CA 105

Brandys, Kazimierz 1916- . . . . **CLC 62**

Branley, Franklyn M(ansfield)
1915-. . . . . **CLC 21**
See also CA 33-36R; CANR 14, 39;
CLR 13; MAICYA; SAAS 16; SATA 4,
68

Brathwaite, Edward Kamau 1930-. . . **CLC 11**
See also BW 2; CA 25-28R; CANR 11, 26,
47; DAM POET; DLB 125

Brautigan, Richard (Gary)
1935-1984 . . . . **CLC 1, 3, 5, 9, 12, 34, 42**
See also CA 53-56; 113; CANR 34;
DAM NOV; DLB 2, 5; DLBY 80, 84;
MTCW; SATA 56

Brave Bird, Mary 1953-
See Crow Dog, Mary
See also NNAL

Braverman, Kate 1950- . . . . **CLC 67**
See also CA 89-92

Brecht, Bertolt
1898-1956 . . . . . . **TCLC 1, 6, 13, 35; DA;
DAB; DAC; DC 3; WLC**
See also CA 104; 133; DAM DRAM, MST;
DLB 56, 124; MTCW

Brecht, Eugen Berthold Friedrich
See Brecht, Bertolt

Bremer, Fredrika 1801-1865 . . . . . **NCLC 11**

Brennan, Christopher John
1870-1932 . . . . **TCLC 17**
See also CA 117

Brennan, Maeve 1917-. . . . . **CLC 5**
See also CA 81-84

Brentano, Clemens (Maria)
1778-1842 . . . . **NCLC 1**
See also DLB 90

Brent of Bin Bin
See Franklin, (Stella Maraia Sarah) Miles

Brenton, Howard 1942-. . . . . **CLC 31**
See also CA 69-72; CANR 33; DLB 13;
MTCW

Brulls, Christian
See Simenon, Georges (Jacques Christian)

Brunner, John (Kilian Houston)
    1934-1995 . . . . **CLC 8, 10**
    See also CA 1-4R; 149; CAAS 8; CANR 2,
    37; DAM POP; MTCW

Bruno, Giordano 1548-1600 . . . . **LC 27**

Brutus, Dennis 1924- . . . . **CLC 43; BLC**
    See also BW 2; CA 49-52; CAAS 14;
    CANR 2, 27, 42; DAM MULT, POET;
    DLB 117

Bryan, C(ourtlandt) D(ixon) B(arnes)
    1936- . . . . **CLC 29**
    See also CA 73-76; CANR 13;
    INT CANR-13

Bryan, Michael
    See Moore, Brian

Bryant, William Cullen
    1794-1878 . . . . . **NCLC 6, 46; DA; DAB;**
                                                          DAC
    See also CDALB 1640-1865; DAM MST,
    POET; DLB 3, 43, 59

Bryusov, Valery Yakovlevich
    1873-1924 . . . . **TCLC 10**
    See also CA 107

Buchan, John 1875-1940 . . . **TCLC 41; DAB**
    See also CA 108; 145; DAM POP; DLB 34,
    70, 156; YABC 2

Buchanan, George 1506-1582 . . . . **LC 4**

Buchheim, Lothar-Guenther 1918- . . . **CLC 6**
    See also CA 85-88

Buchner, (Karl) Georg
    1813-1837 . . . . **NCLC 26**

Buchwald, Art(hur) 1925- . . . . **CLC 33**
    See also AITN 1; CA 5-8R; CANR 21;
    MTCW; SATA 10

Buck, Pearl S(ydenstricker)
    1892-1973 . . . . **CLC 7, 11, 18; DA; DAB;**
                                                          DAC
    See also AITN 1; CA 1-4R; 41-44R;
    CANR 1, 34; DAM MST, NOV; DLB 9,
    102; MTCW; SATA 1, 25

Buckler, Ernest 1908-1984 . . . . **CLC 13; DAC**
    See also CA 11-12; 114; CAP 1;
    DAM MST; DLB 68; SATA 47

Buckley, Vincent (Thomas)
    1925-1988 . . . . **CLC 57**
    See also CA 101

Buckley, William F(rank), Jr.
    1925- . . . . **CLC 7, 18, 37**
    See also AITN 1; CA 1-4R; CANR 1, 24,
    53; DAM POP; DLB 137; DLBY 80;
    INT CANR-24; MTCW

Buechner, (Carl) Frederick
    1926- . . . . **CLC 2, 4, 6, 9**
    See also CA 13-16R; CANR 11, 39;
    DAM NOV; DLBY 80; INT CANR-11;
    MTCW

Buell, John (Edward) 1927- . . . . **CLC 10**
    See also CA 1-4R; DLB 53

Buero Vallejo, Antonio 1916- . . . **CLC 15, 46**
    See also CA 106; CANR 24, 49; HW;
    MTCW

Bufalino, Gesualdo 1920(?)- . . . . **CLC 74**

Bugayev, Boris Nikolayevich 1880-1934
    See Bely, Andrey
    See also CA 104

Bukowski, Charles
    1920-1994 . . . . **CLC 2, 5, 9, 41, 82**
    See also CA 17-20R; 144; CANR 40;
    DAM NOV, POET; DLB 5, 130; MTCW

Bulgakov, Mikhail (Afanas'evich)
    1891-1940 . . . . **TCLC 2, 16; SSC 18**
    See also CA 105; DAM DRAM, NOV

Bulgya, Alexander Alexandrovich
    1901-1956 . . . . **TCLC 53**
    See also Fadeyev, Alexander
    See also CA 117

Bullins, Ed 1935- . . **CLC 1, 5, 7; BLC; DC 6**
    See also BW 2; CA 49-52; CAAS 16;
    CANR 24, 46; DAM DRAM, MULT;
    DLB 7, 38; MTCW

Bulwer-Lytton, Edward (George Earle Lytton)
    1803-1873 . . . . **NCLC 1, 45**
    See also DLB 21

Bunin, Ivan Alexeyevich
    1870-1953 . . . . **TCLC 6; SSC 5**
    See also CA 104

Bunting, Basil 1900-1985 . . . . **CLC 10, 39, 47**
    See also CA 53-56; 115; CANR 7;
    DAM POET; DLB 20

Bunuel, Luis 1900-1983 . . **CLC 16, 80; HLC**
    See also CA 101; 110; CANR 32;
    DAM MULT; HW

Bunyan, John
    1628-1688 . . . . . . **LC 4; DA; DAB; DAC;**
                                                          WLC
    See also CDBLB 1660-1789; DAM MST;
    DLB 39

Burckhardt, Jacob (Christoph)
    1818-1897 . . . . **NCLC 49**

Burford, Eleanor
    See Hibbert, Eleanor Alice Burford

Burgess, Anthony
    . **CLC 1, 2, 4, 5, 8, 10, 13, 15, 22, 40, 62,**
                                              81, 94; DAB
    See also Wilson, John (Anthony) Burgess
    See also AITN 1; CDBLB 1960 to Present;
    DLB 14

Burke, Edmund
    1729(?)-1797 . . . . **LC 7; DA; DAB; DAC;**
                                                          WLC
    See also DAM MST; DLB 104

Burke, Kenneth (Duva)
    1897-1993 . . . . **CLC 2, 24**
    See also CA 5-8R; 143; CANR 39; DLB 45,
    63; MTCW

Burke, Leda
    See Garnett, David

Burke, Ralph
    See Silverberg, Robert

Burke, Thomas 1886-1945 . . . . **TCLC 63**
    See also CA 113

Burney, Fanny 1752-1840 . . . . **NCLC 12, 54**
    See also DLB 39

Burns, Robert 1759-1796 . . . . **PC 6**
    See also CDBLB 1789-1832; DA; DAB;
    DAC; DAM MST, POET; DLB 109;
    WLC

Burns, Tex
    See L'Amour, Louis (Dearborn)

Burnshaw, Stanley 1906- . . . . . **CLC 3, 13, 44**
    See also CA 9-12R; DLB 48

Burr, Anne 1937- . . . . **CLC 6**
    See also CA 25-28R

Burroughs, Edgar Rice
    1875-1950 . . . . **TCLC 2, 32**
    See also AAYA 11; CA 104; 132;
    DAM NOV; DLB 8; MTCW; SATA 41

Burroughs, William S(eward)
    1914- . . . . **CLC 1, 2, 5, 15, 22, 42, 75;**
                                              DA; DAB; DAC; WLC
    See also AITN 2; CA 9-12R; CANR 20, 52;
    DAM MST, NOV, POP; DLB 2, 8, 16,
    152; DLBY 81; MTCW

Burton, Richard F. 1821-1890 . . . . **NCLC 42**
    See also DLB 55

Busch, Frederick 1941- . . . **CLC 7, 10, 18, 47**
    See also CA 33-36R; CAAS 1; CANR 45;
    DLB 6

Bush, Ronald 1946- . . . . **CLC 34**
    See also CA 136

Bustos, F(rancisco)
    See Borges, Jorge Luis

Bustos Domecq, H(onorio)
    See Bioy Casares, Adolfo; Borges, Jorge
    Luis

Butler, Octavia E(stelle) 1947- . . . . . **CLC 38**
    See also AAYA 18; BW 2; CA 73-76;
    CANR 12, 24, 38; DAM MULT, POP;
    DLB 33; MTCW; SATA 84

Butler, Robert Olen (Jr.) 1945- . . . . . **CLC 81**
    See also CA 112; DAM POP; INT 112

Butler, Samuel 1612-1680 . . . . **LC 16**
    See also DLB 101, 126

Butler, Samuel
    1835-1902 . . . . . . **TCLC 1, 33; DA; DAB;**
                                                          DAC; WLC
    See also CA 143; CDBLB 1890-1914;
    DAM MST, NOV; DLB 18, 57

Butler, Walter C.
    See Faust, Frederick (Schiller)

Butor, Michel (Marie Francois)
    1926- . . . . **CLC 1, 3, 8, 11, 15**
    See also CA 9-12R; CANR 33; DLB 83;
    MTCW

Buzo, Alexander (John) 1944- . . . . . . **CLC 61**
    See also CA 97-100; CANR 17, 39

Buzzati, Dino 1906-1972 . . . . **CLC 36**
    See also CA 33-36R

Byars, Betsy (Cromer) 1928- . . . . **CLC 35**
    See also CA 33-36R; CANR 18, 36; CLR 1,
    16; DLB 52; INT CANR-18; JRDA;
    MAICYA; MTCW; SAAS 1; SATA 4,
    46, 80

Byatt, A(ntonia) S(usan Drabble)
    1936- . . . . **CLC 19, 65**
    See also CA 13-16R; CANR 13, 33, 50;
    DAM NOV, POP; DLB 14; MTCW

Byrne, David 1952- . . . . **CLC 26**
    See also CA 127

Byrne, John Keyes 1926-
    See Leonard, Hugh
    See also CA 102; INT 102

Byron, George Gordon (Noel)
1788-1824 . . . . . **NCLC 2, 12; DA; DAB;**
DAC; PC 16; WLC
See also CDBLB 1789-1832; DAM MST,
POET; DLB 96, 110

C. 3. 3.
See Wilde, Oscar (Fingal O'Flahertie Wills)

Caballero, Fernan 1796-1877. . . . . **NCLC 10**

Cabell, James Branch 1879-1958 . . . **TCLC 6**
See also CA 105; DLB 9, 78

Cable, George Washington
1844-1925 . . . . **TCLC 4; SSC 4**
See also CA 104; DLB 12, 74; DLBD 13

Cabral de Melo Neto, Joao 1920-. . . **CLC 76**
See also CA 151; DAM MULT

Cabrera Infante, G(uillermo)
1929- . . . . **CLC 5, 25, 45; HLC**
See also CA 85-88; CANR 29;
DAM MULT; DLB 113; HW; MTCW

Cade, Toni
See Bambara, Toni Cade

Cadmus and Harmonia
See Buchan, John

Caedmon fl. 658-680. . . . . **CMLC 7**
See also DLB 146

Caeiro, Alberto
See Pessoa, Fernando (Antonio Nogueira)

Cage, John (Milton, Jr.) 1912- . . . . . **CLC 41**
See also CA 13-16R; CANR 9;
INT CANR-9

Cain, G.
See Cabrera Infante, G(uillermo)

Cain, Guillermo
See Cabrera Infante, G(uillermo)

Cain, James M(allahan)
1892-1977 . . . . **CLC 3, 11, 28**
See also AITN 1; CA 17-20R; 73-76;
CANR 8, 34; MTCW

Caine, Mark
See Raphael, Frederic (Michael)

Calasso, Roberto 1941- . . . . **CLC 81**
See also CA 143

Calderon de la Barca, Pedro
1600-1681 . . . . **LC 23; DC 3**

Caldwell, Erskine (Preston)
1903-1987 . . . . **CLC 1, 8, 14, 50, 60;**
SSC 19
See also AITN 1; CA 1-4R; 121;
CANR 2, 33; DAM NOV; DLB 9, 86;
MTCW

Caldwell, (Janet Miriam) Taylor (Holland)
1900-1985 . . . . **CLC 2, 28, 39**
See also CA 5-8R; 116; CANR 5;
DAM NOV, POP

Calhoun, John Caldwell
1782-1850 . . . . **NCLC 15**
See also DLB 3

Calisher, Hortense
1911- . . . . **CLC 2, 4, 8, 38; SSC 15**
See also CA 1-4R; CANR 1, 22;
DAM NOV; DLB 2; INT CANR-22;
MTCW

Callaghan, Morley Edward
1903-1990 . . . . . . **CLC 3, 14, 41, 65; DAC**
See also CA 9-12R; 132; CANR 33;
DAM MST; DLB 68; MTCW

Callimachus
c. 305B.C.-c. 240B.C. . . . . **CMLC 18**

Calvino, Italo
1923-1985 . . . . . **CLC 5, 8, 11, 22, 33, 39,**
73; SSC 3
See also CA 85-88; 116; CANR 23;
DAM NOV; MTCW

Cameron, Carey 1952- . . . . **CLC 59**
See also CA 135

Cameron, Peter 1959-. . . . . **CLC 44**
See also CA 125; CANR 50

Campana, Dino 1885-1932. . . . . **TCLC 20**
See also CA 117; DLB 114

Campanella, Tommaso 1568-1639 . . . . **LC 32**

Campbell, John W(ood, Jr.)
1910-1971 . . . . **CLC 32**
See also CA 21-22; 29-32R; CANR 34;
CAP 2; DLB 8; MTCW

Campbell, Joseph 1904-1987 . . . . **CLC 69**
See also AAYA 3; BEST 89:2; CA 1-4R;
124; CANR 3, 28; MTCW

Campbell, Maria 1940-. . . . . . **CLC 85; DAC**
See also CA 102; NNAL

Campbell, (John) Ramsey
1946- . . . . **CLC 42; SSC 19**
See also CA 57-60; CANR 7; INT CANR-7

Campbell, (Ignatius) Roy (Dunnachie)
1901-1957 . . . . **TCLC 5**
See also CA 104; DLB 20

Campbell, Thomas 1777-1844 . . . . **NCLC 19**
See also DLB 93; 144

Campbell, Wilfred . . . . **TCLC 9**
See also Campbell, William

Campbell, William 1858(?)-1918
See Campbell, Wilfred
See also CA 106; DLB 92

Campion, Jane . . . . **CLC 95**
See also CA 138

Campos, Alvaro de
See Pessoa, Fernando (Antonio Nogueira)

Camus, Albert
1913-1960 . . . . **CLC 1, 2, 4, 9, 11, 14, 32,**
63, 69; DA; DAB; DAC; DC 2; SSC 9;
WLC
See also CA 89-92; DAM DRAM, MST,
NOV; DLB 72; MTCW

Canby, Vincent 1924-. . . . . **CLC 13**
See also CA 81-84

Cancale
See Desnos, Robert

Canetti, Elias
1905-1994 . . . . **CLC 3, 14, 25, 75, 86**
See also CA 21-24R; 146; CANR 23;
DLB 85, 124; MTCW

Canin, Ethan 1960-. . . . . **CLC 55**
See also CA 131; 135

Cannon, Curt
See Hunter, Evan

Cape, Judith
See Page, P(atricia) K(athleen)

Capek, Karel
1890-1938 . . . . . **TCLC 6, 37; DA; DAB;**
DAC; DC 1; WLC
See also CA 104; 140; DAM DRAM, MST,
NOV

Capote, Truman
1924-1984 . . . . . . **CLC 1, 3, 8, 13, 19, 34,**
38, 58; DA; DAB; DAC; SSC 2; WLC
See also CA 5-8R; 113; CANR 18;
CDALB 1941-1968; DAM MST, NOV,
POP; DLB 2; DLBY 80, 84; MTCW

Capra, Frank 1897-1991. . . . . **CLC 16**
See also CA 61-64; 135

Caputo, Philip 1941-. . . . . **CLC 32**
See also CA 73-76; CANR 40

Card, Orson Scott 1951- . . . . **CLC 44, 47, 50**
See also AAYA 11; CA 102; CANR 27, 47;
DAM POP; INT CANR-27; MTCW;
SATA 83

Cardenal, Ernesto 1925-. . . . . **CLC 31; HLC**
See also CA 49-52; CANR 2, 32;
DAM MULT, POET; HW; MTCW

Cardozo, Benjamin N(athan)
1870-1938 . . . . **TCLC 65**
See also CA 117

Carducci, Giosue 1835-1907. . . . . . **TCLC 32**

Carew, Thomas 1595(?)-1640. . . . . . . **LC 13**
See also DLB 126

Carey, Ernestine Gilbreth 1908- . . . . **CLC 17**
See also CA 5-8R; SATA 2

Carey, Peter 1943-. . . . . **CLC 40, 55**
See also CA 123; 127; CANR 53; INT 127;
MTCW

Carleton, William 1794-1869. . . . . . **NCLC 3**
See also DLB 159

Carlisle, Henry (Coffin) 1926-. . . . . . **CLC 33**
See also CA 13-16R; CANR 15

Carlsen, Chris
See Holdstock, Robert P.

Carlson, Ron(ald F.) 1947-. . . . . **CLC 54**
See also CA 105; CANR 27

Carlyle, Thomas
1795-1881 . . **NCLC 22; DA; DAB; DAC**
See also CDBLB 1789-1832; DAM MST;
DLB 55; 144

Carman, (William) Bliss
1861-1929 . . . . **TCLC 7; DAC**
See also CA 104; DLB 92

Carnegie, Dale 1888-1955 . . . . **TCLC 53**

Carossa, Hans 1878-1956. . . . . **TCLC 48**
See also DLB 66

Carpenter, Don(ald Richard)
1931-1995 . . . . **CLC 41**
See also CA 45-48; 149; CANR 1

Carpentier (y Valmont), Alejo
1904-1980 . . . . **CLC 8, 11, 38; HLC**
See also CA 65-68; 97-100; CANR 11;
DAM MULT; DLB 113; HW

Carr, Caleb 1955(?)-. . . . . **CLC 86**
See also CA 147

Carr, Emily 1871-1945. . . . . **TCLC 32**
See also DLB 68

Carr, John Dickson 1906-1977 . . . . . . **CLC 3**
See also CA 49-52; 69-72; CANR 3, 33;
MTCW

Chapman, Graham 1941-1989 . . . . . **CLC 21**
See also Monty Python
See also CA 116; 129; CANR 35

Chapman, John Jay 1862-1933 . . . . . **TCLC 7**
See also CA 104

Chapman, Lee
See Bradley, Marion Zimmer

Chapman, Walker
See Silverberg, Robert

Chappell, Fred (Davis) 1936- . . . . **CLC 40, 78**
See also CA 5-8R; CAAS 4; CANR 8, 33;
DLB 6, 105

Char, Rene(-Emile)
1907-1988 . . . . **CLC 9, 11, 14, 55**
See also CA 13-16R; 124; CANR 32;
DAM POET; MTCW

Charby, Jay
See Ellison, Harlan (Jay)

Chardin, Pierre Teilhard de
See Teilhard de Chardin, (Marie Joseph)
Pierre

Charles I 1600-1649 . . . . **LC 13**

Charyn, Jerome 1937- . . . . **CLC 5, 8, 18**
See also CA 5-8R; CAAS 1; CANR 7;
DLBY 83; MTCW

Chase, Mary (Coyle) 1907-1981 . . . . . . **DC 1**
See also CA 77-80; 105; SATA 17;
SATA-Obit 29

Chase, Mary Ellen 1887-1973 . . . . **CLC 2**
See also CA 13-16; 41-44R; CAP 1;
SATA 10

Chase, Nicholas
See Hyde, Anthony

Chateaubriand, Francois Rene de
1768-1848 . . . . **NCLC 3**
See also DLB 119

Chatterje, Sarat Chandra 1876-1936(?)
See Chatterji, Saratchandra
See also CA 109

Chatterji, Bankim Chandra
1838-1894 . . . . **NCLC 19**

Chatterji, Saratchandra . . . . **TCLC 13**
See also Chatterje, Sarat Chandra

Chatterton, Thomas 1752-1770 . . . . . . **LC 3**
See also DAM POET; DLB 109

Chatwin, (Charles) Bruce
1940-1989 . . . . **CLC 28, 57, 59**
See also AAYA 4; BEST 90:1; CA 85-88;
127; DAM POP

Chaucer, Daniel
See Ford, Ford Madox

Chaucer, Geoffrey
1340(?)-1400 . . . **LC 17; DA; DAB; DAC**
See also CDBLB Before 1660; DAM MST,
POET; DLB 146

Chaviaras, Strates 1935-
See Haviaras, Stratis
See also CA 105

Chayefsky, Paddy . . . . **CLC 23**
See also Chayefsky, Sidney
See also DLB 7, 44; DLBY 81

Chayefsky, Sidney 1923-1981
See Chayefsky, Paddy
See also CA 9-12R; 104; CANR 18;
DAM DRAM

Chedid, Andree 1920- . . . . **CLC 47**
See also CA 145

Cheever, John
1912-1982 . . . . . . **CLC 3, 7, 8, 11, 15, 25,**
64; DA; DAB; DAC; SSC 1; WLC
See also CA 5-8R; 106; CABS 1; CANR 5,
27; CDALB 1941-1968; DAM MST,
NOV, POP; DLB 2, 102; DLBY 80, 82;
INT CANR-5; MTCW

Cheever, Susan 1943- . . . . **CLC 18, 48**
See also CA 103; CANR 27, 51; DLBY 82;
INT CANR-27

Chekhonte, Antosha
See Chekhov, Anton (Pavlovich)

Chekhov, Anton (Pavlovich)
1860-1904 . . . . . **TCLC 3, 10, 31, 55; DA;**
DAB; DAC; SSC 2; WLC
See also CA 104; 124; DAM DRAM, MST

Chernyshevsky, Nikolay Gavrilovich
1828-1889 . . . . **NCLC 1**

Cherry, Carolyn Janice 1942-
See Cherryh, C. J.
See also CA 65-68; CANR 10

Cherryh, C. J. . . . . **CLC 35**
See also Cherry, Carolyn Janice
See also DLBY 80

Chesnutt, Charles W(addell)
1858-1932 . . . . **TCLC 5, 39; BLC; SSC 7**
See also BW 1; CA 106; 125; DAM MULT;
DLB 12, 50, 78; MTCW

Chester, Alfred 1929(?)-1971 . . . . **CLC 49**
See also CA 33-36R; DLB 130

Chesterton, G(ilbert) K(eith)
1874-1936 . . . . **TCLC 1, 6, 64; SSC 1**
See also CA 104; 132; CDBLB 1914-1945;
DAM NOV, POET; DLB 10, 19, 34, 70,
98, 149; MTCW; SATA 27

Chiang Pin-chin 1904-1986
See Ding Ling
See also CA 118

Ch'ien Chung-shu 1910- . . . . **CLC 22**
See also CA 130; MTCW

Child, L. Maria
See Child, Lydia Maria

Child, Lydia Maria 1802-1880 . . . . **NCLC 6**
See also DLB 1, 74; SATA 67

Child, Mrs.
See Child, Lydia Maria

Child, Philip 1898-1978 . . . . **CLC 19, 68**
See also CA 13-14; CAP 1; SATA 47

Childers, (Robert) Erskine
1870-1922 . . . . **TCLC 65**
See also CA 113; DLB 70

Childress, Alice
1920-1994 . . **CLC 12, 15, 86; BLC; DC 4**
See also AAYA 8; BW 2; CA 45-48; 146;
CANR 3, 27, 50; CLR 14; DAM DRAM,
MULT, NOV; DLB 7, 38; JRDA;
MAICYA; MTCW; SATA 7, 48, 81

Chislett, (Margaret) Anne 1943- . . . . **CLC 34**
See also CA 151

Chitty, Thomas Willes 1926- . . . . **CLC 11**
See also Hinde, Thomas
See also CA 5-8R

Chivers, Thomas Holley
1809-1858 . . . . **NCLC 49**
See also DLB 3

Chomette, Rene Lucien 1898-1981
See Clair, Rene
See also CA 103

Chopin, Kate
. . . . **TCLC 5, 14; DA; DAB; SSC 8**
See also Chopin, Katherine
See also CDALB 1865-1917; DLB 12, 78

Chopin, Katherine 1851-1904
See Chopin, Kate
See also CA 104; 122; DAC; DAM MST,
NOV

Chretien de Troyes
c. 12th cent. - . . . . **CMLC 10**

Christie
See Ichikawa, Kon

Christie, Agatha (Mary Clarissa)
1890-1976 . . . . . . **CLC 1, 6, 8, 12, 39, 48;**
DAB; DAC
See also AAYA 9; AITN 1, 2; CA 17-20R;
61-64; CANR 10, 37; CDBLB 1914-1945;
DAM NOV; DLB 13, 77; MTCW;
SATA 36

Christie, (Ann) Philippa
See Pearce, Philippa
See also CA 5-8R; CANR 4

Christine de Pizan 1365(?)-1431(?) . . . . **LC 9**

Chubb, Elmer
See Masters, Edgar Lee

Chulkov, Mikhail Dmitrievich
1743-1792 . . . . **LC 2**
See also DLB 150

Churchill, Caryl 1938- . . . **CLC 31, 55; DC 5**
See also CA 102; CANR 22, 46; DLB 13;
MTCW

Churchill, Charles 1731-1764 . . . . **LC 3**
See also DLB 109

Chute, Carolyn 1947- . . . . **CLC 39**
See also CA 123

Ciardi, John (Anthony)
1916-1986 . . . . **CLC 10, 40, 44**
See also CA 5-8R; 118; CAAS 2; CANR 5,
33; CLR 19; DAM POET; DLB 5;
DLBY 86; INT CANR-5; MAICYA;
MTCW; SATA 1, 65; SATA-Obit 46

Cicero, Marcus Tullius
106B.C.-43B.C. . . . . **CMLC 3**

Cimino, Michael 1943- . . . . **CLC 16**
See also CA 105

Cioran, E(mil) M. 1911-1995 . . . . **CLC 64**
See also CA 25-28R; 149

Cisneros, Sandra 1954- . . . . . . **CLC 69; HLC**
See also AAYA 9; CA 131; DAM MULT;
DLB 122, 152; HW

Cixous, Helene 1937- . . . . **CLC 92**
See also CA 126; DLB 83; MTCW

Clair, Rene . . . . **CLC 20**
See also Chomette, Rene Lucien

Clampitt, Amy 1920-1994 . . . . **CLC 32**
See also CA 110; 146; CANR 29; DLB 105

Clancy, Thomas L., Jr. 1947-
See Clancy, Tom
See also CA 125; 131; INT 131; MTCW

Clancy, Tom . . . . CLC 45
See also Clancy, Thomas L., Jr.
See also AAYA 9; BEST 89:1, 90:1;
DAM NOV, POP

Clare, John 1793-1864 . . . . . NCLC 9; DAB
See also DAM POET; DLB 55, 96

Clarin
See Alas (y Urena), Leopoldo (Enrique
Garcia)

Clark, Al C.
See Goines, Donald

Clark, (Robert) Brian 1932- . . . . CLC 29
See also CA 41-44R

Clark, Curt
See Westlake, Donald E(dwin)

Clark, Eleanor 1913-1996 . . . . CLC 5, 19
See also CA 9-12R; 151; CANR 41; DLB 6

Clark, J. P.
See Clark, John Pepper
See also DLB 117

Clark, John Pepper
1935- . . . . CLC 38; BLC; DC 5
See also Clark, J. P.
See also BW 1; CA 65-68; CANR 16;
DAM DRAM, MULT

Clark, M. R.
See Clark, Mavis Thorpe

Clark, Mavis Thorpe 1909- . . . . CLC 12
See also CA 57-60; CANR 8, 37; CLR 30;
MAICYA; SAAS 5; SATA 8, 74

Clark, Walter Van Tilburg
1909-1971 . . . . CLC 28
See also CA 9-12R; 33-36R; DLB 9;
SATA 8

Clarke, Arthur C(harles)
1917- . . . . . . CLC 1, 4, 13, 18, 35; SSC 3
See also AAYA 4; CA 1-4R; CANR 2, 28;
DAM POP; JRDA; MAICYA; MTCW;
SATA 13, 70

Clarke, Austin 1896-1974 . . . . CLC 6, 9
See also CA 29-32; 49-52; CAP 2;
DAM POET; DLB 10, 20

Clarke, Austin C(hesterfield)
1934- . . . . CLC 8, 53; BLC; DAC
See also BW 1; CA 25-28R; CAAS 16;
CANR 14, 32; DAM MULT; DLB 53,
125

Clarke, Gillian 1937- . . . . CLC 61
See also CA 106; DLB 40

Clarke, Marcus (Andrew Hislop)
1846-1881 . . . . NCLC 19

Clarke, Shirley 1925- . . . . CLC 16

Clash, The
See Headon, (Nicky) Topper; Jones, Mick;
Simonon, Paul; Strummer, Joe

Claudel, Paul (Louis Charles Marie)
1868-1955 . . . . TCLC 2, 10
See also CA 104

Clavell, James (duMaresq)
1925-1994 . . . . CLC 6, 25, 87
See also CA 25-28R; 146; CANR 26, 48;
DAM NOV, POP; MTCW

Cleaver, (Leroy) Eldridge
1935- . . . . CLC 30; BLC
See also BW 1; CA 21-24R; CANR 16;
DAM MULT

Cleese, John (Marwood) 1939- . . . . . CLC 21
See also Monty Python
See also CA 112; 116; CANR 35; MTCW

Cleishbotham, Jebediah
See Scott, Walter

Cleland, John 1710-1789 . . . . LC 2
See also DLB 39

Clemens, Samuel Langhorne 1835-1910
See Twain, Mark
See also CA 104; 135; CDALB 1865-1917;
DA; DAB; DAC; DAM MST, NOV;
DLB 11, 12, 23, 64, 74; JRDA;
MAICYA; YABC 2

Cleophil
See Congreve, William

Clerihew, E.
See Bentley, E(dmund) C(lerihew)

Clerk, N. W.
See Lewis, C(live) S(taples)

Cliff, Jimmy . . . . CLC 21
See also Chambers, James

Clifton, (Thelma) Lucille
1936- . . . . CLC 19, 66; BLC
See also BW 2; CA 49-52; CANR 2, 24, 42;
CLR 5; DAM MULT, POET; DLB 5, 41;
MAICYA; MTCW; SATA 20, 69

Clinton, Dirk
See Silverberg, Robert

Clough, Arthur Hugh 1819-1861 . . NCLC 27
See also DLB 32

Clutha, Janet Paterson Frame 1924-
See Frame, Janet
See also CA 1-4R; CANR 2, 36; MTCW

Clyne, Terence
See Blatty, William Peter

Cobalt, Martin
See Mayne, William (James Carter)

Cobbett, William 1763-1835 . . . . . NCLC 49
See also DLB 43, 107, 158

Coburn, D(onald) L(ee) 1938- . . . . . . CLC 10
See also CA 89-92

Cocteau, Jean (Maurice Eugene Clement)
1889-1963 . . . . CLC 1, 8, 15, 16, 43; DA;
DAB; DAC; WLC
See also CA 25-28; CANR 40; CAP 2;
DAM DRAM, MST, NOV; DLB 65;
MTCW

Codrescu, Andrei 1946- . . . . CLC 46
See also CA 33-36R; CAAS 19; CANR 13,
34, 53; DAM POET

Coe, Max
See Bourne, Randolph S(illiman)

Coe, Tucker
See Westlake, Donald E(dwin)

Coetzee, J(ohn) M(ichael)
1940- . . . . CLC 23, 33, 66
See also CA 77-80; CANR 41; DAM NOV;
MTCW

Coffey, Brian
See Koontz, Dean R(ay)

Cohan, George M. 1878-1942 . . . . . TCLC 60

Cohen, Arthur A(llen)
1928-1986 . . . . CLC 7, 31
See also CA 1-4R; 120; CANR 1, 17, 42;
DLB 28

Cohen, Leonard (Norman)
1934- . . . . CLC 3, 38; DAC
See also CA 21-24R; CANR 14;
DAM MST; DLB 53; MTCW

Cohen, Matt 1942- . . . . CLC 19; DAC
See also CA 61-64; CAAS 18; CANR 40;
DLB 53

Cohen-Solal, Annie 19(?)- . . . . CLC 50

Colegate, Isabel 1931- . . . . CLC 36
See also CA 17-20R; CANR 8, 22; DLB 14;
INT CANR-22; MTCW

Coleman, Emmett
See Reed, Ishmael

Coleridge, Samuel Taylor
1772-1834 . . . . . NCLC 9, 54; DA; DAB;
DAC; PC 11; WLC
See also CDBLB 1789-1832; DAM MST,
POET; DLB 93, 107

Coleridge, Sara 1802-1852 . . . . . . NCLC 31

Coles, Don 1928- . . . . CLC 46
See also CA 115; CANR 38

Colette, (Sidonie-Gabrielle)
1873-1954 . . . . . . TCLC 1, 5, 16; SSC 10
See also CA 104; 131; DAM NOV; DLB 65;
MTCW

Collett, (Jacobine) Camilla (Wergeland)
1813-1895 . . . . NCLC 22

Collier, Christopher 1930- . . . . CLC 30
See also AAYA 13; CA 33-36R; CANR 13,
33; JRDA; MAICYA; SATA 16, 70

Collier, James L(incoln) 1928- . . . . . CLC 30
See also AAYA 13; CA 9-12R; CANR 4,
33; CLR 3; DAM POP; JRDA;
MAICYA; SAAS 21; SATA 8, 70

Collier, Jeremy 1650-1726 . . . . LC 6

Collier, John 1901-1980 . . . . SSC 19
See also CA 65-68; 97-100; CANR 10;
DLB 77

Collins, Hunt
See Hunter, Evan

Collins, Linda 1931- . . . . CLC 44
See also CA 125

Collins, (William) Wilkie
1824-1889 . . . . NCLC 1, 18
See also CDBLB 1832-1890; DLB 18, 70,
159

Collins, William 1721-1759 . . . . LC 4
See also DAM POET; DLB 109

Collodi, Carlo 1826-1890 . . . . NCLC 54
See also Lorenzini, Carlo
See also CLR 5

Colman, George
See Glassco, John

Colt, Winchester Remington
See Hubbard, L(afayette) Ron(ald)

Colter, Cyrus 1910- . . . . CLC 58
See also BW 1; CA 65-68; CANR 10;
DLB 33

Colton, James
See Hansen, Joseph

Cox, William Trevor 1928- . . . **CLC 9, 14, 71**
See also Trevor, William
See also CA 9-12R; CANR 4, 37;
DAM NOV; DLB 14; INT CANR-37;
MTCW

Coyne, P. J.
See Masters, Hilary

Cozzens, James Gould
1903-1978 . . . . **CLC 1, 4, 11, 92**
See also CA 9-12R; 81-84; CANR 19;
CDALB 1941-1968; DLB 9; DLBD 2;
DLBY 84; MTCW

Crabbe, George 1754-1832 . . . . . . **NCLC 26**
See also DLB 93

Craddock, Charles Egbert
See Murfree, Mary Noailles

Craig, A. A.
See Anderson, Poul (William)

Craik, Dinah Maria (Mulock)
1826-1887 . . . . **NCLC 38**
See also DLB 35, 163; MAICYA; SATA 34

Cram, Ralph Adams 1863-1942 . . . . **TCLC 45**

Crane, (Harold) Hart
1899-1932 . . . . **TCLC 2, 5; DA; DAB;**
DAC; PC 3; WLC
See also CA 104; 127; CDALB 1917-1929;
DAM MST, POET; DLB 4, 48; MTCW

Crane, R(onald) S(almon)
1886-1967 . . . . **CLC 27**
See also CA 85-88; DLB 63

Crane, Stephen (Townley)
1871-1900 . . . . **TCLC 11, 17, 32; DA;**
DAB; DAC; SSC 7; WLC
See also CA 109; 140; CDALB 1865-1917;
DAM MST, NOV, POET; DLB 12, 54,
78; YABC 2

Crase, Douglas 1944- . . . . **CLC 58**
See also CA 106

Crashaw, Richard 1612(?)-1649 . . . . . **LC 24**
See also DLB 126

Craven, Margaret
1901-1980 . . . . **CLC 17; DAC**
See also CA 103

Crawford, F(rancis) Marion
1854-1909 . . . . **TCLC 10**
See also CA 107; DLB 71

Crawford, Isabella Valancy
1850-1887 . . . . **NCLC 12**
See also DLB 92

Crayon, Geoffrey
See Irving, Washington

Creasey, John 1908-1973 . . . . **CLC 11**
See also CA 5-8R; 41-44R; CANR 8;
DLB 77; MTCW

Crebillon, Claude Prosper Jolyot de (fils)
1707-1777 . . . . **LC 28**

Credo
See Creasey, John

Creeley, Robert (White)
1926- . . . . . **CLC 1, 2, 4, 8, 11, 15, 36, 78**
See also CA 1-4R; CAAS 10; CANR 23, 43;
DAM POET; DLB 5, 16; MTCW

Crews, Harry (Eugene)
1935- . . . . **CLC 6, 23, 49**
See also AITN 1; CA 25-28R; CANR 20;
DLB 6, 143; MTCW

Crichton, (John) Michael
1942- . . . . **CLC 2, 6, 54, 90**
See also AAYA 10; AITN 2; CA 25-28R;
CANR 13, 40; DAM NOV, POP;
DLBY 81; INT CANR-13; JRDA;
MTCW; SATA 9, 88

Crispin, Edmund . . . . **CLC 22**
See also Montgomery, (Robert) Bruce
See also DLB 87

Cristofer, Michael 1945(?)- . . . . **CLC 28**
See also CA 110; DAM DRAM; DLB 7

Croce, Benedetto 1866-1952 . . . . . . **TCLC 37**
See also CA 120

Crockett, David 1786-1836 . . . . **NCLC 8**
See also DLB 3, 11

Crockett, Davy
See Crockett, David

Crofts, Freeman Wills
1879-1957 . . . . **TCLC 55**
See also CA 115; DLB 77

Croker, John Wilson 1780-1857 . . **NCLC 10**
See also DLB 110

Crommelynck, Fernand 1885-1970 . . **CLC 75**
See also CA 89-92

Cronin, A(rchibald) J(oseph)
1896-1981 . . . . **CLC 32**
See also CA 1-4R; 102; CANR 5; SATA 47;
SATA-Obit 25

Cross, Amanda
See Heilbrun, Carolyn G(old)

Crothers, Rachel 1878(?)-1958 . . . . . **TCLC 19**
See also CA 113; DLB 7

Croves, Hal
See Traven, B.

Crow Dog, Mary . . . . **CLC 93**
See also Brave Bird, Mary

Crowfield, Christopher
See Stowe, Harriet (Elizabeth) Beecher

Crowley, Aleister . . . . **TCLC 7**
See also Crowley, Edward Alexander

Crowley, Edward Alexander 1875-1947
See Crowley, Aleister
See also CA 104

Crowley, John 1942- . . . . **CLC 57**
See also CA 61-64; CANR 43; DLBY 82;
SATA 65

Crud
See Crumb, R(obert)

Crumarums
See Crumb, R(obert)

Crumb, R(obert) 1943- . . . . **CLC 17**
See also CA 106

Crumbum
See Crumb, R(obert)

Crumski
See Crumb, R(obert)

Crum the Bum
See Crumb, R(obert)

Crunk
See Crumb, R(obert)

Crustt
See Crumb, R(obert)

Cryer, Gretchen (Kiger) 1935- . . . . . . **CLC 21**
See also CA 114; 123

Csath, Geza 1887-1919 . . . . **TCLC 13**
See also CA 111

Cudlip, David 1933- . . . . **CLC 34**

Cullen, Countee
1903-1946 . . . . . . **TCLC 4, 37; BLC; DA;**
DAC
See also BW 1; CA 108; 124;
CDALB 1917-1929; DAM MST, MULT,
POET; DLB 4, 48, 51; MTCW; SATA 18

Cum, R.
See Crumb, R(obert)

Cummings, Bruce F(rederick) 1889-1919
See Barbellion, W. N. P.
See also CA 123

Cummings, E(dward) E(stlin)
1894-1962 . . . . . . **CLC 1, 3, 8, 12, 15, 68;**
DA; DAB; DAC; PC 5; WLC 2
See also CA 73-76; CANR 31;
CDALB 1929-1941; DAM MST, POET;
DLB 4, 48; MTCW

Cunha, Euclides (Rodrigues Pimenta) da
1866-1909 . . . . **TCLC 24**
See also CA 123

Cunningham, E. V.
See Fast, Howard (Melvin)

Cunningham, J(ames) V(incent)
1911-1985 . . . . **CLC 3, 31**
See also CA 1-4R; 115; CANR 1; DLB 5

Cunningham, Julia (Woolfolk)
1916- . . . . **CLC 12**
See also CA 9-12R; CANR 4, 19, 36;
JRDA; MAICYA; SAAS 2; SATA 1, 26

Cunningham, Michael 1952- . . . . **CLC 34**
See also CA 136

Cunninghame Graham, R(obert) B(ontine)
1852-1936 . . . . **TCLC 19**
See also Graham, R(obert) B(ontine)
Cunninghame
See also CA 119; DLB 98

Currie, Ellen 19(?)- . . . . **CLC 44**

Curtin, Philip
See Lowndes, Marie Adelaide (Belloc)

Curtis, Price
See Ellison, Harlan (Jay)

Cutrate, Joe
See Spiegelman, Art

Czaczkes, Shmuel Yosef
See Agnon, S(hmuel) Y(osef Halevi)

Dabrowska, Maria (Szumska)
1889-1965 . . . . **CLC 15**
See also CA 106

Dabydeen, David 1955- . . . . **CLC 34**
See also BW 1; CA 125

Dacey, Philip 1939- . . . . **CLC 51**
See also CA 37-40R; CAAS 17; CANR 14,
32; DLB 105

Dagerman, Stig (Halvard)
1923-1954 . . . . **TCLC 17**
See also CA 117

de la Mare, Walter (John)
1873-1956 .... **TCLC 4, 53; DAB; DAC; SSC 14; WLC**
See also CDBLB 1914-1945; CLR 23; DAM MST, POET; DLB 162; SATA 16

Delaney, Franey
See O'Hara, John (Henry)

Delaney, Shelagh 1939- .... **CLC 29**
See also CA 17-20R; CANR 30; CDBLB 1960 to Present; DAM DRAM; DLB 13; MTCW

Delany, Mary (Granville Pendarves)
1700-1788 .... **LC 12**

Delany, Samuel R(ay, Jr.)
1942- .... **CLC 8, 14, 38; BLC**
See also BW 2; CA 81-84; CANR 27, 43; DAM MULT; DLB 8, 33; MTCW

De La Ramee, (Marie) Louise 1839-1908
See Ouida
See also SATA 20

de la Roche, Mazo 1879-1961 ...... **CLC 14**
See also CA 85-88; CANR 30; DLB 68; SATA 64

Delbanco, Nicholas (Franklin)
1942- .... **CLC 6, 13**
See also CA 17-20R; CAAS 2; CANR 29; DLB 6

del Castillo, Michel 1933- .... **CLC 38**
See also CA 109

Deledda, Grazia (Cosima)
1875(?)-1936 .... **TCLC 23**
See also CA 123

Delibes, Miguel .... **CLC 8, 18**
See also Delibes Setien, Miguel

Delibes Setien, Miguel 1920-
See Delibes, Miguel
See also CA 45-48; CANR 1, 32; HW; MTCW

DeLillo, Don
1936- .... **CLC 8, 10, 13, 27, 39, 54, 76**
See also BEST 89:1; CA 81-84; CANR 21; DAM NOV, POP; DLB 6; MTCW

de Lisser, H. G.
See De Lisser, Herbert George
See also DLB 117

De Lisser, Herbert George
1878-1944 .... **TCLC 12**
See also de Lisser, H. G.
See also BW 2; CA 109

Deloria, Vine (Victor), Jr. 1933-.... **CLC 21**
See also CA 53-56; CANR 5, 20, 48; DAM MULT; MTCW; NNAL; SATA 21

Del Vecchio, John M(ichael)
1947- .... **CLC 29**
See also CA 110; DLBD 9

de Man, Paul (Adolph Michel)
1919-1983 .... **CLC 55**
See also CA 128; 111; DLB 67; MTCW

De Marinis, Rick 1934-........... **CLC 54**
See also CA 57-60; CAAS 24; CANR 9, 25, 50

Dembry, R. Emmet
See Murfree, Mary Noailles

Demby, William 1922-....... **CLC 53; BLC**
See also BW 1; CA 81-84; DAM MULT; DLB 33

Demijohn, Thom
See Disch, Thomas M(ichael)

de Montherlant, Henry (Milon)
See Montherlant, Henry (Milon) de

Demosthenes 384B.C.-322B.C. .... **CMLC 13**

de Natale, Francine
See Malzberg, Barry N(athaniel)

Denby, Edwin (Orr) 1903-1983..... **CLC 48**
See also CA 138; 110

Denis, Julio
See Cortazar, Julio

Denmark, Harrison
See Zelazny, Roger (Joseph)

Dennis, John 1658-1734........... **LC 11**
See also DLB 101

Dennis, Nigel (Forbes) 1912-1989.... **CLC 8**
See also CA 25-28R; 129; DLB 13, 15; MTCW

De Palma, Brian (Russell) 1940-.... **CLC 20**
See also CA 109

De Quincey, Thomas 1785-1859 ... **NCLC 4**
See also CDBLB 1789-1832; DLB 110; 144

Deren, Eleanora 1908(?)-1961
See Deren, Maya
See also CA 111

Deren, Maya .... **CLC 16**
See also Deren, Eleanora

Derleth, August (William)
1909-1971 .... **CLC 31**
See also CA 1-4R; 29-32R; CANR 4; DLB 9; SATA 5

Der Nister 1884-1950........... **TCLC 56**

de Routisie, Albert
See Aragon, Louis

Derrida, Jacques 1930-........ **CLC 24, 87**
See also CA 124; 127

Derry Down Derry
See Lear, Edward

Dersonnes, Jacques
See Simenon, Georges (Jacques Christian)

Desai, Anita 1937- ...... **CLC 19, 37; DAB**
See also CA 81-84; CANR 33, 53; DAM NOV; MTCW; SATA 63

de Saint-Luc, Jean
See Glassco, John

de Saint Roman, Arnaud
See Aragon, Louis

Descartes, Rene 1596-1650 .... **LC 20**

De Sica, Vittorio 1901(?)-1974 ..... **CLC 20**
See also CA 117

Desnos, Robert 1900-1945....... **TCLC 22**
See also CA 121; 151

Destouches, Louis-Ferdinand
1894-1961 .... **CLC 9, 15**
See also Celine, Louis-Ferdinand
See also CA 85-88; CANR 28; MTCW

Deutsch, Babette 1895-1982 .... **CLC 18**
See also CA 1-4R; 108; CANR 4; DLB 45; SATA 1; SATA-Obit 33

Devenant, William 1606-1649 ...... **LC 13**

Devkota, Laxmiprasad
1909-1959 .... **TCLC 23**
See also CA 123

De Voto, Bernard (Augustine)
1897-1955 .... **TCLC 29**
See also CA 113; DLB 9

De Vries, Peter
1910-1993 .... **CLC 1, 2, 3, 7, 10, 28, 46**
See also CA 17-20R; 142; CANR 41; DAM NOV; DLB 6; DLBY 82; MTCW

Dexter, John
See Bradley, Marion Zimmer

Dexter, Martin
See Faust, Frederick (Schiller)

Dexter, Pete 1943-........... **CLC 34, 55**
See also BEST 89:2; CA 127; 131; DAM POP; INT 131; MTCW

Diamano, Silmang
See Senghor, Leopold Sedar

Diamond, Neil 1941- .... **CLC 30**
See also CA 108

Diaz del Castillo, Bernal 1496-1584 .. **LC 31**

di Bassetto, Corno
See Shaw, George Bernard

Dick, Philip K(indred)
1928-1982 .... **CLC 10, 30, 72**
See also CA 49-52; 106; CANR 2, 16; DAM NOV, POP; DLB 8; MTCW

Dickens, Charles (John Huffam)
1812-1870 ...... **NCLC 3, 8, 18, 26, 37, 50; DA; DAB; DAC; SSC 17; WLC**
See also CDBLB 1832-1890; DAM MST, NOV; DLB 21, 55, 70, 159, 166; JRDA; MAICYA; SATA 15

Dickey, James (Lafayette)
1923-........ **CLC 1, 2, 4, 7, 10, 15, 47**
See also AITN 1, 2; CA 9-12R; CABS 2; CANR 10, 48; CDALB 1968-1988; DAM NOV, POET, POP; DLB 5; DLBD 7; DLBY 82, 93; INT CANR-10; MTCW

Dickey, William 1928-1994 ...... **CLC 3, 28**
See also CA 9-12R; 145; CANR 24; DLB 5

Dickinson, Charles 1951-.......... **CLC 49**
See also CA 128

Dickinson, Emily (Elizabeth)
1830-1886 .... **NCLC 21; DA; DAB; DAC; PC 1; WLC**
See also CDALB 1865-1917; DAM MST, POET; DLB 1; SATA 29

Dickinson, Peter (Malcolm)
1927-.................... **CLC 12, 35**
See also AAYA 9; CA 41-44R; CANR 31; CLR 29; DLB 87, 161; JRDA; MAICYA; SATA 5, 62

Dickson, Carr
See Carr, John Dickson

Dickson, Carter
See Carr, John Dickson

Diderot, Denis 1713-1784 .... **LC 26**

Didion, Joan 1934-..... **CLC 1, 3, 8, 14, 32**
See also AITN 1; CA 5-8R; CANR 14, 52; CDALB 1968-1988; DAM NOV; DLB 2; DLBY 81, 86; MTCW

Dietrich, Robert
See Hunt, E(verette) Howard, (Jr.)

Dillard, Annie 1945-............ CLC 9, 60
See also AAYA 6; CA 49-52; CANR 3, 43;
DAM NOV; DLBY 80; MTCW;
SATA 10

Dillard, R(ichard) H(enry) W(ilde)
1937- .... CLC 5
See also CA 21-24R; CAAS 7; CANR 10;
DLB 5

Dillon, Eilis 1920-1994............ CLC 17
See also CA 9-12R; 147; CAAS 3; CANR 4,
38; CLR 26; MAICYA; SATA 2, 74;
SATA-Obit 83

Dimont, Penelope
See Mortimer, Penelope (Ruth)

Dinesen, Isak........ CLC 10, 29, 95; SSC 7
See also Blixen, Karen (Christentze
Dinesen)

Ding Ling...................... CLC 68
See also Chiang Pin-chin

Disch, Thomas M(ichael) 1940-... CLC 7, 36
See also AAYA 17; CA 21-24R; CAAS 4;
CANR 17, 36; CLR 18; DLB 8;
MAICYA; MTCW; SAAS 15; SATA 54

Disch, Tom
See Disch, Thomas M(ichael)

d'Isly, Georges
See Simenon, Georges (Jacques Christian)

Disraeli, Benjamin 1804-1881 .. NCLC 2, 39
See also DLB 21, 55

Ditcum, Steve
See Crumb, R(obert)

Dixon, Paige
See Corcoran, Barbara

Dixon, Stephen 1936-..... CLC 52; SSC 16
See also CA 89-92; CANR 17, 40; DLB 130

Dobell, Sydney Thompson
1824-1874 .... NCLC 43
See also DLB 32

Doblin, Alfred .... TCLC 13
See also Doeblin, Alfred

Dobrolyubov, Nikolai Alexandrovich
1836-1861 .... NCLC 5

Dobyns, Stephen 1941-............ CLC 37
See also CA 45-48; CANR 2, 18

Doctorow, E(dgar) L(aurence)
1931- ..... CLC 6, 11, 15, 18, 37, 44, 65
See also AITN 2; BEST 89:3; CA 45-48;
CANR 2, 33, 51; CDALB 1968-1988;
DAM NOV, POP; DLB 2, 28; DLBY 80;
MTCW

Dodgson, Charles Lutwidge 1832-1898
See Carroll, Lewis
See also CLR 2; DA; DAB; DAC;
DAM MST, NOV, POET; MAICYA;
YABC 2

Dodson, Owen (Vincent)
1914-1983 .... CLC 79; BLC
See also BW 1; CA 65-68; 110; CANR 24;
DAM MULT; DLB 76

Doeblin, Alfred 1878-1957....... TCLC 13
See also Doblin, Alfred
See also CA 110; 141; DLB 66

Doerr, Harriet 1910- .... CLC 34
See also CA 117; 122; CANR 47; INT 122

Domecq, H(onorio) Bustos
See Bioy Casares, Adolfo; Borges, Jorge
Luis

Domini, Rey
See Lorde, Audre (Geraldine)

Dominique
See Proust, (Valentin-Louis-George-Eugene-)
Marcel

Don, A
See Stephen, Leslie

Donaldson, Stephen R. 1947-...... CLC 46
See also CA 89-92; CANR 13; DAM POP;
INT CANR-13

Donleavy, J(ames) P(atrick)
1926- .... CLC 1, 4, 6, 10, 45
See also AITN 2; CA 9-12R; CANR 24, 49;
DLB 6; INT CANR-24; MTCW

Donne, John
1572-1631 .... LC 10, 24; DA; DAB;
DAC; PC 1
See also CDBLB Before 1660; DAM MST,
POET; DLB 121, 151

Donnell, David 1939(?)-........... CLC 34

Donoghue, P. S.
See Hunt, E(verette) Howard, (Jr.)

Donoso (Yanez), Jose
1924- .... CLC 4, 8, 11, 32; HLC
See also CA 81-84; CANR 32;
DAM MULT; DLB 113; HW; MTCW

Donovan, John 1928-1992 .... CLC 35
See also CA 97-100; 137; CLR 3;
MAICYA; SATA 72; SATA-Brief 29

Don Roberto
See Cunninghame Graham, R(obert)
B(ontine)

Doolittle, Hilda
1886-1961 ..... CLC 3, 8, 14, 31, 34, 73;
DA; DAC; PC 5; WLC
See also H. D.
See also CA 97-100; CANR 35; DAM MST,
POET; DLB 4, 45; MTCW

Dorfman, Ariel 1942-.... CLC 48, 77; HLC
See also CA 124; 130; DAM MULT; HW;
INT 130

Dorn, Edward (Merton) 1929-... CLC 10, 18
See also CA 93-96; CANR 42; DLB 5;
INT 93-96

Dorsan, Luc
See Simenon, Georges (Jacques Christian)

Dorsange, Jean
See Simenon, Georges (Jacques Christian)

Dos Passos, John (Roderigo)
1896-1970 ...... CLC 1, 4, 8, 11, 15, 25,
34, 82; DA; DAB; DAC; WLC
See also CA 1-4R; 29-32R; CANR 3;
CDALB 1929-1941; DAM MST, NOV;
DLB 4, 9; DLBD 1; MTCW

Dossage, Jean
See Simenon, Georges (Jacques Christian)

Dostoevsky, Fedor Mikhailovich
1821-1881 ...... NCLC 2, 7, 21, 33, 43;
DA; DAB; DAC; SSC 2; WLC
See also DAM MST, NOV

Doughty, Charles M(ontagu)
1843-1926 .... TCLC 27
See also CA 115; DLB 19, 57

Douglas, Ellen .... CLC 73
See also Haxton, Josephine Ayres;
Williamson, Ellen Douglas

Douglas, Gavin 1475(?)-1522........ LC 20

Douglas, Keith 1920-1944 .... TCLC 40
See also DLB 27

Douglas, Leonard
See Bradbury, Ray (Douglas)

Douglas, Michael
See Crichton, (John) Michael

Douglass, Frederick
1817(?)-1895 .... NCLC 7, 55; BLC; DA;
DAC; WLC
See also CDALB 1640-1865; DAM MST,
MULT; DLB 1, 43, 50, 79; SATA 29

Dourado, (Waldomiro Freitas) Autran
1926- .... CLC 23, 60
See also CA 25-28R; CANR 34

Dourado, Waldomiro Autran
See Dourado, (Waldomiro Freitas) Autran

Dove, Rita (Frances)
1952- .... CLC 50, 81; PC 6
See also BW 2; CA 109; CAAS 19;
CANR 27, 42; DAM MULT, POET;
DLB 120

Dowell, Coleman 1925-1985........ CLC 60
See also CA 25-28R; 117; CANR 10;
DLB 130

Dowson, Ernest (Christopher)
1867-1900 .... TCLC 4
See also CA 105; 150; DLB 19, 135

Doyle, A. Conan
See Doyle, Arthur Conan

Doyle, Arthur Conan
1859-1930 .... TCLC 7; DA; DAB;
DAC; SSC 12; WLC
See also AAYA 14; CA 104; 122;
CDBLB 1890-1914; DAM MST, NOV;
DLB 18, 70, 156; MTCW; SATA 24

Doyle, Conan
See Doyle, Arthur Conan

Doyle, John
See Graves, Robert (von Ranke)

Doyle, Roddy 1958(?)-............ CLC 81
See also AAYA 14; CA 143

Doyle, Sir A. Conan
See Doyle, Arthur Conan

Doyle, Sir Arthur Conan
See Doyle, Arthur Conan

Dr. A
See Asimov, Isaac; Silverstein, Alvin

Drabble, Margaret
1939- .... CLC 2, 3, 5, 8, 10, 22, 53;
DAB; DAC
See also CA 13-16R; CANR 18, 35;
CDBLB 1960 to Present; DAM MST,
NOV, POP; DLB 14, 155; MTCW;
SATA 48

Drapier, M. B.
See Swift, Jonathan

Drayham, James
See Mencken, H(enry) L(ouis)

Drayton, Michael 1563-1631........ LC 8

Dreadstone, Carl
See Campbell, (John) Ramsey

Dreiser, Theodore (Herman Albert)
1871-1945 . . . . . . **TCLC 10, 18, 35; DA;**
DAC; WLC
See also CA 106; 132; CDALB 1865-1917;
DAM MST, NOV; DLB 9, 12, 102, 137;
DLBD 1; MTCW

Drexler, Rosalyn 1926- . . . . **CLC 2, 6**
See also CA 81-84

Dreyer, Carl Theodor 1889-1968 . . . . **CLC 16**
See also CA 116

Drieu la Rochelle, Pierre(-Eugene)
1893-1945 . . . . **TCLC 21**
See also CA 117; DLB 72

Drinkwater, John 1882-1937 . . . . . . **TCLC 57**
See also CA 109; 149; DLB 10, 19, 149

Drop Shot
See Cable, George Washington

Droste-Hulshoff, Annette Freiin von
1797-1848 . . . . **NCLC 3**
See also DLB 133

Drummond, Walter
See Silverberg, Robert

Drummond, William Henry
1854-1907 . . . . **TCLC 25**
See also DLB 92

Drummond de Andrade, Carlos
1902-1987 . . . . **CLC 18**
See also Andrade, Carlos Drummond de
See also CA 132; 123

Drury, Allen (Stuart) 1918- . . . . **CLC 37**
See also CA 57-60; CANR 18, 52;
INT CANR-18

Dryden, John
1631-1700 . . . . **LC 3, 21; DA; DAB;**
DAC; DC 3; WLC
See also CDBLB 1660-1789; DAM DRAM,
MST, POET; DLB 80, 101, 131

Duberman, Martin 1930- . . . . **CLC 8**
See also CA 1-4R; CANR 2

Dubie, Norman (Evans) 1945- . . . . . . **CLC 36**
See also CA 69-72; CANR 12; DLB 120

Du Bois, W(illiam) E(dward) B(urghardt)
1868-1963 . . . . . . **CLC 1, 2, 13, 64; BLC;**
DA; DAC; WLC
See also BW 1; CA 85-88; CANR 34;
CDALB 1865-1917; DAM MST, MULT,
NOV; DLB 47, 50, 91; MTCW; SATA 42

Dubus, Andre 1936- . . . **CLC 13, 36; SSC 15**
See also CA 21-24R; CANR 17; DLB 130;
INT CANR-17

Duca Minimo
See D'Annunzio, Gabriele

Ducharme, Rejean 1941- . . . . **CLC 74**
See also DLB 60

Duclos, Charles Pinot 1704-1772 . . . . . **LC 1**

Dudek, Louis 1918- . . . . **CLC 11, 19**
See also CA 45-48; CAAS 14; CANR 1;
DLB 88

Duerrenmatt, Friedrich
1921-1990 . . . . . **CLC 1, 4, 8, 11, 15, 43**
See also CA 17-20R; CANR 33;
DAM DRAM; DLB 69, 124; MTCW

Duffy, Bruce (?)- . . . . **CLC 50**

Duffy, Maureen 1933- . . . . **CLC 37**
See also CA 25-28R; CANR 33; DLB 14;
MTCW

Dugan, Alan 1923- . . . . **CLC 2, 6**
See also CA 81-84; DLB 5

du Gard, Roger Martin
See Martin du Gard, Roger

Duhamel, Georges 1884-1966 . . . . **CLC 8**
See also CA 81-84; 25-28R; CANR 35;
DLB 65; MTCW

Dujardin, Edouard (Emile Louis)
1861-1949 . . . . **TCLC 13**
See also CA 109; DLB 123

Dumas, Alexandre (Davy de la Pailleterie)
1802-1870 . . . . **NCLC 11; DA; DAB;**
DAC; WLC
See also DAM MST, NOV; DLB 119;
SATA 18

Dumas, Alexandre
1824-1895 . . . . **NCLC 9; DC 1**

Dumas, Claudine
See Malzberg, Barry N(athaniel)

Dumas, Henry L. 1934-1968 . . . . . **CLC 6, 62**
See also BW 1; CA 85-88; DLB 41

du Maurier, Daphne
1907-1989 . . . . **CLC 6, 11, 59; DAB;**
DAC; SSC 18
See also CA 5-8R; 128; CANR 6;
DAM MST, POP; MTCW; SATA 27;
SATA-Obit 60

Dunbar, Paul Laurence
1872-1906 . . . . . . **TCLC 2, 12; BLC; DA;**
DAC; PC 5; SSC 8; WLC
See also BW 1; CA 104; 124;
CDALB 1865-1917; DAM MST, MULT,
POET; DLB 50, 54, 78; SATA 34

Dunbar, William 1460(?)-1530(?) . . . . **LC 20**
See also DLB 132, 146

Duncan, Lois 1934- . . . . **CLC 26**
See also AAYA 4; CA 1-4R; CANR 2, 23,
36; CLR 29; JRDA; MAICYA; SAAS 2;
SATA 1, 36, 75

Duncan, Robert (Edward)
1919-1988 . . . . **CLC 1, 2, 4, 7, 15, 41, 55;**
PC 2
See also CA 9-12R; 124; CANR 28;
DAM POET; DLB 5, 16; MTCW

Duncan, Sara Jeannette
1861-1922 . . . . **TCLC 60**
See also DLB 92

Dunlap, William 1766-1839 . . . . **NCLC 2**
See also DLB 30, 37, 59

Dunn, Douglas (Eaglesham)
1942- . . . . **CLC 6, 40**
See also CA 45-48; CANR 2, 33; DLB 40;
MTCW

Dunn, Katherine (Karen) 1945- . . . . . **CLC 71**
See also CA 33-36R

Dunn, Stephen 1939- . . . . **CLC 36**
See also CA 33-36R; CANR 12, 48, 53;
DLB 105

Dunne, Finley Peter 1867-1936 . . . . **TCLC 28**
See also CA 108; DLB 11, 23

Dunne, John Gregory 1932- . . . . **CLC 28**
See also CA 25-28R; CANR 14, 50;
DLBY 80

Dunsany, Edward John Moreton Drax
Plunkett 1878-1957
See Dunsany, Lord
See also CA 104; 148; DLB 10

Dunsany, Lord . . . . **TCLC 2, 59**
See also Dunsany, Edward John Moreton
Drax Plunkett
See also DLB 77, 153, 156

du Perry, Jean
See Simenon, Georges (Jacques Christian)

Durang, Christopher (Ferdinand)
1949- . . . . **CLC 27, 38**
See also CA 105; CANR 50

Duras, Marguerite
1914-1996 . . **CLC 3, 6, 11, 20, 34, 40, 68**
See also CA 25-28R; 151; CANR 50;
DLB 83; MTCW

Durban, (Rosa) Pam 1947- . . . . **CLC 39**
See also CA 123

Durcan, Paul 1944- . . . . **CLC 43, 70**
See also CA 134; DAM POET

Durkheim, Emile 1858-1917 . . . . . . **TCLC 55**

Durrell, Lawrence (George)
1912-1990 . . . . **CLC 1, 4, 6, 8, 13, 27, 41**
See also CA 9-12R; 132; CANR 40;
CDBLB 1945-1960; DAM NOV; DLB 15,
27; DLBY 90; MTCW

Durrenmatt, Friedrich
See Duerrenmatt, Friedrich

Dutt, Toru 1856-1877 . . . . **NCLC 29**

Dwight, Timothy 1752-1817 . . . . . . **NCLC 13**
See also DLB 37

Dworkin, Andrea 1946- . . . . **CLC 43**
See also CA 77-80; CAAS 21; CANR 16,
39; INT CANR-16; MTCW

Dwyer, Deanna
See Koontz, Dean R(ay)

Dwyer, K. R.
See Koontz, Dean R(ay)

Dylan, Bob 1941- . . . . . . **CLC 3, 4, 6, 12, 77**
See also CA 41-44R; DLB 16

Eagleton, Terence (Francis) 1943-
See Eagleton, Terry
See also CA 57-60; CANR 7, 23; MTCW

Eagleton, Terry . . . . **CLC 63**
See also Eagleton, Terence (Francis)

Early, Jack
See Scoppettone, Sandra

East, Michael
See West, Morris L(anglo)

Eastaway, Edward
See Thomas, (Philip) Edward

Eastlake, William (Derry) 1917- . . . . . **CLC 8**
See also CA 5-8R; CAAS 1; CANR 5;
DLB 6; INT CANR-5

Eastman, Charles A(lexander)
1858-1939 . . . . **TCLC 55**
See also DAM MULT; NNAL; YABC 1

Eberhart, Richard (Ghormley)
1904- . . . . **CLC 3, 11, 19, 56**
See also CA 1-4R; CANR 2;
CDALB 1941-1968; DAM POET;
DLB 48; MTCW

Elytis, Odysseus 1911-1996..... **CLC 15, 49**
See also CA 102; 151; DAM POET; MTCW

Emecheta, (Florence Onye) Buchi
1944-................ **CLC 14, 48; BLC**
See also BW 2; CA 81-84; CANR 27;
DAM MULT; DLB 117; MTCW;
SATA 66

Emerson, Ralph Waldo
1803-1882 ..... **NCLC 1, 38; DA; DAB;**
DAC; WLC
See also CDALB 1640-1865; DAM MST,
POET; DLB 1, 59, 73

Eminescu, Mihail 1850-1889..... **NCLC 33**

Empson, William
1906-1984 .... **CLC 3, 8, 19, 33, 34**
See also CA 17-20R; 112; CANR 31;
DLB 20; MTCW

Enchi Fumiko (Ueda) 1905-1986.... **CLC 31**
See also CA 129; 121

Ende, Michael (Andreas Helmuth)
1929-1995 .... **CLC 31**
See also CA 118; 124; 149; CANR 36;
CLR 14; DLB 75; MAICYA; SATA 61;
SATA-Brief 42; SATA-Obit 86

Endo, Shusaku 1923-..... **CLC 7, 14, 19, 54**
See also CA 29-32R; CANR 21;
DAM NOV; MTCW

Engel, Marian 1933-1985........ **CLC 36**
See also CA 25-28R; CANR 12; DLB 53;
INT CANR-12

Engelhardt, Frederick
See Hubbard, L(afayette) Ron(ald)

Enright, D(ennis) J(oseph)
1920-.................. **CLC 4, 8, 31**
See also CA 1-4R; CANR 1, 42; DLB 27;
SATA 25

Enzensberger, Hans Magnus
1929-...................... **CLC 43**
See also CA 116; 119

Ephron, Nora 1941-.......... **CLC 17, 31**
See also AITN 2; CA 65-68; CANR 12, 39

Epsilon
See Betjeman, John

Epstein, Daniel Mark 1948- .... **CLC 7**
See also CA 49-52; CANR 2, 53

Epstein, Jacob 1956- .... **CLC 19**
See also CA 114

Epstein, Joseph 1937-............ **CLC 39**
See also CA 112; 119; CANR 50

Epstein, Leslie 1938- .... **CLC 27**
See also CA 73-76; CAAS 12; CANR 23

Equiano, Olaudah
1745(?)-1797 .... **LC 16; BLC**
See also DAM MULT; DLB 37, 50

Erasmus, Desiderius 1469(?)-1536.... **LC 16**

Erdman, Paul E(mil) 1932- .... **CLC 25**
See also AITN 1; CA 61-64; CANR 13, 43

Erdrich, Louise 1954-.......... **CLC 39, 54**
See also AAYA 10; BEST 89:1; CA 114;
CANR 41; DAM MULT, NOV, POP;
DLB 152; MTCW; NNAL

Erenburg, Ilya (Grigoryevich)
See Ehrenburg, Ilya (Grigoryevich)

Erickson, Stephen Michael 1950-
See Erickson, Steve
See also CA 129

Erickson, Steve .... **CLC 64**
See also Erickson, Stephen Michael

Ericson, Walter
See Fast, Howard (Melvin)

Eriksson, Buntel
See Bergman, (Ernst) Ingmar

Ernaux, Annie 1940- .... **CLC 88**
See also CA 147

Eschenbach, Wolfram von
See Wolfram von Eschenbach

Eseki, Bruno
See Mphahlele, Ezekiel

Esenin, Sergei (Alexandrovich)
1895-1925 .... **TCLC 4**
See also CA 104

Eshleman, Clayton 1935-.......... **CLC 7**
See also CA 33-36R; CAAS 6; DLB 5

Espriella, Don Manuel Alvarez
See Southey, Robert

Espriu, Salvador 1913-1985........ **CLC 9**
See also CA 115; DLB 134

Espronceda, Jose de 1808-1842... **NCLC 39**

Esse, James
See Stephens, James

Esterbrook, Tom
See Hubbard, L(afayette) Ron(ald)

Estleman, Loren D. 1952- .... **CLC 48**
See also CA 85-88; CANR 27; DAM NOV,
POP; INT CANR-27; MTCW

Eugenides, Jeffrey 1960(?)-........ **CLC 81**
See also CA 144

Euripides c. 485B.C.-406B.C. .... **DC 4**
See also DA; DAB; DAC; DAM DRAM,
MST

Evan, Evin
See Faust, Frederick (Schiller)

Evans, Evan
See Faust, Frederick (Schiller)

Evans, Marian
See Eliot, George

Evans, Mary Ann
See Eliot, George

Evarts, Esther
See Benson, Sally

Everett, Percival L. 1956- .... **CLC 57**
See also BW 2; CA 129

Everson, R(onald) G(ilmour)
1903-...................... **CLC 27**
See also CA 17-20R; DLB 88

Everson, William (Oliver)
1912-1994 .... **CLC 1, 5, 14**
See also CA 9-12R; 145; CANR 20; DLB 5,
16; MTCW

Evtushenko, Evgenii Aleksandrovich
See Yevtushenko, Yevgeny (Alexandrovich)

Ewart, Gavin (Buchanan)
1916-1995 .... **CLC 13, 46**
See also CA 89-92; 150; CANR 17, 46;
DLB 40; MTCW

Ewers, Hanns Heinz 1871-1943 ... **TCLC 12**
See also CA 109; 149

Ewing, Frederick R.
See Sturgeon, Theodore (Hamilton)

Exley, Frederick (Earl)
1929-1992 .... **CLC 6, 11**
See also AITN 2; CA 81-84; 138; DLB 143;
DLBY 81

Eynhardt, Guillermo
See Quiroga, Horacio (Sylvestre)

Ezekiel, Nissim 1924-............ **CLC 61**
See also CA 61-64

Ezekiel, Tish O'Dowd 1943-....... **CLC 34**
See also CA 129

Fadeyev, A.
See Bulgya, Alexander Alexandrovich

Fadeyev, Alexander............... TCLC 53
See also Bulgya, Alexander Alexandrovich

Fagen, Donald 1948-............. **CLC 26**

Fainzilberg, Ilya Arnoldovich 1897-1937
See Ilf, Ilya
See also CA 120

Fair, Ronald L. 1932-............. **CLC 18**
See also BW 1; CA 69-72; CANR 25;
DLB 33

Fairbairns, Zoe (Ann) 1948- .... **CLC 32**
See also CA 103; CANR 21

Falco, Gian
See Papini, Giovanni

Falconer, James
See Kirkup, James

Falconer, Kenneth
See Kornbluth, C(yril) M.

Falkland, Samuel
See Heijermans, Herman

Fallaci, Oriana 1930-............ **CLC 11**
See also CA 77-80; CANR 15; MTCW

Faludy, George 1913-............. **CLC 42**
See also CA 21-24R

Faludy, Gyoergy
See Faludy, George

Fanon, Frantz 1925-1961..... **CLC 74; BLC**
See also BW 1; CA 116; 89-92;
DAM MULT

Fanshawe, Ann 1625-1680......... **LC 11**

Fante, John (Thomas) 1911-1983 ... **CLC 60**
See also CA 69-72; 109; CANR 23;
DLB 130; DLBY 83

Farah, Nuruddin 1945-....... **CLC 53; BLC**
See also BW 2; CA 106; DAM MULT;
DLB 125

Fargue, Leon-Paul 1876(?)-1947 ... **TCLC 11**
See also CA 109

Farigoule, Louis
See Romains, Jules

Farina, Richard 1936(?)-1966 .... **CLC 9**
See also CA 81-84; 25-28R

Farley, Walter (Lorimer)
1915-1989 .... **CLC 17**
See also CA 17-20R; CANR 8, 29; DLB 22;
JRDA; MAICYA; SATA 2, 43

Farmer, Philip Jose 1918-....... **CLC 1, 19**
See also CA 1-4R; CANR 4, 35; DLB 8;
MTCW

Farquhar, George 1677-1707........ **LC 21**
See also DAM DRAM; DLB 84

Farrell, J(ames) G(ordon)
1935-1979 .... **CLC 6**
See also CA 73-76; 89-92; CANR 36;
DLB 14; MTCW

Farrell, James T(homas)
1904-1979 .... **CLC 1, 4, 8, 11, 66**
See also CA 5-8R; 89-92; CANR 9; DLB 4,
9, 86; DLBD 2; MTCW

Farren, Richard J.
See Betjeman, John

Farren, Richard M.
See Betjeman, John

Fassbinder, Rainer Werner
1946-1982 .... **CLC 20**
See also CA 93-96; 106; CANR 31

Fast, Howard (Melvin) 1914- ...... **CLC 23**
See also AAYA 16; CA 1-4R; CAAS 18;
CANR 1, 33; DAM NOV; DLB 9;
INT CANR-33; SATA 7

Faulcon, Robert
See Holdstock, Robert P.

Faulkner, William (Cuthbert)
1897-1962 ..... **CLC 1, 3, 6, 8, 9, 11, 14,
18, 28, 52, 68; DA; DAB; DAC; SSC 1;
WLC**
See also AAYA 7; CA 81-84; CANR 33;
CDALB 1929-1941; DAM MST, NOV;
DLB 9, 11, 44, 102; DLBD 2; DLBY 86;
MTCW

Fauset, Jessie Redmon
1884(?)-1961 .... **CLC 19, 54; BLC**
See also BW 1; CA 109; DAM MULT;
DLB 51

Faust, Frederick (Schiller)
1892-1944(?) .... **TCLC 49**
See also CA 108; DAM POP

Faust, Irvin 1924-................. **CLC 8**
See also CA 33-36R; CANR 28; DLB 2, 28;
DLBY 80

Fawkes, Guy
See Benchley, Robert (Charles)

Fearing, Kenneth (Flexner)
1902-1961 .... **CLC 51**
See also CA 93-96; DLB 9

Fecamps, Elise
See Creasey, John

Federman, Raymond 1928- ...... **CLC 6, 47**
See also CA 17-20R; CAAS 8; CANR 10,
43; DLBY 80

Federspiel, J(uerg) F. 1931-........ **CLC 42**
See also CA 146

Feiffer, Jules (Ralph) 1929-.... **CLC 2, 8, 64**
See also AAYA 3; CA 17-20R; CANR 30;
DAM DRAM; DLB 7, 44;
INT CANR-30; MTCW; SATA 8, 61

Feige, Hermann Albert Otto Maximilian
See Traven, B.

Feinberg, David B. 1956-1994...... **CLC 59**
See also CA 135; 147

Feinstein, Elaine 1930-............ **CLC 36**
See also CA 69-72; CAAS 1; CANR 31;
DLB 14, 40; MTCW

Feldman, Irving (Mordecai) 1928-.... **CLC 7**
See also CA 1-4R; CANR 1

Fellini, Federico 1920-1993 ..... **CLC 16, 85**
See also CA 65-68; 143; CANR 33

Felsen, Henry Gregor 1916- .... **CLC 17**
See also CA 1-4R; CANR 1; SAAS 2;
SATA 1

Fenton, James Martin 1949-....... **CLC 32**
See also CA 102; DLB 40

Ferber, Edna 1887-1968........ **CLC 18, 93**
See also AITN 1; CA 5-8R; 25-28R; DLB 9,
28, 86; MTCW; SATA 7

Ferguson, Helen
See Kavan, Anna

Ferguson, Samuel 1810-1886..... **NCLC 33**
See also DLB 32

Fergusson, Robert 1750-1774 .... **LC 29**
See also DLB 109

Ferling, Lawrence
See Ferlinghetti, Lawrence (Monsanto)

Ferlinghetti, Lawrence (Monsanto)
1919(?)-........ **CLC 2, 6, 10, 27; PC 1**
See also CA 5-8R; CANR 3, 41;
CDALB 1941-1968; DAM POET; DLB 5,
16; MTCW

Fernandez, Vicente Garcia Huidobro
See Huidobro Fernandez, Vicente Garcia

Ferrer, Gabriel (Francisco Victor) Miro
See Miro (Ferrer), Gabriel (Francisco
Victor)

Ferrier, Susan (Edmonstone)
1782-1854 .... **NCLC 8**
See also DLB 116

Ferrigno, Robert 1948(?)-.......... **CLC 65**
See also CA 140

Ferron, Jacques 1921-1985 ... **CLC 94; DAC**
See also CA 117; 129; DLB 60

Feuchtwanger, Lion 1884-1958 ..... **TCLC 3**
See also CA 104; DLB 66

Feuillet, Octave 1821-1890 ...... **NCLC 45**

Feydeau, Georges (Leon Jules Marie)
1862-1921 .... **TCLC 22**
See also CA 113; DAM DRAM

Ficino, Marsilio 1433-1499 .... **LC 12**

Fiedeler, Hans
See Doeblin, Alfred

Fiedler, Leslie A(aron)
1917-................... **CLC 4, 13, 24**
See also CA 9-12R; CANR 7; DLB 28, 67;
MTCW

Field, Andrew 1938-............. **CLC 44**
See also CA 97-100; CANR 25

Field, Eugene 1850-1895 .... **NCLC 3**
See also DLB 23, 42, 140; DLBD 13;
MAICYA; SATA 16

Field, Gans T.
See Wellman, Manly Wade

Field, Michael .... **TCLC 43**

Field, Peter
See Hobson, Laura Z(ametkin)

Fielding, Henry
1707-1754 ...... **LC 1; DA; DAB; DAC;
WLC**
See also CDBLB 1660-1789; DAM DRAM,
MST, NOV; DLB 39, 84, 101

Fielding, Sarah 1710-1768 .... **LC 1**
See also DLB 39

Fierstein, Harvey (Forbes) 1954- ... **CLC 33**
See also CA 123; 129; DAM DRAM, POP

Figes, Eva 1932-................. **CLC 31**
See also CA 53-56; CANR 4, 44; DLB 14

Finch, Robert (Duer Claydon)
1900-..................... **CLC 18**
See also CA 57-60; CANR 9, 24, 49;
DLB 88

Findley, Timothy 1930- ...... **CLC 27; DAC**
See also CA 25-28R; CANR 12, 42;
DAM MST; DLB 53

Fink, William
See Mencken, H(enry) L(ouis)

Firbank, Louis 1942-
See Reed, Lou
See also CA 117

Firbank, (Arthur Annesley) Ronald
1886-1926 .... **TCLC 1**
See also CA 104; DLB 36

Fisher, M(ary) F(rances) K(ennedy)
1908-1992 .... **CLC 76, 87**
See also CA 77-80; 138; CANR 44

Fisher, Roy 1930-................. **CLC 25**
See also CA 81-84; CAAS 10; CANR 16;
DLB 40

Fisher, Rudolph
1897-1934 .... **TCLC 11; BLC**
See also BW 1; CA 107; 124; DAM MULT;
DLB 51, 102

Fisher, Vardis (Alvero) 1895-1968.... **CLC 7**
See also CA 5-8R; 25-28R; DLB 9

Fiske, Tarleton
See Bloch, Robert (Albert)

Fitch, Clarke
See Sinclair, Upton (Beall)

Fitch, John IV
See Cormier, Robert (Edmund)

Fitzgerald, Captain Hugh
See Baum, L(yman) Frank

FitzGerald, Edward 1809-1883 .... **NCLC 9**
See also DLB 32

Fitzgerald, F(rancis) Scott (Key)
1896-1940 .... **TCLC 1, 6, 14, 28, 55;
DA; DAB; DAC; SSC 6; WLC**
See also AITN 1; CA 110; 123;
CDALB 1917-1929; DAM MST, NOV;
DLB 4, 9, 86; DLBD 1; DLBY 81;
MTCW

Fitzgerald, Penelope 1916-... **CLC 19, 51, 61**
See also CA 85-88; CAAS 10; DLB 14

Fitzgerald, Robert (Stuart)
1910-1985 .... **CLC 39**
See also CA 1-4R; 114; CANR 1; DLBY 80

FitzGerald, Robert D(avid)
1902-1987 .... **CLC 19**
See also CA 17-20R

Fitzgerald, Zelda (Sayre)
1900-1948 . . . . **TCLC 52**
See also CA 117; 126; DLBY 84

Flanagan, Thomas (James Bonner)
1923- . . . . **CLC 25, 52**
See also CA 108; DLBY 80; INT 108;
MTCW

Flaubert, Gustave
1821-1880 . . . . **NCLC 2, 10, 19; DA;**
DAB; DAC; SSC 11; WLC
See also DAM MST, NOV; DLB 119

Flecker, Herman Elroy
See Flecker, (Herman) James Elroy

Flecker, (Herman) James Elroy
1884-1915 . . . . **TCLC 43**
See also CA 109; 150; DLB 10, 19

Fleming, Ian (Lancaster)
1908-1964 . . . . **CLC 3, 30**
See also CA 5-8R; CDBLB 1945-1960;
DAM POP; DLB 87; MTCW; SATA 9

Fleming, Thomas (James) 1927- . . . . **CLC 37**
See also CA 5-8R; CANR 10;
INT CANR-10; SATA 8

Fletcher, John 1579-1625 . . . . . **LC 33; DC 6**
See also CDBLB Before 1660; DLB 58

Fletcher, John Gould 1886-1950 . . . **TCLC 35**
See also CA 107; DLB 4, 45

Fleur, Paul
See Pohl, Frederik

Flooglebuckle, Al
See Spiegelman, Art

Flying Officer X
See Bates, H(erbert) E(rnest)

Fo, Dario 1926- . . . . **CLC 32**
See also CA 116; 128; DAM DRAM;
MTCW

Fogarty, Jonathan Titulescu Esq.
See Farrell, James T(homas)

Folke, Will
See Bloch, Robert (Albert)

Follett, Ken(neth Martin) 1949- . . . . **CLC 18**
See also AAYA 6; BEST 89:4; CA 81-84;
CANR 13, 33; DAM NOV, POP;
DLB 87; DLBY 81; INT CANR-33;
MTCW

Fontane, Theodor 1819-1898 . . . . . **NCLC 26**
See also DLB 129

Foote, Horton 1916- . . . . **CLC 51, 91**
See also CA 73-76; CANR 34, 51;
DAM DRAM; DLB 26; INT CANR-34

Foote, Shelby 1916- . . . . **CLC 75**
See also CA 5-8R; CANR 3, 45;
DAM NOV, POP; DLB 2, 17

Forbes, Esther 1891-1967 . . . . **CLC 12**
See also AAYA 17; CA 13-14; 25-28R;
CAP 1; CLR 27; DLB 22; JRDA;
MAICYA; SATA 2

Forche, Carolyn (Louise)
1950- . . . . **CLC 25, 83, 86; PC 10**
See also CA 109; 117; CANR 50;
DAM POET; DLB 5; INT 117

Ford, Elbur
See Hibbert, Eleanor Alice Burford

Ford, Ford Madox
1873-1939 . . . . . . **TCLC 1, 15, 39, 57**
See also CA 104; 132; CDBLB 1914-1945;
DAM NOV; DLB 162; MTCW

Ford, John 1895-1973 . . . . **CLC 16**
See also CA 45-48

Ford, Richard 1944- . . . . **CLC 46**
See also CA 69-72; CANR 11, 47

Ford, Webster
See Masters, Edgar Lee

Foreman, Richard 1937- . . . . **CLC 50**
See also CA 65-68; CANR 32

Forester, C(ecil) S(cott)
1899-1966 . . . . **CLC 35**
See also CA 73-76; 25-28R; SATA 13

Forez
See Mauriac, Francois (Charles)

Forman, James Douglas 1932- . . . . . . **CLC 21**
See also AAYA 17; CA 9-12R; CANR 4,
19, 42; JRDA; MAICYA; SATA 8, 70

Fornes, Maria Irene 1930- . . . . . . **CLC 39, 61**
See also CA 25-28R; CANR 28; DLB 7;
HW; INT CANR-28; MTCW

Forrest, Leon 1937- . . . . **CLC 4**
See also BW 2; CA 89-92; CAAS 7;
CANR 25, 52; DLB 33

Forster, E(dward) M(organ)
1879-1970 . . . . . **CLC 1, 2, 3, 4, 9, 10, 13,**
15, 22, 45, 77; DA; DAB; DAC; WLC
See also AAYA 2; CA 13-14; 25-28R;
CANR 45; CAP 1; CDBLB 1914-1945;
DAM MST, NOV; DLB 34, 98, 162;
DLBD 10; MTCW; SATA 57

Forster, John 1812-1876 . . . . **NCLC 11**
See also DLB 144

Forsyth, Frederick 1938- . . . . . . **CLC 2, 5, 36**
See also BEST 89:4; CA 85-88; CANR 38;
DAM NOV, POP; DLB 87; MTCW

Forten, Charlotte L. . . . . **TCLC 16; BLC**
See also Grimke, Charlotte L(ottie) Forten
See also DLB 50

Foscolo, Ugo 1778-1827 . . . . **NCLC 8**

Fosse, Bob . . . . **CLC 20**
See also Fosse, Robert Louis

Fosse, Robert Louis 1927-1987
See Fosse, Bob
See also CA 110; 123

Foster, Stephen Collins
1826-1864 . . . . **NCLC 26**

Foucault, Michel
1926-1984 . . . . **CLC 31, 34, 69**
See also CA 105; 113; CANR 34; MTCW

Fouque, Friedrich (Heinrich Karl) de la Motte
1777-1843 . . . . **NCLC 2**
See also DLB 90

Fourier, Charles 1772-1837 . . . . . . **NCLC 51**

Fournier, Henri Alban 1886-1914
See Alain-Fournier
See also CA 104

Fournier, Pierre 1916- . . . . **CLC 11**
See also Gascar, Pierre
See also CA 89-92; CANR 16, 40

Fowles, John
1926- . . . . . . **CLC 1, 2, 3, 4, 6, 9, 10, 15,**
33, 87; DAB; DAC
See also CA 5-8R; CANR 25; CDBLB 1960
to Present; DAM MST; DLB 14, 139;
MTCW; SATA 22

Fox, Paula 1923- . . . . **CLC 2, 8**
See also AAYA 3; CA 73-76; CANR 20,
36; CLR 1; DLB 52; JRDA; MAICYA;
MTCW; SATA 17, 60

Fox, William Price (Jr.) 1926- . . . . . **CLC 22**
See also CA 17-20R; CAAS 19; CANR 11;
DLB 2; DLBY 81

Foxe, John 1516(?)-1587 . . . . **LC 14**

Frame, Janet . . . . **CLC 2, 3, 6, 22, 66**
See also Clutha, Janet Paterson Frame

France, Anatole . . . . **TCLC 9**
See also Thibault, Jacques Anatole Francois
See also DLB 123

Francis, Claude 19(?)- . . . . **CLC 50**

Francis, Dick 1920- . . . . **CLC 2, 22, 42**
See also AAYA 5; BEST 89:3; CA 5-8R;
CANR 9, 42; CDBLB 1960 to Present;
DAM POP; DLB 87; INT CANR-9;
MTCW

Francis, Robert (Churchill)
1901-1987 . . . . **CLC 15**
See also CA 1-4R; 123; CANR 1

Frank, Anne(lies Marie)
1929-1945 . . . . **TCLC 17; DA; DAB;**
DAC; WLC
See also AAYA 12; CA 113; 133;
DAM MST; MTCW; SATA 87;
SATA-Brief 42

Frank, Elizabeth 1945- . . . . **CLC 39**
See also CA 121; 126; INT 126

Frankl, Viktor E(mil) 1905- . . . . **CLC 93**
See also CA 65-68

Franklin, Benjamin
See Hasek, Jaroslav (Matej Frantisek)

Franklin, Benjamin
1706-1790 . . . . . **LC 25; DA; DAB; DAC**
See also CDALB 1640-1865; DAM MST;
DLB 24, 43, 73

Franklin, (Stella Maraia Sarah) Miles
1879-1954 . . . . **TCLC 7**
See also CA 104

Fraser, (Lady) Antonia (Pakenham)
1932- . . . . **CLC 32**
See also CA 85-88; CANR 44; MTCW;
SATA-Brief 32

Fraser, George MacDonald 1925- . . . . **CLC 7**
See also CA 45-48; CANR 2, 48

Fraser, Sylvia 1935- . . . . **CLC 64**
See also CA 45-48; CANR 1, 16

Frayn, Michael 1933- . . . . . . **CLC 3, 7, 31, 47**
See also CA 5-8R; CANR 30;
DAM DRAM, NOV; DLB 13, 14;
MTCW

Fraze, Candida (Merrill) 1945- . . . . . **CLC 50**
See also CA 126

Frazer, J(ames) G(eorge)
1854-1941 . . . . **TCLC 32**
See also CA 118

Gordon, Adam Lindsay
1833-1870 . . . . NCLC 21

Gordon, Caroline
1895-1981 . . . **CLC 6, 13, 29, 83; SSC 15**
See also CA 11-12; 103; CANR 36; CAP 1;
DLB 4, 9, 102; DLBY 81; MTCW

Gordon, Charles William 1860-1937
See Connor, Ralph
See also CA 109

Gordon, Mary (Catherine)
1949- . . . . **CLC 13, 22**
See also CA 102; CANR 44; DLB 6;
DLBY 81; INT 102; MTCW

Gordon, Sol 1923- . . . . **CLC 26**
See also CA 53-56; CANR 4; SATA 11

Gordone, Charles 1925-1995 . . . . . **CLC 1, 4**
See also BW 1; CA 93-96; 150;
DAM DRAM; DLB 7; INT 93-96;
MTCW

Gorenko, Anna Andreevna
See Akhmatova, Anna

Gorky, Maxim . . . . **TCLC 8; DAB; WLC**
See also Peshkov, Alexei Maximovich

Goryan, Sirak
See Saroyan, William

Gosse, Edmund (William)
1849-1928 . . . . **TCLC 28**
See also CA 117; DLB 57, 144

Gotlieb, Phyllis Fay (Bloom)
1926- . . . . **CLC 18**
See also CA 13-16R; CANR 7; DLB 88

Gottesman, S. D.
See Kornbluth, C(yril) M.; Pohl, Frederik

Gottfried von Strassburg
fl. c. 1210- . . . . **CMLC 10**
See also DLB 138

Gould, Lois . . . . **CLC 4, 10**
See also CA 77-80; CANR 29; MTCW

Gourmont, Remy (-Marie-Charles) de
1858-1915 . . . . **TCLC 17**
See also CA 109; 150

Govier, Katherine 1948- . . . . **CLC 51**
See also CA 101; CANR 18, 40

Goyen, (Charles) William
1915-1983 . . . . **CLC 5, 8, 14, 40**
See also AITN 2; CA 5-8R; 110; CANR 6;
DLB 2; DLBY 83; INT CANR-6

Goytisolo, Juan
1931- . . . . **CLC 5, 10, 23; HLC**
See also CA 85-88; CANR 32;
DAM MULT; HW; MTCW

Gozzano, Guido 1883-1916 . . . . **PC 10**
See also DLB 114

Gozzi, (Conte) Carlo 1720-1806 . . **NCLC 23**

Grabbe, Christian Dietrich
1801-1836 . . . . **NCLC 2**
See also DLB 133

Grace, Patricia 1937- . . . . **CLC 56**

Gracian y Morales, Baltasar
1601-1658 . . . . **LC 15**

Gracq, Julien . . . . **CLC 11, 48**
See also Poirier, Louis
See also DLB 83

Grade, Chaim 1910-1982 . . . . **CLC 10**
See also CA 93-96; 107

Graduate of Oxford, A
See Ruskin, John

Graham, John
See Phillips, David Graham

Graham, Jorie 1951- . . . . **CLC 48**
See also CA 111; DLB 120

Graham, R(obert) B(ontine) Cunninghame
See Cunninghame Graham, R(obert)
B(ontine)
See also DLB 98, 135

Graham, Robert
See Haldeman, Joe (William)

Graham, Tom
See Lewis, (Harry) Sinclair

Graham, W(illiam) S(ydney)
1918-1986 . . . . **CLC 29**
See also CA 73-76; 118; DLB 20

Graham, Winston (Mawdsley)
1910- . . . . **CLC 23**
See also CA 49-52; CANR 2, 22, 45;
DLB 77

Grahame, Kenneth
1859-1932 . . . . **TCLC 64; DAB**
See also CA 108; 136; CLR 5; DLB 34, 141;
MAICYA; YABC 1

Grant, Skeeter
See Spiegelman, Art

Granville-Barker, Harley
1877-1946 . . . . **TCLC 2**
See also Barker, Harley Granville
See also CA 104; DAM DRAM

Grass, Guenter (Wilhelm)
1927- . . . . . **CLC 1, 2, 4, 6, 11, 15, 22, 32,**
49, 88; DA; DAB; DAC; WLC
See also CA 13-16R; CANR 20;
DAM MST, NOV; DLB 75, 124; MTCW

Gratton, Thomas
See Hulme, T(homas) E(rnest)

Grau, Shirley Ann
1929- . . . . **CLC 4, 9; SSC 15**
See also CA 89-92; CANR 22; DLB 2;
INT CANR-22; MTCW

Gravel, Fern
See Hall, James Norman

Graver, Elizabeth 1964- . . . . **CLC 70**
See also CA 135

Graves, Richard Perceval 1945- . . . . **CLC 44**
See also CA 65-68; CANR 9, 26, 51

Graves, Robert (von Ranke)
1895-1985 . . . . . . **CLC 1, 2, 6, 11, 39, 44,**
45; DAB; DAC; PC 6
See also CA 5-8R; 117; CANR 5, 36;
CDBLB 1914-1945; DAM MST, POET;
DLB 20, 100; DLBY 85; MTCW;
SATA 45

Graves, Valerie
See Bradley, Marion Zimmer

Gray, Alasdair (James) 1934- . . . . . . **CLC 41**
See also CA 126; CANR 47; INT 126;
MTCW

Gray, Amlin 1946- . . . . **CLC 29**
See also CA 138

Gray, Francine du Plessix 1930- . . . . **CLC 22**
See also BEST 90:3; CA 61-64; CAAS 2;
CANR 11, 33; DAM NOV;
INT CANR-11; MTCW

Gray, John (Henry) 1866-1934 . . . . **TCLC 19**
See also CA 119

Gray, Simon (James Holliday)
1936- . . . . **CLC 9, 14, 36**
See also AITN 1; CA 21-24R; CAAS 3;
CANR 32; DLB 13; MTCW

Gray, Spalding 1941- . . . . **CLC 49**
See also CA 128; DAM POP

Gray, Thomas
1716-1771 . . . . . . **LC 4; DA; DAB; DAC;**
PC 2; WLC
See also CDBLB 1660-1789; DAM MST;
DLB 109

Grayson, David
See Baker, Ray Stannard

Grayson, Richard (A.) 1951- . . . . **CLC 38**
See also CA 85-88; CANR 14, 31

Greeley, Andrew M(oran) 1928- . . . . **CLC 28**
See also CA 5-8R; CAAS 7; CANR 7, 43;
DAM POP; MTCW

Green, Anna Katharine
1846-1935 . . . . **TCLC 63**
See also CA 112

Green, Brian
See Card, Orson Scott

Green, Hannah
See Greenberg, Joanne (Goldenberg)

Green, Hannah . . . . **CLC 3**
See also CA 73-76

Green, Henry . . . . **CLC 2, 13**
See also Yorke, Henry Vincent
See also DLB 15

Green, Julian (Hartridge) 1900-
See Green, Julien
See also CA 21-24R; CANR 33; DLB 4, 72;
MTCW

Green, Julien . . . . **CLC 3, 11, 77**
See also Green, Julian (Hartridge)

Green, Paul (Eliot) 1894-1981 . . . . . . **CLC 25**
See also AITN 1; CA 5-8R; 103; CANR 3;
DAM DRAM; DLB 7, 9; DLBY 81

Greenberg, Ivan 1908-1973
See Rahv, Philip
See also CA 85-88

Greenberg, Joanne (Goldenberg)
1932- . . . . **CLC 7, 30**
See also AAYA 12; CA 5-8R; CANR 14,
32; SATA 25

Greenberg, Richard 1959(?)- . . . . **CLC 57**
See also CA 138

Greene, Bette 1934- . . . . **CLC 30**
See also AAYA 7; CA 53-56; CANR 4;
CLR 2; JRDA; MAICYA; SAAS 16;
SATA 8

Greene, Gael . . . . **CLC 8**
See also CA 13-16R; CANR 10

Greene, Graham
1904-1991 .... **CLC 1, 3, 6, 9, 14, 18, 27,**
37, 70, 72; DA; DAB; DAC; WLC
See also AITN 2; CA 13-16R; 133;
CANR 35; CDBLB 1945-1960;
DAM MST, NOV; DLB 13, 15, 77, 100,
162; DLBY 91; MTCW; SATA 20

Greer, Richard
See Silverberg, Robert

Gregor, Arthur 1923- .... **CLC 9**
See also CA 25-28R; CAAS 10; CANR 11;
SATA 36

Gregor, Lee
See Pohl, Frederik

Gregory, Isabella Augusta (Persse)
1852-1932 .... **TCLC 1**
See also CA 104; DLB 10

Gregory, J. Dennis
See Williams, John A(lfred)

Grendon, Stephen
See Derleth, August (William)

Grenville, Kate 1950- .... **CLC 61**
See also CA 118; CANR 53

Grenville, Pelham
See Wodehouse, P(elham) G(renville)

Greve, Felix Paul (Berthold Friedrich)
1879-1948
See Grove, Frederick Philip
See also CA 104; 141; DAC; DAM MST

Grey, Zane 1872-1939 .... **TCLC 6**
See also CA 104; 132; DAM POP; DLB 9;
MTCW

Grieg, (Johan) Nordahl (Brun)
1902-1943 .... **TCLC 10**
See also CA 107

Grieve, C(hristopher) M(urray)
1892-1978 .... **CLC 11, 19**
See also MacDiarmid, Hugh; Pteleon
See also CA 5-8R; 85-88; CANR 33;
DAM POET; MTCW

Griffin, Gerald 1803-1840 .... **NCLC 7**
See also DLB 159

Griffin, John Howard 1920-1980.... **CLC 68**
See also AITN 1; CA 1-4R; 101; CANR 2

Griffin, Peter 1942- .... **CLC 39**
See also CA 136

Griffiths, Trevor 1935-......... **CLC 13, 52**
See also CA 97-100; CANR 45; DLB 13

Grigson, Geoffrey (Edward Harvey)
1905-1985 .... **CLC 7, 39**
See also CA 25-28R; 118; CANR 20, 33;
DLB 27; MTCW

Grillparzer, Franz 1791-1872 ..... **NCLC 1**
See also DLB 133

Grimble, Reverend Charles James
See Eliot, T(homas) S(tearns)

Grimke, Charlotte L(ottie) Forten
1837(?)-1914
See Forten, Charlotte L.
See also BW 1; CA 117; 124; DAM MULT,
POET

Grimm, Jacob Ludwig Karl
1785-1863 .... **NCLC 3**
See also DLB 90; MAICYA; SATA 22

Grimm, Wilhelm Karl 1786-1859 .. **NCLC 3**
See also DLB 90; MAICYA; SATA 22

Grimmelshausen, Johann Jakob Christoffel
von 1621-1676 .... **LC 6**

Grindel, Eugene 1895-1952
See Eluard, Paul
See also CA 104

Grisham, John 1955- .... **CLC 84**
See also AAYA 14; CA 138; CANR 47;
DAM POP

Grossman, David 1954- .... **CLC 67**
See also CA 138

Grossman, Vasily (Semenovich)
1905-1964 .... **CLC 41**
See also CA 124; 130; MTCW

Grove, Frederick Philip .... **TCLC 4**
See also Greve, Felix Paul (Berthold
Friedrich)
See also DLB 92

Grubb
See Crumb, R(obert)

Grumbach, Doris (Isaac)
1918- .... **CLC 13, 22, 64**
See also CA 5-8R; CAAS 2; CANR 9, 42;
INT CANR-9

Grundtvig, Nicolai Frederik Severin
1783-1872 .... **NCLC 1**

Grunge
See Crumb, R(obert)

Grunwald, Lisa 1959- .... **CLC 44**
See also CA 120

Guare, John 1938- .... **CLC 8, 14, 29, 67**
See also CA 73-76; CANR 21;
DAM DRAM; DLB 7; MTCW

Gudjonsson, Halldor Kiljan 1902-
See Laxness, Halldor
See also CA 103

Guenter, Erich
See Eich, Guenter

Guest, Barbara 1920- .... **CLC 34**
See also CA 25-28R; CANR 11, 44; DLB 5

Guest, Judith (Ann) 1936- .... **CLC 8, 30**
See also AAYA 7; CA 77-80; CANR 15;
DAM NOV, POP; INT CANR-15;
MTCW

Guevara, Che .... **CLC 87; HLC**
See also Guevara (Serna), Ernesto

Guevara (Serna), Ernesto 1928-1967
See Guevara, Che
See also CA 127; 111; DAM MULT; HW

Guild, Nicholas M. 1944- .... **CLC 33**
See also CA 93-96

Guillemin, Jacques
See Sartre, Jean-Paul

Guillen, Jorge 1893-1984.......... **CLC 11**
See also CA 89-92; 112; DAM MULT,
POET; DLB 108; HW

Guillen, Nicolas (Cristobal)
1902-1989 ..... **CLC 48, 79; BLC; HLC**
See also BW 2; CA 116; 125; 129;
DAM MST, MULT, POET; HW

Guillevic, (Eugene) 1907-......... **CLC 33**
See also CA 93-96

Guillois
See Desnos, Robert

Guillois, Valentin
See Desnos, Robert

Guiney, Louise Imogen
1861-1920 .... **TCLC 41**
See also DLB 54

Guiraldes, Ricardo (Guillermo)
1886-1927 .... **TCLC 39**
See also CA 131; HW; MTCW

Gumilev, Nikolai Stephanovich
1886-1921 .... **TCLC 60**

Gunesekera, Romesh.............. **CLC 91**

Gunn, Bill .... **CLC 5**
See also Gunn, William Harrison
See also DLB 38

Gunn, Thom(son William)
1929- .... **CLC 3, 6, 18, 32, 81**
See also CA 17-20R; CANR 9, 33;
CDBLB 1960 to Present; DAM POET;
DLB 27; INT CANR-33; MTCW

Gunn, William Harrison 1934(?)-1989
See Gunn, Bill
See also AITN 1; BW 1; CA 13-16R; 128;
CANR 12, 25

Gunnars, Kristjana 1948-......... **CLC 69**
See also CA 113; DLB 60

Gurganus, Allan 1947-............ **CLC 70**
See also BEST 90:1; CA 135; DAM POP

Gurney, A(lbert) R(amsdell), Jr.
1930- .... **CLC 32, 50, 54**
See also CA 77-80; CANR 32;
DAM DRAM

Gurney, Ivor (Bertie) 1890-1937... **TCLC 33**

Gurney, Peter
See Gurney, A(lbert) R(amsdell), Jr.

Guro, Elena 1877-1913.......... **TCLC 56**

Gustafson, Ralph (Barker) 1909-.... **CLC 36**
See also CA 21-24R; CANR 8, 45; DLB 88

Gut, Gom
See Simenon, Georges (Jacques Christian)

Guterson, David 1956-............ **CLC 91**
See also CA 132

Guthrie, A(lfred) B(ertram), Jr.
1901-1991 .... **CLC 23**
See also CA 57-60; 134; CANR 24; DLB 6;
SATA 62; SATA-Obit 67

Guthrie, Isobel
See Grieve, C(hristopher) M(urray)

Guthrie, Woodrow Wilson 1912-1967
See Guthrie, Woody
See also CA 113; 93-96

Guthrie, Woody.................. **CLC 35**
See also Guthrie, Woodrow Wilson

Guy, Rosa (Cuthbert) 1928-........ **CLC 26**
See also AAYA 4; BW 2; CA 17-20R;
CANR 14, 34; CLR 13; DLB 33; JRDA;
MAICYA; SATA 14, 62

Gwendolyn
See Bennett, (Enoch) Arnold

H. D. .... **CLC 3, 8, 14, 31, 34, 73; PC 5**
See also Doolittle, Hilda

H. de V.
See Buchan, John

Haavikko, Paavo Juhani
1931- . . . . CLC **18, 34**
See also CA 106

Habbema, Koos
See Heijermans, Herman

Hacker, Marilyn
1942- . . . . CLC **5, 9, 23, 72, 91**
See also CA 77-80; DAM POET; DLB 120

Haggard, H(enry) Rider
1856-1925 . . . . TCLC **11**
See also CA 108; 148; DLB 70, 156;
SATA 16

Hagiwara Sakutaro 1886-1942 . . . . TCLC **60**

Haig, Fenil
See Ford, Ford Madox

Haig-Brown, Roderick (Langmere)
1908-1976 . . . . CLC **21**
See also CA 5-8R; 69-72; CANR 4, 38;
CLR 31; DLB 88; MAICYA; SATA 12

Hailey, Arthur 1920- . . . . CLC **5**
See also AITN 2; BEST 90:3; CA 1-4R;
CANR 2, 36; DAM NOV, POP; DLB 88;
DLBY 82; MTCW

Hailey, Elizabeth Forsythe 1938- . . . CLC **40**
See also CA 93-96; CAAS 1; CANR 15, 48;
INT CANR-15

Haines, John (Meade) 1924- . . . . CLC **58**
See also CA 17-20R; CANR 13, 34; DLB 5

Hakluyt, Richard 1552-1616 . . . . LC **31**

Haldeman, Joe (William) 1943- . . . . . CLC **61**
See also CA 53-56; CANR 6; DLB 8;
INT CANR-6

Haley, Alex(ander Murray Palmer)
1921-1992 . . . . CLC **8, 12, 76; BLC; DA;
DAB; DAC**
See also BW 2; CA 77-80; 136; DAM MST,
MULT, POP; DLB 38; MTCW

Haliburton, Thomas Chandler
1796-1865 . . . . NCLC **15**
See also DLB 11, 99

Hall, Donald (Andrew, Jr.)
1928- . . . . CLC **1, 13, 37, 59**
See also CA 5-8R; CAAS 7; CANR 2, 44;
DAM POET; DLB 5; SATA 23

Hall, Frederic Sauser
See Sauser-Hall, Frederic

Hall, James
See Kuttner, Henry

Hall, James Norman 1887-1951 . . . TCLC **23**
See also CA 123; SATA 21

Hall, (Marguerite) Radclyffe
1886-1943 . . . . TCLC **12**
See also CA 110; 150

Hall, Rodney 1935- . . . . CLC **51**
See also CA 109

Halleck, Fitz-Greene 1790-1867 . . NCLC **47**
See also DLB 3

Halliday, Michael
See Creasey, John

Halpern, Daniel 1945- . . . . CLC **14**
See also CA 33-36R

Hamburger, Michael (Peter Leopold)
1924- . . . . CLC **5, 14**
See also CA 5-8R; CAAS 4; CANR 2, 47;
DLB 27

Hamill, Pete 1935- . . . . CLC **10**
See also CA 25-28R; CANR 18

Hamilton, Alexander
1755(?)-1804 . . . . NCLC **49**
See also DLB 37

Hamilton, Clive
See Lewis, C(live) S(taples)

Hamilton, Edmond 1904-1977 . . . . . . CLC **1**
See also CA 1-4R; CANR 3; DLB 8

Hamilton, Eugene (Jacob) Lee
See Lee-Hamilton, Eugene (Jacob)

Hamilton, Franklin
See Silverberg, Robert

Hamilton, Gail
See Corcoran, Barbara

Hamilton, Mollie
See Kaye, M(ary) M(argaret)

Hamilton, (Anthony Walter) Patrick
1904-1962 . . . . CLC **51**
See also CA 113; DLB 10

Hamilton, Virginia 1936- . . . . CLC **26**
See also AAYA 2; BW 2; CA 25-28R;
CANR 20, 37; CLR 1, 11, 40;
DAM MULT; DLB 33, 52;
INT CANR-20; JRDA; MAICYA;
MTCW; SATA 4, 56, 79

Hammett, (Samuel) Dashiell
1894-1961 . . . . CLC **3, 5, 10, 19, 47;
SSC 17**
See also AITN 1; CA 81-84; CANR 42;
CDALB 1929-1941; DLBD 6; MTCW

Hammon, Jupiter
1711(?)-1800(?) . . . NCLC **5; BLC; PC 16**
See also DAM MULT, POET; DLB 31, 50

Hammond, Keith
See Kuttner, Henry

Hamner, Earl (Henry), Jr. 1923- . . . CLC **12**
See also AITN 2; CA 73-76; DLB 6

Hampton, Christopher (James)
1946- . . . . CLC **4**
See also CA 25-28R; DLB 13; MTCW

Hamsun, Knut . . . . TCLC **2, 14, 49**
See also Pedersen, Knut

Handke, Peter 1942- . . CLC **5, 8, 10, 15, 38**
See also CA 77-80; CANR 33;
DAM DRAM, NOV; DLB 85, 124;
MTCW

Hanley, James 1901-1985 . . . CLC **3, 5, 8, 13**
See also CA 73-76; 117; CANR 36; MTCW

Hannah, Barry 1942- . . . . CLC **23, 38, 90**
See also CA 108; 110; CANR 43; DLB 6;
INT 110; MTCW

Hannon, Ezra
See Hunter, Evan

Hansberry, Lorraine (Vivian)
1930-1965 . . . . . . CLC **17, 62; BLC; DA;
DAB; DAC; DC 2**
See also BW 1; CA 109; 25-28R; CABS 3;
CDALB 1941-1968; DAM DRAM, MST,
MULT; DLB 7, 38; MTCW

Hansen, Joseph 1923- . . . . CLC **38**
See also CA 29-32R; CAAS 17; CANR 16,
44; INT CANR-16

Hansen, Martin A. 1909-1955 . . . . . TCLC **32**

Hanson, Kenneth O(stlin) 1922- . . . . CLC **13**
See also CA 53-56; CANR 7

Hardwick, Elizabeth 1916- . . . . CLC **13**
See also CA 5-8R; CANR 3, 32;
DAM NOV; DLB 6; MTCW

Hardy, Thomas
1840-1928 . . . . . . TCLC **4, 10, 18, 32, 48,
53; DA; DAB; DAC; PC 8; SSC 2; WLC**
See also CA 104; 123; CDBLB 1890-1914;
DAM MST, NOV, POET; DLB 18, 19,
135; MTCW

Hare, David 1947- . . . . CLC **29, 58**
See also CA 97-100; CANR 39; DLB 13;
MTCW

Harford, Henry
See Hudson, W(illiam) H(enry)

Hargrave, Leonie
See Disch, Thomas M(ichael)

Harjo, Joy 1951- . . . . CLC **83**
See also CA 114; CANR 35; DAM MULT;
DLB 120; NNAL

Harlan, Louis R(udolph) 1922- . . . . . CLC **34**
See also CA 21-24R; CANR 25

Harling, Robert 1951(?)- . . . . CLC **53**
See also CA 147

Harmon, William (Ruth) 1938- . . . . . CLC **38**
See also CA 33-36R; CANR 14, 32, 35;
SATA 65

Harper, F. E. W.
See Harper, Frances Ellen Watkins

Harper, Frances E. W.
See Harper, Frances Ellen Watkins

Harper, Frances E. Watkins
See Harper, Frances Ellen Watkins

Harper, Frances Ellen
See Harper, Frances Ellen Watkins

Harper, Frances Ellen Watkins
1825-1911 . . . . TCLC **14; BLC**
See also BW 1; CA 111; 125; DAM MULT,
POET; DLB 50

Harper, Michael S(teven) 1938- . . CLC **7, 22**
See also BW 1; CA 33-36R; CANR 24;
DLB 41

Harper, Mrs. F. E. W.
See Harper, Frances Ellen Watkins

Harris, Christie (Lucy) Irwin
1907- . . . . CLC **12**
See also CA 5-8R; CANR 6; DLB 88;
JRDA; MAICYA; SAAS 10; SATA 6, 74

Harris, Frank 1856-1931 . . . . TCLC **24**
See also CA 109; 150; DLB 156

Harris, George Washington
1814-1869 . . . . NCLC **23**
See also DLB 3, 11

Harris, Joel Chandler
1848-1908 . . . . TCLC **2; SSC 19**
See also CA 104; 137; DLB 11, 23, 42, 78,
91; MAICYA; YABC 1

Harris, John (Wyndham Parkes Lucas)
Beynon 1903-1969
See Wyndham, John
See also CA 102; 89-92

Harris, MacDonald . . . . CLC **9**
See also Heiney, Donald (William)

Hillesum, Etty 1914-1943 .... **TCLC 49**
See also CA 137

Hilliard, Noel (Harvey) 1929- ...... **CLC 15**
See also CA 9-12R; CANR 7

Hillis, Rick 1956- .... **CLC 66**
See also CA 134

Hilton, James 1900-1954 .... **TCLC 21**
See also CA 108; DLB 34, 77; SATA 34

Himes, Chester (Bomar)
        1909-1984 .... **CLC 2, 4, 7, 18, 58; BLC**
See also BW 2; CA 25-28R; 114; CANR 22;
    DAM MULT; DLB 2, 76, 143; MTCW

Hinde, Thomas .... **CLC 6, 11**
See also Chitty, Thomas Willes

Hindin, Nathan
See Bloch, Robert (Albert)

Hine, (William) Daryl 1936- .... **CLC 15**
See also CA 1-4R; CAAS 15; CANR 1, 20;
    DLB 60

Hinkson, Katharine Tynan
See Tynan, Katharine

Hinton, S(usan) E(loise)
        1950- .... **CLC 30; DA; DAB; DAC**
See also AAYA 2; CA 81-84; CANR 32;
    CLR 3, 23; DAM MST, NOV; JRDA;
    MAICYA; MTCW; SATA 19, 58

Hippius, Zinaida .... **TCLC 9**
See also Gippius, Zinaida (Nikolayevna)

Hiraoka, Kimitake 1925-1970
See Mishima, Yukio
See also CA 97-100; 29-32R; DAM DRAM;
    MTCW

Hirsch, E(ric) D(onald), Jr. 1928- ... **CLC 79**
See also CA 25-28R; CANR 27, 51;
    DLB 67; INT CANR-27; MTCW

Hirsch, Edward 1950- .... **CLC 31, 50**
See also CA 104; CANR 20, 42; DLB 120

Hitchcock, Alfred (Joseph)
        1899-1980 .... **CLC 16**
See also CA 97-100; SATA 27;
    SATA-Obit 24

Hitler, Adolf 1889-1945 .... **TCLC 53**
See also CA 117; 147

Hoagland, Edward 1932- .... **CLC 28**
See also CA 1-4R; CANR 2, 31; DLB 6;
    SATA 51

Hoban, Russell (Conwell) 1925- .. **CLC 7, 25**
See also CA 5-8R; CANR 23, 37; CLR 3;
    DAM NOV; DLB 52; MAICYA;
    MTCW; SATA 1, 40, 78

Hobbs, Perry
See Blackmur, R(ichard) P(almer)

Hobson, Laura Z(ametkin)
        1900-1986 .... **CLC 7, 25**
See also CA 17-20R; 118; DLB 28;
    SATA 52

Hochhuth, Rolf 1931- .... **CLC 4, 11, 18**
See also CA 5-8R; CANR 33;
    DAM DRAM; DLB 124; MTCW

Hochman, Sandra 1936- .... **CLC 3, 8**
See also CA 5-8R; DLB 5

Hochwaelder, Fritz 1911-1986 ..... **CLC 36**
See also CA 29-32R; 120; CANR 42;
    DAM DRAM; MTCW

Hochwalder, Fritz
See Hochwaelder, Fritz

Hocking, Mary (Eunice) 1921- ..... **CLC 13**
See also CA 101; CANR 18, 40

Hodgins, Jack 1938- .... **CLC 23**
See also CA 93-96; DLB 60

Hodgson, William Hope
        1877(?)-1918 .... **TCLC 13**
See also CA 111; DLB 70, 153, 156

Hoeg, Peter 1957- .... **CLC 95**
See also CA 151

Hoffman, Alice 1952- .... **CLC 51**
See also CA 77-80; CANR 34; DAM NOV;
    MTCW

Hoffman, Daniel (Gerard)
        1923- .... **CLC 6, 13, 23**
See also CA 1-4R; CANR 4; DLB 5

Hoffman, Stanley 1944- .... **CLC 5**
See also CA 77-80

Hoffman, William M(oses) 1939- ... **CLC 40**
See also CA 57-60; CANR 11

Hoffmann, E(rnst) T(heodor) A(madeus)
        1776-1822 .... **NCLC 2; SSC 13**
See also DLB 90; SATA 27

Hofmann, Gert 1931- .... **CLC 54**
See also CA 128

Hofmannsthal, Hugo von
        1874-1929 .... **TCLC 11; DC 4**
See also CA 106; DAM DRAM; DLB 81,
    118

Hogan, Linda 1947- .... **CLC 73**
See also CA 120; CANR 45; DAM MULT;
    NNAL

Hogarth, Charles
See Creasey, John

Hogarth, Emmett
See Polonsky, Abraham (Lincoln)

Hogg, James 1770-1835 .... **NCLC 4**
See also DLB 93, 116, 159

Holbach, Paul Henri Thiry Baron
        1723-1789 .... **LC 14**

Holberg, Ludvig 1684-1754 .... **LC 6**

Holden, Ursula 1921- .... **CLC 18**
See also CA 101; CAAS 8; CANR 22

Holderlin, (Johann Christian) Friedrich
        1770-1843 .... **NCLC 16; PC 4**

Holdstock, Robert
See Holdstock, Robert P.

Holdstock, Robert P. 1948- .... **CLC 39**
See also CA 131

Holland, Isabelle 1920- .... **CLC 21**
See also AAYA 11; CA 21-24R; CANR 10,
    25, 47; JRDA; MAICYA; SATA 8, 70

Holland, Marcus
See Caldwell, (Janet Miriam) Taylor
    (Holland)

Hollander, John 1929- ...... **CLC 2, 5, 8, 14**
See also CA 1-4R; CANR 1, 52; DLB 5;
    SATA 13

Hollander, Paul
See Silverberg, Robert

Holleran, Andrew 1943(?)- .... **CLC 38**
See also CA 144

Hollinghurst, Alan 1954- .... **CLC 55, 91**
See also CA 114

Hollis, Jim
See Summers, Hollis (Spurgeon, Jr.)

Holly, Buddy 1936-1959 .... **TCLC 65**

Holmes, John
See Souster, (Holmes) Raymond

Holmes, John Clellon 1926-1988.... **CLC 56**
See also CA 9-12R; 125; CANR 4; DLB 16

Holmes, Oliver Wendell
        1809-1894 .... **NCLC 14**
See also CDALB 1640-1865; DLB 1;
    SATA 34

Holmes, Raymond
See Souster, (Holmes) Raymond

Holt, Victoria
See Hibbert, Eleanor Alice Burford

Holub, Miroslav 1923- .... **CLC 4**
See also CA 21-24R; CANR 10

Homer
        c. 8th cent. B.C.- ..... **CMLC 1, 16; DA;
                                    DAB; DAC**
See also DAM MST, POET

Honig, Edwin 1919- .... **CLC 33**
See also CA 5-8R; CAAS 8; CANR 4, 45;
    DLB 5

Hood, Hugh (John Blagdon)
        1928- .... **CLC 15, 28**
See also CA 49-52; CAAS 17; CANR 1, 33;
    DLB 53

Hood, Thomas 1799-1845....... **NCLC 16**
See also DLB 96

Hooker, (Peter) Jeremy 1941- ...... **CLC 43**
See also CA 77-80; CANR 22; DLB 40

hooks, bell .... **CLC 94**
See also Watkins, Gloria

Hope, A(lec) D(erwent) 1907- .... **CLC 3, 51**
See also CA 21-24R; CANR 33; MTCW

Hope, Brian
See Creasey, John

Hope, Christopher (David Tully)
        1944- .... **CLC 52**
See also CA 106; CANR 47; SATA 62

Hopkins, Gerard Manley
        1844-1889 .... **NCLC 17; DA; DAB;
                            DAC; PC 15; WLC**
See also CDBLB 1890-1914; DAM MST,
    POET; DLB 35, 57

Hopkins, John (Richard) 1931- ...... **CLC 4**
See also CA 85-88

Hopkins, Pauline Elizabeth
        1859-1930 .... **TCLC 28; BLC**
See also BW 2; CA 141; DAM MULT;
    DLB 50

Hopkinson, Francis 1737-1791 ...... **LC 25**
See also DLB 31

Hopley-Woolrich, Cornell George 1903-1968
See Woolrich, Cornell
See also CA 13-14; CAP 1

Horatio
See Proust, (Valentin-Louis-George-Eugene-)
    Marcel

Horgan, Paul (George Vincent O'Shaughnessy)
1903-1995 . . . . CLC 9, 53
See also CA 13-16R; 147; CANR 9, 35;
DAM NOV; DLB 102; DLBY 85;
INT CANR-9; MTCW; SATA 13;
SATA-Obit 84

Horn, Peter
See Kuttner, Henry

Hornem, Horace Esq.
See Byron, George Gordon (Noel)

Hornung, E(rnest) W(illiam)
1866-1921 . . . . TCLC 59
See also CA 108; DLB 70

Horovitz, Israel (Arthur)   1939- . . . . CLC 56
See also CA 33-36R; CANR 46;
DAM DRAM; DLB 7

Horvath, Odon von
See Horvath, Oedoen von
See also DLB 85, 124

Horvath, Oedoen von   1901-1938 . . . TCLC 45
See also Horvath, Odon von
See also CA 118

Horwitz, Julius   1920-1986 . . . . CLC 14
See also CA 9-12R; 119; CANR 12

Hospital, Janette Turner   1942- . . . . . CLC 42
See also CA 108; CANR 48

Hostos, E. M. de
See Hostos (y Bonilla), Eugenio Maria de

Hostos, Eugenio M. de
See Hostos (y Bonilla), Eugenio Maria de

Hostos, Eugenio Maria
See Hostos (y Bonilla), Eugenio Maria de

Hostos (y Bonilla), Eugenio Maria de
1839-1903 . . . . TCLC 24
See also CA 123; 131; HW

Houdini
See Lovecraft, H(oward) P(hillips)

Hougan, Carolyn   1943- . . . . CLC 34
See also CA 139

Household, Geoffrey (Edward West)
1900-1988 . . . . CLC 11
See also CA 77-80; 126; DLB 87; SATA 14;
SATA-Obit 59

Housman, A(lfred) E(dward)
1859-1936 . . . . . . TCLC 1, 10; DA; DAB;
DAC; PC 2
See also CA 104; 125; DAM MST, POET;
DLB 19; MTCW

Housman, Laurence   1865-1959 . . . . . TCLC 7
See also CA 106; DLB 10; SATA 25

Howard, Elizabeth Jane   1923- . . . CLC 7, 29
See also CA 5-8R; CANR 8

Howard, Maureen   1930- . . . . . CLC 5, 14, 46
See also CA 53-56; CANR 31; DLBY 83;
INT CANR-31; MTCW

Howard, Richard   1929- . . . . . . CLC 7, 10, 47
See also AITN 1; CA 85-88; CANR 25;
DLB 5; INT CANR-25

Howard, Robert Ervin   1906-1936 . . . TCLC 8
See also CA 105

Howard, Warren F.
See Pohl, Frederik

Howe, Fanny   1940- . . . . CLC 47
See also CA 117; SATA-Brief 52

Howe, Irving   1920-1993 . . . . CLC 85
See also CA 9-12R; 141; CANR 21, 50;
DLB 67; MTCW

Howe, Julia Ward   1819-1910 . . . . . TCLC 21
See also CA 117; DLB 1

Howe, Susan   1937- . . . . CLC 72
See also DLB 120

Howe, Tina   1937- . . . . CLC 48
See also CA 109

Howell, James   1594(?)-1666 . . . . LC 13
See also DLB 151

Howells, W. D.
See Howells, William Dean

Howells, William D.
See Howells, William Dean

Howells, William Dean
1837-1920 . . . . TCLC 7, 17, 41
See also CA 104; 134; CDALB 1865-1917;
DLB 12, 64, 74, 79

Howes, Barbara   1914-1996 . . . . CLC 15
See also CA 9-12R; 151; CAAS 3;
CANR 53; SATA 5

Hrabal, Bohumil   1914- . . . . CLC 13, 67
See also CA 106; CAAS 12

Hsun, Lu
See Lu Hsun

Hubbard, L(afayette) Ron(ald)
1911-1986 . . . . CLC 43
See also CA 77-80; 118; CANR 52;
DAM POP

Huch, Ricarda (Octavia)
1864-1947 . . . . TCLC 13
See also CA 111; DLB 66

Huddle, David   1942- . . . . CLC 49
See also CA 57-60; CAAS 20; DLB 130

Hudson, Jeffrey
See Crichton, (John) Michael

Hudson, W(illiam) H(enry)
1841-1922 . . . . TCLC 29
See also CA 115; DLB 98, 153; SATA 35

Hueffer, Ford Madox
See Ford, Ford Madox

Hughart, Barry   1934- . . . . CLC 39
See also CA 137

Hughes, Colin
See Creasey, John

Hughes, David (John)   1930- . . . . CLC 48
See also CA 116; 129; DLB 14

Hughes, Edward James
See Hughes, Ted
See also DAM MST, POET

Hughes, (James) Langston
1902-1967 . . . . . CLC 1, 5, 10, 15, 35, 44;
BLC; DA; DAB; DAC; DC 3; PC 1;
SSC 6; WLC
See also AAYA 12; BW 1; CA 1-4R;
25-28R; CANR 1, 34; CDALB 1929-1941;
CLR 17; DAM DRAM, MST, MULT,
POET; DLB 4, 7, 48, 51, 86; JRDA;
MAICYA; MTCW; SATA 4, 33

Hughes, Richard (Arthur Warren)
1900-1976 . . . . CLC 1, 11
See also CA 5-8R; 65-68; CANR 4;
DAM NOV; DLB 15, 161; MTCW;
SATA 8; SATA-Obit 25

Hughes, Ted
1930- . . . . . . CLC 2, 4, 9, 14, 37; DAB;
DAC; PC 7
See also Hughes, Edward James
See also CA 1-4R; CANR 1, 33; CLR 3;
DLB 40, 161; MAICYA; MTCW;
SATA 49; SATA-Brief 27

Hugo, Richard F(ranklin)
1923-1982 . . . . CLC 6, 18, 32
See also CA 49-52; 108; CANR 3;
DAM POET; DLB 5

Hugo, Victor (Marie)
1802-1885 . . . . NCLC 3, 10, 21; DA;
DAB; DAC; WLC
See also DAM DRAM, MST, NOV, POET;
DLB 119; SATA 47

Huidobro, Vicente
See Huidobro Fernandez, Vicente Garcia

Huidobro Fernandez, Vicente Garcia
1893-1948 . . . . TCLC 31
See also CA 131; HW

Hulme, Keri   1947- . . . . CLC 39
See also CA 125; INT 125

Hulme, T(homas) E(rnest)
1883-1917 . . . . TCLC 21
See also CA 117; DLB 19

Hume, David   1711-1776 . . . . LC 7
See also DLB 104

Humphrey, William   1924- . . . . CLC 45
See also CA 77-80; DLB 6

Humphreys, Emyr Owen   1919- . . . . . CLC 47
See also CA 5-8R; CANR 3, 24; DLB 15

Humphreys, Josephine   1945- . . . . CLC 34, 57
See also CA 121; 127; INT 127

Huneker, James Gibbons
1857-1921 . . . . TCLC 65
See also DLB 71

Hungerford, Pixie
See Brinsmead, H(esba) F(ay)

Hunt, E(verette) Howard, (Jr.)
1918- . . . . CLC 3
See also AITN 1; CA 45-48; CANR 2, 47

Hunt, Kyle
See Creasey, John

Hunt, (James Henry) Leigh
1784-1859 . . . . NCLC 1
See also DAM POET

Hunt, Marsha   1946- . . . . CLC 70
See also BW 2; CA 143

Hunt, Violet   1866-1942 . . . . TCLC 53
See also DLB 162

Hunter, E. Waldo
See Sturgeon, Theodore (Hamilton)

Hunter, Evan   1926- . . . . CLC 11, 31
See also CA 5-8R; CANR 5, 38;
DAM POP; DLBY 82; INT CANR-5;
MTCW; SATA 25

Hunter, Kristin (Eggleston)   1931- . . . CLC 35
See also AITN 1; BW 1; CA 13-16R;
CANR 13; CLR 3; DLB 33;
INT CANR-13; MAICYA; SAAS 10;
SATA 12

James, Dynely
See Mayne, William (James Carter)

James, Henry Sr. 1811-1882 . . . . . **NCLC 53**

James, Henry
1843-1916 . . . . . . **TCLC 2, 11, 24, 40, 47, 64; DA; DAB; DAC; SSC 8; WLC**
See also CA 104; 132; CDALB 1865-1917; DAM MST, NOV; DLB 12, 71, 74; DLBD 13; MTCW

James, M. R.
See James, Montague (Rhodes)
See also DLB 156

James, Montague (Rhodes)
1862-1936 . . . . **TCLC 6; SSC 16**
See also CA 104

James, P. D. . . . . **CLC 18, 46**
See also White, Phyllis Dorothy James
See also BEST 90:2; CDBLB 1960 to Present; DLB 87

James, Philip
See Moorcock, Michael (John)

James, William 1842-1910 . . . . . **TCLC 15, 32**
See also CA 109

James I 1394-1437 . . . . **LC 20**

Jameson, Anna 1794-1860 . . . . . . **NCLC 43**
See also DLB 99, 166

Jami, Nur al-Din 'Abd al-Rahman
1414-1492 . . . . **LC 9**

Jandl, Ernst 1925- . . . . **CLC 34**

Janowitz, Tama 1957- . . . . **CLC 43**
See also CA 106; CANR 52; DAM POP

Japrisot, Sebastien 1931- . . . . **CLC 90**

Jarrell, Randall
1914-1965 . . . . **CLC 1, 2, 6, 9, 13, 49**
See also CA 5-8R; 25-28R; CABS 2; CANR 6, 34; CDALB 1941-1968; CLR 6; DAM POET; DLB 48, 52; MAICYA; MTCW; SATA 7

Jarry, Alfred
1873-1907 . . . . **TCLC 2, 14; SSC 20**
See also CA 104; DAM DRAM

Jarvis, E. K.
See Bloch, Robert (Albert); Ellison, Harlan (Jay); Silverberg, Robert

Jeake, Samuel, Jr.
See Aiken, Conrad (Potter)

Jean Paul 1763-1825 . . . . **NCLC 7**

Jefferies, (John) Richard
1848-1887 . . . . **NCLC 47**
See also DLB 98, 141; SATA 16

Jeffers, (John) Robinson
1887-1962 . . . . **CLC 2, 3, 11, 15, 54; DA; DAC; WLC**
See also CA 85-88; CANR 35; CDALB 1917-1929; DAM MST, POET; DLB 45; MTCW

Jefferson, Janet
See Mencken, H(enry) L(ouis)

Jefferson, Thomas 1743-1826 . . . . **NCLC 11**
See also CDALB 1640-1865; DLB 31

Jeffrey, Francis 1773-1850 . . . . . . **NCLC 33**
See also DLB 107

Jelakowitch, Ivan
See Heijermans, Herman

Jellicoe, (Patricia) Ann 1927- . . . . . . **CLC 27**
See also CA 85-88; DLB 13

Jen, Gish . . . . **CLC 70**
See also Jen, Lillian

Jen, Lillian 1956(?)-
See Jen, Gish
See also CA 135

Jenkins, (John) Robin 1912- . . . . **CLC 52**
See also CA 1-4R; CANR 1; DLB 14

Jennings, Elizabeth (Joan)
1926- . . . . **CLC 5, 14**
See also CA 61-64; CAAS 5; CANR 8, 39; DLB 27; MTCW; SATA 66

Jennings, Waylon 1937- . . . . **CLC 21**

Jensen, Johannes V. 1873-1950 . . . . **TCLC 41**

Jensen, Laura (Linnea) 1948- . . . . . . **CLC 37**
See also CA 103

Jerome, Jerome K(lapka)
1859-1927 . . . . **TCLC 23**
See also CA 119; DLB 10, 34, 135

Jerrold, Douglas William
1803-1857 . . . . **NCLC 2**
See also DLB 158, 159

Jewett, (Theodora) Sarah Orne
1849-1909 . . . . **TCLC 1, 22; SSC 6**
See also CA 108; 127; DLB 12, 74; SATA 15

Jewsbury, Geraldine (Endsor)
1812-1880 . . . . **NCLC 22**
See also DLB 21

Jhabvala, Ruth Prawer
1927- . . . . **CLC 4, 8, 29, 94; DAB**
See also CA 1-4R; CANR 2, 29, 51; DAM NOV; DLB 139; INT CANR-29; MTCW

Jibran, Kahlil
See Gibran, Kahlil

Jibran, Khalil
See Gibran, Kahlil

Jiles, Paulette 1943- . . . . **CLC 13, 58**
See also CA 101

Jimenez (Mantecon), Juan Ramon
1881-1958 . . . . **TCLC 4; HLC; PC 7**
See also CA 104; 131; DAM MULT, POET; DLB 134; HW; MTCW

Jimenez, Ramon
See Jimenez (Mantecon), Juan Ramon

Jimenez Mantecon, Juan
See Jimenez (Mantecon), Juan Ramon

Joel, Billy . . . . **CLC 26**
See also Joel, William Martin

Joel, William Martin 1949-
See Joel, Billy
See also CA 108

John of the Cross, St. 1542-1591 . . . . **LC 18**

Johnson, B(ryan) S(tanley William)
1933-1973 . . . . **CLC 6, 9**
See also CA 9-12R; 53-56; CANR 9; DLB 14, 40

Johnson, Benj. F. of Boo
See Riley, James Whitcomb

Johnson, Benjamin F. of Boo
See Riley, James Whitcomb

Johnson, Charles (Richard)
1948- . . . . **CLC 7, 51, 65; BLC**
See also BW 2; CA 116; CAAS 18; CANR 42; DAM MULT; DLB 33

Johnson, Denis 1949- . . . . **CLC 52**
See also CA 117; 121; DLB 120

Johnson, Diane 1934- . . . . **CLC 5, 13, 48**
See also CA 41-44R; CANR 17, 40; DLBY 80; INT CANR-17; MTCW

Johnson, Eyvind (Olof Verner)
1900-1976 . . . . **CLC 14**
See also CA 73-76; 69-72; CANR 34

Johnson, J. R.
See James, C(yril) L(ionel) R(obert)

Johnson, James Weldon
1871-1938 . . . . **TCLC 3, 19; BLC**
See also BW 1; CA 104; 125; CDALB 1917-1929; CLR 32; DAM MULT, POET; DLB 51; MTCW; SATA 31

Johnson, Joyce 1935- . . . . **CLC 58**
See also CA 125; 129

Johnson, Lionel (Pigot)
1867-1902 . . . . **TCLC 19**
See also CA 117; DLB 19

Johnson, Mel
See Malzberg, Barry N(athaniel)

Johnson, Pamela Hansford
1912-1981 . . . . **CLC 1, 7, 27**
See also CA 1-4R; 104; CANR 2, 28; DLB 15; MTCW

Johnson, Samuel
1709-1784 . . . . . **LC 15; DA; DAB; DAC; WLC**
See also CDBLB 1660-1789; DAM MST; DLB 39, 95, 104, 142

Johnson, Uwe
1934-1984 . . . . **CLC 5, 10, 15, 40**
See also CA 1-4R; 112; CANR 1, 39; DLB 75; MTCW

Johnston, George (Benson) 1913- . . . **CLC 51**
See also CA 1-4R; CANR 5, 20; DLB 88

Johnston, Jennifer 1930- . . . . **CLC 7**
See also CA 85-88; DLB 14

Jolley, (Monica) Elizabeth
1923- . . . . **CLC 46; SSC 19**
See also CA 127; CAAS 13

Jones, Arthur Llewellyn 1863-1947
See Machen, Arthur
See also CA 104

Jones, D(ouglas) G(ordon) 1929- . . . . **CLC 10**
See also CA 29-32R; CANR 13; DLB 53

Jones, David (Michael)
1895-1974 . . . . **CLC 2, 4, 7, 13, 42**
See also CA 9-12R; 53-56; CANR 28; CDBLB 1945-1960; DLB 20, 100; MTCW

Jones, David Robert 1947-
See Bowie, David
See also CA 103

Jones, Diana Wynne 1934- . . . . **CLC 26**
See also AAYA 12; CA 49-52; CANR 4, 26; CLR 23; DLB 161; JRDA; MAICYA; SAAS 7; SATA 9, 70

Jones, Edward P. 1950- . . . . **CLC 76**
See also BW 2; CA 142

Kristeva, Julia   1941- . . . . **CLC 77**

Kristofferson, Kris   1936- . . . . **CLC 26**
  See also CA 104

Krizanc, John   1956- . . . . **CLC 57**

Krleza, Miroslav   1893-1981. . . . . **CLC 8**
  See also CA 97-100; 105; CANR 50;
  DLB 147

Kroetsch, Robert
  1927- . . . . **CLC 5, 23, 57; DAC**
  See also CA 17-20R; CANR 8, 38;
  DAM POET; DLB 53; MTCW

Kroetz, Franz
  See Kroetz, Franz Xaver

Kroetz, Franz Xaver   1946- . . . . **CLC 41**
  See also CA 130

Kroker, Arthur   1945- . . . . **CLC 77**

Kropotkin, Peter (Aleksieevich)
  1842-1921 . . . . **TCLC 36**
  See also CA 119

Krotkov, Yuri   1917- . . . . **CLC 19**
  See also CA 102

Krumb
  See Crumb, R(obert)

Krumgold, Joseph (Quincy)
  1908-1980 . . . . **CLC 12**
  See also CA 9-12R; 101; CANR 7;
  MAICYA; SATA 1, 48; SATA-Obit 23

Krumwitz
  See Crumb, R(obert)

Krutch, Joseph Wood   1893-1970. . . . **CLC 24**
  See also CA 1-4R; 25-28R; CANR 4;
  DLB 63

Krutzch, Gus
  See Eliot, T(homas) S(tearns)

Krylov, Ivan Andreevich
  1768(?)-1844 . . . . **NCLC 1**
  See also DLB 150

Kubin, Alfred (Leopold Isidor)
  1877-1959 . . . . **TCLC 23**
  See also CA 112; 149; DLB 81

Kubrick, Stanley   1928- . . . . **CLC 16**
  See also CA 81-84; CANR 33; DLB 26

Kumin, Maxine (Winokur)
  1925- . . . . **CLC 5, 13, 28; PC 15**
  See also AITN 2; CA 1-4R; CAAS 8;
  CANR 1, 21; DAM POET; DLB 5;
  MTCW; SATA 12

Kundera, Milan
  1929- . . . . **CLC 4, 9, 19, 32, 68**
  See also AAYA 2; CA 85-88; CANR 19,
  52; DAM NOV; MTCW

Kunene, Mazisi (Raymond)   1930- . . . **CLC 85**
  See also BW 1; CA 125; DLB 117

Kunitz, Stanley (Jasspon)
  1905- . . . . **CLC 6, 11, 14**
  See also CA 41-44R; CANR 26; DLB 48;
  INT CANR-26; MTCW

Kunze, Reiner   1933- . . . . **CLC 10**
  See also CA 93-96; DLB 75

Kuprin, Aleksandr Ivanovich
  1870-1938 . . . . **TCLC 5**
  See also CA 104

Kureishi, Hanif   1954(?)- . . . . **CLC 64**
  See also CA 139

Kurosawa, Akira   1910- . . . . **CLC 16**
  See also AAYA 11; CA 101; CANR 46;
  DAM MULT

Kushner, Tony   1957(?)- . . . . **CLC 81**
  See also CA 144; DAM DRAM

Kuttner, Henry   1915-1958. . . . . . . **TCLC 10**
  See also CA 107; DLB 8

Kuzma, Greg   1944- . . . . **CLC 7**
  See also CA 33-36R

Kuzmin, Mikhail   1872(?)-1936 . . . . **TCLC 40**

Kyd, Thomas   1558-1594. . . . . . **LC 22; DC 3**
  See also DAM DRAM; DLB 62

Kyprianos, Iossif
  See Samarakis, Antonis

La Bruyere, Jean de   1645-1696. . . . . **LC 17**

Lacan, Jacques (Marie Emile)
  1901-1981 . . . . **CLC 75**
  See also CA 121; 104

Laclos, Pierre Ambroise Francois Choderlos
  de   1741-1803 . . . . **NCLC 4**

Lacolere, Francois
  See Aragon, Louis

La Colere, Francois
  See Aragon, Louis

La Deshabilleuse
  See Simenon, Georges (Jacques Christian)

Lady Gregory
  See Gregory, Isabella Augusta (Persse)

Lady of Quality, A
  See Bagnold, Enid

La Fayette, Marie (Madelaine Pioche de la
  Vergne Comtes   1634-1693. . . . . . . **LC 2**

Lafayette, Rene
  See Hubbard, L(afayette) Ron(ald)

Laforgue, Jules
  1860-1887 . . . . **NCLC 5, 53; PC 14;**
  SSC 20

Lagerkvist, Paer (Fabian)
  1891-1974 . . . . **CLC 7, 10, 13, 54**
  See also Lagerkvist, Par
  See also CA 85-88; 49-52; DAM DRAM,
  NOV; MTCW

Lagerkvist, Par . . . . **SSC 12**
  See also Lagerkvist, Paer (Fabian)

Lagerloef, Selma (Ottiliana Lovisa)
  1858-1940 . . . . **TCLC 4, 36**
  See also Lagerlof, Selma (Ottiliana Lovisa)
  See also CA 108; SATA 15

Lagerlof, Selma (Ottiliana Lovisa)
  See Lagerloef, Selma (Ottiliana Lovisa)
  See also CLR 7; SATA 15

La Guma, (Justin) Alex(ander)
  1925-1985 . . . . **CLC 19**
  See also BW 1; CA 49-52; 118; CANR 25;
  DAM NOV; DLB 117; MTCW

Laidlaw, A. K.
  See Grieve, C(hristopher) M(urray)

Lainez, Manuel Mujica
  See Mujica Lainez, Manuel
  See also HW

Laing, R(onald) D(avid)
  1927-1989 . . . . **CLC 95**
  See also CA 107; 129; CANR 34; MTCW

Lamartine, Alphonse (Marie Louis Prat) de
  1790-1869 . . . . **NCLC 11; PC 16**
  See also DAM POET

Lamb, Charles
  1775-1834 . . . . **NCLC 10; DA; DAB;**
  DAC; WLC
  See also CDBLB 1789-1832; DAM MST;
  DLB 93, 107, 163; SATA 17

Lamb, Lady Caroline   1785-1828. . **NCLC 38**
  See also DLB 116

Lamming, George (William)
  1927- . . . . **CLC 2, 4, 66; BLC**
  See also BW 2; CA 85-88; CANR 26;
  DAM MULT; DLB 125; MTCW

L'Amour, Louis (Dearborn)
  1908-1988 . . . . **CLC 25, 55**
  See also AAYA 16; AITN 2; BEST 89:2;
  CA 1-4R; 125; CANR 3, 25, 40;
  DAM NOV, POP; DLBY 80; MTCW

Lampedusa, Giuseppe (Tomasi) di . . . **TCLC 13**
  See also Tomasi di Lampedusa, Giuseppe

Lampman, Archibald   1861-1899 . . **NCLC 25**
  See also DLB 92

Lancaster, Bruce   1896-1963. . . . . . . **CLC 36**
  See also CA 9-10; CAP 1; SATA 9

Landau, Mark Alexandrovich
  See Aldanov, Mark (Alexandrovich)

Landau-Aldanov, Mark Alexandrovich
  See Aldanov, Mark (Alexandrovich)

Landis, John   1950- . . . . **CLC 26**
  See also CA 112; 122

Landolfi, Tommaso   1908-1979. . . **CLC 11, 49**
  See also CA 127; 117

Landon, Letitia Elizabeth
  1802-1838 . . . . **NCLC 15**
  See also DLB 96

Landor, Walter Savage
  1775-1864 . . . . **NCLC 14**
  See also DLB 93, 107

Landwirth, Heinz   1927-
  See Lind, Jakov
  See also CA 9-12R; CANR 7

Lane, Patrick   1939- . . . . **CLC 25**
  See also CA 97-100; DAM POET; DLB 53;
  INT 97-100

Lang, Andrew   1844-1912. . . . . **TCLC 16**
  See also CA 114; 137; DLB 98, 141;
  MAICYA; SATA 16

Lang, Fritz   1890-1976 . . . . **CLC 20**
  See also CA 77-80; 69-72; CANR 30

Lange, John
  See Crichton, (John) Michael

Langer, Elinor   1939- . . . . **CLC 34**
  See also CA 121

Langland, William
  1330(?)-1400(?) . . . . . . **LC 19; DA; DAB;**
  DAC
  See also DAM MST, POET; DLB 146

Langstaff, Launcelot
  See Irving, Washington

Lanier, Sidney   1842-1881 . . . . **NCLC 6**
  See also DAM POET; DLB 64; DLBD 13;
  MAICYA; SATA 18

Lanyer, Aemilia   1569-1645 . . . . . . **LC 10, 30**
  See also DLB 121

Lee, Willy
　　See Burroughs, William S(eward)

Lee-Hamilton, Eugene (Jacob)
　　1845-1907 .... **TCLC 22**
　　See also CA 117

Leet, Judith 1935- .... **CLC 11**

Le Fanu, Joseph Sheridan
　　1814-1873 .... **NCLC 9; SSC 14**
　　See also DAM POP; DLB 21, 70, 159

Leffland, Ella 1931- .... **CLC 19**
　　See also CA 29-32R; CANR 35; DLBY 84;
　　INT CANR-35; SATA 65

Leger, Alexis
　　See Leger, (Marie-Rene Auguste) Alexis
　　Saint-Leger

Leger, (Marie-Rene Auguste) Alexis
　　Saint-Leger 1887-1975....... **CLC 11**
　　See also Perse, St.-John
　　See also CA 13-16R; 61-64; CANR 43;
　　DAM POET; MTCW

Leger, Saintleger
　　See Leger, (Marie-Rene Auguste) Alexis
　　Saint-Leger

Le Guin, Ursula K(roeber)
　　1929- ...... **CLC 8, 13, 22, 45, 71; DAB;**
　　　　　　　　　　　　　　　DAC; SSC 12
　　See also AAYA 9; AITN 1; CA 21-24R;
　　CANR 9, 32, 52; CDALB 1968-1988;
　　CLR 3, 28; DAM MST, POP; DLB 8, 52;
　　INT CANR-32; JRDA; MAICYA;
　　MTCW; SATA 4, 52

Lehmann, Rosamond (Nina)
　　1901-1990 .... **CLC 5**
　　See also CA 77-80; 131; CANR 8; DLB 15

Leiber, Fritz (Reuter, Jr.)
　　1910-1992 .... **CLC 25**
　　See also CA 45-48; 139; CANR 2, 40;
　　DLB 8; MTCW; SATA 45;
　　SATA-Obit 73

Leimbach, Martha 1963-
　　See Leimbach, Marti
　　See also CA 130

Leimbach, Marti .... **CLC 65**
　　See also Leimbach, Martha

Leino, Eino .... **TCLC 24**
　　See also Loennbohm, Armas Eino Leopold

Leiris, Michel (Julien) 1901-1990... **CLC 61**
　　See also CA 119; 128; 132

Leithauser, Brad 1953-........... **CLC 27**
　　See also CA 107; CANR 27; DLB 120

Lelchuk, Alan 1938- .... **CLC 5**
　　See also CA 45-48; CAAS 20; CANR 1

Lem, Stanislaw 1921-........ **CLC 8, 15, 40**
　　See also CA 105; CAAS 1; CANR 32;
　　MTCW

Lemann, Nancy 1956-............ **CLC 39**
　　See also CA 118; 136

Lemonnier, (Antoine Louis) Camille
　　1844-1913 .... **TCLC 22**
　　See also CA 121

Lenau, Nikolaus 1802-1850 ...... **NCLC 16**

L'Engle, Madeleine (Camp Franklin)
　　1918- .... **CLC 12**
　　See also AAYA 1; AITN 2; CA 1-4R;
　　CANR 3, 21, 39; CLR 1, 14; DAM POP;
　　DLB 52; JRDA; MAICYA; MTCW;
　　SAAS 15; SATA 1, 27, 75

Lengyel, Jozsef 1896-1975......... **CLC 7**
　　See also CA 85-88; 57-60

Lennon, John (Ono)
　　1940-1980 .... **CLC 12, 35**
　　See also CA 102

Lennox, Charlotte Ramsay
　　1729(?)-1804 .... **NCLC 23**
　　See also DLB 39

Lentricchia, Frank (Jr.) 1940-...... **CLC 34**
　　See also CA 25-28R; CANR 19

Lenz, Siegfried 1926-............ **CLC 27**
　　See also CA 89-92; DLB 75

Leonard, Elmore (John, Jr.)
　　1925- .... **CLC 28, 34, 71**
　　See also AITN 1; BEST 89:1, 90:4;
　　CA 81-84; CANR 12, 28, 53; DAM POP;
　　INT CANR-28; MTCW

Leonard, Hugh................... **CLC 19**
　　See also Byrne, John Keyes
　　See also DLB 13

Leonov, Leonid (Maximovich)
　　1899-1994 .... **CLC 92**
　　See also CA 129; DAM NOV; MTCW

Leopardi, (Conte) Giacomo
　　1798-1837 .... **NCLC 22**

Le Reveler
　　See Artaud, Antonin (Marie Joseph)

Lerman, Eleanor 1952-............ **CLC 9**
　　See also CA 85-88

Lerman, Rhoda 1936-............ **CLC 56**
　　See also CA 49-52

Lermontov, Mikhail Yuryevich
　　1814-1841 .... **NCLC 47**

Leroux, Gaston 1868-1927........ **TCLC 25**
　　See also CA 108; 136; SATA 65

Lesage, Alain-Rene 1668-1747....... **LC 28**

Leskov, Nikolai (Semyonovich)
　　1831-1895 .... **NCLC 25**

Lessing, Doris (May)
　　1919- ..... **CLC 1, 2, 3, 6, 10, 15, 22, 40,**
　　　　　　　　　　94; DA; DAB; DAC; SSC 6
　　See also CA 9-12R; CAAS 14; CANR 33;
　　CDBLB 1960 to Present; DAM MST,
　　NOV; DLB 15, 139; DLBY 85; MTCW

Lessing, Gotthold Ephraim
　　1729-1781 .... **LC 8**
　　See also DLB 97

Lester, Richard 1932-............ **CLC 20**

Lever, Charles (James)
　　1806-1872 .... **NCLC 23**
　　See also DLB 21

Leverson, Ada 1865(?)-1936(?) .... **TCLC 18**
　　See also Elaine
　　See also CA 117; DLB 153

Levertov, Denise
　　1923- ...... **CLC 1, 2, 3, 5, 8, 15, 28, 66;**
　　　　　　　　　　　　　　　　　　PC 11
　　See also CA 1-4R; CAAS 19; CANR 3, 29,
　　50; DAM POET; DLB 5, 165;
　　INT CANR-29; MTCW

Levi, Jonathan.................... **CLC 76**

Levi, Peter (Chad Tigar) 1931-..... **CLC 41**
　　See also CA 5-8R; CANR 34; DLB 40

Levi, Primo
　　1919-1987 .... **CLC 37, 50; SSC 12**
　　See also CA 13-16R; 122; CANR 12, 33;
　　MTCW

Levin, Ira 1929- .... **CLC 3, 6**
　　See also CA 21-24R; CANR 17, 44;
　　DAM POP; MTCW; SATA 66

Levin, Meyer 1905-1981 .... **CLC 7**
　　See also AITN 1; CA 9-12R; 104;
　　CANR 15; DAM POP; DLB 9, 28;
　　DLBY 81; SATA 21; SATA-Obit 27

Levine, Norman 1924-............ **CLC 54**
　　See also CA 73-76; CAAS 23; CANR 14;
　　DLB 88

Levine, Philip 1928-.. **CLC 2, 4, 5, 9, 14, 33**
　　See also CA 9-12R; CANR 9, 37, 52;
　　DAM POET; DLB 5

Levinson, Deirdre 1931-.......... **CLC 49**
　　See also CA 73-76

Levi-Strauss, Claude 1908- .... **CLC 38**
　　See also CA 1-4R; CANR 6, 32; MTCW

Levitin, Sonia (Wolff) 1934- .... **CLC 17**
　　See also AAYA 13; CA 29-32R; CANR 14,
　　32; JRDA; MAICYA; SAAS 2; SATA 4,
　　68

Levon, O. U.
　　See Kesey, Ken (Elton)

Lewes, George Henry
　　1817-1878 .... **NCLC 25**
　　See also DLB 55, 144

Lewis, Alun 1915-1944............ **TCLC 3**
　　See also CA 104; DLB 20, 162

Lewis, C. Day
　　See Day Lewis, C(ecil)

Lewis, C(live) S(taples)
　　1898-1963 ..... **CLC 1, 3, 6, 14, 27; DA;**
　　　　　　　　　　　　　　DAB; DAC; WLC
　　See also AAYA 3; CA 81-84; CANR 33;
　　CDBLB 1945-1960; CLR 3, 27;
　　DAM MST, NOV, POP; DLB 15, 100,
　　160; JRDA; MAICYA; MTCW;
　　SATA 13

Lewis, Janet 1899-.............. **CLC 41**
　　See also Winters, Janet Lewis
　　See also CA 9-12R; CANR 29; CAP 1;
　　DLBY 87

Lewis, Matthew Gregory
　　1775-1818 .... **NCLC 11**
　　See also DLB 39, 158

Lewis, (Harry) Sinclair
　　1885-1951 ..... **TCLC 4, 13, 23, 39; DA;**
　　　　　　　　　　　　　　DAB; DAC; WLC
　　See also CA 104; 133; CDALB 1917-1929;
　　DAM MST, NOV; DLB 9, 102; DLBD 1;
　　MTCW

Author Index

Machiavelli, Niccolo
1469-1527 ...... **LC 8; DA; DAB; DAC**
See also DAM MST

MacInnes, Colin 1914-1976 ...... **CLC 4, 23**
See also CA 69-72; 65-68; CANR 21;
DLB 14; MTCW

MacInnes, Helen (Clark)
1907-1985 .... **CLC 27, 39**
See also CA 1-4R; 117; CANR 1, 28;
DAM POP; DLB 87; MTCW; SATA 22;
SATA-Obit 44

Mackay, Mary 1855-1924
See Corelli, Marie
See also CA 118

Mackenzie, Compton (Edward Montague)
1883-1972 .... **CLC 18**
See also CA 21-22; 37-40R; CAP 2;
DLB 34, 100

Mackenzie, Henry 1745-1831 .... **NCLC 41**
See also DLB 39

Mackintosh, Elizabeth 1896(?)-1952
See Tey, Josephine
See also CA 110

MacLaren, James
See Grieve, C(hristopher) M(urray)

Mac Laverty, Bernard 1942- ...... **CLC 31**
See also CA 116; 118; CANR 43; INT 118

MacLean, Alistair (Stuart)
1922-1987 .... **CLC 3, 13, 50, 63**
See also CA 57-60; 121; CANR 28;
DAM POP; MTCW; SATA 23;
SATA-Obit 50

Maclean, Norman (Fitzroy)
1902-1990 .... **CLC 78; SSC 13**
See also CA 102; 132; CANR 49;
DAM POP

MacLeish, Archibald
1892-1982 .... **CLC 3, 8, 14, 68**
See also CA 9-12R; 106; CANR 33;
DAM POET; DLB 4, 7, 45; DLBY 82;
MTCW

MacLennan, (John) Hugh
1907-1990 .... **CLC 2, 14, 92; DAC**
See also CA 5-8R; 142; CANR 33;
DAM MST; DLB 68; MTCW

MacLeod, Alistair 1936- ..... **CLC 56; DAC**
See also CA 123; DAM MST; DLB 60

MacNeice, (Frederick) Louis
1907-1963 ...... **CLC 1, 4, 10, 53; DAB**
See also CA 85-88; DAM POET; DLB 10,
20; MTCW

MacNeill, Dand
See Fraser, George MacDonald

Macpherson, James 1736-1796 ...... **LC 29**
See also DLB 109

Macpherson, (Jean) Jay 1931- ...... **CLC 14**
See also CA 5-8R; DLB 53

MacShane, Frank 1927- .... **CLC 39**
See also CA 9-12R; CANR 3, 33; DLB 111

Macumber, Mari
See Sandoz, Mari(e Susette)

Madach, Imre 1823-1864 .... **NCLC 19**

Madden, (Jerry) David 1933- .... **CLC 5, 15**
See also CA 1-4R; CAAS 3; CANR 4, 45;
DLB 6; MTCW

Maddern, Al(an)
See Ellison, Harlan (Jay)

Madhubuti, Haki R.
1942- .... **CLC 6, 73; BLC; PC 5**
See also Lee, Don L.
See also BW 2; CA 73-76; CANR 24, 51;
DAM MULT, POET; DLB 5, 41;
DLBD 8

Maepenn, Hugh
See Kuttner, Henry

Maepenn, K. H.
See Kuttner, Henry

Maeterlinck, Maurice 1862-1949 ... **TCLC 3**
See also CA 104; 136; DAM DRAM;
SATA 66

Maginn, William 1794-1842 ...... **NCLC 8**
See also DLB 110, 159

Mahapatra, Jayanta 1928- .... **CLC 33**
See also CA 73-76; CAAS 9; CANR 15, 33;
DAM MULT

Mahfouz, Naguib (Abdel Aziz Al-Sabilgi)
1911(?)-
See Mahfuz, Najib
See also BEST 89:2; CA 128; DAM NOV;
MTCW

Mahfuz, Najib .... **CLC 52, 55**
See also Mahfouz, Naguib (Abdel Aziz
Al-Sabilgi)
See also DLBY 88

Mahon, Derek 1941- .... **CLC 27**
See also CA 113; 128; DLB 40

Mailer, Norman
1923- ...... **CLC 1, 2, 3, 4, 5, 8, 11, 14,
28, 39, 74; DA; DAB; DAC**
See also AITN 2; CA 9-12R; CABS 1;
CANR 28; CDALB 1968-1988;
DAM MST, NOV, POP; DLB 2, 16, 28;
DLBD 3; DLBY 80, 83; MTCW

Maillet, Antonine 1929- ...... **CLC 54; DAC**
See also CA 115; 120; CANR 46; DLB 60;
INT 120

Mais, Roger 1905-1955 .... **TCLC 8**
See also BW 1; CA 105; 124; DLB 125;
MTCW

Maistre, Joseph de 1753-1821 .... **NCLC 37**

Maitland, Frederic 1850-1906 ..... **TCLC 65**

Maitland, Sara (Louise) 1950- ...... **CLC 49**
See also CA 69-72; CANR 13

Major, Clarence
1936- .... **CLC 3, 19, 48; BLC**
See also BW 2; CA 21-24R; CAAS 6;
CANR 13, 25, 53; DAM MULT; DLB 33

Major, Kevin (Gerald)
1949- .... **CLC 26; DAC**
See also AAYA 16; CA 97-100; CANR 21,
38; CLR 11; DLB 60; INT CANR-21;
JRDA; MAICYA; SATA 32, 82

Maki, James
See Ozu, Yasujiro

Malabaila, Damiano
See Levi, Primo

Malamud, Bernard
1914-1986 ..... **CLC 1, 2, 3, 5, 8, 9, 11,
18, 27, 44, 78, 85; DA; DAB; DAC;
SSC 15; WLC**
See also AAYA 16; CA 5-8R; 118; CABS 1;
CANR 28; CDALB 1941-1968;
DAM MST, NOV, POP; DLB 2, 28, 152;
DLBY 80, 86; MTCW

Malaparte, Curzio 1898-1957 ..... **TCLC 52**

Malcolm, Dan
See Silverberg, Robert

Malcolm X .... **CLC 82; BLC**
See also Little, Malcolm

Malherbe, Francois de 1555-1628 ..... **LC 5**

Mallarme, Stephane
1842-1898 .... **NCLC 4, 41; PC 4**
See also DAM POET

Mallet-Joris, Francoise 1930- ...... **CLC 11**
See also CA 65-68; CANR 17; DLB 83

Malley, Ern
See McAuley, James Phillip

Mallowan, Agatha Christie
See Christie, Agatha (Mary Clarissa)

Maloff, Saul 1922- .... **CLC 5**
See also CA 33-36R

Malone, Louis
See MacNeice, (Frederick) Louis

Malone, Michael (Christopher)
1942- .... **CLC 43**
See also CA 77-80; CANR 14, 32

Malory, (Sir) Thomas
1410(?)-1471(?) ...... **LC 11; DA; DAB;
DAC**
See also CDBLB Before 1660; DAM MST;
DLB 146; SATA 59; SATA-Brief 33

Malouf, (George Joseph) David
1934- .... **CLC 28, 86**
See also CA 124; CANR 50

Malraux, (Georges-)Andre
1901-1976 ...... **CLC 1, 4, 9, 13, 15, 57**
See also CA 21-22; 69-72; CANR 34;
CAP 2; DAM NOV; DLB 72; MTCW

Malzberg, Barry N(athaniel) 1939-... **CLC 7**
See also CA 61-64; CAAS 4; CANR 16;
DLB 8

Mamet, David (Alan)
1947- ...... **CLC 9, 15, 34, 46, 91; DC 4**
See also AAYA 3; CA 81-84; CABS 3;
CANR 15, 41; DAM DRAM; DLB 7;
MTCW

Mamoulian, Rouben (Zachary)
1897-1987 .... **CLC 16**
See also CA 25-28R; 124

Mandelstam, Osip (Emilievich)
1891(?)-1938(?) ...... **TCLC 2, 6; PC 14**
See also CA 104; 150

Mander, (Mary) Jane 1877-1949... **TCLC 31**

Mandiargues, Andre Pieyre de ...... **CLC 41**
See also Pieyre de Mandiargues, Andre
See also DLB 83

Mandrake, Ethel Belle
See Thurman, Wallace (Henry)

Mangan, James Clarence
1803-1849 .... **NCLC 27**

Maniere, J.-E.
　See Giraudoux, (Hippolyte) Jean

Manley, (Mary) Delariviere
　　1672(?)-1724 . . . . **LC 1**
　See also DLB 39, 80

Mann, Abel
　See Creasey, John

Mann, (Luiz) Heinrich　1871-1950. . . **TCLC 9**
　See also CA 106; DLB 66

Mann, (Paul) Thomas
　　1875-1955 . . . . **TCLC 2, 8, 14, 21, 35, 44,**
　　　　60; DA; DAB; DAC; SSC 5; WLC
　See also CA 104; 128; DAM MST, NOV;
　　DLB 66; MTCW

Mannheim, Karl　1893-1947 . . . . . . **TCLC 65**

Manning, David
　See Faust, Frederick (Schiller)

Manning, Frederic　1887(?)-1935 . . . **TCLC 25**
　See also CA 124

Manning, Olivia　1915-1980 . . . . . . **CLC 5, 19**
　See also CA 5-8R; 101; CANR 29; MTCW

Mano, D. Keith　1942- . . . . **CLC 2, 10**
　See also CA 25-28R; CAAS 6; CANR 26;
　　DLB 6

Mansfield, Katherine
　. . **TCLC 2, 8, 39; DAB; SSC 9, 23; WLC**
　See also Beauchamp, Kathleen Mansfield
　See also DLB 162

Manso, Peter　1940- . . . . **CLC 39**
　See also CA 29-32R; CANR 44

Mantecon, Juan Jimenez
　See Jimenez (Mantecon), Juan Ramon

Manton, Peter
　See Creasey, John

Man Without a Spleen, A
　See Chekhov, Anton (Pavlovich)

Manzoni, Alessandro　1785-1873 . . **NCLC 29**

Mapu, Abraham (ben Jekutiel)
　　1808-1867 . . . . **NCLC 18**

Mara, Sally
　See Queneau, Raymond

Marat, Jean Paul　1743-1793 . . . . **LC 10**

Marcel, Gabriel Honore
　　1889-1973 . . . . **CLC 15**
　See also CA 102; 45-48; MTCW

Marchbanks, Samuel
　See Davies, (William) Robertson

Marchi, Giacomo
　See Bassani, Giorgio

Margulies, Donald . . . . **CLC 76**

Marie de France　c. 12th cent. -. . . . **CMLC 8**

Marie de l'Incarnation　1599-1672. . . . **LC 10**

Mariner, Scott
　See Pohl, Frederik

Marinetti, Filippo Tommaso
　　1876-1944 . . . . **TCLC 10**
　See also CA 107; DLB 114

Marivaux, Pierre Carlet de Chamblain de
　　1688-1763 . . . . **LC 4**

Markandaya, Kamala . . . . **CLC 8, 38**
　See also Taylor, Kamala (Purnaiya)

Markfield, Wallace　1926- . . . . **CLC 8**
　See also CA 69-72; CAAS 3; DLB 2, 28

Markham, Edwin　1852-1940 . . . . . **TCLC 47**
　See also DLB 54

Markham, Robert
　See Amis, Kingsley (William)

Marks, J
　See Highwater, Jamake (Mamake)

Marks-Highwater, J
　See Highwater, Jamake (Mamake)

Markson, David M(errill)　1927- . . . . **CLC 67**
　See also CA 49-52; CANR 1

Marley, Bob . . . . **CLC 17**
　See also Marley, Robert Nesta

Marley, Robert Nesta　1945-1981
　See Marley, Bob
　See also CA 107; 103

Marlowe, Christopher
　　1564-1593 . . . . . **LC 22; DA; DAB; DAC;**
　　　　　　　　　　　　　　　DC 1; WLC
　See also CDBLB Before 1660;
　　DAM DRAM, MST; DLB 62

Marmontel, Jean-Francois
　　1723-1799 . . . . **LC 2**

Marquand, John P(hillips)
　　1893-1960 . . . . **CLC 2, 10**
　See also CA 85-88; DLB 9, 102

Marquez, Gabriel (Jose) Garcia
　See Garcia Marquez, Gabriel (Jose)

Marquis, Don(ald Robert Perry)
　　1878-1937 . . . . **TCLC 7**
　See also CA 104; DLB 11, 25

Marric, J. J.
　See Creasey, John

Marrow, Bernard
　See Moore, Brian

Marryat, Frederick　1792-1848 . . . . **NCLC 3**
　See also DLB 21, 163

Marsden, James
　See Creasey, John

Marsh, (Edith) Ngaio
　　1899-1982 . . . . **CLC 7, 53**
　See also CA 9-12R; CANR 6; DAM POP;
　　DLB 77; MTCW

Marshall, Garry　1934- . . . . **CLC 17**
　See also AAYA 3; CA 111; SATA 60

Marshall, Paule
　　1929- . . . . **CLC 27, 72; BLC; SSC 3**
　See also BW 2; CA 77-80; CANR 25;
　　DAM MULT; DLB 157; MTCW

Marsten, Richard
　See Hunter, Evan

Marston, John　1576-1634 . . . . **LC 33**
　See also DAM DRAM; DLB 58

Martha, Henry
　See Harris, Mark

Martial　c. 40-c. 104 . . . . **PC 10**

Martin, Ken
　See Hubbard, L(afayette) Ron(ald)

Martin, Richard
　See Creasey, John

Martin, Steve　1945- . . . . **CLC 30**
　See also CA 97-100; CANR 30; MTCW

Martin, Valerie　1948- . . . . **CLC 89**
　See also BEST 90:2; CA 85-88; CANR 49

Martin, Violet Florence
　　1862-1915 . . . . **TCLC 51**

Martin, Webber
　See Silverberg, Robert

Martindale, Patrick Victor
　See White, Patrick (Victor Martindale)

Martin du Gard, Roger
　　1881-1958 . . . . **TCLC 24**
　See also CA 118; DLB 65

Martineau, Harriet　1802-1876. . . . **NCLC 26**
　See also DLB 21, 55, 159, 163, 166;
　　YABC 2

Martines, Julia
　See O'Faolain, Julia

Martinez, Jacinto Benavente y
　See Benavente (y Martinez), Jacinto

Martinez Ruiz, Jose　1873-1967
　See Azorin; Ruiz, Jose Martinez
　See also CA 93-96; HW

Martinez Sierra, Gregorio
　　1881-1947 . . . . **TCLC 6**
　See also CA 115

Martinez Sierra, Maria (de la O'LeJarraga)
　　1874-1974 . . . . **TCLC 6**
　See also CA 115

Martinsen, Martin
　See Follett, Ken(neth Martin)

Martinson, Harry (Edmund)
　　1904-1978 . . . . **CLC 14**
　See also CA 77-80; CANR 34

Marut, Ret
　See Traven, B.

Marut, Robert
　See Traven, B.

Marvell, Andrew
　　1621-1678 . . . . . . **LC 4; DA; DAB; DAC;**
　　　　　　　　　　　　　　　PC 10; WLC
　See also CDBLB 1660-1789; DAM MST,
　　POET; DLB 131

Marx, Karl (Heinrich)
　　1818-1883 . . . . **NCLC 17**
　See also DLB 129

Masaoka Shiki . . . . **TCLC 18**
　See also Masaoka Tsunenori

Masaoka Tsunenori　1867-1902
　See Masaoka Shiki
　See also CA 117

Masefield, John (Edward)
　　1878-1967 . . . . **CLC 11, 47**
　See also CA 19-20; 25-28R; CANR 33;
　　CAP 2; CDBLB 1890-1914; DAM POET;
　　DLB 10, 19, 153, 160; MTCW; SATA 19

Maso, Carole　19(?)- . . . . **CLC 44**

Mason, Bobbie Ann
　　1940- . . . . **CLC 28, 43, 82; SSC 4**
　See also AAYA 5; CA 53-56; CANR 11,
　　31; DLBY 87; INT CANR-31; MTCW

Mason, Ernst
　See Pohl, Frederik

Mason, Lee W.
　See Malzberg, Barry N(athaniel)

Mason, Nick　1945- . . . . **CLC 35**

Mason, Tally
　See Derleth, August (William)

McGuane, Thomas (Francis III)
1939- . . . . **CLC 3, 7, 18, 45**
See also AITN 2; CA 49-52; CANR 5, 24,
49; DLB 2; DLBY 80; INT CANR-24;
MTCW

McGuckian, Medbh 1950- . . . . **CLC 48**
See also CA 143; DAM POET; DLB 40

McHale, Tom 1942(?)-1982 . . . . **CLC 3, 5**
See also AITN 1; CA 77-80; 106

McIlvanney, William 1936- . . . . **CLC 42**
See also CA 25-28R; DLB 14

McIlwraith, Maureen Mollie Hunter
See Hunter, Mollie
See also SATA 2

McInerney, Jay 1955- . . . . **CLC 34**
See also AAYA 18; CA 116; 123;
CANR 45; DAM POP; INT 123

McIntyre, Vonda N(eel) 1948- . . . . . **CLC 18**
See also CA 81-84; CANR 17, 34; MTCW

McKay, Claude
. . . . **TCLC 7, 41; BLC; DAB; PC 2**
See also McKay, Festus Claudius
See also DLB 4, 45, 51, 117

McKay, Festus Claudius 1889-1948
See McKay, Claude
See also BW 1; CA 104; 124; DA; DAC;
DAM MST, MULT, NOV, POET;
MTCW; WLC

McKuen, Rod 1933- . . . . **CLC 1, 3**
See also AITN 1; CA 41-44R; CANR 40

McLoughlin, R. B.
See Mencken, H(enry) L(ouis)

McLuhan, (Herbert) Marshall
1911-1980 . . . . **CLC 37, 83**
See also CA 9-12R; 102; CANR 12, 34;
DLB 88; INT CANR-12; MTCW

McMillan, Terry (L.) 1951- . . . . . **CLC 50, 61**
See also BW 2; CA 140; DAM MULT,
NOV, POP

McMurtry, Larry (Jeff)
1936- . . . . **CLC 2, 3, 7, 11, 27, 44**
See also AAYA 15; AITN 2; BEST 89:2;
CA 5-8R; CANR 19, 43;
CDALB 1968-1988; DAM NOV, POP;
DLB 2, 143; DLBY 80, 87; MTCW

McNally, T. M. 1961- . . . . **CLC 82**

McNally, Terrence 1939- . . . **CLC 4, 7, 41, 91**
See also CA 45-48; CANR 2;
DAM DRAM; DLB 7

McNamer, Deirdre 1950- . . . . **CLC 70**

McNeile, Herman Cyril 1888-1937
See Sapper
See also DLB 77

McNickle, (William) D'Arcy
1904-1977 . . . . **CLC 89**
See also CA 9-12R; 85-88; CANR 5, 45;
DAM MULT; NNAL; SATA-Obit 22

McPhee, John (Angus) 1931- . . . . . . **CLC 36**
See also BEST 90:1; CA 65-68; CANR 20,
46; MTCW

McPherson, James Alan
1943- . . . . **CLC 19, 77**
See also BW 1; CA 25-28R; CAAS 17;
CANR 24; DLB 38; MTCW

McPherson, William (Alexander)
1933- . . . . **CLC 34**
See also CA 69-72; CANR 28;
INT CANR-28

Mead, Margaret 1901-1978 . . . . **CLC 37**
See also AITN 1; CA 1-4R; 81-84;
CANR 4; MTCW; SATA-Obit 20

Meaker, Marijane (Agnes) 1927-
See Kerr, M. E.
See also CA 107; CANR 37; INT 107;
JRDA; MAICYA; MTCW; SATA 20, 61

Medoff, Mark (Howard) 1940- . . . **CLC 6, 23**
See also AITN 1; CA 53-56; CANR 5;
DAM DRAM; DLB 7; INT CANR-5

Medvedev, P. N.
See Bakhtin, Mikhail Mikhailovich

Meged, Aharon
See Megged, Aharon

Meged, Aron
See Megged, Aharon

Megged, Aharon 1920- . . . . **CLC 9**
See also CA 49-52; CAAS 13; CANR 1

Mehta, Ved (Parkash) 1934- . . . . **CLC 37**
See also CA 1-4R; CANR 2, 23; MTCW

Melanter
See Blackmore, R(ichard) D(oddridge)

Melikow, Loris
See Hofmannsthal, Hugo von

Melmoth, Sebastian
See Wilde, Oscar (Fingal O'Flahertie Wills)

Meltzer, Milton 1915- . . . . **CLC 26**
See also AAYA 8; CA 13-16R; CANR 38;
CLR 13; DLB 61; JRDA; MAICYA;
SAAS 1; SATA 1, 50, 80

Melville, Herman
1819-1891 . . . . . **NCLC 3, 12, 29, 45, 49;**
DA; DAB; DAC; SSC 1, 17; WLC
See also CDALB 1640-1865; DAM MST,
NOV; DLB 3, 74; SATA 59

Menander
c. 342B.C.-c. 292B.C. . . . . **CMLC 9; DC 3**
See also DAM DRAM

Mencken, H(enry) L(ouis)
1880-1956 . . . . **TCLC 13**
See also CA 105; 125; CDALB 1917-1929;
DLB 11, 29, 63, 137; MTCW

Mercer, David 1928-1980 . . . . **CLC 5**
See also CA 9-12R; 102; CANR 23;
DAM DRAM; DLB 13; MTCW

Merchant, Paul
See Ellison, Harlan (Jay)

Meredith, George 1828-1909 . . . **TCLC 17, 43**
See also CA 117; CDBLB 1832-1890;
DAM POET; DLB 18, 35, 57, 159

Meredith, William (Morris)
1919- . . . . **CLC 4, 13, 22, 55**
See also CA 9-12R; CAAS 14; CANR 6, 40;
DAM POET; DLB 5

Merezhkovsky, Dmitry Sergeyevich
1865-1941 . . . . **TCLC 29**

Merimee, Prosper
1803-1870 . . . . **NCLC 6; SSC 7**
See also DLB 119

Merkin, Daphne 1954- . . . . **CLC 44**
See also CA 123

Merlin, Arthur
See Blish, James (Benjamin)

Merrill, James (Ingram)
1926-1995 . . . . **CLC 2, 3, 6, 8, 13, 18, 34,**
91
See also CA 13-16R; 147; CANR 10, 49;
DAM POET; DLB 5, 165; DLBY 85;
INT CANR-10; MTCW

Merriman, Alex
See Silverberg, Robert

Merritt, E. B.
See Waddington, Miriam

Merton, Thomas
1915-1968 . . **CLC 1, 3, 11, 34, 83; PC 10**
See also CA 5-8R; 25-28R; CANR 22, 53;
DLB 48; DLBY 81; MTCW

Merwin, W(illiam) S(tanley)
1927- . . . **CLC 1, 2, 3, 5, 8, 13, 18, 45, 88**
See also CA 13-16R; CANR 15, 51;
DAM POET; DLB 5; INT CANR-15;
MTCW

Metcalf, John 1938- . . . . **CLC 37**
See also CA 113; DLB 60

Metcalf, Suzanne
See Baum, L(yman) Frank

Mew, Charlotte (Mary)
1870-1928 . . . . **TCLC 8**
See also CA 105; DLB 19, 135

Mewshaw, Michael 1943- . . . . **CLC 9**
See also CA 53-56; CANR 7, 47; DLBY 80

Meyer, June
See Jordan, June

Meyer, Lynn
See Slavitt, David R(ytman)

Meyer-Meyrink, Gustav 1868-1932
See Meyrink, Gustav
See also CA 117

Meyers, Jeffrey 1939- . . . . **CLC 39**
See also CA 73-76; DLB 111

Meynell, Alice (Christina Gertrude Thompson)
1847-1922 . . . . **TCLC 6**
See also CA 104; DLB 19, 98

Meyrink, Gustav . . . . **TCLC 21**
See also Meyer-Meyrink, Gustav
See also DLB 81

Michaels, Leonard
1933- . . . . **CLC 6, 25; SSC 16**
See also CA 61-64; CANR 21; DLB 130;
MTCW

Michaux, Henri 1899-1984 . . . . . . **CLC 8, 19**
See also CA 85-88; 114

Michelangelo 1475-1564 . . . . **LC 12**

Michelet, Jules 1798-1874 . . . . **NCLC 31**

Michener, James A(lbert)
1907(?)- . . . . **CLC 1, 5, 11, 29, 60**
See also AITN 1; BEST 90:1; CA 5-8R;
CANR 21, 45; DAM NOV, POP; DLB 6;
MTCW

Mickiewicz, Adam 1798-1855 . . . . . **NCLC 3**

Middleton, Christopher 1926- . . . . . . **CLC 13**
See also CA 13-16R; CANR 29; DLB 40

Middleton, Richard (Barham)
1882-1911 . . . . **TCLC 56**
See also DLB 156

Middleton, Stanley 1919-........ **CLC 7, 38**
See also CA 25-28R; CAAS 23; CANR 21,
46; DLB 14

Middleton, Thomas
1580-1627 .... **LC 33; DC 5**
See also DAM DRAM, MST; DLB 58

Migueis, Jose Rodrigues 1901-..... **CLC 10**

Mikszath, Kalman 1847-1910 ..... **TCLC 31**

Miles, Josephine
1911-1985 .... **CLC 1, 2, 14, 34, 39**
See also CA 1-4R; 116; CANR 2;
DAM POET; DLB 48

Militant
See Sandburg, Carl (August)

Mill, John Stuart 1806-1873 ..... **NCLC 11**
See also CDBLB 1832-1890; DLB 55

Millar, Kenneth 1915-1983 .... **CLC 14**
See also Macdonald, Ross
See also CA 9-12R; 110; CANR 16;
DAM POP; DLB 2; DLBD 6; DLBY 83;
MTCW

Millay, E. Vincent
See Millay, Edna St. Vincent

Millay, Edna St. Vincent
1892-1950 ...... **TCLC 4, 49; DA; DAB;
DAC; PC 6**
See also CA 104; 130; CDALB 1917-1929;
DAM MST, POET; DLB 45; MTCW

Miller, Arthur
1915- .... **CLC 1, 2, 6, 10, 15, 26, 47, 78;
DA; DAB; DAC; DC 1; WLC**
See also AAYA 15; AITN 1; CA 1-4R;
CABS 3; CANR 2, 30;
CDALB 1941-1968; DAM DRAM, MST;
DLB 7; MTCW

Miller, Henry (Valentine)
1891-1980 .... **CLC 1, 2, 4, 9, 14, 43, 84;
DA; DAB; DAC; WLC**
See also CA 9-12R; 97-100; CANR 33;
CDALB 1929-1941; DAM MST, NOV;
DLB 4, 9; DLBY 80; MTCW

Miller, Jason 1939(?)- .... **CLC 2**
See also AITN 1; CA 73-76; DLB 7

Miller, Sue 1943-.................. **CLC 44**
See also BEST 90:3; CA 139; DAM POP;
DLB 143

Miller, Walter M(ichael, Jr.)
1923-.................... **CLC 4, 30**
See also CA 85-88; DLB 8

Millett, Kate 1934-............... **CLC 67**
See also AITN 1; CA 73-76; CANR 32, 53;
MTCW

Millhauser, Steven 1943-...... **CLC 21, 54**
See also CA 110; 111; DLB 2; INT 111

Millin, Sarah Gertrude 1889-1968 .. **CLC 49**
See also CA 102; 93-96

Milne, A(lan) A(lexander)
1882-1956 .... **TCLC 6; DAB; DAC**
See also CA 104; 133; CLR 1, 26;
DAM MST; DLB 10, 77, 100, 160;
MAICYA; MTCW; YABC 1

Milner, Ron(ald) 1938-...... **CLC 56; BLC**
See also AITN 1; BW 1; CA 73-76;
CANR 24; DAM MULT; DLB 38;
MTCW

Milosz, Czeslaw
1911- ... **CLC 5, 11, 22, 31, 56, 82; PC 8**
See also CA 81-84; CANR 23, 51;
DAM MST, POET; MTCW

Milton, John
1608-1674 ..... **LC 9; DA; DAB; DAC;
WLC**
See also CDBLB 1660-1789; DAM MST,
POET; DLB 131, 151

Min, Anchee 1957-............... **CLC 86**
See also CA 146

Minehaha, Cornelius
See Wedekind, (Benjamin) Frank(lin)

Miner, Valerie 1947- .... **CLC 40**
See also CA 97-100

Minimo, Duca
See D'Annunzio, Gabriele

Minot, Susan 1956- .... **CLC 44**
See also CA 134

Minus, Ed 1938-................. **CLC 39**

Miranda, Javier
See Bioy Casares, Adolfo

Mirbeau, Octave 1848-1917...... **TCLC 55**
See also DLB 123

Miro (Ferrer), Gabriel (Francisco Victor)
1879-1930 .... **TCLC 5**
See also CA 104

Mishima, Yukio
.... **CLC 2, 4, 6, 9, 27; DC 1; SSC 4**
See also Hiraoka, Kimitake

Mistral, Frederic 1830-1914 ...... **TCLC 51**
See also CA 122

Mistral, Gabriela............ **TCLC 2; HLC**
See also Godoy Alcayaga, Lucila

Mistry, Rohinton 1952-...... **CLC 71; DAC**
See also CA 141

Mitchell, Clyde
See Ellison, Harlan (Jay); Silverberg, Robert

Mitchell, James Leslie 1901-1935
See Gibbon, Lewis Grassic
See also CA 104; DLB 15

Mitchell, Joni 1943-............. **CLC 12**
See also CA 112

Mitchell, Margaret (Munnerlyn)
1900-1949 .... **TCLC 11**
See also CA 109; 125; DAM NOV, POP;
DLB 9; MTCW

Mitchell, Peggy
See Mitchell, Margaret (Munnerlyn)

Mitchell, S(ilas) Weir 1829-1914 .. **TCLC 36**

Mitchell, W(illiam) O(rmond)
1914- .... **CLC 25; DAC**
See also CA 77-80; CANR 15, 43;
DAM MST; DLB 88

Mitford, Mary Russell 1787-1855.. **NCLC 4**
See also DLB 110, 116

Mitford, Nancy 1904-1973......... **CLC 44**
See also CA 9-12R

Miyamoto, Yuriko 1899-1951 ..... **TCLC 37**

Mo, Timothy (Peter) 1950(?)-...... **CLC 46**
See also CA 117; MTCW

Modarressi, Taghi (M.) 1931-...... **CLC 44**
See also CA 121; 134; INT 134

Modiano, Patrick (Jean) 1945-..... **CLC 18**
See also CA 85-88; CANR 17, 40; DLB 83

Moerck, Paal
See Roelvaag, O(le) E(dvart)

Mofolo, Thomas (Mokopu)
1875(?)-1948............**TCLC 22; BLC**
See also CA 121; DAM MULT

Mohr, Nicholasa 1935-............ **CLC 12; HLC**
See also AAYA 8; CA 49-52; CANR 1, 32;
CLR 22; DAM MULT; DLB 145; HW;
JRDA; SAAS 8; SATA 8

Mojtabai, A(nn) G(race)
1938-...................**CLC 5, 9, 15, 29**
See also CA 85-88

Moliere
1622-1673 ..... **LC 28; DA; DAB; DAC;
WLC**
See also DAM DRAM, MST

Molin, Charles
See Mayne, William (James Carter)

Molnar, Ferenc 1878-1952........ **TCLC 20**
See also CA 109; DAM DRAM

Momaday, N(avarre) Scott
1934- ..... **CLC 2, 19, 85, 95; DA; DAB;
DAC**
See also AAYA 11; CA 25-28R; CANR 14,
34; DAM MST, MULT, NOV, POP;
DLB 143; INT CANR-14; MTCW;
NNAL; SATA 48; SATA-Brief 30

Monette, Paul 1945-1995.......... **CLC 82**
See also CA 139; 147

Monroe, Harriet 1860-1936....... **TCLC 12**
See also CA 109; DLB 54, 91

Monroe, Lyle
See Heinlein, Robert A(nson)

Montagu, Elizabeth 1917-........ **NCLC 7**
See also CA 9-12R

Montagu, Mary (Pierrepont) Wortley
1689-1762 .... **LC 9; PC 16**
See also DLB 95, 101

Montagu, W. H.
See Coleridge, Samuel Taylor

Montague, John (Patrick)
1929-................... **CLC 13, 46**
See also CA 9-12R; CANR 9; DLB 40;
MTCW

Montaigne, Michel (Eyquem) de
1533-1592 ...... **LC 8; DA; DAB; DAC;
WLC**
See also DAM MST

Montale, Eugenio
1896-1981 .... **CLC 7, 9, 18; PC 13**
See also CA 17-20R; 104; CANR 30;
DLB 114; MTCW

Montesquieu, Charles-Louis de Secondat
1689-1755 .... **LC 7**

Montgomery, (Robert) Bruce 1921-1978
See Crispin, Edmund
See also CA 104

Montgomery, L(ucy) M(aud)
1874-1942 .... **TCLC 51; DAC**
See also AAYA 12; CA 108; 137; CLR 8;
DAM MST; DLB 92; JRDA; MAICYA;
YABC 1

Montgomery, Marion H., Jr. 1925- .. **CLC 7**
See also AITN 1; CA 1-4R; CANR 3, 48;
DLB 6

Montgomery, Max
See Davenport, Guy (Mattison, Jr.)

Montherlant, Henry (Milon) de
1896-1972 .... **CLC 8, 19**
See also CA 85-88; 37-40R; DAM DRAM;
DLB 72; MTCW

Monty Python
See Chapman, Graham; Cleese, John
(Marwood); Gilliam, Terry (Vance); Idle,
Eric; Jones, Terence Graham Parry; Palin,
Michael (Edward)
See also AAYA 7

Moodie, Susanna (Strickland)
1803-1885 .... **NCLC 14**
See also DLB 99

Mooney, Edward 1951-
See Mooney, Ted
See also CA 130

Mooney, Ted .... **CLC 25**
See also Mooney, Edward

Moorcock, Michael (John)
1939- .... **CLC 5, 27, 58**
See also CA 45-48; CAAS 5; CANR 2, 17,
38; DLB 14; MTCW

Moore, Brian
1921- ...... **CLC 1, 3, 5, 7, 8, 19, 32, 90;**
DAB; DAC
See also CA 1-4R; CANR 1, 25, 42;
DAM MST; MTCW

Moore, Edward
See Muir, Edwin

Moore, George Augustus
1852-1933 .... **TCLC 7; SSC 19**
See also CA 104; DLB 10, 18, 57, 135

Moore, Lorrie .... **CLC 39, 45, 68**
See also Moore, Marie Lorena

Moore, Marianne (Craig)
1887-1972 .... **CLC 1, 2, 4, 8, 10, 13, 19,**
47; DA; DAB; DAC; PC 4
See also CA 1-4R; 33-36R; CANR 3;
CDALB 1929-1941; DAM MST, POET;
DLB 45; DLBD 7; MTCW; SATA 20

Moore, Marie Lorena 1957-
See Moore, Lorrie
See also CA 116; CANR 39

Moore, Thomas 1779-1852........ **NCLC 6**
See also DLB 96, 144

Morand, Paul 1888-1976 .. **CLC 41; SSC 22**
See also CA 69-72; DLB 65

Morante, Elsa 1918-1985........ **CLC 8, 47**
See also CA 85-88; 117; CANR 35; MTCW

Moravia, Alberto....... **CLC 2, 7, 11, 27, 46**
See also Pincherle, Alberto

More, Hannah 1745-1833 .... **NCLC 27**
See also DLB 107, 109, 116, 158

More, Henry 1614-1687............. **LC 9**
See also DLB 126

More, Sir Thomas 1478-1535 .... **LC 10, 32**

Moreas, Jean.................... **TCLC 18**
See also Papadiamantopoulos, Johannes

Morgan, Berry 1919- .... **CLC 6**
See also CA 49-52; DLB 6

Morgan, Claire
See Highsmith, (Mary) Patricia

Morgan, Edwin (George) 1920- ..... **CLC 31**
See also CA 5-8R; CANR 3, 43; DLB 27

Morgan, (George) Frederick
1922- .... **CLC 23**
See also CA 17-20R; CANR 21

Morgan, Harriet
See Mencken, H(enry) L(ouis)

Morgan, Jane
See Cooper, James Fenimore

Morgan, Janet 1945- .... **CLC 39**
See also CA 65-68

Morgan, Lady 1776(?)-1859...... **NCLC 29**
See also DLB 116, 158

Morgan, Robin 1941- .... **CLC 2**
See also CA 69-72; CANR 29; MTCW;
SATA 80

Morgan, Scott
See Kuttner, Henry

Morgan, Seth 1949(?)-1990 .... **CLC 65**
See also CA 132

Morgenstern, Christian
1871-1914 .... **TCLC 8**
See also CA 105

Morgenstern, S.
See Goldman, William (W.)

Moricz, Zsigmond 1879-1942 ..... **TCLC 33**

Morike, Eduard (Friedrich)
1804-1875 .... **NCLC 10**
See also DLB 133

Mori Ogai .... **TCLC 14**
See also Mori Rintaro

Mori Rintaro 1862-1922
See Mori Ogai
See also CA 110

Moritz, Karl Philipp 1756-1793 ...... **LC 2**
See also DLB 94

Morland, Peter Henry
See Faust, Frederick (Schiller)

Morren, Theophil
See Hofmannsthal, Hugo von

Morris, Bill 1952- .... **CLC 76**

Morris, Julian
See West, Morris L(anglo)

Morris, Steveland Judkins 1950(?)-
See Wonder, Stevie
See also CA 111

Morris, William 1834-1896 .... **NCLC 4**
See also CDBLB 1832-1890; DLB 18, 35,
57, 156

Morris, Wright 1910- ... **CLC 1, 3, 7, 18, 37**
See also CA 9-12R; CANR 21; DLB 2;
DLBY 81; MTCW

Morrison, Chloe Anthony Wofford
See Morrison, Toni

Morrison, James Douglas 1943-1971
See Morrison, Jim
See also CA 73-76; CANR 40

Morrison, Jim .... **CLC 17**
See also Morrison, James Douglas

Morrison, Toni
1931- .... **CLC 4, 10, 22, 55, 81, 87;**
BLC; DA; DAB; DAC
See also AAYA 1; BW 2; CA 29-32R;
CANR 27, 42; CDALB 1968-1988;
DAM MST, MULT, NOV, POP; DLB 6,
33, 143; DLBY 81; MTCW; SATA 57

Morrison, Van 1945- .... **CLC 21**
See also CA 116

Mortimer, John (Clifford)
1923- .... **CLC 28, 43**
See also CA 13-16R; CANR 21;
CDBLB 1960 to Present; DAM DRAM,
POP; DLB 13; INT CANR-21; MTCW

Mortimer, Penelope (Ruth) 1918- .... **CLC 5**
See also CA 57-60; CANR 45

Morton, Anthony
See Creasey, John

Mosher, Howard Frank 1943- ...... **CLC 62**
See also CA 139

Mosley, Nicholas 1923- .... **CLC 43, 70**
See also CA 69-72; CANR 41; DLB 14

Moss, Howard
1922-1987 .... **CLC 7, 14, 45, 50**
See also CA 1-4R; 123; CANR 1, 44;
DAM POET; DLB 5

Mossgiel, Rab
See Burns, Robert

Motion, Andrew (Peter) 1952- ..... **CLC 47**
See also CA 146; DLB 40

Motley, Willard (Francis)
1909-1965 .... **CLC 18**
See also BW 1; CA 117; 106; DLB 76, 143

Motoori, Norinaga 1730-1801 .... **NCLC 45**

Mott, Michael (Charles Alston)
1930- .... **CLC 15, 34**
See also CA 5-8R; CAAS 7; CANR 7, 29

Mountain Wolf Woman
1884-1960 .... **CLC 92**
See also CA 144; NNAL

Moure, Erin 1955- .... **CLC 88**
See also CA 113; DLB 60

Mowat, Farley (McGill)
1921- .... **CLC 26; DAC**
See also AAYA 1; CA 1-4R; CANR 4, 24,
42; CLR 20; DAM MST; DLB 68;
INT CANAR-24; JRDA; MAICYA;
MTCW; SATA 3, 55

Moyers, Bill 1934- .... **CLC 74**
See also AITN 2; CA 61-64; CANR 31, 52

Mphahlele, Es'kia
See Mphahlele, Ezekiel
See also DLB 125

Mphahlele, Ezekiel 1919- ..... **CLC 25; BLC**
See also Mphahlele, Es'kia
See also BW 2; CA 81-84; CANR 26;
DAM MULT

Mqhayi, S(amuel) E(dward) K(rune Loliwe)
1875-1945 .... **TCLC 25; BLC**
See also DAM MULT

Mrozek, Slawomir 1930- .... **CLC 3, 13**
See also CA 13-16R; CAAS 10; CANR 29;
MTCW

Mrs. Belloc-Lowndes
See Lowndes, Marie Adelaide (Belloc)

Newman, Edwin (Harold) 1919- . . . . **CLC 14**
See also AITN 1; CA 69-72; CANR 5

Newman, John Henry
1801-1890 . . . . **NCLC 38**
See also DLB 18, 32, 55

Newton, Suzanne 1936- . . . . **CLC 35**
See also CA 41-44R; CANR 14; JRDA;
SATA 5, 77

Nexo, Martin Andersen
1869-1954 . . . . **TCLC 43**

Nezval, Vitezslav 1900-1958 . . . . . . **TCLC 44**
See also CA 123

Ng, Fae Myenne 1957(?)- . . . . **CLC 81**
See also CA 146

Ngema, Mbongeni 1955- . . . . **CLC 57**
See also BW 2; CA 143

Ngugi, James T(hiong'o) . . . . **CLC 3, 7, 13**
See also Ngugi wa Thiong'o

Ngugi wa Thiong'o 1938- . . . . . **CLC 36; BLC**
See also Ngugi, James T(hiong'o)
See also BW 2; CA 81-84; CANR 27;
DAM MULT, NOV; DLB 125; MTCW

Nichol, B(arrie) P(hillip)
1944-1988 . . . . **CLC 18**
See also CA 53-56; DLB 53; SATA 66

Nichols, John (Treadwell) 1940- . . . . **CLC 38**
See also CA 9-12R; CAAS 2; CANR 6;
DLBY 82

Nichols, Leigh
See Koontz, Dean R(ay)

Nichols, Peter (Richard)
1927- . . . . **CLC 5, 36, 65**
See also CA 104; CANR 33; DLB 13;
MTCW

Nicolas, F. R. E.
See Freeling, Nicolas

Niedecker, Lorine 1903-1970. . . . **CLC 10, 42**
See also CA 25-28; CAP 2; DAM POET;
DLB 48

Nietzsche, Friedrich (Wilhelm)
1844-1900 . . . . **TCLC 10, 18, 55**
See also CA 107; 121; DLB 129

Nievo, Ippolito 1831-1861 . . . . **NCLC 22**

Nightingale, Anne Redmon 1943-
See Redmon, Anne
See also CA 103

Nik. T. O.
See Annensky, Innokenty Fyodorovich

Nin, Anais
1903-1977 . . . . . . **CLC 1, 4, 8, 11, 14, 60;
SSC 10**
See also AITN 2; CA 13-16R; 69-72;
CANR 22, 53; DAM NOV, POP; DLB 2,
4, 152; MTCW

Nishiwaki, Junzaburo 1894-1982 . . . . **PC 15**
See also CA 107

Nissenson, Hugh 1933- . . . . **CLC 4, 9**
See also CA 17-20R; CANR 27; DLB 28

Niven, Larry . . . . **CLC 8**
See also Niven, Laurence Van Cott
See also DLB 8

Niven, Laurence Van Cott 1938-
See Niven, Larry
See also CA 21-24R; CAAS 12; CANR 14,
44; DAM POP; MTCW

Nixon, Agnes Eckhardt 1927- . . . . . . **CLC 21**
See also CA 110

Nizan, Paul 1905-1940 . . . . **TCLC 40**
See also DLB 72

Nkosi, Lewis 1936- . . . . **CLC 45; BLC**
See also BW 1; CA 65-68; CANR 27;
DAM MULT; DLB 157

Nodier, (Jean) Charles (Emmanuel)
1780-1844 . . . . **NCLC 19**
See also DLB 119

Nolan, Christopher 1965- . . . . **CLC 58**
See also CA 111

Noon, Jeff 1957- . . . . **CLC 91**
See also CA 148

Norden, Charles
See Durrell, Lawrence (George)

Nordhoff, Charles (Bernard)
1887-1947 . . . . **TCLC 23**
See also CA 108; DLB 9; SATA 23

Norfolk, Lawrence 1963- . . . . **CLC 76**
See also CA 144

Norman, Marsha 1947- . . . . **CLC 28**
See also CA 105; CABS 3; CANR 41;
DAM DRAM; DLBY 84

Norris, Benjamin Franklin, Jr.
1870-1902 . . . . **TCLC 24**
See also Norris, Frank
See also CA 110

Norris, Frank
See Norris, Benjamin Franklin, Jr.
See also CDALB 1865-1917; DLB 12, 71

Norris, Leslie 1921- . . . . **CLC 14**
See also CA 11-12; CANR 14; CAP 1;
DLB 27

North, Andrew
See Norton, Andre

North, Anthony
See Koontz, Dean R(ay)

North, Captain George
See Stevenson, Robert Louis (Balfour)

North, Milou
See Erdrich, Louise

Northrup, B. A.
See Hubbard, L(afayette) Ron(ald)

North Staffs
See Hulme, T(homas) E(rnest)

Norton, Alice Mary
See Norton, Andre
See also MAICYA; SATA 1, 43

Norton, Andre 1912- . . . . **CLC 12**
See also Norton, Alice Mary
See also AAYA 14; CA 1-4R; CANR 2, 31;
DLB 8, 52; JRDA; MTCW

Norton, Caroline 1808-1877 . . . . . . **NCLC 47**
See also DLB 21, 159

Norway, Nevil Shute 1899-1960
See Shute, Nevil
See also CA 102; 93-96

Norwid, Cyprian Kamil
1821-1883 . . . . **NCLC 17**

Nosille, Nabrah
See Ellison, Harlan (Jay)

Nossack, Hans Erich 1901-1978 . . . . . **CLC 6**
See also CA 93-96; 85-88; DLB 69

Nostradamus 1503-1566 . . . . **LC 27**

Nosu, Chuji
See Ozu, Yasujiro

Notenburg, Eleanora (Genrikhovna) von
See Guro, Elena

Nova, Craig 1945- . . . . **CLC 7, 31**
See also CA 45-48; CANR 2, 53

Novak, Joseph
See Kosinski, Jerzy (Nikodem)

Novalis 1772-1801 . . . . **NCLC 13**
See also DLB 90

Nowlan, Alden (Albert)
1933-1983 . . . . **CLC 15; DAC**
See also CA 9-12R; CANR 5; DAM MST;
DLB 53

Noyes, Alfred 1880-1958 . . . . **TCLC 7**
See also CA 104; DLB 20

Nunn, Kem 19(?)- . . . . **CLC 34**

Nye, Robert 1939- . . . . **CLC 13, 42**
See also CA 33-36R; CANR 29;
DAM NOV; DLB 14; MTCW; SATA 6

Nyro, Laura 1947- . . . . **CLC 17**

Oates, Joyce Carol
1938- . . . . . . **CLC 1, 2, 3, 6, 9, 11, 15, 19,
33, 52; DA; DAB; DAC; SSC 6; WLC**
See also AAYA 15; AITN 1; BEST 89:2;
CA 5-8R; CANR 25, 45;
CDALB 1968-1988; DAM MST, NOV,
POP; DLB 2, 5, 130; DLBY 81;
INT CANR-25; MTCW

O'Brien, Darcy 1939- . . . . **CLC 11**
See also CA 21-24R; CANR 8

O'Brien, E. G.
See Clarke, Arthur C(harles)

O'Brien, Edna
1936- . . . **CLC 3, 5, 8, 13, 36, 65; SSC 10**
See also CA 1-4R; CANR 6, 41;
CDBLB 1960 to Present; DAM NOV;
DLB 14; MTCW

O'Brien, Fitz-James 1828-1862. . . **NCLC 21**
See also DLB 74

O'Brien, Flann. . . . . . . **CLC 1, 4, 5, 7, 10, 47**
See also O Nuallain, Brian

O'Brien, Richard 1942- . . . . **CLC 17**
See also CA 124

O'Brien, Tim 1946- . . . . **CLC 7, 19, 40**
See also AAYA 16; CA 85-88; CANR 40;
DAM POP; DLB 152; DLBD 9;
DLBY 80

Obstfelder, Sigbjoern 1866-1900 . . . **TCLC 23**
See also CA 123

O'Casey, Sean
1880-1964 . . . . . . **CLC 1, 5, 9, 11, 15, 88;
DAB; DAC**
See also CA 89-92; CDBLB 1914-1945;
DAM DRAM, MST; DLB 10; MTCW

O'Cathasaigh, Sean
See O'Casey, Sean

Ochs, Phil 1940-1976 . . . . **CLC 17**
See also CA 65-68

O'Connor, Edwin (Greene)
1918-1968 . . . . **CLC 14**
See also CA 93-96; 25-28R

O'Connor, (Mary) Flannery
1925-1964 .... **CLC 1, 2, 3, 6, 10, 13, 15, 21, 66; DA; DAB; DAC; SSC 1, 23; WLC**
See also AAYA 7; CA 1-4R; CANR 3, 41; CDALB 1941-1968; DAM MST, NOV; DLB 2, 152; DLBD 12; DLBY 80; MTCW

O'Connor, Frank .... **CLC 23; SSC 5**
See also O'Donovan, Michael John
See also DLB 162

O'Dell, Scott 1898-1989 .... **CLC 30**
See also AAYA 3; CA 61-64; 129; CANR 12, 30; CLR 1, 16; DLB 52; JRDA; MAICYA; SATA 12, 60

Odets, Clifford
1906-1963 .... **CLC 2, 28; DC 6**
See also CA 85-88; DAM DRAM; DLB 7, 26; MTCW

O'Doherty, Brian 1934- .... **CLC 76**
See also CA 105

O'Donnell, K. M.
See Malzberg, Barry N(athaniel)

O'Donnell, Lawrence
See Kuttner, Henry

O'Donovan, Michael John
1903-1966 .... **CLC 14**
See also O'Connor, Frank
See also CA 93-96

Oe, Kenzaburo
1935- .... **CLC 10, 36, 86; SSC 20**
See also CA 97-100; CANR 36, 50; DAM NOV; DLBY 94; MTCW

O'Faolain, Julia 1932- .... **CLC 6, 19, 47**
See also CA 81-84; CAAS 2; CANR 12; DLB 14; MTCW

O'Faolain, Sean
1900-1991 .... **CLC 1, 7, 14, 32, 70; SSC 13**
See also CA 61-64; 134; CANR 12; DLB 15, 162; MTCW

O'Flaherty, Liam
1896-1984 .... **CLC 5, 34; SSC 6**
See also CA 101; 113; CANR 35; DLB 36, 162; DLBY 84; MTCW

Ogilvy, Gavin
See Barrie, J(ames) M(atthew)

O'Grady, Standish James
1846-1928 .... **TCLC 5**
See also CA 104

O'Grady, Timothy 1951- .... **CLC 59**
See also CA 138

O'Hara, Frank
1926-1966 .... **CLC 2, 5, 13, 78**
See also CA 9-12R; 25-28R; CANR 33; DAM POET; DLB 5, 16; MTCW

O'Hara, John (Henry)
1905-1970 .... **CLC 1, 2, 3, 6, 11, 42; SSC 15**
See also CA 5-8R; 25-28R; CANR 31; CDALB 1929-1941; DAM NOV; DLB 9, 86; DLBD 2; MTCW

O Hehir, Diana 1922- .... **CLC 41**
See also CA 93-96

Okigbo, Christopher (Ifenayichukwu)
1932-1967 ..... **CLC 25, 84; BLC; PC 7**
See also BW 1; CA 77-80; DAM MULT, POET; DLB 125; MTCW

Okri, Ben 1959- .... **CLC 87**
See also BW 2; CA 130; 138; DLB 157; INT 138

Olds, Sharon 1942- .... **CLC 32, 39, 85**
See also CA 101; CANR 18, 41; DAM POET; DLB 120

Oldstyle, Jonathan
See Irving, Washington

Olesha, Yuri (Karlovich)
1899-1960 .... **CLC 8**
See also CA 85-88

Oliphant, Laurence
1829(?)-1888 .... **NCLC 47**
See also DLB 18, 166

Oliphant, Margaret (Oliphant Wilson)
1828-1897 .... **NCLC 11**
See also DLB 18, 159

Oliver, Mary 1935- .... **CLC 19, 34**
See also CA 21-24R; CANR 9, 43; DLB 5

Olivier, Laurence (Kerr)
1907-1989 .... **CLC 20**
See also CA 111; 150; 129

Olsen, Tillie
1913- ..... **CLC 4, 13; DA; DAB; DAC; SSC 11**
See also CA 1-4R; CANR 1, 43; DAM MST; DLB 28; DLBY 80; MTCW

Olson, Charles (John)
1910-1970 ..... **CLC 1, 2, 5, 6, 9, 11, 29**
See also CA 13-16; 25-28R; CABS 2; CANR 35; CAP 1; DAM POET; DLB 5, 16; MTCW

Olson, Toby 1937- .... **CLC 28**
See also CA 65-68; CANR 9, 31

Olyesha, Yuri
See Olesha, Yuri (Karlovich)

Ondaatje, (Philip) Michael
1943- ... **CLC 14, 29, 51, 76; DAB; DAC**
See also CA 77-80; CANR 42; DAM MST; DLB 60

Oneal, Elizabeth 1934-
See Oneal, Zibby
See also CA 106; CANR 28; MAICYA; SATA 30, 82

Oneal, Zibby .... **CLC 30**
See also Oneal, Elizabeth
See also AAYA 5; CLR 13; JRDA

O'Neill, Eugene (Gladstone)
1888-1953 ...... **TCLC 1, 6, 27, 49; DA; DAB; DAC; WLC**
See also AITN 1; CA 110; 132; CDALB 1929-1941; DAM DRAM, MST; DLB 7; MTCW

Onetti, Juan Carlos
1909-1994 .... **CLC 7, 10; SSC 23**
See also CA 85-88; 145; CANR 32; DAM MULT, NOV; DLB 113; HW; MTCW

O Nuallain, Brian 1911-1966
See O'Brien, Flann
See also CA 21-22; 25-28R; CAP 2

Oppen, George 1908-1984 .... **CLC 7, 13, 34**
See also CA 13-16R; 113; CANR 8; DLB 5, 165

Oppenheim, E(dward) Phillips
1866-1946 .... **TCLC 45**
See also CA 111; DLB 70

Orlovitz, Gil 1918-1973 .... **CLC 22**
See also CA 77-80; 45-48; DLB 2, 5

Orris
See Ingelow, Jean

Ortega y Gasset, Jose
1883-1955 .... **TCLC 9; HLC**
See also CA 106; 130; DAM MULT; HW; MTCW

Ortese, Anna Maria 1914- .... **CLC 89**

Ortiz, Simon J(oseph) 1941- .... **CLC 45**
See also CA 134; DAM MULT, POET; DLB 120; NNAL

Orton, Joe .... **CLC 4, 13, 43; DC 3**
See also Orton, John Kingsley
See also CDBLB 1960 to Present; DLB 13

Orton, John Kingsley 1933-1967
See Orton, Joe
See also CA 85-88; CANR 35; DAM DRAM; MTCW

Orwell, George
..... **TCLC 2, 6, 15, 31, 51; DAB; WLC**
See also Blair, Eric (Arthur)
See also CDBLB 1945-1960; DLB 15, 98

Osborne, David
See Silverberg, Robert

Osborne, George
See Silverberg, Robert

Osborne, John (James)
1929-1994 ..... **CLC 1, 2, 5, 11, 45; DA; DAB; DAC; WLC**
See also CA 13-16R; 147; CANR 21; CDBLB 1945-1960; DAM DRAM, MST; DLB 13; MTCW

Osborne, Lawrence 1958- .... **CLC 50**

Oshima, Nagisa 1932- .... **CLC 20**
See also CA 116; 121

Oskison, John Milton
1874-1947 .... **TCLC 35**
See also CA 144; DAM MULT; NNAL

Ossoli, Sarah Margaret (Fuller marchesa d')
1810-1850
See Fuller, Margaret
See also SATA 25

Ostrovsky, Alexander
1823-1886 .... **NCLC 30, 57**

Otero, Blas de 1916-1979 .... **CLC 11**
See also CA 89-92; DLB 134

Otto, Whitney 1955- .... **CLC 70**
See also CA 140

Ouida .... **TCLC 43**
See also De La Ramee, (Marie) Louise
See also DLB 18, 156

Ousmane, Sembene 1923- .... **CLC 66; BLC**
See also BW 1; CA 117; 125; MTCW

Ovid 43B.C.-18(?) .... **CMLC 7; PC 7**
See also DAM POET

Owen, Hugh
See Faust, Frederick (Schiller)

Owen, Wilfred (Edward Salter)
1893-1918 . . . . . TCLC **5, 27; DA; DAB;**
DAC; WLC
See also CA 104; 141; CDBLB 1914-1945;
DAM MST, POET; DLB 20

Owens, Rochelle 1936- . . . . CLC **8**
See also CA 17-20R; CAAS 2; CANR 39

Oz, Amos 1939- . . . CLC **5, 8, 11, 27, 33, 54**
See also CA 53-56; CANR 27, 47;
DAM NOV; MTCW

Ozick, Cynthia
1928- . . . . CLC **3, 7, 28, 62; SSC 15**
See also BEST 90:1; CA 17-20R; CANR 23;
DAM NOV, POP; DLB 28, 152;
DLBY 82; INT CANR-23; MTCW

Ozu, Yasujiro 1903-1963 . . . . CLC **16**
See also CA 112

Pacheco, C.
See Pessoa, Fernando (Antonio Nogueira)

Pa Chin . . . . CLC **18**
See also Li Fei-kan

Pack, Robert 1929- . . . . CLC **13**
See also CA 1-4R; CANR 3, 44; DLB 5

Padgett, Lewis
See Kuttner, Henry

Padilla (Lorenzo), Heberto 1932- . . . CLC **38**
See also AITN 1; CA 123; 131; HW

Page, Jimmy 1944- . . . . CLC **12**

Page, Louise 1955- . . . . CLC **40**
See also CA 140

Page, P(atricia) K(athleen)
1916- . . . . CLC **7, 18; DAC; PC 12**
See also CA 53-56; CANR 4, 22;
DAM MST; DLB 68; MTCW

Page, Thomas Nelson 1853-1922 . . . . SSC **23**
See also CA 118; DLB 12, 78; DLBD 13

Paget, Violet 1856-1935
See Lee, Vernon
See also CA 104

Paget-Lowe, Henry
See Lovecraft, H(oward) P(hillips)

Paglia, Camille (Anna) 1947- . . . . CLC **68**
See also CA 140

Paige, Richard
See Koontz, Dean R(ay)

Pakenham, Antonia
See Fraser, (Lady) Antonia (Pakenham)

Palamas, Kostes 1859-1943 . . . . TCLC **5**
See also CA 105

Palazzeschi, Aldo 1885-1974 . . . . CLC **11**
See also CA 89-92; 53-56; DLB 114

Paley, Grace 1922- . . . . CLC **4, 6, 37; SSC 8**
See also CA 25-28R; CANR 13, 46;
DAM POP; DLB 28; INT CANR-13;
MTCW

Palin, Michael (Edward) 1943- . . . . . CLC **21**
See also Monty Python
See also CA 107; CANR 35; SATA 67

Palliser, Charles 1947- . . . . CLC **65**
See also CA 136

Palma, Ricardo 1833-1919 . . . . TCLC **29**

Pancake, Breece Dexter 1952-1979
See Pancake, Breece D'J
See also CA 123; 109

Pancake, Breece D'J . . . . CLC **29**
See also Pancake, Breece Dexter
See also DLB 130

Panko, Rudy
See Gogol, Nikolai (Vasilyevich)

Papadiamantis, Alexandros
1851-1911 . . . . TCLC **29**

Papadiamantopoulos, Johannes 1856-1910
See Moreas, Jean
See also CA 117

Papini, Giovanni 1881-1956 . . . . . . TCLC **22**
See also CA 121

Paracelsus 1493-1541 . . . . LC **14**

Parasol, Peter
See Stevens, Wallace

Parfenie, Maria
See Codrescu, Andrei

Parini, Jay (Lee) 1948- . . . . CLC **54**
See also CA 97-100; CAAS 16; CANR 32

Park, Jordan
See Kornbluth, C(yril) M.; Pohl, Frederik

Parker, Bert
See Ellison, Harlan (Jay)

Parker, Dorothy (Rothschild)
1893-1967 . . . . CLC **15, 68; SSC 2**
See also CA 19-20; 25-28R; CAP 2;
DAM POET; DLB 11, 45, 86; MTCW

Parker, Robert B(rown) 1932- . . . . . . CLC **27**
See also BEST 89:4; CA 49-52; CANR 1,
26, 52; DAM NOV, POP;
INT CANR-26; MTCW

Parkin, Frank 1940- . . . . CLC **43**
See also CA 147

Parkman, Francis, Jr.
1823-1893 . . . . NCLC **12**
See also DLB 1, 30

Parks, Gordon (Alexander Buchanan)
1912- . . . . CLC **1, 16; BLC**
See also AITN 2; BW 2; CA 41-44R;
CANR 26; DAM MULT; DLB 33;
SATA 8

Parnell, Thomas 1679-1718 . . . . LC **3**
See also DLB 94

Parra, Nicanor 1914- . . . . CLC **2; HLC**
See also CA 85-88; CANR 32;
DAM MULT; HW; MTCW

Parrish, Mary Frances
See Fisher, M(ary) F(rances) K(ennedy)

Parson
See Coleridge, Samuel Taylor

Parson Lot
See Kingsley, Charles

Partridge, Anthony
See Oppenheim, E(dward) Phillips

Pascoli, Giovanni 1855-1912 . . . . . . TCLC **45**

Pasolini, Pier Paolo
1922-1975 . . . . CLC **20, 37**
See also CA 93-96; 61-64; DLB 128;
MTCW

Pasquini
See Silone, Ignazio

Pastan, Linda (Olenik) 1932- . . . . . . CLC **27**
See also CA 61-64; CANR 18, 40;
DAM POET; DLB 5

Pasternak, Boris (Leonidovich)
1890-1960 . . . . . . CLC **7, 10, 18, 63; DA;**
DAB; DAC; PC 6; WLC
See also CA 127; 116; DAM MST, NOV,
POET; MTCW

Patchen, Kenneth 1911-1972 . . . CLC **1, 2, 18**
See also CA 1-4R; 33-36R; CANR 3, 35;
DAM POET; DLB 16, 48; MTCW

Pater, Walter (Horatio)
1839-1894 . . . . NCLC **7**
See also CDBLB 1832-1890; DLB 57, 156

Paterson, A(ndrew) B(arton)
1864-1941 . . . . TCLC **32**

Paterson, Katherine (Womeldorf)
1932- . . . . CLC **12, 30**
See also AAYA 1; CA 21-24R; CANR 28;
CLR 7; DLB 52; JRDA; MAICYA;
MTCW; SATA 13, 53

Patmore, Coventry Kersey Dighton
1823-1896 . . . . NCLC **9**
See also DLB 35, 98

Paton, Alan (Stewart)
1903-1988 . . . . . . CLC **4, 10, 25, 55; DA;**
DAB; DAC; WLC
See also CA 13-16; 125; CANR 22; CAP 1;
DAM MST, NOV; MTCW; SATA 11;
SATA-Obit 56

Paton Walsh, Gillian 1937-
See Walsh, Jill Paton
See also CANR 38; JRDA; MAICYA;
SAAS 3; SATA 4, 72

Paulding, James Kirke 1778-1860 . . NCLC **2**
See also DLB 3, 59, 74

Paulin, Thomas Neilson 1949-
See Paulin, Tom
See also CA 123; 128

Paulin, Tom . . . . CLC **37**
See also Paulin, Thomas Neilson
See also DLB 40

Paustovsky, Konstantin (Georgievich)
1892-1968 . . . . CLC **40**
See also CA 93-96; 25-28R

Pavese, Cesare
1908-1950 . . . . . TCLC **3; PC 13; SSC 19**
See also CA 104; DLB 128

Pavic, Milorad 1929- . . . . CLC **60**
See also CA 136

Payne, Alan
See Jakes, John (William)

Paz, Gil
See Lugones, Leopoldo

Paz, Octavio
1914- . . . . . . CLC **3, 4, 6, 10, 19, 51, 65;**
DA; DAB; DAC; HLC; PC 1; WLC
See also CA 73-76; CANR 32; DAM MST,
MULT, POET; DLBY 90; HW; MTCW

Peacock, Molly 1947- . . . . CLC **60**
See also CA 103; CAAS 21; CANR 52;
DLB 120

Peacock, Thomas Love
1785-1866 . . . . NCLC **22**
See also DLB 96, 116

Peake, Mervyn 1911-1968 . . . . CLC **7, 54**
See also CA 5-8R; 25-28R; CANR 3;
DLB 15, 160; MTCW; SATA 23

Pirandello, Luigi
1867-1936 . . . . . . **TCLC 4, 29; DA; DAB; DAC; DC 5; SSC 22; WLC**
See also CA 104; DAM DRAM, MST

Pirsig, Robert M(aynard)
1928- . . . . **CLC 4, 6, 73**
See also CA 53-56; CANR 42; DAM POP; MTCW; SATA 39

Pisarev, Dmitry Ivanovich
1840-1868 . . . . **NCLC 25**

Pix, Mary (Griffith) 1666-1709 . . . . . . **LC 8**
See also DLB 80

Pixerecourt, Guilbert de
1773-1844 . . . . **NCLC 39**

Plaidy, Jean
See Hibbert, Eleanor Alice Burford

Planche, James Robinson
1796-1880 . . . . **NCLC 42**

Plant, Robert 1948- . . . . **CLC 12**

Plante, David (Robert)
1940- . . . . **CLC 7, 23, 38**
See also CA 37-40R; CANR 12, 36; DAM NOV; DLBY 83; INT CANR-12; MTCW

Plath, Sylvia
1932-1963 . . . . . **CLC 1, 2, 3, 5, 9, 11, 14, 17, 50, 51, 62; DA; DAB; DAC; PC 1; WLC**
See also AAYA 13; CA 19-20; CANR 34; CAP 2; CDALB 1941-1968; DAM MST, POET; DLB 5, 6, 152; MTCW

Plato
428(?)B.C.-348(?)B.C. . . . . . **CMLC 8; DA; DAB; DAC**
See also DAM MST

Platonov, Andrei . . . . **TCLC 14**
See also Klimentov, Andrei Platonovich

Platt, Kin 1911- . . . . **CLC 26**
See also AAYA 11; CA 17-20R; CANR 11; JRDA; SAAS 17; SATA 21, 86

Plautus c. 251B.C.-184B.C. . . . . **DC 6**

Plick et Plock
See Simenon, Georges (Jacques Christian)

Plimpton, George (Ames) 1927- . . . . . **CLC 36**
See also AITN 1; CA 21-24R; CANR 32; MTCW; SATA 10

Plomer, William Charles Franklin
1903-1973 . . . . **CLC 4, 8**
See also CA 21-22; CANR 34; CAP 2; DLB 20, 162; MTCW; SATA 24

Plowman, Piers
See Kavanagh, Patrick (Joseph)

Plum, J.
See Wodehouse, P(elham) G(renville)

Plumly, Stanley (Ross) 1939- . . . . . . **CLC 33**
See also CA 108; 110; DLB 5; INT 110

Plumpe, Friedrich Wilhelm
1888-1931 . . . . **TCLC 53**
See also CA 112

Poe, Edgar Allan
1809-1849 . . . . **NCLC 1, 16, 55; DA; DAB; DAC; PC 1; SSC 1, 22; WLC**
See also AAYA 14; CDALB 1640-1865; DAM MST, POET; DLB 3, 59, 73, 74; SATA 23

Poet of Titchfield Street, The
See Pound, Ezra (Weston Loomis)

Pohl, Frederik 1919- . . . . **CLC 18**
See also CA 61-64; CAAS 1; CANR 11, 37; DLB 8; INT CANR-11; MTCW; SATA 24

Poirier, Louis 1910-
See Gracq, Julien
See also CA 122; 126

Poitier, Sidney 1927- . . . . **CLC 26**
See also BW 1; CA 117

Polanski, Roman 1933- . . . . **CLC 16**
See also CA 77-80

Poliakoff, Stephen 1952- . . . . **CLC 38**
See also CA 106; DLB 13

Police, The
See Copeland, Stewart (Armstrong); Summers, Andrew James; Sumner, Gordon Matthew

Polidori, John William
1795-1821 . . . . **NCLC 51**
See also DLB 116

Pollitt, Katha 1949- . . . . **CLC 28**
See also CA 120; 122; MTCW

Pollock, (Mary) Sharon
1936- . . . . **CLC 50; DAC**
See also CA 141; DAM DRAM, MST; DLB 60

Polo, Marco 1254-1324 . . . . **CMLC 15**

Polonsky, Abraham (Lincoln)
1910- . . . . **CLC 92**
See also CA 104; DLB 26; INT 104

Polybius c. 200B.C.-c. 118B.C. . . . . **CMLC 17**

Pomerance, Bernard 1940- . . . . **CLC 13**
See also CA 101; CANR 49; DAM DRAM

Ponge, Francis (Jean Gaston Alfred)
1899-1988 . . . . **CLC 6, 18**
See also CA 85-88; 126; CANR 40; DAM POET

Pontoppidan, Henrik 1857-1943 . . . **TCLC 29**

Poole, Josephine . . . . **CLC 17**
See also Helyar, Jane Penelope Josephine
See also SAAS 2; SATA 5

Popa, Vasko 1922-1991 . . . . **CLC 19**
See also CA 112; 148

Pope, Alexander
1688-1744 . . . . . . **LC 3; DA; DAB; DAC; WLC**
See also CDBLB 1660-1789; DAM MST, POET; DLB 95, 101

Porter, Connie (Rose) 1959(?)- . . . . . **CLC 70**
See also BW 2; CA 142; SATA 81

Porter, Gene(va Grace) Stratton
1863(?)-1924 . . . . **TCLC 21**
See also CA 112

Porter, Katherine Anne
1890-1980 . . . . . . **CLC 1, 3, 7, 10, 13, 15, 27; DA; DAB; DAC; SSC 4**
See also AITN 2; CA 1-4R; 101; CANR 1; DAM MST, NOV; DLB 4, 9, 102; DLBD 12; DLBY 80; MTCW; SATA 39; SATA-Obit 23

Porter, Peter (Neville Frederick)
1929- . . . . **CLC 5, 13, 33**
See also CA 85-88; DLB 40

Porter, William Sydney 1862-1910
See Henry, O.
See also CA 104; 131; CDALB 1865-1917; DA; DAB; DAC; DAM MST; DLB 12, 78, 79; MTCW; YABC 2

Portillo (y Pacheco), Jose Lopez
See Lopez Portillo (y Pacheco), Jose

Post, Melville Davisson
1869-1930 . . . . **TCLC 39**
See also CA 110

Potok, Chaim 1929- . . . . **CLC 2, 7, 14, 26**
See also AAYA 15; AITN 1, 2; CA 17-20R; CANR 19, 35; DAM NOV; DLB 28, 152; INT CANR-19; MTCW; SATA 33

Potter, Beatrice
See Webb, (Martha) Beatrice (Potter)
See also MAICYA

Potter, Dennis (Christopher George)
1935-1994 . . . . **CLC 58, 86**
See also CA 107; 145; CANR 33; MTCW

Pound, Ezra (Weston Loomis)
1885-1972 . . . . . . **CLC 1, 2, 3, 4, 5, 7, 10, 13, 18, 34, 48, 50; DA; DAB; DAC; PC 4; WLC**
See also CA 5-8R; 37-40R; CANR 40; CDALB 1917-1929; DAM MST, POET; DLB 4, 45, 63; MTCW

Povod, Reinaldo 1959-1994 . . . . **CLC 44**
See also CA 136; 146

Powell, Adam Clayton, Jr.
1908-1972 . . . . **CLC 89; BLC**
See also BW 1; CA 102; 33-36R; DAM MULT

Powell, Anthony (Dymoke)
1905- . . . . **CLC 1, 3, 7, 9, 10, 31**
See also CA 1-4R; CANR 1, 32; CDBLB 1945-1960; DLB 15; MTCW

Powell, Dawn 1897-1965 . . . . **CLC 66**
See also CA 5-8R

Powell, Padgett 1952- . . . . **CLC 34**
See also CA 126

Power, Susan . . . . **CLC 91**

Powers, J(ames) F(arl)
1917- . . . . **CLC 1, 4, 8, 57; SSC 4**
See also CA 1-4R; CANR 2; DLB 130; MTCW

Powers, John J(ames) 1945-
See Powers, John R.
See also CA 69-72

Powers, John R. . . . . **CLC 66**
See also Powers, John J(ames)

Powers, Richard (S.) 1957- . . . . **CLC 93**
See also CA 148

Pownall, David 1938- . . . . **CLC 10**
See also CA 89-92; CAAS 18; CANR 49; DLB 14

Powys, John Cowper
1872-1963 . . . . **CLC 7, 9, 15, 46**
See also CA 85-88; DLB 15; MTCW

Powys, T(heodore) F(rancis)
1875-1953 . . . . **TCLC 9**
See also CA 106; DLB 36, 162

Prager, Emily 1952- . . . . **CLC 56**

Pratt, E(dwin) J(ohn)
1883(?)-1964 . . . . CLC 19; DAC
See also CA 141; 93-96; DAM POET;
DLB 92

Premchand . . . . TCLC 21
See also Srivastava, Dhanpat Rai

Preussler, Otfried 1923- . . . . CLC 17
See also CA 77-80; SATA 24

Prevert, Jacques (Henri Marie)
1900-1977 . . . . CLC 15
See also CA 77-80; 69-72; CANR 29;
MTCW; SATA-Obit 30

Prevost, Abbe (Antoine Francois)
1697-1763 . . . . LC 1

Price, (Edward) Reynolds
1933- . . CLC 3, 6, 13, 43, 50, 63; SSC 22
See also CA 1-4R; CANR 1, 37;
DAM NOV; DLB 2; INT CANR-37

Price, Richard 1949- . . . . CLC 6, 12
See also CA 49-52; CANR 3; DLBY 81

Prichard, Katharine Susannah
1883-1969 . . . . CLC 46
See also CA 11-12; CANR 33; CAP 1;
MTCW; SATA 66

Priestley, J(ohn) B(oynton)
1894-1984 . . . . CLC 2, 5, 9, 34
See also CA 9-12R; 113; CANR 33;
CDBLB 1914-1945; DAM DRAM, NOV;
DLB 10, 34, 77, 100, 139; DLBY 84;
MTCW

Prince 1958(?)- . . . . CLC 35

Prince, F(rank) T(empleton) 1912- . . CLC 22
See also CA 101; CANR 43; DLB 20

Prince Kropotkin
See Kropotkin, Peter (Aleksieevich)

Prior, Matthew 1664-1721 . . . . LC 4
See also DLB 95

Pritchard, William H(arrison)
1932- . . . . CLC 34
See also CA 65-68; CANR 23; DLB 111

Pritchett, V(ictor) S(awdon)
1900- . . . . CLC 5, 13, 15, 41; SSC 14
See also CA 61-64; CANR 31; DAM NOV;
DLB 15, 139; MTCW

Private 19022
See Manning, Frederic

Probst, Mark 1925- . . . . CLC 59
See also CA 130

Prokosch, Frederic 1908-1989 . . . . CLC 4, 48
See also CA 73-76; 128; DLB 48

Prophet, The
See Dreiser, Theodore (Herman Albert)

Prose, Francine 1947- . . . . CLC 45
See also CA 109; 112; CANR 46

Proudhon
See Cunha, Euclides (Rodrigues Pimenta) da

Proulx, E. Annie 1935- . . . . CLC 81

Proust, (Valentin-Louis-George-Eugene-)
Marcel
1871-1922 . . . . TCLC 7, 13, 33; DA;
DAB; DAC; WLC
See also CA 104; 120; DAM MST, NOV;
DLB 65; MTCW

Prowler, Harley
See Masters, Edgar Lee

Prus, Boleslaw 1845-1912 . . . . TCLC 48

Pryor, Richard (Franklin Lenox Thomas)
1940- . . . . CLC 26
See also CA 122

Przybyszewski, Stanislaw
1868-1927 . . . . TCLC 36
See also DLB 66

Pteleon
See Grieve, C(hristopher) M(urray)
See also DAM POET

Puckett, Lute
See Masters, Edgar Lee

Puig, Manuel
1932-1990 . . . CLC 3, 5, 10, 28, 65; HLC
See also CA 45-48; CANR 2, 32;
DAM MULT; DLB 113; HW; MTCW

Purdy, Al(fred Wellington)
1918- . . . . CLC 3, 6, 14, 50; DAC
See also CA 81-84; CAAS 17; CANR 42;
DAM MST, POET; DLB 88

Purdy, James (Amos)
1923- . . . . CLC 2, 4, 10, 28, 52
See also CA 33-36R; CAAS 1; CANR 19,
51; DLB 2; INT CANR-19; MTCW

Pure, Simon
See Swinnerton, Frank Arthur

Pushkin, Alexander (Sergeyevich)
1799-1837 . . . . . NCLC 3, 27; DA; DAB;
DAC; PC 10; WLC
See also DAM DRAM, MST, POET;
SATA 61

P'u Sung-ling 1640-1715 . . . . LC 3

Putnam, Arthur Lee
See Alger, Horatio, Jr.

Puzo, Mario 1920- . . . . CLC 1, 2, 6, 36
See also CA 65-68; CANR 4, 42;
DAM NOV, POP; DLB 6; MTCW

Pym, Barbara (Mary Crampton)
1913-1980 . . . . CLC 13, 19, 37
See also CA 13-14; 97-100; CANR 13, 34;
CAP 1; DLB 14; DLBY 87; MTCW

Pynchon, Thomas (Ruggles, Jr.)
1937- . . . . . CLC 2, 3, 6, 9, 11, 18, 33, 62,
72; DA; DAB; DAC; SSC 14; WLC
See also BEST 90:2; CA 17-20R; CANR 22,
46; DAM MST, NOV, POP; DLB 2;
MTCW

Qian Zhongshu
See Ch'ien Chung-shu

Qroll
See Dagerman, Stig (Halvard)

Quarrington, Paul (Lewis) 1953- . . . . CLC 65
See also CA 129

Quasimodo, Salvatore 1901-1968 . . . CLC 10
See also CA 13-16; 25-28R; CAP 1;
DLB 114; MTCW

Quay, Stephen 1947- . . . . CLC 95

Quay, The Brothers
See Quay, Stephen; Quay, Timothy

Quay, Timothy 1947- . . . . CLC 95

Queen, Ellery . . . . CLC 3, 11
See also Dannay, Frederic; Davidson,
Avram; Lee, Manfred B(ennington);
Sturgeon, Theodore (Hamilton); Vance,
John Holbrook

Queen, Ellery, Jr.
See Dannay, Frederic; Lee, Manfred
B(ennington)

Queneau, Raymond
1903-1976 . . . . CLC 2, 5, 10, 42
See also CA 77-80; 69-72; CANR 32;
DLB 72; MTCW

Quevedo, Francisco de 1580-1645 . . . . LC 23

Quiller-Couch, Arthur Thomas
1863-1944 . . . . TCLC 53
See also CA 118; DLB 135, 153

Quin, Ann (Marie) 1936-1973 . . . . CLC 6
See also CA 9-12R; 45-48; DLB 14

Quinn, Martin
See Smith, Martin Cruz

Quinn, Peter 1947- . . . . CLC 91

Quinn, Simon
See Smith, Martin Cruz

Quiroga, Horacio (Sylvestre)
1878-1937 . . . . TCLC 20; HLC
See also CA 117; 131; DAM MULT; HW;
MTCW

Quoirez, Francoise 1935- . . . . CLC 9
See also Sagan, Francoise
See also CA 49-52; CANR 6, 39; MTCW

Raabe, Wilhelm 1831-1910 . . . . TCLC 45
See also DLB 129

Rabe, David (William) 1940- . . . CLC 4, 8, 33
See also CA 85-88; CABS 3; DAM DRAM;
DLB 7

Rabelais, Francois
1483-1553 . . . . . . LC 5; DA; DAB; DAC;
WLC
See also DAM MST

Rabinovitch, Sholem 1859-1916
See Aleichem, Sholom
See also CA 104

Racine, Jean 1639-1699 . . . . LC 28; DAB
See also DAM MST

Radcliffe, Ann (Ward)
1764-1823 . . . . NCLC 6, 55
See also DLB 39

Radiguet, Raymond 1903-1923 . . . . TCLC 29
See also DLB 65

Radnoti, Miklos 1909-1944 . . . . TCLC 16
See also CA 118

Rado, James 1939- . . . . CLC 17
See also CA 105

Radvanyi, Netty 1900-1983
See Seghers, Anna
See also CA 85-88; 110

Rae, Ben
See Griffiths, Trevor

Raeburn, John (Hay) 1941- . . . . CLC 34
See also CA 57-60

Ragni, Gerome 1942-1991 . . . . CLC 17
See also CA 105; 134

Rahv, Philip 1908-1973 . . . . CLC 24
See also Greenberg, Ivan
See also DLB 137

Raine, Craig 1944- . . . . CLC 32
See also CA 108; CANR 29, 51; DLB 40

Raine, Kathleen (Jessie) 1908- ... **CLC 7, 45**
　　See also CA 85-88; CANR 46; DLB 20;
　　MTCW

Rainis, Janis 1865-1929 .... **TCLC 29**

Rakosi, Carl .... **CLC 47**
　　See also Rawley, Callman
　　See also CAAS 5

Raleigh, Richard
　　See Lovecraft, H(oward) P(hillips)

Raleigh, Sir Walter 1554(?)-1618 .... **LC 31**
　　See also CDBLB Before 1660

Rallentando, H. P.
　　See Sayers, Dorothy L(eigh)

Ramal, Walter
　　See de la Mare, Walter (John)

Ramon, Juan
　　See Jimenez (Mantecon), Juan Ramon

Ramos, Graciliano 1892-1953 ..... **TCLC 32**

Rampersad, Arnold 1941- .... **CLC 44**
　　See also BW 2; CA 127; 133; DLB 111;
　　INT 133

Rampling, Anne
　　See Rice, Anne

Ramsay, Allan 1684(?)-1758 .... **LC 29**
　　See also DLB 95

Ramuz, Charles-Ferdinand
　　1878-1947 .... **TCLC 33**

Rand, Ayn
　　1905-1982 ..... **CLC 3, 30, 44, 79; DA;
　　　　　　　　　　　　　　　DAC; WLC**
　　See also AAYA 10; CA 13-16R; 105;
　　CANR 27; DAM MST, NOV, POP;
　　MTCW

Randall, Dudley (Felker)
　　1914- .... **CLC 1; BLC**
　　See also BW 1; CA 25-28R; CANR 23;
　　DAM MULT; DLB 41

Randall, Robert
　　See Silverberg, Robert

Ranger, Ken
　　See Creasey, John

Ransom, John Crowe
　　1888-1974 .... **CLC 2, 4, 5, 11, 24**
　　See also CA 5-8R; 49-52; CANR 6, 34;
　　DAM POET; DLB 45, 63; MTCW

Rao, Raja 1909- .... **CLC 25, 56**
　　See also CA 73-76; CANR 51; DAM NOV;
　　MTCW

Raphael, Frederic (Michael)
　　1931- .... **CLC 2, 14**
　　See also CA 1-4R; CANR 1; DLB 14

Ratcliffe, James P.
　　See Mencken, H(enry) L(ouis)

Rathbone, Julian 1935- .... **CLC 41**
　　See also CA 101; CANR 34

Rattigan, Terence (Mervyn)
　　1911-1977 .... **CLC 7**
　　See also CA 85-88; 73-76;
　　CDBLB 1945-1960; DAM DRAM;
　　DLB 13; MTCW

Ratushinskaya, Irina 1954- .... **CLC 54**
　　See also CA 129

Raven, Simon (Arthur Noel)
　　1927- .... **CLC 14**
　　See also CA 81-84

Rawley, Callman 1903-
　　See Rakosi, Carl
　　See also CA 21-24R; CANR 12, 32

Rawlings, Marjorie Kinnan
　　1896-1953 .... **TCLC 4**
　　See also CA 104; 137; DLB 9, 22, 102;
　　JRDA; MAICYA; YABC 1

Ray, Satyajit 1921-1992 ...... **CLC 16, 76**
　　See also CA 114; 137; DAM MULT

Read, Herbert Edward 1893-1968.... **CLC 4**
　　See also CA 85-88; 25-28R; DLB 20, 149

Read, Piers Paul 1941- ...... **CLC 4, 10, 25**
　　See also CA 21-24R; CANR 38; DLB 14;
　　SATA 21

Reade, Charles 1814-1884 .... **NCLC 2**
　　See also DLB 21

Reade, Hamish
　　See Gray, Simon (James Holliday)

Reading, Peter 1946- .... **CLC 47**
　　See also CA 103; CANR 46; DLB 40

Reaney, James 1926- .... **CLC 13; DAC**
　　See also CA 41-44R; CAAS 15; CANR 42;
　　DAM MST; DLB 68; SATA 43

Rebreanu, Liviu 1885-1944 .... **TCLC 28**

Rechy, John (Francisco)
　　1934- .... **CLC 1, 7, 14, 18; HLC**
　　See also CA 5-8R; CAAS 4; CANR 6, 32;
　　DAM MULT; DLB 122; DLBY 82; HW;
　　INT CANR-6

Redcam, Tom 1870-1933 .... **TCLC 25**

Reddin, Keith .... **CLC 67**

Redgrove, Peter (William)
　　1932- .... **CLC 6, 41**
　　See also CA 1-4R; CANR 3, 39; DLB 40

Redmon, Anne .... **CLC 22**
　　See also Nightingale, Anne Redmon
　　See also DLBY 86

Reed, Eliot
　　See Ambler, Eric

Reed, Ishmael
　　1938- ... **CLC 2, 3, 5, 6, 13, 32, 60; BLC**
　　See also BW 2; CA 21-24R; CANR 25, 48;
　　DAM MULT; DLB 2, 5, 33; DLBD 8;
　　MTCW

Reed, John (Silas) 1887-1920 ...... **TCLC 9**
　　See also CA 106

Reed, Lou .... **CLC 21**
　　See also Firbank, Louis

Reeve, Clara 1729-1807 .... **NCLC 19**
　　See also DLB 39

Reich, Wilhelm 1897-1957 .... **TCLC 57**

Reid, Christopher (John) 1949- ..... **CLC 33**
　　See also CA 140; DLB 40

Reid, Desmond
　　See Moorcock, Michael (John)

Reid Banks, Lynne 1929-
　　See Banks, Lynne Reid
　　See also CA 1-4R; CANR 6, 22, 38;
　　CLR 24; JRDA; MAICYA; SATA 22, 75

Reilly, William K.
　　See Creasey, John

Reiner, Max
　　See Caldwell, (Janet Miriam) Taylor
　　(Holland)

Reis, Ricardo
　　See Pessoa, Fernando (Antonio Nogueira)

Remarque, Erich Maria
　　1898-1970 .... **CLC 21; DA; DAB; DAC**
　　See also CA 77-80; 29-32R; DAM MST,
　　NOV; DLB 56; MTCW

Remizov, A.
　　See Remizov, Aleksei (Mikhailovich)

Remizov, A. M.
　　See Remizov, Aleksei (Mikhailovich)

Remizov, Aleksei (Mikhailovich)
　　1877-1957 .... **TCLC 27**
　　See also CA 125; 133

Renan, Joseph Ernest
　　1823-1892 .... **NCLC 26**

Renard, Jules 1864-1910 .... **TCLC 17**
　　See also CA 117

Renault, Mary .... **CLC 3, 11, 17**
　　See also Challans, Mary
　　See also DLBY 83

Rendell, Ruth (Barbara) 1930- .. **CLC 28, 48**
　　See also Vine, Barbara
　　See also CA 109; CANR 32, 52;
　　DAM POP; DLB 87; INT CANR-32;
　　MTCW

Renoir, Jean 1894-1979 .... **CLC 20**
　　See also CA 129; 85-88

Resnais, Alain 1922- .... **CLC 16**

Reverdy, Pierre 1889-1960 .... **CLC 53**
　　See also CA 97-100; 89-92

Rexroth, Kenneth
　　1905-1982 ...... **CLC 1, 2, 6, 11, 22, 49**
　　See also CA 5-8R; 107; CANR 14, 34;
　　CDALB 1941-1968; DAM POET;
　　DLB 16, 48, 165; DLBY 82;
　　INT CANR-14; MTCW

Reyes, Alfonso 1889-1959 .... **TCLC 33**
　　See also CA 131; HW

Reyes y Basoalto, Ricardo Eliecer Neftali
　　See Neruda, Pablo

Reymont, Wladyslaw (Stanislaw)
　　1868(?)-1925 .... **TCLC 5**
　　See also CA 104

Reynolds, Jonathan 1942- .... **CLC 6, 38**
　　See also CA 65-68; CANR 28

Reynolds, Joshua 1723-1792 .... **LC 15**
　　See also DLB 104

Reynolds, Michael Shane 1937- .... **CLC 44**
　　See also CA 65-68; CANR 9

Reznikoff, Charles 1894-1976 .... **CLC 9**
　　See also CA 33-36; 61-64; CAP 2; DLB 28,
　　45

Rezzori (d'Arezzo), Gregor von
　　1914- .... **CLC 25**
　　See also CA 122; 136

Rhine, Richard
　　See Silverstein, Alvin

Rhodes, Eugene Manlove
　　1869-1934 .... **TCLC 53**

R'hoone
　　See Balzac, Honore de

Rhys, Jean
1890(?)-1979 .... **CLC 2, 4, 6, 14, 19, 51;
SSC 21**
See also CA 25-28R; 85-88; CANR 35;
CDBLB 1945-1960; DAM NOV; DLB 36,
117, 162; MTCW

Ribeiro, Darcy 1922- .... **CLC 34**
See also CA 33-36R

Ribeiro, Joao Ubaldo (Osorio Pimentel)
1941- .... **CLC 10, 67**
See also CA 81-84

Ribman, Ronald (Burt) 1932- .... **CLC 7**
See also CA 21-24R; CANR 46

Ricci, Nino 1959- .... **CLC 70**
See also CA 137

Rice, Anne 1941- .... **CLC 41**
See also AAYA 9; BEST 89:2; CA 65-68;
CANR 12, 36, 53; DAM POP

Rice, Elmer (Leopold)
1892-1967 .... **CLC 7, 49**
See also CA 21-22; 25-28R; CAP 2;
DAM DRAM; DLB 4, 7; MTCW

Rice, Tim(othy Miles Bindon)
1944- .... **CLC 21**
See also CA 103; CANR 46

Rich, Adrienne (Cecile)
1929- .... **CLC 3, 6, 7, 11, 18, 36, 73, 76;
PC 5**
See also CA 9-12R; CANR 20, 53;
DAM POET; DLB 5, 67; MTCW

Rich, Barbara
See Graves, Robert (von Ranke)

Rich, Robert
See Trumbo, Dalton

Richard, Keith .... **CLC 17**
See also Richards, Keith

Richards, David Adams
1950- .... **CLC 59; DAC**
See also CA 93-96; DLB 53

Richards, I(vor) A(rmstrong)
1893-1979 .... **CLC 14, 24**
See also CA 41-44R; 89-92; CANR 34;
DLB 27

Richards, Keith 1943-
See Richard, Keith
See also CA 107

Richardson, Anne
See Roiphe, Anne (Richardson)

Richardson, Dorothy Miller
1873-1957 .... **TCLC 3**
See also CA 104; DLB 36

Richardson, Ethel Florence (Lindesay)
1870-1946
See Richardson, Henry Handel
See also CA 105

Richardson, Henry Handel .... **TCLC 4**
See also Richardson, Ethel Florence
(Lindesay)

Richardson, John
1796-1852 .... **NCLC 55; DAC**
See also DLB 99

Richardson, Samuel
1689-1761 ...... **LC 1; DA; DAB; DAC;
WLC**
See also CDBLB 1660-1789; DAM MST,
NOV; DLB 39

Richler, Mordecai
1931- ...... **CLC 3, 5, 9, 13, 18, 46, 70;
DAC**
See also AITN 1; CA 65-68; CANR 31;
CLR 17; DAM MST, NOV; DLB 53;
MAICYA; MTCW; SATA 44;
SATA-Brief 27

Richter, Conrad (Michael)
1890-1968 .... **CLC 30**
See also CA 5-8R; 25-28R; CANR 23;
DLB 9; MTCW; SATA 3

Ricostranza, Tom
See Ellis, Trey

Riddell, J. H. 1832-1906 .... **TCLC 40**

Riding, Laura .... **CLC 3, 7**
See also Jackson, Laura (Riding)

Riefenstahl, Berta Helene Amalia 1902-
See Riefenstahl, Leni
See also CA 108

Riefenstahl, Leni .... **CLC 16**
See also Riefenstahl, Berta Helene Amalia

Riffe, Ernest
See Bergman, (Ernst) Ingmar

Riggs, (Rolla) Lynn 1899-1954 .... **TCLC 56**
See also CA 144; DAM MULT; NNAL

Riley, James Whitcomb
1849-1916 .... **TCLC 51**
See also CA 118; 137; DAM POET;
MAICYA; SATA 17

Riley, Tex
See Creasey, John

Rilke, Rainer Maria
1875-1926 .... **TCLC 1, 6, 19; PC 2**
See also CA 104; 132; DAM POET;
DLB 81; MTCW

Rimbaud, (Jean Nicolas) Arthur
1854-1891 ..... **NCLC 4, 35; DA; DAB;
DAC; PC 3; WLC**
See also DAM MST, POET

Rinehart, Mary Roberts
1876-1958 .... **TCLC 52**
See also CA 108

Ringmaster, The
See Mencken, H(enry) L(ouis)

Ringwood, Gwen(dolyn Margaret) Pharis
1910-1984 .... **CLC 48**
See also CA 148; 112; DLB 88

Rio, Michel 19(?)- .... **CLC 43**

Ritsos, Giannes
See Ritsos, Yannis

Ritsos, Yannis 1909-1990..... **CLC 6, 13, 31**
See also CA 77-80; 133; CANR 39; MTCW

Ritter, Erika 1948(?)- .... **CLC 52**

Rivera, Jose Eustasio 1889-1928... **TCLC 35**
See also HW

Rivers, Conrad Kent 1933-1968...... **CLC 1**
See also BW 1; CA 85-88; DLB 41

Rivers, Elfrida
See Bradley, Marion Zimmer

Riverside, John
See Heinlein, Robert A(nson)

Rizal, Jose 1861-1896.......... **NCLC 27**

Roa Bastos, Augusto (Antonio)
1917- .... **CLC 45; HLC**
See also CA 131; DAM MULT; DLB 113;
HW

Robbe-Grillet, Alain
1922- ...... **CLC 1, 2, 4, 6, 8, 10, 14, 43**
See also CA 9-12R; CANR 33; DLB 83;
MTCW

Robbins, Harold 1916- .... **CLC 5**
See also CA 73-76; CANR 26; DAM NOV;
MTCW

Robbins, Thomas Eugene 1936-
See Robbins, Tom
See also CA 81-84; CANR 29; DAM NOV,
POP; MTCW

Robbins, Tom .... **CLC 9, 32, 64**
See also Robbins, Thomas Eugene
See also BEST 90:3; DLBY 80

Robbins, Trina 1938- .... **CLC 21**
See also CA 128

Roberts, Charles G(eorge) D(ouglas)
1860-1943 .... **TCLC 8**
See also CA 105; CLR 33; DLB 92;
SATA 88; SATA-Brief 29

Roberts, Kate 1891-1985 .... **CLC 15**
See also CA 107; 116

Roberts, Keith (John Kingston)
1935- .... **CLC 14**
See also CA 25-28R; CANR 46

Roberts, Kenneth (Lewis)
1885-1957 .... **TCLC 23**
See also CA 109; DLB 9

Roberts, Michele (B.) 1949-........ **CLC 48**
See also CA 115

Robertson, Ellis
See Ellison, Harlan (Jay); Silverberg, Robert

Robertson, Thomas William
1829-1871 .... **NCLC 35**
See also DAM DRAM

Robinson, Edwin Arlington
1869-1935 .... **TCLC 5; DA; DAC; PC 1**
See also CA 104; 133; CDALB 1865-1917;
DAM MST, POET; DLB 54; MTCW

Robinson, Henry Crabb
1775-1867 .... **NCLC 15**
See also DLB 107

Robinson, Jill 1936- .... **CLC 10**
See also CA 102; INT 102

Robinson, Kim Stanley 1952- ...... **CLC 34**
See also CA 126

Robinson, Lloyd
See Silverberg, Robert

Robinson, Marilynne 1944-........ **CLC 25**
See also CA 116

Robinson, Smokey................. **CLC 21**
See also Robinson, William, Jr.

Robinson, William, Jr. 1940-
See Robinson, Smokey
See also CA 116

Robison, Mary 1949- .... **CLC 42**
See also CA 113; 116; DLB 130; INT 116

Rod, Edouard 1857-1910 .... **TCLC 52**

Roddenberry, Eugene Wesley 1921-1991
See Roddenberry, Gene
See also CA 110; 135; CANR 37; SATA 45;
SATA-Obit 69

Roddenberry, Gene . . . . **CLC 17**
See also Roddenberry, Eugene Wesley
See also AAYA 5; SATA-Obit 69

Rodgers, Mary 1931- . . . . **CLC 12**
See also CA 49-52; CANR 8; CLR 20;
INT CANR-8; JRDA; MAICYA;
SATA 8

Rodgers, W(illiam) R(obert)
1909-1969 . . . . **CLC 7**
See also CA 85-88; DLB 20

Rodman, Eric
See Silverberg, Robert

Rodman, Howard 1920(?)-1985 . . . . . **CLC 65**
See also CA 118

Rodman, Maia
See Wojciechowska, Maia (Teresa)

Rodriguez, Claudio 1934- . . . . **CLC 10**
See also DLB 134

Roelvaag, O(le) E(dvart)
1876-1931 . . . . **TCLC 17**
See also CA 117; DLB 9

Roethke, Theodore (Huebner)
1908-1963 . . . . . . **CLC 1, 3, 8, 11, 19, 46;**
                                                      PC 15
See also CA 81-84; CABS 2;
CDALB 1941-1968; DAM POET; DLB 5;
MTCW

Rogers, Thomas Hunton 1927- . . . . . **CLC 57**
See also CA 89-92; INT 89-92

Rogers, Will(iam Penn Adair)
1879-1935 . . . . **TCLC 8**
See also CA 105; 144; DAM MULT;
DLB 11; NNAL

Rogin, Gilbert 1929- . . . . **CLC 18**
See also CA 65-68; CANR 15

Rohan, Koda . . . . **TCLC 22**
See also Koda Shigeyuki

Rohmer, Eric . . . . **CLC 16**
See also Scherer, Jean-Marie Maurice

Rohmer, Sax . . . . **TCLC 28**
See also Ward, Arthur Henry Sarsfield
See also DLB 70

Roiphe, Anne (Richardson)
1935- . . . . **CLC 3, 9**
See also CA 89-92; CANR 45; DLBY 80;
INT 89-92

Rojas, Fernando de 1465-1541 . . . . . **LC 23**

**Rolfe, Frederick (William Serafino Austin
     Lewis Mary)** 1860-1913 . . . . . . **TCLC 12**
See also CA 107; DLB 34, 156

Rolland, Romain 1866-1944 . . . . . . **TCLC 23**
See also CA 118; DLB 65

Rolvaag, O(le) E(dvart)
See Roelvaag, O(le) E(dvart)

Romain Arnaud, Saint
See Aragon, Louis

Romains, Jules 1885-1972 . . . . **CLC 7**
See also CA 85-88; CANR 34; DLB 65;
MTCW

Romero, Jose Ruben 1890-1952 . . . **TCLC 14**
See also CA 114; 131; HW

Ronsard, Pierre de
1524-1585 . . . . **LC 6; PC 11**

Rooke, Leon 1934- . . . . **CLC 25, 34**
See also CA 25-28R; CANR 23, 53;
DAM POP

Roper, William 1498-1578 . . . . **LC 10**

Roquelaure, A. N.
See Rice, Anne

Rosa, Joao Guimaraes 1908-1967 . . . **CLC 23**
See also CA 89-92; DLB 113

Rose, Wendy 1948- . . . . **CLC 85; PC 13**
See also CA 53-56; CANR 5, 51;
DAM MULT; NNAL; SATA 12

Rosen, Richard (Dean) 1949- . . . . **CLC 39**
See also CA 77-80; INT CANR-30

Rosenberg, Isaac 1890-1918 . . . . . . **TCLC 12**
See also CA 107; DLB 20

Rosenblatt, Joe . . . . **CLC 15**
See also Rosenblatt, Joseph

Rosenblatt, Joseph 1933-
See Rosenblatt, Joe
See also CA 89-92; INT 89-92

Rosenfeld, Samuel 1896-1963
See Tzara, Tristan
See also CA 89-92

Rosenthal, M(acha) L(ouis) 1917- . . . **CLC 28**
See also CA 1-4R; CAAS 6; CANR 4, 51;
DLB 5; SATA 59

Ross, Barnaby
See Dannay, Frederic

Ross, Bernard L.
See Follett, Ken(neth Martin)

Ross, J. H.
See Lawrence, T(homas) E(dward)

Ross, Martin
See Martin, Violet Florence
See also DLB 135

Ross, (James) Sinclair
1908- . . . . **CLC 13; DAC**
See also CA 73-76; DAM MST; DLB 88

Rossetti, Christina (Georgina)
1830-1894 . . . . . **NCLC 2, 50; DA; DAB;**
                                              DAC; PC 7; WLC
See also DAM MST, POET; DLB 35, 163;
MAICYA; SATA 20

Rossetti, Dante Gabriel
1828-1882 . . . . **NCLC 4; DA; DAB;**
                                                         DAC; WLC
See also CDBLB 1832-1890; DAM MST,
POET; DLB 35

Rossner, Judith (Perelman)
1935- . . . . **CLC 6, 9, 29**
See also AITN 2; BEST 90:3; CA 17-20R;
CANR 18, 51; DLB 6; INT CANR-18;
MTCW

Rostand, Edmond (Eugene Alexis)
1868-1918 . . . . . . **TCLC 6, 37; DA; DAB;**
                                                              DAC
See also CA 104; 126; DAM DRAM, MST;
MTCW

Roth, Henry 1906-1995 . . . . **CLC 2, 6, 11**
See also CA 11-12; 149; CANR 38; CAP 1;
DLB 28; MTCW

Roth, Joseph 1894-1939 . . . . **TCLC 33**
See also DLB 85

Roth, Philip (Milton)
1933- . . . . . . **CLC 1, 2, 3, 4, 6, 9, 15, 22,**
            31, 47, 66, 86; DA; DAB; DAC; WLC
See also BEST 90:3; CA 1-4R; CANR 1, 22,
36; CDALB 1968-1988; DAM MST,
NOV, POP; DLB 2, 28; DLBY 82;
MTCW

Rothenberg, Jerome 1931- . . . . **CLC 6, 57**
See also CA 45-48; CANR 1; DLB 5

Roumain, Jacques (Jean Baptiste)
1907-1944 . . . . **TCLC 19; BLC**
See also BW 1; CA 117; 125; DAM MULT

Rourke, Constance (Mayfield)
1885-1941 . . . . **TCLC 12**
See also CA 107; YABC 1

Rousseau, Jean-Baptiste 1671-1741 . . . **LC 9**

Rousseau, Jean-Jacques
1712-1778 . . . . . **LC 14; DA; DAB; DAC;**
                                                              WLC
See also DAM MST

Roussel, Raymond 1877-1933 . . . . . **TCLC 20**
See also CA 117

Rovit, Earl (Herbert) 1927- . . . . **CLC 7**
See also CA 5-8R; CANR 12

Rowe, Nicholas 1674-1718 . . . . **LC 8**
See also DLB 84

Rowley, Ames Dorrance
See Lovecraft, H(oward) P(hillips)

Rowson, Susanna Haswell
1762(?)-1824 . . . . **NCLC 5**
See also DLB 37

Roy, Gabrielle
1909-1983 . . . . . **CLC 10, 14; DAB; DAC**
See also CA 53-56; 110; CANR 5;
DAM MST; DLB 68; MTCW

Rozewicz, Tadeusz 1921- . . . . **CLC 9, 23**
See also CA 108; CANR 36; DAM POET;
MTCW

Ruark, Gibbons 1941- . . . . **CLC 3**
See also CA 33-36R; CAAS 23; CANR 14,
31; DLB 120

Rubens, Bernice (Ruth) 1923- . . . **CLC 19, 31**
See also CA 25-28R; CANR 33; DLB 14;
MTCW

Rudkin, (James) David 1936- . . . . . . **CLC 14**
See also CA 89-92; DLB 13

Rudnik, Raphael 1933- . . . . **CLC 7**
See also CA 29-32R

Ruffian, M.
See Hasek, Jaroslav (Matej Frantisek)

Ruiz, Jose Martinez . . . . **CLC 11**
See also Martinez Ruiz, Jose

Rukeyser, Muriel
1913-1980 . . . . **CLC 6, 10, 15, 27; PC 12**
See also CA 5-8R; 93-96; CANR 26;
DAM POET; DLB 48; MTCW;
SATA-Obit 22

Rule, Jane (Vance) 1931- . . . . **CLC 27**
See also CA 25-28R; CAAS 18; CANR 12;
DLB 60

Rulfo, Juan 1918-1986 . . . . **CLC 8, 80; HLC**
See also CA 85-88; 118; CANR 26;
DAM MULT; DLB 113; HW; MTCW

Runeberg, Johan 1804-1877 . . . . . . **NCLC 41**

Santiago, Danny .... CLC 33
See also James, Daniel (Lewis)
See also DLB 122

Santmyer, Helen Hoover
1895-1986 .... CLC 33
See also CA 1-4R; 118; CANR 15, 33;
DLBY 84; MTCW

Santos, Bienvenido N(uqui)
1911-1996 .... CLC 22
See also CA 101; 151; CANR 19, 46;
DAM MULT

Sapper .... TCLC 44
See also McNeile, Herman Cyril

Sappho fl. 6th cent. B.C.-.... CMLC 3; PC 5
See also DAM POET

Sarduy, Severo 1937-1993 .... CLC 6
See also CA 89-92; 142; DLB 113; HW

Sargeson, Frank 1903-1982 .... CLC 31
See also CA 25-28R; 106; CANR 38

Sarmiento, Felix Ruben Garcia
See Dario, Ruben

Saroyan, William
1908-1981 ..... CLC 1, 8, 10, 29, 34, 56;
DA; DAB; DAC; SSC 21; WLC
See also CA 5-8R; 103; CANR 30;
DAM DRAM, MST, NOV; DLB 7, 9, 86;
DLBY 81; MTCW; SATA 23;
SATA-Obit 24

Sarraute, Nathalie
1900- .... CLC 1, 2, 4, 8, 10, 31, 80
See also CA 9-12R; CANR 23; DLB 83;
MTCW

Sarton, (Eleanor) May
1912-1995 .... CLC 4, 14, 49, 91
See also CA 1-4R; 149; CANR 1, 34;
DAM POET; DLB 48; DLBY 81;
INT CANR-34; MTCW; SATA 36;
SATA-Obit 86

Sartre, Jean-Paul
1905-1980 .... CLC 1, 4, 7, 9, 13, 18, 24,
44, 50, 52; DA; DAB; DAC; DC 3; WLC
See also CA 9-12R; 97-100; CANR 21;
DAM DRAM, MST, NOV; DLB 72;
MTCW

Sassoon, Siegfried (Lorraine)
1886-1967 .... CLC 36; DAB; PC 12
See also CA 104; 25-28R; CANR 36;
DAM MST, NOV, POET; DLB 20;
MTCW

Satterfield, Charles
See Pohl, Frederik

Saul, John (W. III) 1942- .... CLC 46
See also AAYA 10; BEST 90:4; CA 81-84;
CANR 16, 40; DAM NOV, POP

Saunders, Caleb
See Heinlein, Robert A(nson)

Saura (Atares), Carlos 1932- .... CLC 20
See also CA 114; 131; HW

Sauser-Hall, Frederic 1887-1961.... CLC 18
See also Cendrars, Blaise
See also CA 102; 93-96; CANR 36; MTCW

Saussure, Ferdinand de
1857-1913 .... TCLC 49

Savage, Catharine
See Brosman, Catharine Savage

Savage, Thomas 1915- .... CLC 40
See also CA 126; 132; CAAS 15; INT 132

Savan, Glenn 19(?)- .... CLC 50

Sayers, Dorothy L(eigh)
1893-1957 .... TCLC 2, 15
See also CA 104; 119; CDBLB 1914-1945;
DAM POP; DLB 10, 36, 77, 100; MTCW

Sayers, Valerie 1952-............ CLC 50
See also CA 134

Sayles, John (Thomas)
1950- .... CLC 7, 10, 14
See also CA 57-60; CANR 41; DLB 44

Scammell, Michael .... CLC 34

Scannell, Vernon 1922- .... CLC 49
See also CA 5-8R; CANR 8, 24; DLB 27;
SATA 59

Scarlett, Susan
See Streatfeild, (Mary) Noel

Schaeffer, Susan Fromberg
1941- .... CLC 6, 11, 22
See also CA 49-52; CANR 18; DLB 28;
MTCW; SATA 22

Schary, Jill
See Robinson, Jill

Schell, Jonathan 1943-........... CLC 35
See also CA 73-76; CANR 12

Schelling, Friedrich Wilhelm Joseph von
1775-1854 .... NCLC 30
See also DLB 90

Schendel, Arthur van 1874-1946 ... TCLC 56

Scherer, Jean-Marie Maurice 1920-
See Rohmer, Eric
See also CA 110

Schevill, James (Erwin) 1920-...... CLC 7
See also CA 5-8R; CAAS 12

Schiller, Friedrich 1759-1805 .... NCLC 39
See also DAM DRAM; DLB 94

Schisgal, Murray (Joseph) 1926-..... CLC 6
See also CA 21-24R; CANR 48

Schlee, Ann 1934-................ CLC 35
See also CA 101; CANR 29; SATA 44;
SATA-Brief 36

Schlegel, August Wilhelm von
1767-1845 .... NCLC 15
See also DLB 94

Schlegel, Friedrich 1772-1829 .... NCLC 45
See also DLB 90

Schlegel, Johann Elias (von)
1719(?)-1749 .... LC 5

Schlesinger, Arthur M(eier), Jr.
1917- .... CLC 84
See also AITN 1; CA 1-4R; CANR 1, 28;
DLB 17; INT CANR-28; MTCW;
SATA 61

Schmidt, Arno (Otto) 1914-1979.... CLC 56
See also CA 128; 109; DLB 69

Schmitz, Aron Hector 1861-1928
See Svevo, Italo
See also CA 104; 122; MTCW

Schnackenberg, Gjertrud 1953-..... CLC 40
See also CA 116; DLB 120

Schneider, Leonard Alfred 1925-1966
See Bruce, Lenny
See also CA 89-92

Schnitzler, Arthur
1862-1931 .... TCLC 4; SSC 15
See also CA 104; DLB 81, 118

Schopenhauer, Arthur
1788-1860 .... NCLC 51
See also DLB 90

Schor, Sandra (M.) 1932(?)-1990 ... CLC 65
See also CA 132

Schorer, Mark 1908-1977 .... CLC 9
See also CA 5-8R; 73-76; CANR 7;
DLB 103

Schrader, Paul (Joseph) 1946-...... CLC 26
See also CA 37-40R; CANR 41; DLB 44

Schreiner, Olive (Emilie Albertina)
1855-1920 .... TCLC 9
See also CA 105; DLB 18, 156

Schulberg, Budd (Wilson)
1914- .... CLC 7, 48
See also CA 25-28R; CANR 19; DLB 6, 26,
28; DLBY 81

Schulz, Bruno
1892-1942 .... TCLC 5, 51; SSC 13
See also CA 115; 123

Schulz, Charles M(onroe) 1922-.... CLC 12
See also CA 9-12R; CANR 6;
INT CANR-6; SATA 10

Schumacher, E(rnst) F(riedrich)
1911-1977 .... CLC 80
See also CA 81-84; 73-76; CANR 34

Schuyler, James Marcus
1923-1991 .... CLC 5, 23
See also CA 101; 134; DAM POET; DLB 5;
INT 101

Schwartz, Delmore (David)
1913-1966 ... CLC 2, 4, 10, 45, 87; PC 8
See also CA 17-18; 25-28R; CANR 35;
CAP 2; DLB 28, 48; MTCW

Schwartz, Ernst
See Ozu, Yasujiro

Schwartz, John Burnham 1965- .... CLC 59
See also CA 132

Schwartz, Lynne Sharon 1939-..... CLC 31
See also CA 103; CANR 44

Schwartz, Muriel A.
See Eliot, T(homas) S(tearns)

Schwarz-Bart, Andre 1928-....... CLC 2, 4
See also CA 89-92

Schwarz-Bart, Simone 1938-........ CLC 7
See also BW 2; CA 97-100

Schwob, (Mayer Andre) Marcel
1867-1905 .... TCLC 20
See also CA 117; DLB 123

Sciascia, Leonardo
1921-1989 .... CLC 8, 9, 41
See also CA 85-88; 130; CANR 35; MTCW

Scoppettone, Sandra 1936-......... CLC 26
See also AAYA 11; CA 5-8R; CANR 41;
SATA 9

Scorsese, Martin 1942- .... CLC 20, 89
See also CA 110; 114; CANR 46

Scotland, Jay
See Jakes, John (William)

Scott, Duncan Campbell
1862-1947 .... TCLC 6; DAC
See also CA 104; DLB 92

Shaw, George Bernard
    1856-1950 ... **TCLC 3, 9, 21; DA; DAB;**
                                    DAC; WLC
    See also Shaw, Bernard
    See also CA 104; 128; CDBLB 1914-1945;
    DAM DRAM, MST; DLB 10, 57;
    MTCW

Shaw, Henry Wheeler
    1818-1885 .... **NCLC 15**
    See also DLB 11

Shaw, Irwin   1913-1984...... **CLC 7, 23, 34**
    See also AITN 1; CA 13-16R; 112;
    CANR 21; CDALB 1941-1968;
    DAM DRAM, POP; DLB 6, 102;
    DLBY 84; MTCW

Shaw, Robert   1927-1978 .... **CLC 5**
    See also AITN 1; CA 1-4R; 81-84;
    CANR 4; DLB 13, 14

Shaw, T. E.
    See Lawrence, T(homas) E(dward)

Shawn, Wallace   1943- .... **CLC 41**
    See also CA 112

Shea, Lisa   1953-................. **CLC 86**
    See also CA 147

Sheed, Wilfrid (John Joseph)
    1930- .... **CLC 2, 4, 10, 53**
    See also CA 65-68; CANR 30; DLB 6;
    MTCW

Sheldon, Alice Hastings Bradley
    1915(?)-1987
    See Tiptree, James, Jr.
    See also CA 108; 122; CANR 34; INT 108;
    MTCW

Sheldon, John
    See Bloch, Robert (Albert)

Shelley, Mary Wollstonecraft (Godwin)
    1797-1851 .... **NCLC 14; DA; DAB;**
                                    DAC; WLC
    See also CDBLB 1789-1832; DAM MST,
    NOV; DLB 110, 116, 159; SATA 29

Shelley, Percy Bysshe
    1792-1822 .... **NCLC 18; DA; DAB;**
                                    DAC; PC 14; WLC
    See also CDBLB 1789-1832; DAM MST,
    POET; DLB 96, 110, 158

Shepard, Jim   1956-............... **CLC 36**
    See also CA 137

Shepard, Lucius   1947-............. **CLC 34**
    See also CA 128; 141

Shepard, Sam
    1943-.... **CLC 4, 6, 17, 34, 41, 44; DC 5**
    See also AAYA 1; CA 69-72; CABS 3;
    CANR 22; DAM DRAM; DLB 7;
    MTCW

Shepherd, Michael
    See Ludlum, Robert

Sherburne, Zoa (Morin)   1912-...... **CLC 30**
    See also AAYA 13; CA 1-4R; CANR 3, 37;
    MAICYA; SAAS 18; SATA 3

Sheridan, Frances   1724-1766........ **LC 7**
    See also DLB 39, 84

Sheridan, Richard Brinsley
    1751-1816 .... **NCLC 5; DA; DAB;**
                                    DAC; DC 1; WLC
    See also CDBLB 1660-1789; DAM DRAM,
    MST; DLB 89

Sherman, Jonathan Marc........... **CLC 55**

Sherman, Martin   1941(?)-......... **CLC 19**
    See also CA 116; 123

Sherwin, Judith Johnson   1936-... **CLC 7, 15**
    See also CA 25-28R; CANR 34

Sherwood, Frances   1940-.......... **CLC 81**
    See also CA 146

Sherwood, Robert E(mmet)
    1896-1955 .... **TCLC 3**
    See also CA 104; DAM DRAM; DLB 7, 26

Shestov, Lev   1866-1938 .... **TCLC 56**

Shevchenko, Taras   1814-1861 .... **NCLC 54**

Shiel, M(atthew) P(hipps)
    1865-1947 .... **TCLC 8**
    See also CA 106; DLB 153

Shields, Carol   1935-......... **CLC 91; DAC**
    See also CA 81-84; CANR 51

Shiga, Naoya   1883-1971... **CLC 33; SSC 23**
    See also CA 101; 33-36R

Shilts, Randy   1951-1994 .... **CLC 85**
    See also CA 115; 127; 144; CANR 45;
    INT 127

Shimazaki, Haruki   1872-1943
    See Shimazaki Toson
    See also CA 105; 134

Shimazaki Toson .... **TCLC 5**
    See also Shimazaki, Haruki

Sholokhov, Mikhail (Aleksandrovich)
    1905-1984 .... **CLC 7, 15**
    See also CA 101; 112; MTCW;
    SATA-Obit 36

Shone, Patric
    See Hanley, James

Shreve, Susan Richards   1939-...... **CLC 23**
    See also CA 49-52; CAAS 5; CANR 5, 38;
    MAICYA; SATA 46; SATA-Brief 41

Shue, Larry   1946-1985............ **CLC 52**
    See also CA 145; 117; DAM DRAM

Shu-Jen, Chou   1881-1936
    See Lu Hsun
    See also CA 104

Shulman, Alix Kates   1932- ...... **CLC 2, 10**
    See also CA 29-32R; CANR 43; SATA 7

Shuster, Joe   1914- .... **CLC 21**

Shute, Nevil...................... **CLC 30**
    See also Norway, Nevil Shute

Shuttle, Penelope (Diane)   1947-..... **CLC 7**
    See also CA 93-96; CANR 39; DLB 14, 40

Sidney, Mary   1561-1621 .... **LC 19**

Sidney, Sir Philip
    1554-1586 ..... **LC 19; DA; DAB; DAC**
    See also CDBLB Before 1660; DAM MST,
    POET; DLB 167

Siegel, Jerome   1914-1996 .... **CLC 21**
    See also CA 116; 151

Siegel, Jerry
    See Siegel, Jerome

Sienkiewicz, Henryk (Adam Alexander Pius)
    1846-1916 .... **TCLC 3**
    See also CA 104; 134

Sierra, Gregorio Martinez
    See Martinez Sierra, Gregorio

Sierra, Maria (de la O'LeJarraga) Martinez
    See Martinez Sierra, Maria (de la
    O'LeJarraga)

Sigal, Clancy   1926-............... **CLC 7**
    See also CA 1-4R

Sigourney, Lydia Howard (Huntley)
    1791-1865 .... **NCLC 21**
    See also DLB 1, 42, 73

Siguenza y Gongora, Carlos de
    1645-1700 .... **LC 8**

Sigurjonsson, Johann   1880-1919... **TCLC 27**

Sikelianos, Angelos   1884-1951 .... **TCLC 39**

Silkin, Jon   1930- .... **CLC 2, 6, 43**
    See also CA 5-8R; CAAS 5; DLB 27

Silko, Leslie (Marmon)
    1948- .... **CLC 23, 74; DA; DAC**
    See also AAYA 14; CA 115; 122;
    CANR 45; DAM MST, MULT, POP;
    DLB 143; NNAL

Sillanpaa, Frans Eemil   1888-1964... **CLC 19**
    See also CA 129; 93-96; MTCW

Sillitoe, Alan
    1928-.......... **CLC 1, 3, 6, 10, 19, 57**
    See also AITN 1; CA 9-12R; CAAS 2;
    CANR 8, 26; CDBLB 1960 to Present;
    DLB 14, 139; MTCW; SATA 61

Silone, Ignazio   1900-1978 .... **CLC 4**
    See also CA 25-28; 81-84; CANR 34;
    CAP 2; MTCW

Silver, Joan Micklin   1935- .... **CLC 20**
    See also CA 114; 121; INT 121

Silver, Nicholas
    See Faust, Frederick (Schiller)

Silverberg, Robert   1935- .... **CLC 7**
    See also CA 1-4R; CAAS 3; CANR 1, 20,
    36; DAM POP; DLB 8; INT CANR-20;
    MAICYA; MTCW; SATA 13

Silverstein, Alvin   1933- .... **CLC 17**
    See also CA 49-52; CANR 2; CLR 25;
    JRDA; MAICYA; SATA 8, 69

Silverstein, Virginia B(arbara Opshelor)
    1937-...................... **CLC 17**
    See also CA 49-52; CANR 2; CLR 25;
    JRDA; MAICYA; SATA 8, 69

Sim, Georges
    See Simenon, Georges (Jacques Christian)

Simak, Clifford D(onald)
    1904-1988 .... **CLC 1, 55**
    See also CA 1-4R; 125; CANR 1, 35;
    DLB 8; MTCW; SATA-Obit 56

Simenon, Georges (Jacques Christian)
    1903-1989 .... **CLC 1, 2, 3, 8, 18, 47**
    See also CA 85-88; 129; CANR 35;
    DAM POP; DLB 72; DLBY 89; MTCW

Simic, Charles   1938-... **CLC 6, 9, 22, 49, 68**
    See also CA 29-32R; CAAS 4; CANR 12,
    33, 52; DAM POET; DLB 105

Simmel, Georg   1858-1918 .... **TCLC 64**

Simmons, Charles (Paul)   1924-..... **CLC 57**
    See also CA 89-92; INT 89-92

Simmons, Dan   1948-............... **CLC 44**
    See also AAYA 16; CA 138; CANR 53;
    DAM POP

Snow, C(harles) P(ercy)
　　1905-1980 . . . . **CLC 1, 4, 6, 9, 13, 19**
　　See also CA 5-8R; 101; CANR 28;
　　　CDBLB 1945-1960; DAM NOV; DLB 15,
　　　77; MTCW

Snow, Frances Compton
　　See Adams, Henry (Brooks)

Snyder, Gary (Sherman)
　　1930- . . . . **CLC 1, 2, 5, 9, 32**
　　See also CA 17-20R; CANR 30;
　　　DAM POET; DLB 5, 16, 165

Snyder, Zilpha Keatley 1927- . . . . . . **CLC 17**
　　See also AAYA 15; CA 9-12R; CANR 38;
　　　CLR 31; JRDA; MAICYA; SAAS 2;
　　　SATA 1, 28, 75

Soares, Bernardo
　　See Pessoa, Fernando (Antonio Nogueira)

Sobh, A.
　　See Shamlu, Ahmad

Sobol, Joshua . . . . **CLC 60**

Soderberg, Hjalmar 1869-1941 . . . . **TCLC 39**

Sodergran, Edith (Irene)
　　See Soedergran, Edith (Irene)

Soedergran, Edith (Irene)
　　1892-1923 . . . . **TCLC 31**

Softly, Edgar
　　See Lovecraft, H(oward) P(hillips)

Softly, Edward
　　See Lovecraft, H(oward) P(hillips)

Sokolov, Raymond 1941- . . . . **CLC 7**
　　See also CA 85-88

Solo, Jay
　　See Ellison, Harlan (Jay)

Sologub, Fyodor . . . . **TCLC 9**
　　See also Teternikov, Fyodor Kuzmich

Solomons, Ikey Esquir
　　See Thackeray, William Makepeace

Solomos, Dionysios 1798-1857 . . . **NCLC 15**

Solwoska, Mara
　　See French, Marilyn

Solzhenitsyn, Aleksandr I(sayevich)
　　1918- . . . . . . **CLC 1, 2, 4, 7, 9, 10, 18, 26,**
　　　　　　　34, 78; DA; DAB; DAC; WLC
　　See also AITN 1; CA 69-72; CANR 40;
　　　DAM MST, NOV; MTCW

Somers, Jane
　　See Lessing, Doris (May)

Somerville, Edith 1858-1949 . . . . . . **TCLC 51**
　　See also DLB 135

Somerville & Ross
　　See Martin, Violet Florence; Somerville,
　　　Edith

Sommer, Scott 1951- . . . . **CLC 25**
　　See also CA 106

Sondheim, Stephen (Joshua)
　　1930- . . . . **CLC 30, 39**
　　See also AAYA 11; CA 103; CANR 47;
　　　DAM DRAM

Sontag, Susan 1933- . . . **CLC 1, 2, 10, 13, 31**
　　See also CA 17-20R; CANR 25, 51;
　　　DAM POP; DLB 2, 67; MTCW

Sophocles
　　496(?)B.C.-406(?)B.C. . . . . **CMLC 2; DA;**
　　　　　　　　　　　DAB; DAC; DC 1
　　See also DAM DRAM, MST

Sordello 1189-1269 . . . . **CMLC 15**

Sorel, Julia
　　See Drexler, Rosalyn

Sorrentino, Gilbert
　　1929- . . . . **CLC 3, 7, 14, 22, 40**
　　See also CA 77-80; CANR 14, 33; DLB 5;
　　　DLBY 80; INT CANR-14

Soto, Gary 1952- . . . . **CLC 32, 80; HLC**
　　See also AAYA 10; CA 119; 125;
　　　CANR 50; CLR 38; DAM MULT;
　　　DLB 82; HW; INT 125; JRDA; SATA 80

Soupault, Philippe 1897-1990 . . . . . . **CLC 68**
　　See also CA 116; 147; 131

Souster, (Holmes) Raymond
　　1921- . . . . **CLC 5, 14; DAC**
　　See also CA 13-16R; CAAS 14; CANR 13,
　　　29, 53; DAM POET; DLB 88; SATA 63

Southern, Terry 1924(?)-1995 . . . . **CLC 7**
　　See also CA 1-4R; 150; CANR 1; DLB 2

Southey, Robert 1774-1843 . . . . **NCLC 8**
　　See also DLB 93, 107, 142; SATA 54

Southworth, Emma Dorothy Eliza Nevitte
　　1819-1899 . . . . **NCLC 26**

Souza, Ernest
　　See Scott, Evelyn

Soyinka, Wole
　　1934- . . . . **CLC 3, 5, 14, 36, 44; BLC;**
　　　　　　　DA; DAB; DAC; DC 2; WLC
　　See also BW 2; CA 13-16R; CANR 27, 39;
　　　DAM DRAM, MST, MULT; DLB 125;
　　　MTCW

Spackman, W(illiam) M(ode)
　　1905-1990 . . . . **CLC 46**
　　See also CA 81-84; 132

Spacks, Barry 1931- . . . . **CLC 14**
　　See also CA 29-32R; CANR 33; DLB 105

Spanidou, Irini 1946- . . . . **CLC 44**

Spark, Muriel (Sarah)
　　1918- . . . . . **CLC 2, 3, 5, 8, 13, 18, 40, 94;**
　　　　　　　　DAB; DAC; SSC 10
　　See also CA 5-8R; CANR 12, 36;
　　　CDBLB 1945-1960; DAM MST, NOV;
　　　DLB 15, 139; INT CANR-12; MTCW

Spaulding, Douglas
　　See Bradbury, Ray (Douglas)

Spaulding, Leonard
　　See Bradbury, Ray (Douglas)

Spence, J. A. D.
　　See Eliot, T(homas) S(tearns)

Spencer, Elizabeth 1921- . . . . **CLC 22**
　　See also CA 13-16R; CANR 32; DLB 6;
　　　MTCW; SATA 14

Spencer, Leonard G.
　　See Silverberg, Robert

Spencer, Scott 1945- . . . . **CLC 30**
　　See also CA 113; CANR 51; DLBY 86

Spender, Stephen (Harold)
　　1909-1995 . . . . . . **CLC 1, 2, 5, 10, 41, 91**
　　See also CA 9-12R; 149; CANR 31;
　　　CDBLB 1945-1960; DAM POET;
　　　DLB 20; MTCW

Spengler, Oswald (Arnold Gottfried)
　　1880-1936 . . . . **TCLC 25**
　　See also CA 118

Spenser, Edmund
　　1552(?)-1599 . . . . **LC 5; DA; DAB; DAC;**
　　　　　　　　　　PC 8; WLC
　　See also CDBLB Before 1660; DAM MST,
　　　POET; DLB 167

Spicer, Jack 1925-1965 . . . . . . **CLC 8, 18, 72**
　　See also CA 85-88; DAM POET; DLB 5, 16

Spiegelman, Art 1948- . . . . **CLC 76**
　　See also AAYA 10; CA 125; CANR 41

Spielberg, Peter 1929- . . . . **CLC 6**
　　See also CA 5-8R; CANR 4, 48; DLBY 81

Spielberg, Steven 1947- . . . . **CLC 20**
　　See also AAYA 8; CA 77-80; CANR 32;
　　　SATA 32

Spillane, Frank Morrison 1918-
　　See Spillane, Mickey
　　See also CA 25-28R; CANR 28; MTCW;
　　　SATA 66

Spillane, Mickey . . . . **CLC 3, 13**
　　See also Spillane, Frank Morrison

Spinoza, Benedictus de 1632-1677 . . . . **LC 9**

Spinrad, Norman (Richard) 1940- . . . **CLC 46**
　　See also CA 37-40R; CAAS 19; CANR 20;
　　　DLB 8; INT CANR-20

Spitteler, Carl (Friedrich Georg)
　　1845-1924 . . . . **TCLC 12**
　　See also CA 109; DLB 129

Spivack, Kathleen (Romola Drucker)
　　1938- . . . . **CLC 6**
　　See also CA 49-52

Spoto, Donald 1941- . . . . **CLC 39**
　　See also CA 65-68; CANR 11

Springsteen, Bruce (F.) 1949- . . . . . . **CLC 17**
　　See also CA 111

Spurling, Hilary 1940- . . . . **CLC 34**
　　See also CA 104; CANR 25, 52

Spyker, John Howland
　　See Elman, Richard

Squires, (James) Radcliffe
　　1917-1993 . . . . **CLC 51**
　　See also CA 1-4R; 140; CANR 6, 21

Srivastava, Dhanpat Rai 1880(?)-1936
　　See Premchand
　　See also CA 118

Stacy, Donald
　　See Pohl, Frederik

Stael, Germaine de
　　See Stael-Holstein, Anne Louise Germaine
　　　Necker Baronn
　　See also DLB 119

Stael-Holstein, Anne Louise Germaine Necker
　　Baronn 1766-1817 . . . . **NCLC 3**
　　See also Stael, Germaine de

Stafford, Jean 1915-1979 . . . **CLC 4, 7, 19, 68**
　　See also CA 1-4R; 85-88; CANR 3; DLB 2;
　　　MTCW; SATA-Obit 22

Stafford, William (Edgar)
　　1914-1993 . . . . **CLC 4, 7, 29**
　　See also CA 5-8R; 142; CAAS 3; CANR 5,
　　　22; DAM POET; DLB 5; INT CANR-22

Staines, Trevor
　　See Brunner, John (Kilian Houston)

Stowe, Harriet (Elizabeth) Beecher
1811-1896 ..... **NCLC 3, 50; DA; DAB; DAC; WLC**
See also CDALB 1865-1917; DAM MST, NOV; DLB 1, 12, 42, 74; JRDA; MAICYA; YABC 1

Strachey, (Giles) Lytton
1880-1932 .... **TCLC 12**
See also CA 110; DLB 149; DLBD 10

Strand, Mark 1934- ...... **CLC 6, 18, 41, 71**
See also CA 21-24R; CANR 40; DAM POET; DLB 5; SATA 41

Straub, Peter (Francis) 1943- ..... **CLC 28**
See also BEST 89:1; CA 85-88; CANR 28; DAM POP; DLBY 84; MTCW

Strauss, Botho 1944- .... **CLC 22**
See also DLB 124

Streatfeild, (Mary) Noel
1895(?)-1986 .... **CLC 21**
See also CA 81-84; 120; CANR 31; CLR 17; DLB 160; MAICYA; SATA 20; SATA-Obit 48

Stribling, T(homas) S(igismund)
1881-1965 .... **CLC 23**
See also CA 107; DLB 9

Strindberg, (Johan) August
1849-1912 ...... **TCLC 1, 8, 21, 47; DA; DAB; DAC; WLC**
See also CA 104; 135; DAM DRAM, MST

Stringer, Arthur 1874-1950 ...... **TCLC 37**
See also DLB 92

Stringer, David
See Roberts, Keith (John Kingston)

Strugatskii, Arkadii (Natanovich)
1925-1991 .... **CLC 27**
See also CA 106; 135

Strugatskii, Boris (Natanovich)
1933- .... **CLC 27**
See also CA 106

Strummer, Joe 1953(?)- .... **CLC 30**

Stuart, Don A.
See Campbell, John W(ood, Jr.)

Stuart, Ian
See MacLean, Alistair (Stuart)

Stuart, Jesse (Hilton)
1906-1984 .... **CLC 1, 8, 11, 14, 34**
See also CA 5-8R; 112; CANR 31; DLB 9, 48, 102; DLBY 84; SATA 2; SATA-Obit 36

Sturgeon, Theodore (Hamilton)
1918-1985 .... **CLC 22, 39**
See also Queen, Ellery
See also CA 81-84; 116; CANR 32; DLB 8; DLBY 85; MTCW

Sturges, Preston 1898-1959 ...... **TCLC 48**
See also CA 114; 149; DLB 26

Styron, William
1925- .... **CLC 1, 3, 5, 11, 15, 60**
See also BEST 90:4; CA 5-8R; CANR 6, 33; CDALB 1968-1988; DAM NOV, POP; DLB 2, 143; DLBY 80; INT CANR-6; MTCW

Suarez Lynch, B.
See Bioy Casares, Adolfo; Borges, Jorge Luis

Su Chien 1884-1918
See Su Man-shu
See also CA 123

Suckow, Ruth 1892-1960 .... **SSC 18**
See also CA 113; DLB 9, 102

Sudermann, Hermann 1857-1928 .. **TCLC 15**
See also CA 107; DLB 118

Sue, Eugene 1804-1857 .... **NCLC 1**
See also DLB 119

Sueskind, Patrick 1949- .... **CLC 44**
See also Suskind, Patrick

Sukenick, Ronald 1932- .... **CLC 3, 4, 6, 48**
See also CA 25-28R; CAAS 8; CANR 32; DLBY 81

Suknaski, Andrew 1942- .... **CLC 19**
See also CA 101; DLB 53

Sullivan, Vernon
See Vian, Boris

Sully Prudhomme 1839-1907 ..... **TCLC 31**

Su Man-shu .... **TCLC 24**
See also Su Chien

Summerforest, Ivy B.
See Kirkup, James

Summers, Andrew James 1942- ..... **CLC 26**

Summers, Andy
See Summers, Andrew James

Summers, Hollis (Spurgeon, Jr.)
1916- .... **CLC 10**
See also CA 5-8R; CANR 3; DLB 6

Summers, (Alphonsus Joseph-Mary Augustus)
Montague 1880-1948 .... **TCLC 16**
See also CA 118

Sumner, Gordon Matthew 1951- .... **CLC 26**

Surtees, Robert Smith
1803-1864 .... **NCLC 14**
See also DLB 21

Susann, Jacqueline 1921-1974 ...... **CLC 3**
See also AITN 1; CA 65-68; 53-56; MTCW

Su Shih 1036-1101 .... **CMLC 15**

Suskind, Patrick
See Sueskind, Patrick
See also CA 145

Sutcliff, Rosemary
1920-1992 .... **CLC 26; DAB; DAC**
See also AAYA 10; CA 5-8R; 139; CANR 37; CLR 1, 37; DAM MST, POP; JRDA; MAICYA; SATA 6, 44, 78; SATA-Obit 73

Sutro, Alfred 1863-1933 .... **TCLC 6**
See also CA 105; DLB 10

Sutton, Henry
See Slavitt, David R(ytman)

Svevo, Italo .... **TCLC 2, 35**
See also Schmitz, Aron Hector

Swados, Elizabeth (A.) 1951- .... **CLC 12**
See also CA 97-100; CANR 49; INT 97-100

Swados, Harvey 1920-1972 .... **CLC 5**
See also CA 5-8R; 37-40R; CANR 6; DLB 2

Swan, Gladys 1934- .... **CLC 69**
See also CA 101; CANR 17, 39

Swarthout, Glendon (Fred)
1918-1992 .... **CLC 35**
See also CA 1-4R; 139; CANR 1, 47; SATA 26

Sweet, Sarah C.
See Jewett, (Theodora) Sarah Orne

Swenson, May
1919-1989 .... **CLC 4, 14, 61; DA; DAB; DAC; PC 14**
See also CA 5-8R; 130; CANR 36; DAM MST, POET; DLB 5; MTCW; SATA 15

Swift, Augustus
See Lovecraft, H(oward) P(hillips)

Swift, Graham (Colin) 1949- .... **CLC 41, 88**
See also CA 117; 122; CANR 46

Swift, Jonathan
1667-1745 ...... **LC 1; DA; DAB; DAC; PC 9; WLC**
See also CDBLB 1660-1789; DAM MST, NOV, POET; DLB 39, 95, 101; SATA 19

Swinburne, Algernon Charles
1837-1909 ...... **TCLC 8, 36; DA; DAB; DAC; WLC**
See also CA 105; 140; CDBLB 1832-1890; DAM MST, POET; DLB 35, 57

Swinfen, Ann .... **CLC 34**

Swinnerton, Frank Arthur
1884-1982 .... **CLC 31**
See also CA 108; DLB 34

Swithen, John
See King, Stephen (Edwin)

Sylvia
See Ashton-Warner, Sylvia (Constance)

Symmes, Robert Edward
See Duncan, Robert (Edward)

Symonds, John Addington
1840-1893 .... **NCLC 34**
See also DLB 57, 144

Symons, Arthur 1865-1945 .... **TCLC 11**
See also CA 107; DLB 19, 57, 149

Symons, Julian (Gustave)
1912-1994 .... **CLC 2, 14, 32**
See also CA 49-52; 147; CAAS 3; CANR 3, 33; DLB 87, 155; DLBY 92; MTCW

Synge, (Edmund) J(ohn) M(illington)
1871-1909 .... **TCLC 6, 37; DC 2**
See also CA 104; 141; CDBLB 1890-1914; DAM DRAM; DLB 10, 19

Syruc, J.
See Milosz, Czeslaw

Szirtes, George 1948- .... **CLC 46**
See also CA 109; CANR 27

Tabori, George 1914- .... **CLC 19**
See also CA 49-52; CANR 4

Tagore, Rabindranath
1861-1941 .... **TCLC 3, 53; PC 8**
See also CA 104; 120; DAM DRAM, POET; MTCW

Taine, Hippolyte Adolphe
1828-1893 .... **NCLC 15**

Talese, Gay 1932- .... **CLC 37**
See also AITN 1; CA 1-4R; CANR 9; INT CANR-9; MTCW

Author Index

Vance, John Holbrook 1916-
See Queen, Ellery; Vance, Jack
See also CA 29-32R; CANR 17; MTCW

Van Den Bogarde, Derek Jules Gaspard Ulric Niven 1921-
See Bogarde, Dirk
See also CA 77-80

Vandenburgh, Jane . . . . **CLC 59**

Vanderhaeghe, Guy 1951- . . . . **CLC 41**
See also CA 113

van der Post, Laurens (Jan) 1906- . . . **CLC 5**
See also CA 5-8R; CANR 35

van de Wetering, Janwillem 1931- . . **CLC 47**
See also CA 49-52; CANR 4

Van Dine, S. S. . . . . **TCLC 23**
See also Wright, Willard Huntington

Van Doren, Carl (Clinton)
1885-1950 . . . . **TCLC 18**
See also CA 111

Van Doren, Mark 1894-1972 . . . . . **CLC 6, 10**
See also CA 1-4R; 37-40R; CANR 3;
DLB 45; MTCW

Van Druten, John (William)
1901-1957 . . . . **TCLC 2**
See also CA 104; DLB 10

Van Duyn, Mona (Jane)
1921- . . . . **CLC 3, 7, 63**
See also CA 9-12R; CANR 7, 38;
DAM POET; DLB 5

Van Dyne, Edith
See Baum, L(yman) Frank

van Itallie, Jean-Claude 1936- . . . . **CLC 3**
See also CA 45-48; CAAS 2; CANR 1, 48;
DLB 7

van Ostaijen, Paul 1896-1928 . . . . . **TCLC 33**

Van Peebles, Melvin 1932- . . . . . . **CLC 2, 20**
See also BW 2; CA 85-88; CANR 27;
DAM MULT

Vansittart, Peter 1920- . . . . **CLC 42**
See also CA 1-4R; CANR 3, 49

Van Vechten, Carl 1880-1964 . . . . . . **CLC 33**
See also CA 89-92; DLB 4, 9, 51

Van Vogt, A(lfred) E(lton) 1912- . . . . . **CLC 1**
See also CA 21-24R; CANR 28; DLB 8;
SATA 14

Varda, Agnes 1928- . . . . **CLC 16**
See also CA 116; 122

Vargas Llosa, (Jorge) Mario (Pedro)
1936- . . . . **CLC 3, 6, 9, 10, 15, 31, 42, 85;
DA; DAB; DAC; HLC**
See also CA 73-76; CANR 18, 32, 42;
DAM MST, MULT, NOV; DLB 145;
HW; MTCW

Vasiliu, Gheorghe 1881-1957
See Bacovia, George
See also CA 123

Vassa, Gustavus
See Equiano, Olaudah

Vassilikos, Vassilis 1933- . . . . **CLC 4, 8**
See also CA 81-84

Vaughan, Henry 1621-1695 . . . . **LC 27**
See also DLB 131

Vaughn, Stephanie . . . . **CLC 62**

Vazov, Ivan (Minchov)
1850-1921 . . . . **TCLC 25**
See also CA 121; DLB 147

Veblen, Thorstein (Bunde)
1857-1929 . . . . **TCLC 31**
See also CA 115

Vega, Lope de 1562-1635 . . . . **LC 23**

Venison, Alfred
See Pound, Ezra (Weston Loomis)

Verdi, Marie de
See Mencken, H(enry) L(ouis)

Verdu, Matilde
See Cela, Camilo Jose

Verga, Giovanni (Carmelo)
1840-1922 . . . . **TCLC 3; SSC 21**
See also CA 104; 123

Vergil
70B.C.-19B.C. . . . . . **CMLC 9; DA; DAB;
DAC; PC 12**
See also DAM MST, POET

Verhaeren, Emile (Adolphe Gustave)
1855-1916 . . . . **TCLC 12**
See also CA 109

Verlaine, Paul (Marie)
1844-1896 . . . . **NCLC 2, 51; PC 2**
See also DAM POET

Verne, Jules (Gabriel)
1828-1905 . . . . **TCLC 6, 52**
See also AAYA 16; CA 110; 131; DLB 123;
JRDA; MAICYA; SATA 21

Very, Jones 1813-1880 . . . . **NCLC 9**
See also DLB 1

Vesaas, Tarjei 1897-1970 . . . . **CLC 48**
See also CA 29-32R

Vialis, Gaston
See Simenon, Georges (Jacques Christian)

Vian, Boris 1920-1959 . . . . **TCLC 9**
See also CA 106; DLB 72

Viaud, (Louis Marie) Julien 1850-1923
See Loti, Pierre
See also CA 107

Vicar, Henry
See Felsen, Henry Gregor

Vicker, Angus
See Felsen, Henry Gregor

Vidal, Gore
1925- . . . . . **CLC 2, 4, 6, 8, 10, 22, 33, 72**
See also AITN 1; BEST 90:2; CA 5-8R;
CANR 13, 45; DAM NOV, POP; DLB 6,
152; INT CANR-13; MTCW

Viereck, Peter (Robert Edwin)
1916- . . . . **CLC 4**
See also CA 1-4R; CANR 1, 47; DLB 5

Vigny, Alfred (Victor) de
1797-1863 . . . . **NCLC 7**
See also DAM POET; DLB 119

Vilakazi, Benedict Wallet
1906-1947 . . . . **TCLC 37**

**Villiers de l'Isle Adam, Jean Marie Mathias
Philippe Auguste Comte**
1838-1889 . . . . **NCLC 3; SSC 14**
See also DLB 123

Villon, Francois 1431-1463(?) . . . . **PC 13**

Vinci, Leonardo da 1452-1519 . . . . . . **LC 12**

Vine, Barbara . . . . **CLC 50**
See also Rendell, Ruth (Barbara)
See also BEST 90:4

Vinge, Joan D(ennison) 1948- . . . . . . **CLC 30**
See also CA 93-96; SATA 36

Violis, G.
See Simenon, Georges (Jacques Christian)

Visconti, Luchino 1906-1976 . . . . **CLC 16**
See also CA 81-84; 65-68; CANR 39

Vittorini, Elio 1908-1966 . . . . . . **CLC 6, 9, 14**
See also CA 133; 25-28R

Vizinczey, Stephen 1933- . . . . **CLC 40**
See also CA 128; INT 128

Vliet, R(ussell) G(ordon)
1929-1984 . . . . **CLC 22**
See also CA 37-40R; 112; CANR 18

Vogau, Boris Andreyevich 1894-1937(?)
See Pilnyak, Boris
See also CA 123

Vogel, Paula A(nne) 1951- . . . . **CLC 76**
See also CA 108

Voight, Ellen Bryant 1943- . . . . **CLC 54**
See also CA 69-72; CANR 11, 29; DLB 120

Voigt, Cynthia 1942- . . . . **CLC 30**
See also AAYA 3; CA 106; CANR 18, 37,
40; CLR 13; INT CANR-18; JRDA;
MAICYA; SATA 48, 79; SATA-Brief 33

Voinovich, Vladimir (Nikolaevich)
1932- . . . . **CLC 10, 49**
See also CA 81-84; CAAS 12; CANR 33;
MTCW

Vollmann, William T. 1959- . . . . **CLC 89**
See also CA 134; DAM NOV, POP

Voloshinov, V. N.
See Bakhtin, Mikhail Mikhailovich

Voltaire
1694-1778 . . . . . **LC 14; DA; DAB; DAC;
SSC 12; WLC**
See also DAM DRAM, MST

von Daeniken, Erich 1935- . . . . **CLC 30**
See also AITN 1; CA 37-40R; CANR 17,
44

von Daniken, Erich
See von Daeniken, Erich

von Heidenstam, (Carl Gustaf) Verner
See Heidenstam, (Carl Gustaf) Verner von

von Heyse, Paul (Johann Ludwig)
See Heyse, Paul (Johann Ludwig von)

von Hofmannsthal, Hugo
See Hofmannsthal, Hugo von

von Horvath, Odon
See Horvath, Oedoen von

von Horvath, Oedoen
See Horvath, Oedoen von

von Liliencron, (Friedrich Adolf Axel) Detlev
See Liliencron, (Friedrich Adolf Axel)
Detlev von

Vonnegut, Kurt, Jr.
1922- . . . . . . **CLC 1, 2, 3, 4, 5, 8, 12, 22,
40, 60; DA; DAB; DAC; SSC 8; WLC**
See also AAYA 6; AITN 1; BEST 90:4;
CA 1-4R; CANR 1, 25, 49;
CDALB 1968-1988; DAM MST, NOV,
POP; DLB 2, 8, 152; DLBD 3; DLBY 80;
MTCW

Wassermann, (Karl) Jakob
1873-1934 . . . . **TCLC 6**
See also CA 104; DLB 66

Wasserstein, Wendy
1950- . . . . **CLC 32, 59, 90; DC 4**
See also CA 121; 129; CABS 3; CANR 53;
DAM DRAM; INT 129

Waterhouse, Keith (Spencer)
1929- . . . . **CLC 47**
See also CA 5-8R; CANR 38; DLB 13, 15;
MTCW

Waters, Frank (Joseph)
1902-1995 . . . . **CLC 88**
See also CA 5-8R; 149; CAAS 13; CANR 3,
18; DLBY 86

Waters, Roger　1944- . . . . **CLC 35**

Watkins, Frances Ellen
See Harper, Frances Ellen Watkins

Watkins, Gerrold
See Malzberg, Barry N(athaniel)

Watkins, Gloria　1955(?)-
See hooks, bell
See also BW 2; CA 143

Watkins, Paul　1964- . . . . **CLC 55**
See also CA 132

Watkins, Vernon Phillips
1906-1967 . . . . **CLC 43**
See also CA 9-10; 25-28R; CAP 1; DLB 20

Watson, Irving S.
See Mencken, H(enry) L(ouis)

Watson, John H.
See Farmer, Philip Jose

Watson, Richard F.
See Silverberg, Robert

Waugh, Auberon (Alexander)　1939- . . **CLC 7**
See also CA 45-48; CANR 6, 22; DLB 14

Waugh, Evelyn (Arthur St. John)
1903-1966 . . . . . . **CLC 1, 3, 8, 13, 19, 27,
44; DA; DAB; DAC; WLC**
See also CA 85-88; 25-28R; CANR 22;
CDBLB 1914-1945; DAM MST, NOV,
POP; DLB 15, 162; MTCW

Waugh, Harriet　1944- . . . . **CLC 6**
See also CA 85-88; CANR 22

Ways, C. R.
See Blount, Roy (Alton), Jr.

Waystaff, Simon
See Swift, Jonathan

Webb, (Martha) Beatrice (Potter)
1858-1943 . . . . **TCLC 22**
See also Potter, Beatrice
See also CA 117

Webb, Charles (Richard)　1939- . . . . . . **CLC 7**
See also CA 25-28R

Webb, James H(enry), Jr.　1946- . . . . **CLC 22**
See also CA 81-84

Webb, Mary (Gladys Meredith)
1881-1927 . . . . **TCLC 24**
See also CA 123; DLB 34

Webb, Mrs. Sidney
See Webb, (Martha) Beatrice (Potter)

Webb, Phyllis　1927- . . . . **CLC 18**
See also CA 104; CANR 23; DLB 53

Webb, Sidney (James)
1859-1947 . . . . **TCLC 22**
See also CA 117

Webber, Andrew Lloyd . . . . **CLC 21**
See also Lloyd Webber, Andrew

Weber, Lenora Mattingly
1895-1971 . . . . **CLC 12**
See also CA 19-20; 29-32R; CAP 1;
SATA 2; SATA-Obit 26

Webster, John
1579(?)-1634(?) . . . . . . **LC 33; DA; DAB;
DAC; DC 2; WLC**
See also CDBLB Before 1660;
DAM DRAM, MST; DLB 58

Webster, Noah　1758-1843 . . . . . . **NCLC 30**

Wedekind, (Benjamin) Frank(lin)
1864-1918 . . . . **TCLC 7**
See also CA 104; DAM DRAM; DLB 118

Weidman, Jerome　1913- . . . . **CLC 7**
See also AITN 2; CA 1-4R; CANR 1;
DLB 28

Weil, Simone (Adolphine)
1909-1943 . . . . **TCLC 23**
See also CA 117

Weinstein, Nathan
See West, Nathanael

Weinstein, Nathan von Wallenstein
See West, Nathanael

Weir, Peter (Lindsay)　1944- . . . . **CLC 20**
See also CA 113; 123

Weiss, Peter (Ulrich)
1916-1982 . . . . **CLC 3, 15, 51**
See also CA 45-48; 106; CANR 3;
DAM DRAM; DLB 69, 124

Weiss, Theodore (Russell)
1916- . . . . **CLC 3, 8, 14**
See also CA 9-12R; CAAS 2; CANR 46;
DLB 5

Welch, (Maurice) Denton
1915-1948 . . . . **TCLC 22**
See also CA 121; 148

Welch, James　1940- . . . . **CLC 6, 14, 52**
See also CA 85-88; CANR 42;
DAM MULT, POP; NNAL

Weldon, Fay
1933- . . . . **CLC 6, 9, 11, 19, 36, 59**
See also CA 21-24R; CANR 16, 46;
CDBLB 1960 to Present; DAM POP;
DLB 14; INT CANR-16; MTCW

Wellek, Rene　1903-1995 . . . . **CLC 28**
See also CA 5-8R; 150; CAAS 7; CANR 8;
DLB 63; INT CANR-8

Weller, Michael　1942- . . . . . . **CLC 10, 53**
See also CA 85-88

Weller, Paul　1958- . . . . **CLC 26**

Wellershoff, Dieter　1925- . . . . **CLC 46**
See also CA 89-92; CANR 16, 37

Welles, (George) Orson
1915-1985 . . . . **CLC 20, 80**
See also CA 93-96; 117

Wellman, Mac　1945- . . . . **CLC 65**

Wellman, Manly Wade　1903-1986 . . **CLC 49**
See also CA 1-4R; 118; CANR 6, 16, 44;
SATA 6; SATA-Obit 47

Wells, Carolyn　1869(?)-1942 . . . . . . **TCLC 35**
See also CA 113; DLB 11

Wells, H(erbert) G(eorge)
1866-1946 . . . . **TCLC 6, 12, 19; DA;
DAB; DAC; SSC 6; WLC**
See also AAYA 18; CA 110; 121;
CDBLB 1914-1945; DAM MST, NOV;
DLB 34, 70, 156; MTCW; SATA 20

Wells, Rosemary　1943- . . . . **CLC 12**
See also AAYA 13; CA 85-88; CANR 48;
CLR 16; MAICYA; SAAS 1; SATA 18,
69

Welty, Eudora
1909- . . . . . . **CLC 1, 2, 5, 14, 22, 33; DA;
DAB; DAC; SSC 1; WLC**
See also CA 9-12R; CABS 1; CANR 32;
CDALB 1941-1968; DAM MST, NOV;
DLB 2, 102, 143; DLBD 12; DLBY 87;
MTCW

Wen I-to　1899-1946 . . . . **TCLC 28**

Wentworth, Robert
See Hamilton, Edmond

Werfel, Franz (V.)　1890-1945 . . . . . . **TCLC 8**
See also CA 104; DLB 81, 124

Wergeland, Henrik Arnold
1808-1845 . . . . **NCLC 5**

Wersba, Barbara　1932- . . . . **CLC 30**
See also AAYA 2; CA 29-32R; CANR 16,
38; CLR 3; DLB 52; JRDA; MAICYA;
SAAS 2; SATA 1, 58

Wertmueller, Lina　1928- . . . . **CLC 16**
See also CA 97-100; CANR 39

Wescott, Glenway　1901-1987 . . . . **CLC 13**
See also CA 13-16R; 121; CANR 23;
DLB 4, 9, 102

Wesker, Arnold　1932- . . **CLC 3, 5, 42; DAB**
See also CA 1-4R; CAAS 7; CANR 1, 33;
CDBLB 1960 to Present; DAM DRAM;
DLB 13; MTCW

Wesley, Richard (Errol)　1945- . . . . **CLC 7**
See also BW 1; CA 57-60; CANR 27;
DLB 38

Wessel, Johan Herman　1742-1785 . . . . **LC 7**

West, Anthony (Panther)
1914-1987 . . . . **CLC 50**
See also CA 45-48; 124; CANR 3, 19;
DLB 15

West, C. P.
See Wodehouse, P(elham) G(renville)

West, (Mary) Jessamyn
1902-1984 . . . . **CLC 7, 17**
See also CA 9-12R; 112; CANR 27; DLB 6;
DLBY 84; MTCW; SATA-Obit 37

West, Morris L(anglo)　1916- . . . . . **CLC 6, 33**
See also CA 5-8R; CANR 24, 49; MTCW

West, Nathanael
1903-1940 . . . . . **TCLC 1, 14, 44; SSC 16**
See also CA 104; 125; CDALB 1929-1941;
DLB 4, 9, 28; MTCW

West, Owen
See Koontz, Dean R(ay)

West, Paul　1930- . . . . **CLC 7, 14**
See also CA 13-16R; CAAS 7; CANR 22,
53; DLB 14; INT CANR-22

Williams, John A(lfred)
1925- .... **CLC 5, 13; BLC**
See also BW 2; CA 53-56; CAAS 3;
CANR 6, 26, 51; DAM MULT; DLB 2,
33; INT CANR-6

Williams, Jonathan (Chamberlain)
1929- .... **CLC 13**
See also CA 9-12R; CAAS 12; CANR 8;
DLB 5

Williams, Joy 1944- .... **CLC 31**
See also CA 41-44R; CANR 22, 48

Williams, Norman 1952- .... **CLC 39**
See also CA 118

Williams, Sherley Anne
1944- .... **CLC 89; BLC**
See also BW 2; CA 73-76; CANR 25;
DAM MULT, POET; DLB 41;
INT CANR-25; SATA 78

Williams, Shirley
See Williams, Sherley Anne

Williams, Tennessee
1911-1983 ..... **CLC 1, 2, 5, 7, 8, 11, 15,
19, 30, 39, 45, 71; DA; DAB; DAC;
DC 4; WLC**
See also AITN 1, 2; CA 5-8R; 108;
CABS 3; CANR 31; CDALB 1941-1968;
DAM DRAM, MST; DLB 7; DLBD 4;
DLBY 83; MTCW

Williams, Thomas (Alonzo)
1926-1990 .... **CLC 14**
See also CA 1-4R; 132; CANR 2

Williams, William C.
See Williams, William Carlos

Williams, William Carlos
1883-1963 .... **CLC 1, 2, 5, 9, 13, 22, 42,
67; DA; DAB; DAC; PC 7**
See also CA 89-92; CANR 34;
CDALB 1917-1929; DAM MST, POET;
DLB 4, 16, 54, 86; MTCW

Williamson, David (Keith) 1942- .... **CLC 56**
See also CA 103; CANR 41

Williamson, Ellen Douglas 1905-1984
See Douglas, Ellen
See also CA 17-20R; 114; CANR 39

Williamson, Jack................. **CLC 29**
See also Williamson, John Stewart
See also CAAS 8; DLB 8

Williamson, John Stewart 1908-
See Williamson, Jack
See also CA 17-20R; CANR 23

Willie, Frederick
See Lovecraft, H(oward) P(hillips)

Willingham, Calder (Baynard, Jr.)
1922-1995 .... **CLC 5, 51**
See also CA 5-8R; 147; CANR 3; DLB 2,
44; MTCW

Willis, Charles
See Clarke, Arthur C(harles)

Willy
See Colette, (Sidonie-Gabrielle)

Willy, Colette
See Colette, (Sidonie-Gabrielle)

Wilson, A(ndrew) N(orman) 1950- .. **CLC 33**
See also CA 112; 122; DLB 14, 155

Wilson, Angus (Frank Johnstone)
1913-1991 .. **CLC 2, 3, 5, 25, 34; SSC 21**
See also CA 5-8R; 134; CANR 21; DLB 15,
139, 155; MTCW

Wilson, August
1945- .... **CLC 39, 50, 63; BLC; DA;
DAB; DAC; DC 2**
See also AAYA 16; BW 2; CA 115; 122;
CANR 42; DAM DRAM, MST, MULT;
MTCW

Wilson, Brian 1942- .... **CLC 12**

Wilson, Colin 1931- .... **CLC 3, 14**
See also CA 1-4R; CAAS 5; CANR 1, 22,
33; DLB 14; MTCW

Wilson, Dirk
See Pohl, Frederik

Wilson, Edmund
1895-1972 .... **CLC 1, 2, 3, 8, 24**
See also CA 1-4R; 37-40R; CANR 1, 46;
DLB 63; MTCW

Wilson, Ethel Davis (Bryant)
1888(?)-1980 .... **CLC 13; DAC**
See also CA 102; DAM POET; DLB 68;
MTCW

Wilson, John 1785-1854......... **NCLC 5**

Wilson, John (Anthony) Burgess 1917-1993
See Burgess, Anthony
See also CA 1-4R; 143; CANR 2, 46; DAC;
DAM NOV; MTCW

Wilson, Lanford 1937- .... **CLC 7, 14, 36**
See also CA 17-20R; CABS 3; CANR 45;
DAM DRAM; DLB 7

Wilson, Robert M. 1944- .... **CLC 7, 9**
See also CA 49-52; CANR 2, 41; MTCW

Wilson, Robert McLiam 1964- ..... **CLC 59**
See also CA 132

Wilson, Sloan 1920- .... **CLC 32**
See also CA 1-4R; CANR 1, 44

Wilson, Snoo 1948-............... **CLC 33**
See also CA 69-72

Wilson, William S(mith) 1932- ..... **CLC 49**
See also CA 81-84

Winchilsea, Anne (Kingsmill) Finch Counte
1661-1720 .... **LC 3**

Windham, Basil
See Wodehouse, P(elham) G(renville)

Wingrove, David (John) 1954-...... **CLC 68**
See also CA 133

Winters, Janet Lewis .... **CLC 41**
See Lewis, Janet
See also DLBY 87

Winters, (Arthur) Yvor
1900-1968 .... **CLC 4, 8, 32**
See also CA 11-12; 25-28R; CAP 1;
DLB 48; MTCW

Winterson, Jeanette 1959-........ **CLC 64**
See also CA 136; DAM POP

Winthrop, John 1588-1649.......... **LC 31**
See also DLB 24, 30

Wiseman, Frederick 1930-........ **CLC 20**

Wister, Owen 1860-1938 .... **TCLC 21**
See also CA 108; DLB 9, 78; SATA 62

Witkacy
See Witkiewicz, Stanislaw Ignacy

Witkiewicz, Stanislaw Ignacy
1885-1939 .... **TCLC 8**
See also CA 105

Wittgenstein, Ludwig (Josef Johann)
1889-1951 .... **TCLC 59**
See also CA 113

Wittig, Monique 1935(?)-.......... **CLC 22**
See also CA 116; 135; DLB 83

Wittlin, Jozef 1896-1976 .... **CLC 25**
See also CA 49-52; 65-68; CANR 3

Wodehouse, P(elham) G(renville)
1881-1975 ... **CLC 1, 2, 5, 10, 22; DAB;
DAC; SSC 2**
See also AITN 2; CA 45-48; 57-60;
CANR 3, 33; CDBLB 1914-1945;
DAM NOV; DLB 34, 162; MTCW;
SATA 22

Woiwode, L.
See Woiwode, Larry (Alfred)

Woiwode, Larry (Alfred) 1941-... **CLC 6, 10**
See also CA 73-76; CANR 16; DLB 6;
INT CANR-16

Wojciechowska, Maia (Teresa)
1927- .... **CLC 26**
See also AAYA 8; CA 9-12R; CANR 4, 41;
CLR 1; JRDA; MAICYA; SAAS 1;
SATA 1, 28, 83

Wolf, Christa 1929- .... **CLC 14, 29, 58**
See also CA 85-88; CANR 45; DLB 75;
MTCW

Wolfe, Gene (Rodman) 1931-....... **CLC 25**
See also CA 57-60; CAAS 9; CANR 6, 32;
DAM POP; DLB 8

Wolfe, George C. 1954- .... **CLC 49**
See also CA 149

Wolfe, Thomas (Clayton)
1900-1938 ..... **TCLC 4, 13, 29, 61; DA;
DAB; DAC; WLC**
See also CA 104; 132; CDALB 1929-1941;
DAM MST, NOV; DLB 9, 102; DLBD 2;
DLBY 85; MTCW

Wolfe, Thomas Kennerly, Jr. 1931-
See Wolfe, Tom
See also CA 13-16R; CANR 9, 33;
DAM POP; INT CANR-9; MTCW

Wolfe, Tom .... **CLC 1, 2, 9, 15, 35, 51**
See also Wolfe, Thomas Kennerly, Jr.
See also AAYA 8; AITN 2; BEST 89:1;
DLB 152

Wolff, Geoffrey (Ansell) 1937- ..... **CLC 41**
See also CA 29-32R; CANR 29, 43

Wolff, Sonia
See Levitin, Sonia (Wolff)

Wolff, Tobias (Jonathan Ansell)
1945- .... **CLC 39, 64**
See also AAYA 16; BEST 90:2; CA 114;
117; CAAS 22; DLB 130; INT 117

Wolfram von Eschenbach
c. 1170-c. 1220 .... **CMLC 5**
See also DLB 138

Wolitzer, Hilma 1930-............ **CLC 17**
See also CA 65-68; CANR 18, 40;
INT CANR-18; SATA 31

Wollstonecraft, Mary 1759-1797...... **LC 5**
See also CDBLB 1789-1832; DLB 39, 104,
158

Zappa, Francis Vincent, Jr.   1940-1993
    See Zappa, Frank
    See also CA 108; 143

Zappa, Frank................... **CLC 17**
    See also Zappa, Francis Vincent, Jr.

Zaturenska, Marya   1902-1982.... **CLC 6, 11**
    See also CA 13-16R; 105; CANR 22

Zelazny, Roger (Joseph)
    1937-1995 .... **CLC 21**
    See also AAYA 7; CA 21-24R; 148;
        CANR 26; DLB 8; MTCW; SATA 57;
        SATA-Brief 39

Zhdanov, Andrei A(lexandrovich)
    1896-1948 .... **TCLC 18**
    See also CA 117

Zhukovsky, Vasily   1783-1852.... **NCLC 35**

Ziegenhagen, Eric .... **CLC 55**

Zimmer, Jill Schary
    See Robinson, Jill

Zimmerman, Robert
    See Dylan, Bob

Zindel, Paul
    1936- ..... **CLC 6, 26; DA; DAB; DAC;**
                                    DC 5
    See also AAYA 2; CA 73-76; CANR 31;
        CLR 3; DAM DRAM, MST, NOV;
        DLB 7, 52; JRDA; MAICYA; MTCW;
        SATA 16, 58

Zinov'Ev, A. A.
    See Zinoviev, Alexander (Aleksandrovich)

Zinoviev, Alexander (Aleksandrovich)
    1922- .... **CLC 19**
    See also CA 116; 133; CAAS 10

Zoilus
    See Lovecraft, H(oward) P(hillips)

Zola, Emile (Edouard Charles Antoine)
    1840-1902 ...... **TCLC 1, 6, 21, 41; DA;**
                            DAB; DAC; WLC
    See also CA 104; 138; DAM MST, NOV;
        DLB 123

Zoline, Pamela   1941- .... **CLC 62**

Zorrilla y Moral, Jose   1817-1893.. **NCLC 6**

Zoshchenko, Mikhail (Mikhailovich)
    1895-1958 .... **TCLC 15; SSC 15**
    See also CA 115

Zuckmayer, Carl   1896-1977....... **CLC 18**
    See also CA 69-72; DLB 56, 124

Zuk, Georges
    See Skelton, Robin

Zukofsky, Louis
    1904-1978 .... **CLC 1, 2, 4, 7, 11, 18;**
                                    PC 11
    See also CA 9-12R; 77-80; CANR 39;
        DAM POET; DLB 5, 165; MTCW

Zweig, Paul   1935-1984........ **CLC 34, 42**
    See also CA 85-88; 113

Zweig, Stefan   1881-1942 .... **TCLC 17**
    See also CA 112; DLB 81, 118

Literary Criticism Series
Cumulative Topic Index

This index lists all topic entries in Gale's *Classical and Medieval Literature Criticism, Contemporary Literary Criticism, Literature Criticism from 1400 to 1800, Nineteenth-Century Literature Criticism,* and *Twentieth-Century Literary Criticism.*

Topic Index

Topic Index

Topic Index

CLC Cumulative Nationality Index

ALBANIAN
Kadare, Ismail **52**

ALGERIAN
Camus, Albert **1, 2, 4, 9, 11, 14, 32, 63, 69**
Cixous, Helene **92**
Cohen-Solal, Annie **50**

AMERICAN
Abbey, Edward **36, 59**
Abbott, Lee K(ittredge) **48**
Abish, Walter **22**
Abrams, M(eyer) H(oward) **24**
Acker, Kathy **45**
Adams, Alice (Boyd) **6, 13, 46**
Addams, Charles (Samuel) **30**
Adler, C(arole) S(chwerdtfeger) **35**
Adler, Renata **8, 31**
Ai **4, 14, 69**
Aiken, Conrad (Potter) **1, 3, 5, 10, 52**
Albee, Edward (Franklin III) **1, 2, 3, 5, 9, 11, 13, 25, 53, 86**
Alexander, Lloyd (Chudley) **35**
Algren, Nelson **4, 10, 33**
Allen, Edward **59**
Allen, Paula Gunn **84**
Allen, Woody **16, 52**
Allison, Dorothy E. **78**
Alta **19**
Alter, Robert B(ernard) **34**
Alther, Lisa **7, 41**
Altman, Robert **16**
Alvarez, Julia **93**
Ammons, A(rchie) R(andolph) **2, 3, 5, 8, 9, 25, 57**
Anaya, Rudolfo A(lfonso) **23**
Anderson, Jon (Victor) **9**
Anderson, Poul (William) **15**
Anderson, Robert (Woodruff) **23**

Angell, Roger **26**
Angelou, Maya **12, 35, 64, 77**
Anthony, Piers **35**
Apple, Max (Isaac) **9, 33**
Appleman, Philip (Dean) **51**
Archer, Jules **12**
Arendt, Hannah **66**
Arnow, Harriette (Louisa) Simpson **2, 7, 18**
Arrick, Fran **30**
Ashbery, John (Lawrence) **2, 3, 4, 6, 9, 13, 15, 25, 41, 77**
Asimov, Isaac **1, 3, 9, 19, 26, 76, 92**
Attaway, William (Alexander) **92**
Auchincloss, Louis (Stanton) **4, 6, 9, 18, 45**
Auden, W(ystan) H(ugh) **1, 2, 3, 4, 6, 9, 11, 14, 43**
Auel, Jean M(arie) **31**
Auster, Paul **47**
Bach, Richard (David) **14**
Badanes, Jerome **59**
Baker, Elliott **8**
Baker, Nicholson **61**
Baker, Russell (Wayne) **31**
Bakshi, Ralph **26**
Baldwin, James (Arthur) **1, 2, 3, 4, 5, 8, 13, 15, 17, 42, 50, 67, 90**
Bambara, Toni Cade **19, 88**
Banks, Russell **37, 72**
Baraka, Amiri **1, 2, 3, 5, 10, 14, 33**
Barbera, Jack (Vincent) **44**
Barnard, Mary (Ethel) **48**
Barnes, Djuna **3, 4, 8, 11, 29**
Barondess, Sue K(aufman) **8**
Barrett, William (Christopher) **27**
Barth, John (Simmons) **1, 2, 3, 5, 7, 9, 10, 14, 27, 51, 89**
Barthelme, Donald **1, 2, 3, 5, 6, 8, 13, 23, 46, 59**

Barthelme, Frederick **36**
Barzun, Jacques (Martin) **51**
Bass, Rick **79**
Baumbach, Jonathan **6, 23**
Bausch, Richard (Carl) **51**
Baxter, Charles **45, 78**
Beagle, Peter S(oyer) **7**
Beattie, Ann **8, 13, 18, 40, 63**
Becker, Walter **26**
Beecher, John **6**
Begiebing, Robert J(ohn) **70**
Behrman, S(amuel) N(athaniel) **40**
Belitt, Ben **22**
Bell, Madison (Smartt) **41**
Bell, Marvin (Hartley) **8, 31**
Bellow, Saul **1, 2, 3, 6, 8, 10, 13, 15, 25, 33, 34, 63, 79**
Benary-Isbert, Margot **12**
Benchley, Peter (Bradford) **4, 8**
Benedikt, Michael **4, 14**
Benford, Gregory (Albert) **52**
Bennett, Hal **5**
Bennett, Jay **35**
Benson, Jackson J. **34**
Benson, Sally **17**
Bentley, Eric (Russell) **24**
Berendt, John (Lawrence) **86**
Berger, Melvin H. **12**
Berger, Thomas (Louis) **3, 5, 8, 11, 18, 38**
Bergstein, Eleanor **4**
Bernard, April **59**
Berriault, Gina **54**
Berrigan, Daniel **4**
Berrigan, Ted **37**
Berry, Chuck **17**
Berry, Wendell (Erdman) **4, 6, 8, 27, 46**
Berryman, John **1, 2, 3, 4, 6, 8, 10, 13, 25, 62**
Bessie, Alvah **23**

Nationality Index

Nationality Index

CLC-95 Title Index

Title Index

ISBN 0-7876-1056-9

90000

9 780787 610562